THE LIFE OF MARK TWAIN
THE MIDDLE YEARS

The Life of
MARK TWAIN

—◆—

THE MIDDLE YEARS
1871–1891

Gary Scharnhorst

UNIVERSITY OF MISSOURI PRESS
Columbia

Library of Congress Cataloging-in-Publication Data

Names: Scharnhorst, Gary, author.
Title: The life of Mark Twain : the middle years, 1871-1891 / by Gary
    Scharnhorst.
Description: Columbia : University of Missouri Press, [2019] | Series: Mark
    Twain and his circle | Includes bibliographical references and index. |
    Identifiers: LCCN 2018049235 (print) | LCCN 2018055461 (ebook) | ISBN
    9780826274304 (e-book) | ISBN 9780826221896 (hardcover : alk. paper)
Subjects: LCSH: Twain, Mark, 1835-1910. | Twain, Mark, 1835-1910--Homes and
    haunts. | Authors, American--19th century--Biography. | Humorists,
    American--19th century--Biography.
Classification: LCC PS1331 (ebook) | LCC PS1331 .S24 2019 (print) | DDC
    818/.409 [B] --dc23
LC record available at https://lccn.loc.gov/2018049235

Typefaces: Clarendon and Jenson

This book was published with the generous support of

The Missouri Humanities Council

and

The State Historical Society of Missouri

Mark Twain and His Circle
Tom Quirk and John Bird, Series Editors

Contents

Contents

Illustrations

THE LIFE OF MARK TWAIN

THE MIDDLE YEARS

◈

CHAPTER 1

Elmira, Hartford, and on the Stump

The farm is perfectly delightful, this season. It is as quiet & peaceful as a South-sea island.

—Samuel Clemens to W. D. Howells, August 9, 1876

IN MARCH 1871 Samuel Clemens faced a daunting future. He had washed out as the managing editor of the Buffalo *Express* and sold his one-third interest in the newspaper at a loss. As a result, he was thousands of dollars in debt. His writing of the book that would become *Roughing It* (1872) had stalled and was months behind schedule. He had grown to loathe Buffalo and its harsh winters, so he had listed his house for sale for ten thousand dollars less than his father-in-law had paid for it little more than a year before. His wife Olivia, a near invalid, suffered from nervous prostration, and their infant son Langdon was chronically ill. Sam's most recent release, *Mark Twain's (Burlesque) Autobiography* (1871), had been a critical and commercial flop. Rumors were afloat, fueled by its failure, that he was written out and reduced to mining slag from an exhausted vein. He depended for a livelihood on royalties from *The Innocents Abroad* (1869) but its sales were fast declining after its initial appearance two years earlier. And Bret Harte, his not-so-friendly rival, had recently emigrated from California and signed the most lucrative contract to date in the history of American letters to write exclusively for the firm of Fields, Osgood and Company, the publishers of the *Atlantic Monthly*. Sam's own prospects seemed dreary to dismal by comparison. He could not have predicted that as soon as Harte signed this contract his career went into a death spiral. As Howells later remarked, when Harte moved east he lost the power of observation.[1] Or, as he might have said, Harte left his eye in San Francisco.

The interlude the Clemenses spent with Olivia's family in Elmira during the spring and summer of 1871 proved to be a welcome but temporary respite from their woes. As he notified his publisher Elisha Bliss and brother Orion two days after their arrival, "We are all here, & my wife has grown weak, stopped eating, & dropped back to where she was two weeks ago. But we've all the *help* we want here." Livy's prognosis had not improved a week

Figure 1. The Langdon mansion in Elmira. Courtesy of the Mark Twain Archive, Elmira College.

later. "My wife has been very sick for two months," Sam informed John Henry Riley, "so I moved her hither on a mattrass [*sic*] & she is slowly recovering, though still in bed. We shall remain here 2 or 3 months, & eventually will move to Hartford & build," though likely not for at least the next year and a half. For weeks her recovery was doubtful and even once it began her recuperation was painfully slow. "Livy as feeble as ever—has not sat up but once or twice for a week," Sam confided to Orion on April 4. She could neither stand nor walk with assistance. "I find myself daily regarding her substantial recovery as farther & farther away," Sam wrote Mary Mason Fairbanks in mid-April. "I cannot see that she has gained a single hair's breadth in 30 days. She is hopeful & confident—but what does she found it on?" Only at the end of the month could Sam finally report that Livy was "making progress. . . . She walks three or four steps by holding on to a chair, & every day she rides a few blocks. She is bright & cheerful," though Sam could not fathom the reason for her optimism. As late as May 2, over six weeks after the family landed in Elmira, he grumbled that Livy was "still confined to her bed & has been over three months."[2]

No sooner had Sam dropped his bags at the Langdon mansion on Main Street than he began to plot a way forward.

He desperately needed to complete his overdue book about the West, which had reached a standstill after only 168 pages of manuscript, about one-tenth the length required for a subscription book. He soon settled into a routine. Most days he escaped the din of the city and the crying of his son by climbing Watercure Hill, two miles east of the city, to the house at Quarry Farm, offered him as a hideaway by his in-laws Theodore and Susan Crane. The retreat stood several hundred feet above the valley, with a view of Elmira, the Chemung River, and the distant blue hills of northern Pennsylvania.[3]

Relieved of nursing duties by the Langdon servants and spared the distractions that plagued him in Buffalo, Sam shortly found his working groove again. He was joined on March 24, less than a week after his arrival in Elmira, by his old Nevada friend Joe Goodman, and the two writers began to worry over their respective projects like stray dogs over bones. Goodman "wrote loads of poetry while I wrote" the yet untitled western narrative, Sam

Figure 2. Quarry Farm, the Clemens family's summer home. Courtesy of the Mark Twain Archive, Elmira College.

testified years later, "& between whiles" they played cards or collected rocks and fossil shells from the quarry on the farm. On his part, Goodman remembered that Sam

> was awfully tickled at my coming and wanted to pay me a salary to remain until he had finished the work, saying he had lost Pacific Coast atmosphere and vernacular, but that I brought it all back to him afresh. I told him I couldn't stop a great while, but that I would stay with him as long as I could, if he would agree not to speak about pay again. So every morning for a month or more we used to tramp together up to the Quarry Farm, about two miles from town, where he was doing his writing in the unoccupied farmhouse.

Sam averaged about twenty pages of sixty to seventy words per page, or about twelve hundred to fourteen hundred words of manuscript per day, according to Goodman. Sam's goal was "from ten thousand to twelve thousand words a week." More to the point, Sam solicited Goodman's opinion of his work in progress. As Goodman would later comment,

> I recollect his giving me the manuscript of "Roughing It" to read one afternoon when I was visiting him. . . . He made a great hit with Innocents Abroad and he was afraid he would not sustain his newly acquired reputation. When I began to read Sam sat down at his desk and wrote nervously. For an hour I read along intently, hardly noticing that Sam was beginning to fret and shift about uneasily. At last he could not stand it any longer and jumping up, he exclaimed "Damn you, you have been reading that stuff an hour and you haven't cracked a smile yet. I don't believe I'm keeping up my lick."

Goodman may fairly be regarded as the godfather of Sam's second travel book, although, as he allowed, "It was a long while before he grew calm enough to accept the assurance of my appreciation of his work."[4]

They briefly considered cowriting a satirical political novel. Sam contacted Isaac Sheldon, the publisher who had issued his *(Burlesque) Autobiography*, to propose the joint project, even though he was still under contract to Elisha Bliss and the American Publishing Company of Hartford for three books. Sheldon was initially receptive to the notion—"I like the idea & it would sell well if it were a good story & had a quiet vein of humor"—and Sam replied with alacrity: "I begin to think I can get up quite a respectable novel, & mean to fool away some of my odd hours in the attempt." Three weeks after leaving Buffalo for Elmira, in other words, Sam had begun to plan a series of ventures to compete with Harte, reestablish his reputation as a humorist, and earn a living. "Joe & I have a 600-page book in contemplation which will wake up the nation," he crowed to Orion. Although their collaboration never advanced beyond the planning stage, the premise bore fruit in *The Gilded Age* (1873), the satirical exposé Sam would coauthor with Charles Dudley Warner two years later.[5]

Meanwhile, he stewed over the prospects for his burlesque of the mythic West. He was "booming along" on the manuscript, he bragged to Orion on April 8, with 570 pages in the can, though "what I am writing now is so much better than the opening chapters . . . that I do *wish* I could spare time to revamp the opening chapters, & even write some of them over again." Irritated by the publication in March of the *(Burlesque) Autobiography* by a rival press, moreover, Bliss tempered Sam's hopes for the new book by admonishing him for saturating the market with his brand of earthy humor: "I do not think there is as much of a desire to see another book from you as there was 3 months ago. Then anything offered would sell, people would subscribe to anything of yours without overhauling or looking at it much. Now they will inspect a Prospectus closer, & buy more on the strength of *it*, than they would have done a few months ago." Despite "pegging away at my book," Sam feared it would "have no success," he fretted to Mary Fairbanks on April 26, because "the papers have found at last the courage to pull me down off my pedestal & cast slurs at me—& that is simply a popular author's death rattle." (Recently, the *Chicago Tribune* had complained that Sam had "no aspirations or abilities in any other direction" than cheap humor and the *Nation* had charged that he "was sometimes rather vulgar and rather low" and, in any case, he was "not refined.") Four days later, however, he waxed confident the book would be "a tolerable success—possibly an *excellent* success if the chief newspapers start it off well." The statement begins to explain his clumsy attempt to micromanage the critical reception of *Roughing It* the next year. Four days later still, he effectively blamed Bliss in advance for bungling the artwork if the book failed to sell: the narrative would be "pretty readable, after all, & if it is well & profusely illustrated it will crowd the [popularity of the] 'Innocents.'"[6]

Fortunately, Sam's reservations about parts of his narrative failed to cramp either his style or his speed of composition. He swore to Bliss in early May that the book was "half done," complete through chapter 15. By mid-May he had finished twelve hundred pages of manuscript, the equivalent of four hundred printed pages, and "consequently am two-thirds done." He planned

> to write as much more as I have already written, & then cull from the mass the very best chapters & discard the rest. I am not half as well satisfied with the first part of the book as I am with what I am writing now. When I get it done I want to see the man who will begin to read it & not finish it. If it falls short of the Innocents in any respect I shall lose my guess. When I was writing the Innocents my daily "stent" was 30 pages of MS & I hardly ever

got beyond it; but I have gone over that nearly every day for the last ten. That shows that I am writing with a red-hot interest. . . . If I keep up my present lick three weeks more I shall be able & willing to scratch out half of the chapters of the Overland narrative—& shall do it.

Sam (over)confidently predicted that the "book will be done soon, now" because he was "now writing 200 [manuscript sheets] a week." But he had also begun to pad the narrative, particularly in chapters 10, 11, and 16, with generous dollops of text ladled into it from such printed sources as John Hyde's *Mormonism: Its Leaders and Designs* (1857), Samuel Bowles's *Across the Continent* (1865), Thomas J. Dimsdale's *The Vigilantes of Montana* (1866), and Catharine V. Waite's *The Mormon Prophet and His Harem* (1866). According to Hamlin Hill, Sam "paraphrased a lot of Dimsdale's material and even transcribed one passage verbatim without citing his source"—hardly the first time he had been guilty of plagiarism.[7]

Sam hand-delivered his latest batch of copy to Bliss in early June, pausing en route at the luxury St. Nicholas Hotel on Broadway in New York, attending Sunday services at the Asylum Hill Congregational Church in Hartford on June 4, and dining that evening with Governor Marshall Jewell of Connecticut before returning to the Langdon mansion in Elmira. When he resumed writing *Roughing It* he continued to pad it with recycled material, including excerpts from sketches he had originally written for the *Galaxy* and the Buffalo *Express*—specifically, five of the "Around the World" letters he had contributed to its columns. He cannibalized chapter 38, about Mono Lake, from the abandoned "Curiosities of California" lecture he had prepared in Buffalo in 1869; and he assembled chapter 49, about gunplay in Virginia City, from *Territorial Enterprise* clippings he had preserved in one of his scrapbooks. Still, as the editors of the Mark Twain Papers observe, "the scrapbooks turned out to be much less useful" than Sam had anticipated. Though he cut and pasted over 130 pages of published passages into the narrative, he "used scarcely anything of his own from the *Enterprise*, and nothing at all of what he had published in the San Francisco *Morning Call*, the *Californian*, and the *Golden Era*." With the publication of his western travelogue, Sam had exhausted all of the usable material in his scrapbooks.[8]

In mid-June Sam was still struggling to finish the final section of the book. It had "been dragging along just 12 months, now, & I am *so* sick & tired of it," he whined to Mother Fairbanks, adding, "If I were to chance another break or another move before I finish it I fear I never *should* get it done." He later told Annie Fields that when he "sat down to write" *Roughing It* he discovered that he needed "a cigar to steady my nerves. I began to smoke [again]" in order to complete the manuscript. He had spent "three weeks writing six chapters," he remembered a decade later, and then he surrendered to his nicotine addiction to conquer his writer's block or his attention deficit disorder. He resumed his custom of smoking three hundred cigars a month and finished the book in ninety days "without any bother or difficulty." "One of the most nervous men in the world" who had "constant difficulty in keeping still," Sam self-medicated.[9]

By early July he had completed sixty-one of seventy-nine chapters; however, he was still short of the eighteen hundred manuscript sheets required for a subscription book of six hundred printed pages and he was running low on sources to crib. In early August he railed to New York and again registered at the St. Nicholas Hotel before continuing to Hartford, where he delivered another batch of printer's copy to Bliss. He remained in Hartford for most of the month, working on the book and hunting for a house to rent. He arranged to lease the home of John and Isabella Hooker at the corner of Forest and Hawthorn Streets in the Nook Farm neighborhood, a 140-acre enclave of artists, intellectuals, and politicians, beginning in October while the owners were traveling in Europe. Both Sam and Livy had stayed in the house in the past and it was available for only a hundred dollars a month payable quarterly. During the month, too, he began to backfill the manuscript with material inserted into the sections already completed. "I wrote a splendid chapter today, for the middle of the book," he notified Livy on August 10. This inset has been conjecturally identified as chapter 53, Jim Blaine's tale of "his grandfather's old ram," which Henry B. Wonham describes as "a magnificently woven shaggy dog story" narrated by a circumlocutious "drunken raconteur who never arrives at his titular subject." Jim Blaine's name evokes the moniker of James G. Blaine, Schuyler Colfax's successor as Speaker of the U.S. House of Representatives. Sam once referred to the Ohio congressman in his notebook as "the most notorious blatherskite in America." As he was reading proofs of some of the early chapters, Sam also queried Alfred Sutro about a tunnel project on the Comstock Lode he was financing. "I'm awful busy on my new book on Nevada & California," Sam noted, but he hoped "you might tell me something about the tunnel that would make an interesting page." After meeting Sutro in New York in late August he added a postscript to chapter 52. "I admire the book more & more the more I cut & slash & lick & trim & revamp it," he bragged. "It is a tedious, arduous job shaping such a mass of MS for the press. It took me two months to do it for the Innocents. But this is another sight easier job, because it is so much better literary work—so much more acceptably written." As he assured Livy in November, "This is a better book than the Innocents, & *much* better written."[10]

W. D. Howells, the editor of the *Atlantic Monthly*, agreed and fairly described *Roughing It* as a "crazy-quilt of homespun fabrics." As Howells allowed, "A thousand anecdotes, relevant and irrelevant, embroider the work; excursions and digressions of all kinds are the very woof of it, as it were; everything far-fetched or near at hand is interwoven, and yet the complex is a sort of 'harmony of colors' which is not less than triumphant." Sam was "as uplifted" by Howells's notice "as a mother who has given birth to a white baby when she was awfully afraid it was going to be a mulatto." A pastiche or bricolage of tall tales, fictionalized autobiography, anecdote, allegory, animal fables, character sketches, factual reporting, mining narrative, and excerpts from other books about the West, his "record of several years of variegated vagabondizing" sometimes followed a meandering narrative flow and occasionally spilled over the banks. Just as Sam devised his lectures to be both entertaining and informative, he was obliged to include "quite a good deal of information in the book," especially about mining, milling, and assaying processes, as he explained in his preface. He halted in the middle of chapter 65, for example, to declare that "this is a good time to drop in a paragraph of information" from a guidebook. He began chapter 52 with a warning that because "I desire, in this chapter, to say an instructive word or two about the silver mines, the reader may take this fair warning and skip, if he chooses," as though the reader could cut a channel through a looping bend in the narrative.[11]

Despite its haphazard development, the story has direction and purpose. *Roughing It* demythologizes the romantic Wild West of ruthless outlaws, red-shirted miners, noble natives, and hardy pioneers that Bret Harte had popularized. Put another way, it is the lineal ancestor of such satirical Westerns as Eliot Silverstein's *Cat Ballou* (1965) and Mel Brooks's *Blazing Saddles* (1974). But Sam's Wild West, populated by desperadoes and confidence men, is also as terrifying as it is entertaining. Simply put, *Roughing It* is not a realistic account of life on the frontier but a tall tale designed to challenge eastern readers' assumptions about the region.[12] Sam reproduced the same pattern of progressive disillusionment or comic deflation that he had exploited to good effect in *The Innocents Abroad*. If, in his earlier travelogue, the churlish narrator—an invented character not to be confused with the author—is disillusioned by the paintings of the Old Masters and Turkish baths, here he is dismayed by barren alkali deserts and frustrated by his failure to strike it rich with a wood ranch and various mines, including a blind lead. If, in *The Innocents Abroad*, he was the stranger who bedeviled his fellow "pilgrims," here he is the naïf who must earn his spurs. To summarize the plot in terms of the allegory related in chapter 5, the narrator is cast initially in the role of a tenderfoot or town dog outwitted by a slinking coyote native to the West. The first half of the book or the first volume of the two-volume edition demonstrates the irrelevance of the attitudes the greenhorns bring with them from "the States." As the second volume opens in chapter 42, however, the narrator abandons the badlands for a regular salary as the city editor of the Virginia City *Territorial Enterprise*. Much as he exchanges his "slouch hat, blue woolen shirt, pantaloons stuffed into boot-tops" for "a more Christian costume" that reflects his newfound respectability, he shifts his perspective. Sam repeatedly developed in his writings over the years this notion of the symbolic function of clothing, as in *The Adventures of Tom Sawyer* (1876), when the hero dons Sunday-school attire and his river-rat companion Huck, a social untouchable, wears cast-off garments "in perennial bloom and fluttering with rags" denoting his outsider status. Whereas the narrator of *Roughing It* had sided with the vernacular types in the first volume, he begins to identify with the bourgeoisie in the second. An innocent initially infatuated with desperadoes and miners, in the latter half, with his initiation more or less complete, he becomes a reporter/observer who subtly condescends to desperadoes and miners. That is, the narrator in the second half no longer shares the point of view of "the boys" but adopts a more documentary format or reportorial style for his story. The shift in perspective might be summarized this way: whereas as an innocent he had been intimidated by the outlaw Spade, as a reporter he welcomes the news of a murder because it supplies him with a story. His transformation is nowhere more evident than in the Buck Fanshaw episode in chapter 47. After the death of Fanshaw, "a stalwart rough" (the very phrase betrays an "attitude of tolerant but condescending amusement") his friend Scotty Briggs calls on a local cleric—"a fragile, gentle, spiritual new fledgling from an Eastern theological seminary"—to plan his funeral. (The two characters are broadly modeled on Sam's friends Tom Peasley, owner of the Sazerac Saloon in Virginia City, and the Episcopalian minister Franklin Rising, secretary of the Storey County Bible Society.) Their dialects are so dissimilar that neither understands the other:

> Briggs: "Are you the duck that runs the gospel-mill next door?"
> The minister: "I am the . . . spiritual adviser of the little company of believers whose sanctuary adjoins these premises."
> Briggs: "What we want is a gospel-sharp. See?"
> The minister: "I am a clergyman—a parson."
> Briggs: "You don't smoke me and I don't smoke you."

Sam's greater use of colloquial speech in *Roughing It* is in fact what primarily distinguishes it from *The Innocents Abroad*.[13]

Ironically, just as Sam revised his dispatches to the San Francisco *Alta California* for inclusion in *The Innocents Abroad*, Sam tamed some of the risqué passages in his posts to the *Sacramento Union* before submitting the manuscript of *Roughing It* to Elisha Bliss. He omitted a passage from his July 1866 letter to the *Union*, for example, about how, when he stumbled upon "a bevy of nude native young ladies bathing in the sea," he "went and undressed and went in myself." In a word, Sam changed his tone as he shifted his audience. No longer targeting an exclusively local and lowbrow readership but a more national and middlebrow one, Sam hit upon a style, particularly in the latter half of the book, that may best be described as a chastened vernacular—Scotty Briggs's dialect mediated through a translator for consumption by the eastern minister, as it were. From the distance of Elmira and Hartford, San Francisco seemed a far country and Sam's own experiences there the riotous living of a prodigal. In chapter 4 of *Roughing It*, Sam re-creates the moment when, at a stagecoach way station en route to Nevada, he "first encountered the vigorous new vernacular of the occidental plains and mountains." Seated at a table with "hostlers and herdsmen," he heard one of them say in a "gruffly friendly voice, 'Pass the bread, you son of a skunk!' No, I forget—skunk was not the word; it seems to me it was still stronger than that; I know it was, in fact, but it is gone from my memory, apparently. However, it is no matter—probably it was too strong for print, anyway." The profanity spoken in a "gruffly friendly" voice that Sam pretends to have forgotten ("son of a bitch") points forward to chapter 2 of Owen Wister's *The Virginian* (1902), where a pair of cowpokes utter the phrase in very different contexts and timbres for different effects. Whereas the hero's best friend uses it as an endearment, when the villain says it to the hero the Virginian responds by drawing his gun and replying, "When you call me that, *smile*."[14]

Notwithstanding its nostalgic veneer, *Roughing It* is the least autobiographical of Sam's travel books. Hamlin Hill refers to Sam's "enormous violation of the facts of his biography" in its construction. He "dramatized many episodes," Gladys Bellamy notes, "and invented others outright when the narrative demanded it. He fictionalized himself, too, and his own adventures." In particular, Sam's account of his life among the rowdies of San Francisco fudges or obscures many of the specific details normally associated with local-color realism. He nowhere names, for example, the luxurious hotels where he lived briefly (the Lick House, the Occidental), the newspaper for which he worked (the *Morning Call*), the theaters he frequented (e.g., Platt's Hall, the Metropolitan), or even the name of the theater where he delivered his first public lecture (Maguire's Academy of Music). Of the six years he lived in the West, the most eventful and unhappiest year, 1866, is dismissed in scarcely two pages. The feud with James Laird and the reasons for his hasty departure from Virginia City are ignored entirely and the months he lived in San Francisco are largely neglected. But the narrative may be read as an accurate barometer of his racial attitudes at the moment of its composition. As usual, he castigated Native Americans, alleging that the Australian bushmen and "our Goshoots [Goshutes] are manifestly descended from the self-same gorilla, or kangaroo, or Norway rat, whichever animal-Adam the Darwinians trace them to." His prejudices against the Chinese were more subtle, however: "They are a harmless race when white men either let them alone or treat them no worse than dogs; in fact they are almost entirely harmless. . . . They are quiet, peaceable, tractable, free from drunkenness, and they are as industrious as the day is long." No Californian "ever abuses or oppresses a Chinaman, under any circumstances," Sam insisted. "Only the scum of the population do it." As Cynthia Wu suggests, Sam "expresses outrage at the treatment of Chinese laborers in California by unsympathetic whites even as it perpetuates the racism behind that kind of abuse."[15]

From his socially privileged perspective, he also satirized such topics as trial by jury and universal suffrage. He had condemned the jury system since the exoneration of Daniel McFarland for the murder of his friend A. D. Richardson in 1869 on the grounds of temporary insanity and his views had not mellowed. As Tom Quirk suggests, Sam's "infuriation with the legal defense plea of temporary insanity bordered on monomania." He even considered dedicating *Roughing It* "to the late Cain . . . in that it was his misfortune to live in a dark age that knew not the beneficent insanity plea." Virtually no killers had been convicted of their crimes in Nevada—in consequence, he argued, of a flawed criminal justice system. Juries had been perverted into "the most ingenious and infallible agency for *defeating* justice that human wisdom could contrive" because it put "a ban upon intelligence and honesty, and a premium upon ignorance, stupidity, and perjury." Such qualified jurors as ministers, mining superintendents, and quartz mill owners were routinely dismissed from the jury pool. Instead, courts impaneled "two desperados, two low beerhouse politicians, three barkeepers, two ranchmen who could not read, and three dull, stupid, human donkeys! It actually came out afterward that one of these latter thought that incest and arson were the same thing." As a result, like Wister in *The Virginian*, Sam sanctioned vigilante justice, as when Captain Ned Blakely, modeled on his friend Captain Ned Wakeman, hangs a murderer on his own authority. Sam was no more upbeat on the topic of universal suffrage. He blamed the ratification of the Nevada state constitution in October 1864 on the rabble who had no stake in the referendum. "The property holders of Nevada voted against the State

Constitution; but the folks who had nothing to lose were in the majority," he complained, "and carried the measure over their heads." As a result, Sam believed, the economy crashed and vaporized his paper fortune in mining stock.[16]

In order to conclude the book, Sam decided—reluctantly, it seems—to include parts of the Sandwich Islands narrative rejected by New York publishers in 1867 and based on thirteen of the twenty-five Sandwich Islands letters he had contributed to the *Sacramento Union* between April and November 1866. "I am now waiting a day or two till I get my old Sandwich Islands notes together," he alerted Bliss on July 10, "for I want to put in 4 or 5 chapters about the Islands for the benefit of New England—& the world." In the end, he inserted not four or five chapters about Hawaii but fifteen, including some thirty thousand words in chapters 74 to 78 that were mostly salvaged from the *Union* letters. When he was asked his opinion of these chapters, King Kalākaua was equivocal: they were "a blending of fact and fiction. He was a clever humorist, and had burlesqued some things, while he had truthfully described others." Sam also augmented the length of the book with three long appendixes copied from printed sources. His decision to extend the geographical reach of the travelogue beyond Nevada precluded him from calling the book "Flush Times in the Silver Mines," one of its working titles. Sam also vetoed one of Bliss's recommendations, "The Innocents at Home." By late August his work on the book was virtually complete save for final proofreading and the rewriting of chapter 20, which one of Bliss's pressmen had misplaced. "I remember the heavy work it was to write it before," Sam commented, and he hoped the man who lost it "had the M.S. stuffed into his bowels. . . . If time presses, just leave the whole chapter out. It is all we can do."[17]

He was unexpectedly summoned back to Elmira on August 30 to attend the sickbed of his son Langdon. He hurried home, not even pausing overnight in New York. "We have scarcely any hope of the baby's recovery," he wrote Orion the next day. "Livy takes neither sleep nor rest. We have 3 old experienced nurses. Three months of overfeeding & surreptitious poisoning with laudanum & other sleeping potions is what the child is dying of." Since moving to Elmira in March and all through Livy's illness, Langdon had been nurtured by a succession of wet nurses and had enjoyed robust health. "The baby is perfectly strong & hearty," Sam informed friends on April 6. Two months later, he again assured his "sainted idiot brother" that "the baby is flourishing." On July 23, however, he revealed to his childhood friend Will Bowen that "the baby is seriously ill," so Langdon's turn for the worse did not come as a complete surprise. Sam had in fact reassured Livy during Langdon's illness that should she die he would "love the baby & have a jealous care over him.—But let us hope & trust that both you & I shall tend him & watch over him till we are helped from our easy-chairs to the parlor to see his children married."[18] Fortunately, the crisis soon passed, but Langdon's precarious health would remain a family concern for the duration of his short life. At the age of sixteen months, he had a vocabulary of a single word ("Pa") and was still unable to walk. During her second pregnancy, Livy expressed the hope that she would not "have as delicate a child next time as little Langdon." Sam ascribed the delays in his son's development to "precocity of development intellectually . . . since it is development of inherited indolence, acquired from his father." Victor Doyno has speculated that Langdon may have been born "with what modern pediatric neurologists identify as 'a bossed forehead,' indicative of a hydrocephalic condition."[19]

Figure 3. Langdon Clemens, 1872.
Courtesy of the Mark Twain
Archive, Elmira College.

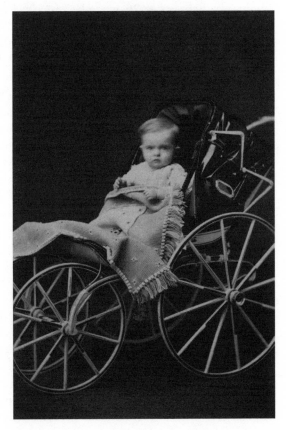

Sam visited Washington, D.C., between September 7 and 9 to file for a patent he was soon granted for an adjustable garment strap he had recently invented—the Washington *National Republican* described it as a new type of suspenders "combining elegance, comfort and convenience." Sam claimed that he was inspired to design the accessory when he met Horace Greeley for the first time. As the *National Republican* reported, "the extraordinary set of [Greeley's] trowsers, half in and half out of his boots, attracted his attention, and he at once set to work to see if he could not devise some plan of making them hang more gracefully." Sam returned via New York and Hartford to Elmira, arriving on September 13. Four days later, he and Livy headed to Buffalo to pack and Livy, in the early stages of her second pregnancy, promptly fell ill again. Sam was frantic, writing on September 22, "We are in a mess—house upside down—my wife sick—can't leave her bed for perhaps a week yet—& yet we must take possession of our house in Hartford Oct. 1." Sam somehow succeeded in crating their furniture and boxing other belongings by September 26, when he and Livy boarded a train for New York. After pausing a week at the St. Nicholas to allow Livy to rest, they at last reached their new home in Hartford on October 3.[20]

The capital of Connecticut, with a population of about thirty-eight thousand, according to the 1870 census, Hartford was "becoming the pleasantest city, to the eye, that America can show," Sam wrote Livy even before their marriage. "I never saw any place before where morality and huckleberries flourished as they do here," he had observed during his first visit to the city in September 1868. The home of the Colt Arms factories and the Pratt & Whitney machine shops, with convenient rail links to Boston and New York, Hartford was so prosperous that its citizens enjoyed the highest per capita income in the country. "I want to be in such a position that I can go to New York or Boston" by train in four hours or so "if I want to," Sam explained. "I don't want to go to either, but I like to have them nearby." Years later he would reflect, "A good deal of experience of men enabled me to choose my residence wisely. I live in the freest corner of the country." Hartford was also the headquarters of Sam's publisher, the American Publishing Company, several other subscription presses, and the Aetna Life Insurance Company, the Phoenix Mutual Life Insurance Company, and other national insurers. The residents of the Nook Farm neighborhood included former U.S. senator Francis Gillette, John Hooker's brother-in-law; Gillette's son William, a future playwright and actor; the author Harriet Beecher Stowe and her husband Calvin; Charles Dudley Warner, co-owner and coeditor of the *Hartford Courant*, and his wife Susan; Charles Dudley Warner's brother George and his wife Lilly, the daughter of Francis Gillette; retired Civil

War general Joseph Hawley, the other co-owner of the *Hartford Courant*; Thomas Perkins and his wife Mary Beecher Perkins, the sister of Harriet Stowe and Isabella Hooker; and the lawyer Charles Enoch Perkins, the son of Thomas and Mary and nephew of Harriet and Isabella. Above all, Hartford was the hometown of Harmony and Joseph Twichell, minister of the Asylum Hill Congregational Church and Sam's best friend for the next forty years. While Sam and Livy remained members, at least nominally, of the Park Church in Elmira, they rented a pew at Asylum Hill. "With his big heart, his wide sympathies, and his limitless benignities and charities and generosities," Sam avowed, Twichell was "the kind of person that people of all ages and both sexes fly to for consolation and help in time of trouble." He was "a good man, one of the best of men, although a clergyman," and "my oldest friend—and dearest enemy on occasion."[21]

Sam was soon at work supervising final production of his new book. He finally settled on a title, *Roughing It*—another of Bliss's suggestions—in mid-October. He had resisted the temptation to name it until it was finished because, he explained to Mary Fairbanks, he had "to write it first— you wouldn't make a garment for an animal till you had seen the animal, would you?" Bliss commissioned True Williams, a local artist and notorious drunk, to illustrate it. Williams contributed over a hundred illustrations, both signed and unsigned, to its pages. As was customary to reduce production costs, Bliss also recycled at least thirty-three plates from such sources as Richardson's *Beyond the Mississippi* (1867), Thomas Knox's *Overland through Asia* (1870), and J. Ross Browne's *Adventures in the Apache Country* (1868). Despite the shortcuts and Bliss's best efforts, the illustrations were not yet finished when *Roughing It* was copyrighted on December 6 and sales canvassing began the next day. Bliss explained that he had "set up to page 300" but none of the plates had been engraved. Sam commissioned one of the most significant sketches, of William Stewart as a bandit sporting an eyepatch, in response to Stewart's supposed theft of a sheaf of mining shares he had promised him. "My revenge will be found in the accompanying portrait," Sam declared. In his autobiography Stewart confirmed the accuracy of this backstory: "When he wrote 'Roughing It' he said I had cheated him out of some mining stock or something like that, and that he had given me a sound thrashing; and he printed a picture of me in the book, with a patch over one eye."[22]

In order to support Livy in the style to which he had become accustomed and to earn his own bread and butter until he began to collect royalties on *Roughing It*, Sam had decided even before leaving Buffalo to speak throughout New England during the fall and winter lecture season under the auspices of the Boston Lyceum Bureau and its manager James Redpath. By mid-May he was "flooded with lecture invitations" and a month later, between writing stints on *Roughing It*, he had prepared two talks. "An Appeal on Behalf of Extending the Suffrage to Boys" was, he insisted, "a good-natured satire" of women's suffrage. Redpath announced publicly in mid-June that "An Appeal" would be the title of Sam's presentation in the fall and such papers as the *Albany Journal, Boston Traveller, Cincinnati Gazette*, New York *Evening Post*, and Washington *Evening News* all carried the news between June 13 and 19. Almost nothing is known about the other lecture, which Sam simply gave the enigmatical title "D.L.H." Orion prematurely announced in the July issue of the *American Publisher*, the monthly newsletter of the American Publishing Company, that both talks were available to be booked by lyceums throughout New England. But Sam discarded both before he had delivered either, and no manuscript of either survives. Redpath proposed that he revive "Our Fellow Savages of the Sandwich Islands" and Sam quickly repudiated the suggestion: "Were you serious in suggesting that rubbishy Sandwich Island hogwash for another campaign?"[23]

Instead, before the end of June he had written a third lecture. "I use no notes in lecturing," he explained to Redpath, "& so I don't dare to try to use more than one lecture during a season. I shall carry the MSS. of another lecture, along, for safety, & shall discard the new one altogether if, after a few trials, it is not a success." The new talk, "Reminiscences of Some Pleasant Characters Whom I Have Met" ("or should the 'whom' be left out?" he asked Redpath in a letter) or "Reminiscences of Some Uncommonplace Characters I Have Chanced to Meet," was a miscellany of memories about some of his acquaintances—"kings, humorists, lunatics, idiots, and all"—including Artemus Ward, Emperor Norton I, King Kalākaua of Hawaii, his *Quaker City* compatriot Reeves Jackson, his newspaper colleague John Henry Riley, and the California miner Dick Stoker. "I shall deliver no lecture" except this one, Sam advised Redpath on June 28. "By the time I have talked it in 12 towns, & got the hang of it, I'll engage to plug the bull's eye with it, every time." He bragged to Orion that it was "the best [lecture] I ever wrote" and to Mary Fairbanks that "I just know [it] will 'fetch' any audience I spout it before."[24]

If he was not yet an A-list celebrity among the lyceums, Sam nevertheless enjoyed sufficient popularity—and thus leverage—to negotiate the ground rules of the tour from a position of strength. In 1868–69 he had traveled from Illinois to New York, often for speaking fees of only $100. As a result, he was sometimes booked to speak in churches or in small country towns. In 1871–72 he expected Redpath to treat him more deferentially. This time around, he offered to lecture for $125 in most places but no less than $250 in Boston. Should he be booked to speak "in Philadelphia, Newark, Pittsburgh, Cleveland, & Detroit," he demanded that they "pay high prices" too. He also insisted on "a big price in Buffalo if I talk there, which I ain't particular whether I talk there or not" after he had been snubbed following a lecture for charity there in March 1870. He also wanted to be priced out of churches—"I never made a success of a lecture delivered in a church yet," he explained. "People are afraid to laugh in a church." He preferred to avoid "candle-lighted halls," "execrable hotels," and "one-horse towns" such as Rondout, New York. In fact, ease of travel was one of his major concerns. "I want to stick to main railroad lines as a rule, avoiding out-of-the way branches as far as practicable," he stipulated. "I don't want to make any steamboat trips, or *any* stage or carriage trips of even 2½ miles—2 miles is too much. To simplify it, I don't want *any* engagements OFF the railroads." As a rule, he asked Redpath to "give me the very *shortest trips* you can, & Heaven will bless you. {Three hours is a healthy stretch—six is FRIGHTFUL.[}]" Nor did he "want to lecture a single rod west of St. Louis in Missouri or Davenport Iowa.—nor south of Washington, D.C." In late July he reiterated these boundaries: "I have been offered $150 a night to talk 30 consecutive nights in Missouri & Kansas, but declined, partly because it was not enough & partly because I don't like so much railroad travel. I may talk in St Louis if my agents have already made a contract to that effect, but I hope they have not; for I have concluded to go no further west than Cleveland." Finally, he and Livy had concluded that he could not "possibly talk after Feb. 2" of the new year, six weeks before Livy's due date. With few exceptions, Redpath met all of these conditions in scheduling the tour—in all, seventy-four performances in fifteen states and the District of Columbia between October 16, 1871, and February 1, 1872.[25]

The tour was, nonetheless, according to the most recent editors of Sam's correspondence, "perhaps the most difficult of his career, chiefly because of his inability to write" a lecture that would pass muster with the public. He left Hartford in company with his brother-in-law Charley Langdon, who had helped in their move, on October 13, only ten days after he and Livy had lighted there, and overnighted (again) at the St. Nicholas Hotel in New York. Fortunately, he did not leave Livy and Langdon to shift for themselves. Orion and Mollie Clemens, as well as such old and new friends as Joe and Harmony Twichell, Alice Beecher Day and her husband John, and George and Lilly Warner, all lived only a few blocks from the Hooker house. And at least one of their servants from Buffalo, the coachman/stableman and jack-of-all-trades Patrick McAleer, had also moved with the furniture to Hartford. The next day Charley returned to Elmira, and Sam slouched toward Bethlehem, Pennsylvania. "I got here at 4 oclock yesterday afternoon," he wrote Livy on October 15. "It is now nearly noon, & still I don't feel moved to begin studying my lecture." As became his custom in the future, he traveled incognito: "I entered an assumed name on the hotel register (learned from Redpath that a reception was intended & sumptuous rooms provided for me,) & so, as simple 'Samuel Langhorne, New York,' I occupy the shabbiest little den in the house & am left wholly & happily unnoticed. It is luxury." He opened with his "Reminiscences" lecture the evening of October 16. It was a spectacular flop from the very beginning. The *Bethlehem Times* complained that, while most of the auditors "were satisfied" merely to see him, they had been neither "instructed nor exactly entertained." Sam spoke next in Allentown, where the Allentown *Chronicle* averred that "the greatest joke he ever perpetrated was his 'lecture' last evening. We do not propose to make an extended notice and merely remark that we prefer *reading* to hearing him." He conceded to Livy that "this lecture will never do. I hate it and won't keep it. I can't even handle these chuckleheaded Dutch with it. Have blocked out a lecture on Artemus Ward, & shall write it next Saturday & deliver it next Monday in Washington."[26]

After another ineffective tryout in Wilkes-Barre the next night—the Wilkes-Barre Luzerne *Union* declared that "one dose of such stuff was sufficient for a generation"—he abandoned "Reminiscences." As he wrote Livy after the lecture, "I shall reach Washington tomorrow night, & then for two days & nights I shall work like a beaver on my new lecture. How I ever came to get up such a mess of rubbish as this & imagine it *good*, is too many for me." He canceled his next two appearances, in Easton and Reading, Pennsylvania, professing "sickness in my family," registered at a Washington, D.C., hotel under an assumed name, and reworked the anecdotes about Artemus Ward in "Reminiscences" into a full-length, ninety-minute talk. He premiered it in Washington on October 23, reading from a script before a standing-room-only audience estimated at two thousand, allegedly the largest audience ever assembled in Lincoln Hall. Sam was relieved if not elated to be rid of the earlier lecture. "I have come square out, thrown 'Reminiscences' overboard, and taken 'Artemus Ward, Humorist,' for my topic," he notified Redpath. "Wrote it here on Friday and Saturday and read it from mss. last night to enormous house. It suits me and I'll never deliver the nasty, nauseous 'Reminiscences' anymore."[27]

But the new lecture was also fraught with problems. His Washington listeners were utterly confused by what they heard; according to the Washington *Star*, "They didn't seem to know whether he was lecturing on 'uncommonplace characters,' as announced, or only one uncommonplace character [Ward]—or whether he was delivering that lecture, or another lecture, or whether there was any other lecture—in fact, they couldn't get the hang of it at all." The *Washington Chronicle* was likewise disappointed. Sam seemed out of practice on the stage, betraying "unfit habits of manner and speech," "eccentricities of bearing," and "*outré* gestures" that distracted from his lackluster performance. "Even the promise of his humor-stamped face seems to fail."[28] When news of Sam's "lamentable failure" in Washington reached Nevada, the *Reese River Reveille* rubbed salt in the wound: the lecturer "is 'played,'" the editors declared. "His wit was genuine on the Pacific slope," but no longer. The editors of the *Brooklyn Eagle* quipped that Bret Harte "seems to have gone East and died out, while Twain seems to have died out and gone East." Not the least of the problems with "Artemus Ward, Humorist" was Sam's failure to distinguish between his own and Ward's humor. Their jokes were so intermingled that the Washington correspondent of the *Boston Advertiser* alleged that Sam's listeners could not determine which yarns were his and which he had lifted from Ward, in effect accusing him, not for the first time, of plagiarism. Sam as much as admitted the force of such criticism in a letter to Livy three weeks after switching to the new lecture. He was "patching" it "all the time—trying to weed Artemus out of it & work myself *in*. What I say *fetches* 'em—but what *he* says don't."[29]

The reviews were no better during the final week in October. While the Wilmington, Delaware, *Every Evening* ("exceedingly pleasant") and Wilmington *Commercial* ("interesting") paid polite lip service to his appearance, the *Delaware Gazette* sniffed that Sam's lecture the evening of October 24 had received "the chilling reception . . . it deserved." After his appearance the next evening in Norristown, Pennsylvania, the *Norristown Independent* carped that Sam's performance "never rose to the dignity of a lecture." The *Norristown Herald and Free Press* not only accused him of fraud but predicted that unless Redpath was "uncommonly skilled," Sam would soon be out of work. Both papers noted that he twice mentioned in the course of his talk that he was underpaid to speak there. The *Berkshire Courier* estimated that "at least three hundred and ninety" of the four hundred auditors in Great Barrington, Massachusetts, the next night "went away dissatisfied and disappointed" with Sam's "plagiaristic lecture," though he reported to Livy that "the lecture went off very handsomely" and had "*convulsed*" the "crowded house."[30] The attendees in Brattleboro, Vermont, the evening of October 30 were similarly dissatisfied, according to the *Manchester Journal*. Everyone who heard the "stale anecdotes and secondhand jokes" seemed "disgusted and disappointed." The *Vermont Phoenix* considered the talk "an insult to the public and a disgrace to the 'bureau' that endorses it." The same lecture that had succeeded in Great Barrington was merely "received with the gentlest & most well-bred smiles & rippling comfort" in Milford, Massachusetts, on October 31, he wrote Livy.[31]

Sam then faced a major test at the Music Hall in Boston on November 1—for which he was paid $250, his highest fee of the season. Though he competed with Wendell Phillips, who was appearing at Tremont Temple a few hundred yards away the same night, Sam attracted an audience of two thousand and mixed reviews the next morning. "We had a packed house," he reported to Livy, "& if the papers say any disparaging things, don't you believe a single *word* of it, for I never saw a lecture go off so *magnificently* before. I tell you it made me feel like my old self again. I wanted to talk a week." As he feared, however, the reviewers were unimpressed by his performance. The *Boston Post* merely commended him for his "genial tribute" to Ward, which "was listened to with delight from beginning to end." According to the *Boston Journal*, Sam "made his hearers laugh, and laugh heartily and often, and that was what he came there for. . . . Taken as a whole the lecture served its purpose admirably." The *Boston Traveller* presumed to distinguish between the two humorists: "The best joke of the many good jokes of Mark Twain's lecture was the fact that the best jokes attributed to Artemus Ward were the lecturer's own productions." The *Boston Transcript* simply noted that the audience listened "with pleasure." The *Boston Advertiser* not only censured Sam's "rambling history of the life" of Ward but printed a synopsis of the lecture, thus damaging its appeal in the region where the paper circulated.[32]

Sam's visit to Boston on this occasion was noteworthy for another reason: He was invited to lunch the next day at Louis P. Ober's French restaurant on Winter Street to welcome Bret Harte to the East, though Harte had arrived eight months earlier. He was hosted—along with Thomas Bailey Aldrich, James T. Fields, Harte, and Howells—by Ralph Keeler, a California émigré, proofreader for the *Atlantic Monthly*, and author of the travel book *Vagabond Adventures* (1870). The cream of Boston literary society dined on steak, mushrooms, and *omelette souse*, and Howells remembered forty years later the

> idle and aimless and joyful talk-play, beginning and ending nowhere, of eager laughter, of countless good stories from Fields [including "a deliriously blasphemous" one about a can of peaches], of a heat-lightning shimmer of wit from Aldrich, of an occasional concentration of our joint mockeries upon our host, who took it gladly; and amid the discourse, so little improving, but so full of good fellowship, Bret Harte's fleeting dramatization of Clemens's mental attitude toward a symposium of Boston illuminates. "Why, fellows," he spluttered, "this is the dream of Mark's life," and I remember the glance from under Clemens's feathery eyebrows which betrayed his enjoyment of the fun.

Howells misread Sam's facial expression. Far from enjoying it, he clearly resented Harte's cheeky comment. Sam soon asked Bliss to send copies of *The*

Innocents Abroad "marked with my compliments" to Aldrich, Howells (who had reviewed it in the *Atlantic Monthly*), and Keeler, but not to Harte, who had helped him edit the manuscript and had reviewed it in the *Overland Monthly*. Rather than fostering their reconciliation, the luncheon exacerbated their estrangement. On a more positive note, Keeler joined Sam on his speaking dates over the next few weeks. "He often went out with me to the small lecture-towns in the neighborhood of Boston," Sam remembered in 1898. "These lay within an hour of town, & we usually started at six or thereabouts, & returned to the city in the morning. It took about a month to do these Boston annexes, & that was the easiest & pleasantest month of the four or five which constituted the 'lecture season.'"[33]

Despite his modest success on the boards in Boston, Sam continued to receive consistently equivocal to hostile reviews, especially in small cities, when he returned to the road. The Exeter, New Hampshire, *News-Letter* ("this plagiaristic lecture . . . is lamentably deficient in originality"), the Malden, Massachusetts, *Mirror* ("a "patchwork" of "anecdotal beads, threaded with a . . . filament of tattered biography"), the Malden *Messenger* ("it was difficult to tell which was Ward and which was Twain"), the *Worcester Gazette* ("rather thin"), and the *Worcester Spy* ("very silly") all disparaged the talk. Sam griped to Livy after his appearance in Worcester that he had just spoken "to 1700 of the staidest, puritanical people you ever saw—one of the hardest gangs to move, that ever was. By George the next time I come here I mean to put some cathartic pills in my lecture." The *Manchester Union* ("some very silly jokes . . . beneath the dignity of a clown in the circus"), the Haverhill, Massachusetts, *Gazette* ("trifling chatter"), and the *Haverhill Bulletin* ("small potatoes") expressed similar opinions. Sam obviously was discouraged by such criticism, grousing to Livy, "Lecturing is hateful, but it must come to an end yet." On the other hand, he enjoyed some home cooking in Hartford on November 8. "No lecturer of the season has had such a hearty welcome" as he enjoyed before a "vast audience" at Allyn Hall. "There is not an abundance of material for a sketch of Artemus Ward," the *Hartford Courant* acknowledged in an unsigned review probably written by Charles Dudley Warner, "but Mr. Clemens made the most of it, and the slender thread of the narrative was a string for endless stories and happy hits."[34]

During the brief intermission in his schedule, Livy was adamant that Sam would not long lecture for a living. Without the help of her husband she had interviewed and hired servants, with whom in turn she managed the house and cared for their son. As Horst Kruse notes, Sam "left the burden of settling in wholly to Olivia." As she wrote him after he left, "I *can not* and I *will not* think about your being away from me this way every year, it is not half living—if in order to sustain our present mode of living you are obliged to do that, then we will change our mode of living." They would practice small economies—for example, "we will board or live in a small cottage and keep one servant, will live near the horse cars so that I can get along without a horse and carriage." Simplify, simplify. Even as she designed the floor plan of their new house, she prepared a family budget. With five hundred dollars a month from her inheritance and Sam's three hundred dollars a month from his "regular work" for the magazines, as well as royalties from his books, she calculated, they could cover their bills. If Sam earned two thousand dollars a year by lecturing "*one month* in New England during the Winter*," they could continue to send Sam's mother Jane Clemens an allowance and afford a few luxuries. After Redpath notified him in July 1872 that he had already received promises of seven or eight thousand dollars in speaking fees for him during the next season, Sam apprised the agent that he planned never to "lecture again more than one month in one season, & then only in the large cities—this, of course, is supposing that I remain pecuniarily able to follow such a course." Though he had "been offered *$10,000* to lecture *one month*, next winter, before the associations of the principal cities, or $5,000 for 12 nights," he declined both offers because he was still working on *Roughing It* "& shall not get it done as soon as I desire, if I drift off to other things." Meanwhile, Livy was consumed with domestic anxieties. She pled with Sam to "teach me a 'don't care' spirit, as regards cooks and the like. . . . I believe there is nothing that sooner ruins the happiness of a family than a worrying woman." Livy clearly bemoaned her green widowhood, regretting Sam's long absences. As she eventually admitted to her mother, "I should like to put my head in your lap and cry just a little bit. . . . I have four servants to manage, I have a glorious husband to try and be a woman for, but sometimes I would like to lie down and give it all up—I feel so incompetent for anything." She realized "that he will make more in the long run by writing than by lecturing, but it is a great temptation to him when they offer him such enormous prices" to tour.[35]

After speaking before "a most delightful & jolly little audience" in Randolph, Massachusetts, the evening of November 10—the house was "two-thirds full," not one-third empty, Sam reported to Livy—he enjoyed a three-day weekend in Boston, a brief respite from the rigors of the road. He dined with the Boston Press Club on Saturday, November 11, crossing paths with Charles Carleton Coffin, a popular Civil War memoirist; Albert A. Folsom, superintendent of the Boston and Providence Railroad; Henry S. Olcott, cofounder and first president of the Theosophical Society; William S. Robinson (aka Warrington), the Boston correspondent of the *Springfield Republican*; and the impresarios Richard M. Field of the Boston Museum and Henry A. McGlenen of the Boston Theatre. He briefly addressed the group, reminiscing about his career as a reporter in the West, according to the *Boston Transcript*, "and, strange to say, the more unfortunate his experiences were, the more uproarious was the laughter which greeted their recital." Unfortunately, it was a "cold-water dinner" without wine or liquor, he complained to Livy, so "the flow of impromptu wit & wisdom" was so flat that "the thing got so melancholy" and the party "broke up at 10.30."[36]

The next day he went to lunch with his new best friends Aldrich, Howells, and Keeler, and Aldrich invited him home for dinner. Lilian Aldrich recalled the catastrophe in her autobiography. She thought he was a no-name drunk, a stray animal who had followed her husband home. Sam "showed marked inability to stand perpendicular, but swayed from side to side, and had also difficulty with his speech; he did not stammer exactly, but after each word he placed a period." The would-be hostess threw a "wet blanket" over the "gay laughter" of the men until "a cold and repellent frost . . . set in" and the visitor left without an invitation to join them in the dining room. Sam never forgave the slight. He privately fumed in 1893 that Lilian was "an idiot—an absolute idiot—and does not know it. She is show, show, show—not a genuine fixture in her anywhere—a manifest and transparent humbug—and her husband, the sincerest man that walks . . . tied for life to this vacant hellion, this clothes-rack, this twaddling, blethering, driveling blatherskite!" As late as July 1908 he insisted that she was "a strange and vanity-devoured, detestable woman! I do not believe I could ever learn to like her except on a raft at sea with no other provisions in sight. I conceived an aversion for her the first time I ever saw her, which was thirty-nine years ago, and that aversion has remained with me ever since. She is one of those people who are profusely affectionate, and whose demonstrations disorder your stomach."[37]

Fortunately, Sam's weekend did not end with his introduction to Lilian Aldrich. On Monday evening, November 13, he lectured a second time in Boston to rosy reviews. According to the *Boston Herald*, his talk "was filled up and running over with humorous incidents and anecdotes, which were related in Twain's own irresistible and mirth-provoking style. Some of the anecdotes were new, and the old ones were almost made new by the manner of recital." Back on the road and despite poor weather, Sam packed the house in Portland, Maine, on November 16. The audience of over two thousand was "highly entertained" by his stories, "told in such a droll way that they never failed to excite laughter," according to the *Portland Advertiser*. The Portland *Eastern Argus* noted that "we never saw an audience enjoy itself more heartily than did Mark Twain's last evening" and Sam advised Livy that the "lecture went off magnificently." After spending the weekend in Hartford with Livy and Langdon, he spoke in Philadelphia the evening of November 20 and, despite inclement weather, he packed the Academy of Music there. Virtually all the tickets had been sold a month before. It was his only appearance, besides Boston, for which he was paid $250, and from all indications the fee was justified. "Throughout the entire lecture the audience was kept in a continuous roar of laughter," according to the *Philadelphia Inquirer*. The *Philadelphia Bulletin* ("his manner is agreeable, and those who have enjoyed his writings were not disappointed either in his appearance or his lecture") and the Philadelphia *Press* ("new and delicious lecture") echoed the praise. The next night he spoke before "the usual Beecher people" at Henry Ward Beecher's Plymouth Church in Brooklyn and his success "heartily pleased the audience, who frequently testified" to their satisfaction by "applause and laughter." Instead of dismissing the lecture as a "patchwork" of loosely strung "beads," as it had been depicted in Malden two weeks earlier, the *Brooklyn Eagle* described it as a "pleasant bundle of stories bound together by a cord of quaint fancy." According to the *Brooklyn Times*, Sam's audience was "heartily pleased" by the talk, which prompted "continuous fits of laughter." The *Brooklyn Union* commended "his quaint, apparently unconcerned manner and comical drawling tone." After the lecture, Moses Beach, another of the pilgrims from the *Quaker City* cruise in 1867, hosted a reception for Sam at his mansion on Columbia Street.[38]

Then followed another week of almost unbroken humiliations. Despite his earlier misgivings, Sam trudged to Rondout, New York, where the local *Freeman* considered the talk "in some degree a disappointment, though funny. Mark was by no means half as humorous as in his last lecture" there three years earlier and further noted, "There was more of Artemus than of Mark in the lecture." Sam was belittled in the Easton, Pennsylvania, *Express* on November 24 as a "lamentable failure" flogging an "abortive lecture." After his appearance in Bennington, Vermont, on November 27 he bragged to Livy about a success of sorts. He had spoken before a "good house, but they laughed too much. A great fault with this lecture is that I have no way of turning it into a serious & instructive vein at will." The *Newark Advertiser* on November 30 declared that Sam had lectured in the Opera House there before "so many empty seats" because many who had "heard him once did not care to suffer the infliction the second time. . . . It was about the dullest entertainment ever given here" and "as a lecturer he does not seem to be a success." Discouraged by this chorus of woe, Sam crossed the Hudson River, registered at the St. Nicholas Hotel (again), and over the next two days began to prepare yet another lecture he gleaned from the manuscript of *Roughing It*. He returned to the boards on December 1 in Oswego, New York, and limped along with the Ward lecture for another week in such towns as Homer and Auburn. He appeared in Geneva on December 4 before "a good house—good in numbers, and appreciative in character." Afterward he was approached by a middle-aged woman who introduced herself as Kitty Shoot, one of his sweethearts back in Hannibal. She seemed to him like a waif "from some vague world I had lived in ages & ages ago—myths—creatures of a dream." But, more to the point, the Geneva *Gazette* was underwhelmed by Sam's lecture, reporting the next day that he appeared "very—*tired,* some might denominate it even less complimentarily." He allegedly declared during this week, too, that he was "so sick" of the Ward lecture, adding, "It makes me g-a-g to think of it." In Syracuse two nights later, however, he pleased an "immense audience" at the Wieting Opera House, according to the Syracuse *Standard*.[39]

After a six-week slog through the lyceums with "Memories of Artemus Ward," Sam finally debuted "Roughing It on the Silver Frontier" before "the largest audience of the season" at Sprague's Hall in Warsaw, New York, on December 7. Sam had reason at first to be encouraged. His friend David Gray puffed in the *Buffalo Courier* the "brilliantly" delivered "*mélange* of passages" culled from his forthcoming book—"grave and gay, descriptive and humorous,—which are in his very best style." Gray predicted "a hearty reception for the new lecture." The reviewer for the Warsaw *Western New Yorker* similarly praised its "descriptive passages of rare beauty" and its "droll, extravagant humor." Sam was so elated by its reception that, during a stop in Buffalo that night, he telegraphed Redpath to "notify all hands that from this date I shall talk nothing but selections from my forthcoming book Roughing it." He wrote him a day or two later that he liked his new lecture "first rate,—better than any I have ever had except the 'Vandal'—three years ago."[40]

But it was a false start. Sam delivered the new talk a second time the evening of December 8 at the Fredonia Normal School with his mother and sister in attendance and bombed. Willard McKinstry of the *Fredonia Censor* reported that "a lean cadaverous-looking speaker" entered and stood "upon the platform for five minutes like a schoolboy who has forgotten his 'piece'" and then delivered "a dismal failure" of a lecture. It was a "thin diet for an evening's entertainment. . . . In appearing this season with . . . such lack of preparation, making a tour 'on his reputation' . . . he does an injustice . . . to himself and the societies employing him." Sam was not deaf to the criticism. As he admitted to Mother Fairbanks the same evening he flopped in Fredonia, he had been "writing a new, tip-top lecture about California & Nevada—been at it all night—am still at it & pretty nearly dead with fatigue." He planned to continue to work on it "in the cars till midnight, & then sleep half the day in Toledo & study the rest. If I am in good condition there, I shall deliver it," but if not he expected to repeat the Ward lecture "two or three nights longer & go on studying. . . . Have already tried the new lecture in two villages" and "made a tip-top success in one, but was floored by fatigue & exhaustion of body & mind & made a dismal failure in the other." He admitted to Redpath that he had been "so tired out" in Fredonia that he "came near going to sleep on the platform."[41]

The evening of December 9 in Erie, Pennsylvania, after realizing that the "Roughing It" talk required more pencil-whipping, he reverted to the Ward lecture. It enjoyed no more success than before he abandoned it. The reporter for the Erie *Observer* penned a brutal notice: Sam had "neither the looks, the voice, nor the manner of a popular lecturer, serious or humorous." He accused Sam of trying to steal Ward's thunder if not the limelight: his performance was a "decided failure,"

> a pitiful attempt to ape the style of Artemus Ward, in which he only succeeded in reaching the standard of a negro minstrel. The genial "showman" was a natural comedian. . . . The impropriety of discussing the life and character of a dead popular favorite in a burlesque vein is manifest to every person of refined taste, and it comes with peculiarly bad grace from a brother humorist who aspires to rank among the first class talent of his profession.

The *Erie Gazette* was scarcely more kind, lambasting Sam's "flat" attempt to impersonate "the inimitable Artemus."[42]

He had better luck at the next stops on his trek across northern Ohio and Michigan. He dined with his friend David Ross Locke (aka Petroleum V. Nasby) in Toledo and his talk at White's Hall in the city the evening of December 11 "was frequently applauded," according to the *Toledo Blade*, and was "one of the most remunerative" in the lyceum course there. He "kept his audience in a continual roar of laughter" the next night in Ann Arbor, and the *Ann Arbor Chronicle*, the University of Michigan campus newspaper, reported that, despite "the manifest boorishness of certain members of the professional departments"—that is, the older students—"all appeared satisfied when the lecture closed." Sam spoke before an "unusually fine audience" at Union Hall in Jackson, Michigan, the next evening. The reviewer for the *Jackson Citizen Patriot* chided the speaker for his "rather monotonous and tiresome" tone and implied by quantifying his fee that he was overpaid: "For this lecture, . . . Mr. Clemens received $125—or nearly two dollars per minute."[43]

Sam recovered the next night in Lansing, where he delivered the "Roughing It" talk before five hundred members of the Students' Lecture Association in Mead's Hall at the State Agricultural College, today Michigan State University. According to a transcript of his remarks printed in the Lansing

State Republican, Sam readily allowed that he was springing a new talk on them without warning: "when I first started out on this missionary expedition, I had a lecture which I liked very well, but by-and-by I got tired of telling that same old stuff over and over again, and then I got up another lecture, and after that another one, and I am tired of that: so I just thought tonight I would try something fresh, if you are willing." The *Chicago Tribune* reported that the "very large" audience was "apparently very appreciative" of the performance although "many of the anecdotes and jokes were familiar" to them. Sam repeated "Roughing It" the next night before a crowd of thirteen hundred at Luce's Hall in Grand Rapids to mixed reviews by the *Grand Rapids Eagle* (which claimed the audience got "their money's worth") and the *Grand Rapids Democrat* ("we think it was a failure, and as far as we could judge, the audience were pretty much of that opinion").[44]

Then something of a disaster occurred in Kalamazoo. Sam packed Union Hall the evening of December 16 with the largest audience since the whiskey warrior John B. Gough had spoken there the year before. The *Kalamazoo Gazette* asserted that no lecturer in the city since Gough "had more perfect control of his subject, himself, and his listeners. A single word sometimes, said in that slow, droll, calculating way, would be like the spark in a powder magazine." But the *Gazette* also conceded that its contemporary, the *Kalamazoo Telegraph*, did "not agree in their estimate of Mark's lecture." And how. "No lecturer that has visited Kalamazoo, unless Gough be excepted, ever drew together a larger or more cultivated audience," the critic for the *Telegraph* began,

and no lecturer, we regret to say, ever more completely disappointed his hearers. The substitute for a lecture which Mr. Clemens foisted upon his audience was an insult to their intelligence and capacity. We have no ill-will toward Mark Twain. On the contrary, we attended the lecture very friendly disposed, have read his writing with pleasure, and regard his "Innocents Abroad" as containing more real humor than any book ever published in America. But we are compelled to pronounce his performance Saturday evening an imposition on both the Young Men's Library Association and the audience who listened to it. This is not Twain's first season on the lecture platform. Heretofore he has demonstrated his ability to give instructive and entertaining lectures, but in resorting to such a makeshift as we heard Saturday night he is guilty of obtaining money from the Society and the public under false pretenses. Capable of furnishing a good lecture, Mr. Clemens had no right to impose upon his hearers any such desultory trash as they were subjected to. They had a right to expect something worth coming out to hear, and if he is too lazy or unmindful to do justice to himself or an audience he ought not to lecture at all. He should have given the lecture he contracted to deliver, or something equally good, in its stead, and not put us off with a rambling, disconnected talk about a hackneyed subject, *sans* wit, *sans* information, *sans* sense.

The press was obliged "to expose such impositions," the *Telegraph* concluded, "and if other journals remain silent, we shall not."[45]

It was not the triumphant note on which Sam had hoped to enter the gates of Chicago, but to Chicago he proceeded nevertheless for a two-night engagement. He entrained from Kalamazoo early in the morning of December 17 and arrived in the Windy City later that day. He was appalled by the devastation still apparent in the city two months after the Great Chicago Fire. "There is literally no Chicago *here*," he remarked to Livy. "I recognize *nothing* here that ever I saw before." He delivered the "Roughing It" lecture before "immense" audiences at the Michigan Avenue Baptist Church the evening of December 18—"every seat in the house, 400 chairs in the aisles, and standing-room for 200 or 300"—and at the Union Park Congregational Church the next night. All of the local newspapers attested to the brilliance of his talks. The *Chicago Times* asserted that his "genius drew together one of the largest as well as the most intelligent audiences that have ever gathered in this city to hear a lecture." The *Chicago Tribune* averred that he was "truly eloquent in his glowing descriptions of California scenery" and, according to the *Chicago Post*, he "convulsed the audience with laughter" with his "droll yarns of life in the bush." The *Chicago Mail* warned that "those who do not hear Twain . . . will have cause for perpetual sorrow." Both the *Tribune* ("his face . . . is as grave and solemn as the visage of an undertaker when screwing down a coffin-lid") and the *Post* (claiming Sam exhibited the countenance of a "bereaved Vermonter who had just come from the death-bed of his mother-in-law and is looking for a sexton") remarked on his physiognomy onstage. After his first appearance in the city, he entertained several Chicago journalists at the home of Reeves Jackson and his new wife, the former Julia Newell, both of them his friends from the *Quaker City* voyage. Jackson had recently been appointed surgeon-in-chief of the Woman's Hospital of the State of Illinois and, while in the city, Sam donated twenty-five dollars to the hospital.[46] Unfortunately, the *Chicago Tribune* printed almost verbatim the version of "Roughing It on the Silver Frontier" he delivered in Chicago. As a result, the commercial value of the lecture was virtually destroyed in the region. Worse yet, the *Cincinnati Gazette* reprinted the lecture from the *Tribune*, effectively expanding the territory where its value had depreciated. Sam considered such reporting the equivalent of theft of his intellectual property. "If these devils incarnate only appreciated what suffering they inflict with their infernal synopses, maybe they would try to have humanity enough to refrain," he groused to Livy.[47]

As an upshot of the publication of the text of "Roughing It," Sam again delivered his Artemus Ward lecture to audiences in most of the eight Illinois towns remaining on his itinerary through the end of the year—with predictable results. The *Cairo Bulletin* cited a "local authority" who disparaged the "silly, senseless mass of stale witticisms" Sam foisted on an audience in Aurora, adding that he had perpetrated a "huge and merciless" joke on the audience and charged "$100 for such an effort." Sam spoke the next night in Princeton, Illinois, and the local paper there objected that he only "passably told" Ward's anecdotes and that his performance was "not in any way up to the standard of the original storyteller."[48]

Sam spent most of his four-day hiatus over Yuletide back in Chicago polishing and memorizing his "Roughing It" talk. "I have worked hard all day yesterday—& till late last night—& all day again & till *now*—on my lecture—& it is re-written—& is *much* more satisfactory," he wrote Livy on Christmas Day. The next day he reported from Champaign that his "new lecture is about licked into shape, & this afternoon, after trimming at it all day I memorized one-fourth of it. Shall commit another fourth tomorrow, maybe more." He had "entirely rewritten & memorized my lecture," he assured his mother, "& have at last got it so that I could even 'fetch' that frozen Fredonia audience with it now, without a bit of trouble." The *Chicago Tribune* "*printed* my new speech in full," he bellyached to Mother Fairbanks, "& I had to sacrifice most of my sleeping time for 5 days & nights in the getting up of an entirely *new* lecture." He also deplored the "execrable hotel" where he had registered in Champaign so he checked out to find a better one. As a result, he slept in a chair in an unheated room in Tuscola. "I made an ass of myself leaving a mean hotel at midnight to hunt up a good one 20 miles away," he admitted to Livy the next day. "Hunted up the hotel myself & carried my own baggage. Found *every* bed in the house occupied. . . . My splendid overcoat earned its cost—every cent of it." The next day he traveled to Danville and registered at the St. James Hotel before all the rooms were filled. That evening he apparently switched back to his "Roughing It" talk, though the Danville *Commercial* noncommittally stated that "like every other lecture, some appreciated it and others did not." The reporter was apparently lukewarm toward literary humor: "Take Doesticks, Billings, Twain, Fat Contributor . . . most of what they say is chaff." Livy tried to comfort him from afar: "I am so sorry that you have been annoyed by those reporters again." After speaking in Paris, Illinois, the evening of December 30, Sam closed the year on a glum note. As he wrote Livy, "I never want to go through such a terrific siege again."[49]

But the new year began on much the same note as the old one had ended. He delivered "Roughing It" under the auspices of the YMCA at Association Hall on North Illinois Street in Indianapolis the night of January 1, 1872, to mixed reviews. Whereas the Indianapolis *People* averred that the lecture "read better than it was spoken," the Indianapolis *Journal* commended the "matchless, indescribable, whimsical, and intrepid humorist" for speaking before "a large, refined, and very appreciative audience." On his part, Sam harbored no doubt that he had exceeded expectations. As he wrote Redpath the next day, he "had a splendid time with a splendid audience in Indianapolis last night—a perfectly jammed house, just as I have had all the time out here." Lest he be misunderstood about his future plans, he added that he despised "the 'Artemus Ward' talk & won't talk it anymore." The "Roughing It" lecture "was unquestionably the most successful in Mark Twain's repertoire for the season," as Fred Lorch has noted.[50] With the turn into the new year, Sam's speaking tour became a promotional tour for the forthcoming book.

Not that he sold many advance copies at his next stop. Sponsored by the local Christian Associations, he delivered the "Roughing It" lecture at the packed Opera House in Logansport, Indiana, the evening of January 2. As Paul Fatout remarks, however, the Logansport *Sun* "roasted the lecturer to a rich and crispy brown." No one unfit to be a "candidate for a lunatic as(s)-ylum, or who meant to be sarcastic, would dignify the performance by calling it a lecture," the reporter alleged, and Sam's "anecdotes and witticisms were mostly old and stale." As a speaker, Sam was "a 'magnificent' fizzle, or a first-class humbug." In any event, the *Sun* concluded, "let us have no more such performances under the auspices of the Christian Associations."[51]

After completing the western leg of his road show, he began to follow a slow eastward arc toward Hartford and home. He registered at the Beckel House in Dayton, Ohio, and spoke there to "hearty laughter and frequent applause" before a "whopping house" the evening of January 4. The next night he addressed an "appreciative" audience in Columbus. "It is impossible to imitate on paper his gestures and manner of speaking," the *Ohio State Journal* observed. "One must hear him to realize the effect of what he says." After the lecture, rather than rise at 2:00 a.m. to catch a train to Wooster, he chartered a locomotive for seventy-five dollars to carry him ninety-five miles to his next lecture date. There he delivered a talk, according to the *Wooster Republican*, "abounding in humorous and graphic description" to "a fair audience" in Arcadome Hall. But Sam, on his part, was not so sanguine. As he wrote Livy from Wooster, "I *do* hate lecturing & I shall try hard to have as little as possible of it to do hereafter." Two months later he had not forgotten or forgiven "the vexation, the profanity & the unspeakable indignation of that long day & the talking to the dullest & stupidest of audiences that memorable night. A place so out of the way that my usual telegraphing cost me $18 that day!" In Salem, Ohio, two nights later, Sam's lecture failed to please his audience, according to the Salem *Republican*, because "no one could tell when he told the truth or when he was indulging in fiction"—a curious critique of a humorous talk. Before he was finished "his hearers had lost confidence in his sayings, and did not *expect* to be told anything on which they could rely." Sam was no less disgusted with his audience. As he wrote Livy after his appearance in Salem, "slowly this lecturing penance drags toward the end. Heaven knows I shall be glad when I get far away from these country communities of wooden-heads. Whenever I want to go away from New England again, lecturing, please show these letters to me & bring me to my senses. How I do chafe & sweat when I count up the Dutch audiences I have yet to play the fool before." Two nights later at Washington Hall in Wheeling, West Virginia, "crowded with the most intelligent and refined people of the city," according to the *Wheeling Intelligencer*, Sam was welcomed by "almost continuous laughter and applause." The Wheeling *Register* added that "after listening to his inexhaustible fund of stories, his exquisite humor and style," its reporter believed "that the world would be better if we had more Mark Twains." Sam, too, was gratified by his reception in Wheeling from "the livest, quickest audience I almost ever saw in my life."[52]

He arrived in Pittsburgh in the afternoon of January 11 and spoke before the "largest audience that had ever attended a lecture" at Library Hall that evening. "Great numbers were turned away—couldn't get in," he bragged to Livy; "stage was jam-full; all the private boxes full." The local newspapers were generous in their praise for his performance the next day. The *Pittsburgh Commercial* commended his "telling jokes, humorous hits, and apparently unconsciously delivered sallies of wit which convulsed the entire audience in the most uproarious laughter." The *Pittsburgh Gazette* similarly lauded his "compound of brilliant description and hard material facts. . . . The effort financially to the managers, happily to the lecturer, and enjoyably in the highest degree to the people, was a signal success." Three days later, however, after Sam apparently complained that some local reporters had "stole the *good* (?) points out of his recent lecture and published them," the screw turned. The *Gazette* suddenly asserted that Sam was "a much overestimated clown. He has little originality and less genuine humor. He would hardly fill the bill for a police reporter on a first class journal." This critic implied that Sam's lecture had been gleaned from "the almanac literature of the day," thus "he is anxious that no word he speaks on the stage should be published," and concluded that the sponsors of his lecture should apologize for "the gross fraud perpetrated on the intellectual community by introducing such a mountebank as Mark Twain."[53]

Even before the *Gazette* reversed course and expressed skepticism about his speaking abilities, Sam had soured on his prospects for critical success in small-town Pennsylvania. Kittanning, where he spoke on January 12, was "a filthy, stupid, hateful Dutch village, like *all* Pennsylvania," he informed Livy. To judge from the reviews of his performance in Harrisburg on January 18, his mood had not lifted after crossing the state. Sam addressed a standing-room only audience in the main hall of the courthouse—according to the *Harrisburg Patriot*, "the only vacant space left when the lecturer commenced was his mouth, and that nobody crowded down his throat was astonishing." But the *Patriot* also conceded that "half of the finer points of the lecture" were lost on "those who have never been" to Nevada. The Harrisburg *Mercury* remarked in passing that Sam's lecture had been "a grand success oratorically and facetiously" but the *Harrisburg Telegraph* begged to differ. "Before the close" of Sam's talk, many in the audience "heartily wished they had not come." "Roughing It" was, in the opinion of this reviewer, "the roughest excuse for a lecture we ever heard. The peculiar drawling style of the lecturer does not add to the interest of the subject—many of the jokes were very far-fetched, and the lecture itself was as devoid of interesting matter as it well could be. It was indeed all 'chaff,' hardly a good seed in the lot. Any person hearing Mark Twain once won't desire to hear him soon again."[54]

Sam likely failed to read this review in the *Telegraph* because he wrote Livy the next day that all the recent towns where he had appeared "insist on my coming back." Certainly his claim applied to Lancaster, where he spoke the evening of January 19. He had "a magnificent time" there before a "brilliant" capacity crowd, he bragged, and the Lancaster *Intelligencer* ("convulsed them with laughter by his humorous sketches") and the Lancaster *Express* ("never appeared before a finer and more appreciative audience") concurred. He was now in the home stretch of his detested campaign. His appearance in Carlisle, Pennsylvania, on January 22 was "more largely attended than any of the previous ones in the course" there, with about six hundred people present according to the *Carlisle Herald*. The next evening at the Maryland Institute in Baltimore, he "kept his audience in the best humor for over one and a half hours," the *Baltimore Sun* reported. At a critical juncture in the lecture, thinking "there was a large number" of people seated on the platform behind him, he gestured over his shoulder and joked that he had "brought some specimens" of the border ruffian with him. But only two persons were there, one of them Mayor Joshua Vansant. He railed to New York the next day, registered at the St. Nicholas Hotel, and spoke that evening in Steinway Hall before a crowd of two thousand, arguably "the most enormous audience ever collected at any lecture in New York," at a benefit for the Mercantile

Library Association. Before the doors were even opened, an estimated thirteen hundred dollars in tickets had been sold. In an unpublished essay written a few months later, Sam recalled that the association "got up a 'good old-fashioned' course that was perfectly saturated with morals & instruction, & at the end of it came out wise & holy, but—in debt. I went there with my 'degrading influence,' & with a single stalwart effort cleared off the debt & left twelve or fifteen hundred dollars in the committee's coffers." The local dailies also hailed his performance the next morning. The *New York Times* reported that the "lecture was a decided success, and much gratified all who heard it" and that the effort "seemed to require no effort at all on the part of the humorous story-teller." The *New York Herald* praised his "exceptionally funny" talk. John Hay, who had earned a reputation as a dialect poet with his *Pike County Ballads* (1871), delivered a decisive assessment of his friend's talents in the *New York Tribune*: "There was hardly a minute of silence during the hour. Peals of laughter followed every phrase. . . . He is the finest living delineator of the true Pike accent. . . . He is a true humorist, endowed with that indefinable power to make men laugh which is worth . . . more than the highest genius or the greatest learning." While in the city, Sam apparently also visited the famous medium James Vincent Mansfield. In a passage deleted from chapter 48 of *Life on the Mississippi* (1883), he remembered a séance ten years earlier when "with a couple of friends" he inquired "after my brother, lost in the *Pennsylvania*" disaster. In this version of the incident, he received through the medium answers to his questions that consisted of nothing but "sloppy twaddle" and added that if "this man is not the paltriest fraud that lives, I owe him an apology."[55]

Exploiting a five-day gap in his schedule, Sam returned to Hartford, probably the next day, his first trip home since his brief visit in mid-November. The evening of January 28 he attended a performance of the Fisk University Jubilee Singers, a choir of former slaves, at the Asylum Hill Church. The reviewer for the *Hartford Courant*, probably Charley Warner, observed that it was "the first time that we at the north have heard the genuine songs of their race, executed with their faith and their feeling. It was like a revelation. . . . One heard in those strange and plaintive melodies the sadness and the hope of a trusting and a really joyous race." A year later, Sam recalled that he

heard them sing once, & I would walk seven miles to hear them sing again. You will recognize that this is strong language for me to use, when you remember that I never was fond of pedestrianism. . . . I think these gentlemen and ladies make eloquent music—and what is as much to the point, they reproduce the true melody of the plantations, and are the only persons I ever heard accomplish this on the public platform. The so-called "Negro minstrels" simply misrepresent the thing; I do not think they ever saw a plantation or ever heard a slave sing. I was reared in the South, and my father owned slaves, and I do not know when anything has so moved me as did the plaintive melodies of the Jubilee Singers. It was the first time for twenty-five or thirty years that I had heard such songs, or heard them sung in the genuine old way—and it is a way, I think, that white people cannot imitate—and never can, for that matter, for one must have been a slave himself in order to feel what that life was and so convey the pathos of it in the music.

Over the years, Sam heard the Jubilee Singers perform five times, and he championed their talent to the end of his life. As he wrote in March 1875, he thought the music of the Fisk Jubilee Singers "utterly beautiful . . . and it moves me infinitely more than any other music can."[56]

Sam returned to the platform before a full house in Jersey City, New Jersey, the night of January 30. The Jersey City *Journal*, while conceding that "Mark is no orator," nevertheless declared that "he is an amusing talker with a droll drawl, a nasal twang, and an indescribably odd fashion of 'standing around' and moving his hands and his features as if he didn't know what to do with them." More important, he "made people laugh, and that was what he came for, but we would rather read his fun than have it from him by word of mouth." Following the lecture, he ferried back across the Hudson to New York and overnighted at the St. Nicholas. The next evening he lectured in Paterson, New Jersey. The Paterson *Press* lauded his talk as an "inimitable mixture of fact and fancy, seriousness and fun, absurd pathos and sentiment." Finally, he ended his regular speaking tour the evening of February 1 in Troy, New York. According to the Troy *Press*, Rand's Hall was "jammed" and Sam again kept his listeners "constantly convulsed with laughter." He hurried back to Hartford the next day to celebrate his second wedding anniversary with Livy. But at least he had closed on an upbeat note "the most detestable lecture campaign that ever was—a campaign," he wrote Mother Fairbanks, "which was one eternal worry with contriving new lectures & being dissatisfied with them. I think I built & delivered 6 different lectures during the season."[57]

Nor had it been particularly remunerative. Except in Boston and Philadelphia ($250) and Newark ($200), he was paid a modest fee of $125 or $150 per engagement. Through the end of January his income from the tour totaled slightly less than $10,000, but he ended the campaign with less than $1,500 to show "for all that work & misery," he complained, because he had "squandered it thoughtlessly paying debts." Or as he explained to Livy, "It has all gone & is going, for those necessaries of life—debts. Every night the question is, Well, who does *this* day's earnings belong to?—&

away it goes." In all, he had liquidated some $4,000 of accumulated lia-
bilities. "You are the last on my list," he notified Redpath. "Shall begin to
pay you in a few days and then I shall be a free man again." He insisted to
Mary Fairbanks, "I ain't going to ever lecture any more—unless I get in
debt again."[58]

Four days later Sam was back in New York, again registering at the St.
Nicholas, to attend Horace Greeley's sixty-first birthday celebration. Several hundred national and civic leaders assembled at a private home on Fifty-
Seventh Street, among them P. T. Barnum, Samuel Bowles, Noah Brooks,
William Conant Church, David Croly, Anna Dickinson, Mary Mapes
Dodge, Edward Eggleston, Murat Halstead, Joseph R. Hawley, John Hay,
and Whitelaw Reid. During the evening Sam chatted with Bret Harte, an
indication that they were finally reconciling. In any case, as the star author
of the American Publishing Company, Sam soon urged Bliss to contract
with Harte for a novel, eventually published under the title *Gabriel Conroy*
(1875), and Harte shared with Twain details of his financial negotiations
with several publishers so that neither of them would underprice the other
and ruin the market.[59]

Though Sam's speaking tour had nominally ended in Troy the evening of
February 1, Redpath had scheduled him to deliver "Roughing It" twice later
in the month in cities only a few hours distant from Hartford. The first of
these dates, at the Opera House in Danbury, Connecticut, on February 21,
was "a failure and a disappointment," according to the *Danbury News*. "The
evening was so dreadfully tedious, and the humor was so wickedly sparse,
that the people became tired, and not a few disgusted." The critic even took
an ad hominem swipe at the speaker: Sam resembled "a person who had
served long and faithfully in a brickyard without any fore-piece to his cap"
and he was "not a beautiful man."[60]

Rather than return to Hartford after his talk, Sam continued to New
York to attend a dinner at the St. James Hotel the evening of February 23
to celebrate the installation of Richard Henry Stoddard as editor of the
monthly magazine *Aldine*. The dozens of guests included Vice President
Schuyler Colfax; the novelist Julian Hawthorne, son of Nathaniel; the poet
E. C. Stedman; the Reverend De Witt Talmage, whom Sam had once attacked in his *Galaxy* column for his classism; the travel writer Bayard Taylor; and a cadre of the usual suspects, including John Hay and Whitelaw
Reid. After the dinner, Sam "excused himself from making a speech" by
delivering "a felicitous speech of some length, abounding with touches of
humor peculiar to himself," according to the *New York Tribune*, and it was

greeted "with shouts of laughter." "I have made a great many happy *impromptu* speeches," Sam declared, but at least "I had time to prepare them." He spent the night at the St. James before returning to Hartford.[61]

During this final week in February the Clemenses were visited by Joe Goodman and his wife, who were passing through Hartford en route back to the West. Goodman remembered later that Sam's manners had reverted to normal in the year since they had met in Buffalo. Thomas Wentworth Higginson had dined with the Clemenses at the Hooker home soon after they settled in Hartford and "heard him say grace at table," which "was like asking a blessing over Ethiopian minstrels. But he had no wine at his table and that seemed to make the grace a genuine thing." When Goodman saw him in Hartford, however, Sam no longer asked Livy "for permission to smuggle whisky" into the house. Instead,

> It stood on the sideboard as boldly as in a bar room. And when we sat down at table and I bowed my head in silence, there was no blessing forthcoming. I sought the first opportunity to inquire of Mark what the omission meant. He said he had tried his best to keep up the practice of saying grace to please his wife, but that it had come to seem too much like mockery to him, and he had asked her to relieve him from playing the part of a hypocrite, and she had agreed it was probably as well that he should, and so they had dropped it.

Sam denied the existence of hell and the divinity of Christ, he wrote Orion, though he still professed to revere Christ as "a sacred Personage."[62] As for Livy, rather than the Christian converting the skeptic, the opposite had occurred. In the rural vernacular, she had "backslid."

Sam delivered his "Roughing It" lecture in Amherst, Massachusetts, the evening of February 27. When Redpath scheduled the engagement in late January, Sam was displeased, whining to the agent that "it looks like the infernalest misfortune that I have got to go there & talk after being out of practice three whole weeks. I shall make a botch of it, for I use no notes whatever, & my memory is execrable." The day before he left Hartford for Amherst he announced to Redpath, "If I had another engagement I'd rot before I'd fill it." His regrets became self-fulfilling prophecy. "We do not know whether the audience had expected too much of the funny Mark Twain from reading his funny book, or whether two hours of nonsense is more than people care for at once or not," the student newspaper at Amherst College observed, "but true it is that they had heard enough of him when he was done." The *Amherst Record* similarly judged his performance "a first-class failure" with "some good hits" but "nearly all of it we had already read." After the lecture Sam enjoyed "a choice collation consisting of oysters, tongue, cold meats, and the like" at the Amherst House. The reception on his behalf "was very enjoyable to all parties, and, in the opinion of some, Mark appears to better advantage at the festive board than upon the platform." Back in Hartford the next evening, Sam and Joe Goodman called on the actor Frank Mayo, their mutual friend from Virginia City, in town to perform at the Opera House.[63] Sam then turned his attention to the most pressing issue on his agenda—the publication and sale of *Roughing It*.

CHAPTER 2

Roughing It in London and Hartford

I am not an ass; I am only the saddle of an ass.

—"The Facts Concerning the Recent Carnival of Crime in Connecticut"

THOUGH THE BOOK had been copyrighted in the United States in December 1871, the first copies of *Roughing It* arrived from the bindery on January 30, 1872, coincident with the close of Sam Clemens's speaking tour. A copy was finally deposited in the Library of Congress on February 19 and the official publication date was set for February 29. In order to secure copyright in Great Britain, Routledge and Company issued the book in London shortly before the American edition was put on the market, thus protecting it from reprinting by Canadian pirates. Sam cooperated fully with publisher Elisha Bliss in the prepublication sales campaign for the book. He published three excerpts from it in the *American Publisher* between May 1871 and January 1872. One of them, the passage about a Pony Express rider that appeared in chapter 8, he considered "by all odds" the "finest piece of writing I ever did." In addition, Sam helped prepare the prospectus or "dummy" of specimen chapters of *Roughing It* that Bliss's book agents exhibited to potential buyers. The agents began to canvass for subscribers in late November 1871, three months before the book became available.[1]

Sam also made a tactical but foolish decision to restrict the number of copies sent to newspapers and magazines for review. He worried that the book would be such a disappointment that widespread publicity of its publication would hamper sales; he "was *afraid* of & didn't want" the "prompt notoriety" of dozens of book notices in papers across the country and in England. He reminded David Gray years later "how I felt about 'Roughing It'—that it would be considered pretty poor stuff, & that therefore I had better not let the press get a chance at it."[2] As a result, review copies of the book were sent only to selected venues, such as the *Atlantic Monthly* and *Hartford Courant*, where Sam could depend on W. D. Howells and Charles Dudley Warner to puff it; to the *Boston Transcript*, where his friends would applaud it; and to the *New York Tribune*, where he expected Whitelaw Reid to assign it to a critic who would favorably blurb it.

At least initially, the critical reception of *Roughing It* went according to this plan, if not entirely to Sam's satisfaction. Howells and Warner predictably praised the book in the *Atlantic* ("singularly entertaining") and *Courant* ("the best picture of frontier mining life that has been written"). Joseph E. Babson (aka Tom Folio) announced in the *Boston Transcript* that the book "will be read not so much for its wisdom as for its wit" and pronounced Sam "almost . . . a comic Plutarch." But Sam underestimated the fund of goodwill he had accrued with Reid at the *Tribune*. To be sure, its longtime book editor, George Ripley of Brook Farm fame, puffed *Roughing It* as "one of the most racy specimens of Mark Twain's savory pleasantries." But the compliment fell short of the rave review Sam expected from the most influential newspaper in the country and his skin was thinner than a potato's. He carped that the *Tribune* had permitted the book to be appraised "by the profound old stick who has done all the Tribune reviews for the last 90 years. The idea of setting such an oyster as that to prating about Humor!" Ripley was, he fumed, as unqualified to comment on *Roughing It* as Josh Billings would be "to write a critique on the *Iliad*." Fortunately, Louise Chandler Moulton, the Boston correspondent of the *Tribune*, also noticed the book in her column on June 10. "For pure fun," according to Moulton, "I know of nothing which has been published this year to compare with 'Roughing It.' . . . It is funny everywhere; perhaps it is funniest of all when he sojourns in Salt Lake City, and learns to understand the Mormons through the revelations of their Gentile neighbors." Sam was mollified for the moment. "I am *content*, now that the book has been praised in the Tribune," he observed in a note of thanks to Moulton, "& so I think you will that honest glow of gratitude that comes into a mother's eyes when a stranger praises her child." But he was not pleased that Bliss had followed his advice and limited the number of venues to which he sent copies for review. He complained to Moulton that his publisher had not sent "a copy of my book to any newspaper to be reviewed, but is only always *going* to do it—so I seem to be publishing a book that attracts not the slightest mention."[3]

In fact, including the comments in the *Atlantic*, *Courant*, *Transcript*, and *Tribune*, *Roughing It* received only twenty-three known critical notices, some of them likely commissioned by book agents. Many of them were perfunctory, as in the St. Louis *Missouri Democrat* ("equal to Mark's *Innocents*"); the Auburn, Massachusetts, *Bulletin* ("brimful of characteristic humor"); the Portland, Maine, *Press* ("one of the best [books] of the season"); the San Francisco *Morning Call* ("full of humor and atrocious woodcuts, even more grotesque than the text"); the *Nashville Union and American* ("irresistibly droll"); and Tom Hood's London *Fun* ("will thoroughly re-establish the reputation of the author of *The Jumping Frog*"). The Quincy, Illinois, *Whig* both extolled the work in March ("certain of a hearty welcome") and denigrated it in December ("unnecessarily and certainly distastefully rough"). The *San Francisco Examiner* offered no comment on the book but reprinted an excerpt of about three hundred words.[4]

On the whole the book was well received. The New York *Independent* commended it "to all who enjoy the wild Western drollery of which Mark Twain is the ablest living master" and the *Portland Transcript* in Maine declared that it was "one huge joke." Some reviewers drew the inevitable comparison to *The Innocents Abroad* (1869), as in the London *Examiner*: Sam's new book was "in some respects superior to" the earlier travelogue, "more consecutive and less fragmentary, but both are almost equally racy and entertaining." The West Coast notices were particularly favorable, as in the *Overland Monthly* (a "vein of broad, robust humor crops out . . . on almost every page"), the *Sacramento Union* ("there is a good deal of stuff in this book, and a great deal too that is amusing"), the *San Francisco Bulletin* ("a spicy, interesting, and instructive book, abounding in brave though brilliant exaggerations"), and the San Francisco *Alta California* ("the information conveyed is so mingled with genuine dry wit and hearty humor, with so many good things so well told, that the reader will never wish to put it down till the very last page is reached"). At worst, some reviews were ambivalent, such as the *Cincinnati Gazette* ("one may not always approve the taste of what is said, yet he can rarely record his dissent without a smile") and the *Utica Herald and Gazette* (which noted that Sam "is not our favorite author" but "there is no doubt that this book will find thousands of readers, and that it will afford them all amusement"). Only the Manchester, New Hampshire, *Guardian* struck an unambiguously sour note: "Mark Twain . . . often falls into the slang of transatlantic journalism, and displays also its characteristic inability to distinguish between the picturesque and the grotesque." Mary Mason Fairbanks was dissatisfied with the book, too. She would not approve of any of his books until he had written something uncharacteristically genteel. "I'm just crazy to have him write one book of *polite literature*," she admitted to Sam's wife Olivia, because "I want him to show the world more of his rich, brilliant imaginings." In late August 1872, in the midst of his doomed campaign for the presidency as the candidate of the Liberal Republicans and only three months before his death, Horace Greeley also expressed a harsh opinion of Sam, in particular of *Roughing It*: "I can't appreciate wit stretched out to three or four hundred pages; wit should be like a flash, but when a man attempts to sustain it all through a large book he generally fails. . . . I think [Artemus Ward] is the best of that class of writers." Still, seventeen years later Sam would contribute twenty dollars to the Greeley Statue Fund.[5]

Despite the paucity of reviews of *Roughing It* in major venues, it achieved commercial success roughly commensurate with its critical reception, though sales numbers differ dramatically depending on the source. Sam claimed that Bliss's book peddlers had enrolled forty-three thousand subscribers before it was issued, and the binding and shipping records of the American Publishing Company tend to corroborate this figure. By the end of February 1872, 10,855 orders had been filled and, as the *Hartford Post* reported, the bindery was shipping some "600 or 800" copies daily. By the end of March, a month after the date of publication, the bindery had shipped 23,645 copies, and in early April Sam received a royalty check in the amount of $10,562 for first-quarter sales. He sent his brother Orion $1,000 of this amount for his help on the book. By the end of May sales totaled 46,122 and a month later 67,395. Sam was more convinced than ever that subscription sales were more lucrative than trade publication. His readers were blue-collar factory hands and farmers who "never go to a bookstore; they have to be hunted down by the canvasser. When a subscription book of mine sells 60,000, I always think I know whither 50,000 of them went. They went to people who don't visit bookstores." But sales of *Roughing It* began to plummet in July, when only 2,645 copies were shipped, and only about 5,000 more copies, bringing the total to slightly over 75,000, were sold by the end of 1872. As usual, Sam found a scapegoat in Bliss. He attributed the decline to the substandard engravings in the book, the shoddy paper on which it was printed, and, strangely, to the "original lack of publicity" it received. Still, *Roughing It* earned its author about $20,600 during its first year in print. Traffic in the book did not improve through the end of the decade. Bliss shipped only 7,831 copies in 1873 and 5,132 in 1874. When Sam informed Dan De Quille that "something over 100,000 copies" of *Roughing It* had been sold by March 1875, the actual total was fewer than 90,000. In a January 1885 interview Sam estimated aggregate sales at 150,000, but this figure, too, was a gross exaggeration, because by December 1879, when company records end, *Roughing It* still had not passed the 100,000 mark.[6]

Of course, the company records may not have been entirely reliable. The contract Sam signed with Bliss in July 1870 for the volume that became *Roughing It* provided him with a royalty of 7½ percent on gross sales of the book in all editions. Sam had demanded half the profit above cost of manufacture, and

> [Bliss] said with enthusiasm that that was exactly right, exactly right. He went to his hotel and drew the contract and brought it to the house in the afternoon. I found a difficulty in it. It did not name "half profits," but named

a 7½ per cent royalty instead. I asked him to explain that. I said that that was not the understanding. He said "No, it wasn't," but that he had put in a royalty to simplify the matter—that 7½ per cent royalty represented fully half the profit and a little more, up to a sale of a hundred thousand copies; that after that, the Publishing Company's half would be a shade superior to mine.

Trouble is, Sam trusted Bliss to calculate all production expenses—paper, printing, binding, fees for illustrations and engravings, shipping costs, and so forth. And, according to Hamlin Hill but unbeknownst to Sam at the time, Bliss apparently kept two sets of books, one of which inflated production costs in case the company accounts were ever audited. Orion Clemens, stuck in a dead-end job as factotum and flunky in the offices of the American Publishing Company, alerted his brother in early March 1872, soon after *Roughing It* was issued, that he was the victim of Bliss's brand of bookkeeping. According to Orion, Bliss had illustrated the book with recycled engravings rather than commissioning new ones and exaggerated their price in the ledgers he used to calculate Sam's half-profits, printed the book on cheap paper, and stitched it with inferior bindings. Sam was initially dubious about the credibility of Orion's accusations but confronted Bliss regarding the matter on March 12. Sam recalled in his autobiography that the publisher had again beguiled him "into the belief that in changing the agreed wording of the contract for *Roughing It* from 'half profit over and above cost of manufacture' to a specified royalty" he was acting in good faith. Instead, Bliss "was setting a trap for me, whereby he expected to rob me," a "trick which succeeded."[7]

He should have known better. Bliss had fired Orion shortly after he met with Sam, but Sam was blind to the truth. He figured Orion deserved to be dismissed because, he wrote their sister Pamela, he "did a thing which was utterly inexcusable—it was the act of a half-witted child, & I could not say a word when he was discharged, notwithstanding he did this foolish thing with an honest intent to do me a brotherly service—& came almighty near *ruining* me." Rather than detect a cause for concern in Orion's dismissal, Sam found a silver lining in it. "Remember only that it has wrought one good: It has set you free from a humiliating servitude," he wrote his brother. He preferred to trust Bliss over breaking with him. The more he thought over their talk, he wrote the publisher on March 20,

the better I am satisfied. But I *was* troubled a good deal, when I went there, for I had worried myself pretty well into the impression that I was getting a smaller ratio of this book's profits than the spirit of our contract had authorized me to promise myself; indeed, I was so nearly convinced of it that if you had not been so patient with my perplexities, & taken the pains to show me by facts & figures & arguments that my present royalty gives me fully half & possibly even more than half the net profits of the book, I would probably have come to the settled conviction that such was not the case.

Nevertheless, Sam proposed to alter their contract "in such a way that it shall express that I am to receive half the profits."[8]

When Bliss refused, Sam considered filing suit against the company for breach of contract, and his lawyer brother proposed a potential legal tactic. Orion was convinced that Sam could break his agreement with the American Publishing Company, noting that

> on the basis of fraud you can prove concerning the printing of *Roughing It.* . . . Imagine the effect . . . on Bliss when he finds Hinckley [Bliss's accountant] subpoenaed to testify as to borrowed engravings, the amount of paper received from the paper mill for *Roughing It*; the testimony of the paper man as to its quality; of the *Churchman* pressman as to the country newspaper style of printing the cuts, etc. of the binder as to the quality of the binding, and how many he bound so. Bliss can see then that there is only needed to be added the testimony of some prominent engravers, book-binders, and book publishers in the trade, at Boston and New York, to overwhelm with devastating ruin the subscription business and the American Publishing Company in particular. . . . This indirect quiet threat would be so terrible that he would never bring a suit against you if you simply went quietly along and wrote your next book which you have contracted with him to publish, and put it into the hands of somebody else to publish just as if you had never made any contract at all with Bliss to publish it.

Sam next consulted his attorney and neighbor Charles E. Perkins, though he was not much help in the matter. "I was going to law about it," Sam recounted three years later, but after Perkins "heard me through, he remarked that Bliss's assertion [of the equivalency of 7½ percent royalty and half-profits] being only verbal & not a part of a written understanding, my case was weak—so he advised me to leave the law alone—& charged me $250 for it." Orion, too, soon discouraged Sam from suing Bliss on the grounds that he did not believe "there was any chance for enough to be made that way to justify such a proceeding." He recommended merely that Sam "use the fraud you can prove concer[n]ing the printing of Roughing It to give a court of chancery jurisdiction so as to protect you against Bliss interfering with your putting your next book into some other publisher's hands. . . . His hands are not clean. They are stained with fraud." Sam opted not to litigate the issue, though he regretted this decision eight years later, when he finally concluded that his supposedly batty brother had been right all along. Had Perkins "listened to my urgings & sued the company for ½ profits on 'Roughing It,' at the time you cipherded on cost," he conceded to Orion in 1880, "Bliss would have backed down & would not have allowed the case to go into court."[9]

In the end there is little doubt that Sam had been fleeced. As Hill, who carefully studied the balance sheets of the American Publishing Company, bluntly asserts, Bliss "was coldly calculating, he was happy to cheat both authors and customers with a repertory of the worst tricks of salesmanship, and he apparently juggled books with the skill of a master accountant." Or as Hill elsewhere explains, Sam's "7½ per cent on *Roughing It* . . . represented only half" of what he "believed it represented. He received twenty-seven cents a volume, on an average, for *Roughing It* in its various bindings. His royalty on the 96,083 copies sold up to the end of December 1879 would therefore have been about $26,000. At fifty cents a copy, which probably represented half-profits, he should have received over $48,000 for that number of copies." That is, Sam lost about $22,000 on this single book, to say nothing about his losses on the next several. He failed to realize for most of the decade of the 1870s that "7½ per cent did not represent one-fourth of the profits. But in the meantime I had published several books with Bliss on 7½ and 10 per cent royalties, and of course had been handsomely swindled on all of them. . . . Bliss had been robbing me ever since the day that I had signed the 7½ per cent contract" for the Western book. He estimated in his autobiography that Bliss had conned him out of a total of $30,000.[10]

"We are getting to work, now, packing up, & fixing things with the servants, preparatory to migrating to Elmira," Sam notified Mother Fairbanks in early March, immediately after the release of *Roughing It*. Sam, Livy, and Langdon left Hartford on March 14, spent two nights at the St. Nicholas Hotel in New York, and reached Quarry Farm the evening of March 16. Their departure was precipitated by Livy's approaching accouchement and they arrived none too soon. Olivia Susan Clemens was born early in the morning of March 19. Named for her grandmother, mother, and aunt, Susy was born prematurely, like her father and brother, and weighed barely four pounds. Unlike Langdon, however, Susy was healthy from birth, though her parents were compelled to hire a wet nurse. "The new baby flourishes, & grows strong & comely apace," Sam wrote Charley and Susan Warner on April 22. "She keeps one cow 'humping herself' to supply the bread of life for her." In early May the family made a visit to Abel and Mary Mason Fairbanks in Cleveland to show off the new baby, returning to Elmira on May 14.

The next day Sam sounded a cautious note about Langdon's health in a note to Orion. His son had come down with "a heavy cough & the suffering & irritation consequent upon developing six teeth in nine days. He is as white as alabaster and is weak; but he is pretty jolly about half the time." Susy was, on the other hand, "as fat as butter, & wholly free from infelicities of any kind."[11]

On a "raw, cold morning" during the third week of May Sam went "for an airing" in an open barouche accompanied by his son. Livy's custom was "to drive out each morning with Langdon" but when she was indisposed Sam took him instead. "I should not have been permitted to do it," he told Albert Bigelow Paine years later. "I was not qualified for any such responsibility as that." Langdon "was well wrapped about with furs and, in the hands of a careful person, no harm would have come to him. But I soon dropped into a reverie and forgot all about my charge." When he at length realized that "the carriage-robes had dropped away from the little fellow . . . I hurried home with him. I was aghast at what I had done, and I feared the consequences. I have always felt shame for that treacherous morning's work and have not allowed myself to think of it when I could help it." By May 24, according to Susan Crane, Langdon was "miserable" with a "severe cold"—"tonsilitis or something of the sort," Sam thought—but his condition seemed to improve over the next few days. Susy was baptized in the presence of her grandmother on May 26, and two days later, after a local doctor pronounced Langdon on the mend, the family left for home by way of New York. In a biography of her father written when she was thirteen, Susy observed that "mamma" thought "the journey might do him good," no doubt echoing what her parents told her about the brother she never knew. While en route to Hartford on May 29, as Lilly Warner wrote her husband, Sam telegraphed for Dr. Cincinnatus Taft, the family homeopath, to meet them at their house, "the boy being taken very sick." "For two or three days his cold grew worse" until on June 1 Langdon was diagnosed with diphtheria or membranous croup. The next morning "he gave up his life-long struggle to live & died quietly in his mother's arms." He was only nineteen months old.[12]

Neither Sam nor Livy chronicled the events of the next three days, though Lilly Warner and Susan Crane remarked on them in their letters and journals. "Of course everybody thinks what a mercy that he is at rest—but his poor devoted mother is almost heart-broken," Lilly wrote her husband on June 3. "Mr. Clemens was all tenderness but full of rejoicing for the baby—said he kept thinking it wasn't death for him but the beginning of life. She will see it all by & by, but can't yet, & it is such a mercy that they have the little baby." The parents decided to bury their child beside Livy's father in Woodlawn Cemetery in Elmira, and Livy had planned to attend the interment, but by the next day she had "given up going, overcome by the wishes of the Dr. & everybody else. We all felt that it would be almost wild for her to go in her poor state of health." Instead, Joseph Twichell conducted a brief memorial service in the parlor of the Clemens home. He "read from the Bible & made a simple & most appropriate prayer." Afterward, in the midst of a rainstorm, Susan and Theodore Crane accompanied Langdon's body to Elmira. "It was hard to leave Livy in her desolation," Sue wrote, "but she said it was best." Sam remained with her. The next day, June 5, the Cranes arrived with the coffin and "with dear friends laid the pure beautiful sleeper near his grandfather just as the sun was going down."[13] His grave was only the second in the family plot.

Much as he had blamed himself for his brother Henry's death in 1858, Sam took responsibility for his son's death in 1872. As his second daughter Clara Clemens noted in 1931, "If on any occasion he could manage to trace the cause of some one's mishap to something he himself had done or said, no one could persuade him that he was mistaken. Self-condemnation was the natural turn for his mind to take, yet often he accused himself of having inflicted pain or trouble when the true cause was far removed from himself." The record bears out this assertion. "I was the cause of the child's illness," Sam avowed in March 1906. "I doubt if I had the courage to make confession at that time. I think it most likely that I have never confessed until now." In fact, he assumed guilt for a crime when none was incurred. He once spoke to Howells about Langdon and admitted with "unsparing self-blame" that "I killed him" because he had "taken the child out imprudently and the child had taken the cold which he died of." Howells "never heard him speak of his son except that once, but no doubt in his deep heart his loss was irreparably present." Susan Crane told Albert Bigelow Paine in 1911 that "Mr. Clemens was often inclined to blame himself unjustly" for the death of his son, though the family "never thought of attributing Langdon's death to that drive."[14] Nor should the child's illness be blamed on the chill he received on that May morning. Membranous croup is caused by a bacterial, not viral, infection unrelated to wintry weather, though this etiology was unknown to medical science at the time. Put another way, diphtheria is not a common cold in extremis or a form of pneumonia but an entirely different type of disease.

Sam and Livy responded in markedly different ways to Langdon's death. Though he blamed himself, Sam to all outward appearances seems not to have mourned for his son. Only eleven days later—and thirteen days after the birth of his own daughter Jessamy—Bret Harte arrived in Hartford for an extended visit, presumably at Sam's invitation. On July 6 Sam, Livy, Susy, and a nursemaid left to spend the remainder of the summer at the ocean resort Fenwick Hall in New Saybrook, Connecticut, fifty miles and two hours by train south of Hartford on Long Island Sound. Whether by design or coincidence, Cincinnatus Taft registered at Fenwick Hall the same day. Though the Clemenses ostensibly went there for the sea air and a change of scenery, Sam savored these weeks as if he were on holiday. He played billiards and "took part in the *tableaux vivants* staged in the hotel's parlor, entertaining the guests" the evening of July 29 "with an inimitable personation of Mrs. Jarley, the wax-works exhibitor in Dickens's *Old Curiosity Shop.*" According to the *Hartford Courant*, he became "a great favorite with the ladies, and really the lion of the house." He also contemplated where he might travel—alone—to begin his next travel book. In late July he decided to "spend my winter either in the rural part of England or in Cuba & Florida—the latter most likely." Two weeks later he had determined to vacation in England because "I think a Book on Great Britain w[oul]d be ever so much more interesting than one on Cuba at present." Livy's mother came to New Saybrook to stay with her daughter and Susy, and on August 21, the day after dining with John Hay and other friends at the Union League Club, Sam sailed from New York Harbor aboard the Cunard luxury liner *Scotia* for Liverpool. "I do miss him so much and yet I am contented to have him away," Livy admitted to Mother Fairbanks. He was apparently unable to share her sorrow for their son, and the Atlantic crossing provided little solace. "I can't say that I have been enjoying myself, greatly, lost in a vast ship where our 40 or 50 passengers flit about in the great dim distances like vagrant spirits," he mused in a letter to Livy.[15]

On her part, Livy was inconsolable. "Mamma became very very ill" after Langdon's death, Susy wrote at thirteen, "but with a great deal of good care she recovered." Despondent and miserable, Livy grieved for her son. "Seeing the Mothers with their children does make me so homesick for Langdon— it seems as if I could not do without him," she wrote Orion's wife Mollie Clemens in early July from New Saybrook. Three weeks later, she expressed to Susan Crane a wish to decorate her son's grave in Elmira, which she had not yet visited, "as if it was all I could do and I longed to do that—He was so rarely beautiful, this house is full of children but there is none like him." Her thoughts had taken a morbid turn, for she admonished Sue not to "think of me as always sad, I am not so I have great comfort in those are left to me, only I feel so often as if my path way was to be from this time forth lined with graves."[16]

Sam reminisced in his autobiography that in the late summer of 1872, "I took a sudden notion to go to England and get materials for a book about that not-sufficiently known country. It was my purpose to spy out the land in a very private way and complete my visit without making any acquaintances. I had never been in England, I was eager to see it, and I promised myself an interesting time." He landed at Queenstown on August 30, at Liverpool the next day, and he registered at the historic Langham Hotel at Portland Place in London on September 2. He called directly on his English publishers, the Routledges, whom he had never met in person, and they had "never heard any one talk who in the least resembled him," according to biographer Paine. Sam's "first hour in England was an hour of delight," he jotted in his journal. "These are the best words I can find, but they are not adequate"; they were "not strong enough to convey" his initial impressions.[17] At the time he was still considered a minor-league wit in England, a literary comedian inferior to Bret Harte and Artemus Ward, roughly of the same caliber as Josh Billings and Orpheus C. Kerr, though he was soon to burnish his reputation.

The news of Sam's arrival in London soon circulated by word of mouth, whereupon he was welcomed by the social and literary elites with unexpected and lavish hospitality. The clergyman and novelist Charles Kingsley, the pre-Raphaelite painter Sir John Millais, and the novelist Charles Reade all called on him at his hotel. As the London *Telegraph* reported,

> The auspicious rumour that an American man of letters had come to see what he should see was buzzed about; and when it became known that this illustrious visitor was "Mark Twain," one of the latest and most successful of those comic writers who dissemble their graces and accomplishments beneath a humorous eccentricity of spelling, and who discover a truly international spirit in their mingling of Yankee rhetoric with Cockney rhymes, great was the desire to identify the face of the distinguished *littérateur*.

During his first week in London, Sam formed a fast friendship with Tom Hood, editor of the humor magazine *Fun*. The evening of September 6 he was Hood's guest at a meeting of the Whitefriars Club at the Mitre Tavern on Fleet Street. Ambrose Bierce, another guest of the club, was invited to speak and related a story about Sam's visit to the offices of the San Francisco *News-Letter* in 1868, while he was in the city to complete the manuscript of *The Innocents Abroad*. According to Carey McWilliams, Sam "never cracked a smile and merely appeared to be bored with the story," thus upstaging Bierce. In a brief speech in response to a toast in his honor, Sam claimed that he in fact had discovered the English doctor David Livingstone in the African jungle, though Henry Stanley had received "all the credit." He assured his listeners that he was "simply here to stay a few months, and to see English people and to learn English manners and customs, and to enjoy myself." By the close of the meeting Sam had been elected an honorary member of the club—a "mark of respect which had been accorded to few strangers," according to the South London *Press*. Sam was pleased with his debut performance before an audience of clubbable Londoners. It was a "very good speech," he wrote Livy, though "the shorthand reporters did not get it exactly right." Unfortunately, the address was roundly panned back in the United States by those papers that deigned to notice it. The Washington, D.C., *Star* snorted that it was "much too silly to have come from the author of *The Innocents Abroad*. If genuine it is evident that the London air has had a very depressing effect upon Mark's intellect." The *Chicago Tribune* similarly declared that " 'Mark Twain's' first speech in England" had been "in considerably bad taste."[18]

Sam's social calendar filled so quickly that he had scant time to transact the single item of business that required his presence in London. On September 7 Sam and Tom Hood called on John Camden Hotten, the publishing pirate who had issued *The Innocents Abroad* and *The Jumping Frog and Other Humourous Sketches* in 1870, though Sam concealed his identity. Hotten wrote Bierce that the visitor looked "glum" and "stern." Two weeks later, Sam protested in a letter to the editor of the London *Spectator* about Hotten's habit of adding a half dozen chapters to the books he pirated from him. "My books are bad enough just as they are written," Sam joked. "Sometimes when I read one of those additional chapters constructed by John Camden Hotten, I feel as if I wanted to take a broom-straw and go and knock that man's brains out. Not in anger, for I feel none. Oh! not in anger; but only to see, that is all." George Smalley, the London correspondent for the *New York Tribune*, chortled that he was keen "on high moral grounds to see Mr. John Camden Hotten put in the pillory." Sam paid Hotten, whom he once called "the missing link" between "man and the hyena," a second visit a few weeks later to offer to review for accuracy the next of his books the publisher wished to pirate. He did not expect to be compensated for the favor or remunerated with royalties on sales of the book. He merely wished to ensure that Hotten—"this creature, this vegetable, this candle-end, this molluck, this fungus, this bug, this pill, this vertebraed and articulated emetic"—did not include in it spurious chapters that would damage his reputation.[19]

Meanwhile, Sam found few opportunities to take notes for his projected travel book. "Confound this town, time slips relentlessly away & I accomplish next to nothing. . . . Too much company—too much dining—too much sociability," he admitted to Livy on September 11. He had not "even written in my journal for 4 days—don't get time." He was so infatuated with his new friends that, only nine days after arriving in London, he allowed in a sudden burst of Anglophilia that he "would rather live in England than America—which is treason." "I came here to take notes for a book, but I haven't done much but attend dinners & make speeches," he confessed on

November 6. Sam eventually realized his plan to write a satirical travelogue about England was impractical for the same reason the Holy Land chapters of *The Innocents Abroad* were mostly unfunny: he found a dearth of comic material, almost nothing to travesty. "These English men & women take a body right into their inner sanctuary," he apprised Mary Fairbanks on November 2, "& when you have broken bread & eaten salt with them once it amounts to *friendship*." He wrote his mother at nearly the same moment that he had "had a jolly good time" and "made hundreds of friends." And he was loath to offend his friends. "I could not leave out the manners & customs which obtain in an English gentleman's household without leaving out the most interesting feature of the subject," he explained. "They are admirable; yet I would shrink from deliberately describing them in a book, for I fear that such a course would be, after all, a violation of the courteous hospitality which furnished me the means of doing it." He might have satirized England in "a half-hearted way," he explained, but a "man with a humpbacked uncle mustn't make fun of another man's cross-eyed aunt." As late as 1879 in an interview with the New York *World*, Sam defended his failure to write a satirical travelogue about the mother country along the lines of *The Innocents Abroad*: "I couldn't get any fun out of England," he insisted. It was "too grave" a nation, and

> its gravity soaks into the stranger and makes him as serious as everybody else. When I was there I couldn't seem to think of anything but deep problems of government, taxes, free trade, finance—and every night I went to bed drunk with statistics. I could have written a million books, but my publisher would have hired the common hangman to burn them. One is bound to respect England . . . but she is not a good text for hilarious literature.

Instead of researching a humorous book during this first trip to England, Sam mostly played the tourist. As early as September 11, in company with Tom Hood, he visited the Crystal Palace in Sydenham, Newgate Prison, the Tower of London, and St. Paul's Cathedral. With James R. Osgood he spent September 12 "driving about Warwickshire in an open barouche." They toured the Kenilworth Castle ruins, Warwick Castle, and "the Shakspeare celebrities in & about Stratford-on-Avon." He traveled to Brighton ("one of the favorite better-class watering places") to tour the Royal Pavilion and the new Brighton aquarium ("a wonderful place" and "a majestic curiosity to me") with Hood; Henry Lee, the editor of *Land and Water*; and Edmund Routledge. While there, James Mortimer, editor of London *Figaro*, "tried to crowd me into writing for his paper," albeit to no avail. Sam lunched with the English comic actor John L. Toole on September 16 and he was the guest of Routledge at a meeting of the Savage Club the evening of September 21.

There he met the actor Henry Irving and Moncure D. Conway, an American Unitarian minister and the London correspondent of the *Cincinnati Commercial*. Among other club members in attendance were Hood and Henry Stanley. Toole, who presided at the meeting, seated Sam at the head table and, "when the repast was over," Conway reported,

> Toole arose and invited us to fill our glasses. A large proportion of the fifty or sixty persons present did not know that any distinguished guest was present until this unusual invitation to fill glasses was given. The necessity of repairing to the theaters has made it the rule that there shall be no toasts or speeches to prolong the dinners, except at the Christmas or anniversary banquet. All now set themselves to know what was up. Toole then said: "We have at our table Mark Twain." At these words a roar of cheers arose, and for some moments the din was indescribable.

Attired in "full evening dress—swallow-tail coat, white cravat, and all that," Sam delivered another brief post-prandial address, his second since arriving in London.[20] "I cannot express to you what entire enjoyment I find in this first visit to this prodigious metropolis," he began. "Its wonders seem to me to be limitless. I go about as in a dream" to gaze on such sites as "the statuary in Leicester Square," the punch line to an inside joke: Leicester Square at the time was in shambles, with the equestrian statue at its center in pieces. "I go to that matchless Hyde Park and drive all around it," he likewise declared. Another inside joke: cabs and carriages were not allowed in Hyde Park. He had "been to the Zoological Gardens," he announced, adding that he had "never seen such a curious and interesting variety of wild-animals in any garden" except the Jardin Mabille in Paris. He had also "been to the British Museum" and advised his auditors "to drop in there some time when you have nothing to do for—five minutes—if you have never been there." He equated the monuments to Lord Wellington in Dublin and Lord Nelson in Trafalgar Square with the memorial to Prince Albert, the queen's consort, in Kensington Gardens—a sarcasm that drew a hearty laugh. He similarly proclaimed that the "Albert memorial is the finest monument in the world and celebrates the existence of as commonplace a person as good luck ever lifted out of obscurity,"[21] an "assertion with which many of the Englishmen in the audience would have concurred, even if it would have been impolitic for them to say it aloud." "'The Library at the British Museum I find particularly astounding," Sam also remarked. "I have read there hours together, and hardly made an impression on it." Conway pronounced this address "the best after-dinner speech we had ever heard."[22]

After the banquet Sam left with friends to attend a performance of Lord Byron's play *Good News* starring Toole at the Gayety Theater. He apparently returned to the club after the theater, as he remembered in his autobiography, and "had something to eat again; also something to drink," and enjoyed "a very hospitable and friendly and contenting and delightful good time" into the wee hours of the morning. He reported to Livy the next day that he had "made a speech at the Savage Club last night. Had a very good time there." The novelist Charles Reade, who was seated near Sam, objected to Sam's remarks, however, complaining to Conway that "that accent! that accent!" grated on his ears. Mary Fairbanks hastened to congratulate Sam on his social triumph among the Savages: "Your little 'after dinner' at the Club was *nice*. Keep doing the *nice* things. Say nothing irreverent—make your wit exquisite (as you know how) not broad—touch lightly, rather tenderly upon *departed* goodness, even if it was not greatness (see Albert memorial) and then I'll just settle back to my knitting and dream of your glory." Thirty-five years later, Sam still remembered the "very hospitable and friendly and contenting and delightful good time" he had enjoyed.[23]

His reputation had preceded him. So popular was he in England that George Dolby, who managed Charles Dickens's 1869 lecture tour in America, proposed to arrange a similar sortie for Sam throughout Great Britain. "I have not the least idea of doing it—certainly not at present," Sam assured Livy. "I can't be hired to talk here, because I have no time to spare." Yet, as he noted in another letter to her, "invitations to lecture in the cities & towns of England & Scotland" continued to land on his desk, and "the gratifying feature of it is that they come not from speculators or cheap societies, but from self-elected committees of *gentlemen*, who want to give me their hospitality in return for the pleasure they say my pen has given them." And indeed the demands on his time did not subside. At the invitation of H. L. Bateman, the manager of the Lyceum Theater, whom he had known in St. Louis in 1853, Sam attended a performance of a new period piece by W. G. Wills based on the life of Charles I and starring Henry Irving—he remarked in his journal that it was "a curious literary absurdity"—and the evening of September 25 he went to the Royal Albert Hall to hear a production of Handel's *Messiah* featuring the operatic soprano Thérèse Tietjens and a chorus of seven hundred voices. He later described the building as "a huge and costly edifice, but the architectural design is old, not to say in some sense a plagiarism; for there is but little originality in putting a dome on a gasometer." During the performance, "Sir John Bennett, the sheriff of London, called in our box & invited me to a trial at the Old Bailey tomorrow," he wrote Livy, "& also to the election for Lord Mayor on Saturday, & also to the Sheriff's dinner on the same day—not a private dinner, strictly speaking, for there are to be 450 others present."[24]

Thus he was present at Guildhall on September 28 to witness the installation of the new sheriffs and lord mayor of London. He also attended the Inauguration Banquet of Sheriffs at the Freemasons' Tavern that evening as Bennett's guest and subsequently recorded two very different versions of events there. First his apocryphal account: He had "received an invitation" to

> one of those tremendous dinners where there are from eight to nine hundred invited guests.... When we took our seats at the tables, I noticed that at each plate was a little plan of the ball with the position of each guest numbered, so that one could see at a glance where his friend was seated by learning his number. Just before we fell to, someone—the Lord Mayor, or whoever was bossing the occasion—arose and began to read a list of those present—No. 1, Lord So-and-so; No. 2, the Duke of Something-or-other, and so on. When this individual read the name of some prominent political character or literary celebrity, it would be greeted with more or less applause. The individual who was reading the names did so in so monotonous a manner that I became tired, and began looking about for something to engage my attention. I found the gentleman next to me on the right a well-informed personage and I entered into conversation with him. I had never seen him before, but he was a good talker, and I enjoyed it. Suddenly, just as he was giving me his views upon the future religious aspect of Great Britain, our ears were assailed by a deafening storm of applause. Such a clapping of hands I never heard before. It sent the blood to my head with a rush, and I got terribly excited. I straightened up and commenced clapping my hands with all my might. I moved about in my chair and clapped harder and harder. "Who is it?" I asked the gentleman on my right. "Whose name did he read?" "Samuel L. Clemens," he answered. I stopped applauding. I didn't clap any more. It kind of took the life out of me, and I sat there like a mummy and didn't even get up and bow.[25]

The facts, of course, are far more prosaic.

In the account he wrote his wife and friends, he arrived alone at the tavern, where "nobody seemed to know me—so I passed modestly in, & took the seat" that he had been assigned beside Bennett. Before the soup was served, his host asked him to reply extemporaneously to the toast to "literature." When Bennett came to Sam's name during the roll call of the guests—"my name being No. 75 in a list of 250"—the audience erupted in

> such a storm of applause as you never heard. The applause continued, & they could not go on with the list. I was never so taken aback in my life—never stricken so speechless—for it was totally unlooked-for on my part. I thought I was the humblest in that great titled assemblage—& behold, mine was the *only* name in the long list that called forth this splendid compliment. I did not

know what to do, & so I sat still & did nothing. By & by the new sheriff, in his gorgeous robes of office, got up & proposed my health, & accompanied it with the longest & most extravagantly complimentary speech of the evening, & appointed me to respond to the toast to "literature."

He "got up & said" something about his failure to prepare anything to say, ironically, "& made a good deal of a success." He bragged to Elisha Bliss in a letter written later that night that he had been "received in a sort of tremendous way, tonight, by the brains of London," though he admitted a week later to Charley Warner that he had been "an ass to make a speech at such an awfully swell affair at 15 minutes notice."[26]

Over the next month he became even more pressed for time. In early October he made a brief excursion to Oxford, including "an hour round about Magdalen College," and gushed to Livy that "there is nothing even in New England that equals it for pure loveliness, & nothing outside of New England that even remotely approaches it." His schedule was so cluttered with engagements that, he informed Conway, "I find myself in inextricable fetters for some weeks to come—not a day clear, that I can see from this till the hour I expect to sail." Sam crossed paths in mid-October with two old acquaintances, the travel writer J. Ross Browne and George Turner, the former Nevada Supreme Court justice. According to Browne, he was "just the same dry, quaint old Twain we knew in Washington. I believe he is writing a book over here. He made plenty of money on his other books." Sam's schedule had become so crowded that he decided to return to England the following year. "I have been thinking & thinking," he advised Livy, "& I have decided that one of 2 or 3 things *must* be done: either you must come right over here for 6 months; or I must go right back home 3 or 4 weeks hence & both of us come here April 1st & stay all summer. But I am not going abroad any more without you." Livy agreed to return to England with him in a twelvemonth, whereupon Sam extended an invitation to Susan and Theodore Crane to "come over in the spring with Livy & me, & spend the summer." He reiterated his desire to "live here if I could get the rest of you over."[27]

In the meantime, Sam spent as much time sightseeing as possible. He noted that the work of Gustave Doré, on display at the artist's gallery on Bond Street, "fascinated me more than anything I have seen in London yet." He considered *The Christian Martyrs* the "strangest & the loveliest" painting there, and he was so impressed by *Christ Leaving the Praetorium*—"the greatest picture that ever was painted"—that he ordered an engraving of it for eighty dollars. Accompanied by Canon Charles Kingsley, Sam toured Westminster Abbey, particularly Poet's Corner and the Chapel of St. Edward the Confessor, "the holiest ground in the British Empire." He later recounted the particulars of this late-night visit in "A Memorable Midnight Experience" (1872), one of the few surviving fragments of his unfinished English travel book. During the climactic coronation scene in *The Prince and the Pauper* (1882), moreover, Edward VI emerges miraculously from this chapel in a symbolic resurrection to reclaim his royal station.[28]

Sam tried "to see as many *people* as I can" as his first trip to England wound down. The evening of October 21 he attended a banquet at Willis's Rooms, St. James Square, hosted by the Royal Geographical Society in honor of Henry Stanley. The day "lives with me forever," he later told an interviewer. "I went there to meet my old friend, Mr. Stanley, and he was good enough to bring some 75 or a 100 of his friends to greet me," he remembered. "There was not one of the men present who had not earned his claim to personal distinction." The explorer had returned from Africa less than three months earlier, though his claim to have found David Livingstone had been disputed and he had come under fire. Sam was cheered by the efforts of the society to recognize Stanley's achievement. "I think the most tremendous piece of manliness of modern times was the conduct of the Royal Geographical Society" at the dinner paying tribute to him; Sam "sat opposite the President & was flanked by various dignitaries." He then accepted an invitation to join a stag hunt near the village of Wargrave near Henley-on-Thames for several days and missed a Whitefriars Club meeting held in his honor the evening of November 1. "I got it into my head that Friday was Thursday so I staid in the country stag-hunting a day too long," he wrote James Redpath, and "when I reached the club last night nicely shaved" he discovered "that the dinner was *the night before*." He soon compensated for his absence. The evening of November 4 he was present at the inauguration dinner for the lord mayor—elect, Sir Sydney Waterlow, in the hall of the Stationers' Company; the next night, he met "a familiar face every other step" at the opening of the new Guildhall Library and Museum; two days later, he was Henry Lee's guest at a Linnean Society dinner; and the evening of November 8 he was present at another lord mayor's dinner when "the Lord High Chancellor of England, in his vast wig & gown, . . . walk[ed] me arm-in-arm through the brilliant assemblage, & welcome[d] me with all the enthusiasm of a girl." He assured Mother Fairbanks that, though he was regularly invited to feast with friends, he was watching his waistline: "I go to the dinners, public & private, & steer clear of wine & food, & so I have just as good a time as ever chaffing & talking & making little speeches."[29]

Both J. Ross Browne and Moncure Conway socialized with Sam during the final weeks of his trip, when his health had begun to suffer from overindulgence. Browne mentioned on October 29 that he saw Sam "every day and have long talks with him. He looks very badly." According to Conway, Sam was so driven hither and yon he seemed "to be growing rapidly thinner and paler. Day after day he drags himself still an hour later in the afternoon from his bed at the Langham, where efforts at sleep have ceased to restore his relaxing energies." He was "already complaining," moreover, "that his London dinners have long since ceased to digest." Before leaving London, Sam assured "those societies in London and other cities of Great Britain under whose auspices I have partly promised to lecture" in a letter to the *Times* of London that he planned to "spend with my family the greater part of next year" in England "and may be able to lecture a month during the autumn."[30] At last, on November 11 Sam railed to Liverpool and that evening spoke at the Liverpool Institute. The next day he boarded the new Cunard steamship *Batavia* under the command of Captain John E. Mouland and embarked for America and another adventure in midocean. Among his fellow passengers was Edward Waldo Emerson, son of the Sage of Concord.[31]

The ship sailed into a hurricane in the North Atlantic fifteen hundred miles from shore. "We encountered a fearful gale," Sam recalled later, "that is known to have destroyed a great many vessels, and is supposed to have made away with a great many more that have never been heard of up to this day. The storm lasted two days with us; then subsided for a few brief hours; then burst forth again." During the squall, on the open sea and driven off course, the *Batavia* "came upon a dismasted vessel, the wooden bark *Charles Ward*," wrecked on November 18 while en route from Quebec for Sunderland. Of its original crew of twenty, eleven sailors had been washed overboard. Mouland launched a lifeboat that succeeded in rescuing the remaining nine men in an hour. "I do not know when anything has alternately so stirred me through and through and then disheartened me, as it did to see the boat every little while get almost close enough and then be hurled three lengths away again by a prodigious wave," Sam reported. "Our people managed to haul the party aboard, one at a time, without losing a man." Sam facetiously claimed some credit for the rescue because as the lifeboat was maneuvering into position he stood on the deck "without any umbrella, keeping an eye on things and seeing that they were done right, and yelling whenever a cheer seemed to be the important thing. . . . I would do it again under the same circumstances." On November 27, the day after the ship docked in New York, Sam told the *New York Tribune* that Mouland "risked his life many times to rescue shipwrecked men—in the days when he occupied a subordinate

position." All of the passengers aboard the *Batavia* signed a letter written by
Sam to thank the captain for his bravery and nautical skills:

> You have brought us safely through a remarkable voyage, and one which once
> or twice seemed to promise disastrous results to ship and passengers. Your
> courageous bearing and your cheery words and countenance all through the
> storms that beset us inspired us with a hope and a confidence that not even
> the deliberate villainy of a barometer could vanquish. . . . We are sailors
> enough to know and appreciate the necessity to us all of your intelligent head
> and your superb seamanship in those troubled hours—we are sailors enough
> for that, although it is doubtful if one of us can tell the mizzen foretopsail
> jibboom from the binnacle gaskets of the maintopgallantmast bulkhead.

In a more earnest expression of their gratitude, on November 20, while still
at sea, the passengers signed a second petition drafted by Sam urging the
Royal Humane Society of London to recognize Mouland and the first officers of the *Batavia* for their "gallant achievement" and their petition was
granted. The Humane Society conferred medals on Mouland and the officers and sailors involved in the rescue as well as cash rewards "suited to their
official grade"—in the case of the crewmen, seven British pounds or thirty-
five dollars in gold, the equivalent of two months' wages. Sam only quibbled
with the amount of the money, which as he noted amounted to less than the
cost of "sending moral tracts to Timbuctoo. . . . Not that I object to sending
moral tracts to Timbuctoo; far from it; I write the most of them myself, and
gain the larger part of my living in that way. I would grieve to see Timbuctoo
redeemed, and have to lose its custom. But why not start a Humane Society
[in the United States] besides?"[32]

Sam returned to the United States three weeks after the election that returned Ulysses S. Grant to the White House. He had supported the Republicans sotto voce during the campaign even before he departed for England,
particularly in a pseudonymous sketch printed in the *Hartford Courant* titled "The Secret of Dr. Livingstone's Continued Voluntary Exile," in which
he explained that Livingston had opted to remain secreted in Africa when
he learned that Horace Greeley was running for president and his candidacy
had been endorsed by the Ku Klux Klan. Sam also wrote to congratulate
Thomas Nast of *Harper's Weekly* for helping to reelect Grant with his editorial cartoons and win "a prodigious victory" for "Civilization & progress."[33]

On November 29, only two days after Sam debarked in New York after almost three months in England, Greeley suddenly died. As a result,
Sam inadvertently landed in the middle of a political muddle. The owner-
editor of the *New York Tribune* had failed to anoint a successor. By rights of

seniority, Whitelaw Reid, the associate editor, should have assumed the job, but he did not own the paper. He became the interim editor but the majority stockholders shopped the job around, at length offering the position to Sam's friend (and Reid's enemy) Schuyler Colfax, the former Speaker of the House and vice president of the United States. As a result, Reid resigned from the *Tribune* on December 16. When Colfax unexpectedly declined the editorship, probably because of his complicity in the unfolding Crédit Mobilier scandal, Reid enlisted Sam's help in a public relations effort to "save" the Great Moral Organ. Reid organized a cadre of investors, including the robber baron Jay Gould, who loaned him a half million dollars, enough to buy a half interest in the newspaper. It was a classic case of playing with fire but Reid reve(a)led in the *Tribune* on December 23 that he had acquired financial and editorial control of the paper. The same day this editorial appeared, Sam sent a hackneyed satirical lyric about the controversy entitled "The New Cock Robin" to the *Hartford Post*. The third of five stanzas is the pertinent one:

> *Who's to be Editor of the Tribune?*
> I, says Whitelaw Reid!
> On, great Pegasus, my steed,
> I charge the felon Tweed!
> Of all his filthy breed,
> That with a ghoul-like greed
> On our credit's corpse did feed,
> The metropolis I freed.
> Of Reform I took the lead—
> To the West, with ardent speed
> Bent my way. And in the hour of need,
> In Cincinnati sowed the seed
> Of a movement that decreed
> Corruption's death. Alas! the reed—
> Oh, weaker still!—the *weed*—
> We leaned on, broke—indeed
> The time was past, I rede,
> For "Liberal" virtue to succeed.
> Now I promised naught. I'm key'd
> Up to honor's pitch. I'll bleed
> Before I'll ever draw a bead
> In monopoly's defence. Give heed
> To my words. On which basis Whitelaw Reid
>   Is content to be that Editor.

Five days later, as if to thank him for his support, Reid invited Sam to submit "something . . . over your own signature within the next week" to the *Tribune.* "Say your say on any topic on which you want to say it. I cannot pay you the prices which those subscription publishers pay, but I can pay enough to make it worth your while and you will value a great deal more than the money the fact that you are doing a kindness." On January 3 Sam sent him a pair of brief essays about the splendors of the Sandwich Islands and the case for their annexation by the United States. His cover letter doubled as a note of congratulations: "the Lord knows I grieved to see the old Tribune wavering and ready to tumble into the trough of common journalism, and God knows I am truly glad you saved it. I hope you will stand at its helm for a hundred years." (In fact, Reid owned the paper until his death in 1912.) After printing both of the pieces, Reid sent Sam a check for a hundred dollars and intimated that the pages of the *Tribune* were open to him at his pleasure: "wont you do something more for us when you see a chance? It won't hurt you a bit to freshen up people's recollection of you as a newspaper writer."[34]

Sam notified James Redpath even before leaving England in November 1872 that he hoped never to lecture again. "When I yell again for less than $500 I'll be pretty hungry," he warned his agent, "but I haven't any intention of yelling at any price." A false report circulated in December that he would tour over the winter with a lecture titled "England and What I Saw There." He refused overtures from the ever-persistent Redpath to speak once in Philadelphia for four hundred dollars and at Livy's behest he declined offers for five hundred to eight hundred dollars per appearance to speak "for 20 or 30 nights" later in the season. He was finally persuaded to speak in Brooklyn, Jersey City, and New York in early February—"he was seduced into it by the large prices they offer him," Livy wrote her mother, specifically "half the gross proceeds" or upwards of "five and six hundred dollars a night." He also agreed to lecture pro bono in Hartford the evening of January 31, 1873, to benefit David Hawley's City Mission. Hawley, a layman, had operated the mission since 1851 with support from private donors. "Father Hawley knows of a great many widows and little children here who suffer from cold and hunger every day and every night, yet the means he is able to gather up fall far short of being enough to relieve them," Sam announced on January 29 in the *Hartford Post.* He composed a similar card for the *Hartford Courant.* He was careful to stipulate that Hawley's charity was not wasted on "able-bodied tramps who are too lazy to work" but dedicated to what he called the "deserving poor." The entire box office proceeds "shall go into Father Hawley's hands," Sam assured his readers, and all related expenses—rent of Allyn Hall, advertising, and so forth—had been covered by donors and volunteers. Sam admitted that he planned to speak about "Our Fellow Savages of the Sandwich Islands," the same lecture he had delivered on behalf of the Young Men's Institute in November 1869, "because Father Hawley's need is so pressing that I have not time to prepare a new lecture; I happen to be just fixed and primed for this Sandwich Island talk, for the reason that I have been rubbing it up to deliver before the New York Mercantile Library some ten days hence." In an editorial the same day, the *Courant* promised their subscribers that all of the recipients of Hawley's benevolence were needy, including "the families of men who are temporarily out of employment, who cannot get money for the rent, for flour, for coal. We are not writing of the bummers and of professional beggars, but of the respectable poor who are overtaken by misfortune, sickness, want of work." The editorial concluded by commending Sam for his altruism: "Having declined to deliver here for pay the lecture he is about to deliver in New York, he offers to put it at the service of the city mission." The lecture was, predictably, a commercial and critical success. Despite ten inches of new snow in the city, a capacity audience of over fifteen hundred filled the hall, ticket sales totaled fifteen hundred dollars, and both the *Courant* and the *Post* commended the substance of the speech. It was not only a "greatly improved" version of his old Sandwich Islands lecture but "by far the best of the lecturer's efforts here." The *Post* reviewer reported that "the audience listened with great attention throughout, evidently enjoying the lecturer's eloquence, his vivid descriptions, and his serious comments, and the wit, humor and jokes, about equally."[35]

The next day, February 1, Sam railed to New York, where he registered at the St. Nicholas Hotel, to begin his abbreviated speaking tour. First, however, he attended a meeting of the Lotos Club that evening as Reid's guest. Sam Bowles, Bret Harte, John Hay, and Henry Watterson, editor of the *Louisville Courier-Journal* and Sam's distant cousin by marriage, were also present. Sam joked during a brief speech that Reid "had grown so accustomed to editing a newspaper that he could not distinguish between truth and falsehood," that "Hay had written so many ribald verses that [Sam] was always compelled to disown his acquaintance when presiding at meetings of the YMCA," and he "censured Bowles for his shameful failure as a banker in Paris." Sam closed by inviting the members to attend his talk at Steinway Hall the following Wednesday evening. "I make it a rule of life never to miss any chances, especially on occasions like these," he added, "where the opportunity for converting the heathen is luxuriously promising." He was soon elected a member of this exclusive "ace of clubs," as he called it, and he was the guest of honor at a club dinner three weeks later. In the future he often made the club billiard room his de facto office when he visited New York.[36]

As promised, Sam reprised his Sandwich Islands lecture at Steinway Hall in New York under the auspices of the Mercantile Library Association the evening of February 5. The hall "scarcely ever had within its walls so large a number as was last night assembled" to hear Sam speak, according to the New York *World*, and an estimated thousand more were turned away for lack of space. The hall was so packed that some auditors, including the humorist Petroleum V. Nasby, were seated on the stage. He was greeted by the crowd with "frequent applause and bursts of laughter" and by "a similar appreciative attention upon the more serious portions of the lecture." The *Times* averred that Sam "kept the audience convulsed with laughter" and the *Tribune* joined the chorus of praise: "After you have laughed at his wild extravagances for an hour, you are astonished to perceive that he has given you new and valuable views of the subject discussed. Every sentence may be burlesque, but the result is fact. And what insures his success as a teacher is that his manner is so irresistibly droll that it conquers at the first moment the natural revolt of the human mind against instruction." The New York *Mail* added that Sam "concluded with an eloquent and poetical description of the dreamy tropical land." Two nights later at the Academy of Music in Brooklyn, the result was much the same. In its review the *Brooklyn Union* compared Sam to Charles Lamb and François Rabelais and the *Brooklyn Eagle* reported that he ended his lecture "amid loud applause." Sam again spoke at Steinway Hall the evening of February 10 and he gleefully averred later that his half of the profits from the two appearances there amounted to thirteen hundred dollars. "I lectured 2 nights in Steinway Hall once, for half of the gross receipts," he bragged. "We packed the house both nights at a dollar a head. The rent of the hall was either $200 or $250 per night, & the advertising little or nothing, because there was not time to do much." Sam lectured at the Tabernacle in Jersey City on February 14 to a "large audience," was accorded a lengthy ovation at the end, and received a favorable notice the next day in the Jersey City *Journal* (his listeners "laughed and laughed, until their sides ached"). He returned to Hartford suffering from a severe cold and, in truth, a purse that was lighter than he had expected. Nine months later, Sam concluded that the Mercantile Library had filched seven hundred dollars from him after the lectures in Steinway Hall. As Orion explained the larceny, "There were 2000 or 2500 people at each lecture. He was to have had half and they were to pay all expenses. The tickets were a dollar and they paid him $1300 for the two lectures. Now they want him to lecture again and he wants to tell them they are thieves."[37]

As soon as he returned from England, Sam jumped into several literary projects. On December 2 he "went to work on my English book," which had been given such working titles in the press as "John Bull," "English Notes," and "Upon the Oddities and Eccentricities of the English." That day he "turned out 36 pages of satisfactory manuscript" of sixty or seventy words per page, though "the baby kept me awake so much" that night he found "the inspiration . . . vanished & gone" the next day. By February he had completed hundreds of pages of manuscript, and the New York correspondent of the *Chicago Tribune* reported that "those who have seen the MS. say it will be indescribably funny." Thomas Nast, famous for his editorial cartoons in *Harper's Weekly*, volunteered to illustrate the book when it was finished and Sam was interested. "I do hope my publishers can make it pay you to illustrate my English book," he replied. "Then I should have good pictures"—a tacit acknowledgment that *Roughing It* had limped on the art leg. He advised Bliss that "Nast appears to be doing nothing in particular. I want him, solitary & alone, to illustrate this next book, it being an essentially *American* book, & he will enjoy doing it. Nast only has just one *first-class* talent (caricature,) & no more—but this book will exercise that talent, I think."[38] Several excerpts from the projected book were eventually published, including "A Memorable Midnight Experience" and "Rogers" in *Mark Twain's Sketches, No. 1* (1874) and "Some Recollections of a Storm at Sea" in the Cleveland *Bazaar Record* (1876). "A Storm at Sea" was widely reprinted and "Rogers" was even translated into German by Udo Brachvogel in 1882. Three other excerpts from the incomplete English travelogue, "The Albert Memorial," "Old Saint Paul's," and "The British Museum," appeared posthumously in *Letters from the Earth* (1962).[39]

Sam also turned, however tentatively, to a project that would gradually develop into *The Adventures of Tom Sawyer*. In 1868 he had started to develop a juvenile novel, the "Boy's Manuscript" published by Bernard DeVoto in *Mark Twain at Work* (1942). Some circumstantial evidence suggests that Sam also jotted notes for an ur-*Sawyer* while in New Saybrook during the summer of 1872. While in London in the fall of 1872, as he remembered in his autobiography, he told Henry Irving and W. G. Wills about how the hero whitewashed the fence "and thereby captured on cheap terms a chapter; for I wrote it out when I got back to the hotel while it was fresh in my mind." When he returned to Hartford, he resumed scribbling on the manuscript and completed a draft of the first five chapters, including the whitewashing scene, in January 1873. While this episode is unrelated to any of the multiple story lines in the finished novel, it serves as a paradigmatic episode, illustrating Tom's genius at merging the childhood and adult worlds of work and play.[40]

Meanwhile, Sam and his neighbor Charles Dudley Warner, author of such collections of familiar essays as *My Summer in a Garden* (1870) and

Back-Log Studies (1872), decided to collaborate on a novel simply to prove
to their wives that they could write one—or so the story goes. According to
Charles Warren Stoddard, Sam and Warner "were walking to church one
Sunday in Hartford. Said Warner: 'Let us write a novel!' Mark wondered
what in the world there was to write a novel about, but promised to think the
matter over." But the origin story of *The Gilded Age*—the very title became
a generic term for the period between the end of the Civil War and the end
of the century—is much more complicated than this simple statement. As
Bryant Morey French allows, there are several "conflicting accounts of just
how Warner and Twain decided to collaborate." As early as 1878 a tale circulated in the press that was demonstrably incorrect on many points: "One
evening in the summer of 1874 Warner and his wife dropped in upon Mark
Twain." Warner declared that "it's atrocious what bosh is written for American novels now." Sam supposedly agreed: "I have for a long time felt that I
could write a better story than any American novelist." When their wives
ridiculed the idea, Sam invited his neighbor to help him prove them wrong:
"Let's write a story, Warner, and show these women what we can do." Warner replied "that he once knew a man who would make a first-rate character
for a novel." They then finished the manuscript "in just a month."[41] Trouble
is, this genetic history of *The Gilded Age* is too similar to the legend about
James Fenimore Cooper and the origin of his novel *Precaution* (1820) to be
credible.

Still, the journalist E. J. Edwards in 1910 and Albert Bigelow Paine in 1912
recapitulated this account, with minor differences. According to Edwards,
Livy Clemens and Susan Warner "began to twit" Sam for his "accidental hit"
with *The Innocents Abroad* and "ended up by defying him to write another
work like it," so he recruited Warner to assist him. According to Paine, "The
husbands were inclined to treat rather lightly the novels in which their wives
were finding entertainment" and "on the spur of the moment Clemens and
Warner agreed that they would do a novel together." Sam had contemplated
a novel about James Lampton and his family since August 1870, when he
asked his sister Pamela to write him with "every little trifling detail" about
how Cousin Jim and his family "look & dress & what they say, & how the
house is furnished—& the various ages & characters of the tribe." Certainly
he and Warner were at work on *The Gilded Age* by January 1873 and Sam
remembered four years later that he had written the opening chapters, fifty-
five pages of manuscript, at a single sitting. Sam planned his part of the novel
from the first to focus on the character of the affable buffoon Eschol Sellers,
whom he modeled on Lampton. "The real Colonel Sellers, as I knew him in
James Lampton," Sam reflected, "was a pathetic and beautiful spirit, a manly
man, a straight and honorable man, a man with a big, foolish, unselfish heart

in his bosom, a man born to be loved; and he was loved by all his friends, and by his family worshiped." But in his bluster, bombast, and sublime oblivion Colonel Sellers was also a takeoff on Colonel Culpepper Starbottle, a stock character in Bret Harte's recent short fiction. Within a couple of weeks Sam had written the first eleven chapters of the novel, or 399 pages of manuscript, before he turned the writing task over to Warner. Each of the collaborators "had a veto on anything the other wrote." And fortunately so: Sam admitted that "some of my errors in this book would have been simply outrageous but Warner criticized them faithfully & so I re-wrote 200 pages of my MS & cooled the absurdities down to a reasonable temperature." Sam claimed, after the publication of the novel, that he wrote "32 of the 63 chapters *entirely* and part of 3 others beside," though he also allowed that "there is scarcely a chapter that does not bear the marks of the two writers of the book." He insisted unequivocally on a single "solemn stipulation": "if there was any love making in the book I was not to be asked to do it."[42]

The authors worked together privately on the story for three months. "Every night for many weeks," Sam advised Mary Mason Fairbanks, "Livy & Susie Warner have collected in my study to hear Warner & me read our day's work; & they have done a power of criticising, but have always been anxious to be on hand at the reading & find out what has been happening to the dramatis personae since the previous evening." Livy's cousin Hattie Paff (née Lewis) spent a month in Hartford during the winter of 1873 and similarly recalled in 1897 that Sam and Charley would each "write during the day in his own study, and in the early twilight Mr. W[arner] would come over and he & Mr C[lemens] with no light save that given by the glowing grate would talk about the book, and later when the lights were brought in, each would read what he had written, so that I heard nearly all of that book before it went to the printers." Their progress was briefly disrupted by the weeklong visit of the Scottish author George MacDonald and his family. According to Paff, "It was a rare treat to listen while [MacDonald] and Mr C[lemens] talked—for both were at their best." In early April Warner finally informed Whitelaw Reid that he and Sam were collaborating on a novel: "No one here, except our wives, knows anything of it. We conceived the design early in the winter, but were not able to get seriously at work on it till sometime in January. . . . We have hatched the plot day by day, drawn out the characters, and written it so that we cannot exactly say which belongs to who; though the different styles will show in the chapters." Warner's hint that the authors wanted the book publicized in the *New York Tribune*—this even before the manuscript was finished, much less under contract—was apparently too subtle for Reid. Sam contacted the editor a few days later to urge him to commission a shill to puff the book: "we want a mere mention, *now* with either exceedingly complimentary additions, or pitiless abuse accompanied with profanity. . . . We think a pretty good deal of this novel I can tell you; even the paper it is written on cost eleven dollars." Reid passed the letter to John Hay with instructions to prepare "a rollicking bit" of news about the novel for the next Saturday edition. On April 19, true to form, Hay revealed to *Tribune* readers that Sam and Warner "have written a novel in partnership! It will be published about the end of the Summer." Hay was unclear about the plot of the novel, only that it "deals with the salient features of our American life of to-day; and, as might easily be divined, is in the nature of a satire. It is no holiday work. It deals with every aspect of modern society, and we are authorized to announce"—Hay here quoted Sam almost verbatim—"that the paper on which it is written cost eleven dollars."[43]

Sam was dismayed by the tenor of this notice. He had written Reid a lighthearted request to announce the book, but he had hardly expected the *Tribune* to follow suit with a lighthearted promo. In writing Reid (again), his disappointment was palpable. "In speaking facetiously instead of seriously," he carped,

> I am afraid you have hurt us. I wanted you to do us a genuine good turn & give us a fair & square good send-off. . . . [W]e wanted the *first* mention to come from the *Tribune*, so that it might start from the most influential source in the land & start *right*. And now you give us a notice which carries the impression to the minds of other editors that we are people of small consequence in the literary world, & indeed only triflers; that a novel by us is in no sense a literary event. . . . Now I hold that a novel from us is a literary *event*, (though it may sound pretty egotistical) & it deserved from you two stickfuls of *brevier*, gravely worded, & an honorable place in your chief editorial columns. I am not a man of trifling literary consequence.

Nor was he above calling in a favor. Some weeks earlier Reid had asked him to contribute to the paper and

> I put down this novel in the midst of a chapter & put in two whole days on the S[andwich] I[slands] letters. . . . Now confound you when I want you to do something for me, you shove my novel at the world as if neither it nor its father amounted to much! This isn't fair—I swear it is not fair. . . . Our novel will have some *point* to it & will *mean* something, & I think it will not be snubbed & thrown aside, but will make some men talk, & may even make some people *think*. All I claim is that it is the literary event of the season—& that I stick to. . . . Now just see if you can't do us a real outspoken good turn that will leave a strong wholesome impression on the public mind—& then command our services, if they can be of use to you.

Two days later, in reply to a telegram from Reid, Sam wrote again: "I want the Tribune to say it *right* & say it powerful—& then I will answer for the consequences."[44]

Reid obliged. The *Tribune*—almost certainly Hay again—not only announced the title of the novel in its columns on April 23 but added (once again almost in Sam's exact words) that *The Gilded Age* "is likely to prove the chief literary event of the season. It is an unusual and a courageous enterprise for two gentlemen who have already won honorable distinction in other walks of literature to venture upon untrodden paths with a work so ambitious and so important as this is likely to be." In a letter to Reid, Sam expressed his delight at this "bully" notice: "If any man is deceived by that he will be deceived in the happy direction, at any rate—and that is what we want."[45]

But still he was dissatisfied. Sam wanted Reid to commission Ned House, who had read the manuscript of the novel during a visit to Hartford in late April, to write a detailed review of *The Gilded Age* for the *Tribune* as soon as it was published. House "liked the Gilded Age, & wanted to do it a favor," Sam reminisced in 1890. "He proposed to review it in the *New York Tribune* before some other journal should get a chance to give it a start which might not be to its advantage." He had discovered, or so he claimed, "that the latest review of a book was pretty sure to be just a reflection of the *earliest* review of it; that whatever the first reviewer found to praise or censure in the book would be repeated in the latest reviewer's report, with nothing fresh added," so he was careful to finagle an early favorable notice or two. Moreover, he believed that "if one don't secure publicity and notoriety for a book the instant it is issued, no amount of hard work and faithful advertising can accomplish it later on."[46]

Reid declined the offer, however, because he feared (correctly) that House would merely puff the book. House reported to Sam, in fact, that Reid had "abused him & charged him with bringing a dishonorable proposal from Warner & me. That seemed strange; indeed unaccountable, for there was nothing improper about the proposition." Reid in turn recorded his side of the story in mid-May:

> I hear [Sam] says that he has a quarrel with *The Tribune*. If so, it is simply that *The Tribune* declined to allow him to dictate the person who should review his forthcoming novel. His modest suggestion was that Ned House should do it. . . . There is a nice correspondence on a part of the subject which would make pleasant reading; and if Twain gives us trouble, I'm very much tempted to make him a more ridiculous object than he has ever made anybody else.

Sam soon learned Reid's reasons for refusing to cooperate, "which was simply that he considered House a 'blatherskite,' and wouldn't have anything to do with him." Sam broke off their friendship and they never resumed it. As he put it to Warner, Reid "is a contemptible cur, and I want nothing more to do with him. I don't want the Tribune to have the book at all. Please tell Bliss *not to send a copy there under any circumstances.* If you feel at any time like explaining, you may tell Reid or anyone that I desired this." Reid, he claimed, was fully "capable of stealing peanuts from a blind pedlar." Orion was shocked to learn around this time that "Reid is an enemy of Sam." He had assumed "that he was a warm personal friend." When the two men again began to cross paths some twelve years later, they maintained a discreet distance. They "met at people's tables, and smiled and passed the time of day, but neither of us has much enjoyed even those slight love passages." Ironically, but perhaps predictably, Sam eventually fell out with House, too. "In justice to Reid," he conceded in his autobiography, "I found out that he was right concerning Edward H. House. Reid had labeled him correctly; he was a blatherskite."[47]

The coauthors "finished revamping & refining the book" on May 5, Sam wrote his brother and sister, "& we are well satisfied with it." Warner constructed the woof and Sam supplied the warp, or as he divulged in a letter to the editor of the New York *Graphic,* Warner "worked up the fiction & I have hurled in the facts. I consider it one of the most astonishing novels that ever was written. Night after night I sit up reading it over & over again & crying." Sam anticipated that it would "be published early in the fall." On May 19 they signed a contract with Bliss to publish the novel, the first work of fiction ever issued and distributed by a subscription press. The agreement granted each of them a 5 percent royalty, and they obtained a dramatic copyright on the title and plot of *The Gilded Age* the same day. Meanwhile, Sam recruited his friend J. Hammond Trumbull, "the most learned man in Hartford," a philologist and fellow member of the Monday Evening Club of Hartford and the Lotos Club of New York, to supply epigraphs for each chapter in Chinese, Sanskrit, Sioux, and dead languages with forgotten alphabets. A list of translations of these epigraphs was appended to the book in 1890 and enabled Sam to extend its copyright.[48]

The authors had labored for months under the misapprehension "that we were writing one coherent yarn" when in fact "we were writing two *incoherent* ones." Sam admitted later that their "ingredients refused to mix, & the book consisted of *two* novels—& remained so, incurably & vexatiously, [in] spite of all we could do to make the contents blend." Whereas Warner composed a conventional and sentimental domestic romance set in the genteel society of upper-crust Philadelphia, Sam drafted a more realistic satire of government fraud and political corruption set in Washington, D.C. At best, like parallel tracks, the plotlines either failed to intersect or they intersected only on occasion and by accident. At worst, the discrete stories warred for preeminence and concluded with nearly as many loose ends as a frayed rope. The authors apologized to the reader in an appendix for failing to resolve the fate of one character and for abandoning another with this explanation: "His life lay beyond the theatre of this tale." Some circumstantial evidence also suggests that neither Sam nor Charley Warner relished their collaboration when it was over. Sam told his personal secretary years later that he "became irked by the association" and, according to press reports, Warner's friends believed that his coauthorship of the novel "was a source of mortification to him." Sam treated Warner like the junior author, delegating to him the tasks of supervising the proofreading and selecting the illustrations for the American edition. Certainly Sam accused Warner privately of bungling "his description of Laura as a school-girl," and he later excused Mother Fairbanks for disliking the novel because, he assumed, she had "been reading Warner's chapters." Lest it seem like the potboiler calling the kettle black, Warner similarly wrote his friend Thomas Wentworth Higginson soon after publication that he had decided not to send a review copy to him. "You would not care for it," Warner explained, "and I have already found out that it is not much of a novel. It is rather of a raw satire on recent disagreeable things. You would only waste time on it." In an interview in 1886 Warner conceded that "neither of us thought much of the literary merit of *Gilded Age*, although it brought us in a great deal of money."[49]

For eighteen months Sam had been maturing as a political satirist. In September 1871 he published in the *New York Tribune* an ingenious parody of the Westminster Shorter Catechism, which he had no doubt been compelled to memorize as a Presbyterian schoolboy. The orthodox communicant was required to reply to the question "What is God?" by reciting this line: "There are three persons in the Godhead; the Father, the Son, and the Holy Ghost; and these three are one God, the same in substance, equal in power and glory." To the question "Who is God?" Sam's "Revised Catechism" specified this answer: "Money is God. Gold and greenbacks and stock—father, son, and the ghost of the same—three persons in one: these are the true and only God, mighty and supreme; and William Tweed is his prophet"—effectively desacralizing the Holy Trinity and lambasting the New York Democratic machine Tammany Hall as well. In December 1872, the month before starting to collaborate with Warner on *The Gilded Age*, he roasted New York mayor A. Oakey Hall, a creature of Tammany Hall, in a letter to the *Hartford Post* as a "piece of animated putridity." In April 1873, the same month he and Warner completed a draft of the novel, Sam protested in a letter to the editor of the *New York Tribune* the practice of bribing congressmen—that is, paying them "over again for work which they had already been paid to do."[50] He addressed the contemporary political scene in his share of the novel from precisely this jaded point of view.

The strength of the story lies in its topical satire, not the convoluted plot, which defies simple synopsis. Howard Baetzhold in fact has called it "one of the most curious melanges of farce, sentimental romance, and slashing satire ever written." It begins as a roman à clef. Though Squire Silas Hawkins, modeled on John Marshall Clemens, owns a vast tract of land in East Tennessee, he moves his family, including two adopted children, Henry Clay and Laura, to Missouri at the urging of the dreamy Colonel Sellers. The schemes to form the Columbus River Slackwater Navigation Company and build the Salt Lick Extension to the Pacific Railroad for commercial purposes mirror, respectively, James Marshall Clemens's pet projects, the Salt River Navigation Company and the Hannibal and St. Joseph Railroad. On his deathbed ten years later, Squire Hawkins admonishes his wife to hold onto the Tennessee land because eventually, he believed, their children would be fabulously rich. The land "furnished me a field for Sellers and a book," Sam reminisced in his autobiography. "Out of my half of the book I got $20,000, perhaps something more,"[51] ironically contradicting his claim elsewhere that Fentress County, Tennessee, resembled Nazareth because nothing good ever came out of it.

After the death of Squire Hawkins in chapter 9, the narrative morphs into a social satire, a study in political scandal, or a series of plotlines ripped from the headlines. The corrupt Senator Abner Dilworthy schemes to purchase sixty-five thousand acres of the Hawkins land for use as a trade school for freed slaves (an archetypal oxymoron) much as Senator Samuel Pomeroy of Kansas greased passage of a bill appropriating several acres of public land in Nashville to Fisk University. The proposal sounds honorable in the abstract—"the Knobs Industrial University would be a vast school of modern science and practice, worthy of a great nation"—but it is, of course, nothing more than a ruse for graft. Sam also satirized in the Indigent Congressman's Retroactive Appropriation the so-called Salary Grab Act passed by Congress on March 3, 1873, which raised the salaries of the president, Supreme Court justices, and members of Congress.[52] Laura Hawkins—named for Sam's childhood sweetheart—metamorphoses from an innocent ingénue in the first half of the novel into a soiled dove and femme fatale in the final chapters. She lobbies on behalf of the land appropriation and recklessly marries a bigamist, whom she murders in revenge for his faithlessless. Tried for the crime, she is exonerated by reason of temporary insanity on the strength of an expert defense witness who "was paid a thousand dollars for looking into the case." Sam used the episode as a hook on which to hang another editorial on the injustice of the insanity defense. He scorned the mental acuity of the jurors—"low foreheads and heavy faces they all had; some had a look of animal cunning, while the most were only stupid"—who decided Laura's fate. This part of the novel may be read as a parody of the postwar, formulaic "reconciliation novel," best exemplified by John W. De-Forest's *Miss Ravenel's Conversion* (1867), in which a former Northern soldier and an unreconstructed Southern belle fall in love and marry, typifying the reunion of the American nation after the War. In Sam's story, the double agent Laura Hawkins upon her acquittal turns in desperation "to that final resort of the disappointed of her sex, the lecture platform" (a stab at Anna Dickinson, the best-known female lecturer of her generation), only to suffer an embarrassment during her first appearance onstage and to die in mysterious circumstances, an apparent suicide, in divine retribution for her sin. In all, according to Bryant French, *The Gilded Age* reads like a parody of a sensation novel, with elements of disaster, suspense, "unknown parentage, adoption, false marriage, murder, self-sacrificing devotion."[53]

But more to the point, *The Gilded Age*, especially Sam's part of it, is a political satire that targeted Boss Tweed's corrupt political machine, the celebrated trial of Laura Fair in San Francisco for the murder of her ex-lover Alexander P. Crittenden, and the Pomeroy voter fraud controversy that disgraced the U.S. senator from Kansas. The duplicitous Dilworthy ends his political career in shame after he is caught buying votes to secure his re-election. According to Albert R. Kitzhaber, Sam "altered the facts" of the Pomeroy case "very little" in his depiction of the Dilworthy scandal. Claus Daufenbach adds that "chapters 53, 57, and 59 of the novel are drawn almost verbatim from the published reports" of the Pomeroy investigation.[54] In the Knobs Industrial University scenario, Sam foregrounded the Crédit Mobilier bribery scandal that destroyed the political career of Schuyler Colfax, the vice president of the United States, implicated Grant's private secretary and two members of his cabinet, and threatened Grant's presidency. While Sam nowhere refers to Colfax's role in the scandal, he caricatures his old Nevada acquaintance James Nye in the character of Senator Balloon (originally named "Bly") and General Ben Butler in General Sutler of Massachusetts.

Though hardly the hero of the novel, Colonel Sellers became its most memorable character. Sometimes considered a first cousin to Dickens's Wilkins Micawber, the improvident but inveterate optimist in *David Copperfield*, Sellers was in Sam's original conception of him above all a gentleman. "He is always genial, always gentle, generous, hospitable, full of sympathy with anything that any creature has at heart—he is always courtly of speech

& manner & never descends to vulgarity," Sam insisted to Warner in July 1873. "He must not be *distorted or caricatured* in any way in order to make a "funny" picture. Make him plain & simple." Similarly, he wrote Henry Watterson that Sellers was "a close study of a certain mutual kinsman" and "he had drawn him to the life, 'but for the love of Heaven' he said, 'don't whisper it, for he would never understand, or forgive me, if he did not thrash me on sight.'" In his autobiography, Sam insisted that he had "merely put him on paper as he was; he was not a person who could be exaggerated. The incidents which looked most extravagant . . . were not inventions of mine, but were facts of his life." Yet, as Sellers's surname suggests, he was a consummate salesman and a creature of the cash nexus. As the *New York Tribune* put it, he personified "the genial speculator who borrows ten cents while he divulges his scheme involving as many millions—but he is nevertheless a living and distinctive type of real American and peculiarly American character."[55] Fortunately, Cousin Jim apparently never learned that he was the inspiration for the colonel.

But his namesake surely objected. "Eschol Sellers was originally named 'Rollin Stone,'" Sam remembered later, but

> Mr. Warner did not like it and wanted it improved. He asked me if I was able to imagine a person named "Eschol Sellers." Of course I said I could not, without stimulants. He said that away out West, once, he had met, and contemplated, and actually shaken hands with a man bearing that impossible name—"Eschol Sellers." He added—"It was twenty years ago; his name has probably carried him off before this; and if it hasn't, he will never see the book anyhow. We will confiscate his name. . . Eschol Sellers is a safe name—it is a rock."

During the first week the novel was in press, George Eschol Sellers of Bowlesville, Illinois, appeared at the offices of the American Publishing Company in Hartford and threatened a libel suit for ten thousand dollars in damages should the authors of *The Gilded Age* fail to change the name of the character in the book. Warner later protested that he "never saw Col Escoll Sellers of Illinois nor did Mr. Clemens, nor did we ever hear of him till the book was published." Before more than a few thousand copies of the novel had been printed, Warner replaced "Eschol" with "Beriah."[56]

Ironically, Sam filed suit in the state of New York against a publishing pirate for twenty-five thousand dollars in damages soon after he and Warner finished the novel. In mid-April, as he testified in his sworn affidavit, "a stranger whose card bore the name of B. J. Such called at night at my house in Hartford, and said that he wanted to get me to write a sketch for an advertising pamphlet which he was about to publish. He said it would contain sketches by many authors. He showed me a proof plan of the work, which contained pictures which I now recognize in the completed pamphlet now before me." Benjamin Such offered Sam a thousand dollars to write a sketch for inclusion in this pamphlet, but Sam replied that he had no time because

> I was very busy on a book. He urged me further and finally asked if I had a reprint sketch which was not well known. I said I had and showed him a London edition of certain sketches of mine [*A Curious Dream and Other Sketches*], telling him he might use any of them free of charge. But I never authorized him to use two of them or more. . . . Gave him the book and told him I would prefer that he should use one of the sketches.

While traveling on May 15, the day before he dictated this statement, Sam had encountered a newsboy on the train selling a pamphlet containing five of his sketches "with this extraordinary feature in the title-page: 'Revised and selected for this work by Mark Twain!' I would not have given Mr. Such permission to use five of my sketches and use my name in his title page as he has done for $50,000. . . . Yet this man, a stranger to me, has seen fit to think I would give him such a privilege without the payment of a cent." As soon as he arrived in New York, Sam retained the legal services of Simon Sterne, senior partner in the firm of Sterne, Hudson, and Straus. He demanded twenty-five thousand dollars in damages and an injunction against the continued sale of the pamphlet.[57]

The suit was predicated not on a charge of copyright violation but on trademark infringement. "He does not sue under the Copyright Law, but claims that under the Trademark Law he has given a mercantile value to the name 'Mark Twain' which he alone has the right to use," the New York *Commercial Advertiser* explained. On June 11 Chief Justice Daniel P. Ingraham of the New York Supreme Court granted a permanent injunction against the sale of Such's pamphlet. "The sketches were the property of plaintiff," Ingraham ruled, "and he is entitled to an order restraining their publication without his consent. The agreement only contemplated the use of one sketch, and there was no authority to publish that one as revised by the author." But Ingraham did not base his decision on Sam's ownership of the Mark Twain trademark nor did he award him any punitive damages. Such was assessed only ten dollars in court costs. Nevertheless, Sam was convinced that the case validated his exclusive right to use his pseudonym. If a pseudonym could be registered as a trademark, he figured, an author who signed published writings with the brand would own rights to the intellectual property in perpetuity. As Loren Glass explains, Sam's "attempts to trademark his pen name" presume "a new model of U.S. authorship—one that legitimates literary property less as a mark of intellectual labor than as an index of cultural recognition." Or, as Sam claimed a couple of years later, "I won a suit on uncopyrighted matter by pleading my *nom de plume* as trademark." And in 1882 he asserted, "I won a trademark suit in New York once, but I never expect to win a copyright suit anywhere." The ruling in *Clemens v. Such* proved in the long run to be a Pyrrhic victory. As Herbert Feinstein concludes, the outcome "led Clemens to imagine for the rest of his life that a talismanic property inhered in his trademark (or trade name) 'Mark Twain' and that his pseudonym transcended the copyright laws determining the rights of more ordinary authors." When in June 1875 a pirate tried to sell "certain literary rubbish of mine" that was ostensibly "unprotected," Sam inserted a card in the *Hartford Courant* "to inform all interested parties that *all* of my rubbish is amply protected." Or as he jotted in his notebook as late as April 1879, "it occurred to me that a trademark case decided in my favor . . . in New York (about 1873) *really established international copyright.*"[58] Sam never clearly understood the differences between the two concepts.

On a happier note, Sam and Livy's plans for their new house began to assume tangible form. Livy notified her husband in early December 1871, while he was still on his speaking tour, that she had "been drawing a plan of our house" to be built within their budget. "We will put if it is necessary the 29000 into house, grounds, and what new furniture we may need," she wrote. But "if after a time we find that the estate is not worth a living to us, we will change entirely our mode of living—That probably will not be discovered for three or four or perhaps the eight years—we shall involve nobody and discomfort nobody, we will not be in debt for our house." They purchased a building lot near the home of Harriet Beecher Stowe for thirty-one thousand dollars from Hartford attorney Franklin Chamberlin on January 16, 1872. The lot was bounded on the north by Farmington Avenue, on the east by Forest Street, and on the west by Park River, formerly known as Hog River for the effluence dumped into it by the slaughterhouses along its shores. The stream no doubt reminded Sam of Bear Creek in the Hannibal of his boyhood. "Have just bought the loveliest building lot in Hartford," Sam bragged in mid-January, with measurements of "544 feet front on the Avenue & 300 feet deep," and "paid for it with first six months" of royalties on the sale of *Roughing It*. He reveled from the start in the prestige of his purchase. "Mr. Clemens seems to glory in his sense of possession," Livy wrote her family, because "he goes daily onto the lot, has had several falls trying the lay of the land by sliding around on his feet."[59]

Sam and Livy contracted with the architect Edward Tuckerman Potter at the recommendation of Lilly and George Warner, whose house and others in the neighborhood had been designed by him. (Sam's chariness about Potter may be suggested by the assignment of his surname to the vagrant Muff Potter in *The Adventures of Tom Sawyer*. While the name might evoke a pauper destined for burial in a "Potter's field," Sam arguably meant to refer derisively to the architect.) Elinor Mead Howells reported that, soon after moving into their house, the Clemenses were "greatly dissatisfied" with it because the garish exterior was "too much like a church." Its architectural style has been variously labeled over the years as "red brick Queen Anne," "high Victorian gothic, "steamboat gothic" (though there is no evidence that the design was meant to evoke the profile of a steamboat), "a cross between a Mexican adobe hut and a Swiss cottage," "Mark Twain in brick and mortar," and "English Violet" after the style of the French architect Eugène Viollet-le-Duc. Justin Kaplan rather ostentatiously characterized it as "part steamboat, part medieval stronghold, and part cuckoo clock." Sam was content to describe it simply as "eclectic." "There are nineteen different styles in it," he observed, "and folks can take their pick. It wouldn't do to call it 'mongrel' for that would be offensive to some." Livy had submitted her sketches to Potter, with floor plans for a mansion with a cellar and three stories above ground, dimensions at the foundation of 105 by 62 feet, featuring five lavatories with running water and nineteen other rooms, as well as central gas heating, and a veranda or "ombra" (Italian for "shade") circling most of the structure. The construction plans also included a greenhouse and a two-story stable or carriage house. Among Livy's most controversial decisions was "to turn [the] house around," with the kitchen, pantry and servants' quarters facing toward Farmington Avenue.[60]

Sam and Livy initially budgeted the house to cost between $55,000 and $60,000 (well over a million in twenty-first-century dollars), including land, construction, and furnishings, though the price soon expanded to fill the available space like gas in a vacuum. The total cost has been fairly estimated at $122,000. Sam calculated the cost in his autobiography at $167,000. However, the value of the property was assessed for tax purposes in 1875 at $84,450 and in 1877 at $66,650. Much as Sam raced to complete *The Gilded Age* in the spring of 1873 before the family left for England in mid-May, Livy hurried to finalize the blueprints of the house. "I think probably the architects [*sic*] plan of our house will come this week and I shall be exceedingly glad to get it," she wrote her sister Sue in late March. The construction company excavated the cellar for the house before the family sailed.[61] Sam and

Livy authorized their lawyer Charles E. Perkins to represent them with the architect and builders during their absence. By contract, the house was to be completed a year later but, like many of Sam's books, it would be finished long past the deadline.

CHAPTER 3

Round Trip

Persons who think there is no such thing as luck—good or bad—are
entitled to their opinion, although I think they ought to be shot for it.

—*Autobiography of Mark Twain*

IN MAY 1873 Samuel L. Clemens made good on his promise to escort Olivia
to England. His purpose in returning was threefold: to introduce his wife to
the mother country; to research his next travel book, a project that would
soon be abandoned; and to secure imperial copyright on *The Gilded Age*,
which had just been published in the United States. Joining the three Clemenses were Livy's Elmira friend Clara Spaulding, daughter Susy's nurse
Nellie Bermingham, and Sam's personal secretary Samuel Thompson. On
May 15 Sam led the party of six from Elmira to New York City. They were
greeted there by Mary Mason Fairbanks, who overnighted with Livy in their
cabin aboard ship while Sam slept at the St. Nicholas Hotel. Sam also consulted with the Irish playwright Dion Boucicault, who was angling to adapt
The Gilded Age for the stage. He was underwhelmed by the proposal, however. Boucicault "in some minor respects is an ass," he wrote Charles Dudley
Warner. "If you describe the outside of your trunk to him he can tell you
what it's got in it. I will not consent to his having more than one-third for
dramatizing the book." Boucicault soon lost interest in the project. On May
17, less than two weeks after completing the manuscript of *The Gilded Age*,
nine days after signing a contract with Elisha Bliss to publish it, and the day
after filing suit against Benjamin J. Such, Sam sailed with his family on the
Batavia, once again under the command of John Mouland. "Capt. Mouland
is just about perfection," Livy wrote her mother. "He has done every thing
that he possibly could to make us comfortable and to make things pleasant
for us. . . . He grows more & more delightful the better one knows him—We
would not come back with anyone else on any account if it is possible to come
with him."[1]

Sam and his entourage landed in Liverpool on May 27. "We felt so dirty
and forlorn when we reached Liverpool and found that we had got to remain there two days in order to get washing done," Livy wrote her sister

Sue, "that we decided to come right on to London." They railed to London the next day—"the ride was the most charming that I ever could imagine," Livy mused—where they rented rooms at Edwards's Royal Cambridge Hotel in Hanover Square. She added, "Our appartments [*sic*] are perfectly delightful, I expected to find them rather barren looking but was very happily disappointed—Our food is excellent, delicious bread and butter and everything palatable, we do feel so cozy and comfortable as we sit down to our meals." Among their first callers were Benjamin Disraeli, a novelist and the once and future prime minister of Great Britain, who lodged on the same floor of their hotel; George W. Smalley, the London correspondent of the *New York Tribune*; and Sam's publisher Edmund Routledge. Sam also renewed his friendship with Joaquin Miller, a western American poet and playwright. "We see Miller every day or two, & like him better & better all the time," Sam confided to Mother Fairbanks. Through Miller's agency Sam also met the British publisher Richard Bentley, Lord Houghton (aka Richard Monckton Milnes), a poet and Labour Party politician, and Lord Elcho (aka Francis Charteris, Tenth Earl of Wemyse). Miller laughed that Sam was as "shy as a girl" when he was introduced to "the learned and great who wanted to take him by the hand."[2]

From the first, Sam and his clan experienced some tumult in their family life, even though they had registered at a quiet family hotel. "There was little routine" to their days, Thompson remembered. Occasionally Sam "would dictate in the morning. But there were callers, excursions, and sightseeings." He heard the Fisk University Jubilee Singers perform at least once and probably twice at the Hanover Square Rooms in May. He long remembered the afternoon "when their 'John Brown's Body' took a decorous, aristocratic English audience by surprise and threw them into a volcanic eruption of applause before they knew what they were about." He was delighted when the singers earned accolades in England because "their music so well deserved such a result." According to Thompson, Sam "had never before seen a cultured English audience so enthusiastic in applause." Their success was proved, too, by the "companies of imitators trying to ride into public favor by endeavoring to convey the impression that they are the original Jubilee Singers." Livy reported to her sister on May 31 that she and Sam had driven to Temple Bar, seen "the City gates, went through Drury lane," and attended a performance of *Man and Wife*, adapted from a novel by Wilkie Collins, at the Prince of Wales Theater. She gushed two weeks later to Sam's mother and sister that they had since visited St. Paul's Cathedral, Westminster Abbey, and Westminster Hall and had "taken rides in the Parks." Sam also attended the races in Berkshire on Ascot Cup Day, June 12, and Madame Ristori's performance in *Elizabeth* at the Theatre Royal on June 18. George Dolby renewed his effort to persuade Sam to lecture during his residence in England. "I have tried to make up my mind" to "lecture on the Sandwich Islands here," Sam reflected on June 19, "but I can't—so I have dismissed the subject from my mind at present & don't know whether I shall talk or not." The evening of June 22 Sam and Livy dined at the Chelsea home of Charles Dilke, at the time a young member of Parliament from the Liberal Party. There Sam again encountered the American journalist Kate Field, the Dilkes' houseguest, whom he had forgotten since their first meeting in Buffalo two and a half years earlier. Field reported in her London correspondence with the *New York Tribune* that the dinner had lasted until well after midnight and she had enjoyed the company of "an American by the singular name of Mark Twain." At subsequent dinners at Dilke's home, Sam also met the poet Robert Browning; Ricciotti Garibaldi, son of the Italian revolutionary; and Segismundo Moret, Spanish ambassador to the Court of St. James.[3]

Ironically, when Field and Sam dined together in Chelsea on June 22 they were rival journalists covering the visit to England of the Shah of Persia. Field held by far the more prestigious appointment: she had been recruited by Whitelaw Reid to report events for the *New York Tribune*, whereas Sam had been hired by G. W. Hosmer, the London representative of the *New York Herald*, "to help write up the Shah . . . at £20 a column, gold" or one hundred dollars for each of the five articles he contributed to its pages. Sam never mentioned Field in any of his dispatches to the *Herald*, though Field teased in hers that Sam was "endeavoring to instil civilization into the Shah by sitting on the floor and playing draw poker" with him. According to Field's reports, Sam claimed "that his august pupil makes wonderful progress in this great American game, and will soon be able to play against the American Minister or the brilliant editor of the *Louisville Courier-Journal*," Henry Watterson.

In any case, on June 17 Sam railed to Dover and crossed the English Channel to Ostend. The residents of the Belgian town "speak both the French and the Flemish with exceeding fluency, and yet I could not understand them in either tongue," he joked in his first dispatch. The next day he caught a glimpse of "the King of Kings" and wrote a brief portrait of him: "He was a handsome, strong-featured man, with a rather European fairness of complexion; had a mustache, wore spectacles, seemed of a good height

THE NEW HEATHEN CHINEE.
MARK TWAIN TEACHES THE SHAH THE AMERICAN GAME OF DRAW POKER.

Figure 4. Caricature of Samuel Clemens playing cards with the shah of Persia, *Frank Leslie's Illustrated Newspaper*, July 26, 1873.

and graceful build and carriage, and looked about forty or a shade less." In the afternoon of June 18 Sam recrossed the Channel with the British flotilla accompanying the shah and devoted most of his second report to the "picturesque naval spectacle," particularly to the ironclads *Audacious*, *Devastation*, and *Vanguard*, the "enormous five-masted men-of-war, great turret ships, steam packets, pleasure yachts. . . . All the ships were in motion—gliding hither and thither, in and out, mingling and parting—a bewildering whirl of flash and color." Sam's next three columns covered the events honoring the shah in London and Portsmouth, including a reception and military exhibition at Windsor Castle; a ball at Guildhall, even though the esteemed visitor did not dance; an opera at Covent Garden Theatre, where the shah wore "all his jewels" and a "shaving brush in his hat front"; a naval show; another grand ball at the Southsea Assembly Rooms, where Sam and Livy were invited guests; and a concert at Albert Hall.[4]

Sam did not see any of his dispatches in print until early August, after an excursion to northern England, Ireland, and Scotland, when much to his dismay he discovered that they had been rewritten by the editors. After he read the first of them he complained to his friend Edmund Yates, the editor of the London *World*, "I am sincerely grieved to see that the *Herald* people have added a paragraph to one of my letters which puts me in a bad light. They describe me & the London correspondents as cheering the Shah at Ostend & conducting ourselves in anything but a proper way. It was a careless thing in the *Herald* people to do." But they continued to tamper with his prose. "The *Herald* folks rung some very vile & offensive sentences into my account" of the shah's visit, he whined. Worse yet, Elisha Bliss had tentatively planned to reprint all of the letters in a pamphlet so Sam telegraphed him to cease and desist. He followed the telegraph with a letter of explanation: "I find by reading over those Herald letters that I don't like them at all—& besides, the *Herald* people have added paragraphs & interlineations, & not pleasant ones, either. . . . Curse those letters!" Forty years later, in his autobiographical dictation, he still resented the insult. His reports "seemed to the *Herald* to lack humor," he recalled, "a defect which the New York office supplied from its own resources, which were poor and coarse and silly beyond imagination."[5] Sam never reissued any part of them in any forum.

Still, they damaged his reputation, as he feared when he discovered they had been mutilated. The dispatches were roundly scorned upon their first printing (and only appearance until 1923, when Albert Bigelow Paine collected them in *Europe and Elsewhere*). The *Raleigh Sentinel* objected to "the manner of Mark Twain" pandering to the shah. The New York *Commercial Advertiser* editorialized that "America will never forgive the Shah for his unhappy influence upon Mark Twain." The *Charleston News and Courier* opined that Sam's "account of the Shah's visit to England is as dull and wearisome as a third-rate funeral procession." The *Richmond Whig* ("conspicuous failure") and *Brooklyn Eagle* ("excessive dullness") joined the chorus of criticism. Unbeknownst to Sam, Whitelaw Reid at the *New York Tribune* sniggered over Sam's quandary in a letter to Kate Field: "You do not need to be told that most of the stuff he has done for the *Herald* is very poor, because you have seen it. It won't hurt you to know that your letters, on the other hand, have received more praise than any you ever wrote for us before."[6] In his contest with Field in this particular case, Sam finished last.

As if their days were not hectic enough, on June 25 the Clemenses moved six blocks from Edwards's Royal Cambridge to the Langham Hotel, where Sam had stayed the year before. The private house, according to Thompson, "was not so convenient for some things; for instance there was no billiard room, and billiards was Clemens' chief exercise." Or, as Sam put it, "My wife likes Edwards' Hotel; & so would I if I were dead; I would not desire a more tranquil & satisfactory tomb." And, more bluntly: "I prefer a little more excitement." At the Langham they rented, he wrote Joseph Twichell on June 29, "a luxuriously ample suite of apartments on the third floor, our bedroom looking straight up Portland Place, our parlor having a noble array of great windows." Their rooms soon became a kind of salon. Moncure Conway visited Sam and "found the great American humorist comfortably at home in an elegant private parlor, in the center of which a dinner was spread for two. Mark looks pale and careworn. His beautiful, charming wife appeared exquisitely graceful playing with the infant Twain." Among the writers, artists, and politicians who called on Sam were Robert Browning, Charles Dilke, Lord Houghton, Charles Kingsley, John Millais, David Dunglas Home, the novelist Ivan Turgenev, and the Anglo-Irish journalist and politician Lord Wyndham, Fourth Earl of Dunraven.[7]

When he was not hosting celebrities and other friends in his rooms at the Langham, Sam became a coveted guest at myriad dinners and parties, usually in company with Livy. "We seem to see nothing but English social life," he boasted to Mother Fairbanks. "We seem to find no opportunity to see London sights." He was invited to meetings of the Whitefriars, the Savage Club, and the Athenaeum Club. He compared the Athenaeum clubhouse when he first entered it to a well-appointed private library; it was a "very dignified, composed place with a dim religious light. All manner of books—tables full of them. Luxurious chairs. Huge reading room." He crossed paths during these weeks with "many pleasant people," including the lawyer and future jurist Sir Henry James; the American expatriate, humorist, and folklorist Charles Godfrey Leland (aka Hans Breitmann); the novelist George Meredith; the historian John Lothrop Motley; and the dramatist Arthur Pinero. On June 15 he was the guest of honor at a dinner at the Langham hosted by J. M. Bellew, a fellow passenger aboard the *Batavia* the month before, where he likely met the genre painter W. P. Frith and the novelists Anthony Trollope and Wilkie Collins among "the fourteen gentlemen distinguished in literature and art and on the stage" in attendance. Sam and Livy attended a private dinner hosted by George Smalley at the Cosmopolitan Club on July 2, where he met Thomas Hughes, the author of *Tom Brown's School Days* (1857), and Herbert Spencer.[8]

On July 4 Sam and Livy were present at a conclave of American expatriates in London celebrating Independence Day, with U.S. Ambassador Robert Schenck presiding, where Sam echoed his remarks aboard the *Quaker City* in June 1867 on the occasion of Hannah Duncan's birthday: "I say better one decade of this period than the 900 years of Methusaleh. There is more done now in a year than he ever saw in all his life."[9] He also took another swipe at trial by jury, noting that "its efficiency is only marred by the difficulty of finding twelve men every day who don't know anything and can't read. And I may observe that we have an insanity plea that would have saved Cain." The next day, at the invitation of Trollope, Sam and Livy attended the Saturday evening salon of the novelist Lady Thomas Duffus Hardy. Two evenings later, Trollope hosted a dinner at the Garrick Club to honor Joaquin Miller with Sam and Thomas Hughes in attendance. Trollope pointedly excluded Kate Field from the invitation list on the basis of her gender, writing her that "two of the wildest of your countrymen . . . dine with my club. Pity you have not yet established the rights of your sex or you could come and meet them and be as jolly as men." The Clemenses spent the next three days, July 8–10, sightseeing in Warwick and Stratford-on-Avon, the hometown of William Shakespeare, at the invitation of its mayor Charles E. Flower. Moncure Conway acted as their guide. Livy "was an ardent Shakespearian," Conway remembered in his autobiography, and Sam was

> determined to give her a surprise. He told her that we were going on a journey to Epworth, and persuaded me to connive with the joke by writing to Charles Flower not to meet us himself but send his carriage. On arrival at the station we directed the driver to take us straight to the church. When we entered and Mrs. Clemens read on Shakespeare's grave "Good friend for Jesus sake forbeare," she started back exclaiming, "Heavens, where am I!" Mark received her reproaches with an affluence of guilt, but never did lady enjoy a visit more.

Sam signed the guest album at Anne Hathaway's cottage, which at the time P. T. Barnum was negotiating to buy and move lock, stock, and barrel to the United States. Sam thanked Flower for his hospitality a couple of days later. "No episode in our two months' sojourn in England," he allowed, "has been . . . so altogether rounded & complete" and he soon donated five guineas, over five hundred dollars in modern money, toward the construction of the Shakespeare Memorial Theater in Stratford. On July 11 Sam traveled to Richmond Park, southwest of the city, to the grave of the poet James

Thomson. He arrived back in London in time to attend the Lord Mayor's Ball at the Mansion House that evening along with eight hundred other guests. On July 16 Sam and Livy were welcomed by George MacDonald to a garden party at his home, the Retreat, in Hammersmith on the Thames in West London. The Jubilee Singers entertained, at least the third time that Sam heard them perform.[10]

So busy was he that in mid-July Sam dismissed his secretary Thompson with a generous severance. He had had no time to write anything except the mediocre shah letters for the *New York Herald*, and he had finally decided not even to take notes for a travel book about England. Thompson remembered, as he wrote Sam in 1909, that after a few weeks "you found the public and social tax on your time interfered with literary work and that you might as well dispense with my services. Your memory was that I was to expect less than ten dollars a week. However, you gave me twenty pounds," the equivalent of a hundred dollars, for eight weeks' employment.[11]

To escape temporarily the "tax" on their time—"six weeks of daily lunches, teas, and dinners away from home"—Sam and Livy left for Scotland with Susy and nurse Nellie in tow on July 19 and paused in York, midway between London and Edinburgh, for a few days to bask in their anonymity and tour St. Mary's Abbey. They carried no letters of introduction and "for full 24 hours no one has called, no cards have been sent up, no letters received, no engagements made, & none fulfilled," Sam wrote Livy's mother, adding,

> All of which is to say, we have been 24 hours out of London, & they have been 24 hours of *rest* & quiet. Nobody knows us here—we took good care of that. In Edinburgh we are to be introduced to nobody, & shall stay in a retired, private hotel, & go on resting. For the present we shall remain in this queer old walled town, with its crooked, narrow lanes, that tell us of their old day that knew no wheeled vehicles.

The Clemens party arrived in the Scottish capital no later than July 25, registered at Veitch's Hotel on George Street, "and prepared to have a comfortable season all to ourselves," Sam recalled. But as luck would have it, Livy immediately fell ill and required medical attention. Sam knew the name of only one physician in the city and him only by reputation: John Brown, the author of *Rab and His Friends* (1859), a heart-warming boy-meets-dog story. Brown was still practicing medicine, Sam learned, so he called at his home on Rutland Street to fetch him to the hotel. Livy soon recovered and, for the next month, Brown and the Clemenses "were together every day, either in his house or in our hotel," and Sam was unusually grateful. "I am very glad," he confessed to Brown, "to know that I reached so high a place with you—& all the more so because we hold you in such love & reverence. Livy, my wife, has never conceived so strong & so warm an affection for any one since we were married as she has for you." According to Sam's dictation in February 1906, "[Brown's] was a sweet and winning face—as beautiful a face as I have ever known. Reposeful, gentle, benignant—the face of a saint at peace with all the world and placidly beaming upon it the sunshine of love that filled his heart." Sam thought Brown was

> the loveliest creature in the world. . . . We made the round of his professional visits with him in his carriage every day for six weeks. He always brought a basket of grapes and we brought books. The scheme which we began with on the first round of visits was the one which was maintained until the end—and was based upon this remark, which he made when he was disembarking from the carriage at his first stopping place to visit a patient, "Entertain yourselves while I go in here and reduce the population."

On his part, Brown also cherished the friendship. "Had the author of *The Innocents Abroad* not come to Edinburgh at that time we in all human probability might never have met, and what a deprivation that would have been to me during the last quarter of a century!" he declared. He considered Livy "a quite lovely little woman, modest and clever," with "eyes like a Peregrine's," and he thought Susy, whom he nicknamed "Megalopis" for her large eyes, Livy's "ludicrous miniature." In a concession to Walter Scott, Sam bought the twelve-volume Abbotsford edition of the Waverly novels and, in the spirit of the purchase, he and Livy fit into their schedule visits to local landmarks associated with Scott's life and writings, including Scott's hometown Abbotsford and Melrose. During their excursion to Melrose, they dined with Alexander Russell, editor of the Edinburgh *Scotsman*. Three months later, Sam remarked that he knew "Russell very well." Sam and Livy also toured the Trossachs nature park and Arthur's Seat, "a ruined palace of Mary Queen of Scots," in mid-August, leaving Susy in the care of her nursemaid in Edinburgh. Ned House visited the city and touched Sam for a loan of three hundred dollars so that he could sail to Japan. In Edinburgh Sam wrote the first six chapters of the burlesque "Diary of Shem in the Ark"; he would work on it intermittently for the rest of his life, never completing it, though it developed over the years into a "Diary of Methuselah" and a "Noah's Ark" narrative and it obviously influenced Sam's "Adam's Diary" (1893) and *Eve's Diary* (1905).[12]

During their trip to Great Britain, to judge from all available evidence, Sam and Livy went on an extravagant spending spree. Between late May and early September, by his estimate, they blew through $10,000 (about $200,000 in modern currency) in travel, living, and incidental expenses—"& the end is not yet!" In Edinburgh they stumbled across "an old carved oak mantelpiece in a kind of general junk-shop and hospital for disabled furniture." Some fourteen feet tall, it had been salvaged from Ayton Castle near the city and featured "the armorial carvings of its original owner." Livy "was greatly taken with it and wanted to own it and put it into the house which we were then building in Hartford" so they bought and shipped it to the United States, where it was mounted over the fireplace in the ground-floor library of their new home. Sam had the year of its installation (1874) engraved in the oak and hung a brass plate on it with a motto from Ralph Waldo Emerson's essay "Domestic Life" (1870): "The ornament of a house is the friends who frequent it."[13] Livy resisted the temptation to lavish even more money on home furnishings. "If I was sure our house would not exceed $20[000] or 25000," she admitted to her mother, "I would spend more here, because we shall want the things when we get into our new house, but our expenses are so heavy and we cannot feel sure what the house will cost until it is finished, so I do not think it best." Instead she devised a plan. When the family returned to London, "if Mr Clemens does some traveling through rural England with Mr [Joaquin] Miller," she would move into a small apartment "and live just as cheaply as possible"—not to economize but "so that I can have the money to spend."[14]

The Clemenses left Edinburgh on August 25, as Livy wrote her sister Sue, "with sincere regret," in large part because Livy feared "that we shall probably never see" John Brown again. She was prescient. While they lingered in Glasgow for a couple of days, Sam wrote an essay, "'Party Cries' in Ireland," about religious sectarianism. The family then suffered a rocky ferry trip across the Irish Sea to Belfast on August 28. All in the party except Sam "suffered more in that one day than in the ten days crossing the Atlantic," according to Livy. While in the city Sam befriended Frank Finlay, son-in-law of Alexander Russell and owner-editor of the Belfast *Northern Whig*, the principal daily in northern Ireland; he soon considered Finlay "one of the closest friends I have." He also toured the Purdysburn Mental Hospital, though he disapproved of the personal liberties allowed the inmates. The family railed south to Dublin on September 2, where they registered at the historic Shelbourne Hotel, then again ferried across the Irish Sea to Liverpool, Chester, and Shrewsbury on September 6. There they were entertained for two days at Condover Hall, an Elizabethan manor house, by Reginald Cholmondeley, uncle of novelist Mary Cholmondeley, whom Sam had apparently met during his travels in England the year before. Brown had urged Sam to accept the invitation. As Sam recounted their conversation in chapter 15 of *Following the Equator* (1896), which disguises Cholmondeley under the alias Bascom and Condover Hall as Bascom Hall, Brown described Cholmondeley as "a man of genius, a man of fine attainments, a choice man in every way, a rare and beautiful character. He said that Bascom Hall was a particularly fine example of the stately manorial mansion of Elizabeth's days, and that it was a house worth going a long way to see . . . ; that Mr. B. was of a social disposition; liked the company of agreeable people, and always had samples of the sort coming and going." Sam and Livy returned to London and the Langham Hotel on September 8. They had decided during the final leg of the trip to return to the United States no later than October 25 because they were weary of the rigors of travel. Livy was also two months pregnant. Sam scribbled a friend that he planned to "stay right here in this hostelry till Oct 24." He added, however, that he and Livy were "building a house in America, & London is a good enough place to buy little odds & ends in for it, & so I have sent for more money & am going to continue to collect the odds & ends calmly & with courage."[15]

Soon enough he had reason to worry. The financial markets in the United States were shaky when Sam sent for more money and they collapsed shortly after the money arrived by wire. Jay Cooke and Company, one of the largest banks in the world, defaulted on its debt on September 13 and the brokers on Wall Street were plunged into panic on Black Thursday, September 18. The New York Stock Exchange locked its doors on September 20 and did not reopen for ten days. Meanwhile, Sam was as unnerved as a New York stockbroker. "The financial panic in America has absorbed about all my attention & anxiety since Monday evening [September 22]," he wrote John Brown. He estimated that he had lost six hundred pounds sterling, or three thousand dollars, the equivalent of about sixty thousand modern dollars, in the crash. A day or two later he was notified that his bank, Livermore, Clews and Company, had suspended payment. "After we went to bed," Livy wrote her mother,

> Mr Clemens could not sleep, he had to return to the parlor and smoke and try to get sleepy—He said the reason that he could not sleep was that he kept thinking how stupid he had been not to draw out our money after he heard that J. Cook & Co. had failed. . . . We do wish that we knew how you are all feeling at home financially, it seems as if this terrible pannic [sic] must effect all business men. You know if the firm is cramped Mr Clemens can lecture and get money to pay our debts and get us home—Now Mother don't you and Charlie laugh at that, lecturing is what Mr C. always speaks of doing when their [sic] seems any need of money—Just think here we are among friends who would quickly lend us money if we needed it.

Sam long believed that Livermore, Clews and Company defrauded him; Henry Clews "choused me out of a good deal of money . . . as coolly as ever any other crime was committed in this world," he claimed.[16]

Still, Livy was not nearly so troubled as Sam by the financial shellacking they suffered in the Panic of 1873. She happily traveled to Brighton in late

September 27 to tour the aquarium, "a perfectly wonderful place I did enjoy it so very much, it was like an enchanted land," she wrote her mother. She added in the same letter that she and Sam planned to travel to Paris with Henry Lee on October 1 to sightsee and shop for the house. Sam had written Lee "after the loss of the money to wait, not to make the arrangements about Paris until he saw us again, but Mr Lee did not get the word and the arrangements were all made—I think probably it will not make any great difference."[17]

After resisting for months Dolby's entreaties to lecture in London, Sam finally consented under financial duress. Before leaving for Paris on September 30 he asked the agent to schedule dates for him to deliver "Our Fellow Savages of the Sandwich Islands" after he returned from the Continent on October 7. The next week in Paris is a literal blank in the record. There is no impression of it except for one letter Livy wrote her sister on October 4: "I am blue & cross and homesick—I suppose what makes me feel the latter strongly is that we are contemplating staying in London another month." She was distressed by the prospect of postponing their return to the United States because she had suffered "socially more than he," W. D. Howells later explained. "She had sat after dinner with ladies who snubbed and ignored one another and left her to find her own amusement." Sam had traveled to England in part to reside there as a condition of securing British copyright on *The Gilded Age* when it was published by Routledge, but Bliss to date had not sent any proof of the American edition so, as Livy lamented, "if [Sam] goes home before the book is published here he will lose his copyright."[18]

Back in London, Sam launched a weeklong lecture series—six performances in London at the Queen's Concert Rooms, aka the Hanover Square Rooms—beginning the evening of October 13. Dolby's choice of venue was strategic: Charles Dickens, Franz Joseph Haydn, Franz Liszt, and Niccolò Paganini had all performed in the hall, which had opened in 1774 with a seating capacity of about nine hundred. Moncure Conway expressed surprise that Dolby had booked Sam to appear in "the most fashionable hall in London" and "charge high prices for admission" rather than, "like Artemus Ward and other American entertainers, at Egyptian Hall or some popular place," but it may have been the only venue available on short notice. Or Dolby chose it for its snooty cachet and excellent acoustics. Because he charged high prices, "the hall was crowded with fashionable people in evening dress" every night. Sam adapted the talk to his upscale audience, slightly revising "Our Fellow Savages," for example, by omitting his description of the statue of a skinless man in the introduction, his offer to illustrate cannibalism by devouring a baby, and his comment about a cannibal who wondered "how a white man would go with onions." Both Sam and Dolby promoted the lectures unstintingly during the week before Sam debuted. In a letter to the editor of the London *Standard* dated October 7, Sam piqued interest in his appearances by declaring his intention to serve the public:

> In view of the prevailing frenzy concerning the Sandwich Islands, and the inflamed desire of the public to acquire information concerning them, I have thought it well to tarry yet another week in England and deliver a lecture upon this absorbing subject. . . . I do it because I am convinced that no one can allay this unwholesome excitement as effectually as I can, and to allay it, and allay it as quickly as possible, is surely the one thing that is absolutely necessary at this juncture. I feel and know that I am equal to this task, for I can allay any kind of an excitement by lecturing upon it. I have saved many communities in this way.

Moncure Conway recalled later that Sam "raised a roar" by declaring "he had selected the subject because he had observed the frantic excitement about those Islands filling every English breast." Sam was quoted often in the British press, as when he declared that "only three more miracles remain to be done, viz., the fitting up of a cabin inside a whale, and thus solving the north-west passage" and opening the Polar Sea "in comfort and security; the resuscitating of Dante and sending him on a new tour through the lower regions as a special correspondent; and the draining of the Dead Sea and the rediscovery of Sodom and Gomorrah!" On his part, Dolby placed advertisements for Sam's lectures in the leading newspapers beginning on October 9. Nevertheless, according to Charles Warren Stoddard, "nobody expected him to draw an audience unless he could be advertised at least three months in advance." But against all odds "he drew. He drew better every night. The week's business was something astonishing."[19] By the end of the week, people were turned away.

Moreover, the reviewers were almost unanimous in their admiration for the lecturer and the lecture. Sam spoke without a lectern or props, merely a table with a water pitcher and tumbler. As usual, he employed no one to introduce him; he merely wandered onto the stage and introduced himself. He spoke for eighty to ninety minutes without a script, pictures, or music. And like Dickens, he proved to be a consummate actor on the boards. He was a smash success in the opinion of all but the most provincial of newspapers. Before a full house on opening night that included, according to the London *Cosmopolitan*, "a large and select assembly, embracing many of the wits, the journalists, the authors, the celebrities, and . . . the beauties of London," as well as the American showman P. T. Barnum, Sam amazed the critics. The London *Standard* considered the talk "not only brimful of humor" but "remarkable for the shrewd observation which the lecturer evinced of men and the events of the day; and it contained no small amount of information." Sam was lauded as "an actor of no mean powers, and were he to take to the stage instead of to the reading desk, it is a question whether some actors that we wot of might not find in him a very formidable competitor for public favor." The London *Observer* commended his "literary eccentricities" and his "singularly enjoyable abilities as a public lecturer." The London *Sportsman* averred that "if his books are humorous, his lectures are ten times more so, and if his printed jokes are laughable they possess the inestimable advantage of increased raciness when heard from his own lips." No less enthusiastic were *Once a Week* ("a word painter of no mean caliber"), the *Times* of London ("his quaint dry manner and curious accent provoked much amusement"), *Bradford Observer* ("repeatedly and loudly applauded"), *Lloyd's Weekly Newspaper* ("humorous anecdotes and quaint touches of satire"), the Darlington *Northern Echo* ("No amount of verbatim reporting or glowing description could give you a fair idea of the charmingly novel mannerism and marvelously happy story-telling ability of this singularly eccentric American genius"), and Tom Hood in *Fun* ("a more genuine intellectual treat has not been presented to the public for years"). The London *Examiner* applauded Sam's "dry manner, his admirable self-possession, and perfectly grave countenance," all supposed characteristics "of the American humorous lecturer." Similarly, the London *Evening Post* acclaimed the "vein of humour peculiarly American" that "permeates the lecture" and added that "there was a unanimous expression of satisfaction" by the audience, which by the "heartiest applause" twice recalled the speaker for bows. The London *Daily News* also reported that the speaker "possesses all the *insouciance* and *aplomb* which is generally ascribed to American lecturers," he "apparently came upon the stage assured of the success which he so speedily obtained," and he "was greatly cheered on retiring." On Friday, October 17, the final evening of Sam's engagement, the packed house was "well pleased with him, and warmly testified it." Only the *Sheffield & Rotherham Independent* ("to the ordinary reader" the acerbic wit in the lecture "will be quite invisible") and the *Manchester Guardian* ("he embodied in his lecture too large a proportion of admitted facts") were adverse in their criticism.[20]

Several reviewers drew the inevitable comparisons between Sam and Artemus Ward, such as the London *Graphic* ("a lecture of the Artemus Ward type"), often but not always in Sam's favor. One of the illustrated London papers suggested that the lecture was "as full of good stories as a plum-pudding ought to be of plums" and that it was "the freshest and most amusing entertainment London has enjoyed since poor Artemus Ward delighted the town." The London *Echo* made the same point ("since the days of Artemus Ward, there has been no one to animate . . . American drollery until Mark

Twain"), as did the London *Spectator* ("an entertainment perhaps ever more generally popular than Artemus Ward's inimitable lectures") and the London correspondent for the Buffalo *Commercial* ("there are compensating qualities in his fun which render him as a whole as successful a 'show' . . . as was the poor fellow who came over here to make us laugh while he was coughing his way to an early grave"). But in a second review of Sam's lecture, the London *Daily News* struck a slightly dissenting note, referring to Sam as "a leading professor" of "that school of jesting" that included humorists such as Ward. At its best, this critic opined, "it is irresistible; even at its worst, it is popular," but "we doubt whether it is destined to amuse the world for long; or whether anything more than ashes will be felt when its fire goes out." He considered Bret Harte "a true poet" despite the joke in the United States that Harte had reversed the path of the sun by rising in the west and setting in the east.[21]

Sam ended his week at the Queen's Concert Rooms with a matinee performance on Saturday, October 18. He had already laid plans with Dolby to resume his London lectures on December 1. First, however, he was obliged to escort Livy, Susy, Clara Spaulding, and Nellie back to Hartford. He closed his afternoon performance by thanking his audience for their kindness:

> I won't keep you one single moment in this suffocating atmosphere. I simply wish to say that this is the last lecture I shall have the honor to deliver in London until I return from America, four weeks from now. I only wish to say . . . I am very grateful. I do not wish to appear pathetic, but it is something magnificent for a stranger to come to the metropolis of the world to be received so handsomely as I have been. I simply thank you.

Afterward, the Clemenses railed to Liverpool, where Sam spoke before a packed house at the Liverpool Institute the evening of October 20. According to the New York *Graphic*, "thousands were unable to obtain admission to the hall." The *Liverpool Express* complained that the lecture was "an odd combination of grotesque and jerky drollery" and the *Liverpool Journal* followed suit, lamented his "air of improvisation," "strong American accent," and "low, rather droning monotone." But at the finale, according to the *Liverpool Mercury*, "the audience cheered him to the echo and recalled him to the platform."[22] The next day, the Clemenses embarked aboard the *Batavia*, again captained by John Mouland, for their return to the United States.

Sam alluded a quarter century later to his visit to England and Scotland in mid-1873 in one of his gloomiest dream narratives, titled "The Great Dark" (1898) by Bernard DeVoto and first published in *Letters from the Earth* (1962). In this aborted fragment of a semiautobiographical story, avatars of

Sam and Livy are named Henry and Alice Edwards; they are homunculi aboard a microscopic ship adrift in a drop of water and their lives are surreal. Henry attempts to remind his wife about details of a former excursion before "the great dark" descended upon them:

> "It was seven years ago. We went over in the *Batavia*. Do you remember the *Batavia*?"
> "I don't Henry."
> "Captain Moreland. Don't you remember him?"
> "To me he is a myth, Henry."
> "Well, it beats anything. We lived two or three months in London, then six weeks in a private hotel in George Street, Edinburgh—Veitch's. Come!"
> "It sound pleasant, but I have never heard of these things before, Henry."
> "And Dr. John Brown, of *Rab and His Friends*—you were ill, and he came every day; and when you were well again he still came every day and took us all around while he paid his visits, and we waited in his carriage while he prescribed for his patients. And he was so dear and lovely. You *must* remember all that, Alice."
> "None of it, dear; it is only a dream."

In this dystopian fantasy, Sam/Henry recalls the trip to England and Scotland only to have Livy/Alice stifle all memory of it—if it occurred at all. Written soon after Sam emerged from personal bankruptcy and was again living abroad, the tale both evokes and represses the portentous events of 1873 when Livy suffered a medical emergency, their Hartford house was under construction and over budget, the costs of furnishing it were ruinous, and Sam was compelled to stride the London stage nightly in order to recoup some of his losses in the Panic and to keep the proverbial wolf from the door—or, in other words, when his bank account was first overextended, then depleted, then inaccessible. The financial anxieties Sam suffered for the remainder of his life, his obsessive worry over money, his recurring fear of spiraling into debt and bankruptcy all bubbled to the surface during this trip. As if he had knotted a thread around his finger, he always remembered the financial crisis precipitated by the Panic of 1873. Like Alice Edwards, he would have preferred to believe from a distance of twenty-five years that the nightmare had never happened.[23]

"The first three days were stormy, and wife, child, maid, and Miss Spaulding were all sea-sick 25 hours out of the 24, and I was sorry I ever started," Sam wrote John Brown during the voyage. "We have plowed a long way over the sea, and there's twenty-two hundred miles of restless water between us, now, besides the railway stretch." When they landed in New York the evening of November 2, they were met by Sam's brother Orion, Livy's mother, and Charley Langdon, who helped them clear customs. As usual, the clan registered for the night at the St. Nicholas Hotel. Orion wrote Mollie the next day that Susy "runs about and talks a little, and is exceedingly pretty, having a rather broad face with color in her cheeks." Their Hartford house, nothing more than a hole in the ground when they left, had been roofed by the time they returned.[24]

However eager they were to hurry home, Sam and Livy took time the next afternoon to attend a matinee performance of *Hamlet* starring Edwin Booth at Booth's Theater. The tragedy reminded Sam of an idea that Joe Goodman had once proposed to him: to add a modern character to the play, "a bystander who makes humorous modern comment on the situations," and transform it into a comedy. Invited backstage after the final curtain, Sam mentioned the premise to Booth, who "laughed immoderately."[25] Sam was so inspired by the notion that he apparently tried to script a "burlesque *Hamlet*" soon afterward. "I have written a 5-act play, with only one (visible) character in it," he reported to Mother Fairbanks. "It may never be played—but you shall read it—it is at least novel & curious." He wrote Howells in 1881 that "I did the thing once—nine years ago; the addition was a country cousin of Hamlet's. But it did not suit me, & I burnt it."[26] He would eventually try again.

Sam and Livy, with Susy and Nellie, returned home on December 4. They were accompanied by Livy's mother, who remained with her daughter when Sam returned to England. After lingering in Hartford for only three days, he railed to New York on December 7, apparently spent the night at the home of his friend Dan Slote, and embarked on the Inman steamer *City of Chester* the next morning. He booked the ship for comfort, not company, and assured Livy he was unlikely to suffer from mal de mer during the voyage. Whereas the *Batavia* was 316 feet long, the *City of Chester* "is nearly 500" and thus "does not rock & pitch,—so we do not need racks on the table; there are no staterooms anywhere near,—so you eat in peace & hear no nasty sounds of vomiting in your vicinity." It was "a lovely ship," with a smoking room and speed. The *Batavia* "left considerably ahead of us, but we overtook her in half an hour & swept by her as if she were standing still. She looks like a yawl beside this vast vessel." Sam suffered from insomnia during the cruise—"sleep would only tire me," he complained to Livy—so for recreation he read Samuel Richardson's monumental *Clarissa* (1748), originally published in seven volumes and at nearly a million words one of the longest novels in the English language. The ship docked at Queenstown on November 17, at Liverpool the next day, and Sam arrived back at the Langham in London on November 19.[27]

Why did Sam repair to England to acquire British copyright on *The Gilded Age* when he might have secured it more conveniently by establishing temporary residence in Montreal? Routledge finally had received proof from Bliss and the book was in production, but it would not be issued for three more weeks. Why did he return to London to lecture when he had standing offers from James Redpath to speak anywhere in the United States at any price he might name? Certainly he no longer planned to write a travelogue about England. The conclusion is inescapable that, in the full bloom of his Anglophilia, he simply relished the camaraderie, his entrée to the upper crust of English society. "I am by long odds the most widely known & popular American author among the English," he had insisted during his first trip to the mother country,[28] and he reveled in the hero worship.

Before leaving London three weeks earlier, Sam had hired Charley Stoddard for three months "at $15 a week & board & lodging" to act as his private secretary upon his return. In the end Stoddard refused to accept any salary and Sam "had to finally smuggle it to him through Dolby" after he left England. In truth, the only job performed by Stoddard, a man with "no worldly sense," as Sam explained to Howells, was "to sit up nights with me & dissipate."[29] Sam wanted "a comrade in the semiseclusion of his apartments at the Langham," Stoddard explained, "and it was settled that I was to join him." They lived in "a beautiful suite" and enjoyed "a kind of gorgeous seclusion" broken only when they entertained friends. Sam adopted a custom at the Langham that the surgeon aboard the *City of Chester* had recommended to him: three Old Fashioneds a day, one each "before breakfast, before dinner, & just before going to bed." In fact, according to Stoddard, during these weeks Sam became "adept at cocktail making—knew the art to perfection." He would "bring out a bottle of Bourbon whiskey . . . some Angostura bitters, sugar, lemons, and the other 'fixin's,' and proceed to mix a cocktail for each of us." Then the two men

> drank in silence and were supremely happy for some moments. Then Mark, arousing from a revery, would turn to me and say in that mellow, slowly-flowing voice of his: "Now you make one, Charlie." With genuine embarrassment I would protest. I used to say: "Mark, you know that I cannot make one: I never could. It is not an art that can be acquired. It is a gift, a birthright, and there are not many who are so richly endowed as you. There is no recipe in the wide, wide world that even followed religiously would come within a thousand miles of that you lately offered me."

And he was right. Stoddard remembered for the rest of his life Twain's "mournful refrain, 'Too much bitters! Too much bitters!'" He forewarned Livy in one of his last letters before returning to the United States in January "to have, in the bath-room, when I arrive, a bottle of Scotch whisky, a lemon, & some crushed sugar, & a bottle of *Angostura bitters*."[30]

By the end of the six weeks they lived together in the Langham Hotel, Stoddard "learned much of his life that is unknown even to his closest friends," he recalled, and "I could have written his biography." They conversed many nights until the wee hours of the morning: "How the hours flew by, marked by the bell clock of the little church over the way! One—two—three in the morning, chimed on a set of baby bells, and still we sat by the sea-coal fire and smoked numberless peace-pipes, and told droll stories, and took solid comfort in our absolute seclusion." The two men bonded during these weeks, and Sam expressed affection for Stoddard for the rest of his life, one of the few protracted friendships he never renounced. He honored the "poor, sweet, pure-hearted, good-intentioned, impotent Stoddard" in a letter to Howells in September 1876, and even as late as 1900, in his autobiography, he lauded him as "the purest male I have ever known in mind and speech." Sam predictably confided to Stoddard, given the deepening global depression and his precarious finances. As Stoddard would later note, Sam

was always afraid of dying in the poorhouse. The burden of his woe was that he would grow old and lose the power of interesting an audience, and become unable to write, and then what would become of him? He had trained himself to do nothing else. He could not work with his hands. There could be no escape. The poorhouse was his destiny. And he'd drink cocktails and grow more and more gloomy and blue until he fairly wept at the misery of his own future.

"I used to go to sleep night after night with that word of woe in my ears," Stoddard recollected, "that Mark would die in the poorhouse." Sam's fear of pauperism was so palpable that he warned Livy from England that during the "hard times this winter . . . there will be a multitude of tramps & prowlers about." He urged her to treat them kindly but not too well: "Send Father Hawley a cheque for $50" and "give them soup-tickets [to David Hawley's mission] when they ask for food."[31]

The twelve weeks Sam was separated from Livy during her third pregnancy proved the truth of the adage "abstinence makes the heart grow fonder." After they had been apart for five weeks, he wrote her from the Langham that, when he returned, "Expedition's the word"—apparently a private code for intercourse that, as Leland Krauth observes, "appropriated the terms of adventurous travel." Sam's ardor had not diminished when, on New Year's Day 1874, he admitted to Livy that he was "wild to see you." He imagined their reunion in his next daily letter: "ringing the bell, at midnight—then a pause of a second or two—then the turning of the bolt & 'who is it?'—then ever so many kisses—then you & I in the bathroom, I drinking my cocktail

& undressing & you standing by—then to bed, and—everything happy & jolly as it should be." No intimate conversation with Stoddard—they had "been talking & keeping a lonely vigil for hours"—could substitute for her affection. "I want *you*—& nobody else. I do love you so." Two days later, however, Sam was more craven than craving in a note to Joe Twichell, who had written that Livy was "lovelier than ever." He replied, with more than a hint of affectation, that he was "right down grateful that she is looking strong and 'lovelier than ever.' I only wish I could see her look her level best, once—I think it would be a vision."[32]

Stoddard's only task as Sam's secretary was "to scrap-book the daily reports of the great trial of the Tichborne Claimant for perjury." An illiterate butcher and sailor, Arthur Orton had emigrated from Australia and appeared in England in 1866 claiming to be Sir Roger Tichborne, the long-lost heir of the Tichborne title, estate, and fortune. He was charged with perjury and convicted in one of the longest trials in English legal history, lasting 188 court days, from April 1873 until February 1874. Sam was fascinated by the trial and directed Stoddard to clip the articles about the trial and preserve them in six scrapbooks still extant among the Mark Twain Papers. "I was in London when the Claimant stood his trial for perjury," he reminisced in 1897. Though there is no evidence he or Stoddard actually witnessed any part of the legal proceedings in person, Sam attended one of the claimant's receptions

> in the sumptuous quarters provided for him from the purses of his adherents and well-wishers. He was in evening dress, and I thought him a rather fine and stately creature. There were about twenty-five gentlemen present; educated men, men moving in good society, none of them commonplace; some of them were men of distinction, none of them were obscurities. They were his cordial friends and admirers. It was "Sir Roger," always "Sir Roger," on all hands; no one withheld the title, all turned it from the tongue with unction, and as if it tasted good.

The legitimate Tichborne heirs spent $400,000, Sam averred, "to unmask the Claimant and drive him out; and even after the exposure multitudes of Englishmen still believed in him. It cost the British Government another $400,000 to convict him of perjury; and after the conviction the same old multitudes still believed in him; and among these believers were many educated and intelligent men; and some of them had personally known the real Sir Roger." The eyewitnesses were divided as to the identity of the claimant. Three hundred of them swore that he was Roger Tichborne, Sam noted in his journal, and about as many more swear positively that he is not. . . . I talked with a gentleman who is very cultivated man, with an acknowledged place in science [who] had a conversation with Claimant. Says that he is low, vulgar, cockney-speaking butcher. Then I talked with member of aristocracy who is known all over the world as a very able man, and he said that there is nothing vulgar or low about the Claimant. Refined—every inch a gentleman. No cockney in his speech.[33]

At the conclusion of the trial in April, Orton was found guilty of perjury and sentenced to fourteen years in prison.

Shortly after the Tichborne Claimant's trial ended, Sam was contacted by Jesse Leathers, who solicited his support of his claim to be the rightful Earl of Durham. Leathers's plea for recognition as heir to the Durham estate would rival Orton's cause célèbre. As it happened, however, Sam's tepid offer of assistance backfired. Starting in September 1875, Leathers actually hounded Sam with occasional appeals for money to enable him to pursue his pipe dream. But Sam never met his fourth cousin face-to-face nor did he encourage his quixotic quest: "You ask me what I think of the chances of the American heirs. I answer frankly that I think them inconceivably slender. The present earl of Durham has been in undisputed possession thirty-five years; his father, the first earl, held possession forty-three years. Seventy-eight years' peaceable possession is a pretty solid wall to buck against before a court composed of the House of Lords of England." In 1881 Sam suggested that Leathers pen his autobiography rather than engage in a court battle. As he allowed to James R. Osgood, he expected Leathers to "write a gassy, extravagant, idiotic book that will be delicious reading, for I've read some of his rot; and it is just the sort of windy stuff which a Kentucky tramp who has been choused out of an English earldom would write. By George I believe this ass will write a serious book which will make a cast-iron dog laugh." Unfortunately, neither Osgood nor Howells was interested in "the Earl's literary excrement" after he evacuated it, though it charmed Sam "like *Fanny Hill*. I just wallowed in it." When the penniless Leathers died of consumption in the New York City jail six years later, Sam wrote his epitaph in a private letter, nothing that "there was something very striking, and pathetically and grotesquely picturesque . . . about this long, and hopeless, and plucky, and foolish, and majestic fight of a foghorn against a fog."[34]

In any event, the trial of the Tichborne Claimant stoked Sam's interest in stories about false heirs. By his own admission, it stirred the p(l)ot of *The Prince and the Pauper* (1882). The Tichborne case gave the lie to the chief criticism of the novel, he argued, which "was its utter improbability. That the identity of the boys could be thus mixed up and sorted out wrong was regarded as so entirely impossible as to destroy all interest in the romance."[35] The case also influenced the composition of a play, *Colonel Sellers as a Scientist*, that Sam wrote in collaboration with Howells in 1883; chapters 34–39 of *Adventures of Huckleberry Finn* (1885), in which the Duke and Dauphin falsely assert a claim to the estate of Peter Wilkes; and his late novel *The American Claimant* (1891), which features a character modeled on Jesse Leathers named Simon Lathers in a cameo role.

Even before Sam reopened his lectures in the Queen's Concert Rooms, he resumed his privileged social life among the London elite. "In England," Howells recalled, "rank, fashion, and culture rejoiced in him. Lord mayors, lord chief justices, and magnates of many kinds were his hosts; he was desired in country houses, and his bold genius captivated the favor of periodicals which spurned the rest of our nation." Shortly after his arrival Sam dined at the Hotel Albemarle on Piccadilly Circus with his manager Dolby, a "large and ruddy" fellow "full of life and strength and spirits, a tireless and energetic talker, and always overflowing with good-nature and bursting with jollity." The "gladsome gorilla" Dolby neatly complemented the "pensive poet" Stoddard. Sam also mended relations with publisher Andrew Chatto, John Camden Hotten's successor. The evening of November 29, ten days after his return to London, he attended the inaugural meeting of the St. Andrew's Society at the Salutation Tavern on Newgate Street at the invitation of Tom Hood. Before about a hundred guests, including the lord mayor of London, he delivered the toast "to the Guests." Alerted in advance, he wrote his speech on a scroll of manuscript—an old trick he had first used to good effect in Carson City in 1864—and read to the audience from it that he was entirely surprised and unprepared to speak. He jokingly reminisced about the five weeks he had passed the previous summer in Scotland:

> I remember when in Edinburgh I was nearly always taken for a Scotchman. . . . I had my clothes some part colored tartan, and I rather enjoyed being taken for a Scotchman. I stuck a big feather in my cap, too, and the people would follow me miles. They thought I was a Highlander, and some of the best judges in Scotland said they had never seen a Highland costume like mine. What's more, one of the judges fined me for wearing it—out of mere envy, I suppose. But any man may have a noble, good time in Scotland, if they only think he's a native. For breakfast you may have oatmeal poultice—I beg pardon, I mean porridge. Then for dinner you have the Scotch game—the blackcock, the spatchcock, the woodcock, the Moorcock.

He spent his days in Scotland aping the natives, he said, by "drinking slogans of whisky and smoking bagpipes."[36]

The night of December 1, St. Andrew's Day, a holiday honoring the patron saint of Scotland, Sam restarted his Sandwich Islands lectures on Hanover Street. Afterward he responded to a toast at the annual meeting of the Scottish Corporation of London at Freemasons' Tavern on Great Queen's Street. On this occasion, before an audience of about five hundred, he saluted "the Ladies" and, according to the London *Cosmopolitan*, again made the speech of the evening by celebrating the achievements of some of the most famous women in history:

> Who was more patriotic than Joan of Arc? Who was braver? Who has given us a grander instance of self-sacrificing devotion? Ah, you remember, you remember well, what a throb of pain, what a great tidal wave of grief swept over us all when Joan of Arc fell at Waterloo! Who does not sorrow for the loss of Sappho, the sweet singer of Israel. Who among us does not miss the gentle ministrations, the softening influence, the humble piety of Lucretia Borgia? Who can join in the heartless libel that says woman is extravagant in dress when he can look back and call to mind our simple and lowly mother Eve arrayed in her modification of the Highland costume?

The London *Times* commended his "characteristic and most humorous speech, which was loudly and repeatedly cheered." Sam even subscribed five guineas, over five hundred dollars in modern money, toward the charitable work of the corporation.[37]

The following week, Sam lunched with Stoddard and Charles Kingsley at the Cloisters, Westminster Abbey, and after his lecture the evening of December 11 he attended the second annual festival of the London Morayshire Club at St. James' Hall on Piccadilly Circus with Lord Viscount MacDuff in the chair. As usual, he responded to a toast, this time giving his reply "to Visitors" before an audience of "150 gentlemen," as the *Aberdeen Journal* put it. He announced plans to return to Scotland "next week or the week after to lecture" so he "was learning the language now" and had "mastered six or eight of the words." The speech "was received with prodigious applause," he reported to Livy, "but I thought if Livy were only here, I would enjoy it a thousand times more."[38]

"It was a dangerous experiment to think of renewing the season after the interval of a month," Stoddard reported in his London correspondence with the *San Francisco Chronicle*, but Sam "opened his new season to good business" on December 1. Dolby certainly had a hand in his success. He reproduced Sam's photo on posters plastered all over the city. His picture was so ubiquitous, Sam wrote, that "it seems as if 3 people out of every 5 I meet on the street recognize me." Though his schedule initially required no travel, the pace of his appearances was arduous. As Fred Lorch re-creates the calendar of speaking dates, Sam lectured each evening through December 5 and at two afternoon matinees, resumed his appearances on December 8, and performed every night through December 20, as well as at four matinees, for a total of twenty-four lectures in twenty days. As in October, the critics were kind. The London *Telegraph* averred that the audience on reopening night "listened with the same interest and sustained enjoyment which were so strongly manifested by the auditory on the previous occasions." The *Morning Post* agreed: Sam "kept the large audience in the greatest good humour" and added that he would "repeat his exceedingly amusing and interesting lecture, under Mr. George Dolby's management, until further notice."[39]

Sam and Charley Stoddard soon settled into a daily routine. They breakfasted on toasted muffins at "half-past twelve sharp" and read the mail and a dozen newspapers over cigars. Then they took a walk—"a lazy stroll through the London parks" or "a saunter among the byways of the city in search of the picturesque." Then came the "lazy hour before dinner, perhaps the pleasantest in the day," when there was "chat or long intervals of dreamy silence by the fireside, or music at the piano." After dinner Sam dressed for his lecture and they "strolled down the street to Hanover Square, arriving about half-past seven." At precisely eight o'clock Sam stepped from the wings onto the stage. After the lecture, he "always felt amiable" and there "followed an informal reception. The green room seemed cheerful enough with a dozen or more delightful people, saying a dozen delightful things all in a breath." He signed autographs and smoked cigars. Finally, they walked home with Dolby "to the big sitting-room at the Langham, with easy chairs wheeled up before the fire, with pipes and plenty of 'Lone Jack'" tobacco. Dolby and Sam spun yarns—sometimes "indelicate" ones—'till midnight" to entertain Stoddard, who "would lie down on a couch and sleep and interrupt the conversation with a species of snores."[40]

Still, some circumstantial evidence suggests that all was not well. Stoddard admitted that audiences were "sometimes a little dull" at the Queen's Concert Rooms, an apparent reference to attendance rather than to the tenor of the lectures themselves. Sam complained to Livy in mid-December that his "houses fell right down till they contained only £14 & £17!" The equivalent of seventy and eighty-five dollars, these amounts indicate that little more than a hundred people were in the audience for each of these performances. The liberal politician John Bright noted in his diary for December 2, 1873, that Sam's Sandwich Islands lecture was "amusing but flimsy." The cleric H. R. Haweis recalled that on the evening he heard Sam:

the audience was not large nor very enthusiastic. I believe he would have been an increasing success had he stayed longer. We had not time to get accustomed to his peculiar way, and there was nothing to take us by storm. . . . He spoke more slowly than any other man I ever heard, and did not look at his audience quite enough. I do not think that he felt altogether at home with us, nor we with him. We never laughed loud or long. . . . I got no information out of the lecture, and hardly a joke that would wear, or a story that would bear repeating.

In a column dated December 15 the London correspondent of the *New York Herald* asserted that Sam "made a great hit at first, but I am afraid has rather overdone it by lecturing every night," and the *Bradford Observer* remarked that his lectures had "met with indifferent success." Above all, there is the reason Sam suspended his platform appearances on December 6 and 7. During the hiatus, Sam revised his old "Roughing It" lecture apparently because the Sandwich Islands talk had exhausted its appeal. George Grossmith, most famous today for his performances in the comic operas of W. S. Gilbert and Arthur Sullivan, soon began to impersonate Sam onstage —the sincerest form of flattery—delivering this lecture.[41]

"Roughing It on the Silver Frontier" revived interest in hearing the original Clemens. The papers puffed the lecture in a new round of reviews. Sam bragged to Livy the first evening he delivered it that he had "never enjoyed delivering a lecture, in all my life, more than I did tonight. It was so perfectly jolly." He was pleased by his performance despite a heavy fog that invaded the Rooms and clouded the gaslights. Stoddard compared the hall to a smokehouse. From his position in the audience he spied onstage "a shadowy dresscoat, supported by a pair of shadowy trousers, girdled by the faint halo of the ineffectual footlights." The speaker was an "apparently headless trunk," and the audience "invisible to the naked eye." From the stage, too, Sam remembered that "the audience did look so vague, & dim, & ghostly! The hall seemed full of a thick blue smoke." The first words he uttered to the crowd were "Ladies & gentlemen, I *hear* you, & so I know that you are here—& I am here, too, notwithstanding I am not visible."[42]

The next day, the London papers were nearly unanimous in their praise. The notice in the *Morning Post* was "most excellent," Sam thought. He had received an "exceedingly flattering" reception from a packed house, according to the *Post's* critic, and he had dwelled in his deadpan delivery "with what, for him, is enthusiasm upon the scenic charms which abound in California." According to the *Times*, Sam depicted Silverland as "the most objectionable place on the face of the earth," so "his sustained irony" reached perfection "when, at the end of his description of horrors, he grimly expresses a hope that he has not said anything which might tend to depopulate England through a vast emigration to Nevada." *Vanity Fair* heralded his performance in its column "At the Play," noting, "Mark Twain is not a play" but "he is as good as a play" and "he keeps his audience in a constant state of merriment." The *Telegraph* ("the tendency of the speaker was always toward the droll instead of the didactic"), *Standard* ("must be heard to be appreciated"), *Orchestra* ("altogether *sui generis*—a wonderful mixture of eloquence, nonsense, and ironical humour"), *Era* ("excessively droll manner"), *Sportsman* ("wonderful power of humour"), *Observer* ("humorously original and singularly enjoyable"), and *Figaro* ("has scored one again in his new lecture") all joined the chorus of praise. Frank Finlay, who had traveled to London to hobnob with Sam, pictured his "steady deliberative gravity," his skill at "remaining stonily impassive" while "hardly changing his position, never moving the muscles of his face," in the Belfast *Northern Whig*.[43] Only the *Daily News* and the *Evening Globe* expressed reservations. The former grumbled that Sam left his audience "entirely in the dark as to the locality to which he intended to introduce them," though conceding that "he began and concluded his lecture last evening amidst loud applause." The latter groused that the new lecture was "well received, but scarcely so heartily as the famous lecture on the Fiji Islands." (*Sic*: the lecture was apparently not that famous.) His auditors "seemed to become accustomed to [his] tricks of style, and to find them less amusing the oftener they were repeated. He has some genuine humour; but it is of an elementary kind, consisting for the most part of grotesque exaggeration."[44]

Sam sent a pair of complimentary tickets to George Smalley, who rewarded him with a brief blurb in his next column and a letter of thanks. "Mrs. Smalley and I agreed in thinking the lecture capital, both in itself and in the manner of its delivery, which was simply inimitable," Smalley wrote in the letter, although he noted, "I was sorry to see you so wretchedly noticed in the Daily News,—what a donkey the man must be to be able to spoil things so." Moncure Conway had listened to the lecture with the Smalleys "& laughed till the bench shook" and he sent Sam his own letter of congratulations on December 10. He deemed the new lecture "even better than the Sandwich one, and that is saying a great deal."[45]

Much as Sam had advertised his October lectures with a comic letter to the editor of the London *Standard*, he promoted his "Roughing It" talk by addressing a "delightfully amusing letter" to the London *Post*, the venue that had hyped it the day before. "I find that there is one attraction which I forgot to provide" his audiences, he began, "and that is the attendance of some great member of the Government to give distinction to my entertainment." He could hardly expect one of "those great personages" to attend a mere amusement, however, so he had arranged to borrow some wax figures of "a couple of kings and some nobility" to display in the Rooms. But then a catastrophe occurred: "In attempting to move Henry VIII to my lecture hall, the porter fell down stairs and utterly smashed him all to pieces; in the course of moving William the Conqueror, something let go and all the saw-dust burst out of him, and he collapsed and withered away to nothing before my eyes. Then we collared some dukes, but they were so seedy and decayed that nobody would ever have believed in their rank."[46] Dolby soon added Wednesday and Saturday matinees to Sam's speaking schedule to accommodate the renewed demand for tickets.

Sam originally expected to tour northern England and Scotland with his lectures after ringing down the curtain at the Queen's Concert Rooms. "I shall lecture only one week longer in London—closing Dec. 20," he notified Livy in mid-December, "& then shall talk in 4 or 5 cities outside," leaving on December 22. He finished his bookings at the Rooms as planned and celebrated that evening over dinner with the Smalleys and his friends Frank Finlay and John Russell Young. A day or two later he and Stoddard breakfasted with their old California friend Prentice Mulford. Meanwhile, Dolby was unable to book arenas on satisfactory dates in the provinces and thus canceled lectures in Glasgow, Edinburgh, Belfast, Dublin, Cork, and Manchester. The impresario "found that every hall and theatre throughout the two kingdoms" was "full of holiday shows," Alexander Russell reported in the Edinburgh *Scotsman*, "and that he cannot get even a church to talk in till near the end of January. Mark Twain is not able to wait till then." Only three lectures remained on Sam's itinerary: in Leicester on January 8 and in Liverpool the next two nights.[47]

Unexpectedly, Sam faced a lull in his schedule: no deadlines or speaking dates for two entire weeks. The evening of December 22—coincidentally, the same day the British edition of *The Gilded Age* was issued in three volumes by Routledge—he was the guest of honor at a private feast at the Westminster Club with a few friends, including Dolby and Stoddard. In response to a toast to his health, he declared that he had

> lectured all through the fog, and all through the fine weather in London, and
> have completed my mission of instruction and moral elevation. But now that
> it is all over, I am sorry rather than glad, for I never have seen audiences that
> were quicker to see a point and seize it than those I have had in London and

Liverpool, and in this the comfort of lecturing lies. I have always had an idea before that British risibles were hard to move.

Sam and his friends retired after the banquet to the New Gallery on Argyll Street to hear F. C. Burnand read from his book *Happy Thoughts* (1869), a compilation of humorous anecdotes. Much to Sam's consternation, the opera glasses in the theater were "all leveled at *me*. I didn't mind it for a time, but when it had lasted an hour & a half I began to get a little fidgetty & ill at ease." Finally Dolby broke the ice, telling Sam in a stutter that if he "were Burnand, I would have you on the stage behind a curtain & charge these da-da-dam people an extra shilling for a sight." Sam was also a guest at a holiday reception hosted by the actress Emily Fowler, the leading lady of the Olympic Theater in London, at her mansion on Langham Street. Among the other invitees were the composers Julius Benedict and Arthur Sullivan, the playwrights Westland Marston and James Planché, and the Duke of Beaufort and Sir George Orby Wombwell. In the course of the evening the Prince of Wales dropped by for half an hour.[48]

Sam and Stoddard left London on December 24 and railed to Salisbury for Christmas. They were entertained there by the lawyer, philanthropist, and amateur antiquarian William Blackmore, who escorted them through his museum "full of antiquities collected and housed at an expense of fifty thousand dollars" and hosted "a grand dinner" on Christmas Eve "to which fifteen gentlemen sat down," Stoddard noted. Among the guests were Henry William Pullen, author of *The Fight at Dame Europa's School* and vicar-choral of Salisbury Cathedral, and the archeologist Edward Thomas Stevens. Sam and Stoddard registered at the historic White Hart Hotel, a short walk from the cathedral, where they "attended the grand Christmas" service the next morning. In the afternoon they drove eight miles out of town to Stonehenge, "one of the most mysterious & satisfactory ruins I have ever seen," as Sam put it. On December 26 they rode to Old Sarum, "where the Saxons used to meet." Sam was "feeling rather ill after all this dining," according to Stoddard, so they left Salisbury for Ventnor, on the southern tip of the Isle of Wight, to recuperate from their holiday before heading back to London on December 29.[49]

Sam returned to a full dance card. He attended a New Year's Eve party at the home of Shirley Brooks, the editor of *Punch*, where he marked the occasion with Burnand, actor and comedian Arthur Cecil, cartoonist and author George du Maurier, Sir John Tenniel, and Edmund Yates. The next day he reported that his social calendar was booked through the following week. He dined with Dolby the evening of Sunday, January 4, and spent "a good part" of the next day, he wrote Joe Twichell, "browsing through the

Royal Academy Exhibition" of Edwin Landseer's animal paintings. His critical tastes were maturing, to judge from his comments about such canvases as *The Challenge, The Combat, The Sanctuary, A Random Shot,* and *The Connoisseurs.* He was cultivating a realist aesthetic rather than a romantic one, commending Landseer for his depiction of "animals' flesh and blood" so that "if the room were darkened ever so little, and a motionless living animal placed beside the painted one, no man could tell which was which." On January 7 he and Stoddard entrained to Leicester, where Sam delivered his Sandwich Islands lecture and read the "Jumping Frog" story at Temperance Hall. In Liverpool, where he and Stoddard registered at the historic Adelphi Hotel, he again delivered his Sandwich Islands lecture—perhaps for the final time—on January 9 and closed his English engagements the following evening with "Roughing It," again reading the "Jumping Frog" story as an afterpiece. His performances were well attended—"we had full houses here & a jolly good time with them," he reported—and he was, according to Stoddard, "most cordially received," with a curtain call at the close. "Mark takes new laurels home with him—English laurels that are not so apt to fade as ours." Of his last performance, the *Liverpool Post* declared the next morning,

> As it is altogether impossible to retell Mr. Twain's stories without spoiling them, we shall make no attempt to indicate the means by which he last night provoked incessant mirth. Suffice it that his sallies were as unexpected, his moralisings as much governed by the rule of contraries, his stories as rich in comic incident, and his serious descriptions as full of poetry and glow, as the corresponding features of his previous lecture.

According to Stoddard, on January 12, the night before his departure, Sam "sank into a sea of forebodings. His voice was keyed in a melancholy minor. . . . his last words were, that if ever he got down in the world—which Heaven forbid—he would probably have to teach elocution; but this was at five o'clock in the morning."[50]

Sam boarded the Cunard steamer *Parthia* the next day and arrived in Boston on January 26. He was back in the bosom of his family in Hartford and no doubt sipping whiskey cocktails the next day.

CHAPTER 4

Market Twain

Man is part angel, part rat; mainly rat.

—Samuel Clemens, quoted in William Gibson, *The Art of Mark Twain*

THE CANVASSING FOR subscriptions for *The Gilded Age* began in early October 1873. The novel was formally published in England by Routledge on December 22 and in the United States by the American Publishing Company the following day. Elisha Bliss marketed the book as the latest novel by Mark Twain, downplaying Charles Dudley Warner's contribution, to judge by the prospectus carried door-to-door by the book agents, which consisted largely of pages from the first eleven chapters. Over twelve thousand copies of the American edition had been released by the end of the year. Initial sales were extremely encouraging; over thirty-five thousand copies had been distributed by the end of February 1874, earning royalties of $5,337 for each author. But purchases of the book then plunged. By the end of the year the novel had barely sold fifty thousand copies in the United States, and six years later only six thousand more. Sales in England were even more discouraging. Routledge's initial print run consisted of only eighty-five hundred copies and the firm did not issue a second printing until 1877. One factor inhibiting sales was the financial panic in September 1873 and the global economic depression that followed. Sam speculated in the immediate aftermath of publication that "but for the panic our sale would have been doubled."[1] Over the long run, however, he found a more convenient scapegoat: Elisha Bliss.

Though Sam repeatedly insisted that his "interest in a book ceases with the printing of it," in truth his interest waned only after the marketing of it. He carped that Bliss had produced a "rather rubbishy looking book," particularly its "wretched paper & vile engravings," and that the publisher had too freely distributed it to the press. "I see distinct evidence that if *The Gilded Age* had been kept away from the newspapers, it would have given satisfaction & its early sales would not have been 'knocked,'" Sam complained. In the case of *Roughing It*, he had convinced Bliss to limit the number of review copies sent to newspapers and then blamed Bliss's failure to publicize the book for its drop in sales. In this case, he charged Bliss with mailing too many copies to hostile reviewers. Sam may never have known a more legitimate reason to blame Bliss for the falloff in sales. The company dumped remaindered copies of the novel onto the retail market just before Christmas, disguising them as pirated printings with a bogus title page, both exploiting the holiday trade and deceiving the agents who believed they had exclusive contracts to sell the book.[2]

Of course, another possible reason for the decline in the popularity of the novel was that it deserved its fall from favor. W. D. Howells, the most influential and unrepentant champion of Sam's genius for over forty years, confessed to Warner less than a week after the novel's publication that he was disappointed by it. "Up to the time old Hawkins dies [in chapter 9] your novel is of the greatest promise—I read it with joy," he explained, "but after that it fails to assimilate the crude material with which it is fed, and becomes a confirmed dyspeptic at last." In Howells's view, all of the characters, including Colonel Sellers, failed to "fulfill their early promise." He offered to withhold his opinion from the public and, he admitted, "I should prefer to do so; though I should be able to praise parts of it with heartiness and sincerity."[3] Howells never reviewed the book in the *Atlantic Monthly*. Nor, for that matter, did the *New York Tribune*, the most prestigious paper in the country, or such parlor magazines as *Scribner's* and *Harper's Monthly*.

Sam's Scottish friends John Brown and George MacDonald were no more impressed by the novel than Howells. MacDonald averred in a letter to Sam that he was "delighted with the courage and honesty of the book" even as he admitted that he did "not think the action quick enough." Brown similarly professed to admire the novel—it was "so full of good sense & good feeling & good fun & good knowledge of men and things." Brown's remark delighted Sam "because some of our newspapers have set forth the opinion that *Warner* really wrote the book & I only added my name to the title-page in order to give it a large sale. It is a shameful charge to make." But Brown was more measured in his comments to John Forsyth, chaplain and professor at the U.S. Military Academy at West Point, written while Sam was aboard the *Parthia* bound for Boston: "Mark Twain is home—a queer fellow, but with excellent stuff in him—& his wife is simply delicious—beautiful & good. What do you think of his last novel? It is powerful but unequal—& lacks the true storytelling knack."[4]

The almost eighty known published reviews of the novel in Britain and the United States were certainly mixed, on the whole containing more darkness than light. Sam remarked with characteristic hauteur that it was both "the best abused & one of the best written books of the age," but on balance it damaged his reputation. One of the first reviews of *The Gilded Age* in a major venue, the New York *Graphic* on December 23, the day of its publication,

hit a sour note. It was written by David Croly, the editor of the *Graphic*
and son of Jane Cunningham Croly (aka Jennie June), one of the founders
of the famous New York women's club Sorosis. "Regarded either as a novel
or an exponent of the wit and humor of the two authors, *The Gilded Age* is
a failure," Croly opined. "It is simply a rather incoherent series of sketches
with fragmentary characterization and chaotic plot," and "the two most brilliant humorists in America . . . have written a book in which we look almost
in vain for the traces of either's pen." As late as 1906 Sam still harbored a
grudge: "When Charles Dudley Warner and I were about to bring out 'The
Gilded Age,' the editor of the *Daily Graphic* persuaded me to let him have
an advance copy, he giving me his word of honor that no notice of it should
appear in his paper until after the *Atlantic Monthly* notice should have appeared. This reptile published a review of the book within three days afterward." Sam was so offended by this notice that he instructed his publishers
never to send the paper another review copy of any of his works.[5]

But as Sam had feared, the tone was set. Critical opinion of the novel, despite its satire of political corruption during the administration of President
Ulysses S. Grant, was largely unaffected by either geographical region or political affiliation. The major exception to this rule was the *Chicago Tribune*,
a staunchly Republican paper, whose reviewer trashed the book mercilessly
or, as Sam put it, spoke "of it in terms of the severest censure." Not only did
the critic assail "the mongrel"—"a book so utterly bald, so puerile, so vicious"
that he deemed it "a fraud on the reading public"—but he indulged in ad
hominem attack. The authors had "willfully degraded their craft, abused
the people's trust," and deserved "a stern condemnation." Then the coup de
grâce: "Stupidity can be forgiven, but deliberate deceit—never." Other critics spread the rumor that the novel was "a gigantic practical joke," that it was
not even written by the authors whose names appeared on the title page. In
this scenario, the "two notorious wits" had recruited a cadre of "several obscure" newspaper reporters to dash off the story. The prank "was to be kept
a profound secret till three hundred thousand copies of the work were sold."[6]

Still other reviewers reasoned that the book was merely knocked out to
make a buck—that is, ironically, to satisfy the same crass desire for wealth
that the authors presumed to mock. "The story is dreadfully attenuated, and
the padding is so evident," claimed the *San Francisco Bulletin*, "that one cannot help the suspicion that that the dominant motive in writing the book"
was profit. The Washington, D.C., *Star* remonstrated that the authors had
traded upon their "fair reputations" and finished the novel without truly
ending it. The St. Louis *Post-Dispatch* flayed the authors for earning forty
thousand dollars in the exercise: "Almost any man would experience a sense
of guilt in defrauding the public with such a book." The Boston *Literary*

World seconded the motion: "The book has a strong savor of lucre; it was evidently written to sell, and in the hope of gaining a liberal heap of that money whose worship it purports to ridicule." This particular critic believed that Sam was vulgar enough to stoop so low but wondered "how a man of Mr. Warner's literary reputation could lend his name to such cheap and feeble stuff." Ironically, Warner had admitted to James R. Osgood while he and Sam were collaborating that they hoped their "high art" would be "rewarded with several dollars."[7] Some reviewers evaded comment on the book by referring only to the authors' pedigrees, such as the London *Saturday Review* ("the name of Mark Twain will be a sufficient recommendation"), the *Cleveland Herald* ("we do not propose to say just what the book is about"), and the *Sacramento Union* ("their reputation indorses it"). Others began to read it but admittedly failed to finish it—for example, the *New Orleans Republican* ("no one . . . can take up this book without disappointment, and when he lays it down will never lift it again"), the *Ohio Farmer* ("one feels no disposition" to continue this "mongrel work" after "reading the first few pages"), and (again) the Boston *Literary World* ("we have read enough of the book to convince us that it is not worth reading").[8]

Then there were the critics who damned the novel with faint praise. The *New York Herald* published a brief review a day before the official publication and concluded rather ambiguously that "it will scarcely be too highly praised." The *Springfield Republican* attempted to straddle the fence, asserting both that "better satires . . . of our recent national life have never been put before the public" and that "the story as a story doesn't amount to much." The Alexandria, Virginia, *State Journal* hailed it as "the book of the period" without specifying the length of the period. The San Francisco *Alta California* thought that "some chapters are almost trashy but they do not occupy a large part of the book." In the Boston monthly *Old and New*, Frederic Beecher Perkins, the brother of Sam's Hartford lawyer Charles E. Perkins, the father of Charlotte Perkins Gilman, and the head of the Boston Public Library, tepidly observed that "for two men situated as the authors of *The Gilded Age* are situated, it is a remarkably well-executed work." The *Galaxy* praised the "consistently burlesque air" given the book "by quotations from non-existent languages at the beginning of chapters," and the *Literary World* capitulated to the last resort of a critic desperate to flatter a book: "The only feature of it that we can conscientiously praise," he declared, "is the illustrations." But even this topic was disputed. The *St. Louis Republican* condemned the "miserable cuts" and, according to *Hearth and Home*, most of the illustrations were "execrable." The same reviewer, however, commended the satire ("pungent enough to have grown on a red-pepper plant") and gave a positive spin to the rambling story ("fun enough in the book to make the fortune of half a dozen novels"), which to meet the length required of a subscription book the authors had padded like a refurbished sofa. The London *Graphic* concurred, noting that "the stage is overcrowded with characters and the authors do not seem to know how to manage them." Not to be outdone, the London *Athenaeum*, the grand damn of British magazines, criticized both the "preposterous mottoes" and the sprawling plot ("far too many characters . . . [enough] materials in this one book for several novels").[9] Even the character of Colonel Sellers was targeted by some critics. In another review that essentially maintained two opposing points of view, the *Independent* allowed that the best feature in the book was "the character of Eschol Sellers, the extravagantly visionary bummer; but even he is disgusting." The *Hartford Times*, Sam's hometown paper, while conceding that *The Gilded Age* was "the most entertaining book of the season," protested that Sellers was "overdrawn." Sam's friends at the Edinburgh *Scotsman* intimated that the authors had plagiarized the character from Dickens, arguing that Sellers bore "too close a resemblance to Micawber" in *David Copperfield* and the London *Morning Post* similarly noted that the character seemed to be "founded on recollections, unconscious, perhaps," of "Dickens's 'Micawber,' adequately Americanised."[10]

On the whole, the British press panned the novel. The London *Figaro* condemned it in its January 15, 1874, issue. The London *Graphic* judged it "a failure." The London *Standard* remarked that the novel "must make the world wonder how the Americans could ever have objected to a single word in *Martin Chuzzlewit*." The critic for the *Spectator* expressed relief "that the writers are not English." The *Morning Post*, so favorably inclined toward Sam during his lectures at the Queen's Concert Rooms, sniffed that the authors had adopted "a somewhat higgledy-piggledy way of dealing with the incidents," though to "some persons" the novel "may not be without its amusing side." The criticisms were echoed by some papers in the colonies—for example, the Melbourne *Australasian* ("desultory and disconnected"), *Otago Times* ("too flimsy to bear re-telling" and "excessively wire-drawn"), and New Zealand *Evening Post* ("we have read the book, and we should probably have written more favorably of it had we not done so").[11]

On the other hand, the novel was received by other papers in Australia and New Zealand with surprising enthusiasm, such as the *Melbourne Argus* ("must take high rank in contemporary literature"), Melbourne *Age* (it had "crisp" and "refreshing" dialogue and an "interesting" plot), *Brisbane Courier* ("a really delightful book" and "one of the keenest satires on modern American life"), *Australasian* (the book depicted "the morals and manners of society in the United States much as Juvenal in his satires"), *Sydney Empire* ("bold, trenchant, and unsparing"), Brisbane *Queenslander* ("as a study of American life and character it must take high rank in contemporary literature"), and *Auckland Star* (its "genial humour" mingled with "caustic satire").[12]

Of course, some notices of the novel in the United States were favorable, a few excessively so. The review in the Boston *Saturday Evening Gazette*, for example, was filled with superlatives, as though the critic had just stepped from a hyperbolic chamber ("the book is one of the most readable ever written"). According to the New Orleans *Southwestern Advocate*, it promised to be the "greatest literary sensation of the time." The assertions in the *Boston Transcript* ("some of the most vivid and natural characterizations of any book recently published"), *Boston Globe* ("one of the most comprehensive novels of American life we have ever read"), *San Francisco Chronicle* ("quite worthy of anything that Mark Twain previously produced"), and New York *Sun* ("will add new reputation to the author") were no less inflated. The reviewers for the *Baltimore Sun* ("shows the hand of a master"), New York *Golden Age* ("no one would imagine that the novel was the work of more than one hand"), Philadelphia *Press* ("more of a true American novel than any story produced for a long time"), and *Portland Oregonian* ("in some respects more amusing than either of Clemens' former volumes and is in all respects superior to them in point of literary merit") seem to have read a different book, evidence if nothing else of the validity of reader-response theory. The "entire conservative and religious Press, with scarcely an exception," eulogized the novel—for example, the *Syracuse Journal* described the novel as a sort of satirical wackadoodle that "hits about every head that shows itself prominently above the surface of society, politics, and finance." The Alexandria, Louisiana, *Caucasian* averred that "those who have not read *The Gilded Age* have a treat in store for themselves." The editors of the *Congregationalist* avowed that they wished "some tract society would see that it is widely circulated at Washington."[13]

Finally, some U.S. venues expressed vehemently hostile opinions about the novel. The *Shreveport Times* evoked superlatives of a negative sort, pronouncing it "the greatest literary fraud of this gilded age." The *Boston Advertiser* declared that the authors' attempt to construct a plot augured ill for their literary futures. Their depiction of scandal "is revolting to the last degree. . . . It is not 'a story of today' [the subtitle of the novel] but a caricature of today." Just as derogatory were the *New York Herald* ("entitled to no rank at all"), New York *World* ("its plot is slight, ill-connected, and thoroughly inartistic"), *Cincinnati Times* (exhibits "neither the brilliant wit of Mark Twain nor the meditative sweetness of Mr. Warner"), and *St. Louis Republican* ("acres of margin swell this book like the Connecticut River and its literary strength is as wishy-washy and muddy"). Harold Frederic, future author of *The Damnation of Theron Ware* (1896), scorned the novel in the *Utica Observer* as an "ill-constructed and hasty work."[14]

Perhaps the most objective assessment of the book, one that elides super-latives at both extremes, was penned by Edward L. Burlingame for *Appleton's Journal*. In June 1866, at the age of eighteen, Burlingame had met Sam when he accompanied his father to Hawaii. For the younger Burlingame, the clumsiness of the plot did not detract from its satiric force. *The Gilded Age* was "good in episodes from which to make a novel—unsatisfactory as a combination of them. It is like a salad-dressing badly mixed, wherein one comes upon the mustard in lumps, the salt in masses, pools of vinegar, and collections of oil which might have softened the whole. The ingredients are capital, the use of them faulty, so it seems to us." In extenuation of the novel's faults, Warner explained to Burlingame after this review appeared that "the book was written at the close of last winter, when we were disgusted with Congress and with some other things. We went at it in rather a grim temper, trying to hit and hit hard, and pretty well conscious that we were violating most of the laws of art, and that we could only be saved by the discovery of some faltering new ones."[15]

One of the most halcyon periods in Sam's life began when he landed back in the United States in late January 1874. The markets had stabilized so that his investments were no longer bleeding red ink; Olivia was suffering fewer complications than with her earlier pregnancies; *The Gilded Age* was selling well, at least for the moment (by some estimates, as many as fifty thousand copies in its first year in print); and the house they were building on Farmington Avenue was in the final stage of construction. "If there is one individual creature on all this footstool who is more thoroughly and uniformly and unceasingly *happy* than I am," Sam crowed to John Brown in late February, "I defy the world to produce him and *prove* him." That same week he boasted to Mary Mason Fairbanks, "I am the busiest white man in America—& much the happiest."

Sam railed to Boston on February 16 to attend a farewell dinner hosted by the Boston publisher William F. Gill at the St. James Hotel for Wilkie Collins, who had been lecturing in the United States. He mingled in distinguished company: among the other guests were Ralph Waldo Emerson, James T. Fields, Oliver Wendell Holmes, W. D. Howells, Henry Wadsworth Longfellow, E. P. Whipple, John Greenleaf Whittier, and Vice President Henry Wilson. Sam delivered a brief postprandial speech in which he declared that during his missionary expedition to England he had preached "good morals" to his audiences. At the dinner Sam also met the Unitarian minister and writer Thomas Wentworth Higginson, who thought him "something of a buffoon, though with earnestness un-derneath." Sam carried the manuscript of his burlesque Hamlet to Boston to show James Redpath, who apparently persuaded him to remain in the city an extra day so that he might speak at a Massachusetts Press Association dinner honoring Charles Kingsley, who had just arrived in the United States to launch his own tour under Redpath's management, and to introduce Kingsley prior to his lecture about Westminster Abbey at Tremont Temple the next evening. Sam delivered a similar talk, about his friendship with Kingsley, on both occasions. In response, Kingsley remembered "wandering through Westminster Abbey" with Sam the year before.[16]

Redpath had been hectoring Sam to return to the platform for months. In May 1873, on the eve of his second trip to England, Sam offered to "possibly lecture in 3 or 4 large eastern cities—but nowhere else" upon his return in October. In December 1873, back in England to appear at the Queen's Concert Rooms and to await imperial copyright on *The Gilded Age*, he proposed to Redpath "to talk in Steinway hall on a Thursday & Friday evenings, Saturday afternoon (& *possibly*) Saturday night" when he landed in the United States. "Then talk possibly Monday and Tuesday in Boston & *retire permanently* from the platform"—or, as he sometimes called it, the "scaffold." Sam repeated this basic position two weeks later. He expected to lecture "3 nights in New York" in the winter "& then I retire from the platform *permanently*. I think I will try to eke out a meagre subsistence upon my permanent annual income of £8,000, & try to sit at home & in peace & do nothing." But when he arrived back in Hartford in late January Livy was opposed to another temporary separation and Sam (in his own words) assured her that "there isn't money enough in America to hire me to leave you for one day." Redpath finally persuaded him to speak in Boston once or twice, though plans were still unsettled on February 23. If he was scheduled to lecture, Sam, ever the self-promoter, informed the manager that "it would be a good item to start afloat that I have been offered $20,000 to lecture 30 times, & *declined*. {Privately, the *truth* is, I was offered *$25,000* to lecture 30 times, but it is a good deal wiser to tell the public only about as much of a thing as they can believe without straining too much. Part of the truth is often a deal more effective than the whole of it.}" In the end he delivered an abbreviated version of his "Roughing It" lecture in a crowded Horticultural Hall the evening of March 5. Among those in the crowd were Howells and publisher Osgood. He "was in excellent humor," according to the *Boston Herald*, and though the anecdotes were "the same as are contained in the book of the same title," the audience did not seem to notice. Sam concluded by announcing to the crowd they had witnessed his last appearance onstage.[17]

He returned to Hartford the next day in advance of weekend guests— Thomas Bailey Aldrich and his wife Lilian, Howells, and Osgood. Sam and Charley Warner met their friends on the platform in Springfield, where they transferred trains, and escorted them the remaining thirty-five miles to Nook Farm. Howells and Osgood stayed with the Warners, while the Aldriches lodged with Sam and Livy. Lilian Aldrich remembered that the eight of them "dined the evening of our arrival at the Warners'" and "never again can there be such talk as scintillated about the table that night." Sam referred no less than three times in his autobiography to Tom Aldrich's "brilliant" wit, and Howells recalled that "in the good fellowship of that cordial neighborhood we had two such days as the aging sun no longer shines on in his round. There was constant running in and out of friendly houses where the lively hosts and guests called one another by their Christian names or nicknames, and no such vain ceremony as knocking or ringing at doors." Their daily regimen seemed "quite an ideal" to Howells. "They live very near each other, in a sort of suburban grove, and their neighbors are the Stowes and Hookers, and a great many delightful people." The most vivid impression Sam left on "us two ravenous young Boston authors [he was a year and a half older than Howells, two months older than Osgood] was of the satisfying, the surfeiting nature of subscription publication." Sam maintained to Howells that *The Innocents Abroad* (1869) "sells right along just like the Bible" and "he lectured Aldrich and me on the folly" of trade publication. "Anything but subscription publication is printing for private circulation," Sam had insisted.[18]

Neither Howells nor Lilian Aldrich had met Livy before and each of them recorded a favorable first impression of her. Howells wrote that she was "a delicate little beauty, the very flower and perfume of *ladylikeness*, who simply adores [Sam]—but this leaves no word to describe his love for her." Mrs. Aldrich thought Livy a "white and fragile flower" who had married a "novel Westerner." Though he professed to disdain practical jokes, Sam played one on the Aldriches the next morning, no doubt partly in retaliation for the cool reception he had received from Lilian Aldrich the first time he met her. He scolded Tom Aldrich for the noise he and his wife had made in the guest bedroom just above the master bedroom, complaining that it had disturbed the pregnant Livy, who "needs her rest." Sam implied that he had overheard them engaged in loud sex. They vociferously apologized to both Sam and Livy, who (not part of the joke) replied naively that the Clemenses' bedroom was on the other side of the house and she had slept soundly all through the night. On her part, Livy shared Sam's disdain for Lilian Aldrich. She wrote to her mother that Elinor Howells was "not a bit like Mrs. Aldrich. She is exceedingly simple in her dress. . . . She is *exceedingly* bright—very intellectual—sensible and nice." The evening of March 9, the night before the visitors returned to Boston, the group of

Figure 5. Samuel Clemens's self-portrait, sent to Thomas Bailey Aldrich, 1874, from *The Life of Thomas Bailey Aldrich*, 1908.

eight "voted at dinner that the company would not disband until the genial morn appeared and that there should be at midnight a wassail brewed," according to Lilian. During the revelry, she alleged, they ran so low on drink that Sam walked to a saloon and reappeared "in an incredibly short time . . . excited and hilarious, with his rapid walk in the frosty air—very wet shoes, and no cap." Justin Kaplan inferred that Sam "tried the whiskey at the saloon where he bought the ale" but he failed to consider the source: Lilian Aldrich thought Sam was drunk the first time she met him.[19]

In April 1874 the "chronically litigious" Samuel Clemens—the lawsuits filed by and against him during the course of his career were as numerous as dragon's teeth—was involved in two legal cases, though neither of them went to trial. On April 8 the New York *Evening Post* printed an item to the effect that Sam had been honored with a "complimentary supper" in Hartford and paid for it from his own pocket—just the type of self-advertisement he might have sponsored had it not cost money. The item was widely copied across the nation, and Sam was outraged that he was the butt of a joke, humiliated by fake news. He contacted a friend of the staff of the New York *World* on April 9 to deny the allegation and added that he planned to file a libel suit. He reiterated the point the next day in letters to his brother Orion and Redpath, asking the lecture manager to "send me all the newspapers you can find containing" the item. "I will try hard," Sam fumed, "to make some newspaper sweat for this." He had thought of a strategy by April 11 and solicited Redpath's advice: "How would it do to go for a blatant, characterless paper, & place the damages at *three dollars*, as just representing all the harm that such a paper is able to do a body? I think I'd enjoy that." Fortunately, cooler heads prevailed. In the end, Sam brought no suit. Instead he denied in a letter to the editor of the *Hartford Courant* printed on April 14 that he had ever "been complimented with a dinner or a supper, & so I wondered how that item got its start." He dismissed the contretemps as an April Fools' joke gone awry. On April 15 the *Evening Post* calmed the brewing tempest in a teapot, acknowledging that the "concocted story" was "as innocent of reality as it was of malice."[20]

A more serious issue erupted in late April when a huckster fleeced the residents of Dubuque, Iowa, by posing as the brother and advance man for Mark Twain, who was ostensibly coming there to lecture. As a celebrity well known for his public performances, Sam was often misrepresented over the years—always to his dismay—by charlatans who tried to cash in on his reputation. As the *Chicago Inter Ocean* recounted the tale, on April 15 "a cute, sleek chap" alighted in the city, "gave out that he was the brother" of Sam, and advertised "a lecture to be delivered" by the "great humorist" on Monday evening, April 20. The hustler "became quite a lion, ran up bills at various places, and generally made himself quite 'numerous.' Some 200 or 300 persons invested their regular seventy-five cents apiece in the lecture and duly assembled to hear it" on the appointed night. "After waiting half an hour" the audience sent word to the impostor "Charles Clemmens" to ask "where the lecturer was," but the bogus agent had fled with the box office receipts and his hotel and other bills unpaid. Some of the victims pursued, captured, and returned him to the city, where he was jailed overnight and arraigned the next day. But he was released on the grounds the state failed to show that he was *not* Mark Twain's brother! The *Dubuque Herald* dubbed this judicial decision "the worst burlesque on Iowa law and our municipal authority that has yet come to hand." The rest of the story proves the truth of the adage that, as (Groucho?) Marx held, history repeats itself, first as tragedy, second as farce. Though the culprit, whose real name was Jared S. Strong, was re-arrested for defrauding printers, booksellers, and hostelers, he was released again on the grounds that "there was no presumptive guilt sufficient to hold him."

Meanwhile, Sam learned of the matter on April 24 and immediately instructed his Elmira attorney to contact T. S. Wilson, the Dubuque sheriff, to "have the fellow re-arrested and prosecuted." He sent a letter to the editor of the *Dubuque Herald* the same day, printed in the paper on April 28, expressing the hope "that the full rigor of the law will be meted out to this small villain. He professes to be my brother. If he is, it is a pity he does not know how to spell the family name." A Dubuque deputy sheriff and a private detective failed to recapture Strong, however. In a letter postmarked May 5 to Sam's attorney, Sheriff Wilson pled for money to pay their personal expenses while they continued their pursuit of the malefactor. If the good people of Dubuque had been duped by a huckster, Sam was a mark targeted by shysters. Sam replied with a check for $26.90 to reimburse law enforcement for the cost of telegrams. He offered a fitting conclusion to this comedy of errors in a letter to Orion: "A loafing vagabond swindles Dubuque in my name & that spiritless & dirty community let him go. I employ a lawyer here to plan the rascal's capture, & the first move he makes [contacting an inept sheriff] proves him a fool. A [deputy] sheriff starts after the culprit & *he* turns fool—& rascal, I judge."[21] For once, his assessment of the situation seemed commensurate with the facts.

Sam was cursed by impersonators on at least three other occasions. "In a good many places men have appeared, represented that they were Mark Twain and have corroborated the claim by borrowing money and immediately disappearing," he complained in 1889. "Such personators do not always borrow money. Sometimes they seem to be actuated by a sort of idiotic vanity." A false Twain was booked to lecture at the Academy of Music in Chicago in early July 1875, though he apparently evaporated into the ether before he could be arrested. Similarly, Sam was impersonated during an entire speaking tour in Australia in 1881 until the impostor literally died, prompting him to joke later that he was buried "in Melbourne or somewhere out there . . . by proxy." And in late July 1888 a fake Twain sold out Toland Opera House in London, Ohio, before he too disappeared into the night.[22]

Under the best of circumstances, Sam preferred to summer at Quarry Farm than to simmer in Hartford. With Livy in the final trimester of her pregnancy and with her history of miscarriages and premature births, the

Clemenses hurried there from an excess of caution early in the spring of 1874. On March 20 Sam advised Howells that Livy was "an invalid yet but is getting along pretty fairly." Shortly after hosting Mary Mason Fairbanks and her teenage daughter Mollie—who impressed Sam "as the darlingest, daintiest, sweetest vision" of maidenhood he had seen in a "long, long time"—and after terminating the rental agreement on the Hooker house, the clan left Hartford on April 15 and spent two nights in New York at the new Windsor Hotel on Fifth Avenue. While in the city Sam and Livy dined with Dan Slote, Fairbanks, and her son Charles, who remembered later that he "almost forgot to eat, in my enjoyment of the conversation." The Clemenses arrived at the Langdon mansion on Main Street in Elmira on April 17 and attended a performance of *Rip Van Winkle* starring Joe Jefferson at the Elmira Opera House the evening of May 4, though Livy "got herself pretty full of back-aches." The next day, in anticipation of Livy's confinement, they moved to Quarry Farm. There they could depend upon the care and attention of three servants—the washerwoman Charlotte, the cook and former slave Mary Ann Cord, and Mary Lewis, the wife of their African American tenant farmer John Lewis—as well as Susy's German nursemaid Rosina Hay, Nellie Bermingham's successor.[23]

On June 8, the seventh anniversary of the departure of the *Quaker City* for Europe and the Holy Land, Clara Clemens, christened after Clara Spaulding, was born at the farm. Livy was attended by Rachel Brooks Gleason, only the fourth woman physician in the United States and one of the directors of the Elmira Water Cure, downhill from Quarry Farm. Sam gloated to Joseph Twichell that the baby was "the great American Giantess—weighing 7¾ pounds, & all solid meat." Livy was unable to nourish the baby, however, and Clara was allergic to cow's milk, condensed milk, and pabulum. "Two or three times the baby has threatened to wink out like a snuffed candle, at 5 minutes notice," Sam wrote Orion when Clara was seven weeks old, "& each time the trouble was laid to prepared food." Sam and Livy hired a series of wet nurses, including Mary Lewis; a nursemaid named Maggie O'Day; and Mary McAleer, the wife of the Clemenses' coachman Patrick McAleer, but "each time the wet nurse went dry or something happened.—We have fled to wet nurses four times & to-day we are after two others downtown. Livy is about worn out; the present wet nurse is pumped out; & my profanity is played out—for it no longer brings healing & satisfaction to the soul." Finally, they turned to Maria McManus or McLaughlin, the "wife of a worthless Irishman," who remained a year until the Bay [baby] was weaned. Once, Sam discovered, Maria had invaded his cache of beer and "drank 200 bottles of the 252," and "it was the dryest month I ever spent since I first became a theoretical teetotaler." Yet Sam always regarded Maria with unqualified admiration. She was as "healthy as iron" and

> had the appetite of a crocodile, the stomach of a cellar, & the digestion of a quartz-mill. Scorning the adamantine law that a wet-nurse must partake of delicate things only, she devoured anything & everything she could get her hands on, shoveling into her person fiendish combinations of fresh pork, lemon pie, boiled cabbage, ice cream, green apples, pickled tripe, raw turnips, & washing the cargo down with freshets of coffee, tea, brandy, whisky, turpentine, kerosene—anything that was liquid; she smoked pipes, cigars, cigarettes, she whooped like a Pawnee & swore like a demon; & then she would go upstairs loaded as described & perfectly delight the baby

with a milk cocktail equivalent to infant forty-rod "but which only made it happy & fat & contented & boozy." Clara thrived on Maria's milk, Sam remembered thirty years later, because "no other milk had so much substance to it."[24]

Livy's sister Susan Crane, anticipating the distractions of a newborn, had built "the loveliest study" for Sam to write on a bluff a hundred yards from the main house. "It is octagonal," he bragged to Twichell,

> with a peaked roof, each octagon filled with a spacious window, & it sits perched in complete isolation on top of an elevation that commands leagues of valley & city & retreating ranges of distant blue hills. It is a cosy nest, with just room in it for a sofa & a table & three or four chairs—& when the storms sweep down the remote valley & the lightning flashes above the hills beyond, & the rain beats upon the roof over my head, imagine the luxury of it! It stands 500 feet above the valley & 2½ miles from it.

Sue Crane had designed the study to resemble the pilot house of a Mississippi steamboat and from its vantage point Sam surveyed the Chemung River bisecting the town and the topography of northern Pennsylvania. The gazebo was a retreat almost as secluded as the cabin at Walden Pond or, at the very least, "it is remote from *all noise*," Sam bragged. "On hot days I spread the study wide open, anchor my papers down with brickbats & write in the midst of hurricanes." He worked there almost every summer until 1891, and it was where he composed most of *The Adventures of Tom Sawyer* (1876), *The Prince and the Pauper* (1881), *Adventures of Huckleberry Finn* (1885), and *A Connecticut Yankee in King Arthur's Court* (1889). The only better setting for an author, Sam argued in years to come, was solitary confinement in prison, "the one perfect condition for perfect performance." Only John Bunyan,

Figure 6. Clemens family gathering, fall 1874 (*left to right*): Susy Clemens in the lap of Rosina Hay; Samuel Clemens; Susan Crane; Theodore Crane; Olivia Clemens; Clara Clemens; Katy Leary; "the table waitress, a young negro girl"; Auntie Cord; and "the little baby's American nurse-maid." In the distance are Olivia Lewis Langdon's coachman and Samuel Clemens's study. Courtesy of the Mark Twain House and Museum, Hartford, Connecticut.

Figure 7. The Quarry Farm study from overhead. Courtesy of the Mark Twain House and Museum, Hartford, Connecticut.

Miguel de Cervantes, Sir Walter Raleigh, and a few other authors enjoyed such "opportunities for working."[25]

Sam devoted much of his writing season in 1874 to *The Adventures of Tom Sawyer*, which he had started but laid aside in the summer of 1872. He had prepared an outline for the novel, though it hardly resembled the finished text: "1. Boyhood & youth; 2 y[outh] & early manh[ood]; 3 the Battle of Life in many lands; 4 (age 37 to [40?]) return & meet grown babies & toothless

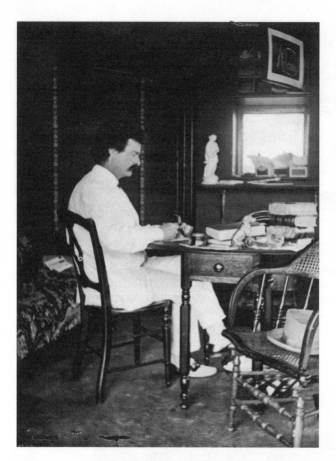

Figure 8. Samuel Clemens at work in his Quarry Farm study, ca.
1880. Courtesy of the Mark Twain Archive, Elmira College.

old drivelers who were the grandees of his boyhood. The Adored Unknown
a [illegible] faded old maid & full of rasping, puritanical vinegar piety." Set
in a fictionalized Hannibal named St. Petersburg after the capital of czarist
Russia, *Tom Sawyer* is less a boy book in the vein of Jacob Abbott's Rollo
series, Horatio Alger's *Ragged Dick* (1888), or even T. B. Aldrich's *The Story
of a Bad Boy* (1870) than a satire of the tradition. After all, Sam named his
hero after the steamboatman's term for a submerged log, a hazard on the
river. Two generations before Edgar Lee Masters's *Spoon River Anthology*
(1915), Sherwood Anderson's *Winesburg, Ohio* (1919), or Sinclair Lewis's
Main Street (1920), and though he omitted all suggestions of gambling and

prostitution along the river, Sam inaugurated the "revolt from the village" in American literature. He worked on the story intermittently through September 2. He modeled the grave-robbing scene in chapter 9 on a comparable chapter in Dickens's *A Tale of Two Cities* (1859), though in general he based the episodic plot on childhood memories. "I have been writing fifty pages of manuscript a day, on an average, for some time, now," he wrote John Brown. "But night before last I discovered that that day's chapter was a failure, in conception, moral, truth to nature & execution—enough blemishes to impair the excellence of almost any chapter—& so, I must burn up the day's work & do it all over again. It was plain that I had worked myself out, pumped myself dry." Ascribing agency to a work of fiction as if it were a stubborn animal, he acknowledged thirty years later that "a book is pretty sure to get tired, along about the middle." But it was only necessary to pigeonhole it when the "tank ran dry, well knowing that it would fill up within the next two or three years, and that then the work of completing it would be simple and easy." In his autobiography, Sam described the moment that he suffered a block in the midst of writing *Tom Sawyer*:

> At page 400 of my manuscript the story made a sudden and determined halt and refused to proceed another step. Day after day it still refused. I was disappointed, distressed and immeasurably astonished, for I knew quite well that the tale was not finished and I could not understand why I was not able to go on with it. The reason was very simple—my tank had run dry; it was empty; the stock of materials in it was exhausted; the story could not go on without materials; it could not be wrought out of nothing.

He had reached a stop on page 403 of the manuscript, the point near the end of chapter 15 when Tom leaves Huck and Joe Harper on Jackson's Island and swims over to St. Petersburg to deliver a message to his aunt. The message? That he had not drowned but was playing pirates with the boys on the island and was about to embark for "the Battle of Life in many lands." But in the end Sam decided not to take the story in this direction because he realized Tom was too conventional a character to run away. Or as he later wrote Howells, "By & by I shall take a boy of twelve & run him on through life (in the first person) but not Tom Sawyer—he would not be a good character for it." Sam understood intuitively, as Henry Nash Smith observes, that he "would ultimately need a hero more hostile toward the dominant culture than Tom Sawyer." Rather than continue the narrative he had planned, Sam pigeonholed the manuscript "& went to playing billiards for a change." By the spring of 1875 the cistern had refilled—"there was plenty of material now, and the book went on and finished itself, without any trouble," he notified Howells. In the interim, Sam "stopped to fool" with a play about Colonel Sellers.[26]

Sam and Charley Warner had the foresight to secure dramatic copyright to *The Gilded Age* while the novel was still in manuscript. Sam once even claimed that, while in England in late 1873, he "began to map out the play" but he had no more time for it than for his travelogue about Britain. On April 30, 1874, however, he learned that Gilbert B. Densmore, the drama critic of the San Francisco *Golden Age*, had dramatized the novel and that a production starring John T. Raymond had recently been staged six times at the California Theater in the Bay City to modest success. From his retreat in Elmira Sam filed an injunction barring further performances of the play and on May 5 he opened negotiations with Charley Warner for exclusive dramatic rights to their novel. Apparently "only my portions of the book are used in the play," he wrote Warner, so it appeared to be

> a one-character play, like Rip Van Winkle. The one character is Sellers. Now what I want to propose is this: & it seems fair to me. You make over to me your ownership in our dramatic copyright (duly in writing,) so far as it concerns characters created by me in the Gilded Age, & I will convey to you my dramatic ownership in all the characters created by you. You can then use your characters in a drama, if you wish to, & I will buy this play of Densmore, re-write it if it is worth it—or burn it, & write one myself & enjoin D[ensmore] from playing his.[27]

Warner agreed to these terms, though no money exchanged hands. The deal may have led to a brief breach between the collaborators, particularly because Sam incorporated into his own script some material that originated in Warner's part of the novel.[28]

Certainly there was plenty of money to be made on a popular play. Bret Harte had long argued that playwriting was "vastly most profitable" than fiction writing, especially before tough copyright laws were enacted. A "good popular play," Harte contended, "ought to give me certainly $3,000 a year for a year or two." Stage plays earned royalties from audiences at every performance, a source of income immune to literary piracy. As a result, Sam was involved in writing over twenty plays during his career, and Sam, Harte, Howells, and Henry James as a group authored "more than sixty plays, either alone or in collaboration," according to Brenda Murphy.[29]

After enjoining the further production of Densmore's melodrama, Sam maneuvered to buy the San Franciscan's now worthless script. He had "an itching desire to see Colonel Sellers on the stage—the only character in the book that I thought much of." He was quick to recognize the moneymaking potential of the project, which would enable him to escape the financial black hole that had absorbed so much of his time and money since the Panic of 1873. He offered Densmore two hundred dollars for a copy of "his *manuscript*, not his copyright—for he had none, his rights being annulled by my prior copyright. He took me up in such a prompt and gentlemanly way that he rather got the best of my human nature," so Sam sent Densmore an additional two hundred dollars for his cooperation. Densmore was "fully satisfied" with the arrangement, thanked Sam for "the very handsome manner in which you have acted," and surrendered all presumption of ownership in his work. "The character [of Sellers] is distinctly yours," he conceded, "the arrangement of incidents become yours by purchase, and I never have nor ever shall put forward any claim to having had a hand in the work." Moreover, Densmore allowed that he "did not for a moment suppose that my name would appear as joint author." Coincidentally, before Sam enjoined the production of the play in San Francisco, John T. Raymond had traveled to New York and not only sent his copy of the script to Sam at Densmore's direction but asked Sam to "write me a play with Colonel Sellers as the chief character," the first among equals in an ensemble cast.[30]

Sam shopped around his dramatization of *The Gilded Age* even before he had written it. According to both Henry Watterson and the New York impresario Daniel Frohman, Sam first offered the part of Colonel Sellers to the tragedian Edwin Booth, who declined it. In May 1874 he approached Lawrence Barrett, who rejected the role because his repertoire was full but suggested Raymond who, he remarked, "is a good actor" and "ambitious of success." Not that Barrett was overly optimistic about the commercial prospects of Sam's comedy; royalties for most stage productions ranged "from ten to one hundred dollars per night," he explained. "Your play would command at least $50 a night in New York, and $30 elsewhere." Privately, Sam thought that the only actor "who could have played the whole of Colonel Sellers," not just his comic side, was Frank Mayo, his friend from Virginia City. But by default he turned to Raymond, who negotiated face-to-face with Sam for rights to the play, probably in New York in mid-June when the family was en route to Elmira. According to a report in the New York *Sunday Mercury*, Raymond "requested an interview with Mr. Clemens in person" and they "met by appointment" and reached an agreement "on a mutually satisfactory basis." They would share profits equally, the same arrangement Sam thought he had negotiated with Bliss on his books, whereupon, Raymond added, "Mr. Clemens then set to work and produced a dramatization of 'The Gilded Age.'"[31]

"I worked a month at my play" in the study at Quarry Farm, Sam reported to Howells, rewriting Densmore's script "three separate and distinct times."

In the course of reworking the story, he replaced "Beriah," Sellers's first name in the novel, with "Mulberry" because a Beriah Sellers had surfaced to object to the use of his moniker. Sam's adaptation also omitted most of the political satire of the novel and focused on the subplot featuring Laura Hawkins and the scheme to buy the family's Tennessee land for use as an industrial school for manumitted slaves. In other words, the play was a shotgun marriage of farce and melodrama: while Sellers comically schemes to reap a fortune from a corrupt Congress, Laura, betrayed by the man she loves, kills him and is tried for murder. Sam used "little of [Densmore's] language and but little of his plot." To be sure, no copy of Densmore's script is known to survive, so it is impossible to determine exactly how fully Sam revised it. From all indications, however, he kept the structure of Densmore's play and changed the dialogue, in the end retaining only language in Densmore's script that had originally appeared in the novel. "I was by no means averse to saying that the play was written by the pair of us," he allowed, "but there was so little of Densmore's handiwork left in it that it did not seem worthwhile." More to the point, Sam continued, "All the characters and incidents used in this play are *my own creation*—but I value none of them *except Colonel Sellers* and what he says and does. No man can claim Sellers or a word that proceeds out of his mouth but me. . . . I furnished all the characters in this play, and I put in their mouths almost every individual word they utter." So, Sam asked, who wrote the play based on *The Gilded Age?* "I supposed *I* wrote it, but perhaps there may be people who are better informed about my matters than I am myself." Sam completed his dramatization in mid-July and submitted it for copyright within the week. His agreement to lease the play to Raymond was publicized a few days later. Sam admitted to Howells that he did not "think much of it, as a drama, but I suppose it will do to hang Col. Sellers on, & maybe even damn him. *He* will play tolerably well, in the hands of a good actor." Two months later, he was more equivocal: "It is simply a *setting* for the one character, Col. Sellers—as a *play* I guess it will not bear a critical assault in force."[32]

On September 2, the same day he laid aside the manuscript of *Tom Sawyer,* Sam sent a pair of sketches to Howells to consider for publication in the *Atlantic Monthly,* the leading parlor magazine in the country. In his cover letter Sam offered "Some Learned Fables for Good Old Boys and Girls," a parody of Sunday-school fiction along the lines of "The Story of a Bad Little Boy" (1865), a piece originally published in the *Californian.* Should Howells "come to like it" he could buy it for a pittance but, Sam advised, "hurl it back with obloquy if you don't." As an apparent afterthought, Sam also enclosed "A True Story, Repeated Word for Word as I Heard It," an experiment in black dialect he had transcribed from a conversation on the porch at Quarry Farm with Mary Ann Cord, though it had "no humor in it. You can pay as lightly as you choose for that, if you want it, for it is rather out of my line. I have not altered the old colored woman's story except to begin it at the beginning, instead of the middle, as she did—& traveled both ways." Howells was aghast by the former submission, his timid acceptance policy conditioned by the disastrous publication of Harriet Beecher Stowe's "Lady Byron Vindicated," the revelation of the poet's incestuous relationship with his half-sister Augusta Leigh in the August 1869 issue of the magazine. The monthly circulation of the *Atlantic* had plummeted from a high of about forty thousand in 1869 to twenty-one thousand in 1874, and Howells was struggling to recover readers. "A little fable like yours wouldn't leave [the *Atlantic*] a single Presbyterian, Baptist, Unitarian, Episcopalian, Methodist or Millerite *paying* subscriber," he confessed to Sam, because "all the deadheads would stick to it and abuse it in the denominational newspapers. Send your fable to some truly pious concern like Scribner or Harper, and they'll extract it into all the hymnbooks. But it would ruin *us*." Sam eventually included it in *Sketches New and Old* (1875).[33]

Howells was, however, delighted by the "colored one," as he put it, "which I think extremely good and touching with the best and realest kind of black talk in it." "A True Story" is a poignant tale that punctures the stereotype of the "contented darky." Only two figures are portrayed in the narrative: Sam, here in the guise of Misto C——, and the former slave Cord, here renamed Aunt Rachel after the biblical matriarch who weeps for her lost children. (Sam had mentioned in passing in chapter 55 of *The Innocents Abroad* that he had spent "some little time" at the biblical Rachel's reputed tomb near Bethlehem.) Aunt Rachel "was of mighty frame and stature; she was sixty years old" and "a cheerful, hearty soul." Misto C—— naively asks her, "how is it that you've lived sixty years and never had any trouble?" The question prompts Rachel to relate the story of the husband and seven children she lost in slave sales before the Civil War. "We loved dem chil'en jist de same as you loves yo' chil'en," she declares in debunking the racist notion that black people can't love their children as much as whites.[34] Miraculously, Aunt Rachel is reunited after the war with her youngest son Henry, whom she identifies "by means of scars on his wrist and forehead"; that is, like Stowe's Uncle Tom and Frederick Douglass in his *Personal Narrative* (1845), Rachel's son is a type of the crucified Christ. Faithful to his title, Sam insisted to Howells that he had "not altered the old colored woman's story" except to order the sequence of events.[35]

The importance of "A True Story" in the Mark Twain oeuvre can hardly be overestimated. It represented a breakthrough in Sam's career, if only because it was not humorous, and established his bona fides as one of the leading American writers—not merely one of the leading humorists—of his generation. As Tom Quirk explains, it was "the first piece Twain published in the *Atlantic Monthly* and the first time he had used a vernacular narrator to tell a socially and morally serious story." It "gave him literary and cultural authority." Sam tinkered with Rachel's speeches in order to re-create them as accurately as possible. "I amend dialect stuff by talking & talking & *talking* it till it sounds right—& I had difficulty with this negro talk," he confided to Howells. That is, "A True Story" and Sam's similar but decidedly inferior sketch, "Sociable Jimmy," narrated by a black child and published six weeks later in the *New York Times*, were early rehearsals for Jim's voice in *Huckleberry Finn*. The character of Aunt Rachel anticipates other noble black women who figure in Sam's writings, such as Roxana in *The Tragedy of Pudd'nhead Wilson* (1894), Katrina in "No. 44, The Mysterious Stranger" (ca. 1903–5), and Aunty Phyllis in "The Refuge of the Derelicts" (1905–6). Her lamentation for her lost children foreshadows Jim's guilt and regret for his treatment of his daughter 'Lizbeth in *Huckleberry Finn* and for Huck's own realization that Jim "cared just as much for his people as white folks does for their'n."[36] Sam later reenacted the separation of families by slave sale in chapter 37 of *Huck Finn*, chapter 21 of *A Connecticut Yankee*, and chapter 3 of *Pudd'nhead Wilson*.

Howells recognized the genius in the sketch when he first read it. Ten days after he accepted it for publication in the *Atlantic*—and even as he was hurrying it into print in the November issue—he wrote Sam that the "little story delights me more and more: I wish you had about forty of 'em." Before the end of the month he was soliciting other tales like it: "Couldn't you send me some such story as that colored one, for our Jan'y number—that is, within a month?" Howells lobbied for a rate of payment for "A True Story" hitherto unprecedented in the history of the magazine "in the highest recognition of [Sam's] writing as literature": twenty dollars per printed page or a total of sixty dollars, "a sum we could ill afford." Even as early as 1874 Sam had been paid more by other magazines and newspapers but, Howells added, "no acceptance, then, or later, ever made him happier."[37]

More to the point, "A True Story" epitomized for Howells the practice of literary realism. John W. DeForest, author of the pioneering realist novel *Miss Ravenel's Conversion from Secession to Loyalty* (1867), urged Howells in January 1875 to "tell Mark Twain to try pathos now & then. His 'True Story,'—the story of the old negress,—was a really great thing." Howells subsequently remarked that the sketch was "by far the most perfect piece of work" Sam collected in *Sketches New and Old*: "The rugged truth of the sketch leaves all other stories of slave life infinitely far behind and reveals a gift in the author for the simple dramatic report of reality which we have seen equaled in no other American writer." Ironically, he added, no more than two or three reviewers "recognized A True Story for what it was, namely, a study of character as true as life itself, strong, tender, and most movingly pathetic in its perfect fidelity to the tragic fact." Howells's summary of the cockeyed contemporary reception of the sketch was fair. The critics seemed to assume that black dialect was inherently funny. The New York *Evening Post* ("much truth and humor"), *New York Times* ("amusing"), and *New York Herald* ("semi-humorous, semi-serious") all misconstrued the sketch in their notices. Louise Chandler Moulton, usually an unapologetic champion of Sam's work, allowed that she did not "care much" for the story because it was "not funny at all." Still, the piece was widely copied across the country in such newspapers as the *Albany Journal, Baltimore Bulletin, Chicago Inter Ocean, Chicago Times, New Orleans Republican*, and *Newport Mercury*. The *Western Christian Advocate* fairly regarded it as "a faithful sketch of a Southern negro woman. . . . The humorist scarcely appears at all in his own person, but he puts the character he draws in a very clear light." The next year, upon the reprinting of "A True Story" in *Sketches New and Old*, Sam mailed a copy of the book to Aunty Cord inscribed "with his kindest regards, & refers her to page 202 for a well-meant but libelous portrait of herself & also the bit of personal history which she recounted to him once at 'Quarry Farm.'"[38]

After his summer in Elmira, Sam again declined an offer from James Redpath to lecture fifty nights during the winter season for six hundred dollars a night. "I have run about the world long enough," he advised Redpath. "I mean to live and die at home, now, if I starve at it. I love you, but I cannot lecture anymore." Instead he devoted his time to other projects, including the Sellers play. Raymond commenced a weeklong tryout of *The Gilded Age* in Rochester on August 30, 1874, to mediocre reviews and minuscule audiences. The *Rochester Union and Advertiser* ("simply an incoherent jumble of scenes and acts, without any sequence or continuity whatever") and the *Rochester Democrat and Chronicle* (which noted that the script "makes no pretensions to the skillful unfolding of scenes in due subordination to an artistic climax") panned the play. Or as the *New York Tribune* later indicated, Sam's "play was at first about as hopeless a piece of rubbish as—well, his novel." Though the Rochester audiences "were pleased" with Raymond's performances, the actor conceded that "they were not large enough to please me." Sam had hoped to attend, but he was prevented from traveling from Elmira by illness in his family. Raymond moved the production to Buffalo, his hometown, and on September 7 began a second weeklong tryout at the

Academy of Music there. Sam attended the first-night performance with instructions from the star to fix the script.

Figure 9. John T. Raymond and Samuel Clemens, ca. 1874. Collection of Gary Scharnhorst.

Sam was no play doctor; for that matter, he was no playwright. Nor did he seek the assignment, though his royalties depended on repairing the defects. As he wrote John Brown on September 4, "I would about as soon spend a night in the Spanish Inquisition as sit there & be tortured with all the adverse criticisms I can contrive to imagine the audience is indulging in. But whether the play be successful or not, I hope I shall never feel obliged to see it performed a second time." To his surprise, he was called to the curtain at the end of the fourth act on opening night. He spoke only a few words. "I didn't expect to be called out here tonight, and so I didn't prepare a speech," he protested. "Had I known I was to be called upon I should certainly have written out something. [As the local Buffalo reporter transcribed his speech, Sam's "emotion overcame him" at this point "while the audience applauded uproariously."] I sincerely hope none of you will ever write a play to be produced upon the opening night. When a play is produced upon the opening night the effect upon the author is almost too much for him to stand." The next day, both the *Buffalo Express* (the play was "weak and unsatisfactory" in "its present unfinished state") and the *Buffalo Courier* ("not quite complete and Mr. Clemens' presence in the city now is with reference to ascertaining how far it falls short of meeting the popular requirements") expressed muted criticism. The Buffalo correspondent of the *New York Clipper*, a theatrical paper, was more outspoken and fed a narrative the actor was beginning to frame: "Raymond's creation of Colonel Sellers stamps him as a comedian of great ability. The play itself will admit of much improvement; there is substance for a good piece, but it needs an entire reconstruction."[39]

In Raymond's chronicle of events, he intervened decisively before the production flopped. Rather than depend upon Sam to mend the play, he "fixed up the stage business as I thought most effectively." Then, in a rush of hubris, "I did a rash thing." He borrowed a few hundred dollars, rented the New Park Avenue Theater in New York for a week, hired and rehearsed a cast, and premiered the play the evening of September 16, 1874, scarcely two weeks after it had been roundly derided in Rochester and a week after it had been slighted in Buffalo. Livy and Sam spent a week in New York in mid-September at the Hoffman House, located at Broadway and Twenty-Sixth Street, a few blocks from the theater. While she shopped for furnishings for the new house, he drilled actors in the play. As he wrote Orion, "I staid on the stage 2 to 4 hours several days in succession showing them how I thought the speeches ought to be uttered. The consequence was the play went right through without a hitch on the very first night. They are better actors than I am, but of course I wanted the play played *my* way unless my way was radically wrong." The theater was packed for the premiere, not because of the inherent appeal of the play but because Raymond had papered the house with free tickets. Sam attended and at Raymond's request again delivered a curtain speech at the end of the fourth act, just before the murder trial of Laura Hawkins. "Mark lounged out to the foot-lights," according to the actor. "He was as solemn as a mule. During the whole of his twenty minutes' speech he never cracked a smile, while the audience were roaring as an audience never roared before at a fusillade of inexpressibly funny hits." As Bryant French has explained, Sam's peroration was "a clever showman's trick . . . intended to enhance the satire of the play," though he also not so subtly criticized Raymond's portrayal of Sellers. As he explained to the audience,

I have written this piece in such a way that the jury can bring in a verdict of guilty or not guilty, just as they happen to feel about it. I have done this for this reason. If a play carries its best lesson by teaching what ought to be done in such a case, but is not done in real life, then the righteous verdict of guilty should appear; but if the best lesson may be conveyed by holding up the mirror and showing what is done every day in such a case but ought not to be done, then the satirical verdict of not guilty should appear. I don't know which is best, strict truth and satire, or a nice moral lesson void of both. So I leave my jury free to decide. I am killing only one man in this tragedy now, and that is bad, for nothing helps out a play like bloodshed. But in a few days I propose to introduce the smallpox into the last act. And if that don't work, I shall close with a general massacre. I threw all my strength into the character of Colonel Sellers, hoping to make it a very strong tragedy part and pathetic. I think this gentleman [Raymond] *tries* hard to play it right and make it majestic and pathetic; but his *face* is against him.

When the curtain rose on the final act, according to Raymond, "the applause was deafening. Every hit took. That night one thousand people advertised Sellers, his mules, hog, corn, and eye-water speculations. From that time on we could not keep people away." The play that Rochester and Buffalo had ignored "became the piece-de-resistance of the dramatic season," the New York *Sunday Mercury* reported.[40]

The reviews in New York and other regional papers the next day were mostly complimentary. William Winter, the veteran drama critic of the *New York Tribune*, suggested that the play, "though excessively thin in texture," might serve to inaugurate a tradition of indigenous American drama "resting not on the piles driven into the mud and slime of French sensationalism, but founded on American society and manners." Winter asserted that the play evinced "practically no merit whatever except as a vehicle for the actor." He concluded with a backhanded compliment, however: "Mr. Raymond won a genuine success, and certainly Mr. Clemens's drama is not a failure." The *New York Times* judged the play "a truly American work. It is of native authorship, color, motive, flavor, and humor." This reviewer also disputed the commonplace comparison of Wilkins Micawber to Mulberry Sellers because "Micawber's imagination is feeble compared to that of Col. Sellers." The *New York Herald* suggested that the play "fills a void in drama of purely American life that has been long felt" and that it achieved a "most pronounced" success. The *Baltimore Bulletin* declared Raymond "an immense hit" in a play that not only had "taken the town by storm" but had been "hailed as an embodiment of purely American humor." Even Sam's nemesis, the New York *Graphic*, credited him with fashioning a silk purse from a sow's ear. From his half of a "rather poor novel" he "constructed a very fair play," or at least a leading character in Sellers, "a purely American creation" who "will hold possession of the stage for many years to come." *Wilkes' Spirit of the Times* ("one of the most entertaining [plays] that we have witnessed in a long time") and the New York *Commercial Advertiser* ("the legitimate metropolitan dramatic sensation of the day") were both complimentary.[41]

Raymond's reputation as a brilliant comic actor and de facto creator of the Sellers character was only enhanced when, ten days after the play premiered in New York, Ulysses S. Grant, former commanding general of the Union army and former president of the United States, attended a performance. With Generals James Barnet Fry, George S. Green, and Rufus Ingalis in his entourage, he "joined heartily in the applause and laughter," according to the *Evening Post*, and afterward personally congratulated the star backstage. When he heard about the incident, Howells wrote Sam that he was "glad to see that even President Grant recognized the excellence of the Sellers character in your play."[42]

Some months later, on the evening of May 1, 1875, Howells attended a performance of *The Gilded Age* at the Globe Theater in Boston and devoted the whole of the "Drama" section of the *Atlantic Monthly* for June 1875 to a review of it. Though he had chosen not to review the novel on which the play was based, Howells pleaded the case for *The Gilded Age* as a work of dramatic realism. "The play is true, in its broad way, to American conditions," he asserted, "and is a fair and just satire upon our generally recognized social and political corruptions." Moreover, he situated Raymond in the school of realistic actors because, he insisted, as an actor he "does not merely represent; he becomes, he impersonates, the character he plays." Howells apparently was aware that Raymond had recently made a well-publicized visit to the Pittsburgh criminal courts to glean some new ideas for the trial scene in the last act of the play.[43]

Other notices fed the narrative that Raymond circulated in the months and years to come: that he single-handedly salvaged the play and that Sam had contributed next to nothing to the endeavor, not even the starring role, which existed in the script only as a skeleton. The New York *Evening Express*, for example, applauded Raymond for proving to be a "thorough and admirable" artist while it indicted the script, "the work of a wit and writer of magazine articles rather than the work of a writer of plays." The *Chicago Tribune* argued that the play had been "written by Mark Twain" but "published by John Raymond, with his copyright mark on every page." The Philadelphia *North American* credited Raymond exclusively "for the success of the dramatic version of Mark Twain's 'The Gilded Age,' for a more absurd mess of twaddle than this work . . . would be hard to find." The *Arcadian*, a New York theater magazine, dismissed the "very weak and unsatisfactory" plot and dialogue of the script and credited Raymond with "all the success which [the play] promises to bring him." The *New York Republic*, in a notice dripping with irony, suggested that Sam had attempted "to omit characters altogether as a weak extravagance" and that Raymond, by failing "to comprehend the central idea of the dramatist," had "spoiled" the play by acting in it. As the New York correspondent of the London *Athenaeum*, Sam's sometime rival Kate Field praised the performance of her friend Raymond in the starring role. Raymond, she wrote, "convulses fine audiences at the Park Theatre by a real American characterization of Col. Sellers" and "I don't see how comedy can be more naturally and beautifully acted than it is by Mr. Raymond."[44]

The original September production of *The Gilded Age* scheduled for the Park Avenue Theater eventually stretched into early January 1875. In all, Raymond performed in the play over a hundred times at the theater, including matinees. When the play became a hit, he claimed most of the credit. That is, he adopted the same perspective toward Sam that Sam took toward Bliss and other middlemen of literary production. As the lessee of the script, Raymond not only starred in the comedy but produced and directed it. According to Densmore, the actor originally "had no faith in the play" as performed in San Francisco in April 1874. Raymond claimed in November 1874, however, that "Densmore's play was a very excellent one"—that is, Raymond implied that he could have thrived as Sellers even acting in Densmore's version, that he had not required Sam's help to triumph in the role, and that as a rising star in the theatrical firmament he was the reason the play had succeeded. His attitude was painfully apparent the night of December 23, 1874, when the cast celebrated the one hundredth representation of *The Gilded Age* onstage in New York. The Park Theatre was "crammed from pit to dome" on the occasion. Sam and his family, including Livy's mother and the Cranes, had traveled to the city to join in the festivities, and after the fourth act Sam was again called before the curtain to speak. He thanked the cast, read (inexplicably) the anecdote about the "genuine Mexican plug" from *Roughing It*, and retired to applause. Sam's friend Brander Matthews, later a professor of dramatic literature at Columbia University, was in the audience and remembered that "this was not one of his happiest addresses, since it consisted of little more than his recital of the story." Sam "had little skill as a playwright," according to Matthews, who thought the play "disjointed" and its characters "juxtaposed in haphazard fashion." Raymond also addressed the audience and, without the pretense of false modesty, declared—to laughter, though he was not being facetious—that "of one thing I can assure you: that Mr. Twain's play would not have amounted to much if he had not found a man to act the part" of Sellers.[45] Sam would soon reply in kind.

The longer *The Gilded Age* kept the stage, however, the more reviewers reviled it. "Mark Twain's play is bad—execrably bad," noted the New York *Commercial Advertiser* after it had been staged a few hundred times, "but it happened that the most prominent character was so grotesquely drawn that he appealed directly to the American sense of the ridiculous; therefore everybody laughed, and in the general guffaw came success. Thus it has happened that one silly play has made a great success." This reviewer blamed Sam for almost single-handedly impeding the progress of American theater. He "did what he could to ruin the American drama," and since *The Gilded Age* had become a hit, "every playwright who sought to make his work a success has made one central character around which all the rest must revolve."[46]

Andrew Wheeler (aka Nym Crinkle) of the New York *World* represented the best barometer of the critical climate when *The Gilded Age* was produced. Wheeler disparaged the "essentially undramatic" plot but hailed Raymond's "impersonation" of Sellers, a "contribution at once valuable and unique to the American stage," and disparaged the dramatist's "want of constructive art." On opening night in 1874 Sam welcomed Wheeler's notice, telegraphing the editor of the *World* that he wished to "thank Wheeler cordially for doing that thing up so thoroughly & handsomely." But for the rest of his career Wheeler tried to compensate for his temperate review in the *World*. "I cannot for the life of me imagine where the notion originated that Mark Twain is, or by any possibility can become, a dramatist," he announced in August 1877. "His 'Colonel Sellers' is, without exception, the most absurd, the most irrational, and the most inartistic drama that ever succeeded by means of sheer absurdity and a clever actor." Wheeler denounced "Mark Twain's rubbishy play" with a vengeance when it was revived at the Park Theatre in January 1878:

> Without doubt, if plot, interdependence of characters, truth to nature, and fidelity to art are at all essential to a play, this is one of the worst ever written. But it is also one of the absurdist and that has preserved it for the delectation of generations, much as the quality of absurdity has preserved Mark Twain himself. . . . Col. Sellers [as the play had been retitled] is destitute of wit or probability. . . . Its author is incapable of making a plot; he is, oddly enough, destitute of any sense of the pathetic and anything like reverence. His wild American humor, here as in most of his other works, blinds him to all the requirements of literary and decent art. . . . But if Mark Twain wrote the worst possible play, Mr. Raymond has certainly worked, with many natural advantages, . . . to make it the most popular. . . . Had this part of Col. Sellers been committed to any other actor than [Raymond], the play would long ago have been forgotten.

Wheeler still later reiterated his criticism in similarly harsh terms:

> The more the play smelled to heaven with its literary and dramatic rankness, the more heaven-favored John [Raymond] appeared for surviving it and surmounting it. His humor was the true and fecund principle of nature herself, which embroiders even a dung heap with posies. The story of that play was incredible, foolish, and weak. The plot was manufactured like a patent scrapbook, ready gummed, that any current incident might adhere to it. The pathos, painfully intended, was always ignorantly undiscovered. And the wit was trampled all over with Mark Twain's hoof marks, and was vulgar, irreverent, and coarse.

Wheeler predicted unhappily that Raymond's "enduring portraiture" of Sellers "will meet with the same hearty recognition in England as it has met with here." But nearly a decade later, he reiterated his censure of Sam's lack of playwriting talent: Mark Twain "is as destitute of the dramatic instinct as a parish clerk." While *Colonel Sellers* was "one of the funniest hodge-podges ever put on our boards, and, I believe one of the most successful," it "was as far from being a drama as is a comic counting house almanac."[47]

Sam was unwittingly trapped in a quadruple bind. First, he was the butt of widespread criticism for scripting an inferior dramatization of a lousy novel. The play continued to receive hostile reviews so long as it kept the stage. Second, Sam was accused of stealing the character of Mulberry Sellers from Charles Dickens. "But for Dickens' happy idea in conceiving the character of Wilkins Micawber," one of his foes charged, "Mark Twain would not now be reaping a golden harvest out of the character of Col. Sellers." Third, he was also suspected of merely slapping his name on Densmore's script, much as he allegedly had affixed his name to Warner's on the novel *The Gilded Age* and passing it off as his own, though this argument never extended so far as to blame Densmore for writing a bad play. The *New York Herald* resurrected this claim in its response to his curtain speech on December 23:

> It would have been a graceful act on the part of Mr. Twain to have publicly acknowledged his indebtedness to his co-laborer in the dramatization of the "Gilded Age," Mr. Densmore, but the opportunity was let slip. It, therefore, becomes the duty of the press to call public attention to the fact that the first dramatization of "The Gilded Age" was made by a Californian newspaper writer named Densmore, and that the present play is but a modification of his work. . . . We consider that his partnership in the creation of the play should be publicly acknowledged.

Fourth, Raymond presumed that as the star he was the true "creator" of Sellers. He occasionally ad-libbed a line onstage that, if it drew a laugh, was added to the play permanently. Or as Albert Bigelow Paine observed, the actor "believed he had created a much greater part than Mark Twain had written."[48]

In the most obvious sense, Sam and Raymond's disagreement over which of them owned Sellers was manifest in a clash over how the character ought to be represented onstage. Raymond portrayed him as a low comic type, whereas Sam always believed "that there was a tragic element in the Colonel's character." As Henry Watterson put it, "from the first and always [Sam] was disgusted by Raymond's portrayal." Howells opined that Raymond "conceived the character wonderfully well and he plays it with an art that ranks him to that extent with the great actors; but he has in nowise 'created' it. If anyone 'created' Colonel Sellers it was Mark Twain." On his part, Sam wrote Howells that "the finer points in Sellers's character are a trifle above Raymond's level." He professed to be unconcerned "if the world *does* hail Raymond as the gifted creator of Sellers. The actual truth is that *nobody* created Sellers—I simply put him on paper as I found him in life . . . & any scrub of a newspaper reporter could have done the same thing." Nevertheless, Sam roasted the actor unmercifully in his autobiography:

> The real Colonel Sellers was never on the stage. Only half of him [the farcical part] was there. Raymond could not play the other half of him; it was above his level. That half was made up of qualities of which Raymond was wholly destitute. For Raymond was not a manly man, he was not an honorable man nor an honest one, he was empty & selfish & vulgar & ignorant & silly, & there was a vacancy in him where his heart should have been.

He paid the actor a backhanded compliment elsewhere in his autobiography: Raymond "was great in humorous portrayal only. In that he was superb, he was wonderful," but "in all things else he was a pygmy of the pygmies."[49]

More specifically, their quarrel may best be illustrated by their different perspectives on the so-called turnip scene. Sam long argued that, as a cub pilot in the mid-1850s, he once went to supper at the home of Cousin Jim Lampton in St. Louis and was fed raw turnips and cold water. He depicted the meal in both the novel and the play and he always insisted he meant to evoke pathos in the scene. Or as he wondered in his curtain speech on opening night in New York, "how more forcibly could you represent poverty and misery and suffering than by such a dinner, and of course if anything would bring tears to people's eyes that would." But Raymond played the scene for laughs. He ate "those turnips as if they were the bread of life, and so of course the pathos is knocked clear out of the thing." Raymond's audiences "used to come near to dying with laughter over the turnip-eating scene," Sam conceded, but "in the hands of a great actor that piteous scene would have dimmed any manly spectator's eyes with tears and racked his ribs apart with laughter at the same time." On his part, Raymond ridiculed the notion that a serious actor could have played the colonel. Raymond had learned that Sam "had intended the character of Sellers for Edwin Booth or Lawrence Barrett," adding, "Fancy Edwin Booth sitting down to that turnip dinner."[50] Raymond never altered his conception of the character.

The Gilded Age ran in New York until January 9, 1875, when Raymond took the show on the road. The first stop on the tour, coincidentally, was the Allyn House in Hartford, where it was performed the evenings of January 11 and 12. Sam and Livy declined the opportunity to see the play again, though they invited Raymond; his wife, the actress Marie Gordon; and Kate Field, who had joined the road typecast in the role of Laura Hawkins, to lunch on January 11. Sam and Livy's niece Annie Moffett described the formalities to her brother, Sam's namesake: "Yesterday Mr & Mrs Raymond and Miss Kate Field lunched with us. Lunch was to be at three. The first course was soup, the second quails & rice croquets, third, chicken croquets and salad, . . . fourth strawberry short cake, fifth orange ice, lastly fruit & coffee." Sam rented a box for Joe Twichell and his wife Harmony at the Allyn House that evening and Annie accompanied them to see the play. "The house was crowded," Raymond was "perfect as Colonel Mulberry Sellers," she reported, and "Miss Field did much better than we feared she would do, in the shooting scene [in the fourth act] she was very good indeed." But without a doubt Field was woefully miscast in the part. In act 1, according to the script, Laura is sixteen years old, and in acts 2 through 5 she is twenty-five. Field was thirty-seven at the time. It was the first time she had played the part in public and the notice of her debut in the *Hartford Courant* was restrained, to be sure:

> Miss Kate Field, the well-known writer and lecturer, made her first appearance in the play last night in the character of Laura. Miss Field is as yet so inexperienced on the stage that she is entitled to charitable criticism. During the first part of the evening she was evidently nervous, and her talking savored somewhat of recitation. But in the Washington scene [the fourth act] she forgot herself in her character and exhibited decided histrionic ability, although she can hardly flatter herself on a great success.

Of her second performance the *Courant* observed, "Miss Kate Field's personation of *Laura Hawkins* was better than on the first evening. Then she labored under the disadvantages of a first appearance in the character, a position more trying to a recent debutante than to one long familiar with the stage." In all, the *Courant* called the play "one of the most enjoyable entertainments ever put upon the boards," crediting Sam and Raymond equally. Sam also sent Raymond a letter for him to read before the curtain both nights. "I cannot come to the theater on either evening," he wrote, "because there is something so touching about your acting that I can't stand it."[51] So much for Raymond's assertion on the stage of the Park Theatre nineteen days earlier that the play "would not have amounted to much" had he not starred in it.

Unfortunately, Field attempted to burnish her public reputation by exaggerating her middling stage success in Hartford at Sam's expense. More specifically, she attributed to Sam a favorable comment about her acting that he simply did not utter nor did he even see her onstage. Her misguided effort to legitimize her performance in *The Gilded Age* by invoking his authority was a foolish mistake by any standard and he predictably responded with disgust. Field played the part of Laura Hawkins in Raymond's company only a few times, all in January 1875, in Hartford; Springfield, Massachusetts; Brooklyn; and Newark. In Springfield the play was favorably reviewed by Samuel Bowles, editor of the *Springfield Republican*, Field's friend and Sam's erstwhile foe. The next day, January 14, to publicize her achievements on the boards to date, Fields sent a list of three blurbs about her acting, two of them from Bowles's notice, to the *Newark Morning Register*, the *New York Herald*, and the *New York Tribune*. As she noted to Jeannette Gilder, one of the editors of the *Register*, "I've made a success and here are my vouchers which you can use. Have acted the part three times and improve nightly. Great houses." All three papers printed one or more of the "vouchers," and the *Tribune* published all three of them in its January 19 issue under the title "Miss Kate Field in the Country." Only one had not appeared in print before: "Miss Field played her part admirably and made a most happy success. [Mark Twain]." This "voucher" was a sentence excerpted from a confidential communication Sam had sent Marie Gordon, Raymond's wife, during the two-day run of the play in Hartford. As Sam explained later, in "a private note" he had paid "Miss Field as good & as hearty a compliment as I could, considering the fact that I was speaking from mere *hearsay evidence*, but I perceive" from the sentence cited in the *New York Tribune* "that my remark has been considerably improved & strengthened since I uttered it. I do not mind being quoted in full, but I must protest against a cutting down of my words which makes me seem to say a very great deal more than I did say or had any moral right to say." The same day "Miss Kate Field in the Country" appeared in the *Tribune*, Sam addressed a note to his journalist friend Jerome Stillson, the former managing editor of the New York *World*, to protest her unauthorized use of his name and words. "The only inference one can draw" from the item, he began, "is that I was an eyewitness of Miss Field's performance. But in truth I never have seen the lady play at all." Sam hoped his letter would be published. "This woman is the most inveterate sham & fraud & manipulator of newspapers I know of; & I didn't think she would ever be smart enough to get a chance to use me as a lying bulletin board to help her deceive the public, but by cutting down & printing a private note to Mrs. Raymond she really has got the best of me, after all."[52] Stillson no longer worked at the *World*, however, so Sam's letter was never printed in the paper. Field likely never knew that she was spared a major embarrassment. She continued to perform in *The Gilded Age* through late January, though the reviews of her acting did not improve. She finally left the stock company with no ill will.

Andrew Wheeler erred in predicting that *The Gilded Age* would enjoy "the same hearty recognition in England" that it had received in the United States. On the contrary; during its abbreviated run in London in late July 1880 the play was universally scorned by the London *Graphic* ("altogether wanting in that ingenuity of design which might reasonably have been expected"), London *Era* ("pitiful stuff" that is "beneath contempt"), London *Examiner* ("an intolerably dull piece"), London *Times* ("not a play at all"), and *Glasgow Herald* ("feeble"). The London correspondent of the Melbourne *Argus* considered it "quite the worst [play] I have ever seen on any stage." On her part, Field attributed Raymond's failure in London not to his acting but to the topical humor in Sam's script. As she wrote the New York *Graphic*,

> If "Colonel Sellers" has not been as well received here as in the United States, it is partly because the play has been so ingeniously cast as to bring out its shortcomings in full relief. Then the humor is often so local as to be incomprehensible to Cockneys. . . . Mr. Raymond's acting has taken immensely. His appearance is the signal for genuine and hearty laughter. It is unfortunate that he should not have a play better suited to English taste.

As for the part of Laura Hawkins, it "does not awaken enthusiasm," Field complained. That is, if the play flopped in London, it was more the fault of the playwright than the actor. On his part, Sam was "more than charmed" by Raymond's failure there, as he wrote Joe Twichell. He only wished the actor had suffered humiliation sooner. "My malignity was so worn out & wasted away with time & the exercise of charity," he admitted, "that even Raymond's death would not afford me anything more than a mere fleeting ecstasy, a sort of momentary pleasurable titillation, now—unless, of course, it happened in some peculiarly radiant way like burning, or boiling, or something like that." An Australian production of *The Gilded Age*, apparently staged with Raymond's assent if not his assistance, was a modest success on tour in Australia during the spring and summer of 1878 but similarly bombed when staged at the Theatre Royal in Sydney in early October and closed there after only two performances.[53]

The conflict between playwright and actor eventually degenerated into a dispute over money. After Raymond took *The Gilded Age* on tour, Sam bragged to Charley Langdon that his half of the profits amounted to nine hundred dollars a week in major cities such as Baltimore, Boston, Brooklyn, Chicago, Cincinnati, Philadelphia, St. Louis, and Washington, and an average of between four and five hundred dollars a week in smaller cities such as Hartford, New Haven, Providence, Springfield, Trenton, Troy, and Wilmington. He crowed to Howells in October 1876 that his "clear profit on Raymond's first week in Philadelphia" was over sixteen hundred dollars. Certainly his contract with Raymond enabled him to recover from the financial setbacks he suffered in the wake of the Panic of 1873 and to finish construction on the Hartford house. But fractures in their relations developed when Raymond was on tour with the play because Sam hired an agent to accompany the troupe and report his share of the box office on a daily postcard. The precaution seemed warranted because Raymond was, according to M. A. DeWolfe Howe, "hopelessly given 'to saving at the spigot and losing at the bung-hole.'" Howells remembered that the "postals used to come about dinner-time, and Clemens would read them aloud to us in wild triumph. One hundred and fifty dollars—two hundred dollars—three hundred dollars were the gay figures which they bore, and which he flaunted in the air before he sat down at table." But Raymond was irked by the arrangement and once, in late August 1875, refused to permit Sam's agent to examine the accounts. When Sam telegraphed to protest, Raymond angrily replied, "To say [your telegram] made me angry is to put a mild form to it and if you had been here I would have expressed to you *personally* my opinion of one whose dealings through life must have been of a very singular kind to cause him to suspect mankind as you do." Raymond claimed that he had faithfully "paid over to the author of the play the sum of forty thousand dollars" for "what is in reality a very ordinary play." The next month, the actor protested the terms of their contract. Raymond was "convinced that, while he was doing all the work," Sam "was reaping half the profits, and this struck him as not being quite fair." Sam was initially adverse to any adjustments in the contract, but he and Raymond finally agreed to submit to arbitration. The umpires met in the

St. James Hotel with the principals present and were persuaded that, while Sam's "work was done long ago," Raymond's labor "still continued and was as necessary" to Sam's "pecuniary success as it was to his own." In the end, Sam agreed to accept a quarter of the profits. Despite the reduction in his share, Sam bragged that the play the next summer still "paid me $23,000 clear"—that is, it was earning more money than all of his books combined— and in 1881 he estimated his total income from the play at $70,000. Walter Meserve, a theatrical historian, estimated Sam's total proceeds from the play during its thousand performances over fourteen years at "well over $100,000."[54]

Sam's profits from *Colonel Sellers* emboldened him to sink money into another foolish investment. In June 1874 his old friend Senator John Percival Jones of Nevada organized the Hartford Accident Insurance Company with an initial offering of $200,000 in stock. Sam bought $50,000 worth, with $12,500 invested up front and a like amount due soon thereafter, though Jones guaranteed him against loss. Better had Jones insured Sam against risk mismanagement. On June 20 Sam was elected to the company board of directors and nine days later he railed from Elmira to New York, where he registered for three nights at the St. Nicholas Hotel, before continuing to Hartford to consult with Bliss, inspect the construction site on Farmington Avenue, and pay Jones for his stock. He returned to New York on July 4 en route to Hartford, where a few weeks later, as a representative of the company, he spoke at a banquet at the Allyn House honoring the English insurance underwriter Cornelius Walford:

> Certainly there is no nobler field for human effort than the insurance line of business—especially accident insurance. Ever since I have been a director in an accident insurance company, I have felt that I am a better man. Life has seemed more precious. Accidents have assumed a kindlier aspect. Distressing special providence have lost half their horror. I look upon a cripple, now, with affectionate interest—as an advertisement. I do not seem to care for poetry any more. . . . But to me, now, there is a charm about a railway collision that is unspeakable. There is nothing more beneficent than accident insurance. I have seen an entire family lifted out of poverty and into affluence by the simple boon of a broken leg. I have had people come to me on crutches, with tears in their eyes, to bless this beneficent institution. In all my experience of life, I have seen nothing so seraphic as the look that comes into a freshly mutilated man's face when he feels in his vest pocket with his remaining hand and finds his accident ticket all right. And I have seen nothing so sad as the look that comes into another splintered customer's face, when he found he couldn't collect on a wooden leg.

Unfortunately, after only eighteen months the Hartford Accident Insurance Company "went to pieces and I was out of pocket twenty-three thousand dollars," though Jones eventually reimbursed Sam.[55]

Sam and Livy left their daughters at Quarry Farm in early August in the care of the Cranes and a wet nurse. They first visited Sam's mother and sister in Fredonia, then David Gray and his wife in Buffalo, overnighting in Canandaigua, New York, before returning to Elmira on August 14. Livy was exhausted by the travel just two months after giving birth to Clara: "I brought Mrs. Clemens back from her trip in a dreadfully broken down condition," Sam reported to Howells. Sam also behaved foolishly during a reception in his honor in Fredonia. Irritated that his mother and sister Pamela, who were members of the Women's Christian Temperance Union, served only nonalcoholic fruit punch in their home, "his thoughts grew black and blacker," his grandniece recalled, "until a terrible thunderstorm broke over the head of a local banker." Not until a week later, the day after returning to Elmira, did he beg their pardon:

> I came away from Fredonia ashamed of myself;—almost too much humiliated to hold up my head & say good-bye. For I began to comprehend how much harm my conduct might do you socially in your village. I would have gone to that detestable oyster-brained bore & apologized for my inexcusable rudeness to him, but that I was satisfied he was of too small a calibre to know how to receive an apology with magnanimity. . . . I am mainly grieved because I have been rude to a man who has been kind to you—& if you ever feel a desire to apologize to him for me, you may be sure that I will endorse the apology, no matter how strong it may be. I went to his bank to apologize to him, but my conviction was strong that he was not man enough to know how to take an apology & so I did not make it.

It was a curious response to a sensitive situation. Sam was not sorry for his tirade per se but only because it might damage the reputation of his kinfolk in the neighborhood. He failed to beg the pardon of the person he had offended because he feared his act of contrition would not be received "with magnanimity." Instead he urged his mother and sister to express his regret and he would "endorse" their apology; he was "grieved" but unbowed. A year later, Sam defiantly wrote Pamela that he hated "the very name of total abstinence. I have taught Livy at last to drink a bottle of beer every night; & all in good time I shall teach the children to do the same."[56]

The Clemenses left Elmira on September 10, spent a week shopping for carpeting and other home furnishings in New York, where they again registered at the Hoffman House, and arrived in Hartford on September 19. Their house was finished save for interior detailing on the ground floor. As Livy wrote her mother, "We are perfectly delighted with everything here and do so want you all to see it." Sam added at the bottom of this letter that he had been

> bullyragged all day by the builder, by his foreman, by the architect, by the tapestry devil who is to upholster the furniture, by the idiot who is putting down the carpets, by the scoundrel who is setting up the billiard-table (& has left the balls in New York), by the wildcat who is sodding the ground & finishing the driveway (after the sun went down), by a book *agent*, whose body is in the back yard & the coroner notified. Just think of this thing going on the whole day long, & I a man who loathes details with all his heart! But I haven't lost my temper, & I've made Livy lie down *most* of the time; could anybody make her lie down *all* the time?

Upon their arrival in the city, they settled into several upstairs rooms. The carpenters and plumbers were "all on the first floor," he explained, "so we have taken up quarters on the second story, sleeping in a guest room, eating in a nursery & using my study for a parlor." They had gas and water in this apartment, "so we are pretty comfortable," he wrote Orion. Or as he notified Howells on September 20, "we are in part of the new house. Goodness knows when we'll get in the rest of it—full of workmen yet." Under the circumstances, he could not write. He had neither the quiet nor the solitude he enjoyed in his octagonal study at Quarry Farm, only the distractions of a house in disarray. He had "one or two things in my head that might do" for his next writing project, he explained to Howells on October 3, "but the trouble is I can't hope to get them out while the house is still full of carpenters." There seemed to be no end in sight. "These carpenters-devils are here for time & eternity; I am satisfied of that," he added. "I kill them when I get opportunities, but the builder goes & gets more." He had only one solution: "I have retired from the literary field & shall contemplate & curse carpenters henceforth & try to subsist on it." Sam and Livy were eager to flaunt their dream house, however. On December 6 Livy wrote Howells that they hoped "to be entirely settled by Christmas and after that we shall be anxious to see you here."[57]

They happily furnished and showcased the interior of their home in a flourish of conspicuous display. They installed the mantel from Ayton Castle in the first floor library, which was paneled in carved black oak, lined with bookshelves, adorned with statuary, and had windows that, according to Albert Bigelow Paine, "looked out over the valley with the little stream

in it, and through and across the tree-tops." Next to the library in one
direction was a spacious guest room or, as they dubbed it, the "mahogany
room." At the rear of the library was located a glass-enclosed, semicircular
conservatory, which was supplied with plants from the greenhouse. According to Howells, "the plants were set in the ground, and the flowering
vines climbed up the sides and overhung the roof above the silent spray of
the fountain companied by Callas and other waterloving lilies." The dining
room fireplace featured a window in the chimney so that guests could see
snow apparently fall into the flames—"like a magic trick," according to the
Hartford Times.

All these rooms opened with folding doors to create a space for receptions
and other large gatherings. On the second floor were guest rooms, the nursery, Livy's parlor, and Sam's study. The third floor featured a billiard parlor
with a private veranda.

Paine also mentioned the "Oriental rugs and draperies, and statuary
and paintings" throughout the house and the "unexpected little balconies,
which one could step out upon for the view." The exterior of the house,

Figure 10. The Hartford house dining room. Courtesy of the Library of Congress.

Figure 11. The Hartford house billiard room. Courtesy of the Library of Congress.

asymmetrical from every angle, with its decorative brickwork, "three turrets and multiple chimneys, its bright roof of colored tile," was no less impressive. Mary Mason Fairbanks, who toured the house with the architect Edward Potter while it was still under construction, was awed. She admitted that "adjectives begin to fail me" as she labored to describe the house and environs to the readers of the *Cleveland Herald*. In his *Autobiography* (1905), Moncure Conway compared the mansion to an English country home. As Sam reported to Livy when he inspected the construction site in early July 1874, "You may look at the house or the grounds from any point of view you choose, & they are simply exquisite. It is a quiet, murmurous, enchanting *poem* done in the solid elements of nature." In time, he even ascribed a sort of sentience to the structure: "it had a heart, and a soul, and eyes to see us with; and approvals, and solicitudes and deep sympathies; it was of us, and we were in its confidence, and lived in its grace and in the peace of its benediction." In all, he and Livy spent twenty-one thousand dollars on fixtures and furnishings and seventy thousand dollars on construction of a house standing on five and a half acres of land worth thirty-one thousand dollars.[58]

Figure 12. The Hartford house on Farmington Avenue. Courtesy of the Library of Congress.

They staffed the house and grounds with six and sometimes seven servants: a nursemaid for the children, a coachman, a butler, a housemaid, a
launderer, a cook, and—when necessary—a wet nurse, seamstress, or gardener. The children's longtime German nurse Rosina Hay, who remained
with the family twelve years, moved with them into the house. Sam fired
the coachman Patrick McAleer in spring 1872 for habitual drunkenness but
rehired him in June 1874. Sam had tried to replace him but, as he explained
to Orion, "we prefer Patrick to everybody else, when he is straight—& his
wife seems to keep him straight now." During the twenty-two years he was
in the Clemenses' employ, McAleer and his wife Mary raised eight children,
mostly in the apartment above the carriage house, on his salary of fifty-five
dollars a month. Moreover, in the spring of 1875 Sam hired George Griffin,
born into slavery in Virginia, as his butler. As Sam often remarked, Griffin arrived at the Hartford mansion to wash windows and remained eighteen years. According to Howells, Sam preferred a black butler because "he
could not bear to order a white man about, but the terms of his ordering
George were those of the softest entreaty which command ever wore." By
all accounts, Griffin was "handsome, well built, shrewd, wise, polite, always
good-natured, cheerful to gaiety, honest, religious, a cautious truth-speaker,

devoted friend to the family, champion of its interests." He was a deacon in the African Methodist Church, "no profanity ever soiled his speech, and he neither drank nor smoked." He exhibited only two vices, according to Sam: like the young George Washington, he could not tell a lie—until Sam trained him to "stand at that front door and lie to an unwelcome visitor"— and he was a habitual gambler. He became wealthy not on his salary of thirty dollars a month but from wagering and loan-sharking.[59]

CHAPTER 5

Afoot

It is easier for a rich man to go through a camel
than it is for either of them to crowd through the eye of a needle.

—Samuel Clemens to "Laura," undated

Sam clemens and Joseph Twichell customarily hiked every Saturday
from their Nook Farm homes to a lookout on Talcott Mountain, eight miles
to the southwest, and back. They were sometimes joined by Charles Dudley
Warner or students from the Chinese Educational Mission or the Asylum
for the Deaf and Dumb. "Get him out on a walk into the country in pleasant
weather, let the spirit of utterance be quickened in him," Twichell observed
about Sam, "and you have him at his best." The "true charm of pedestrianism
does not lie in the walking, or in the scenery, but in the talking," Sam allowed
in *A Tramp Abroad* (1880). "The walking is good to time the movement of
the tongue by, and to keep the blood and the brain stirred up and active; the
scenery and the woodsy smells are good to bear in upon a man an unconscious and unobtrusive charm and solace to eye and soul and sense; but the
supreme pleasure comes from the talk." Twichell also cherished these opportunities to chat and to bathe their "souls and bodies in the delicious tinted
light of the wood paths of Talcott Mountain." Sam declared that Twichell
"sometimes gains ideas" for his sermons from his companionship while he
"obtains information from his pastor" that he worked "into comical and humorous stories." They sometimes returned to Hartford "after one of these
jaunts," he recalled, "with the jaw ache, but never footsore."[1]

On one of these hikes, probably on November 7, 1874, Sam and Twichell
struck on the notion of walking the next week from Hartford to Boston, a
distance of about ninety-five miles, along the old stage turnpike "through a
lot of quiet, pleasant villages, away from the railroads." W. D. Howells had
invited them to dine at his house while they were in Boston and Twichell
was scheduled to preach in Newton, Massachusetts, on Sunday morning,
November 15; and so, with little planning or foresight, they decided to leave
from the East River Bridge in Hartford the following Thursday morning

and "walk to Boston, just loafing along the road" merely "for the sake of talking and swapping experiences." They hoped to complete the hike over three days. Sam notified James Redpath, who promptly released the news of the "great pedestrian excursion" to the Associated Press.[2]

Sam was delighted by the publicity stunt. Edward Payson Weston had made competitive walking a national craze, as faddish as the fifty-mile hike a century later. Weston famously hoofed some twelve hundred miles from Portland, Maine, to Chicago in twenty-six days in 1867, and he circled St. Louis backward on foot, a distance of about two hundred miles, in forty-one hours in 1871. The feat Sam and Twichell attempted in mid-November 1874 was routinely compared with Weston's treks, though Sam insisted to an interviewer that he was "not anxious to take Weston's laurels away." The first day they trudged twenty-eight miles in ten hours through East Hartford and the "quiet, pleasant villages" of Buckland, Vernon, and Tolland. "The day is simply *gorgeous*—perfectly matchless," he wrote his wife Olivia. "And the *talk*! Our jaws have wagged ceaselessly & every now & then our laughter does wake up the old woods—for there is nothing to restrain it, there being nobody to hear it." They stopped at a roadhouse in Westford, Connecticut, about 7:00 p.m., about an hour before sunset, to spend the night. The route was so little traveled, Sam added, "that you don't have to be skipping out into the bushes every moment to let a wagon go by, because no wagon goes by." In his journal Twichell referred to the inn as "a low tavern, but the best that was to be had." More to the point, the innkeeper was so "sublimely profane" he responded to "any sort of mild remark" with "a perfect avalanche of oaths," much to Sam's amusement. "The funniest scene I ever saw," Sam noted in his journal in May 1878, "was when my poor parson struck up a talk with the hostler." Twichell tried to persuade the fellow to temper his sacrileges by explaining that he was a Christian minister, whereupon the fellow launched into a diatribe about local church affairs "torch-lighted with indelicacies from end to end, which flickered lambent through a misty red hell of profanity rent and torn at four-foot intervals all down the line by sky-cleaving rock explosions of gorgeous blasphemy!" Sam later resolved to transcribe as much of the conversation as he remembered "with dashes to represent swearing & obscenity" and in 1882 he included an account of the hosteler's "crimson lava-jets of desolating & utterly unconscious profanity" in the manuscript for *Life on the Mississippi* (1883) before omitting it in revision. He eventually included the fragment in his unpublished "The Innocents Adrift" manuscript. "The man had . . . no thought of offending," Sam allowed; "he was using his natural speech" and "doing his honest best, in his simple, untaught way, to entertain us—& with me he was succeeding." But Twichell was not thankful and not happy.[3]

Before retiring on Thursday night, Sam and Twichell agreed that their walk "had developed into everything but a pleasure trip and was actually hard work." They decided to abandon their pedestrian experiment, tramp no farther than the nearest train depot, and rail to Boston. Early on a bitterly cold Friday morning they plodded another seven miles to North Ashford, where they persuaded the proprietor of an inn, C. M. Brooks, a Yale University graduate and a former New York attorney, to carry them in his buggy to the Webster, Massachusetts, rail station. Interviewed about Sam and Twichell later, Brooks recalled that Sam "limped rather painfully and carried with him an air of being generally fagged out" when he arrived, complained that he was "suffering greatly from having walked so far in new shoes," and asked "for a room where he might lie down quietly" for a few minutes. Sam had not slept the night before. He "had a pain through my left knee," he said, that nearly incapacitated him, and moaned that his "lameness was like walking on stilts—as if he had wooden legs with pains in them." While Sam napped, Twichell "told our host who [Sam] was, and who *we* were, and then he [the host] wanted to have us go in and see his lately paralyzed wife which we did for about 5 m[inutes], but then retreated, the lady being quite unable to converse and looking 'gashly.'" Around noon they left for Webster in "a narrow seated buggy behind the slowest horse I ever saw," Twichell noted. "It was a very cold tedious ride of 10 m[iles] and we suffered the acutest hardship of the whole trip in taking it. Mr. Brooks wouldn't accept a cent of pay" for the service but charged three dollars "for the man who owned the horse." Sam telegraphed Redpath from the station: "We have made thirty-five miles in less than five days. This demonstrates that the thing can be done. Shall now finish by rail. Did you have any bets on us?" Redpath, of course, released this message to the press. Sam telegraphed Howells that they would arrive in Boston around 7:00 p.m., completing "the first of a series of grand annual pedestrian tours from Hartford to Boston."

Upon reaching the city, they registered at Young's Hotel.[4] There they found a note from Howells urging them to hurry to his home on Concord Avenue in Cambridge. When they arrived around 9:00 p.m. they found a dinner party in progress and the philosopher and historian John Fiske, Nathaniel Hawthorne's daughter Rose, and the sculptor Larkin Mead, Elinor Howells's brother, gathered in the parlor. "I never saw a more used-up, hungrier man than Clemens," Howells remembered. He "immediately began to eat and drink of our supper. . . . I can see him now as he stood up in the midst of our friends, with his head thrown back, and in his hand a dish of those escalloped oysters without which no party in Cambridge was really a party." The erstwhile travelers "had a royal time till midnight," Sam wrote Livy, when they returned to their hotel "and went joyfully to bed." The next day Sam hosted a dinner for Thomas Bailey Aldrich, Howells, Mead, James R. Osgood, and Twichell. On Sunday evening, November 14, he again dined with Howells, and the next day Sam and Twichell attended a late-morning meeting of the Radical Club, where they met Cyrus Bartol and heard Edward Morse, professor of zoology and anatomy at Bowdoin College, deliver "a very interesting lecture on Evolution," according to Twichell. They then lunched with Howells, called on James Russell Lowell, visited the new Memorial Hall at Harvard University, and left on the 9:00 p.m. train to return to Hartford. Twichell considered the day "on some accounts the most pleasant experience of my life." On November 17 Sam wrote to thank Howells for his hospitality, reporting, "Mrs. Clemens gets upon the verge of swearing, and goes tearing around in an unseemly fury when I enlarge upon the delightful time we had in Boston, and she not there to have her share." He joked with Howells after their aborted trek that "Twichell & I invariably descend in the public estimation when discovered in a vehicle of any kind." His hike with Twichell, as it happened, was a rehearsal for their walking tours of Bermuda in 1877 and Germany and Switzerland in 1878, excursions that Sam would chronicle in "Some Rambling Notes of an Idle Excursion" (1877) and *The Tramp Abroad*.[5]

The most momentous conversation Sam shared with Twichell on one of their weekly hikes to Talcott Mountain occurred on Saturday, October 24. That morning Sam had declined an offer from Howells to contribute to the January 1875 issue of the *Atlantic*. "I find that I can't," he protested. The carpenters were still finishing the interior of the house on Farmington Avenue and as a result, Sam claimed, "my head won't 'go.'" His hike with Twichell, however, cleared his mind. "I take back the remark that I can't write for the Jan. number," he wrote the editor later the same day. "Twichell & I have had a long walk in the woods & I got to telling him about old Mississippi days of steamboating glory & grandeur as I saw them (during 5 years) *from the pilot house*. He said 'What a virgin subject to hurl into a magazine!' I hadn't thought of that before. Would you like a series of papers to run through 3 months or 6 or 9?—or about 4 months, say?" Sam acknowledged later that when he proposed the series to Howells "the vague thought in my mind was that 6 might exhaust the material & 9 would be pretty sure to do it." In the end Sam contributed seven essays published in the magazine between January and August 1875 under the title "Old Times on the Mississippi."

Ironically, Howells had recently ended negotiations with Bret Harte, who had demanded five hundred dollars for his forgettable story "The Fool of Five Forks." It eventually appeared in the feuilleton of the Sunday *New York Times* in September 1874 and he was paid four hundred dollars for it. That is, Harte effectively priced himself out of the *Atlantic* market; his writing never again appeared in the magazine.[6] Instead, Howells filled the space in the *Atlantic* that Harte might have claimed with Sam's "Old Times" articles.

In truth, Sam had been contemplating a book about the Mississippi since at least January 1866, when he lived in San Francisco, and as recently as November 1871, while he was on his lecture tour through the Northeast, he had cautioned Livy that when he finally began "the Mississippi book, *then* look out! I will spend 2 months on the river & take notes, & I bet you I will make a standard work." He believed, as first a riverboat pilot and then a professional author, he was uniquely qualified to tell the story. "No one could write that life but a pilot," he once told an interviewer, "because no one else but a pilot entered into the spirit of it. But the pilots were the last men in the world to write its history." Sam submitted the first of the "Old Times" papers to Howells a month after proposing the series with instructions to "cut it, scarify it, reject it, handle it with entire freedom," and the editor happily welcomed it. "The piece about the Mississippi is capital—it almost made the water in our ice-pitcher muddy as I read it," he replied to Sam on November 23, and he promised not to "meddle much with it, even in the way of suggestion. The sketch of the low-lived little town [Hannibal] was so good that I could have wished there was more of it." Howells "fancied a short hurried and anxious air" in the prose and Sam explained, with only a slight hint of paranoia, that he was "seriously afraid to appear in print often—newspapers soon get to lying in wait for me to blackguard me. You think it over & you will see that it will doubtless be better for all of us that I don't infuriate the 'critics' to[o] frequently." He fished for a compliment from Howells a few days later. He had finished the first three installments and started a fourth,

> and yet I have spoken of nothing but of Piloting as a science so far; and I doubt if I ever get beyond that portion of my subject. And I don't care to. Any muggins can write about Old Times on the Miss. of 500 different kinds, but I am the only man alive that can scribble about the piloting of that day—& no man ever has tried to scribble about it yet. Its newness pleases me all the time—& it is about the only new subject I know.

Howells tried to reassure him in his next letter: "If I might put in my jaw at this point, I should say, stick to actual fact and character in the thing, and give things in *detail*. *All* that belongs to the old river life is novel and is now mostly historical. Don't write *at* any supposed Atlantic audience, but yarn it off as if into my sympathetic ear. Don't be afraid of rests or pieces of dead color." Sam replied, "It isn't the Atlantic audience that distresses me; for *it* is the only audience that I sit down before in perfect serenity (for the simple reason that it don't require a 'humorist' to paint himself stripèd & stand on his head every fifteen minutes)." He implicitly compared his calculated (mis)behavior before *Atlantic* readers to the antics of the king in the Royal Nonesuch he would recount in *Adventures of Huckleberry Finn* a decade later. Despite his anxiety about appearing before an upscale audience, Sam found a channel while writing "Old Times." As he explained to Howells in January 1875, "The piloting material has been uncovering itself by degrees . . . until it has exposed such a huge hoard to my view that a whole book will be required to contain it."[7]

The January 1875 issue of the *Atlantic*, containing the first installment of "Old Times" as well as an essay by Oliver Wendell Holmes, the opening chapter of Henry James's novel *Roderick Hudson*, and poetry by Henry Wadsworth Longfellow, was issued on December 15, 1874. Sam's friend John Hay, "a most pleasant comrade" who had been raised on the banks of the Mississippi in Warsaw, Illinois, congratulated Sam on the article the next day. "It is perfect," Hay wrote, "no more nor less. I don't see how you do it. I knew all that, every word of it—passed as much time on the levee as you ever did, knew the same crowd and saw the same scenes,—but I could not have remembered one word of it all. You have the greatest gifts of the writer, memory and imagination." The New York *Evening Post* averred that Sam's description of the arrival of a steamer was "exceedingly good." According to the *Chicago Inter Ocean*, the initial installment was "funny, but vulgar," though this opinion did not deter the paper from reprinting an excerpt from the March installment of "Old Times" two months later. Louise Chandler Moulton opined in the *New York Tribune* that Sam's essay was "in the best vein of the best of American humorists." Moulton added that in the April installment of "Old Times," Sam proved "with every page what flexible idiomatic English he is capable of writing."[8]

The evening of December 15, 1874, the same day the January 1875 issue of *Atlantic Monthly* appeared, Henry O. Houghton and Melancthon M. Hurd, owners and publishers of the magazine, and Howells, its editor, hosted a dinner at the Parker House in Boston for twenty-eight contributors (all men) to celebrate the publication of the first number of its thirty-fifth volume. Houghton sat at the head of the table and Howells at its foot. Sam was invited, even though he had only published two *Atlantic* articles to date. The other guests included three aging transcendentalists—Christopher Cranch, James Freeman Clarke, and Frank Sanborn—as well as Thomas Bailey Aldrich, James T. Fields, Holmes, Henry James, Osgood, George Parsons

Lathrop, Francis Parkman, and George E. Waring. William Cullen Bryant, Emerson, Longfellow, Lowell, and John Greenleaf Whittier all sent letters of regret.[9] Sam and Henry James each sat near Howells, but apparently on opposite sides of the table. Bret Harte, once hailed as the savior of the *Atlantic*, was conspicuously absent.

As a newcomer to this most exclusive of clubs, Sam reveled in the festivities. In toasting Howells's health, Houghton declared he was "an editor of such singular modesty that he had been known to reject his own contributions." Early in the proceedings Sam spoke on the topic of "The President of the United States and the Female Contributors"; he pretended to be "staggered by the magnitude" of the subjects and asked if he might discuss them "one at a time," then launched into what the *New York Tribune* called "an inimitable and utterly unreportable speech." He concluded to laughs that the dinner had been "as good as he should have got at home." After the banquet, Sam, Aldrich, and Howells retired to Sam's room, where they "sat up talking . . . till two o'clock in the morning."[10] After breakfasting with Howells the next day, Sam returned to Hartford and the manuscript of "Old Times on the Mississippi."

Howells and Houghton counted on "Old Times" to increase the circulation of the *Atlantic*, still reeling from the Lord Byron incest debacle in 1870, but these hopes were dashed when Sam's articles were widely copied in major newspapers from coast to coast, effectively suppressing sales of the magazine. Among these papers were the *Boston Advertiser, Chicago Tribune, Hartford Courant, New York Times, San Francisco Bulletin, Sacramento Union, St. Louis Democrat*, and Washington, D.C., *Star*. The series was frequently pirated in such provincial or regional papers as the *Bangor Whig and Courier*; Lowell, Massachusetts, *Citizen and News*; *Memphis Appeal*; New Orleans *Republican*; Portland, Maine, *Press*; *Trenton State Gazette*; Virginia City, Nevada, *Territorial Enterprise*; and Worcester, Massachusetts, *National Aegis*. Four papers in Cincinnati alone—the *Commercial, Enquirer, Gazette*, and *Times*—reprinted installments. As a result, the "subscription list was not enlarged in the slightest measure" by "Old Times," according to Howells, and the *Atlantic* "languished on the newsstands as undesired as ever."[11]

In the first five installments Sam humorously recounted his decision to become a steamboatman and "learn" the river—all its shapes, bends, islands, depths, snags, sandbars, and reefs between St. Louis and New Orleans and back again. Because he was composing a serial for a magazine rather than planning a book for subscription publication, James M. Cox notes, Sam wrote these pages "completely freed from the conventions of the travel book." The cub pilot disappears from the final two parts or, as Edgar M. Branch suggests, these chapters "are essentially postscripts." In the June installment

Sam recapitulated the history of the Western Boatmen's Benevolent Association—a chapter reprinted in some labor journals—and the final segment included a brief history of steamboat racing and a capsule geological history of the river. Sam suggested to Howells that because "No. 6 closes the series," he might omit "No. 7 entirely & let the articles end with the June No. On the whole I should think that would be the neatest thing to do. I retire with dignity, then, instead of awkwardly. There is a world of river stuff to write about, but I find it won't cut up into chapters worth a cent. It needs to run right along, with no breaks but imaginary ones." Had Howells followed Sam's advice, Cox adds, "the structural lesion" in "Old Times" between the first six parts and the seventh "would not have been evident; but with the addition of the seventh sketch enough weight was added beyond the break in structure to make the lesion visible." For the record, none of the seven sections of "Old Times" was a lead article in the *Atlantic* and, for the forty-eight pages the series filled in the magazine, Sam was paid less than a thousand dollars.[12]

The newspapers that deigned to notice the essays during these months were almost universally complimentary—for example, the *Boston Advertiser* ("one of the most graphic pictures of river life ever penned"), *San Francisco Bulletin* ("his best writing so far"), Portland *Press* ("very funny and philosophical"), *St. Louis Republican* ("some of the most thoroughly artistic lying yet"), and *Milwaukee Sentinel* ("a descriptive power that is very unusual in his common, humorous writings"). The *Cincinnati Star* commended the "scenes and incidents of a kind, probably, never before touched upon by any writer." The *Chicago Inter Ocean* observed accurately enough that Sam seemed "to regret that he ever left the pilot business." Only the New York *Evangelist* expressed reservations, and then about the anticlimactic June installment: "Mark Twain "goes on with 'Old Times on the Mississippi' to little purpose."[13]

An idyllic reconstruction of Sam's adolescence and early maturity, "Old Times" exploits a number of trends well established in his writings and inaugurates others that would recur in his later work. Much as *Roughing It* (1872) omits all mention of the crime that thrived in the mining camps and in San Francisco, "Old Times" ignores the vice that flourished on the river. Like the tenderfoot in *Roughing It*, the cub pilot of "Old Times" reflects on his callow boyhood. Each of the narrators traces his initiation to adulthood, in *Roughing It* by becoming a reporter, in "Old Times" by learning "to read the face of the water as one would cull the news from the morning paper" or memorizing it "like A B C" or mastering "the language of this water." But in learning to pilot, the narrator also loses all sense of "the grace, the beauty, the poetry" of the "majestic river." Sam's next three novels, each a variation of a boy's book—*The Adventures of Tom Sawyer* (1876), *The Prince and the Pauper* (1881), and *Adventures of Huckleberry Finn* (1885)—may also be fairly described as bildungsromans insofar as they recount rites of passage. In both *Roughing It* and "Old Times," moreover, the narrator is hazed as part of his initiation: in the former by the "boys" who trick him into listening to Jim Blaine's tale of his grandfather's old ram and in the latter by pilot Bixby, who leaves his cub at the wheel of a steamboat during an imaginary crisis. Sam also continues to rewind his life as though it were a film. Much as he re-created events in 1867 in *The Innocents Abroad* (1869) and happenings in 1861–66 in *Roughing It*, he reimagined his early manhood in 1857–61 in "Old Times." In his next major work, he would continue on this course: he would depict scenes and events in Hannibal in the mid-1840s in *The Adventures of Tom Sawyer*. In "Old Times," however, for the first time he cites no documentary sources such as newspaper clippings or a personal journal; his story is less historical than personal.[14]

On February 19, 1875, sixteen leading citizens of Hartford, including the minister Nathaniel Burton and Yung Wing of the Chinese Educational Mission, publicly invited Sam to deliver another lecture on behalf of David Hawley's City Mission. "Two winters ago," their letter read, "you gave a lecture here in behalf of our city poor, which was pecuniarily, and otherwise, a memorable success. The fact that while still comparatively a stranger among us you manifested such willingness to assist in a time of great necessity, suggests to us the possibility that now that you are an established citizen of Hartford, you may be willing to help the same good cause again." According to the *Hartford Courant*, "Father Hawley is sadly in need of money owing to the combined pressure of hard times and bad weather." Sam agreed on the condition that

> the expenses of this enterprise shall be paid out of four or five private pockets (mine to be one of them), to the end that *all* of the money that comes in at the door shall go to Father Hawley's needy ones, unimpaired by taxes on its journey. I am glad to know that you are going to put the tickets at one dollar; for what we are after, now, is *money* for people who stand sorely in need of bread & meat, & so the object justifies the price. As this will probably be the last time I shall ever have the opportunity of hearing sound wisdom & pure truth delivered from the platform, I wish to buy a ticket to this lecture, & I herewith send money for the purchase.

"As this is honestly the last lecture I ever expect to deliver," Sam explained to a friend, "I would like to see it corral as much cash as possible." The *Courant* promised that Sam's talk "will be one never before delivered in Hartford" and expressed the hope that "there will be as many dollars received at the door as there are sitting places in the Opera House." In one of the most genuinely charitable acts of his life, Sam spoke on "Old Pioneering Times in the Silver Mining Region" before "one of the largest and finest audiences of the season" at the Opera House the evening of March 5.[15]

As usual, the *Courant* lauded his performance the next day:

> The lecture abounded in graphic description and amusing anecdote, and was delivered in the remarkably comical manner which is peculiar to Mark Twain. No lecture that we have ever heard has been more provocative of mirth. The audience were kept the whole evening in one perpetual burst of laughter. No newspaper report could begin to reproduce its genuine and wholesome humor, or indicate how extraordinarily funny were some of its incidents. The lecture is without doubt the best Mr. Clemens has yet delivered in this city.

The box offices receipts totaled over twelve hundred dollars, a beneficence soon acknowledged by Hawley, who expressed his "heartfelt thanks to the lecturer for his generous offering." A month later, on April 7, Sam again performed pro bono at the Connecticut Retreat for the Insane in Hartford. According to Twichell, who accompanied him, he "delivered to a hall full of patients and visitors his 'Nevada' Lecture—with great success." A few months later Sam contributed a sentiment to an album to be auctioned on behalf of the Massachusetts Infant Asylum Fair and offered to donate his own children to the enterprise.[16]

On March 11 the Howellses arrived in Hartford for a weekend with Sam and Livy in their new house. Elinor and Livy, who met for the first time, became fast friends. Each of the women was in delicate health and required "peace & rest." As Kenneth S. Lynn has noted, they "were alike in more ways than one and it is not surprising that they developed a deeply sympathetic understanding of each other," especially in light of the bond their husbands had forged. From all indications, the get-together went swimmingly and the Clemenses invited Charles and Mary Perkins, Joe and Harmony Twichell, and George and Lilly Warner to dinner to meet their friends. Twichell noted in his journal afterward that he had spent the "most delightful evening with some of the best people in the world." Howells wrote his father that they enjoyed "a really charming visit, not marred by anything. The Clemenses are whole-souled hosts, with inextinguishable money, and a palace of a house." Ever the consummate guest, Howells also sent a note to Sam on March 15 expressing his gratitude for the Clemenses' hospitality. The consummate host (most of the time), Sam promptly replied in equal measure, "all that was necessary to make that visit perfect was to know that you & Mrs. Howells enjoyed it. Sunday morning Mrs. Clemens said, 'Nothing could have been added to that visit to make it more charming, except *days*.'" Sam thanked Howells, too, for an added bonus: "I had got intellectual friction enough out of your visit to be able to go to work," apparently on the pigeonholed manuscript of *Tom Sawyer*, and "wrote 4000 words yesterday."[17]

In the spring of 1875 Sam was intrigued by the latest trial of the century. In November 1872 Victoria Woodhull had published an article in her weekly paper charging that Henry Ward Beecher, the most celebrated clergyman in America, had committed adultery. An advocate of free love, Woodhull was incensed less by Beecher's violation of his marriage vows than by his hypocrisy for publicly opposing sexual freedom while privately practicing it. His alleged partner in crime was Elizabeth Tilton, a parishioner and the wife of Theodore Tilton, Beecher's former associate at the Plymouth Church and managing editor of Beecher's paper, the *Independent*. Woodhull, who based the story on oral evidence, was arrested with Beecher's blessing on a charge of mailing obscene material, though she was acquitted at trial on a technicality. The scandal divided the Beecher family, with Isabella Beecher Hooker, a disciple of Woodhull, convinced of her brother's guilt, and his other siblings, including Catherine Beecher, Thomas K. Beecher, and Harriet Beecher Stowe, either choosing the better part of valor or rallying to his defense. Sam Clemens from the beginning considered Henry Ward guilty as charged. "I think the silence of the Beechers is a hundred fold more of an *obscene publication* than that of the Woodhulls," he wrote Livy's mother when the scandal was still new, "and the said silence is a thousand-fold more potent in convincing people of the truth of that scandal than the evidence of fifty Woodhulls could be. *Silence has given assent* in all ages of the world—it is a law of *nature*, not ethics—and Henry Ward Beecher is as amenable to it as the humblest of us." The Plymouth Church convened an inquiry into the affair and Tilton filed a brief explicitly accusing Beecher of "criminal intimacy." Tilton was then charged with libel, a suit Sam assumed falsely that Beecher had engineered. Had Beecher taken such an action "in the *first* place," Sam groused to Twichell,

> no doubt it would have been better. And by George it's *Tilton* that is on trial, at last!—& before a packed jury. Beecher's own people say it is Tilton that is on trial. I like the idea of a man insulting my wife & then I being tried for the heinous offense of complaining about it. But I have no sympathy with Tilton. He began by being a thundering fool & a milksop, & ends by being a hopeless lunatic—& a lunatic of that poor kind that hasn't even spirit enough to be

interesting. Mr. Tilton never *has* been entitled to any sympathy since the day
he heard the news & did not go straight & kill Beecher & then humbly seek
forgiveness for displaying so much vivacity.[18]

In Sam's opinion, Tilton would have been justified in killing Beecher on the
basis of primal law. After his arrest on July 28 Tilton was released on his
own recognizance, and the suit was dropped in early August.

On August 22 the Plymouth Church examining committee released a
statement exonerating Beecher of all charges of impropriety and excommu-
nicating his accuser. Sam referred sarcastically later to "the worn stub of the
Plymouth white-wash brush." On August 24 Tilton in turn sued Beecher on
a civil charge of adultery or "criminal conversation" or "alienation of affec-
tions." The trial began in Brooklyn City Court in January 1875, and for Sam
the scandal epitomized the "incredible rottenness" in American morality.
As he wrote Orion in late March, "The nation is not reflected in Charles
Sumner," the honorable senator from Massachusetts, "but in Henry Ward
Beecher, Benjamin Butler, Whitelaw Reid, Wm. M. Tweed." To observe
the proceedings firsthand, Sam and Twichell railed to Brooklyn on April
13, stayed overnight with their friend Dean Sage, a businessman, essayist,
and Twichell's former classmate at Yale, and were present for the start of
Beecher's cross-examination on April 15. According to the New York *Sun*,
Sam "shambled in, loose of coat and joints, and got a seat near the plaintiff's
table." Also in the courtroom that day were David Croly, editor of the New
York *Graphic*; Gertrude Kellogg, one of the actors who played Laura Hawkins in John Raymond's troupe; and Robert Todd Lincoln, the martyred
president's son. Croly jumped at the chance to solicit Sam's opinion about
the presidential candidacy of Samuel J. Tilden, the Democratic Party governor of New York, though Sam sidestepped the question: "No—oh! No you
don't. You can't make me commit myself. If I was foreman of the jury here it
might be profitable for me to express my opinions, but, as it is, I won't." After
they dined at Delmonico's with John Hay and Sage that evening, Sam and
Twichell returned to Hartford.[19] The trial ended on June 2 with a hung jury,
which voted nine–three to acquit Beecher.

The scandal never became grist for Sam's fiction mill, though he never
forgot about it either. He owned a copy of a pamphlet titled *The Beecher
Trial* reprinted from the *New York Times* for July 2, 1875, after the case was
closed. Sam was "tremendously worked up" by the trial, Howells remembered, and he "believed the accused guilty, but when we met some months
after it was over, and I tempted him to speak his mind upon it, he would
only say the man had suffered enough; as if the man had expiated his wrong,
and he was not going to do anything to renew his penalty. I found that very

curious, very delicate." Sam's sympathy for Beecher was no doubt encouraged by Twichell, who noted in his journal the day Beecher died a dozen years later that it was "to me an occasion of inexpressible sorrow. . . . So passes the greatest man I ever knew." Sam's private secretary Isabel Lyons noted in her diary for February 27, 1906, that he had "discussed the famous Beecher trial" over dinner that day and declared again that "guilty or not, Beecher should have publicly denied the charge the day after it appeared in the press for the honor of the woman"—a point he reiterated in his marginalia in *Sixty Years with Plymouth Church* (1907) by Stephen M. Griswold, his fellow *Quaker City* passenger:

> Beecher made the stupendous & irremediable mistake of remaining stubbornly & persistently silent until all sane people believed him guilty. A prompt denial in the beginning would have convinced the entire nation; but when at last he made it, not many persons outside Plymouth Church believed him. . . . That Mr. Beecher's denial was a falsehood there is small room for doubt; he should have told that honorable lie in the beginning, when it would have saved Mrs. Tilton.[20]

Two days after attending a session of the Beecher trial, Sam railed to Cambridge with plans to mark the centennial of the revolutionary battles in Concord and Lexington with Howells. Though the two men had special invitations to the celebrations that included rail tickets from Boston, they chose instead to depart from the North Cambridge station near Howells's home. Unfortunately, the local trains stopping there were packed to overflowing, with passengers even cramming the roofs of the cars. Unable to hire a hack of any kind, stranded "on the sidewalk in the peculiarly cold mud of North Cambridge," they slowly walked back to Howells's house and pretended that they had already returned from Concord, though Elinor Howells saw through the ruse. As Howells concluded, "I think the humor of this situation was finally a greater pleasure to Clemens than an actual visit to Concord would have been." Livy wrote Elinor a day or two later that Sam had "such a good time with you and Mr Howells, he evidently has no regret that he did not get to the centennial." On his part, Sam joked to Mary Mason Fairbanks that he "staid 3 days" in Boston "at a fearful expense of valuable time, to see the Concord Centennial, but it did not come there."[21]

Sam was no more fortunate in celebrating the centennial of the nation in Philadelphia in July 1876. He had been commissioned to write a brief biographical sketch of Francis Lightfoot Lee of Virginia, a signer of the Declaration of Independence and the Articles of Confederation, and to read it during the Congress of Authors convening in Independence Hall on July 2.

His utterly forgettable, uncharacteristic essay was subsequently published in the *Pennsylvania Magazine of History and Biography*. Sam spent most of a day at the centennial fair, where he was struck by the West Point cadets he met, but "then I got discouraged & returned home. I became satisfied that it would take me two, or possibly 3 days, to examine such an array of articles with anything like just care & deliberation."[22]

As a part-time surrogate father to his nephew and namesake, Sam Clemens was charged by his sister Pamela with arranging for her son Sam Moffett's appointment to one of the U.S. military academies—Annapolis or West Point. "I have pleasant letters from Secretary of War & Secy. of Navy," he notified Pamela. "Sammy can begin his [preparatory] studies" because "he will be appointed next year." He was still pulling strings seven months later. "I saw Gov. [Marshall] Jewell," the U.S. postmaster general and former governor of Connecticut, he again wrote Pamela in April 1875, "& he said he was still moving in the matter of Sammy's appointment & would stick to it till he got a result of a positive nature one way or the other." Certainly Sam admired the schools for instilling intellectual and physical discipline in the corps. He visited West Point informally at least three times between 1876 and 1880 and he was invited for a formal inspection of the grounds by the officers on February 28, 1881. On this occasion Sam read to the cadets, including "How I Escaped Being Killed in a Duel" (1873), for "as much as an hour and a half and produced extreme delight," according to Joe Twichell, who accompanied him. Sam jotted in his notebook that Annapolis and West Point were "institutions to be proud of" and courage was taught there just as dueling was taught in Heidelberg. He remembered how the cadets had impressed him at the Congress of Authors and he wanted "to see the boys at West Point" again. In the last chapter of *Tom Sawyer*, Judge Thatcher pledges that Tom "should be admitted to the National military academy," just as, in real life, Sam was maneuvering for Sammy's admission.[23] Neither the judge nor Sam delivered on his promise, however: Tom fails to attend a military school in any of the Tom and Huck sequels, and Sammy was not admitted to either of the academies.

Sam resumed work on *Tom Sawyer* in early spring of 1875. Rather than launch his hero on the "Battle of Life in many lands," he continued Tom's adventures in St. Petersburg—the boys' resurrection in the midst of their funeral sermon, the whipping Tom suffers after lying to protect Becky Thatcher, the school declamation, Muff Potter's exoneration at trial for the murder of Dr. Robinson, the treasure hunt with Huck, Tom and Becky's escape from the cave, the recovery of the Murrell gang's loot, and the death of Injun Joe. Sam completed a draft of the novel on July 5 and asked Howells to read it. He "didn't take the chap beyond boyhood," he explained, because "he would just be like all the one-horse men in literature & the reader would conceive a hearty contempt for him." After all, he insisted, *Tom Sawyer* was "*not* a boy's book, at all. It will only be read by adults. It is only written for adults." He solicited Howells's advice, whether "I am right in closing with him as a boy," and urged him to "point out the most glaring defects for me." Howells expressed interest in serializing the novel in the *Atlantic* after "Old Times" ran its course but Sam doubted "if it would pay the publishers to buy the privilege, or me to sell it. You see I take a vile, mercenary view of things—but then my household expenses are something almost ghastly." A few months earlier he had written to the publisher Houghton, "I find that trying to support a family is a thing which compels one to look at all ventures with a mercenary eye. I hope to see a day when I can publish in a way which shall please my fancy best and not mind what the banking result may be— but that time has not come yet." Or he might have said, as Herman Melville wrote Nathaniel Hawthorne in June 1851, "The calm, the coolness, the silent grass-growing mood in which a man *ought* always to compose,—that, I fear, can seldom be mine. Dollars damn me."[24]

Howells offered several suggestions for revision, not the least that Sam omit the last chapter of the manuscript, which detailed Huck's new life with the Widow Douglas. Sam dutifully deleted it. Howells also recommended that his friend temper some of the language, such as changing the "foul slops" of a chamber pot to "water," and "reeking" to "drenched." Whereas in the manuscript a poodle, after sitting on a pinch bug in church, went "sailing up the aisle with his tail shut down like a hasp" (Howells's comment: "awfully good but a little too dirty"), the poodle in the novel simply went "sailing up the aisle." Sam also modified Aunt Polly's complaint in chapter 1 that Tom was "full of cussedness" to "full of the Old Scratch" and he canceled a reference to how the widow would "gag" when Huck "spit." Howells eventually also urged him to market the novel as a boy's book rather than a novel exclusively for adults. "It's altogether the best boy's story I ever read," he observed. "I think you ought to treat it explicitly *as* a boy's story. Grown-ups will enjoy it just as much if you do; and if you should put it forth as a study of boy character from the grown-up point of view, you'd give the wrong key to it." Sam concurred, albeit a bit reluctantly: "Mrs. Clemens decides with you that the book should issue as a book for boys, pure & simple, & so do I. It is surely the correct idea." In his preface to the novel, Sam noted that it was "intended mainly for the entertainment of boys and girls," though he hoped "it will not be shunned by men and women on that account." He also acquiesced, however, to the omission of this preface from the British edition of the novel "so that it will not profess to be a book for youth." A quarter century later, he jotted a note in his journal that "I have never written a book for boys; I write for grown-ups who have been boys." Elisha Bliss, who steadfastly believed Tom Sawyer was "a boy overwhelmingly fascinating to grown up readers," refused to target the juvenile market only. He refrained from branding it as a book for children in the dummy he prepared for the canvass.[25]

Sam's decision to tailor the story to appeal to a broad market required a final minor revision to the text. In the final pages of the novel, Huck complains about "the rigorous system in vogue at the widow's" and objects in particular to the "compulsory decencies" he is expected to heed. The servants, he says, "comb me all to hell." Neither Livy nor her mother had objected to the passage when Sam read the chapter aloud to them. "I was glad," he admitted to Howells, "for it was the most natural remark in the world for that boy to make (& he had been allowed few privileges of speech in the book); when I saw that you, too, had let it go without protest, I was glad." But "since the book is now professedly & confessedly a boy's & girl's book, that dern word bothers me some, nights, but it never did until I had ceased to regard the volume as being for adults." The prudish Howells hastened to agree. "I'd have that swearing out in an instant," he wrote Sam the next day. "I suppose I didn't notice it because the locution was so familiar to my Western sense, and so exactly the thing that Huck would say. But it wont do for the children." The even more prudish Sam revised the passage to read "they comb me all to thunder" or, as he assured Howells, "I tamed the various obscenities until I judged that [they] no longer carried offense."[26]

During the spring and summer of 1875 Sam also repaid a long-owed favor by facilitating the publication of Dan De Quille's *The Big Bonanza*, a history of the Comstock Lode. De Quille, his friend and former colleague on the staff of the Virginia City *Territorial Enterprise*, wrote Sam from Nevada that he had completed a draft of the book and Sam in turn called on Elisha Bliss on March 24 to recommend the project. De Quille, he informed Bliss, "is a good man to write a stirring & truthful book" on the topic "because he has been city editor on that paper more than 14 years, & knows it *all*—& everybody." The same day, Sam encouraged De Quille to "come & stay in my house while you read your proofs." He advised him to "meddle with no Western publisher" and "make bargains of no kind until you get my letters." Within days he had also improved his offer to De Quille to come to Hartford and revise his manuscript. He promised to put him up

> at the best hotel, & every morning I will walk down, meet you half way, bring you to my house & we will grind literature all day long in the same room; then I'll escort you halfway home again. Sundays we will smoke & lie. When you need money you will know where to get it. If ever you feel delicate about

taking it of me, there's the publisher, who will cheerfully advance it. . . . If you prefer to write at night, you may write all night here, if you want to—there's a most noble divan in my study to stretch your bones on when you get tired. Besides, when it comes to building a book I can show you a trick or two which I don't teach to everybody, I can tell you!

He encouraged De Quille to "bring Joe [Goodman] along with you. What is the use of his staying out there till May?" Recalling how he had scribbled on *Roughing It* while Goodman wrote poetry across the table at Quarry Farm in the spring of 1871, Sam joked that the owner-editor of the *Territorial Enterprise* "can tell you what an inspiration it is to write in the same room with another fellow." Sam assured De Quille that he "need never pay me back any borrowed money unless you get it out of the book" and explained that he could not invite him to "eat & sleep in my house all the time you are here" because "my wife's health is so unsettled that at times we can't venture to have company."[27]

On May 16 the Virginia City paper reported that De Quille had departed for the East and "may possibly prepare his volume under the roof of Mr. Clemens' elegant cottage at Hartford." The New York *Evening Post* copied the item on May 25, two days before De Quille's arrival in Hartford, where he registered at the Union Hall Hotel on Farmington Avenue near Union Station, about a mile from Sam's house. They worked on their respective manuscripts—De Quille on *The Big Bonanza*, Sam on *The Adventures of Tom Sawyer*—for the next two months. Though both books were completed in the summer of 1875, neither was published by the American Publishing Company until the following year. Sam tried to push Bliss to "rush Dan's book into print, by New Year's, if possible, and give *Tom Sawyer* the early spring market," but *The Big Bonanza* was not published until July 1876, followed by *Tom Sawyer* in December. Bliss was unforgivably dilatory in supervising their production. According to Goodman, De Quille "put his book in the hands of a publisher who never was known" to adhere to either the letter or the spirit of a contract "in his life. The same publisher kept Mark Twain waiting thirteen months over time for his *Roughing It*." Goodman feared, when *The Big Bonanza* finally appeared, that De Quille would respond as Sam had—"that Dan will grow rich, leave the sagebrush, and make a void in the *Enterprise* that cannot be filled." Nevertheless, some "authorities" blasted Sam for subverting a rival, not Bliss for lassitude. The *Carson Appeal* was blunt in its assessment: "Twain did not invite Dan to his house in Hartford but allowed him to stay at a hotel not far distant. Twain's house cost $200,000 and had about twenty spare rooms in it. The failure of De Quille's book was directly due to the double dealing of Twain, whose abominable meanness in all the walks of life is proverbial with all who know him." Rather than "assisting his old friend," Sam "was a positive injury to him." Though "it is not often that a genius is selfish or small hearted . . . Mark Twain presents a conspicuous exception to the rule." To be sure, Sam cautioned Bliss that he would "be mighty sorry to see *Tom Sawyer* issue when any other book of the firm is either being canvassed or within six months of *being* canvassed."[28] But there is no evidence that Sam tried to stall the publication of De Quille's work or otherwise sabotage its success. On the contrary, he contributed a highly complimentary introduction it.

On account of Livy's delicate health, the Clemenses opted to vacation in 1875 at the ocean rather than in the hills above Elmira. On July 31, with De Quille in their company, the family left Hartford for Newport, Rhode Island, some ninety miles east. They took rooms at Bateman's Point, which De Quille described as "a sort of half-hotel, half farm-house kept by Seth Bateman, a descendent of one of the original settlers of the place." From all indications Sam enjoyed his six-week vacation, though he later disparaged Newport in his autobiography as a "breeding place—that stud farm, so to speak, of aristocracy of the American type." According to De Quille, Sam was "very indolent" while on holiday, though he read "about a thousand pages" of the *Big Bonanza* manuscript and "said it was all right." He reportedly played baseball every afternoon with a group of boys and went bowling on an old alley in the hotel.[29] Along with his old friend and now disgraced former vice president Schuyler Colfax, he picnicked with the members of the chic Town and Country Club, among them Thomas Wentworth Higginson, Julia Ward Howe, and George E. Waring, an urban reformer who designed the first modern sewer systems. Maud Howe Elliott, Julia's daughter, remembered that Sam "was a tall, strongly built man, with keen hawklike nose and bushy eyebrows. His white broad-cloth dress suit, with shoes to match, always made him noticeable among a crowd of conventional evening coats. He was a brilliant, aggressive speaker, who sometimes startled his audience by jokes some thought ill-timed."[30] The evening of August 23 Sam spoke at the Opera House in Newport under the auspices of the Bellevue Dramatic Club on behalf of local charities. Though he had been scheduled to read excerpts from *The Innocents Abroad*, he read instead "How I Edited an Agricultural Paper" (1870) and "How I Escaped Being Killed in a Duel." The *Newport News* reprinted his talk nearly word for word, and the *Providence Journal* reported that he was "the hero of the evening," that he "delighted his hearers," and that often during his talk the "laughter was immense." As usual, however, he was also criticized by his cohorts for failing to be a mere humorist. "Mark Twain is a disappointment to his Newport fellow sojourners," the *Boston Traveller* declared, because "he does not get off so many jokes as they naturally expected." The Clemenses returned to Hartford by September 8.[31]

Sam and Livy returned to the Boston area a few weeks later. They called on Emerson in Concord, lunched with Longfellow at Craigie House, and visited with Lowell in Cambridge on October 31. Howells accompanied them but, as he admitted, "I do not think Longfellow made much of him, and Lowell made less." Sam was apparently too uncouth for their refined tastes, though Howells made the point more diplomatically: "I cannot say just why Clemens seemed not to hit the favor of our community of scribes and scholars, as Bret Harte had done . . . but it is certain he did not, and I had better say so."[32]

In the interim between Raymond's production of *The Gilded Age* in September 1874 and the publication of *Tom Sawyer* in England in June 1876, Sam compiled a long-planned sampler of his short writings under the title *Sketches New and Old* (1875). The contents were in fact more old than new: all but seven of the sixty-three items in it were recycled, most of them from the *Galaxy* or *Buffalo Express*, others copied from the *Golden Era* and the *Territorial Enterprise*, with "The Celebrated Jumping Frog of Calaveras County" (1865) and "A True Story" (1874) gathered from the *Saturday Press* and the *Atlantic*. "I destroyed a mass of sketches" while compiling the collections, he wrote Howells, "& can now heartily wish I had destroyed some more of them."[33]

Unfortunately, Sam was denied permission to reprint in the book a piece he had written a year earlier, an insult that refocused his attention on copyright issues. He had contributed without compensation a comic essay, "An Encounter with an Interviewer," to a compilation of original works by members of the Lotos Club entitled *Lotos Leaves* and published by William F. Gill, host of the Wilkie Collins farewell banquet Sam had attended in February 1874. Gill copyrighted the collection in his name so Sam applied to him in April 1875 for permission to reprint the essay—and Gill denied his request. When Gill announced plans in May to reprint the essay in one of his own collections, Sam admonished him: "Don't do it." Sam noted that he had been "burnt once" and "that is enough. I shall be a very very old fool before I repeat the courtesy (i.e. folly) of giving my permission to print a sketch of mine in any book but mine." He bolstered his warning with a threat: Benjamin J. Such had discovered "in a United States Court, to his serious pecuniary cost, that my sole ownership of my matter is perfect and impregnable—I mean all of my matter—every single page I ever wrote"—a statement that contains two serious factual errors. The judgment in *Clemens v. Such* did not grant Sam a trademark on his pseudonym in perpetuity, nor was Such punished by a substantial fine. Still, Sam gave Gill "fair warning that if a single line of mine appears in one of your books I will assuredly stop that book with an injunction. I beg you to believe me when I say that I do not do this in any fractious or unamiable spirit toward you or your editor, but solely & only because I think it injurious to me to come prominently into print any oftener than I am professionally *obliged* to do." As he wrote to Howells, he was prepared to assail "the puppy Gill on infringement of trademark. To win one or two suits of this kind will set literary folks on a firmer bottom." When Gill then proposed reprinting "An Encounter with an Interviewer" without attributing it to Mark Twain, however, Sam was effectively checkmated. If Gill reprinted the essay "without printing my name anywhere in his book he will do himself no good & me no serious harm—& neither will he be violating trademark, I suppose." But Gill reneged. Despite promising to remove Sam's pseudonym from the book, he merely removed it from the list of contributors on the spine and retained it on the contents page and on the first page of the essay. In response, Sam demanded that Osgood sue Gill "for *violating my trademark*—copyright not to be mentioned." He was unwilling to compromise except on these terms: "Gill to pay me $500 cash & sign a paper confessing in soft language that he is a detected liar & thief." Under legal threat the publisher removed the nom de plume from subsequent reprintings of the book, though he left the essay in it. "Of course this destroys the possibility of my suing him for violating trademark," Sam allowed, "& I don't wish to sue him for anything else." But he saved his ire for his attorney: the pettifogger was "a lame & impotent d——d fool to compromise with Gill with Gill's mere *word* as the only security that he would keep his promise? The more I see of lawyers, the more I despise them. They seem to be natural born *cowards*, & on top of that they are God damned idiots."[34]

Among a trio of noteworthy previously unpublished pieces Sam gathered in *Sketches New and Old* were "Some Learned Fables for Good Old Boys and Girls," the parody of Sunday-school fiction Howells had declined the year before, and "The Experiences of the McWilliamses with Membranous Croup," the first of three domestic comedies featuring fictionalized avatars of Sam and Livy. The McWilliams stories, published in 1875, 1880, and 1882, foreshadow James Thurber's depiction of the "battle of the sexes" in such humorous tales as "A Couple of Hamburgers" (1935) and "The Catbird Seat" (1942). All three McWilliams stories proceed from the same premise: Mortimer McWilliams, a mildly henpecked husband, tells a stranger about a recent quirk in his wife Caroline's behavior—specifically, her overreaction to a child's illness, her panic during a thunderstorm, and her obsession with a malfunctioning burglar alarm.

The first of these stories was incongruously based on Sam's daughter Susy's exposure to diphtheria, the same disease that killed Langdon Clemens. Sam wrote Osgood on January 13, 1875, that Livy had "made me promise that I wouldn't absent myself from home until this epidemical & dreadful membranous croup has quitted the atmosphere hereabouts. It kills somebody's child every day & all the mothers are in a state of fright which nobody can realize who hasn't seen it. Our small Susie was threatened last night, & I never have seen Mrs. Clemens so scared before." This lethal outbreak of the croup provides the entrée to Sam's humorous tale. The "frightful and incurable disease" was "ravaging the town and driving all mothers mad with terror," Mortimer declares, and when their daughter Penelope coughs twice in her sleep Caroline orders her husband to build a fire, move the child's crib away from a window, turn down the heat, administer cough medicine, smear her with goose grease, and finally to "go for the doctor" and "tell him he must come, dead or alive." Mortimer obeys: "I dragged that poor sick man from his bed and brought him. He looked at the child and said she was not dying. This was joy unspeakable to me but it made my wife as mad as if he had offered her a personal affront. Then he said the child's cough was only caused by some trifling irritation or other in the throat."[35]

Sketches New and Old also included a travesty in translation titled " 'The Jumping Frog' in English, then in French, then Clawed Back into a Civilized Language once more by Patient, Unremunerated Toil." Marie-Thérèse Blanc (aka Th. Bentzon) had translated the jumping frog sketch from idiomatic English into faultless French and published the result in the July 15, 1872, issue of the *Revue des deux mondes*. The exercise was, at the least, culturally chauvinistic and it was prefaced with a patronizing headnote questioning the popularity of Sam's sketch, "the roars of laughter it has aroused," and its numerous reprintings. Sam was simultaneously amused and outraged by the insult. "Got a French version of the Jumping Frog—fun is no name for it," he wrote Livy when he read it. "I am going to translate it literally French construction & all, (apologizing in parenthesis where a word is too much for me) & publish it . . . as the grave effort of a man who does not know but what he is as good a French scholar as there is—& sign my name to it, without another word. It will be toothsome reading." Sam's retranslation became a tour de force in literature anthologies. Whereas he had written in "The Celebrated Jumping Frog," for example, "I don't see no p'ints about that frog that's any better 'n any other frog," Madame Blanc had written "Je ne vois pas que cette grenouille ait mieux qu'aucune grenouille," which in Sam's retranslation becomes "I no saw not that that frog had nothing of better than each frog's." As Sam's original has it, " 'Maybe you don't,' Smiley says. 'Maybe you understand frogs and maybe you don't understand 'em; maybe you've had experience, and maybe you ain't only a amature, as it were. Anyways, I've got my opinion, and I'll resk forty dollars that he can outjump any frog in Calaveras County.'" Sam's retranslation from Madame Blanc's standard French back into English is pure gibberish: "'Possible that you not it saw not,' said Smiley; 'possible that you you comprehend frogs; possible that you not you there comprehend nothing; possible that you had of the experience, and possible that you not be but an amateur. Of all manner (de toute maniere) I bet forty dollars that she batter in jumping, no matter which frog of the county of Calaveras.'"

"If that isn't grammar gone to seed," Sam added in his own voice, "then I count myself no judge." Ironically, Alphonse Daudet later read Madame Blanc's translation, which "was reputed to be excessively humorous, called 'Le Grenouille Sautant,'" but he "failed to see any fun in it." According to Sam's friend Hjalmar Hjorth Boyesen, Daudet complained, "'You see the story is just about a man who loaded a poor frog with shot and then made a bet as to how high the frog could jump.' 'Well,' I said, 'don't you think that's rather funny?' He responded, 'No; I feel too sorry for the poor frog.'" Daudet insisted more than once that he could not appreciate Sam's humor: "I have tried my hardest. I have said to myself: 'Everybody laughs at him. What can be the matter with me?' But there I sit perfectly silent. Impossible to laugh, impossible to smile. Mark Twain, to me, is a sealed book." On his part, Sam ignored Daudet's criticism and, in an interview in Paris in 1895, he even purported to have forgotten his name: "This Frenchman is a great critic and is an authority on all literary matters. I don't remember his name, because I never remember names, but he is an authority."[36]

Osgood had tried to persuade Sam to publish a book with his firm in 1872, and Sam had been tempted to accept his offer. In reply to the overture, he admitted that he "*would* like to publish a volume of sketches through your house, but unfortunately my contracts with my present publisher tie my hands & prevent me." After compiling *Sketches New and Old*, disappointed with the production and marketing of *Roughing It* (1872) and *The Gilded Age* (1873) by the American Publishing Company, he tested Bliss's temperament again. On a visit to Bliss's office on February 11, 1875, Sam announced that he "had got all my old sketches culled & put together & a whole lot of new ones added, & that I had about made up my mind" to publish them through Osgood's firm, whereupon Bliss "went to his safe & brought back a contract *four years old* to give him all my old sketches, with a lot of new ones added!—royalty 7½ percent! I had totally forgotten the existence of such a contract—totally." Though Sam might have considered Bliss's move a form of extortion, the publisher mollified the author by offering to compromise: they signed an addendum to the contract, raising Sam's royalty to 10 percent on any sales beyond the first fifty thousand copies of the projected collection.[37] This sales number was not reached until long after both men were dead.

Bliss then fumbled the copyright filing. He deposited a title page for *Sketches New and Old* with the copyright office of the Library of Congress on July 25, 1875, but he neglected to include two copies of the book, an oversight that would have annulled the filing had anyone noticed. The first bound copies of *Sketches New and Old* arrived in Hartford on September 25, although Bliss invested little time or money in promoting it. Sam arranged for Howells to review the volume in the December issue of the *Atlantic Monthly*. Howells sent an advance copy of his notice to Sam in mid-October and solicited his comments. Sam replied that it was "perfectly superb" and "nothing ever gratified me so much before." Howells lauded Sam's artistry by praising his "growing seriousness of meaning in the apparently unmoralized drolling," though many of the pieces in the book were a decade or more old. All of the other reviews that have come to light were cursory—for example, the *Hartford Times* ("fun alive"), *Hartford Courant* ("a better antidote for dyspepsia than the drug store can furnish"), *New York Times* ("most amusing"), *Saturday Review* ("the kind of book to take up while a patient is waiting for a dentist"), *New York Tribune* ("more noteworthy illustrations and better typography than in the common subscription volumes"), *Mining & Scientific Press* ("brimful of Mark's peculiar humor"), *Moore's Rural New-Yorker* ("will cause many to laugh exceedingly"), and *San Francisco Bulletin* ("something more than a mere 'funny writer'"). Schuyler Colfax alerted Sam that he had read the sketch "Political Economy" with "side-splitting emotions, & then read it to our family circle, who laughed till they cried." Sales of the book were disappointing, however, totaling only about twenty-seven thousand copies during its first year in print.[38]

Sam learned in early March 1876 that his Scottish friend John Brown's health was failing but in order to retire Brown required a fund of at least five thousand British pounds to "render him independent of money cares for the future." Brown's friends asked that money be raised "quickly" and "that it be done *without publicity*." Sam had already promised to deliver the latest iteration of his "Roughing It" lecture on March 22 before the Kent Club at the Yale Law School, so he offered to "talk it in N.Y. while it is fresh in my mind" on behalf of "a friend of mine who is in need," as he wrote James Redpath. "I want Chickering Hall—& will *wait* till I can get it if you think it the best place." He wanted to speak two or three times "& then fold my tent & skip home." Redpath scheduled him to appear four times in the New York area—three afternoons at Chickering Hall on March 28, 29, and 31, and the afternoon of March 30 at the Brooklyn Academy of Music. He also spoke during a reception at the New York Press Club the same evening.[39]

The abbreviated lecture tour in New York and Brooklyn was no more than a qualified failure. The talk at Chickering Hall the afternoon of March 28 was well received by the New York *Graphic* ("old and good") and the *New York Herald* ("a most amusing lecture") but it was panned by the New York *World*. He walked onto the stage with inexplicable glee at the size of "the misled audience" and, the *World* added, the lecture "had no value whatever and it had no moral lesson either. There was no apparent reason for calling it a lecture." During one of the talks Sam "had just reached the middle of his lecture, and was going on with flying colors," he told James Fields, when he recognized William Cullen Bryant in the audience. No one had told him that the distinguished poet was present, and "I was sure he saw the failure I was making, and all the weak points in what I was saying, and I couldn't do anything more—the old man just spoiled my work." Even Sam's informal remarks were derided. While the *New York Times* noted that he delivered a brief, informal, "funny address" at the club reception, other press outlets reported that Sam "apologized for the poorness of his speech" afterward and that "the apology was quite called for and appropriate." Nor were his other three talks at Chickering Hall and in Brooklyn profitable. He told Annie Fields that the box office receipts were disappointing and that, while "he had never lectured there before without making a great deal of money," this time "he barely covered his expenses." Instead, he contributed forty pounds (the equivalent of about thirty-nine hundred modern dollars) from his own pocket to Brown's pension fund, which eventually exceeded seven thousand pounds and enabled the doctor to retire comfortably.[40]

In the spring of 1876 Sam struck on another quick and easy scheme to boost his literary reputation and improve his cash flow: a "blindfold novelette." As he and Howells planned it, each of twelve authors would write a story using the same skeleton plot, unaware of the others' versions, and Howells would print them serially in the *Atlantic*. The stories would not make up a collaborative novel like *The Silver Fiend*, serialized in the *Weekly Occidental* in 1864, or *The Whole Family* (1908), which were long works composed incrementally by a series of authors yet were essentially the same story written in different styles. "I wrote my skeleton novelette yesterday and today," Sam notified Howells on April 22. At about eighty-six hundred words, he added, "it will make a little under 12 [printed] pages." He showed his manuscript, eventually titled "A Murder, a Mystery, and a Marriage," to Livy, who pronounced it "'good.' Pretty strong language—for her." The project stalled, however, when Howells was unable to recruit other contributors.

Sam decided in August to simplify the outline. His Buffalo friend David Gray thought that, if executed, the idea would make "a rattling stir" and "a mighty strike." But "with only 8 pages to tell the tale in, the plot must be less elaborate." As Sam conceded, "the hanging & the marriage" should not occur on the same day. In mid-October they were still trying to assemble a roster of potential authors but with little success. Sam wrote Howells,

> I see where the trouble lies. The various authors dislike trotting in procession behind me. I vaguely thought of that in the beginning, but did not give it its just importance. We must have a new deal. . . . My plot was awkward & overloaded with tough requirements. Warner will fill up the skeleton—for one. No doubt Harte will; will ask him. Won't Mr Holmes? Won't Henry James? Won't Mr. Lowell, & some more of the big literary fish? If we could ring in one or two towering names beside your own, we wouldn't have to beg the lesser fry very hard. Holmes, Howells, Harte, James, Aldrich, Warner, [John T.] Tro[w]bridge, Twain—now there's a good & godly gang.

If they failed to interest American authors in the project, Sam would contact the editors of *Temple Bar* in London "& see if I can't get the English Authors to do it up handsomely. It would make a stunning book to sell on railway trains."[41] All of the plans fell through, however, and Sam's manuscript of his installment in the "blindfold novelette" was not published in the *Atlantic* until the summer of 2001.

James T. Fields and Annie Fields visited the Clemenses in Hartford the last weekend of April 1876, when a pair of significant events in Sam's life happened to converge. Sam had been an avid supporter of the recently organized Hartford Dramatic Association, which rented an "elegant hall in Hamersley's block" with seating for about three hundred. Sam appeared there in a stage play for the only time in his life as Peter Spyk, a Dutch farmer, in an amateur theatrical production of James Robinson Planché's one-act vaudeville *The Loan of a Lover* the evenings of April 26 and 27, 1876, when the Fieldses were in town. Characteristically, Sam was dissatisfied with the part as written, so he revised it. "By re-writing Peter Spyk," he explained to Augustin Daly, "I managed to change the language & the character to a degree that enabled me to talk the one & represent the other after a fashion." He reiterated the point to Moncure Conway: "I've been playing Peter Spyk in 'The Loan of a Lover' (I re-wrote the part, stupefying it a little more & making it unconsciously sarcastic in spots,) & we made a considerable success of it." The *Hartford Courant* concurred: as the role was "amended and acted by Mr. Clemens, the fellow is not incidentally stupid; he is the model blockhead, irresistible in the comicalities that his stupidity leads him into, and wandering in the course of the vagaries incident to his dull mind through a series of mental processes that fairly convulsed the audience." Worse yet, Sam ad-libbed lines while performing, much to the consternation of the other cast members. According to the husband of the female lead, he indulged

> a propensity to go on with his talk after the other person's cue came. He would put in lines, which, while very funny to those on the other side of the footlights, were decidedly embarrassing to his fellow actors. At one point I remember he began to tell the audience about the tin roof which he had just put on an ell of his new house and rambled on for a while, ending up that particular gag by asking Gertrude, very much to her embarrassment, if she had ever put a tin roof on *her* house.

Never one to conform carelessly to community standards, Sam refused to censor the melodic "damns" from his dialogue in a play for adults as he had deleted the "hells" from *Tom Sawyer*. "If I cannot swear in heaven," he once wrote, "I shall not stay there." Nevertheless, according to Lilly Warner, he "was inimitable as a slow young dutchman" and Annie Fields believed that had he chosen "to adopt the professor of actor" he would have been "as successful as [Joe] Jefferson," the star of *Rip Van Winkle*. "It is really amazing to see what a man of genius can do besides what is usually considered his legitimate sphere." According to Albert Bigelow Paine, the actor Henry Irving once told Sam that he had "made a mistake by not adopting the stage as a profession. You would have made even a greater actor than a writer."[42]

The morning of April 28, the day after Sam's second performance in *The Loan of a Lover*, Annie Fields described Sam's daughters Clara and Susy in her journal as "exquisite, affectionate children, the very fountain of joy to their interesting parents." The following morning, Annie found Sam alone in the drawing room. "He greeted me apparently as cheerfully as ever," she recalled, "and it was not until some moments had passed that he told me they had a very sick child upstairs. From that instant I saw, especially after his wife came in, that they could think of nothing else." Susy had spiked a fever during the night, and her parents "were half-distracted with anxiety. Their messenger could not find" the family doctor, Cincinnatus Taft, "which made matters worse. However, the little girl did not really seem very sick, so I could not help thinking they were unnecessarily excited. The effect on them, however, was just as bad as if the child were really very ill." Lilly Warner similarly thought Susy did not seem very sick, despite Sam and Livy's concern. Fields and Warner may have misjudged the severity of Susy's malady or they may have been correct in thinking Sam and Livy overly alarmist. In either case, Sam reported to Howells a few days later that "Susie is just recovering from about the savagest assault of diphtheria a child ever did recover from" and the next day he repeated the news to Conway: "Susie escaped death by a hair last week. Diphtheria, of the worst form."[43]

Sam's curiosity in the dramatic arts was piqued by his weekend on the boards, and before James and Annie Fields left Hartford he expressed to them his interest in traveling to Boston the next weekend to see Anna Dickinson in her acting debut at the Globe Theater. Hattie Lewis remembered that Sam and Dickinson "did not get along well together. They seemed to be always trying to test each other's right to be famous." In March 1873, for example, Dickinson had privately criticized Sam for earning "not short of $200,000" with his "stuff," enough "to disgust one with one's kind." In any case, Sam railed to the city on May 8—without Livy, who was caring for Susy in the aftermath of her bout with diphtheria—and registered at the Parker House, rented a proscenium box at the theater for that evening, and invited the Aldriches and the Howellses to share it with him. Among the other celebrities in the audience that night were Emerson, Julia Ward Howe, Longfellow, and Whitelaw Reid. Sam fully expected Dickinson to bomb and was not disappointed. Dickinson had composed the play *A Crown of Thorns*, based on the life of Anne Boleyn, though she had never written a play before. In the lead role, as Howells wrote Augustin Daly the next day, she "was sorrowfully bad" and "the heaps of cut flowers" presented to her by her fans "only made the gloom heavier." Over thirty years later, Howells recalled that Sam had traveled to Boston "to witness the aesthetic suicide of Anna Dickinson," who "ranted and exhorted through the five acts, drawing ever nearer the utter defeat of the anticlimax." Sam told Lilly Warner that Dickinson's voice "was the worst thing—*dreadful* a squeal & a shriek," "her gestures were awkward, her walk bad," and "her face old."[44] Dickinson was, in fact, only thirty-three at the time.

The reviewers the next day largely agreed with Sam's hostile opinion. William Winter, the veteran theatrical critic for the *New York Tribune*, set the tone for the cacophony of complaints: "In art she was callow" and her "voice was often nasal and thin." The *New York Herald* was the most critical of all, warning that Dickinson in one histrionic set piece "behaved as if she was delivering a woman's suffrage address." The actress dismissed this notice with an ethnic slur, scorning the Irish "brogue and bigotry" of the *Herald*. Only the *Boston Post* pronounced the production "a magnificent success."[45] Not surprisingly, *A Crown of Thorns* closed on May 20 after less than two weeks on the stage.

Howells had launched a recurring feature in the *Atlantic Monthly* in January 1877 entitled "Contributors' Club" that was basically a column of unsigned op-eds on a variety of subjects. Sam was an original contributor, and his paragraph excoriated Dickinson's performance seven months later. "On her first appearance I found the spectacle of her failure so cruel that it was impossible to look at it steadily," he noted anonymously. He blamed the fiasco on Dickinson's conceit, her refusal to study the art of acting before presuming to star onstage. "On the whole," he observed,

> I consoled myself for Miss Dickinson's defeat. It was not peculiarly arrogant in her to attempt the highest prize of the theatrical art; that is what *débutantes* of mature years nearly always do; but the thing is arrogant in itself. If Miss Dickinson had gone humbly to some accomplished actor and begged to know in what subordinate walk of the profession she might hope, with anxious and assiduous study, to succeed, and she had tried that and failed, I should have felt sorry for her. But I bear her present defeat with fortitude.

Sam did not easily forgive or forget. "Talent is useless without training, thank God," he wrote Mary Fairbanks, "as Anna Dickinson may yet discover before she gets done trying to skip to the top-round of tragedy at a bound."[46] Dickinson finally retired permanently from the stage in 1882 after she failed commercially and critically in the lead role of *Hamlet*.

At one point during the Fieldses' visit to Hartford in April 1876, the talk turned to American politics and Sam vented his views to his guests without reserve. According to Annie Fields, the supposed champion of democracy and the common folk had "lost all faith in our government. This wicked ungodly suffrage, he said, where the vote of a man who knew nothing was as good as the vote of a man of education and industry; this endeavor to equalize what God had made unequal was a wrong and a shame. He only hoped to live long enough to see such a wrong and such a government overthrown." These convictions, though seemingly out of character, were hardly new; they had in fact been brewing for several years in parallel with Sam's Anglophilia. He had expressed them over three years before at a meeting of the Monday Evening Club, a group of Hartford professional men "of large intellectual calibre and more or less distinction" who assembled in a member's home every two weeks between May and October to discuss current events before adjourning at 10:00 p.m. to supper and cigars. Founded in 1869 by Horace Bushnell, the so-called Emerson of Hartford, whom Sam called a "theological giant" and "that noble old Roman," the club boasted among its members such local luminaries as Reverends Nathaniel Burton, Francis Goodwin, and Edwin Pond Parker; Charles Hopkins Clark; Henry Ferguson, one of the survivors of the *Hornet* disaster in 1866; Generals William B. Franklin and Joseph Hawley; William Hamersley; Charles E. Perkins; former Hartford mayor Henry C. Robinson; George Williamson Smith, the president of Trinity College; Calvin Stowe; J. Hammond Trumbull; Joe Twichell; and Charley Warner. Wives of the members were welcome to accompany their husbands to these meetings—and to socialize in a different room. As Sam explained in his autobiography, "it was their privilege . . . to keep still; they were not allowed to throw any light upon the discussion." Bushnell, who literally wrote these rules, was not particularly enlightened on the woman question. He considered women's suffrage "a reform against nature—an attempt to make trumpets out of flutes and sunflowers out of violets."[47]

Sam was admitted to membership in the club in February 1873 and read his first paper before the group, "License of the Press," the evening of March 31. He was not an unqualified defender of the First Amendment despite his early career as a journalist. On the contrary, the topic aroused his elitist instincts. The "more than free" press was "licensed to say any infamous thing it chooses about a private or a public man, or advocate any outrageous doctrine it pleases," he charged, and "stupid people—who constitute the grand overwhelming majority of this and all other nations"—believe what they read in the paper. In consequence, American public opinion, "that awful power," was moulded "by a horde of ignorant, self-complacent simpletons who failed at ditching or shoemaking and fetched up in journalism on their way to the poorhouse." Less than two years later, on February 15, 1875, Sam read his second paper before the club, "Universal Suffrage." While he endorsed the right of women to the franchise, he refused to advocate the right of *all* women—or of all men—to vote. Feeling that only the most qualified citizens should be allowed the right, he disparaged the notion that the vote of "a fool or a scoundrel" should be counted equally with that of "a president, a bishop, a college professor, a merchant prince." Thus the title for his paper: he was vigorously opposed to universal suffrage. Though the talk in its entirety is lost, its substance may be inferred from his essay "The Temperance Insurrection" (1874), in which Sam indicted a political system that denied native-born, educated women the vote "while every ignorant whiskey-drinking foreign-born savage in the land may hold office, help to make the laws, degrade the dignity of the former and break the latter at his own sweet will." The votes of qualified women, he believed, would offset the influence of "the scum of the country" who "assemble at the 'primaries,' name the candidates for office from their own vile ranks, and, unrebuked, elect them."[48]

Sam refined his opposition to universal suffrage in the utopian/dystopian fantasy "The Curious Republic of Gondour," published without signature in the *Atlantic Monthly* for October 1875. To paraphrase George Orwell in *Animal Farm* (1945), in Gondour everyone has a vote, but some have more votes than others. That is, rather than a democracy premised on the idea of one person, one vote, Gondour is a meritocracy or political oligarchy where the rich and educated classes enjoy plural or weighted votes that easily out-number the single votes of people in "the ignorant and non-taxpaying class-es." As Sam told Annie Fields in April 1876, "It is too late now . . . to restrict the suffrage; we must increase it." The nation of Gondour (an anagram of "go round") had once "tried universal suffrage pure and simple, but had thrown that form aside" because it delivered "all power into the hands" of the poor and uneducated. The people eventually struck on a remedy: not "the de-struction of universal suffrage" but "the enlargement of it." Every person had a constitutional right to vote that could not be revoked but some people exercised "from one to nine additional votes" for special qualifications such as higher education and/or property ownership—and learning trumped wealth. "For the first time in the history of the republic . . . money, virtue, and intelligence" instead of the rabble wielded political influence. In Sam's imaginary Gondour, "brains and property managed the state." In lieu of a spoils system, civil servants in Gondour "ascended to their several positions through well-earned promotions." As Sam explained to Annie Fields, "This is the only way I see to get out of the false position into which we have fall-en." His friend Julian Hawthorne was disappointed by the piece, however. "I read it," Hawthorne complained, "without finding a single sentence that sounded like Mark or is worthy of him."[49]

Sam's political opinions did not change appreciably in future months. The next year he wrote Mary Fairbanks's daughter Mollie that he thought "Republican government, with a sharply restricted suffrage," was "just as good as a Constitutional monarchy with a virtuous & powerful aristocracy" and that "unrestricted suffrage" was "founded in wrong & is weak & bad & tyrannical." Sam admitted, "I am . . . trying my best to win you & the rest of the rising generation over to an honest & saving loathing for universal suffrage" and confessed he hated "all shades & forms of republican govern-ment." Howells, who insisted that Sam "was always beautifully and unfal-teringly a republican," apparently never heard his friend fulminate on this topic. Ironically, Sam was occasionally mentioned as a potential candidate for political office. He had joked in his *Galaxy* column as early as December 1870 about running for governor of New York. But in May 1875, according to the *Hartford Courant*, some citizens were urging Sam to become an inde-pendent candidate for mayor, though others attributed the rumor to "soft-ening of the brain." The Virginia City *Territorial Enterprise* heaped ridicule on the notion: "If Mark would look after city affairs as he does after his own he would make a thrifty, careful mayor," but "it is a pity to see a man come down so much in the world. Think of a man who was once reporter on the *Enterprise* accepting such an office as Mayor of Hartford."[50]

◆

Not that he abstained from election year politicking in 1876. He confided to Howells that, should Samuel Tilden be elected president, "I think the entire country will go pretty straight to Mrs. Howells's bad place." Tilden's local supporters invited Sam to "a Tilden flag-raising and 'give counsel.' He declined to attend and gave them counsel in the kindest manner" in light of Tilden's dismal Civil War record: "not to raise the flag." On August 18 Sam announced his support for the Republican presidential candidate Rutherford B. Hayes, governor of Ohio and Elinor Howells's cousin, whose platform included a plank to abolish political patronage. Though he had earlier tried to secure patronage jobs for his brother Orion and Charles Warren Stoddard, Sam was an ardent advocate of civil service reform, even joining a Civil Service Reform Club with General William B. Franklin, William Hamersley, Charles Perkins, and Joe Twichell.[51]

As soon as news of Sam's endorsement of Hayes appeared in the *New York Tribune*, Howells contacted him to enlist his help on the campaign. "I honestly believe that there isn't another man in the country who could help him so much as you," he suggested. Sam replied, "I am glad you think I could do Hayes any good, for I have been wanting to write a letter or make a speech to that end." Sam was a novice in the Sturm und Drang of politics, or, as he wrote Howells, "It seems odd to find myself interested in an election. I never was before." But he seemed to find his way intuitively. He arranged an interview with the *New York Herald*, printed on August 28, in which, attired "in a summer dress of snowy white," he contrasted the two major candidates. On the one hand, Hayes "talks right out upon the important issues. You cannot mistake what he means concerning civil service, second term, and the honest payment of the national debt." As Louis J. Budd noted, Sam had by this time "become as firm a hard-money man as any Hartford banker." On the other hand, Sam told the *Herald*, "If you can understand what Mr. Tilden means it is only because you have got more brains than I have." He wanted a chief executive "who can not only tell a buzzard when he sees it but will promptly wring its neck. I feel satisfied that Mr. Hayes is such a man; I am not satisfied that Mr. Tilden is." He was confident Hayes would be elected, moreover, because his foolhardy brother Orion had announced his support for Tilden, a decision "that made Mr. Tilden's coming defeat . . . inflexibly & implacably & absolutely certain. I can always tell which party's funeral is appointed if I can find out how my brother has made up his mind to vote. For some inscrutable reason God never allows him to vote right." Sam first exhibited mugwumpish sympathies during this campaign season.

"When you get below the politician scum—or above it, perhaps one ought to say," he told an interviewer in August, "you will find that the solid men in both parties are equally good and equally well meaning."[52] Better to be independent and vote for the most qualified candidate.

On the last day of September Sam presided at a Republican Party meeting at Allyn Hall in Hartford to rally support for Hayes, his running mate William Wheeler, and Sam's friend and former Connecticut governor Joseph Hawley, who was running for Congress. Sam and Hawley arrived at the hall in a parade. Among the Hartfordians in the crowd were Harriet Beecher Stowe, Twichell, and Charley Warner. "I never have taken any part in a political canvass before, except to vote," Sam declared at the start of the festivities, but Hayes had promised to "institute an honest and sensible system of civil service" to replace the current "idiotic" system "born of General Jackson and the Democratic party." In the future "under Mr. Hayes," Sam predicted, "excellent" civil servants would be rewarded and retained "through a just system of promotion." After the rally Sam was selected president of the local Hayes-Wheeler club. His speech was printed in its entirety on the front page of the *New York Times*, which also reported that it was "received with much favor," and it was reprinted in the *Chicago Tribune*. Howells applauded Sam's speech, which was "civil service reform in a nutshell. You are the only Republican orator quoted without distinction of party by all the newspapers and I wish you could have gone largely into the canvass." The speech was also a lightning rod for criticism. The *Boston Transcript* editorialized that Sam should have been led "from the platform by the ear" like a misbehaving child and the *Baltimore Gazette* dismissed it as little more than a distraction: Republicans relied on "sensational speakers to bolster up their courage," with "[James G.] Blaine to do the bullying, [Robert G.] Ingersoll to do the blasphemy," George S. Boutwell "to falsify the figures," and "Mark Twain to do the low-comedy business." The party bosses had "put up this humorist to harlequin away the damning record of their party," and while the public "may laugh over this Jack Pudding's antics" the laugh would become "a little merrier when the humorist declares his remedy for the evils that he capers over lightly with his cap and bells" was to elect Hayes and Wheeler.[53]

The first weekend in November 1876 Bret Harte landed on the stoop of Sam's Hartford house, partly to escape his creditors in New York. Joe Twichell noted in his journal that on Sunday, November 5, Harte attended the Asylum Hill Church with Sam. On Election Day, November 7, Harte was "tranquil" and "serene"; he was, Sam remembered, "doubtless the only serene and tranquil voter in the United States." Harte explained that he would not vote for either Hayes or Tilden for president because he had been promised a foreign consulate by friends of both candidates. In the era before the secret ballot, Harte "was going to be taken care of no matter how the contest might go" and "his interest in the election began and ended there." Sam claimed later that he told Harte "that the New York Custom house was the right place for him, & that I thought him an unfit person for our foreign service. I would think so yet, only the Custom house has latterly become too clean a place for such a dirty bird as he is." He regarded Harte's claim as nothing more than an "after-breakfast lie to whet up his talent for the day's villainies; & besides, I judged that his character was so well known that he would not be able to succeed in his nefarious design."[54] Soon enough he learned otherwise.

Though Tilden won a majority of the vote, Hayes was handed the election through manipulation of the results in the Electoral College. On November 8, as the polls reported results, Sam telegraphed Howells a parody of the first lines of a hymn from the *Plymouth Collection*: "I love to steal a while away from every cumbering care and while returns come in today lift up my voice & swear." Sam was initially relieved by this outcome—"Here's a shout for Hayes!" he wrote Howells. Four months after the inauguration, Sam was still elated. "It's been a long time since we've had anybody to feel proud of and have confidence in," he declared, a not-so-subtle criticism of former president Ulysses S. Grant and the political vultures who surrounded him. "I mean to take my fill now while the meat's hot and the appetite ravenous." In retrospect, however, Sam recognized the crass political dealings that enabled Hayes to become president for what they were. In his autobiographical dictation in 1907, he reflected bitterly on "one of the Republican party's most cold-blooded swindles . . . the stealing of the Presidential chair from Mr. Tilden."[55]

At Quarry Farm during the summer of 1874 Sam read Theodore Crane's copy of William E. H. Lecky's *History of European Morals from Augustus to Charlemagne* (1869). He glossed in the margins that it was "so noble a book, & so beautiful a book, that I don't wish it to have even trivial faults." According to Lecky's pre-Freudian concept, conscience was "more often the source of pain than of pleasure" so anyone "who possessed such a temperament would be happier if he were to 'quench that conscientious feeling, which . . . prevents him from pursuing the course that would be most conducive to his tranquility.'" In other words, the person who could repress this faculty, the innate monitor of right and wrong, or better yet "kill" the conscience, would be happy as a result. Lecky's argument informs Sam's characterization of Huck Finn, who on Jackson's Island in *Tom Sawyer* "sleeps the sleep of the conscience-free and the weary" while the more perfectly behaved boys Tom and Joe Harper are troubled in their sleep; and who in *Huck Finn* wages war on the conscience: "If I had a yaller dog that didn't know no more than a person's conscience does I would pison him. It takes up more room than a person's bowels, and yet ain't no good, nohow."[56]

To be sure, Sam was never a systematic thinker. As Tom Quirk has observed, "As a philosopher, Twain would have made a good third baseman; as a metaphysician, a first-rate pastry chef." But in his third paper before the Monday Evening Club, titled "The Facts Concerning the Recent Carnival of Crime in Connecticut," read on January 24, 1876, Sam illustrated Lecky's ideas about human conscience. Twichell jotted in his journal the night of the meeting that Sam's paper was "about ¾ of an hour long" and "described an interview between himself and his conscience—very finely written—serious in its intent though vastly funny and splendidly, brilliantly read." Sam had urged Howells to come to Hartford to hear his "exasperating metaphysical . . . literary extravaganza," predicting that "it will bring out considerable discussion among the gentlemen of the Club."[57]

In his allegory Sam personified his conscience as "a shrivelled, shabby dwarf" no more "than two feet high" and "about forty years old" who speaks in a drawl. Moreover, this "vile bit of human rubbish seemed to bear a sort of remote and ill-defined resemblance to me!" In conventional Freudian terms, the narrator is the ego and the dwarf the supervisory superego. The dwarf contemplates the narrator "with his weasel eyes," then raises a moral question, whether or not to give charity to tramps who swarmed the country during the economic depression of the 1870s. Sam had long been opposed to such generosity, but the deformed doppelgänger frames the situation as a dilemma: if he freely feeds a tramp or gives a tramp work, the dwarf objects on the grounds that he is encouraging vagrancy; but if he turns the tramp from his door, he is equally guilty of cruelty. The narrator finally realizes that the only way to live without distress is to annihilate his conscience, "my lifelong foe." He tears the dwarf "to shreds and fragments" and rends "the fragments to bits." He casts

> the bleeding rubbish into the fire. . . . At last, and forever, my Conscience was dead! . . . Since that day my life is all bliss. Bliss, unalloyed bliss. Nothing in all the world could persuade me to have a conscience again. I settled all my old outstanding scores, and began the world anew. I killed thirty-eight persons during the first two weeks—all of them on account of ancient grudges. I burned a dwelling that interrupted my view. I swindled a widow and some orphans out of their last cow. . . I have also committed scores of crimes, of various kinds, and have enjoyed my work exceedingly.

Howells was so impressed by the narrative that he quickly printed it as the lead article in the June 1876 issue of the *Atlantic Monthly*, the same number that contained the first installment of Henry James's novel *The American*. Howells recommended Sam's piece to Oliver Wendell Holmes upon its publication because "it seems to me to go deeper than anything else he has written, and it strongly moved me from its serious side." He later wrote that "under the fun" it was "an impassioned study of the human conscience. Hawthorne or Bunyan might have been proud to imagine that powerful allegory, which had a grotesque force far beyond either of them." The New York *Evening Post* opined that the allegory "shows a decided advance upon Mr. Clemens's part as a literary artist" and "if readers will forget that its author has been in the habit of saying and writing amusing things" they would discover "an unexpected power upon his part to write something better worth remembering than any of his amusingly extravagant stories." Put another way, the *Post* noted, "we have a new Mark Twain who promises to be even better than the old one." The *Louisville Courier-Journal* ("the most artistic sketch of his that we have ever read") and the *Christian Union* ("admirable in design and execution") were similarly effusive. Mary Fairbanks was exceedingly pleased by the sketch. The "Carnival of Crime," she observed, "has some most delicate, metaphysical touches and I never was so sure of your having a live conscience, as since you have proclaimed its death." As usual, at least one dissenting voice was raised: the Boston *Literary World* judged the allegory "not worth the space it occupies. . . . A more tedious composition it has never been our lot to read."[58]

Sam's plans for *Tom Sawyer* included a major sales campaign for it in England. Moncure Conway had lectured in Hartford under the auspices of the local Unitarian society in January 1876, staying with the Clemenses for a few days, and Sam recruited him to place the novel with a London publisher in exchange for a royalty of 5 percent on its profits in Britain. As he wrote Conway, "I want you to take my new book to England & have it published there by someone . . . before it is issued here." Conway jumped at the chance. "Mark Twain has written a remarkable book called 'Tom Sawyer,'" he wrote his wife Ellen from Hartford on January 18. While Sam had no dispute with Routledge, the company that had issued *Roughing It* and *The Gilded Age* in England, he wanted Conway to shop around the manuscript and negotiate more favorable terms than Routledge offered. In fact, he originally wanted his English publisher to accept a 10 percent royalty on sales, with Sam to pay all production costs, but Livy persuaded him to contract with a press to issue the book without an investment up front. A traditional contract for a flat percentage of profits "simplifies everything; removes all risk; requires no outlay of capital; makes the labor easy for Mr. Conway."[59] Conway carried a copy of Sam's manuscript with him back to England when he sailed a few days later.

Sam personally delivered the manuscript of the novel to Bliss in early November 1875 and he expected that it would be issued in the United States by the American Publishing Company between mid-May and early June 1876. True Williams completed 160 "rattling pictures for it" by January 18 and Sam heartily approved of them, unlike Williams's drawings in *Sketches New and Old*. "Poor devil, what a genius he has," Sam added in a note to Howells, "& how he does murder it with rum. He takes a book of mine, & without suggestion from anybody builds no end of pictures just from his reading of it." Sam considered "many of the pictures . . . considerably above the American average, in conception if not in execution." Howells had asked Sam the previous November to "give me a hint" when the novel was scheduled to appear "and I'll start the sheep to jumping in the right places" with a review in the *Atlantic*. He advised Sam in January to "get Bliss to hurry out *Tom Sawyer*. That boy is going to make a prodigious hit." Sam sent him a set of galley proofs on March 20 so that he could prepare his notice and urged Bliss to begin his canvassing for sales in May and issue the novel in time to tap the spring market. According to the *Boston Transcript* in late April, however, the book had been delayed so that "it may be issued simultaneously in England and America."[60]

In truth, as Sam confided to Conway, he was worried that the moment was not ripe for its appearance. He thought the literary market so dull "that this is no time to adventure a new book. I am determined that Tom shall outsell any previous book of mine, & so I mean that he shall have every possible advantage." He advised Bliss to delay its publication until fall 1876 and "make a Boy's Holiday Book of it." Then, in June, Sam postponed its appearance when he learned that the company had nine other books scheduled for publication that summer, including De Quille's *The Big Bonanza*, Harte's *Gabriel Conroy*, and Warner's *Moslems and Mummies*. On June 24 Sam reproached Bliss for the glut of new volumes he had planned. "I think that the present extended business is a considerable detriment to my pocket," he groused. "If the directors will cut the business down two-thirds & the expenses one half," move into cheaper offices, and publish only one or two books a year, "I think it will be an advantage to all concerned, & I feel persuaded that I shall sell more books." The same day Sam addressed a similar message to Bliss's board of directors. As a major stockholder, he was a de facto member of the board from 1873 until 1881, though, as Hamlin Hill adds, "he was never advised in time of the company's meetings and never attended one." Still, he reminded his fellow directors that his own books "were almost the only ones that should have been published by the Company. I say 'almost,'" because in the intervals between the canvassing of his own works the sales of "other books" could "pay expenses." In any event, Sam believed the company had overreached:

> We are now publishing several books which I think would make considerable money if our expenses were more moderate, for they are good books & are doubtless very popular. . . . I have a selfish interest at stake. *Tom Sawyer* is a new line of writing for me, & I would like to have every possible advantage in favor of that venture. When it issues, I would like it to have a clear field, & the *whole* energies of the company put upon it; & not only this, but I would like the canvassers to distinctly understand that no new book would issue till *Tom Sawyer* had run 6, or even 9 months.

Sam's relationship with Bliss, always vexed, predictably suffered when he second-guessed the publisher's judgment. Sam complained so often about the neglect of his books that Bliss eventually got wind of his protests and challenged him. "I do not know as you are aware of the condition of the Co. or not," he acidly noted. "You have never been present at any of the meetings and have never asked for information of me." In any event, Bliss regretted that Sam "found it necessary to talk against my management outside of our board as I have several times heard you have." Even "poor drunken" True Williams "taunts me with what you tell him," Bliss noted, and another employee "gets letters from N.Y. stating what he says you told there—For myself I care nothing, but it seems poor policy to injure the stock this way, and our stock is too valuable to be made to suffer."[61]

Whether or not Sam's rumormongering damaged the stock value of the company, his reply was conciliatory. In his defense, he maintained, "I am solicitous about *Tom Sawyer*—more so than I would be about another book, because this is an experiment. I want it run by itself, if possible, & pushed like everything." He proposed that Bliss offer a bonus to the canvasser(s) "who shall sell the largest number of Tom Sawyers in six months." Nothing came of the idea nor did Sam's complaints prompt Bliss to alter any of his plans. In September Sam was still uncertain when his novel would appear. "I haven't issued *Tom Sawyer* here, yet," he wrote Charley Stoddard. He was "waiting for a livelier market. Shall issue right after the Presidential election." Charley Warner also griped that Bliss's publication of his book had been delayed. Like Sam, he was "waiting for the fall rise. I fear we shall none of us get rich out of it."[62]

Meanwhile, Conway had placed the manuscript of *Tom Sawyer* with the London publisher Chatto & Windus, and Andrew Chatto put the novel into production as soon as the contract details with Sam were settled. Chatto notified Conway on March 29, 1876, that the manuscript was "in the printer's hands to be set up." Conway received the first proofs on April 11 and returned the last of them to Chatto with his corrections on May 3. Still laboring under the misapprehension that U.S. publication of *Tom Sawyer* was imminent, Howells drafted a notice of the novel for publication in the *Atlantic*. As he indicated, *Tom Sawyer* exemplified "a fidelity to circumstance which loses no charm by being realistic in the highest degree and which gives incomparably the best picture of life" along the Mississippi River in the antebellum period "as yet known to fiction." The local color was "excellent," he declared, and overall "the story is a wonderful study of the boy-mind." In early April, Howells mailed proof of this notice to Sam, who replied that it was "splendid" and "will embolden weak-kneed journalistic admirers to speak out & will modify or shut up the unfriendly." Sam in turn notified Conway on April 9 that "a week from now the *Atlantic* will come out with a mighty handsome notice of the book . . . but the book won't issue till 2 or even 4 weeks later." He assured his London agent that "first publication in England cannot impair my American copyright" and he apologized to Howells for giving him the go-ahead to print his mistimed review. Howells was unruffled. "Never mind about Tom Sawyer," he replied to Sam's note of regret. "I rather like the fun of the thing; besides I know I shall do you an injury someday, and I want a grievance to square accounts with." Sam instructed Bliss to excerpt Howells's review in the prospectus sent to drummers and in his advertisements "for I think it will have a good effect."[63]

Chatto's edition of the novel was released on June 9, though it was not illustrated because Bliss had failed to forward the plates of Williams's drawings. As usual, Sam blamed Bliss, not his own temporizing, for the preemptive publication of the British edition. "We fixed a date for *Tom Sawyer* to issue," he later acknowledged to Chatto; "Bliss was behindhand, you were not." Before the end of the year Chatto issued an illustrated edition featuring 111 of Williams's sketches, or about two-thirds of the total number that appeared in the authorized American edition. As Sam's London agent, Conway proofread the novel and penned the first review of it, in the London *Examiner* for June 17 ("the kind of art in which Mark Twain is pre-eminent in our time"). The notice set the tone for most of the other notices in Britain— for example, in the *Edinburgh Scotsman* ("nothing in it of an unwholesome kind"), *Illustrated London News* ("the faithful portrayal of boy-life"), London *Standard* ("a capital boy's book"), *British Quarterly Review* ("full of roaring fun"), London *Times* ("abounds" in "drollery"), *Spectator* ("will amuse many readers"), *Academy* ("very amusing in parts"), *Newcastle Chronicle* ("a bright, most readable, and informing book"), London *Post* ("a story which boys will gloat over and which their seniors will read"), *Pall Mall Gazette* ("a tale full to overflowing of exciting and impossible scenes"), and *Athenaeum* (the humor was "always genuine and sometimes almost pathetic"). Only a couple of reviewers struck slightly sour notes: the *Saturday Review* ("the story is marked by the extravagant and too often vulgar humour of the writer") and the *Westminster Review* ("Mark Twain's wit too often depends on mere mannerism").[64]

As the London correspondent of the *Cincinnati Commercial*, Conway also hyped the book in his next column, dated June 10, which filled forty-six column inches of the June 26 issue of the newspaper. There he declared it "the most notable work which Mark Twain has yet written and will signally add to his reputation" and, more important, in a clever marketing gambit he printed several selections from the novel, including the passages about whitewashing the fence, the pinch bug in church, and the death of Injun Joe. These excerpts were immediately copied in dozens of newspapers around the world, stirring an appetite for the book that Howells's *Atlantic* review had only whetted. Between June and August 1876, in fact, over two dozen newspapers in the United States reprinted extracts from *Tom Sawyer* that originally appeared in Conway's column months in advance of its publication by Bliss. "I've found out where the wildly-floating extracts that puzzled me so much come from," Sam wrote Conway a month after his notice appeared in the *Commercial*. "From your Cincinnati letter, you shrewd man! I happened to run across the entire letter in a Hartford paper, extracts & all."[65]

Though at the time they seemed astute forms of prepublication publicity, Howells's review in the *Atlantic Monthly* and the frequent reprinting of extracts from the novel boomeranged. On July 25 the *Toronto Mail*, edited by Charles Belford, printed an excerpt from *Tom Sawyer*, much like dozens of other North American newspapers—but with a difference. The *Mail* printed a passage from the Belford Brothers' pirated edition of the novel, issued less than a week later. In other words, much to Sam's dismay, Howells's early review and the widespread circulation of Conway's extracts had the ironic effect of promoting sales of cheap Canadian editions priced for as little as fifty cents. The three Belford brothers—Alexander, Charles, and Robert— were "flooding America with a cheap pirated edition of *Tom Sawyer*," Sam wrote Conway on November 2, three months after the British edition was first issued. He estimated that Belford would sell a hundred thousand copies "over the frontier" and kill "my book dead" before Bliss could publish the authorized U.S. edition, adding that Bliss's delinquency "cost me ten thousand dollars."[66]

Conway assured Sam that the Belfords' proceedings were "entirely spontaneous & highhanded" and, no doubt at his behest, Andrew Chatto telegraphed the Belfords on November 15 that "Tom Sawyer is English copyright," in effect ordering them to withdraw their pirated edition. The Belfords replied with a salute to the Jolly Roger: "We should be very sorry to conflict with your interest in any way in Canada. We know Americans are in the habit of taking out copyright in England, but we doubt if it would hold there: we are well advised that it gives no right in Canada. We shall be glad, however, to hear further from you on the subject." They then added insult to injury by asking Howells to send them all of Sam's future contributions to the *Atlantic Monthly* for publication in *Belford's Monthly*, a magazine the firm was launching in Canada. The brothers indicated a willingness to pay "liberally" for the privilege, then added that, of course, "the law allows us *to pirate* them." Sam's response to this proposal was unequivocal: "The miserable thieves couldn't buy a sentence from me for any money." He soon proposed to Howells that the editor send duplicate proofs of his *Atlantic* articles gratis to the *Canadian Monthly* to preclude future piracy by the Belfords. In order to thwart the swashbuckling publishers, he attempted over the next couple of years to "simutane," or publish his articles simultaneously in Australia, Canada, England, and the United States.[67]

The parsimony of the Belfords stands in stark contrast with the generosity of the German publisher Bernhard von Tauchnitz, who sought and received Sam's permission in September 1876 to include *Tom Sawyer* in his Collection of British and American Authors series sold on the Continent. Baron Tauchnitz was famous for paying royalties to authors even in the absence of international copyright. As Sam wrote Tauchnitz, "That you have recognized my moral right to my books gratifies me but does not surprise me, because I knew before that you were always thus courteous with authors"; he was, miracle of miracles, a rare publisher "who puts moral rights above legal ones, to his own disadvantage." Tauchnitz first listed *Tom Sawyer* in his catalog of American novels in October 1876 and paid Sam for the privilege. Among the German readers of the novel, perhaps surprisingly, was Friedrich Nietzsche.[68]

The degree of copyright protection granted *Tom Sawyer* under Canadian law remains unclear. Sam depended upon legal advice from Bliss, who after consulting with lawyers informed him on December 11 that "to hold a copyright in Canada taken out in England, it is necessary to have it recorded in Canada also within 60 days of its publication in England—or it is lost. I fear your copyright in Canada is worthless." Alexander Belford had exploited a loophole in British copyright. Under the law, Canadian publishers might import foreign reprints and were required to pay royalties "only if the author had entered his copyright with the customs department of the colony." Because no international copyright prohibited American publishers from pirating English copyright books, Belford was printing copies of *Tom Sawyer* in the United States and shipping them to Canada for sale there and for export back to the States. In the end, Sam had little legal recourse. He passed along the news to Conway. "The Canadian 'Tom Sawyer' has actually taken the market away from us in every village in the Union," he groused two days after Bliss finally issued the American edition. Moreover, any U.S. book dealer was "privileged to sell a pirated book until we give him personal and distinct notice that that book is copyrighted." Disgusted by the perfect storm that had infringed upon his copyright, he announced, "if I can make a living out of plays, I shall never write another book."[69] After all, Raymond was still paying him quarter profits on every performance of *The Gilded Age*.

He considered a lawsuit, though he preferred that Conway and Chatto file it in London because they could "prosecute Belford more conveniently" under English law than Sam could arraign him across the border. He recommended that they consult with Simon Sterne, "the lawyer that won that other decision" (*Clemens v. Such*) that, Sam believed, protected his trademark pseudonym. He was willing to foot the bill. In the end he did not seek legal redress or restitution for the piracy of *Tom Sawyer*. Though under imperial copyright he might have obtained an injunction restraining the reprinting of the novel in Canada, the damage was done: Sam's loss of sales could not be repaired and the Canadian penalty for illegal reprinting was slight. Over two years later, he commenced suit in a U.S. district court in Chicago against the Rose-Belford Publishing Company of Toronto, the successor to Belford Brothers, for illegally smuggling a hundred copies of *Tom Sawyer* into the United States on April 15, 1879. Judge Henry W. Blodgett forbade their sale but required Sam to file a bond in the sum of eleven thousand dollars "to pay all damages arising from the seizure, if it shall be found to be illegally made."[70] It was a shot across the bow that anticipated copyright battles to come.

In the end Sam had little recourse except one: to notify personally as many American booksellers as possible that they were peddling a pirated work. His brother Orion sprang into action in Keokuk: he presented written notice to the book dealer D. G. Lowry that he was selling illegal copies of the novel and filed a successful suit in a U.S. circuit court against him. Lowry was the only person ever prosecuted for violating Sam's *Tom Sawyer* copyright. Orion also seized the remaining copies of the novel in Lowry's shop and cautioned the owners of three other stores in the city not to carry unauthorized editions of the book. To Sam's chagrin, he then sent Bliss a bill for services rendered in the amount of fifty dollars. Bliss paid him fifteen.

But Sam continued to throw some work his way, as when Orion represented Bloodgood Cutter, the "poet lariat" of the *Quaker City*, in some bond cases against the City of Keokuk.[71]

In the wake of the commercial success of *The Gilded Age* Sam suggested that Howells dramatize *Tom Sawyer* and, if he chose, "alter the plot entirely." Howells declined because he had no time to devote to the project and he could not "enter into the spirit of another man's work sufficiently to do the thing you propose." Sam tried his hand at adapting the novel, even copyrighting the idea on the basis of a one-page synopsis on July 21, 1875. He planned at one point to end the play with the reunion of "General Sawyer, Rear-Admiral Harper, Bishop Finn," and "the celebrated detective" Sid Sawyer fifty years later, but his script was woefully impractical for the stage, requiring over thirty-five scene changes.[72]

Ironically, shortly after completing a sentimentalized account of his boyhood in *Tom Sawyer*, Sam lambasted his Hannibal friend Will Bowen for wallowing in nostalgia. In a recent letter Bowen had invited Sam to "recall some of the old feeling that distance & time & other duties have perhaps dimmed a little." Sam reacted with unexpected acrimony. "For more than twenty years you have stood dead still in the midst of the dreaminess, the melancholy, the romance, the heroics, of sweet but sappy sixteen," he wrote Bowen. "Man, do you know that this is simply mental & moral masturbation? It belongs eminently to the period usually devoted to *physical* masturbation, & should be left there & outgrown. Will, you must forgive me, but I have not the slightest sympathy with what the world calls Sentiment—not the slightest." He conceded to their mutual friend Jacob Burrough that the letter likely "made [Bowen] mad," but he was adamant: "There is one thing which I can't stand, & *won't* stand, from many people. That is, sham sentimentality—the kind a school-girl puts into her graduating composition; the sort that makes up the Original Poetry column of a country newspaper; the rot that deals in 'the happy days of yore,' 'the sweet yet melancholy past,' with its 'blighted hopes' & its 'vanished dreams'—& all that sort of drivel."[73] Sam and Will Bowen did not correspond again for a dozen years.

After completing *Tom Sawyer* but before its release, Sam agreed to an abbreviated reading tour managed by Major James B. Pond, a Medal of Honor recipient for his service during the Civil War, who had become James Redpath's partner in the Redpath Agency. Sam opened at the Academy of Music in Brooklyn the evening of November 13 on a program with the soprano Emma Thursby. While he detested joint bookings, he delivered a version of his "Roughing It" lecture featuring Colonel Jack and Colonel Jim, "the

Nevada mushroom nabobs," before "a throng of most fashionable Brooklyn residents," according to the New York *Sun*, and "was very funny." The *Brooklyn Eagle*, however, was less complimentary: "The never varying drawl in which Mr. Clemens clothes his utterances soon becomes unspeakably wearisome and is in no wise relieved by his studied awkwardness and conscious ungracefulness. Read, Mark Twain is inimitable; heard, he is simply an imitator, and a poor one at that." The next evening Sam read "An Encounter with an Interviewer" and "The Experience of the McWilliamses with Membranous Croup" at the Academy of Music in Philadelphia interspersed with several musical performances by others. The "immense audience" greeted him "with a burst of applause" and, according to the *Philadelphia Times*, he "kept the audience in a roar from the beginning to the end." Unfortunately, T. B. Pugh, the manager of the academy, paid him only three hundred dollars for his appearance, an amount Sam considered niggardly, and pretended "he couldn't afford any more" on account of the "vast sum" the musicians cost. Sam scorned Pugh's explanation: "I could get up a better concert with a barrel of cats."[74]

After a weeklong layoff, Sam appeared at the Boston Music Hall with Thursby and the Mendelssohn Quintette Club the evenings of November 21 and 22. Despite inclement weather on the second night, "a great crowd turned out to hear" him, according to the *Providence Press*, and they "laughed until they cried, almost, and then took breath and laughed again." The *Boston Advertiser* echoed the opinion: Sam "was funny and everybody was so ready to laugh that the explosion was instantaneous upon every point made." Two nights later, Sam, Thursby, and the quintet performed before "an immense audience" at the Academy of Music in Chelsea, north of Boston, where he read "An Encounter with an Interviewer" and the McWilliams piece and, as an encore, "How I Escaped Being Killed in a Duel." The next night Sam and Thursby concluded the barnstorming tour before a crowded house of about two thousand at the Music Hall in Providence. Both the *Providence Press* and *Journal* were reserved in their praise of Sam's performance, however. The *Press* wondered why "people should have laughed till their sides ached at Mark Twain's nonsense" and the *Journal* noted that while his readings "called forth such peals of laughter as are strange in that hall," many in the audience listened "stolidly through the recitations."[75]

In the spring of 1876 Sam founded the Saturday Morning Club, a group of about a dozen "charming lasses of 16 to 20 yrs. old," as he put it, who met every Saturday morning from October to June to discuss current events and hear speakers. It was both a type of auxiliary of the Monday Evening Club and a precursor of the Aquarium, the club for adolescent girls or "angelfish" whom he would befriend thirty years later. He was often the host and speaker. Bret Harte visited Hartford during the week of December 5 and upon his arrival he read aloud to the family a four-part love story entitled "Thankful Blossom" commissioned by Charles A. Dana of the New York *Sun*. Dana had agreed to pay Harte $150 for the tale but promised him $250 "if he finished it in time" to print the last installment on Christmas Eve. As Sam tells the story in his autobiography, on Friday night, December 8, Harte drank two quarts of whiskey and finished the manuscript before breakfast the next morning, earning the bonus. Sam "wondered what a story would be like that had been completed in circumstances like these," so he invited Harte to read it to the members of the Saturday Morning Club. "I was booked to talk to the lassies but I asked Harte to take my place," he remembered. Though the second half of the story "was written under the unpromising conditions which I have described," Sam thought "that it belongs at the very top of Harte's literature." Over the next several months he invited Boyesen, James T. Fields, General William B. Franklin, Joseph Hawley, Howells, Bayard Taylor, and Charley Warner to address "our Young Girls."[76]

CHAPTER 6

Delectable Land

Tom Sawyer is simply a hymn put into prose form to give it a worldly air.

—Samuel Clemens to W. R. Ward, September 8, 1887

SOME THIRTEEN MONTHS elapsed between Sam Clemens's delivery of the *Tom Sawyer* manuscript to publisher Elisha Bliss and its American publication on December 8, 1876. The authorized U.S. edition was in fact the fifth printing of the novel, after Chatto & Windus's original and illustrated editions in England, Bernhard von Tauchnitz's edition on the Continent, and the Belford Brothers' Canadian piracy. It was also both expensive and thin for a subscription book. As a result, according to Hamlin Hill, it was "doomed commercially" from the start and became "the least successful of all Twain's first six major books." Compared to first-year sales of nearly seventy thousand copies of *The Innocents Abroad* (1869), sixty-five thousand of *Roughing It* (1872), and over fifty thousand of *The Gilded Age* (1873), the authorized American edition sold only about thirteen thousand copies during its first two months in print, fewer than twenty-four thousand during its first year, and only about thirty-five thousand copies by 1885. Two notable readers of the novel were Theodore Dreiser, who fondly remembered devouring *Tom Sawyer* as a Hoosier schoolboy, and Henry Watterson, who congratulated Sam when he read the novel: "It is immense!"[1]

The strange circumstances of its release not only suppressed U.S. sales but also quashed interest among critics. Few reviewers deigned to notice it. Charles Dudley Warner declared the novel in the *Hartford Courant* "an advance on anything that Mr. Clemens has before done" and a few other critics agreed—for example, the *Baltimore Sun* ("the book is in Twain's peculiar vein of humor"), *Springfield Republican* ("Mark Twain's very best literary work"), *Hartford Post* ("the characters are drawn with a firm hand"), *San Francisco Chronicle* ("one of the best books ever written by the genial Mark Twain"), *San Francisco Bulletin* ("vividly realistic"), San Francisco *Alta California* ("full of humorous and acute delineation of the follies, superstitions and peculiarities of boys, girls, and older people"), *Boston Globe* ("a masterly reproduction of boy life and feeling"), and *New Haven Journal and Courier* ("overflows with rare and quaint humor"). The New York *World* mistakenly assigned mercenary motives to Sam for the prior publication of the book in Canada, misconstruing its piracy there by the Belfords ("if 'Mark' had not proved himself unpatriotic enough to sell his wares first to a 'Kanuck' we should possibly have dwelt longer upon this book"). Surprisingly, given its modern reputation as an idyll of boyhood, the novel was often criticized for its sensationalism, its "blood-and-thunder." The *New York Times* grumbled, "We should have liked Tom Sawyer better with less . . . Injun Joe and 'revenge,' and 'slitting women's ears,' and the shadow of the gallows," though the critic also praised Sam's depiction of Huckleberry Finn, an "admirable character" drawn "with the hand of a master." Both the *Hartford Times* ("those who imagine this to be a tame story for little boys will discover their mistake on reading it") and the New York *Evening Post* ("unsafe to put the book into the hands of imitative youth") were more scornful. The *Christian Secretary* dismissed it as no better than a juvenile dime novel, noting that "the last few chapters are extremely sensational" and "one cannot help regretting that so fine a fellow as Tom lies and smokes." The Australian reviewers were both anonymous and near unanimous in their critiques of the novel—for example, the *Sydney Herald* ("a book of questionable tendency"), *Adelaide Observer* ("the boy deserved to be flogged and despised for the manner in which he played upon his best friends for his own amusement"), and *Brisbane Courier* (Tom "deserved a good deal of punishment for his escapades"). Only the Melbourne *Australasian* qualified its criticism; though Tom "is never deterred from any wrong-doing by compunction as to the number of fictions he will have to invent to escape punishment," the critic conceded that the book would be "a source of amusement to adult readers."[2]

Apart from the *New York Times* reviewer, no one objected in print at the time to Sam's racist portrayal of Injun Joe. In fact, Sam almost never treated Indians sympathetically in his fiction. Helen Harris has fairly concluded that while he "has been called the 'champion of the oppressed,' when he wrote of the Native American he was unfailingly hostile"; Injun Joe in particular is "a horrible stereotype of the devilish Native." Unfortunately, this stereotypical view of Indians was all too commonplace. The British edition of *Tom Sawyer* was published only two weeks before the Battle of the Little Bighorn in Montana, which inflamed public opinion on the topic of Native rights. W. D. Howells visited the Centennial Fair in Philadelphia in mid-May 1876 and commented on the exhibition of Indian dress and other artifacts in his essay "A Sennight of the Centennial," written at almost the same moment *Tom Sawyer* was issued in England. One of the most progressive and tolerant Americans of his era, Howells nevertheless expressed a conventionally jaundiced opinion of Native Americans. As he observed of the American Southwest in an utterly dispassionate tone,

> If the extermination of the red savages of the plains should take place soon enough to save this peaceful and industrious people [the Moquis] whom they have harassed for hundreds of years, one could hardly regret the loss of any number of Apaches and Comanches. The red man, as he appears in effigy and in photograph in this collection, is a hideous demon, whose malign traits can hardly inspire any emotion softer than abhorrence. In blaming our Indian agents for malfeasance in office, perhaps we do not sufficiently account for the demoralizing influence of merely beholding those false and pitiless savage faces; moldy flour and corrupt beef must seem altogether too good for them.

In context, Sam's racist characterization of Injun Joe was normal, not exceptional. He was at best conflicted about the "Indian problem." He wrote Howells the next year that he preferred "a humanitarian" leader of the Bureau of Indian Affairs who might contain Native Americans on reservations, but in 1885, two years before passage of the disastrous Dawes Act, he endorsed assimilation and de facto cultural genocide: "I expect to see, before I die, all the Indian tribes disbanded and the members of them settled as citizens, holding their private property; all reservations abolished, and an end of all this bloody, guilty Indian question." Sam's argument for eradicating reservations was not entirely malevolent, however, but simply a recognition that, as Helen Hunt Jackson documented in *A Century of Dishonor* (1881), many of the treaties were ignored and whites "frequently encroached upon" Native lands anyway. Sam envisioned a genuinely malign possibility in *A Connecticut Yankee in King Arthur's Court* (1889), in which he referred to the people of Camelot as "white Indians." The novel closes with a reversal of George Armstrong Custer's defeat and an extermination of the so-called Indians during "the last stand of the chivalry of England" in the Battle of the Sand Belt.[3]

Sam suggested in the final paragraph of *Tom Sawyer* that he might eventually continue the saga of his boys and he devoted part of the summer of 1876 to the task. After leaving Hartford on June 15, overnighting at the St. James Hotel in New York, and arriving at the Langdon mansion in Elmira a day or two later, the Clemenses moved to Quarry Farm by the end of the month and Sam set to work in his study, which was located, as he joked to Howells, "1,000,000 miles from New York." His first move was a false start: the continuation of an untitled "double-barreled novel" he eventually abandoned and destroyed. Then he began the sequel to *Tom Sawyer*. On August 1 he mentioned *Adventures of Huckleberry Finn* for the first time in a note to Moncure Conway: "I am booming along with my new book—have written ⅓ of it & shall finish it in 6 working weeks." On August 9 he informed Howells that "a month ago" he had started "another boys' book—more to be working than anything else. I have written 400 pages on it—therefore it is nearly half done. It is Huck Finn's Autobiography. I like it only tolerably well, as far as I have got, and may possibly pigeonhole or burn the MS when it is done." In fact, he wrote 446 manuscript pages that summer, basically through the middle of chapter 18, before he left Elmira with his family to return to Hartford the second week of September. That is, during the summer of 1876 Sam composed chapter 15 of the novel in which, as Henry Nash Smith suggests, the author discovered "unsuspected meanings in what he had thought of as a story of picaresque adventure." Separated from Jim on the river in an overnight storm, Huck plays a Tom Sawyer–like prank on him. When they are reunited in the morning, Huck pretends that Jim has merely had a nightmare. But when Jim spies branches and leaves on the raft, ocular proof of the storm, he scolds Huck for trying to "make a fool uv ole Jim wid a lie. Dat truck dah is *trash*; en trash is what people is dat puts dirt on de head er dey fren's en makes 'em ashamed." Huck reports that Jim then "got up slow and walked to the wigwam, and went in there without saying anything but that. But that was enough. It made me feel so mean I could almost kissed *his* foot to get him to take it back. It was fifteen minutes before I could work myself up to go and humble myself to a nigger; but I done it, and I warn't ever sorry for it afterwards, neither."[4] This passage set the tone for most of the remainder of the novel. In the next chapter, Huck is afflicted for the first time with a pang of conscience for assisting a runaway slave.

Sam interrupted his work on the novel in chapter 18, several pages into the Buck Grangerford subplot, after the raft has been struck by a steamboat and Huck asks Grangerford to define a "feud," and he did not resume it for almost four years. Thus the questions Kenneth S. Lynn has posed: Why did Sam stop with Huck's question "What's a feud? . . . What was the problem . . . that so stubbornly resisted solution?" Simply put, Jim and Huck have floated past Cairo in the night and so there is no reason to continue their voyage downstream. Moreover, the vessel has apparently been smashed into splinters in a steamboat collision. "She come smashing straight through the raft," Huck reports. Jim dives overboard from the raft when it is struck, disappears from the narrative at this juncture, and is apparently killed. Or, as Tom Quirk has phrased the issue, "it is by no means clear that [Sam] intended at this time to resurrect either the raft or Jim. Certainly the easiest way out of his dilemma was to get rid of Jim altogether." The long pause in the composition illustrates once again the dangers of Sam's improvisational method of writing. He simply did not yet know what should come next. The difficulty was akin to the snag in *Tom Sawyer* when he decided not to launch his hero from Jackson's Island on "the Battle of Life in many lands."[5]

During an interlude between projects in August 1876, at virtually the same moment that the American edition of *Tom Sawyer*, his most decorous novel, began to be delivered to buyers, Sam was writing his most profane fiction, *1601: Conversation as It Was by the Social Fireside in the Time of the Tudors*. As he described it in his autobiography, "The piece is a suppositious conversation which takes place in Queen Elizabeth's closet in that year, between the Queen and Shakspeare, Ben Jonson, Francis Bacon, Beaumont, Sir Walter Raleigh, the Duchess of Bilgewater," and Sir Nicholas Throckmorton. In the year 1601 Raleigh was forty-nine, William Shakespeare thirty-seven, Jonson twenty-seven, and Francis Beaumont seventeen. Four of Elizabeth's maids of honor listen to the discussion, including "a sweet young girl 2 years younger than the boy Beaumont." Sam had been reading such books as Marguerite of Navarre's *Heptameron* (1558), *The Diary of Samuel Pepys* (1825), and Thomas D'Urfey's *Wit and Mirth; or, Pills to Purge Melancholy* (1719), preliminary research for a project that would eventuate in Sam's *The Prince and the Pauper* (1881). He was saturated "with archaic English to a degree which would enable me to do plausible imitations of it" and thus "I contrived that meeting of the illustrious personages in Queen Elizabeth's private parlor, and started a most picturesque and lurid and scandalous conversation between them. . . . I put into the Queen's mouth, and into the mouths of those other people, grossnesses not to be found outside of Rabelais, perhaps. I made their stateliest remarks reek with them, and all this was charming to me—delightful, delicious." He spent a day in his study at Quarry Farm writing the "conversation" as a risqué letter to Joseph Twichell "when I ought to have been better employed."[6]

A tour de force of scatological humor, the dramatic dialogue is ostensibly transcribed by Elizabeth's misogynistic cupbearer in what Guy Cardwell has termed "ersatz Elizabethan" and Howells publicly called an "Elizabethan breadth of parlance." Howells was privately more direct: his friend had "a sewer running through him." Sam admitted, "If there is a decent or delicate word findable in it, it is because I overlooked it." Ironically, *1601* is one of only three of Sam's works—the others are *The Gilded Age* and *The Tragedy of Pudd'nhead Wilson* (1894)—to register human sexual desire. In the course of the conversation, the reader learns, the Duchess of Bilgewater (a play on

Bridgewater and a malapropism that recurs in *Huck Finn*) had been "roger'd by four lords before she had a husband." The bawdy bard relates the tale of

> a certain emperor of such mighty prowess that he did take ten maidenheddes in ye compass of a single night, ye while his empress did entertain two and twenty lusty knights between her sheetes, yet was not satisfied; whereat ye merrie Countess Granby saith a ram is yet ye emperor's superior, sith he wil tup above a hundred yewes 'twixt sun and sun; and after, if he can have none more to shag, will masturbate until he hath enrich'd whole acres with his seed.

When David Gray visited Elmira the weekend of August 19, Sam showed him the "unfinished sketch of Elizabeth's time." Gray was entertained "pretty exhaustively" by it and advised Sam to have it printed privately and leave it behind "when I died, and then my fame as a literary artist would last." Sam told Albert Bigelow Paine years later that he "sent [the completed manuscript of *1601*] anonymously to a magazine, and how the editor [Howells?] abused it and the sender!" Then he shared it with Twichell, who "came within an ace of killing himself with laughter (for between you and me the thing was dreadfully funny. I don't often write anything that I laugh at myself, but I can hardly think of that thing without laughing). That old Divine said it was a piece of the finest kind of literary art." On August 31, after finishing the manuscript, Sam wrote that he had finally "passed my sentimental worms & have no longer the moral belly-ache."[7] A week later the family left Elmira for New York, where they again registered at the St. James Hotel, and arrived back in Hartford on September 11.

The manuscript of *1601* circulated privately for years. In 1880 Sam sent a copy to John Hay, who declared it a "masterpiece," passed it around Washington, D.C., and sent a copy to a Cleveland friend with a cover letter. Sam's manuscript was "a serious effort to bring back our literature and philosophy to the sober and chaste Elizabethan standard," Hay wrote semiseriously. "He has not yet been able even to find a publisher. . . . I send it to you as one of the few lingering relics of that race of appreciative critics, who know a good thing when they see it. Read it with reverence and gratitude and send it back to me." Sam also sent copies to his brother Orion, though he admonished him to "*keep no copy of it*," and to his sister Pamela, to whom he conceded that "it should only be shown to people who are learned enough to appreciate it as a very able piece of literary art. Heretofore it has only been shown to Bishops, Presidents of colleges, &c., & has always compelled their applause; but Orion does not run with that sort of people." Dean Sage printed a dozen copies in Brooklyn and Ned House a limited edition of the sketch in Japan. Sam also obliquely alluded to *1601* in chapter 17 of *A Connecticut*

Yankee when the Yankee overhears lewd stories told at court "that would almost have made Queen Margaret of Navarre or even the great Elizabeth of England hide behind a handkerchief."[8]

The first formal though surreptitious publication of *1601* occurred in 1882 at the U.S. Military Academy at West Point under the vigilant eye of Sam's friend Lieutenant Charles Erskine Scott Wood, who was the director of the small press there and the adjutant to the superintendent. Sam had visited West Point in early February and left a manuscript copy of the sketch that the generals, including William Tecumseh Sherman and Stewart Van Vliet, passed around. "Its circulation is quietly enlarging," Sam bragged to Wood, though he expected to "get into trouble with it yet before I die." He conceded that there were "errors in it, also, heedlessness in antiquated spelling," but because he was "too much driven just now" to fix them—he was in the midst of writing *The Prince and the Pauper*—he authorized Wood "to make any and all corrections" he thought appropriate. Wood recalled that when he read it he decided to print it on rough-edged, coffee-stained paper for effect. As a playful "species of forgery," the booklet would appear "to the eye" to be "contemporaneous with the pretended 'conversation.'" After all, Wood noted, "[Sam's] only object was to secure a number of copies, as the demand for it was becoming burdensome." Wood's only other changes were emendations of spelling. Otherwise, "the text is exactly as written by Mark." Wood produced an edition of fifty copies, fifteen of them still in Sam's possession when he died. Scott admitted in 1939 that, had his use of a government printing press to produce the risqué booklet been discovered, he "would have expected to be court-martialed."[9]

Critical opinion of *1601* is predictably uneven. There is literally no consensus about its (lack of?) merit. Paine warily pronounced it "a genuine classic, as classics of that sort go." Whereas Franklin Meine hailed it as "the most curious masterpiece of American humor," DeLancey Ferguson dismissed it as a work of adolescent humor "of small importance. It owes most of its fame to its surreptitious circulation." Albert E. Stone considered it "mild pornography" and Edward Wagenknecht "the most famous piece of pornography in American literature," while Maxwell Geismar argued that it was "hardly so much pornography as erotica," and the editor William Marion Reedy regarded it as "scatological rather than erotic." Walter Blair asserted that it was "playfully obscene," Ed Folsom and Jerome Loving deemed it "mock-pornographic," and J. D. Stahl suggested that "it may be obscene." Wood, its original editor and publisher, framed the issue well: "Anyone who ever knew Mark heard him use [vulgarity] freely, forcibly, picturesquely in his unrestrained conversation," adding that in *1601* Sam expressed "a sense of real delight in what may be called obscenity for its own sake." In his autobiography Sam posed a related question: "I wonder if it would be as funny to me now as it was in those comparatively youthful days when I wrote it. . . . We used to laugh ourselves lame and sore over the cup-bearer's troubles. I wonder if we could laugh over them now?"[10]

Sam kicked off the holiday season of 1876 by attending the first Christmas party hosted by Sorosis, an early and influential women's club, and its president Jane Cunningham Croly (aka Jennie June) at Delmonico's the evening of December 21. The next night Sam delivered what is widely regarded as his most popular after-dinner speech at Delmonico's before an all-male audience of over two hundred at the seventy-first annual banquet of the New England Society of New York. The occasion was Forefather's Day, the anniversary of the landing of the Pilgrims in 1620. "The banquet was all that could be expected," the *Boston Advertiser* reported, "and was conspicuous by an entire absence of baked beans and brown bread." Among those present were Frédéric Auguste Bartholdi, architect of the Statue of Liberty; Chauncey Depew, president of the New York Central Railroad; and Mayor William H. Wickham. Toward the end of the evening Sam delivered an "abundantly droll and witty" talk entitled "The New England Weather" that, the *New York Times* noted the next day, "provoked a storm of laughter." The text of the speech is unremarkable on the printed page, reading like an uninterrupted rant about the unpredictability of the New England climate. Sam alleged, for example, that "in the spring I have counted one hundred and thirty-six different kinds of weather inside of four and twenty hours." The humor of "his best after-dinner speech," according to the *Brooklyn Eagle*, was rooted in his delivery, "the perfection of drawling, careless, impromptu speaking." He had gradually honed his ability to speak without a text, first replacing the script with a card with hieroglyphics, eventually depending on a few marks on his fingernails to suggest talking points, until he was able to deliver his speeches without extraneous aids. Back in Hartford on New Year's Eve, Sam and Livy joined a group of friends, including Hjalmar Hjorth Boyesen, at Charley and Susan Warner's house. At midnight, "after much pleasant storytelling (M.T. was at his best)," Twichell reported, "we sang together 'Nearer My God to Thee' and I led the company in prayer, all uniting at the close in the Lords Prayer."[11]

Livy decided in late 1876 that her famous husband should have a formal portrait painted and, at the recommendation of friends, she contacted the artist Frank Millet, who had recently completed a commission to paint murals with John LaFarge at Trinity Church in Boston. A few months later, during the Russian-Turkish War, Millet would serve as a war correspondent for the

New York Herald and the London *Daily News* and, as Sam later noted, "won 4 decorations." Millet arrived at the mansion on Farmington Avenue early in the new year 1877 and soon "captured the fervent admiration of the whole family," according to Paine. No doubt Sam's friendship with Millet eventually became the basis of his story "Is He Living or Is He Dead?" (1893) and the theatrical adaptation *Is He Dead?* (1908), about a starving artist named François Millet who fakes his death so that the value of his paintings will appreciate. Sam posed until Millet finished the portrait on January 17. "He devoted a couple of diligent weeks to the portrait and made a good one," Sam recounted in his autobiography, "if you don't count the hair." Sam's shock "was fairly long" when the sitting began, he explained, and after several days "I went to the barber to have it trimmed." Millet "nearly wept with despair when he saw his subject sheared of the auburn, gray-sprinkled aureola," Paine added. "As there was no hair, he had to manufacture it, and his effort was a failure," Sam said of Millet in 1907. "I have the portrait yet, but the hair it wears is not hair at all; it is tarred oakum, and doesn't harmonize with the rest of the structure."[12] The painting hangs today in the Hannibal Free Public Library, a gift from Clara Clemens Gabrilowitsch.

Figure 13. Frank Millet portrait of Samuel Clemens, January 1877. Photograph by Danny Henley. Courtesy of the Hannibal Free Public Library, Hannibal, Missouri.

Sam also helped raise money for several aid organizations during these months. On December 14 he served as the auctioneer at a church fair in Hartford that sold a twelve-piece "Jabberwock" collection of carved animals based on those imagined by Lewis Carroll in the *Alice* books. With current governor Richard Hubbard and ex-governor Marshall Jewell, he helped organize a Hartford charity ball held on January 23, 1877, and two weeks later he read "An Encounter with an Interviewer" and "How I Escaped Being Killed in a Duel" on the same bill as the elocutionist A. P. Burbank on behalf of sick and injured members of the New York Press Club. Sam's performance before a full house in Steinway Hall "kept the audience in constant laughter" and, according to the *New York Times*, was "a gratifying success."[13]

Sam long believed that Orion's biography was ripe with literary possibilities or, as he once wrote Howells, "a field which grows richer & richer the more he manures it with each new top-dressing of religion or other guano." He often considered chronicling his brother's life and wanted to "make it effective, too, by merely stating the bald facts." He began a draft in late March 1877, he reported to Howells, "& am charmed with the work. I have started him at 18, printer's apprentice, soft & sappy, full of fine intentions & shifting religions & not aware that he is a shining ass. Like Tom Sawyer he will stop where I start him, no doubt—20, 21 or along there; can't tell; am driving along without plot, plan, or purpose—& enjoying it." In the partial manuscript and notes Sam wrote before Livy persuaded him to abandon the project, the protagonist reads the Koran, is converted to Islam, and resolves to "have a harem"; he "argues with whiskey sellers and slave-owners and dealers on immorality of their trades" until "they take away their printing and advertising," and "makes a convert or so to anti-slavery and then becomes pro-slavery himself again."[14]

Sam's greatest publishing success in 1877–78—and his only profitable invention ever—was a scrapbook with adhesive on the pages, an application of the same principle as gummed envelopes. Its greatest asset was that, as Paine put it, it "did not contain a single word that critics could praise or condemn." Sam described it to Elinor Howells as "my last & least objectionable work." He had thought of this "great humanizing and civilizing invention" while vacationing in New Saybrook, Connecticut, in the summer of 1872. He patented the self-pasting scrapbook in June 1873, though he delayed marketing it for several years because, between trips to England and supervising the stage production of *The Gilded Age*, "I can't stand being under discussion on a play & a scrap-book at one & the same time!" In the fall of 1876, however, he decided to entrust publication of the scrapbook to his friend Dan Slote, who owned a stationery manufactory. "I have invented & patented a new Scrap Book," he wrote Slote,

> not to make money out of it, but to economise the profanity of this country. You know that when the average man wants to put something in his scrapbook he can't find his paste—then he swears; or if he finds it, it is dried so hard that it is only fit to eat—then he swears; if he uses mucilage it mingles with the ink, & next year he can't read his scrap—the result is barrels & barrels of profanity. This can all be saved & devoted to other irritating things, where it will do more real & lasting good, simply by substituting my self-pasting Scrap Book for the old-fashioned one. If Messrs. Slote, Woodman & Co. wish to publish this Scrap Book of mine, I shall be willing. You see by the above paragraph that it is a sound moral work, & this will commend it to editors & clergymen, & in fact to all right feeling people.

This letter was subsequently used to advertise the product in such magazines as *American Stationer*, the *Journal of Education*, and *Scientific American*, and the scrapbook enjoyed brisk sales from the start. Slote sold over twenty-six thousand copies of it in the first half of 1877 alone, and it generated a profit of twelve thousand dollars in the first half of 1878. Over a hundred thousand copies were routinely sold each year between 1878 and 1884, earning Sam "an income as large as any salary I ever received on a newspaper," he bragged. Its sales were "booming," he wrote Mary Mason Fairbanks in February 1878, "& promises to kill all the other Scrap-books in the world. Dan can't keep up with the orders; he is adding new machinery." Sam joked with an interviewer in 1882 that the invention "cost me years of hard study and sleepless nights," though of course he confessed to Fairbanks that it actually "cost me five minutes' thought in a railway car one day." Five days after sending this note, he composed another comic testimonial that Slote printed in ads:

> During many years I was afflicted with cramps in my limbs, indigestion, salt rheum, & enlargement of the liver, & periodical attacks of inflammatory rheumatism complicated with St. Vitus's dance, my sufferings being so great that for months at a time I was unable to stand upon my feet without assistance, or speak the truth with it. But as soon as I had invented my Self-Pasting Scrap Book & begun to use it in my own family all these infirmities disappeared. In disseminating this universal healer among the world's afflicted ones you are doing a noble work; & I sincerely hope you will get your reward—partly in the sweet consciousness of doing good, but the bulk of it in cash.

Incredibly, *Mark Twain's Scrapbook* and its blank pages were reviewed in two major magazines. *Harper's Monthly* fairly called it "a capital invention, especially for children," and Robert Underwood Johnson, in a "mock-serious notice of it" in *Scribner's*, described it as "a book to which readers could easily become attached." The scrapbook became so popular that in 1881 the official White House records of President James Garfield's assassination and death were preserved in a number of volumes of it.[15] The product was still available for purchase over a generation after it first went on sale.

Sam struck on another way to publicize the scrapbook. In early February 1878 he mailed Slote "a little bundle of stuff" to reprint in an inexpensive, 140-page promotional circular for it. Entitled *Punch, Brothers, Punch*, it was the only printed volume Sam published between September 1877 and March 1880. It contained nine items, including his 1870 "Map of Paris," his speech on New England weather, and the leaflet's titular poem, a precious little jingle that was Sam's meager contribution to the then current craze for horsecar verse. The second printing featured his autograph facsimile on the title page, the first of his books to do so and a form of self-advertising coming into vogue. Like his *(Burlesque) Autobiography*, moreover, the pamphlet skirted the clause in his contract that required him to publish all his books exclusively with the American Publishing Company. It was not received with critical favor, however. "The only thing absolutely new" in it, complained the New York *Sun*, "is the puff of the scrapbook," Sam's playful letters to Slote reprinted on the end pages, which were "worded with great skill from a mercantile point of view." The *San Francisco Chronicle* contested even this point: the "efforts at advertising" were "too cheap to be commendable."[16]

As the inventor of the self-pasting scrapbook, Sam became a victim of his own success. In July 1878, as Slote, Woodman and Company seemed ready to ramp up its production, Slote asked to borrow five thousand dollars from Sam. "I gave him the five thousand dollars," Sam remembered, whereupon the company "failed inside of three days." The collapse came as a surprise to the business community in the city. As the *New York Tribune* reported on July 19, the firm "had excellent credit, a large trade," and was "well known throughout the country." All was not lost, according to the *Tribune*: its liabilities "will not exceed $100,000" and Slote liquidated the company debt for only twenty or thirty cents on the dollar. Sam was Slote's creditor in the amount of $6,794, but he was unfazed at first by his friend's bankruptcy. He regarded Slote's misfortune as an opportunity to invest in the company. "Slote wants to take the scrapbook & run it by himself," he wrote Frank Fuller in mid-August 1878. To facilitate the deal he bought 80 percent of the stock in the reorganized Daniel Slote and Company for an additional $20,000 in cash and contracted with Slote to manufacture and market the scrapbook for one-third of the profits. As for the nearly $6,800 Sam was owed when Slote, Woodman and Company failed in July 1878, Slote pledged that he would repay it in full, though he never gave Sam a note to this effect. Slote's unpaid loan stuck like a bone in Sam's craw and as late as September 1882 he reiterated to Charles L. Webster that Slote had verbally agreed to make the loan a "debt of honor."[17]

Like a long-smoldering dump fire, Sam's feud with C. C. Duncan, the titular captain of the *Quaker City* during his voyage to Europe and the Holy Land in 1867, suddenly erupted into flames early in 1877. Duncan fanned the coals to life from the sanctuary of a Brooklyn church the evening of January 11, 1877, when before an audience of about three hundred he mocked Sam's account of the voyage in *The Innocents Abroad*. Duncan had long been disturbed by Sam's portrayal of him in the book and had occasionally tried to retaliate over the years. In his address, printed the next day in the New York *World*, Duncan accused his antagonist of repeated misbehavior while intoxicated during the excursion. On his part, Sam initially refused to engage in a war of words. Had he chosen to do so, the New York *Evening Post* editorialized, he might have shredded Duncan's reputation and reduced him to an object of ridicule, especially because "Duncan's anger appears to have arisen without due provocation." Instead Sam held his fire and kept his powder dry. Duncan had finagled a federal government appointment as shipping commissioner of the Port of New York in 1872 and in that office he was expected to collect fees and duties from ships that docked in New York Harbor; assist distressed sailors, especially if they had been illegally impressed or "shanghaied" into service; and transfer all funds over and above the cost of administering his office to the U.S. Treasury. Instead he was accused by the Ship Owners Association in a report to the Senate Committee on Commerce of a series of crimes, including the payment of lavish salaries to his sons, "renting his offices from the Seamen's Association, of which he is President, at a price four times greater than is just," and returning almost no money to the Treasury. The New York newspapers occasionally reported on the allegations leveled against the shipmaster, but nothing changed as a result.[18]

Like a beast of prey crouching in the weeds, Sam was quick to pounce. The day after the Ship Owners' report became grist for the local newspapers, Sam drafted a letter to the New York *World* that began by decrying "the absurd nature of our civil service system" for permitting a person like Duncan "to obtain a high & responsible position" and "to keep such a position after getting it." Sam deleted entire paragraphs from this unsent draft, including one that asserted that

> in "appropriating" other people's money, Captain Duncan is a thief; that in grossly over-paying his sons, he is treacherous to his official duty;—otherwise, a sneak; that in being "arbitrary & unjust" in his decisions, he is a tyrant; that in "refusing to recognize exemptions specified in the law," he is a shabby rascal; that in misusing his authority to rent offices from himself (for he is mainly the "Seamen's Association") at four times their value, he is a fraud.

Sam also accused Duncan of rank hypocrisy. He had been "a rabid total abstinence gladiator for forty years," but while in Italy during the *Quaker City* cruise he "primed himself daily with the cheap wines of the country." Then "when he got home, he denied it. He denied it flatly. It seems to me that a person who would act like that would almost prevaricate, upon a pinch."[19] For better or worse, Sam shelved this version.

In a second draft, printed in the *World* on February 18, he softened his language slightly. It began genially enough—"I see by your report of a lecture delivered in your neighborhood very recently that a bit of my private personal history has been revealed to the public"—before inserting a knife and twisting it: "The lecturer was headwaiter of the Quaker City Excursion of ten years ago. I do not repeat his name for the reason that I think he wants a little notoriety as a basis for introduction to the lecture platform, and I don't wish to contribute." He then explained his derisive reference to Duncan's rank aboard ship. As soon as the ship was fairly at sea, Daniel Leary, owner of the vessel, demoted Duncan and promoted Ira Bursley, its executive officer, raising the issue of Duncan's real role on the ship. "As he was not a passenger and had now ceased to be an officer," his post "was something of a puzzle." But because "he still had authority to discharge" waiters, the passengers concluded "that he must naturally be the headwaiter." As for Duncan's charges that Sam was a proverbial loose cannon during the voyage: Why bother "about what a man's character was ten years ago"? Sam insisted that his own character "was simply in course of construction then. I hadn't anything up but the scaffolding, so to speak. But I have finished the edifice now and taken down that worm-eaten scaffolding. I have finished my moral edifice, and frescoed it and furnished it." On the other hand, Duncan over the past decade had proven

> to be wholly without principle, without moral sense, without honor of any kind. I think I am justified in believing that he is cruel enough and heartless enough to rob any sailor or sailor's widow or orphan he can get his clutches upon; and I know him to be coward enough. I know him to be a

canting hypocrite, filled to the chin with sham godliness, and forever ooz-
ing and dripping false piety and pharisaical prayers. I know his word to be
worthless.

Sam closed his letter as he had opened the first draft, by lamenting a civil
service that allowed such a person as Duncan "to worm himself into an office
of trust and high responsibility" and then "remain in it."[20]

A week later, in yet another letter to the editor of the New York *World*,
Sam criticized in detail the maritime law Duncan both championed and
exploited in his office as shipping commissioner. The law, he charged, was
written by Duncan and "is plainly and simply a Black Flag" that sanctioned
his looting and plundering. Its very title Sam deemed "a blistering sarcasm:
'An Act for the Further Protection of Seamen.'" Instead, "it ought to have
been entitled 'An act for the creation of a pirate and for the multiplication
of tramps.'" While the law provided the commissioner with an annual salary of $5,000 for "superintending," Duncan had "charged the country more
than $160,000 in four years for that needless service by pocketing the fees."
Sam concluded with yet another attack on Duncan's character: he was "a
man whose stock in trade is sham temperance, sham benevolence, religious
hypocrisy, and a ceaseless, unctuous drip of buttery prayers." Privately Sam
wrote a friend two days after this letter was printed that Duncan "is one
of the vilest men that exists today." In an undated and unpublished essay,
Sam poked fun at Duncan's "noisy and offensive piety at prayer meetings, his
incompetence as an officer, his prevarication in denying that he had drunk
daily 'the cheap wines' of Italy, and his status as 'a glittering & majestic em-
bezzler.'" Ten years earlier, the *Quaker City* nighthawks "all thought him
only a harmless, over-pious hypocrite & tuppeny fraud" before he revealed
his true colors.[21]

On his part, Duncan was not amused, though he claimed to be Sam's
muse. "I am sorry Twain has made such a fool of himself," he declared in
an open letter to the public. "I have even felt kindly towards him, and am
sure he ought to be very grateful to me; for but for me he would never have
immortalized himself by his Innocents Abroad." More to the point, Duncan apparently threatened to sue Sam for libel in the amount of $10,000,
though they quietly settled the dispute out of court. "The villain got only
$300 out of me instead of $10,000," Sam reported to Howells, "& his lawyer got *that*. My lawyer's bill & some little items, added to the $300, only
swelled my expense to $800—so I got off admirably well." But their feud
had not ended. Sam urged Mother Fairbanks, who was planning to write a
book about the *Quaker City* excursion, to "always refer offensively to Capt.
Duncan" in it. If she would, Sam offered to contribute an introduction "&

when it comes my turn . . . I will give him a lift that will enable him to find out what Mars's new moons are made of."[22]

Bret Harte once penned "a play with a perfectly delightful Chinaman in it—a play which would have succeeded if anyone else had written it," Sam reminisced in his autobiography. He was one of the few people who enjoyed Harte's *Two Men of Sandy Bar* when he and Livy saw it at the Fifth Avenue Theater in early September 1876 during its brief New York run. He wrote the playwright a facetious note the next day that he "did not laugh once" because Harte had sold rights to the script "for a sum you should have received for three months' performance of it." He wrote Howells that "Harte's play can be doctored till it will be entirely acceptable & then it will clear a great sum every year. . . . The play entertained me hugely, even in its present crude state." He was particularly enthralled by the minor character Hop Sing, a Chinese laundryman and a "perfectly delightful" and "wonderfully funny creature" who appears onstage for five minutes and delivers a total of nine lines (e.g., "Me washee shirtee"). Languishing in debt, Harte proposed to Sam that they collaborate on a play "& divide the swag" and Sam jumped at the chance. As he wrote Howells on October 11, "I am to put in Scotty Briggs (see Buck Fanshaw's Funeral, in *Roughing It*), & he is to put in a Chinaman [who] is to be *the* character of the play, & both of us will work on him & develop him. Bret is to draw a plot, & I am to do the same; we shall use the best of the two, or gouge from both & build a third."[23] The result was the most disastrous collaboration in the history of American letters.

The project was plagued from the start by a pair of problems. Harte was broke and depended upon Sam's loans and largess to pay his bills so long as they worked together. Harte had antagonized the New York drama critics during the run of *Two Men of Sandy Bar*, moreover, by alleging that they charged bribes to puff new plays. These self-anointed custodians of culture were scarcely inclined to praise his next project, even if it was cowritten with Mark Twain. In any case, Harte and Sam outlined the scenario between games of billiards and shots of whiskey in the Hartford house, Sam remembered, and then Harte drafted the play "while I played billiards, but of course I had to go over it to get the dialect right." Harte "worked rapidly, and seemed to be troubled by no hesitations or indecisions; what he accomplished in an hour or two would have cost me several weeks of painful and difficult labor, and would have been valueless when I got through. But Harte's work was good, and usable; to me it was a wonderful performance." They spent a fortnight plotting the play and eight days filling in the outline. Sam's neighbor Isabella Beecher Hooker peeked into the billiard room the day after Thanksgiving 1876 and noted in her diary that "there were bottles of spirits near. I felt a new distrust of such companionship." She also risked Sam's ire by joking with him about a cheap lampshade that Livy had bought. "He was vexed & said something about things going around the neighborhood." By her own admission, Hooker mocked him: "I said oh that was handsomely said but really as a matter of fact I thought one often paid a high price for a homely article under such circumstances—which he didn't seem to like & again spoke of being talked about. When I said why it was all a joke as I heard it . . . his eyes flashed & he looked really angry." On December 13 Sam informed Conway that he and Harte had completed a new play, "which we expect great things from, tho' of course we may be disappointed." On December 30 the collaborators signed a contract and on January 5 they hired Charles Parsloe, the Anglo actor who had played Hop Sing in *Two Men of Sandy Bar*, to star as the eponymous hero in *Ah Sin*. ("Is the name of your play 'Arse in'?—sounds like a sitz bath," Frank Fuller asked Sam later.) The contract specified that the three of them, actor and coauthors, would share equally the profit from the play and that "Parsloe would pay them $25 every time he ad-libbed" a line the playwrights disapproved, a precaution Sam had learned by harsh experience with John T. Raymond in performances of *The Gilded Age*.[24]

From all indications, Sam and Harte were pulling together in harness as late as February 22, 1877. After completing a draft of *Ah Sin* they were "plotting out" another play, Sam wrote Howells that day. During the ensuing week, however, their friendship abruptly ended. On February 27, for example, Sam declared to his sister Pamela that he was "in a smouldering rage" over "the precious days & weeks" he had wasted with Harte. The crux of their disagreement, as often is the case in such partnerships, was money. Harte tried to borrow a few hundred dollars from Sam, who refused the loan but offered his collaborator a salary of twenty-five dollars a week and board to finish the second play with him—an insult Harte promptly spurned. In a letter to Sam on March 1, 1877, from New York, Harte detailed the issues at stake in their dispute from his perspective. He accused Sam of conspiring with Elisha Bliss to cheat him out of royalties he was owed on his novel *Gabriel Conroy* (1875), of offering Parsloe "the very sum you refused to advance your *collaborateur*" to travel to San Francisco and "study Chinese character," and of insulting him with an offer of a meager salary to collaborate on another play. "I think that if I accepted it, even *you* would despise me for it," Harte remonstrated. "I can make about $100 per week for a few weeks here at my desk." He charged Sam with attempting to exploit "my poverty, but as a shrewd man, a careful man, a provident man, I think you will admit that in my circumstances the writing of plays with you is not profitable. . . . I think I'll struggle on here on $100 per week—and not write any more plays with you." As for the script of *Ah Sin*, Harte asked Sam not to mar it "any more by alterations until it is rehearsed" and asked him "to allow me some understanding of the characters I have created." Sam scribbled a note on the back of this letter that he had only "read two pages of this ineffable idiotcy." But by his own admission he failed to polish the script of *Ah Sin* as much as it required. "I learned something from the fatal blunder of putting Ah Sin aside before it was finished," he admitted to Howells. He and Harte "didn't trim & polish [the play] at all" because they had quarreled "& we shall live to repent it, too." Not that he accepted any of the blame: "it was wholly [the fault] of that natural liar, swindler, bilk, & literary thief, Bret Harte, son of an Albany Jew-pedlar. I shall shed no tears if that play should fail, in October. It *ought* to—I know *that* pretty well."[25]

The apparent nub of their estrangement was not, as Sam alleged thirty years later, Harte's criticism of Livy's interior decoration. He seems to have confused Harte in this case with Isabella Hooker.[26] As Sam claimed in 1907, Harte had made snide comments "about the furniture of the bedroom, and about the table-ware, and about the servants, and about the carriage and the sleigh, and the coachman's livery." Throughout his visit he repeatedly delivered "sparkling sarcasms about our house, our furniture, and the rest of our domestic arrangements." In the billiard room, "he contributed the last feather: it seemed to be a slight and vague and veiled satirical remark with Mrs. Clemens for a target; he denied that she was meant, and I might have accepted the denial if I had been in a friendly mood, but I was not." In reply, as the story goes, Sam chewed him out. Harte was "a born bummer and tramp, . . . a loafer and an idler," he supposedly told him. "Nine-tenths of your income is borrowed money—money which, in fact, is stolen, since you never intended to repay any of it." Whatever the reason for their rift, the disagreement ended their friendship. They rarely crossed paths again, though each of them took occasional verbal potshots at the other for the rest of his life. Meanwhile, Parsloe joined forces with Sam against Harte. One day early in March 1877 Parsloe passed Harte on Broadway and ducked his questions about the progress of the play. Parsloe told him he already knew everything he needed to know, whereupon Harte blushed and stalked away. "To have the annoyance with Harte that I have," Parsloe complained to Sam, "is too much for a beginner." Ironically, on April 6, soon after completing a draft of his farce, Sam attended a performance of *Hamlet* starring Edwin Booth at Roberts Opera House in Hartford—and profusely apologized in a note the next day for interrupting the actor in his dressing room while he was relaxing after the play.[27]

The collaborators assiduously avoided each other when *Ah Sin* went into rehearsal. Whereas Harte skipped the run-throughs in Baltimore in April but attended the premiere in Washington in May, Sam supervised the rehearsals in Baltimore but skipped the premiere. "I had a delightful afternoon," he wrote Livy on April 23, because "I left behind me" for a day or two "those 2 men who have not been absent from my thoughts (& my hate) for months—Raymond & Harte." He granted interviews, including one with his friend George Alfred Townsend (aka Gath), to promote the play. "Ain't [Charles Parsloe] a lost and wandering Chinee by nature?" he told Townsend. "See those two front teeth of Parsloe, just separated far enough to give him the true Mongol look"? He explained to a reporter for the *Baltimore Gazette* that "we've got a good character in Ah Sin; whether it is in the right setting is another matter." He spent the night of April 30 at the Arlington Hotel in Washington but "found I was not absolutely needed" at the theater, he told Howells, so he called at the White House to see President Rutherford B. Hayes. He carried a letter of introduction Howells had given him, but William Rogers, Hayes's private secretary, mistook him for the eccentric entrepreneur George Francis Train and refused him entry, so he caught an early train back to Hartford.[28]

The finished script of *Ah Sin* was mostly Sam's, though the cast of characters was cannibalized largely from Harte's story "A Monte Flat Pastoral" (1874). Sam wrote Howells that he had "left hardly a foot-print of Harte in it" and no fragments of dialogue in Harte's handwriting appear in the prompt copy of the play that survives. But Sam admitted that the play was still "full of incurable defects: to wit, Harte's deliberate thefts & plagiarisms, & my own unconscious ones." He charged that Harte had never "had an idea that he came by honestly. He is the most abandoned thief that defiles the earth." He reiterated the point to Conway: "I have left precious little of Harte in 'Ah Sin,' & what there is he stole from other people. He is an incorrigible literary thief—& always was." But if Sam deleted most of Harte's contributions to the play, how could it have been filled with Harte's "incurable defects"? That is, Sam claimed to have erased Harte's share of the script but nevertheless blamed Harte for its failure. Never mind that Ah Sin exists mostly in the margins of a yellowface minstrel melodrama that defies brief summary. Sam's version of "the heathen Chinee" is a mere caricature who is mocked in the first scene as a "moral cancer" and an "unsolvable political problem." The title character is little more than a repulsive stereotype and the butt of racial violence. As Margaret Duckett observes, "almost every character in the play at some time speaks scornfully" of him, "much of the humor is at his expense," and "his frequent beatings and cuffings" are but "clumsy antecedents of the jokes" perpetrated on Jim in *Adventures of Huckleberry Finn* (1885). The script, which was unpublished until 1961, is a mishmash of stale jokes. As Frederick Anderson remarks, while the play "is not the poorest work by either man, it is not far from it."[29]

Ah Sin was staged for the first time before a packed house at the National Theatre in Washington the evening of May 7, 1877. Though he had first proposed the play, Harte was entirely excluded from all plans for its production. Even the complimentary passes he gave his friends were refused by the ushers. Sam sent a pair of speeches, "one to deliver in the event of failure of the play and the other if successful." The audience "voted the play a success." Harte congratulated the cast backstage before leaving the theater confident the play was a triumph and telegraphing the producer John T. Ford to "thank your people for their honest endeavor and clever interpretation of the varied characters." On his part, Ford notified Sam that he "ought to be here" to mend the play: "Your presence will be worth 10,000 men." That evening, Augustin Daly noted in his log, "Play went very well with the audience." In attendance were Senator Blanche Bruce of Mississippi; Nelly Sartoris, the daughter of Ulysses S. Grant; Governor Pinckney Pinchback of Louisiana; and General William T. Sherman. By chance, Andrew Chatto, the English publisher, was in the audience; he and Sam met personally for the first time, and the two of them chatted the next day at the Lotos Club. Dion Boucicault, John Brougham, John T. Raymond, and E. A. Sothern also sat in boxes near the stage. Raymond later called *Ah Sin* the "worst play I ever saw." Nevertheless, the box office receipts for the first night totaled about six hundred dollars and, for the weeklong tryout, over two thousand. At the end of the week, Sam instructed his lawyer Charles Perkins to post "any moneys received" from the play to his bank account, including Harte's share, crediting it toward "his indebtedness to me," and to inform Harte, should he inquire, that he had "gone off on a sea voyage." The next day Harte telegraphed Sam to request his share of the box receipts "if any."[30] There were none.

The initial reviews of the play during its tryouts in Washington between May 7 and 12 and at Ford's Theater in Baltimore between May 14 and 19 were mixed. Such papers as the Washington *National Republican* ("many passages which were unexcelled by anything in the other works of the two authors"), *Baltimore Bee* ("one of the most amusing and successful productions in the country's dramatic annals"), Denver *Rocky Mountain News* ("ingeniously constructed"), and *San Francisco Bulletin* ("evoked great laughter and applause from a densely crowded audience") were surprisingly upbeat. The *New York Clipper* ("the play lacks action" and "seems weak") and the *San Francisco Bulletin* ("toilsome jokes and farfetched puns") were less impressed.

Harte tried to doctor the comedy when it was staged in Washington, though Parsloe resisted his attempts to intervene in the production, so the cast made some improvements in the script on their own.[31]

No sooner had Sam returned from overseeing rehearsals of *Ah Sin* in Baltimore than he planned another excursion with Joe Twichell, this one to Bermuda. He needed a sea voyage, he explained to Sue Crane, "to get the world & the devil out of my head so that I can start fresh at the farm early in June." On May 16 the two friends sailed on a night boat from New Haven and the next day they embarked from New York on the steamer *Bermuda* for Sam's "first actual pleasure trip" in his life. The ship docked the morning of May 20 at Hamilton, the capital of the British territory. Though Sam had paused there briefly in 1867 on the return voyage of the *Quaker City*, he described it now as "a wonderfully white town; white as snow itself. White as marble; white as flour." He and Twichell went to extraordinary lengths to travel incognito. They "brought no letters of introduction; our names had been misspelt in the passenger-list; nobody knew whether we were honest folk or otherwise." Sam "traveled under an assumed name & was never molested with a polite attention from *anybody*." They registered under cognomens—in Sam's case, S. Langhorne—at a private boardinghouse where they were assigned "large, cool, well-lighted rooms on a second floor, overlooking a bloomy display of flowers and flowering shrubscalia."[32]

During the four days Sam and Twichell spent in Bermuda—"three bright ones out of doors and one rainy one in the house"—the friends "roamed about Bermuda day & night & never ceased to gabble & enjoy"; drove to the town of St. George's; visited Devil's Hole, a collapsed sea cavern; and attended a racially integrated Episcopal church service. Sam reveled in the cleanliness of the main island. "Nowhere is there dirt or stench, puddle or hog-wallow, neglect, disorder, or lack of trimness and neatness," he wrote. "The roads, the streets, the dwellings, the people, the clothes—this neatness extends to everything that falls under the eye. It is the tidiest country in the world." The prosperity of the Bermudians also pleased him, though he "felt the lack of something in this community—a vague, an indefinable, an elusive something" that was missing until "after considerable thought we made out what it was—tramps," his favorite flogging horse.[33]

Sam and Twichell embarked on the *Bermuda* for their return to New York on May 24 and, the first day out from Hamilton, the ship encountered the bark *Jonas Smith* adrift without nautical instruments. Sam was intrigued by the plight of the crew and wrote a letter to the editor of the *Hartford Courant* about the tramp steamer upon his return, though by that time the ship had been assisted by a revenue cutter. The *Bermuda* landed back in New York on

Sunday, May 27, and, in retrospect, Sam's only regret was that Howells had not joined them on the trip. "If you had gone with us & let me pay the $50 which the trip, & the board & the various nick-nacks & mementoes would cost," he wrote his friend, "I would have picked up enough droppings from your conversation to pay me 500 per cent profit in the way of the *several* magazine articles which I could have written, whereas I can now write only one or two & am therefore largely out of pocket by your proud ways." Twichell, too, expressed his appreciation to Sam for sponsoring his holiday. "I'm afraid I shall not see as green a spot again soon," he wrote. "And it was your invention and your gift. And your company was the best of it. Indeed, I never took more comfort in being with you than on this journey, which, my boy, is saying a great deal." He had "derived very marked physical benefit from the recreation and rest." Sam had enjoyed the trip no less than Twichell, as he acknowledged in reply: "It was much the joyousest trip I ever had, Joe—not a heartache in it, not a twinge of conscience."[34]

Sam soon turned his jottings about the trip into a series of four travel essays under the title "Some Rambling Notes of an Idle Excursion" published in the *Atlantic Monthly* between October 1877 and January 1878. They might better have been called "a matter-of-fact record of an uneventful trip." The sketches were mostly ignored but occasionally disparaged. "The amusing passages are like stepping-stones in a brook," the *New York Times* averred, "fordable, to be sure, but not fordable dryshod." Everett Emerson observes that the series "bears few of the earmarks of a travelogue by Mark Twain." Though he liked the final two installments "ever so much," Sam harbored doubts about the first two and adjured Howells "to squelch them, even with derision & insult," if the editor shared the author's reservations.[35]

On June 6, little more than a week after Sam returned from Bermuda, the Clemens family left Hartford to summer at Quarry Farm where, Sam wrote Tom Aldrich, he hoped "to write a book of some sort of other to beat the people with." Sam completed "Some Rambling Notes" for the *Atlantic* on June 26 and began a new project the next day, a play he gave such working titles as "Balaam's Ass," "Clews," "Cap'n Simon Wheeler," and "Simon Wheeler, Amateur Detective," in which he resurrected the narrator of the jumping frog sketch in the guise of a bumbling gumshoe. He was enthralled by detective stories—particularly the fiction of Arthur Conan Doyle and Edgar Allan Poe—and such "true crime" narratives as Allan Pinkerton's *The Somnambulist and the Detective* (1875). As he once wrote in his notebook, "What a curious thing a 'detective' story is. And was there ever one that the author needn't be ashamed of, except 'The Murders in the Rue Morgue?'"[36] In midcareer Sam composed seven tales according to the detective formula. Four of them—the "Cap'n Simon Wheeler" play (1877) and novel (1878–79), "The Stolen White Elephant" (1878), and "A Double-Barreled Detective Story" (1902), a parody of the Sherlock Holmes stories—burlesque the genre, while *Pudd'nhead Wilson* (1894), *Tom Sawyer, Detective* (1896), and the unfinished "Tom Sawyer's Conspiracy" (1897) subscribe to it.

Sam had considered writing the Simon Wheeler farce since the fall of 1876, when he outlined the plot to the producer and playwright Chandos Fulton of the Park Theatre. Fulton considered it "the germ of a good acting play" and in March 1877, while he was shopping for a script for two comedians, he remembered Sam's story. "It strikes me there was the material there," he wrote Sam, "one the detective, the other the man of disguise." The following June the moment seemed ripe to compose the play Sam had described to Fulton. "Today I am deep in a comedy which I began this morning," he advised Howells on June 27. His "principal character, that old detective—I skeletoned the first act & *wrote* the second, to-day; & am dog-tired, now. Fifty-four close pages of MS in 7 hours." He dashed off a 250-page rough draft in forty-two hours of working time, six and a half days "of booming pleasure," and deposited a copy of the screwball comedy for copyright on July 20. "Never had so much fun over anything in my life—never such consuming interest & delight," he reported to Howells—and bragged when he finished polishing the script on July 6 that his "old fool detective pervades the piece from beginning to end." He calculated that the melodrama would be worth fifty thousand dollars if it succeeded on the boards. "She reads in 2 hours & 20 minutes & will play not longer than 2¾ hours," he wrote.[37]

A precursor of Tom Stoppard's *The Real Inspector Hound* (1962), *Simon Wheeler, Amateur Detective* burlesques many of the conventions of the formulaic parlor mystery. Wheeler believes he is trained to solve crimes because he is a student of the genre, telling his doting wife, for example, that if she had "read as many detective tales as I have, you'd know that pretty much *all* the murders are committed by left-handed people" and asking witnesses such questions as "when she was a child did she stuff her dolls with *rags* or *sawdust?*" and "did her ancestors eat cold pie for breakfast?" In the course of his investigation he dresses in disguise as a woman and a sailor and speaks in black dialect, an Irish brogue, and Choctaw. "When I've finished working up this case," he announces, "it'll be worthy a chapter in one of Allen Pinkerton's great detective books!" The villain in the play is Jack Belford (named for the unauthorized Canadian publishers of *Tom Sawyer*), who is an escaped convict, a beggar, a desperado, and a "black-souled pirate." The presumed murder victim turns out not to be dead and in fact is the primary suspect disguised as a tramp. He reveals his true identity in the final scene, when he is reunited with his long-suffering bride-to-be.[38]

Sam had written the play with the popular comic actor Sol Smith Russell in mind for the leading role, though Russell was unavailable. Sam railed to New York on July 7, the day after completing the script, to search for another thespian who might play the part. As he wrote his mother, "If I can't find a considerably better [actor] than Raymond is or ever was, I shall come back home & weep." But his search was unsuccessful. He decided to "let [the play] lie & ripen under correction some months yet before producing it. I have a vast opinion of the chief character in it." He weighed the possibility of starring in the role himself "in New York or London, but the madam won't allow it. She puts her 2½ down with considerable weight on a good many of my projects." He eventually submitted the script to Dion Boucicault, who responded that it was "ever so much better than Ah Sin"—faint praise indeed—and that "the Amateur detective is a bully character." Similarly, John Brougham read the play and, while agreeing that it contained quartz "in abundance, only requiring the necessary manipulation to extract the gold," he thought it was "altogether too diffuse in its present condition for dramatic representation." Though Howells expressed interest in rewriting the play, Sam belatedly decided not even to send him a copy of it "because I couldn't find a single idea in it that could be useful to you. It was dreadfully witless & flat. It knew it would sadden you & unfit you for work." In the end, as Howard Baetzhold concludes, the play "was stillborn for lack of a producer," and Sam eventually discarded it. Even the editors of the *Mark Twain–Howells Letters* concede that it was "quite phenomenally bad."[39]

On July 16 Sam left New York for Hartford to investigate reports of an attempted burglary at his house the night of July 12. He soon determined that, rather than a prowler, the intruder was Willie Taylor, the beau of the housemaid Lizzie Wells, who to facilitate his surreptitious entries had disabled a burglar alarm on a basement door near her room. According to the *Boston Herald*, Wells, "a buxom English girl, with a handsome form and a bright, cheerful face," confessed to Sam that she was "lost irretrievably" and professed to be pregnant. Sam quickly arranged their marriage. He procured a license in their names, summoned Twichell and a policeman to be present when he confronted Taylor, a "tall muscular, handsome fellow of 35," and gave him an ultimatum either to marry the woman or face jail time. Had Taylor refused, Sam reported to Livy, he planned "to lock the door & say 'You either leave this room a married man or you leave it with an officer, & charged with being in this house at midnight in March with a dishonest intent—take your choice.'" The coercion worked and the couple wed in the parlor of the mansion. "Lizzy cried through the service & the prayer," Sam wrote Livy, "& then her husband put his arm about her neck & kissed her &

shed a tear & said 'Don't cry.'" While it was obvious that Lizzie had been dismissed from their employ, it was not so obvious that she was not pregnant. Sam gave the couple two hundred dollars as a gift, paid the minister, and celebrated the ceremony with the other servants and Twichell in the dining room with champagne and cake. He returned to New York the next day and, with their nest egg, the newlyweds opened a restaurant in Hartford.[40]

The circumstances surrounding Wells and Taylor's nuptials supplied Sam with material for a pair of stories. He premised "The McWilliamses and the Burglar Alarm" (1882), his third McWilliamses tale, on the malfunctioning alarm that permits repeated intruders to enter the McWilliamses' house at night. After sleeping "nine years with burglars," Mortimer concludes, he told his wife "that I had had enough of that kind of pie; so with her full consent I took the whole thing out and traded it off for a dog, and shot the dog." In May 1891 Sam jotted in his notebook the premise of the second tale he based on the incident: "How we made an honest woman of the English servant girl." In "Wapping Alice," completed in 1907 though unpublished until 1981, Sam recast Wells and Taylor as "wapping" (or "thumping") Alice and Bjurnsen Bjuggersen ("bugger") Bjorgensen—or, as John R. Cooley interprets the sexual shorthand of their names, "Slice Waps, Bjorn Bjuggers." Sam introduced a plot twist in this second version of tale. As the narrator reveals in its opening paragraphs, Alice "had a secret. It was this: she was not a woman at all, but a *man*." That is, "Wapping Alice" is "a gay transvestite story" that culminates "in a 'shotgun' same-sex marriage," the logical end of Sam's many tales of cross-dressing and gender bending. Unsurprisingly, his efforts to peddle the manuscript to the New York *World*, *Cosmopolitan*, and *Harper's Monthly* were unsuccessful.[41]

Back in New York on July 18 Sam registered at the St. James Hotel and again began to supervise rehearsals of *Ah Sin* in preparation for the debut of the play at Augustin Daly's Fifth Avenue Theater, two blocks away, the evening of July 31. He "coached those actors" in "that close, hot oven" at least four hours a day over the next two weeks. He crossed paths with Harte in the lobby of the hotel a few days before the premiere. Harte had been doctoring the script and one evening "came into the lobby of the hotel" to deliver his revisions to Parsloe, as Sam recounted in his autobiography. He was "dressed in an ancient gray suit so out of repair that the bottoms of his trowsers were frazzled to a fringe; his shoes were similarly out of repair, and were sodden with snow-slush and mud, and on his head, and slightly tipped to starboard, rested a crumpled and gallus little soft hat which was a size or two too small for him." Harte begged a dollar from Sam to pay a messenger to hand the script to Parsloe before disappearing back into the night.[42]

Expecting that her husband would deliver a curtain speech and sit for several interviews with the New York press on opening night, Livy cautioned not to "say harsh things about Mr Harte, don't talk against Mr Harte to people," and "don't let anybody trap you into talking freely of him." Harte was "so miserable," she remarked, that "we can easily afford to be magnanimous." Livy's warnings resonate with those of Miss Watson in *Huck Finn*, who scolded the *sauvage* hero: "Don't put your feet up there, Huckleberry," and "Don't scrunch up like that, Huckleberry—set up straight." Sam assured his wife the next day that "Harte has not put in an appearance." He added on July 30 that he thought "the 3 first acts will go off nicely—& that is the main point; if the curtain goes down handsomely on the 3d act, all will be well"— this because he planned to address the audience at the close of act 3. He did not expect the curtain to fall happily on act 4, however, because he had been unable "to drill the people into doing it right. There will be gaps of silence, & mistakings of cues that will be pretty distressing. Still, we are having a much more thorough rehearsal that we had of Col. Sellers. Daly stays right by & attends strictly to business. He makes them do a scene over three or four times, till they get it right." Sam also notified Livy that he had already written his curtain speech and planned to wear a white linen summer suit when he delivered it. "If I wear a swallow-tail it is plain I *expected* to be called out, maybe *wanted* to be," he explained. "My! but the laundry here does make my white linen lovely! The driven snow doesn't beg*in* [to compare] with it."[43]

Ostensibly called to the curtain by applause at the end of act 3 on opening night and costumed in a white linen suit—perhaps the first occasion that he wore the iconic attire in public—Sam delivered a speech rife with anti-Asian rhetoric that framed the play as a cautionary tale about the so-called Yellow Peril:

> Whoever sees Mr. Parsloe in this piece sees as good and natural and consistent a Chinaman as he could see in San Francisco. I think his portrayal of the character reaches perfection. The whole purpose of this piece is to afford an opportunity for the illustration of this character. The Chinaman is going to become a very frequent spectacle all over America, by and by, and a difficult political problem, too. Therefore it seems well enough to let the public study him a little on the stage beforehand.

Without mentioning Harte by name, Sam fired a volley across the bow of his "cordial enemy" during the speech, declaring the play "a work of great labor and research, also of genius and invention—and plagiarism." No doubt Sam meant to imply that he had contributed the "genius and invention," Harte the "plagiarism." He added that the more material he deleted from the script, "the better it got." *Ah Sin*, he asserted, would be "one of the best plays in the world today" if someone "cut out the rest of it." Some of the reviewers in the audience considered his curtain speech better than the play. According to the *Spirit of the Times*, Sam was "one of the funniest story-tellers and speech-makers in the world, but it is a question with us if his first-night speeches are as prudent as they are funny. People are always sure to say, 'Why didn't he make us laugh like that with his play?'" Sam telegraphed Livy after the premiere that the production had been a success,[44] but as often was the case he spoke too soon.

Unfortunately, some scholars in recent years have attempted to defend Sam's blatant racism in both his speech and his portrayal of Ah Sin by suggesting they should be read against the grain. While his *"seemingly* condescending speech could easily *seem* to suggest that the play offers mockery of the Chinese," according to Selina Lai-Henderson, "it actually mocks the American anxiety over the presence of this cultural other." As for the play, Hsin-yun Ou contends, it "represents Ah Sin as a trickster figure . . . a highly subversive character, clever and mischievous, surviving in a dangerous world through the use of trickery." The play "generally adopts the gaze of a Chinese character to satirize white Americans" and to represent "power relations between different ethnicities on the West Coast" in the 1870s. This tortured argument is too clever by half. The play makes most sense if it is simply and straightforwardly understood as pandering to the racist sympathies of its audience by staging an odious stereotype of the "inscrutable Chinaman." Or as Cynthia Wu insists, Ah Sin "is overtly—rather than quietly—racist."[45]

There is no repairing the bigotry inherent in the play, even as some of the opening-night reviewers recognized. The New York *Spirit of the Times* not only panned the production ("few plays of the American stamp can be mentioned whose literary execution is so bad, whose construction is so ramshackly, and whose texture is so barren of true wit") but ridiculed the title character. The New York *Dramatic News* reiterated the point that Ah Sin is a stereotypical Chinaman who, "for two hours and a half, waltzes through all manner of impossible incidents and situations, merely to give him a chance of saying 'Merican man' every five minutes" in pidgin English. The New York *World* disparaged the lead character as nothing more than "a contemptible thief and imperturbable liar." Andrew Wheeler, who had moved his soapbox from the *World* to the *Sun*, roasted the play ("trifling and unreal" and "devoid of art and literary ability") and particularly the leading character ("shallow and false"). "Ah Sin steals everything he can lay his hands upon," Wheeler ranted. "Does Mark Twain mean to tell us that that is characteristic of the Mongolian race?" Sam considered the notice in the New York

Evening Post a "fair sample" of the reviews in general: Ah Sin "lies because it is his nature" and the play overall "is not remarkable either as a literary work . . . or as a dramatic composition." The *New York Herald* ("the literary merit of the play is small and its tone is low") and *Hartford Times* ("not of much account") were no more measured in their criticisms. The *New York Times* ("not so bad a piece as might have been anticipated") and William Winter in the *New York Tribune* ("richly flavored with delicious absurdities") damned with faint praise. Yet Sam welcomed the ridicule. As he explained to Conway, the critics "all abuse the play, & that fills the house." Thirty years later in his autobiography Sam blatantly misrepresented the critical reception of *Ah Sin*. When "the piece was staged," he claimed, the reviewers "praised my share of the work with quite a suspicious prodigality of approval, and gave Harte's share all the vitriol they had in stock." On the contrary, Parsloe reported to Sam on August 20 that Wheeler of the *Sun*, for one, "pitches into you and I and leans a little" toward Harte.[46]

The evening of August 1 Sam attended the second performance of *Ah Sin* before scurrying back to Quarry Farm, "glad the troublesome thing was off my hands." Soon after his arrival, he and Livy spent a couple of days in Ithaca, thirty-five miles north of Elmira, as guests of the businessman and philanthropist Henry W. Sage, father of Dean Sage. While in the city Sam read some of his short pieces "to a select and appreciative audience" in Sage Hall at Cornell University. On August 3 he reported to Howells that the play was "a-booming at the Fifth Avenue [Theater]. The reception of Col. Sellers was calm compared to it. If Bret Harte had suppressed his name (it didn't occur to me to suggest it) the play would have received as great applause in the papers as it did in the Theatre. The criticisms were just; the criticisms of the great New York dailies are always just, intelligent, & square & honest." He expected to receive a windfall in profits from the production. "There was as much money in the house the first 2 nights as in the first 10 of Sellers," he bragged. As had been the case in Washington in May, Sam also appropriated Harte's third of the box office receipts. He instructed his lawyer Perkins to credit both his and Harte's shares to his account "& tell me the amount. Harte shan't have a cent till his entire indebtedness to me is paid. . . . If Harte inquires, tell him that is my verdict." On August 6 Sam sent slightly different signals about the play. He wrote Conway that it was "proving a bigger success even than 'Col. Sellers' was," with "*exceedingly* enthusiastic" audiences. But he betrayed his doubts about its merits even while bragging about its popularity to Mollie Fairbanks: the "dreadful play" seemed "to be a real success, since it keeps on filling the theatre [in] this hot weather." It drew "like a blister," he reported to his painter friend Frank Millet. On his part, Harte struggled to get news of the production after it opened in New York.

As if on cue, he contacted Augustin Daly for information: "I don't want any accounts from you or Parsloe, only a simple expression of your opinion as to whether the play was or was not successful, and as one of its authors, this does not seem to me to be an inconsistent request or calculated to wound anybody's—say Parsloe's—sensitive nature." In August, while the play was still "a-booming at the Fifth Avenue," Parsloe proposed to buy out Harte's interest in the play but Harte rashly refused the offer.[47]

He should have sold his stake. After its initial burst of popularity, *Ah Sin* quickly exhausted its appeal. Daly tried his hand at doctoring the script to no avail. It played at the Fifth Avenue for less than five weeks before steadily shrinking houses and closed there on September 1 with "considerable loss." That night Daly noted in his account book that the box office receipts for the thirty-fourth and final performance totaled only $163, adding, "End of summer season. The worst of the worst that 'ever was.'"[48] The two authors were scheduled to share the stage of the theater on the last night, but neither of them appeared.

As stipulated in his contract with the coauthors, Parsloe took the play on the road, accompanied by an agent to monitor ticket sales and report them to Sam and Harte. His first stop was St. Louis, where *Ah Sin* ran at Ben de Bar's Opera House from September 4 to 8. Ironically, it played opposite John T. Raymond in *The Gilded Age* at the nearby Olympic Theater. (While Parsloe highlighted "Mark Twain and Bret Harte" as the authors of his play, Raymond's advertising did not so much as mention Sam's name.) The initial reviews in St. Louis, as in New York, hailed the "decided hit" made by *Ah Sin*, but it played through the week to "rapidly diminishing houses" and after only five days the St. Louis *Globe-Democrat* pronounced it "a failure." Parsloe next took the play to Towanda, Pennsylvania, and upstate New York, where he staged it in Binghamton, Elmira, Hornellsville, Ithaca, and Rochester between September 13 and 22. He then carried it back to New York, to the déclassé Grand Opera House for a week. After this booking Parsloe dropped out of sight for a month. The play was not even earning enough to cover expenses. Before reviving it, he solicited a subsidy from Sam to help underwrite production costs but Sam declined. "'Ah Sin' is a most abject & incurable failure!" he acknowledged to Howells on October 15. "I'm sorry for poor Parsloe, but for nobody else concerned." The play was staged at the working-class Bowery Theater in New York between October 29 and November 4, in Pittsburgh from November 5 to 10, and in Cincinnati from November 12 to 17, where it died not with a bang but a whimper. As the *Cincinnati Commercial* remarked, "Parsloe played 'Ah Sin' till it played out."[49]

On the surface *Ah Sin* seemed to advocate discriminatory policies toward Asians. In truth, however, Sam favored open immigration. That is, his racist characterization of the titular character is all the more abject in light of his backing for the Chinese Educational Mission headquartered in Hartford. Established in 1872 by the Chinese government and directed by Yung Wing, the first Chinese native to earn a college degree in the United States, the mission over a period of eight years sponsored Western education in the sciences and military of over a hundred young Chinese men. Joe Twichell and the Asylum Hill Church were instrumental in the work of the mission and Sam supported it with both time and money. The Clemenses hosted a reception for Yung on October 26, 1877, at their home, where Sam and Joe Hawley "sang negro religious songs," according to Twichell. Sam was soon afterward quoted to the effect that "the Chinese question is largely a pretext of political demagogues. It is very much what the 'negro question' used to be for the demagogues of Connecticut."[50] But Sam had been no less culpable of demagoguing the issue.

Would but the story ended here. Even before the final curtain rang down on *Ah Sin*, Sam resolved to make trouble for Harte. When his former friend was rumored in the summer of 1877 to be in line for a diplomatic position, Sam urged Howells to sabotage the appointment. "Three or four times lately I have read items to the effect that Bret Harte is trying to get a Consulship," he wrote Howells on June 21, 1877. He urged Howells to

> prevent the disgrace of literature & the country which would be the infallible result of the appointment of Bret Harte to any responsible post. Wherever he goes his wake is tumultuous with swindled grocers, & with defrauded innocents who have loaned him money. He *never* pays a debt but by the squeezing of the law. He borrows from all new acquaintances, & repays none. His oath is worth little, his promise nothing at all. He can lie faster than he can drivel false pathos. He is always steeped in whisky & brandy; he gets up in the night to drink it cold. No man who has ever known him respects him. Harte is a viler character than [the corrupt former Consul General to Egypt] Geo. Butler, for he lacks Butler's pluck & spirit. You know that I have befriended this creature for seven years. I am even capable of doing it still—while he stays at home. But I don't want to see him sent to foreign parts to carry on his depredations.

Later the same day Sam thought better of his appeal to Howells and asked him to ignore his letter. As he explained, "I had to have an outlet to my feelings—I saw none but through you—but of course the thing would be disagreeable to you. I must try to get somebody to plead with the President who is in the political line of business & won't mind it." He added that "when we were writing the play together" he told Harte "that nobody would appoint him to an office, or ought to." Howells assured Sam in his reply that he thought "there is no danger of the national calamity you feared, and I don't believe there ever was much." But privately, Howells backed Harte for a government job. The appointment "would be a godsend" to Harte, he confided to Hayes. Or as the editors of the *Mark Twain–Howells Letters* note, Howells "would help Harte if he could, but he would not risk his friendship with Clemens for Harte's sake."[51]

Not that Harte's appointment ended the campaign of personal vilification Sam orchestrated from Hartford. In January 1878 he planted a derogatory story in a hometown newspaper of President Hayes, apparently with the cooperation of his friend Murat Halstead, that slandered him. The New York correspondent of the *Cincinnati Commercial* quoted Sam, albeit not by name, to the effect that Harte "was absolutely devoid of a conscience. If his washerwoman had saved $500 by long years of careful industry, he would borrow it without the slightest intention of repaying it." This smear was widely copied in papers across the country, though it failed to prevent Hayes's appointment of Harte in May 1878 to a minor consular post in Crefeld, Germany. Even after Harte's nomination was announced, however, Sam complained to Howells that he felt "personally snubbed" that Hayes had "silently ignored my testimony" and he then leveled another barrage of accusations: Harte was "a liar, a thief, a swindler, a snob, a sot, a sponge, a coward, a Jeremy Diddler, he is brim full of treachery." How did he know? "By the best of all evidence, personal observation." Sam asked Howells "what German town he is to filthify with his presence" so that he could warn the local authorities. Two years later he (seriously?) proposed a club whose only object would be "to impair & eventually destroy the influence" of Harte—"not from any base feeling, but from a belief that this is a thing required in the interest of the public good." In 1906, four years after Harte's death, Sam's anger still had not subsided. He libeled his onetime collaborator in his autobiographical dictation: "In the early days I liked Bret Harte," he admitted, "but by and by I got over it. So also did the others. He couldn't keep a friend permanently. He was bad, distinctly bad; he had no feeling, and he had no conscience. . . . He was an incorrigible borrower of money; he borrowed from all his friends; if he ever repaid a loan the incident failed to pass into history." Sam's hatred for Harte was rekindled as late as 1907, when he refused to come to the aid of Harte's destitute daughter Jessamy.[52]

At sunset on August 23 Sam's brother-in-law Charley Langdon's "young & comely" wife Ida, their daughter Julia, and nursemaid Norah left Quarry Farm to drive to downtown Elmira, some two and a half miles downhill. Their buggy was drawn by a "spry gray" horse. "Ida was seen to turn her face toward us across the fence & intervening lawn," Sam recounted, and

"Theodore [Crane] waved good-bye to her, for he did not know that her sign was a speechless appeal for help. The next moment Livy said, 'Ida's driving too fast downhill!'" More correctly, the frisky gray was a runaway. Sam and Crane ran down the hill after the buggy, fearing the worst. As Sam recalled,

> My last glimpse showed it for one instant, far down the descent, springing high in the air out of a cloud of dust, & then it disappeared. As I flew down the road, my impulse was to shut my eyes as I turned them to the right or left, & so delay for a moment the ghastly spectacle of mutilation & death I was expecting. I ran on & on, still spared this spectacle, but saying to myself "I shall see it at the turn of the road; they never can pass that turn alive." When I came in sight of that turn I saw two wagons there bunched together—one of them full of people. I said, "Just so—they are staring petrified at the remains." But when I got amongst that bunch, there sat Ida in her buggy & nobody hurt, not even the horse or the vehicle! Ida was pale but serene. . . . A miracle had been performed—nothing less.

The miracle worker was John Lewis, the Cranes' African American tenant farmer, who had been laboring up the hill with a load of manure in his wagon. "Lewis has worked mighty hard & remained mighty poor," Sam wrote Howells. "At the end of each whole year's toil he can't show a gain of fifty dollars. He had borrowed money of the Cranes till he owed them $700—& he being conscientious & honest, imagine what it was to him to have to carry this stubborn, hopeless load year in & year out." When he saw "the frantic horse plunging down the hill toward him" at full gallop,

> Lewis turned his team diagonally across the road just at the "turn," thus forming a V with the fence—the running horse could not escape that, but must enter it. Then Lewis sprang to the ground & stood in this V. He gathered his vast strength, & with a perfect Creedmoor aim he seized the gray horse's bit as he plunged by, & fetched him up standing! It was downhill, mind you; ten feet *further* downhill neither Lewis nor any other man could have saved them, for they would have been on the abrupt "turn," then. But how this miracle was ever accomplished at all, by human strength, generalship & accuracy, is clear beyond my comprehension—& grows more so the more I go & examine the ground & try to believe it was actually done.

Later that evening, after Lewis finished his chores, he arrived back at the farm "hunched up on his manure wagon & as grotesquely picturesque as usual." He "found his supper spread, & some presents of books there," including several inscribed copies of Sam's volumes, "& certain very complimentary letters, & divers & sundry bank notes of dignified denomination pinned to these letters and fly-leaves." The Cranes forgave his debt to them,

Sam donated fifty dollars to the pot, and the next day Sue Crane presented Lewis with "a new, sumptuous gold Swiss stem-winding stopwatch." Sam had been asked whether "this would be a wise gift" and replied with more than a hint of racial condescension that it was "the very wisest of all; I know the colored race, & I know that in Lewis's eyes this fine toy will throw the other more valuable testimonials far away into the shade." In acknowledging the gifts, Lewis wrote a letter that, Sam suggested, in parts rose "to the dignity of literature": "I beg to say, humbly, that inasmuch as divine providence saw fit to use me as a instrument for the saving of those presshious lives, the honner conferd upon me was greater than the feat performed."[53]

The news of Lewis's heroism was reported in the Elmira press and widely copied. In 1902 Sam told the story to an interviewer for the *Ladies' Home Journal* and added that he still held Lewis "in high and grateful regard."

Sam contributed to a pension fund for Lewis when he retired, and when he died in July 1906, Susan Crane recounted the circumstances: "He was always cheerful and seemed not to suffer much pain, told stories, and was able to eat almost everything. Three days ago a new difficulty appeared, on account of which his doctor said he must go to the hospital for care such as

Figure 14. Samuel Clemens and John Lewis, 1902. Courtesy of the Mark Twain House and Museum, Hartford, Connecticut.

it was quite impossible to give in his home. He died on his way there. Thus it happened that he died on the road where he had performed his great deed."[54]

Sam's respect for Lewis endured long after the Clemenses returned to Hartford on September 5. Over the years he repeatedly tried to work the story of Lewis's heroism into his fiction. Howells had advised him to convert the Wheeler play into a novel in October 1877, and Sam soon worked a version of Lewis's story into chapter 4 of the novelized *Simon Wheeler, Detective*, although Tom Quirk observes that "in that fiction he made the hero of the episode white, not black." His exploit seemed providential and "many people climbed the hill to look at the spot where the impossible feat had been performed." In a passage deleted from *Pudd'nhead Wilson*, the slave Jasper stops a runaway buggy with his bare hands, an almost impossible feat, and for the next three days was "the talk of the town." Chapter 11 of the unfinished tale "The Refuge of the Derelicts" (written 1905–6) similarly includes a scene drawn along the lines of Lewis's heroic act. In this case, Uncle 'Rastus stops the runaway buggy, "the newspapers applauded it," and "for several days the people climbed up from the town to look at the spot and wonder how the incredible thing was done."[55]

Sam maintained a discrete silence on the subject of his (lack of a) Civil War record for nearly twenty years. While other literary men of his generation had evaded military service, they usually had a good excuse. Henry James had injured his back and Howells had served as the U.S. consul in Venice, appointed to the post by Abraham Lincoln. Sam omitted from *Roughing It* all mention of his two weeks of retreating and subsequent desertion from the Marion Rangers. He was so uneasy about his (lack of) military experience that, as Forrest G. Robinson suggests, "his treatment of it was invariably defensive." But by 1877 he could no longer evade the issue. The New York *World* editorially questioned Sam's loyalty in its January 25, 1877, issue: "Has Mark Twain taken the iron-clad oath, or is he an unreconstructed rebel?" The *World* briefly reviewed his military history, noting that the "Ralls County Rangers appear to have been a Confederate organization," expressed the hope that Sam never "lifted a fratricidal hand against Gen. Joe Hawley," and concluded that "surely an explanation is in order. Perhaps it was all a joke." This editorial was widely soon reprinted in such papers as the *Portland Oregonian*. The San Francisco *Alta California* reported in February that journalists had begun to "unearth" Sam's early biography, "showing that in June 1861 he joined the Ralls' County Rangers, a regiment of Missouri Rebels. They haven't got half the story yet."[56]

At a banquet the following October 2 at Allyn Hall for the Hartford Putnam Phalanx of the Ancient and Honorable Artillery Company of Boston,

Sam for the first time publicly discussed his war experiences. The speech, a preliminary version of his essay "The Private History of a Campaign That Failed" (1885), was quoted across the country and temporarily inoculated him against a charge of treason. Before an audience that included former governor Nathaniel Banks of Massachusetts, Joe Hawley, current governor Richard Hubbard of Connecticut, and Henry Robinson, Sam "described with serious simplicity," according to the *New York Tribune*, his "stirring campaign" in Missouri with a ragtag band of Confederate irregulars. Sam "delivered his speech in his droll and inimitable manner, which fairly convulsed the company with laughter and kept the hall in a continuous roar of hilarity," the *Boston Journal* reported.[57] But his remarks failed to squelch permanently the whispers about what he did in the war and he revisited the issue again eight years later.

Howells and his daughter Winifred visited the Clemenses in Hartford for several days in mid-December 1877. They arrived on December 11 and Howells lectured on Edward Gibbon before a packed house at Seminary Hall the next evening. Sam introduced him: "The gentleman who is now to address you is the editor of the *Atlantic Monthly*. He has a reputation in the literary world which I need not say anything about. I am only here to back up his moral character." According to the *Hartford Courant*, the audience maintained a "breathless silence" throughout the lecture, which Howells had polished to an "exquisite finish." The Saturday Morning Club held a special meeting the next day, a Thursday, at Sam's house to hear Howells talk "most charmingly about Venice." The next evening Sam and Livy hosted a dinner in Howells's honor attended by the Twichells. No doubt during these several days Sam and Howells discussed such matters as the final installment of "Some Rambling Notes of an Idle Excursion," scheduled for publication in the *Atlantic* on December 1; Sam's telephone romance "The Loves of Alonzo Fitz Clarence and Rosannah Ethelton," forthcoming in the March 1878 issue of the magazine; and the novelization of "Simon Wheeler," a fragment he had started in several different ways, none of them satisfactory. Sam eventually abandoned this project. "I have given up writing a detective novel," he wrote Howells in January 1879; "I can't write a novel, for I lack the faculty."[58] He would cannibalize the manuscript for the feud plot in *Huckleberry Finn*, with Judge Griswold and his daughter Milly in the aborted novel transformed into Colonel and Sophia Grangerford.

But they obviously did not discuss in any detail the after-dinner speech Sam planned to deliver at the seventieth birthday celebration in honor of the poet and abolitionist John Greenleaf Whittier at the Brunswick Hotel in Back Bay Boston the evening of December 17. He was expected to deliver a talk like "The New England Weather," which had earned him a measure of fame among the Brahmins a year earlier. Howells remembered later that Sam thought he had been "particularly fortunate in his notion" for his speech before the brightest stars in the American literary firmament and "had worked it out in joyous self-reliance"—that is, without consulting him. The fifty-eight men of letters at table savored such haute cuisine as consommé Printanier Royal, saddle of English mutton à la Pontoise, vol au vent of oysters à l'Américaine, boiled chicken halibut à la Navarine, potatoes à la Hollandaise, squabs en compote à la Française, terrapin stewed Maryland style, canvasback ducks, sorbet au kirsch, charlotte russe, and six wines— Sauternes, sherry, Chablis, Mumm's Dry Verzency champagne, claret, and burgundy. The *Boston Advertiser* claimed that "the company was without doubt the most notable that has ever been seen in this country within four walls."[59]

After the tables were cleared about 10:00 p.m., women were admitted to the room, and three hours of speeches began with Howells in the toastmaster's chair. Midway through the program, Howells introduced Sam Clemens,

> the good friend of us all, . . . the humorist whose name is known wherever our tongue is spoken and who has perhaps done more kindness to our race, lifted from it more crushing care, rescued it from more gloom, and banished from it more wretchedness than all the professional philanthropists that have lived; a humorist who never makes you blush to have enjoyed his joke; whose generous wit has no meanness in it, whose fun is never at the cost of anything honestly high or good, but comes from the soundest of hearts and the clearest and the clearest of heads.

By most accounts, Sam then bombed. In the ten-minute speech he related an imaginary episode set in the foothills of the California Sierras some thirteen years earlier. He had visited the cabin of a "jaded, melancholy" miner who had recently been victimized by three tramps who answered to the names Ralph Waldo Emerson, Oliver Wendell Holmes, and Henry Wadsworth Longfellow—all of whose namesakes were present in the Brunswick dining room. "Mr. Emerson was a seedy little bit of a chap, red-headed," according to Sam. "Holmes was as fat as a balloon; he weighed as much as three hundred, and had double chins all the way down to his stomach." Longfellow "was built like a prize fighter. His head was cropped and bristly, like as if he had a wig made of hairbrushes" and he sported a cauliflower nose that "lay straight down his face, like a finger with the end joint tilted up." These "littery people" had cheated at cards and drank all the miner's whiskey, all the while misquoting the verse of the authors they impersonated and misidentifying titles of their work—such as Emerson's "Brahma," Holmes's "The

Chambered Nautilus," and Longfellow's "A Psalm of Life"—until "Long-fellow" tried to steal their host's only pair of boots on his way out the door. According to the *Boston Globe*, when Sam finished his speech he returned to his seat and lit a pipe. Henry Nash Smith contends that Sam's performance revealed his "latent hostility" toward the older New England literary elite. He ridiculed the revered poets by casting them as low Western types, much as he had twitted the sacred cows of the Forty-Niners in "The Pioneers' Ball" (1865). Sam also infringed in his speech on Bret Harte's stock-in-trade, the California mining camps.[60]

The many analyses of Sam's Whittier birthday speech have all over-looked a crucial detail in the context of its delivery. Sam was preoccupied with the so-called tramp menace. At the same moment Whittier's seventi-eth birthday was celebrated in Boston, a "tramp conference" was convening in Baltimore to discuss solutions to the problem of "indigent, non-working outlaws" who roamed the countryside. One of the proposed remedies was incarceration in jails or confinement in almshouses, much as the poor laws permitted foragers or "bummers" to be imprisoned in England. Michael Denning has noted that the pejorative term *tramp* was "a category con-structed in the wake of the 1873 depression and the 1877 railroad strikes to designate migratory and unemployed workers; indeed, it was ideolog-ical naming of the new phenomenon of unemployment." At the annual meeting of the American Social Science Association in September 1877, Francis Wayland, the dean of Yale Law School, delivered "A Paper on Tramps" in which he declared that when "we utter the word *tramp* there arises straightaway before us the spectacle of a lazy, incorrigible, cowardly, utterly depraved savage." In other words, by 1877 the term *tramp* had be-come ideologically and emotionally charged. Horatio Alger's juvenile novel *Tony the Tramp*, serialized in the *New York Weekly* during the summer of 1876, was retitled *Tony the Hero* when it was printed in book form in 1880. Rather than a synonym for the relatively neutral words *vagabond* or *home-less*, the term *tramp* connoted "bum." This evolving meaning of the word may begin to explain the umbrage the speech provoked when he flippantly characterized Emerson, Holmes, and Longfellow in his Whittier speech as deadbeats in the California outback.[61]

Sam's speech was commended the next day by most of the reporters in the room, including Sylvester Baxter of the *Boston Herald* and Delano God-dard of the *Boston Advertiser*. Goddard reported that "the amusement of the audience was intense, while the subjects of the wit, Longfellow, Emerson and Holmes, enjoyed it as much as any." According to the *Boston Globe*, the speech inspired "the most violent bursts of hilarity. Mr. Emerson seemed a puzzled about it, but Mr. Longfellow laughed and shook, and Mr. Whittier seemed to enjoy it keenly." The *Boston Traveller* attested that Sam's remarks provoked a roar of mirth and the *Boston Transcript* asserted that "there was no mistaking the hearty fun elicited by the droll attitude in which these literary lights were represented." The *Boston Journal* averred that the speech "aroused uproarious merriment," and the Portland, Maine, *Press* testified that "the funniest if not the wittiest speech was made by Mark Twain." The *New York Times* ("one of his most humorous of speeches") and *Hartford Times* ("a peculiarly droll speech") both lauded it. The *Chicago Times* split the difference between praise and vilification: Sam's address was both "drivel" and "the best speech of the night." The Boston correspondent of the *Chicago Tribune* stated that while Sam "was telling his yarn," Whittier's lips were shaped in an "odd, quizzical pucker," that "every now and then he would shake his shoulders with laughter, as if he was a little ashamed," and that Emerson and Longfellow "laughed as much as anybody." Although Sam implied in his autobiography that the party ended soon after his speech, in fact the festivities continued for another hour, ending at about 1:00 a.m., after Emerson, Holmes, Longfellow, and Whittier had left, with readings or addresses by seven more men, including Thomas Wentworth Higginson, George Waring, and Charley Warner. As Smith concludes, "There was nothing approaching a visible scandal" at the end of the evening. Henry O. Houghton was "delighted" by Sam's performance and the next day sent him a congratulatory note.[62]

Sam was so pleased with his speech that he shared his manuscript with the local press. It was widely copied, especially in New England, and within the next three days it appeared in the *Boston Journal, Post, Globe, Advertiser,* and *Transcript*; the *New York Times* and *Graphic*; the *Hartford Courant* and *Times*; the *Chicago Inter Ocean*; the Portland, Maine, *Press* and *Transcript*; the *Cincinnati Gazette*; and the *Philadelphia Bulletin*; and before the end of the month in the *Chicago Tribune*; Lowell, Massachusetts, *Citizen*; St. Louis *Globe-Democrat*; *Milwaukee Sentinel*; *New Orleans Picayune*; Washington *Capital*; and *Galveston News*.[63] Much of the immediate press coverage, rather than focusing on Sam's speech, lamented the exclusion from the dinner of women contributors to the *Atlantic* and especially the wine served during the meal "given in honor of a Quaker teetotaler." The day after the dinner, the Executive Committee of the Women's Christian Temperance Union adopted a resolution "to express to Messr H. O. Houghton & Co. the deep pain and regret felt by the members of this Union."[64]

Whatever dismay the attendees at the Whittier dinner may have felt about Sam's speech was not immediately evident; it smoldered for a week before exploding in the papers. The *Worcester Gazette* was the only newspaper of record to protest immediately the tenor of his comments:

> Mark Twain made a speech at the Atlantic dinner last night which was in bad taste. We refer to it, because Mark's sense of propriety needs development and it is not his first offence. He told a story in which Messrs. Longfellow, Emerson and Holmes were represented as crowding their society upon a California miner, guzzling his whiskey and cheating him at cards. It was, of course, meant to be a piece of incongruous absurdity, and although the idea was not at all original, it might have seemed funny in some circles when told with Mark's drawl but men who have attained the years and fame of Longfellow and Emerson are entitled to some degree of respect amongst a company of their friends. The offence is easier to feel than describe, but it is one which if repeated would cost Mark Twain his place among the contributors to the *Atlantic Monthly*, where indeed his appearance was in the beginning considered an innovation.

The *Boston Transcript* took the hint and, not to be outdone, reversed its opinion of Sam's talk in its December 19 edition. Instead of commending the "hearty fun" of the address, the *Transcript* announced that "the general verdict seems to be that Mark Twain's speech, though witty and well worked-up, was in bad taste and entirely out of place. As one critic puts it, 'if the three gentlemen named in his remarks had been entertained in New York, and a speaker had said what Twain did, Boston would have been insulted.'"[65]

Once the *Transcript*, the gray lady of Boston newspapers, criticized Sam's speech, other papers from the Eastern Seaboard to the Mississippi Valley joined the fray as though lying in ambush with sharpened quills. The *Boston Herald* complained that his talk, "though not reaching obscenity or blasphemy, was yet so out of place in such an assembly as to indicate a stupidity which people have not generally associated with the name of its author." The *New York Herald* growled that "Mark Twain evidently overdid it this time" and the rumor soon circulated that Longfellow had challenged Sam to a duel. Some of the harshest censure was leveled by the *Springfield Republican*, which fretted that Sam's speech was "too long if it had been good; and it was not good, it was vulgar," and dismissed the talk as "high-flavored Nevada delirium tremens." The paper amplified its scorn a week later, comparing Sam to "a wild Californian bull" in a china shop and asking, "is it not well to inquire whether the popularity of this man ought not to have already reached a climax? Literary men in America, where so much is tolerated, ought to aim higher than the gutter, no matter what they have of talent, or even genius."[66]

The *Republican* added that "indignation over Mark Twain's speech was great-er in up-country Massachusetts and in the Middle West than in Boston." The *Chicago Tribune* agreed: "Everywhere, upon all sides, there has arisen a cry of disgust and reprobation." True enough. This tempest in a Boston tea-pot grew into a full-fledged cause célèbre in the provincial newspapers, such as the *Cincinnati Commercial* ("even a King's jester should know when it will do to shake his cap and bells in the royal presence"), the *Cincinnati Gazette* ("the introduction of a circus clown in motley would be quite as congruous"), the *Cleveland Plain Dealer* (Sam was a "clown to the intellectual exquisites of Boston"), the St. Louis *Post-Dispatch* ("he would have made the apostles appear ridiculous at the last supper"), and the Washington *Capital*, in a brief notice probably written by Bret Harte to settle old scores ("the effort was as flat and stale as unbottled beer after an hour's exposure"). The hullaballoo extended to the Denver *Rocky Mountain News* ("Julia Ward Howe said some time ago that the *Atlantic* was losing caste and lowering its tone by admitting the Twain papers to its pages"), the *Chicago Advance* ("what will the histo-rian of American literature a hundred years from now make of it when he shall dig it out of the rubbish of musty newspapers?"), and the San Francisco *Argonaut*, where Ambrose Bierce facetiously hoped that "the daring joker" would not be lynched by the Bostonians because "it would be irregular and illegal, however roughly just and publicly beneficial." The *New York Tribune* referred derisively to Sam's "profane gymnastics at the Boston Valhalla" and the *Independent* warned ominously that "when Boston spanks, she spanks hard and long." Overall, the *New York Times* deemed aspects of the contro-versy to be "funnier than Mark Twain's speech."[67]

In truth, as Smith argues, "the panic that followed" mostly originat-ed in Howells's overreaction to Sam's faux pas: "The two friends churned themselves into a state of mind which bore little relation to external reality at the time and distorted their memories of what happened." Simply put, Howells—whose reputation as the editor of the august *Atlantic Monthly* was at risk—was embarrassed and convinced Sam that he should be ashamed. But the Whittier speech was more a two-day feature story than a public re-lations disaster. Or as the *Chicago Times* editorialized, "the funniest thing" about the overblown scandal that followed Sam's speech was the way it af-fected Howells, who "thinks Twain is immense; took him up from the first, rushed him into the *Atlantic*, floated him in *Atlantic* society. Howells . . . is suddenly obliged to sit and swallow all this bilge water from his favorite contributor, in the presence of such fine company, too; has to see the man he has endorsed degrade himself to the rank of a buffoon. It must have been tough for Howells." In an effort to repair the damage, Howells sent notes of regret to his friends before Sam mailed any apologies. He explained to

Charles Eliot Norton that before Sam "had fairly touched his point, he felt the awfulness of what he was doing, but was fatally helpless to stop. He was completely crushed by it, and though it killed the joy of the time for me, I pitied him. . . . [H]is performance was like an effect of demoniacal possession. The worst of it was, I couldn't see any retrieval for him." Norton replied by "expressing just the right feeling toward you," Howells reported to Sam, and Francis J. Child, the first professor of English at Harvard University and "one of the most fastidious men," read the speech in the newspaper and "saw no offense in it." Still, Howells warned Sam on Christmas Day 1877 that "everyone with whom I have talked about your speech regards it as a fatality," though he oddly counseled him not "to dwell too morbidly on the matter." He eventually modeled an episode in his novel *The Rise of Silas Lapham* (1885), in which the titular hero in a drunken stupor disrupts a fashionable dinner party, upon Sam's awkward performance at the Whittier celebration. Howells's most recent biographers observe that "why Twain's joking offended Howells—what made him so unforgiving—is hard to pin down."[68]

Howells's panic was contagious. Sam expressed no overt remorse for his speech until December 23, nearly a week after the dinner, when Howells communicated his alarm. When on occasion Sam was publicly embarrassed, as in this instance, he backpedaled. He declined invitations to appear a week later at the Forefathers' Dinner in Boston, to the reunion and banquet of the Associated Pioneers of California in New York, and to the Union Veterans Club in Chicago. "My sense of disgrace does not abate. It grows," Sam wrote Howells on December 23, for the first time responding to the brouhaha. He feared that

> my misfortune has injured me all over the country; therefore it will be best that I retire from before the public at present. It will hurt the Atlantic for me to appear in its pages now. It seems as if I must have been insane when I wrote that speech & saw no harm in it, no disrespect toward those men whom I reverenced so much. And what shame I brought upon *you*, after what you said in introducing me! It burns me like fire to think of it. The whole matter is a dreadful subject—let me drop it here—at least on paper.

This letter from "poor Clemens . . . almost breaks my heart," Howells admitted to Charley Warner. But as he assured Sam the same day he received his note, "I have no idea of dropping you out of the Atlantic, and Mr. Houghton has still less, if possible. You are going to help and not hurt us many a year yet." Still, as Sam anticipated, as soon as his comic sketch "The Loves of Alonzo Fitz Clarence and Rosannah Ethelton" appeared in the March 1878 issue of the magazine, the *Boston Journal* brusquely asserted it approached "nearer to stupidity than anything" Sam had yet written.[69]

Howells also acceded to Sam's wish a week after the dinner that he apologize to the poets. "Your letter was a godsend," Sam replied, "& perhaps the welcomest part of it was your consent that I write to those gentlemen; for you discouraged my hints in that direction that morning in Boston." Charley Warner, who was present at the dinner, tried to lift Sam's spirits, but Joe Twichell was so demoralized by the "scandal" that, as Sam wrote to Howells, "he confessed that he would rather take nearly any punishment than face Livy & me. He hasn't been here since!" Sam later told an interviewer, "I thought I was going to do one of the gayest things in my whole career. But things happened differently, and before I left I had turned that dinner into a funeral." Twichell confided to his diary that although Sam "worked hard at it beforehand, wrote every syllable—& thought it was the best thing he had ever done," in consequence of its "irreverence" the speech produced "a disagreeable impression." According to Twichell, Sam "saw before he was done speaking that he had made a fatal blunder. Anybody could have told him that before, that had the chance, for he was shockingly out of taste, but he didn't know it."[70]

On December 27, ten days after the dinner, Sam wrote identical letters to Emerson, Holmes, and Longfellow to express his contrition:

I come before you, now, with the mien & posture of the guilty—not to excuse, gloss, or extenuate, but only to offer my repentance. If a man with a fine nature had done that thing which I did, it would have been a crime—because all his senses would have warned him against it beforehand; but I did it innocently & unwarned. I did it as innocently as I ever did anything. You will think it is incredible; but it is true, & Mr. Howells will confirm my words. . . . But when I perceived what it was that I had done, I felt as real a sorrow & suffered as sharp a mortification as if I had done it with a guilty intent. This continues. That the impulse was innocent, brings no abatement. As to my wife's distress, it is not to be measured; for she is of finer stuff than I; & yours were sacred names to her. . . . I *had* to write you, for the easement of it, even though the doing it might maybe be a further offense. But I do not ask you to forgive what I did that night, for it is not forgivable; I simply had it at heart to ask you to believe that I am only heedlessly a savage, not premeditatedly; & that I am under as severe punishment as even you could adjudge to me if you were required to appoint my penalty. I do not ask you to say one word in answer to this; it is not needful, & would of course be distasteful & difficult. I beg you to consider that in letting me unbosom myself you will do me an act of grace that will be sufficient in itself. I wanted to write such a letter as this that next morning in Boston, but one of wiser judgment [Howells] advised against it, & said Wait.

The next day Sam dutifully reported to Howells, as though to a moral monitor, that he had apologized to the poets. He was undecided whether to send a copy of his letter to Whittier, though

> the offense was done also against him, being committed in his presence, & he the guest of the occasion, besides holding the well nigh sacred place he does in this people's estimation; but I didn't know whether to venture or not, & so ended by doing nothing. It seemed an intrusion to approach him, & even Livy seemed to have her doubts as to the best & properest way to do in the case. I do not reverence Mr. Emerson less, but I somehow I could approach him easier. . . . I haven't done a stroke of work since the Atlantic dinner; have only moped around. But I'm going to try tomorrow. How could I ever have—Ah, well, I am a great & sublime fool. But then I am God's fool, & all His works must be contemplated with respect.

Sam's outreach to Emerson, Holmes, and Longfellow was reported in the *Boston Herald* a few days later in an item probably written by Sylvester Baxter in consultation with Howells. The apology was "so utterly abject and forlorn that all will forgive Mark from the bottom of their hearts." The author of the item had not seen a copy of the letter, the *Herald* allowed, but understood "that he said to them in substance that he was a fool, and he knew it, but that God made him a fool, and couldn't help himself, and that they ought to have a little compassion on him for God's sake, if not for his own."[71]

Each of the poets responded to Sam's apology with grace and humor. Ellen Emerson, not her father, testily replied to Livy, not Sam, that the night of the dinner her father "did not hear Mr Clemens's speech he was so far off," though when her mother read the speech to him the next day he was "amused." In any case, "he never quite heard, never quite understood it, and he forgets easily and entirely." Still, Ellen Emerson stressed that when she, her brother, and her mother "read this speech it was a real disappointment. I said to my brother that it didn't seem good or funny." On his part, Longfellow assured Sam that he was "a little troubled that you should be so much troubled about a matter of such slight importance. The newspapers have made all the mischief. . . . I do not believe that anybody was much hurt." Holmes struck a similar note in his reply: "It grieves me to see that you are seriously troubled about what seems to me a trifling matter," he answered. "It never occurred to me for a moment to take offence, or to feel wounded by your playful use of my name." The premise of Sam's anecdote was, Longfellow wrote, "a very amusing one and with a little less of broad farce about it might have pleased everybody as it did so many. Any man who knows your *bonhommie* and evident kindness of disposition would never think of supposing you meant to strike anything with the heat-lightning of your wit and humor."[72]

After the poets absolved him of guilt for insulting them, Sam aggressively defended his behavior at the Whittier dinner. Howells remembered that he asserted "with all his fierceness" that "I don't admit that [the speech] *was* a mistake.'" In early February 1878 Sam admitted to Mother Fairbanks that

> very likely the Atlantic speech was in ill taste; but that is the worst that can be said of it. I am sincerely sorry if it in any wise hurt those great poets' feelings—I never wanted to do that. But nobody has ever convinced me that that speech was not a good one—for me; above my average, considerably. I could as easily have substituted the names of Shakspeare, Beaumont & Ben Jonson, (since the absurd *situation* was where the humor lay,) & all these critics would have discovered the merit of it, then. But my purpose was clean, my conscience clear, & I saw no need of it.

The editorial cartoonist Thomas Nast read a transcript of the address in a newspaper and told Sam that it was "very much the best speech & the most humorous situation" he had ever contrived. When Longfellow died in 1882, Sam was reminded of the Whittier dinner when, as he acknowledged to Howells, he had felt "like an unforgiven criminal" and would "never be as miserable again as I was then." But, he insisted, his speech was "just as good as good can be. It is smart; it is saturated with humor. There isn't a suggestion of coarseness or vulgarity in it anywhere." In his authorized biography of Whittier in 1884, Francis H. Underwood observed that the speech "was audacious and perhaps in questionable taste; but nothing more comic was ever conceived."[73]

Only in Sam's and Howells's memoirs printed after the turn of the century did they assert that they understood on the night of the dinner the magnitude of Sam's offense. That is, the modern mythology surrounding Sam's "hideous mistake" mostly accreted around the event over many years. The hyperbolic accounts of the principal actors in the disaster published long after the fact should be discounted like penny stocks in a bubble economy. Even after his embarrassment subsided, Sam continued to pick at the wound for no good reason. He had supposed his "gay oration" at the dinner "would be the gem of the evening," he reminisced on January, 11, 1906, adding,

> I had written it all out the day before, and had perfectly memorized it, and I stood up there at my genial and happy and self-satisfied ease, and began to deliver it. . . . The expression of interest in the faces turned to a sort of black frost. I wondered what the trouble was. I didn't know. . . . [I was] always hoping—but with a gradually perishing hope—that somebody would laugh,

or that somebody would at least smile, but nobody did. I didn't know enough
to give it up and sit down, I was too new to public speaking.

This last excuse was, of course, absurd. By 1877 Sam had been lecturing
professionally for over a decade. Nevertheless, he explained, "I went on with
this awful performance, and carried it clear through to the end, in front of
a body of people who seemed turned to stone with horror. . . . When I sat
down it was with a heart which had long ceased to beat. I shall never be as
dead again as I was then." Sam reread the speech twice and concluded that
"unless I am an idiot, it hasn't a single defect in it from the first word to the
last. It is just as good as good can be. It is smart; it is saturated with humor.
There isn't a suggestion of coarseness or vulgarity in it anywhere." The censure he suffered, he allowed, "pretty nearly killed me with shame during that
first year or two whenever it forced its way into my mind." His shame was "so
intense, and my sense of having been an imbecile so settled, established and
confirmed, that I drove the episode entirely from my mind." But he refused
to retreat from his position. "What could have been the matter with that
house?" he asked. "It is amazing, it is incredible, that they didn't shout with
laughter, and those deities the loudest of them all." If only he could re-create
the conditions when he spoke before "those beloved and revered old literary
immortals," he claimed, "I would take that same old speech, deliver it word
for word, and melt them till they'd run all over that stage." He even pondered the possibility of repeating the talk "before the Twentieth Century
Club of Boston or at a banquet of newspapermen in Washington," though
Howells discouraged the idea.[74]

Less than two weeks later, Sam reversed his decision. After reviewing the
speech another couple of times, he decided it was "gross, coarse." To his own
surprise, he "didn't like any part of it, from the beginning to the end," though
he could not "account for this change" in his attitude. "My instinct said, formerly, that it was an innocent speech, and funny. The same instinct, sitting
cold and judicial, as a court of last resort, has reversed the verdict. I expect
this latest verdict to remain." A month later he told an interviewer that he
was unprepared to recount "those painful events" in detail, though he would
"publish a full account" in his autobiography. "The feeling of remorse for
the part I took on that festive occasion has gone away now," he explained.
"But I confess that for two years after that dinner I used to kick myself regularly every morning for half an hour on account of what I had done." But
three months later, he noted on a transcription of his autobiographical dictation that he had given the speech "a final & vigorous reading—*aloud*—&
dropped straight back to my former admiration of it." Sam's private secretary Isabel Lyon noted in her diary at the time that Sam had chuckled "with

delight" while reading the speech and vowed to print it "before I die." He made good on this promise. He not only inserted the text of the speech into his dictation for January 11, 1907, but he also included this section of his autobiography in an excerpt published in the December 1907 issue of the *North American Review*.[75]

Smith speculates that this chapter influenced Howells's account of the Whittier dinner in *My Mark Twain* (1910). Certainly Howells remembered the speech more glumly than did its most cynical contemporary critics. After his introduction of Sam, Howells reminisced, "the amazing mistake, the bewildering blunder, the cruel catastrophe was upon us." As soon as "the scope of the burlesque made itself clear," he averred, "there was no one there, including the burlesquer himself, who was not smitten with a desolating dismay. . . . Nobody knew whether to look at the speaker or down at his plate. I chose my plate. . . . And so I do not know how Clemens looked, except when I stole a glance at him, and saw him standing solitary amid his appalled and appalling listeners, with his joke dead on his hands." In the throes of senility Emerson listened "with a sort of Jovian oblivion of the nether world"; Holmes jotted notes on his menu "with a well-feigned effect of preoccupation"; and Longfellow regarded the speaker "with an air of pensive puzzle." Unlike the journalists present at the Brunswick Hotel in December 1877, Howells recollected not mirth in the dining room but an oppressive silence that weighed "many tons to the square inch" finally broken "by the hysterical and blood-curdling laughter of a single guest, whose name shall not be handed down to infamy." The joke fell flat because, according to Howells, Sam had failed to gauge "the species of religious veneration" in which the poets were held and had underestimated the difficulty of poking even good-natured fun at these men in their presence while "expecting them to enter into the delight of it." Sam "must have dragged his joke to the climax and left it there" but Howells could not remember. He only recalled sitting afterward in a room of the Parker House, "where Clemens was not to sleep, but to toss in despair," and Charley Warner's comment, "Well, Mark, *you're* a funny fellow." Still, Howells admitted, he had "often wondered how much offence there really was" in the speech. "I am not sure but the horror of the spectators read more indignation" into the "hapless drolling than they felt."[76] Unfortunately, Howells's flawed version of events shaped the narrative surrounding the Whittier speech more than any other account for generations to come.

CHAPTER 7

Grand Tour

I have found out there ain't no surer way to find out whether you like people or hate them than to travel with them.

—*Tom Sawyer Abroad*

SAM AND LIVY began to plan a months-long grand European tour in the summer of 1877, long before the debacle at the dinner honoring John Greenleaf Whittier. Livy wrote her mother early in 1877 that Sam was "determined to go to Germany next Summer" but she preferred to delay the trip until the summer of 1878 "if we have money enough." As usual, Livy carried the point. Sam informed Mary Mason Fairbanks in September 1877 that they planned to leave the United States the following spring "& settle down in some good old city of Germany, & never stir again for 6 months." The desire soon became an idée fixe: "I want to find a German village where nobody knows my name or speaks any English, and shut myself up in a closet two miles from the hotel and work every day without interruption until I shall have satisfied my consuming desire in that direction." Even on the eve of his departure Sam told reporters, "I am going to the most out-of-the-way place in Germany I can find, fifty miles away from any railroad."[1]

At the age of forty-two, Sam faced a midlife crisis. He had written almost nothing for publication since "Old Times on the Mississippi" in 1875. He had been embarrassed by the Whittier birthday speech and he had suffered financial reverses. He wanted to "breathe the free air of Europe and lay in a stock of self-respect and independence," he noted in his journal, to stop feeling "so cowed" and "deferential to all sorts of clerks and little officials." As he confessed to his mother,

Life has come to be a very serious matter with me. I have a badgered, harassed feeling a good part of my time. It comes mainly of business responsibilities & annoyances, & the persecutions of kindly letters from well-meaning strangers—to whom I must be rudely silent or else put in the biggest half of my time bothering over answers. There are other things, also, that help to consume my time & defeat my projects. Well, the consequence is, I cannot write a book at home. This cuts my income down. Therefore, I have about made up my mind to take my tribe & fly to some little corner of Europe & budge no more until I shall have completed one of the half dozen books that lie begun, upstairs.

Among the projects Sam had pigeonholed were the sequel to *Tom Sawyer*, the novelization of the Simon Wheeler play, a burlesque diary of Shem in the ark, and a fictionalized life of his brother Orion. He and Livy arranged for Clara Spaulding and Rosina Hay to accompany them to Europe and hired Patrick McAleer to care for the house and grounds in their absence. "For two or three years," Sam wrote Charles Warren Stoddard, "the coachman & family will stand guard at the stable with the horses & keep the conservatory blooming & the hanging flower-baskets flourishing in the balconies." Sam also promised to cover Joseph Twichell's expenses if his friend would join him on a walking tour through parts of southern Germany and Switzerland. But their departure also "threw three people out of work," Livy lamented, including their longtime butler George Griffin.[2]

In the weeks before they embarked they maintained a hectic routine. Sam, Livy, and Lilly Warner attended a performance of W. D. Howells's drawing room comedy *A Counterfeit Presentiment* starring Lawrence Barrett at the Hartford Opera House the evening of January 2, 1878. Howells had published the play seriatim in the *Atlantic Monthly* between August and October 1877 and Sam was enchanted when he saw it performed. "I laughed & cried all the way through it," Sam reported to his friend. "The dialogue is intolerably brilliant; one hadn't time to see where one lightning-burst struck before another followed. I cannot remember when I have spent so delightful an evening in a theatre." He only wished that he could replicate Howells's achievement in his Simon Wheeler script with his "old fool of a detective mooning & meddling along."[3]

With his writing blocked and Livy's revenue from the family coal business in decline as a result of labor strikes and the economic depression, Sam briefly contemplated a lecture tour with his friend Thomas Nast like the one Nast had proposed to him in 1867, Nast "to draw pictures & I to do all the talking; he to portray & I to explain." He spun his fantasy for the cartoonist as though the money was tangible and ripe for the taking. He had continued to receive and refuse "the same old offers" to speak year after year—"$500 for Louisville, $500 for St Louis, $1,000 gold for 2 nights in Toronto, half gross proceeds for New York, Boston, Brooklyn, &c." He might have scheduled a solo tour, he explained to Nast, but he desisted because "traveling alone is so heart-breakingly dreary" and "*shouldering the whole show* is such a cheer-killing responsibility." But he would "enormously enjoy meandering around, (to *big* towns—don't want to go to little ones)—with you for company." He proposed in a letter to the caricaturist on November 12, 1877, to "put all the ducats religiously into two equal piles," pay a bureau "2 per cent of gross receipts to *engage halls & arrange dates & route* for us," retain an agent "to tend door—& shoulder all details, at $70 or $75 per week, he to pay his own expenses," and to charge "a dollar a ticket, & only in towns capable of furnishing from eight to 1200-dollar audiences." They might launch the raid upon the lyceums on February 1 "& perform 100 times[.] call the gross result $100,000 for 4 months & a half, & the profit from $60,000 to $75,000." Such an itinerary would still allow Sam, Livy, and the rest of the family to sail for Europe by mid-June. "I know you & I could pack [Steinway Hall in New York] 6 nights & 2 matineés—& double that time in a smaller hall," he wrote, concluding his spiel. "We could clear $3000 apiece for a Steinway week with no trouble at all. We can pack Music Hall in Boston (it seats near about 2500) 2 nights & one matinée, or run a week in a smaller hall. . . . I could easily pick out & add 25 one-thousand dollar towns scattered about New England & along that route. You & I can cram any house in America as full as it can hold." Nast resisted the temptation, however. As Sam explained in a letter to Mother Fairbanks, Nast hated the platform and there was "not money enough in the world to hire him to show his face to an audience again."[4]

With an income from his pen inadequate to support his family, during a hiatus between lecture tours and in lieu of living on Livy's diminished dividends Sam turned to speculating for a livelihood. His old friend Frank Fuller convinced him to invest in the New York Vaporizing Company and a new type of steam generator that could ostensibly extract virtually all energy from coal. The machine failed to work, however, and Sam lost five thousand dollars on the venture. But he "had become an enthusiast on steam" and "took some stock in a Hartford company which proposed to make and sell and revolutionize everything with a new kind of steam pulley. The steam pulley pulled thirty-two thousand dollars out of my pocket in sixteen months, then went to pieces, and I was alone in the world again, without an occupation." Because he had been burned on the generator and pulley deals he claimed to want "nothing further to do" with wildcat speculations. He had twenty-three thousand dollars liquid "which I had no particular use for" when an agent of Alexander Graham Bell tried to sell him "a couple of tons of stock" in a gadget called the telephone. He balked because Bell had not yet been granted an ironclad patent on the invention. The agent "insisted that I take five hundred dollars' worth. He said he would sell me as much as I wanted for five hundred dollars; offered to let me gather it up in my hands and measure it in a plug hat; said I could have a whole hatful for five hundred dollars." But still Sam declined. Had he bought the stock, he admitted in 1907, he would have been able to "pay off our national debt now and let the country take a fresh start."[5]

Though he declined the opportunity to invest in the telephone, he installed one in his house during the winter of 1877–78. It was "the only telephone wire in town, and the *first* one that was ever used in a private house in the world," he bragged. It connected to only one location: the editorial offices of the *Hartford Courant* a mile and a half away. In the wake of the Lizzie Wells–Willie Taylor imbroglio in July 1877 and the threat of intruders in the neighborhood of Nook Farm, Livy

> was afraid something might happen, so she suggested a telephone about the time they first became communicative. I contracted for the thing and had one end fastened to the house, but for a while I didn't know what to do with the other end. You see the farm lies some distance out of Hartford, and is sometimes difficult of access at night time. Well, to be on the safe side of thing[s], I asked the chief of police to hold the other end, as the doctor, or clergyman, or I might be wanted home. Police headquarters shut up too early, he said. However, I was allowed to fix the troublesome terminus at the *Courant* shop, which is open all night.

Sam's direct telephone connection to the *Courant* offices in turn sparked a rumor that he had been hired by the newspaper. The New York *Sun* reported in a spurious interview on January 7, 1878, that he had become its editor. He intended to transform the paper, so the story went, into "a semi-political, semi-humorous journal" supporting the policies of President Rutherford B. Hayes, Sam's own candidacy for governor of Connecticut, and the candidacy of Marshall Jewell for U.S. senator. The item was copied from coast to coast. When Orion got wind of the story, he begged Sam for a job: "Can't you try me again? Put me at *anything* you think I can do, if it is setting type, collecting, or sweeping out and running errands at any wages you please." One of Sam's friends at the Virginia City, Nevada, *Territorial Enterprise* even endorsed his gubernatorial nomination: "He would make an impressive State Executive if he could keep his face in a profound and somber aspect long enough to have it enameled." The *Enterprise* article in turn elicited Sam's reply to his old friend Rollin Daggett, the new editor of the paper, denying the rumor. "No doubt the *Sun's* report grew out of the fact that my house is connected with the *Courant* office by telephone," he explained to Daggett. The "telephone is a great convenience to me when I want to send for something in a hurry" but "no editorials pass through the telephone either way." On January 26 the New York *Sun* printed a second spurious interview with Sam denying the accuracy of the earlier one.[6]

Sam was also irritated during the weeks preceding their departure for Europe by the fallout from a temperance revival held between January 7 and February 8, 1878, at the Rink in Hartford led by Dwight L. Moody and his musical director Ira D. Sankey. Though Sam once insisted that he had "always avoided the Moody & Sankey revivals," he had in fact attended one of their meetings in Boston in March 1877. A year later, Joe Twichell participated in several of the evening meetings in Hartford and, following one of these gatherings, he apparently went to a drugstore, "bought a bottle of lager beer & drank it on the premises." After Moody and Sankey left Hartford for greener pastures, a local preacher "exposed" the incident and, as Sam wrote Jane Clemens, "a tempest of indignation swept the town." Fortunately, the outrage was aimed at the parochialism of the revivalists. "Our clergymen & everybody else said the 'culprit' had not only done an innocent thing, but had done it in an open, manly way, & it was nobody's right or business to find fault with it," Sam explained to his mother. He attributed the provincialism of the evangelicals to "the fact that we never have any temperance 'rot' going on in Hartford." Predictably, when he was asked to donate money to Moody's cause, he refused, though he later used the incident with good effect in *Adventures of Huckleberry Finn* (1885), where the sham king of France admits he had been "a-running' a little temperance revival . . . when somehow or another a little report got around last night that I had a way of puttin' in my time with a private jug on the sly."[7]

Before embarking for Germany, Sam also lined up another pair of writing projects he hoped to complete while abroad. He outlined the idea for a new novel in his notebook on November 23, 1877: "Edward VI and a little pauper exchange places by accident a day or so before Henry VIII's death. The Prince wanders in rags and hardships and the pauper suffers the (to him) horrible miseries of princedom, up to the moment of crowning in Westminster Abbey, when proof is brought and the mistake rectified." It was just the sort of story that Mother Fairbanks had admonished him to write, a story shorn of the backwoods slang and vulgarity that she felt had tarnished his writings. On February 5, 1878, he gleefully assured her that he was working on a "historical tale, of 300 years ago, simply for the love of it—for it will appear without my name—such grave & stately work being considered by the world to be above my proper level." It would eventually appear under the title *The Prince and the Pauper* (1881). He had been gathering background from sixteenth-century British histories "for a year & a half," he told her—no mention here of his *1601*, written in the summer of 1876—and had drafted a couple of hundred pages. He had read the manuscript "half a dozen chapters at a time" to the young women in the Saturday Morning Club and noted that "they profess to be very much fascinated with it; so do Livy, & Susie Warner." It was admittedly "a wide departure from my accustomed line" and, in fact, the least characteristic of his novels, so much so that he would not complete it for another two and a half years. He briefly weighed the possibility of releasing it through Dan Slote's company. As Slote wrote him on February 2, 1878, "Should the Amer Publishing Co ever let go their grip we can get 'good and even' on your future writings." On March 8, 1878, a month before sailing, however, Sam secretly contracted with Frank Bliss, Elisha's son and the treasurer of the American Publishing Company, for a travelogue about his upcoming European trip, a project that would eventually be titled *A Tramp Abroad* (1880). The younger Bliss was planning to break with his father's firm and start his own subscription house. Sam was more convinced than ever that Elisha Bliss had cheated him by paying him a royalty on his books rather than half profits, and Frank Bliss guaranteed him 10 percent of gross sales or half of the profits, whichever was more. The contract stipulated that Frank would "keep a true and correct record of the cost of preparing the plates for said book both of text and engravings and of every article needed in order to be in a state of preparation to make the book" in order to calculate exact profits, and "if at the end of the first year one half of said gross profits exceeds the amount of said royalty for said year," Sam was to receive "the amount of such excess in addition to said royalty." In other words, the contract promised everything that Sam had demanded from Elisha Bliss but been denied for the past decade. Privately Sam assured Frank Bliss that he had never "mentioned your contract & mine to anybody," and he continued to insist publicly that his next book would be "published by the same fortunate beings who have published my other works," a claim that was technically correct because Frank had been an officer of the American Publishing Company yet misleading because Sam had contracted with the rival start-up Frank planned to launch.[8]

By mid-March the Clemenses had moved back into the second floor study and adjacent bedroom of the mansion—the same suite of rooms they occupied in 1874 when the house was in the final stages of construction—to allow workers to "box up the furniture & carpets of the rest of the house & put the place into the state of desolation meet for our two-years' absence from it." By March 20, as Sam notified Howells, the pictures were "gone from the walls, the carpets from the floors, the curtains, the furniture, the books—everything has vanished away to the storage warehouse, & the place is empty, desolate, & filled with echoes." Sam and Livy had decided not to rent the house but to leave it vacant in case they returned from Europe early.

He had been pleasantly surprised to learn—by telephone from the *Courant* office—that the poet and travel writer Bayard Taylor, the newly designated U.S. minister to Prussia, would sail on the same ship with them in mid-April. Sam hastened to congratulate him: "Your appointment was as welcome news to us as it was to the whole country—& now comes a report that you are to sail with your family in the *Holsatia*" of the Hamburg-America line, "a ship in which we engaged a couple of rooms a week or ten days ago." Sam paid $450 in gold for the transatlantic fares of four adults and two children, eagerly anticipated Taylor's company during the voyage, and accepted with alacrity an invitation to attend a "proposed testimonial to my esteemed friend & (to-be) fellow-passenger" at Delmonico's in New York the evening of April 4.[9]

It was Sam's first public appearance since his Whittier speech in Boston over three and a half months earlier. The other guests included Henry Bellows, Noah Brooks, and Horatio Stebbins from Sam's San Francisco days; August Belmont and George Waring of Newport; Howells; Osgood; E. C. Stedman; and New York editors David Croly, Richard Watson Gilder, and Whitelaw Reid. Sam was slated to talk and had written a speech but, in his anxiety, forgot it and thus spoke extemporaneously for only a few moments. In the wake of the Whittier ruckus, he was careful to avoid all controversial topics:

> I have been warned that a dinner to our Ambassador is an occasion which demands, and even requires, a peculiar caution and delicacy in the handling of the dangerous weapon of speech. I have been warned to avoid all mention of international politics, and all criticism, however mild, of countries with which we are at peace, lest such utterances embarrass our Minister and our Government in their dealings with foreign States. In a word, I have been cautioned to talk, but be careful not to say anything. I do not consider this a difficult task.

He was "so jaded & worn" by preparing for the journey to Europe "that I found I could not remember 3 sentences of the speech I had memorized, & therefore got up & said so & excused myself from speaking."[10]

The Taylor banquet was remarkable for another reason. As Sam recounted the story in his autobiography, he was seated next to the Wall Street banker T. B. Musgrave, "a gentleman whose society I found delightful" but who harbored a grievance against Bret Harte. Musgrave had "gladly" loaned Harte money over the years and Harte in return not only "affectionately dedicated" his novel *Gabriel Conroy* (1876) to him but "always gave his note" until the debt totaled about three thousand dollars. Musgrave confided to Sam "that Harte's notes were a distress to him, because he supposed that they were a distress to Harte. Then he had what he thought was a happy idea: he compacted the notes into a bale and sent them to Harte on the 24th of December '77 as a Christmas present; and with them he sent a note begging Harte to allow him this privilege because of the warm and kind and brotherly feeling which prompted it." In reply, "Harte fired the bale back" the next day "with a letter which was all afire with insulted dignity" but "nothing in it about paying the notes sometime or other."[11]

Sam returned to Hartford after the dinner at Delmonico's, arriving in the afternoon of April 7, to finish packing for the trip. On April 10 he and his entourage of five—Livy, six-year-old Susy, three-year-old Clara, Clara Spaulding, and Rosina Hay—railed from Hartford to New York. "I've got 6 people in my care, now," he joked to his mother, "which is just 6 too many for a man of my unexecutive capacity. I expect nothing else but to lose some of them overboard." They registered at the Gilsey House on Broadway at East Twenty-ninth Street, a short hack ride from the ferry to Hoboken, New Jersey, and sailed for Hamburg the next afternoon from the Hoboken dock. Among the well-wishers who bid them farewell were Howells, Reid, Slote, Stedman, and Charles Dudley Warner. As usual, Sam regaled the reporters at the scene with a few wisecracks. When asked the difference between Taylor the diplomat and Sam the writer, he responded,

> Mr. Taylor goes abroad with a purpose, I with none. Mr. Taylor goes to represent his country, I to represent myself. Mr. Taylor goes to do business, I to loaf. How long shall I stay? I can't tell. I left my house in Hartford just as it is, so I can come back at any time. Perhaps that is the best way to do if you want to stay a good while. If you rent your house for a year or so, you know, you want to come back in three months. I am going to write something when I get settled. I can't write when I am interrupted—burn three pages out of every four, and begin over again. In Germany, where I can't understand a word they say, I can settle down and write it off.

Like the *Quaker City* in June 1867, the *Holsatia* sailed south for only a few miles through New York Harbor before it anchored overnight near Sandy Hook to await calmer seas. Murat Halstead, who had planned to accompany his family as far as the Verrazano Narrows, return to shore aboard an escort steamer, and follow them six weeks later to conduct some business in Paris, instead decided on the spur of the moment to join them when his wife Mary became seasick. He might "attend to his business there about as well now" as later, he reasoned, so he borrowed a pair of pants from Sam and a greatcoat from Taylor to complement his wardrobe on the cruise.[12]

The spring weather during their two-week crossing of the North Atlantic was "devilish," Sam remarked to Howells, with a daily "afternoon hell" in the ship. One day, Sam reported, "we sighted an iceberg in the morning & a water-spout in the afternoon." Another day, according to Livy, "we had waves 20 ft high, they looked sometimes as if they would engulf us," and "when we were on deck they were just grand but when we were below they seemed frightful." The ship docked briefly at Plymouth on April 22 and the Clemenses disembarked "in the beautiful, the *very* beautiful city of Hamburg" three days later. Sam promised to meet Taylor soon in Berlin, but they never saw each other again. On December 19, eight months into his tenure as U.S. consul, Taylor died suddenly of edema.[13]

The family stayed five days at the Hotel Kronprinz, near the Elbe River docks and the main Hamburg train station, where they booked a room for Rosa and the children, a single room for Clara Spaulding, and a suite with parlor and alcove for Sam and Livy. "What a paradise this land is!" Sam wrote Howells. "What clean clothes, what good faces, what tranquil contentment, what prosperity, what genuine freedom, what superb government! And I am so happy, for I am responsible for none of it. I am only here to enjoy. How charmed I am when I overhear a German word which I understand." Nor was he "accosted by a beggar" the entire time the family lingered in Hamburg.[14]

Sam and his entourage slowly migrated to the southwest over the next week, overnighting in Hanover, where Sam and Clara Spaulding attended a performance of the comic opera *Roberto il Diarolo*; Göttingen, Kassel, and Wilhelmshöhe; and Frankfurt, where the family toured the Goethe Geburtshaus in the Altstadt and again crossed paths with Frank Mason, the U.S. consul general there and former editor of the *Cleveland Leader*. "I and mine had spent a good deal of time with [Mason] and his family in Frankfort in '78," Sam recalled in his autobiography. "He was a thoroughly competent, diligent, and conscientious official." Their courier "had the effrontery" to propose an outing to the birthplace of Mayer Rothschild in the Jewish ghetto, though Sam nixed the suggestion: "2 or 300 years ago, they'd have skinned this Jew in old Frankfurt, instead of paying homage to his birthplace," he observed in his journal, "but it is an advance—we have quit loathing Jews & gone to worshiping their money." At least for the moment, Sam relished his anonymity on the Continent. "I have such a deep, grateful, unutterable sense of being 'out of it all,' " he gloated. "I think I foretaste some of the advantage of being dead. Some of the joy of it. I don't read any newspapers or care for them." Though Samuel Clemens was unknown to the German public, Mark Twain was available to German readers in a half dozen translated editions, and he was nearly as popular as his archnemesis Bret Harte.[15]

On May 5 Sam and the clan railed from Frankfurt to Heidelberg, their immediate destination, where they registered the first night at the Hotel Schrieder, across the street from the central station on the edge of the Altstadt. The village boasted a population of about twenty-three thousand and was home to the Universität Heidelberg, founded in 1386 and one of the great centers of learning in the world, with a faculty of about 100 and an all-male student body of about 750, including some fifty American and British students. When the weather grew too warm for comfort the next day, Sam sought alternative accommodations. For less than $250 a month Sam rented a suite of rooms in the Schloss-Hotel, a posh residential guest-house on a precipice overlooking the Neckar River. He detected "only two sounds" from the bluff: "the happy clamor of the birds in the groves and the muffled music of the Neckar tumbling over the opposing dikes." From "a billowy upheaval of vivid green foliage, a rifle-shot removed" arose the carefully maintained ruin of Heidelberg Castle, "the Lear of inanimate nature—deserted, discrowned, beaten by the storms, but royal still, and beautiful."[16]

When he sent word to Livy and Clara Spaulding a mile away to join him, they took a "charming" carriage ride up the hillside that "reminded us often of the drive to the farm, because we seemed going up so very high." Sam crowed to Howells that the hotel, built only seven years earlier, was

> divinely located. From this airy perch among the shining groves we look down upon Heidelberg Castle, & upon the swift Neckar, & the town, & out over the wide green level of the Rhine valley—a marvelous prospect. We are in a cul de sac formed of hill-ranges & river we are on the side of a steep mountain; the river at our feet is walled, on its other side . . . by a steep and wooded mountain-range which rises abruptly aloft from the water's edge; portions of these mountains are densely wooded; the plain of the Rhine, seen through the mouth of this pocket, has many & peculiar charms for the eye.

The view from the glass-enclosed balconies of their rooms was entrancing.

Figure 15. Panorama of Heidelberg, Germany, ca. 1908. Photograph by William Herman Rau. Courtesy of the Library of Congress.

As Sam gushed,

> The picture changes from one enchanting aspect to another in ceaseless procession, never keeping one form half an hour, & never taking on an unlovely one. To look out upon the Rhine Valley when a thunderstorm is sweeping across it is a thing sublime. Every day there is a new spectacle in the way of a sunset, a new vision that the sun-rise brings, & when the moonlight drapes the Castle, town, bridges & valley, it is truly soothing & satisfying to the outlooker. And then Heidelberg on a dark night! It is massed, away down there, almost right under us, you know, and stretches off towards the valley. Its curved & interlacing streets are a cobweb, beaded thick with lights—a wonderful thing to see; then the rows of lights on the arches bridges, & their glinting reflections in the water. . . . The hotel grounds join & communicate with the Castle grounds; so we & the children loaf in the winding paths of those leafy vastnesses a great deal.

Livy too was charmed by the site. It was "just the place for the children," she wrote her mother, with woods "filled with wild flowers." As Sam would later write in *A Tramp Abroad*, "I have never enjoyed a view which had such a serene and satisfying charm about it as this one gives. One thinks Heidelberg by day—with its surroundings—is the last possibility of the beautiful; but when he sees Heidelberg by night, a fallen Milky Way" with its thousands of gas jets lighting the city, "he requires time to consider upon the verdict."

Figure 16. The Schloss-Hotel, Heidelberg, from across the river, engraving, from *A Tramp Abroad*, 1880.

The vista was eerily reminiscent, moreover, of the view of Hannibal and the Mississippi River from Lover's Leap.[17]

They lingered in the university town for eleven weeks. "The summer semester was in full tide," Sam remembered, so "the most frequent figure in and about Heidelberg was the student." When he registered with the local authorities to obtain his residency permit or *Aufenthaltserlaubnis*, he listed his profession as "Philologist and artist." In a reversion to his interest in the code duello in Nevada, he was especially intrigued by the student corps and their tradition of dueling. Through the agency of Edward M. Smith, the U.S. consul in Mannheim, he was admitted to the students' dueling hall on

May 17 and witnessed eight sword fights. Two spectators fainted, he noted in his journal, and one of the duelists "had a piece of his scalp taken. The others faces so gashed up & floor all covered with blood." He also noted that in Germany "you can't tell" by facial scars "whether a man is a Franco-Prussian war hero" or "merely has a university education." But in the end Sam defended the gory rite: "There is blood and pain and danger enough about the college duel to entitle it to a considerable degree of respect," he insisted in chapter 6 of *A Tramp Abroad*. The Clemenses occasionally hiked a few hundred yards east from their hotel along the Wolfsbrunnenweg to a hunting lodge that traced its origins back to the fifteenth century where Sam dined on "splendid trout." They traveled at least once to Worms, some twenty miles distant, where Martin Luther defied a papal edict to renounce his heretical teachings in 1521. One day Smith ushered Sam to three an-tique stores, "my pet detestation," to shop for curios but, as he fulminated in his notebook, "I wouldn't have such rubbish in the house. I do hate this antiquarian rot, sham, humbug; cannot keep my temper in such a place & *never* voluntarily enter one." Sam and Livy railed ten miles to Mannheim on May 24 to see *King Lear* performed in German. He "never understood a word but the thunder & lightning," though he thought "Lear's great speeches sounded mighty flat" in a more guttural tongue. He returned to Mannheim on May 30 to attend a "shivaree," Richard Wagner's opera *Lohengrin*, with Smith ("the racking and pitiless pain of it remains stored up in my memory alongside the memory of the time that I had my teeth fixed"). Wagner ever after was a special target of Sam's (sat)ire. When a "great chorus composed entirely of maniacs" suddenly appeared onstage and began to yodel on cue, for two minutes he "lived over again all that I had suffered the time the or-phan asylum burned down." He later famously quoted his friend Bill Nye's line: "Wagner's music is better than it sounds." In truth, Sam admired some Wagner pieces—in particular, the bridal chorus or wedding march from *Lo-hengrin*. To his "untutored ear" it was "almost divine music."[18]

Meanwhile, along with Livy, Spaulding, and the children, Sam studied German, with its gendered nouns and separable verbs, and it became an almost inexhaustible target of his mockery. He marveled that in German grammar "a tree is male, its buds are female, its leaves are neuter." In Ger-man, he protested, "a young lady has no sex, while a turnip has." He imag-ined such a conversation as this one:

Gretchen: "Wilhelm, where is the turnip?"
Wilhelm: "She has gone to the kitchen."
Gretchen: "Where is the accomplished and beautiful English maiden?"
Wilhelm: "It has gone to the opera."

In a part of his essay "The Awful German Language," originally published as appendix D to *A Tramp Abroad*, Sam spoofed speech in which "fish is *he*, his scales are *she*, but a fishwife is neither," permitting such idioms as "the poor Fishwife, it is stuck fast in the Mire; it has dropped its Basket of Fishes" and "one Scale has even got into its Eye, and it cannot get her out." He opened "The Awful German Language" by announcing, "I went often to look at the collection of curiosities in Heidelberg Castle and one day I surprised the keeper of it with my German. I spoke entirely in that language. He was greatly interested; and after I had talked a while he said my German was very rare, possible 'unique'; and he wanted to add it to his museum." On another occasion, when Sam tried to offer directions to an inquiring tourist in his best German, the visitor "put up his hands and solemnly said, 'Gott im Himmel!'" (Sam grew fond of not only German beer, especially Pilsner, but German profanity.) As for the difficulty of the language, he insisted that "a gifted person ought to learn English in thirty hours, French in thirty days, and German in thirty years" and that God invented eternity "to give some of us a chance to learn German." Separable verbs? Sam had a host of one-liners. The Germans "take part of a verb and put it down here, like a stake, and they take the other part of it and put it away over yonder like another stake." He knew a man who "would rather decline 2 drinks than one German verb." Fraktur type? "It is easier for a cannibal to enter the Kingdom of Heaven through the eye of a rich man's needle," he claimed, "than it is for any other foreigner to read the terrible German script." Livy struggled with the language, too, though Rosina Hay spoke German exclusively to the children in the nursery. As a result, Sam bragged, Susy and Clara "speak German as well as they do English. Susy often translates Livy's orders to the servants."[19]

In fact, Sam acquired over time a modest competence in the complexities of both written and spoken German. Howells remembered that Sam knew German "pretty well," and he certainly understood the language well enough to read the daily papers, Johann Wolfgang von Goethe's and Friedrich Schiller's poetry, and Arthur Schopenhauer's *Die Welt als Wille und Vorstellung* in the original German. His private library included Martin Luther's German translation of the Bible, and while researching *Life on the Mississippi* (1883) Sam read at least two books by German authors, Friedrich Gerstäcker and Ernst von Hess-Wartegg, who had traveled through the Mississippi River valley. He translated Heinrich Heine's "Die Lorelei" and "Du bist wie eine Blume" and poetry by Heinrich Hoffmann into English. He even tried his hand at writing some plays in German, including the bilingual "Meisterschaft" in 1888—a play, ironically, that features contrived conversations gleaned from German phrase books.[20]

About a month after the family settled in Heidelberg, Sam finally started to write the travelogue he had promised Frank Bliss. "I have waited for a 'call' to go to work," he wrote Howells on May 26. "Well, it began to come a week ago; my notebook comes out more and more frequently every day since." He rented a room on the upper floor of a house across the river for five dollars a month "so as to be away from home attractions & distractions," and began "regular, steady work" the next day. He had been "making notes ever since we left home," Livy reported to her mother, "so he has a good deal of material to work from." The walk every morning through the castle grounds and the town, across the Old Bridge, and upriver to his study "gives me very pleasing exercise, & just enough of it," he wrote his friend David Gray. "I have begun writing a book about Germany, in the sort of narrative form which I used in Innocents, Roughing It & Bermuda stuff. I think I shall enjoy the work when I get fairly into the swing of it." The return to the hotel up the mountain in the heat of the afternoon soon wore on him, however, so after a week he took a room for the same monthly rent on the second story of the Molkenkur inn—remodeled but still standing today—atop the Königstuhl and hiked there almost every forenoon. "I start to climb the mountain every morning about 10 or a little after," he reported to Charley Warner. "I loaf along its steep sides cogitating and smoking; rest occasionally and peer out through ragged windows in the dense foliage upon the fair world below; then trudge further to another resting-place, and finally I reach my den about noon." He worked three or four hours, then spoke "the most hopeless & unimprovable German with the family till 5" before returning to his hotel. "It is a sehr schönes Aussicht [very beautiful view] up there," he wrote Bayard Taylor. "The exercise of climbing up there is invigorating, but devilish."

Sam, Livy, and the children spent hours around the castle "knitting, embroidering, smoking, & hearing the music" performed there each evening. "The grounds about the castle here are perfectly wonderful," Livy wrote her brother Charley on July 21. For a diversion, Sam advised the readers of A Tramp Abroad, "you could stroll to the Castle and burrow among its dungeons, or climb about its ruined towers, or visit its interior shows," including "the great Heidelberg Tun," a "wine-cask as big as a cottage." Despite the local distractions, by mid-July Sam had completed about "400 pages of MS—that is to say, about 45 or 50,000 words, or one-fourth of a book," he notified Frank Bliss, "but it is in disconnected form & cannot be used until joined together by the writing of at least a dozen intermediate chapters."[21] Livy also exulted in the tranquility of the village, though she missed her Hartford home: "I enjoy it as much as possible here," she wrote her mother, though "I would rather live just where I do than any place that I know of—and I only hope that we will always have money enough so that we can continue to live there." From Livy's lips to Sam's ear. Two weeks later, on June 27, he triumphantly reported to Howells that, in fact, *"we've quit feeling poor! Isn't that splendid?"* Their European expatriation, ironically, enabled them to live within their means. At least they saved on pew rental in Hartford when they were abroad, he sometimes joked. "Yesterday," Sam announced to Howells, "we fell to figuring & discovered that we have more than income enough, from investments, to live in Hartford on a generous scale."[22]

Though he had initially reveled in his anonymity on the Continent, Sam soon rediscovered its perils. In the United States and England he enjoyed the privileges of fame, but in Germany, he complained, "I am utterly unknown & must stand around & wait with Tom Dick & Harry—& lucky if not received at last with rude impertinence." After his arrival in Heidelberg was announced in the *Heidelberger Zeitung*, however, he was invited to address the students in the Anglo-American Club on the Fourth of July. The invitation was tendered personally by twenty-three-year-old Frank Harris, later a well-known journalist, who left the Schloss-Hotel in disgust after a visit when Sam attacked Bret Harte as a "disgrace to literature." Harris vowed never "to see that man again; never again do I want to talk to him." Still, Sam delivered a first draft of "The Awful German Language" at the meeting of the club on Independence Day 1878. He stumbled over declensions ("meinem Freunde—no, meinen Freunden—meines Freundes—well, take your choice") and joked about the placement of German verbs at the end of declarative statements ("I don't know what wollen haben warden sollen sein hätte means, but I notice they always put it at the end of a German sentence—merely for general gorgeousness, I suppose"). Unfortunately, Livy complained, when Sam's presence in the town became well known the Clemenses' evenings in the gardens were "entirely spoiled" because they were frequently met by some of the students, especially when Clara Spaulding was with them.[23]

On May 23 Sam renewed his invitation to Joe Twichell to join his family in Germany "about Aug. 1st for a two months visit" and enclosed a check for three hundred dollars to cover his travel expenses. Twichell received the letter and the money on June 8. "Really our bounties are extraordinary," he noted that day in his journal. "This is a most handsome offer. And I must of course, accept it." He immediately replied, "Nothing replenishes me as travel does. Most of all I am to have my fill, or a big feed anyway, of *your company*—and under such circumstances! To walk with you, and talk with

you, and sleep with you, and say my prayers with you, and see things with
you, for weeks together—why, it's my dream of luxury. I can't tell you how
it 'rises the cockles of my heart' to think of it. The fact is, Mark, I'm in love
with you." On his part, Sam allowed to Charley Warner that he had "bully-
ragged" Twichell into the trip, "perfectly aware that nineteen-twentieths of
the pecuniary profit & advantage are on my side" because he wanted to incorporate details of their walking tours into his travelogue and, of course, he
desired "the social advantage" of Twichell's company. After hiring the porter
of the Schloss-Hotel, Georg Burk, to serve as the family courier at a salary
of fifty-five dollars a month and expenses, the Clemenses left Heidelberg
on July 23 by train for Baden-Baden where, as Livy allowed, it would again
be "ever so pleasant to know no one and to be utterly unknown." As Sam
recalled in *A Tramp Abroad*, "We had a pleasant trip of it, for the Rhine valley is always lovely." He would claim in 1884 that he again wanted to "pack
up out household tribe & spend next summer at the Schloss Hotel" and,
according to Katy Leary, Livy's room in the Hartford mansion was adorned
with "a beautiful picture of Heidelberg" as long as she lived there.[24]

Compared to the university town, Baden-Baden was a disappointment.
Still engrossed in furnishing the Hartford house, Livy spent much of her
time in the shops. But in his travelogue Sam depicted the city ambivalently,
noting that the town "sits in the lap of the hills, and the natural and artificial
beauties of the surroundings are combined effectively and charmingly," but
he also observed "sham, and petty fraud, and snobbery." Still, "the baths
are good." He took the waters there in a nod to his mother's hydrotherapy
and claimed that after "a fortnight's bathing" his "twinges of rheumatism"
had disappeared. In a play on the words of the popular German song "Ich
hab' mein Herz in Heidelberg verloren" (I left my heart in Heidelberg), Sam
insisted that "I left my rheumatism in Baden-Baden." Privately, however, he
groused that the weather there was "dismally cold & rainy" with occasional spells of "hellish heat." Even the Black Forest was "too close to B[aden-
Baden] to be endurable. Still, by going to it one gets out of B." The family
was eager indeed to leave the town on excursions. As soon as they settled in
the town, they embarked on a carriage trip through the Black Forest villages
of Forbach, Schoenmuenzach, and Allerheilgen. Sam contrived a new civic
motto: "See Naples & then die.—but endeavor to die *before* you see B.B." He
joked that in the Hôtel de France he had "sent for soap & the waiter brought
soup." Twichell rendezvoused with the family in Baden-Baden on August 1
and the next day Sam and Joe walked to Schloss-Favorite, about six miles
north. Two days later, on Sunday, August 4, they hiked to Ebersteinburg,

Zum Neuhaus, and Gernsbach, a round-trip of about twelve miles. They drank beer along the way, attended a village church, and dined before returning. As Sam observed in his journal, "It is pleasant to be in a country where you break the Sabbath without sin." On these treks they "became very familiar with the fertilizer in the Forest" and soon ventured to judge "a man's station in life by this outward and eloquent sign." When they "saw a stately accumulation" of manure, they concluded that a banker lived nearby. "When we encountered a country-seat surrounded by an Alpine pomp of manure, we said, 'Doubtless a duke lives here.'" Manure was "evidently the Black Forester's main treasure," and they learned to appreciate its worth as a measure of wealth. On August 5 they tramped to Achern and took a carriage to Ottenhöfen, "a very pretty village" where they lunched on fried trout and beer at the Hotel Pflug, then hiked to Allerheiligen by 6:00 p.m. and Oppenau by 8:30.[25]

The next day Sam returned to Heidelberg by train with Twichell specifically to witness "one of the sights of Europe," the "illumination of Heidelberg Castle." Much of the castle had been destroyed by French soldiers during the Thirty Years' War. Its most heavily damaged part was the Powder Tower, which collapsed when cannon fire exploded the magazine within. The castle was again damaged when it was struck by lightning in 1764. Sam no doubt knew these details when he depicted the destruction of Merlin's tower in chapter 7 of *A Connecticut Yankee in King Arthur's Court* (1889), where the Yankee crams the magician's turret full of gunpowder, then ignites it with a bolt of lightning he attracts with a metal rod. Since the early nineteenth century, moreover, the destruction of Heidelberg Castle by the French has been reenacted with a fireworks display twice every summer by local chamber of commerce types. In Appendix B of *A Tramp Abroad*, Sam described the event as he observed it the night of August 6, 1878. As usual, the hills and riverbanks around the town were crowded with thousands of spectators. From their vantage at Lang's Hotel across the river, Sam and Twichell saw that

> every detail of the prodigious ruin stood revealed against the mountainside and glowing with an almost intolerable splendor of fire and color. For some little time the whole building was a blinding crimson mass, the towers continued to spout thick columns of rockets aloft, and overhead the sky was radiant with arrowy bolts which clove their way to the zenith, paused, curved gracefully downward, then burst into brilliant fountain-sprays of richly colored sparks. The red fires died slowly down, within the Castle, and presently the shell grew nearly black outside.... While we still gazed and enjoyed, the ruin was suddenly enveloped in rolling and rumbling volumes of vaporous green

fire; then in dazzling purple ones; then a mixture of many colors followed. . . . For a while the whole region about us seemed as bright as day.

This scene no doubt inspired Sam's representation of a pair of "miracles" Hank Morgan performs in *A Connecticut Yankee*. Just as Sam described in *A Tramp Abroad* the "ivy-mailed battlements" of Heidelberg Castle, Merlin's ancient stone tower is in the novel "clothed with ivy from base to summit, as with a shirt of scale mail." The faux bombardment of Heidelberg Castle Sam described in *Tramp* illuminates the town "as bright as day," much as Merlin's stronghold in *Yankee* explodes in a "fountain of fire that turned night to noonday." Just as "vast sheaves" of rockets are "vomited skyward" from the castle towers in the travelogue, Hank Morgan ignites "a hogshead of rockets and a vast fountain of dazzling lances of fire vomited itself toward the zenith" in the novel.[26]

On August 7 Sam and Twichell began a four-day tour of the Neckar River towns between Heidelberg and Heilbronn along the "romantic road," traveling mostly by carriage, train, and boat. More specifically, they traveled by train upriver from Heidelberg to Neckargemünd, which was as far as the spur line had been built in 1878; by carriage from Neckargemünd to Hirschhorn, a distance of about ten miles; and then by boat another thirty miles to Weinsburg, Bad Wimpfen, and Heilbronn. There they "found a good hotel and ordered beer and dinner" and "took a stroll through the venerable old village. It was very picturesque and tumble-down, and dirty and interesting." Reversing course, they traveled downriver by small boat "7 or 8 miles to Jagsfeldt," according to Twichell, "where we stopped for lunch and took another boat." Sam records in *A Tramp Abroad* their (fanciful?) negotiation with the boat owner. He was unable to comprehend Sam's broken German, so Twichell "faced this same man, looked him in the eye, and emptied this sentence on him, in the most glib and confident way: 'Can man boat get here?'" The "mariner promptly understood" because, Sam explained, "all the words except 'get' have the same sound and the same meaning in German [Kann Mann Boot geht hier?] that they have in English." About this time, too, when Sam mentioned "some rather private matters" within earshot of some locals, Twichell cautioned him to "speak in German" because someone overhearing their conversation "may understand English." The afternoon of August 9 the travelers floated downriver past Eberbach to Hirschhorn, where they registered overnight at the Zum Naturalisten and visited the ancient castle and ruined church nearby. The next day they drifted downriver to Neckarsteinach and Dilsberg, where they again toured the village and a local castle atop a steep hill overlooking the river, then back to Neckargemünd, where they ditched the skiff and took the train back to

Heidelberg. Twichell wrote his wife the next day that "coarse as [Sam] is in streaks, he is a genuinely loveable fellow. As to the whiskey, most of the time he doesn't take any, and drinks no more wine and beer than I should, if I indulged, as I feel I might without sin. Anybody here would call him temperate. Really I am enjoying him exceedingly and take delight in being with him." They even knelt in prayer together before retiring for the night.[27]

In chronicling the return trip in chapters 14 through 19 of *A Tramp Abroad*, Sam imagined their journey downriver not by skiff but log raft. Or as he declared in the travel book,

> Germany, in the summer, is the perfection of the beautiful, but nobody has enjoyed the utmost possibilities of this beauty unless he has voyaged down the Neckar on a raft. The motion of a raft is the needful motion; it is gentle, and gliding, and smooth, and noiseless; it calms down all feverish activities, it soothes to sleep all nervous hurry and impatience; under its restful influence all the troubles and vexations and sorrows that harass the mind vanish away, and existence becomes a dream, a charm, a deep and tranquil ecstasy.

Huck Finn makes much the same point: "Other places do seem so cramped up and smothery, but a raft don't. You feel mighty free and easy and comfortable on a raft." The fictional trip in *A Tramp Abroad* ends when the raft hits a pier of the Old Bridge in Heidelberg and goes "all to smash and scatteration like a box of matches struck by lightning," much as Huck and Jim's raft is crushed beneath the paddlewheel of a steamboat at the approximate point where Sam had stopped writing *Huck Finn* two years earlier.[28]

Meanwhile, Livy, her daughters, and Rosina Hay, accompanied by Georg Burk, enjoyed an excursion of their own. They left Baden-Baden on August 8 and traveled across the Rhine to Strasburg "to see the Cathedral," once the tallest building in the world and a consummate example of late Gothic architecture. They then headed south and east to Zurich and Lucerne, where they registered at the Schweizerhof on August 11 and where Sam and Twichell joined them late the next evening. Sam soon discovered that the beauty of Lake Lucerne "had not been exaggerated." The city, moreover, was "a charming place. It begins at the water's edge, with a fringe of hotels, and scrambles up and spreads itself over two or three sharp hills in a crowded, disorderly, but picturesque way, offering to the eye a heaped-up confusion of red roofs, quaint gables, dormer windows, toothpick steeples, with here and there a bit of ancient embattled wall bending itself over the ridges, worm-fashion, and here and there an old square tower of heavy masonry." The day after their reunion, the entire family and Rosina enjoyed, as Livy put it, "a little ride on the lake" in a steamboat to Flüelen and "a most enjoyable afternoon." On August 15 the family journeyed fifteen miles by boat across the lake to the foot of the Rigi Kulm, the highest peak in the Rigi range. It was "an imposing Alpine mass, six thousand feet high, which stands by itself, and commands a mighty prospect of blue lakes, green valleys, and snowy mountains—a compact and magnificent picture three hundred miles in circumference," Sam related in his travelogue. While he and Twichell hiked up a trail, Livy and the children rode the funicular railroad to the hotel on the summit, where she drank a glass of wine and took a nap. By the time the men arrived, a storm had settled on the slopes and Sam had suffered a rheumatic attack. So much for the purportedly medicinal waters of Baden-Baden. At eleven the next morning, Sam and Twichell joined the family in descending the mountain "by rail. It was a good deal like coming down a ladder by rail. I did not like it," Sam complained. By half past one they had returned to Lucerne, with Livy reporting that they had "had a very satisfactory time."[29]

Over the next several days Sam and Twichell prepared for the longest walking tour of their lives: an excursion, as Sam described it, "from Interlaken, by the Gemmi [Pass] and Visp, clear to Zermatt, on foot!" On August 21 Sam and his family left Lucerne in a four-horse diligence for Interlaken, forty miles away, where they registered at the Jungfrau Hotel, "one of those huge establishments which the needs of modern travel have created in every attractive spot on the continent." The windows in their rooms opened to a "superb view" of "the mighty dome," the mountain named "virgin" in German, "softly outlined" against the southern sky "and faintly silvered by the starlight." Sam sketched the Jungfrau in his notebook during his brief stay in Interlaken, though he admitted the sketch "gives me a bellyache." He conceded, "I do not regard this as one of my finished works, in fact I do not rank it among my Works, at all; it is only a study." Both his original drawing and a slightly more modest version of it reproduced in *A Tramp Abroad* resemble a woman's breast (thus the name of the mountain) with a clear image of a nipple. (He similarly compared the onion domes of the Frauenkirche in Munich to "cow-teats.")

Livy wrote Sue Crane from the hotel that the Clemenses' rooms "face the Yung Frau [*sic*] & it is pleasant to watch the snow and the clouds on the mountains, but it is not at all comparable to Lucerne—there is no lake just here where we are."[30]

On the morning of August 23 Sam and Joe left Livy, Susy, Clara, and the servants in Interlaken and traveled by buggy—a concession to Sam's rheumatism—through the Kiental and Frutigen to Kandersteg at the foot

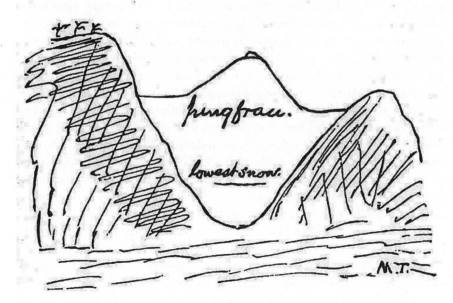

Figure 17. *The Jungfrau*, by "M.T.," August 1878, from *A Tramp Abroad*, 1880.

of the Gemmi Pass. On August 24 they "skirted the lonely little lake called the Daubensee" and trudged over the pass to Leukerbad. Much as he remembered retreating in time by climbing the volcanoes in Hawaii in 1866, Sam wrote to Livy that evening,

> Joe & I have had a most noble day. Started to climb (on foot) at 8.30 this morning among the grandest peaks! Every half hour carried us back a month in the season. We left them harvesting 2d crop of hay. At 9 we were in July & found ripe strawberries; at 9.30 we were in June & gathered flowers belonging to that month; at 10 we were in May . . . ; at 11.30 we were in April (by the flowers); at noon we had rain & hail mixed, & wind & enveloping fogs, & considered it March; at 12.30 we had snow-banks above us & snow-banks below us, & considered it February.

During the next few days they walked and railed through the Rhone Valley to Visp and St. Niklaus. At three in the afternoon on August 27, nine hours by foot from Saint Niklaus, they reached Zermatt near the Matterhorn, where they registered at the Cervin Hotel. Sam was awed by the "tall sharp peak" of the massif, describing in Whitmaniacal prose "his vast wreaths of white cloud circling about his summit & floating away from it in rolling & tumbling volumes twenty-mile wreaths floating slanting toward the sun." Still, he was disgusted by the squalor in the villages of this "wretched canton." The "narrow ill paved alleys or streets" of St. Niklaus and Zermatt, he noted, ran foul with "liquid dung," filthy fluid he euphemistically termed "fertilizer-juice" in *A Tramp Abroad*. "The only clean members of the family," he insisted, "are the cattle." The morning of August 30, after day trips to the Gornergrat and the Gorner glacier, Sam and Twichell left Zermatt in a wagon and a rainstorm to retrace their steps to St. Niklaus, then tramped seven miles downhill to Visp, where they registered at the Hôtel du Soleil. The next day they traveled by rail to Bouveret and by boat across Lake Geneva to Lausanne, where they rejoined the family at the Hôtel Beau Rivage.[31]

After resting two days, Sam led the group on a thirty-mile steamer excursion to the chateau of Chillon at the eastern end of the lake. The island castle had been made famous by Lord Byron's narrative poem *The Prisoner of Chillon* (1816), which dramatized the travail of François Bonnivard, the Genevois patriot jailed there. But Sam regarded it as a "humbug," nothing more than a tourist trap built "around the living rock to fit Byron's poem. This dungeon is much cleaner & pleasanter than Visp or any of those places." Sam repeated much the same point in his travelogue. His "pilgrimage" to "the place where poor Bonnivard endured his dreary captivity three hundred years ago" relieved him of "some of the pain I was feeling on the prisoner's account." The "dungeon was a nice, cool, roomy place, and I cannot see why he should have been dissatisfied with it." It was, after all, a more suitable lodging than "a St. Nicholas private dwelling, where the fertilizer prevails, and the goat sleeps with the guest, and the chickens roost on him and the cow comes in and bothers him." Sam betrayed in such passages his unrelenting bias against Catholicism. He repeatedly contrasted the "poverty and dirt and squalor" he encountered in the Catholic cantons of central Switzerland with the relative cleanliness of the Protestant cantons. Even the "Protestant glaciers," he averred, had nary a speck of dirt on them because they were routinely whitewashed.[32]

Sam and Twichell took a final Alpine trip during their last days together on the Continent. They railed to Martigny on September 4, stayed overnight at the Hôtel Clerc, and hiked the next day for over eight hours past Tête-Noire to Argentière, France. Footsore, they hired a diligence to carry them the final six miles to Chamonix, at the foot of Mont Blanc, where they registered at the Hôtel d'Angleterre. They devoted the entire day of September 6 to climbing the Montenvert eminence, first "to the Hôtel des Pyramides, which is perched on the high moraine which borders the Glacier des Bossons," as Sam reported in *A Tramp Abroad*, then to the Hôtel du

Montenvert, which commanded a view of "the great glacier, the famous Mer de Glace." They descended by a different route, the steep and rocky Mauvais Pas or "villainous path," which the Baedeker guide cautioned "elderly travellers and those subject to giddiness" to avoid.[33]

The next morning Sam and Twichell left aboard one of the diligences that regularly ran the fifty miles between Chamonix and Geneva, where they rejoined the other Clemenses at the Hôtel de l'Ecu de Genéve. Twichell left the city the following afternoon for Liverpool and a steamer back to America. "We do hate so desperately to have Mr. Twichell go," Livy declared to her sister Sue, because "we have enjoyed his being with us so much, and we have such fondness & such deep respect for him." On his part, Twichell no less than Livy lamented the end of his "most delightful and ever memorable" vacation. "My heart was mighty heavy . . . when the train moved out of Geneva after I bade you goodbye," the minister acknowledged in a note to Sam. He soon assured his friend that he preferred to travel with no one but him in the future. Sam, too, bemoaned the close of this chapter in their friendship. "I was so low-spirited at the station yesterday," he wrote Twichell on September 9, "& this morning when I woke, I couldn't seem to accept the dismal truth that you were really gone, & the pleasant tramping & talking at an end. Ah, my boy, it has been such a rich holiday to me; & I feel under such deep & honest obligations to you for coming." Two years later, on the anniversary of Twichell's departure, Sam remembered the "pleasant tramping and talking" they had shared. On occasion he could be a doe-eyed sentimentalist. As late as 1899, Twichell declared that their tour of Switzerland had been "the incomparable and unapproachable vacation of all my experience. Oh, what a splendid outing that was!"[34]

Sam had been so impressed with Chamonix during his visit that he returned there with Livy on September 10. They had "a wonderfully enjoyable trip," Livy wrote her mother, "although it was a rather wearing one." They left their daughters with Rosina Hay, rode in a two-horse wagon for nine hours one way, remained a day, and returned to Geneva on September 12. Otherwise, the remainder of their visit to the city was uneventful. The local attractions were "not numerous," Sam complained in *A Tramp Abroad*. "I made one attempt to hunt up the houses once inhabited by those two disagreeable people, Rousseau and Calvin," he allowed, "but had no success." Privately he was even more disparaging. The "principal features of Swiss scenery," he noted in his journal, were "Mont Blanc and the goiter."[35]

Sam and Livy's visit to Geneva in 1878 was most memorable, however, for the music box they bought there for four hundred dollars. Their housemaid Katy Leary remembered years later that "they always had music during dinner. They had a music box in the hall" of the Hartford house, and their butler George Griffin "would set that going at dinner every day." Encased in walnut wood and fashioned by the firm of Samuel Troll Fils, the box could be programmed to play as many as ten songs with full instrumentation. Sam struggled for months to select them. "I thought I had ten favorite tunes, but easily found I had only four," he admitted in a chapter omitted from *A Tramp Abroad*. "It took me eight months to furnish the other six." Even to-day only six of the songs on the playlist can be identified: three Wagner arias ("The Wedding March" from *Lohengrin*, "The Pilgrim's Chorus" from *Tannhäuser*, and "The Lorelei" from *Das Rheingold*); Guiseppe Verdi's "Miserère" from *Il Trovatore*; the Russian national anthem; and "The Last Rose of Summer." Sam considered including two lyrics by Robert Burns, "Bonnie Boon" and "Auld Lang Syne." These selections belie Sam's oft-professed dislike for classical music. "I detest it," he once insisted. "Not mildly, but with all my heart. . . . If base music gives me wings, why should I want any other? But I do. I want to like the higher music because the higher & better like it." Unfortunately, the music box Sam and Livy purchased in Geneva was damaged when it was finally delivered to Hartford: "When I at last opened the blessed thing in America, the first turn of the crank brought forth an agonizing jingle and squawk and clatter of bells, gongs, drums, and castanets, with never a solitary strain of flute or fiddle! It was like ordering a serenade of angels, and getting a shivaree in place of it." Sam eventually arranged for the apparatus to be repaired at great expense by a clockmaker.[36]

After Twichell left them, Sam led his family on a tour of Italy despite his mixed feelings about revisiting "the home of art & swindling" and of "religion & moral rottenness." He noted his ambivalence in his notebook: "One dreads going into Italy because of its reputation. What small & frivolous & trivial countries these are over here." Livy's mother was concerned for the Clemenses' safety, especially given the threat of cholera in late summer. "We shall make enquiries and if it does not seem entirely safe we shall not go until winter," Livy assured Olivia Lewis Langdon in mid-August. "I would not dream of running any risk, that I knew to be a risk" that might endanger her daughters. "We only planned to go to Venice in September and not that until the middle of the month then Florence and not Rome until the 1st of Nov. and not at all if there had not been frost so that it should seem entirely safe." She reiterated a month later that "we shall of course be very carefull in every way" while in Italy. On September 14 they railed sixty miles in four hours—"the Swiss trains go upward of three miles an hour," Sam grumbled—from Geneva to Chambéry, France, "the quaintest old town out of Heilbronn." They paused there an extra day "to break our journey into Italy," Livy explained. She was still recovering from "the accumulation of weariness" following her hasty trip to Chamonix. After only two days in Chambèry, however, she began to share her husband's aversion to the French. "I am more and more thankful that I am an American," she wrote her mother. "I believe the old puritan education [produces] better men and women." She echoed the thought months later: "How I should hate to bring up the children here—I am afraid it would take more strength of mind than I possess to draw the line where it ought to be drawn." The family traveled another 140 miles from Chambèry to Turin, Italy, on September 16. They departed around 10:00 a.m. on a "fast express which makes 4 miles an hour—the other trains make only 3¼," Sam joked. "By 11 we were out of sight of Chambery." They arrived in Turin about 7:00 p.m. and registered at the "Hotel d'Europe—wonderful rooms—great parlor with walls & windows upholstered in red silk damask 4 sofas upholstered in the same stuff." Though they remained there only two nights, Sam formed a distinctly favorable impression of the city. It was "the very liveliest town we have seen since Hamburg," he noted in his journal, "in its pavements, squares, arcades & commercial palaces." He was particularly impressed by the large and "architecturally imposing" public buildings.[37]

They left Turin by rail the morning of September 18 and arrived four hours later in Milan. They registered at the venerable Hotel de Ville, which, Sam complained, swarmed "with mice and fleas, and if the rest of the world were destroyed it could furnish dirt enough to start another one." Nor was its table d'hôte tolerable: "The food would create an insurrection in a poorhouse." But its "excellent reputation still keeps its dreary rooms crowded with travelers." They spent most of a week in the city "in the vast and beautiful" newly opened shopping mall, Galleria Vittorio Emanuele II, though they also tarried "an impressive hour in the noble cathedral," which Sam had toured during the *Quaker City* excursion almost twelve years earlier. He had commended the "bas-relief of birds and fruits and beasts and insects" that bordered its central door in *The Innocents Abroad* (1869), and he was no less fascinated this time by the "same old door-frame" with "its wonderful life-like carvings of snakes, insects, fruits &c. Could look at it weeks without tiring. It must be very bad art." And, of course, the family "visited the picture-galleries and the other regulation 'sights' of Milan—not because I wanted to write about them again, but to see if I had learned anything in twelve years." Fortunately, his taste in art had improved with time. In one of the galleries he bought a watercolor portrait of a young woman by the impressionist Daniele Ranzoni. Sam named it *Emmeline*—perhaps after his friend Emeline Beach, certainly the same name he gave to poor Emmeline Grangerford in *Huck Finn*—and it hung in the house in Hartford as long as the Clemens family lived there. In *The Innocents Abroad* he had pronounced amateurish copies better than the original paintings by the Old Masters. While the originals "were still unpleasing to me," by 1878 they appeared "truly divine contrasted with the copies." Lest he seem to have mellowed, Sam added elsewhere in his notebook that there were "artists in Arkansas to-day who would not have had to paint signs for a living if they had had the luck to live in the times of the old masters." Some of the canvases on exhibition in Milan, he thought, were as bad as J. M. W. Turner's *Slave Ship*. "They give you the belly-ache," like his sketch of the Jungfrau. He had seen the Turner painting in Boston a year earlier and compared it to a "cat having a fit in a platter of tomatoes." On September 20 he revisited Leonardo da Vinci's *Last Supper* in the Church of Santa Maria delle Grazie and, while expressing no explicit judgment of the picture on this occasion, his opinion may be inferred from this note in his journal: the experience "was well worth the trouble because we heard the military bugle" outside in the courtyard.[38]

They left Milan on September 24 and paused for a "rainy, sour, cold, drea-ry" night in Bellagio on Lake Como. They found a fireplace in their room at the Grand Bretagne Hotel and "right away we had the first wood fire we had seen since we left our own house. This made the day cheery." After a ten-hour train ride the next day, they arrived in Venice. They located their hotel, the Grand Britannia, which, according to Livy, "we did not find very comfortable," then "took our supper, which was poor, & went to bed." She was cold and homesick, she complained, though she was appeased the next day. The City of Bridges was "fascinating" and "thoroughly charming," she reported to her mother. "I sit now before a open window that opens on to a little piazza, where I can look right on to the Grand Canal."[39]

Sam spent most of the next three weeks playing the tourist (again). He was fascinated by the "gaudy scarecrow" of St. Mark's Cathedral, "partly be-cause it is so old and partly because it is so ugly," he observed in *A Tramp Abroad*. The adjacent campanile resembled "a mere brick factory chimney," he thought. He visited the Doge's Palace to view the paintings, particular-ly Tintoretto's massive, "three-acre [*sic*: eighty-foot] 'Il Paradiso,'" which contained hundreds of figures, "and they are all doing something." He also satirized the breezy style of art critics in reporting these visits in the travel-ogue by extolling the merits of Leandro Bassano's "immortal Hair Trunk," which in fact is nothing more than an inconspicuous detail in Bassano's *Pope Alexander III and the Doge Ziani* (ca. 1605) in the Hall of the Council of Ten. He considered Antonio Zona's *Meeting of Titian and Young Veronese* (1861), a modern painting in classical style in the Accademia di Belle Arti, the "loveliest picture" in the city. Despite his occasional qualms about Vene-tian life, Sam wrote Howells, a former U.S. diplomat there and the author of *Venetian Life* (1866), that he wished his friend were still consul there, "for we want to stay a year & would do so in that case."[40]

On her part, Livy shopped for furniture, bric-a-brac, knickknacks, and gimcracks to fill the Hartford house. William M. Gibson estimates that she "spent nearly five thousand dollars on household furnishings—a staggering sum," equivalent to about $130,000 in modern money, during the sixteen months she was abroad. Eventually they felt the pinch in their pocketbook. They may have "quit feeling poor" in June 1878 but they began to feel poor again in January 1879. "We are feeling very poverty stricken just now," Livy wrote her mother, because they had "spent so much in Italy—I don't know as we have done right, but it is such a temptation when things seem so reasonable and you get such a good premium on your letter of credit. Venice was the place where we spent the most money on the furniture that I wrote you about." Among her purchases were glassware from Salviati's and "a most wonderful old carved bedstead that was a great beauty—that we got for our room" for $200. Sam described it in his autobiography in 1906, perhaps even while lying on it: it was an "old elaborately carved black Venetian bedstead—the most comfortable bedstead that ever was, with space enough in it for a family, carved angels enough surmounting its twisted columns and its headboard and footboard to bring peace to the sleeper, and pleasant dreams." According to Albert Bigelow Paine, the ornate bed came from "an old Venetian palace" and "would become a stately institution in the Clemens household." After her brother Charley reported a decline in dividends paid by J. Langdon and Company in March, however, Livy conceded that "we bought a good deal in Italy which of course we should not have bought if we had known that times were going to be so bad—but unless business is ruinous I think we shall be glad when we get home that we have got them." But she also wondered "why we feel depressed at the prospect of not having money—it seems to me that it is not so much because we cannot have the things that we want as it is that we dread changing our manner of life and how very foolish and weak minded that is in people as young as we are." Sam ruefully confessed to Mother Fairbanks that "we are in Europe mainly to cut down our expenses, & we are doing it the best we can."[41]

While in Venice, Sam found a simple way to trim expenses: he abruptly fired Georg Burk, the courier, for incompetence. "I had thought it best to hire one," he explained in *A Tramp Abroad*, "as we should be in Italy" and "we did not know the language." Unfortunately, "neither did he." Sam later joked that he knew "only one ass in the world who is ass enough to have hired a 'currier' to conduct him through a certain country while knowing that that currier did not know the language of that country. There has never been but one ass of that sort; there will never be another." Sam wrote Twichell that

Burk was a "worthless idiot," and after discharging him he had "developed into a pretty fair sort of courier myself." In addition, Burk had swindled Rosina Hay out of ten marks, roughly equivalent to a week's working-class wage at the time.[42]

Sam and Livy yearned again for anonymity, or at least fewer claims on their time, by mid-October. For example, they were entertained along with other Americans by John Harris, the local U.S. consul, at his first-floor apartment on the Grand Canal. "We find altogether too much social life in Venice for our comfort," Livy complained to her mother on October 13, and too many people recognized them on the street. The family fled Venice four days later by train for Florence, where they registered at the New York Hotel. Livy was mollified, alerting her mother on October 21 that "Florence is much more restful than Venice, because we have no social demands."[43]

They remained there for eleven humdrum days, though the biographical record is largely silent on Sam's activities during this period. Only his trips to the art galleries left much of a mark. He mocked the "sappy & gushy & chuckleheaded & theatrical" paintings in the Pitti Palace collection and he was particularly outraged by Titian's *Venus of Urbino* in the Uffizi,[44] which he described in his notebook as "grossly obscene" and "wholly sensual." The figure on the canvas, he asserted, "is thinking bestialities. She inflames & disgusts at the same moment. . . . Young girls can be defiled by looking at V[enus]." He elaborated his attack in *A Tramp Abroad*, unleashing a diatribe about the painting, labeling it "the foulest, the vilest, the obscenest picture the world possesses," not merely because "she is naked and stretched out on a bed" but because her left hand touches her pudenda. "I saw young girls stealing furtive glances at her," he added. "I saw young men gaze long and absorbedly at her; I saw aged, infirm men hang upon her charms with a pathetic interest. . . . Without any question it was painted for a bagnio" or brothel.[45]

On October 28 the family railed to Rome, registered at the Hotel d'Allemagne on the Piazza di Spagna, and again settled into a routine. "I don't think I have gathered any matter before or since your visit worth writing up," he notified Twichell on November 3, adding, "though I do wish you were in Rome to do my sight-seeing for me. Rome interests me as much as East Hartford could, and no more." Sam, Livy, and Clara Spaulding toured the Pantheon, the Sistine Chapel, and the Raphael Rooms and Loggie in the Palace of the Vatican, and on November 1 they attended High Mass at St. Peter's. As Livy wrote her mother, "We have enjoyed Rome immensely & wish so very much that we were going to spend three months here." Meanwhile, Sam again gritted "my ineffectual teeth" over the Old Masters. He speculated that "the first thing a statue dug up in the Campagna does is to go shopping &

buy an offensive & obscene fig leaf"—"the statue that advertises its modesty with a fig-leaf brings its modesty under suspicion," he once insisted—and was amused when, after a life drawing class, he saw a nude model adjust her skirt to hide her ankle. On the whole, he mused, "Rome seems to be a great fair of shams, humbugs, & frauds. Religion is its commerce & its wealth, like dung in the Black Forest." Mostly he savored his two weeks in Rome by befriending the American expatriate painter Elihu Vedder. On November 4 Sam "spent all day in Vedder's lofty studio" on Capo le Case and passed a "very pleasant evening" with him and the painter Casimir Griswold, "spinning yarns & drinking beer in a quiet saloon" on Via della Croce. Livy likewise thought Vedder had "immense genius" and "a large amount of pictures" on "an infinite variety of subjects." She wrote her mother, "I felt as if I could spend two thousand dollars" in his studio "if I had it to spend." In any case, Sam and Livy purchased one of Vedder's paintings, *Young Medusa*, for $250 before they left Rome. They hung it in the library of the Hartford house above the mantel they had bought in Scotland in August 1873.[46]

On November 11 the Clemenses retreated to Florence for two days, where Sam took special pleasure in viewing the "splendid torchlight processions crossing the 2 Arno bridges to see the King, at the Pitti Palace." The family then overnighted in Bologna and Trent en route to Munich, where they arrived at their winter quarters "in drizzle & fog" on November 15 after "a solid 12-hour pull through the loveliest snow-ranges & snow-draped forests" of the Tyrol. "I brought the tribe through from Rome," Sam bragged. "We never had so little trouble before. The next time anybody has a courier to put out to nurse, I shall not be in the market." At the recommendation of Charley Warner, they had booked rooms months in advance in Caroline Dahlweiner's pension on Karlstrasse. Dahlweiner was sufficiently well known to Americans passing through Munich that Helen Hunt Jackson had published a profile of her, "A German Landlady," in the *Atlantic Monthly* for October 1870. As usual, however, Livy was initially dissatisfied with the housing conditions. "Munich did seem the horriblest place, the most desolate place, the most unendurable place!" Sam wrote Howells, "& the rooms were *so* small, the conveniences so meagre, & the porcelain stoves so grim, ghastly, dismal, intolerable! So Livy & Clara sat down forlorn, & cried, & I retired to a private place to pray." Sam and Livy "decided that we would rest 24 hours, then pay whatever damages were required, & straightway fly to the south of France." As in Venice, however, the next morning "the tribe fell in love with the rooms, with the weather, with Munich, & head over heels in love with Fräulein Dahlweiner. We got a larger parlor—an ample one—threw two communicating bedrooms into one, for the children, & now we are entirely comfortable." Livy was soon reconciled to the domestic arrangements. "We are living very cheaply here in a pension," she admitted to Mollie Clemens, and while "in certain ways we lack for the comforts that we are accustomed to at home ... the thought that we are living so much less expensively than at home is a comfort." Over the weeks she variously lauded Munich as "an attractive looking place," a "fascinating interesting city," and a "queer old town." Both Livy and Sam continued to fret over the threat of cholera, especially the risk to their daughters. Livy assured her mother that "the children drink no water except with a little red wine" to disinfect it, and Sam worried that Munich was such "a damp, dark, muddy place" that the water was "full of fever."[47]

Sam rented a workroom in the home of the widow Krotz on Nymphenburgerstrasse, about a mile from the pension, on November 19. "The walk to & from that place gives me what exercise I need & all I take," he informed his mother and sister. As he was transferring his manuscripts there the next day, however, he discovered that he had mislaid his Switzerland notebook. "If it remains lost," he wrote Twichell, "I can't write any volume of travels, & shan't attempt it, but shall tackle some other subject." When "the confounded thing turned up" after a few days, "down went my heart into my boots" because he could not beg off from writing the book Frank Bliss had contracted to publish. Sam's third travel book was unique because unlike *The Innocents Abroad* it was not based on previously published newspaper columns and unlike *Roughing It* (1872) it was not written retrospectively but begun during the trip and composed from notes.[48]

For the next several weeks, almost every morning when "some member of the family isn't sick," Sam would "bundle up in furs & tramp a mile to my den" at about 11:00 a.m. He "went solidly to work—tore up a great part of the MS" he had composed in Heidelberg—"wrote and tore up,—continued to write and tear up,—and at last, reward of patient and noble persistence, my pen got the old swing again!" Livy wrote Mollie Clemens in mid-December that Sam hoped "to have certainly one and perhaps two books ready when we go home" the following fall. He discarded some four hundred pages of manuscript in all and began the book afresh along the lines of "a new and better plan" he formed after Twichell had joined him in August. "I have instructed Twichell to keep the title and plan of the book a secret," he confided to Frank Bliss. "I will disclose them to you by letter, presently, or through Twichell—but I do not want them to get into print *until the book is nearly ready to issue from the press.*—They are in themselves a joke—and a joke which the public are already prepared for is no joke at all." Sam had decided to structure the story about a European walking tour around a running gag: hardly anyone ever walks or "tramps." The narrator might dress "in pedestrian costume, as a general thing, & *start* on pedestrian tours," but he mounts "the first conveyance that offers"—carriage, coach, train, farm wagon, skiff, buggy, riverboat, it made no difference—"making but slight explanation or excuse & endeavoring to seem unconscious that this is not legitimate pedestrianizing." Even the drift of the narrative mimicked the nature of his ramble, "a lazy, delightful, irresponsible high-holiday time on the road" without a care for "whither I went, or how long it took me to go, or whether I saw anything or found out anything when I got there." In other words, he explained, "My book has caught the complexion of the trip" and it would be "a book written by one loafer for a brother loafer to read." As Leland Krauth notes, *A Tramp Abroad* is one of Sam's "most daring and innovative travel pieces, simply because he does in it what no one had done before: he writes a parody of the grand tour or a travel narrative in which *nothing happens*." Sam also entitled the book with a pun. (So much for his professed dislike of this brand of humor.) As he explained in an unused preface to *A Tramp Abroad*, "When I chose my book's title, I only intended it to describe the nature of my journey, which was a *walk*, through foreign lands, that is, a tramp." But "in using the word Tramp," he realized, he was "describing the walker as well as the walk."[49]

By subscribing to the *Hartford Courant* while living in Europe, Sam remained au courant about the status of the "tramp nuisance" in the United States. On February 2 he began, but apparently failed to finish, a letter to the editor of the *Courant* in which he commented on the unwise and unwarranted (in his opinion) hospitality shown to "tramps" in the city. The piece also illustrates the increasingly toxic connotations of the term *tramp*. The local jail in Hartford no longer housed tramps overnight in exchange for a few hours' community service, a new policy of which Sam approved. "Any community which will allow tramps to be assisted by its citizens will be sure to have a plentiful harvest of tramps," he alleged. But "for three-quarters of a century Bavaria has had the reputation of being the only country in Europe uncursed by tramps" because the authorities put all indigents to work at hard labor and forbade "all forms of begging." Sam noted that he had lived in Munich "two months & a half, now, & have walked a mile to my work & a mile back again, every day during that time, through a densely populated part of the city, yet I have never once been accosted by a beggar,—have never once seen a person who looked like a beggar." When Hartford adopted a similar course of action, Sam predicted, "the tramps will as soon go to any other place beginning with H as Hartford. Meaning short-syllable places beginning with H."[50]

By mid-January 1879 he had finished about nine hundred pages of manuscript, "which need no tearing," he wrote Twichell. "They suit me very well.

So the book is half finished." He had completed the first ten chapters and on January 25 he narratively "stepped my foot out of Heidelberg for the first time," chronicling "our first pedestrian tour" to Heilbronn, a trip expected to "take 100 MS pages or more." The book, he hoped, "may really be finished before I ever get to Switzerland." He assured Frank Bliss on February 9 that he was "making pretty good & steady progress, though I continue to tear up MS." Then he actually counted the average number of words per manuscript sheet "& found that I had written only 65 to 70 words on a page, instead of 100! Consequently I was only ⅓ done. I had been writing 30 pages a day, & allowing myself Saturdays for holiday." He had toyed with the idea of portraying a character named the Grumbler, a foil to the narrator like Mr. Brown in his *Sacramento Union* letters from Hawaii in 1866, who would lambaste German customs, cuisine, art, and grammar. In the end, however, Sam introduced a Twichell-like companion named Harris who joins the narrator on his tramp and appears in most of the chapters. As Russell Banks observes, Harris plays the role of Sancho Panza to the narrator's Don Quixote. Twichell accompanied Sam on his European tour for only six weeks of the fourteen months he was abroad but, Sam acknowledged, Harris figured "in 440 of the 531 pages the book contains!"[51]

"I want to make a book which people will *read*," he emphasized to Howells in late January, but he admitted in the same letter that he was too easily distracted to remain in the "calm judicial good humor" necessary to entertain them. "I *hate* travel, & I *hate* hotels, & I *hate* the opera, & I *hate* the Old Masters," he inveighed, and "in truth I don't ever seem to be in a good enough humor with *anything* to satirize it; no, I want to stand up before it & *curse* it, & foam at the mouth,—or take a club & pound it to rags and pulp." In the end, *A Tramp Abroad* was a crazy quilt of shards, fragments, random anecdotes, and loose memoranda written at various times and only loosely organized into a coherent narrative. In the original version of the raft trip downriver from Heilbronn to Heidelberg, for example, he planned to "pick up useful passengers here & there" who would, like Chaucer's Canterbury pilgrims, "tell me the legends of the ruined castles" along the Neckar. While he failed to deploy this device, Sam "manufactured" several legends "to fit the ruined castles." He "tore up two or three of them, but the rest have the right ring to them." He "invented quite a nice little legend for Dilsberg Castle" in chapter 19 and concocted a legend of the "spectacular ruin" in chapter 17, a parody of medieval romance. The hero of this legend, Sir Wissenschaft (or "science"), a forerunner of the eponymous hero of Sam and Howells's play *Colonel Sellers as a Scientist* (1883), slays a dragon with a fire extinguisher. Sam also comically retold four folktales lifted from F. J. Kiefer's *The Legends of the Rhine from Basle to Rotterdam* (1870), including the stories of the Lorelei and "The

Knave of Bergen." He "borrowed" both passages of text and illustrations—or, as Huck says, "I called it borrowing, because that was what pap always called it; but Tom said it warn't borrowing, it was stealing"—from Edward Whymper's *Scrambles amongst the Alps* (1871) and consulted such sources as Thomas W. Hinchliff's *Summer Months among the Alps* (1857) and A. G. Girdlestone's *The High Alps without Guide* (1870). In chapter 47 ("Queer European Manners") Sam defended American manners against the aspersions of "critical and polished" Europeans.[52] In addition, he padded the length of the book with "The Great French Duel," stories about a ludicrous pistol fight between pusillanimous members of the National Assembly, printed separately in the *Atlantic Monthly* for February 1879; "The Man Who Put Up at Gadsby's," about a frustrated office seeker in Washington, D.C., originally published in the Virginia City *Territorial Enterprise* in March 1868; and "Nicodemus Dodge," about a practical-joking apprentice printer in Missouri. He likewise incorporated into chapter 3 a minor masterpiece, "Baker's Blue Jay Yarn," a tall tale about a bird that discovers a knothole in the roof of an abandoned cabin and attempts to fill it with acorns—a self-reflexive, comic allegory about Sam's writing of the book in which it appears. The blue jay, like Sam, struggles to prepare for the winter by undertaking a seemingly interminable task.

Sometimes more interesting than what Sam included in the book is what he omitted from it. At one point, according to his notebook, he planned a chapter about German water closets so revolting it was "not to be read aloud." He similarly wanted to incorporate a piece he had originally written for "Some Rambling Notes of an Idle Excursion" (1877) about a passenger who travels in a heated baggage car with a carton of Limburger cheese and a crate full of guns he confuses with a coffin. He is sickened when he mistakes the stench of the cheese for the odor of a corpse. Howells had persuaded him to exclude "The Invalid's Story" from the *Atlantic* when "Some Rambling Notes" was serialized and, as Sam wrote Twichell, he was "mighty glad Howells declined it. It seems to gather richness & flavor with age." But he was sufficiently cautious on the point to check with Howells again. "I have rung in that fragrant account of the Limburger cheese & the coffin-box full of guns," he notified the editor. "Had I better leave that out? Give me your plain, square advice, for I propose to follow it."[53] Howells's reply, if any, does not survive but Sam again omitted the story. It was finally published in *The Stolen White Elephant Etc.* (1882) along with several other pieces omitted from *A Tramp Abroad* but too good to waste ("Paris Notes," "Legend of Sagenfeld in Germany," "Concerning the American Language").

Still another piece written for but omitted from the book, "The Great Revolution in Pitcairn," was inspired by a well-publicized visit to the South

Pacific island chain by a British ship in the fall of 1878. The essay may also be considered a companion piece to "The Curious Republic of Gondour" (1875) because it similarly betrays Sam's increasing cynicism and disillusionment with democratic institutions and universal suffrage. When the HMS *Bounty* mutineers originally scuttled the ship there in 1790, the island inhabitants basked in a kind of idyllic innocence until an American opportunist, Joshua Hill, was elected president of the island nation and began to govern tyrannically. In 1838 Hill was deposed, the islands recognized as a British colony, and all citizens over the age of seventeen granted the vote. Forty years later, on September 8, 1878, British rear admiral Algernon Frederick Rous de Horsey landed on the island and reported to the admiralty that the residents "live together in perfect harmony and contentment." But in rewriting De Horsey's statement in "The Great Revolution," Sam perpetuated a minor hoax, adding this line to it: "One stranger, an American, has settled on the island, *a doubtful acquisition.*"[54] In effect, he rewrote the Genesis account of the Fall in "The Great Revolution," published in the *Atlantic Monthly* for March 1879, with an American interloper in the role of Satan. The Edenic island is invaded by a stranger named Butterworth Stavely, who subverts the government and manipulates the innocents into electing him magistrate and crowning him Emperor Butterworth I. At length the people revolt, oust the emperor, and restore "the old useful industries and the old healing and solacing pieties."[55]

Yet another story Sam composed in Munich during the winter of 1878–79 but omitted from *A Tramp Abroad* was inspired by the theft of the body of the department store magnate A. T. Stewart from the graveyard of St. Mark's Church-in-the-Bowery in New York the night of November 7, 1878. The grave robbers held the corpse for ransom, reportedly for twenty thousand dollars. For the next several days the press was abuzz with details about the crime, particularly the investigation by Inspector George W. Dilks and Captain Thomas F. Byrnes,[56] the chief of detectives, though by early December public interest in the story had waned. Stewart's body was never recovered. "When the detectives were nosing around after Stewart's loud remains," Sam explained to Howells in January 1879, "I threw a chapter into my present book in which I have very extravagantly burlesqued the detective business—if it is possible to burlesque that business extravagantly." "The Stolen White Elephant" parodies not Arthur Conan Doyle's Sherlock Holmes's stories but, like Sam's "Simon Wheeler" novel and play, the genre of "true crime" stories in vogue at the time. He even lifted a Pinkerton detective named Bullet from his Wheeler narrative, renamed him Blunt, and dropped him into his new story. In Sam's account, an albino elephant from Siam (an ambiguous trope: a type of sacred animal in Eastern cultures, a euphemism for a useless possession elsewhere) named Jumbo disappears upon its arrival in New York and defies all attempts by bumbling detectives (including one Captain Burns) to track it. The squads of police searching for the "dim vast mass" glimpse it in New Haven, in New Jersey, in Pennsylvania, in upstate New York, in Brooklyn, and even in the city of New York, only finally to find it dead in the basement of NYPD headquarters.[57]

The Clemenses kept a low profile during the three and a half months they resided in Munich, perhaps to allow Sam more time to work, perhaps because their budget did not allow for much socializing. He never told Frau Krotz that he was Mark Twain, for example, though he spoke German with her every day. "We have only about twenty five hundred dollars left of our letter of credits and we have sent for another because we did not want to run short," Livy notified her mother. Sam was amenable to extending their stay six months, he wrote Olivia Lewis Langdon in mid-January, because he found Germany "very pleasant"—"even the dirt, now that we are used to it & don't mind seeing it caked around. It is the greatest country for Art & dirt in the world." They at least twice attended the opera, performances of Verdi's *Il Trovatore* the last week of December 1878 and François Adrien Boieldieu's *Die Weisse Frau* or *The White Lady* in mid-January 1879. As in Venice, Sam also fraternized with some American diplomats, among them G. Henry Horstmann, the U.S. consul in Munich, and Samuel H. M. Byers, the U.S. consul in Zurich. Byers noted in his diary that he "saw Mark Twain several times" in Munich and "one night had the pleasure of taking him to the American Artists' Club," whose members included the students Frank Duveneck and Toby Rosenthal. The "largest beer schooner" in the room sat on a table in front of his chair and the consul "was amazed to see him empty it almost before he sat down." Sam read "The Awful German Language" to the artists and students and, Byers concluded, "the smoke, and the beer, and the jokes went on till midnight." Byers remained in touch with Sam and a dozen years later Charles L. Webster and Company published a collection of his verse.[58]

Despite the interruption it required in his writing, Sam and Livy concluded they would leave Munich because, as pleasant as their stay had been, they did not want to extend it through the spring. They had, moreover, been invited to Frank Millet's wedding in Paris on March 11. Sam "buckled in & wrote 400 pages" in eight days to bring his work "close up to half-way" by February 27, when the family and their nine trunks departed. They "had a most comfortable day in the cars" despite falling snow, Livy wrote her mother; overnighted in Strasburg, "where we found pleasant rooms with open fires"; and arrived in Paris at dusk on February 28. They registered first at the

Grand Hôtel St. James on the rue Saint-Honoré, near the Place Vendôme and the Louvre, but their parlor was so spacious that the fireplace failed to heat it. Sam was more forthright in his notebook: "This is the very hatefulest room I have seen in Europe" because it was *"cold, & raw & unwarmable."* On March 4 they moved a few blocks to the Hôtel de Normandie on the rue de l'Echelle, near the avenue de l'Opera, the Tuileries, the Théâtre Français, and the Royal Palace. "We are very nicely situated here," Livy wrote Sam Moffett, "but it is a much more expensive place than we intended to stop in" and "we could not suit ourselves better although we looked about a good deal." A week later she struck the same note in a letter to her mother: "I wish that we were living less expensively at home as well as here," she admitted. "When times seem hard I always regret that we have such an expensive establishment—I seem only able to save at the spigot and the waste goes on at the bung just the same." Sam agreed, writing Elisha Bliss that their expenses in Paris were "something perfectly gaudy." Still, Livy bought several antique Persian rugs for the Hartford house, though they struck Sam as "a shabby and unpleasant property," and in May, when the Fairbankses were suffering financial reverses and Mother Fairbanks touched Sam for a loan, he sent her a check for a thousand dollars.[59]

The marriage of Frank Millet and the Boston aristocrat Elizabeth Greely Merrill was one of the social events of the season for the American colony in Paris. As soon as they were settled in the City of Light, Sam and Livy called on Millet at his studio on rue de l'Orient atop Montmartre just east of the Sacré-Coeur Basilica. The painter had invited Sam to be one of his witnesses and among the other guests at the wedding were the artists Leslie Pease Barnum and William Gerney Bunce, showman P. T. Barnum, U.S. consul general Lucius Fairchild, the sculptor Augustus Saint-Gaudens, and the architect Stanford White. Whereas Livy's gift to the happy couple was a set of china, Sam "contributed a stick of firewood decorated with pretty ribbons, and of course it ranked as jewelry, as any one will know who had to pay for wood fires in the French capital in those days." It was, he joked at the time, "the costliest thing I could find in Paris." Rather than rent a room where he might write, as in Heidelberg and Munich, Sam was given the keys to Millet's studio the day after the wedding to use as a study while the artist and his bride were on their honeymoon. But as soon as he was ready to work he caught a cold, suffered from dyspepsia and rheumatism, and was more or less bedridden for a month.[60]

He had hoped to finish the travelogue in Paris, he wrote Mary Fairbanks in March, because he planned "to work six days in the week here, uninterruptedly for the next 2 or 2½ months." He had had "a dismal time for months over this confounded book, working hard every time I got a chance,

& tearing up a lot of the MS next time I came to read it over." Though he sometimes fit at least part of a day's work into his schedule, he failed in fact to make much progress during these months. In May he insisted to Mother Fairbanks that he worked six days a week because "nothing short of it will ever finish this book." On June 10 he notified Joe Twichell that he had "written matter enough for the book, but have weeded out & discarded a fourth of it & am banging away to supply the deficiency." The manuscript was not yet finished when he returned to the United States in September. One problem was the inclement weather in Europe. The "damnable & interminable winter" of 1879 not only was severe but lasted well into the spring, with a cold snap in late May and a "raw, cold rain" as late as June 1. "We had 4 steady months of rain & cold weather in Paris," Sam noted.[61] (The coldest winter he ever spent was a winter in France?)

More to the point, Sam and Livy's dance card filled quickly after the Millet-Merrill wedding. That is, they jumped back into the social maelstrom and surrendered the relative anonymity they had painstakingly protected in Munich. "I hope we are not going to see a great many people here in Paris, but I begin to be a little afraid because we have not begun as moderately as I could wish," Livy admitted five days after the wedding. "One reason why I don't want to be invited out is that in that case I should be compelled to have new clothes or decline the invitations—I have no dress that I could wear if invited out in the evening." The same day Livy addressed this note to her mother, she and Sam were invited by General Edward Noyes, the U.S. minister to France and a former governor of Ohio, "to drive in the Bois de Boulogne with him"; and she reported they had received a visit from the artist Bunce, from whom they eventually bought a watercolor painting. "We live in such a perfect whirl of people these days," Livy wrote her mother two months later, "that it seems utterly impossible to do anything." As Sam recalled to Howells in March 1883, "We got ourselves ground up in that same mill" in Paris. "It is a kind of foretaste of hell." In order to escape the tumult, Sam noted, "one must live secretly and cut himself utterly off from the human race, or life in Europe becomes an unbearable burden and work an impossibility."[62]

Hardly hiding his light under a bushel, however, Sam delivered a pair of after-dinner speeches during his first weeks in Paris. At a meeting of the Stanley Club at the Continental Hotel in late March he was invited to the podium and spent three quarters of an hour explaining why he was not "able to say anything at all."

> When I look around upon this brilliant assembly, I feel disappointed to think what a nice speech I might have made, what fine topics I might have found in

Paris to speak about among these historic monuments, the architecture of Paris, the towers of Notre Dame, the caves, and other ancient things. Then I might have said something about the objects of which Paris folks are fond—literature, art, medicine, [then, taking a card from his vest pocket as if to glance at his notes,] and adultery.

Sometime in April he addressed the Stomach Club, an all-male group of English and American artists and writers whose members included Saint-Gaudens and the painter Edwin Austin Abbey. As Paine notes with an excess of delicacy, Sam's talk that night "has obtained a wide celebrity among the clubs of the world, though no line of it, or even its title has ever found its way into published literature." The speech was in fact entitled "Some Thoughts on the Science of Onanism" on "that species of recreation called self-abuse" or masturbation, so named for Onan in Genesis 38, who "spilled his seed on the ground." Among Sam's many risqué remarks was this one: "The signs of excessive indulgence in this destructive pastime are easily detectible. They are these: A disposition to eat, to drink, to smoke, to meet together convivially, to laugh, to joke, and to tell indelicate stories—and mainly, a yearning to paint pictures"—an obvious jibe at Abbey. Despite his censure of the pub(l)ic display of Titian's *Venus of Urbino*, his salacious imagination and fondness for masturbation humor sometimes surfaced in his private notebooks, as in this entry: "Girl used sausage & threw it out of window—beggar picked it up—said must be rich folks here, put butter on sausage."[63]

As though starved for publicity back in the United States, Sam also launched a mock candidacy for president akin to the modern joke candidacies of Pigasus, Pat Paulsen, and Stephen Colbert. In a sense, he shared the comic ambition of Tom Sawyer ("there were some that believed he would be President, yet, if he escaped hanging") or followed the absurd precedent of his Hartford neighbor Isabella Hooker, who anticipated that as a divinely appointed president she would inaugurate a feminist millennium. In an unused preface to *A Tramp Abroad* Sam also quipped that, with the increase in the number of tramps, "by and by they may be in the majority; in that day a Tramp will be elected President of the United States: I seem to have a future before me." In a flippant letter from Paris to the editor of the New York *Evening Post* published on June 9 he announced that he had "pretty much made up my mind to run for President. What the country wants is a candidate who cannot be injured by investigation of his past history." Thus Sam preempted his putative enemies by confessing "in advance to all the [fictitious] wickedness I have done"—for example, "I treed a rheumatic grandfather of mine in the winter of 1850" and "I ran away at the battle of Gettysburg," though he failed to identify which army he deserted. "The rumor that I buried a dead aunt under my grapevine was correct," he added, because "the vine needed fertilizing" and "my aunt had to be buried." Nor was he "a friend of the poor man. I regard the poor man, in his present condition, as so much wasted raw material. Cut up and properly canned, he might be made useful to fatten the natives of the cannibal islands and to improve our export trade."[64] Sam would occasionally throw his proverbial hat into the political ring similarly in the future.

The Clemenses routinely entertained or were entertained over the months by such Americans in Paris as Abbey, Fairchild, the Millets, Saint-Gaudens, and the poet and journalist Lucy Hooper. Quite by chance, Sam and Moncure Conway one day crossed paths on the Champs Élysées and Conway promptly transferred his rooms to the Hôtel de Normandie, where he "had the happiness of making myself useful to [Livy] in seeing Paris." Sam was "working steadily" on his manuscript during the evenings so "could not go with us to theatres." On Mardi Gras, Sam and Conway "started out in a voiture and looked in on a dozen fancy balls." On March 21 Sam accompanied Conway and Noyes to a reception hosted by French president Jules Grévy that was also attended by Leon Gambetta, president of the Chamber of Deputies. The same month he attended masked balls at the American circus, the Paris Opera, and the Tivoli as well as an art exhibition at the Palais de l'Industrie. He dined one evening with D. D. Home, the Scottish medium, and the Earl of Dunraven, a Tory politician, and he sat for an extensive interview on April 25 with the Paris correspondent of the New York *World*. On April 30 Sam and ex-governor and former senator Reuben E. Fenton of New York were featured guests at a dinner Noyes hosted in honor of Edwin W. Stoughton, former U.S. minister to Russia, and Horace Maynard, U.S. minister to Turkey. Hjalmar Hjorth Boyesen and his wife Lillie passed through Paris in the spring, staying at the Hôtel de Normandie, and on May 8 Sam and Boyesen took tea with the Russian expatriate novelist Ivan Turgenev ("great in literature & equally great in brave & self-sacrificing patriotism") at his home in Bougival. Four days later, Turgenev returned the favor and, as Sam jotted in his notebook, "brought me one of his books. Gave him Tom Sawyer." He subsequently had Chatto & Windus send Turgenev copies of *Roughing It* and *The Innocents Abroad*. As Boyesen recalled later, Turgenev considered Sam "a real American—the first American who conforms to [his] notion of what an American ought to be" and *Roughing It* "one of the best books written in America; and for its author he had the kindliest feeling." A few days later the family rode about eight miles to Nanterre, northwest of Paris, to see the festival of La Rosière. During this particularly hectic period, Livy was so overwhelmed by social obligations that

she admitted to her mother that "I think every day, well this will be the last[.
W]e shant have as many [visitors] again."[65]

But their social obligations continued to multiply. On June 8, Clara
Clemens's fifth birthday, Sam accompanied Clara Spaulding and General
Fairchild to Longchamps in Bois de Bologne to watch the Grand Prix de
Paris, though he omitted his write-up about the horse race from *A Tramp
Abroad*; it did not appear in print until 2010.[66] On June 30, Livy reported,
they "drove to Vincennes and wandered about there in the woods for half
an hour"; on July 3 they dined with Walter Frances Brown, a young American artist who studied with the painter and sculptor Jean-Léon Gérôme and
who had been hired to help illustrate *A Tramp Abroad*; and on July 4, as they
were packing to leave Paris, the Clemenses picnicked in the Parisian suburb
of Saint-Cloud with "Gen & Mrs Fairchild & some of their friends," Livy
reported to her mother. She added a postscript: "Gen Fairchild reminds us
all a good deal of Father." On July 23 the family returned with the Fairchilds
to Saint-Cloud to take a sightseeing ride in a tethered balloon. "What good
times we had that day," Sam remembered a year later, though in 1882 he
also described the experience as "the frightfullest time I ever saw." He had
already decided not to work any more until he got home, according to Livy,
because he was so preoccupied with the rush of other matters. He surrendered to the melee of living abroad.[67]

Around this time Thomas Bailey Aldrich and his wife Lilian sauntered
through the city, and Tom chaffed Sam for his relative unpopularity among
French readers. Together in a bookstore on the rue Saint-Honoré, Aldrich
mentioned to Sam that he had "asked this shopkeeper if he has any more of
the works of Aldrich, and he says no," but "he says he has several shelves full
of the works of Mark Twain, and more of them in the basement. I'm afraid
you are not appreciated in France." Sam seems to have retaliated at a dinner
party hosted by Madame Thérèse Blanc, author of the ill-fated translation
of Sam's jumping frog story, and her mother, the Countess d'Aure. Apparently at the Aldriches' suggestion, Sam and Livy were also invited, though
Livy demurred, probably because she owned no suitable dress for such a
formal dinner. She admonished her husband, in her absence, to "resist all
inclination to rise before the dinner was half over and take his usual prome-
nade round and round the table." Lilian Aldrich remembered, however, that
halfway through the dinner Sam suddenly rose from his chair and began
to march around the room, "holding his large white napkin in his hand and
using it as an Admiral might his flag, were he making code signals to his
squadron," before returning to his seat. She probably misunderstood Sam's
behavior. He later remarked in his notebook that, in his opinion, the French
aristocracy enjoyed "atrocious privileges" and during what Mrs. Aldrich

considered a "brilliant" dinner he took umbrage at some perceived slight and made a scene. A few months later, Sam admonished Tom Aldrich to aspire to higher literary station and compared Aldrich's apprenticeship prior to his appointment as editor of the *Atlantic Monthly* to "sucking bay rum & make-believe forty-rod out of a sugar-teat in solitude."[68]

In any event, Sam came down with a virulent case of Francophobia during his residence in Paris. As he noted in his journal, "Scratch an F[renchman] & you find a gorilla" or "a savage" or scratch "a F[rench]w[oman] & you find a harlot" or "the F[renchman] is the connecting link between monkey & human being." He wrote several chapters for *A Tramp Abroad* assailing the French but deleted them in revision and they did not appear in print until 1962. In the great chain of being, he observed, "the Frenchman is . . . the conspicuous inferior of the Comanche," hardly a compliment to either group. "The most attractive feature of the French national character, he added, was "its admirable and unapproachable docility." Though he had spoken kitchen French since his piloting days on the Mississippi, he now regarded the language as "a mess of trivial sounds." Or as Jim famously asks Huck, "Why doan' [a Frenchman] *talk* like a man? Answer me *dat*." In other words, Sam considered French "the language for lying compliment, for illicit love" and "double meanings, a decent & indecent one."[69]

He was most dismayed by French libertinism and punctuated his notebook with slanders on the character of the Gauls. France "has been governed by concubines for 1000 years," he asserted. "France has neither winter nor summer nor morals—apart from these drawbacks it is a fine country." "'Tis a wise Frenchman that knows his own father," he claimed, and "every man in France over 16 years of age & under 116 has at least 1 wife to whom he has never been married. This occasions a good deal of what we call crime and the French call sociability." He was appalled by the ostensible immorality of racy French novels ("37 cases of adultery, & they all live happy to the end") and apparently to satisfy his curiosity he read Émile Zola's *L'Assommoir* (1877). He later disparaged the "semiannual inundation from Zola's sewer," vilifying his *La Terre* (1877) as "a tumultuous & ghastly nightmare," arguing that it "beat any French book I ever saw before" in its "filth." He even belittled the relatively benign fiction of "that French idiot" and "rampaging French lunatic" Jules Verne. Ironically, Sam jotted in the same notebook some risqué one-liners (for example, "Couldn't tell whether the short man had a sore throat or piles") and included a couple of newlywed gags, one about an "old maid" on her honeymoon who complains she "never *could* [fornicate] worth a dam on a steamboat," another about a legend tattooed on a bride's stomach: "Try Helmbold's Balsam Coperia." Another was a punch line to a gag about venereal disease: "have *you* noticed that wart?—you're the millionth man."[70]

Even before departing on his European trip, Sam began a regimen of study about the French Revolution. He had read Thomas Carlyle's *The French Revolution: A History* (1837), "one of the greatest creations that ever flowed from a pen," periodically since 1871. During the summer of 1877 he again read it, as well as Alexandre Dumas's *Storming the Bastille* (1853), some chapters of Hippolyte Taine's *The Ancient Régime* (1876), and Charles Duke Yonge's *Life of Marie Antoinette* (1876), the "slovenliest piece of literary construction I ever saw," which, he claimed, "succeeds in making you loathe [the queen] all the way through & swing your hat with unappeasable joy when they finally behead her." While in Paris in the spring of 1879 he reread Charles Dickens's *A Tale of Two Cities* (1859). He was more convinced than ever that the Revolution had been, as he wrote in *A Tramp Abroad*, "hideous but beneficent," and observed in his notebook, "The Reign of Terror showed that without distinction or rank the [French] people were savages. . . . For 1000 years this savage nation indulged itself in massacres—every now & then a big massacre or a little one."[71] These entries serve as a prelude to Sam's comments about the Reign of Terror in *A Connecticut Yankee* a decade later when he had become even more radicalized.

In early July Sam hired Joseph N. Verey for two dollars a day to serve as their courier during a hasty tour of the Low Countries. Unlike Georg Burk, Verey "spoke eight languages, and seemed to be equally at home in all of them; he was shrewd, prompt, posted, and punctual; he was fertile in resources, and singularly gifted in the matter of overcoming difficulties; he not only knew how to do everything in his line, but he knew the best ways and the quickest; he was handy with children and invalids; all his employer needed to do was to take life easy." Livy shared Sam's opinion; Verey "proved to be *perfect*," she wrote her mother. "We had no care whatever" because "he managed everything so splendidly," adding, "we have wished during all these days that we had him last Fall [as] we should have had so much more pleasure in our Switzerland and Italian trip." On July 10 they entrained two hundred miles from Paris to Brussels, "a dirty, beautiful (architecturally) interesting town," and the next day Sam "heard the most majestic organ music & men's voices, ever listened to" in the cathedral there; "[n]ever have heard anything that rose to the sublimity of those sounds." On July 12 they proceeded another thirty miles to Antwerp and the next day attended High Mass in the cathedral, where Sam admired Peter Paul Rubens's altarpiece *The Elevation of the Cross*, though he thought Rubens's Christ was so contorted he seemed "to be an acrobat." The family also socialized with the officers of the steamer USS *Trenton* and the gunboat *Alliance* anchored in the Scheldt River. They traveled on July 14 to Rotterdam and registered at the Victoria Hotel. Sam was impressed by the countryside, "so green & lovely, & quiet & pastoral & homelike," and, as usual, by the "very pretty & fresh & amiable & intelligent" Dutch damsels. The next day they railed fifty miles to Amsterdam, where they spent two nights at the Hotel Doelen. Sam delighted in Rembrandt's paintings in the Rijksmuseum, especially *The Night Watch*, and Livy bought "a beautiful etching" of it for twenty dollars to hang in the Hartford house. On July 17 the family railed through Haarlem to the Hague, where they toured the gallery of the Mauritshuis and viewed Rembrandt's *School of Anatomy*, then traveled two days later to the port city of Vlissingen, or Flushing, where they caught the night boat to England.[72]

"We had a comfortable passage, very smooth sea, none of us were sea sick, but crossing the channel is not pleasant at the best," Livy wrote her mother the next day from the Brunswick House Hotel on Hanover Square in London. Sam soon made his return to England well known, which sparked another barrage of invitations. The afternoon of July 23 he sat on the platform at Willis's Rooms on St. James's Square with several other dignitaries—including the German revolutionary Karl Blind; the liberal British politicians John Bright, David Fawcett, and Sir David Wedderburn; and Moncure Conway—to hear Lalmohun Ghose, a distinguished Bengali barrister and future president of the Indian National Congress, discuss the "grievances of the people of India." They dined with the Conways at their London house Inglewood, where Sam played with a toy jumping frog, and on July 26 at George and Louisa MacDonald's home in Hammersmith they met Charles L. Dodgson (aka Lewis Carroll), the author of the *Alice* books. Sam remembered that Dodgson "was the stillest and shyest full-grown man I have ever met" besides Joel Chandler Harris. The conversation among MacDonald and his guests "went briskly on for a couple of hours but Carroll sat still all the while except that now and then he answered a question. His answers were brief. I do not remember that he elaborated any of them." Sam apparently did not know that Carroll was reticent to speak in groups because he stuttered. On his part, Carroll noted in his diary that he had "met Mr. Clements (Mark Twain), with whom I was pleased and interested."[73]

On July 28 they began a long-planned second visit to Condover Hall, Reginald Cholmondeley's country estate near Shrewsbury, where six years earlier they had stayed for two days. "We remained a week in that house," Sam recalled, "& learned much. Sometimes there were a dozen guests, sometimes two dozen," including the painter John Millais. The welcome respite from the bustle of London was, as Paine observes, "one of the happiest chapters of their foreign sojourn," though it left virtually no record. They left on August 2 for Oxford, where the family parted ways for a few days: Rosina Hay returned with the children to London and Sam and Livy were joined by the English actor Edward Wyndham, who escorted them through the town. "Oxford is so beautiful the grounds about the colleges are something marvelous," Livy wrote her mother. "How I do wish you could see them, the old, old stone buildings with the ivy on them and often with our woodbine on them." The Clemenses returned to London and their children on August 4.[74]

Bret Harte remained a pebble in Sam's shoe. "The more I think of the matter the more I am satisfied that the President never appointed" Harte to the American consulate in Crefeld, Germany, he wrote Howells from the Hôtel de Normandie in Paris. Secretary of State William Evarts, he suspected, "simply *crowded* that shameless scoundrel in." Presumably at the request of the author, Andrew Chatto had sent Sam a copy of *An Heiress of Red Dog and Other Tales* (1879), Harte's latest book. "I have read it twice," Sam admitted to Howells, first "through tears of rage over the fellow's inborn hypocrisy & snobbishness, his apprentice-art, his artificialities, his mannerisms, his pet phrases," the second time detecting "a most decided brightness on every page of it—& here & there evidences of genius." Ironically, in the title story in the collection, Harte extended a veiled apology to Sam. In the wreck of their collaboration on *Ah Sin* two years earlier, Harte apparently repented the haste with which he had ended their friendship. The lead character in the story, Peggy Moffat of Calaveras County, California, seems to represent Sam, whose most famous tale was set in Calaveras County and whose sister Pamela was surnamed Moffett. The offspring of a "deceased humorist," she "suddenly [springs] into opulence and celebrity" and is courted by a "handsome, graceless vagabond" like Harte, "a cyclone of dissipation" named Jack Folinsbee. When he proposes marriage, Peggy Moffat offers him a twenty-five-dollar weekly allowance, exactly the same deal Sam had offered Harte to write another play with him; and Folinsbee tells her "to go to —— with her money," much as Harte had rejected Sam's offer. In the end, however, Folinsbee concedes Moffat's right to spend her money as she chooses; that is, Harte acknowledges Sam's identical right.[75]

Unfortunately, the veiled apology failed to repair the rift between them; Sam either failed to recognize the apology or refused to accept it. In any case, he ranted repeatedly during these months about Harte's failings as a writer. He pictured in late May 1879 a fictional "meeting of Bret Harte's characters" who are indignant "for being so misrepresented" by the author, who merely imagined "the one good deed possible to each of us" and set "the whole world to snuffling over us." Sam complained privately to Howells that Harte "rings in *Strasse* when street would answer every purpose, and *Bahnhof* when it carries no sharper significance to the reader than 'station' would," exactly as in chapter 30 of *A Tramp Abroad* he carped that some asinine authors "think they 'adorn their page' when they say *Strasse* for street, and *Bahnhof* for railway station." In a later notebook entry he derided "Harte's saintly wh[ore]s and self-sacrificing sons of b[itches]" such as Mother Shipman and the gambler Jack Hamlin in "The Outcasts of Poker Flat" (1869). Sam was particularly disturbed by Harte's tin ear for dialect. As he wrote in an unsigned "Contributor's Club" column in the *Atlantic Monthly* for June 1880, "no human being, living or dead, ever had experience of the dialect which he puts into his people's mouths. Mr. Harte's originality is not questioned; but if it ever shall be, the caviler will have to keep his hands off that dialect, for that *is* original."[76]

In this context, a story about Sam around this time, an anecdote usually considered apocryphal, seems perfectly plausible. According to an oral tradition recorded by the humorist Finley Peter Dunne (aka Mr. Dooley) before his death in 1936, Sam crossed paths with the expatriate novelist Henry James at a dinner in London. James supposedly asked Sam, "Do you know Bret Harte?" to which Sam replied, "Yes, I know the son of a bitch." Certainly the Clemenses and Clara Spaulding met both James and the expatriate painter James Whistler at a London dinner in August 1879 soon after their return from Condover Hall. James and Livy chatted before the meal and, she reported, "he was exceedingly pleasant and easy to talk with." James escorted Clara to the table and "enjoyed him very much." On his part, James wrote Howells on August 19 that he had "lately seen several times our friend Clemens." With more than a hint of condescension—the attitude Livy feared—James added that Sam "seems to me a most excellent pleasant fellow—& what they call here very 'quaint.' Quaint he is! & his two ladies charming."[77]

As for Whistler, Livy remarked that "he did not attract me." But Sam saw an etching of Whistler's *Battersea Beach*, a "view from his window on the Thames in Chelsea," in a shop near the Haymarket Theatre and, he wrote Chatto on August 7, they concluded they would buy it for Clara Spaulding.[78]

Back in London, Sam attended a performance of *H.M.S. Pinafore* at the Opera Comique in Westminster and afterward told W. S. Gilbert and Arthur Sullivan that it "was sure to be a great success"; and he accompanied Rosina Hay and his daughters to the Royal Aquarium. On a "raw & cold" Sunday, August 17, he and Livy attended services at the Metropolitan Tabernacle in a drenching rain to hear the renowned C. H. Spurgeon, a Particular Baptist and unreconstructed Calvinist. Neither of them was edified. Livy wrote her mother that she "was not at all impressed by the sermon or the prayers or the singing." Sam recorded his more detailed reactions in his notebook: "1st hour, lacking 1 minute, taken up with two prayers, two ugly hymns, &

Scripture-reading. Sermon ¾ of an hour long. A fluent talk. Good, sonorous voice. Topic treated in the unpleasant, old fashion." He concluded that "Spurgeon was not at his best, to-day, I judge—he was probably even at his worst."[79]

The next morning the family left on a final, hurried three-day tour of the Lake District. The highlight of the trip was Sam's brief visit with Charles Darwin at Grasmere. Sam had read and annotated the first volume of Darwin's *The Descent of Man* upon its release in 1871 and alluded to his theory of natural selection in chapter 19 of *Roughing It.* Upon Darwin's death in 1882 he was pleased to learn that the naturalist "always read himself to sleep with my books." According to Howells, Sam was "glad that he had contributed to the repose of that great man." Darwin told Thomas Wentworth Higginson, too, that "he always kept" Sam's work "by his bedside for midnight amusement." In another iteration of the yarn, when E. P. Parker, a Hartford clergyman and member of the Monday Evening Club, visited Darwin, the naturalist pointed "to a table with a reading-lamp and three books on it" and said, "I don't want anyone to disturb that table, for those are Mark Twain's books, and they are the only books I read; I read myself to sleep with them at night, and I read myself awake with them in the morning." When Parker told this to Sam, the story goes, he "felt very much flattered" because he and Darwin shared a common trait: both had "done much to disillusion people." Sam eagerly read *The Life and Letters of Charles Darwin* upon its publication in 1887 "to see what was said" about him, but could not find his name, though he came across a statement that "quite reconciled him to the omission": that "Darwin had suffered from atrophy of the brain for a long time" before his death "and hadn't been able to read any decent literature." In his autobiography, Darwin observed that he suffered a "curious and lamentable loss of the higher æsthetic tastes" as a result of "atrophy of that part of the brain . . . on which the higher tastes depend."[80]

Livy hoped to extend the trip to the Lake District another hundred miles to Edinburgh to see John Brown. "She urged me, she begged me, she implored me to take her to Edinburgh to see Doctor John," Sam allowed, "but I was in one of my devil moods, and I would not do it. I would not do it because I should have been obliged to continue the courier in service until we got back to Liverpool. It seemed to me that I had endured him as long as I could. I wanted to get aboard ship and be done with him." On August 21 the family railed to Liverpool, Verey returned to London, and Sam wrote an apology to the doctor from the Washington Hotel. "We have been promising ourselves a sight of you" for weeks, he began, but "our short sojourn of three or four weeks on English soil" had been "frittered gradually away & we were at last obliged to give up the idea." Sam conceded in his autobiography that he was to blame that Livy "never saw Doctor John in life again." They dallied in Liverpool for two days, and then boarded the newly commissioned Cunard steamer *Gallia*, "a very fine ship." Coincidentally, they sailed with Sam's friend the Earl of Dunraven, "an uncommonly clever fellow." During the transatlantic voyage, the body of a passenger who had died en route was packed in ice and stored in a lifeboat, and Sam added a grisly note to this news in his notebook: "the hilarious passengers sing & laugh & joke under him" as "the melting ice drips on them." The family landed in New York on September 2 after a tour that had lasted nearly eighteen months. "We were fed like princes," Sam told the reporters at the dock, and "made a comfortable voyage. We have been in some seas that would have made the old *Quaker City* turn somersaults, but this ship kept steady through it all." The New York *Mail* reported that Sam had been "the life of the voyage." When asked if he had written a book while abroad, he replied that he had "nearly finished" one, "all but the last two or three chapters. The first half of it, I guess, is finished, but the last half has not been revised yet; and when I get at it I will do a good deal of rewriting and a great deal of tearing up. I may possibly tear up the first part of it, too, and rewrite that." He noted that his publisher wanted him "to stay in New York and revise it . . . but I cannot possibly do that. I am going to start tomorrow morning for Elmira, where we will stay for some time." The family returned with twelve trunks and twenty-two parcels full of furnishings for the Hartford house and Sam was trapped for six hours passing through customs, which he finally cleared at 8:00 p.m., because "the ship was loaded mainly with my freight." Sam forwarded the cargo north and, after relaxing three days at the Gilsey House, the family headed west to reunite with Livy's mother.[81]

CHAPTER 8

Coin of the Realm

There is a fascination about writing, even for my waste-basket, which is bread & meat & almost whisky to me.

—Samuel Clemens to Hjalmar Hjorth Boyesen, April 23, 1880

SAMUEL CLEMENS WAS unable to return to work on the manuscript of his European travelogue for several weeks. "My book is not finished," he admitted to Frank Bliss from Elmira on September 8, but "I shall finish it here." He had asked Patrick McAleer to retrieve the manuscript from one of the trunks forwarded to Hartford and send it to him. "There is nearly matter enough," he assured Bliss, "but I shall probably *strike out* as well as *add*." As usual, however, he was distracted by other demands on his time. The Hartford Flag Committee solicited a donation to pay for the transfer of the old Connecticut battle flags to the new state capitol and Sam readily complied with a check for twenty-five dollars. "Out of the poverty left on hand by an interminable European trip, I very gladly put up the enclosed," he wrote in his cover letter, joking that he would "subtract this sum from the pew rent" at Joseph Twichell's church. In mid-September Sam visited his family in Fredonia, New York, where he met Charles L. Webster, a civil engineer, realtor, and the new husband of Annie Moffett, Sam's sister Pamela's daughter. Sam was impressed with "his energy, capacity & industry" but he worried that his nephew and namesake Sammy Moffett had inherited through Pamela the Clemens family indolence. Sammy seemed on a path to become "another Orion. This may be a false alarm & I hope it is—but isn't it really time Sam was getting at something?"[1]

A few days after Sam and Livy a returned to Elmira they headed "with bag- & baggage" and manuscript "to the serene hill-top" at Quarry Farm. He wrote W. D. Howells on September 15, 1878, that he hoped "to finish my book here before migrating" back to Hartford but when he returned to work on it he continued to slash and revise chapters. He wrote Twichell two weeks later that he had "been knocking out early chapters for more than a year now . . . because they hindered the flow of the narrative; it was a dredging process. Day before yesterday my shovel fetched up three more chapters and laid them, reeking, on the festering shore-pile of their predecessors, and now I think the yarn swims right along, without hitch or halt. I believe it will be a readable book of travels."[2] But it was still short by several thousand words of the length usually required for a subscription book. Even when finished it never rolled smoothly over the submerged rocks and other hazards; it stagnated in swamps, languished in bogs, and surged in rapids.

His progress on the manuscript was interrupted again when he agreed to introduce his friend Joseph Hawley, one of the founders of the Republican Party, at a political rally at the Elmira Opera House on October 18. The invitation "was a great surprise to me," Sam admitted, "for I had supposed the man was comparatively well known. I shall remain, of course, & shall do what I can to blow the fog from around his fame." He took time away from the book to write his speech. Hawley, he declared, "never sends a tramp empty-handed from his door, but always gives him a letter of introduction to me" and "as a member of Congress he has upheld our excellent President's hands; his voice and his vote have always been for the best good of his country." Livy thought the speech needed "a snapper on the end of it, for it flats out, as it is," so at her suggestion he added a sentence at the close that he had written about John Hay: "Such a man in politics is like a vase of attar of roses in a glue factory—it may modify the stench if it doesn't destroy it." At her urging, too, he changed a word: he had originally written "stink" instead of "stench." A few days after the rally the Clemenses left Quarry Farm, overnighted in New York, and finally returned to Hartford the weekend of October 24, only to discover that many of the items they had bought in Europe and shipped home were broken. "Our unpacking room looks like a furniture hospital," Sam lamented to Hjalmar Hjorth Boyesen.[3]

His first order of business was to rehire their butler George Griffin, who rejoined the coachman-caretaker Patrick McAleer on the domestic staff. "George is going to live with his wife again," Sam wrote Joe Twichell, "unless we get a cook to his taste. I *want* him to live with his wife; it curtails her immoralities." The family "could not spare" Griffin, Sam explained, because "mixed up with his three or four million vices he has two or three invaluable & absolutely unreplaceable virtues—so we have kept him all these years & shall probably go on keeping him till Satan sends for him."[4]

His second order of business was to renegotiate his publishing agreement with Elisha Bliss. The company Bliss's son Frank had hoped to launch—and with whom Sam had signed a contract—never materialized so Sam contacted the elder Bliss to discuss a deal with him. He had feared for years, he recalled in his autobiography, that "this animal had been swindling me." He "was not satisfied" with the "fixed royalties" he had received on his earlier books and "I did not believe in their 'half profit' pretenses; that this time he must put the 'half profit' in the contract and make no mention of royalties—otherwise I would take the book elsewhere." Bliss replied that "he was perfectly willing to put it in, for it was right and just, and that if his directors opposed it and found fault with it he would withdraw from the concern and publish the book himself." Sam and the younger Bliss agreed to transfer their contract to the elder Bliss and Frank resumed his duties as treasurer of the American Publishing Company. Elisha Bliss even agreed, should Sam return to the fold, to promote and publish his book exclusively for a period of nine months.[5] All seemed well. The potential unpleasantness among all three parties had apparently been smoothed over and Sam went back to work.

He submitted most of the manuscript to Bliss the second week of November and Bliss began to advertise the "large and handsome volume" and to canvass for subscribers before the end of the month. Sam told an interviewer that he planned "to commence another book" (*The Prince and the Pauper*) as soon as *A Tramp Abroad* was released, with a third book (*Adventures of Huckleberry Finn*) to follow "as soon as possible."[6]

Sam failed to notice, so he claimed later, that the contract for *A Tramp Abroad* "was with Elisha Bliss as a private individual and the American Publishing Company was not mentioned in it." Bliss ostensibly bragged to Sam later that he used the contract the two of them signed as a bargaining chip in his own negotiations with his board of directors. He offered to sell it to the company, Sam declared in his autobiography, "for three-fourths of the profits above cost of manufacture"—a percentage not only more than Sam's half profits on the book but a share that would have guaranteed the company lost money on every copy sold. As an alternative, Bliss delivered an ultimatum to his board: his and his son's salaries "must be continued at the present rate." If Bliss's account of these events was true, Sam concluded, "it was without doubt the only time during Bliss's sixty years that he opened his mouth without a lie escaping through the gaps in his teeth."[7]

Then yet another matter distracted his attention from the book. Sam was invited by General William E. Strong, a veteran of the Armies of the Potomac and the Tennessee, to respond to the toast "The Ladies" at the Chicago Grand Army of the Republic Festival (or, more formally, the Citizens' Reception and Grand Re-Union of the Army of the Tennessee) in mid-November. The celebration was organized to honor Ulysses S. Grant after his triumphant postpresidential round-the-world tour and, not so coincidentally, to promote Grant's incipient and ultimately failed campaign for a third term as president. "My sluggish soul needs a fierce upstirring" and it would "get it when Grant enters the meeting-place," Sam wrote Howells. He doubted he could attend because the "book isn't done yet. But I would give a heap to be there." He even drafted a letter to Strong declining the invitation with his regrets. Grant's "progress across the continent is of the marvelous nature of the returning Napoleon's progress from Grenoble to Paris," Sam mused, and he expected that "the crowning spectacle" in Chicago "will be our great captain's meeting with *his* Old Guard—& that is the very climax which I wanted to witness." Before mailing this note Sam reconsidered and offered instead to reply to the toast "The Babies." As he wrote the Civil War brevet general Joseph Blackburn Jones, he had often rejoined at banquets over the years to the "Ladies" toast but he had never "responded to the *Babies* & I judged I might be able to throw considerable light on that topic. I thought that if somebody made a good speech on Woman, a speech on Babies would follow after it with a happy appropriateness." The organizing committee in Chicago agreed, whereupon Sam accepted the invitation to attend the festival. He wrote Strong, "I think it is worthwhile to add the Babies to the show. Mainly, you see, it is *new*—the Babies have never yet had the slightest mention at a banquet since Adam invented them. Plainly, this is not right." He notified Jones that he would "come with my (impromptu) speech all tucked away in my memory" but he asked that he not be scheduled to speak late. "I want to have a good time," he affirmed, but "how can I have a good time if I have to sit there two or three hours in the family way with my Babies & not knowing whether I'm going to miscarry or not?" Then he promptly repented his decision. "I jumped into that Chicago business without sufficient reflection," he wrote to Thomas Bailey Aldrich on November 7, "& now that formidable winter-trip is before me & has to be taken." He planned to depart the following day "in order to be ahead of the prodigious railway crowds." Though he dreaded the journey, he allowed he would "rather make two like it than miss the excitement."[8]

Sam arrived in Chicago on Monday morning, November 10, and registered at the Palmer House, the site of most of the reunion events. That evening he sampled performances at three theaters with "a lot of newspaper men," including Sam Steele and Henry Fisher of the *Chicago Times*, and "staid but a few minutes at two" but "saw a whole act at the third. It was the first act of Pinafore, admirably done by children" at Haverly's Theatre. That night he assured Livy, who was monitoring his drinking, that he was "in bed at 10 o'clock. Drank 11 gallons of Appolinaris water & 1 glass of lager during the evening; drank one Scotch whisky in bed, read 2 hours, & went to sleep without needing the other punch." The next day at noon he was awakened by his *Quaker City* friend A. Reeves Jackson, who escorted him to his Chicago home for "an hour's visit with Mrs. Jackson," the former Julia Newell, another of his fellow passengers on the *Quaker City*. As he walked down Michigan Avenue back to his hotel, Sam met Colonel Fred Grant, "an erect, soldierly looking young gentleman," who invited him to a private reception for his father that he was hosting for "a few friends" on Friday afternoon, November 14, "& I said I would." He then accompanied Jackson back to the Palmer House, "& we played billiards from 7 till 11.30 PM and then went to a beer mill to meet some twenty Chicago journalists." They "talked, sang songs & made speeches till 6 o'clock this morning. Nobody got in the least degree 'under the influence,'" or so he claimed. Among the revelers was Melville Stone, the founder and publisher of the *Chicago Daily News*. Five months later Sam recalled in a letter to Stone the "wassail-bout" and "sociable good time in a beer-hostelry at midnight" they had enjoyed. "As far as I was personally concerned," he noted, the evening "had but one blemish about it—the daylight came with a too indecent celerity."[9]

The official festivities honoring the former president began the afternoon of November 12 with a parade of tens of thousands of Union veterans down State Street led by General Phil Sheridan in full dress uniform, which Grant, Sam, the governor of Illinois, the mayor of Chicago, and other dignitaries observed from a reviewing stand constructed on the steps of the Palmer House especially for the occasion.[10] Sam was awed by the pageantry; he wrote Howells,

> Imagine what it was like to see a bullet-shredded old battle-flag reverently unfolded to the gaze of a thousand middle-aged soldiers, most of whom hadn't seen it since they saw it advancing over victorious fields when they were in their prime. And imagine what it was like when Grant, their first commander, stepped into view while they were still going mad over the flag, and then right in the midst of it all somebody struck up "Marching through Georgia." Well, you should have heard the thousand voices lift that chorus & seen the tears stream down. If I live a hundred years I shan't ever forget these things, nor be able to talk about them. I shan't ever forget that I saw Phil Sheridan, with martial cloak and plumed chapeau, riding his big black horse in the midst of his own cannon; by all odds the superbest figure of a soldier *I* ever looked upon!

On the reviewing stand, Mayor Carter Harrison introduced Sam to Grant and they chatted briefly. At Haverly's Theatre at the corner of Dearborn and Monroe that evening, Sam sat cheek by jowl on the stage with thirty or so other grandees, most of them military heroes—Christopher Auger, Grant, John A. Logan, John Pope, John Schofield, Sheridan, and William Tecumseh Sherman—and he made a very brief speech before a standing-room-only audience of over two thousand. For much of the evening the stoic

Grant "never moved a muscle of his body for a single instant" until "at last a speaker made such a particularly ripping & blood-stirring remark about him that the audience rose & roared & yelled & stamped & clapped an entire minute—Grant sitting as serene as ever—when Gen. Sherman stepped to him, laid his hand affectionately on his shoulder, bent respectfully down & whispered in his ear. Then Grant got up & bowed, & the storm of applause swelled into a hurricane." After this reception, Sam attended a meeting of night crawlers called the Owl Club, though once again he hastened to assure Livy that he only remained at the gathering "till 3 this morning & drank little or nothing. Went to sleep without whisky." The next morning he, Reeves Jackson, and several journalists breakfasted at the Tremont House at the corner of Lake Street and Dearborn, hosted by Franc B. Wilkie, one of the editors of the *Chicago Times*. According to the *Cincinnati Commercial*, Sam was "in an unusually felicitous mood."[11]

The climax of the weekend festivities occurred the evening of November 13 with a dinner in the banquet hall of the Palmer House with six hundred men in attendance, including Colonel Robert Anderson of Fort Sumter fame, the publisher George W. Childs, General George Crook, and the Chicago department store magnate Marshall Field. The meal and the fifteen postprandial speeches, mostly delivered by a veritable who's who of Union generals, including James Garfield, Grant, Pope, Schofield, and Sherman, lasted almost nine hours. But of all the speakers, Sam most revered Robert Ingersoll, "the Great Agnostic," disciple of Thomas Paine, and former infantry colonel, who as the twelfth of fifteen orators that evening stood on a table well after midnight and electrified the audience with his eloquent remarks in response to the toast "The Volunteer Soldiers of the Union Army." Ingersoll's "first sentence or two showed his quality," according to Sam. The federal volunteers "broke the shackles from the limbs of slaves, from the souls of masters, and from the Northern brain," Ingersoll proclaimed. "The soldiers were the saviors of the Republic. They were the liberators of man." Then Ingersoll delivered the coup de grâce: the soldiers "battled that a mother might own her own child." The language "was so fine" and "the delivery was so superb that the vast multitude rose as one man and stood on their feet, shouting, stamping, and filling all the place with such a waving of napkins that it was like a snowstorm." Even the transcript of the speech in the *Chicago Tribune* the next morning indicated that this line was followed by "loud and prolonged applause."[12]

Sam gushed to Livy the next day that Ingersoll's address was "the supremest combination of English words that was ever put together since the world began." On reading all the speeches the next day in the local papers, he realized how dull they looked in cold type "but how the lightnings glared around them when they were uttered & how the crowd roared in response!" Similarly, he exulted to Howells,

> Bob Ingersoll's music will sing through my memory always as the divinest that ever enchanted my ears. . . . The words look like any other print, but Lord bless me, he borrowed the very accent of the angel of Mercy to say them in, & you should have seen that vast house rise to its feet, & you should have heard the hurricane that followed. That's the *only* test!—people may shout, clap their hands, stamp, wave their napkins, but none but the master can make them *get up on their feet.*

Sam wrote Ingersoll to request a copy of his "peerless Chicago speech" and on December 13 he read it to the young women of the Saturday Morning Club "& told them to remember that it was doubtful if its superior existed in our language." On his part, Ingersoll replied to Sam not only with a copy of his remarks but with a copy of his book *The Ghosts and Other Lectures* (1878). "I am devouring" the published talks, Sam replied to Ingersoll, because their opinions "found a hungry place and they content and satisfy it to a miracle." Though the two men rarely met in person, Sam unabashedly admired Ingersoll for the rest of his life. When the famous freethinker died in 1899, Sam wrote Ingersoll's niece that, with one exception, "I have not grieved for any death as I have grieved for his. His was a great and beautiful spirit, he was a man—all man from his crown to his foot soles. My reverence for him was deep and genuine; I prized his affection for me and returned it with usury." A year later, he declared that he had held Ingersoll "in as high honor as I have held any man living or dead." Howells, too, recalled that Sam had "greatly admired Robert Ingersoll, whom he . . . regarded as an evangel of a new gospel—the gospel of free thought."[13]

Sam was the fifteenth and final speaker that night in Chicago at "the greatest of all American banquets," as he described it six years later. He was preceded by retired brevet brigadier general Thomas Clement Fletcher's reply to the toast "Woman." Fletcher "killed *all* the enthusiasm by delivering the flattest, insipidest, silliest of all responses to 'Woman' that ever a weary multitude listened to," Sam reported to Livy. "There wasn't a sign of applause & the man ended almost in funereal silence." Despite his request to Strong to schedule him earlier in the evening, Sam had been booked last to hold the audience and he did not disappoint. He addressed the audience in the dining hall sometime after 3:00 a.m. and, like Ingersoll, he stood on a table to be heard. "The crowd gave me a good round of applause," he recalled, "but it was only on account of my name, nothing more," because "they were all tired & wretched." He began: "We haven't all had the good-fortune to be ladies; we haven't all been generals, or poets, or statesmen; but when the toast works down to the babies—we stand on common ground." The audience "let my first sentence go in silence," he wrote Livy, "till I paused & added 'we stand on common ground'—then they burst forth like a hurricane & I saw that I *had* them! From that time on, I stopped at the end of each sentence & let the tornado of applause & laughter sweep around me." Sam Medill, managing editor of the *Chicago Tribune*, reported that for the next ten minutes Sam elicited "laughter," "roars," and "convulsive screams" over thirty times. One of the reporters on the scene remembered seventeen years later that "from the beginning to the end" the talk was punctuated with "uproarious laughter. No speech of the many brilliant ones of that night compared with this." In his conclusion, Sam referred to the "Farragut of the future," "the future renowned astronomer," "the future great historian," and "the future President" who were, as he spoke, lying in their cradles, adding,

> And in still one more cradle, somewhere under the flag, the future illustrious Commander-in-Chief of the American armies is so little burdened with his approaching grandeurs and responsibilities as to be giving his whole strategic mind, at this moment, to trying to find some way to get his big toe into his mouth, an achievement which, meaning no disrespect, the illustrious guest of this evening turned his attention to some 56 years ago [a pause here] and if the child is but a prophecy of the man, there are mighty few who will doubt that he *succeeded*.

Steele claimed later that Sam's attendance at a juvenile production of *H.M.S. Pinafore* two nights earlier inspired the final line of his speech. In the wake of the controversy over his talk at the birthday dinner for John Greenleaf Whittier less than a year before, Sam ran quite a risk by inviting his listeners to imagine a former president and general of the Army of the United States, a transcendent national hero, as a babe sucking his toe. But the snapper worked. While Sam's closing remarks seem rather banal on the page today, the men in the room in Chicago at nearly four in the morning on November 15 went wild with laughter. "The house came down with a crash," he bragged to Livy.[14]

Sam's speech especially impressed Grant, who had sat impassively, "like a graven image," through hours of speeches honoring him in a textbook example of *Sitzfleisch*. "But I fetched him!" Sam bragged to Livy. "I broke him up, utterly! He told me he laughed till the tears came & every bone in his body ached. . . . The audience *saw* that for once in his life he had been knocked out of his iron serenity." Invoking a series of military metaphors, as though the general was a rival to be vanquished, Sam crowed to Howells,

Gen. Grant sat at the banquet like a statue of iron & listened without the faintest suggestion of emotion to fourteen speeches which tore other people all to shreds, but when I lit in with the fifteenth & last, his time was come! I shook him up like dynamite & he sat there fifteen minutes & laughed & cried like the mortalest of mortals. But bless you I had measured this unconquerable conqueror, & went at my work with the confidence of conviction, for I knew I could lick him. He told me he had shaken hands with 15,000 people that day & come out of it without an ache or pain but that my truths had racked all the bones of his body apart.

Hundreds of people congratulated Sam on his speech, he reported to Livy. "Ladies, Tom, Dick & Harry—even the policemen—captured me in the halls & shook hands, & scores of army officers," including Generals Pope and Schofield, "paid their compliments." Sherman told him, "Lord bless you, my boy, I don't know how you do it—it's a secret that's beyond me—but it was great—give me your hand again." Ingersoll "put his arms about me & said 'Mark, if I live a hundred years, I'll always be grateful for your speech—Lord, what a supreme thing it was!' But I told him it wasn't any use to talk, *he* had walked off with the honors of that occasion by something of a majority." If he seemed excited, Sam added in his note to Livy, "it is the intoxication of supreme enthusiasm." He only wished "that you were there to be lifted into the very seventh heaven of enthusiasm, as I was." It was one of the most memorable nights of his life, he wrote his brother Orion. "I never shall see its like again. I never shall hear such speeches any more in this life—I don't b[e]lieve the human tongue can improve on them. And I had a triumph."[15]

The next day Sam attended the private reception for General Grant at the home of Grant's son Fred to which he had been invited and he left Chicago at 5:15 on the Pennsylvania Central train for the East. He arrived back in Hartford early in the morning of November 17 after, as he put it to Howells, "a solid week of unparalleled dissipation." So much for his assurances to Livy that he had curbed his drinking. "I was up all night Monday, Tuesday, Wednesday and Thursday nights & was in bed only four & five hours a day during three of those days." Still, the trip had been well worth the trouble. "I doubt if America has ever seen anything quite equal to it; I am well satisfied I shall not live to see its equal again."[16]

Sam returned to a still unfinished manuscript and myriad distractions. One of them he easily dismissed. James B. Pond, who had opened his own lecture bureau in New York, offered to organize a speaking tour for Sam, who demurred. "If I could spare the time, & had the inclination, and nothing was in the way," he replied, "I would willingly do it for $7,000 a night." He was also urged by Dan Slote to invest in a new form of lithography called Kaolatype, a patented chalk-plate process that Slote expected would revolutionize the engraving industry. According to Albert Bigelow Paine, the idea was ingenious: "A sheet of perfectly smooth steel was coated with a preparation of kaolin," china clay, hard mud, or fine-grained sand, "and a picture was engraved through the coating down to the steel surface. This formed the matrix into which the molten metal was poured to make the stereotype plate or die for printing." Even before departing for Europe, Sam had assured Livy that he had "that engraving invention fixed so I can take it & pay for it when I get back," and while in Paris over a year later he contacted Frank Bliss about using Kaolatype to produce the illustrations for his next travel book. "It looks like excellent wood engraving," he told Bliss, "whereas *all* these other processes are miserably weak & shammy." Upon Sam's return from Europe, Slote pressed him for venture capital and five days after returning from Chicago he admitted to Frank Fuller that he was "about to start in on another ten thousand dollar venture—a patent. Want to come in?—in case it continues to look good? Slote is to run it." Slote visited Sam in Hartford on November 25 to cement the deal. Sam's lawyer Charles Perkins discouraged him from investing on the grounds that the new process "was risky, although it promised mighty-well & seemed to have a deal of money in it." But in the end the temptation proved too great; in mid-February 1880 Sam bought four-fifths of the patent for twenty thousand dollars. He told Orion, of all people, that he believed the invention "will utterly annihilate & sweep out of existence one of the minor industries of civilization, & take its place—an industry which has existed for 300 years." Sam conceded he might be "mistaken in this calculation, but I am not able to see how I can be." He then formed the Kaolatype Engraving Company, appointed himself president, Perkins vice president, and Slote treasurer and capitalized it in the amount of twenty-five thousand dollars: a thousand shares at twenty-five dollars per share. To finance the operation, Sam loaned the company three thousand dollars a month for three months, after which time he hoped "she'll be able to run herself" for a "good long spell." He planned to sell no rights for a year and "if the thing is then a success, we will sell some rights; if isn't a success, rights couldn't be *given* away."[17]

He was also invited by the publishers of the *Atlantic Monthly*, Henry Houghton and James R. Osgood, to a breakfast in Boston on December 3, 1879, to mark Oliver Wendell Holmes's seventieth birthday. It was similar to the dinner two years earlier to celebrate Whittier's seventieth birthday, albeit with two major differences: as a breakfast rather than a dinner no wine was served and the guest list included women. The Holmes breakfast was even scheduled for the Hotel Brunswick on Boylston Street, the same venue as the Whittier fete. Howells had invited Sam to stay at Redtop, his new home in Belmont, but as Sam explained to his friend the same day he returned from Chicago, "the dozen closing chapters of my book have got to be tackled now & stuck to without interruption till they are all written & completed—& this bars me out of the Holmes breakfast & my visit with you." He described his resolve to finish the travelogue as "my confinement with this book," as though its composition was a type of pregnancy or the manuscript itself a child in utero. He would appear before the Brahmins for the first time since the Whittier dinner, moreover, so he initially declined the Holmes breakfast invitation. "I thought it wisest not to be there at all," he wrote Howells on November 28, but Charles Dudley Warner "took the opposite view, & most strenuously," so he switched gears. "My book is really finished at last," he decided, and "every care is off my mind, everything is out of my way—so I have accepted the invitation." Never mind that three days later he admitted that the book was "not as near done as I thought it was, by considerable many chapters" and that there was "five weeks' solid work to be done on it." By then he could not withdraw his acceptance without further embarrassment. In fact, he doubled down by suggesting that he "shall claim the right" to speak at the breakfast "if anybody talks" there, "else it would be confoundedly awkward for me," though he also assured Howells that he could read his speech in advance "& strike out whatever you choose."[18]

Sam decamped for Boston on December 2 to attend the event the next morning. The guests, once again, were the cream of New England literary culture. Among the women contributors to the *Atlantic* present were Rose Terry Cooke, Julia Ward Howe, Helen Hunt Jackson, Sarah Orne Jewett, Lucy Larcom, Louise Chandler Moulton, Elizabeth Stuart Phelps, and A. D. T. Whitney. To emphasize the presence of women at the event, Houghton escorted Harriet Beecher Stowe to her seat. Dozens of Sam's friends and acquaintances were also present, among them Thomas Bailey Aldrich, Henry W. Bellows, Edward Burlingame, Ralph Waldo Emerson, James T. Fields, Thomas Wentworth Higginson, Howells, George Parsons Lathrop, Henry Wadsworth Longfellow, Frank Millet, Charles Eliot Norton, E. C. Stedman, Charley Warner, and John Greenleaf Whittier. Sam met the historian Francis Parkman for the first time at the breakfast and Bret Harte once again was conspicuous in his absence. After the guests had dined on such morsels as filet of sole, roasted oysters, and roast quail stuffed with truffles, Howells again introduced Sam to the crowd, though his remarks were more reserved than at the Whittier dinner: "We would now like to hear something from Mark Twain." Sam's brief comments at the breakfast were utterly inoffensive and even self-deprecating. He freely complimented

Holmes, "the first great man who ever wrote me a letter," and he joked that he had often been told that "I had nearly a basketful [of brains], though they were rather reserved as to the size of the basket." The *New York Tribune* noted that Sam's "witty remarks were frequently checked by ebullitions of mirth." Two newspapers expressed relief that Sam had not violated the proprieties: the *Christian Union* noted that attendees were "spared the rough buffoonery of Mark Twain" and the *Literary World* asserted that there was "no rude break of good taste such as marked the former occasion."[19]

Sam returned to Hartford the next day after "an awful good time" with Howells. But at the Belmont depot, when he apparently attempted to telegraph Livy that he would be home that afternoon, Sam was treated with "insolent neglect by the young lady in charge" so he "told her he should report her to her superiors, and (probably to her astonishment) he did so" with Howells's collusion. Sam was "very much obliged for the trouble you have taken in the telegraphic matter," he wrote his friend on December 9. "I think the employment of 'young ladies' to do a servant's work in a waiting-room is a mistake." Soon "the poor girl came to me in terror and in tears," Howells recalled, "for I had abetted Clemens in his action and had joined my name to his in his appeal to the authorities. She was threatened with dismissal unless she made full apology to him and brought back assurance of its acceptance. I felt able to give this and, of course, he eagerly approved."[20] But this episode set a precedent in some of Sam's future dealings with surly hack drivers and horsecar conductors.

Sam finally finished a draft of *A Tramp Abroad*, that "most infernally troublesome book," on January 7, 1880, carried the last 288 manuscript pages to Elisha Bliss, "told him that was the very last line I should ever write" on it, and left the next day with Livy but without Susy and Clara for Elmira, "very much against Livy's desire." As Sam explained to Howells, "The wear and tear of settling the house broke her down" after they returned from Europe "and she has been growing weaker and weaker for a fortnight." Livy had complained to her mother about the difficulties of reorganizing a house "that has stood empty for eighteen months—the pots & kettles are all rusty, the laundry chimney would not draw," and "in fact all the chimneys smoked. . . . Every thing, every where in confusion." Neither Sam nor Livy mentioned another factor in Livy's fatigue: at the age of thirty-four, she was three months pregnant.[21] Six days before their departure for Elmira, Sam and Livy hired another maid, whom they named Wapping Alice because she hailed from the Wapping district of London,[22] not to be confused with their former housemaid Lizzie Wells, about whom Sam wrote the story he entitled "Wapping Alice" over a quarter of a century later.

During their two weeks in Elmira, Livy hired Katy Leary, the twenty-four-year-old daughter of Irish immigrants, as her personal maid and seamstress.[23] "I was settin' in the library" of the mansion on Main Street, Leary remembered, when "this wonderful, wonderful woman appeared, and she startled me with all her beauty—she was like an angel, almost. She wore a white silk dress and her hair was perfectly plain." Livy invited her "to come and live with me," and Leary jumped at the opportunity. "It was my duty to keep buttons on [Sam's] shirts," she elsewhere recalled, "and he'd swear something terrible if I didn't. If he found a shirt in his drawer without a button on, he'd take every single shirt out of that drawer and throw them right out of the window, rain or shine—out of the bathroom window they'd go." Clara Clemens recollected that Katy Leary and George Griffin "used to fight in such picturesque language that Father often threatened to put them in print. Yet, in spite of the descriptive names they called each other when quarreling, they were at other times the best of friends." Leary remained a part of the family for the next thirty years and, as her biographer Mary Lawton remarked, she "was a potent influence, all over the premises. Fidelity, truthfulness, courage, magnanimity, personal dignity, a pole-star for steadiness."[24]

Sam basked in the "unutterable joy" of finishing *A Tramp Abroad*, or as he put it "of getting that Old Man of the Sea off my back, where he has been roosting more than a year & a half. Next time I make a contract before writing the book, may I suffer the righteous penalty & be burnt, like the injudicious believer." He had "been fighting a life-and-death battle with this infernal book and *hoping* to get done some day," he added. The book of 580 printed pages required 2,600 pages of manuscript, and Sam had written nearly 4,000 and burned or pigeonholed the balance. Bliss immediately put the book into production and Sam "read proof of the *middle* chapter" on January 18. He reported to Moncure Conway that a "big edition has already been sold by subscription in the past 2½ months," though he was not yet sure of the publication date. Not that the matter Sam added to the manuscript during the four months after he returned to the United States—basically accounts of the ascent of Mont Blanc through sightseeing in Italy—materially improved *A Tramp Abroad*. He skipped lightly over their stops in Florence, Rome, and Paris and summarized the nine-day tour to the Low Countries in a single misleading sentence: "From Paris I branched out and walked through Holland and Belgium, procuring an occasional lift by rail or canal when tired, and I had a tolerably good time of it 'by and large.'" He dismissed the month in England in only four words. Hamlin Hill concludes that the last chapters of the book were "even more chaotic" than the chapters that preceded them. Or as Everett Emerson observes, "nothing holds the book together except the binding."[25]

It was issued from "the jaws of three steam presses" in Hartford on March 13 in a first printing of twenty-five thousand copies. Sam was torn between embargoing the critics and promoting the book aggressively. He demanded, on the one hand, that no review copies be sent out before the end of the month. As he explained to Howells, he was "afraid of the general press, because it killed the 'Gilded Age' before you had a chance to point out that there were merits in that book." The travelogue enjoyed favorable word-of-mouth advertising, however. "No book of mine has made so much talk here, since *The Innocents Abroad*," he gloated, "and to my infinite surprise and delight, it is strongly *complimentary* talk." Nor did the formal silence hinder sales. "I believed that I was writing a book which few would read & everybody execrate," Sam wrote Boyesen after it had been in print for a month, "& now, to my stupefying surprise, I hear good words about the book on all hands—& it has sold 35,000 copies & all the steam presses & binderies in Hartford are still hard at work on it, night & day." *A Tramp Abroad* sold roughly fifty thousand copies by mid-June—"which is 7,000 more than any previous book of mine achieved in the same length of time," Sam noted—and some sixty-two thousand copies by the anniversary of its publication. It was so well received that Sam quipped that even he had begun to respect it. "When it reaches a hundred thousand [in sales] I will throw prejudice aside & sit down & read it myself." By his own estimate, he earned "25 cents a word for every word" in the book. It was one of his most widely reviewed works and not so coincidentally the best-selling of all his books during his life. It earned about forty thousand dollars during its first year in print, proving that half profits far exceeded a 10 percent royalty, as he emphasized to Frank Bliss. Elinor Howells thought it was "the wittiest book she ever read," according to her husband, who added that he thought "there is *sense* enough in it for ten books. That is the idea which my review will try to fracture the average numbscull with." As promised, Howells lauded the work in the *Atlantic Monthly* for May, calling it the "delightful work of a man of most original and characteristic genius" and noting that Sam's "humor springs from a certain intensity of common sense, a passionate love of justice, and a generous scorn of what is petty and mean." Howells added, "At the bottom of his heart he has often the grimness of a reformer" and "the 'average American' will find much to enlighten as well as to amuse him," though he also struck a slightly tepid note: "This book has not the fresh frolicsomeness of *The Innocents Abroad*; it is Europe revisited, and seen through eyes saddened by much experience of *tables d'hôte*, old masters, and traveling Americans." Still, this notice pleased Sam "exceedingly." When it appeared, he wrote David Gray, "the surprise of it took my breath away." Once released, *A Tramp Abroad* was occasionally noticed favorably, as in the *Brooklyn Eagle* (a "masterly success in exposing the falsities of the guide book"), San Francisco *Alta California* ("fully equal to any other from Twain's pen"), *Scranton Free Press* ("all this knowledge is combined with sparkling wit"), and *Cleveland Herald*, in a notice likely written by Mary Mason Fairbanks ("Mark Twain has the happy faculty of combining much valuable information with most amusing stories").[26]

On the other hand, it was panned as often as it was puffed—for example, in the *Chicago Tribune* ("a too evident straining to attain a gnat of fun"), *San Francisco Bulletin* ("lacks the freedom and lawless abandon, the sublime audacity, the unctuous and spontaneous humor, the irresistible drollery" of *The Innocents Abroad*), and *San Francisco Chronicle* ("the greater part of the 631 pages are absolutely dull and stupid"). Harold Frederic roasted it in the *Utica Observer*: *The Innocents Abroad* is to *A Tramp Abroad*, Frederic suggested, "what the sparkling, iridescent champagne which the host pours out to his friends is to the flat, sour stuff the servant drains from the bottle the next morning."[27]

Although Elisha Bliss put *A Tramp Abroad* into production in Hartford many weeks prior to its U.S. publication in mid-March, he failed to coordinate its appearance with the book's release by Chatto & Windus in England the following month. As a result, Andrew Chatto was unable to secure British copyright on the book and Sam blasted him for the delay on April 23. "It is through his own carelessness that he is out behind us with the new book," Sam groused to Howells. Conway hastened to correct him from London: "Bliss did not do his duty" in forwarding proof to Chatto "until the work was out in America." Chatto also insisted that Bliss had gone to press in March "without giving us sufficient notice." In any event, the Canadian pirates were lying in ambush. Charles Belford warned, according to Sam, "that he will glut the market at half-a-dollar [per pirated copy] within ten days after we issue; proclaims that he has bought advance-sheets right along from pressmen & understrappers in the three printing-offices" in the United States, "attending to the matter in person here under an assumed name." Within two months of its release by the American Publishing Company, seven unauthorized reprints had been issued in Canada. "Our friends the Canadian pirates . . . were on the market almost as soon as we were," Sam whined to Chatto. He facetiously notified Conway in April, about the same time the book appeared in England, that he had decided to race "north to kill a pirate. I must procure *some* way, else I cannot get down to work again." In the end, Sam estimated that "they hurt us to the extent of 20,000 copies, perhaps." Nevertheless, he received a check from Bliss the next summer in the amount of nearly nineteen thousand dollars for first-quarter sales of the book.[28]

Sam was so flummoxed by the thieves' inroads on his income, however, that in May he proposed to his old Nevada friend Rollin Daggett, now a congressman, that he sponsor a law "making the selling of pirated books a penal offense, punishable by fine & imprisonment, like dealing in any other kind of stolen goods." He resorted to his old Western vernacular, moreover, in making his appeal to Daggett:

> [W]hat a silly & son-of-a-bitch of a law the present law against book-piracy is. I believe it was framed by an ~~goddamd~~ idiot, & passed by a Congress of ~~goddamd~~ muttonheads. . . . My books sell at $3.50 a copy, their Canadian counterfeit at 25 & 50 cents. If I could sieze [*sic*] *all* the Canadian counterfeits I could no more use them to my advantage than the Government could use bogus notes to *its* advantage. The *only* desirable & useful thing, in both cases, is the utter *suppression* of the counterfeits. The government treats *its* counterfeiters as *criminals*, but mine as erring gentlemen. What I want is that *mine* shall be treated as criminals too.

Daggett replied from Washington, D.C., within the week that in an election year "Congress *couldn't* be persuaded to bother about Canadian pirates" when "*all* legislation must have a political & Presidential bearing." Not that this answer placated Sam. Before the end of May he sent Daggett a draft of a change to the criminal code to punish pirates. "Not a soul can be hurt by the proposed amendment," he insisted, "except Canadians & a set of American scoundrels who prey upon & devour our own authors & publishers by selling stolen literary goods. Is there anybody *but* these villains who can find the least fault with the proposed amendment?"[29]

Ironically, the Chatto & Windus edition of *A Tramp Abroad*, though issued without copyright protection a month after the American edition appeared, was widely reviewed in Australia, England, and New Zealand. On balance, it was appraised more favorably in the British Commonwealth than in the United States by such journals as the *British Quarterly Review* ("delightful"), London *Congregationalist* ("this *most entertaining* volume"), London *Graphic* ("full of clever remarks" and "a worthy sequel" to *The Innocents Abroad*), London *Standard* ("certainly equal, if not in some respect superior, to any other continuous effort that has flowed from his pen"), London *Morning Post* ("his good humour and his flow of spirits are inexhaustible"), Cardiff *Western Mail* ("one of Mark Twain's best"), and London *Daily News* ("his exuberant drollery, his boisterous exaggerations, his sly good-tempered sarcasms, his ingeniously amusing parodies"). William Ernest Henley in *Athenaeum* declared that Sam had "a keen, sure sense of character and uncommon skill in presenting it dramatically." The travelogue was lauded no less in the colonies by the *Adelaide Observer* ("a worthy companion to *The Innocents Abroad*"), *Sydney Mail* and Melbourne *Herald* ("quite equal to any of his other productions"), *Melbourne Argus* ("as a piece of pleasant fooling his book is most commendable"), Melbourne *Australasian* ("a good deal of graphic description of a very faithful kind"), Rockhampton *Capricornian* ("numerous amusing sketches"), Perth *Inquirer and Commercial News* ("very amusing"), *Auckland Star* ("his masterpiece"), and *New Zealand Herald* ("full of American humour and freshness").[30]

As usual, however, there were also dissenting voices. Among them were the London *Spectator* ("bears evidence of having been patched and pieced together from all sorts of odd and old materials"), *Edinburgh Scotsman* ("a little wearisome"), *Pall Mall Gazette* ("the humour is apt to degenerate into mere striving to be funny"), London *Times* ("savours somewhat objectionably of book-making"), and *Westminster Review* ("somewhat of a nuisance"). Predictably, the trenchantly anti-American *Saturday Review* panned the book ("some astoundingly stupid would-be-humorous remarks"). The author of this notice was probably Leslie Stephen, the father of Virginia Woolf and Vanessa Bell. In any event, as Sam later wrote Andrew Chatto, the *Saturday Review* would not "compliment the holy Scriptures if an American had written them."[31]

Even before Elisha Bliss issued *A Tramp Abroad*, Sam resumed work on *The Prince and the Pauper*, the children's novel dedicated to his daughters and set in sixteenth-century England he had been researching and writing intermittently since 1877. By mid-September 1879 he had "carried the little 'Pauper' along" to the moment in chapter 11 when "the ragged little true prince, trying to force his way" into the Guildhall to "assert his rights, was hustled, hooted, bruised, & driven away by the mob." Sam expressed for the first time in this episode his abhorrence of mob violence, a recurrent theme in his later fiction and a product of his reading Thomas Carlyle's *The French Revolution: A History* (1837). Five months later he advised Orion that he was "grinding away now, with all my might, & with an interest which amounts to intemperance, at the 'Prince & the Pauper.'" He wrote Howells enthusiastically a week later. He had added over 100 pages of manuscript since resuming his work on "my historical tale of 'The Little Prince & the Little Pauper,'" bringing the total to 326,

"& if I knew it would never sell a copy my jubilant delight in writing it would not suffer any diminution." He "even fascinated" Livy "with this yarn for youth. My stuff generally gets considerable damning with faint praise out of her, but this time it is all the other way." He sent Howells a précis of the narrative:

> It begins at 9 a.m., Jan. 27, 1547, seventeen & a half hours before Henry VIIIs death, by the swapping of clothes *and places*, between the prince of Wales & a pauper boy of the same age & countenance . . . and after that, the rightful small king has a rough time among tramps & ruffians in the country parts of Kent, whilst the small bogus king has a gilded & worshiped & dreary & restrained & cussed time of it on the throne—& this all goes on for three weeks—till the midst of the coronation grandeurs in Westminster Abbey Feb. 20, when the ragged true king forces his way in but cannot prove his genuineness—but the bogus king, by a remembered incident of the first day is able to prove it *for* him—whereupon clothes are changed & the coronation proceeds under the new & rightful conditions.

In the most obvious sense, the novel is a study in environmental determinism or the significance of training in the shaping of character. Sam had flirted with the notion from the very earliest stages of his career. As Jim Smiley explains in the jumping frog sketch, "all a frog wanted was education, and he could do most anything."[32]

This notion is even more evident in *The Prince and the Pauper*. Tom Canty and the Prince of Wales are, in effect, identical twins. They not only are indistinguishable physically but were also born on the same day. The only difference between them is circumstantial: Tom Canty has been raised in abusive conditions in the slums of Offal Court by "a couple of fiends." John Canty, his father, is a forerunner of Pap Finn. On the other hand, Prince Edward is a child of royal privilege groomed to be king. Yet his fantasy of freedom from constraint and convention is as vain and frustrating as Tom's pipe dream of wealth and status and his father, King Henry VIII, is, according to Tom Towers, "as insensitive to the frustrations" of his son "as the drunken pauper John Canty is to the needs of his." Less obviously, Sam wrote *The Prince and the Pauper* with serious political purpose. As he explained to Howells, his idea was "to afford a realizing sense of the exceeding severity of the laws of that day by inflicting some of their penalties upon the king himself & allowing him a chance to see the rest of them applied to others—all of which is to account for certain mildnesses which distinguished Edward VI's reign from those that preceded & followed it." More to the point, he wanted to prove that the ecclesiastical blue laws of seventeenth-century Connecticut were not as severe or oppressive as

English statutes of the same period. His primary documentary source for his argument was his friend J. Hammond Trumbull's *The True-Blue Laws of Connecticut and New Haven*, issued in 1876 by the American Publishing Company. Trumbull was a fellow member of the Monday Evening Club and the philologist who had supplied the epigraphs for *The Gilded Age*. Sam considered him "the most learned man in the United States. He knew everything—everything in detail that had ever happened in this world, and a lot that was going to happen, and a lot that couldn't ever possibly happen." Trumbull had written his history of the Connecticut blue laws in reply to the ultra-Tory Samuel Peters's indictment of them in *The General History of Connecticut* (1781), in which Peters argued that "the Religion of the first settlers at New-Haven was fanaticism turned mad" and included legal proscriptions on baking mince pies and kissing children on Sunday. According to Trumbull, Peters's list of early Connecticut blue laws was "unadulterated mendacity." In fact, compared to the laws in force in England during the reign of James I, "the Connecticut constitution of 1638–9 is the foundation of the republican institutions of the colony and state." Whereas 31 offenses were punishable by death in England in 1603, with the number increasing to 123 in 1819, for example, the Connecticut legal code in 1642 specified only 12 capital offenses, eventually rising to 14. This contrast is central to Sam's depiction of British society in *The Prince and the Pauper*. He declared in his general note to the novel that the "humane and kindly" Connecticut blue laws represented "the first *sweeping departure from judicial atrocity* which the 'civilized' world had seen." As he revealed in the footnotes to the novel, he cited Trumbull's summaries of the English penal code in chapter 15, where a counterfeiter of pennies and an alleged witch are threatened with execution; in chapter 23, where the prince is falsely convicted of theft and threatened with hanging; and in chapter 27, where the prince—who became the first Protestant king of England—witnesses firsthand the inhumane treatment of prisoners, including two Baptist women burned at the stake. In addition to Trumbull's reference to this event, Sam found a similar account of social injustice in Robert Ingersoll's lecture "The Ghosts." In England in 1716, Ingersoll declared, a Mrs. Hicks and her nine-year-old daughter were executed "for selling their souls to the Devil" and "raising a storm by pulling off their stockings and making a lather of soap." Despite these pointed critiques of folly and intolerance, Sam's political conservatism is implicit in his refusal to challenge the legitimacy of constitutional monarchy and his social conservatism is explicit in his criticism of mendicancy, the "tramps & ruffians" whom the prince encounters in the countryside. That is, the novel seems to argue for benevolent despotism, an enlightened King Edward VI, rather than for democratic rule.[33]

In addition to Trumbull's book, Sam cited several other historical sources in the novel. Among them were a pair of guidebooks, John Timbs's *Curiosities of London* (1868) and J. Heneage Jesse's *London: Its Celebrated Characters and Remarkable Places* (1871), and a pair of English histories, Raphael Holinshed's *Chronicles of England* (1577) and James Anthony Froude's multivolume *History of England* (1850–70). He gleaned some details about the life of Edward VI from David Hume's *History of England* (1762) and about the London underclass from Richard Head and Francis Kirkman's *The English Rogue* (1665).[34] In another case of deliberate plagiarism, Sam transferred almost verbatim the set speech of a beggar in chapter 7 of *The English Rogue* to chapter 18 of *The Prince and the Pauper*:

The English Rogue, chapter 7	*The Prince and the Pauper*, chapter 18
For Gods sake some tender hearted Christians, cast through your merciful eyes one pitiful look upon a sore, lame, and miserable wretch: Bestow one penny or half-penny upon him that is ready to perish, &c.	O' God's name cast through your merciful eyes on pitiful look upon a sick, forsaken, and most miserable wretch; bestow one little penny out of thy riches upon one smitten of God and ready to perish![35]

Sherwood Cummings also detects borrowings from Hippolyte Taine. In *The Ancient Régime*, for example, Taine alludes to mendicants and "gutterscum" who "invade a farm-house to sleep there, intimidating the farmers and exacting whatever they pleased," much as Sam mentions in *The Prince and the Pauper* vagrants who "invaded a small farm house and made themselves at home while the trembling farmer and his people swept the larder clean to furnish a breakfast for them."[36] As for the premise of the novel, in August 1908 Sam erroneously claimed that the donnée was "suggested by that pleasant and picturesque little history-book," *The Little Duke* (1854) by Charlotte M. Yonge. Paine corrects the record, contending that Sam's interest in Edward VI began when he read Yonge's *The Prince and the Page* (1866), which includes a chapter titled "The Beggar and the Prince" and features a disguised French princess passing as a peasant.[37]

Sam modeled the prince's protector Miles Hendon on the character of Don Caesar de Bazan in Victor Hugo's *Ruy Blas* (1838). The play had been performed in English translation since at least 1864, with one of the productions starring Sam's friend Frank Mayo, and Sam referred to it in his *Galaxy* column in September 1870. He described Hendon as the prince's "fantastic Don-Caesar-de-Bazan of a Champion" in a letter to David Gray in mid-September as he was writing the book, and he compared Hendon to "a sort of Don Caesar de Bazan in dress, aspect, and bearing" in the novel.[38] The plot consists in large part of Edward VI's trek through the kingdom in company with Hendon, much as Sam and Joe Twichell had toured parts of central Europe and most of the region around Hartford on foot. Additionally, during his exile from the palace the refugee king is schooled in the injustice of the law, a plot twist Sam deployed again when King Arthur and Hank Morgan travel incognito through Camelot in *A Connecticut Yankee in King Arthur's Court* (1889).

One other influence on Sam's composition of the novel was *Yorick's Love*, Howells's translation from Spanish of Manuel Tamayo y Baus's *Un drama nuevo* (1867). Sam and Livy attended a performance of this play, starring Lawrence Barrett, in Hartford the evening of March 10, 1880. "The magnificence of it is beyond praise," he prattled to the playwright. "The language is so beautiful, the passion so fine, the plot so ingenious, the whole thing so stirring, so charming, so pathetic! . . . The 'thee's' & the 'thou's' had a pleasant sound, since it is the language of the Prince & the Pauper." Sam took care to re-create early modern English in *The Prince and the Pauper* just as he crafted seven distinct southwestern U.S. dialects in *Huck Finn*. Before completing the novel, Sam saw Howells's play a second time at the Park Theatre in New York.[39]

He laid aside the manuscript of *The Prince and the Pauper* in late March to work on *Huckleberry Finn*. As Henry Nash Smith contends, Sam had decided since last working on it to shift the direction of the narrative: "He now launched into a satiric description of the society of the prewar South." Jim's escape from slavery had become largely superfluous to the story. He resumed Huck's story where the Grangerford-Shepherdson feud threatens to erupt into violence, a subplot borrowed from the unpublished Simon Wheeler novel. (Much as Judge Griswold admits to Hale Dexter "I do not remember—that is, I never knew" what started the Griswold-Morgan blood-feud, Buck Grangerford confesses to Huck that even the adults "don't know now what the [Grangerford-Shepherdson] row was about in the first place.") In a sense, too, the feud chapters—like the Johnson County War in Owen Wister's *The Virginian* (1902) a generation later—capture the tension between farmers or grangers and ranchers or shepherds in an agrarian economy. The uneasy truce between the families is epitomized by the separation of the families in church, where the men listen to sermons on "brotherly love and such-like tiresomeness" with their rifles at arm's length and the aisle between them a demilitarized zone.[40]

Huck declares in chapter 17 that the Grangerfords are "mighty nice" people and live in "a mighty nice house" but by the end of chapter 18 the elopement of Sophia Grangerford and Harney Shepherdson triggers a paroxysm of carnage. Suddenly homeless again, Huck with his bachelor freedoms might have lit out for the Territory at this stage of the narrative but the novel was only half written. Instead, Sam thought of a way to continue Huck's adventures on the river. Unlike the raft that is crushed to splinters at the end of the Neckar River excursion in *A Tramp Abroad*, Sam decided that the raft on which Jim and Huck float downriver is "only *crippled* by steamer" and, moreover, Jim survives the collision with the steamboat and rejoins Huck for more escapades. "You mean to say our old raft warn't smashed all to flinders?" Huck asks Jim, who replies, "She was tore up a good deal—one en' of her was; but dey warn't no great harm done." But Jim's resurrection raises a related question: Why would a fugitive slave resume his flight south after passing the confluence of the Mississippi and Ohio Rivers at Cairo? Sam solved this problem with a sort of ragged genius in chapter 19 by introducing a pair of scam artists who commandeer the raft and masquerade as the Duke of Bridgewater (or Bilgewater) and the lost Dauphin of France. His satire of royalty in the depiction of these "low-down humbugs and frauds" was based on his recent reading about the French Revolution.[41]

Sam added two additional chapters to *Huck Finn* after the hooligans join the cast before he finally "knocked off" his work on the manuscript in Hartford in early May. He had no intention "to go to work again till we go away [to Elmira] for the summer, 5 or 6 weeks hence," he advised Howells. In chapter 21 the rapscallion who impersonates the king delivers a revival sermon and collects eighty-seven dollars for the avowed purpose of proselytizing among the pirates of the Indian Ocean. As the king explains, "heathens don't amount to shucks alongside of pirates to work a camp-meeting with." In chapter 22 Huck witnesses the murder of the Bricksville town drunk Boggs by Colonel Sherburn, an incident based on the Hannibal shooting of Sam Smarr by William Owsley in 1845. Sam again shelved the novel at this point, with an angry lynch mob headed toward Sherburn's house, "snatching down every clothes-line they come to to do the hanging with."[42]

In spring 1880 Sam had four different projects on the boards: *The Prince and the Pauper*, *Adventures of Huckleberry Finn*, and the never-finished "Captain

Stormfield's Visit to Heaven" and "The Diary of Shem in the Ark." "It is my habit to keep four or five books in the process of erection all the time, and every summer add a few courses of bricks to two or three of them," he explained in 1887, "but I cannot forecast which of the two or three it is going to be. It takes seven years to complete a book by this method, but still it is a good method." His docket was so full that he suggested to Orion in February 1880 that he "write two books which it has long been my purpose to write" were his deck clear. In truth, the concepts were variations on the same theme—"The Autobiography of a Coward" and "Confessions of a Life That Was a Failure." For either of the two projects, Sam explained,

> My plan was simple—to take the absolute facts of my own life & tell them simply & without ornament or flourish, exactly as they occurred, with this difference, that I would turn every courageous action (if I ever performed one) into a cowardly one & every success into a failure. . . . Tackle one of these books & simply tell your story to *yourself*, laying all hideousnesses utterly bare, reserving nothing. Banish the idea of an audience & all hampering things. If the book is well done, there's a market for it.

Sam cited Jean-Jacques Rousseau's *Confessions* (1782) and Giacomo Casanova's memoirs (1822) as examples of the type of chronicle his brother should tackle. Orion was smitten with the idea and began to write "The Autobiography of an Ass" the same day he received Sam's proposal. He "wrote a hundred pages or so" about his childhood and adolescence "with a startling minutia of detail and frankness," according to Paine, one of only four people known to have read any part of the manuscript. (The other three were Sam, Howells, and Sam's private secretary Isabel Lyon.) Orion "mailed them to his brother for inspection" with a promise to send him a chapter per day until the book was finished.[43]

Sam was initially supportive. He expected Orion's memoirs to be, Paine averred, "one long record of fleeting hope, futile effort, and humiliation. It is the story of a life of disappointment; of a man who has been defeated and beaten down and crushed by the world until he has nothing but confession left to surrender." The "simple narrative" of the opening pages was "all that [Sam] had dreamed it would be" and he complimented Orion in early May. "It is a model autobiography," he wrote his brother, then offered some advice:

> Continue to develop your own character in the same gradual, inconspicuous & apparently unconscious way. The reader, up to this time, may have his doubts, perhaps, but he can't say decidedly, "This writer is not such a simpleton as he has been letting on to be." . . . Keep him in that state of mind. If, when you shall have finished, the reader shall say, "The man *is* an ass, but I

really don't know whether he knows it or not," your work will be a triumph. Stop *re-writing*. I saw places in your last batch where re-writing had done formidable injury. Do not try to find those places, else you will mar them further by trying to better them. It is perilous to revise a book while it is under way. All of us have injured our books in that foolish way.

He ended with a final recommendation: "when you recollect something which belonged in an earlier chapter, do not go back, but jam it in *where you are*. Discursiveness does not hurt an autobiography in the least." As if to prove the point, Sam applied this principle to his own memoirs a quarter of a century later. Meanwhile, their sister Pamela thanked Sam for "the high opinion you express of Orion's book."[44]

Sam went so far as to send sections of Orion's autobiography to Howells in June to consider for publication in the *Atlantic Monthly*. In his cover letter he insisted that, in his opinion, bits of it were "absolutely delicious." Howells was diplomatic in declining the submission: "I have read the autobiography with close and painful interest. It wrung my heart, and I felt haggard after I had finished it." The best parts of it were those related to Sam's boyhood, Howells noted; "they will be valuable material hereafter. But the writer's soul is laid *too* bare: it is shocking. I can't risk the paper in the Atlantic." Orion blamed his brother for failing to place any part of the narrative with a press after encouraging him to undertake it but he also refused to slacken the pace of his writing. He often sent ten to twenty pages of manuscript a day to Sam, who soon lost interest in it. The sheaf of manuscript Orion mailed on May 31, 1880, for example, included "a skip of 28 years," from 1851 to 1879, when he was excommunicated from the Presbyterian Church in Keokuk. "If I can get my religious ideas widely read," Orion maintained, "I am willing to let the public think of me personally as they please." But as Paine griped, Orion "drifted off into theological byways; into discussions of his excommunication and infidelities, which were frank enough, but lacked human interest." Rather than badger Orion with daily or weekly installments of text, Sam urged him "to let his manuscript accumulate, and to send it in one large consignment at the end." As a result, on January 18, 1882, Orion sent Sam a complete, 2,523-page manuscript retitled "The Autobiography of a Crank." Sam was disappointed in the narrative as a whole, however. As he told Rudyard Kipling in 1890, he persuaded "a man painfully given to speaking the truth on all occasions—a man who wouldn't dream of telling a lie," to "write his autobiography for his own amusement and mine. He did it. The manuscript would have made an octavo volume but, good honest man though he was, in every single detail of his life that I knew about he turned out, on paper, a formidable liar." Sam claimed in his own autobiography in

April 1906 that Orion in his life story "was constantly making a hero of himself" and "constantly forgetting to put in the episodes which placed him in an unheroic light. I knew several incidents of his life which were distinctly and painfully unheroic, but when I came across them in his autobiography they had changed color." Sam read some eight hundred pages of the manuscript and told Pamela that he "found but little to preserve." In November 1883 Sam demanded that Orion swear that for an entire year he would "make no proposition of a business or literary nature" to him "in writing, by telegraph, or other vehicle"; neither would Orion "ask [Sam's] advice concerning any business or literary project of mine" nor "submit any piece of writing to him for judgment or criticism"; nor would he lecture. Sam claimed in April 1906 that he "destroyed a considerable part" of the manuscript and in July 1907 virtually all of it that remained was stolen with Paine's bag in Grand Central Station. Though Paine cites the manuscript occasionally in *Mark Twain: A Biography* (1912), only a few leaves survive among the Mark Twain Papers.[45]

Sam loafed for most of the spring of 1880, especially after he decided to postpone all but essential literary labor until he arrived at Quarry Farm in late June. He and Livy planned "to spend a week secretly in a Boston hotel, by & by," he wrote Howells in early March, "& hope you & Mrs. Howells will not be sorry to hear it." Unfortunately, the trip was delayed for over a month. Meanwhile, Sam contributed a sentiment to an autograph collections to benefit the Irish Relief Fund and he spoke "before a large audience" in Hartford on April 2 on behalf of Republican Party candidates in the upcoming city election. The day before the election, he delivered a paper, "On the Decay of the Art of Lying," before the Monday Evening Club. "Lying is universal—we *all* do it; we all *must* do it," he announced. "Therefore, the wise thing is for us diligently to train ourselves to lie thoughtfully, judiciously." The entire family, including the children and Rosina Hay, traveled to Boston on April 12 "to give Livy a week's rest & change of aggravations—usually styled 'change of scene.'" They spent parts of two days and a night with the Howellses in Belmont and enjoyed "a good time" at James and Annie Fields's home on Beacon Hill before returning to Hartford. The evening of May 11 he read from his work in the drawing room of Armsmear, the home of Elizabeth Colt, widow of the founder of Colt's Patent Fire-Arms Manufacturing Company, on behalf of the Decorative Arts Society of Hartford, of which Livy was an active member. Similarly, he served on a committee that organized a bazaar held on June 5 to benefit the Union for Home Work, which sponsored reading rooms, a day nursery for working mothers, sewing and cooking schools, a lending library, and other charities. Among the other committee members were such pillars of the community as newly elected mayor Morgan Bulkeley, General William B. Franklin, William Hamersley, General Joe Hawley, and Charley Warner. Sam also contributed to the fair newspaper a chapter he deleted at Howells's urging from *The Prince and the Pauper* entitled "A Boy's Adventure."[46] Over the ensuing months Sam also contributed both ten dollars and "A Tale for Struggling Young Poets" to the paper of the Buffalo Homeopathic Fair; twenty-five dollars and a set of his books to the Florida, Missouri, schools; and ten dollars to the Union Veteran Corps fair in Washington.[47]

The family finally left for Elmira and Quarry Farm on June 15, 1880, and railed to New York, where they overnighted at the Gilsey House. Sam saw part of a performance of *Hazel Kirke* starring Georgia Cavyan and Effie Ellsler at the Madison Square Theater and the next morning the clan entrained for Elmira in a special sleeping car Sam hired because Livy, now almost eight months pregnant, needed "to lie down a good deal." Had they not had an entire car to themselves, Sam reckoned, "Livy & the children would have found the ten-hour trip wholly unendurable. This is the first time Livy ever made that trip without arriving in a played-out condition. She shall always go by special car hereafter, until we bust." After a couple of weeks with Livy's mother at the Langdon mansion on Main Street, the Clemenses moved up East Hill to the farm. Sam was unable to write uninterruptedly even in his study on the bluff overlooking the Chemung River valley "for one can't work during a lying-in season," though he had reeled off an additional hundred manuscript pages of *The Prince and the Pauper* and "one or two magazine articles" by July 19. One of the tales, "Edward Mills and George Benton," in which Sam again deployed the device of twinning ("Baby Mills took care of his toys; Baby Benton always destroyed his in a very brief time"), reads like a preliminary study for the characters of Tom Driscoll and Chambers in *The Tragedy of Pudd'nhead Wilson* (1894). This "telling satire on the mawkish sympathy felt for criminals and worthless wretches," the *Boston Herald* noted, also echoes Sam's critique of the "sappy women" with "their permanently impaired and leaky water-works" who petition the governor to pardon Injun Joe in the final pages of *Tom Sawyer*.[48]

Jane Lampton Clemens (aka Jean), named for Sam's mother, was born at Quarry Farm on July 26. Livy's doctor Rachel Brooks Gleason and Sam were both initially concerned about the health of the new mother, though she was soon out of danger. He announced to his sister Pamela that at about seven pounds Jean was "as fat as a watermelon, & just as sweet & good, & often just as wet," and he reported to Howells that she "arrived perfectly sound but with no more baggage than I had when I was on the river." She was "the prettiest & perfectest little creature we have turned out yet. Susie & Bay [Clara] could not worship it more if it were a cat." In a note to Elinor

Howells a month later, to be sure, Sam lightly canceled a line in which he compared Jean to "an orange that is a little mildewed in spots." Ironically, the same day Jean was born, Mary Fairbanks wrote Sam to nudge him along on his novel: "The time has come for your *best* book. I do not mean your most taking book, with the most money in it, I mean your best contribution to American literature. I have thought of it a great deal of late and wished the thought & wish would inspire you my boy." E. P. Parker offered Sam similar counsel that betrayed an all too common bias against humor writing:

> Your rank as a writer of humorous things is high enough—but, do you know—Clemens—that it is in you to do some first-class serious or sober work. Now let me say *to* you what I have repeatedly said *of* you—that I know no American writer of your generation, who is capable of writing such forcible, sinewy, racy English as you. You are abundantly capable of turning out some work that shall bear the stamp of your individuality plainly enough, and at the same time have a sober character and a solid worth & a permanent value. It might not pay in "shekels," but it would do you vast honor, and give your friends vast pleasure.

It was, of course, dreadful advice. While *The Prince and the Pauper* was one of Sam's most carefully planned and plotted novels, it was also one of his poorest. Even he conceded that by surrendering to literary convention and conventional pieties he had strayed from the deep channel. Joe Goodman, after learning that Sam was writing "a story of remote English life," struck a prudent note of caution in his next letter: "I'm very impatient to see it, for of all things I have been anxious that you should try your hand at another novel. But what could have sent you groping among the driftwood of the Deluge for a topic when you would have been so much more at home in the wash of today?"[49]

Only after mother and baby were safe and healthy did Sam return to work on the novel. "I wrote the first half of the climax chapter of 'The Little Prince and the Little Pauper' three days ago," he wrote Ned House on August 31, and he expected that "another week's work will finish that book." As usual, he underestimated the amount of writing that remained. He added a chapter to the manuscript on September 11 and finished a draft three days later, though he continued to tinker with it. The family left Elmira on September 27 to return to Hartford via New York, where they again stayed at the Gilsey House and shopped for toys at the Schwartz Toy Bazaar (later FAO Schwartz). Once again, Sam exercised caution in making travel arrangements. "I have chartered a special car—a sleeper for a daylight train— for the better conservation of Mrs. C's health on that long trip," he explained to David Gray, "& I don't know but it might have been an economy to charter some New York hotel, too, seeing we are to remain there a day or two for Madam to rest."[50]

Back in the Connecticut capital, Sam hit the ground running his mouth. The presidential campaign between the Democrat Winfield Hancock and the Republican James A. Garfield was in full swing and Sam rallied to Garfield's flag, though he had been critical of Garfield's complicity in the Crédit Mobilier scandal in 1873. The dark-horse candidate Garfield secured the nomination at the Republican National Convention in Chicago in early June, and on June 15, the same day his family left Hartford for Elmira for the summer, Sam wrote Howells that "Garfield suits me thoroughly & exactly. I prefer him to Grant"—or, more precisely, he preferred Garfield to the Republican Party hacks who had promoted Grant's candidacy in their own self-interest. "The presidency can't add anything to Grant—he will shine on, without it. It is ephemeral, he is eternal." Ironically, Sam's brother-in-law Charley Langdon had been a Grant delegate to the convention.[51] Though denied the nomination, Grant stumped for Garfield, including stops in Connecticut. As a member of the reception committee that welcomed Grant to Hartford, Sam railed to Boston on October 14, a day before the other members, to see Howells and Ned House. He registered at the Brunswick Hotel in the Back Bay neighborhood and joined the delegation that escorted the former president to the city on October 16. He introduced Grant at a rally in Bushnell Park that afternoon with a speech that was mostly political boilerplate. He referred to Grant's willingness upon his election in 1868 to resign his "great office of the General of the Army" and the salary for life it guaranteed to risk "the chance mercies of a precarious existence" after leaving the White House. By campaigning for Garfield he was "mightily contributing toward saving your country once more, this time from dishonor and shame and from commercial disaster." Addressing Grant directly, Sam assured him, "Your country stands ready from this day forth to testify her measureless love and pride and gratitude toward you in every conceivable *inexpensive* way." This final line, Sam bragged to Howells, "invoked the loudest shout, & the longest, & the most full-hearted that was heard in Hartford that day. It started in laughter but ended in a thunder of endorsement." As in Chicago eleven months earlier, "Grant came near laughing his entire head off."[52]

Sam followed his introduction of Grant with an address at a Republican rally at the Hartford Opera House the evening of October 26, a week before Election Day, before an audience of nearly twenty-five hundred. In his speech he launched an ironic defense of "tariff reform," the repeal of the protective tariff proposed by the influential Democratic congressman Fernando

Wood, a former mayor of New York and creature of Tammany Hall. "I am going to vote the Republican ticket, myself, from old habit," Sam allowed, but he wanted to persuade his listeners "to vote the Democratic ticket, because if you throw the government of this country into the hands of the Republicans they will unquestionably kill that Wood tariff project. But if you throw this government into the hands of the Democrats, the Wood tariff project will become the law of the land and every one of us will reap his share of the enormous benefits resulting from it." The "chief benefit" would be cleaner air because all the factories would close. Workers would enjoy "a long holiday season" and "the streets of the North would be adorned with soft, rich carpets of grass." Everyone would be a tramp, and tramps could, in the paradise promised by universal suffrage, "outvote anything that can be devised to hamper us." Sam appealed even to the Irish Democrats in the opera house by warning that reduced tariffs would restore England as their oppressor—"perhaps the deepest plunge into demagoguery" he ever took, according to Louis J. Budd. Two nights later, Sam also addressed a crowd at a German Republican meeting on behalf of Garfield.[53]

On election night, November 2, Sam tracked the returns with Joe Twichell and other fellow Republicans at the Opera House until midnight. The *Hartford Courant* reported the next day that ten thousand people filled the streets of the city awaiting the results. "When the news was all in" and with Garfield's victory secure, Sam delivered his third political speech of the season, a funeral oration over the Democratic Party, which he personified as

> a footsore political wanderer, a hoary political tramp, an itinerant poor actor familiar with many disguises, a butcher of many parts. In the North he played "Protection" and "Hard Money." In the West he played "Protection," "Free Trade," "Hard Money," and "Soft Money," changing disguises and parts according to the exigencies of the occasion. In the South he played "Tariff for Revenue"; in the North and West he played "The Apostle of Freedom," and mouthed the sacred shibboleths of liberty with cruel and bloody lips.

The *Chicago Tribune* reported that "almost every sentence was greeted with roars of laughter" and, as Sam noted, in the course of the evening the assembly sang the hymn "Praise God from Whom All Blessings Flow" in "a mighty chorus."[54] Who would have guessed that, four years hence, he would abandon the Republican Party and endorse the Democratic candidate for president?

Four days after Garfield's election, Sam addressed the Middlesex Club, a group of staunch Republicans, at Young's Hotel in Boston. Among the others present were his Hartford friend Marshall Jewell, chair of the Republican National Committee, and former Massachusetts governors George S.

Boutwell and Nathaniel P. Banks. During his brief speech, he cracked wise that in the "biggest triumph" of the canvass Republican voters in Connecticut had "elected seven sheriffs out of eight" running for the office "and that is as it should be, because the criminals and officers ought to be of opposite parties." He also correctly predicted that the state would send a Republican to the U.S. Senate and "that man will be that good soldier, and wise man and pure man, that able man and statesman, General Joe Hawley, unquestionably the ablest and most eminent man in Connecticut except me."[55]

When the humorist Robert Burdette of the Burlington, Iowa, *Hawkeye* lectured in Hartford the evening of December 10, 1880, he was introduced onstage by Sam and stayed overnight at the Clemens home. Burdette afterward published a glowing report of the hospitality he received at Sam's fireside. He had "never been in a home more beautifully home-like than this palace of the king of humorists," he reported, and "the humor and drollery that sparkle in [Sam's] conversation is as utterly unaffected and natural as sunlight." Sam also noted in his journal one of Burdette's ribald remarks over the weekend: "Texas girl lassos wild horse & rides home; Boston girl captures codfish & rides him home astride. Burdette—'This accounts for the peculiar smell of the codfish.'" Burdette also remarked later on Sam's insatiable tobacco habit: "he loves a good cigar even better than Grant does."[56]

A cigar in his mouth or between his fingers was a quintessential part of Sam's persona. His grandniece Jean Webster thought he was "the smokiest man she had ever met" and "when I used to climb on his knee I classified him among the men of my childish acquaintance as the one most like a human furnace." Charles H. Clark, his Hartford friend, recalled that Sam smoked "from half-past eight in the morning to half-past ten at night, stopping only when at meals." Clark calculated that each cigar lasted "about forty minutes" and that Sam consumed "from fifteen to twenty cigars every day." By his own estimate, Sam smoked ten per day during the nine months of the year he lived in Hartford and increased the number to fifteen during the summer months in Elmira when he worked, "and if my interest reaches the enthusiastic point, I smoke more. I smoke with all my might, and allow no intervals." In January 1875, when he was ill "for the first time in 21 years," as he wrote Howells, he exploited the opportunity to "take my meals in bed, neglect all business without a pang, & smoke 18 cigars a day." Nicotine was a stimulant to Sam's writing or, as he explained in 1882, "I find cigar smoking to be the best of all inspirations for the pen and, in my particular case, no sort of detriment to the health." His incessant smoking in the house no doubt contributed to Livy's heart problems. Perhaps the most frequent commentator on Sam's tobacco habit, however, was Howells. After a visit to Cambridge in November 1876, for example, Howells admitted that "the smoke and the Scotch and the late hours almost kill[ed]" him and Elinor; "but we look each other in the eye when [you] are gone, and say what a glorious time it was, and air the library." In his memoir of Sam, Howells also recalled that

> whenever he had been a few days with us, the whole house had to be aired, for he smoked all over it from breakfast to bedtime. He always went to bed with a cigar in his mouth, and sometimes, mindful of my fire insurance, I went up and took it away, still burning, after he had fallen asleep. I do not know how much a man may smoke and live, but apparently he smoked as much as a man could.

So familiar to the public was Sam as a smoker that a tobacco company produced a Mark Twain brand of cigars with advertising that featured a portrait of him. Joe Goodman asked "if he derived any revenue" from the use of the image and Sam admitted he did not and had even tried to stop it but discovered that a celebrity "had no property right in his own likeness, except in special copyrighted reproductions."[57]

In failing health, Elisha Bliss retired from the American Publishing Company in May 1880 and died of heart disease on September 28, two weeks after Sam finished a draft of *The Prince and the Pauper*. Within a month Sam finally saw a balance sheet detailing the income from sales of all his books issued by the company and their production costs and discovered that Bliss had routinely swindled him since 1870, exactly as Orion alleged. Had Sam been paid half profits as he had demanded rather than a percentage of sales, he would have earned tens of thousands of dollars in additional royalties on the third of a million copies of his books Bliss had peddled over the previous decade. "I have lost considerably by all this nonsense—sixty thousand dollars, I should say," he wrote Orion on October 24. He later inflated this figure to a hundred thousand dollars. Hamlin Hill has meticulously calculated that Sam's losses—the difference between half profits and what he was actually paid while under contract to the American Publishing Company—totaled about forty-nine thousand dollars. "If Bliss were alive I would stay with the concern and get it all back," Sam resolved at the time, "for on each new book I would require a portion of that back pay." As a reward to Orion for alerting him to Bliss's dishonesty, he had resolved as early as spring 1875, if possible, to grant his brother a "regular pension without revealing the fact that it *is* a pension" and in the fall of 1880 it became possible. He expected to recover twenty thousand dollars of what he was owed in royalties on *A Tramp Abroad*, so he decided not only to cancel Orion's debt but to send him the interest on this amount in installments of seventy-five dollars a month in perpetuity. He assured Orion that henceforth he was "living not on bor-rowed money but on money which you have squarely earned, & which has no taint nor savor of charity about it."[58]

That is, Sam replaced one polite fiction, that he was merely loaning Orion money, with another, that he was paying Orion a pension he had earned. "He needn't blush to receive it," he advised their sister Pamela. "If I had listened to him long ago, I could have been giving him the income from $50,000 without missing it all this time. However, I have swept away his past indebt-edness. He owes no man a cent—at least he owes *me* nothing." He advised his brother again a year later that he was "not receiving a pension but an in-come fairly & righteously derived from money saved to me by your exposure of Bliss's swindling methods." By virtue of this bequest, Sam also evaded any obligation he may have felt to shelter Jane Lampton Clemens under his own roof. "We dare not invite her to stay with us," Sam insisted to Orion in March 1882, while his mother and sister were visiting Hartford and plan-ning their futures after Fredonia, "for with three children & a lot of servants, Livy has already as heavy a burden as she can possibly wag under; to add a care & a solicitude would be to add the one thing more than she could bear up under." In the end, Jane Clemens moved to Keokuk to live with Ori-on and Mollie while Pamela joined her son Sammy in Berkeley. Sam sent Orion, Mollie, and his mother a monthly stipend of $125, eventually raised to $200, and maintained this allowance until 1891 (even after his mother's death in 1890), when in consequence of his own financial duress he reduced it to fifty dollars.[59]

Sam's generosity toward Orion was matched by his fury with Elisha Bliss and his firm. Bliss "was a fool," he declared to Chatto, "& if he were not dead I would add that he was also a persistent liar & a rascal; but I never allow myself to say harsh things about a dead person." Sam's bitterness had not abated a quarter century later; Bliss "was a tall, lean, skinny, yellow, tooth-less, bald-headed, rat-eyed professional liar and scoundrel," he asserted in February 1906, and

> I never heard him tell the truth, so far as I can remember. He was a most repulsive creature. When he was after dollars he showed the intense earnest-ness and eagerness of a circular-saw. In a small, mean, peanut-stand fashion, he was sharp and shrewd. But above that level he was destitute of intelligence; his brain was a loblolly, and he had the gibbering laugh of an idiot. It is my belief that Bliss never did an honest thing in his life when he had a chance to do a dishonest one. I have had contact with several conspicuously mean men, but they were noble compared to this bastard monkey.

Bliss was so dishonest, Sam alleged, that he "could overshadow and blot out a whole continent" with his lies. He "told the truth once, to see how it would taste, but it overstrained him and he died." Sam professed compassion for Bliss only to the extent that "if I could send him a fan I would." The American Publishing Company "swindled me out of huge sums of money in the old days," he wrote George Washington Cable in June 1883, but he thought "there was only one thief in the concern and he is shoveling brimstone now."[60]

Convinced that he had been cheated for years, Sam ended his long relationship with the company. "I removed my purity from that mephitic atmosphere" or "severed our relations in a fine large leather-headed passion," as he put it in his autobiography. His decision cost Frank Bliss a quarter of a million dollars in hypothetical profits over the years, according to Sam's own calculations. Instead, he contracted in November with his friend James R. Osgood, "the loveliest man in the world," to issue *The Prince and the Pauper*. Osgood had been interested in publishing Sam's works for a decade and he had in fact released a small print run of *A True Story and the Recent Carnival of Crime* to the trade market in 1877. Under the terms of their new agreement, Osgood would receive royalties on sales of the novel, 5 percent of the first fifty thousand copies and 7½ percent thereafter, and Sam would pay to produce the book, including design and illustrations, in essence reversing the normal arrangement of author and publisher. Osgood became little more than a book agent and accountant. "My contract for the 'Little Prince' is made—& *this* time it is no fool of a contract," Sam assured Orion in November 1880. He asked his brother to "keep it mum, for I have changed my publisher—a thing which I do not want the Am. Pub. Co. to suspect for some months yet," much as he had negotiated a secret deal with Frank Bliss two years earlier and demanded that his friends conceal the news. Or as he advised Osgood soon after they agreed to terms, "I'm not ready for [Bliss] to begin to smell a rat." He estimated that he had earned to date about $125,000 from his books, but that "the sum ought to have been over $400,000, and that he had just discovered that he had printed his books on a wrong basis; that he ought to have published the books himself and paid his publishers a percentage for selling them, instead of letting them pay him a percentage for writing them." In other words, the publisher should be "hireling and not the author." Sam advised Joel Chandler Harris to adopt this strategy: "Make your book at your own expense & pay some publisher ten per cent to sell it for you. On a sale of 50,000 copies this will pay your publisher $15,000, & yourself $35,000 or close upon it." He was delighted by the deal he had struck with Osgood, who was "a fine man every way; he knows his business; & it is less bother to publish a book with him than a pamphlet with another man."[61]

Ironically, around the time he became a de facto publisher of his own books, Sam experienced an about-face on the issue of international copyright that lasted over a year. He had testified on behalf of copyright legislation since 1872, but in the fall of 1880 he realized that the absence of international copyright mostly punished British authors who were pirated in the United States, and the passage of copyright laws would redound to the benefit of only a handful of American writers pirated in Canada and England. "My notions have mightily changed, lately," he admitted to Howells in October 1880, scarcely three weeks after his discovery that Bliss had been cheating him for years. As long as American publishers could pirate foreign authors, the country would be "flooded with the best of English literature at prices which make a package of water closet paper seem an 'edition de luxe' in comparison," he wrote to the surprise of Howells. "I can buy a lot of the great copyright classics, in paper, at from 3 cents to 30 cents apiece. These things must find their way into the very kitchens & hovels of the country." Maintaining the status quo ought to render the United States

> the most intelligent & the best-read nation in the world. International copyright must becloud this sun & bring on the former darkness and dime-novel reading. Morally, this is all wrong—governmentally it is all right; for it is the *duty* of governments—& families—to be selfish, & look out simply for their own. International copyright would benefit a few English authors, & a lot of American publishers, & be a profound detriment to 20,000,000 Americans; it would benefit a dozen American authors a few dollars a year, & there an end.

As Sam argued in an interview, "If English publishers rob American authors of $8000 a year, under the present system American publishers rob foreign authors of at least $100,000 a year." He offered only a thin rationale for international copyright: "I would like to see [it] succeed out of simple justice to the foreign authors." Though he failed to mention it, Sam enjoyed another advantage in the absence of copyright: free advertising for his books when newspapers reprinted excerpts from them. During this paradoxical period in 1880 Sam opposed free trade in favor of protective tariffs and opposed international copyright in favor of a publishing free-for-all. In the script of the play *Colonel Sellers as a Scientist* (1883), written in collaboration with Howells, the title character, when asked if he favors copyright legislation, replies, "No sir! The American people demand cheap literature, and they shall have it if they have to steal it."[62] By the end of the decade, however, Sam's positions on these issues were reversed: he favored both free trade and copyright laws to protect intellectual property. He was nothing if not inconsistent.

On November 30, 1880, his forty-fifth birthday, Sam reflected on the watershed moment in a note to his friend and business adviser Franklin G. Whitmore, one of the members of the Friday Evening Club who met every week at Sam's house for billiards, cigars, and cocktails: "I stand to-day on the mid-summit of life & am for the first time looking down upon the country beyond, while the sun in the zenith has begun to tilt westward toward his setting." Like Dante at the halfway point of his life in canto 1 of the *Inferno*, Sam suggested that "from this day forth" both of them should "cease from scoffing at the old; for we be of that lot ourselves."[63]

CHAPTER 9

◆

Behind the Scenes

—*Dam* business of *all* sorts!—that's my only religious creed.

—Samuel Clemens to Moncure Conway, May 1, 1880

Sam clemens began to flex his political muscle immediately after James Garfield's election by redeeming a few chits with the politicos. He "took the liberty to write a long letter to John Hay (ostensibly) but really for General Garfield's eye," recommending Ned House, crippled and living in Japan, for the Japanese mission, and in late November 1880 he began to boost W. D. Howells, who was preparing to resign as editor of the *Atlantic Monthly*, for U.S. envoy to either the Netherlands or Switzerland. He started a petition he hoped would be signed by a host of literary types, including Higginson, Longfellow, Osgood, and Stowe, to be sent to the president-elect "without Howells' knowing anything about it" to recommend the appointment. "We can get an array of bully signatures which would not only convince" Garfield, he wrote Osgood, "but come derned near amounting to a command." Howells's only liability, Sam wrote Longfellow, was "the high respectability of his relationships."[1] That is, he ran with too reputable a crowd.

The very existence of the Chinese Educational Mission, headquartered in Hartford, directed by Chinese émigré and Yale University alumnus Yung Wing and actively supported by Joseph Twichell, was threatened in the last days of 1880, moreover, and Sam intervened to the extent possible to save it. The Chinese government, reducing its foreign expenses and contracting its outreach to the West, had recalled the 120 students it sponsored in Hartford and other New England towns. Among them were several classmates of William Lyon Phelps, who was raised in the Nook Farm neighborhood of Hartford and later served as professor of English literature at Yale. Many of the boys had graduated from local prep schools and were attending college. Yung Wing believed that the decision to recall the students might be reversed by Li Hung Chang, the viceroy and leader of progressives in China, who had welcomed Ulysses S. Grant in Tientsin during his round-the-world tour a year before. At Yung's request, Twichell agreed to ask Sam to arrange a meeting with Grant to urge him to intervene with Li. Though the open-door policies of the Chinese Educational Mission were at odds with the xenophobia implicit in his play *Ah Sin*, Sam assented.[2]

Incredibly, the strategy seemed to succeed, though it merely postponed the inevitable for a few months. Twichell and Sam discussed the matter with Grant at the Fifth Avenue Hotel in New York on December 21, 1880. "Grant took in the whole situation in a jiffy," Sam wrote Howells, "& before Joe had more than fairly got started, the old man said: 'I'll write the Viceroy a letter—a separate letter—& bring strong reasons to bear upon him; I know him well, & what I say will have weight with him; I will attend to it right away.'" Grant only asked Twichell to provide him with some talking points. As soon as Grant mailed his letter, he notified Sam that "Li Hung Chang is the most powerful and most influential Chinaman in his country. He professed great friendship for me when I was there, and I have had assurances of the same thing since. I hope . . . that the decision to withdraw the Chinese students from this country may be changed."[3]

During this audience with Grant, Sam also took the opportunity to pitch another project to him: as one of the directors of the American Publishing Company, he wanted the general to write his memoirs for the press, but Grant demurred. As Sam wrote,

> His inborn diffidence made him shrink from voluntarily coming before the public and placing himself under criticism as an author. He had no confidence in his ability to write well; whereas we all know now that he possessed an admirable literary gift and style. He was also sure that the book would have no sale, and of course that would be a humility too. I argued that the book would have an enormous sale, and that out of my experience I could save him from making unwise contracts with publishers, and would have the contract arranged in such a way that they could not swindle him, but he said he had no necessity for any addition to his income.

"I couldn't get General Grant to promise to write that book," Sam admitted later to House, "but he sat down & spun out a lot of secret national history that would make a stunning chapter; says he *does* want to write *that* out before it gets too dim in his memory."[4]

Yung Wing reported to Twichell the following March that Grant's letter to the viceroy had "done its work" and "the mission has passed its most critical crisis." He asked Twichell to "see our friend Mr. Clemens and tell him confidentially what good he is capable to doing" and Sam in turn conveyed the news to Grant: "Your letter to Li Hung Chang has done its work & the Chinese Educational Mission in Hartford is saved. The order to take the students home to China was revoked by the Viceroy three days ago—by cable." Twichell crowed that "we succeeded easily beyond our expectation, thanks largely to Clemens's assistance." Unfortunately, the decision was overturned the following July, when the mission was abolished and the students again ordered to return to China.[5]

Sam was also a featured guest at a dinner meeting of the Papyrus Club, a group of journalists and men of letters, at the Revere House in Boston the evening of February 24, 1881. Among the eighty attendees were his friends Thomas Bailey Aldrich, Howells, George Waring, Charles Dudley Warner, and E. P. Whipple. Among the others present whom he may have met for the first time were the novelist Robert Grant and the poet John Boyle O'Reilly. After the dinner Sam delivered a brief humorous speech in which he claimed to have been mistaken once by a black railroad porter for the hirsute general George McClellan.[6]

Sam also spoke his mind repeatedly around this time about a local Hartford issue: polluted water. Ever alert to his civic responsibilities, he had complained about the drainage in the streets as early as 1876 in a pair of pseudonymous letters to the editor of the *Hartford Courant*. The basements in the homes on Niles Street had flooded, he complained, and nearby lakes had been contaminated with toxic runoff and effluvia from sewers. The next year Sam invested, at Frank Fuller's suggestion, in a still for purifying water, though the device was never built. He occasionally ranted about the decisions by the city fathers that transformed the Park River (formerly the Hog River) into an open sewer and Hartford from "a conspicuously healthy city into a conspicuously unhealthy one." In September 1880 Sam objected to the quality of water in the Hartford pumps and mains. In an unsent letter to the editor of the *Hartford Courant*, he alleged that the city was "well stocked with sufferers from malaria" on account of "our bad sewerage & foul & stagnant water courses." He modestly proposed to warn visitors to Hartford about the condition of the malodorous water by flying a "black flag with skull & cross-bones" from the dome of the state capitol. The Clemenses stopped drinking the tap water in their home, preferring an imported German mineral water.[7] At the Hartford train depot a few years later, Sam joked with a reporter that he never drank "anything strong, but I will take a glass of apollinaris—just a little apollinaris without the water, and with about three fingers of whisky in place of the apollinaris." Sam also tried to address the water issue by contracting with a plumber to fix or replace the pipes in his Farmington Avenue house during the spring and summer of 1880. Coincidentally, the same month the plumbers went to work Sam bought a strip of land along the south boundary of the Hartford property from his neighbor Franklin Chamberlin "& the very next day, just within the bounds of that strip, we struck a spring of cold, sweet, limpid & abundant water," though it was never pumped into the house.[8]

In early November 1881, in company with General William Franklin and Richard Gatling, Sam hosted a delegation of French army officers who toured Colt's Patent Fire-Arms Manufacturing Company's armory and then dined at the Hartford Club. Ten days later, on November 17, he entertained the lecturer and war reporter Archibald Forbes and R. S. Smyth of Melbourne, an Australian lecture agent, at his Farmington Avenue home. That evening he introduced Forbes, who delivered his lecture "The Inner Life of a War Correspondent" in Hartford. "It seems peculiarly fitting," Sam declared, "that a soldier should introduce a soldier to his audience." He noted that he had served "more than two years now as honorary member of the Connecticut Militia; and in that time have dared, suffered all that they have suffered—fought, bled, and died; so I can speak as gallantly as the best of them." Like Sam, Forbes had "smelt the breath of dissolution on many a field and is as familiar with it as is our angel of death who presides over the malarious mission of our river Sty." His clever conflation of the Hog River / Sty River / River Styx, the boundary between earth and hell, was deliberate, of course. "During four weeks Hartford hasn't dared to quench its thirst with a drop of water," he complained to Howells in April 1880, "for the pipes deliver only a fearfully-stinking fluid which is thick with rotten fish—one has to hold his breath whilst he washes his face." In June 1886, in another unsent letter to the editor of the *Hartford Courant*, he swore that he "had to hold my nose when washing in the morning because the water stunk so; & had to give over washing my teeth because the taste of rotten fish was so strong in the water that it turned my stomach." The problem, he learned, was decaying fish and tadpoles trapped in the water pipes by the spring freshets. As late as October 1888 he complained that "a lot of sewers" empty into the streams "right under our noses. It's unpleasant, of course—the 'bouquet,' I mean. . . . The richest city in the world for its size can't afford sewers and uses hog troughs. We get all of New Britain's sewage, you know; but did you know that we're going to have West Hartford's too, right away? And I've been told they are going to siphon the Farmington sewage over the hill to us."[9]

Sam completed a draft of *The Prince and the Pauper* in September 1880, though he continued to tweak the novel for several weeks. In early February 1881, at Sam's invitation, Ned House visited the Clemenses in Hartford with a young Japanese woman named Koto—some question remains whether she was his adopted daughter or his common-law wife—and House read the manuscript.[10] House later swore that Sam asked him to "correct" it, much as he had invited Howells to suggest revisions, but Sam dismissed the claim. "Mr. House was never invited to edit the book for me," Sam insisted later. "He asked if he might read the manuscript while lying bedridden for several weeks simply to satisfy his own curiosity." In any case, House suggested some minor changes and Sam thanked him.[11] Sam also made three critical decisions prior to publication. First, he chose not to issue *The Prince and the Pauper* in one volume with *Adventures of Huckleberry Finn*. After all, the two novels were dramatically different and pitched to dissimilar audiences. Moreover, *Huck Finn* was only half finished and required, Sam figured, another "two or three months' work."[12] Next, he concluded that he should publish *The Prince and the Pauper* with his nom de plume attached to it instead of concealing his authorship. He had originally planned to "smuggle" the book into press "with my name suppressed" but "I was persuaded not to do so by my family because they liked it." He subsequently regretted the decision, however, because "the signature Mark Twain is a kind of trademark. The public buying a book by Mark Twain expects to get a book of a certain type"—specifically, "low comedy." He believed "it was not quite fair to my readers to publish a book of quite another type under that signature." He also wanted "to test the value of the book on its own merits." But he ultimately concluded to "put my name to it & let it help me or hurt me as the fates shall direct." Finally, he chose not to serialize the story in the juvenile magazine *St. Nicholas*, though he received overtures from its editor Mary Mapes Dodge, because it would have dampened its sales in book format, on which he earned profit and Osgood royalties. Both Sam's wife Olivia and Lilly Warner recommended serialization for the sake of publicity but Osgood thought the move a mistake. A novice in subscription publication, Osgood nevertheless diddled over the manuscript for months, unsure how to recruit a sales force. Eventually, Sam urged him simply to hire Elisha Bliss's book agents. On August 15, 1881, Sam agreed to terms with Chatto & Windus for an English edition to be printed from advance sheets of the American edition, then waited for Osgood to deliver on his promises.[13]

Meanwhile, Sam continued to invest in Kaolatype, hoping to exploit its commercial potential as an engraving process. In particular, he thought the process could be adapted to "mould hard brass with sharp-cut lines & perfect surfaces. But every brass-expert laughed at the idea & said the thing was absolutely impossible." In the fall of 1880 he hired a young German metallurgist, Charles Sneider, "who believed he could do it. I have had him under wages for 3 months, now, night & day, & at last he has worked the miracle." In November 1880 Sam "contracted to pay him $5,000 when he is able to put his patents into my hands & assign me a one-third ownership in them for America & Europe, & pay him $150 a month" and expenses "to go on & perfect his methods." He was optimistic he would soon realize a fortune from the process. He attended an oyster dinner at the Tile Club on

West Tenth Street in New York at midnight on December 20 and alerted Dan Slote in advance that, while he was in the city, he wanted to "talk & afterwards look in on Sneider at his shop."[14]

Sam initially delegated to Slote all responsibility for his investments in the self-pasting scrapbook and Kaolatype. "Just make the trades yourself, Dan," he wrote Slote in January 1881. "I started in to be a Figure-Head President [of the engraving company] & that's what I *am*." By March, however, he was disenchanted with Slote's slipshod management. The recent income from the scrapbook, he grumbled, "gravels me because while they have been paying me about $1800 or $2000 a year, I judge it ought to have been 3 times as much." He eventually discovered that Slote had been selling "*regular* scrap-books," for which Sam received no royalties, rather than the patented ones. The amount Slote remitted him on scrapbook sales dwindled from twelve thousand dollars during the first half of 1878 to only eight hundred dollars for the first half of 1884.[15]

In desperation Sam recruited Charles L. Webster, his nephew by marriage, to manage his business affairs. His niece Annie Moffett had married Webster over the objections of her mother. Still, as Sam's sister Pamela wrote Mollie Clemens, "Annie thinks everything of C.W. I believe he does of her." Sam anointed Webster in March as his subordinate at an annual salary of eighteen hundred dollars, though Pamela privately expressed reservations about his character. "I have always believed that C[harley]'s moral nature was weak and underdeveloped with lower instincts in the ascendant," she cautioned. "I remind you of this not to prejudice you against him but to put you on your guard, both for his sake and your own." When Sam's brother Orion waved a red flag to warn Sam about Webster's supposed moral lassitude, Sam replied in high dudgeon: "when Ma's pocket shall have suffered as much from your mismanagement of her Tennessee land as it has from his, it will be time for him to begin to belch holy indignation upon you." He threw caution to the wind by granting Webster in April 1881 the right to exercise "complete authority over Kaolatype & its concerns already vested in you. You will take entire control of the property & employes of the Company; you will hire whom you please, discharge whom you please; all moneys received & disbursed must pass through your hands, & you will be held responsible." He cast a vote of confidence in Webster the following October by assuring him that, so far as he was concerned, he was no "more capable of a selfish or unjust act toward me than your Aunt Livy is." Sam paid his nephew a rare compliment the next month: "You have wrought admirably, from the beginning, in everything you have undertaken" and "although I *do* lose my temper 30 times a day on an average," he begged him always to remember he was disinclined "to let it out on you." Webster assured his uncle in turn that his "smallest wish shall be gratified no matter how much it discommodes me," a pledge he would subsequently regret. He had become by then little more than Sam's errand boy. After two more years, Sam admonished his nephew that "I don't want anything to do with" commercial matters because Webster was "to take care of my business, not make business for *me* to take care of."[16]

Webster initially rose to the challenge. A few days after assuming his duties, he reported to his uncle "fraudful misrepresentations" in the management of Kaolatype. In mid-April he spirited two plates, "one of iron & one of glass," made by the process to a brass foundry. As soon as "the hot metal struck the cold iron plate," he reported to Sam, "it sputtered & flew & washed the kaolatype all away leaving not a vestige of the design" and "the glass one was shattered to atoms and came out in a large conglomerate mass of broken glass, sand, brass, & kaolatype." It "looked as though it had been through the Chicago fire and would sell well as a relic." In late April Webster notified Sam that Sneider had been "casting plates & pulling the wool over Slotes eyes magnificently." In early May 1881 Webster confronted Sneider, who refused to demonstrate Kaolatype in operation. He soon determined that Sneider was an unrepentant charlatan and Slote was "either a knave or a fool" in conspiring to "bleed" money from Sam "under the guise of friendship. . . . Everything points to a deliberate plan to *live* on you as long as you could be kept in the thing." All of the engravings Sam had seen that had allegedly been cast in Kaolatype had in fact been produced in the conventional way. On May 11 Slote anxiously admitted to Webster that the budding scandal "would ruin him & his firm if this thing was not hushed up." "The bubble has burst," Webster wrote Sam on May 18, and "Sneider has confessed . . . that the whole thing was a swindle from the beginning. . . . Sneider says he's going to commit suicide," though he assured Sam there was "no fear of that . . . as long as there's any money left in the country to steal." Sneider had perpetrated "a wicked fraud deliberately planned and as deliberately carried out to rob you." Sam was ready to sue Sneider for "obtaining money under false pretenses" and to ask Slote if he would "bear one half the expenses of the suit" to prove, if not his innocence, at least his ignorance. As he allowed to Webster,

> that contract of ours with Sneider was *based* upon a lie & a fraud—viz., that Sneider had *already* invented the process. He brought the (apparent) proofs of this, & exhibited them. If the process could be protected by patent, there would be no question of its *value*. . . . But it was all a lie, for Sneider had invented nothing new; he was working by old methods—& at the same time not succeeding with them. He pretended that the specimens he brought were

made by the process described in the patents afterward issued to him, but such was not the case.

Slote refused to be drawn into the suit, so Sam plotted a strategy with Webster: "to finish with Sneider & then tackle Dan." On May 19 Sneider confessed to the swindle and assigned the Kaolatype patents to Sam, though later in the day Webster saw Slote "drinking with Sneider," reinforcing his suspicion the two had conspired to defraud his uncle. When the time came, Sam insisted, Slote would be required to surrender all his stock in Kaolatype, "repay every dollar which the late swindle cost," and give his note "for three thousand dollars with interest from eighteen seventy eight" for the money "obtained by fraudful representations." Only belatedly did a question occur to him that he should have asked three years earlier: "If [Kaolatype] had $3,000 worth of plant, why did it need $1,000 a month to run it when it had already been in operation 2 years?" Slote was "frightened, & he has good reason," Sam figured, though he thought he held an ace in the hole. He wanted Slote either to "restore my 10 per cent royalty on Scrap Books or do something which shall come nearer the equivalent of it than the present royalty does."[17]

On his part, Webster urged his uncle to padlock the engraving company and to stop throwing good money after bad but Sam was not so easily dissuaded. Sneider may have been a fraud but Sam remained convinced that Kaolatype was commercially viable. "The day that Kaolatype arrives at a point where it pays its own expenses," he promised his nephew, "you are to have $900 of its stock. Meantime, I wish to give you $100 of its stock, now, anyhow, & make you Vice President & Treasurer—also Manager." When Webster persisted in advising him to close the business, Sam was adamant: "You wish to know when I shall 'close up'? When the business pays me $5,000 a year clear profit. Not before. The brass alone shall pay me more than that before I am done with it." Privately Webster was alarmed by how his employer-uncle "lets money slip through his hands" and worried presciently that "he will be a poor man yet, if he keeps this up, although he makes more money now than he knows what to do with."[18]

Despite all the evidence that Kaolatype was impractical, Sam still harbored grandiose dreams of its many commercial applications. He was convinced that "there was a fortune ready for the man who can find a way to cast fine nice brass book-stamps." Four months after Sneider confessed to deception, Sam still planned to "patent the *general* idea of applying Kaolatype to the casting of brass; & also at the same time patent the application of K[aolatype] to the casting of metal cylinders for calico & wallpaper printing, &c." As soon as those patents were granted, he mused to Webster, "I suppose we shall have to think of patenting them in England, France, Germany & Canada." But then another thought struck him: "I should try to sell a foreign interest to Osgood, so as to cover the expenses & have a partner who could take care of the foreign end." He conceded that there was "heavy competition for Kaolatype" in print shops and publishing houses, "but none at all for the brass end of it." Lest he seem too promiscuous with his ideas for making money, he advised Webster to "read this [letter] till you are *sure* of its several points, then burn it." Obviously Webster failed to comply. But a year later Sam tried to sell "a fourth, fifth, or sixth interest" in the process to Osgood and added that "this is the first time I have ever offered any part or portion of the thing for sale." Osgood did not rise to the bait, though a week later, apparently blind to the truth, Sam assured Webster that "K[aolatype] is doing well & will yet do first-rate" and "K[aolatype] flourishes, better & better."[19]

Slote died on February 13, 1882, at the age of fifty-three at his mother's home in New York. Bloodgood Cutter, the "poet lariat" of the *Quaker City* voyage, attended the funeral. After the obsequies Sarah Slote burned most of the letters her husband had received from Sam over the years. Had he "died thirteen months earlier, I should have been at the funeral, and squandered many tears; but as it is, I did not go and saved my tears," Sam wrote Mary Mason Fairbanks. Slote "stole from me during at least seven years unsuspected by me. I did not find him out then, but a sharper man than I am [Webster] did." Slote was "not a robber. There is a sort of robust dignity about robbing. He was only a pick-pocket." He had exploited their friendship and Sam had come, he said, "very near sending him to the penitentiary."[20]

After Slote's death, Webster determined that Slote had been skimming profits on sales of the patented self-pasting scrapbooks, paying Sam but a fraction of the royalties he was owed. "There never was any verbal or other agreement to reduce my share below one-third of the profits on the Scrap Books," Sam replied. He had been an easy mark. "Slote took advantage of my utter confidence in his honesty to cheat me"; he "knew he was lying when he said that those figures represented one third of the profits" and "knew I was ass enough to believe him." Mother Fairbanks scolded him in her reply: "Dan Slote was your friend—for years, you believed in him and trusted him, and seemingly he served you with a willing fidelity. It was a conspicuous, a notable friendship—made so by your book [*The Innocents Abroad*] it is true, but consistently sustained by after years of mutual service and sympathy."[21]

Kaolatype was small potatoes, Pamela wrote in December 1881, "compared to another enterprise Sam has set Charley to work on. This is some new invention. They want to start with a capital of five hundred thousand dollars, a stock company." One day in late April 1880 Dwight Buell, owner of a jew-elry store on Main Street in Hartford, offered to sell Sam some stock in a typesetting machine under construction at the Colt's Arms factory that "was about finished." On Webster's recommendation, Sam bought "$2,000 of the stock. I was always taking little chances like that, and almost always losing by it, too." A native of Rochester, James Paige had invented an automat-ed typesetter, for which he received a patent in December 1874, moved to Hartford the next year, and rented space in Colt's factory, where he tinkered endlessly with his prototype. It was a work in progress. Unfortunately, it would always be a work in progress. "Sometime afterward" Sam visited the factory to see the machine. "I went promising myself nothing," he noted,

> for I knew all about type-setting by practical experience, and held the settled and solidified opinion that a successful type-setting machine was an impos-sibility, for the reason that a machine cannot be made to think, and the thing that sets movable type must think or retire defeated. So the performance I witnessed did most thoroughly amaze me. Here was a machine that was re-ally setting type and doing it with swiftness and accuracy, too. Moreover, it was distributing its case at the same time. The distribution was automatic; the machine fed itself from a galley of dead matter and without human help or suggestion, for it began its work of its own accord when the type channels needed filling, and stopped of its own accord when they were full enough. The machine was almost a complete compositor.

The operator of the Paige compositor, even at this relatively early stage in its development, set type "at the rate of 3,000 ems an hour, which, counting distribution, was but little short of four casemen's work."[22] In other words, automated typesetting promised to dramatically increase worker productiv-ity and dramatically decrease employment in the print industry.

Soon enough Sam was obliged to explain the reasons he favored mecha-nization at the cost of jobs. In this case his sympathies were all on the side of the capitalists. The Paige machine, he bragged, "does not get drunk. He does not join the Printers' Union. He does not distribute a dirty case, he does not set a dirty proof. A woman can operate him." But the increase in productiv-ity was in nowise passed along to the workers in the form of increased wages or other benefits, at least in Sam's reckoning. The Paige "does the work of 5 men," Sam noted in his journal, and "therefore the new wages should be 1/5 of the old; 9 cents per 1,000 on morning papers." His calculations were oc-casionally callous to the point of cruelty; the New York *World* employed 185 compositors in its shop in May 1888 and they might be replaced with only 37 machines. With a fivefold increase in productivity, a typesetter would earn "as much as [he or she] did before" only by maintaining a breakneck pace like

workers on an accelerated assembly line. While theoretically a skilled compositor might work fewer hours to earn a living, such a benefit did not figure
into Sam's calculations nor was he an advocate of the eight-hour workday.[23]

But, he rationalized, mechanized typesetting would not eliminate jobs in
the long run; in fact, it would increase employment, though his predictions
on this point fluctuated wildly. "Every great invention takes a livelihood
away from 50,000 men—& within ten years *creates* a livelihood for *half a
million*," he insisted to Howells in March 1887. As books and magazines became less expensive to produce, he figured, more openings would be created
for "binders, papermakers, sales agents, etc." For every worker displaced by
the Paige, he expected in early 1889 that "10 will *get* work, through it." As he
explained in chapter 10 of *The American Claimant* (1891), "17,900 persons
today" performed the equivalent labor of "thirteen millions of persons" fifty
years earlier; that is, by Sam's calculations in 1891, workers were on average
over seven hundred times as productive as workers in 1841. "My machine is
bound to throw out of work 65,000 men in the United States," he conceded,
"but it will lead to the employment of many more than sixty-five thousand
men by the impulse which it will give to the multiplication of printed matter.
There will be more men wanted in paperworks and in the manufacture of
printers' ink, and more women and girls in binderies."[24]

Sam was so impressed by the Paige typesetter when he witnessed it in operation that he immediately invested an additional three thousand dollars in
its stock. "I never saw such an inspired bugger of a machine," he wrote John
Russell Young. "A man who owns a newspaper can't look at this creature un-
moved. Anybody can set type with it; nobody can get it out of order; & as for
the distributing, it attends to that itself, automatically, & without waiting to
be notified." He dubbed the typesetter "a mechanical marvel" that made "all
the other wonderful inventions of the human brain sink pretty nearly into
the commonplace." Much as he had once stumbled across an apparent field
of gold nuggets glittering on the ground in the mining fields of Washoe, he
believed that he need do nothing "to protect the $5000 invested in that ma-
chine; it is safe, there, & is very much the best investment I have ever had. I
want an opportunity to add to it—that is how I feel about it." In November
1881 Sam had another marketing idea: to travel with Webster "to England
& put Kaolatype . . . into good hands there . . . & also sell a hundred or so of
those typesetters, if we can get a fair enough commission for it." For better
or worse, Sam's lawyers cautioned him that the compositor was "not ready to
be presented to investors."[25]

Sam and Livy became patrons of the arts, or at least of an artist, early in
1881. In January Josephine (aka Hattie) Gerhardt invited Sam to examine a

clay statue her husband Karl, a self-taught sculptor and draftsman in Pratt
& Whitney's machine shop, had executed. When he visited their second-
floor apartment a couple of days later, he saw a life-size figure—"a graceful
girlish creature, nude to the waist"—and then "this young wife posed herself
alongside the image & so remained." Sam was charmed by "this girl's innocence & purity—exhibiting her naked self, as it were, to a stranger & alone,
& never once dreaming that there was the slightest indelicacy about the matter. And so there wasn't; but it will be many a long day before I run across
another woman who can do the like & show no trace of self-consciousness."
Sam asked three of his artist friends—James Wells Champney, Augustus
Saint-Gaudens, and John Quincy Adams Ward—to evaluate Gerhardt's talent and all agreed that "the stuff is in him, sure." Champney urged Sam to
"send him to Paris" to study "two years; then if the promise holds good, keep
him there three more—and warn him to study, study, work, work, and keep
his name out of the papers." Sam loaned Gerhardt three thousand dollars so
that he could study for five years at the École des Beaux-Arts in Paris, where
he was taken under the wing of François Jouffroy, the onetime instructor of
Saint-Gaudens, and Sam expected him to become "a rattling sculptor." The
Gerhardts sailed for Europe on March 4, scarcely more than a month after
Sam first met them. He claimed that his financial assistance to Gerhardt
"had very little sentiment in it, from my side of the house, and no romance."
He merely asked the aspiring sculptor eventually to repay the loan if possible
"without inconvenience." Sam's relationship with Hattie Gerhardt, however,
was flirtatious. As she wrote him privately in May 1881, "I do not like to
have you fond of anyone else but me."[26]

By early 1881 the plumbing repairs in the Hartford house had escalated
into a full-blown home remodeling, much to Sam's dismay. He had built a
"noble wood fire" in his study one winter day—"that is, part of it is wood,"
he explained to a friend. "The back log is a plumber. He came up here &
interrupted me when I was writing about the scenery. Whenever you catch
a plumber, you just make a back-log of him: I always do. Ignorant people
say a plumber isn't useful—this is because they do not know how to apply
a plumber." Sam was convinced that he was routinely bilked by them and
he joked in *The Prince and the Pauper* that he could not understand why the
royal food taster at the court of Edward VI was not replaced by "a dog or a
plumber."[27]

In any event, what began as the simple replacement of pipes soon became
a wholesale renovation of the house. With the first twelve thousand dollars in profits he expected to realize from Kaolatype, Sam bought another
hundred feet of land east of their property in mid-March 1881 to prevent

Chamberlin ("a rectum," as Sam once described him) from building a house there that would have obstructed their view. Had the "utility of our invention" been in doubt, he would have permitted his neighbor

> to go on digging his blamed cellar, & build a house right in our faces & shut off our eastward prospect—& in effect, block up the front of our house. If the utility of our invention was *not* doubtful, I could afford to say to him, "You can't build there—discharge your workmen immediately; deed me the land; & send in your bill." Well, his terms were twelve thousand dollars—rather too much, but he had me where the hair was short.

Sam "wanted to be pretty *certain*" of the success of Kaolatype before committing to the purchase. The same day he was convinced of the practicality of Kaolatype he notified his sister Pamela that he planned to build a factory in New York for brass-casting work and Chamberlin transferred the deed to the Hartford land.[28]

Sam and Livy commissioned an architect to draw plans to expand the kitchen and front hall and paid contractors eighteen thousand dollars to remodel the house and landscape. "The masons & bricklayers are hard at work tearing down & enlarging the kitchen," he reported in late May. "Plumbers are all over the house uprooting & re-arranging all the pipes; Mrs. Clemens is head over heels in the work of ordering & superintending the snaking-up of carpets, storing of pictures, etc." Sam's second-floor study was transformed into a schoolroom for Susy and Clara—he eventually moved his workspace first to the loft over the stable and then to the billiard room on the third floor of the mansion—and two additional bathrooms were built in the basement. The ground around the greenhouse was lowered to enhance the prospect from the house, and the driveway was relocated a hundred feet to the east. Sam and Livy hired Associated Artists of New York, owned by Louis Comfort Tiffany, son of the New York jeweler, to redecorate the interior with hand-painted wallpaper, stained glass, new fireplace tiles, and mahogany paneling with silver stenciling. Sam hoped "to sheathe our *library* walls & ceiling with the elegant brass plates" fashioned by Kaolatype. In all, they spent an additional thirty thousand dollars, over and above the money spent on home furnishings in Europe, to buy the chunk of land from Chamberlin and to remodel.[29]

Sam was again a featured speaker at the twelfth annual reunion of the Society of the Army of the Potomac at Allyn Hall in Hartford on June 8, 1881, the fourteenth anniversary of the departure of the *Quaker City* for Europe and the Holy Land and the seventh birthday of his daughter Clara. Among the attendees were former Connecticut governors Hobart Bigelow and

Marshall Jewell; Generals Ambrose Burnside, Joe Hawley, Nelson A. Miles, Horace Porter, and William Tecumseh Sherman; Secretary of War Robert Todd Lincoln; and Sam's friend Joe Twichell. In his response to "The Benefit of Judicious Training" toast after dinner, Sam critiqued in hilarious detail Napoleon Bonaparte's military strategy when he lost the Battle of Water-loo, repeating what he claimed the cadets at the U.S. Military Academy at West Point had told him. First, the French commander should not have fetched his "reserves from the start." He should not have "assaulted with his bomb-proofs and ambulances and embrasures" when he might have used heavy artillery. Then "he retired his right by ricochet—which uncovered his pickets—when his only possibility of success lay in doubling up his centre, flank by flank, and throwing out his *chevaux de frise* by the left oblique to relieve the skirmish line and confuse the enemy."[30]

The next morning Sam and Twichell left Hartford with Lincoln and Sher-man to attend commencement ceremonies at West Point. During this visit to the military academy, Sam bunked with the post adjutant, Lieutenant Charles Erskine Scott Wood; read from his works before the cadets' literary society; and sat on the dais in Schofield Hall during graduation on June 10.[31]

As soon as Sam returned from West Point, the Clemenses left Hartford for Montowese House in the resort town of Branford, Connecticut, on Long Island Sound near New Haven, where the family enjoyed "a luxuriously lazy & comfortable time" for the next two months. Sam and Livy returned to Hartford on June 13 to inspect the renovations on their house and to meet the southern local colorist George Washington Cable at Charley Warner's home. "We all lunched together & 'Mark' & Mr. Warner were ever so fun-ny," Cable reported to his wife Louise. Afterward Cable sent a copy of one of his books, probably his novel *Madame Delphine* (1881), to Sam, who read it in one sitting. "The charm of it, & the pain of it, & the deep music of it are still pulsing through me," he wrote Cable in his letter of thanks. Sam remembered, too, that the family was relaxing "at a little watering place on Long Island Sound" on July 2, the day President James Garfield was shot by Charles Guiteau. Garfield died from the wound ten weeks later and was succeeded by Chester A. Arthur. Sam was scheduled to speak at a benefit for Sanderson Academy in Ashfield, Massachusetts, while Garfield lay dy-ing, but he canceled his appearance on the grounds that "nonsense would be out of place" under the circumstances. Sam and Livy hosted Joe Twichell and three of his children at Montowese House for a few days and Howells for a day in mid-July—"Branford seems to have agreed with Mr. Clemens," Elinor Howells wrote Livy after her husband's return to Boston—and Sam read from his work before "a large and appreciative audience in the large parlor" of the hotel a week later. While still at the coast in late July he also reviewed proof of 150 illustrations Osgood had commissioned for *The Prince and the Pauper*. "I like them far better than any that have ever been made for me before," Sam gushed to the Gerhardts. "They are as dainty & rich as etchings."[32]

The family left Branford on August 4 to spend the remainder of the summer in Elmira, pausing in Newport and New York en route. Sam worked on a couple of projects during the next eight weeks, both of which he eventually abandoned. Howells had proposed that Sam write a burlesque etiquette book as early as May 1879 and reiterated the suggestion in March 1881: "Such a book . . . put into the trade would go like wildfire. Think what a chance to satirize the greed, solemn selfishness and cruel dullness of society! It's a wonderful opportunity, and you were made for it." Sam agreed that the idea was "a mighty good one." He planned to include a model suicide note like the model thank-you letters found in other etiquette books. Some of the fragments of what he wrote eventually reached print in *Letters from the Earth* (1962). For example, in a chapter outlining proper decorum at funerals, Sam recommended that when "a blood relation sobs, an intimate friend should choke up, a distant acquaintance should sigh," and "a stranger should merely fumble sympathetically with his handkerchief."[33]

Sam also took another stab while at Quarry Farm at his burlesque *Hamlet*. Again he based his satire on the premise that Shakespeare omitted a character from the cast—in this case Hamlet's foster brother, a Danish subscription book agent named Basil Stockmar, who wanders into Elsinore only to be dumbfounded by the stilted blank-verse speeches and courtly manners of the characters. "The events at Elsinore happened as I have written them," Sam insisted in his preface. "Shakespeare transposed and distorted the facts, and I cannot conscientiously allow these gross historical mistakes to pass uncorrected." In a review of the advance sheets, the San Francisco *Post* noted that "some of the passages are intensely funny and in others the humour is forced, with a tendency to slang; but as a whole the innovation is very laughable and the thing will no doubt attract large audiences wherever the piece is played." While the play was expected to be produced in New York during the winter of 1881–82, it instead disappeared from view. The *Chicago Inter Ocean* speculated that Sam's "natural stock of humor is running out when he is put to the strait of burlesquing sacred themes to amuse the vulgar." Joe Goodman wrote Sam that he had discussed the concept of a satirical *Hamlet* with the tragedian Lawrence Barrett, who also "thought it would be a sort of sacrilege." But, Goodman added, "you and I know such talk is all fudge. Anything is legitimate sport and game—and especially Shakespeare, who cribbed right and left and ridiculed nearly everybody and everything by turns."[34] A trace of Sam's burlesque *Hamlet* survives in the duke and king's mock Shakespearean soliloquy in chapter 21 of *Huckleberry Finn* (1885).

After Sam made a quick trip to Buffalo to visit David Gray, the family left Quarry Farm in mid-September and paused at the Gilsey House in New York en route back to Hartford. Though Elinor Howells assured Livy that she would soon be "settled in your own house after all those repairs," they returned to a house "full of joiners, masons, & plumbers" who had promised that a finish date of October 1 would "be the best they can do." On October 9 Sam moaned that the family was still trapped "in our carpetless & dismantled home, living like a gang of tramps on the second floor" with "the rest of the house in the hands of mechanics & decorators." The family finally reoccupied the library and the dining room on the first floor in late December 1881 and Tiffany completed the interior decoration two months later. On January 28, 1882, Sam at last notified Howells that "all our rooms are finished and inhabitable." He was predictably perturbed by such disruptions in his routine. "O *never* revamp a house!" he admonished Ned House. "Leave it just as it was & then you can economise in profanity." He joked that when all the work was finished he still "had three hundred dollars in the bank which the plumber didn't know anything about." In all, Sam spent over $100,000 in 1881, including $46,000 in investments, some of it in remodeling, and all but $5,000 of it in ventures "from whose bourne no dollar would ever return."[35]

Sam finally received page proofs of *The Prince and the Pauper* in August 1881, though he was aggravated by the changes in the text introduced by the copy editors and printers. "Let the printers follow my punctuation—it is the one thing I am inflexibly particular about," he admonished Benjamin Ticknor, Osgood's junior partner. "I like to have my punctuation respected. I learned it in a hundred printing-offices when I was a jour printer; so it's got more real variety about it than any other accomplishment I possess & I reverence it accordingly. . . . Sometimes I even spell words erroneously; but I do it purposely, & out of hatred of the dictionary, & I want the copy followed in those cases too." As it happened, Sam's rebukes fell on semideaf ears. Many of the changes he demanded were simply not made, though he never stopped demanding them. "I am sending Chapter VI back unread," he wrote Osgood on August 23. "I don't want to see any more until this godamded idiotic punctuating & capitalizing has been swept away & my own restored. I didn't see this chapter until I had already read Chap. VII— which latter mess of God-forever-God-damned lunacy has turned my hair white with rage."[36] He sent a set of proofs to Howells in October 1881 and urged him to "slash away, with entire freedom; & the more you slash, the better I shall like it & the more I shall be cordially obliged to you." Howells liked the novel "immensely" and approved the "whole intention" of the tale, adding that it was "such a book as I would expect from you, knowing what a bottom of fury there is to your fun." Howells found some passages "rather strong milk for babes," however, and forwarded to Sam four pages of suggested revisions. Some of his recommendations were minor, mostly at the level of line editing, including the deletion of "such words as devil, and hick (for person) and basting (for beating)." Others were more substantive, such as abridging the descriptions of English court ceremonies and omitting entirely a chapter about Edward VI's whipping boy.[37] Over the next three months, Sam deleted material according to Howells's suggestions and added "over 130 new pages to the prince's adventures in the rural districts." He thought the manuscript would make "fully as bulky a book as *Tom Sawyer*," long enough (barely) for subscription publication. He finished revisions in late January 1881 and announced that he liked "this tale better than *Tom Sawyer*—because I haven't put any fun in it," that it was "done as well as I can do it," and so he would never change a word of it.[38]

At Sam's urging, if not his direction, Howells puffed the novel in the *New York Tribune* prior to its publication. Whitelaw Reid, who had denied House the opportunity to review *The Gilded Age* in 1873, was traveling in Europe and John Hay was temporarily filling his chair. "I have written to Hay and he has commissioned me [to] write a review" of *The Prince and the Pauper*, Howells advised Sam on September 11. In an excess of caution, Hay advised Reid that he had taken into account "your disapproval of Mark in general and your friendship for Howells—and decided for the benefit for the Tribune." Should Howells's review displease Reid, Hay suggested to his boss, "wait for [Sam's] next book and get Bret Harte to review it. That will be a masterpiece of the skinner's art." Reid chastised Hay for commissioning Howells's notice on September 25, three weeks after Hay wrote to solicit his counsel:

> It isn't good journalism to let a warm personal friend & in some matters literary partner write a critical review of him in a paper wh[ich] has good reason to think little of his delicacy & highly of his greed. So, if you haven't published it yet, I w[ou]ld think of this point before doing so. If you have, there's no harm done. But, as you remember we agreed years ago, a new book by Twain is *not* (as he modestly suggested) a literary event of such importance that it makes much difference whether we have our dear friend Howells write the review or whether indeed we have any review.

Osgood finally copyrighted the novel in the United States on October 13 and issued a prospectus to book agents six days later.[39]

Despite Reid's warning, Hay published Howells's notice without signature in the *Tribune* for October 25. In his cover letter Howells assured Hay that he had reviewed the novel "solely in the interest of that unappreciated serious side of Clemens's curious genius. . . . The book has a thousand blemishes and triumphs over them." The substance of his comments proves the claim. Howells called it "a satire on monarchy" and "a manual of republicanism which might fitly be introduced" as a civics textbook in schools. In a foreshadowing of his remarks about *A Connecticut Yankee in King Arthur's Court* (1889) eight years later, Howells averred that it "breathes throughout the spirit of humanity and the reason of democracy." Ironically, his only quibble, given Sam's recurring complaints about Harte's dialect, was with Sam's attempts at Elizabethan vernacular, which "sometimes wavers between theatrical insistence and downright lapse into the American of Arthur's Presidency." Still, Sam was "vastly" pleased with Howells's notice, even as he failed to place a similar review by House in the *Atlantic Monthly*. He and Bliss wanted to engineer a favorable critical reception of the book by sending "other copies to personal friends in the press" but Sam's legal adviser Franklin Whitmore discouraged them.[40]

On November 25, the day after Thanksgiving, Sam left Hartford for Boston and Montreal in order to establish Canadian residency, or at least the appearance of it, for the purpose of securing British copyright on the book. It was his first prolonged trip north of the border. After registering at the Windsor Hotel in Montreal, he had little to do except shelter in place. He enjoyed a sleigh ride on November 28 and "inspected a lot of Catholic churches, French markets, shop windows, &c." but after filing the paperwork for copyright he seems to have mostly played billiards and read Francis Parkman's *The Jesuits in North America in the Seventeenth Century* (1867). Osgood joined him in Montreal no later than November 30; they were guests that day of Samuel Dawson of the firm of Dawson and Brothers, Sam's Canadian publisher; and they celebrated the appearance of *The Prince and the Pauper* from the presses of Chatto & Windus in London on December 1. It was the decisive event of the trip because it meant (they thought) that Sam had obtained imperial copyright. They then took a three-day excursion to Quebec City, where Sam was disgusted with his room at Russell's Hotel, "the foulest hotel in some respects in Am[erica]," he wrote Livy. "Everything in the hotel is of the date of Champlain, or even of Cartier, & thoroughly worn out." But the pulchritude in Quebec caught his eye. "So *many* pretty girls," he remarked in his journal. "Never so many in one town before—beauty of girls, & of little children of both sexes so common as to be almost monotonous. . . . The dresses are short."[41]

Osgood returned to Boston after their trip to Quebec but Sam lingered in Montreal for a few days to enjoy the highlight of his two-week "residency" in Canada: a banquet in his honor at the Windsor Hotel the evening of December 8. The dinner was open to the public and attended by some 150 citizens who each paid three dollars for the privilege. Louis Fréchette, the poet laureate of Canada, recent recipient of the Montyon Prize of the Académie française in Paris, and brother of W. D. Howells's son-in-law, welcomed him with a poem ("le plus grant des philosophes") printed on the menu. Sam also replied to a toast in his honor. He described his speech to Livy the day before delivering it as "good easy-flowing nonsense, and will *go*, if there are enough English people present to understand it. But anyway I'm safe because I wind up in French—if one may call it that." He began by explaining his reasons for traveling to Montreal: "I came here to place myself under the protection of the Canadian law and secure a copyright. I have complied with the requirements of the law. I have followed the instructions of some of the best legal minds in the city, including my own, and so my errand is accomplished." But he was also candid in his criticism of literary piracy. He hoped "that a day will come when, in the eye of the law, literary property will be as sacred as whiskey." He paused to praise Fréchette, "an author who has earned and worthily earned and received the vast distinction of being crowned by the Academy of France," and joked that he had "seen the cab which Champlain employed when he arrived" in Quebec and "the horse which Jacques Cartier rode when he discovered Montreal." He ended with a few sentiments in hilariously broken French. Sam left Montreal a day or two later and arrived back in Hartford by December 12.[42]

He received an unpleasant surprise less than a week later. His application for an imperial copyright for *The Prince and the Pauper* was denied by the Canadian Department of Agriculture and Arts on the grounds that two weeks in Montreal and Quebec City hotels constituted only an "elective domicile." Had Sam stated in the paperwork that he was a permanent resident of Canada—that is, if he had flagrantly lied—the Ottawa government "would have been bound to take his assertion," the Washington, D.C., *Critic* editorialized. The decision to deny Sam an imperial copyright was "really extraordinary," according to the *Springfield Republican*, "for although everybody sees at once that such a sojourn is a mere fiction of residence, it has nevertheless repeatedly been accepted by the Dominion and copyrights granted accordingly." Sam must have "too honestly stripped the tenuous veil from his object in visiting Montreal" with his speech at the banquet "or he made too many bad jokes about Montreal cabmen, Toronto publishers, and other choice Canadian institutions." In any case, his response to the toast in his honor apparently provoked a backlash. He should, the *Republican* noted, "beware of his tongue,—it has proved a very embarrassing organ before now."[43]

Sam tried to put the best face possible on the contretemps by insisting that, whatever the Canadian government ruled, he had obtained "both imperial and Canadian copyright" on *The Prince and the Pauper* by simply being on Canadian soil on December 1, the day the British edition of the novel was issued by Chatto & Windus. "I applied formally for Canadian copyright and failed to get it. But this did not cripple my case," Sam rationalized. His trip to Canada was not entirely in vain. He had protected his rights, he had retained Canadian counsel to prosecute "any who might pirate the book," and his "experiment" had also "established the fact, as far as it can be established without the decision of a court, that 'elective domicile' is not sufficient in a copyright matter."[44]

Figure 18. Thomas Nast's caricature *Innocence Abroad (In Search of a Copyright)*, Harper's Weekly, January 21, 1882.

Unfortunately, Sam's understanding of the law was woefully uninformed. He had obtained imperial copyright, he asserted, but not Canadian copyright. That is, he protected *The Prince and the Pauper* from sales in Canada of Canadian reprints, but not "from the importation into Canada of foreign reprints" or the sale of editions imported into Canada or from Canada into the United States. As the *New York Times* explained, Sam erred "in supposing that he secures the same protection in the Dominion from an imperial copyright as he would from a copyright issued in Canada." In addition to the authorized Dawson Brothers edition of the novel, at least two pirated editions were issued, one of them by the Belford Brothers of Toronto. As good as his word, Sam filed suit the following year in federal court in Boston against a bookseller for hawking copies of the Belford edition of *Sketches New and Old* (1875) and in Chicago against Belford, Clarke and Company for violating his trademark by pirating *Sketches, The Prince and the Pauper*, and other works. By accusing Belford of trademark rather than copyright violations, however, he effectively conceded that the books were not adequately protected by copyright, exactly as the *New York Times* had maintained. The federal judge in Chicago, Henry W. Blodgett, ruled in January 1883 that the books were not protected by Sam's trademark nom de plume either. As Blodgett noted in his decision,

> It does not seem to me that an author or writer has any better or higher right in a *nom de plume*, or assumed name, than he has in his Christian or baptismal name. When a person enters the field of authorship, he can secure to himself the exclusive right to his writings by a copyright under the laws of the United States. If he publishes anything of which he is the author or compiler, either under his own proper name or an assumed name, without protecting it by copyright, it becomes public property, and any person who chooses to do so has the right to republish it and to state the name of the author in such form in the book, either upon the title page or otherwise, as to show who was the writer or author thereof. . . . No pseudonym, however ingenious, novel, or quaint, can give an author any more rights than he would have under his own name.

Blodgett added that this case was the first attempt that had come to his attention to consider a nom de plume as a trademark. As a result, his decision became a crucial precedent in copyright case law. In the short run, protected by neither copyright nor trademark, Sam's works were "open to republication by anyone." Whatever extrastatutory privilege Sam believed adhered to his pseudonym as a result of the *Clemens v. Such* case in 1873 was effectively negated by the judicial decision in *Clemens v. Belford*. As Victor Doyno observes, in the wake of Blodgett's decision and in the absence of a coherent international copyright law, "an American author wishing to protect his or her copyright" was required to take four steps "in rapid succession: register the title in the United States, publish the book with one set of plates in England, publish with another set of plates in America, and publish with a third set of plates in Canada within ten days of the British publication while 'residing' in Canada."[45]

Admittedly, Blodgett's decision was controversial, stirring arguments on both sides of the question. As Herbert Feinstein testifies, the afternoon edition of the *Chicago Daily News* on January 10, 1883, criticized Sam for pressing his suit: "It is not probable that the name will be disgraced, and in future Mr. Clemens ought to feel grateful, because in future much of the stale wit that has borne his *nom de plume* and has been attributed to him will be blessed with a doubtful parentage." Yet the same paper in its evening edition editorially excoriated the judicial decision, "which legalizes piracy" or made thievery "respectable." Not that Sam suffered the judgment gladly. In chapter 24 of *Huck Finn*, written in the summer of 1883, the fraudulent king masquerades under the name Blodgett while attempting to swindle the Wilks sisters.[46]

Before the end of the year, Sam also engaged in a number of bitter spats with his critics. To be sure, some "authorities" had been predicting his demise for years, especially after his speech in honor of the birthday of John Green-leaf Whittier in 1877. Sam had "had his day," the *San Francisco Bulletin* announced in October 1878, while he was traveling in Italy. "It is a little more than ten years since he appeared before the public, and during that time he has enjoyed a degree of success hardly paralleled in the history of literature. It is now, however, gone like a dream, and it will be well for him if he has laid up enough of the bounties of fortune to place him in an independent situation." In the wake of the critical flop of *A Tramp Abroad* (1880), the columnists began to vilify him. The joke went around, after Sam moved his study to the loft of the carriage house at the mansion, that the book read as if it was "written in a stable by an author thoroughly at home there." The New York *Graphic* alleged that Sam was "played out" and that his recent books were "selling poorly." The New York *Sun* even spread a rumor that he was a lunatic, suffering from melancholy and delusions, fancying that he was the editor of the *Hartford Courant* and/or a deacon in Twichell's church, often standing on a box in his yard like an Egyptian obelisk on its pedestal—this at the same moment that fund-raising to build the pedestal for the Statue of Liberty in New York Harbor had stalled. The hoax concluded with sarcastic reassurance: "Happily, these attacks do not last as a rule more than ten days or a fortnight."[47] These rumors were so distorted by time and distance that

Australian journalists reported over two years later that Sam had "lost his reason" and "been placed under restraint." The *San Francisco Bulletin*, which had once championed his genius, asserted in November 1882 that he was "supposed by many sober-minded people to be a crank." The *Louisville Post* proclaimed that he was "an imbecile and vulgarian and 'out of place in the East among men of culture.'" The country was "getting very weary" of Sam's brand of humor, according to the *St. Louis Post-Dispatch*, which unleashed an ad hominem attack on him. He had been "a second-class pilot on the Western rivers and went into humor because the pay was better and the work not so exhausting. His style is bad, his matter bad, and his humor was worn out three years ago. His later books are simply a rehash of the earlier ones." In fact, Sam was "a standing monument to the success which will always attend literary dishonesty." E. W. Howe, author of *The Story of a Country Town* (1883), concluded that Sam's career was "nearly at an end. The paragraphists have commenced to pelt him, and they will finish him before they get through. His wit has been watered until it is without flavor." The *Pall Mall Gazette* sniffed that Sam was "nothing but a clown." *Ideal* magazine lamented that at times he was "so coarse he is not fit for polite society" and he exhibited no qualities "to redeem his coarseness, his irreverence, his want of refinement." In a poll of its readers published in April 1884 the *Critic* listed Sam only fourteenth among living American literary "immortals"— though only men or those of the "sterner sex" were eligible for inclusion in the voting—behind the three surviving Fireside Poets (Holmes, Lowell, and Whittier) and such luminaries as Thomas Bailey Aldrich, Cable, Edward Everett Hale, Harte, Howells, Henry James, and E. C. Stedman. The Hartford correspondent of the *Boston Herald* sniped that Sam had overestimated his appeal and would "learn some lessons which will abate his conceit" as soon as more of his "twaddle" appeared in print. He had ostensibly "made more money out of mere trash than any other writer in the records of literature, and what reputation he at first won has been for some years on a decline." Convinced that this correspondent was connected with the American Publishing Company, Sam urged Osgood to "set your detective forces to work" and identify the culprit so that he might "begin suit against that concern" and "waltz into that gang with affectionate enthusiasm."[48]

Nothing came of this empty threat, but Sam was understandably more driven than ever to protect his privacy. "I cannot abide those newspaper references to me & my matters," he wrote Orion. Eventually he learned to ignore them. He requested "fair play, nothing more," in a letter to the editor of the *Boston Herald* in early July 1885. "I can't reply when the newspapers make misstatements about me. It wouldn't do—the public would quickly tire of it." Later in the month he reiterated, "I am quite willing to let the minor imaginary crimes that are now and then charged against me in the newspapers pass unchallenged so long as the large real ones which I daily commit, and seldom repent of, are not found out." Privately he was even more sanguine. The jackleg journalist Henry Clay Lukens eventually charged in the April 1890 issue of *Harper's* that Sam was merely a beneficiary of luck, not talent, the "one man of all our newspaper harlequins whom Good Luck chose for its pampered idol." Sam retorted that his "inflexible rule" was "to be satisfied & content with anything & everything" that might be said about him in public "so long as it confines itself to statements that are not true." He had "never seen an opinion of me in print which was as low down as my private opinion of myself."[49]

The ongoing controversy over Sam's presumed loss of power and popularity, however, set the stage for another public charge of plagiarism against him in December 1881. In his tale "A Curious Experience," he portrayed a teenage reader of dime novels and blood-and-thunder fiction who inadvertently convinces the narrator he is a Confederate spy. The frame opens with this statement: "This is the story which the Major told me, as nearly as I can recall it." A correspondent of the *Critic* soon wrote to complain:

> I am an admirer of the writings of Mr. Mark Twain, and consequently, when I saw the table of contents of the November number of the *Century*, bought it and turned at once to the article bearing his name. . . . When I began to read it, it struck me as strangely familiar, and I soon recognized the story as a true one, told me in the summer of 1878 by an officer of the U.S. Artillery.

The correspondent concluded with a question: Did Sam expect "the public to credit this narrative to his clever brain?" Even more thin-skinned than usual, Sam was outraged by the suggestion he had filched the tale or purposefully misled his readers. He addressed an angry letter to the editor of the *Critic*:

> Your correspondent is not stupid, I judge, but purely & simply malicious. He knew there was not the shadow of a suggestion, from the beginning to the end of "A Curious Experience," that the story was an *invention*; he knew he had no warrant for trying to persuade the public that I had stolen the narrative & was endeavoring to palm it off as a piece of literary invention; he also knew that he was asking his closing question with a base motive—else he would have asked it of me, by letter, not spread it before the public.

Sam also turned his guns on the editor who had included the letter in the magazine. "I have never wronged you in any way," he fumed, "& I think you had no right to print that communication; no right, neither any excuse. As to publicity answering that correspondent, I would as soon think of bandying words in public with any *other* prostitute." But he soon repented the haste and anger in which he wrote. The editor of the *Critic* and thus the recipient of his letter was not Joseph Gilder, as he thought, but Jeannette Gilder, Joseph's sister and cofounder of the magazine with him, and Sam was abashed when he discovered his mistake a month later. But even then he failed to express his regrets to her directly. As he wrote to Hjalmar Hjorth Boyesen,

> I beg you to offer my thoroughly sincere apologies to Miss Gilder, & say to her that no injury, real or imaginary, could provoke me to write a letter like that to any member of her sex, high or low, rich or poor. I never have done such a thing, & I know myself well enough to know that I never shall. Confound it, I did the very thing I was complaining of other people about—rushed in without right information when right information was easy to get.[50]

In order to combat the adverse publicity and help repair Sam's reputation, Howells published a full-scale defense of his friend, his "burning resentment of all manner of cruelty and wrong," and literary realism in general in the September 1882 issue of the *Century*. It was the first article of its kind. Sam's "purely and wholly American" humor, he wrote, "is as simple in form and as direct as the statesmanship of Lincoln or the generalship of Grant." But Sam was also "an artist of uncommon power as well as a humorist." As Howells admonished the reader, "if he leaves out of the account an indignant sense of right and wrong, a scorn of all affectation and pretense, an ardent hate of meanness and injustice, he will come indefinitely short of knowing Mark Twain." Howells sent a copy of the article in proof to Sam, who readily approved it: "Of *course* it pleases *me*—that goes without saying—& I hope the public will be willing to see me with your eyes. I shouldn't ask anything better than that. Well, I am mighty glad you had time & the disposition to write it."[51]

The Prince and the Pauper was finally issued in the United States by Osgood on December 12, 1881. The initial sales by subscription were disappointing, however. Osgood had hoped to limit the cost of production to no more than 45 cents per copy, though the cost of the initial print run of twenty-five thousand copies was $17,500 or about 70 cents per copy, and after all reprintings the cost per copy only dropped to about 60 cents—one of the reasons Sam earned little money on the book and soon became disenchanted with Osgood's management style. Only three weeks after publication, in fact, Sam was scheming with Osgood to dump copies of the novel on the trade market in violation of contractual agreements and the norms of subscription publication. "We can't keep the books out of the stores—& moreover, we don't want to," he explained to Osgood. "We only want to *let on* like everything that we *do* want to—otherwise the canvassers would sail into us."

Sam proposed in the same letter that they retail his next book in the market as "our own general agents in N. Y., Phila and Boston." They "could work the bookstores and divide the swag"—this last phrase the same one Sam had used five years earlier to describe his collaboration with Harte on *Ah Sin*. Five weeks later, on February 12, 1882, Sam was even more explicit about the ploy: "It might be a good thing to cut under the unfaithful gen[era]l agents by shoving books into the stores at a little cheaper terms than *they* can afford—doing this either openly or clandestinely as shall seem most judicious." Such a duplicitous trick not only subverted the book agents who had contracted with the press to sell the book door-to-door but also reduced gross revenue. A subscription book "will sell two or three times as many copies as it would in the trade," Sam continued to insist, "and the profit is bulkier because the retail price is greater," but he was willing to dump remaindered copies when a print run exceeded demand. In all, he only cleared some $17,000 on initial sales of the novel, a small fraction of the $100,000 the family spent in 1881. Fortunately, Sam and Livy did not depend on the profit on *The Prince and the Pauper* for a livelihood. Their joint total income for the year from all sources totaled about $250,000. Still, their expenses were so exorbitant that Sam briefly flirted with the possibility of launching another lecture series in London the following spring or summer. Andrew Chatto supported the notion, expressing "not the slightest doubt of the success of the venture," but Sam soon dropped the idea.[52]

Whereas *A Tramp Abroad* had been a smash sales success and a critical disappointment, *The Prince and the Pauper* was a commercial calamity and a critical triumph. To be sure, it faced stiff competition in the book market because it was released during the same holiday season as Howells's *Dr. Breen's Practice* and Henry James's *The Portrait of a Lady*. But many of Sam's personal friends lauded the book. Predictably, Mother Fairbanks declared it "your masterpiece in fineness" and E. P. Parker, again exhibiting a bias against humor writing, announced in the *Hartford Courant* that Sam had "finally fulfilled the earnest hope of many of his best friends" by writing "a book which has other and higher merits than can possibly belong to the most artistic expression of mere humor." Even Sam's fellow humorist John Henton Carter (aka Commodore Rollingpin) believed that *The Prince and the Pauper* "was his best and would outlive any of the others that he had written." Joel Chandler Harris opined that "all that is really vital in the wild humor of Mark Twain is here, but it is strengthened and refined. . . . The wild western burlesquer, the builder of elephantine exaggerations and comicalities has disappeared, and in his stead we have the true literary artist." Harriet Beecher Stowe considered *The Prince and the Pauper* "the best book for young people that was ever written," she told Sam in April 1887, and the next month she told him that she was reading it "for the sixth time"—evidence, according to Sam, that "she was already losing her mind." Aldrich, Howells's successor as editor of the *Atlantic Monthly,* commissioned a review by Boyesen, who was predictably effusive: Sam had "written a book which no reader, not even a critical expert, would think of attributing to him" but "it will be accorded a rank far above any of the author's previous productions." *The Prince and the Pauper* was "certainly not by the Twain we have known for a dozen or more years as the boisterous and rollicking humorist, whose chief function has been to diffuse hilarity with mirth in its most demonstrative forms." On the other hand, Joe Goodman, with his preference for extravagant humor, was disenchanted with the novel. It was, Goodman wrote Sam, "the first of your works in which I have ever been disappointed. Aside from the clear-cut English and an occasional bit of elegant description or quiet humor, there are no evidences of your handiwork in the volume. It might have been written by anybody else—by a far less masterly hand, in fact. You went entirely out of your sphere. The laboriousness is apparent everywhere." Goodman reminded Sam that his "forte is existing people and things" and that "no one but a mere romancer should travel out of his age."[53]

These divided opinions were mirrored in other reviews of the novel. Many publications were loud in their praise—for example, the *Boston Journal* ("a finer grade of work and a more delicate quality of humor"), *Boston Advertiser* ("Mark Twain never appeared to better advantage"), *Boston Herald* ("an achievement like this would be a triumph for any author"), *Boston Transcript* ("a quality so refined and yet so searching"), *Hartford Courant* (in the ultimate appraisal of his fiction it is sure to rank very high"), *New York Herald* ("characterized by a manly love of truth, a hatred of humbug, and a scorn for cant"), *Harper's Monthly* ("a generous and ennobling moral"), *Sacramento Union* ("some excellent examples of keen satire"), and Washington *Critic* (the book exhibited "the finer element in Mark Twain's nature"). The *San Francisco Bulletin* was more equivocal, calling it "a book which is not exquisite fun." Among the American venues that noticed the book, only the *Century* was inhospitable, writing that "we do not think his 'new departure' is a conspicuous success" and "some of the fun sprinkled through the story grates on the ear."[54]

The reviews in the British Commonwealth, too, were "surprisingly complimentary," Sam bragged to Andrew Chatto. "Even the 'London Times' stoops to flatter," he wrote; the paper had called it "a remarkably ingenious and sensible story." Among the other papers that joined the chorus were the London *Graphic* ("its humour is delicate; its fun joyously real; and its pathos tender and deep"), London *Congregationalist* ("a tale which young people in particular will find of thrilling and absorbing interest"), *Spectator* ("an ingenious idea, which has been well worked out"), London *Standard* ("a serious tale of absorbing interest"), *Nonconformist* ("delicate fancy as well as lively humour"), London *Morning Post* ("a queer, wild story"), London *Daily News* ("perhaps there is no living writer who has a more marked individuality than Mark Twain"), and *Leicester Chronicle* ("the best Christmas book issued this season"). A pair of Scottish papers also hailed the novel: the *Edinburgh Scotsman* ("one of the most delightful boys' books") and *Glasgow Herald* ("full of clever work"). Even the major quarterlies applauded the novel, including the *Quarterly Review* ("mingled humor and pathos"), *British Quarterly Review* ("almost accomplished the impossible"), and *Westminster Review* (the author had turned "from comic accounts of travel and general American buffoonery to the task of writing a serious historical novel"). The book was lauded in Australia in the Melbourne *Leader* ("marked by qualities which the popular humorist has not before been suspected of possessing") and *Brisbane Courier* ("an exceedingly nice story") and in New Zealand in the *Lyttelton Times* (Sam had "devoted one of the autumnal days of his literary life to breaking a lance in the sacred cause of humanity"). Like the *Century* in the United States, however, many of the predictable venues panned it, including the *Academy* ("a ponderous fantasia on English history . . . singularly deficient in literary merit") and "an enraged idiot" (as Sam called the critic) in the *Athenaeum* ("the flattest and worst" of "Clemens's many jokes").[55]

The evening of December 22, 1881, the 261st anniversary of the landing of the Pilgrims, the New England Society of Pennsylvania hosted its first annual dinner at the Continental Hotel in Philadelphia. Among the guests were Senator William P. Frye of Maine and Governor Henry M. Hoyt of Pennsylvania, and Sam delivered the featured after-dinner speech. Almost exactly four years after the Whittier birthday celebration, he again ran the risk of offending his audience, in this case by ridiculing "the Mayflower gang" they were there to honor, though this talk received much less publicity. The president of the society had declared in his opening address that Plymouth Rock had been "put there especially for the Pilgrims by the Lord" and Sam rushed to correct this misapprehension. "Those Pilgrims were a hard lot," he acknowledged. "They took good care of themselves, but they abolished everybody else's ancestors. I am a border ruffian from the state of Missouri; I am a Connecticut Yankee by adoption. In me you have Missouri morals, Connecticut culture." But all of Sam's ostensible forebears—Indians, Quakers, witches, and slaves alike, he claimed—were exterminated by the forebears of the men in the room.

> Your ancestors—yes, they were a hard lot; but, nevertheless, they gave us religious liberty to worship as they required us to worship and political liberty to vote as the church required. . . . Hear me, I beseech you; get up an auction

and sell Plymouth Rock! . . . Sell it before it is injured by exposure or at least throw it open to the patent medicine advertisements and let it earn its taxes. Yes, hear your true friend—your only true friend—list to his voice. Disband these societies, hotbeds of vice, of moral decay; perpetuators of ancestral superstition. Here on this board I see water, I see milk, I see the wild and deadly lemonade. These are but steps upon the downward path. Next we shall see tea, then chocolate, then coffee—hotel coffee. A few more years—all too few, I fear—mark my words, we shall have cider!

As incestuous a relative to the Whittier speech as this address may seem in cold type, it was, according to press reports, received with "hearty applause" and "continual laughter." Bruce Michelson concludes that on this occasion Sam got "the tone right." But it once more triggered a backlash among editorialists far from Philadelphia who read but did not hear his remarks. "At public dinners," according to the *New Haven Register,* Sam was "growing a little bit sacrilegious and decidedly strained." The *Chicago Inter Ocean* agreed that his "recent public exhibit" again almost made "a wreck" of his reputation and the *Cleveland Plain Dealer* averred that Sam was "clever in some respects but he has chosen to lower himself to the plane of a literary buffoon."[56]

In the first days of 1882 Sam was so sensitive to the critical aspersions recently hurled at him in the press that for a time he planned to retaliate. In early January Charley Warner intimated to him "that the N.Y. Tribune was engaged in a kind of crusade against me." Since Reid's return from his wedding journey in Europe, Warner alleged, "the Tribune had been flinging sneers & brutalities" at Sam "with such persistent frequency 'as to attract general remark'" and another friend charged "that the attacks were not merely 'frequent' but 'almost *daily*.'" How should Sam respond? "I set about contriving a plan to accomplish one or the other of two things: 1. Force a peace; or 2. Get revenge." The latter alternative appealed to Sam more than the former. Or as he notified Osgood on January 7, "I am meditating a little assault of a rather venomous nature upon Whitelaw Reid." He devoted the next three weeks to researching an exposé of Outlaw Reid, the derisive nickname Ulysses S. Grant had given the editor, and "went to New York and sat three hours taking evidence while a stenographer set it down." He consulted John Russell Young, the former managing editor of the *Tribune,* who told Sam that Reid was "a gigantic donkey—with none of the donkey's redeeming qualities," and he began to take notes for a hatchet job to be published anonymously. Reid was "the skunk of our species" and "purely and simply a Guiteau with the courage left out," he wrote as the trial of Garfield's assassin was concluding in Washington. By borrowing money to buy a half interest in the *Tribune* from Jay Gould, Sam believed, Reid had become a mere lackey of the robber baron. In a word, Gould "owned him." Reid was guilty of "double-facedness & treachery toward Grant," though they were both prominent Republicans; he "chased after all the rich girls in California"; and, like the young George Washington, he could not tell a lie, as when he admitted that "I have no <stones> nuts." Sam then added a touch of phallic humor: Reid "envied the Stones of Venice." Sam noted that Reid's "character was unique," punning on "eunuch." He planned to dedicate the iconoclastic biography "to the Remote Darwinian" because Reid was the "Missing Link," an atavist or evolved gorilla. To judge by the size of his feet, Reid should have been "9 ft high." In Sam's phrenological reading of Reid's skull, the editor exhibited "selfish organs . . . so heavy they weigh down back of head & tilt his face upward." After his marriage to the daughter of a millionaire, Sam asserted, Reid had reached the "dignity of pall-bearers at <rich> capitalist's funerals." Sam planned to reproduce in the book as many as a dozen steel portraits of Reid "as a sort of idiot, from infancy up." Sam fell "thoroughly in love with this work; for I saw that I was going to write a book which the very devils & angels themselves would delight to read & which would draw disapproval from nobody but the hero of it." Livy, however, was "bitter against the whole thing" from the start.[57]

She insisted that Sam verify the claims against Reid before proceeding further with his nefarious designs so on January 21 he asked Webster to "copy off & send to me every remark which the Tribune has made about me *since the end of October,* up to the present date. Keep your own counsel; say nothing to anybody about this. As I understand it, these remarks have usually been brief original paragraphs on the inside pages & *borrowed* slurs on the other pages." Sam also subscribed to the paper and began to monitor its columns. But his petty scheme soon dissipated like noxious smoke in a gust of wind. Webster found little evidence of the "prodigious bugaboo" Reid had allegedly mounted against him—nothing more than a couple of asides to the effect that Sam had been denied Canadian copyright and that he had spoken at a public banquet while "domiciled" in Montreal, an item "touched with an almost invisible satire." To "offset that one jest," Sam conceded, "the Tribune paid me one compliment" for his speech in Philadelphia on Forefather's Day. He was waylaid by the paucity of evidence of Reid's perfidy. As he wondered to Howells, "Can you conceive of a man's getting himself into a sweat over so diminutive a provocation? I am sure I can't. What the devil can those friends of mine have been thinking about to spread those three or four harmless things out into two months of daily sneers and affronts?" The *Tribune* "didn't say anything that could annoy me or justify me in retaliating—so of course I have had to pigeon-hole my notes. I didn't destroy them; it would not be wise nor far-sighted to do that." But he never returned to the project. His "three weeks' hard work" had gone to naught while he "could have earned ten thousand dollars with infinitely less trouble." Howells, whom Osgood had urged to discourage Sam from pursuing his "dynamitic life of Reid," was relieved by the news, though he had "had an abiding faith that you would get sick of your enterprise." After Sam's death Howells reflected on the close call and how "the editor's life was spared. The wretch never knew how near he was to losing it, with incredible preliminaries of obloquy and a subsequent devotion to lasting infamy." Not that Sam ever really reconciled with Reid. In his autobiographical dictation for August 27, 1907, he was ruthless in his characterization of Reid, even after his adversary had been nominated for vice president on the Republican ticket with Benjamin Harrison in 1892:

> He is narrow, and hard, cold, calculating, unaffectionate, except toward his family and a very small circle of especial friends; his dislikes are strong and steady and lasting, and he is unforgiving. . . . He is disliked by many, liked by few, envied by a multitude, and admired by nobody. He is a typical American product—a product hardly producible elsewhere, but easily producible among us. He is a good sample of what money, push, steady-going energy, pertinacity, and a reasonably good business talent—unsubject to damaging excitements and gushing enthusiasms—can do for a man in our republic.

Lest Sam betray his true opinion of Reid in 1882, however, he carefully covered his tracks. As soon as he abandoned the revenge biography, he wrote Reid to extend a kind hand: "I have told you many times, these many years, that I am always ready & glad to help you . . . just as far as I am able. A friendship that can say less, is not a friendship to be valued."[58]

Not that he was hypocritical in all his relations. Ned House and Koto returned to the Clemens home on January 30, 1882, whereupon House was felled by an attack of gout. He was bedridden for "about two weeks; and most of the time *mighty* sick," Sam remembered. House was so tortured by pain "that he drank laudanum in startling quantities." Reid considered House's condition "the nearest to a living death of any case I have ever seen, and . . . the most pitiful." On February 3, while House was still a houseguest, Sam also hosted a dinner party in honor of the Canadian poet Louis Fréchette. Twichell jotted in his journal that Sam "*never was* so funny as this time. The perfect art of a certain kind of storytelling will die with him."[59]

A month later Sam also lobbied Grant on behalf of Howells's father. After Garfield's death, the elder Howells, the U.S. consul in Toronto, feared he would be removed from office by President Arthur. The younger Howells asked Sam to appeal to Grant to intervene, much as Sam and Twichell had asked the former president to intercede on behalf of the Chinese Educational

Mission in December 1880. Sam and Howells rendezvoused in Hartford on March 8 and traveled to New York to petition Grant personally, meeting with him by appointment in his Wall Street office two days later. Howells recalled that his fellow Buckeye was "very simple and very cordial" and spoke with "the soft, rounded, Ohio River accent to which my ears were earliest used from my steamboating uncles." As soon as the two men stated their business, Grant promised to contact Arthur "and he did so that day; and my father lived" to retire voluntarily from the consular service. Sam was gratified: he merely wanted Grant's "assistance in keeping Howells's father from being turned out of his Toronto consulate; and with his usual prompt and indestructible generosity, he came to the rescue." Afterward Grant invited Sam and Howells to join him for a modest lunch of baked beans and coffee. They "were of about the railroad-refreshment quality," Howells remembered, "but eating them with Grant was like sitting down to baked beans and coffee with Julius Caesar, or Alexander, or some other great Plutarchan captain."[60]

Howells returned to Boston after the meeting while Sam railed to Washington on March 13 to plead the case for international copyright with some of "the bright lights there." He urged Congress to enact protections by treaty rather than legislation, though nothing came of this "deep, deep copyright scheme." The *Boston Herald* ridiculed his quixotic mission, editorializing that if he wished to assert "copy, or any other, rights" he should renounce "the Canadian residency he had claimed" in his vain attempt to secure imperial copyright to *The Prince and the Pauper* and become a "naturalized" U.S. citizen. Sam might have anticipated such abuse. "Whenever a copyright law is to be made or altered," he later remarked, "the idiots assemble."[61]

CHAPTER 10

❖

Down the River and Far Away

Traveling by boat is the best way to travel unless one can stay at home.

—Samuel Clemens, interview, July 9, 1886

WHEN W. D. Howells visited Hartford on March 8, 1882, prior to appealing to former president Ulysses S. Grant to help save William Cooper Howells's consular job, Samuel Clemens shared with him his dream of a grandiose lecture tour. A "traveling menagerie" of speakers, including the two of them, Thomas Bailey Aldrich, George Washington Cable, and Joel Chandler Harris, would barnstorm across the country in a private railcar with "a cook of our own and every facility for living on the fat of the land." At every stop, each of them would "read two minutes or so" onstage and "pose as 'the happy family'"—the name of an exhibit of natural predators living together in a cage at P. T. Barnum's dime museum in New York in 1875. Sam, as ringmaster of the circus, would guarantee each of the others at least seventy-five dollars a day and expenses. But both Aldrich and Howells left for Europe "and the others couldn't join us for one reason or another," so the notion of a traveling "menagerie" had to be abandoned. "I suppose I might have gone out on some such expedition all by myself," Sam later reflected in an interview, "but I'm afraid it wouldn't be pleasant. I want somebody to keep me in countenance on the stage, and to help me impose on the audience. But more than that, I want good company on the road and at the hotels. A man can start out alone and rob the public, but it's dreary work, and it's a cold-blooded thing to do."[1]

Instead he lowered his expectations by planning a return to the river, a trip he had considered almost every year for a decade. In late November 1874 Sam proposed to his lecture agent James Redpath that they rail west about May 1 and "make a lagging journey" down the river—a trip that would have enriched his memories prior to writing "Old Times on the Mississippi"— meanwhile "paying expenses & making money by talking 'Roughing It' thrice in New York, once in Cleveland, twice in Chicago, once in Louisville, twice in St. Louis, once in Memphis, & twice in N[ew] Orleans." Redpath declined, but three weeks later Howells tepidly offered to travel with Sam, and Sam urged James R. Osgood to join the party: "[D]on't you want to take a pleasure trip about that time? I wish you would go. Think of the gaudy times you & Howells & I would have on such a bender!" In the end, Sam regretfully canceled the trip. "If I live a year," he vowed to Howells, "I will make one more attempt to go down the river, for I shall have lived in vain if I go silent out of the world."[2] In the spring of 1882 Sam transformed his proposed "orgy" (as Tom Sawyer might have called it) into a barnstorming field trip to research his long-planned Mississippi book, his first trip to the river valley since his 1868 trip to St. Louis to see his mother and sister. He signed a pair of contracts with Osgood on April 10 to supply copy for a collection of miscellany titled *The Stolen White Elephant Etc.* and to develop "Old Times on the Mississippi" into a book (which became *Life on the Mississippi*), stipulating a submission date of October 1. He lunched with Aldrich, Howells, and Osgood in Boston on April 10 and that afternoon traveled with Howells to Concord to visit the ailing Ralph Waldo Emerson before returning to Hartford. On April 17 Sam left Hartford for New York, where he again spent the night at the Hotel Brunswick and dined at the Union League Club with Osgood and William Laffan of the New York *Sun*. He also convened in the city with his erstwhile companions on the trip, Osgood and Roswell Phelps, a young stenographer for the Continental Life Insurance Company of Hartford. Sam had hired Phelps for a hundred dollars a month and expenses plus a dollar for every thousand words of transcription, and he would later bestow his surname upon Aunt Sally and Uncle Silas in *Adventures of Huckleberry Finn* (1885) and *Tom Sawyer, Detective* (1896).[3]

The trio left the next morning, headed west through Pittsburgh for Indianapolis, and transferred there to a train bound for St. Louis, where they arrived that evening. That is, they followed the same route Howells had traveled the year before when he railed to Crawfordsville, Indiana, to research the divorce court scene in his novel *A Modern Instance* (1882). The same day Sam, Osgood, and Phelps were aboard the train, Howells penned a sarcastic note to Sam: "I am sorry that Osgood is with you on this Mississippi trip; I foresee that it will be a contemptible half-success instead of the illustrious and colossal failure *we* could have made it." They took rooms at the Southern Hotel—"plain & substantial—one may say *bald*, sterile in decoration," as Sam described it—on the corner of Fourth Street and Walnut near the waterfront. "My movements must be kept secret, else I shan't be able to pick up the kind of book-material I want," he wrote Joel Chandler Harris. "To escape the interviewers" he registered under a fictitious name, C. L. Samuel, reversing the order of his initials and using his given name as a surname.[4]

The men spent only one night in St. Louis, however, because Sam "got to meeting too many people who knew me. We swore them to secrecy &

left by the first boat." Among the people who recognized him were the actor Lawrence Barrett, who was starring in *Yorick's Love* at the Saint Louis
Grand Opera House and who "stumbled on us" at the Southern Hotel,
where Barrett was also staying. They fled on the 876-ton packet *Gold Dust*,
"a vile, rusty old steamboat, but she was the only one that was going down
the river that day." Ironically, Sam was also recognized on the boat by an
old shipmate, probably John W. Langlois, who had served with him aboard
the *Aleck Scott* in 1858–59. Sam and his mates had planned to lay over in
Memphis before proceeding to New Orleans but when his cover was blown
they headed directly for Vicksburg, Mississippi, pausing en route at Cape
Girardeau, Missouri. There Sam hunted up Jacob Burrough, his St. Louis roommate twenty-seven years earlier, who had become an attorney. "It
would be nonsense to stop at Memphis now," he explained to his wife Livy,
"& fall a prey to the newspapers; so we shall stick to this boat" all the way to
Vicksburg. He gave a different reason to the readers of *Life on the Mississippi*:
"We were so pleasantly situated, that we did not wish to make a change." But
at Memphis, rather than sleep on the boat, the three men registered at the
Peabody Hotel near the harbor, Sam again as C. L. Samuel and Osgood as
J. R. Johnson, and they were not recognized.[5]

Sam was struck by how the lower Mississippi had been transformed since
the Civil War. "The river is so thoroughly changed that I can't bring it back
to mind even when the changes have been pointed out to me," he told Phelps.
"It is like a man pointing out to me a place in the sky where a cloud has been.
I can't reproduce the cloud." Napoleon, Arkansas, once a thriving port town
of two thousand residents at the confluence of the Arkansas and Mississippi
Rivers, had been "washed entirely away by a cut-off and not a vestige of it
remains—except one little house and the chimney of another which were
out in the suburbs once." Hat Island, where Horace Bixby had crossed "the
intricate and dangerous" reef at dusk in 1857, had entirely disappeared; and
Goose Island was "all gone but a piece about big enough for dinner." The "big
corn-fields when I was [a] pilot" were now in "the channel of the river"; Sam
did not "recognize any part of it at all." The lower Mississippi was also in the
late stages of a destructive flood season. Sam predicted in *Life on the Mississippi* that the flood of 1882 "will doubtless be celebrated in the river's history
for several generations before a deluge of like magnitude shall be seen. It put
all the unprotected low lands under water, from Cairo to the mouth; it broke
down the levees in a great many places, on both sides of the river," and in
some regions when the river crested it "was *seventy miles* wide!"[6]

Their progress downriver was desultory. They stopped "every 2 or 3 miles"
and had "a most serene & enjoyable time," Sam noted. "Osgood says he has
never enjoyed any trip more. We were 6 hours & a quarter coming 23 miles,

this morning," he wrote Livy on April 25, "because we made so many land-ings. We are only 70 miles above Vicksburg, now, (where we stop,) but we shall be 12 or 14 hours making it." The *Gold Dust* landed at Vicksburg at 1:00 a.m. on April 26 and, in a passage later omitted from *Life on the Mis-sissippi*, Sam recalled that he, Osgood, and Phelps "were content to remain aboard the *Gold Dust* that night & gossip with the officers—more especially as we should part company with them on the morrow & end a companion-ship which had been exceedingly close & delightful." Later that day, while strolling around the town, Sam visited the editorial offices of the *Vicksburg Herald*, where he made a distinct but not propitious impression. According to a columnist for the newspaper, he looked "like a man who had just escaped from a lunatic asylum, whose only sense was in the perfect realization of that fact, and whose every energy was concentrated in an effort to dodge his keeper. With his long, bushy hair, indifferent colored mustache, shaggy eye-brows, restless, nervous temperament, drawling gait and speech, slouch hat and $6.50 suit of clothes of a baggy fit" he exhibited "the eccentricity which is the 'revenue stamp' of genius."[7]

The three men left Vicksburg on April 26 aboard the *Charles Morgan* and docked the next day in Natchez, Mississippi, and for a half hour in Ba-ton Rouge, Louisiana, where Sam viewed with disdain the recently rebuilt castellated Gothic state capitol. He ridiculed the "imitation castle," which boldly endorsed a "maudlin Middle-Age romanticism" akin to the decadent Walter Scottism he despised. After the *Morgan* arrived in New Orleans the morning of April 28, a fellow passenger complained in the local press that Sam "wasn't at all sociable. He traveled *incog*[*nito*] and never got out of the feeling that he was being pursued and hunted." The trio registered at the lux-urious St. Charles Hotel, today the site of the Place St. Charles. Sam found the hotel bar much as he remembered it from a quarter century earlier, with its "cool porch," "sawdusted floor," and "mint-julep suckers."[8]

With the local author George Washington Cable as their concierge and tour guide, the three men promptly jumped into "a whirlpool of hospitality—breakfasts, dinners, lunches, cock-fights, Sunday schools, mule-races, lake-excursions, social gatherings, & all sorts of things," Sam reported to Livy. The day of their arrival they went sightseeing in a carriage through the French Quarter, where they visited the old St. Louis Hotel ("hasn't been swept for 40 years") at the corner of St. Louis and Chartres Streets, attended the mule races benefiting the Southern Art Union at the fairgrounds, and spent the evening in the West End dining on "a ground-veranda over the water" of Lake Pontchartrain on pompano ("delicious as the less criminal forms of sin"), and returned to their hotel around 10:00 p.m. Ironically, Sam was more familiar with the streets of the city than with the natural bends and curves of the river. "The New Orleans of today in all respects is the N.O. of 40 or 50 years ago," he marveled. "They use the electric lights here pretty lavishly. Canal st[reet] has more lights of the kind than I ever saw before; and several adjoining streets are so lighted. There are 4 miles of electric lights on the river front."[9]

On Sunday, April 30, they met Joel Chandler Harris, who arrived at Sam's invitation by train to join the soiree. As Cable's daughter recalled the occasion, Harris was scheduled "to arrive from Atlanta at seven o'clock Sunday morning; so we got up and received him. We were able to detect him among the crowd of arrivals" at the St. Charles Hotel by the description they had been given: "He was said to be undersized, red-haired, and somewhat freckled." The Sabbatarian Cable escorted the group to the Prytania Street Presbyterian Church. Sam's opinion of the ceremony may be inferred from Grace King's observation five years later during a visit to Hartford that "one of his funniest hits was an imitation of the sermon Cable took him to hear." Cable then ushered the men incongruously to a cockfight, which Sam considered an "inhuman sort of entertainment." That evening they attended an African American service at the First Street Methodist Episcopal Church (aka Winan's Chapel). Sam confided to his journal, however, that the experience "was a failure" because it was "too good for literature" and, besides, a "white woman preached."[10]

May Day was mostly devoted to socializing. In the morning the four men breakfasted with the editors of the *New Orleans Picayune* and spent the afternoon at Cable's home on Eighth Street, where they read aloud to Cable's family. Harris was present "but was too bashful to read," plus the neighborhood children "were grievously disappointed to find he was white & young," so Sam recited some of "my own stuff" as well as several of Harris's Uncle Remus stories, concluding with "Brer Rabbit and the Tar Baby." According to Howells, "no one could read *Uncle Remus* like [Sam]; his voice echoed the voices of the negro nurses who told in his childhood the wonderful tales." Cable read some of his own sketches and recited from his novel *The Grandissimes* (1880). That evening one of Cable's friends, the attorney James B. Guthrie, hosted a reception for them attended by twenty-five guests. "We are still booming along in the sociabilities," Sam wrote Livy, "& find it a pretty energetic business & rather taxing to the strength." Sam was declared "the lion of the past week" by the *New Orleans Picayune*, which noted that "lots of people have had him to breakfast, lunch, and dinner." As in London in 1872 and 1878–79, he was so "involved in the social life of the town" that he "but lamely accomplished" the work at hand. "I had hoped to hunt up and talk with a hundred steamboatmen," he later remembered, but "I got nothing more than mere five-minute talks with a couple of dozen of the craft." He was so eager to escape demands on his time that he was "reduced to lying," as he put it, about other commitments. Part of the problem was the dearth of steamboats still plying the river. One tugboat "now brings down barges containing 6000 tons of grain—stuff which in my time would have come down in 4 or 5 steamboats," he noted in his journal, and the once-bustling docks were now "a wide and soundless vacancy" and "dead past resurrection." In place of "a solid mile of wide-awake" steamboats he now saw "half a dozen sound-asleep" vessels. In the billiard rooms and saloons of the port cities the rivermen with their "swell airs and graces, and ostentatious displays of money, and pompous squanderings of it" were conspicuous by their absence.[11]

The pace of activities began to slow the next day. In the morning, Harris departed for Atlanta and Sam steered a steam-tug owned by Captain Burr Wood, the *W. M. Wood*, "up & down the river a couple of hours at a tremendous rate." Certainly he spent some time along the docks and probably crossed paths with his old friend Captain John A. Stevenson. In the evening Sam and Osgood were the guests of honor at a "charmingly informal" dinner at John Strenna's restaurant on Bourbon Street in the French Quarter where, as Sam recalled in *Life on the Mississippi*, pompano was prepared to its "last possible perfection." Their host was Edward A. Burke, a former Confederate infantry major, Louisiana state treasurer, and owner of the New Orleans *Times-Democrat*. Sam entertained the group by spinning yarns and Cable by singing.[12]

On Wednesday, May 3, he finally crossed paths with his former master Horace Bixby, "the man whom, of all men, I most wished to see." Bixby had just arrived in the city aboard his latest Anchor Line command, the *City of Baton Rouge*, a behemoth at twenty-three hundred tons and a length of over 290 feet, with six bridal chambers and a pilothouse that was, according to Coleman O. Parsons, "nickel-plated, sound-tubed, steam-heated, and partly electrified." It once raced upriver from New Orleans to Memphis in a near-record time of two days, twenty hours, and thirty-eight minutes. At the spry age of fifty-six, Bixby cut the same figure his ex-cub remembered: "the same tight curls, the same springy step, the same alertness, the same decision of eye and answering decision of hand, the same erect military bearing." He and Sam spent the day together and traveled in the same clique the next three days.[13]

Sam had hoped to view Bayou Teche, due west of New Orleans, during his stay, but the river had flooded the district. Instead, he inspected the jetties below New Orleans. He and Osgood joined a party of fifteen, including Bixby and his wife, all of them guests of Captain Wood, and journeyed on the *Wood* about fifty miles south of the Crescent City to former governor Henry Clay Warmoth's Magnolia Plantation in Plaquemines Parish, where they spent the night. Below the city the tugboat passed a boat boneyard, "a number of decayed, ram-shackly, superannuated old steamboats," Sam reported, all of them "built, and worn out, and thrown aside, since I was here last." At the plantation, a former home of Confederate general P. G. T. Beauregard, the "tall, witty, self-possessed" Warmoth led them on a tour of his twenty-six hundred acres of fig and orange groves and sugar cane.[14]

Back in New Orleans on May 6, his last day in the city, Sam visited Washington Artillery Hall, a few blocks from the St. Charles Hotel. There he watched the Sweet Sweepers, a "broom brigade" of twenty-four young women, march and drill. As he cracked wise in his notebook, "To storm *breast works* defended by such sweet troopers would be very difficult." He also saw the massive (ten-by-twelve-foot) painting by Everett B. D. Julio, *Last Meeting of Robert E. Lee and Stonewall Jackson at Chancellorsville* (1869). As irreverent as usual, however, Sam refused to genuflect to this tribute to the Lost Cause. He suggested that in the moment Julio depicted, Jackson was asking Lee for a match.[15]

At 5:00 p.m. on that "delightfully hot day," Sam, Osgood, and Phelps left New Orleans for the return upriver. He wrote Livy with the details of his itinerary: "We leave this evening for St Louis, direct, in the *City of Baton Rouge*, Horace Bixby master . . . & shall arrive there next Friday, remain a few days, then a day in Hannibal, Keokuk, Quincy; then straight up to St Paul & across country to home." Cable played a practical joke on Sam as the boat was boarding. He planted a stranger at the gangplank who breathlessly informed Sam that he had read all of his writings and enjoyed best of all "The Heathen Chinee," Bret Harte's famous poem.[16] By the next evening, after only twenty-two and a half hours en route, the boat docked in Natchez, three hundred miles upriver—"much the swiftest passage I have ever made over that piece of water," Sam reported. The next morning it arrived in Vicksburg, by the morning of May 10 in Memphis, the following day in Cairo, and the next morning in St. Louis. "We had a delightful trip in that thoroughly well-ordered steamer," Sam recalled, "and regretted that it was accomplished so speedily." Osgood left St. Louis for Chicago on business, perhaps related to the suppression by the Boston district attorney of the sixth edition of Walt Whitman's *Leaves of Grass*, which he had issued the previous year, and Phelps headed back to Hartford to resume his duties at the insurance company. Sam visited the Merchants Exchange Building and state capitol and joined Bixby at the Planters' Hotel for cocktails and, as his old mentor put it, "a good last talk over old times and old acquaintances." Sam wrote Bixby later that to his "sore disappointment" they had not spent more time together and that "the most pleasant part of my visit with you was after we arrived in St. Louis." He overnighted at the Southern Hotel before leaving the next afternoon aboard the *Gem City* on a sentimental journey back to his hometown.[17]

He stepped ashore in Hannibal the next morning, a Sunday, with "the feeling of one who returns out of a dead-and-gone generation." None of his family still lived there and no one met him at the dock. No longer a sleepy village, Hannibal had grown into a rail center with a population of fifteen thousand. "Alas! everything was changed," he realized. He walked around the town alone, past his boyhood home, to the Park Hotel at Fourth Street and Center, where he registered, "but when I reached third or fourth st[reet]s the tears burst forth, for I recognized the mud. *It*, at least, was the same— the same old mud." The next day he was driven around by his childhood friend and schoolmate John Garth, now the president of the Farmers & Merchants Bank in Hannibal, who insisted that Sam spend his nights at his "spacious and beautiful" country estate Woodside three miles from town. The three days he loitered around the town, "examining the old localities and talking with the gray heads who were boys and girls with me thirty or forty years ago" were "delightful" but solemn, as he reported to Livy. He awoke every morning "with the impression that I was a boy—for in my dreams the faces were all young again, and looked as they had looked in the old times," he wrote in *Life on the Mississippi*. "But I went to bed a hundred years old, every night—for meantime I had been seeing those faces as they are now." Privately, he was even more pensive and poignant. "That world which I knew in its blossoming youth is old and bowed and melancholy," he wrote the day of his departure from Hannibal. "Its soft cheeks are leathery and wrinkled, the fire is gone out in its eyes, and the spring from its step. It will be dust and ashes when I come again. I have been clasping hands with the moribund— and usually they said, 'It is for the last time.'"[18]

Sam cruised upriver aboard the side-wheeler *Minneapolis* on May 17 to Quincy, Illinois, and then Keokuk, where he briefly visited his brother Orion and his wife Mollie.[19] "I am desperately homesick," Sam admitted to Livy, and he was dreading "this hideous trip to St. Paul." But he had promised to travel back to New York with Osgood "and must stick it out; otherwise I would take the train at once and break for home." Moreover, he had never before traveled so far north on the upper Mississippi. The *Minneapolis* landed on May 18 at Muscatine and Davenport, Iowa, where he was rejoined by Osgood; the next day at Dubuque; and they arrived in St. Paul the morning of May 21, where they registered at the Metropolitan. Sam was charmed by the topography of the upper river, particularly the bluffs around St. Paul, "where the rough and broken turreted rocks stand up against the sky above the steep, verdant slopes. They are inexpressibly rich and mellow in color; soft dark browns mingled with dull greens—the very tints to make an artist worship."[20]

Coincidentally, three of Sam's eminent acquaintances died during his brief Mississippi valley tour—Charles Darwin on April 19, Ralph Waldo Emerson on April 27, and Dr. John Brown on May 11. He noted in his journal his admiration for Darwin ("glad to have seen that mighty man") and Emerson ("so glad I visited him 2 or 3 weeks before"). But he reserved his greatest grief for the doctor, and wrote Brown's son that he had been "three thousand miles from home, at breakfast in New Orleans, when the damp morning paper revealed the sorrowful news among the cable dispatches. There was no place in America, however remote, or however rich or poor or high or humble, where words of mourning for your honored father were not uttered that morning." Coincidentally, only four months after cruising downriver to Vicksburg, the *Gold Dust* exploded and sank near Hickman, Kentucky, with twenty fatalities; and in September 1883 the *Gem City* was ravished by a fire that injured Sam's friend Langlois, who survived the explosion of the *Gold Dust* to become Bixby's head clerk aboard the *City of Baton Rouge* in 1890.[21]

After the spring warmth of New Orleans, Sam was benumbed by the frigidity of Minnesota. St. Paul was as "cold as the very devil" and a few flakes of snow fell. Though the two travelers had originally planned to return east by boat through the Great Lakes—"I go by water because I don't like the railroads," Sam had told an interviewer in St. Louis scarcely a week earlier—they left St. Paul by rail early in the afternoon of May 22 and arrived in New York the evening of May 24. Osgood spent that night at the Hotel Brunswick and soon reported that he and Sam had enjoyed "a glorious time" in the Midwest. Alerted that two-year-old Jean was ill with scarlet fever, Sam hurried to Hartford and arrived the next morning.[22]

He returned to a house under quarantine. "We have had scarlet fever in the house ever since I reached home," he wrote a friend in early July, and he notified Frank Fuller the same week that his "house will be under strict quarantine for several weeks." Jean was nursed by Livy, Sam, and Rosina Hay and attended as usual by Cincinnatus Taft, widely regarded as the leading physician in town. "No one else allowed in that part of the house," Sam wrote his mother, "& nobody allowed to enter the front door." Though they had originally planned to leave for Elmira in mid-June, Jean's illness postponed the Clemenses' departure until July 13 and, Sam claimed, delayed the completion of *Life on the Mississippi* "twice as long." He complained, not very graciously, that "the six weeks which Jean robbed me of happened by accident to be the very most valuable 6 weeks of my entire life." He wrote few letters, "attended to no business, not even matters of the vastest importance" during these weeks. Jean suffered later in life from epilepsy likely caused by this episode of fever. Sam's health was also compromised for the next several months by a series of maladies, including malaria apparently contracted during his Mississippi trip.[23]

Sam's return from his Mississippi Valley tour nearly coincided with the publication by Osgood in the United States and by Chatto & Windus in England in June 1882 of *The Stolen White Elephant Etc.* As sundry an assortment of odds and ends as a mismatched set of dishes, the volume contained such discordant pieces as Sam's "Speech on the New England Weather"; some fragments omitted from *A Tramp Abroad* (1880), including "The Stolen White Elephant" and "The Invalid's Story"; and "Some Rambling Notes of an Idle Excursion." He was so dubious of its appeal—he dismissed it in his autobiography twenty-four years later as "a collection of rubbishy sketches"— that he allowed Osgood to issue it through the regular channels of the book trade rather than by subscription. "The appearance of the volume marks an important change in the policy of the author as to the mode of publication," the *Boston Transcript* commented on June 3. "The present volume goes into the trade and can be had of any bookseller." But even this marketing gambit was not universally approved. The *Chicago Tribune* groused that Sam's latest volume had been issued by "a respectable publisher instead of offering booksellers a premium on dishonesty in order to obtain for their shelves" copies of a subscription book. Even Sam's hagiographer Albert Bigelow Paine allowed that it was "not an especially important volume" and Everett Emerson has granted that, in his view, of all Sam's books "it is the least distinguished."[24]

Moreover, the reviews of the volume were mixed. On the one hand, Lilian Whiting favorably compared the collection to its 1875 predecessor, *Sketches New and Old*, calling it "quite as racy and witty and entertaining." Joel Chandler Harris observed in the *Atlanta Constitution* that Sam "only the other day . . . was journeying up and down the Mississippi in search of material for a new volume," commended the "pungent" and "keen blade" of his satire, and suggested that the best sketch in the volume was "Some Rambling Notes." Similarly, the *Sheffield & Rotherham Independent* asserted that the "delightful book" represented "Mark Twain at his best" and hailed "An Idle Excursion" as the "best of all" the items. The *Leeds Mercury* asserted that "perhaps the most funny thing in this funny book is 'An Encounter with an Interviewer'"; the London *Morning Post* noted that "incomparably the best thing" in the "most amusing volume" was "The Invalid's Story"; and the *Athenaeum* commented that "The Invalid's Story" illustrated "the author at his best and strongest" and selected other sketches for special acclaim. Other publications were equally complimentary—for example, the *Boston Advertiser* ("more than mere burlesques"), *San Francisco Chronicle* ("much genuine fun and delicate sarcasm"), London *Academy* ("decidedly amusing"), London

Congregationalist ("brimful of amusing and interesting matter"), *Westminster Review* ("an amusing collection of stories and talk"), and *Nation* (humor of "a universal and comprehensive character"). The Washington, D.C., *Star*, without commenting on the contents, at least found its production values praiseworthy; the volume was "gotten up in much better style than any of [Sam's] books heretofore published."[25]

On the other hand, many critics indicted the forced humor of the sketches, including *Cottage Hearth*, which claimed Sam was "trying too hard to be funny," and the Philadelphia *North American*, which felt the humor was "sometimes strained." Others simply dismissed the collection as evidence that the wellspring of Sam's humor had run dry, among them the *New York Tribune* ("the reader turns the leaves of this volume, hour after hour, without the least temptation to smile"), *San Francisco Bulletin* ("the pump begins to suck"), Chicago *Dial* ("some falling little short of dullness"), London *Graphic* ("a sad falling-off," particularly evident in the "inherent repulsiveness" of "The Invalid's Story"), *Independent* (the book proved "the immense difficulty of sustaining the reputation of a professional humorist"), *Our Continent* ("inexpressibly dreary"), Melbourne *Australasian* ("various in respect of merit"), and *St. Joseph Gazette* ("a dozen newspapers in America have been made famous by obscure paragraphists of much brighter merit than his"). The Boston *Saturday Evening Gazette* charged that Sam had not only "badly overworked" his vein of humor recently but lacked "what may be termed literary judgment, as Boston people had conspicuous proof" from Sam's speech at the Whittier birthday dinner in 1877. "That he is to rank with the great writers of the country we do not believe. The idea of his greatness is a kind of whimsical conceit in the minds of one or two of his brother authors, which has its basis chiefly in the complete novelty of his work to them." The *Denver Tribune* resented the mere imputation that it should review the book. Sam had "managed to get richer than most people in his line of business" by practicing "penury and stinginess" so "if he wants newspaper puffing he should pay for it, just as other business men do." Eugene West was even more relentless in the *Chicago Times*: if Sam had "no better, purer humor to give to the reading public . . . he ought, out of pure sympathy for the people, . . . stop writing or publishing this washy stuff." He had "made a wo[e]ful failure as a humorist" and was "successfully swindling the public on his reputation." Readers had "learned both to distrust his honesty and ability as a writer." In the end, Osgood sold only about ten thousand copies of *The Stolen White Elephant Etc.* during its first six months in print.[26]

Sam devoted most of the months at Quarry Farm to drafting the manuscript of *Life on the Mississippi*, settling into a routine he maintained the entire summer: He worked in his study on the bluff above the farmhouse six days a week from just after breakfast until 4:00 p.m. and he discouraged visitors from interrupting him by posting a sign on his door: "Step Softly! Keep Away! Do Not Disturb the Remains!" On Sundays he walked into the city to see friends and play billiards. Livy allowed in mid-August that she had "never seen him when he worked with so much difficulty" and at the end of the day "his head [was] so sore & tired that he cannot bear to have the simplest question asked him, or be compelled to talk at all, so our evenings are mostly spent in playing cribbage." Sam complained to Joseph Twichell that he was "full of malaria," his brain "stuffy & cloudy nearly all the time. Some days I have been five hours writing two note-paper pages" or a total of 150 words. By early September he discovered that, though he had written 50,000 words on the manuscript, he was still some 30,000 words short of a complete draft "whereas a few days ago I thought it was only a third of that—dismal miscalculation!"[27]

At Sam's request, Osgood arranged for twenty-five "local histories of Mississippi towns & a lot of other books relating to the river" to be sent to him in late July. He exploited these works to good effect in the narrative, though not always with complete and proper attribution. To pad the book to the length necessary for subscription publication, he copied sources wholesale, among them Henry B. Fearon's *Sketches of America* (1819), Basil Hall's *Travels in North America* (1829), Frances Trollope's *Domestic Manners of the Americans* (1832), Captain Frederick Marryat's *A Diary in America* (1839), Henry Rowe Schoolcraft's *The Myth of Hiawatha* (1856), and Francis Parkman's *La Salle and the Discovery of the Great West* (1869). In parts of the manuscript he later omitted, he cited both Alexis de Tocqueville's *Democracy in America* (1835) and Lady Wortley's *Travels in the United States, Etc., during 1849 and 1850* (1851). In all, Sam acknowledged his debt to sixteen works and copied ten books verbatim but, as Dewey Ganzel has documented, "not always with 'credit given.'" He also inserted into the book several quotations from the New Orleans *Times-Democrat*, dated both during and after his Mississippi excursion, and incorporated some scraps of narrative left over from *A Tramp Abroad* and *The Stolen White Elephant Etc.*, such as "The Professor's Yarn" and Karl Ritter's tale of criminal detection and revenge. In an aside to the reader, Sam admitted that he included this tale "merely because it is a good story, not because it belongs here—for it doesn't."[28]

The structure of the book was in the end more pastiche or hodgepodge than patterned mosaic or linear narrative. Like many of Sam's books, it is a hybrid text, part bildungsroman, part travelogue, part literary miscellany, part novel of the road (or, in this case, the river). A rambling text like *A Tramp Abroad*, *Life on the Mississippi* is filled with eddies, undertows, and whirlpools. Sam opened with two chapters of historical and topological data, culled the five-thousand-word "raftsmen's passage" from the unfinished manuscript of *Huckleberry Finn* for chapter 3, then divided each of the seven "Old Times" installments—constituting about a fourth of the entire work—in half and reprinted them as chapters 4–17. He added to this material the never-told account of his tenure on the *Pennsylvania*, his feud with Brown, and the explosion of the boat and death of his brother Henry in chapters 18–20. The single-page chapter 21, "A Section in My Biography," bridges memoir to travelogue, the history of his trip down and up the river in 1882 in chapters 22–60. But, as he complained to his nephew Charley Webster on September 19, "my book drags like the very devil. Some days I cannot write a line." The manuscript was still incomplete when the family railed from Elmira to New York nine days later, overnighted at the Hotel Brunswick, and arrived back in Hartford the next day.[29]

After the family returned home, Sam worked even harder to finish the narrative. His best books wrote themselves, he often claimed; his role was merely that of an amanuensis. The books that caused him the most difficulty were travelogues, such as *A Tramp Abroad* and *Life on the Mississippi*, which required as much research as imagination. As he reported to Howells on October 3, he had worked that day from nine in the morning until after midnight and he was determined to continue this routine "until the thing is done, or break down at it. The spur and burden of the contract are intolerable to me. I can endure the irritation of it no longer." Though he had similarly struggled to complete the manuscript of *A Tramp Abroad*, he complained to Howells the next month that he had "never had such a fight over a book in my life before. And the foolishest part of the whole business is that I started Osgood to editing" the "apparently interminable book" while he was still writing its final chapters. But, he added,

> at last I have said with sufficient positiveness that I will finish the book at no particular date; that I will not hurry it; that I will not hurry myself; that I will take things easy and comfortably, write when I choose to write, leave it alone when I so prefer. The printers must wait, the artists, the canvassers, and all the rest. I have got everything at a dead standstill, and that is where it ought to be, and that is where it must remain; to follow any other policy would be to make the book worse than it already is. I ought to have finished it before showing [it] to anybody, and then sent it across the ocean to you to be edited, as usual.

Sam's method of writing the book at times resembled Penelope's weaving at her loom. "I have been on the home stretch, with three quarters of the course behind me, for two full months, and I have been laboriously jogging along all those two months; but what I write on one day I tear up the next," he wrote Ned House in early December, "so I make but little permanent advance toward the goal. In the work I have suffered for months with literary gout; all pain and no getting on." He sent a partial manuscript to Osgood on December 29, 1882, to satisfy a self-imposed deadline he had set. But even this attempt to assuage his publisher's anxiety was worrisome. Sam had called on his copyist "to see what was the delay" in transcribing a fair copy and discovered that "she is laid up with the persistent enemy of this book, *scarlet fever*." Much as the French and Italians had tried to prevent the spread of cholera in 1867 by sanitizing letters when they were mailed, Sam's manuscript was "removed from her room & disinfected with carbollic [sic] acid," though he cautioned Osgood to "give it another good disinfecting before you meddle with it or let your children get hold of it." In early January 1883, with the manuscript still unfinished, Sam notified his nephew Webster that he had lost all patience with the project and would have nothing to do with its printing and distribution: "I will not interest myself in *anything* connected with this wretched God-damned book." Finally, on January 15, he announced to Cable in exasperation that he had "just finished my book at last."[30]

Whereas Sam could focus on his writing in seclusion at Quarry Farm, after his return to Hartford in late September his social calendar filled with distractions. Between late September and mid-January as he struggled to finish *Life on the Mississippi*, he and Livy hosted the opera star Christina Nilsson and the tragedian John McCullough in their home, and former Connecticut governor Marshall Jewell invited Sam to a dinner party in honor of Postmaster General Timothy Howe. As usual, too, Sam was in demand as an after-dinner speaker, as when a regiment of soldiers, the Worcester Continentals, visited Hartford on October 19 and Mayor Morgan Bulkeley asked him to welcome them at a formal dinner at Allyn Hall attended by some five hundred people. As Sam declared in the course of his address, "There is much here to see—the State House, Colt's factory, and where the Charter Oak was. And we have an antiquity here—the East Hartford bridge."[31]

George Washington Cable visited Hartford a week later at Sam's invitation. "I want you to choose your own date and come; we are ready for you now any time," he advised Cable on October 5. Cable arrived in time to attend a meeting of the Monday Evening Club on October 23 and a midnight dinner of the Somerset Club on Beacon Street in Boston, and left a very favorable impression at both gatherings. Sam lauded his conversational powers to Howells in his next letter: "He is a marvelous talker on a deep subject. I do not see how even Spencer could unwind a thought more smoothly or orderly, and do it in a cleaner, clearer, crisper English. He astounded Twichell with his faculty." He raved no less about Cable's character: "when it comes down to moral honesty, limpid innocence, and utterly blemishless piety, the Apostles were mere policemen to Cable." At the Somerset Club, Osgood and the poet John Boyle O'Reilly were drunk; the Boston industrialist Charles Fairchild, whom Sam had met through Howells, "responsively loaded"; and Aldrich and Sam "properly fortified." Cable told Livy afterward that Sam "seemed to have been entertaining himself with horses" at an "orgy."[32]

A year earlier Sam had been obliged to decline an invitation to address the New England Society of New York because he was engaged to speak the same evening at the dinner of the New England Society of Pennsylvania. Despite the modest backlash that speech had provoked, the New York society renewed its invitation to Sam to entertain its members after dining at Delmonico's the evening of December 22, 1882. The guest list of nearly three hundred gentlemen included a veritable who's who of national celebrities: Joseph Choate; Governor Alonzo B. Cornell of New York; Chauncey Depew; Mayor William R. Grace of New York; former president Grant; General Horace Porter; and Elihu Root, later U.S. attorney for the Southern District of New York, U.S. secretary of state, and recipient of the Nobel Peace Prize in 1912. Sam again replied to the toast to "Women" and, as the *New York Times* reported, his remarks "kept the tables in a roar for a quarter of an hour." Despite the all-male audience, however, Sam again flirted with trouble by focusing his entire speech on the difference between the dress of "the savage woman of Central Africa and the cultivated daughter of our high modern civilization." The African woman "when dressed for home, or to go to market, or go out calling, does not wear anything at all but just her complexion" and "it always fits." The "fair daughter of civilization and high fashion," however, "dressed at her utmost best, is a morsel of exquisite and beautiful art and expense."[33]

Excepting only the Whittier birthday address, it was the most controversial speech of Sam's career. All of the papers that deigned to notice it took their cue from the *New York Tribune*, which remarked that it contained "humor so low in tone, so coarse in suggestion, so trite in allusion, so foreign to the spirit of the occasion" that it rank(l)ed with barroom humor or the ribaldry of minstrel show end men. The *New Orleans Picayune* grieved that "the most [Sam] can do now is to make drunken men laugh by after-dinner drivel" and the *Macon Telegraph* asserted that not only had he "become the veriest of frauds," but his after-dinner speeches ought to be "outlawed." The St. Louis *Globe-Democrat* urged him to retire from the podium because "his recent efforts at wit" had been "lamentable failures. If he continues to decline, he will in a year or two be dull enough to write editorials for the *Missouri Republican*." The joke made the rounds that the Mark Twain gold mine in Colorado was so named because the prospectors were required to dig through layers of trash to reach pay dirt. To judge from such responses, he had irreparably damaged the tender sensibilities of dozens of military men and professional politicians. On his part, Sam was unflappable. "When an audience do not complain, it is a compliment," he wrote Cable, "& when they *do* it is a compliment, too, if unaccompanied by violence."[34]

Before the end of 1882 Sam was again forced to defend his copyrights in a New York state court. He discovered on September 19 that J. S. Ogilvie and Company, Street and Smith, and others had used his name "to sell stuff which I never wrote," including *Bad Boy's Diary* ("I would not be the author of that witless stuff . . . for a million dollars") and had reprinted corrupt versions of two of his sketches, "Curing a Cold" and "My Watch," in a pamphlet entitled *Ha! Ha! Ha!* Sam instructed his lawyer Daniel Whitford of the New York firm of Alexander & Green to prosecute the "Ogilvie bastards" on "some charge or other," perhaps forgery. Whitford notified Sam less than a week later that he did "not think the publication of the Clemens literary name or trademark in the advertisement or on the book renders the parties liable to indictment for forgery in any degree," though he filed suit against the pirates in the Court of Common Pleas in New York on September 29, charging them with violation of copyright. Neither suit was contested and Sam was awarded judgment on February 17, 1883—though the victory was another Pyrrhic one. While the defendants were "perpetually enjoined and restrained" from advertising, publishing, or selling the books in question, no monetary damages were awarded the plaintiff in either case and Sam was obliged to pay his own legal fees. He also misconstrued the basis for his victory, thinking the verdict was founded on infringement of his trademark, and he fairly itched to press the point. "I have won two trademark suits [B. J. Such and Ogilvie] & lost a third [Belford Brothers]," he wrote in January 1883. "I will not believe that the U.S. Supreme Court will decide against me until I have tried." The next time his work was pirated, he advised Andrew Chatto a month later, he planned "to bring another trademark suit. I have taken legal advice on the subject. It is believed that this device will win." If he could protect his writing under "the existing trademark laws, authors (& literature of *all* kinds) will then be sheltered utterly from injury."[35] This approach was misdirected, however, and he never won another suit against a publishing pirate.

Early in 1883 Sam framed for the first time the mechanistic philosophy that would bedevil him for the rest of his life. The previous June he had asked in his notebook, " Is *any*body or any action ever unselfish? (Good theme for

Club essay.)" He tried to address the question in a paper entitled "What Is Happiness?" that he read before the Monday Evening Club on February 19. An early version of his "bible," *What Is Man?* (1906), his answer was hardly consoling. In response to his reading in William E. H. Lecky's *History of European Morals* (1869), Sam proposed that the human creature is "merely a machine automatically functioning." The desire to attain happiness and avoid pain, according to Lecky, is the primary motive to every human act. The only reason to behave virtuously is "that on the whole such a course will bring us the greatest amount of happiness." Sam glossed this notion in the margin of the book: "Sound and true." In short, "All our acts, reasoned and unreasoned," both those judged good and bad, "are selfish," and the basis for all such moral judgments are conditioned by experiences that "begin in infancy; we never get a chance to find out whether we have any that are innate or not." Thus the germ of his doctrine of environmental determinism. The staid Republicans who belonged to the Monday Evening Club were appalled by such heresy and, according to Paine, "jeered" and "denounced it as a manifest falsity." Sam remembered in his autobiography that

> there was not a man there who didn't scoff at it, jeer at it, revile at it, and call it a lie—a thousand times a lie! . . . The Club handled me without gloves. They said I was trying to strip man of his dignity, and I said I shouldn't succeed, for it would not be possible to strip him of a quality which he did not possess. They said that if this insane doctrine of mine were accepted by the world life would no longer be worth living; but I said that that would merely leave life in the condition it was before.[36]

Sam's beliefs in an indifferent universe and human impotency only grew with the years. Even in 1883, the same year he delivered "What Is Happiness?" before the club, he jotted in his notebook a pair of thoughts that foreshadow the fatalism of his late fragment "The Great Dark," written in 1898: "Life in the interior of an iceberg. . . . Iceberg drifts in a vast circle, year after year" and "I think we are only the microscopic trichina concealed in the blood of some vast creature's veins, and it is that vast creature God concerns himself about and not us."[37]

Even after Sam thought he had finished *Life on the Mississippi*, it was not ready for the printers. He had, in fact, overshot the target length by over twenty thousand words so he decided to prune and paraphrase some material. Even after trimming the manuscript by some fifteen thousand words, the book still contained over twelve thousand words lifted from other sources. He asked Osgood in mid-January 1883 to suggest initial cuts subject to his final approval. Only the "Old Times" chapters printed in the *Atlantic* in 1875 were off-limits to both blue pencil and scissors. "You must glance through all" the other proof-slips, he directed Osgood, especially descriptions of their downriver trip, to find sections that might be omitted—in particular his descriptions of "some Southern assassinations," or lynchings.[38]

Nowhere was his revanchism more apparent than on the topic of lynch law. In the 1860s while living in Nevada and in the early 1870s while writing *Roughing It* (1872), with its portrayal of corrupt juries, the murder of Jack Slade, and Captain Ned Blakely's extrajudicial hanging of Bill Noakes, he tolerated and even approved capital punishment in general and vigilante justice in particular. His opinions had not changed significantly by the early 1880s. To be sure, he observed in his journal in 1879 that "I disfavor capital punishment" but he would have been hard-pressed to prove it by his public declarations. In fact, when the body of a poisoned twenty-year-old woman, Jennie Cramer, was found near New Haven in August 1881, he thirsted for the blood of her killers: "Give the Malley boys a shot & a good strong one—for they are guilty, no matter what the evidence may fail to prove. They ought to be taken from Court & lynched—if I were kin to the girl I would kill them on the threshold of the court." He expressed approval of lynching in the manuscript of *Life on the Mississippi*, though in a paragraph omitted during revision. Southern juries "fail to convict" criminals, he alleged,

> even in the clearest cases. That this is not agreeable to the public is shown by the fact that very frequently such a miscarriage of justice so rouses the people that they rise, in a passion, & break into the jail, drag out their man & lynch him. . . . But this hundred or two hundred men usually do this act of public justice with masks on. They go to their grim work with clear consciences, but with their faces disguised. They know that the law will not meddle with them . . . & they know that the community will applaud their act.

Sam's deletion of this passage, which seems to endorse the terrorist tactics of the Ku Klux Klan, illustrates less his tendency to pander to Southern readers than his fear of alienating Northern ones.[39] Sam apparently still championed vigilante justice when necessary to maintain law and order, even if those who executed it wore masks to shield their identities.

In another slice of text he omitted from *Life on the Mississippi*, Sam remarked on the eradication of slavery in the South since he last lived there. But his comments again betray the orthodoxy and arrogance of his opinions. "I missed one thing in the South—African slavery," he noted. "That horror is gone, and permanently. Therefore, half the South is at last emancipated, half the South is free. But the white half is apparently as far from emancipation as ever." According to Sam in another deleted passage, "the Negroes are now free but the whites are slaves—to one political party," the bloody-shirt-waving

Democrats. That is, he joked about the "crackers" and poor whites who were still oppressed by a corrupt political regime in the former Confederacy in contrast to the freed slaves, as if Jim Crow laws, crop-lien farming, and the convict lease system did not exist in the South after Reconstruction. More to the point, as Arlin Turner argues, *Life on the Mississippi* "pictures the ex-slaves along the Mississippi River in 1882 as shiftless, mendacious darkies, conventionally taken to be appropriate objects of the white man's laughter, practical jokes, and scorn," a view that "differed little from the dominant view in the South at the time." In his notebook around this time, Sam also envisioned a nativist's worst nightmare, a dystopian nation a century hence: either reverse Jim Crow with "Negro supremacy—the whites under foot" or "the Pope here & an Inquisition. The age of darkness back again."[40]

In the spring of 1883 George Washington Cable launched a second career as a public speaker with a lecture, "Creole Women," punctuated with readings from *The Grandissimes* delivered at the Prytania Street Presbyterian Church in New Orleans, the University of Mississippi, and Johns Hopkins University. On March 10 several Hartfordians, including Sam, William B. Franklin, William Hamersley, Joe Hawley, E. P. Parker, Henry C. Robinson, J. Hammond Trumbull, Joe Twichell, and Charles Dudley Warner, formally invited Cable to speak at Unity Hall in their city the evening of April 4 while he was touring the East. A week in advance, Sam puffed the appearance of "the gifted southerner" by inserting a card in the *Hartford Courant*. He testified from experience that Cable was "a reader and speaker whose matter is of the finest quality and whose arts of delivery are of distinguished excellence" and declared that "Mr. Cable is the only master in the writing of French dialects that the country has produced; and he reads them in perfection." This sentence appeared in the manuscript of his forthcoming *Life on the Mississippi*. He might as easily have quoted another line in the book: Cable was "the South's finest literary genius."[41]

Cable arrived in Hartford on April 2 to a full calendar of events over the next three days. Though he stayed with George and Lilly Warner, he spent much of his time with Sam, who invited several of his New York friends to Hartford to meet him, including Richard Watson Gilder, Laurence Hutton, and George Waring. The evening of April 4, before a house so packed the ushers placed chairs in the aisles and with Gilder, Hutton, Osgood, Trumbull, Waring, and Warner seated on the platform, Sam introduced Cable with an "immensely funny" speech. According to eighteen-year-old William Lyon Phelps, who was in the audience that evening, Cable was paralyzed with stage fright. He rose to the podium "and could not even open his mouth" until Sam thrust a copy of one of Cable's books into his hands "and told him to read." In the course of the hour, Cable recited from both *Old Creole Days* (1879) and *The Grandissimes* and, as advertised, lectured on Creole women. The reviewer for the *Hartford Courant*—probably Warner—commended Cable's performance the next day: he spoke "in a simple, unaffected manner, as if he were talking with friends in a drawing-room, in a fine and small voice, but sweet and penetrating," and his reading was "so absolutely simple that we hesitate to apply the word dramatic to it, and yet the effect was dramatic." Cable was paid $125 and was so pleased by his recital that he pronounced it a "decided success" to his wife Louise and announced to his mother that a "new future appears to be opening before me." Privately, however, he worried that he had not been heard throughout the hall and that Sam "was not satisfied" with his presentation. In fact, Sam was merely disappointed by Cable's selection of readings; otherwise, he thought Cable acquitted himself well. "He knows how to read—there ain't any question about it," he wrote Osgood.[42]

After the reading, Sam hosted a supper for Cable at the Hartford Club, attended by all the men on the platform during the performance as well as Roswell Smith of the Century Company and Joe Twichell. Cable reported to Louise they enjoyed an "abundance of innocent fun." The next morning, Cable read his story "Posson Jone" at a special Thursday meeting of the Saturday Morning Club of young women at Charles Perkins's house where, as Sam put it, Cable "scored a rattling victory" and "carried his house by storm." At Cable's request, Sam again introduced him and jocularly represented him "as an impostor & charlatan." His reading, as Cable crowed afterward, "was the greatest success I have ever made in my life." The young women who were present told him that "in the 5 years of their corporate existence they had never had such an entertainment." Sam then accompanied Cable to a special Thursday noontime meeting of the Monday Evening Club, more specifically a luncheon in Cable's honor at the Hartford Club—"the maddest, merriest three hours—the wittiest uproar that *ever* I heard in my life. It beat the Boston dinner" at the Somerset Club the previous October. That evening, Charley and Susan Warner hosted yet another event in Cable's honor at their home, where he again read "Posson Jone" and "some other good selections." Sam predicted accurately that, despite Cable's disappointing performance at Unity Hall the night before, he would "score another triumph" at the Warners' dinner, "his stock" would soar, "& the memory of his defeat will be sponged out & forgotten." Cable wrote his wife on April 7, after leaving Hartford, that she could not "imagine the depth of eager solicitude that Chas. D[udley] W[arner] & Clemens" had shown him during his brief visit.[43] Nor could he have guessed before his arrival that in fact he had just spent two days auditioning to join Sam on a speaking tour the next year.

Sam was never more clubbable than during these months. A billiards afi-
cionado, he introduced the cue master Maurice Vignaux to an audience of
about five hundred at an exhibition on March 5, 1883, in the Columbian
Room of Madison Square Hall in New York. While he was in town he dined
with the members of the Kinsmen at Hutton's home the evening of March 9
along with Edwin Austin Abbey, Lawrence Barrett, Julian Hawthorne, William Laffan, Brander Matthews, Frank Millet, and Elihu Vedder.[44] A once
and future playwright, he also mingled in theatrical circles with many of the
same men. He attended a dinner honoring the Italian actor Tommaso Salvini at the Hotel Brunswick in New York the evening of April 26. The guests
included Barrett, Judge Charles P. Daly, Theodore Low De Vinne, President
Daniel Coit Gilman of Johns Hopkins, Hawthorne, Hutton, Henry James,
Robert Underwood Johnson, George Parsons Lathrop, Marshall Mallory,
Matthews, Millet, Osgood, Stedman, Augustus Saint-Gaudens, and Charley Warner. Sam was likewise present at a banquet the evening of December
17 hosted by Osgood and Charles Fairchild at the Somerset Club on Beacon
Street for the British actor Henry Irving while he was playing in *Louis XI* at
the Boston Theater. Among the others present were Aldrich, Howells, and
Warner. As Hawthorne remembered, Sam delivered a short speech: "Henry," he said, "we've seen you play 'Louis XI,' and we liked it; it's a good play,
and you did it well. But you mustn't stop there, Henry; you must be ambitious; you must go higher; you must fulfill the expectations of your friends.
We believe, Henry, that you've got it in you to play 'Louis XII.'" The morning
of April 29, 1884—two days after his final performance of the season and
the same day he departed for England—Irving hosted a farewell breakfast at
Delmonico's for seventy of his closest friends, another who's who of stars in
the American theatrical and literary firmament, among them Sam, Aldrich,
Edwin Booth, Dion Boucicault, Charles A. Dana, Chauncey Depew, Hawthorne, Hutton, Lathrop, Matthews, Millet, James Pond, Whitelaw Reid,
Lester Wallack, Warner, and William Winter.[45]

During the second week of May 1883, on the eve of publication of *Life on the
Mississippi*, Sam and Osgood traveled to Canada to secure British copyright
of the book. Sam expected to be north of the border for only a week or ten
days. Unfortunately, he was stricken with food poisoning from a Vermont
mince pie as soon as he arrived. Still, as he wrote Livy from the Windsor
Hotel in Montreal on May 8, "Osgood thinks we need not stay in Canada
beyond the 14th" in order to establish residency and file the requisite paperwork. The dominion copyright was duly granted to Chatto & Windus in
London on May 12 and Canadian copyright to Dawson Brothers in Ottawa
without complication three days later. Sam returned to Hartford no later

than May 17. "I have acquired a Canadian copyright at last," Sam gloated to Cable. "We have gone about at it ignorantly and wrong-end first heretofore. But this time I believe we have made no mistakes. We have done everything plainly, and squarely, have evaded no laws, wronged nobody, and yet I think our Canadian copyright is as good and strong as our English one."[46] It was; *Life on the Mississippi* was never pirated.

Before Sam returned to the United States he was invited to attend the five-day meeting of the Royal Society of Canada in Ottawa beginning on May 22 as the guest of the Marquess of Lorne, the governor-general of Canada. He railed to New York on May 20 to spend several days with Osgood at a billiards tournament—this when billiards was a spectator sport—before traveling back to Ottawa on May 23. He regretted that he had not arrived a day sooner or, as he wrote Livy from Rideau Hall (aka Government House), "fun isn't any name for it!" After the Royal Society conference ended, he lingered in Ottawa a few more days. On May 28 he ran the Chandiere Slides on the St. Lawrence River on a raft along with the marquess, his wife and Queen Victoria's daughter Princess Louise, and Lord John Hervey. When word reached the United States that Sam was frolicking with the marquess and the princess, some American journalists were shocked. The Carson City *Appeal* marveled at the "difference between the present career of the self-ish humorist and the time that he would regularly be refused credit for a drink in a Carson saloon." The *Philadelphia News* was no less dumbfounded: "Mark Twain is going downhill very fast. At last accounts he was in Canada hobnobbing with royalty." Sam was indifferent to the carping of the critics. He "spent a week with the Marquiss & the Princess Louise & had as good a time as *I* want" and returned to Hartford, after an absence of nearly a month, at the end of May.[47]

The *Boston Herald* printed a prepublication announcement of *Life on the Mississippi* on March 11 ("largely a labor of love"), and at Sam's direction Osgood ordered fifty thousand copies to be printed. A copy was deposited in the Library of Congress on May 17 and others began to be distributed the same day. But from the first, sales of the book limped under the weight of a pair of problems. Profusely illustrated, the book was expensive to produce, costing about sixty cents per copy. Sam had hoped to reduce expenses by copying illustrations by Kaolatype, but Osgood's engravers balked, judging the process impractical and rendering Sam's fifty-thousand-dollar invest-ment worthless. Moreover, Osgood still had not mastered the subtleties of subscription publication and the aggressive brand marketing it required, though *Life on the Mississippi* was peddled under similar terms as *The Prince and the Pauper* (1881). By contract, the publisher received royalties of 5 percent of gross sales on the first fifty thousand copies, 7½ percent thereafter, and Sam paid production costs and pocketed the balance. In the fall of 1882 Sam appointed Webster the general agent for sales of *Life on the Mississippi* in New York State and ordered him to study "the methods & mysteries of General-Agency right away." Sam no doubt was grooming Webster to succeed Osgood. Just as the canvassing was about to begin in January, Sam warned Osgood that Bliss "usually issued with upwards of 40,000 orders & only 20,000" books to fill the orders. In this case he preferred to print as many copies as he hoped to sell. "We must give Webster all the thunder-&-lightning circulars & advertising enginery" he might need in the lucrative northeastern U.S. sales territory. He expected to "sell 100,000 copies of the book in 12 months, & shan't want him complaining that we are the parties in fault if the sale falls short of it."[48]

The reviewers on both sides of the Atlantic and Pacific were virtually unanimous in their praise for the book, seldom uttering a discouraging word. It was the first of Sam's works to be noticed in *Harper's Monthly* ("amusing and interesting medley of fact and fiction") and was hailed in the *Hartford Courant* ("one of his best and most entertaining works"), *San Francisco Bulletin* ("very entertaining"), *Boston Transcript* ("most graphic"), *Chicago Tribune* ("one of the best, if not *the* best, this writer has given to the public"), *New York Herald* ("side-splitting fun, tender pathos, rollicking incident"), *Cincinnati Commercial* ("one of the author's juiciest productions"), *San Francisco Chronicle* ("the best book Mark Twain has written since *The Innocents Abroad*"), *Critic* ("a good deal of solid reading and genuine information"), *New Haven Journal and Courier* ("an exceedingly interesting account of 'piloting' on the Mississippi"), New York *Evening Post* ("a descriptive and historical work"), *Chicago Inter Ocean* ("racy descriptions of real people"), *New York Tribune* ("contains a little of everything,—from a cyclopaedia to a comic almanac"), *Nation* ("the best part of the book . . . relates to the Mississippi pilot, a creature as extinct as the dodo"), *Atlantic Monthly* ("thorough and racy"), *Overland Monthly* ("unquestionably . . . entertaining"), St. Louis *Globe-Democrat* (predicting it would attract "considerable interest"), *Milwaukee Sentinel* ("thoroughly readable"), *Atlanta Constitution* ("mainly made up of fun and statistics"), *Sacramento Union* ("contains a good deal of useful information"), and by Lafcadio Hearn in the New Orleans *Times-Democrat* ("in some respects, the most solid book that Mark Twain has written"). Only the *Hartford Times* struck a sour note and then only about the illustrations: "a more shabby set of catchpenny wood-cuts we have not met with." John Hay, who grew up in Warsaw, Illinois, only about seven miles downriver from Keokuk, commended Sam privately: "I don't see how you do it. I knew all that, every word of it—passed as much time on the levee as you ever did, knew the same crowd & saw the same scenes,—but I could not have remembered one word of it all. You have the two greatest gifts of the writer, memory & imagination. I congratulate you." Even recent scholars describe Sam's book with superlatives. Stanley Brodwin has called *Life on the Mississippi* "the greatest of Twain's travel books" and Jeffrey Melton refers to it as "Twain's most personal travel book."[49]

The critics in the British Commonwealth were no less enthusiastic. Robert Brown in *Academy* judged it "the best account of social life on the Mississippi with which we are acquainted" and the London *Graphic* declared it "an admirable specimen of [Sam's] powers as a serious writer of history." The *Derby Mercury* averred that *Life on the Mississippi* was "one of the most enjoyable" of Sam's works and that Mark Twain was a "name which will live in the history of literature." The London *Congregationalist* ("there are passages in this book which are equal to anything he has ever written, if, indeed, they are not superior"), *Leeds Mercury* ("Mark Twain is just the pilot for voyagers on such a river"), London *Morning Post* (the author "numbers among his readers a considerable percentage of the educated population of this country"), and Adelaide *South Australian Register* (the book "will rank among the best of the author's productions") followed suit. Among British reviewers, only the *British Quarterly Review* ("extravagances, perversions, inversions") and W. E. Henley in the hypercritical *Athenaeum* ("a disappointment") expressed reservations.[50]

Despite Sam's high hopes for the book and the laudatory reviews it received, *Life on the Mississippi* bombed commercially. He had hoped to exploit the economies of scale with a large press run but the strategy backfired. "We printed and *bound* 50,000 Mississippi's," he remembered, but "the orders stopped at 32,000." He ordered Osgood to dump the remainder on the trade market on November 1 because "the big sale" in subscriptions "is always before the issue. . . . *The orders that come after the ISSUE of a subscription book don't amount to a damn.*" Of course, Sam blamed Osgood for overprinting the edition; he blasted the publisher for binding ten thousand copies, "which he knew there was no sale for," though Osgood had merely followed his instructions. Sam insisted that the book would "not have failed if [Osgood] had listened to me" and that *The Prince and the Pauper* and *Life on the Mississippi* were "the only books of mine which have ever failed. The first failure was not unbearable—but this second one is so nearly so that it is not a calming subject for me to talk upon." He claimed he had lost fifty thousand dollars on the latter volume because "the sale which should have been" eighty thousand was only thirty thousand so he demanded that Osgood settle for a lower royalty "based upon the fact—and it is unquestionably a fact"—that "the publisher who sells less than 50,000 copies of a book for me has merely injured me, he has not benefitted me." Privately, Sam fumed that had Osgood "the copyright on the Bible" his "gang" was so stupid they would have found a way to publish it "as to lose money." In his own defense, Osgood argued that the failure of the book was "not due to lack of intelligent, conscientious & energetic effort on our part." In any event, Sam's publishers were hardly immune from financial travail. On May 2, 1885, less than two years after issuing *Life on the Mississippi*, James R. Osgood and Company—like Daniel Slote and Company in 1878—suspended business, declared bankruptcy, and settled its debts for about thirty cents on the dollar. Sam wrote Osgood on May 5 that he was "exceedingly sorry to hear the bad news & shall hope the suspension will be only temporary." The same day he lamented to Howells that he had known Osgood "was on the very verge" of insolvency the year before but he "continued to hope—but not expect that he would pull through." Unlike Slote's bankruptcy, however, Osgood's failure did not signal the end of his friendship with Sam. They had not quarreled, Sam wrote Howells, "but I think we are pretty completely dissatisfied with each other." Or as he reminisced in his autobiography, "Osgood was one of the dearest and sweetest and loveliest human beings to be found on the planet anywhere but he knew nothing about subscription publishing and he made a mighty botch of it." He was merely a "most incapable publisher," not a scoundrel like Slote or Elisha Bliss. Osgood "was a sociable creature" with whom he routinely played billiards but he paid fifty-six thousand dollars in productions costs on *Life on the Mississippi* before "the first copy issued from the press" and "it took a year to get the fifty-six thousand back into my pocket, and not very many dollars followed it." Or as Hamlin Hill has concluded, "Osgood proved that an honest man had no place in the subscription-book business."[51]

To spare the family the strain of travel after a difficult winter during which Livy and Clara had suffered from diphtheria and Susy from scarlet fever, the Clemenses and their servants traveled to Elmira in June on a private sleeping car. Sam hoped Livy's mother could "nurse her back to health." Ironically, as soon as they arrived at Quarry Farm, during the most inspired summer of his career, Sam knocked out a short story that has never been published—deservedly so, according to Howells. A longtime devotee of the *Arabian Nights' Entertainment*, Sam continued Scheherazade's tales in the "1002d Arabian Night," in which she finally bores Sultan Shahriyar to death. "The opening passages are the funniest you have ever done," Howells allowed, but he thought the rest of the story, though only twenty thousand words, resembled Jim Blaine's tale of his grandfather's old ram in *Roughing It*. Like Blaine, Scheherazade is afflicted with a severe case of "prolixity." In Howells's view, "this burlesque falls short of being amusing. . . . It was not your best or your second-best" and he urged Sam to shelve it. Undeterred, as usual, Sam suggested to Webster that they issue it "anonymously, in a 15 or 20 cent form, right after Huck."[52] It has never appeared in print.

Sam resumed work on *Huckleberry Finn* soon after his arrival at Quarry Farm. As he wrote Karl and Josephine Gerhardt in Paris on July 2, "We have been here on the hill a week or more & I am deep in my work & grinding out manuscript by the acre—stick to it the whole day long." When he had last pigeonholed the manuscript in the spring of 1880, the Bricksville mob with bared faces in daylight was headed to Colonel Sherburn's house, armed with clotheslines to lynch him, and Sam had not yet decided on the direction he wanted to take the story. He considered either permitting Sherburn to escape or to "let them lynch him" but in the end he sided with neither the aristocrat who has killed Boggs in cold blood nor the mob hell-bent on vigilante justice. During the three years since he last laid the manuscript aside, Sam's opinion of lynch law had changed. Southern mob justice after the war consisted of "a hundred masked cowards" in the night, a transparent allusion to the brutal tactics of the Ku Klux Klan based on Sam's growing conviction as the result of his trip to the South in 1882 that the KKK epitomized the worst possible perversion of American justice. He exposed his increasing concern about the Klan when, in his notebook late in 1887, he added a stroke to his prospective picture of the American South in 1910. In a reversal of Jim Crow laws, "whites of both sexes have to ride in the smoking car (& pay full fare,) . . . The colored brother has succeeded in having severe laws against miscegenation passed. There is no such thing as a free ballot. The whites have to vote as they are told, or be visited by masked men & shot, or whipped, & house burned & wife & d[aughter] [stripped] turned out in their night clothes." Though T. S. Eliot asserted later that "there is no exaggeration of grammar or spelling or speech" in the novel, "no sentence or phrase to destroy the illusion that these are Huck's own words," Sherburn's speech belies the claim. Sam speaks directly through the colonel when he confronts the rabble: "The idea of *you* lynching anybody! It's amusing. The idea of you thinking you had pluck enough to lynch a *man*!"[53]

Sam was so prolific during the summer of 1883 that he added some seventy thousand words to *Huckleberry Finn* and completed a rough draft of the novel. "We are having a delightful time here," Livy reported on July 16. "Mr Clemens is at work—and I never saw him in better working condition, or with more enthusiasm for his work." Sam reveled in the serenity of the farm; as he bragged to Howells on July 20,

> I haven't piled up MS so in years as I have done since we came here to the farm three weeks and a half ago. Why, it's like old times, to step right into the study, damp from the breakfast table, and sail right in and sail right on, the

whole day long, without thought of running short of stuff or words. I wrote 4000 words to-day and I touch 3000 and upwards pretty often, and don't fall below 1600 any working day. And when I get fagged out, I lie abed a couple of days and read and smoke, and then go it again for 6 or 7 days. I have finished one small book, and am away along in a big one that I half-finished two or three years ago. I expect to complete it in a month or six weeks or two months more. And I shall like it, whether anybody else does or not.

Sam wrote Orion that "this summer it is no more trouble to me to write than it is to lie." In late August he boasted that he had completed "two seasons' work in one & haven't anything left to do now but revise." Whereas he had worked four or five hours a day, five days a week, in past summers, he worked about eight hours a day, six and sometimes seven days a week, this summer and accumulated "eight or nine hundred MS pages in such a brief space of time that I mustn't name the number of days."[54]

Most of these final chapters of the novel recount the king and duke's scheme to defraud the Wilks sisters and Tom and Huck's rescue of Jim from the ash-hopper at the Phelps farm.[55] Of all Sam's major works, *Huck Finn* is the least dependent on literary sources and, with rare exceptions, it is almost entirely free of autobiographical references.[56] To be sure, Sam probably gleaned Jim's account of his daughter 'Lizbeth's loss of hearing in chapter 23 from the deafness suffered by one of the seven children of his coachman Patrick McAleer. All seven contracted scarlet fever between February and April 1883 and two of them nearly died.[57] Part of his task during this summer, too, was backfilling the narrative, particularly in the latter half of chapter 12 and chapters 13 and 14, the sections about the thieves aboard the *Walter Scott* and Huck and Jim's dialogues about King Sollermun and Frenchmen.

Then there are Sam's deletions from the manuscript. In order to reduce it to a size comparable to *The Adventures of Tom Sawyer* (1876), he readily agreed with Webster in April 1884 that they should omit from *Huck Finn* the raftsmen's passage included in *Life on the Mississippi*. It was a digression in the novel and, as Sam admitted, it could be "left wholly out."[58] Moreover, as Sam admitted to Robert Underwood Johnson, the associate editor of the *Century*, he would have incurred the wrath of publishers had he "knowingly & intentionally" sold "the same chapter of Huck Finn twice."[59] He also excised a chapter in which Jim, after he and Huck meet by accident on Jackson's Island, relates a morbid story about a medical student and a corpse. This anecdote remained unpublished until it appeared under the title "Jim and the Dead Man" in the *New Yorker* in 1985.

Even more telling are the working notes for the novel Sam fortuitously chose to ignore. In order to disguise Jim in the novel, Huck paints Jim in blueface, dresses him in drag, and hangs a sign around his neck that he is a "sick A-rab" to ward off strangers. In his notes, Sam considered an even more extreme alternative: "Turn Jim into an Injun. Then exhib[it] him for gorilla—then wild Arab &c." like the grotesques Sam had seen in Barnum's dime museum in New York in 1853. Sam considered ending the book with the lynching of a "free nigger," presumably Jim, and he weighed other options for "adventures": Huck confronts a congregation of alligators; attends a quilting bee, a house-raising, a candy pull, a "Negro campmeeting," or a country cotillion; and escapes a village fire. Most outrageously of all, a backwoods farmer gives Huck and Tom an escaped elephant he bought at auction and they ride him around the bayous of Louisiana "& make no end of trouble." In any case, Sam notified Andrew Chatto on September 1, two weeks before leaving Elmira to return to Hartford, he had "just finished writing a book and modesty compels me to say it's a rattling good one, too." The story had risen considerably in his estimation since he began it in the summer of 1876, when he thought he might "possibly pigeonhole or burn the MS when it is done."[60]

Is *Adventures of Huckleberry Finn* a racist novel? The best answer: yes and no. Parts of it, such as the scene in which Jim is a "sick A-rab" in blueface, are irredeemably racist. John H. Wallace's alleges that the novel is "the most grotesque example of racist trash ever written." But it is far less overtly racist than Thomas Nelson Page's *Red Rock* (1898), Thomas Dixon's *The Clansman* (1905), and Edgar Rice Burroughs's *Tarzan of the Apes* (1912). Was Samuel Clemens a racist? By modern standards, the most honest answer is a qualified yes. Guy Cardwell concludes that Sam was never "free of racial bias" and Tom Quirk fairly asserts that "by nearly any reckoning Samuel Clemens was something of a racist, though the form [his racism] took was typically paternalistic rather than actively prejudicial." Ironically, the same terms might be used to describe the racial politics of such revered antislavery activists as Harriet Beecher Stowe; that is, the vexed questions about the racism of a novel or a novelist are inevitably infected by a presentist bias. But this much may be affirmed with reasonable confidence: *Huck Finn* is fundamentally not an antislavery novel, given that it was published sixteen years after formal ratification of the Thirteenth Amendment to the U.S. Constitution, nor is it a race novel like Howells's *An Imperative Duty* (1891), Frances E. W. Harper's *Iola Leroy* (1892), or Sam's *The Tragedy of Pudd'nhead Wilson* (1893). To judge from reviews, *Huck Finn* was not read through a racial lens until the mid-twentieth century. Or as Peter Messent notes, "what now seems extraordinary is that Twain's contemporaries, as far as we can tell, did not read the book in those [racial] terms." Philip Foner's statement that "Jim is the real hero" of *Huck Finn* is as misguided a critical claim as Wallace's charge that it is "racist trash." Jim makes only a cameo appearance in the opening chapters of the novel and disappears entirely in chapters 16 and 17.[61]

To be sure, the novel punctures several racial stereotypes. Like Sam's earlier sketch "A True Story," it belies the racist belief that black parents cannot love their children as much as white parents love theirs. Jim escapes from Miss Watson and risks punishment because he fears she will sell him down the river and he is desperate to keep his family intact. In the Wilks episode, Sam depicts the rending of slave families by auction and the anguish suffered by the parents. Far from a comic type, Jim also functions as a trickster figure who, in the hairball incident in chapter 4, tricks Huck into giving him a counterfeit quarter he can spend. After Tom tries to persuade Jim in chapter 2 that he had been ridden around the world by witches, "Jim was most ruined for a servant" and takes a vacation from work.[62]

Then there is the issue of the recurrent use of the racial epithet *nigger* and its cognates, which appear in the novel 213 times. On the one hand, as Lionel Trilling and others have argued, the epithet is "the only word for a Negro that a boy like Huck would know in his place and time." On the other hand, the term was undeniably abhorrent, however commonplace. As Ralph Waldo Emerson noted in his journal in 1845, "The man of the world annihilates the whole combined force of all the antislavery societies of the world by pronouncing it." Often neglected in scholarship is the extent to which Sam subverted the profanity of the word by invoking it ironically. For example, when Huck appears at the Phelps farm in chapter 32 Aunt Sally, who mistakes him for Tom Sawyer, asks why he has been so late in arriving. Huck explains that he has been delayed when a boiler on his steamboat exploded. She asks, "Good gracious! anybody hurt?" He answers, "No'm. Killed a nigger"—to which she replies, "Well, its lucky; because sometimes people do get hurt." Whether or not Huck is ironic—how do we determine the intent of fictional characters?—the author's intent is certainly ironic.[63]

An even more obvious example appears in chapter 6, in which Pap Finn—a bottom-feeder, as his "fish-belly white" complexion suggests—spouts the views of a white supremacist. His character was modeled on the real-life Jimmy Finn, another Hannibal drunk, who "was a monument of rags and dirt; he was the profanest man in town; he had bleary eyes, and a nose like a mildewed cauliflower; he slept with the hogs in an abandoned tanyard." Pap vilifies a "mulatter" in Ohio, a "p'fessor in a college" who "could talk all kinds of languages, and knowed everything." Sam may be alluding to either Daniel Payne, the onetime president of Wilberforce University, or John G. Mitchell, who taught languages at Wilberforce in the 1860s. To Pap's dismay, Payne is even eligible to vote:

> "Thinks I, what is the country a-coming to? It was 'lection day, and I was just about to go and vote myself if I warn't too drunk to get there; but when they told me there was a State in this country where they'd let that nigger vote, I drawed out. I says I'll never vote agin. Them's the very words I said; they all heard me; and the country may rot for all me—I'll never vote agin as long as I live. And to see the cool way of that nigger—why, he wouldn't a give me the road if I hadn't shoved him out o' the way."

This speech can only be read as an ignorant and racist rant; certainly it cannot be read as the straightforward opinion of the author. "Pap's indignation at the Negro's right to vote," David L. Smith asserts, "is precisely analogous to the Southern backlash against the enfranchisement of Afro-Americans during Reconstruction." Moreover, the final fourth of the novel, the so-called evasion chapters or the narrative of Jim's captivity, seemingly allegorizes post-Reconstruction racial politics. Jim's predicament, trapped in the hut by the ash-hopper at the Phelps farm, "reflects that of the Negro of the Reconstruction, free at last and thoroughly impotent, the object of devious schemes and a hapless victim of constant brutality," according to Neil Schmitz. "If we read the evasion as an allegory of the plight of the black in the post-Reconstruction South, Tom Sawyer emerges as the type of contemporary southerner who, wrapped in his sense of principle and tradition and drawing moral strength therefrom, was determined to reverse the gains that freed slaves had made."[64]

While at Quarry Farm during the summer of 1883 Sam also invented an English history game he hoped to turn into a cash cow. On July 19 he wrote Orion, he took a day off from work and devoted it to designing an amusement "for the instruction of the children" without requiring them to study. He measured "817 feet of the road-way in our farm grounds, with a foot-rule, and then divided it up among the English reigns" from William the Conqueror in 1066 to Queen Victoria in 1883, "allowing one foot to the year. I whittled out a basket of little pegs and drove one in the ground at the beginning of each reign, and gave it that King's name. . . . I measured all the reigns exactly as many feet to the reign as there were years in it. You can look out over the grounds and see the little pegs from the front door—some of them close together," like Richard II (two feet), Oliver Cromwell (two feet), James

II (three feet), "and some prodigiously wide apart," like Elizabeth (forty-five feet), Edward III (fifty feet), Henry III (fifty-six feet), George III (sixty feet), and Victoria (forty-six feet and counting). "It gives the children a realizing sense of the length or brevity of a reign," Sam explained to Orion, and by the time he fell asleep that night he "had contrived a new way to play my history game" with cards and a cribbage board.[65]

Two days later he wrote both Howells and Twichell about the game and, to Sam's consternation, he received by return mail a note from Twichell that he liked the idea so much he handed part of Sam's letter to Charley Warner to print in the *Hartford Courant* "and I'm going to do it before you will have time to prevent me; so don't fret a minute." Sam telegraphed Twichell in a vain attempt to stop him "but my letter was already in print & on its wide way about the world." The item appeared in the *Courant* on July 24 and was soon copied from sea to shining sea, from the *Brooklyn Eagle* to the *San Francisco Bulletin*. Twichell's action threatened to spoil Sam's plans to patent and market the game and to publish "an illustrated small book" for children based on it. Even Howells was alarmed by Twichell's effrontery and urged Sam to patent or copyright the game "before someone else gets hold of it; I see the newspapers have exploited it." In the meantime, the incident nearly caused a rupture in their friendship. Sam excoriated Twichell for violating his privacy and perhaps depriving him of a moneymaking scheme. "I wrote him a letter which was pretty much all English," he advised Howells in mid-August, "& he hasn't replied yet, after all these weeks." He thought at the very least that Twichell ought to apologize.[66]

Sam's "all English" letter no longer survives but its tone and contents may easily be inferred. He sent a copy of Twichell's letter to his family in Keokuk to caution them to "avoid this damned fool's example. I shall never thoroughly like him again." Twichell finally replied on September 8 and not only failed to apologize but professed to be "entirely impenitent." As he wrote Sam,

> You made a great fuss about my letting Charley [Warner] print that little extract from your letter; and abused me brutally for it. I suppose it was because you wanted to pick a quarrel with me. If that was it, you'll have to try again, old fellow. . . . It was a good sin that I committed. That extract has gone and is going the rounds, as I wanted it to and knew it would.

It certainly was "a mighty sight better" than some of Sam's interviews that circulated in the press during his trip to the Mississippi River valley during the spring of 1882. But, Twichell allowed, "if you wish I will subscribe a vow never to do anything of the kind again. I'm as safe as Howells henceforth."

Sam was not entirely mollified. Twichell "writes me a chipper letter ... chaff-ing at my concern," he reported to Ned House, "& saying he is still calmly convinced that he did the right thing. We shall remain friends, but I shan't answer his letter just the same." The two men would not correspond again for over a year.[67]

◈

CHAPTER 11

Backstory

> You are my businessman; & business I myself will *not transact.* . . .
> I *won't* talk business—I will perish first. I hate the very idea of busi-
> ness, in all its forms.
>
> —Samuel Clemens to Charles L. Webster, June 29, 1883

IN THE SPRING of 1883 Samuel Clemens became entangled in another legal
dispute with his longtime nemesis Charles C. Duncan, the ex-ersatz captain
of the *Quaker City*, who had continued for years to (mis)appropriate port fees
in his office as U.S. shipping commissioner for the City of New York. The
New York Times reported on June 9, 1883, that U.S. Attorney Elihu Root
had reopened an investigation into Duncan's alleged misuse of public funds.
According to Root, "excessive salaries were paid by the Commissioner to
his sons as deputies." Though receipts of the office averaged about $20,000
per year, a total of no more than $2,000 or $3,000 had been remitted to the
U.S. Treasury during the previous decade. In 1882, for example, the office
received $22,531 in fees and its payroll totaled $19,673, with nearly $16,000
paid to Duncan and three of his sons. Root reported to Judge William James
Wallace that "their father is paying them for the performance of such duties
very much more than they would receive for services of a similar character"
in private business.[1]

Sam was interviewed the same day this story broke by a *Times* stringer
from New Haven, Henry Holloway, who solicited his reaction to it. Sam
was predictably entertained by Duncan's troubles and for thirty minutes or
so he hurled charges like mortar rounds. "I should think that after a while
he'd conclude to put a little genius into his rascality and try to hoodwink
the public as his little game of robbery goes on. It don't become a scoundrel
to be an ass," he began. In the course of his quoted comments he referred to
Duncan as "an old piece of animated flatulence." He added that

> if Duncan will persist in his wicked ways somebody ought to have a guardian
> appointed for him—a guardian with sense enough to throw a little gauze over
> the work of the gouge. . . . The *Times* says that just about $2,000 has been
> turned over to the Government's Treasury by Capt. C. C. Duncan during

389

the 10 years he has been Shipping commissioner. There must be some mistake here. If a single penny in any year, or by any means, has fallen into the Treasury, a doleful error has occurred. Old Duncan never intended it, and I'll wager this new white duck suit I put on this morning that when the old man read the *Times* this morning and saw that a little cash had glided out of his grip, he hurried downtown to cook up some job by which he could make the hoggish Government hand that cash back again. . . . So he and his three sons appropriated to themselves $15,944 of the Government's funds for the work they profess to have done last year. That's monstrous. There's no joke in that. It's scoundrelly, its nauseating, bald, barefaced robbery; but it's Duncan, through and through. . . . Enough brains could not be found in a C. C. Duncan family to run the kitchen of a Sixth Ward restaurant respectably.

At the conclusion of his remarks Sam, as usual, delivered the coup de grâce: "Judas Iscariot rises into respectability" compared to Duncan. The day after his tirade appeared in print, the *New Haven Journal and Courier* reported that Sam had "let himself loose in a very long, very aggressive, and very humorous interview" with the *Times*.[2]

On his part, Duncan was unamused and immediately filed a libel suit against the *New York Times* or more exactly against George Jones, treasurer of the New York Times Corporation, seeking $100,000 in damages. Duncan claimed that he "never at any time has been guilty of any of the wrongful, dishonest, or unlawful acts charged or insinuated in the libel; that, during that time, he has received and paid over to seamen entitled thereto sums of money aggregating over $11,000 without the loss or misappropriation of a single dollar." Sam scrambled to construct a legal defense if, as was rumored in the papers, he was personally implicated in the suit. He instructed his nephew Charley Webster, who had sent him a copy of the *Times* containing the interview, to "say nothing to anybody until you hear from me again. You did not send me that paper." He was planning to repudiate the article, to claim he had been misquoted, and he needed plausible deniability that he had reviewed the text prior to its publication or seen it until several days after it appeared. He also asked Webster to "let me know, as soon as Duncan actually sues *me*—a thing which I am not expecting to happen." A few days later he again wrote Webster with instructions about how to proceed: "Say nothing at all to Jones" because "I cannot be a witness on his side." To preclude legal liability, he planned to testify on behalf of plaintiff Duncan that the interviewer—not the interviewee—had libeled him. "There is not a sentence in the interview that ever issued from my mouth," he insisted to Webster. "There are two or three *parts* of sentences, but no complete one. As a rule the interviewer has invented both the ideas & the language." Sam also contacted Charles Dudley Warner at the *Hartford Courant* to plant a story consistent with the legal defense he was building on alternative facts: "It is doubtful if Mr. Clemens knew anything of the so-called interview until he saw it in print." He reiterated to his California friend Noah Brooks, a reporter for the *Times*, that there was not "*a solitary sentence, in that interview, that was uttered by me.* There are two or three trifling spots where the idiot has got the *substance* of what I said, though in no place the exact language." If he was "called to testify" he would swear that "the great bulk of the interview is reportorial invention & damned poor invention at that." He retained counsel, once again Daniel Whitford of the New York firm of Alexander & Green, and passed instructions to Whitford through Webster. "Tell Mr. Whitford," he enjoined his nephew, "that if I can be allowed to testify on my own behalf, I will go on the stand & point out each & every word in the printed interview that was actually uttered by me, & will show that *20 words* will cover the whole; & I will swear that all the rest was the interviewer's own—invented it *himself.*" If Duncan knew that Sam was cooperating with him, "possibly he will drop his prosecution of me & strengthen his Times suit by summoning me as a witness against the Times—a chance I should not be sorry to have." In any case, Sam bluntly told Whitford in July, "Duncan has no case against me." George Jones rightly felt betrayed and told Webster that Sam had a reputation for "getting into scrapes & then backing down, that that is characteristic of him." The lawyers for the *Times* tried to turn the tables on him. According to Whitford, *Times* attorney Benjamin Franklin Einstein offered Duncan a deal: if the port commissioner would call off his libel suit, the paper would prove Sam was culpable after all.[3]

Sam had inadvertently opened a proverbial box of Pandoras and within a week U.S. Attorney Root and Judge Wallace of the U.S. Circuit Court had opened parallel investigations into Duncan's accounts. The father and sons "seem to have run affairs on a flexible, elastic, go-as-you-please, keep-all-you-can, system of bookkeeping and financiering," the *New York Tribune* reported, "and the particular mystery about it, of which the court proposes to take cognizance and seek explanation, is the singular uniformity with which the number of Duncans employed and their salaries and expenses annually increase in such exact proportion to the fees" they collected, "leaving nothing for the Government" they ostensibly served. The investigation eventually revealed corruption in the office of the shipping commissioner that was even worse than suspected. During the decade between August 1872 and January 1883 Duncan received over $361,000 in fees, and less than $500 of that amount "found its way into the national Treasury."[4]

Sam was deposed in the case in Elmira on August 22, the same week he completed a draft of *Huckleberry Finn,* in an effort to prove "malice on the part of the defendant in publishing said alleged libel." He was accompanied by two lawyers and, according to news reports, "sat very composedly in an armchair, occasionally puffing at his cigar" and answering questions in a "calm and deliberate manner." During the deposition, he carefully walked back his libelous assertions about Duncan. He held a clipping of his interview with the *New York Times* and "went over it, sentence by sentence, almost line by line, telling what he had said and what he had not said." He had, he conceded, "used the expression 'animated flatulence' but not in the sense" it appeared in the paper and in fact "there was very little in the interview" that he admitted to saying.[5]

The libel suit was brought to jury trial on March 3, 1884, before Justice Edgar M. Cullen in the Kings County Supreme Court of New York and lasted a week. In his opening remarks, plaintiff's attorney Robert Benedict declared that the animus evident in the *New York Times* article "was caused by [Duncan's] efforts to break up the organized robbery of sailors" by the shipowners. Duncan testified that he was entitled by law to hire his clerks and paid them "no salary over $4000 a year." In defense of the newspaper, the *Times* lawyers contended that the newspaper's reports about Duncan, rather than libelous, were a matter of public record. His malfeasance in office had been exposed by congressional inquiry and detailed in the press. Moses S. Beach, Duncan's former fellow parishioner at the Plymouth Church in Brooklyn and a fellow passenger on the *Quaker City* cruise sixteen years earlier, appeared as a character witness on Duncan's behalf. Another of Duncan's clerks supplied evidence that in 1873 Duncan had embezzled over $3,000 from the port commissioner's coffers. Sam's deposition was read into the record on March 7 and in rebuttal Holloway testified that he had transcribed their conversation accurately, "showed his notes to Mr. Clemens" afterward, and that Sam had "said a good deal more than what appeared in the article."[6]

The trial ended on March 8 when the jury found in favor of the plaintiff and awarded him six cents in damages on each of two counts rather than the $100,000 he had demanded—or, as the *New York Times* chortled, "that he had precisely 12 cents' worth of character and that it had been damaged to the full amount of its value." After carefully sifting the evidence for a week, the jury decided that the language in the interview was not libelous. As for the accusation that Duncan had defrauded the federal government, the jury tacitly found him guilty as charged. The *Times* editorialized the day after the verdict that "this corrupt and dishonest man is unfit longer to hold the office of Shipping Commissioner." Duncan did not agree. So far as he was concerned, he wrote Sam, the verdict merely proved "that I was in no way damaged by the hasty remarks you are alleged to have made to a N.Y. Times reporter and as proof of my willingness to abide by their [the jury's] decision and desire to return to our former friendly relations I beg leave to ask for three of your signatures one for myself and one for each of my two boys."[7] There is no record that Sam complied with Duncan's request.

The authorities soon angled to dismiss Duncan from his post. On March 20, less than two weeks after the trial ended, the *Times* reported that Judge Wallace had assumed jurisdiction of "any action relating to Capt. Duncan's continuance in office." The *Times* also effectively declared Sam a persona non grata, referring to him in its continuing coverage of the story as merely "a Connecticut person" or "a Connecticut man." Duncan was finally removed from office by Wallace on May 12. As the judge explained, his "salary and emoluments were fixed at $5000" a year but he concocted "a scheme for administering his office which was . . . illegitimate as a radical departure from that contemplated by law" and "utterly repugnant to all notions of economy and decency." Basically, according to Wallace, Duncan had calculated that the work of the office in any given year was "worth just enough to exhaust the fees collected in that year." The ruse required that salaries—at least those of his sons—fluctuate so that "they always absorb" all available receipts. As the *Times* explained, "It was the Duncan policy that no guilty dollar should escape." In a word, according to the *San Francisco Bulletin*, Duncan was guilty of nepotism and "was not a suitable man for the office." Even so, as late as 1890 Duncan was still delivering paid speeches about Sam's antics during the *Quaker City* cruise.[8]

W. D. Howells spent a memorable fortnight with Sam in Hartford in mid-November 1883. Matthew Arnold had arrived in New York on October 15, 1883, to begin a lecture tour of the United States that included a stop in the Connecticut capital. Arnold had lobbed a cannonball or two in Sam's direction in his essay "A Word about America" in the May 1882 issue of *Nineteenth Century* and reprinted in the July number of the *Eclectic* magazine, dismissing the "Quinionian humour of Mr. Mark Twain" that, according to the apostle of high culture, appealed only to the "Philistine of the more gay and light type" and implying that Sam was nothing more than a "rowdy Philistine." Soon after Arnold landed in Boston on October 30 he called on Howells at his home on Beacon Hill, only to learn from Elinor Howells that her husband was visiting Sam in Hartford. According to Albert Bigelow Paine, Arnold "seemed surprised" and asked, "Oh, but he doesn't like *that* sort of thing, does he?" In reply she rebuked him for his snootiness: "He likes Mr. Clemens very much and he thinks him one of the greatest men he ever knew." Arnold arrived in Hartford on November 14 and was honored with an "immense reception" at the home of his host David Clarke, where he met Governor Thomas Waller and Senator Joe Hawley of "this sterling old State of Connecticut and everyone thence downwards," including Sam and Howells. As Howells recounted the story thirty-five years later, Arnold was immediately attracted to Sam. "I do not remember just how their instant encounter was contrived by Arnold's wish," he recalled, "but I have the impression that they were not parted for long during the evening." Sam and Livy invited Arnold, as well as Howells, E. P. Parker, and Joseph and Harmony Twichell to their home for tea the next afternoon, before Arnold's lecture that evening. Twichell noted in his diary that the event was "a great pleasure," that Arnold made "a most favorable impression," and that he was "a gentler, more sympathetic person than his writings would lead some people to expect." On his part, Howells professed a memory lapse: "I cannot say how they got on or what they made of each other. If Clemens ever spoke of Arnold, I do not recall what he said." In his hagiography, Paine added a few strokes to the amusing scene. Sam had been "at his humorous best" during the tea and "had kept a perpetual gale of laughter going." Afterward, Arnold "seemed dazed" by Sam's performance and "repeated some of the things" the "remarkable creature" had said "as if trying to analyze their magic." Then he asked Parker, "Is he never serious?" to which Parker replied, "Mr. Arnold, he is the most serious man in the world."[9]

If only the anecdote were true. Arnold wrote after his lecture that he had "seen no American yet, except [Charles Eliot] Norton at Cambridge, who does not seem to desire constant publicity and to be on the go all day long." For the record, Arnold reprinted without change his comment about Sam's "Quinionian humour" in *Civilization in the United States* (1888). For the record, too, Arnold crossed paths with Sam one more time, specifically on the evening of November 22, in Providence, Rhode Island, the night before his lecture in Newport, when Clarke hosted another dinner in his honor.[10] In any case, Sam's close encounters with Arnold in Hartford and Providence in the fall of 1883 were harbingers of controversies to come.

Howells was visiting Sam in Hartford at the time of Arnold's visit in order to collaborate on a play, a sort of sequel to *The Gilded Age* tentatively titled "Orme's Motor" or "The Steam Generator" and loosely based on the idiosyncrasies of Sam's brother Orion, James Lampton, and Sam's distant cousin Jesse Leathers, the self-crowned Earl of Dunham. They had been flirting with the idea of writing a script together since the summer of 1875. They outlined a very early version of the play in Boston the second week of March 1877 but neither was satisfied with the result. Sam wrote Livy on March 11, "We drop back now to the original proposition—Howells to write the play, dropping in the skeleton of Orme's speeches, I to take him later & fill him out." In early June 1878 Howells confided to Sam that he "would ten times rather write plays than anything else" and hoped to "tackle" their script again soon. In January 1879 Sam regretted that they had abandoned "that play embodying Orion which you began. It was a mistake to do that." In September 1879 Sam again suggested they "get together & grind out a play." More to the point, he wrote, "I see Orion on the stage, always gentle, always melancholy, always changing his politics & religion, & trying to reform the world, always inventing something and losing a limb by a new kind of explosion at the end of each of the four acts." Howells conceded that he had "more than once" retrieved from his files "the skeleton of that comedy of ours and viewed it with tears" but he was reticent "about helping to put your brother into drama. You can say that he is your brother, to do what you like with him; but the alien hand might inflict an incurable hurt on his tender heart." He returned the "skeleton" to his files.[11]

Two years later Sam proposed to Howells they revive the project under the working title "Colonel Sellers in Age," modeling the titular character less on Orion than on James Lampton and Jesse Leathers. He suggested that they feature the colonel forty years later, at the age of seventy-five, still cherishing a delusion that he belongs in the British House of Lords, still scheming to get rich quick with ludicrous inventions. Sam urged Howells to center the play on "this coarse old ass," volunteering to "re-write the Colonel's speeches & make him properly vulgar & extravagant. For this service I would require only ¾'s of the pecuniary result" since he had originally invented the character—a stipulation to which Howells apparently acceded. On March 8, 1882, the evening before Sam and Howells traveled to New York to petition Ulysses S. Grant to save William Cooper Howells's consular job, they discussed the play. The younger Howells, whose daughter Winifred was suffering from anorexia or "neurasthenia," was planning an extended European tour for her health, however. In October, still without a single sentence of their play on paper, Howells invited Sam to spend the winter with him in Italy, where they might collaborate on their "great American Comedy of 'Orme's Motor,'" which, Howells professed to believe, "is to enrich us beyond the dreams of avarice." At the very least, he averred, they "could have a lot of fun writing it and you could go home with some of the good old Etruscan malaria in your bones, instead of the wretched pinch-beck Hartford article that you are suffering from now." Sam again affirmed that they would indeed "write that play."[12]

They agreed in the spring to devote two weeks in the fall to the collaboration. The brothers George and Marshall Mallory, co-owners of the Madison Square Theater on the Great White Way, were eager to stage a play by Howells, who in turn wanted to write one that "would run like Scheherazade, for a thousand and one nights." Elinor Howells joked with her husband "that she would do anything for money" and urged him to visit Sam whenever he liked. He arrived in Hartford in early November 1883. Sam had "no definite idea of what he wanted to do" with the play, however, so he proposed that each of them "jot down a scenario overnight and compare our respective schemes the next morning." According to Howells, Sam's story line "was as nearly nothing as chaos could be" whereas "he liked my plot," in which Sellers is "a man crazed by his own inventions and by his superstition that he was the rightful heir to an English earldom." They spent "a jubilant fortnight" embroidering their ideas in three acts that both thought uproariously funny. They "would work all day long" on their individual scenes and, as with Sam's collaboration with Charley Warner on *The Gilded Age*, read what they had written every evening over dinner. "No dramatists ever got greater joy out of their creations," Howells bragged. "We cracked our sides laughing over it as it went along. We thought it mighty good, and I think to this day that it was mighty good." He was so pleased that he cackled to Edmund Gosse on December 9 that he had just completed "a play with Mark Twain from which I hope big money. It seems to me now at least very droll."[13]

In retrospect, Howells's optimism seems utterly unwarranted. Sellers in his newest incarnation is a pompous ass and quite obviously mad. He has invented a ship's table that converts into a lifeboat, a phonograph that spews profanity to save sailors the trouble of shouting during a storm at sea and print shop foremen the need to curse at workers, a "nihilist bomb" camouflaged as a sugar plum to be served for dessert at the tables of aristocrats, and a device that would enable houses to be heated and illuminated with sewer gas (this soon after Sam had the plumbing in his house replaced). "In five years from now you won't see a house lighted with anything but sewer gas," Sellers quips. He finagles "to get it adopted in the President's house," much as the White House had recently been equipped with flush toilets. Sellers has also devised a fire extinguisher that spits Greek fire and functions on the "principle of vaccination." He enters with it strapped to his back in act 1 and nearly sets his apartment ablaze. Most outlandishly, he has developed a device that materializes the dead (he thinks) and figures to staff all the armies and the police departments of the world with zombies and has even—much as Sam calculated to the nearest quiddity how many typesetters the Paige compositor would throw out of work—computed the worth of this gadget: "I will supply 16,020,000 men for $200 billion a year or I will sell the entire crop, and warrant them to outlast the solar system, for the bagatelle of sixty billion dollars cash on the nail." A zombie army is "the grandest invention of the age," he announces, and "there's no end of money in it." Sam and Howells finished a draft of the play by mid-November, though Howells continued to tinker with the script for a couple of weeks.[14]

Their effort to market it was fraught with difficulties, of course. Sam nurtured a visceral distrust of nearly all middlemen of literary production: publishers, producers, editors, actors, booksellers, proofreaders, lawyers, lecture agents, and sometimes even artists, stenographers, collaborators, and typesetters. While George Mallory had been an impetus behind the project, Sam initially resisted the temptation to send him a copy of the script. He had long boosted the theatrical career of William Gillette, Lilly Warner's younger brother, by arranging for him to be cast in a minor role in *The Gilded Age* in 1875 and, after attending a performance of his play *The Professor* in Hartford on January 9, 1880, by investing three thousand dollars to subsidize its production. Gillette was then hired by the Mallory brothers to manage the Madison Square Theater, where *The Professor* was staged in July 1881 "& achieved a handsome success," Sam crowed. The brothers soon bought a controlling interest in the play. By September 1883, however, Gillette was "having no end of trouble" collecting the money he was owed by the Mallorys and he complained to Sam, who in turn drafted but apparently did not send the brothers an outraged letter: "You have a contract with Mr. Will Gillette; & I am aware that you are trying (as usual with you) to sneak out of the performance of its conditions. I am personally interested in the matter; therefore I suggest to you couple of piety-mouthing, hypocritical thieves & liars that you change your customary policy this time." Clearly Sam was not predisposed to grant the Mallory brothers the right of first refusal to his new play.[15]

Rather than capitulate to the Mallorys, Sam and Howells submitted the script of *Colonel Sellers as a Scientist* to John T. Raymond. As Sam explained, Raymond impersonated Sellers well and no more than "thirty actors in the country" could "do it better." Moreover, he had "a sort of sentimental right to be *offered* the piece—though no moral or legal or other kind of right." In one breath, he hoped Raymond would lease the play for four hundred dollars a week and perform it throughout his next season and, in the next breath, he wished "*to God he would not take it*" because he believed Raymond was a thief. Should the actor rise to the bait, Sam insisted to Webster, he wanted an exclusivity clause in the contract as well as a time limit by which Raymond must begin to stage it. He advised Webster and Whitford to record all their conversations with Raymond in shorthand because the actor "would stand with his foot on the steps of the throne of God & lie" and "he knows that I know that as a liar he has not his equal, either in hell or out of it." On his part, Raymond was intrigued by the offer but noncommittal. He had recently added a new play to his repertoire, the comedy *For Congress* (1884), and did not need another one. He might audition *Colonel Sellers as a Scientist* with a series of one-night stands in the provinces but then he could pay only minimal royalties. He might be willing to lease the play for $250 a week, but first he wanted the authors to make some revisions. Sam, meanwhile, consulted the actor Lawrence Barrett, who believed it would "be a mistake on Raymond's part if he lets this play go to somebody else." Four hundred dollars a week might be more than an actor of Raymond's caliber "should be asked to pay," Sam conceded, "but at the same time it is as low as I can afford." Then a startling instruction to Webster: "If the book business interferes with the dramatic business, drop the *former*—for it doesn't pay salt; & I want the latter rushed"—this only four months after Sam completed the manuscript of the as-yet-unpublished *Adventures of Huckleberry Finn*.[16]

While Raymond dawdled, Howells showed George Mallory a copy of the script in order to gauge his interest. Sam was incensed that Howells failed to specify contract terms before allowing Mallory to see it—one of the few times he was irritated by Howells during their forty-year friendship. Nor was Sam appeased when Mallory lowballed an offer for the play: a third of the profits to the theater owners, another third paid to the comedian Nat Goodwin to star in it, and the other third to be divided between the playwrights. If Mallory had initially proposed these "brilliant terms," Sam fumed, he would have been spared "the opportunity of examining the play." Howells agreed, ridiculing "the widow's thirds offered us by the Mallorys." Webster soon notified the brothers that Sam did not think the Sellers play "would be sufficiently profitable to any of us" under their plan.[17]

Raymond seemed to hold all the cards. He "declared himself delighted with the piece" on the condition it was reworked, according to Howells, and in late May 1884 Sam capitulated to Raymond's offer to lease it for $250 a week. The actor sailed to England in early July for a two-month holiday and upon his return he began discreetly to publicize the comedy. Unfortunately, his self-promotion smacked of further negotiations with the authors in the newspapers. "Raymond has a new play by Mark Twain and W. D. Howells which he will *probably* produce next season," the *Boston Herald* reported on

August 3. In an interview with the *New York Herald*, the actor observed that he intended "to open my engagement at the Star Theatre" on Broadway in May 1885 "with the production of 'The New Colonel Sellers,' by Messrs. Mark Twain and W. D. Howells." But a week later he notified Howells that he would stage the play only if the authors "leave out materialization and the earldom." Howells refused and Sam concurred. "Of course we couldn't re-write that play," Sam allowed, because "it wouldn't pay at all to do that." He similarly conceded to Webster that he and Howells could not "re-write the play; but Raymond's ideas are good, & if we had had them in the beginning we could have used them to good advantage." Confronted by their refusal to accede to his demand, Raymond withdrew his offer. He wrote Webster from the Grand Pacific Hotel in Chicago on September 9 that he had reread the script "and am convinced that in its present form it would not prove successful," though "if the play is altered and *made* longer I should be pleased to read it again." Both Sam and Howells were resigned to his decision. "Hang Raymond, let him go—he is no good," Sam wrote. He had concluded, at Howells's suggestion, to salvage the project by turning the play into a novel. On his part, Howells consoled his writing partner: "Never mind about the play. We had fun writing it, anyway." Yet the question remains: Was Raymond's decision to withdraw his offer another bargaining ploy, yet another attempt to reach the best deal possible with the authors? A week later the *Boston Herald* again reported that "a gentleman who has read the new play written for John T. Raymond by W. D. Howells and Mark Twain says that it is in a very funny strain, Raymond representing a sort of inventive crank and being on the stage most of the time." Two months later, deep into the theater season, Raymond again declared in an interview that he carried in his trunk a script "that promises well, prepared by Mark Twain and W. D. Howells, presenting more particulars about the private life of my old friend Colonel Mulberry Sellers, wherein that sanguine speculator details some new schemes of a very remarkable nature and calculated to revolutionize the worlds of commerce, politics, and mechanics. The new ideas of the Colonel are extremely funny and appeal directly to the American sense of the ridiculous."[18]

After completing the manuscripts of *Huck Finn* and, with Howells, *Colonel Sellers as a Scientist*, Sam entered a fallow period in his career. He continued to work at his craft for the next several months but in the end he had little to show for it. He began his Hawaii novel and, as he notified Howells in early January 1884, "My billiard table is stacked up with books relating to the Sandwich Islands: the walls are upholstered with scraps of paper penciled with notes drawn from them." On January 24 he claimed to be "shirking all other duties in order to give the whole remnant of my mind to a most painstaking revision" of the text, though he soon abandoned the project and the fate of the manuscript is unknown.[19]

Sam filled his time with other activities, such as fund-raising for charity, especially the Decorative Arts Society of Hartford and the Union for Home Work. During the harsh winter of 1883 Sam, Elizabeth Colt, and Harriet Beecher Stowe organized a Carnival of Authors with a goal of clearing five thousand dollars for the Union. Sam and Stowe autographed books and led a parade with Sam costumed as Leo Hunter from Charles Dickens's *Pickwick Papers*. In early September a group of Hartford men, including Sam and Franklin Whitmore, registered at the Montowese House in Branford, Connecticut, and went duck hunting. Sam and Livy attended a performance of Robert Montgomery Bird's *The Gladiator* starring John McCullough at Roberts Opera House, the same play Sam had seen at the Broadway Theater in New York in 1853 with Edwin Forrest in the lead.[20]

The Clemenses regularly entertained and were entertained by friends that during these months, too, visiting the Howellses and Thomas Bailey Aldrich and his wife Lilian in Boston and Laurence Hutton while in New York for a breakfast honoring Edwin Booth. At a benefit evening for Ludwig Barney at the Thalia Theatre in New York, Sam mingled with Daniel Frohman, Julian Hawthorne, Laurence Hutton, Sarah Orne Jewett, George Parsons Lathrop, Brander Matthews, and Frank Mayo. Sam and Livy in turn hosted the Aldriches, Thomas Beecher, George Washington Cable, Joel Chandler Harris, W. D. Howells, Mary Murfree, and E. C. Stedman in Hartford. According to the *Springfield Republican*, their home became "the literary headquarters of the city." The Clemenses also hosted a dinner for Lathrop attended by Stowe and the Twichells. Joe Twichell remembered that Stowe "was in the mood for it" and reminisced about "the old antislavery days. We were conscious of a great reverence toward her." It was "a delightful evening—especially in the pleasure of hearing Mrs. Stowe talk."[21]

While on another of his speaking tours, Cable performed in Hartford the evening of January 26 and awoke the next morning in a guest room of the Clemens house with what he insisted was "biliousness" accompanied by "neuralgia of the lower jaw." He canceled his public appearances for the next three weeks to recover. The Clemenses hired a nurse and summoned Francis Bacon, former professor of surgery at the Yale Medical School and one of the leading physicians in Connecticut, but as Katy Leary remembered "that old blooming doctor never knew what was the matter with Mr. Cable. He was doctoring him all the time for a sore throat." Cable had in fact come down with a simple case of mumps—a readily communicable childhood disease.[22]

Sam hastened to assure Cable's tour manager James Pond that Cable was in no serious danger, though he was not expected to "be out of bed for several weeks." However, Pond seemed to think that either Cable was a hypochondriac or Sam was exaggerating the severity of his illness. Sam replied testily, "Why is it so difficult that Cable is sick, or can become sick? . . . Mr. Cable is sick in bed, and has been for five days. I make this statement in the earnest hope of being able to convince somebody, anybody: and I make it in the belief that it ought to be trustworthy, for surely I have nothing to gain by misrepresenting the matter." On her part, Livy issued almost daily updates to Louise Cable on her husband's medical condition. "If you could see how bright he is today," she wrote on February 1, "it would delight your heart and put it at rest." Five days later she reiterated that the patient was "still better than yesterday, slept all night last night, sat up yesterday & today. Eats with appetite and I think will very soon be himself again." The teetotaling Cable later explained that "while my stomach was in a very delicate condition my physician prescribed champagne with my food in such limited quantity as a medical man would and I insisted on using it more sparingly than it was prescribed." Cable assured his wife—with an ambiguous turn of phrase—that he had "enjoyed Mr. Clemens' company not a little." In the course of their conversations Sam occasionally was "ferocious & funny" on the topic of publishers and, of course, he "proposed a little literary scheme for him & I & 3 or 4 others"—specifically, a speaking tour. Cable bragged to Louise almost gleefully that Sam "seems to warm to me more & more." He had sufficiently recovered by February 16 that he and Sam tried to visit Grant in New York—where they dined at the Union League Club with Clarence Buel, one of the editors of the *Century*—to pitch a plan for the relief of Ohio River flood victims, only to discover that the former president was ill and unavailable.[23]

Meanwhile, Sam continued to nurture projects that never ripened. After abandoning the Hawaii novel, he began another theatrical adaptation of *The Adventures of Tom Sawyer* (1876) in four acts that he completed on January 29, three days after Cable wilted in his guest room, and copyrighted it on February 1 on the basis of a synopsis. On February 8 he assured Webster that it was "a *good* play—a good *acting* play" and two days later Cable reported from his sickbed that Sam had "finished the play he was writing when I fell ill." Sam had a bright idea he thought would guarantee its success: to "have all the boys & girls played by grown people." He wanted Louis Aldrich to play Tom Sawyer and his friend C. T. Parsloe, the star of *Ah Sin*, to play Huck Finn. He offered the script to the impresario Augustin Daly on February 17 and Daly declined it ten days later. "I fear that Tom Sawyer would not make a success at my theatre," Daly demurred. Moreover, he disagreed "that grown up people may successfully represent the boys & girls of your piece. Tom might be played by a clever comedian as a boy—but the other parts would seem ridiculous in grown peoples hands." Undeterred as usual, within a couple of days Sam sold rights to his script to Barton & Miles of the Bijou Opera House in New York. They hired the child actor Mollie Revel to star as Tom and they tried out the play in Yonkers and Hartford with negligible success. Sam eventually abandoned the project and conceded that the novel "cannot be dramatized. One might as well try to dramatize any other hymn."[24]

With Cable still confined to the guest room, Sam also began a dramatic adaptation of *The Prince and the Pauper* (1881). Cable reported to Louise that his host was "in splendid working trim," though his inference was not warranted by the evidence. "I am now writing a new play by myself," Sam informed Webster on February 10, and if he finished it to his liking he was willing even to offer it to the Mallorys without preconditions in the hope that they might reach "terms for it which will be mutually satisfactory." Sam copyrighted the script on February 28 and George Mallory rejected it soon thereafter. "Somehow I couldn't make [the play] go," Sam admitted years later. "I had written books, and knew I could write books as well as anyone. But I couldn't make the play." Sam also shared a copy of the script with Howells, who thought "the parlance is not sufficiently 'early English'" and the script "altogether too thin and slight. You have a good outline but you ought to fill it in from the book with more life and incident." Will Gillette also read the script, advised Sam "that neither the living nor the dead could act the play as [he] had planned it," and volunteered to help Sam revise it. Gillette thought that it represented the "backbone of a good piece—very striking and interesting" but required "a considerable amount of dressing up and rearranging" to "bring out the points." Gillette "went so far as to draft the plot for the play, making liberal alterations of the text of the book," Sam told an interviewer later, but he eventually abandoned the project.[25]

Fully recovered from the mumps, Cable left Hartford in mid-February and resumed his reading tour in Philadelphia a day or two later. He was gone but not forgotten, to judge from the illnesses he left behind. Sam joked with Ned House that Cable had "280 times more fuss over his little pains than you did over your big ones." Cable's nurse and all three of the Clemens daughters contracted the mumps after his departure. Susy in particular agonized in early March for four "hellfiredest days & nights" and "suffered 13 times more than Cable did (whose pains lasted but 2 days), & yet has not made as much fuss in the 4 days as he used to make in 15 minutes."[26] The math may have changed but Sam's point—that Cable had been an impatient patient under a welcome roof—remained the same.

Still, Cable was grateful for the Clemenses' hospitality and the medical attention he received in their home and thanked Sam even before he departed. "Blessed be your hall & your board," he wrote, and "blessed be your guest chamber, your larder & your cellar & angels attend you, your sweet wife & your lovely children." Six weeks later, he also played the fool by perpetrating a famous if frivolous prank. While recuperating in Hartford, Cable noticed that Sam was pestered every day by requests in the mail for his signature. Sam's strategy for coping with what Walt Whitman called the "autograph monster" was to "write out a few hundred cards now and then" and give them to his secretary to mail. He joked privately that once his "autograph sold for $42,480. (It was signed to a check.)" But what if Sam were to receive dozens of appeals for his autograph all at once? Cable sent 150 form letters to Sam's friends suggesting that they solicit his signature and time their mailings and telegrams so that most or all of their requests arrived on April Fools' Day.[27]

On April 1, as planned, Sam received "appalling piles" of applications for his signature and the letters continued to arrive for days afterward from such folks as Moses Beach, Henry Ward Beecher, Noah Brooks, Jeannette Gilder, Richard Watson Gilder, Julian Hawthorne, John Hay, Henry Irving, Clara Louise Kellogg, George Parsons Lathrop, Brander Matthews, Frank Millet, Helena Modjeska, James R. Osgood, James Pond, Napoleon Sarony, Horace Scudder, Ellen Terry, George Waring, and Charley Warner. Some of the autograph hounds expressed a particular reason they needed an autograph. Thomas Bailey Aldrich jokingly requested one because, he explained, he admired *Gabriel Conroy* (a Bret Harte novel); General Gardner Blodgett solicited one to present to a consumptive contemplating suicide; Hjalmar Hjorth Boyesen wished to add to his collection of autographs of "all the great criminals"; Henry F. Gillig desired an autograph he could trade for Tennyson's; Robert Underwood Johnson asked for one to give to a lame boy; and Dean Sage requested one for a young lady who admired Harte's "The Heathen Chinee" (1870). A few of these fiends, according to Sam, demanded more than a mere signature. Clarence Buel of the *Century* solicited a signature attached to the manuscript of a humorous article, Laurence Hutton ordered an autograph as well as one of Sam's children, Major Joel Kinney of Cincinnati needed one at the bottom of a blank check, and E. C. Stedman wanted a few manuscript pages from *Roughing It* (1872). Bloodgood H. Cutter's request arrived in the form of sixteen lines of stricken verse:

> Friends, suggest in each one's behalf
> To write, and ask your autograph
> To refuse that, I will not do,

After the long voyage I had with you.
That was a memorable time
You wrote in Prose, I wrote in Rhyme
To describe the wonders of each place
And the queer customs of each race.
That is in my memory yet
For while I live, I'll not forget.
I often think of that affair
And the many that were with us there
As your friends think it for the best
I ask your Autograph with the rest
Hoping you will it to me send
It will please and cheer your dear old Friend.

A dozen years after the *Quaker City* excursion, according to Sam, Cutter was "the same mildewed idiot. His friends call him a lunatic—but that is pretty fulsome flattery; one cannot become a lunatic without first having brains."[28]

As for the prankster, Cable was unrepentant but relieved the gag had worked. He figured that Sam "was a mad man about the first of the month but I don't see what he has particularly to growl about." He confided to Louise that "the whole American literary guild is laughing over the Mark Twain joke." Twichell noted in his diary that Sam "was pleased with the joke, and well he might be, for it was a great compliment." But Sam also got the last laugh. Cable was "a very particular friend of mine and for that reason would not play jokes on me," Sam mused to an interviewer. Moreover, as "a poet by nature and breeding" Cable "hasn't really got practical sense enough in him to invent a joke."[29]

In order to avoid autograph hounds and interviewers, Sam occasionally traveled under pseudonyms, as when he sailed under the name S. Langhorne to Bermuda in 1877 and under the name C. L. Samuel to the lower Mississippi in 1882; he registered at the Everett Hotel in New York under the name "James P. Jones" in January 1884 and at the Lafayette Hotel in Philadelphia under the name "J. B. Smith" in September 1884. He also scorned interviews unless they were in his self-interest. As a wordsmith, why should he "give 'em away?" he queried Hamlin Garland in July 1883. "I *sell* 'em. It's my grub; it's the only way I've got to earn a dishonest living." Considered as commodities, words were gold and Sam was disinclined to lavish them upon reporters for free. "Why don't you ask me for a shirt?" he inquired. "What is the difference between asking me for the worth of a shirt & asking me for the shirt itself? Perhaps you didn't know you were begging." Or as he concluded, "the proper place for journalists who solicit literary charity is on the street corner with their hats in their hands." He considered requiring journalists to pay to interview him on the grounds that they wanted something to publish to earn their salaries.[30]

In April 1884 Sam and Webster began to plan the rollout of *Huck Finn*. Sam briefly considered entrusting the manuscript to Osgood, but he blamed the publisher for the resounding commercial failures of *The Prince and the Pauper* (1881) and *Life on the Mississippi* (1883). "I have never for a moment doubted that you did the very best you knew how—it is impossible to doubt that," he wrote Osgood in ending their business relationship, "but there were things about the publishing of *my* books which you did not understand. You understand them now but it is I who have paid the costs of the apprenticeship." He also weighed the possibility, more briefly, of contracting again with the American Publishing Company in order to recoup some of the money the dead Elisha Bliss had swindled from him. His terms for the new book included a 60 percent share of profits. The firm declined.[31]

So Sam established his own subscription publishing house and not only hired Webster to run it but named it for him. The articles of incorporation of Charles L. Webster and Company specified that Sam would be paid 60 percent of the profits from his books, and the initial plan was to sell and distribute only his books. Webster agreed on March 20, 1884, to accept an annual salary of $2,500, a third of the first $60,000 of profits per year, and a tenth of all profits above $60,000. As owner of the company, Sam would receive all remaining monies. He immediately put Webster to school. In mid-April he mailed the manuscript of *Huck Finn* to his nephew and outlined his demands in his next several letters. He urged him "to look out for the Canadian pirates. Bliss used to swear that they laid in with pressmen & printing-office boys & bought advance sheets of one of my books & got the book out before we did." He reiterated literally dozens of times that the book was only to be issued only "when a big edition" of at least thirty, forty, or even fifty thousand copies had been sold. "The Tramp issued with 48,000," he remembered on April 14, setting the bar as high as possible. He refused to set a firm publication date until the entire first printing had been subscribed. "It must wait till they are sold, if it is seven years," the same length of time Jacob agreed to work before marrying Rachel in the book of Genesis. "Keep it diligently in mind," Sam decreed,

> that we dont issue *Huck Finn* till we have made a big sale. Get at your canvassing early and drive it with all your might, with an intent and purpose of

issuing on the 10th (or 15th) of next December (the best time in the year to tumble a big pile into the trade)—but if we haven't 40,000 orders then, we simply postpone publication till we've *got* them. It is a plain, simple policy, and would have saved both of my last books if it had been followed. There is not going to be any reason whatever why this book should not succeed—and it shall and *must*.

If, in fact, they could publish by December 15, Sam mused, they could "dump books the same day and catch the holiday trade," though such a move would violate their contracts with book agents.[32]

Sam was amenable to cutting corners if the risk was worth the reward. After the failure of his last two books (or three, including *The Stolen White Elephant Etc.*) and his profligate spending, he was nearly broke. He privately admitted his money woes to the Gerhardts in May: "We have made but few investments in the last few years which have not turned out badly. Our losses during the past three years have been prodigious. Three or four more of such years would make it necessary for us to move out of our house & hunt for cheaper quarters." They had money enough for household expenses but, he added, "I must settle down to work & restore things to the old condition." The family traveled from Hartford to New York on June 17 but Sam could not afford to engage an entire sleeping car for the family on the railroad to Elmira as he had in the past so he arranged instead for a "large compartment" in a drawing room car. Sam admonished Webster to practice even "minor economies" in the management of Webster and Company (e.g., "Instruct your clerks to use the telegraph less freely"). On the one hand, he oversaw the production and distribution of *Huck Finn* and sometimes micromanaged the company. He asked Webster on May 7, for example, whether he had yet selected paper for printing the book that "had been offered you at 7¢ which you could hardly tell from 8¢ paper." He candidly told an interviewer in July 1885 that "I am Webster & Co., myself, substantially" and repeated the point two months later to General William Tecumseh Sherman: "I am Charles L. Webster & Co.—at least I am 90 per cent of that firm." On the other hand, he protested that he was too busy to be bothered with the day-to-day operation of the business. "It is not my function" as president of the company "to help arrive at conclusions in business matters," he chided his nephew. He had no talent for diplomacy and he flew "off the handle altogether too easily." The upshot was that nothing should be submitted to him "except in a completed and determined form—then my function comes in: and it is merely and solely to *approve* or *disapprove*."[33] Put simply, Sam wanted authority without responsibility.

This (mis)management style is evident in the selection of the illustrator of *Huck Finn*. The sales canvass could not begin until a graphic artist had drawn a few images for the prospectus. Sam had been impressed by some sketches that he had seen in *Life* magazine and, he wrote Webster, "*that* is the man I want to try." At Sam's direction, Webster commissioned E. W. Kemble, a twenty-three-year-old self-taught cartoonist, to prepare 175 pen-and-ink pictures for the novel for which he was paid a thousand dollars. Though Sam had never met Kemble, he supervised his work. "Let Kemble rush," he wrote Webster in April, because "time is already growing short. As fast as he gets through with the chapters, take them & read & select your matter for your canvassing book." Three weeks later, Sam quibbled about Huck's physiognomy in one of Kemble's preliminary sketches: "the boy's mouth is a trifle more Irishy than necessary." Three additional weeks later, Kemble submitted a set of illustrations and Sam was hypercritical of them. "Some of the pictures are good," he conceded, "but none of them are [*sic*] very *very* good. The faces are generally ugly & wrenched into over-expression amounting sometimes to distortion. As a rule (though not always) the people in these pictures are forbidding & repulsive." He judged much of Kemble's work "careless & bad." The frontispiece, of Huck holding a dead rabbit in one hand and a smoothbore in the other, had "the usual blemish—an ugly, ill-drawn face," he caviled. "Huck Finn is an exceedingly good-hearted boy & should carry a good & good-looking face." The "best I can say," he noted, was that the illustrations could have been worse. "The pictures will do—they will just barely do & that is the best I can say for them." The next batch of sketches, according to Sam, was "most rattling good. They please me exceedingly." He only demanded the omission of one of them—"the lecherous old rascal kissing the girl at the campmeeting" in chapter 20. "It is powerful good, but it mustn't go in—don't forget it. Let's not make *any* pictures of the campmeeting. The subject won't *bear* illustrating. It is a disgusting thing, & pictures are sure to tell the truth about it too plainly."[34] But by the same token Sam approved a picture of the king naked and painted in stripes hopping about the stage in "The Burning Shame." Ironically, Joel Chandler Harris considered Kemble's drawings "too doggoned flip" and many modern scholars object to them on the grounds they perpetuate racist stereotypes of the "minstrel darky" and represent a countertext to the novel. Kemble's first portrayal of Jim in chapter 2 of the novel basically recapitulates a caricature of a black man he had drawn for *Life*, one of the sketches that had attracted Sam to Kemble in the first place. The similarity of the two images, according to Henry B. Wonham, suggests that Sam's choice of Kemble "represented a conscious effort to insert his narrative of antebellum life into the rapidly emerging contemporary graphic discourse on racial and ethnic identity."

Figure 19.
Caricature of a
black man by E.
W. Kemble, *Life*,
September 6,
1883.

Kemble in later years became a specialist in African American caricature, publishing popular collections of racist cartoons under such titles as *Kemble's Coons* (1897) and *Comical Coons* (1898). Significantly, Sam never criticized any of his sketches of Jim or other black characters.[35]

Nor was Sam easily reconciled to the work of Webster's production team. The typesetters, he allowed, "don't make a very great many mistakes; but those that do occur are of a nature to make a man curse his teeth loose." He wished a special scourge upon the proofreader. Most of the galleys were

Figure 20. Jim as illustrated by E. W. Kemble, from chapter 2 of *Adventures of Huckleberry Finn*, 1885.

JIM.

"clean & beautiful & a pleasure to read; but the rest of it was read by that blind idiot whom I have cursed so much & is a disgraceful mess." He was convinced that some parts of the proof had not been compared to original copy in the print shop and he was more incensed the nearer the date of publication approached. "Charley, your proof-reader is an idiot; & not only an idiot, but blind; & not only blind, but partly dead," Sam fussed. "Some of the spacing—*most* of it, in fact—is absolutely disgraceful; but this goddamned ass never sees it. By God he can't see *anything*; he is blind & dead & rotten &

ought to be thrown into the sewer." Fortunately, Sam persevered. He added some of the most vernacular phrasing in the novel at the proof stage. Huck's reference to the king's "humbug and hogwash" in the manuscript becomes his dismissal of the king's "soul-butter and hogwash" in the final text. Sherburn's laugh "that's fitten for a funeral—the kind that makes you feel crawly" in the manuscript becomes the kind of laugh "that makes you feel like when you are eating bread that's got sand in it" in the book.[36]

At Quarry Farm during the summer of 1884 Sam added yet another abandoned manuscript to his pile of recent failures. Three weeks after his arrival in Elmira, he began a sequel to *Adventures of Huckleberry Finn* premised on Tom's desire near the end of that novel to head west for "howling adventures amongst the Injuns, over in the Territory, for a couple of weeks or two." Just as he had requested books about travel on the Mississippi from Osgood before working on *Life on the Mississippi*, he asked Webster on July 6 to send him Randolph Barnes Marcy's *Thirty Years of Army Life on the Border* (1859) as well as any "other *personal narratives* of life & adventure out yonder on the Plains & in the Mountains" he might run across, "especially life *among the Indians*. See what you can find. I mean to take Huck Finn out there." Webster soon sent him several books, including Henry Bradshaw Fearon's *Sketches of America* (1819); perhaps Washington Irving's *Astoria* (1836); probably Francis Parkman's *The Oregon Trail* (1849); Richard Irving Dodge's *The Plains of the Great West* (1876) and *Our Wild Indians* (1882); and Buffalo Bill's autobiography, *The Life of Honorable William F. Cody* (1879).[37]

Sam completed about twenty-two thousand words or almost nine chapters of the projected novel, which he tentatively titled "Huck Finn and Tom Sawyer among the Indians." In the fragment, Huck, Tom, and Jim join a wagon train headed west and soon befriend a young girl, a Becky Thatcher type named Peggy Mills, and the rest of the Mills family. While the boys are fetching water one day, the wagon train is attacked by Sioux and all of the emigrants are massacred except Peggy and Jim, who are captured. Tom and Huck are joined in their pursuit of the captives by Peggy's sweetheart Brace Johnson, an Indian hater—a stock type in Western fiction, such as Ishmael Bush in James Fenimore Cooper's *The Prairie* (1827) and the Jibbenainosay in Robert Montgomery Bird's *Nick of the Woods* (1837), which Sam had first read no later than 1859 and cited in chapter 55 of *Life on the Mississippi*. The story is again narrated by Huck, who remarks that Johnson "didn't talk very much; and when he talked about Injuns, he talked the same as if he was talking about animals." The plot actually anticipates by some seventy years the John Ford movie *The Searchers* (1956), with John Wayne in the role of Ethan Edwards (Brace Johnson) and Natalie Wood in the role of Debbie

Edwards (Peggy). The fragment breaks off when Tom, Huck, and Johnson discover a blood-soaked piece of Peggy's dress and four stakes in the ground, evidence that she has been gang-raped. Tom and Huck's dream of the pastoral West ends in atrocity and horror and Sam reached a narrative dead end. "This is the first summer which I have lost," Sam grumbled to Webster on September 1. "I haven't a paragraph to show for my 3-months' working-season." In fact, other than revising the proof of *Huck Finn*, he had nothing to show for the previous twelve months of writing except a mound of useless manuscript—and twenty-six galley sheets of "Huck and Tom among the Indians" set on the Paige typesetting machine.[38]

On September 9 and 10 Sam attended performances of Buffalo Bill's Wild West at the Elmira Driving Park and "enjoyed [the show] thoroughly. It brought back to me the breezy, wild life of the great plains & the Rocky Mountains & stirred me like a war song." He happily overlooked the contrivances in William F. Cody's Western simulacrum, graciously pronouncing it "genuine" with its "cowboys, vaqueros, Indians, stage-coach, costumes & all," and "wholly free from sham & insincerity." In fact, the Wild West was no more realistic than a dime novel Western, though in the wake of his work on "Huck and Tom among the Indians" Sam tolerated the fantasy. In any event, he left with the family two weeks later for the Hotel Brunswick in New York en route to a more genteel routine in Hartford, arriving on September 14, and he never resumed his Wild Western tale.[39]

Sam concocted yet another way to help publicize *Huck Finn* at little expense—and, incidentally, to nurture Karl Gerhardt's budding career—while at Quarry Farm during the summer of 1884. Gerhardt had exhausted his stipend to study in Paris and returned to the United States, leaving Hattie and their daughter Olivia (named for Olivia Clemens) in Paris until he could find work. Consummate at self-promotion when it would sell books or tickets, Sam hired Gerhardt in August to sculpt a clay bust of him and, to save time posing, he sat for a shirtless photo at an Elmira studio.

Sam thought so highly of the finished casting that he sent a photograph of it to Webster and suggested they use it as a second frontispiece to the novel. Webster was amenable, especially when he learned that including a heliotype of the bust would increase production costs by only about two cents per volume.[40]

The promotional schemes initially seemed to work. The canvassers collected nine thousand advance orders for *Huck Finn* by early September. But in late November, even before the release of the novel, the sales campaign nearly ground to a halt. Literally in the middle of the Christmas season, the best time of the year to market books, the company was embroiled in

Figure 21. Samuel Clemens posing shirtless for the Karl Gerhardt bust, 1884. Courtesy of the Mark Twain Papers and Project, Bancroft Library, University of California–Berkeley.

Figure 22. Karl Gerhardt bust of Samuel Clemens, frontispiece, *Adventures of Huckleberry Finn*, 1885. Courtesy of the Mark Twain Papers and Project, Bancroft Library, University of California–Berkeley.

a scandal that damaged its reputation and postponed its U.S. publication by two months. As Sam explained to a reporter, someone in the stereotyping department of J. J. Little and Company mutilated one of Kemble's illustrations. More specifically, with one stroke of an awl he drew a penis on a picture of Uncle Silas Phelps in chapter 32, giving the cut "an indecent character never intended by the author or engraver."

Some 250 copies of the prospectus with this mutilated drawing were sent to book agents before the error was detected. Webster was in San Francisco organizing the canvass in California when the story broke on the front page of the New York *World* on November 27. The news was immediately picked up by papers across the country, including the *New York Tribune* on

Figure 23. Mutilated illustration in the first printing of *Adventures of Huckleberry Finn*, 1885.

November 29 and the *Chicago Tribune* on November 30. Both the Carson City *Appeal* and the *San Francisco Bulletin* alleged that the damaged image was nothing more than another cheap publicity stunt orchestrated by Sam to advertise the book. The discovery of the gaffe was "made in the nick of time" to save the entire first printing of thirty thousand copies "from destruction" at a loss "of at least $25,000," according to Webster.[41] He meanwhile telegraphed New York to order a postponement in publication, recalled all copies of the mock-up, arranged for a corrected illustration to be tipped into them before they were returned to the canvassers, and offered a $500 reward for the identification and conviction of the troublemaker. "We have traced this matter as far as possible," he averred, adding,

> The original drawing, photo-engraving and stereotype plates are all right. The proofs were first examined by the printers' proof-reader, next by Mr. Clemens, then by W. D. Howells, and finally by myself, and were found to be correct. Stereotype plates were then made, proofs taken therefrom, read, and found correct, and sent to the printers for publication. I am satisfied that the printers know nothing of the matter. . . . I believe the alteration was made in the press-room, where there are about fifty hands employed.[42]

The culprit was never identified, though Webster and Sam considered suing the engraving company for damages.

Sam also negotiated with Cable and Pond during the summer of 1884 for a four-month speaking and book tour the next winter. Both *Huck Finn* and Cable's new novel *Dr. Sevier*, which would feature prominently in their programs, were scheduled for publication during the lyceum season. Each of the authors insisted upon several conditions in the contract. Sam demanded a Christmas recess so that he could spend the holiday with his family in Hartford. He initially offered Cable a salary of $350 a week plus expenses. He demanded that James Pond or his brother Ozias accompany them and "attend to everything which comes under the head of *business*—halls, route, printing, prices, &c., deciding all business questions himself, & asking no advice of me." The circus had to be booked into six to ten small towns "before it appears in any metropolis" so that the performers could polish their program prior to entertaining any large audiences. Pond's agency was to be paid 10 percent of the profit for services rendered and would provide Sam a regular account of "receipts & disbursements & pay over to me daily what is coming to me." The route of the tour would be arranged so that Sam would be in Canada when *Huck Finn* was published there so that he could secure Canadian copyright. They were not to be booked to read before the hometown folks in either Elmira or Hartford. On his part, Cable had recently moved with his family from New Orleans to Simsbury, Connecticut, to escape Southern censure of his progressive racial opinions. Unlike Sam, Cable was the sole provider for his family and had recently quit his job to earn his living as a full-time lecturer and writer. He demanded a salary of $450 a week plus expenses and a promise that he would not be expected to perform or travel on Sundays. Sam acceded to Cable's salary demand on July 8 ("O damnation, I would rather pay Cable $450 a week & his expenses" than pay Thomas Nast $300 a week). Sam wanted to travel with someone companionable, "somebody to keep me in countenance on the stage and to help me impose on the audience. But more than that, I wanted good company on the road and at the hotels" and Cable fit the bill. Pond publicly announced the upcoming tour on July 20. In Pond's circular the two men received equal billing and agreed to share roughly equal time on the stage "so that the pathos of the one would alternate with the humor of the other." Sam calculated that the tour would earn a profit of $25,000 to $30,000 and he would receive two-thirds to three-fourths of it. He and Cable rendezvoused in New York on September 26 to pose together for a publicity photograph.

The mice and men seemed to have planned well. As usual, Sam pledged that this was his final speaking tour. "'This trip's my *last*—forever & ever," he insisted.[43]

One additional form of prepublication publicity for *Huck Finn* required no capital outlay: Sam sold three installments of the novel to the *Century* for $700. It was not paid advertising but advertising for which he was paid, much as Tom Sawyer hoodwinked his friends into whitewashing his fence and rewarding him for the privilege. Nearly a dozen chapters of the novel, representing over a fourth of the entire text and accompanied by several of Kemble's illustrations, were serialized in the magazine in advance of U.S. book publication between December 1884 and February 1885. They were subsequently reprinted in newspapers around the world, including the *New York Tribune*, New York *Sun*, *Chicago Times*, *Chicago Herald*, *Cleveland Herald*, *Cleveland Plain Dealer*, *Portland Oregonian*, and *Trenton Times* in the United States; the Brisbane *Queenslander*, *Melbourne Times*, *Adelaide Observer* and *Journal* in Australia; and the Auckland *Star* in New Zealand.[44]

To be sure, the squeamish editor Richard Watson Gilder bowdlerized the selections he printed in his parlor magazine with a heavy editorial hand, albeit with Sam's consent. The editor of an American family magazine needed to avoid whatever would "too greatly shock the proprieties," Gilder

Figure 24. Samuel Clemens
and George Washington Cable
publicity photo, September 26,
1884. Courtesy of the Clifton
Waller Barrett Collection,
Special Collections, University
of Virginia Library.

later explained to Bret Harte. Gilder remarked to Sam that he had ex-
punged a few expressions "not adapted to our audience" (e.g., "hogwash,"
"mush," "to be in a sweat," "by jings") or, as he put it, he omitted "a few
cuss words." He also chose to overlook such episodes as the murder of
Boggs; Sherburn's taunt of the lynch mob; the king's ribaldries in the Royal Nonesuch, which Sam had modified "considerably to make it proper
for print" in the book; and the duke's parodic Shakespearean soliloquy,
though he included the chapters detailing the Shepherdson-Grangerford
feud. As Sam acknowledged to Gilder in mid-October when he reviewed
proof of the December installment, "I think you have made a most excellent selection" and "I should not have done so well if the matter had been
left to me." More problematically, Gilder also omitted the scene, crucial

to Huck's maturation, in which Jim confesses his unwitting cruelty to his daughter, whom he does not yet realize is deaf. All three sanitized excerpts from *Huck Finn* ran in issues with installments of Howells's *The Rise of Silas Lapham* and essays in the Battles and Leaders of the Civil War essay series. The January 1885 issue also contained Cable's "The Freedman's Case in Equity," a plea for the civil rights of manumitted slaves. Sam was initially impressed by Cable's piece and wrote Livy that he was "a *great* man; & I believe that if he continues his fight for the negro (& he will,) his greatness will come to be recognized." Ten days later, however, Sam jeered that Cable was "one of the most spoiled men, by success in life, you ever saw." The February 1885 issue—in which, according to Bernard DeVoto, "American journalism attained its highest reach"—also included Howells's "A Florentine Mosaic," Grant's "The Battle of Shiloh," the opening installment of Henry James's *The Bostonians*, and Stedman's tribute to Oliver Wendell Holmes.[45] Ironically, however, none of the works by Sam, Cable, Grant, Howells, James, or Stedman was the lead article in any of the three issues, casting doubt on Gilder's editorial acumen. He was not such an astute judge of the giants of American literature as he was overwhelmed by submissions from them.

In an inauspicious start to the critical history of *Huck Finn*, the magazine and newspaper notices of the installments in the *Century* were restrained. The *New England Farmer* dismissed the "very silly story" in the December issue. The *Boston Herald* carped that the third excerpt, devoted to the shenanigans of the grifters, was "pitched in but one key and that is the key of a vulgar and abhorrent life," though the Sydney *Herald* commended the same passage for "overflowing with [Sam's] peculiar funning." The *Springfield Republican* fretted that the extracts not only "disfigured the *Century*" but revealed "how offensive the whole thing must be." The *Cleveland Leader and Herald* offered little incentive to prospective buyers because "the cream of the book" had appeared in the magazine. Only a pair of friends writing privately to Sam hinted at its brilliance. Stedman congratulated him on the "King Sollermun" passage in the January number, a satire of royal privilege and white racial superiority: "To my mind it is not only the most finished and condensed thing you have done but as dramatic and powerful an episode as I know in modern literature." The journalist and editor William L. Alden was even more effusive. "I have read the extracts from the book in the *Century* & enjoyed them more than I ever enjoyed any magazine articles anywhere," he wrote Sam on February 28, 1885. Two weeks later, after he had read the entire novel, Alden declared that *Huck Finn* was "the best book ever written."[46]

❖

Every four years between 1860 and 1880, only Republican candidates were elected to the presidency (though some questions might be raised about the 1876 canvass). Though Sam's political opinions evolved over time, they were not as capricious as the wind. He occasionally affected indifference, as when he informed an interviewer in March 1877 that he was "neither a Republican nor Democrat—for any length of time. Vacillation is my forte." When James G. Blaine was nominated for president by the Republicans in early June 1884, however, Sam fled the party. Based on his coziness with railroad interests, Blaine was by reputation a prime example of a corrupt politician and Sam refused to support him. Instead, he was drawn to the Democratic candidate Grover Cleveland, the governor of New York, who had been sheriff of Erie County, New York, when Sam lived in Buffalo. Cleveland was also burdened with a scandal in his past, however: by his own admission, he had fathered a child out of wedlock. The New York *World* noted as early as July that, while a Republican, Sam "might be influenced to vote for Cleveland in consequence of the attacks upon the latter's moral character." Sam was undisturbed by the supposed stain on Cleveland's reputation. As he wrote to Howells, "To see grown men, apparently in their right mind, seriously arguing against a bachelor's fitness for President because he has had private intercourse with a consenting widow! Those grown men know what the bachelor's other alternative was [prostitution] & tacitly they seem to prefer that to the widow." As he put it even more succinctly, "Cleveland violated 1—Blaine 9" of the Ten Commandments.[47]

No longer a party loyalist, Sam declared that he was "a mugwump and a mugwump is pure from the marrow out." He was overheard in a hotel lobby in October 1889 insisting that he was "a Mugwump, now and forever, one and indivisible." In a speech in November 1893 he declared, "I was born a Mugwump, and I shall probably die a Mugwump." The nickname, derived from the Algonquin word *mugquomp* or chief, was bestowed derisively by stalwart Republicans upon the disaffected progressives who bolted from the party in 1884 and, like the Know-Nothings of an earlier generation, the label not only stuck but was soon embraced by those who wore it. From the moment he learned of Blaine's nomination, as Sam professed in his autobiography, he insisted "that no party held the privilege of dictating to me how I should vote" and "if party loyalty was a form of patriotism, I was no patriot"; and given the ordinary meaning of the term, "I didn't think I was much of a patriot anyway." A political partisan, he wrote in 1884, was nothing more than a "meek and docile, cringing and fawning, dirt-eating and dirt-preferring slave." In truth, Sam did not change his opinions on the issues so much as the Republican Party changed its convictions and the Democratic Party its platform. As John G. Sproat notes, the centrist Cleveland "stood squarely on the same principles," such as tariff and civil service reform, that "the majority of Republicans advocated." Branded a turncoat, Sam replied at a mugwump rally in Allyn Hall shortly before the election, "What, then, is it that we have changed our opinions about? Why, about Mr. Blaine. That is the whole change." He had not "deserted" the Republican Party nor its "code of principles" but the party had "deserted itself." Though he later championed Cleveland and his policies, Sam in the fall of 1884 was more inclined simply to cast a vote against Blaine than a vote for the Democrat. Indeed, he considered casting a write-in vote for Senator George F. Edmunds of Vermont, a Republican, less than two weeks before the election on November 4.[48]

Still, Sam's declaration of political independence came at a price. He was disappointed by the acquiescence to Blaine's candidacy of such friends as Joe Hawley and Charley Warner. The *Hartford Courant*, long a bulwark of Radical Republicanism under their leadership, once expressed the same "uncomplimentary opinions about [Blaine] as I did then and as I do today" but they "have turned their coats and they now admire Blaine; and not calmly, temperately, but with a sort of ferocious rapture." As Sam recalled in his autobiography, "For two years the *Hartford Courant* had been holding Blaine up to scorn and contumely." As he wailed to Howells, "Even *I* do not loathe Blaine more than they do" in private, yet they "are eating their daily crow in the paper for him." Two months later, on the eve of the election, Sam changed the type of scavenger bird in his metaphor but not his larger argument: all the local Republicans "are & have for years been bitter against Blaine; but they are party-slaves & nearly all will vote for him. . . . Lord, the amount of buzzard these shabby people are gorging these days!" Ironically, Sam claimed to be a convert to Hawley's style of principled politics: his friend had warned for years that Blaine was unqualified for the presidency and Sam claimed to be simply "a Mugwump constructed by General Hawley."[49]

Sam and Howells disagreed on the principles at stake in the election, however. Howells decided he would rather vote "for a man *accused* of bribery" than "a man *guilty* of what society sends a woman to hell for." As he wrote to Sam on September 4, two months before the election, "I shall vote for Blaine." He did not believe the Republican was as sinister a figure as his critics portrayed him and the accusations against him had not been proven. "As for Cleveland," he added, "his private life may be no worse than that of most men but as an enemy of that contemptible, hypocritical, lop-sided morality which says a woman shall suffer all the shame of unchastity and man none, I want to see him destroyed politically by his past." As Sinclair Lewis asserted in his Nobel Prize acceptance speech in 1930, Howells notoriously espoused the moral code "of a pious old maid whose greatest delight was to have tea at the vicarage." Sam was understandably unsettled by the prospect that his friend would cast his vote for "the filthy," "paltry scoundrel," and "nickel-plated statesman." He advised Howells,

> I don't ask you to vote at all. I only urge you to not soil yourself by voting for Blaine. . . . It is not necessary to vote for Cleveland; the only necessary thing to do, as I understand it, is that a man shall keep himself clean, (by withholding his vote for an improper man) even though the party and the country go to destruction in consequence. It is not parties that make or save countries or that build them to greatness—it is clean men, clean ordinary citizens, rank and file, the masses.

As James S. Leonard notes, during the campaign of 1884 Sam "apparently rejected party politics permanently." Louis J. Budd likewise observes that his turn to mugwumpery "was a big step" toward Sam's eventual composition of *A Connecticut Yankee in King Arthur's Court* (1889).[50]

Nor did Sam and Twichell exactly see eye to eye on the question of Cleveland's character. To be sure, Twichell could not support Blaine and in mid-October, along with Sam, the Episcopal minister Francis Goodwin, the linguist William D. Whitney, and about a hundred other men he signed an "Appeal to the Republican Voters of Connecticut." The petition listed many of the accusations of corruption that had been leveled over the years at Blaine and argued that his defeat might save the Republican Party "by freeing it from the control of the camp followers and office-seekers who have too often dictated its policy." As a result, Twichell incurred the ire of many members of his congregation who thought he should keep out of the fracas. "The displeasure which my political action in regard to Mr. Blaine excited among my friends and parishioners was considerable as I had anticipated it would be," he noted in his journal. "I received a number of letters expressing strong disapproval of my course, though nearly all of them were entirely kind in their tone." The row was sufficiently infamous that the *Boston Herald* mentioned it on October 19: "The Rev. Mr. Twichell . . . has had it intimated to him that the majority of his people don't like his course. Rumor has it that a private conference of some of these gentlemen has been held, with a view to calling a church meeting and passing resolutions denouncing Mr. Twichell for taking too prominent a part in politics."[51]

Sam's prominence as a mugwump spokesman was underscored when he introduced Carl Schurz, the former Civil War general, senator from Missouri, and secretary of the interior, before an audience of about three thousand at a Cleveland rally in Allyn Hall in Hartford the evening of October 20, two weeks before the election. The very occurrence of this event had stirred controversy. Loyal Blaine supporters had protested that the invitation to Schurz had been signed by "a large number of republicans as yet in good party standing" and, significantly, Twichell's name was missing from the list of signatories. The stalwart *Hartford Courant* entirely ignored the gathering in its coverage of local news. With a foretaste of the brazen views that would mark his final years, Sam insisted in his speech of introduction that his opinion of Blaine had not been influenced by Democratic propaganda but "is due to the comments of the Republican press before the nomination. Not that they have said bitter or scandalous things, because Republican papers are above that, but the things they said did not seem to be complimentary, and seemed to me to imply editorial disapproval of Mr. Blaine and the belief that he was not qualified to be President of the United States."[52]

With his outspoken ideas, Sam no doubt risked ostracism from the parlors of polite Hartford. At a regular meeting of the Monday Evening Club, Sam, Francis Goodwin, and Twichell had revealed over "a supper-table debate" to "the astonishment and indignation of everybody, the ladies included," that they were "traitors" to the Republican Party and "were going to keep our votes in our pockets." In the end, Sam voted for Cleveland, even though he recognized that as president he would not challenge Jim Crow laws or the racial status quo that effectively disenfranchised black voters in the South. Like Twichell, he had vowed publicly in early October to vote the Republican ticket with the exception of Blaine, though he confessed privately to Ned House five days before the polling that he planned to "vote the entire democratic ticket, from President down to town constable." (On his part, Twichell voted for the Prohibition candidate for president.) As Ralph Waldo Emerson declared in "Self-Reliance," after all, "A foolish consistency is the hobgoblin of little minds." In the end Cleveland carried New York by one-tenth of 1 percent of the popular balloting and thus received all of its thirty-six electoral votes, providing his margin of victory in the Electoral College, and Sam credited the mugwumps in the state for determining the winner:

> We, the mugwumps, a little company made up of the unenslaved of both parties, the very best men to be found in the two great parties—that was our idea of it—voted sixty thousand strong for Mr. Cleveland in New York and elected him. Our principles were high and very definite. We were not a party; we had no candidates; we had no axes to grind. . . . When voting, it was our duty to vote for the best man, regardless of his party name. We had no other creed. Vote for the best man—that was creed enough.

Nor did Sam regret his decision to renounce the Republican Party. A year later he assured President Cleveland that every mugwump in Hartford "who voted for you last fall would vote for you again today." In a talk entitled "Party Allegiance" that he delivered before the Monday Evening Club on December 5, 1887, he adamantly defended his supposed apostasy and replied to the allegation that mugwumps were disloyal Republicans. "This infamous doctrine of allegiance to party plays directly into the hands of politicians of the baser sort," he contended, and he described as mugwump heroes such statesmen as "Washington, Garrison, Galileo, Luther, Christ." As he wrote in his journal a few months later, "People seem to think they are citizens of the Republican party & that that is patriotism & sufficiently good patriotism. I prefer to be a citizen of the United States." Or as he insisted in his autobiography, "In the community, I was regarded as a Republican but I had never so regarded myself."[53]

But he closed the campaign season on a note of resignation. "I am leaving home now to infest the platform for 4 months," he moaned to Ned House after repeatedly protesting over the years that he would never again stride the stage. "Think of the insanity of it! I wish I hadn't promised; but it is too late now to cry about it."[54]

CHAPTER 12

Lecture Tour

> I am frightened by the proportions of my prosperity.
> It seems to me that whatever I touch turns to gold.
>
> —*Mark Twain: A Biography*

SAMUEL CLEMENS CAST his vote for Grover Cleveland on November 4, 1884, and railed with Livy to New Haven the next day for the first of his ninety-four joint readings with George Washington Cable, his first speaking tour in over a dozen years. He and Cable were on the road together for most of the next four months, performing in sixty-eight cities from Minneapolis in the west, Louisville in the south, Montreal in the north, to Boston in the east. His raid on the lyceums with Cable only dimly resembled the debauch with Cable, W. D. Howells, and others he had envisioned in 1882. As Sam had specified, he and Cable performed seven times in the first eight days (excepting only Sunday, November 9, out of consideration for Cable's strict Sabbatarianism) in relatively small cities and towns as they polished their act before appearing before large audiences. "When we first started out," he admitted to an interviewer at the time, "I didn't think I should like the business. I had been off the platform for about fifteen years." He was more candid in his autobiography: "It was ghastly! At least in the beginning."

With Livy present, Sam read from his forthcoming *Adventures of Huckleberry Finn* before a "large and cultivated audience" at the New Haven Opera House and Cable recited selections from his new novel *Dr. Sevier*, including "Mary's Night Ride," which would become his routine program. The *New Haven Journal and Courier* declared their performance "a success in every particular." Cable wrote his wife Louise the next day that their first appearance had been "an emphatic success." The three of them went for tea at the home of Francis Bacon, the physician who had treated Cable for a sore throat instead of mumps ten months earlier. After their recital in East Orange, New Jersey, the following evening, when Sam read for the first time from the script of *Colonel Sellers as a Scientist*, Cable again reported they had enjoyed "a great success" and the *East Orange Gazette* commended their "very novel and pleasing entertainment." At the Opera House in Springfield,

Massachusetts, the evening of November 7, however, their program was repeatedly interrupted, according to Cable, by "brass music & fire-works in front of the hall" and "vast crowds blocking the streets and cannon firing directly in the rear of the house." With Livy once again in the audience, Sam read from both *Huck Finn* and *Colonel Sellers as a Scientist*, though Cable conceded his recitation was "not his very best." Sam, comparing their speaking tour to a military campaign, complained that Springfield was "the only town where we have suffered a defeat." They regrouped at matinee and evening performances the following day at Blackstone Hall in Providence. The *Providence Journal* reported that Sam "delighted the audience" with a selection about human rematerialization from the play and Cable boasted that he left the stage during "a tremendous clatter of applause." Sam met him and exclaimed "superb! superb!" Not only was Sam "greatly pleased with my work, as I am with his," but they divided the honors and the stage time as nearly evenly "as two men well could." After a Sunday recess, the carnival erected its tent in Melrose, Massachusetts, where additional seats were needed to accommodate the crowd. A stringer for the *Boston Journal* reported that Sam recited "his bits of fun with his usual slow, cool, almost unvarying tone, moving about the stage scarcely any, and using few gestures." In Lowell, Massachusetts, on November 11 Sam reverted to his standard program, relating "The Tragic Tale of the Fishwife" and "A Trying Situation" from *A Tramp Abroad* (1880), the ghost story "The Golden Arm," and the "King Sollermun" anecdote from *Huck Finn*. With his more progressive racial views, Cable persuaded Sam to change the title of this part of the playbill from "Learning a Nigger to Argue" to "How Come a Frenchman Doan' Talk Like a Man?" The Music Hall in Waltham, Massachusetts, was "well filled" the next evening, and the audience welcomed Sam's "highly amusing sketches" with "almost incessant applause."[1]

On November 13 the barbarians finally stormed the barricades of the sold-out Music Hall in Boston. Before an audience of twenty-two hundred, Howells among them, Sam repeated his program. Howells was characteristically delighted by his performance. "You are a great artist, and you do this public thing so wonderfully well that I don't see how you could ever bear to give it up," he wrote Sam the next day. "I thought that the bits from *Huck Finn* told the best—at least I enjoyed them the most. That is a mighty good book, and I should like to hear you read it all. But everything of yours is good for platform reading." The reporters for the local papers shared Howells's enthusiasm, including the *Boston Advertiser* ("superbly droll and outrageously extravagant"), *Boston Transcript* ("highly successful"), *Boston Herald* ("excellent in every respect"), *Boston Globe* ("his drollery is perennial, always fresh and always entertaining"), *Boston Traveller* ("kept their auditors in an uproar"), and *Boston Post* ("one of the most successful entertainers of the time"). Sam bragged to an interviewer a few days later that the audience in Boston was "delighted with our efforts to please them." The twenty-four-year old Hamlin Garland reviewed one of Sam's performances in Boston with approbation: "Never the ghost of a smile. Is an excellent elocutionist. Sighs deeply at times, with an irresistibly comic effect. His hair is gray and thick, his face a fine one." While in the city, Sam and Howells helped to rescue a woman, a "poor demented would-be suicide" who tried to jump into the Charles River, though they were required to complete so much paperwork afterward that Sam admitted he did not "want to save any more women from drowning—in Boston." Nevertheless, Cable wrote Louise, "We had a great time" in Beantown.[2]

Not so the next few days. After a huge crowd in Boston, the tour was plagued by disappointing attendance in Brockton, Massachusetts; a Saturday matinee back in Boston; and at the Music Hall in Plainfield, New Jersey, prompting Sam to advise James Pond that "louder advertising" was "absolutely necessary" to promote their appearances, including men with sandwich boards "to patrol the streets." Livy joined Sam at the Everett House in New York and attended his and Cable's two-hour performance before a sold-out Chickering Hall the evening of November 18. Sam opened his part of the program with what at first glance appeared to be a valedictory speech:

> It is eight or nine years since I bade goodby forever to the lecture platform in this very hall. Since that time some things sad and some things joyous have happened to us all, to the country and to all the nations of the earth. I will not stop now to enumerate them. They say lecturers and burglars never reform. I don't know how it is with burglars—it is now so long since I had intimate relations with these people—but it is quite true of lecturers. They never reform. Lecturers and readers say they are going to leave the lecture platform never to return. They mean it, they mean it. But there comes in time an overpowering temptation to come on the platform and give truth and morality one more lift. You can't resist. I got permanently through eight or nine years ago. I may quit again.

After a moment, he added, "Well, there's no telling. I'll make no more promises." He then declaimed the "King Sollermun" chapter from *Huck Finn*. The next day the *New York Herald* commended the "philosophical little darkey" featured in the excerpt and added that "there was nothing actually immoral" in Sam's performance; the *New York Tribune* noted that Sam's "stories were punctuated with laughter every few words"; and the New York *Graphic* praised the "unique" entertainment. The *New York Times* reported that Sam ridiculed "such ridiculous matters as aged colored gentlemen, the German language, and himself" and when recalled for an encore he read another passage from the *Huck Finn* advance sheets. Livy returned to Hartford the next day, though she was sufficiently concerned about Sam's incipient scorn for Cable's shirtsleeve religiosity after they had been on the road for only two weeks that she cautioned him not "to get awry with Mr Cable; he is good and your friend" and to "be careful how you refer to Mr. Cable in public—even in fun. This may be an entirely unnecessary warning—still I must say it." Lew Wallace, the author of the best-selling *Ben-Hur* (1880), attended the second performance at Chickering Hall the evening of November 19 and Sam regretted that Livy was not there to meet him. Sam was so delighted by the audience enthusiasm, he told the New York *World*, he wanted to extend the tour "to California, if I can manage it."[3]

As Sam and Livy were leaving the theater after his first reading at Chickering Hall on November 18, they fortuitously met Richard Watson Gilder and joined him for supper. They were at Gilder's home "an hour or two," Sam recalled in his autobiography, "and in the course of the conversation Gilder said that General Grant had written three war articles for the *Century* and was going to write a fourth. I pricked up my ears."[4] If Ulysses S. Grant was writing his memoirs, who better to publish them than Sam's new firm, Charles L. Webster and Company? In truth, the former president and general was in dire financial straits. He had resigned his commission when he was elected president and thus forfeited both his military salary and his pension and former presidents were not eligible at the time for pensions. Moreover, the Wall Street investment firm of which he was a partner, Grant & Ward, had collapsed on May 6, 1884, as the result of a Ponzi scheme run by Ferdinand Ward, the so-called Young Napoleon of Finance. The liabilities of the firm totaled almost $17 million, its assets were less than $100,000, and Ward had fled the country to avoid prosecution. Grant was writing essays about his war experiences for the *Century* for $500 per article because he desperately needed the money for day-to-day living. By the close of 1884 the ex-president was in ominous circumstances, nearly bankrupt with less than $1,000 in the bank and suffering from a malady publicly described as "chronic superficial inflammation of the tongue" but soon to be diagnosed as throat cancer.[5]

The morning of November 20, before leaving New York for the next stop on his reading tour, Sam visited Grant at his home on East Sixty-Sixth Street near Central Park. He learned from the general that he had been offered a contract by the Century Company for his autobiography that would pay him a standard 10 percent royalty on sales without an advance. Sam was astounded by the terms. The proposal, he thought, was worse than stingy; it was "the most colossal bit of cheek the 19th century can show; & also the most cold-blooded attempt to rob a trusting & inexperienced man since Ward's performances." Though he had never intended Webster and Company "to publish anybody's books but my own," the chance to issue "Grant's memorable book" changed his mind. Sam offered a better deal on the spot: a royalty of 20 percent on sales or 70 percent of the profits plus a $10,000 advance.[6] Grant was inclined to accept Gilder's proposal because it had been made first, but Sam reminded him that he had urged Grant over two years earlier to publish his memoirs with the American Publishing Company. Sam suggested that the general ask the Century people to meet his terms and "if they were afraid to accept them, he would simply need to offer them to any great publishing house in the country." He was publishing *Huck Finn* and developing the best-equipped distribution network in the country. While they did not immediately accept Sam's proposition, Grant and his son Fred decided to temporize until they had investigated the benefits of each bid. Before Sam left New York for his "long western tour on the platform" with Cable, he was confident, as he notified his nephew Charley Webster, that "we have the book," though he advised Webster to continue "to call at the General's house and watch the progress of events." Grant soon consulted with his friend George W. Childs, editor and publisher of the Philadelphia *Public Ledger*, who recommended that he "give the book to Clemens." On November 23, only four days after Sam described the advantages of subscription publication, Grant wrote Childs that upon "re-examining the Contract prepared by the Century people I see that it is all in favor of the publisher, with nothing left for the Author. I am offered very much more favorable terms by the Charles L. Webster & Co." As James Pond later remarked, "No one but Mark could see the profit" in Grant's memoirs.[7]

Back on the road on Thursday, November 20, Sam and Cable read in Newburgh, sixty miles north of New York City on the Hudson River. Cable crowed to Louise that they "had a little audience & no end of fun. They kept calling us back." They headed the next day to Philadelphia, where they read in Association Hall to "a most noble big audience & a most prodigious good time," Sam boasted to Livy. The *Philadelphia Inquirer* reported that while "the great humorist recited" the "tears ran down his listeners' cheeks" and the *Philadelphia Press* added that his reading "convulsed" the audience and "set everybody in roars." Then they were back to the Brooklyn Academy of Music for two shows before "huge houses" on Saturday, with Henry Ward Beecher and Dean Sage in attendance. Sam's "manner was inimitable," the *Brooklyn Eagle* reported, when he read a scene from *Colonel Sellers as a Scientist*. After a Sunday break, Sam and Cable railed to Washington, D.C., registered at the Ebbitt House near the White House, and appeared at the

Congregational church before a capacity crowd of twelve hundred. The audience the first night, according to the Washington *Critic*, "was composed of the most intellectual of the city's population" and Sam entertained them by reading "Encounter with an Interviewer" ("brought shrieks of laughter"), a selection from *Colonel Sellers as a Scientist*, and the "The Golden Arm." Cable gushed that the horde "went off like gunpowder the moment it was touched; a *delicious* audience. The brightest, quickest, most responsive that we have yet stood before."[8]

The attendees the next night were even more exclusive, hailed in the press as the "most brilliant audience assembled in Washington for many years," including President Chester A. Arthur and his daughter Ellen, U.S. marshal for the District of Columbia Frederick Douglass, Secretary of State Frederick Frelinhuysen, Secretary of the Navy William Chandler, Postmaster General Frank Hatton, and Secretary of War Robert Todd Lincoln. Sam bragged afterward that Arthur was "the first president I ever read before." The two men had long shared a mutual admiration from a distance. In the spring of 1882, before Arthur became a lame-duck president, he told Joe Hawley that he would like someday to meet Sam and in August 1883 Sam wrote that in his opinion "it would be hard indeed to better President Arthur's administration." Arthur and Douglass met backstage in Sam's dressing room that evening and Cable exclaimed upon seeing the two together, "Think of it! A runaway slave!" On his part, Sam in his next letter to Livy dwelled less on the celebrities dotting the landscape than the box office receipts ("$750 in the house") and the joie de vivre of the crowd. "We did make them shout, from the first word to the last," he wrote, with Cable in the role of the straight man and Sam as the slapstick comedian. "I say 'we,' for the honors were exactly equal—as they are pretty much always are, now." Cable shared this view, prattling to Louise, "I think it's a great thing to be able to hold my own with so wonderful a platform figure" as Sam. The next evening at Association Hall in Philadelphia, according to the *Philadelphia Inquirer*, the "audience was kept rollicking with laughter at the droll yarns of America's prince of humorists, the ever-comical Mark Twain." The *Philadelphia News* reported that "no rivalry" existed "between these friends." On the contrary: "The combination is a happy one."[9] Would that it remained so.

Sam and Cable took a day off on Thursday, November 27, to celebrate Thanksgiving with the cartoonist Thomas Nast and his family at their home in Morristown, New Jersey. Sam apparently consumed five plates of oysters at dinner and, as he wrote Livy the next day aboard a southbound train, they "stayed all night with Tom Nast & family, & had a most noble good time." He famously spent part of the night stopping the pendulums in some of the clocks in Nast's house and carrying other clocks outdoors so that he could sleep undisturbed. As Katy Leary recounted, "Nast drew a funny picture about Mr. Clemens in his nightshirt, putting out them clocks."[10]

The duo performed the next two nights before large audiences at the Concert Hall of the Academy of Music in Baltimore, one of their few excursions into former slave territory (they never appeared south of the Mason-Dixon line). Sam was greeted "with laughing applause and his funny recitations were much enjoyed," the *Baltimore Sun* reported, and he made "the house roar as only a Southern audience can," according to Cable. On Sunday, November 30, they dined with Cable's friend Daniel Coit Gilman and Sam visited Ross Winans, a millionaire inventor and entrepreneur whom he had met in Newport the summer before, at his home on St. Paul Street. They left

Figure 25. Thomas Nast caricature of Samuel Clemens and George Washington Cable, *Harper's Monthly*, September 1912.

Baltimore by train shortly after midnight early Monday morning, December 1, to keep a date the next night in Adams, Massachusetts. In Albany at noon the next day, while changing trains, they were invited to the state capitol to meet President-Elect Cleveland. When they arrived, Sam was introduced to Cleveland and then Sam introduced Cable. The three of them lunched and "had a quite jolly & pleasant brief chat," Sam wrote Livy. Cleveland claimed to "have seen me often in Buffalo" when both of them lived there, "but I didn't remember him, of course, & I didn't say I did." Sam and Cable invited Cleveland to attend their lecture in Troy that evening and the governor "expressed great regret" that his scheduled meeting with the New York delegation to the Electoral College prevented him from making the trip.[11]

Sam caught a cold as a result of the inclement weather and the frenetic travel so that, despite an audience of fourteen hundred in Troy, he was "hoarse and weak-voiced" and enjoyed only a "feeble" success. The *Troy Times* allowed that he barely "managed to make himself heard." His rendition of "The Golden Arm," which depends on a "snapper" at the close, "fell almost flat," Cable wrote Louise, "by reason of *persons* (2 or 3) rising in the audience just at the crucial moment. It was outrageous & I don't wonder M.T. came off the platform angry." Sam was mollified only when Cable proposed that each of them would in future pause to "poke unmerciful fun at anyone who dares to rise in the audience while we are speaking." The next evening at the opera house in Ithaca, New York, they opened to "a quiet, undemonstrative audience and presently had them clean out of themselves," Cable chuckled. Afterward Sam went to a beer hall "and found about forty students from Cornell University" with whom he imbibed. At Syracuse the following night, the hall "was not entirely" full and Sam and Cable received a cool reception but they "soon warm[ed] them up." In Utica on Friday, December 5, "the audience was large & the evening a bright and successful one, fully up to our high mark," and at a matinee in Rochester the next afternoon the audience was small "but appreciative to a degree." That evening, despite a torrential rain, they spoke before "a large house" and had "great fun." The *Rochester Herald* praised their "very unique and happy entertainment." But for the first time both Sam and Cable betrayed hints of an estrangement. Cable lamented to Louise that Sam was not "a man of prayer & worship"— suggesting that he had urged Sam to join him at church and his companion had declined. From Cable's perspective, Sam desecrated the Sabbath when the next day, rather than attend Christian services, he was "handsomely entertained" by the Rochester Lodge of Elks. In fact, Sam sat for an interview with the *Rochester Herald* at his hotel on Sunday and the reporter was dismayed to discover his room "in an alarming state of disorder. Articles of clothing, books, letters and various other things were scattered about it in the most promiscuous fashion. The humorist's capacious valise, which lay open upon a center table, looked as though it had been struck by a cyclone." Sam was capable of committing the sin of sloth without so much as leaving the hotel. During the interview, moreover, Sam explained the reason he had invited Cable to join him on tour: "I'd just as soon stand on a platform two hours as anywhere else but I prefer to have somebody to share the responsibility of entertaining an audience. One of us counteracts the other, you know. A counter-irritant often produces good results."[12] Soon enough Cable became just an irritant.

Their weekend in Rochester was memorable for another reason. While they were browsing in a bookstore, Cable bought a copy of Thomas Malory's *Le Morte d'Arthur* (1485) for Sam, apparently for his spiritual edification. Sam had perused a juvenile edition of the work edited by Sidney Lanier in 1880 but he apparently had not read the unexpurgated romance before he received this copy. Cable remembered that Sam pored over it "a day or two, when I saw come upon his cheekbones those vivid pink spots which . . . meant that his mind was working with all its energies." Sam and Cable began to speak "the quaint language of [Malory's] book in talk in the cars & hotels," to call themselves "Sir Mark" and "Sir George," and they nicknamed James Pond's brother Ozias, who was accompanying them on the tour, Sir Sagramore, Knight of the Lake. On December 14, a week after Cable gave him a copy of Malory's book, Sam ordered another copy to present to Pond. Sam was so infatuated with the story that, he observed in his journal, "I began to make notes in my head for a book." Among the notes he jotted down within a day or two was one for a comedic skit usually regarded as the germ of a one-joke novel that evolved into *A Connecticut Yankee in King Arthur's Court* (1889):

> Dream of being a knight errant in the middle ages. Have the notions & habits of thought of the present day mixed with the necessities of that. No pockets in armor. No way to manage certain requirement of nature. Can't scratch. Cold in the head—can't blow—can't get at handkerchief, can't use iron sleeve. Iron gets red hot in the sun—leaks in the rain, gets white from frost and freezes me solid in winter. Suffer from lice and fleas. Make disagreeable chatter when I enter church. Can't dress or undress myself. Always getting struck by lightning. Fall down, can't get up.

Sam was so enthralled by Malory's romance that he recommended it to his twelve-year-old daughter Susy. "It is the quaintest and sweetest of all books," he wrote her, and "is full of the absolute English of 400 years ago." Twenty-one years later, he told Albert Bigelow Paine that when he "read those quaint and curious old legends I suppose I naturally contrasted those days with ours, and it made me curious to fancy what might be the picturesque result if we could dump the nineteenth century down into the sixth century and observe the consequences." He considered Malory's tale "one of the most beautiful things ever written in English."[13]

After their normal Sunday off in Rochester on December 7, Sam and Cable traveled via Niagara Falls to Toronto the next day, arriving at 4:30 p.m. and registering at the plush Rossin House before two nights of readings at the packed twenty-five-hundred-seat, glass-enclosed Horticultural Pavilion. Though Cable insisted to Louise that they had received "roars of British applause" such as he had "never heard" outside of New Orleans, and though Sam claimed to Livy that both of them "had a gorgeously good time" and he had seen "ladies swabbing their eyes freely & undisguisedly" after Cable declaimed "Mary's Night Ride," in fact Cable flopped north of the border if one judges from the unanimous opinion of reviewers for the five daily Toronto papers. His Creole dialect stories and songs simply did not translate well to a Canadian audience, according to the *Mail* ("Cable is not so successful in enlisting the sympathies of the audience"), *Telegram* ("Cable made a limited hit"), *World* ("Cable uses up his audience in the first round"), *Evening News* (some in the audience "were evidently impatient with him" and expressed their displeasure "by tapping their walking sticks on the floor"), and *Globe* ("with careful practice he would read better than he does"). Years later Sam privately affirmed the judgment of Cable: "With his platform-talent he was able to fatigue a corpse." On the other hand, Sam was greeted the first night by a "storm of applause" and "for some moments could not proceed" until the din subsided. Both the *Mail* ("continual ripple of laughter") and the *Globe* ("the house was convulsed with laughter") remarked on the stark contrast between Sam's and Cable's performances. The two men seem to have laid low during their stopover in the city. They attended only a single social event: a visit on Tuesday to the studio of the portrait painter A. Dickson Patterson.[14]

Sam's British publishers, Chatto & Windus in England and Dawson Brothers in Canada, scheduled *Huck Finn* for release on Wednesday, December 10, and for copyright reasons the author was obliged to be present on Canadian soil at the close of the business day of issue. He and Cable apparently railed together to Niagara Falls, Canada, and Cable continued the additional twenty miles to Buffalo, where they were scheduled to appear at the Concert Hall the next two nights. Sam lingered in Canada until 5:00 p.m. before rejoining him in Buffalo. Sam's homecoming of sorts was not all that he might have wished. The Concert Hall was "little more than half filled," according to the reporter for the *Buffalo Courier*, probably Sam's friend David Gray, and Sam and Cable were victims of poor acoustics; only people as far back as the middle of the house heard them clearly. Still, according to the *Buffalo Times*, "a more delighted, amused, thoroughly satisfied audience never filled the auditorium of any building in Buffalo" and Sam ad-libbed his initial remarks with the self-assurance of a veteran entertainer. He presented Cable, the dog in this dog-and-pony show, to the sparse crowd with words that were by turns sincere, satirical, and a bit insulting: "Let me introduce a man whom you regard—whom I regard—as the greatest living modern writer of ancient fiction; a man in whom all genius, all honor, all integrity, all virtue—and all vice—combine to make the perfect man. I forgot, his name is George W. Cable." When Sam's turn to speak came, he waxed vaguely nostalgic but without a trace of sentimentality: "I notice many changes since I was a citizen of Buffalo fourteen or fifteen years go. I miss the faces of many old friends. They have gone to the tomb—to the gallows—to the White House. Thus far the rest of us have escaped; but be sure our own turn is coming. Over us, with awful certainty, [looms] one or the other of these fates." As the *Courier* noted, Sam's comments were accorded "a gurgle of low laughter." After the show on the second evening, he and Cable were invited to a reception of the Thursday Club, a group Sam presumed "of 3 or 4 gentlemen" who convened "in a quiet way." He discovered instead, as he grumbled to Livy, that "it was the Hartford Club of Buffalo," some "25 gentlemen & half a dozen ladies—much clatter of talk, & 2 great tables spread. I ate not a bit, & spent 2 of the infernalest weariest hatefulest hours that ever fell to my lot." He had been unknowingly enticed into another unpaid public appearance when all he wanted was rest. "It will be a long day before I sample *anybody's* hospitality again," he fumed. Worse yet, he and Cable left Buffalo shortly after midnight in order to travel about three hundred miles from one end of Lake Erie to the other in time to appear the next night in Ann Arbor, Michigan. "When I was out with Cable in 1885," Sam once told an interviewer, "we experienced the hardest work I have ever known. It was made up of the most absurd railway jumps from one lecture point to another."[15]

Reviewers in the Commonwealth enthusiastically welcomed *Adventures of Huckleberry Finn* upon its publication in mid-December 1884 with nary a hint of the controversies that would dog its reception in the United States a few months later. Among the venues that praised it were the *Westminster Review* ("abundance of American humour of the best sort"), *British Quarterly Review* ("lively and fresh"), London *Post* ("fun of a peculiarly fresh, bright kind"), *Montreal Star* ("thoroughly interesting and mirth-provoking book"), London *Congregationalist* ("quaint humour," "abundant common sense," and "genial sympathy"), Otago, New Zealand, *Star* ("as full of incident as any of Fielding's or Smollet's without their coarseness"), and *Athenaeum* (in his most recent books Sam "has been carried away by the ambition of seriousness and fine writing" but in *Huck Finn* "he returns to his right mind"). Brander Matthews hailed it in the normally hostile *Saturday Review* as "one of the indisputable masterpieces of American fiction." Matthews was impressed by the realism of Sam's portrayal of the "admirably drawn" Jim and concluded that "in no other book has the humourist shown so much artistic restraint." Sam was elated by this "fine notice." In the years to come, the novel would also be acclaimed by such British readers as Walter Besant ("there is no character in fiction more fully, more faithfully presented than the character of Huckleberry Finn"), Andrew Lang (a "great American novel"), and Robert Louis Stevenson ("incredibly well done").[16]

In a return engagement at University Hall in Ann Arbor the evening of December 12 the audience of three thousand was "phenomenal," Sam wrote Livy. The odd couple recited without a hitch except for one small problem: Cable's half of the program, especially his rendition of "Mary's Night Ride," had begun to consume increasing amounts of platform time, partly because he deliberately slowed the pace of his delivery and partly because he began to perform encores upon the slightest provocation. "How I do love to read the Night Ride," he had written Louise from Washington in late November, "but it is a good half-day's work crowded into seven minutes." Within a month it had doubled in length, to Sam's disgust. He complained to James Pond that in New Haven "the 'night ride' was 7 minutes long—it is now 13." In Ann Arbor that night, Cable raved to Louise, "'Mary's Night Ride' received a double encore" and as a result "we were [*sic*: Cable was] kept 30 minutes longer on the platform than we had expected to be." Sam had been upstaged: Cable's name "draws a sixteenth part of the house, & he invariably does two-thirds of the reading," he complained. More and more, rather than sharing the stage equally, Sam wanted Cable to be an opening act and to sing at intermission—to occupy the stage no more than one-third of the time. "He may have 35 or 38 minutes on the platform" during the two-hour show "& no more."[17]

After traveling all day, they performed Saturday evening, December 13, at Powers' Opera House in Grand Rapids before "one of the largest audiences that ever greeted any lecturer that has appeared there in many years." Cable reported, however, that the crowd "had to be lifted out of its apathy and estrangement" because of the cold weather. Sam similarly mentioned to Livy that they had confronted "a perfectly frightened & frozen audience, & gradually & surely thaw[ed] them out & rouse[d] them up." The next day the *Grand Rapids Democrat* commended their "very pleasant entertainment." Sam had also decided to abandon Cable to his own devices and to travel with Ozias Pond on the Sabbath rather than lose sleep by leaving after midnight Monday morning in order to arrive in time for the next evening's engagement. "Cable would land in —— in a minute if he were to go a mile on Sunday" and "consequently he leaves [Grand Rapids] at 5 tomorrow [Monday] morning, & is on the road *the entire day*" in order to reach Toledo by show time. Instead, Sam and Pond railed to Jackson, Michigan, on Sunday, registered at the Hibbard House for the night, and left for Toledo midmorning the next day. Unfortunately, Sam and Cable appeared in Toledo before "a thin audience," though they "kept the audience in a constant giggle," according to the *Toledo Blade*. Afterward the humorist David Ross Locke (aka Petroleum V. Nasby) took them to "a pleasant supper of birds &c." at his club. Cable was unimpressed by the gruff Locke, with his "disheveled hair, knotted forehead, heavy middle and dowdy dress," deeming him "a coarse man of the harder world."[18]

Sam and Cable performed at Whitney's Opera House in Detroit the next evening. Sam declined to be interviewed prior to his appearance because, he explained to a reporter, he was tired from traveling and needed to nap. According to reviews the next day in the *Post* ("infinitely droll looking"), *Evening News* ("his style is conversational, easy and flowing"), and *Free Press* ("audience laughed so heartily"), the reading was a success, though the *Free Press* also recommended that Cable surrender "the funny business entirely to Twain." The next night they registered at the Forest City House in Cleveland and entertained a "crowded audience" at Case Hall that was "entertained by a genuine and wholesome wit," though Sam's drawl reminded a critic of "a little buzz-saw slowly grinding inside a corpse." Sam had earlier refused to be scheduled to appear in either Hartford or Livy's hometown but they read at the Opera House in Elmira the evening of December 18. As the *Elmira Advertiser* reported, on account of "the extreme cold weather" the audience was small but "composed of the most refined and intellectual people of the city." After this performance, the road show disbanded for Christmas. Sam headed to Hartford, Cable to his new home in Simsbury, Connecticut, and Ozias Pond to New York. Two days later Sam admitted to James Pond that he regretted the decision to hire Cable: "I thought Cable would be a novelty, but alas he has been *everywhere*, & is a novelty nowhere. I wish I could pay him $200 a week to withdraw."[19] He filled part of the time during the holiday performing in amateur theatricals at the house, specifically in Livy's adaptation of *The Prince and the Pauper* with his daughters in lead roles.

During the recess Sam filed yet another lawsuit, in this case against a firm that advertised *Huck Finn*—before it had been issued in the United States—for sale at a cut-rate price, threatening the book agents' market as well as his own royalties as author and his profit as publisher. On December 23 he sent Webster a clipping from a sales catalog for the Boston publisher Estes & Lauriat that announced his novel was "now ready" and advertised it for sale for $2.25, fifty cents less than the canvassers offered it to subscribers. "Charley," he wrote in his cover letter, "if this is a lie, let Alexander & Green sue them for damages instantly." If it was, as it appeared, "a purely malicious lie," its "purpose was to injure me, who have in no way harmed them." Within the week, Sam's attorneys had filed for an injunction in the U.S. Circuit Court of Massachusetts to block further marketing of the novel by Estes & Lauriat on the ground that the firm could only obtain copies of the book "by collusion and conspiracy with plaintiff's agents and by inducing them to break their lawful contract with plaintiff to sell only to subscribers." Still smarting from Sam's betrayal of the paper in the libel suit filed by Charles C. Duncan in 1883, the *New York Times* headlined its story about this filing "Put Him on the Witness Stand." In an attempt to conciliate Sam, Dana Estes assured him on December 31 that the company had not violated any agreements: "We did not seek to purchase the book. It was freely offered us. By what course of reasoning a person who purchases a book of another who has bought and paid for it, paying him a reasonable profit upon his purchase, can be said to conspire with the other against a third party, we cannot see."[20] Estes insisted that Sam's quarrel was with his canvassers, not with the firm that purchased from the canvassers.

As usual, Livy appealed to the better angels of Sam's nature. She felt that Estes & Lauriat should have been "allowed an explanation" before "they should first see the matter in the newspaper. . . . How I wish that you were less ready to fight and more ready to see other peoples side of things." If Sam responded to Estes's letter, she admonished him, "write civilly." To his credit, Sam tried to negotiate with his antagonists. "I assuredly have no quarrel against you for selling at any price you please any book of mine which you have 'bought & paid for,'" he replied to Estes. "My quarrel is that you advertise for sale at a low price a book of mine which you have *not bought & do not possess*." For "your sake," he wrote Livy, "I telegraphed my lawyers to compromise with them on lenient terms." He offered "to discontinue the suit if E & L would withdraw the offensive advertisement & pay all my law expenses—which E & L declined to do; whereupon I telegraphed my lawyers to make it as sultry for them as possible." Still, Estes & Lauriat tried to ease hostilities. Their lawyer wrote Sam's lawyer on January 9 that Estes & Lauriat would fill all thirty-one of the orders they had received to date for *Huck Finn* but they would sell no more and that their advertisement for the novel had been withdrawn. "I do not see what more you can desire and the matter seems to me too trivial to prepare affidavits and go to hearing upon," the lawyer concluded. "Let me hear from you as to whether this agreement not to circulate the advertisement is not satisfactory to you."[21]

Obviously it was not. In mid-January both parties filed documents in the case before Judge Le Baron Colt of the U.S. Circuit Court. Webster's affidavit quoted the contracts that every book agent for the company signed agreeing "that no copy shall directly or indirectly be sold or delivered to the book trade in any of its branches." The next day, January 15, the *Boston Journal* took a shot at Sam without mentioning him by name: "If the extracts from 'Huckleberry Finn' already published [in the *Century*] are fair samples of the whole book, we cannot see why Estes & Lauriat want to for sell it less than the subscription price. A man ought to pay $2.75 for the privilege of reading the book. It will teach him a lesson." Then Webster was required to file a second deposition, presumably at the behest of Estes & Lauriat, to explain the sale of remaindered copies of *Life on the Mississippi* (1883) through the trade market little more than a year earlier—a sales tactic undertaken at Sam's order. In effect, he had been caught in a lie. Webster squirmed to answer the question. "After the canvass of the last named book [*Life on the Mississippi*] had ceased some of said books were sold to the trade," he conceded. Webster further noted that "if they were so sold it was contrary to the spirit of the agreement between said Clemens and his publishers and without the authority of said Clemens"—but before he signed the document Webster scratched out this latter statement.[22]

Not surprisingly, Judge Colt ruled in favor of the defendants on February 10. Simply put, he decided that Estes & Lauriat enjoyed the right to resell books legally obtained at any price they chose. In legalese, there was "no privity of contract" between Webster and Company and Estes & Lauriat, so the plaintiffs could not hold the defendants liable because Webster's agents sold books in violation of their contracts. How Webster and Company could maintain its price of the book in the wake of this decision "remains to be seen," the *New Haven Journal and Courier* observed. Soon the local Boston press added insult to injury. The *Boston Courier* gloated that Estes & Lauriat had earned the dubious privilege of selling "Mark Twain's much talked of and thoroughly vulgar and morally unwholesome book, 'Huckleberry Finn.'" The *Boston Traveller* speculated that the lawsuit had been another publicity stunt, given that the novel could not be sold "to people of average intellect at anything short of the point of the bayonet." The *Adelaide*

Observer compared the scheme to "the actresses' old ruse of having their diamonds stolen." As usual, Sam replied in kind. "A Massachusetts judge," he wrote in a letter to the editor of the *Boston Advertiser,*

> has just decided in open court that a Boston publisher may sell not only his own property in a free and unfettered way but also may as freely sell property which does not belong to him but to me; property which he has not bought and which I have not sold. Under this ruling I am now advertising that judge's homestead for sale and, if I make as good a sum out of it as I expect, I shall go on and sell out the rest of his property.

Sam elsewhere invoked the same analogy to argue for authors' rights: "The proper way to treat a copyright is to make [intellectual property] exactly like real estate in every way." In the end, ironically, the controversy was an inconsequential bubble on the surface of Sam's erratic temper. Not only did it fail to damage appreciably the subscription sale of *Huck Finn,* as Sam feared, but a year later by his own testimony he had "made up with Estes & Lauriat & ended that quarrel."[23]

The post-Christmas leg of Sam's reading tour with Cable, complicated by severe weather, was even more arduous than the fall road show. They rendezvoused at the upscale Monongahela House in Pittsburgh and resumed their readings at the Cumberland Presbyterian Church on December 29. Over the holiday Sam struck on another tactic to limit Cable's platform time: he introduced a forty-five-minute recitation from the final chapters of *Huck Finn* that he declaimed in two parts with an intermission of Creole songs performed by his partner. "It's the biggest card I've got in my whole repertoire," Sam boasted to Livy. "It went a-booming. . . . This is merely the episode where Tom & Huck stock Jim's cabin with reptiles, & then set him free, in the night, with the crowd of farmers after them with guns." Ever accommodating, Cable agreed that the new feature on the program was "fine—& great." The praise he received from reviewers over the next weeks for the so-called evasion scene, often disparaged in modern criticism of the novel, helps to explain Sam's own fondness for it. The *Pittsburgh Commercial Gazette* reported that the two men "met with unrestrained levity" despite Sam's departure from the announced program, which "was one of the jokes of the evening." The *Pittsburgh Times* found the change refreshing, "as thoroughly enjoyable as it was completely different." Cable assured Louise that they "had a good time in Pittsburgh," though he added that some of the papers "must have taken some grudge against us; for they made offensive reports of the affair." The *Pittsburgh Dispatch* was particularly disparaging, suggesting that Sam and Cable resembled a pair of cartoon characters. The reporter compared Cable to "an elf" beside the "raw-boned" Sam Clemens, though he judged both of them execrable readers. In his opinion, there was "nothing funny" about the evasion scene and the "whole performance was a hippodrome," or circus. He also found offensive the very notion of a tour to promote a new book: "The unbecomingness and the charlatanism of an author's going around the country reading from the proofs of a book he is about to publish are degrading to literature. How Mr. Clemens could allow himself to do it is past comprehension."[24]

The next evening, after a ten-hour train trip, the two men delivered "a very tiresome & unsatisfactory" performance, or so Sam considered it, at the Grand Opera House in Dayton. Sam wore an "awfully wrinkled" suit and looked as uneasy in it as a country farmer according to the *Dayton Journal* but the large audience was "apparently highly pleased" with the duo. The best thing on the program was Sam's "droll" reading of the evasion chapters from *Huck Finn*, which was, the *Dayton Democrat* reported, "very funny and well rendered." In Hamilton, Ohio, the next night, New Year's Eve, "a man with creaking shoes stalked out of the hall in the midst" of Sam's reading so he shouted to the fellow "in the most benevolent & persuasive tone, 'take your shoes off, please; take your shoes off' to the great delight of the applauding audience." The following evening, in their first border-state performance in a month, they appeared before "a hearty, quick-witted audience" at the courthouse in Paris, Kentucky. Sam agreed with Cable's assessment of southerners, that "they laugh themselves all to pieces. They catch a point before you can get it out—& then if you are not a muggins, you *don't* get it out; you leave it unsaid." The listeners "applauded him until their palms were sore and until their feet were tired." The Parisians "burst into such a storm" of hilarity that Sam began to chuckle—the only time during the entire four-month tour, Cable claimed, that he saw Sam laugh onstage at his own humor. The Paris *Kentuckian* described Sam as a "sort of living and moving anecdote" who possessed a baritone voice "like an old fashioned country preacher" in contrast to Cable's alto-soprano.[25]

The trio traveled to Cincinnati on January 2 and, as a joke, registered at the St. Nicholas Hotel as "J. B. Pond and two servants." Much to Sam's chagrin, however, when they sent their clothes to be washed, Cable "piled out a whole trunkful—all saved up since we were on the road last" in December—laundry to be cleaned at Pond's expense and the cost deducted from Sam's share of the profits. Sam "called Pond's attention to it, & he said he would not permit that; he would make [Cable] pay for that wash out of his own pocket." Pond added that, according to the domestic staff at the Everett House in New York, "when C[able] is paying his own expenses, he starves himself; & when somebody else is paying them his appetite is insatiable."

Sam and Cable performed at the fifteen-hundred-seat Odeon Hall the evenings of January 2 and 3 and a matinee on January 3, though the headliner (as Sam no doubt thought he was) had hardly stepped onstage "when the incoming people grew so troublesome from their number" that he paused middelivery and waited for the late arrivals to find their seats. He had not even finished his opening number when "a piano somewhere in the building, behind & above the stage, began to resound in most spirited fashion" and, before the end of the show, "a lady had to be carried out ill."[26] Nevertheless, according to the *Cincinnati Enquirer*, the lecturers' engagement was a financial success and their entertainments were "highly satisfactory to all who attended." After their performance, Sam and Cable were guests of honor at a reception hosted by the Literary Club of Cincinnati. When Sam was introduced, according to the *Cincinnati Commercial*, "somebody called out 'Speech,' whereupon the humorist, with an injured look, remarked, 'The gentleman who said 'speech' is certainly not a public speaker or he wouldn't expect a man who already preached twice in one day to convert the people of this great city—and I am convinced that I have converted thousands." He spent Sunday, January 4, socializing without a wingman. He breakfasted with Murat Halstead, editor of the *Cincinnati Commercial*; spent three hours touring the famous Rookwood Pottery; dined with its founder, Maria Longworth Nichols; and then "spent a most shouting good lovely 3½ hours" at the home of Pitts Burt, one of the potters.[27]

The next morning, January 5, the troupe left on the 8:15 a.m. train for Louisville, and upon arriving registered at the luxurious Galt House at First and Main Streets. They were guests at the Louisville Press Club and the Pendennis Club that afternoon before their appearance in the evening at Liederkranz Hall. The reviewer for the *Louisville Courier-Journal*, probably Henry Watterson, Sam's distant cousin by marriage, pronounced his performance "indescribable as it is inimitable." After the readings on both that night and the next, Sam dined at the Pendennis with Watterson. They were joined the first night by Cable, who was so appalled by Watterson's vulgarity ("talks shamelessly about getting drunk &c. &c.") that he declined to accompany them the next evening. Sam and Cable performed on January 7 at the Plymouth Church in Indianapolis before "one of the finest audiences that could be gathered," which relished "the most unique and thoroughly enjoyable entertainment ever given" in the city, according to the *Indianapolis Journal*. Sam was "simply indescribable"; similarly, the *Indianapolis News* considered their recitation "one of the pleasantest evenings of the season"; and the *Indianapolis Sentinel* lauded the performance of the "greatest of humorists." Sam learned later that Vice President Thomas Hendricks had been in the audience.[28]

After a nine-hour journey, Sam and Cable appeared at Chatterton's Opera House in Springfield, Illinois, the next evening. The *Illinois State Journal* observed "that few audiences have congregated there composed of more intelligent and cultivated people." Sam, Cable, and Pond left Springfield at 6:35 the next morning much to the disgust of Sam, "who despises early rising," Pond noted in his journal. As their train was crossing the bridge into St. Louis, the engine and baggage car derailed "and for a moment it looked as though we were all going to be smashed up. The cars wrenched terribly and crashed into one another with great violence." Sam panicked, though he explained later that "he would rather fall on top of the train than have the train fall on him." After walking across the bridge and registering at the Southern Hotel, he and Cable appeared the next two evenings and at a Saturday matinee in Mercantile Library Hall, where Sam first lectured in 1867. The first night they were welcomed by an audience of about seven hundred and the reviews in the local papers the next day were at odds. The *Globe-Democrat* complained that neither speaker "could take a prize in an oratorical contest," but the *Missouri Republican* reported that their performance was "highly enjoyable." James Lampton visited Sam at the hotel during this visit, and Cable recognized him from Sam's description of Colonel Sellers in *The Gilded Age*. Lampton's daughter recalled that her father "went down to the old Southern Hotel to greet his kinsman and found him, as usual, at 11 o'clock in the morning, sitting up in bed reading and smoking."[29] Sam never saw Cousin Jim again.

As the trio was preparing to leave the hotel on Monday, January 12, for Quincy, Illinois, Sam "vented his anger" at the early morning departure, according to Pond, "by squaring off with the window shutter and knocking it completely out in one round. Cable and I looked on with bated breath but didn't interfere." Sam and Cable read that evening at the local opera house, which was filled to capacity despite the frigid weather. Once again the reviews in the papers were contradictory. Whereas the *Quincy Journal* panned their performance ("we cannot conscientiously set a very high estimate upon the Twain-Cable entertainment"), the *Quincy Herald* commended it ("the entertainment was enjoyable and appreciative throughout").[30]

Next came Sam's homecoming in Hannibal on January 13. The audience was "not as large as in other places," according to Pond, but the sentimental journey was worth the trouble. "You can never imagine the infinite great deeps of pathos that have rolled their tides over me," Sam wrote Livy from his hometown. "I shall never see another such day. I have carried my heart in my mouth for twenty-four hours. And at the last moment came Tom Nash—cradle-mate, baby-mate, little-boy mate—deaf & dumb, now, for near 40 years, & nobody suspecting the deep & fine nature hidden behind his sealed lips." Sam tarried in Hannibal as long as possible and arrived the next day in Keokuk, just in time to appear with Cable at the Opera House there. Sam's mother, brother Orion, and Orion's wife Mollie were present for his performance, of course, which was so successful that the reviewer for the *Gate City* noted that some in the audience "almost fell from their seats." During his talk, which "convulsed the audience," he remarked "that he had grown handsomer of late." Cable and Pond left Keokuk at 4:00 a.m. the next morning for Burlington, Iowa, forty miles upriver. Sam lingered with his family in Keokuk until midafternoon, though he expressed no regret. He later thanked Orion "for a most pleasant sojourn in Keokuk. . . . I had a *perfect* 24 hours there."[31]

In part because his train was "dreadfully belated" by snow, Sam arrived in Burlington an hour and a half after the curtain rose. Cable was obliged "to lift a stone-dead audience out of the grave & put life and mirth in them & keep their spirits rising." Sam took the stage, though he abridged his performance because he felt "handicapped by the hellish circumstances." When he finally appeared, the *Burlington Hawkeye* reported, he explained that he had delayed his departure from Keokuk to remain with "the only mother he had" because "he might never see her again." His explanation appeased the audience, who "went home in the best of humor." He acknowledged later that he did not "like to think of the Burlington performance."[32]

Sam compensated for the failure the next two days in Chicago, where he and Cable registered at the Grand Pacific Hotel downtown and appeared two nights and an afternoon before large audiences at the Central Music Hall at the corner of State and Randolph Streets. Sam devised yet another ploy to restrict Cable's stage time: to require him to begin his evening reading at exactly 8:00 p.m. rather than wait ten minutes after the hour for the entire audience to be seated. As a result, Sam bragged to Livy, he "talks 15 minutes to an *assembling* house . . . so there isn't too much of C[able] anymore." Both the *Chicago Tribune* ("kept his hearers in a perpetual roar") and the *Inter Ocean* ("quaint style") saluted Sam's performances, but perhaps just as significantly the duo enjoyed the largest box office receipts of their tour. Their audience of eight hundred on Saturday night, January 17, paid $1,216 to see them, the only time on their schedule that ticket sales exceeded the $1,000 threshold in revenue, despite subfreezing temperatures. Sam "played my new bill, containing The Jumping Frog of Calaveras County (cut it down & told it in 13 minutes—quickest time on record) & Tom & Huck setting Jim free from prison—25 minutes." Cable also regarded their final performance in Chicago "one of the greatest successes, if not the very greatest, artistic and pecuniary success of our season."[33]

After their routine Sunday break and despite "intense cold," Sam and Cable appeared before a large audience at the First Methodist Church in Evanston, Illinois, on Monday, January 19. According to the *Evanston Index*, Sam "was at his best." The next evening, they performed in Janesville, Wisconsin, where the *Janesville Recorder* declared they were "both stars of no little magnitude in their specialties." They left for Madison shortly after noon the next day and, despite a temperature of twenty-two below zero, "had a packed house in the M[ethodist] E[piscopal] church" there and enjoyed "one of the most perfect evenings we have ever had." Shortly after midnight, with the temperature at forty-two degrees below zero, they boarded a train for La Crosse, Wisconsin, where they arrived at 9:00 a.m. They were welcomed that Tuesday evening by a packed house and, as Ozias Pond noted in his journal, the audience "seemed to have a good time." They left just before noon the next day for St. Paul, Minnesota, registered at the Grand Hotel there, and spoke that evening before a "very enthusiastic" and "highly entertained" audience of about a thousand at Market Hall. The next day they transferred their luggage seventeen miles to the West Hotel in Minneapolis and performed at the Grand Opera House before large crowds in both the afternoon and the evening. The *Minneapolis Tribune* reported that "perhaps the funniest thing of the evening" was Sam's recitation from the evasion chapters of *Huck Finn*. Cable was delighted by the "eager audience— the most eager to start with that we've ever had," though Sam groused to Webster from Minneapolis on their Sunday off that he "ought to have staid at home and written another book. It pays better than the platform." They traveled on Monday to Winona, Minnesota, where they had "a fair audience" on "a very satisfactory evening" at the Philharmonic Hall.[34]

They left the morning of January 27 at 5:00 a.m. for a return engagement in Madison, where they again filled the basement of the Methodist Episcopal church. Rather than critique their performances, the *Wisconsin State Journal* contrasted their appearances. Cable was stiff and proper, "the embodiment of refinement and culture" with "delicately moulded features," while Sam was slovenly with "a thick mass" of unkempt hair and a "careless" stance onstage. During their stop in Madison, Sam and Cable called on former Wisconsin governor Lucius Fairchild, Sam's friend from Paris. In Madison, too, Ozias Pond suffered a mild heart attack from the stress of hectic travel in freezing weather. Sam was also suffering from the physical demands of the tour and complained to an interviewer that "the trip blocked out for us is too long." He and Cable left the younger Pond in Milwaukee, their next stop, and telegraphed James Pond to join them there, though the older brother could not simply abandon his Boston office on the spur of the moment to manage their tour for the next month. "Now can't you & Mark get on with a perfectly honest, industrious man, who would be your slave, who only has to take care of you & settle the houses[?]" Pond asked Cable on January 30. "If I go away during Feb. I can do nothing but take care of you and Mark & the other business has to be neglected." Sam insisted on his arrival tout de suite in an urgent telegram from Chicago on February 2, and Pond replied not to him but to Cable, the more reasonable of the two men:

> Mark's telegram is very severe & takes the pluck out of me. I don't ask him to take on inexperienced men. . . . [I]f Mark insists that no one but myself will do then I lose the only chance I have to make my summer expenses. . . . I don't complain, but I do feel that Mark ought not to ask me to sacrifice my whole prospect, especially when I can be more value where I am, & any good honest man can settle when contracts are already made & all business done before you arrive in a town.[35]

In the end, Pond joined the tour only in cities no more than a day's travel from Boston.

After speaking the evenings of January 28 and 29 at the Academy of Music in Milwaukee, the first night before a modest audience, the second before "one of the finest, largest, and most fashionable audiences ever assembled" within its walls, according to the *Milwaukee Journal*, the barnstormers railed a hundred miles southwest to Rockford, Illinois, for a one-night stand. Cable reported to Louise that he had "not seen so many bright & so many pretty faces looking toward the footlights since last Saturday" in Chicago, but Sam made the mistake of taking a warm bath "just before going on the platform, & it stupefied [him]. We did well enough," he allowed, "but not superbly." After traveling all night to Davenport, Iowa, the pair "made a great triumph" at the local opera house the next evening. Sam felt "old & seedy & wretched" before the show, but instead of bathing he "drank a big cup of black coffee & went on the stage as fine as a fiddle." On his part, Cable bragged to Louise that both he and Sam "were in superb trim and the house was full of extremely bright people from parquet to pit." The audience recalled each of them for three encores. Sam "has a heart as tender as a child's; as loving as a woman," he wrote Louise. "He dreads to look upon suffering, but cannot hide the sympathy he feels for those who are affected. . . . I shall never forget his quaint, kind ways, and shall always love him as one most desiring *the love of his friends*."[36] But a crisis ensued after their performance. The weather was "squally" Saturday evening, Sam reported to Livy, and they were warned "that unless we left [Davenport] that night at 11, we could not meet our Chicago engagement Monday evening. Cable calmly said 'I cannot travel on

Sunday.' I was furious. I said 'You *will* travel on Sunday, just the same,—*this* time.' He said, 'It is in my contract that I am not to travel on Sunday, & I shall not do it.'" A decade later Sam still recalled his despair "when in the depth of winter" while on tour he had "to travel from point to point in all kinds of weather except good weather." According to Sam's account of his confrontation with Cable in Davenport, Sam replied, "I am not going to be made a plaything of in order to humor the corpse of a superstition of the Middle Ages"—a retort unlikely to have persuaded Cable to accede to his demand. He considered Cable "a Christ-besprinkled psalm-singing Presbyterian," a denomination not known for compromising.[37]

Sam fumed not merely for the four weeks that remained of the tour but for years afterward about Cable's "idiotic Sunday-superstition." It was, he stormed to Livy, "the most beggarly disease, the most pitiful, the most contemptible mange that ever a grown creature was afflicted withal" and he "would throttle a baby that had it." He was more irritated by it than he had been by the pilgrims' refusal to travel on Sundays eighteen years earlier during the *Quaker City* excursion. "I do not believe that any vileness, any shame, any dishonor is too base for Cable," he raged to Livy, "provided by doing it he can save his despicable Sabbath from abrasion. In him this superstition is lunacy—no, idiotcy—pure & unadulterated. Apart from this & his colossal self-conceit & avarice, he is all great & fine: but *with* them as ballast, he averages as other men." Cable had tolerated Sam's impiety and myriad distractions during the tour, a political rally outside the arena in Springfield, banging steam pipes in Baltimore, and a piano recital in Cincinnati, but he refused to break the Sabbath. Two weeks earlier, to be sure, Sam had lingered in Keokuk so long he had arrived ninety minutes late and unprepared for their appearance in Burlington and Cable had performed alone most of the evening. But from his perspective, Cable's refusal to travel on Sunday to keep a date in Chicago was different: it was liable to cause him trouble if not cost him money. He was still seething a week later. "The only time the man ever grows nervous, the only time he ever shows trepidation, is when some quarter of a minute of his detestable Sabbath seems threatened," he stormed. "Since I have been with this paltry child, I have imbibed a venomous & unreasoning detestation of the very *name* of the Sabbath." Over two years later he told his friend Grace King that Cable spent the day in Davenport "Psalm singing in three churches" while Sam "played billiards till midnight in a saloon" with Pond, "winning his agent's money from him." Livy sympathized with her husband, of course. "I am sorry that Mr Cable should be so bigoted about Sunday," she allowed, "but Sunday is good in spite of his bad use of it or our use of it. What a pity that he should be so determined as to make everyone else most uncomfortable."[38]

Ironically, despite his failure to travel on Sunday, Cable arrived in Chicago in time for their Monday performance, the first of two additional readings in a return engagement at the Central Music Hall. The *Chicago Tribune* commended the "irresistible" humor of the evasion scene Sam read the first night and, after the second night, Sam crowed to Livy that he and Cable had "appeared four times before big audiences here & made a ten-strike every time. The ghost story was simply immense. I made those 1600 people jump as one individual."[39]

They checked out of the Grand Pacific Hotel the afternoon of February 4 and headed to South Bend, Indiana, where they read that night at Good's Opera House. The size of the crowd was disappointing—"from a Chicago audience of 1600 people to South Bend with . . . 350 people is not cheering"—but among their auditors were Charles Warren Stoddard, Sam's old friend, now a professor of English literature at Notre Dame University, and Thomas Walsh, the president of the university. Though the South Bend *Tribune* reported that Sam's readings from *Huck Finn* "kept his listeners in a roar," the *South Bend Times* was unimpressed by their performance. Cable's recitations "possessed a sameness that made them . . . monotonous" and Sam's "drawling, devil-may-care way" of speaking prompted many in the audience to fear "that it was their fate to be bored." The reviews of their reading at the Academy in Fort Wayne the next night were similarly lukewarm. According to the *Fort Wayne News*, Cable "grew tiresome toward the close of the entertainment," unlike Sam, who is "never tiresome," and the *Gazette* opined that Cable "is not cut out for dialect recitations, even though they be from his own works." The *Sentinel*, on the other hand, commended Sam: "no person knows how to mingle the sublime and ridiculous better than he does." On the whole, Cable was alliteratively disgusted by the "dreary, dismal taverns, and dingy, dirty platforms & auditoriums" in South Bend and Fort Wayne, whereas Sam reported to Livy that he "had a most delightful time with the Fort Wayne audience last night. I enjoyed every moment of my time on the stage."[40]

The road show left Fort Wayne the next morning before 6:00 a.m. and spent almost six hours traveling 115 miles to Lafayette, Indiana, where Sam and Cable appeared that evening at the Grand Opera House to mixed reviews. The *Lafayette Journal* reported that both Cable and Sam were "geniuses" and "masters" of the platform, though the *Courier* was harshly critical of Cable for the "dreary barrenness" of his selections and his "insipid" reading of them. By contrast, "volcanic flashes of uproarious mirth dart from [Sam's] eyes, consuming the last remnant of the pall-like gloom left in the house by Cable." The poet and essayist Maurice Thompson, author of *The Witchery of Archery* (1878) and Howells's friend, called at the Lahr House after the performance and Sam "was exceedingly glad to see him," though "he staid till midnight." Sam was pleased with their return engagement the next evening at the Plymouth Church in Indianapolis. "I have learned my trade at last," he wrote Livy. "I know how to read my stuff. At last I can stand on a platform & do the thing right. I did make 'em shout last night." The audience was "tickled to death" with the evasion story, according to the *Indianapolis Journal*. Afterward, however, Sam complained to Livy that Cable was not "worth a penny over $200" a week in salary. "He is not a novelty anywhere. He has apparently been in every town in the country just about twice; & that is as often as he is wanted. Especially as he offers his same old stuff all the time." He whined in his notebook that "Cable costs me $550 to $600 a week—that is, $450 a week & expenses"—and Cable was still padding his expenses. "He is not worth the half of it." Sam quibbled with the very meaning of "expenses," which should have included only "food, lodging & transportation" but conceivably might cover "police court expenses" if Cable went "to thrashing people."[41]

Sam even began to blame Cable for his own shortcomings on the platform. "It is Cable's fault that I have done inferior reading all this time," he insisted to Livy. "He has hogged so much of the platform-time that I have always felt obliged to hurry along at lightning speed in order to keep the performance within bounds." Cable "always stole ⅔ of the platform-time when we were out together," he complained a dozen years later. Worse yet, on a Saturday night after reading from a pulpit rather than a podium, Cable engaged Sam in "a discussion of the duty of practicing religion." He routinely nagged Sam to join him at church on Sundays. As he wrote Louise in the iambic pentameter of Christian hymnody, "Would to God I might prevail to take him there."[42]

After passing a Sunday at the Dennison House in Indianapolis, they performed at Comstock's Opera House in Columbus, Ohio, on February 9 before "the handsomest people you ever saw," according to Sam. He "made them shout & tore them all to pieces till half past 10, & not an individual deserted till the thing was over." Despite the hostile weather—it "rained & stormed all day & is spitting snow tonight," Cable wrote Louise—the house was packed and hospitable. On his part, Sam carped to Livy after the show that the "pious ass" Cable "allows an 'entirely new program' to be announced from the stage & in the papers, & then comes out without a wince or an apology & jerks that same old Night Ride on the audience again." Worse yet, "that infernal Night Ride of Mary's has grown from 6 minutes (in New Haven) to *fifteen*! And it is in *every* program." Still, the *Columbus Times* commended the program: "Everything they gave was so original that it would be a difficult task to decide which should claim the greatest merit." After speaking in Delaware, Ohio, on February 10, Sam and Cable appeared under the auspices of the Union Library Association at the First Congregational Church in Oberlin the next evening. Surprisingly, Cable received the more favorable reviews in the *Oberlin News* ("proved himself the peer of his companion in the humorous while he excelled in the pathetic") and the Oberlin College paper ("Twain's humor was distasteful"). Cable graciously refused a call from the audience for an encore on this occasion. As he explained to Louise without realizing the irony of his statement, "Mark *never* objects to my declining an encore."[43]

Sam and Cable spent all day on February 12 traveling 140 miles to Detroit on account of the inclement weather. Cable walked onstage at Whitney's Opera House twenty minutes past the hour and, he reported to Louise, even then he "was inconvenienced by the tardy incoming of a special train from another town that brought about a hundred auditors. Strange to say I went to the work fresh & bright & from the very start did, by verdict of all, the finest evening's reading thus far in my experience." Sam received the more favorable notices for his performance this evening, however. As the *Detroit Post* suggested, Sam struck just the right note of levity, and "his manner heightens the effect of everything he says, because it seems to be utterly unfitted for public readings."[44]

They slipped across the Detroit River into Canada the next day and appeared at the YMCA hall in London, Ontario, that evening. To judge from the review in the *London Advertiser*, Cable again outperformed Sam: "Cable is the most artistic," according to the critic, and "Twain is entertaining, but he is not doing his best work." The paper said of Sam that, on the contrary, "he is grotesque and glories in it." Sam spent the following afternoon tobogganing with seventy students from Helmuth Female College who had attended the reading. Cable was flummoxed by the scene of the "girls waving and hurrahing and he swinging his hat and tossing kisses right and left." That night they arrived in Toronto after dark, again registered at the Rossin House, "dressed in haste," hurried to Horticultural Pavilion, "& read to a thin audience." Cable was disappointed by an auditorium "dotted noticeably with empty seats when we had looked for a crowded house." After another Sunday layover, they "came within an ace of missing" their engagement in Brockville, Canada, spending "11½ hours making a 7-hour trip" there for an appearance Monday evening. Sam complained in his letter to Livy that day that Cable "has never bought one single sheet of paper or an envelop in all these 3 months—sponges all his stationery . . . from the hotels. His body is small, but it is much too large for his soul. He is the pitifulest human louse I have ever known."[45]

They were welcomed upon their arrival in Montreal on February 18 with a reception hosted by the Athenaeum Club at the Windsor Hotel that lasted until 6:00 p.m. and, Cable reported, "was the most elaborate affair I have ever had part it. I don't think I could have shaken less than two hundred and fifty hands." He and Sam read that evening and the next before capacity audiences at the Queen's Hall, and the *Gazette* reviewed their performance the first night, noting that "only one Mark Twain in the world . . . can write such genuine fun." While in the city, Sam was initiated into the Old Toque Bleue Snowshoe Club. As Cable described the ceremony, Sam was "lifted from his feet in the midst of a tightly huddled mass of young athletes, laid out at full length on their hands and then . . . thrown bodily into the air almost to the ceiling, caught upon their hands as he came down, thrown up again, caught again, thrown again—so four, five times amid resounding cheers." Cable was impressed. "Put Montreal down as one of the brightest, liveliest and most charming cities—at least in winter—that can be," he wrote Louise.[46]

After reading in Saratoga, New York, the next day, Sam and Cable railed to New York City on February 20, registered at the Everett House, and appeared at a "well filled" Academy of Music in Brooklyn the following evening. Both of them "were in excellent humor," the *Brooklyn Eagle* reported. After a rare midweek day off—Sam probably spent it in Hartford—they returned to the stage in New Haven on February 23; Orange, New Jersey, on February 24 ("very poor—i.e. the audience was slim"); and Newark on February 25 ("one of the finest nights we have had for some ten days"). They appeared in Philadelphia before an audience of three thousand in the Academy of Music the next evening and Cable boasted that whereas he "had great success" Sam "was not up to high water mark" because "he seems tired out." When Sam announced that as the last piece of the evening he would recite "The Golden Arm," according to the Philadelphia *North American*, "a number of people" stood to leave—one of Sam's pet peeves. He stared at them and to embarrass them declared from the stage that "if they wanted to catch a train they should go right ahead. 'If anybody wants to go out I don't care,' he said, dryly, but nobody else seemed inclined to leave." On the other hand, the reporter for the *Philadelphia Inquirer* noticed no decline in his performance. As usual, when Sam "described a ludicrous scene the audience was convulsed with laughter." The more plausible explanation for Sam's diffidence was that the tour was drawing to a close and he was simply exhausted by travel and exasperated with Cable. As he wrote Howells from Philadelphia, his "four-months platform campaign" had taught him

that Cable's gifts of mind are greater and higher than I had suspected. But— That "But" is pointing toward his religion. You will never, never know, never divine, guess, imagine, how loathsome a thing the Christian religion can be made until you come to know and study Cable daily and hourly. Mind you, I like him; he is pleasant company; I rage and swear at him sometimes, but we do not quarrel; we get along mighty happily together; but in him and his person I have learned to hate all religions. He has taught me to abhor and detest the Sabbath-day and hunt up new and troublesome ways to dishonor it.

The evening of February 27, after speaking at Oratorio Hall in Baltimore, he told a local reporter in a miracle of understatement that he had "stood the test"—or torment—of the tour "very well." After engagements in sixteen states, the District of Columbia, and two Canadian provinces, Sam and Cable shuttered the show with matinee and evening performances in Washington, D.C., on February 28 before large audiences. They spent the next day with Lieutenant Albion V. Wadhams of the U.S. Navy and his wife Carrie Henderson, Cable's friends from New Orleans. Cable bragged to Louise that he had persuaded Sam to attend church with him that morning "at last!"—no doubt a goodwill gesture from Sam in deference to their imminent parting. Cable headed to New Orleans and Sam railed to New York on March 2 and stayed three nights at the Everett Hotel, spending much of his time with Grant, before returning to Hartford three days later. Box office receipts from the tour, by Pond's accounting, totaled slightly over forty-six thousand dollars. After all the bills were paid, after Cable's salary of about eight thousand dollars and expenses and Pond's commissions were deducted, Sam's share of the profits amounted to about fifteen thousand dollars.[47]

Unfortunately, the story of the campaign does not end with the division of spoils. In early May, some ten weeks after their circus folded its tent, Sam spoke too freely about Cable to the New York correspondent of the *Boston Herald* and his comments made national news. His remarks were quite specific in their allegations—so specific that, as Arlin Turner observes, some of the details could only have originated with him. First, Sam charged that Cable had rebuffed an invitation to speak on behalf of the Decorative Arts Society of Hartford unless he was paid an honorarium and he had declined to participate at an authors' reading in New York on behalf of international copyright. Sam was certainly irritated by Cable's refusal. Had he been consulted, Sam insisted to Pond, "I never would have allowed these people to invite Cable; it was the infernalest mistake that was ever made; I could have *told* them they'd get a slap in the face from him." Or as he wrote Howells, "in order to find room for his greatness in his pygmy carcase, God had to cramp his other qualities more than it was judicious." Next the reports accused Cable of parsimony during his tour with Sam, that "Cable did not spend the price of a postage stamp during the trip. The agreement was that his expenses should be paid, and he quickly adopted the habit of ordering the most expensive things at hotels and of leaving Clemens to pay even the horse car fares when they were out together." Finally, Cable had caused no end of trouble with his "Sabbath keeping" or petty piety. A second article in the *Herald* denied the rumor that Sam and Cable had resorted to "personal conflict," perhaps "even fisticuffs," to settle their differences, but again asserted that the tour had ended acrimoniously and repeated the allegation that Cable had charged "the partnership account" for "so highly luxurious a thing as champagne and so lowly a one as the blacking of his boots."[48] These articles were widely reprinted across the country in such papers as the *Philadelphia News*, *Ithaca Journal*, *Milwaukee Sentinel*, and New Orleans *Times-Democrat*.

Cable was, of course, quick to protest. The statements in the *Herald*, he wrote its editor, were "slanderous and libelous. They do not spare even my trusted friends, but make them, by implication, party to slanders of which they are absolutely incapable. No gentleman could have offered them for publication, and I wonder how you could have thought them worthy of room in your paper." The "matter" in its columns "was not news, but gossip." It was "the first careful slander upon my private character that I have ever known" and "neither contained nor was accompanied privately by any authority for its statements." For the record, Cable addressed each of the allegations: An art school in Hartford had asked him "to take part in a public reading, and, as my standing contract with my agent requires, I referred them to him, and he consented, but they could not accept the date he gave them." He had declined to read at the benefit for copyright because "my wife's health did not permit me to leave her side" when the event was scheduled. As for ordering expensive meals in hotels and charging them to the lecturing agency, their stays were "almost invariably at hotels on the American plan" with meals included in the price of the room. He conceded only that "by the letter of my contract I was under no circumstances to be required to travel much or little or any part of Sunday," not that he apologized for insisting upon that condition. He likewise contacted Sam to assure him that, should any of his denials be misconstrued or garbled in the press, he had made no statements "either openly or covertly" intimating "anything unpleasant about you to my friends or anybody else." In fact, he added, "if you care to know it, I esteem you more highly since our winter's experience than I ever did before & should deeply regret if scandal mongers were to make an estrangement between us. Of course I do not believe that you have said ought against me that was not intended as a friend's fair criticism among friends." Sam replied cavalierly—and ironically, given his own inclination to take umbrage at even small offenses—dismissing the contretemps as nothing more than fake news. "My dear boy," he began, on a note of condescension (Cable was, after all, nine years younger than he),

> don't give yourself any discomfort about the slander of a professional newspa-
> per liar—we can*not* escape such things. I do assure you that this thing did not
> distress me, or even disturb the flow of my talk (got it at breakfast some days
> ago), for one single half of a half of a hundredth part of a second; in the same
> length of time it went out of my mind & was forgotten. To take notice of it
> in print is a thing which would never have occurred to me. Why, dear friend,
> flirt it out of your mind, straight off.

Despite Cable's denials and rebuttals, however, the dust-up survived like ra-
dioactive fallout with an afterlife. Two weeks later, the *Chicago Daily News*
quoted "a gentleman" who traveled with Sam and Cable (apparently James
Pond) who claimed that Cable was a cheapskate, "the most penurious man
he ever met," and that Sam was "liberal almost to a fault; if he was out with
a crowd of congenial spirits, he would insist upon paying for everything."[49]

Two years later, in an apparent attempt to silence the persistent rumors
that the two men had become estranged, Sam visited Cable at his home in
Northampton, Massachusetts. Sam publicly denied the claim a decade later
that he and Cable had fallen out. He told an interviewer in August 1895 that
they were "of exactly opposite temperaments, and on that account perhaps
became not only close friends but the most congenial of traveling companions." Privately, too, Sam assured Cable, "I liked you in spite of your religion," though he tactfully focused his compliments on their time together on
trains: "I have always said, & still maintain, that as a railroad-comrade you
were perfect—the only railroad-comrade in the world that a man of moods
& frets & uncertainties of disposition could travel with, a third of a year,
& never weary of his company. We *always* had good times in the cars, &
never minded the length of the trips—& my, but they *were* sockdolagers for
length!" Yet another decade later, at Sam's seventieth birthday celebration,
Cable declared with grace and wit that Sam liked him "well enough" save
for his religion. "Well, I am bound to declare the exception well taken. The
longer I live the less I am satisfied with my religion myself." Cable added
that his tour with "the man of solemn jest" had been one of the highlights of
his life. He had learned that "the power of his marvelous and overwhelming
humor lay in the fact that it was always well grounded, that it was always
the standard-bearer of truth or, at least, a majestic conviction of right and of
human sympathy."[50]

While passing through New York on February 26, 1885, en route to an appearance that evening in Philadelphia, Sam called on General Grant "simply

to inquire after his health" and was shocked to see how emaciated he had become. The rumors that he was dying of throat cancer had never been officially confirmed, though Grant's physician told Sam that his "condition was the opposite of encouraging." The general had completed only about half of the second volume of his memoirs. The previous December 6 Charley Webster had offered Grant a fifty-thousand-dollar advance on sales of his memoirs but had received no response; on February 3, Webster had sweetened the deal, offering Grant 70 percent of profits on the book, but he still had received no reply. During Sam's visit in late February, however, Grant assured him that he planned to commit to the firm, though he asked for a day or two of grace so that he could first notify Roswell Smith of the Century Company of his decision. The next day, at the nadir of his family's fortunes, Grant formally contracted with the upstart Webster and Company to publish his memoirs. The agreement specifically priced the cost of a clothbound two-volume set at seven dollars. As Paine reflected, the firm became overnight "the most conspicuous publisher in the world." Smith congratulated Sam on his acquisition. According to Sam, Smith told him he was "glad on GG's account that there was somebody with pluck enough to give such a figure." Grant had wanted Smith to guarantee "*a sale of twenty-five thousand sets*" and Smith had declined.[51]

In truth, the decision was the culmination of long negotiations. Sam had suggested to Grant that he circulate the Webster and Company offer "to the Century & other great publishing houses, & *close with the one that offered him the best terms.* He did it" and, according to Sam, his terms were matched by several firms, including the Century Company, "& two firms *exceeded* my offer. But none of them could exceed my *facilities* for publishing a subscription book—nor *equal* them, either—a fact which I proved to the satisfaction of General Grant's lawyer; & that is why I got the book." Smith submitted a bid for the contract expecting, according to his colleague Robert Underwood Johnson, "to adjust it to the General's wishes after consultation." Or as Sam remembered in his autobiography, "The Century people were willing to accept the terms which I had proposed to the General but they offered nothing better." Too late, Smith learned that the general had accepted Sam's offer. Johnson subsequently confirmed at least part of Sam's account. Colonel Fred Grant advised him "that his father's decision had been influenced chiefly by the fact that Mr. Clemens had convinced him that the book should be issued by subscription and that his own firm had been successful publishers of subscription books, while the Century Co. had done but little in that line." Had they better understood the strength of the position from which Sam was bargaining, "we should have been able to meet the situation. We were at a disadvantage" in that Sam "knew our terms and we did not know his."[52]

Some of Webster's rivals alleged that Sam had connived to secure the contract, and specifically that he had bribed the general by promising jobs with Webster and Company to either or both of Grant's sons Buck and Jesse. The New York correspondent of the *Boston Herald*—the same columnist who stirred trouble by reporting on the row between Sam and Cable in May—claimed in March that the Century Company had nearly completed all arrangements for printing Grant's memoirs, including the reproduction of maps and other illustrations, when "in stepped Mark Twain and spoiled it all" by proposing "to take his son Jesse into the enterprise of publishing and circulating the autobiography." The *Herald* cited Jeannette Gilder, the New York correspondent of the Boston *Saturday Evening Gazette*, who confirmed that Webster had tendered a job to the younger Grant, "which makes it more attractive to the general. The Century company would probably have published the Grant autobiography if it had not been for the 'son' clause; but that put a new aspect on the thing, and while it was perfectly natural for Gen. Grant to want to see his son fixed in business, it was not so natural for the Century company to want to be forced into a bargain of this sort." Sam promptly denied both the published report that he had obtained the contract by devious means and the gossip that his successful bid for the book had "created any ill feeling between the Century company and General Grant." Neither of Grant's sons ever worked for Webster and Company, and William W. Ellsworth of the Century Company later corroborated the latter claim: "There never was any feeling in our office against Mark Twain for taking away the Grant book. He continued to write for the *Century*," contributing "The Private History of a Campaign That Failed" to the December 1885 number and excerpts from *A Connecticut Yankee in King Arthur's Court* to the December 1889 number, "and he was on the best of terms with everyone about the place." At worst, in September 1888 Sam described the state of his relationship with the Century Company as "armed neutrality."[53]

But the *Boston Herald* continued to claim as late as June 1885 that Sam had interfered with an understanding Grant had reached "with the Century Company that they should issue the work" and that the prospectus issued by Webster to his book agents contained material belonging to Century that had not yet appeared in the magazine. As a result, "they have demanded a reimbursement of the money already paid [Grant] for the contributions, and if they do not get it, there will be a lawsuit for damages." Sam was compelled again to insist that he had "done nothing underhanded in this whole business. Every step has been taken in the broad daylight, & nothing concealed. Neither have I done anything unfair or in any way dishonorable." He conceded that the prospectus of the *Memoirs* Webster sent his canvassers contained three pages of material that belonged to the Century Company "&

should not have been in it at all; but it got there through ignorance, not deliberate purpose. They have not 'demanded reimbursement,' they will bring no 'lawsuit for damages.'" He regretted that he seemed "to be fast getting the reputation in the newspapers of being a pushing, pitiless, underhanded sharper—but I don't quite deserve it." Grant and Century had reached no "understanding" and, moreover, had Grant accepted Century's offer he would have earned only about $175,000 on sales of a quarter million sets of his autobiography, whereas Webster's offer "would amount to $350,000" in royalties paid to him. "He had the wisdom to decline the Century offer," Sam concluded, "& to this day I can't help thinking he was right." Sam estimated the profits earned by Webster and Company on Grant's memoirs at between $110,000 and $115,000. The papers that were "daily bewailing my dog-in-the-manger conduct" failed to understand that Sam had merely advised the general on "what terms to require of the Century people."[54]

On March 3, five days after signing the contract with Webster and Company and literally in the last minutes of the Forty-Eighth Congress, Grant was restored by legislative fiat to the rank of general of the army and retired at an annual salary of $13,500. In effect, the action provided a modest income to his wife and soon-to-be widow Julia. With royalties on his memoirs and a military pension, Grant did not leave his family penniless at his death. Sam was present in Grant's New York home when the former president received the news. He wrote Livy the next day that "the effect upon him was like raising the dead." Twenty years later Sam recalled to Paine, however, that "every face there betrayed strong excitement and emotion except one— General Grant's. He read the telegram, but not a shade or suggestion of a change exhibited itself in his iron countenance. The volume of his emotion was greater than all the other emotions there present combined, but he was able to suppress all expression of it and make no sign."[55]

CHAPTER 13

Gilded Cage

I hate all public mention of my private history, anyway. It is none of the public's business.

—Samuel Clemens to Orion Clemens, December 8, 1887

THE FIRST PRINTING of thirty thousand copies of *Adventures of Huckleberry Finn* was released in the United States by Charles L. Webster and Company on February 18, 1885. Its publication had been announced over a year in advance in such papers as the *Boston Advertiser, Boston Herald,* and *Brooklyn Eagle* and in January 1885 Sam Clemens suggested venues where Webster should send review copies. On January 23 he instructed his nephew Charley Webster to forward unbound proof to prominent magazines like the *Atlantic Monthly* and the *Century;* three days later, he urged him to send advance sheets to a panoply of magazines "*now*—& ask [R. W.] Gilder if he can't review it in next *Century.*" (Even after printing three excerpts from *Huck Finn* in the *Century,* even before Sam outbid the Century Company for Ulysses S. Grant's memoirs, Gilder was loath to commission an early review of the novel and none appeared in the magazine until the following May.) On January 27 Sam demanded that Webster "send no copy of the book to *any* newspaper until after the Century or the Atlantic shall have reviewed it" because "a favorable review by an authority" would set the tone for all subsequent notices. Webster was rankled by these repeated directives. After all, wasn't he the publisher? "You seem to have a mighty poor opinion of my business capacity," he replied on January 30. Nevertheless, he agreed to comply with Sam's "directions in regard to withholding books for review" until either the *Century* or the *Atlantic* had noticed it. On February 8, ten days prior to release, Sam panicked because the novel should already "have been reviewed in the March Century & Atlantic!—how we have been dull enough to go & overlook that? It is an irreparable blunder." To compensate for the lack of early notices in major journals, Sam suggested "we could flood the country with press copies . . . without waiting for the magazines," in effect reversing his earlier edict. On February 10 Sam ordered Webster to "send immediately copies (bound & unbound)" to the major Boston, Hartford, and New York dailies. He admitted that, unfortunately, he was "not able to see anything that can save Huck Finn from being another defeat." Webster exhibited no little irritation upon receiving this barrage of commands. "In regard to the press notices of the book: That was not overlooked," he reminded Sam. "You told me in the start that press notices *hurt* the last book before it was out and that this year we would send *none* until the book was out." Webster assured his uncle that "Huck is a *good* book" and that he was "working intelligently and *hard* and if it don't sell it won't be your fault or mine but the extremely hard times." Moreover, he had "never yet made a business mistake that I am aware of and it is not probable that I shall commence on this book."[1]

Given the enormous prepublication publicity it garnered, *Huck Finn* was "preforeordestinated" to succeed. With the controversy over the mutilated illustration, the suit against Estes & Lauriat for listing it for sale, publication of the raftsman's chapter in *Life on the Mississippi* (1883), the excerpts published in the *Century*, and Sam's readings from the novel during four months on tour, it was, the San Francisco *Alta California* declared, "probably the best advertised book" of the age. The *San Francisco Bulletin* similarly averred that "no book has been put on the market with more advertising" than *Huckleberry Finn*. Webster carefully monitored demand for the book because, as he wrote Sam two weeks prior to publication, "I am not going to fall into [James R.] Osgood's mistake and have 15,000 copies on hand unsold. I have my paper ready and 30,000 printed and can bind 5,000 copies in a *week* if I wish." Webster reported subscription orders of the novel totaling about thirty-nine thousand copies by mid-March 1885, over fifty thousand copies in early May, and over sixty thousand copies in early September. Only three months after publication, Webster handed his uncle a check for $54,500, for which Sam took the credit. He was persuaded that, as he later asserted in his autobiography, "as a publisher I was not altogether a failure." On the contrary, he bragged to Webster a month after the date of issue that "Huck certainly *is* a success."[2]

The novel was initially more a commercial than a critical triumph, however. It certainly was not heralded as either an American classic or Sam's masterpiece save in rare circumstances. His old Nevada friend Tom Fitch scolded him shortly after its publication: "You have money enough. Instead of 'potboilers' why dont you write another such a book as 'Prince & Pauper?'" Many of the earliest published reviews were among the most brutal. The *Boston Globe* indicted Sam's use of dialect ("on the very second page" the "uneducated urchin" who narrates the story "is made to say 'commence'" rather than "begin"). Robert Bridges in *Life* magazine suggested sarcastically that the scene in which Pap "writhes in a fit of delirium tremens" is "suited to amuse the children on long, rainy afternoons" and the Royal Nonesuch, featuring "a nude man, striped with the colors of the rainbow," would be an appropriate reading "at Lenten parlor entertainments and church festivals." The New York *World* bewailed the story of "a wretchedly low, vulgar, sneaking, and lying Southern country boy," concluding that such "cheap and pernicious stuff" should rank as humor "is more than a pity." The novel was nothing more than "a piece of careless hackwork," with "two or three unusually atrocious murders in cold blood thrown in by way of incidental diversion." In response Sam wrote in his notebook, "If you want to rear a family just right for sweet & pure society here & Paradise hereafter, banish Huck Finn from the home circle & introduce the N.Y. World in his place." The *Boston Traveller* trashed the novel in an outbreak of adjectives: it was "singularly flat, stale and unprofitable" and an "extraordinarily senseless publication." This reviewer even condemned the frontispiece, the heliotype of Karl Gerhardt's bust of Sam: "the taste of this gratuitous presentation is as bad as is the book itself." Other hostile early notices appeared in the *New Haven Journal and Courier* ("Mark Twain has written some poor stuff but none much poorer than 'Huckleberry Finn'"), *Boston Herald* ("vulgar and abhorrent"), and *Boston Transcript* ("so false, as well as coarse, that nobody wants to read it after a taste of it"). Even the *Arkansaw Traveler* found Sam's "vulgar humor" offensive. Some of the severest strictures on the novel, Sam acknowledged, were leveled by the *Boston Advertiser*, which launched the first in a series of attacks on it in mid-March in which the reviewer described the narrative as "wearisome and labored," its humor as "monotonous," and accused Sam of "coarseness and bad taste." Then the coup de grâce, an unkind cut by a jaundiced critic: tepid approval of the illustrations ("admirable in their way"). Sam attributed this hostile notice in his notebook to an unnamed reviewer who was attempting to exact "revenge upon me for what was simply & solely an accident. I had the misfortune to catch him in a situation which will not bear describing." The Melbourne *Australian* not only asserted that "the sap seems to have gone out" of Sam's humor, leaving "little more than a dry residuum," but its reviewer was also the first to decry the evasion chapters, noting that "the fun is exhausted long before the end is reached."[3]

Fortunately, a few other early critics added a pinch of leaven to their loaf. The New York *Sun* commended the "beautiful moral" that "decorates nearly every one of its shining pages," as well as Sam's unprecedented use of colloquial language and vernacular dialect; the *Detroit Free Press* declared *Huck Finn* "the brightest and most humorous work he has ever written"; the Port Jervis, New York, *Evening Gazette* opined that "the reputation of the author will not suffer by comparison" of the novel with any of his earlier works; the *Baltimore Sun* considered its best chapters "those relating to the frauds of the

'King' and the 'Duke'"; the *Montreal Gazette* concurred that it was "worthy of Mark Twain's imagination and pen"; and the Napa, California, *Register* applauded Sam's reversion "to his old style of writing." All of the papers in Hartford extolled Sam's new book—for example, the *Post* ("as a storehouse ... of dialect, even more than as a book of humor"), the *Courant*, in a review probably written by Charles Dudley Warner ("extraordinary power"), and the *Times* ("teaches, without seeming to do it, the virtue of honest simplicity, directness, truth"). Several of the papers in San Francisco reviewed it, too, though a couple of them were slightly ambivalent. The *Argonaut* termed the novel "amusing" and praised especially "the variety of dialects spoken by the characters." The *Alta California* thought the book was filled with "genuine humor" and "written in Mark Twain's best style." The *Call* pronounced the novel "at times immensely amusing" and concluded that it "fully sustains Mr. Clemens's well-earned reputation." The *Call* also noted that E. W. Kemble's frontispiece depicted Huck wearing a single suspender, a lower-class marker. The most favorable of the notices in San Francisco appeared in the *Chronicle* and was likely written by George Hamlin Fitch, the staff book critic. It pronounced *Huck Finn* "the most amusing book Mark Twain has written for years," a tour de force in which "the most unlikely materials are transmuted into a work of literary art," and its author "the Edison of our literature. There is no limit to his inventive genius." Only the *Examiner* qualified its approbation. Though regarding the novel as "a potboiler in its baldest form" and "a string of incidents ingeniously fastened together" with "very little of literary art" uniting the episodic plot, it also was "an amusing story if such scrap-work can be called a story." The *Cleveland Leader and Herald* paid it a similar backhanded compliment: *Huck Finn* was "little if at all worse than earlier works by the same author." As for the *Atlantic* and the *Century*, on which Sam was banking for puffs: the former magazine in April, more than a month after the release of the novel, merely asserted that Sam "could not have related" its incidents "more amusingly" and Thomas Sergeant Perry a month later contended in the latter that Huck's "courage, his manliness in every trial, are an incarnation of the better side of the ruffianism that is one result of the independence of Americans." Perry was also the second reviewer to deprecate the evasion chapters that close the novel, the bane of modern critics: "the long account of Tom Sawyer's artificial imitation of escapes from prison is somewhat forced."[4]

Conspicuous by his lack of public comment on the novel was W. D. Howells, one of the most prolific literary critics of the period. His favorable opinion of it is not at issue: he repeatedly wrote Sam how impressed he was with *Huck Finn*; he volunteered to read the proofs; and he asked Webster in December 1884 when the book would appear because he "might like to write" about it. His public silence on the subject is easily explained. When the novel was released, Howells had no regular editorial job and, in fact, he published no reviews of any books during calendar year 1885. To be sure, he had no magazine affiliation when he reviewed *The Prince and the Pauper* in the *New York Tribune* in 1881 but his failure to comment publicly about *Huck Finn* in 1885 should not be construed as a mark against the novel. In fact, Howells enthusiastically approved the book, writing Sam privately that

> the Southwest lives in that book, as it lives nowhere else, with its narrow and rude conditions, its half savage heroism, its vague and dim aspiration, its feuds and its fights, its violence, its squalor, its self-devotion, all in shadow of that horrible cloud of slavery darkening both the souls and the minds of men. There are moments of almost incredible pathos in the book . . . and also of a lofty joy, which is not the less sublime because of the grotesque forms it takes.[5]

The worst was yet to come. *Adventures of Huckleberry Finn* disappointed the custodians of genteel culture who had hoped Sam had finally learned to tame his vulgarities and blood-and-thunder sensationalism. On March 16 the Committee of the Public Library of Concord, Massachusetts, composed of five white men, voted unanimously to remove the novel from its shelves. The hometown of Bronson Alcott, Ralph Waldo Emerson, and Henry David Thoreau, the summer resort destination of thousands of Americans and the site of the annual Concord School of Philosophy banned the book and ignited a critical firestorm. Moreover, the heirs of Emerson and Alcott were complicit in the prohibition. Edward Emerson, Sam's fellow passenger aboard the *Batavia* in 1872, was one of the members of the committee that voted to remove it and Louisa May Alcott, daughter of Bronson and the author of *Little Women* (1869), sniffed that "if Mr. Clemens cannot think of something better to tell our pure-minded lads and lasses," he ought to "stop writing for them." The proscription was not only a premeditated insult, but planned to inflict the greatest humiliation possible on Sam. The news was carried by wire to every corner of the country and it appeared the next day in papers from Boston, Hartford, and Washington, D.C., to St. Louis, Kansas City, Los Angeles, and San Francisco. Two of the members of the committee testified for the record. "While I do not wish to state it as my opinion that the book is absolutely immoral in its tone," one of them said, "still it seems to me that it contains but very little humor and that little is of a very coarse type. If it were not for the author's reputation the book would undoubtedly meet with severe criticism. I regard it as the veriest trash." The other asserted that he had "examined the book and my objections to it are these: It deals with a series of adventures of a very low grade of morality; it is couched in the language of a rough, ignorant dialect, and all through its pages there is a systematic use of bad grammar and an employment of rough, coarse, inelegant expressions. It is also very irreverent" and "trash of the veriest sort." Coincidentally, the day after the novel was expelled from the Concord Library the steamboat *Mark Twain* literally exploded in the middle of the Mississippi River near Mound City, Arkansas, killing five men.[6] It could have been an omen.

The terms of the debate over the merits of the book suddenly shifted. The discussion became less about the quality of the novel than about the rationale for censoring it, though the alignments among the papers in favor of or opposed to its removal remained largely unchanged. The *Boston Transcript* thought the action of the committee "entirely superfluous" because the novel "would doubtless have disappeared into a philological sinkhole without bothering to push it." Many papers expressed support for the prohibition, including the *Cleveland Leader and Herald* ("a just criticism"); St. Albans, Vermont, *Messenger* ("Mark Twain has become what the old soldier would term a 'spent ball'"); *Richmond Whig* ("a Huckleberry beyond the persimmon"); and Boston *Literary World* ("we are glad to see . . . this action at Concord"). The *Boston Journal* noted without a scintilla of evidence but with a gender stereotype that the Concord censor was "a woman who prefers a book of purity rather than of fame." The Lowell, Massachusetts, *Courier* betrayed a familiarity with the interior decoration of Sam's Hartford home while still supporting sanctions on the book. As the *Courier* noted, the fireplace in Sam's library bore the inscription, "The ornament of a house is the friends who frequent it." The Concord Library "might put up a sign to the effect that 'the merit of a library is the books which are kept out of it.'" Even the New York State Reformatory considered removing the novel from its library collection on the grounds it was a corrupting influence on the inmates.[7]

The two papers most outspoken in support of the ban were the *Boston Advertiser* and *Springfield Republican*. The *Advertiser* continued its assault on the book, asserting that its eviction from the Concord Library was a bellwether of literary taste,

> an indication that in matters of humor the tide has turned at last, and that the old school of coarse, flippant, and irreverent joke makers is going out, to return no more. "Huckleberry Finn" is little, if at all, worse than earlier works by the same author, but the public taste has improved and the opportunity to revolt from the Mark Twains who have ruled so long has been seized with avidity. . . . Mark Twain and his followers have added to that exaggeration which is the normal trait in American humor the corroding element of burlesque. Nothing has been sacred with them, and over subjects dignified by age, tragedy, and romance they have cast the slimy trail of the vulgar humorist.

The *Advertiser* expressed the hope that "now that his last effort has failed so ignominiously" Sam would devote his talent in future to tasks "in some manner more creditable to himself and more beneficent to his country." The *Republican* leveled an ad hominem attack on the author. "It is time that this influential pseudonym should cease to carry into homes and libraries unworthy productions," the paper contended. "Mr. Clemens is a genuine and powerful humorist, with a bitter vein of satire on the weaknesses of humanity which is sometimes wholesome, sometimes only grotesque, but in certain of his works degenerates into a gross trifling of every feeling. The trouble of Mr. Clemens is that he has no reliable sense of propriety." To illustrate the point, the editorialist dredged up Sam's "notorious speech at an Atlantic dinner" seven years earlier. *Huck Finn*, he added, was "no better in tone than the dime novels which flood the blood-and-thunder reading population" and had a comparable demoralizing effect. This paragraph was widely copied in such papers as the *Boston Traveller, Providence Bulletin, Cincinnati Commercial Gazette,* and *Critic.*[8]

Sam was inured to this brand of criticism. He suggested to Webster on April 4, two days after the *Advertiser* endorsed the ban on *Huck Finn*, that "we may as well get the benefit of such advertising as can be drawn from it. So, if the idea seems good to you, add this new page—this 'Prefatory Remark,' & insert it right after the copyright page in all future editions":

> Huckleberry Finn is not an imaginary person. He still lives; or rather, *they* still live; for Huckleberry Finn is two persons in one—namely, the author's two uncles, the present editors of the *Boston Advertiser* & the *Springfield Republican*. In character, language, clothing, education, instinct, & origin, he is the painstakingly & truthfully drawn photograph & counterpart of these two gentlemen as they were in the time of their boyhood, forty years ago. The work has been most carefully & conscientiously done, & is exactly true to the originals, in even the minutest particulars, with but one exception, & that a trifling one: this boy's language has been toned down & softened, here & there, in deference to the taste of a more modern & fastidious day.

Sam countermanded the order the next day after Livy forbade publication of the remark.[9]

Several journals alleged that the Concord committee had effectively, if not deliberately, conspired to advertise the book. Among them were the *Boston Journal*, Boston *Commonwealth*, Washington *Critic*, *Hartford Courant*, and St. Louis *Post-Dispatch*. Sam savored the condemnations of the novel at precisely this point. "The Committee of the Public Library of Concord, Mass.," he wrote Charley Webster the day after the ban was announced, "have given us a rattling tip-top puff which will go into every paper in the country. They have expelled Huck from their library as 'trash and suitable only for the slums.' That will sell 25,000 copies for us sure." Put another way, the rude appeal of the Royal Nonesuch ("women and children not admitted") antici-pated the succès de scandale of *Huck Finn*.[10]

Predictably, of course, many critics were incensed by the interdict. Frank B. Sanborn, a Concord native, refused to "subscribe to the extreme censure" on *Huck Finn*—which, he insisted, was "no coarser than Mark Twain's books usually are." He argued, like many critics today, that the novel "should per-haps be left unread" by youngsters "but the mature in mind may read it." Joel Chandler Harris doubted that "the critics who have condemned the book" had read it: "It presents an almost artistically perfect picture of life and char-acter in the southwest, and it will be equally valuable to the historian and to the student of sociology." Harris also wrote to the editors of the *Critic*, in celebration of Sam's fiftieth or "jubilee" birthday in November 1885, that there was not "in our fictive literature a more wholesome book than 'Huck-leberry Finn'" because the reader learns in it lessons "of honesty, justice and mercy." Sam thanked Harris "particularly for the good word about Huck, that abused child of mine, who has had so much unfair mud flung at him." The *Sacramento Union* was matter-of-fact in its defense of the novel: it was "the most humorous" and "the most original" of all Sam's writings, "a popu-lar work in a vein of broad low comedy," and did not deserve the ignominy it had been allotted. The *San Francisco Chronicle*, likely again in the person of Fitch, mounted the most aggressive defense of the book, ridiculing its "ab-surd" banning in Concord. The library authorities had misunderstood Sam's intended audience, considering it a story "written for boys, whereas we ven-ture to say that upon nine boys out of ten much of the humor, as well as the pathos, would be lost." To "people who are impervious to a joke" the novel would seem "dreary, flat, stale and unprofitable. But for the great body of readers it will furnish much hearty, wholesome laughter." Even the evasion chapters made up "a well-sustained travesty of the escapes of great criminals" and "there is not a line in it which cannot be read by a pure-minded woman." Sam thoroughly approved of this editorial. As he wrote his sister Pamela in mid-April, two weeks after it appeared, "The Chronicle understands those idiots in Concord are not a court of last resort & I am not disturbed by their moral gymnastics. No other book of mine has sold so many copies within 2 months after issue as this one has done."[11]

Ironically, some critics mocked the Concordians for their fastidious-ness no less than others censured Sam for his vulgarity. In St. Louis, where the offices of the *Journal of Speculative Philosophy* were located and where its editor William T. Harris lived, the *Post-Dispatch* nevertheless snorted that with its ban on the novel Concord cemented its "reputation of being the home of speculative philosophy and of practical nonsense." The New York *Sun* grieved that "Concord has pampered its Oversoul at the expense of its understanding." The *Boston Globe* proposed that to prevent the Concord Library committeemen from proscribing his next book Sam should add "a little more whenceness of the hereafter among his nowness of the here" and the New York *World* argued that the novel already contained "no end of Henceness of the Which and Thingness of the Unknowable."[12]

Sam received many private compliments on the novel that never registered in the public debate, of course. The Hoosier poet James Whitcomb Riley wrote Sam a week after the release of the American edition that his writings featuring "real characters" speaking "varied dialects" had long "interested and delighted me." Much as he had congratulated Sam upon the publication of the first installment of "Old Times on the Mississippi" in 1875, John Hay expressed to him his delight in reading *Huck Finn* in 1885. Hay appreciated especially the documentary dimensions of Sam's writings. "Without them I should not know today the speech and the way of living with which I was familiar as a child," he mused. "Huck Finns and Tom Sawyers were my admired and trusted friends—though I had to cultivate them as the early Christians did their religion—in out of the way places. I am glad to meet them again in your luminous pages." In addition to reviewing the novel in the columns of the *Atlanta Constitution*, Joel Chandler Harris sent Sam a personal letter of congratulations, stressing that *Huck Finn* "will yet come to be recognized" as a realistic "picture of life and as a study in philology" and declaring it "the most original contribution that has yet been made to American literature." Robert Louis Stevenson wrote John Addington Symonds in February 1885 that the novel "contains many excellent things," above all the story "of a healthy boy's dealings with his conscience."[13]

As usual, Sam enjoyed the last laugh. In late March 1885 he was elected an honorary member of the Concord Free Trade Club. He surely interpreted the action of the free traders—presumably mugwumps, certainly not stalwart Republicans—as they intended it: as a critique of the restrictions placed on the "trade" or free exchange of his most recent book by their fellow townsmen on the library committee. Sam replied to his election in an open letter that Howells helped him compose and that was published behind enemy lines in the *Boston Advertiser* on April 2. He had recently been deluged with honors by the Village of Concord, he acknowledged, including one bestowed upon him by "a committee of the public library of your town," which had

> condemned and excommunicated my last book and doubled its sale. This generous action of theirs must necessarily benefit me in one or two additional ways. For instance, it will deter other libraries from buying the book; and you are doubtless aware that one book in a public library prevents the sale of a sure ten and a possible hundred of its mates. And secondly, it will cause the purchasers of the book to read it, out of curiosity, instead of merely intending to do so, after the usual way of the world and library committees, and then they will discover, to my great advantage and their own indignant disappointment, that there is nothing objectionable in the book after all.

Sam's honorary membership in the Free Trade Club of Concord, he averred, was "worth more than all the rest" of the awards granted him in Massachusetts "since it indorses [sic] me as worthy to associate with certain gentlemen whom even the moral icebergs of the Concord library committee are bound to respect."[14]

As usual, too, his humor was too subtle and nuanced for some of the chumps slouched in their editorial chairs. The *Springfield Republican* noted that Sam "carefully avoids defending himself from the criticism justly made upon his latest book and simply rejoices in the fact that he is going to make money out of it." He "ought to be ashamed of 'Huckleberry Finn,' but he boastfully declares that he is not" in his "extraordinary communication" to the Free Trade Club. The *Boston Globe* was no less obtuse in its response. Sam's letter proved that he could "return thanks for favors in a paragraph that has no object except to advertise himself." He had become merely "a walking sign, a literary sandwich, placarded all over with advertisements of his wares." Those who refused to join him on his ego trip "are made objects of ridicule. His letter to the Free Trade Club is the latest effort in this direction."[15]

Adventures of Huckleberry Finn became a commercial success and an American classic only after weathering a series of critical storms. Banned in Concord and Worcester in 1885, it was removed from the library of Jane Addams's Hull House in Chicago and public libraries in Denver and Omaha in 1902, Des Moines in 1904, and Brooklyn in 1906. In 1907 Sam joked that "when a Library expels a book of mine and leaves an unexpurgated Bible lying around where people can get hold of it, the unconscious irony delights me."[16] *Huck Finn* became "the only one of my own books that I can ever read with pleasure," he told an interviewer in 1891, "because I know the dialect is true and good." In another interview in 1896 he said, "Long after it had been wholly erased from the pages of my memory, I took it up and read it to my daughter [Jean], who was ill. It was new to her; it was new to me." After the turn of the twentieth century, readers were no longer obliged to apologize for Sam's (or Huck's) (mis)behavior. In 1902 Sam bragged that "Huck's morals have stood the strain in every English, German, and French-speaking community in the world for seventeen years." Booker T. Washington asserted that no one could read *Huck Finn* closely "without becoming aware of" the author's "deep sympathy" for Jim. Sam learned in 1907 that the socialist William Morris "was an incurable Huckfinomaniac." The curmudgeonly H. L. Mencken weighed the novel on a critical scale in 1909 and declared that it was worth "the complete works of Poe, Hawthorne, Cooper, Holmes, Howells and James with the entire literary output to date of Indiana, Pennsylvania, and all the States south of the Potomac thrown in." He later described it as "perhaps the greatest novel ever written in English" and Sam as "the true father of our national literature." The comment anticipates Ernest Hemingway's famous assertion in *Green Hills of Africa* (1935) that "all modern American literature comes from one book by Mark Twain called *Huckleberry Finn.* . . . [I]t's the best book we've had. . . . There was nothing before. There has been nothing as good since."[17]

Grant had been preparing his memoirs long before contracting with Webster and Company to publish them, and he delivered the manuscript of volume 1 to the press in mid-March 1885. His cancer was already advanced, however, and he was only able to write in fits and starts for a half hour at a time. The general was "failing steadily & the disease is incurable," Sam wrote Andrew Chatto on March 11. Nevertheless, Webster's army of book agents—they would eventually number nine thousand—had begun their canvass immediately and, with subscriptions in Iowa and Michigan for twenty thousand sets, production of the first volume began in April, with Webster contracting with J. J. Little and Company of New York for the printing. Webster predicted that the memoirs would "outsell any book ever issued save the bible and Shakespeare" and Sam forecast that "the sale will exceed that of any book that has ever been published in America." They were both right. The book agents were instructed to foster the impression that Grant received all profits from sales and by May 1 subscribers had ordered sixty thousand sets. Sam predicted that sales in the United States and Europe by the end of the canvass would total about five hundred thousand and he was not far wrong. He was so confident in the success of the venture that he borrowed two hundred thousand dollars, half of it from Samuel Dunham, a Hartford businessman, to finance production and distribution. The debt was "a mighty load," Sam admitted to Howells in October 1885, before "the relief money" began to arrive. "From now till the first of January every dollar is as valuable to me as it could be to a famishing tramp." But Sam's gamble was also publicly applauded. He "had to risk his entire fortune in the enterprise," the *Pall Mall Gazette* reported, "but he pluckily refused to shirk the chances of loss."[18]

Sam was a frequent guest in Grant's home during the final months of the general's life. During one of the first of these visits, on March 20, he was accompanied by Karl Gerhardt, who had sculpted a small clay bust of Grant from a photograph. Grant's family, especially his wife Julia, was impressed and, in the general's presence, Gerhardt finished it in a single sitting. As Sam observed in his autobiography, "To my mind this bust has in it more of General Grant than can be found in any other likeness of him that has ever been made since he was a famous man. I think it may rightly be called the best portrait of General Grant that is in existence." More to the point, Sam soon contracted with the family to sell reproductions of the bust in both terra-cotta and bronze through the Grand Army of the Republic's veterans association. On March 23 he arranged for the Hartford firm reproducing the bust to "pay Gerhard[t] 65 or 70 per cent of the profit" on every one sold, a royalty apparently to be shared with the Grants. Sam also insisted on maintaining a sharp distinction between the two concerns, "the book agencies & the bust agencies." Unfortunately, the rumor soon circulated that Grant's family was colluding with Sam to profit from the general's illness. The *Albany Journal*, for example, avowed that "Grant did not at first like to have his bust put out in that manner, but the counsel of his wife prevailed. She is a woman of far greater force and potency in her family than is generally imagined. The bust venture is her own affair in connection with Twain." Sam was quick to deny the report, though not entirely convincingly, claiming that "neither Mrs. Grant nor any other member of Gen. Grant's family has any pecuniary interest in [the enterprise] whatever—not a single farthing's worth." But why would the Grant family, especially the general, agree to cooperate if only the sculptor profited? In any event, the busts, especially those in bronze, were financial failures. Lamentably, Sam was also quoted by an interviewer in early April in a way that made him seem like a money-grubber callous to Grant's suffering. The general "is not going to live long; his race is run" and "there is no escape from his disease," he reportedly said. "Were he to be spared to live, his book" would be popular, "but his death will increase that demand tenfold."[19]

Sam was certainly attentive to Grant's condition in late March and April, when the general suffered a health crisis and nearly died. Sam was the only visitor admitted to the house on Sixty-Sixth Street in New York on March 26 and he returned on March 30 and 31, though he apparently was not admitted to the general's bedroom. "I am here on a whole raft of business," he insisted to Brander Matthews, "& people will be coming to me all day by appointment to get themselves swindled," but in truth he was in the city to monitor Grant's condition and his progress on his memoirs. He returned again on April 8 and had a "friendly chat" with Grant's son Fred but again "did not see the general." The next day Sam "held a hasty conversation" with Fred Grant and told reporters as he was leaving that "the General had passed a very restful afternoon." In order to camouflage his ownership of Webster and Company—and thus his fiduciary interest in the general's health—he publicly maintained the polite fiction that this visit was "a personal errand" undertaken "as a friend of Mr. Webster, who is General Grant's publisher." He was the first caller at the house on April 19 and as he departed he again told those on death watch in the street that "the General was feeling very well." Two days later he visited the house in the morning and "had a long talk with the General," who had by this time obviously passed the crisis.[20]

Then occurred a predicament of another sort. On April 29 the New York *World* printed an item, no doubt planted by Grant's aide Brevet-General Adam Badeau that Badeau was in fact the ghostwriter of Grant's memoirs and Grant was merely supervising his work. As the *World* alleged, "Grant has furnished all of the material and all of the ideas in the memoirs, but Badeau has done the work of composition. The most the General has done upon the book has been to prepare the rough notes and memoranda for its various chapters." In truth, Badeau was Grant's research assistant on the project and he was paid $5,000 for his help, but he doubled the ante, demanding half of the first $20,000 in royalties to continue his work. It was a blatant attempt at extortion: he was in no sense the author of Grant's autobiography. That is, Badeau was attempting to shake down the family and the general rose to the challenge. Grant published an open letter in the *World* denying that Badeau had written any part of his memoirs and repeatedly stating, "The composition is entirely my own." After Grant's death Badeau nevertheless sued the family for breach of contract and demanded an additional $10,000 in compensation for services rendered. Julia Grant offered $8,000 to resolve the dispute but Badeau refused to compromise. Eventually, on October 31, 1888, Grant's widow paid Badeau $11,254 to settle the nuisance suit. Meanwhile, Sam tried to mollify Badeau by contracting with him on January 25, 1887, to publish his book *Grant in Peace* and pay him a 10 percent royalty or thirty cents per copy sold. Then Webster attempted to amend the contract with a codicil specifying that "nothing objectional to Mrs. Grant should appear in the work," thus proposing to permit the defendant in Badeau's suit the right to approve everything the plaintiff wrote in his book. When Badeau balked at the codicil, Webster refused to publish *Grant in Peace*, whereupon in March 1889 Badeau sued Webster for $22,500 for breach of contract.[21] They settled out of court and Badeau eventually published his book with a rival press.

Coincidentally, Sam was visiting New York when the *World* broke the story that Grant was not the author of his autobiography. Upon arriving in the city, according to Susy Clemens, her father "went right up to Gen. Grants from the station" while she and her mother remained at Everett House. That evening the three of them attended a performance of the burlesque musical *Adonis* at the Bijou Theater and the next morning, while Livy shopped, Sam, Susy, and James Pond went to the Westminster Dog Show at Madison Square Garden and crossed the new Brooklyn Bridge via trolley. Afterward Sam and Susy visited Grant, who was, according to Sam, "looking and feeling far better than he had looked or felt for some months." He worked on his memoirs that weekend, "the first time he had done any work for perhaps a month." Sam was, of course, outraged by Badeau's "intrepid lie" in the *World* that day, as he described it to Fred Grant. He urged the family to file a libel suit "at once; damages placed at nothing less than $250,000 or $300,000; no apologies accepted from the World, & no compromise permitted for anything but a sum of money that will cripple—yes, *disable*—that paper financially. The suit ought to be brought in the general's name & the expense of it paid out of the book's general expense account." By May 3 Sam had reconsidered his advice to the Grants to sue the *World*. The false story had not been copied in any newspaper, as far as Sam could tell, and so it apparently "fell dead & did no harm." A libel suit "would be a waste of energy & money" and serve merely as an "advertisement for that daily issue of unmedicated closet-paper," he allowed to Charley Webster.[22]

Sam was "right glad to see" in May 1885 that Grant and Webster had forged a cordial working relationship and that his nephew had "tackled the vastest book-enterprise the world has ever seen with a calm cool head & capable hand." Or as Sam remarked to William Tecumseh Sherman, Webster had exhibited "much the best generalship I have ever seen" in steering Grant's memoirs through the press. Sam was "astonished" when he examined the manuscript of the first volume and "said that there was not one literary man in one hundred who furnished as clean a copy as Grant." After completing the first volume of the memoirs, however, Grant "did not feel equal to the task of completing the work" so Webster recommended that the general dictate to a stenographer "an account of the surrender of Lee at Appomattox. He demurred at first, saying that he never had dictated a letter in his life." But Webster persisted. He agreed to accompany the stenographer to Grant's house every day, "remain while the general dictated for about two hours," then deliver a transcript of his remarks back to Grant to be edited. At Grant's first sitting he dictated nine thousand words, some "50 pages of foolscap" about the wilderness and Appomattox, "never pausing, never hesitating for a word, never repeating," belying the claim in the *World* that he was too ill to continue work on his memoirs. In late May, Grant "dictated 10,000 words at a single sitting, & he a sick man!" Sam marveled. "It kills me these days to do half of it!" Sam also noted with regret that he too often engaged in small talk or "cheerful nonsense" with Grant while the general was "under sentence of death with that cancer. He says he has made the book too large by 200 pages—not a bad fault—a short time ago we were afraid we would *lack* 400 of being enough." A few weeks before his death, Grant lost his voice and halted his dictation. As Sam wrote Henry Ward Beecher, he "was not quite done yet, however:—there was no end of little plums & spices to be stuck in, here & there; & this work he patiently continued, a few lines a day, with pad & pencil, till far into July."[23]

In late spring Grant's health had so deteriorated—his weight had dropped below 125 pounds—that his physicians urged him to escape the city for the summer. On June 16 the Grants moved into a bungalow owned by the banker and philanthropist Joseph W. Drexel adjacent to the Balmoral Hotel on Mount McGregor, a summer resort in the Adirondacks twelve miles north of Saratoga Springs, New York. The general summoned Sam to the resort by telegraph on June 27—less than a week after the Clemens family arrived in Elmira for the summer—for what would be a final visit and, after an all-day journey, he arrived after dark on June 29. Grant's family was "all full of apprehensions with regard to the General; & I think that from what I hear the apprehensions are just," he wrote Livy, "yet the General is as placid, serene, & self-possessed as ever, & his eye has the same old humorous twinkle in it, & his frequent smile is still the smile of pleasantness & peace. Manifestly, dying is nothing to a really great & brave man." Sam stayed at the Worden Hotel in Saratoga Springs and rode in a buggy an hour each way to the bungalow for a couple of days. Grant's granddaughter Julia remembered that Sam with his frowzled hair and strict mien "frightened me dreadfully." Once, she noted, "he came upon me in the garden where I was playing and as he spoke to me I turned" and "fled screaming to the cottage-door without replying." Though the general was unable to speak above a whisper, Sam thought "he would live several months. He was still adding little perfecting details to his book—a preface, among other things." Sam even found time for a little sightseeing between visits with Grant. The view from the mountain—"wide & level, & green, & checkered with farms & splotched with groves like cushions of moss"—reminded him of the panorama of the Rhine valley from the Schloss-Hotel in Heidelberg.[24]

Grant "made no braver fight in the field than he made on his death-bed," Sam averred. The general finished polishing the manuscript of his memoirs on July 19 and died five days later.[25]

On board a train in Binghamton, New York, Sam learned the news two hours after Grant's death. "I think his book kept him alive several months," he observed in his journal. "He was a very great man—& superlatively good." In an elegiac tribute to the general he penned that day for the *Hartford Courant*, Sam quoted Thomas Malory's *Le Morte d'Arthur* (1485), comparing Grant to Sir Lancelot, "the flower of Christian Chivalry, the knight without a peer," citing a passage in his honor "whose noble and simple eloquence had not its equal in English literature until the Gettysburg Speech took its lofty place beside it": "thou were the kindest man that ever strake with sword" and "thou were the sternest knight to thy mortal foe that ever put spear in the rest."[26]

Lamentably, Grant's death precipitated a number of internecine disputes during the ensuing months. With Sam's encouragement, if not at his suggestion, the family commissioned Gerhardt to cast a death mask. Sam subscribed five hundred dollars for this purpose soon after visiting the general for the last time, though he pledged Gerhardt to secrecy. He wanted to deny "the shabbier half of the world a chance to say General Grant's publisher is craftily trying to advertise himself." But on July 18, apparently at the suggestion of the family, Sam also cautioned Gerhardt, who hovered over the cottage like a vulture over carrion, to avoid all appearance of impropriety. "You are in danger of wearing out your welcome" with the Grants, he admonished the sculptor. "Now *don't* let that happen. . . . The General sick all these months, the family distressed, worried—a stranger present whose projects are of a sort to get into print & add to the worry—don't you see, it is a most easy thing for you to become a burden & one too many." Nevertheless, Gerhardt quarreled with the Grants immediately after the general's death over ownership of the mask. Gerhardt deposited it in a vault in New York, in effect holding it for ransom. Fred Grant threatened to sue him and Julia Grant offered to pay for it, but as Sam explained to Charley Webster, "his price is too high." Sam wanted Gerhardt simply to present the mask to the Grants and to avoid at all costs the "degrading scandal" of a court battle that would drag Grant's name "out of the rest & peace of the grave." Sam finally struck on a solution: he had loaned Gerhardt nine or ten thousand dollars over the years and cosigned notes for eight thousand more—"seventeen or eighteen thousand altogether; a sum which he cannot expect to pay me for years, if he loses the mask." He proposed that Gerhardt "hand over the mask to Mrs. Grant & I will give him a receipt in full for all he owes me & assume also the payment of the outstanding obligations." On December 21, 1885, the artist presented the mask to Julia Grant. The Grant family would not learn until eleven years later, however, that Gerhardt kept a duplicate.[27] Gerhardt enjoyed a modest career through the end of the 1880s, when his commissions evaporated. In later years he worked as a bartender in the French Quarter in New Orleans, and he died in rural Louisiana in 1940.[28]

On August 6, 1885, Sam visited the Grant family at the Fifth Avenue Hotel, where he crossed paths with former president Rutherford B. Hayes; Phil Sheridan; William Tecumseh Sherman and his brother, Senator John Sherman of Ohio; and Stewart Van Vliet. Later, at the Lotos Club on Fortieth Street at Fifth Avenue, he "talked army life & anecdotes & Grant & the war" with Generals Sherman and Van Vliet "for an hour, over whisky & cigars, & had a very good time." Sherman "spoke in terms of prodigious praise of Gen. Grant's military genius," Sam noted in his journal. Two days later, from the office of Webster and Company on Union Square and then from the Lotos Club headquarters on Fifth Avenue, Sam observed Grant's five-hour-long "very grand & impressive" funeral cortege and the procession of tens of thousands of Civil War veterans marching along Broadway to city hall. Grant's burial site became an issue after his death—a contest among cities competing for what would undoubtedly become a tourist site—and Sam joined the debate over where his body should be interred. The most frequently mentioned contenders were New York City and Washington, D.C., with a riptide of public sentiment favoring the national capital. But, Sam interjected, "we should select a grave which will not merely be in the right place now but will still be in the right place 500 years from now." He feared that "a century hence" Washington would no longer be the seat of government, whereas "as long as American civilization lasts New York will last. I cannot but think she has been well and wisely chosen as the guardian of a grave which is destined to become almost the most conspicuous in the world's history. Twenty centuries from now New York will still be New York, still a vast city, and the most notable object in it will still be the tomb and monument of Gen. Grant."[29] While his argument may have influenced the decision to build Grant's Tomb in Riverside Park in Manhattan, he was, to be fair, a more accurate prophet of sales of Grant's autobiography than of Grant's place in American history.

Webster and Company published the first volume of Grant's memoirs on December 1, 1885, and the second on May 10, 1886, to great critical acclaim and commercial success. By October 1, 1885, two and a half months before volume 1 was issued, the company reported that over 250,000 sets had been sold; three weeks later that number climbed to over 300,000 sets. By the end of the month, Sam gleefully noted, twenty steam presses were "going night & day" and "if we could get 37, we could print a complete volume every second." By December 1, eight binders were in production on the work, nearly a thousand tons of paper had been used in printing, 200,000 copies of volume 1 had been shipped, and Sam anticipated that by December 10 another 125,000 would be mailed. By the end of production, according to Sam, over thirty-five thousand sheep-, goat-, and calfskins; over twenty-five miles of cloth a yard wide, and sixty-nine thousand pounds of paste were used to bind the book "& the gold-leaf on the backs of the books cost $21,639."[30]

In all, some 350,000 sets were sold, a figure that represents purchases by about 3 percent of all Americans. Sam paid Grant's heirs over $450,000 in royalties, including checks to Julia Grant for $200,000 on February 27, 1886, and $150,000 on October 11, 1886—the most money paid for a single book in literary history to that date. Webster and Company earned about $100,000 in profits. But after receiving the first $361,000, the Grant family and Fred Grant in particular claimed to have been shortchanged by Webster and Company in the amount of $104,000 based on an audit by his accountant of the company ledgers. Ironically, much as Sam had indicted Elisha Bliss for inflating production costs on several of his books in order to reduce the royalties he was owed, Fred Grant on July 22, 1887, contested Webster's inclusion of legal expenses among production costs of the *Personal Memoirs* and threatened to sue. That is, Grant accused Webster and Company of cheating on royalties in exactly the same way that Sam had accused the American Publishing Company of cheating him. The parties eventually resolved their differences, the company paying the Grants most of the money they believed they were owed.[31]

Much as he took credit for the unexpectedly large sales of *Huck Finn*, Sam claimed to have engineered the sensational sales of Grant's memoirs. "What I hate as much as anything is to have the public regard me as unwise in business," he told the New York *World* in 1898, three years after he declared personal bankruptcy. "I consider that the contrary was proved by the way I published General Grant's book in 1885, which could not have been done by a bad businessman." Sam on occasion cherished his reputation for ruthlessness. The *San Francisco Chronicle* alerted its readers in June 1885 that he had managed the publication of Grant's memoirs with remarkable shrewdness and estimated his net worth at $425,000. In May 1886 *Theatre* magazine pronounced him "a clever, sagacious, hard-headed man of business" who "seldom makes a blunder in trade" and who "will soon be one of the richest publishers in America." Such comments, he chortled, "will eventually convince everybody that I am the shrewdest, craftiest & most unscrupulous business-sharp in the country & now that I am become a publisher that is the kind of reputation I need." But he was equally proud of the literary quality of Grant's memoirs, which he considered "a great, unique and unapproachable literary masterpiece. There is no higher literature than these modest, simple Memoirs. Their style is at least flawless, and no man can improve upon it."[32]

To build on the success of Grant's autobiography, Sam proposed to Webster that they issue a uniformly bound Great War Library series of Civil War memoirs and related books by and about Samuel W. Crawford, Winfield Scott Hancock, George B. McClellan, Phil Sheridan, William Tecumseh Sherman, and other generals. In addition to his proposal to publish Adam Badeau's *Grant in Peace*, Sam considered an overture for a biography of Grant from Grant's son Fred that would begin "where the Autobiography left off" and end with his death. Webster was unable to lock down the project, however. "I have offered Col Grant ½ profits on his book up to 50,000 and if it sold more than 50,000 to give him 60% of the profits," he notified Sam in late October 1885, but the younger Grant "was not pleased with the offer [and] said he had had a better offer from other publishers than we gave on the Gen[era]l's book." Fred Grant's biography of his father never appeared. The son also floated the possibility of publishing General Grant's diary of his round-the-world trip in the *North American Review*, a report Sam disputed in an unsent letter to the editor of the New York *Sun* signed with the pseudonym "D. Wahrheit" (or *Die Wahrheit*, "the truth"): "people who expect to see that Diary in the North American Review within the next three years can make up their minds that they are going to be disappointed." Sam also considered Julia Grant's proposal to edit a collection of her forty-year correspondence with the general, though Jesse Grant insisted on a partnership share in Webster and Company as a condition of its publication—another bald-faced attempt at extortion—though nothing came of this idea either. In fact, Webster and Company failed to earn a significant profit on any other war book. By the fall of 1888 the market for these works had been exhausted like an overplanted field. Sam suggested to Webster as early as February 1886 that they postpone the publication of Julia Grant's edition of the letters for a year to "let the Grant-feeling recuperate & get new life."[33] Her edition of the correspondence never appeared and although she later wrote an autobiography it was not published during her life.

In fact, the only books of the eighty-eight published by Webster and Company that earned significant profits were the first two: *Huck Finn* and

Grant's *Memoirs*. Sam became a victim of their success, convinced that he had an intuitive sense of what would sell. Rather than rely on any kind of market research, he selected books for publication on the basis of his hunches and the favors he granted to friends. Or as Howells observed, the profit he earned on *Huck Finn* and Grant's autobiography "tempted him to launch on publishing seas where his bark presently foundered." Webster and Company published *McClellan's Own Story* in 1886, Charley Webster reported to Sam in December that it was "selling well," and it apparently earned a small profit, but Sam privately disparaged its author, who had been removed by Lincoln as general in chief of the U.S. Army in November 1862 after the Battle of Antietam. He wrote Livy in July 1887 that Prince Metternich's memoirs, which he was reading at the time, "removed the obloquy from his name," but McClellan's story "deepens that upon *his* & justifies it." In August 1886 Sam was eager to publish Phil Sheridan's two-volume *Personal Memoirs* and in May 1888 he told a reporter that "the publication of Sheridan's memoirs will prove almost as important a contribution to history and to literature as General Grant's" but Fred Hall, Webster's successor as manager of the company, admitted in October that the company would need "to hustle everlastingly to get rid of 75,000 sets of Sheridan." Webster and Company took a flyer on *Tenting on the Plains* (1887) by Elizabeth Custer, the widow of George Armstrong Custer, but it did little better than break even.[34]

Years later, as the company was careening toward bankruptcy and Sam was frantically trying to salvage what remained of his personal fortune, he described Grant's memoirs as "that terrible book which made money for everybody concerned but me." The enormous amounts of cash that were at stake in the immediate aftermath of its publication spawned numerous disputes, some of which ballooned into court cases. In essentially a replay of the litigation against Estes & Lauriat for selling *Huck Finn* at a reduced price, Webster and Company sued the Philadelphia department store magnate John Wanamaker for marketing five hundred sets of Grant's autobiography at a discount. Wanamaker advertised the memoirs in the Philadelphia *Press* for May 15, 1886, with a statement critical of Webster's subscription method of selling it: "We fully believe that the family of General Grant is a loser through the restrictions put on the sale of his book. Of course the people are losers; the book-stores are losers. And who are the gainers? Book-pedlers and book-pedler publishers; nobody else. We are doing what we can to repair the mischief. If the book had been published to suit the market, we believe a million copies of it might have been sold." Four days later, Wanamaker increased its price for a clothbound set to $5.50 with an apology: "Wish we could make them lower. Could, but for the unfortunate manner of publication." Sam was so miffed by the effort to undersell him that he urged

Webster to file suit against Wanamaker, the founder of the Bethany Sunday School in 1858—"otherwise I will go down there & rise up in his Sunday School & give him hell in front of his whole 3000 pupils." He was particularly offended by the sanctimony exhibited by Wanamaker, "that pious son of a dog" and "uncopious butter-mouthed Sunday school slobbering sneak-thief." The suit went to trial on August 4 before Judge William Butler of the U.S. Circuit Court in Philadelphia and Sam attended the proceedings. As in the Estes & Lauriat case, Webster's lawyers contended that Wanamaker had bought the book "by some means unknown and sold it at the store for a sum less than the subscription rate." As in the Estes & Lauriat case, the judge denied Webster's motion for an injunction to restrain sales of the book on the grounds that Wanamaker had no privity of contract to bind sales. Sam groused that the department store magnate "wouldn't be satisfied if he had the contract to furnish hell with fuel!"[35]

In order to expedite production of Grant's memoirs, moreover, Charley Webster outsourced to other shops some of the printing assigned to J. J. Little and Company. In consequence, Little sued for breach of contract and, although he offered to settle his claim for $800 and company lawyer Whitford advised Webster to accept the deal, he refused. Little received a judgment for nearly two thousand dollars plus interest in June 1887 and Webster appealed the decision. "I think we would have won the suit had Mr. Webster's testimony been a little different," Fred Hall admitted to Sam, but on the witness stand Charley "talked more than was required." After losing the appeal, rather than blame Webster for failing to settle at the outset, Sam faulted Whitford: "He is simply a damned fool—in Court—and will infallibly lose every suit you put into his hands." In early 1891 Webster and Company finally paid Little almost $3,000, including accumulated interest, to satisfy the judgment.[36]

In four other cases, however, Webster and Company was successful in pressing suits against subscription agents who violated their contracts. On June 1, 1886, the company charged Adolph W. Berg with larceny in Tombs Police Court in New York. Berg had submitted false names of thirty-seven subscribers and in turn sold the volumes to bookstores, including Brentano's in Union Square. Joseph M. Stoddart Co., the agent for the Carolinas, the District of Columbia, Maryland, and the Virginias, defaulted on payments totaling $12,624 and Webster obtained a judgment for $13,200 on April 12, 1887. The Hubbard Brothers, agents for Delaware, New Jersey, eastern New York, and Pennsylvania, were successfully sued by Webster, who was awarded $31,799 and eventually settled out of court for $25,000 "in cash and property." R. T. Root, the agent for Iowa, similarly defaulted on a debt of about $31,000 and offered to settle in June 1888 for $8,000. In the end, Webster collected from Root only about $9,000, most of which was paid to Julia Grant.[37]

Sam was so enthralled by the prospects for Civil War literature in the spring of 1885, when Grant was completing his autobiography, that he briefly considered writing a story featuring "Huck & Tom & Jim" set during his own "M[iss]o[uri] campaign" with the Marion County Rangers in 1861. The tale would include a scene in which a "Union officer accosts Tom & says his name is U.S. Grant." Instead, Robert Underwood Johnson in March 1885 commissioned Sam to "write out your experiences in the Rebel Army" for the Battles and Leaders of the Civil War essay series in the *Century*. Johnson reiterated the request in May that Sam submit a "little article on your experiences in the Rebel Army, making it, as far as possible, characteristic of the state of things in Missouri early in the war." Sam enlisted in the project even more enthusiastically than he had joined the Rangers. "I would like mighty well to be in the Century war series," he replied to Johnson's invitation. "The fact is, the War Series is the greatest thing of these modern times & nobody who is anybody can well afford to be unrepresented in it." The series, which featured an article per issue between November 1884 and November 1887, was a sales bonanza, increasing circulation of the *Century* from 127,000 to 225,000 copies per month. The four-volume collection of these essays, issued by the Century Company in 1887–88, quickly became a standard reference work about the war—one of the sources, for example, that Stephen Crane consulted while writing *The Red Badge of Courage* (1896). At one point, Sam harbored the vain hope that he might convince Johnson to publish "the Century's warbook" by subscription with Webster and Company—another indication he had not burned his bridges with the Century Company during his negotiations for Grant's memoirs. In any case, when Sam's offbeat manuscript landed on Johnson's desk in November 1885, he thanked Sam for sending the "excellent—'roarious" piece.[38]

Sam's purpose in writing "The Private History of a Campaign That Failed"—the working title was "My Campaign against Grant"—was twofold: both to tap into the popular fascination with war stories and to erect a buffer around his brief service in a Confederate militia. He had tried to protect his reputation in October 1877 with his speech for the Hartford Putnam Phalanx of the Ancient and Honorable Artillery Company of Boston published under the title "Mark Twain's War Experiences." He never attended a reunion of Southern soldiers and in 1881 he even contributed ten dollars to a fund to assist the widow of the martyred abolitionist John Brown. But during his tour of the Mississippi Valley with James Osgood in the spring of 1882 he was, according to a news item widely copied around the country, welcomed "down south as a patriot" who had served in the rebel army "under General Sterling Price. This is a bit of an episode in Mr. Twain's career upon which he has not expatiated lovingly to his northern friends." By early 1885, while on "the lecturing war-path" with George Washington Cable and especially after contracting with Grant for his memoirs, Sam became an inviting target of both Union loyalists for his service in a Confederate militia and unreconstructed rebels for his desertion from a Confederate militia. On January 17, two days after Sam left Keokuk, while on tour with Cable, the *Gate City* printed an unsigned account of his war experience, concluding that he had "quit the [Confederate] army" because he could no longer ride a mule and so "because of a mule" the South lost "a valiant soldier." In March 1885, incredibly, the rumor began to circulate that Sam, as one of William Quantrill's raiders, had even participated in the massacre of civilians in Lawrence, Kansas, in August 1863—drivel so outrageous that Sam did not bother to deny it. Then in July 1885, only days before Grant's death, he was notified by a letter mistakenly sent to him rather than to Samuel Clements of Elma, New York, that he was entitled to a military pension. In his response, he joked that he had "often wanted a pension" but because "the only military service I performed during the war was in the Confederate army, I have always felt a delicacy about asking" for it. He would admit to serving in a Confederate militia, as Jerome Loving notes, but only if "he made it funny." At the same time, Neil Schmitz contends, "he had, in some way, to report his Civil War experience, to answer their implicit question": What did he do in the war? Or more specifically, why was a former Confederate militiaman exploiting for profit General Grant and his family? The St. Louis *Post-Dispatch* stated the problem bluntly: "The Grant Memoirs continue to have a phenomenal sale despite the fact that they are published by an ex-Confederate soldier."[39]

In "The Private History" Sam answered the questions about his military experience that occasionally erupted into print, albeit with more fiction than fact. As Arthur G. Pettit bluntly states, the essay is Sam's apology for his "brief flirtation with treason." In a sense, the essay parodies the other articles in the Battles and Leaders series by such distinguished commanders as Grant, Joe Johnston, James Longstreet, and George Meade, and it was the only piece in the series that was not subsequently reprinted in the compilation of *Century* essays because it was too obviously fictionalized. Sam even proposed to Robert Underwood Johnson that he "put it into the book and leave it out of the magazine," in which case "I will sell it to you for two dollars; and if you crowd me I will take less. I think its defects might be lost in the smoke and thunder of the big guns all around it in the book; but in the narrower and peacefuller field of the magazine I think myself it will look like mighty poor weak stuff." As he wrote James Redpath four days after submitting the manuscript of "The Private History" to Johnson, moreover, it was the only article "I mean to publish over my signature for at least a year."[40]

Sam's version of events in his comic apologia resembles nothing so much as another adventure of Tom Sawyer's gang, though he had been twenty-five years old when he soldiered. The enlistees or "the boys" equate bivouacking with camping out like Tom, Huck, and Joe Harper on Jackson's Island. In this deromanticizing or comic deflation of war, the "first hour was all fun" when half the troop went swimming and the other half fishing. To this point, "The Private History" is not a war story but a tale of boys at play. Mason's Farm, where the boys take an oath of allegiance, is yet another redaction of Patsy and John Quarles's farm, the model for the Phelps farm in *Huck Finn*. Sam sleeps in a corn crib swarming with rats in Mason's barn much as Jim is confined in an ash-hopper swarming with rats at the Phelps farm. "The Private History" was also illustrated for the *Century* by E. W. Kemble, the same artist who illustrated *Huck Finn*. The Rangers express no opinions about the cause of the war and the essay omits all mention of slavery. To be sure, "The Private History" ends on a pathetic note, an imaginary account of the boys' murder of a stranger they mistake for a Union spy and the author's heavy-handed moral to the story: "I was not rightly equipped for this awful business; that war was intended for men and I for a child's nurse. I resolved to retire from this avocation of sham soldiership while I could save some remnant of my self-respect." The disillusioned Sam then lights out from the war much as Huck escapes to the Territory—and, ironically, much as Natty Bumppo flees to the West on the last page of *The Pioneers* (1823) by Sam's bête noire James Fenimore Cooper.[41]

Howells, for one, enjoyed the essay. "I read your piece about the unsuccessful campaign with the greatest delight," he wrote Sam. "It was immensely amusing, with such a bloody bit of heartache in it, too." The *Bangor Whig and Courier* ("perfect type of a satirical war paper"), *Kansas City Times* ("the most agreeable specimen of that sort of literature that has appeared"), and *Memphis Appeal* ("has a special appeal as showing the fluctuations of opinion at the breaking out of the war and the entirely amateur character of some of the early campaigns") all commended the essay. But on the whole it seemed to stir as much controversy as it stilled. The *Boston Herald*, *Chicago Tribune*, *Washington Post*, and other papers remarked on "the fact, heretofore not generally known," that Sam had been "a rebel guerilla in Missouri early in the Civil War." The *Boston Advertiser* similarly noted that some "Eastern literary papers" had only "just discovered that Mark Twain" had been "a rebel bushwhacker"—an item that was reprinted around the world.[42]

For the first time in years, Sam wrote almost nothing for publication during the summer of 1885. The family arrived in Elmira on June 19 and stayed at the mansion on Main Street with Livy's mother until June 27, when they drove to Quarry Farm with two wagonloads of luggage. The Cranes had built a playhouse on the lawn that the girls named Ellerslie after the home of the hero in Jane Porter's *Scottish Chiefs* (1810). A precocious student, Susy read Friedrich Schiller's tragedy about Joan of Arc, *Die Jungfrau von Orleans* (1801), aloud in the original German to her mother that summer. On his part, Sam played lawn tennis and croquet with his daughters and read modern fiction, though often to his displeasure. "I can't stand Geo Eliot & Hawthorne & those people; I see what they are at a hundred years before they get to it, & they just tire me to death," he admitted to Howells. He had "dragged through three chapters" of Eliot's *Daniel Deronda* (1876), "losing flesh all the time, & then was honest enough to quit." Nor could he tolerate Thomas Hardy's "haggard, hideous" *Far from the Madding Crowd* (1874). He pondered several projects, including "an essay on wit and humor" and a couple of Huck and Tom sequels, including one set on a Mississippi steamboat in which Huck, Tom, and Jim's deaf daughter sail down the river to New Orleans and another in which Mother Goose, Hans Brinker, Tom Bailey, Mowgli the Jungle Boy, the Prince and the Pauper, and Tom and Huck all appear together. He also considered editing a series of books for Webster and Company on "Picturesque Incidents in History & Tradition"—he offered to publish a contribution to it by his nephew Sam Moffett to it—though nothing came of any of these ideas.[43]

A loving father but not a patient or doting one, Sam often delegated his parental duties to Livy and a succession of governesses and, as they grew older, to boarding schools and sanitariums. But not always. Nor was he as uninvolved in disciplining them as he sometimes pretended. Sam was well known for his "hair-trigger temper" in his family circle no less than in his social circle. Upon meeting Sam in 1882 the editor of the Marlborough, Massachusetts, *Times* remarked that "below his necktie Mr. Twain is as personable a man as any. The terror is all above his neck." As his daughter Clara remembered, "Every member of our family was provided with a healthy temper but none of us possessed one comparable to the regal proportions of Father's. When his escaped into the open, it was a grand sight," though she hastened to add that her father "almost never permitted his wrath to rise toward my mother." The same cannot be said about his wrath toward his daughters. Susy was, even as an infant, "addicted to sudden and raging tempests of passion," Sam wrote. When she was only three and a half years old, he remembered in 1876, he and Livy "resorted to flogging. Since that day there has never been a better child. We had to whip her once a day, at first; then three times a week; then twice, then once a week; then twice a month. She is nearly 4½ years old now & I have only touched her once in the last 3 months. 'Spare the rod & spoil the child' was well said—& not by an amateur." In January 1877 Sam noted in his journal, Clara "got what may be called about her first thrashing," and a year and a half later, six days before her fourth birthday, he wrote Susan Crane that he "thrashed the Bay today for tramping on the grass in a gentleman's grounds. But I only had my trouble for my pains; she was thinking about something else & did not know when I was through." When Jean was only 2½, Sam "gave her a lecture about some bad behavior and then spanked her. The result was disastrous" so "I whipped her again, after vainly trying to get her to say 'Please'" and eventually "whipped her a third time."[44]

Sam hid his role as family disciplinarian, however, in an essay he composed at Quarry Farm during the summer of 1885 and published in the *Christian Union* for July 16. A month earlier the editors of the paper had printed a piece about a two-year-old toddler and his father, who in response to his misbehavior angrily whips him, and they had asked rhetorically, "What Ought John to Have Done?" Sam's 1,250-word reply contains, as Michael J. Kiskis observes, "his fullest public comments on child-rearing." "I am a fortunate person," Sam began, because he had "been for thirteen years accustomed, daily and hourly, to the charming companionship of thoroughly well-behaved, well-trained, well-governed children." He credited Livy for their conduct. What should the father have done in the scenario sketched by the *Christian Union?* Nothing. He ought to

> have kept still. Then the mother would have led the little boy to a private place, and taken him on her lap, and reasoned with him, and loved him out of his wrong mood, and shown him that he had mistreated one of the best and most loving friends he had in the world; and in no very long time the child would be convinced, and be sorry, and would run with eager sincerity and ask the father's pardon. And that would be the end of the matter.

If "it did not turn out in just this way" and "the child grew stubborn," only then would he be promised a spanking at "the proper time"—that is, "when both mother and child have got the sting of the original difficulty clear out of their minds and hearts and are prepared to give and take a whipping on purely business principles—disciplinary principles—and with hearts wholly free from temper." That was exactly how Livy would have handled the situation, Sam insisted. Livy's "first and foremost object was to make the child understand that he is being punished for *his* sake," Susy remembered,

> and because the mother so loves him that she cannot allow him to do wrong; also that it is as hard for her to punish him as for him to be punished and even harder. Mamma never allowed herself to punish us when she was angry with us she never struck us because she was enoyed at us and felt like striking us if we had been nauty and had enoyed her, so that she thought she felt or would show the least bit of temper toward us while punnishing us, she always postponed the punishment until *she* was no more chafed by our behavior.

Livy occasionally administered corporal punishment, usually paddling with a paper cutter or letter opener, though on at least one occasion she "whipped Bay with the heavy stem of one of [Sam's] pipes." When she prepared to spank her older daughter with the same pipe stem a few days later, Susy "said with simple pathos that she wished we had brought the *paper cutter* from home, 'because she was better acquainted with it.'" "After the whipping was over," Susy added, "mamma did not allow us to leave her until we were perfectly happy, and perfectly understood why we had been whipped. I never remember having felt the least bit bitterly toward mamma for punishing me. I always felt I had deserved my punishment and was much happier for having received it."[45]

In his *Christian Union* article, Sam claimed that Livy alone was responsible for disciplining their daughters and that the punishments she administered were measured. Spankings "are not given in our house for revenge; that are not given for spite, nor ever in anger," he insisted. Moreover,

> the interval between the promise of a whipping and its infliction is usually an hour or two. By that time both parties are calm, and the one is judicial, the other receptive. The child never goes from the scene of punishment until it has been loved back into happy-heartedness and a joyful spirit. The spanking is never a cruel one, but it is always an honest one. It hurts. If it hurts the child, imagine how it must hurt the mother.

Sam concluded the essay by admitting he had never before "made a single reference to my wife in print" except "once in the dedication of a book; and, so, after these fifteen years of silence, perhaps I may unseal my lips this one time without impropriety or indelicacy." He admitted, too, that he was submitting the essay to the magazine "without her knowledge and without asking her to edit it. This will save it from getting edited into the stove."[46]

Figure 26. The Clemens family on the "ombra" of the Hartford home, ca. 1882. Collection of Gary Scharnhorst.

Sam harbored misgivings about publishing the article before Livy had seen it. As Susy recalled, he even "went down to New York"—he registered at the Hotel Normandie at Thirty Eighth and Broadway on July 4—"to see if he couldn't get it back before it was published but it was too late and he had to return without it." He gave a copy of the manuscript to Susan Crane and to his daughters to read but warned them not to mention it to Livy "till it came out." Susy thought the "article was a beautiful tribute to mamma and every word in it true." When the issue of the magazine with Sam's article in it "reached the farm," Sam told Susy and Clara to show it to her "and we all stood around mamma while she read it." She was, according to Susy, initially "surprised" and "pleased privately," but after she realized "that this article was to be read by everyone that took the *Christian Union*" she "was rather shocked and a little displeased." Susy's father and mother agreed never again "to hear or be spoken to on the subject."[47]

In the legend of Saint Mark, moreover, Sam was a kindly cat and dog lover who, according to Edward Wagenknecht, "did not know how to be unkind to any animal." Not exactly. His grandniece Jean Webster recalled an occasion when one of his dogs "had disobeyed him and he started to discipline it, much to my own grief, as the dog was a great pet of mine. I was only a little girl but I had a temper of my own, and when my grand uncle started to whip his dog I interfered."[48]

While 1885 was Sam's *Wunderjahr*, with the publication of *Huck Finn* in the United States, the final months of his reading tour with Cable, and the release of the first volume of Grant's memoirs, his reputation was simultaneously under attack. Apart from the brouhaha over his service in the Marion Rangers, he was accused of underhanded business practices and worse. The *Washington Star* contended that he had "proved his ability to be very dreary as well as very funny" and "takes advantage of every occasion to push himself into notice." The Washington *National Tribune* charged that he was "one of the most greedy and selfish of men" and the always hostile Carson City *Appeal* claimed that Dan De Quille had "more genuine humor in his little finger than Mark Twain ever had in his whole selfish carcass."[49] To combat such allegations, Sam tried to repair his public image by volunteering time and donating money to several charities and philanthropic groups. "The surest way for a business man" to defend his reputation, he believed, "is to give a handsome donation to some charitable concern or distress fund" because "the newspaper men will, in a glowing paragraph, immediately laud the spirit that prompted the gift." Sam entertained the members of the New York Teachers' Association at a standing-room-only crowd in Steinway Hall in late March 1885, three weeks after the end of his reading tour. The "schoolmarms" and "young lady teachers" (as the *New York Herald* termed the audience) enjoyed "the tale of Huck Finn and Tom Sawyer's brilliant achievement" in rescuing Jim.[50]

Sam also became a fixture on the club scene in Boston, New York, and Philadelphia. On March 23 Sam and Livy railed to Boston to visit the Howellses, who hosted a reception for them the next afternoon and Sam and Howells attended a dinner meeting of the new Tavern Club in the evening. A week later, Sam crashed a Tile Club dinner meeting hosted by Laurence Hutton to welcome Henry Irving back to New York. He "would certainly have been invited had his presence in the city been known," Hutton allowed. "He had arrived from Hartford late in the afternoon" with Livy to shop for Easter, learned about the "unusual dinner-party," and "decided that it was too good a thing to lose. So he dressed hurriedly, walked in without ceremony just as the feast began, drew up a chair by the side of his hostess, helped himself to her oysters, and for the rest of the evening was the life of the party," upstaging the guest of honor. A memento of the evening, a menu

autographed by Sam, Edwin Booth, Richard Watson Gilder, Julian Hawthorne, and Brander Matthews, still survives among the Mark Twain Papers. On April 9 Sam read "Tale of the Fishwife and Its Sad Fate" at a benefit
performance for the Actors' Fund Fair at the Academy of Music in Philadelphia. "It was a superb performance & of prodigious variety," he reported
to Livy. "It began shortly after noon & lasted till 4. There were 4,000 people
present, & they sat it through." The event raised about thirty-four hundred
dollars for the fund. He afterward banqueted and delivered an after-dinner
speech at the Clover Club.[51]

On April 23, the same weekend Badeau alleged in the New York *World*
that he had ghostwritten Grant's memoirs, Sam spoke at the New York Association of Cornell University Alumni dinner at Morelli's Restaurant on
West Twenty-Eighth Street, delivering a toast to "the Politician." Among
the other guests were Henry Ward Beecher; Alonzo B. Cornell, oldest son
of the founder of the university and former governor of New York; and
Cornell president Andrew Dickson White. Sam read at benefits for the
American Copyright League at Madison Square Theater the afternoons
of April 28 and 29, along with Beecher, Hjalmar Hjorth Boyesen, Edward Eggleston, Hawthorne, Howells, George Parsons Lathrop, and E. C.
Stedman, that raised seventeen hundred dollars for the league. As Howells wrote him, "You simply straddled down to the footlights, and took that
house up in the hollow of your hand and tickled it." On his part, Sam soon
congratulated Howells on his performance. "You sent even your daintiest
and most delicate and fleeting points home to that audience," he wrote, "but
you couldn't read worth a damn a few years ago. I do not say this to flatter."
He next traveled with Susy to Poughkeepsie, where he spoke at Founder's
Day ceremonies at Vassar College the evening of May 1, the anniversary of
the birthday of Matthew Vassar, before a "great garden of young and lovely
blossoms." "Papa read in the chapel," Susy wrote in her biography of her
father. "It was the first time I had ever heard him read in my life—that is in
public." She heard him declaim parts of *A Tramp Abroad* (1880) and "The
Golden Arm," the ghost story "he heard down South when he was a little
boy," and although she had heard it before "he startled the whole room full
of people" and she "did not much wish to hear it" ever again. So eager was he
to receive favorable publicity that, two weeks later, he sat among other local
celebrities on stage at Roberts Opera House during a lecture by Chauncey
Depew to benefit the Connecticut Indian Association.[52]

At the invitation of Elizabeth Colt, Charley Perkins, E. P. Parker, and
Charley and Susan Warner, Sam also appeared at a pair of benefit readings

on behalf of the Decorative Arts Society of Hartford at Unity Hall on the evening of June 5 and the afternoon of June 6. In appreciation, Mrs. Colt invited Sam and Livy to a lavish dinner at her mansion Armsmear on June 16. In August, along with Lawrence Barrett, Edwin Booth, Oliver Wendell Holmes, Charley Warner, John Greenleaf Whittier, and others, he also publicly donated to a fund to help buy a horse and buggy for the aging poet Walt Whitman. "I have a great veneration for the old man," he wrote Whitman's friend and attorney Thomas Donaldson, "& would be glad to help pay his turnout's board, year after year, & buy another when it fails." Sam also received kudos for reading at a charity benefit in Pittsfield, Massachusetts, the morning of October 7. Eventually, however, Sam's efforts to speak or to arrange for guest speakers in Hartford began to pall. "You know the burnt child shuns the fire," he explained to James Pond a few days after Christmas 1887. "I'm a burnt child. It will be a mighty long day before I ever have even the remotest thing to do with a Hartford entertainment again. I have assisted in one way or another at as many as thirty & they've all left more or less uncomfortable memories behind. No lecture & no reading makes its salt in Hartford & the most unsagacious thing a body can do is to come here & crucify himself on the platform."[53]

Between August 24 and 29, 1885, accompanied by Dean Sage and his wife Sara, Sam and Livy visited Onteora Park, a restricted (i.e., closed to Jews) artists' colony in the Catskill Mountains near Tannersville, New York, founded by the textile designer Candace Wheeler. Among their fellow guests there was Elizabeth Custer, who later commended Sam's "genial flow of characteristic speech." She likewise admired his "lovely wife": "It is a relief when we know a genius to whom a whole continent is indebted to find that his wife is an ideal wife for any man." Sam enjoyed this visit to the Catskills, where there was "just enough rain, just enough sunshine; just enough people, & just the right kind; just enough exercise, just enough lazying around." In all, "it *was* a good time we had there," though he later joked that the walls in the cabins "were so thin that one could hear a lady in the next room changing her mind." The family returned to Quarry Farm for two weeks before leaving on September 15 for New York, where they lingered a few days at the Normandie Hotel before landing back in Hartford on September 18.[54]

Sam was a convert to the cause of civil rights for African Americans relatively late in life. As late as November 1878, at the age of forty-three, he endorsed a flagrantly racist and xenophobic opinion Howells had printed on the "Contributor's Club" pages in the *Atlantic Monthly.* "I think that the man who wrote the paragraph beginning at the bottom of page 643," he wrote Howells from Munich, "has said a mighty sound and sensible thing." Here is that paragraph:

> Disenfranchise all men not born in the country and all negroes, and rule them with an inflexible but kindly rule; take such measures as would stop [im]migration; suppress nine in ten of the newspapers; sweep away the present system of public schools and substitute for them *dame* schools, in which the three R's, with sewing, good manners, decency, and deference would be taught.

By the early 1880s, however, Sam was convinced that white folks owed reparations to former slaves and their descendants. His argument was based not on economics (i.e., slave labor built the nation) but on a flawed Lamarckian belief that black folks inherited traits acquired through generations of ancestral oppression. Admittedly, that is, Sam's case for reparations was rooted in a benign racial paternalism. His belief in the transmission of acquired characteristics enabled him to subscribe to a theory of racial degradation that was, at bottom, naive and patronizing. He believed, in effect, that Native Americans and African Americans had suffered so many "decades and generations of insult and outrage" that they had become debased stock and deserved tolerance and compassion. As he wrote Karl Gerhardt on May 1, 1883,

> On every sin which a colored man commits, the just white man must make a considerable discount, because of the colored man's antecedents. The heirs of slavery cannot with any sort of justice be required to be as clear and straight and upright as the heirs of ancient freedom. And besides, whenever a colored man commits an unright action, upon his head is the guilt of only about one tenth of it and upon your head and mine and the rest of the while race lies fairly and justly the other nine tenths of the guilt.

His conviction that African Americans continued to suffer injustices was galvanized in the spring of 1881 by a national cause célèbre: Johnson C. Whittaker, only the second black cadet admitted to the U.S. Military Academy at West Point, had been slashed and beaten by white cadets in early April 1880 but was accused by authorities of inflicting his own injuries to avoid examinations. A court of inquiry concluded the next month that "if attacked he should have resisted and called for help; that he might have released himself readily; that he was feigning insensibility when found; that he wrote the note of warning to himself; and committed the so-called out-rage upon himself." After a yearlong court-martial before a military tribunal, Whittaker was found guilty and expelled for conduct "unbecoming an offi-cer and gentleman." His expulsion coincided, significantly, with Sam's first formal inspection tour of the academy. Sam suspected that as a "mulatto" Whittaker was simply found guilty of being "colored" by the one-drop rule and therefore unfit for an army commission. Howells recalled his response to the verdict: "'Oh yes,' Clemens said, with bitter irony, 'it was that one part black that undid him.' It made him a 'nigger' and incapable of being a gentle-man. It was to blame for the whole thing. The fifteen parts white were guilt-less.'" The question of Whittaker's guilt anticipates Sam's ironic treatment of the usurper Tom's culpability for killing Judge Driscoll in *Pudd'nhead Wilson* (1894). Whittaker was posthumously commissioned over sixty years after his death by President Bill Clinton in 1995.[55]

As part of his own payment of reparations, Sam donated time and money to a variety of causes to benefit African Americans, especially during his flush times in the early and mid-1880s, such as funding the art education in Paris of still-life painter Charles Ethan Porter and subsidizing the tuition of students at Lincoln University, a historically black school in eastern Penn-sylvania. Among them was A. W. Jones, though Sam stopped supporting him when Jones decided to pursue postgraduate studies in theology. Sam refused to stipulate fields of study for the students he helped, of course, but he had "hoped [Jones] would make choice of some useful occupation" and having "disappointed me, & I feel no further interest in him."[56]

From 1885 until 1887 Sam also paid the board at Yale Law School of Warner McGuinn, a graduate of Lincoln University who later enjoyed a distinguished career as a civil rights attorney. While at Yale to address the Kent Club of the law school in December 1885, Sam met McGuinn, who solicited his help and Sam in turn sought the advice of Francis Wayland, the dean of the school: "Do you know him? And is he worthy? I do not believe I would very cheerfully help a white student who would ask a benevolence of a stranger, but I do not feel so about the other color. We have ground the manhood out of them, & the shame is ours, not theirs, & we should pay for it." In 1917 McGuinn won a case that overturned a law permitting racial segregation in housing in Baltimore. As an eminent black lawyer, moreover, he mentored Thurgood Marshall. As founder and first chief counsel of the Legal Defense Fund of the National Association for the Advancement of Colored People, Marshall successfully argued the landmark *Brown v. Board of Education of Topeka* case before the U.S. Supreme Court in 1954 that outlawed racial segregation in public facilities and he became the first African American to sit on the Supreme Court, serving from 1967 until 1991. That is, Sam was a patron, if only indirectly, of the modern U.S. civil rights movement.[57]

Albert Bigelow Paine asserted in authorized biography, moreover, that Sam "would read for a negro church when he would have refused a cathedral." At least the first half of this statement is true. Sam considered his fund-raising for black churches another form of reparation. On March 10, 1881, two weeks after reading Joel Chandler Harris's story about Uncle Remus and the tar baby for charity in Joseph Twichell's church, he read it again at a black church in Hartford on the same program with a black choir that performed jubilee songs. When he was invited in September 1884 to lecture at a local church to help pay a building debt, he was initially irritated by "the exceedingly cool wording of the request"—until Livy noted that the congregation was black and the minister simply did not "know how to write a polished letter—how should he?" She suggested Sam "consider every man colored till he is proved white"—sound advice under the circumstances. Five years later, he read "The Decay of the Art of Lying," which he had first delivered at a meeting of the Monday Evening Club in April 1880, at a benefit for the organ fund of the black Talcott Street Congregational Church in Hartford and his performance "went exceedingly well—unexpectedly so." In April 1886, when asked for a contribution to the Kirkwood Street African Methodist Episcopal Church in Dover, Delaware, he sent a check.[58]

In the wake of the sales success of *Huck Finn* and Grant's memoirs, Sam jumped at the chance in the spring of 1886 to publish the authorized biography of Pope Leo XIII by Father Bernard O'Reilly. He and Webster each exercised veto authority over books issued by Webster and Company but the pope's biography seemed a no-brainer and Sam hoped to harvest a bumper crop of book orders. As early as March 16 the *Boston Herald* marveled at the coup the upstart company had executed. That "the Sovereign Pontiff and Vicar of Christ" had agreed to submit "his biography to Mark Twain's publishing house 'as a commercial enterprise' surpasses the most audacious travesty of Mark Twain's books. As a stroke of 'business' it is probably supreme in its way." The Vatican signed the contract with Webster and Company the next month and, Sam crowed to Livy, "the Pope's book is ours & we'll sell a fleet load of copies." He was convinced that every Catholic in Christendom would buy a copy and he arranged for it to be simultaneously printed in six languages. He fully expected the book to "outsell the Koran and the Bible."[59]

Webster and his wife Annie sailed to Italy in late June to consult with His Holiness about details and to publicize the book in advance of publication.

During their private audience in mid-July Webster presented the pontiff with a "leather-bound, gold-lettered" copy of Grant's memoirs and the pope conferred upon him the title of Chevalier of the Order of Pius IX. Webster reported to Sam that, though a Protestant, he had "succeeded beyond any human expectations" and Sam congratulated him: "You did well to go to Rome & you did wisely to spend money freely." Sam was pleased that Webster had procured "so much advertising so cheaply" and he hoped that news of Webster's interview with the pope would be featured in the prospectus for the biography because "it is a valuable card." By the close of the calendar year Sam was still optimistic ("the Pope's book looks as good if not better than ever") and the following March 1, when canvassing began, he joked that the prospectus for the biography "would sell a Choctaw Bible, it is so handsome."[60]

Then ensued the unexpected calamity. Neither Sam nor Howells had foreseen the fatal flaw in their scheme: "We did not consider how often Catholics could not read, how often, when they could, they might not wish to read. The event proved that, whether they could read or not, the immeasurable majority did not wish to read *The Life of the Pope*." No one cared that Charley had been knighted or that he had presented the pope with a gold-lettered copy of Grant's autobiography. The book landed in the market with a resounding thud; fewer than a hundred thousand copies were sold. In August 1887 Sam admitted to Webster that the outlook for the company was "disturbing. I suppose the Pope's book" and George McClellan's autobiography "together will not more than pay the expenses of the last year & a half." Or as Howells recalled, "His sanguine soul was utterly confounded and soon a silence fell upon it where it had been so exuberantly jubilant." His hunches were not such reliable barometers of sales appeal after all.[61]

CHAPTER 14

Bucking the Tiger

There are two times in a man's life when he should not speculate: when
he can afford it, & when he can't.

—*Pudd'nhead Wilson's Calendar*

SAMUEL CLEMENS'S ZEAL for investment or speculation did not abate either at the height of his affluence or after it began to wane. As he put it, "I
must speculate in something, such being my nature." After the debacle of
Kaolatype, Sam threw money into such harebrained inventions as a por-
table mosquito net, a fire-extinguishing hand grenade, and a spiral hat pin.
He patented a bedsheet clamp and an adjustable garment strap though, unlike the self-pasting scrapbook, he never put them into production. He purchased stock in the Crown Point Iron Company, the Denver & Rio Grande
Railroad, and the Hartford Engineering Company, all of which lost money.
In 1882, according to his account books, Sam had about a hundred thousand dollars in outstanding investments in twenty-three stocks and bonds,
many of them transportation stocks. Another investment that soured on his
hands: three hundred shares in the Oregon & Transcontinental Railroad, a
gamble that followed a trajectory similar to his other rolls of the dice. Sam
bought two hundred shares in the company on margin at seventy-five dollars
a share in January 1883, doubled down on his bet by buying an additional
hundred shares in September, and also sold the lot in May 1884 at a loss of
about nineteen thousand dollars. Fred Kaplan estimates that, in all, Sam
lost about a hundred thousand dollars in the stock market, about one and a
half million dollars in modern money.[1]

Sam's business (mis)fortunes were evident, too, in his relations with the
American Publishing Company quite apart from the reduced royalties paid
him for his first six books. He received a 10 percent dividend on his five thousand dollars' worth of stock in the company in 1873 but nothing further over
the next eight years. He resigned from its board of directors in May 1881
and sold his two hundred shares of company stock, whereupon the company
paid three dividends over the next year and a half. Sam's failed investment
in the Independent Watch Company of Fredonia, New York, in 1881–82

followed a familiar pattern, both replaying the failures of Kaolatype and other ventures and foreshadowing the larger scandal of the Paige typesetter. Sam had long been fascinated with watchmaking, particularly a handmade Swiss watch owned by a jeweler in New Haven he examined in January 1876. In a product endorsement later published to advertise the brand, he claimed the Matile watch "comes nearer to being a human being than any piece of mechanism I ever saw before. In fact, it knows considerably more than the average voter. . . . It ciphers to admiration; I should think one could add another wheel and make it read and write; still another and make it talk. . . . On the whole I think it is entitled to vote—that is, if its sex is the right kind." In anthropomorphizing the artificial intelligence of the watch, Sam betrayed the source of his attraction to the typesetter, which featured an arm motion that mimicked the work of a human typesetter. Having been a printer in his adolescence like Sam, W. D. Howells testified that the Paige compositor "was so wonderful that it did everything but walk and talk." Sam's friend and financial adviser Henry Huttleston Rogers later contended that the machine was the "mechanical replication of a human being." Significantly, Sam occasionally compared the operation of the typesetter to the workings of a watch. "The machine was as perfect as a watch when we took her apart the other day," he observed on one of the innumerable occasions when James Paige undertook to "repair" or "improve" the mechanism, "but when she goes together again . . . we expect her to be perfecter than a watch."[2] Though he gendered the machine as female in this case, he often gendered it as male.

On the surface Sam's faith in the future of a mechanical compositor was entirely warranted. Publishing was a growth industry during the period the Paige was in development. The number of newspapers almost doubled, to about seven thousand, during the 1870s and by 1890 there were over twelve thousand dailies and weeklies in the United States. The number of magazines also doubled during the 1870s to about twenty-four hundred and ballooned to about thirty-three hundred by 1885 and forty-four hundred in 1890—that is, the total number of magazines published in the United States increased about fourfold in the quarter century after the Civil War. Many factors—technological, economic, demographic, and legal—combined to boost sales of the printed word during the era, including the invention of the mechanical typesetter and the typewriter; the decline in the price of paper, especially newsprint; the passage of the Postal Acts of 1879 and 1885; the growth in population and real income due to immigration and industrialization; increased literacy as the result of compulsory elementary education; and expansion of the public library system.[3] Had Kaolatype and the Paige typesetter proved practical, Charles L. Webster and Company would have owned two essential components of a vertically integrated corporation, like an airline that acquires a travel agency or a car manufacturer that merges with a tire company. Moreover, who would have better understood the appeal of a mechanical compositor than a former manual typesetter?

In any event, at Charley Webster's urging in March 1881 Sam invested five thousand dollars in the Independent Watch Company. Webster touted the stock without knowing that the company directors, his friends the Howard brothers, were running a Ponzi scheme. The swindle became obvious six months later when the company declared a dividend without earning any profits, whereupon Sam launched his own scheme to recover his investment. He prepared a bogus advertisement for Charley Webster to carry to Fredonia, offering to sell five thousand dollars in worthless stock in the Independent Watch Company to the highest bidder. He instructed Webster to publish it "and spread it over Fredonia in the form of handbills" unless the Howards refunded his money, whereupon "they squared" the account "very promptly." Sam appreciated Webster's diplomacy in blackmailing "the Watch thieves. It was an ugly job well carried through. The Howards were wise to hold their temper & come to our terms; for if they hadn't we would have made it warm for them & the rest of the directors on that fraudulent dividend." As late as 1885, during the canvass for Ulysses S. Grant's memoirs, Sam was pleased with his nephew's job performance. Webster had managed the business capably and "with a superb record; & with all its array of business-inventions, -ingenuities & -triumphs, he has not made a single business-misstep."[4]

But all of this past is prologue to the Paige calamity. Katy Leary recalled that Sam was so infatuated with the prospects of the typesetter that he expected eventually to "buy all New York. He was asking how much it would take to buy all the railroads in New York, and all the newspapers, too.... He thought he'd make millions and own the world, because he had such faith in it." The Farnham Typesetter Company of Hartford withdrew its financial support from Paige in 1882 after almost a decade and a total investment to that date of about ninety thousand dollars, though for reasons apparently unrelated to the (im)practicality of the machine. William Hamersley, among its earliest backers, the president of the Farnham Company and the Hartford city attorney who first enticed Sam to invest in it, remained one of Paige's strongest supporters. Sam also helped finance Paige's operating expenses after the Farnham Company divested and he received stock in return. "I'd rather have $250,000 in non-assessable stock" in the typesetter "than $100,000 *cash*," he insisted. At a stockholders' meeting in April 1883 the members of the board of directors were charged with raising a million dollars to capitalize the manufacture of the machine and Paige was required "to stand up & distinctly say he knew the machine to be now flawless," Sam reported. He and Hamersley tried to raise money, hence Sam's meeting with the venture capitalist Ross Winans in November 1884 while he was in Baltimore during his reading tour with George Washington Cable. In May 1885 he pitched the investment in Albany to Dean Sage without success. A week later, Sam met the railroad robber baron Jay Gould and his son George at their Western Union offices in New York to tout the stock, albeit to no avail. "Damned insignificant people," he wrote in his notebook afterward.[5]

Far from a cutthroat capitalist, Sam had over time become increasingly sympathetic to the rights of workers. Under more jejune circumstances during the Great Railroad Strike of 1877, he had been largely indifferent to labor strife in Pennsylvania and West Virginia; the riots in the rail yards in July that year "neither surprised nor greatly disturbed me," he noted, "for where the government is a sham, one must expect such things." While in Paris in 1879, in apparent reference to the Paris Commune of 1871, Sam scorned labor radicals: "Communism is idiotcy. They want to divide up the property. Suppose they did it—it requires brains to keep money as well as make it. In a precious little while the money would be back in the former owner's hands & the Communist would be poor again." But by the mid-1880s he recognized the role of organized labor as a counterforce to capital. When the Knights of Labor struck Gould's Union Pacific and Missouri Pacific railroads in March 1886, Sam extolled the strength of organized labor. In "The New Dynasty," a paper he read before the Monday Evening Club on March 22, two days after strikers began to burn railway bridges in Texas, three days before the Hartford chapter of the Knights of Labor proposed nominating him for mayor, and to the everlasting dismay of his Republican friends, Sam argued that labor unions would be a buffer against radicals, "our permanent shield and defence against the Socialist, the Communist, the Anarchist, the tramp, and the selfish agitator for 'reforms.'" Not that his convictions on the topic were cast in concrete. Six weeks later, on May 4, at a labor rally at Haymarket Square in Chicago called to protest the police killing of strikers at the McCormick harvester factory the day before, eight people died violently and over a hundred were injured. Eight of the organizers of the protest were arrested, though none of them was ever implicated in the actual bloodshed. Seven of them were convicted and sentenced to death and four of them were hanged the following November. Howells vehemently objected to the prosecution, conviction, and execution of the "anarchists" for their political opinions in a famous letter to the *New York Tribune* in which he appealed "for the mitigation of their punishment." On his part, Sam sympathized with the police. He donated ten dollars to the "relief of families of police officers, killed or injured in the discharge of duty" during the "riot."[6]

In early April 1885 the moment seemed ripe to put the Paige machine on the market. As Sam wrote Webster, the typesetter was "in lucrative shape at last," meaning it could attract investment capital, and was "in perfect working order," able "to submit itself to any test an expert chooses to apply." Like a tragic hero, Sam was a victim of hubris. The device was still subject to interminable delays, repairs, and improvements. Over the next five years Paige added a number of accessories to the prototype of the machine, including a mechanical justifier, a motor, an air blast to remove dust, and a type tester, which, Sam boasted, "permits no type to enter the machine (while distributing) without its *strength* being tested by the application to it of six times as much impact as it will afterward get in the machine." Sam considered adding the justifying mechanism fifteen years after marketing the basic model so that he could patent it anew and "thus give the mach[ine] another 17-year lease of life." But as Charles Gold explains, "what Paige did, as Clemens watched in fascination, bemusement, and eventually consternation, was to make the machine so complex it could never function reliably." The basic model was never mass-produced because it was always in a state of incremental improvement. "Business sanity would have said, put it on the market as it was, secure the field, and add improvements later," Sam later admitted. "Paige's business insanity said, add the improvements first and risk losing the field."[7]

Paige's invention faced stiff competition from several rivals, particularly the Mergenthaler Linotype, all of them in development. Like the Paige, the Mergenthaler was operated by a typist at a keyboard, but whereas the Paige transferred movable type one letter or space at a time in imitation of a human compositor, the Mergenthaler struck impressions of letters in copper sheets used as molds for hot lead a line at a time, hence the name "line o' type." The Paige was also more intricate, the prototype eventually weighing over three tons, standing six feet high, nine feet long, and four feet wide and containing some eighteen thousand moving parts, including eight hundred shaft bearings that required constant lubrication.

When it worked properly, its operator could set upwards of four thousand ems per hour—twice the capacity of the Linotype machine. But the Linotype was cheaper to manufacture, more durable, broke no type, required fewer repairs, and thus was more practical. Still, if he could lease a thousand

Figure 27. The Paige typesetter, *Scientific American*, March 9, 1901.

Paige machines, Sam calculated, he would collect $2,500,000 annually. In his more extravagant fantasies, he imagined that the typesetter would earn $55 million annually in worldwide sales and rentals. He dreamed of becoming a publishing tycoon, what Andrew Carnegie was to steel or John D. Rockefeller to oil—or, in an unconscious act of self-parody, what Mulberry Sellers was to eye ointment. As the colonel declares in the theatrical version of *The Gilded Age* (1873), he planned to "sell 50,000 bottles" of his "Infallible, Imperial, Oriental, Optic Liniment" for sore eyes the first year at a profit of "$24,000. 200,000 the second year, clear profit $96,000—third year sell a million bottles, clear profit, four hundred & ninety odd thousand dollars." Little wonder that Howells claimed that the Paige typesetter satisfied Sam's own irrepressible "Colonel Sellers nature."[8]

Sam was simply blind to the contrast between the two machines. He was convinced that the Paige was "a mechanical miracle; when a body sees it work, he says 'it's poetry'; & yet it is so simple & sure that a crossing-sweeper can put down his broom & set type on it." The Mergenthaler was "a most ingenious & capable marvel of mechanism" but "so is a racehorse" and "he can't run no competition with a railroad." As Sam wrote Webster in July 1885, "I have been ciphering on the type-setter. Eight of them will do the N.Y. Sun's work, & reduce its composition-bills from $80,000 a year to $25,000. The truth is 6 or 7 machines will do it, but I don't want you to state that—call it eight & be on the safe side." He figured he could manufacture and lease the machines for $2,500 a year, which would reduce the cost of typesetting the paper from $1,600 to $750 or $800 a week. Six months later, his friend William Laffan, business manager of the New York *Sun*, warned him about the approaching debacle: "I saw the Baltimore [Mergenthaler] machine set type," Laffan reported on January 25, 1886, and he predicted "that every daily in [New York] will be set up by that machine inside of twelve months," including the *Sun*. "I have applied and secured 2d place on the list" behind the *Tribune*. "This is confidential," he advised Sam, "but you'd better haul in your lente [slowness] and festina [hasten] like hell."[9]

Instead, two weeks later, Sam signed a contract that eventually sealed his financial doom. Ironically, at the same moment Webster and Company was at the height of its success, with no outstanding debt, $260,000 in the bank (though most of it owed to Julia Grant), and money "coming in every day." At a meeting in Sam's billiard room on January 20 with Hamersley, Paige offered to sell a half interest in the machine for $30,000, the amount he claimed he needed to finish it, and Sam rose to the bait. Hamersley drew a contract, dated February 6, 1886, stipulating that Sam would pay Paige's expenses to a limit of $30,000 plus an annual salary of $7,000 until he earned a net yearly profit of that amount from the invention. When a prototype was completed, Sam and Hamersley would raise the capital to mass-produce it and Sam would receive a substantial block of stock in the corporation organized to manufacture and market it. Meanwhile, Paige retained ownership of the physical property and patents.[10]

Franklin Whitmore, Sam's legal adviser, "did not altogether approve of the new contract," according to Paige, because it was too open-ended. It committed Sam to a long-term investment in the machine; still, he was undeterred. As he explained in his autobiography, "When I took hold of the machine Feb. 6, 1886, its faults had been corrected" and even an inexperienced operator "could turn out about 3,500 ems an hour on it; possibly 4,000. There was no machine that could pretend rivalry to it." He pinned his hopes on the imminent completion of a perfected model because with it he could persuade "a thousand men worth a million apiece to go in with me." He did not yet realize that Paige's lucrative salary was an incentive for the inventor to tinker indefinitely on the machine or, conversely, a disincentive for him ever to finish it. Nor did he understand that the contract guaranteed him nothing in return—no equity in a company, no ownership of patents—merely a 45 percent stake in a hypothetical future corporation. Nevertheless, he insisted that he "had no fears or doubts" of the wisdom of his investment. As Charles Gold has concluded, "the game was over by early in 1886," though Sam did not grasp this truth.[11]

As Sam's business responsibilities multiplied, he expanded his staff in April 1886 by promoting the twenty-six-year-old Fred J. Hall, one of Webster's subalterns, to a junior partnership in the company at an annual salary of $1,500 and a share of profits. In Webster's absence, beginning with his trip to Rome to consult with the pope, Hall was to "have the entire active management and control of said business." In the short run, too, Hall was in charge of identifying potential buyers of the Paige compositor, a clear indication of the intersection between Webster and Company and Sam's investment in the typesetter, two businesses that should have been separated. As Sam wrote Hall in August 1886, he wanted to obtain for marketing purposes "the name & address of every *daily* newspaper in the U.S & Canada that contains fully *2 pages of new matter daily*," including country dailies, and "a list of the several printers' union (*compositors'* unions) in the U.S.; & where they are located, & how many members each contains." He was optimistic the Paige would soon be completed and he was ready to target potential customers. "I am building a type-setting machine which will be finished by next spring," he notified Andrew Chatto, "& will doubtless put an end to hand-setting. . . . I have been at work at this thing four years, & have spent many shekels on it."[12]

But after a year little had changed. The infusion of $30,000 in cash depleted, Paige confessed "that the machine was still incomplete" but said that "four thousand dollars more would finish it and that with ten thousand dollars he could finish and exhibit it" to investors. Paige offered the machine as collateral for a loan and Sam agreed to advance the money. As he noted in his autobiography, "I went on footing the bills" at the rate of about $4,000 a month" with gusts to five thousand. The project was routinely over budget and past deadline. "When Paige thinks a thing will cost $100," he conceded to Whitmore in August 1887, "*that* is proof that it will cost $1,000." Yet only five days later he wrote Whitmore than he thought the end of tinkering on the machine was in sight. "We will make a good strong steady pull, & all in good time, b'gosh, we'll *arrive.*" Yet Christmas 1887 was not merry. Forced to skimp on holiday gifts, Sam sent his brother Orion and sister Pamela $15 each to "buy some inconsequential trifle that will help you to remember that we remember you." He admitted to his brother that he, Livy, and the children were

> scrimping like devils this year, on account of the type-setter, or we would send check enough to buy a horse, or part of one. I almost think the type-setter will be finished some day or other; anyway the bills are $1000 a month heavier the last 4 months than they ever were in the 17 preceding ones, & we've got 8 more men at work than we ever had before—got all that *can* work on it in fact; so this gives things a mighty cheerful business-like aspect & makes us believe we are within 3 or 4 months of land, at last.

Despite Paige's recurrently broken but persistent promises and Sam's repeatedly dashed but never-ending hopes, the two men always met "on effusively affectionate terms," Sam allowed in 1890, "and yet he knows perfectly well that if I had his nuts in a steel-trap I would shut out all human succor and watch that trap till he died."[13]

Sam had written next to nothing for publication since completing *Adventures of Huckleberry Finn* over two years earlier. As usual, however, his personal schedule was hectic: visits to Hartford by Lawrence Barrett, Laurence Hutton, and his wife Eleanor Varnum Mitchell Hutton in early March 1886; a trip to New York with Livy, daughter Clara, and Daisy Warner, the daughter of Lilly and George, in mid-April to attend a performance of Gilbert and Sullivan's *Mikado* at the Fifth Avenue Theater; a dinner a week later in honor of Edwin A. Abbey at the home of Francis Hopkinson Smith; an Authors' Club of New York dinner at which Sam delivered the speech "Our Children and Great Discoveries"; and a visit by Howells and his daughter Mildred the first weekend in May. Even daughter Susy noticed the length of her father's fallow season, noting in her biography of him that she and her mother had been "very much troubled of late because papa, since he had been publishing General Grant's books, has seemed to forget his own books and works entirely." Coincidentally, Sam wrote Webster the very next day that he had "begun a book, whose scene is laid far back in the twilight of tradition; I have saturated myself with the atmosphere of the day & the subject, & got myself into the swing of the work. If I peg away for some weeks without a break, I am safe; if I stop now for a day, I am unsafe, & may never get started right again." Two months earlier, in fact, he had returned to the notes he had taken after reading Thomas Malory's *Le Morte d'Arthur* while on tour with Cable. The premise of the book was simple, as he outlined it to Howells: a

Hartford man, the superintendent of Colt's Arms factories, is cracked on the head with a crowbar and awakens thirteen centuries earlier in Camelot. Howells thought the idea "capital. There is a great chance in it." Sam had not mentioned to Howells that the Yankee upon awakening is welcomed to Camelot by a "fair slip of a girl about ten years old" who is naked save for a sexually symbolic "hoop of flame-red poppies" around her head. "It was as sweet an outfit as ever I saw, what there was of it."[14]

By March Sam had completed the opening frame set in the present in Warwick Castle, which he had visited with James R. Osgood in September 1872, and the first three chapters. He borrowed a stock device, the transcription of an ancient manuscript about strange and foreign adventures—a device he would deploy again in *Personal Recollections of Joan of Arc* (1896)— from H. Rider Haggard's *King Solomon's Mines* (1885). He likewise lifted a bizarre plot contrivance, an eclipse, from Haggard's sensation novel. He modeled Camelot, a "town sleeping in a valley by a winding river," on antebellum Hannibal. He transported from Malory to these pages several of the Knights of the Round Table, including Sir Galahad, Sir Kay the Senechal, and Sir Launcelot of the Lake, as well as King Arthur, Queen Guenever, and Merlin the magician. In Sam's original conception, the modern technocrat Morgan serves as a foil to the sorcerer Merlin, "the champion of hard unsentimental common-sense and reason" versus "the champion of the frivolous black arts" in order to contrast "the English life of the whole of the Middle ages with the life of modern Christendom and modern civilization—to the advantage of the latter, of course." In all, the novel when completed contained four entire chapters and parts of five additional chapters or several hundred words of verbatim quotes "borrowed" from Malory but only one footnote to *Le Morte d'Arthur*. He told Mary Mason Fairbanks privately that he thought it would be the last book he ever wrote and that he did not plan to publish it: "I expect to write three chapters a year for thirty years; then the book will be done. I am writing it for posterity only; my posterity: my great-grandchildren. It is to be my holiday amusement for six days every summer the rest of my life." He assured Mother Fairbanks that he would "leave unsmirched & unbelittled the great & beautiful *characters* drawn by the master hand of old Malory." Even in these early pages, however, Guenever tosses "furtive glances at Sir Launcelot that would have got him shot in Arkansas, to a dead certainty." He assured Fairbanks that "the story isn't a satire peculiarly,"[15] though of course it became in its subsequent development as much a satire of nineteenth-century England and America as of the idyllic Middle Ages depicted in *Le Morte d'Arthur* and Alfred, Lord Tennyson's *Idylls of the King*. After writing these initial chapters in 1886, Sam ran aground and pigeonholed the manuscript for almost a year and a half.

❖

During the mid-1880s Sam was increasingly frustrated with the failure of Congress to adopt meaningful international copyright legislation to protect both American and foreign authors. He joined the American Copyright League, founded in 1882 by George Parsons Lathrop, and the Authors' Club of New York, a group of working writers established in 1883 by Brander Matthews. Yet he was pessimistic that the rights of writers in the world market would soon change. "I am 47 years old, and therefore shall not live long enough to see international copyright established; neither will my children live long enough," he complained in late 1883. He expressed a willingness in March 1884 to attend the international copyright conference in Berne, Switzerland, the following August. In January 1885, while on tour with Cable, he told an interviewer that the status quo was "morally wrong. We have now an established literature of our own, and should not attempt to rob foreign authors of the fruits of their labor. It is unjust, to say the least." Though he had once opposed international copyright on the grounds that the absence of regulation enabled American readers to buy cheap books, he eventually if reluctantly concluded that morally "these cheap books are the costliest purchase that ever a nation made."[16]

By December 1885 Sam had lost faith in the Authors' Club as an advocacy group because its rolls had swelled to include archeological students at one extreme and the multimillionaire industrialist Andrew Carnegie at the other. When the popular poet Will Carleton, nominated for membership, seemed liable to be blackballed for no good reason, Julian Hawthorne, a member of both the Authors' Club and the American Copyright League, rallied to Carleton's defense and lobbied other members of the club on his behalf. As Hawthorne wrote Sam,

> I was at the Authors' Club last night for the first time in eighteen months. It happened to be election night and Will Carleton, the alleged poet, was among the candidates. I don't myself care for his poetry but I voted for him, because he is par excellence an American author, a man who has done honest work and gained solid and wide recognition. And there was another reason. The Club has latterly been filling up with men who, because they have passed through a street in which there was a bookstore, are called "authors." Nobody has known anything about them, good or bad, except that they have not published books: but their proposer will say "he is a good fellow," and of course his election will bring $15 to the Club.

Carleton had received the requisite four-fifths of the members' votes but "the men who had voted against him" challenged the results, whereupon the executive council "went into session and determined that the election must be held over again next meeting." Hawthorne was outraged and determined

> to do all I can now to get Carleton elected over again. In this I am wholly impartial: I don't know him and don't read his books: but such transactions as those of last night will ruin the Club if they are allowed to stand. I write to you, because I have every confidence in your sense and sincerity. I daresay you may hate Carleton, or that his poetry causes you to vomit: but I imagine that will not prevent you from voting for him on general principles. If you can't come down and do it yourself, I wish you would send me your proxy. This is the first electioneering document I ever penned and the first election in which I ever voted. Such things are contrary to my inclinations and instincts.

The manipulation of the voting "was a little too much for me, and, for the first and last time, I mean to protest," Hawthorne concluded. Sam replied a week later. He was troubled too. He agreed with Hawthorne "in all your points—except one," he allowed. "You think certain conduct will ruin the club; whereas I think that that sort of procedure has already ruined it. It isn't an Author's club at all. It is no more an Author's club than it is a horse-doctor's club. Its name is a sarcasm. I would like to see a new one started—on a sane plan." Whether or not Sam assigned his proxy vote on "the Carleton question" or voted in person, Carleton was reelected to membership in the club at the next meeting, Hawthorne was elected to its executive council, and Sam remained a member.[17]

In mid-November 1885, at about the same time this tempest was raging, Sam was invited to represent the American Copyright League in an audience with President Grover Cleveland at the White House. "One must not refuse an office of that kind, when asked," he explained to Livy, because "a man who prides himself on his citizenship can't refuse it." After registering at the Ebbitt House on November 19, he joined Robert Underwood Johnson of the *Century* and George Walton Green, chief of the Author's League, in a visit to the president. After "the first remark or two made on international copyright," Sam noted in his journal, "I wandered into a speech." He tarried the next several days in New York on business related to Grant's memoirs, though he took most of a day off on November 25 to play billiards and dine with Charles A. Dana, editor and part owner of the New York *Sun*. He returned to Hartford two days later to celebrate Livy's fortieth birthday with a dinner for twelve, including the actor Joseph Jefferson and Joe and Harmony Twichell.[18]

Over the next few weeks he waded into a morass, a convergence of three issues with his positions on two of them radically at cross-purposes: the development of the Paige typesetter, which when perfected would inevitably cost some printers their jobs; his advocacy of labor rights, prompted in part by the rise of the Knights of Labor; and his support for some kind of international copyright, represented at the moment by two competing bills in Congress. The difference between the Chace Bill, authored by Senator Jonathan Chace of Rhode Island, and the Hawley Bill, authored by Sam's friend Senator Joseph Hawley of Connecticut, was the so-called manufacturing or printing clause. In the simplest sense, the Chace Bill included a proviso that required foreign works protected by U.S. copyright be typeset in the United States—that is, it also protected the interests of American publishers and printers—and the Hawley Bill did not include such a stipulation. Sam preferred the Chace Bill but the American Copyright League backed the Hawley Bill. In short, as if to prove the adage that "no man can serve two masters," Sam faced competing if not incompatible demands in his roles of venture capitalist, publisher, author, and advocate of worker rights. There is little wonder that E. C. Stedman once introduced Sam as an amalgam "of Harper & Brothers and Edwin Booth," the roles of publisher and performer intertwined.[19]

Sam was caught in a double bind epitomized by a speech he delivered at a dinner of the Typothetae, a group of master printers, at Delmonico's in New York the evening of January 18, 1886. He had been invited to speak by Douglas Taylor, senior partner in the New York printing firm of Taylor and Company, and among the attendees were Will Carleton, Richard Watson Gilder, Osgood, Stedman, and Charley Webster. In his speech Sam reminisced about his experiences as a printer's devil in Hannibal thirty years earlier. In another rejected version of the speech, however, he had hailed "the type-setting art" as "the source and impulse of all intellectual life" with the implication, as Gregg Camfield suggests, that the Paige compositor "would be a similar benefaction, though it would cost many printers their jobs." Rather than speak from the perspective of either the managers in suits or the workers in aprons, Sam chose to skirt the issues of class and entertain the assembly with old bromides and Ambrose Bierce, for one, was enraged. "Mark the Jester" had been replaced by "Mark the Money-Worm," his speech an "atrocious desecration" of his role as public satirist. It should have been dismissed as "an epitaph, an affidavit, an indisputable proof that Samuel Clemens, Esquire, of Hartford, Connecticut was masquerading in the motley of Mark Twain."[20]

Sam was similarly conflicted when he returned to Washington, D.C., in late January 1886, again as a delegate of the Copyright League, along with Gilder, James Russell Lowell, Horace Scudder, and others, to testify on successive days before a joint meeting of the Senate Committee on Patents and the House Committee on the Judiciary. According to the *Boston*

Herald, Sam "disappointed the audience by not being funny." Neither was he decisive. Instead he betrayed his divided loyalties. The first witness, James Welsh, president of the Philadelphia Typographical Union No. 2, an affiliate of the Knights of Labor, opposed the Hawley Bill because it did not include a printing clause and Sam was persuaded by his argument. As Robert Underwood Johnson remembered, when Sam was called to testify and to the dismay of the delegation of authors, he "began by saying that he had been warned by Mr. [George Walton] Green that it would not be well to touch upon" the vexed question of the printing clause. He proceeded to qualify his support for the Hawley Bill and to boost the Chace proposal: "I am afraid that the Hawley bill in its original form, pure and simple, would work a great injustice to men who have vested rights in that direction," among them "publishers, printers, binders, and so on," he declared. "I cannot see any objection to the insertion of a clause which shall require that the books of a foreign author when copyrighted here shall be printed on this soil." Not that his equivocation made any difference: the Senate Committee on Patents sent a bill to the floor of the Senate on May 21 but it died there as the result of a filibuster. While in the capital, Sam also lunched with Hawley; met Henry Adams at the home of their mutual friend John Hay; chatted with Senator John P. Jones of Nevada and Generals William B. Franklin and Winfield Scott Hancock, the latter a former Democratic candidate for president who unexpectedly died a week later; and joined his colleagues on a visit to the home of Senator John A. Logan of Illinois, a former Civil War general and Republican vice presidential candidate. Within the next few months Sam not only considered publishing Logan's memoirs but issued *Reminiscences of Winfield Scott Hancock* by his widow, Almira Russell Hancock, in Webster and Company's Great War Library series.[21]

The competing commitments Sam faced in early 1886 also came to a head in the pending appearance of *Mark Twain's Library of Humor*, a project he superintended as both publisher and its ostensible editor. The *Library* was long in preparation, originating when the Philadelphia publisher George Gebbie in July 1880 proposed that Sam compile a humor anthology modeled on William Evans Burton's *The Cyclopaedia of Wit and Humor* (1866). In the spring of 1881, after his resignation from the editorship of the *Atlantic Monthly*, Howells agreed to cooperate with Sam in compiling an encyclopedia of humor for a stipend of five thousand dollars. On April 17 Howells explained that he could not "work at it except in the most leisurely way" because he "did not know exactly how hard this work will be" and "I don't know how big a book you wish to make," though he hired Charles Hopkins Clark, managing editor of the *Hartford Courant*, to assist him and perform most of the drudge work. On May 20, 1881, Sam contracted with Osgood to publish the anthology. To be sure, the *Library* was not a high-priority project. "I told Clark the other day to jog along comfortably and not get in a sweat," Sam wrote Howells on March 1, 1883. "I said I believed you would not be able to enjoy editing that library" as long as "you have your own legitimate work to do." A year later, when Howells requested partial payment for his editorial work on the *Library* to date, Sam temporized: "I am like everybody else—everything tied up in properties that cannot be sold except at fearful loss. It has been the roughest twelve-month I can remember, for losses, ill luck, & botched business." After Osgood declared bankruptcy in May 1885, Sam resolved to publish the *Library* under the Webster imprint. Howells continued to work periodically on the project until October 1885, when he contracted to write exclusively for Harper & Brothers, surrendered the *Library*, and requested payment of two thousand dollars over and above the five hundred he had already been paid. Sam again hesitated because he was in the midst of issuing Grant's memoirs and running the business on credit: "I am not in financial difficulties, and am not going to be. I am merely a starving beggar standing outside the door of plenty—obstructed by a Yale time-lock which is set for Jan. 1st." Howells was paid for his work on the *Library of Humor* two months later, but the episode hints at the fragility of Sam's fortunes.[22]

Sam scheduled the sale of the volume for the next year—this at the very juncture he testified before Congress about copyright in his conflicting roles of author and publisher. He admitted in March 1886 that the *Library* was "finished and ready" and he had "spent nearly ten thousand dollars in its preparation; but it is pigeon-holed indefinitely to make room for other people's more important books." This claim was only partly true. Its publication was delayed mostly because Webster and Company needed to secure permission to reprint dozens of articles. Sam was initially reticent to assume responsibility for the project after Osgood's bankruptcy because of the legal liability he would incur. As he warned Charley Webster, "the publisher may be sued for damages for using copyrighted matter without obtaining consent—in which case Osgood would have to pay 30 percent of such damage; whereas if you publish [the *Library*] I must pay *all* the damages. Not much danger of such a suit, but of course there is *some*." Among his other duties, Webster spent the next several months gathering the necessary agreements. As late as June 1887, only seven months before the release of the anthology, Sam instructed his nephew to "get H[oughton] M[ifflin] & Co's terms for the use of the matter we want." He suggested paying ⅔ of a cent per word "for that second-hand matter." Should "Houghton, Syphillis & Co." demand more in fees than they offered, Sam proposed "to use the matter without their consent and let them sue me" for damages.[23] As a publisher he was amenable to violating authors' copyrights, though as an author he was jealously protective of his own. In late 1887 and early 1888 Sam and Brander Matthews also engaged in a brief but spirited public debate in the *Princeton Review* over the merits of international copyright that briefly strained their friendship. Matthews was critical of English copyright protections of American authors, whereas Sam—who had once excoriated Canadian pirates—incongruously blamed the mess on Congress, not the thieves.

Some scholars have suggested that, much as he was a nineteenth-century progressive on matters of race, Sam became a protofeminist under the influence of Livy and other women in his circle. Yet the contents of *Mark Twain's Library of Humor*, once it was finally released, reinforced the prevailing opinion, perhaps best stated by the humorist Charles Godfrey Leland in 1904, that "there has never yet appeared in literature a single, original female Humorist." Of 144 pieces by forty-eight authors, only six articles by six women appeared in the *Library*, among them Sam's friends Mary Mapes Dodge and Harriet Beecher Stowe, who was hardly well known for her humor writings.[24]

Sam's all-too-normal chauvinism was all too apparent in his dealings with Kate Field, with whom he had last had contact in 1875. His attitude toward Field was consistently that of a Victorian patriarch: he treated her with undisguised condescension both privately and publicly, in both his own voice and anonymously. Even late in life, he dismissed Field, Anna Dickinson, and Olive Logan as exemplars of a new type of female lecturer "who "hadn't anything to say, and couldn't have said it if they had had anything to say; women who invaded the platform to show their clothes. They were living fashion-plates." In March 1886 Field wrote Sam to solicit his interest in a book she was writing. "You represent a big publishing house. I am writing a history of Mormonism which I think will be entertaining as well as enlightening. Such a book is fit only, it seems to me, to be sold by subscription. Does it appeal to you from a business point of view? I think I know what I am writing about." In fact, the *Salt Lake Tribune*—the leading "Gentile" or non-Mormon newspaper in Utah—once editorialized that any book Field might write on Mormonism "ought to be of more value than any former book on this subject." In his reply to Field, Sam allowed how he opposed the Mormon Church, much as he harbored reservations about all organized faiths. But he would not endorse any abridgment of religious freedom. "Your notion and mine about polygamy is without doubt exactly the same," he explained,

> but you probably think we have some cause of quarrel with those people for putting it into the religion, whereas I think the opposite. Considering our complacent cant about this country of ours being the home of liberty of

conscience, it seems to me that the attitude of our Congress and people toward the Mormon Church is matter for limitless laughter and derision. The
Mormon religion *is* a religion: the negative vote of all of the rest of the globe
could not break down that fact; and so I shall probably always go on thinking
that the attitude of our Congress and nation toward it is merely good trivial
stuff to make fun of. Am I a friend to the Mormon religion? No. I would like
to see it extirpated, but always by fair means, not these Congressional rascalities. If you can destroy it with a book,—by arguments and facts, not brute
force,—you will do a good and wholesome work.

If his "business decks were clear," he might be persuaded "to publish such
a book" as Field's, but "they are not clear now" and "it is hard to tell when
they will be. They are piled up with contracts which two or three years, and
possibly four, will be required to fulfil." Nor did Sam cease his patronizing remarks about Field after she died in 1896. In his sketch "Villagers of
1840–3" (1897), a roster of people he remembered from his boyhood, Sam
mentioned her as the epitome of the brassy and flamboyant woman journalist. Among the characters he describes in the sketch is Ella Hunter, "a loud
vulgar beauty from a neighboring town—one of the earliest chipper and self
satisfied and idiotic correspondents of the back-country newspapers—an
early Kate Field."[25]

During the winter and spring of 1886, Sam and Howells weighed an offer
to stage *Colonel Sellers as a Scientist*—an endeavor ultimately aborted in a
comedy of errors that turned out to be funnier than the play. On February
17 the elocutionist A. P. Burbank contacted Sam to inquire about the status
of the script and whether, if Burbank could find a producer, he might acquire
rights to it. The two men had been acquainted for a decade, meeting for the
first time at an entertainment sponsored by the New York Press Club in
early February 1877. Sam initially threw cold water on the idea:

'Tain't worth your while to join the procession of them that thought they
wanted it, but concluded they didn't. Still, if you want to waste your time, go
ahead; but I'm darned if I'm going to let you waste mine, old friend! Repair
unto my agent [Webster] & if he has got a copy of the play, business can be
talked; but if he hasn't, he is not to apply to me for it, for I won't take the trouble to hunt. I have said I would cleave the skull & play with the bowels of the
next man who ventured to mention that play to me, but you are a friend & I
spare you just this once.

Meanwhile, Sam advised Webster to discourage Burbank's proposal, too:
"Our interests and those of our clients are too large to be jeopard[iz]ed for

the few dollars that might be squeezed out of a play (a play which isn't worth a damn and is going to fail.) . . . I won't allow that play to be played this year or next upon *any* terms."[26] But Howells was more sanguine. Why not allow Burbank to try?

Sam and Howells finally decided to doctor the script before giving it to Burbank. They met in New York the evening of April 22, when they both attended the Authors' Club dinner at the Gilsey House, and agreed to meet again in Hartford on May 2 and invite Burbank to join them. They were pleased by Burbank's interpretation of the role of Sellers and, buoyed by their opinion, the erstwhile actor signed a two-week lease with Daniel Frohman, the manager of the Lyceum Theater in New York, and announced that the play would premiere there on May 24. Burbank agreed to share any profits with the authors. Meanwhile, desperate to salvage the project, Sam railed to Boston with Howells on May 3 and, on the day of his arrival, Howells reiterated that "as it stands" he feared not only "the thing will fail" but that "it would be a disgrace to have it succeed" and he began to revamp the script. "I've just read over the 3d Act and reviewed the whole play in my mind," he wrote Sam on May 5, and he had reluctantly reached the same conclusion as John Raymond almost two years before. "It *is* a lunatic whom we've pictured and while a lunatic in *one* act must amuse, I'm afraid that in three he would simply bore." Like Raymond, he was convinced that the play was incoherent, consisting of nothing more than a preposterous character and "a lot of comic situations." After originally "firmly, furiously" believing in its merits, Howells had a change of heart and was now convinced he and Sam should suppress the play. "Neither of us needs the money it might make very badly, though we would like it," he reflected, "and it wont make us any reputation, even if it succeeds." The playwrights made some changes "to our satisfaction" the next day but by May 11 a "cold fit came upon" Howells. Haunted by the prospect of professional humiliation, he surrendered to the obvious. *Colonel Sellers as a Scientist*, now renamed *The American Claimant*, was a turkey in the straw and he urged Sam to withdraw the script: "Here is a play which every manager has put out-of-doors and which every actor known to us has refused, and now we go and give it to an elocutioner. We are fools." But Sam had traveled with Twichell to the U.S. Military Academy at West Point for the weekend and the letter failed to reach him for several days, so Howells withdrew the play on his own authority. The *Boston Journal* reported on May 13, in an item dated the day before, that the play had "been indefinitely postponed" because when it "was rehearsed it became evident that it needed much alteration" and that Frohman had "received a check for a considerable sum for allowing" the lease of his theater "to be rescinded."[27]

The backstory is slightly more complicated. Sam and Howells were on the hook for scrapping the production. From all indications, Burbank was good-tempered about the annulment of their agreement so long as the playwrights paid the cancellation fee. Burbank negotiated a compromise with Frohman, who agreed to settle for seven hundred dollars. Howells proposed to Sam that each of them pay half because "the folly was mine as much as yours." Sam welcomed this offer like a bull greets a red flag; he refused to "shoulder a solitary ounce of the 'folly'" and insisted upon piling "every ounce of it" onto Howells. The incident nearly precipitated a spat—as close as the two men ever came to one—though Sam eventually agreed to pay his share of the fee and Howells washed his hands of the project.[28]

Much as he had spent a leisurely summer in Elmira and Quarry Farm in 1885, Sam expected "to enjoy a solid old-fashioned loaf" there in 1886. He floated the story that he planned to retire from professional writing—"if I perform any more literary work in future it will be only to 'keep my hand in,'" he told an interviewer, because "there is more money in being a publisher." He also planned to spend several days in Keokuk at a family reunion. His mother's memory "is wholly faded out and gone," he wrote Howells in May, "and now she writes letters to the school-mates who had been dead forty years, and wonders why they neglect her and do not answer." He hoped to visit her again before she was no longer able to recognize him.[29]

The family left Hartford for New York on June 15, overnighted at the Gedney House in the theater district on Broadway, and arrived in Elmira the next day. On June 21 they departed Elmira and paused in Niagara Falls, registering at the Cataract House, where Sam, Livy, and her parents had sojourned in late July and early August 1869. Rather than journey by train, Sam preferred to travel as much as possible by boat. They embarked from Buffalo on the Great Lakes steamer *India* on June 22, landing six days later in Duluth, where they registered at the St. Louis Hotel. Susy noted in her diary on June 26 that the family was en route "to Keokuk to see Grandma Clemens, who is very feeble and wants to see us, and pertickularly Jean who is her namesake. We are going by way of the lakes, as papa thought that would be the most comfortable way." They arrived on June 29 in Minneapolis, where they took rooms at the Ryan Hotel. The *Minneapolis Tribune* remarked on Sam's appearance in the hotel lobby: "a quiet man of medium height, attired in alligator slippers, a light gray suit, and a pearl colored high hat. In his mouth he had the stem of a corn cob pipe." After an excursion to Minnehaha Falls, the family railed to St. Paul and boarded the steamboat *War Eagle* for Keokuk, arriving on July 2. He repeated to a reporter his claim that this part of the river was much more charming than the Mississippi below St. Louis: "One finds all that the Hudson affords—bluffs and wooded highlands—and a great deal in addition. Between St. Paul and the mouth of the Illinois River there are over 400 islands, strung out in every possible shape. A river without islands is like a woman without hair. She may be good and pure, but one doesn't fall in love with her very often." Outfitted in a white duck suit, Sam delivered a Fourth of July oration at Rand Park on July 3—the Fourth was a Sunday—and, according to the St. Louis *Globe-Democrat*, "delighted a vast concourse of people by his happy and pointed remarks."[30] The Clemenses lingered in Iowa until July 7, enduring "four or five days & nights of hell-sweltering weather." Sam saw "my aged mother in life" for the last time on this trip. "Her memory was decaying; indeed, for matters of the moment it was about gone; but her memories of the distant past remained and she was living mainly in that far away bygone time." To flee the heat they railed to Chicago, where they registered at the Richelieu Hotel. Livy fell ill, so Sam entertained his daughters, accompanying them to a Battle of Shiloh panorama the afternoon of July 8. That evening Sam and the children walked a block north of their hotel on Michigan Avenue to the Exposition Building to hear the Chicago Symphony Orchestra but they arrived late and, after listening outside the hall to part of Beethoven's Symphony Number 5 in C Minor, they returned to the hotel.[31]

Back in Elmira on July 10, Sam spent the balance of the summer at leisure, though he read from his writings for the inmates of the Elmira Reformatory on July 21; vacationed from his summer vacation for a few days at Long Beach, New York; and attended the trial of department store magnate John Wanamaker, against whom Webster and Company had brought suit for marketing Grant's autobiography at a discount, in Philadelphia in early August. He wrote Franklin Whitmore from Elmira on September 16 that the family had enjoyed "an unimaginably delightful summer" and told a reporter the next day that he was "not at work; not doing a single thing; just loafing; that's all. I made up my mind that I would loaf all summer, and I intended to do it." The same day Sam sat for this interview, the family left Quarry Farm for New York, where they stayed a week at the Murray Hill Hotel near Grand Central Station on Forty-Second Street. They detoured for a day to Spring Lake Beach, New Jersey, and returned to Hartford on September 27.[32]

Sam worked on the "Captain Stormfield Visits Heaven" narrative intermittently throughout his career. He originally outlined a version of the story in 1869 and drafted it a year or so later, but in his own estimation "it was not a success." In 1872–73 he revised it but still "*it* wouldn't do." He explained the problem in his autobiography: "There are some books that refuse to be written. They stand their ground year after year and will not be persuaded. It isn't because the book is not there and worth being written—it is only because the right form for the story does not present itself. There is only one right form for a story and if you fail to find that form the story will not tell itself." In July 1874 he published a comic spin-off of the story in the *New York Herald* in the form of a burlesque advertisement for a grand tour of the stars in the tail of the Coy Coggia comet, then visible in the night sky. According to "A Curious Pleasure Excursion," a parody of the *Quaker City* prospectus and others like it, Sam and P. T. Barnum had chartered the comet and built a million staterooms in its tail. First-class travel cost a mere two dollars per fifty million miles and the comet flew at a cruising speed of twenty million miles per day. Barnum "the great showman" was delighted by the piece and appreciated the free publicity—not that he needed it. "Your *comet* article," he wrote Sam, "added much to my notoriety at home and abroad." As a token of his gratitude, Barnum hosted the Clemenses the night of October 11, 1875, at Waldemere, his mansion overlooking Long Island Sound near Bridgeport, Connecticut.[33]

In the spring of 1878 Sam returned to the Stormfield narrative. As he wrote Orion on March 2, he had discussed the premise with Howells, who urged him to "drop the idea of making mere magazine stuff of it," write it as a book, and "publish it first in England" with a blurb by Arthur Penrhyn Stanley, the Dean of Westminster, to "draw *some* of the teeth of the religious press" before reprinting it in the United States. Sam replied on June 27, 1878, that he had decided to open "all sorts of heavens" with a gate for each type of soul, including a barkeeper who is welcomed "with artillery salutes, swarms of angels in the sky, & a noble torch-light procession." He worked this idea into the manuscript of his novel *Simon Wheeler, Detective* around the same time: at the gates of heaven the hero spies people of many faiths, including Buddhists, Catholics, Muslims, and Quakers. A year later Sam decided to depict heaven as "an absolute monarchy with many viceroys" rather than "a leatherheaded Republic with the damnation of unrestricted suffrage." In October 1881 he resumed writing "Wakeman's adventures in heaven— merely for the love of it; for laws bless you, it can't ever be published"—and in an even later version of the story, his heaven is "heated with hot-air registers connected with hell." In any case, Sam told his daughter Susy in February 1886, when he still counted upon untold millions from the Paige typesetter, that "the only book that he had been pertickularly anxious to write was one locked up in the safe downstairs"—the unfinished "Captain Stormfield." This story had already been percolating for seventeen years and "could have been finished in a day at any time during the past five years," he admitted to Jeannette Gilder, but "there seemed to be no hurry, & so I have not hurried." The truth was more prosaic. According to Joe Goodman, Sam postponed publication of the tale because he worried that his heresies might "hurt his literary reputation; that the public wasn't yet advanced enough for that sort of thing."[34]

Sam read the introduction and first chapter of "The Autobiography of Sir Robert Smith of Camelot," the early working title of *A Connecticut Yankee in King Arthur's Court*, at the monthly meeting of the Military Service Institution on Governor's Island in New York Harbor the evening of November 11, 1886. Among the four hundred people in the audience were Generals John Schofield and William Tecumseh Sherman; General Sherman's brother John Sherman, senator from Ohio and former Secretary of the Treasury; and journalists from several New York and Boston dailies and the *Washington Post*. Sam had been invited by General James Barnet Fry to address the group the previous July and he "didn't know of that club's custom of having reporters at some of its meetings." When he rose to the podium, he admitted later, "I think I was about the worst scared man in the United States." He explained by way of introduction that the fragment of his next novel "which by your courtesy I am to read here tonight, is a story—a satire, if you please—which I began to write some time ago, and which is not finished," whereupon he read some passages and summarized the plot. Sam was stunned to read plentiful excerpts from his presentation in the local papers the next day:

> There was the chapter I had read printed almost verbatim but that wasn't all. There was printed in full a rather carefully written synopsis of the whole scheme of the book as I had plotted it out. I thought there was no use of my going on with the work. For the moment I imagined that the book pirate . . . would seize my synopsis and specimen chapter, write the book for me, kindly forge my name on the title-page and help himself to big profits from the spurious edition. I had put myself in a horrible position.

The same day excerpts from the novel appeared in the press, Sam visited General Fry, Julia Grant, and William Laffan, and the following day he returned to Hartford with Livy's mother, who met him in New York and spent the winter with the Clemenses in Hartford.[35]

Sam's social life in the winter and spring of 1886–87 was punctuated by visits to and from friends. Henry Stanley delivered his lecture "Through the Dark Continent" in Hartford the evening of December 8, 1886. Sam invited the African explorer and his Welsh artist-wife Dorothy Tennant to stay at the mansion, hosting a dinner for him, and, according to Twichell, "a late supper which was followed by talk till a late hour." The next evening Sam introduced Stanley before his lecture at Tremont Temple in Boston, commending him in particular for his "indestructible Americanism." With such celebrities as the Confederate war hero Colonel John S. Mosby, the pugilist John T. Sullivan, and James Pond, Sam also attended a reception for Stanley after his talk at the Boston Press Club. In thanking Sam for his hospitality a few days later, Stanley congratulated him on his "good & perfect little wife!" and his "family immeasurably excellent in quality—! Oh my friend rejoice in your happiness."[36]

Sam spent the second week of February 1887 in New York. After registering at the Victoria Hotel on February 8, he consulted with Webster at the company offices; joined the reorganized Authors' Club, whose members included Thomas Bailey Aldrich, Hjalmar Hjorth Boyesen, George William Curtis, Julian Hawthorne, Howells, Lathrop, Matthews, Stedman, Richard Henry Stoddard, and Charley Warner; and likely inspected the new club rooms on West Twenty-Fourth Street. The revised by-laws limited membership to 120 men and explicitly excluded any applicant "who is not the author of a published book proper to literature or who has not a recognized position in other kinds of distinctively literary work." On at least one occasion, probably this one, Sam retreated after a meeting of the club with Aldrich, Hawthorne, Howells, and Stedman to the Hoffman House across the street "for liquid refreshment." The evening of February 10 he spoke at the New York Stationers' Board of Trade banquet in the Hotel Brunswick. Among the 135 other attendees were Lyman Abbott, a minister and editor of the *Christian Union*, and publishers J. S. Ogilvie, whom Sam had sued for copyright infringement in 1882, and Charles Scribner. He excerpted his remarks from his forthcoming essay "English as She Is Taught," based on his correspondence with Brooklyn schoolteacher Caroline Le Row. Sam facetiously blamed the stationers "for selling the nonsensical school books from which parrot rules [of grammar] are drummed into children." Teaching had devolved into "worthless cramming," he alleged, and he illustrated the point with some definitions of words by Le Row's students: "Auriferous—pertaining to an orifice. Ammonia—the food of the gods. Equestrian—one who asks questions. Republican—a sinner mentioned in the Bible. Demigod—a vessel containing beer and other liquids." According to a Washington columnist, the speech "had the effect of stirring up considerable discussion" about cramming among public school students. The essay published in the April issue of the *Century* contained a few more gems (e.g., "Eucharist—one who plays euchre" and "Plagiarist—a writer of plays"). In an unsigned notice of this article, Oscar Wilde averred that it threw "an entirely new light" on "the American child." Sam received a check for $250 in payment for the piece and forwarded it to Le Row, though he had never met her. He also granted her permission to reprint the essay as an introduction to her book *English as She Is Taught* (1887).[37]

Sam delivered his talk on the teaching of English again six weeks later at an authors' reading in Boston to benefit the Longfellow Memorial Fund. He stayed overnight at the Howell's home on Beacon Hill and enjoyed "a rousing good time" before the event at Annie Fields and Sarah Orne Jewett's house on Charles Street near Boston Common and the Public Garden. But he was a reluctant participant in the "witch's Sabbath" that began at two in the afternoon of March 31 at the Boston Museum. Charles Eliot Norton presided and the other readers were Thomas Bailey Aldrich, George W. Curtis, Thomas Wentworth Higginson, Oliver Wendell Holmes, Julia Ward Howe, W. D. Howells, and James Russell Lowell, though Sam claimed in his autobiography that he "was the only one who was qualified by experience to go at the matter in a sane way"; and among the dignitaries in the audience were Fields, Edward Everett Hale, Jewett, Lucy Larcom, and Louise Chandler Moulton. Every seat in the theater was occupied, Lilian Aldrich recalled, "and in every available place the people stood wedged one against another, while the crowd still seeking admission reached far out into the street." At his request, because he was booked to appear in New Haven that evening, Sam led off the program. He was introduced by Norton, who invited him to "give a taste of his precious, patent champagne-mandragora" before fleeing to the train station. He learned later, however, "that at 6 o'clock half the audience had been carried out on stretchers and that the rest were dead—with a lot of readers still to hear from." Howells remembered that Sam was at the top of his game: "He was the most consummate public performer I ever saw and it was an incomparable pleasure to hear him" on the platform. "When he read his manuscript to you, it was with a thorough, however involuntary, recognition of its dramatic qualities." After speaking for ten minutes Sam ended with a jibe at the next speaker, Holmes, as a "profligate and amusing writer" and hurried from the stage. "My train was to leave Boston" at 4:00 p.m., he told an interviewer in 1907, and though he fled the theater "the moment I had finished my brief stunt" he had "barely time left" to catch it. That evening he addressed the Kent Club of Yale Law School at the New Haven City Hall, where he again read selections from *English as She Is Taught*.[38]

Two days later, back in Hartford, Sam spoke at the Trinity College gymnasium exhibition. As usual, he promised James Pond afterward that he would "never hoof a platform again." At the close of his brief remarks he joked that he once had a bookkeeper who, when he stopped exercising, "lost sixteen pounds and stole $30,000." His attempt at levity was, unfortunately, all too true. On March 11 Frank Scott, the cashier and chief accountant of Webster and Company—and treasurer of the Roseville Athletic Association—had been arrested at his home in New Jersey on a charge of embezzlement. Within the week Scott had confessed to robbing the firm of about twenty-five thousand dollars, most of it from the sale of Grant's memoirs, a theft that had begun as soon as he was hired in July 1885. Webster was inclined to leniency, given that Scott was a husband, a father of three children, and a first offender. If Scott would agree to be extradited to New York and plead guilty, Webster was "willing to use every means in his power to have his punishment made as light as possible." Sam, on the other hand, wanted to throw the book at him, to prosecute him to the fullest extent of the law, evict his family from their home, and confiscate and sell it, which is apparently what happened. Webster and Company obtained a deed to a house in Roseville the following November. In a charitable moment, Sam renegotiated Webster's contract, agreeing the same day he spoke at Trinity College to raise his annual salary by eight hundred dollars to compensate for the share of profits he lost through Scott's defalcation. He soon regretted his generosity, however, blaming Webster for "negligence" and "stupidity and mismanagement" for failing to prevent the crime. In the end, Scott pled guilty at trial on April 22 and was sentenced to six years of hard labor in Sing Sing. At the time, Sam considered the punishment "six years well earned." Later he protested that the wrong man had been convicted: "It ought to have been Webster." In his notebook Sam ranted about how his nephew had (mis)handled the problem. When the crime was discovered, he wrote to an imaginary Webster, "you had 3 times the office-force necessary for your (absence of) business, yet in spite of my appeals I was obliged to get *my* information about the defalcation from your sentimental newspaper interviews, in which you posed as a suffering but magnanimous hero & decided to be lenient in Court with a thief who hadn't robbed you but *had* robbed me. You have a rare faculty for being generous at other people's expense." Nevertheless, in November 1890 Sam and Webster together successfully petitioned Governor David Hill of New York to commute Scott's sentence for the sake of his family.[39]

The evening of April 8, a week after his comments at Trinity College, Sam was the featured speaker at the twenty-second reunion banquet of the Union Veterans Association of Maryland at the Hotel Rennert in Baltimore. He had been asked, he said, to "clear up a matter" that "had long been a subject of dispute and bad blood": "the true dimensions of my military services in the Civil War." In fact, in his speech Sam merely rehashed the final incident in "The Private History of a Campaign That Failed," the supposed murder of the stranger, with a similar purpose: to buffer his reputation against allegations of disloyalty to the Union. "Tonight the Union veteran of Maryland clasps hands with the rebel veteran of Missouri," he assured his audience at the beginning, and he closed the circle in his final line: "I acted for the best when I took my shoulder out from under the Confederacy and let it come down."[40]

Five days later Sam was back in New York to attend a pair of events. At a midnight supper party to mark the hundredth performance at Daly's Theater of *The Taming of the Shrew*, the longest run of a Shakespearean comedy in the United States to date, he related an anecdote about the obstacles he once overcame to meet the impresario Augustin Daly. He was introduced by General Sherman and among those in the audience were the stars of the play, John Drew and Ada Rehan, as well as General Fitz John Porter, Bronson Howard, Laurence Hutton, Elihu Vedder, Lester Wallack, and William Winter. The next day, April 14, the twenty-second anniversary of the death of Abraham Lincoln, Sam attended Walt Whitman's lecture on Lincoln at the Madison Square Theater. He was seated in the audience among a host of luminaries, including John Burroughs, Andrew Carnegie, Richard Watson Gilder, John Hay, Lowell, Augustus Saint-Gaudens, and Stedman. Six weeks later Sam contributed fifty dollars toward the construction of a cottage for Whitman. "What we want to do," Sam wrote their mutual friend Sylvester Baxter of the *Boston Herald*, "is to make the splendid old soul comfortable, & do what we do heartily & as a privilege." Whitman replied to Sam with "my special deep-felt personal thanks for your kindness & generosity to me."[41]

When Sam spoke at the ninth annual reunion banquet of the Army and Navy Club of Connecticut at Central Hall in Hartford on Ulysses Grant's sixty-fifth birthday, April 27, 1887, he improved the occasion by publicly chiding Matthew Arnold for his patronizing review of Grant's memoirs. In the January issue of *Murray's* magazine, Arnold had disparaged Grant's writing. He had "found a language all astray" in it, "an English without charm and without high breeding." He was particularly critical of the general's grammar, his misuse of "shall" and "will," "should" and "would." That is, the Oxford don exhibited precisely the type of snobby pedantry Sam had ridiculed in *English as She Is Taught*. In truth, Sam had not read Arnold's essay but only a critique of it by General James B. Fry in the April issue of the *North American Review*. The only sentence in his speech that he quoted from Arnold was one Fry had quoted in his piece. Still, Sam retaliated with a vengeance, charging Arnold with his own sort of "grammatical crimes" and lauding Grant's verbal art as "surpassing the art of the schools." According to the *Hartford Courant*, Sam "was interrupted with applause after every sentence and it was sometime after he had finished before order was restored."

As if to emphasize that the soldier was the equal of the scholar, he spent the next weekend at West Point, where he watched an artillery drill with William Tecumseh Sherman, John Sherman, and Richard Gatling, the inventor of the Gatling gun, and read *English as She Is Taught* to the assembled cadets. In fact, Sam visited West Point twice in the spring of 1886. On April 2 he had read for an hour and a half in the mess hall, including Huck's colloquy with Jim about Sollermun, "with as great success as on the occasion of our previous visit," Twichell reported. Afterward he entertained some of the cadets in the room of John J. Pershing, later the commander of the American Expeditionary Force in Europe during World War I.[42]

During the winter of 1886–87, at Livy's urging Sam also began to recite the poems of Robert Browning for an hour every Wednesday morning to a gathering of their friends in the library or billiard room of the Hartford mansion, one of dozens of Browning clubs organized across the country at the time. Sam had long read Browning to the family, Katy Leary remembered, but in November 1886 he became the instructor of a class that included Livy, Harmony Twichell, Susan and Lilly Warner, and occasional visitors. In March 1887 he informed Mother Fairbanks, who had organized a similar club in Cleveland, that he was "pretty proud of my Browning class" and that he prepared "30 or 40 pages of new matter for each sitting. It takes me much longer to learn to read a page of Browning than a page of Shakespeare." Originally he had prefaced his recitations with a brief lecture— that is, until the class objected. "They say that my reading imparts clear comprehension—& that is a good deal of a compliment." Or as he bragged, "put me in the right condition & give me room according to my strength & I can read Browning so Browning himself can understand it." The moral? "Don't explain your author; read him right & he explains himself." Mary Bushnell Cheney, the daughter of Horace Bushnell, remembered Sam's recitations in exactly this light. They were "not oratorical and aimed at no effects of cadence." Sam was "free from self-consciousness" and he "attempted only to let those sentences speak for themselves as the author meant them." In February 1887 Sam jotted on the flyleaf of his copy of Browning's *Dramatis Personae* (1884) some comments on his approach to reciting his verse: "One's glimpses & confusions, as one reads Browning, remind me of looking through a telescope (the small sort which you must move with your hand, not clockwork). You toil across dark spaces which are (to *your* lens) empty; but every now & then a splendor of stars & suns bursts upon you and fills the whole field with flame." His nephew Jervis Langdon, son of Charley and Ida, remembered that Sam's auditors "invariably demanded" that he recite "three favorites, 'How They Brought the Good News from Ghent to Aix,' 'Up at a Villa, Down in the City,' and, for climax, 'The Battle for Naseby,' which he delivered with supreme eloquence and emotion." In the spring of 1887, moreover, Sam invited Hiram Corson, professor of English literature at Cornell University, the leading Browning expert in the United States and the author of *An Introduction to the Poetry of Robert Browning* (1886), to meet with the class. Sam's reputation as a Browning reader also attracted guests to his home, including the New Orleans writer Grace King, who listened to him declaim passages from *The Ring and the Book* during the summer of 1887. "To him there were no obscure passages to be argued over, no guesses at meaning," King observed. "His slow deliberate speech and full voice gave each sentence its quota of sound and sense followed naturally and easily. He understood Browning as did no one else I ever knew." Candace Wheeler, too, thought Sam read Browning's verse "in a way which raised the standard of reading or recitation immeasurably." He also recited from Browning the evening of September 11, 1888, at "a private home to 130 people, the ladies in the majority," and at Smith College in November 1888.[43]

A. P. Burbank still aspired to star in *Colonel Sellers as a Scientist*, but he should have curbed the desire. Instead, he persuaded Sam to revise the script one last time and to finance a series of one-night stands in "country towns free from metropolitan criticism" in September 1887. Howells happily "relinquished gratis all right and title I had in the play." Burbank borrowed an array of props from Thomas Edison, including a "swearing phonograph" and a telephone, and premiered *The American Claimant*, or *Mulberry Sellers Ten Years Later* in New Brunswick, New Jersey, the evening of September 10 before an invited audience, followed by road performances in Syracuse and Rochester. These out-of-town tryouts were a financial misadventure, losing about $800. Nevertheless, Sam gambled another $230 to stage it at the Lyceum Theater in New York the afternoon of Friday, September 23.[44]

In its first and only performance in the city, the farcical comedy opened and closed to ruthlessly hostile reviews. Sam's friend William Winter, in one of the more restrained critiques, declared that it was "a little ghastly" and "cannot be long lived." The *New York Times* declared that because Sam wrote the piece, "it may be inferred that it is not a play. Mr. Clemens lacks something, maybe it is patience, perhaps it is talent, that a playwright should possess"; in his attempts at playwriting Sam had never demonstrated "that he comprehends the meaning of the word 'dramatic'" and *The American Claimant* was "as much like a play as a school exhibition dialogue." Andrew Wheeler (aka Nym Crinkle) confessed in the New York *Mirror*

that the manner in which the theater exposed Mark Twain's absolute empti-
ness gave me a new respect for the theater. He has been figuring successfully
for a long time in literature as a brilliant man. He couldn't do it on the stage.
His attempt to be a playwright reminded me of a comic singer's attempt to
play Hamlet. . . . Your mere funny man cannot do all things. He can't conduct
a funeral and he can't make a play. . . . I never saw mere humor so tiresome,
so undramatic, so imbecile. You can't dramatize a comic almanac. You can
make the public swallow any amount of rubbish if you put it on the Elevated
newsstands, but you put it on the boards for half an hour and see the result.

The New York *Evening Post* leveled its criticism at both playwright and star:
"Mr. Twain is an excellent humorist who knows nothing about playwriting
and Mr. Burbank is an amusing lecturer who knows nothing about acting."
The New York *Sun* ("tedious lengths of silly sentiment and witless doings")
and *New York Clipper* ("an utter and irredeemable failure," with Sellers "portrayed as an idiot" and the other characters as "dummies") were no more
complimentary. *Theatre* was harsh in its denunciation: "a miserable lot of
twaddle with neither dramatic construction nor reason" and "a more silly
conglomeration of rubbish . . . has not been seen on a respectable stage." The
New York *World* reviewer expressed his opinion in a piece of doggerel verse
entitled "A Petition":

> Mark Twain
>> In vain
> You try to write a play;
>> Your part
>>> In art
> Was never built that way.
>> 'Tis slush
>>> And mush
> You put upon the boards;
>> Each act,
>>> In fact,
> Built up of foolish words.
>> O Twain,
>>> Restrain
> Your wild dramatic craze.
>> Reflect—
>>> Expect
> No word of critic's praise;

For when
Your pen
Attempts to make a plot
It runs
To puns
And other stupid rot.
Excuse
My muse
For speaking out so plain;
But, Mark,
Please hark,
Don't write a play again.

The *New York Herald* was no less critical ("weak in dramatic construction, lacking notably in action and variety of incident"), albeit with a difference: the reviewer wondered why the fact of Howells's coauthorship had been suppressed: the play "was originally understood to be by Messrs. Samuel L. Clemens (Mark Twain) and W. D. Howells but was accredited to Mark Twain alone" on the program. Of all the adverse comments about the production, Burbank was most aghast at this violation of etiquette. "You cannot be more annoyed than I am about the association of Howells' name with the play," he admitted to Sam. "I said and reiterated it, that Mr. Howells had *no connection whatever* with the play and that his name must not be mentioned." On his part, Frohman was more amused than aggrieved by the failure of *The American Claimant*, more anxious to be paid for the onetime use of his theater than that despondent Burbank would not be leasing it for the long term: "A week passed and I did not receive any money" for the rental "so I said to Mark Twain: 'If your company does not pay me for my losses on this play I will keep it on,' whereupon he instantly hustled around and made up with his colleagues the required sum and so the play was stopped."[45]

Not that it was dead yet. When Sam's friend W. A. Croffut of the *Washington Post* asked about the play in late October, Sam replied that it might require "doctoring here and there." It more sensibly needed a euthanasist. Croffut added that it was "without dramatic parts or story. It is mainly a monologue—immensely funny but lacking movement." In an apparently unsent draft of a letter to Burbank written at about the same time, Sam admonished the would-be actor to "go to Sheol," then to "go to the other place. My future is uncertain; & if the worst comes to the worst" it would be a comfort to know that the play was not "as bad as it could have been." Two years later, in reply to an inquiry from Howard Taylor, a former compositor on the staff of the Virginia City *Territorial Enterprise*, Sam attempted to leverage the surrender of theatrical rights to *Colonel Sellers as a Scientist* by coupling them with the sale of theatrical rights to *A Connecticut Yankee*. Sam proposed to sell Taylor the dramatic rights to his latest novel if he would cast Burbank in the leading role of his adaptation, an attempt to persuade Burbank to abandon his rights to the earlier play. Nothing came of the idea because Howells objected. Yet Howells, still captivated by its humor, offered the script as late as January 1890 to the actor James A. Herne, who briefly considered revising and performing it, and Sam discussed the viability of staging the play with Augustin Daly as late as February 1892.[46]

As if he did not already have a number of irons in the fire, Sam urged Ned House to dramatize *The Prince and the Pauper* (1881) in the winter and spring of 1887. According to Sam, House professed (falsely) to be the author of "the bulk of 'Arrah no Pouge,'" an 1864 play usually attributed to Dion Boucicault, and in January 1884, after collaborating with Howells on *Colonel Sellers as a Scientist*, Sam expressed his wish to House that "*you* were here to write plays with." Sam repeatedly claimed over the years that he had originally composed the story of Edward VI and Tom Canty as a drama rather than a novel. Further, he had tried his own hand at adapting the novel to the stage "& made a bad botch of it," he explained to House on December 17, 1886, "but *you* could do it. And if you will, for ½ or ⅔ of the proceeds, I wish you would." House replied on December 24 that he would be "well pleased to undertake a dramatization" and "could start in a day or two." Sam's attorneys subsequently claimed that this letter was ambiguous, "full of qualified phrases," that House indicated in it he "would be pleased to do something" but for his "physical limitations which rendered of doubtful value or utility his services in placing the play even after it should be written." A few days later Sam had a couple of copies of the novel sent to House in New York and mailed him a copy of his own "absurd P. and P. dramatization," though House later insisted he never read it. Early in the new year, probably during the second week of February while in New York on business, Sam met with House, who had decided that the dual roles of prince and pauper should be performed by a single child actor, and he invited House to Hartford where they would "put the play in shape"—or so House remembered. In April and early May, he claimed later, he addressed at least six letters to Sam about the script, including one on May 7 in which the poverty-stricken playwright asserted that

> the complete scheme of the play developed with an effectiveness that I had not expected to arrive at so soon. The mere writing of the scenes and acts ought not now to occupy a great deal of time. But it may take a mighty long

time to find the right person to fill the double part. . . . I would rather have it put off two or three years than let it be intrusted to incompetent hands. . . . I can't tell you, my dear Mark, what a comforting thing it is to have this piece of good fortune in prospect. It takes a load of care away from me, as you can well imagine.

If House sent these letters to Sam, the originals have disappeared.[47]

In any event, House, his companion Koto, and his Japanese servant Ejiro Miromiya arrived in Hartford in mid-May and lived at the mansion until the Clemenses returned in September from their summer in Elmira. Sam and House discussed the play during this period, as they had both agreed to do, though they signed no formal contract. House testified later that on June 13 he read a complete act 1 to Sam, who "expressed his approval in energetic and enthusiastic terms, exclaiming at intervals: 'That's a play' and 'I see that on the stage.'" House told the *Boston Herald* two years later, "When I read the play to Mr. Clemens, he was pleased with it and offered me liberal terms. In fact, the terms were so liberal that I should have hesitated to accept them." Others were present during the reading, House remembered, "and can testify that the act was wholly written, that Mr. Clemens came to my room for the express purpose of hearing it, and that he remained there, listening and discussing the subject, during the best part of an afternoon." House promised to finish the script over the summer and reported to Sam on August 29 that he had completed a script of "the whole five acts" save for "the closing of Act V," though he had not copyrighted it. But Sam was indifferent, according to House, who "again and again tried to interest Clemens in the play and to induce him to go into the question of putting it before managers." But Sam "would not discuss it" and "appeared irritated if urged to do so against his inclination." In fact, House testified, Sam asked not to be consulted in the preparation of the script, much as Sam had ordered Webster to avoid bothering him with business details. "From the moment when the dramatization was first arranged," House told the press, Sam's "chief desire was that no care or burden of business should fall upon him. He wished to do nothing, to hear of nothing, that should make it necessary for him to take any active part in the affair."[48] When House complied, Sam construed his silence as a loss of interest in the project. The entire affair, from this perspective, was nothing more than a huge misunderstanding.

Sam remembered events very differently. When he visited House in New York in February 1887, he recalled, "I was looking for a dramatist for 'The Prince and the Pauper,' and this principal author of Boucicault's great play seemed to me to be the very man I wanted; so I proposed that House dramatize the book." But House "was indifferent and declined." Nor had he invited House to Hartford to write the play a few weeks later. On the contrary, from House's letters—again, they have vanished—"it appeared that his landlord was a desperado and the lives of the Houses in danger" so he had bidden the "friendless and forsaken cripple," Koto, and servant to Hartford to live in his Farmington Avenue house temporarily. "The reason we invited him to come to us," Sam insisted, was that "he & Koto were being brutally treated by their landlord & were afraid of bodily assault" so he had offered them "an asylum." As Sam averred, "House thinks he wrote an act of the play while he was in our house" but "if he did, he crowded it into two or three pages of paper, for he showed me no more than that. It was a skeleton of part of an act" with "some trifles of conversation put in to indicate the drift of the act," and "I was to do the filling-in myself, not he." Sam was later even more specific: "The sketched contained hardly more than fifteen lines of dialogue." He "praised the skeleton" and he "exchanged some commonplaces" with House, he recollected. "The interview was at an end in fifteen minutes, and if the subject was ever mentioned again by either of us during the year and five or six months that he remained in Hartford afterward, I have not the slightest recollection of it." Sam lost interest in the project, he later insisted, because House "gradually abandoned the matter & ceased to speak of it." In any case, Sam swore that House never "wrote a complete act" so far as he knew and that he "never received any letter from Mr. House saying the play was finished." Or as he advised Dean Sage, "I tried my level best to get that man to agree to dramatize the Prince & Pauper, but I failed, & then after his brief attempts here in the house I totally *dropped* the matter" and "so did he."[49]

At the same time House and his entourage were living in the Clemens mansion, Grace King was staying with Charley and Susan Warner in their Nook Farm home. To judge from King's diary and her memoirs, she and Sam became fast friends. King remembered a two-hour walk she took with Sam and Twichell, "just meandering through the winding roads up and down the hill, under the grand forest trees, and all around the little lake." In private Sam was "not at all refined," she thought; he would pad around in slippers with a pipe and munch on food "like a corn-field darkey." Yet she also discovered that "under his great shock of grey hair lies a very profound vigorous intellect"; Sam was "a genius in disguise of a humorist; in old times he would have been a righteous buffoon." She was enthralled by his casual conversation because, as she put it, "he talks just as he writes," though she admitted "his anecdotes are always a little risqué." On June 7 King accompanied Sam,

Livy, and the Warners on a weekend trip to Olana, the home of the painter Frederic Edwin Church overlooking the Hudson River. "It was an ideal holiday, in a Garden of Eden without the Garden of Eden's unprotection from weather," Sam wrote Church afterward in his note of thanks.[50]

The evening of Sunday, June 19, two days before departing for New York en route to Elmira for the summer, the Clemenses hosted a formal dinner for King and Lucius Fairchild, their friend from Paris and former Union general and three-term governor of Wisconsin. "We dressed *en grande tenue,*" King recalled, "I in my best, a pretty, long trailing crêpe, made by one of the New Orleans best modistes." Among the guests were Charley Clark, Karl Gerhardt, Ned and Koto House, and the Warners. Sam and Livy spared no expense to entertain in style. "The table was beautiful—round with an exquisite cut glass bowl in the centre filled with daisies, ferns and grasses—a bunch of white roses was at each one's plate," according to King. Sam ushered her to the dining room and Fairchild escorted Livy. The dinner talk soon turned to the Civil War and the conciliatory politics toward the South of Grover Cleveland. King, an ardent Southerner, took offense at Fairchild's rabid republicanism, though she held her tongue. Sam turned the conversation by regaling the guests with stories, including one of Joe Twichell's: A temperance minister visits an old woman in his congregation, who offers him a glass of wine. He declines and explains that he is "a teetotaler." The woman replies, "So am I, but I'm not a fool." After the dinner Sam and Livy were mortified and apologized to King for Fairchild's bad manners.[51]

As usual, the family vacationed in the summer of 1887 at Quarry Farm, leaving Hartford on June 21, spending a week in New York, and arriving in Elmira on June 29. Sam devoted his working months at the farm to reading and writing, indulging in particular his taste for history and biography with Thomas Babington Macaulay's *The History of England from the Accession of James II* (1849), *The Memoirs of the Duke of Saint-Simon on the Reign of Louis XIV and the Regency* (1857), Prince Metternich's *Memoirs* (1880), George Standring's *The People's History of the English Aristocracy* (1887), and rereading for the umpteenth time Thomas Carlyle's *History of the French Revolution* (1837). This time, however, the *History* was not the same book. "When I finished Carlyle's French Revolution in 1871, I was a Girondin," he wrote Howells, the champion of the Haymarket anarchists. "Every time I have read it since, I have read it differently—being influenced & changed, little by little, by life & environment (& Taine & St. Simon): & now I lay the book down once more, & recognize that I am a Sansculotte!—And not a pale & characterless Sansculotte, but a Marat," a radical revolutionary. "Carlyle teaches no such gospel: so the change is in *me*—in my vision of the evidences."[52]

Sam's changed perspective is discernible in the seismic shift in tone of the sixteen-plus chapters he added that summer to the manuscript of *A Connecticut Yankee*. For example, whereas Sam's hero had observed in chapter 2 that "the speech and behavior" of the sixth-century nobles "were gracious and courtly," in chapter 4 as he stands "naked as a pair of tongs" before the gentry of Camelot he is shocked to discover that "many of the terms used in the most matter-of-fact way by this great assemblage of the first ladies and gentlemen in the land would have made a Comanche blush." In chapter 13 the Yankee hails "the ever memorable and blessed [French] Revolution, which swept a thousand years of such villainy away in one swift tidal-wave of blood." As Sam explains in the voice of his Yankee, "there were two 'Reigns of Terror,'" the brief "Terror of the Revolution" and the "older and real Terror" that lasted a thousand years and "which none of us has been taught to see in its vastness or pity as it deserves." Or as he elaborates in chapter 20, "all gentle cant and philosophizing to the contrary notwithstanding, no people in the world ever did achieve their freedom by goody-goody talk and moral suasion: it being immutable law that all revolutions that will succeed must *begin* in blood, whatever may answer afterward." The people of Camelot needed "a Reign of Terror and a guillotine." He wrote these chapters in white heat fueled by his reading. "Within the past 3 days I have got head over heels in a book & am writing without rest or stop—steam at high pressure," he wrote Franklin Whitmore on July 21. "As the book is worth thirty or forty thousand dollars when finished, I can't afford to stop to read agreements, write letters, or anything else." By mid-August he was so consumed by the narrative that when he stopped working at the end of a day, "everything seems confused & I can't get my bearings." Though he had completed only about five hundred manuscript pages or a third of the novel when he left Elmira for Hartford on September 13, he hoped to finish his "uncommonly bully book" by the end of the year. "But it may never go to press," he again asserted, "for it is a 100,000-copy book, if Huck Finn was a 50,000-copy book, & I shall wait until I see at least an 80,000-copy sale ahead before I publish."[53]

Despite his hectic writing schedule, Sam still found time for baseball. His love for the game blossomed in Elmira during the summer of 1887. It germinated in May 1875, when he attended a contest in Hartford between a local team and the Bostons. The event is well known not for his enjoyment of it, however, but because his umbrella was stolen and he advertised for its return:

TWO HUNDRED AND FIVE DOLLARS REWARD—At the great baseball match on Tuesday, while was engaged in hurrahing, a small boy walked off with an English-made brown silk UMBRELLA belonging to me, and forgot to bring it back. I will pay $5 for the return of that umbrella in good condition to my home on Farmington avenue. I do not want the boy (in an active state) but will pay two hundred dollars for his remains.

Sam played baseball every afternoon later that summer of 1875 while on vacation at Bateman's Point near Newport. He alluded to baseball in his sketch "Methuselah's Diary" (1875), recorded the box score of a game in his notebook sometime in the mid-1870s, and protested the fixing of games in a two-sentence letter to the editor of the *Hartford Times* in June 1877. His enthusiasm for the sport exceeded his ability to play it, however. In February 1887 he subscribed to an "amusement association" in Hartford that sponsored a new baseball club and on Saturday, July 2, he and Thomas K. Beecher umpired a five-inning game between a pair of local teams, the Alerts and Unions, at the Maple Avenue Grounds in south Elmira that was covered by New York and Boston reporters. Sam wore a white duck suit, black slippers, and straw hat and, sharing in a long baseball tradition, he spit on a flat stone that apparently served as home plate to start the game. "Foul lines were generally ignored," according to the *New York Tribune*, and the New York *Sun* reported that "of all the utterly incompetent, shiftless, and ignorant umpires that ever tangled up the proceedings of a pair of ball clubs," Sam and Tom Beecher "were the worst." At one point, Sam ruled that "cripples will be removed from the field at once and substitutes put into their places" and during the late innings he apparently called balls and strikes from the grandstand. Still, *Sporting Life* magazine noted a year later that Sam was "an enthusiast regarding baseball and attends all the games played at Hartford" and, in a passage he subsequently deleted from *A Connecticut Yankee*, Sandy heaves rocks at Hank while he umpires a game.[54]

CHAPTER 15

Vanity Fair

The man who is a pessimist before 48 knows too much;
if he is an optimist after it, he knows too little.

—Sam Clemens to Joseph Twichell, March 14, 1905

IN THE SPRING of 1887 Samuel Clemens picked a fight with his nephew
and nominal publisher over the management of Charles L. Webster and
Company, blaming him for the selection of books the firm published (or
failed to publish), delays in issuing some volumes, the splashes of red ink in
its accounting ledgers, its move to larger and more expensive office space on
East Fourteenth Street in New York, and the size of its bloated office staff.
To be sure, Sam had betrayed some signs of dissatisfaction earlier, as in January 1885 when he declined to loan his nephew forty-five hundred dollars
to finance the purchase of a brownstone uptown on 126th Street. (Webster
found another lender and bought the house and by December 1886 he was
building a fourteen-room summer home at Far Rockaway, Long Island.)
Years later Sam complained to his sister Pamela that his publishing company "was insanely managed from the day it got the [Ulysses S.] Grant book"
in February 1885, though at the time he either applauded Webster's successes or acquiesced to what he subsequently considered his failures. To be
sure, Webster probably hired more employees than he needed; he bragged in
December 1886 that he supervised "the finest subscription publishing office
in the world," a "pretty busy place" with "about 14 clerks." It was apparently
as busy and chaotic as a fire drill. Sam wrote his brother Orion in the fall of
1887 that "there was no more system in the office than there is in a nursery
without a nurse. But I have spent a good deal of time there since & reduced
everything to exact order & system—insomuch that even Webster can run
it now—& in most particulars he is a mere jackass." Webster dumped all of
the remaindered copies of *Life on the Mississippi* (1883) on the trade market "for more than cost" in April 1887, "a splendid sale," he reported—and
Sam initially agreed. "Thank goodness the Mississippi is out of the way at
last," he replied to Webster. "I was very tired looking at the pile." But then
he reconsidered. He had acquired the copies from James R. Osgood at his

own expense so from his perspective they were his private property and the proceeds from their sale should not have been credited to the firm. Worse, he later alleged that, rather than selling the remaindered copies for a slight profit, Webster gave them away. Worse yet, the practice of dumping books into the trade market eventually backfired when, in the spring of 1888, some book agents refused to sell Webster and Company subscription volumes on any terms because, as Fred Hall reported, the firm failed to honor their contracts with the agents to prevent retail stores from carrying them.[1]

After the disappointing sales of the biography of Pope Leo, Sam pinned his hopes for a blockbuster best seller on the autobiography of Henry Ward Beecher. In mid-January 1887 Sam approved a five-thousand-dollar advance and half profits to Beecher because "his wide reputation entitles him to that." He anticipated that the book would "sell first-rate—tip-top" because "½-profits from us is as good as 75 per cent from any other house" and if Beecher failed to earn forty thousand dollars in royalties it would be his own fault. In mid-February Sam predicted that Beecher's book would sell quite well if he "heaves in just enough piousness." No doubt he also counted on Beecher's account of the Elizabeth Tilton scandal to spur sales. But less than a month later, on March 8, Beecher died suddenly of a cerebral hemorrhage. On March 16 Sam admitted to Orion that "the loss of the Autobiography" was a "*real* financial discomfort" and "a clear loss of $100,000" to the firm. He also acknowledged to Joe Twichell that it was a pity "so insignificant a matter as the chastity or unchastity of Elizabeth Tilton could clip the locks of this Samson & make him as other men, in the estimation of a nation of Lilliputians creeping & climbing about his shoe-soles." Webster and Company renegotiated the contract with the Beecher family, who eventually returned the advance. In place of the autobiography, Henry Ward's brother William and son-in-law Samuel Scoville assembled a Beecher biography, though Sam was frustrated with its progress. "If those people cannot be frightened into completing the Beecher book in three weeks," he complained on September 2, "I think the book will not only fail but will so clog our hands as to heavily damage one or two *other* books." Though the biography was published in 1888, it "brought only a moderate return," as Albert Bigelow Paine put it diplomatically.[2]

In January 1887 Sam's friend William Laffan of the New York *Sun* offered William Walter's *Oriental Ceramic Art* to Webster and Company and Sam again jumped at the opportunity. He expected the catalog, illustrated with images of artifacts in Walter's collection and text by Laffan, to be "a greenback-mine" worth "a couple of dozen B[eecher] autobiographies" and he urged Webster to reach a deal that included a "proper division of the swag." But he grossly overestimated the appeal of the volume: "I see a probable three quarters of a million dollars' profit in L[affan]'s proposed book. There's a dead-certain half-million, I judge." So he suggested that Webster offer Laffan "*one-quarter* of said swag, we to take the ¾. If that doesn't seem satisfactory, maybe the offer of a third will." In his autobiographical dictation twenty years later, however, Sam alleged that Webster failed to act on his advice and the available evidence tends to substantiate the charge. Laffan asked Sam the following summer, "When can Webster talk figures on that Baltimore book?" Sam relayed the question to his nephew, who failed to reply.[3] The catalog was eventually published in 1897, three years after Walter's death, by D. Appleton and Company, featuring over a hundred color plates and over four hundred black-and-white photographs.

The comic actor Joe Jefferson offered his autobiography to Webster and Company in the spring of 1887 and suffered a similar fate. "We've *got* to keep places open for great books" because "they spring up in the most unexpected places," Sam admonished his nephew on May 11. He planned to "read the MS for 'literary quality'" and then send the manuscript to New York "to be read for pecuniary quality." He urged Webster to negotiate terms with Jefferson, as if the decision to publish the book had already been made. By May 28 Sam reported that Jefferson's narrative was "delightful reading & I see that it has this additional great advantage: it is quite largely a book of *foreign travel* & the illustrations can be made to show up that feature prominently." He estimated total sales of the volume at twenty to fifty thousand copies and recommended that Jefferson be offered "forty per cent of the profits" or an 8 percent royalty. But then Webster disappeared from the day-to-day management of the company for the entire summer of 1887. Because of the "long silence," Jefferson signed a contract with the Century Company, which released the book in 1890. "Webster did not decline" it, Sam complained in 1906. "He simply ignored it." Sam claimed that he had "accepted several excellent books but Webster declined them every time and he was master. But if anybody offered *him* a book, he was so charmed with the compliment that he took the book without examining it. He was not able to get hold of one that could make its living."[4]

Early in 1887 Sam's friend E. C. Stedman proposed a multivolume *Library of American Literature* to be coedited with Ellen Mackay Hutchinson for publication by Webster and Company. "But Stedman didn't bring the book to me," Sam remembered in June 1906. "He took it to Webster," who "was delighted and flattered" and "accepted the book on an 8 per cent royalty." But by contract both Sam and Webster needed to sign off on every project. Sam wrote his nephew on March 1 that he thought "well of the Stedman book but I can't somehow bring myself to think *very* well of it." Sam no doubt gave his blessing to the project, however. Not only did Webster and Company contract for the ten-volume *Library* (which eventually swelled to eleven volumes) with the support of both principals in the company but the firm paid eight thousand dollars for plates of the first five volumes. The contract between Webster and the editors also included a clause best described as a poison pill that eventually doomed the company despite the sale success of the series. As Sam observed later, the clause "secured the lingering suicide of Charles L. Webster and Company" by front-loading most of the expense, including all production costs and royalties on sales, prior to delivery of the volumes and payment by the subscribers. The set cost buyers thirty-three dollars, payable in three-dollar monthly installments, and therein lay the problem. This method of sale depleted the company's operating capital much more rapidly than it was recouped in payments. As a result, the firm was required, as Paine explained, "to borrow most of the money required to build these books." In 1889 alone the cost to produce the *Library of American Literature* exceeded collections by twenty-two thousand dollars. By March 1891 the company was owed over thirty thousand dollars by customers but was in debt about a hundred thousand dollars for expenses, royalties, and commissions. "The faster installment orders came in, the faster our capital shrank, until our prosperity became embarrassing," Fred Hall recalled.[5]

Sam also blamed Webster for the long-delayed publication of *Mark Twain's Library of Humor*. After W. D. Howells and Charley Clark submitted the copy for the *Library*, Sam reworked the table of contents, organizing the articles not by "authors, times, and topics" but by the principle of free association "on which he built his travels and reminiscences and tales and novels," Howells recalled. He also commissioned E. W. Kemble to draw nearly two hundred illustrations for the volume, though for the most part Sam disliked the images. The months Webster required to secure reprint permissions and the weeks Kemble needed to prepare the sketches substantially delayed publication of the book. Sam was anxious that it appear as soon as possible, given the company's cash flow problems. He groused in his notebook in December 1887 that the *Library* "ought to have issued & sold 100,000, fall of '86." He begged Webster to put the volume into production "without waiting for pictures," if necessary, "& push it through" in order to issue it on December 15. He was confident that the *Library* would sell fifty thousand copies with illustrations and thirty thousand copies without them. He had notified Orion on September 5, 1887, that the *Library of Humor* was "going into the works now & I have appointed the day & cleared the field for it." He added two days later that Webster's mismanagement of the accounts had caused him to borrow a hundred thousand dollars with interest to cover expenses and he admitted to Andrew Chatto two weeks later that 1887 had been an "off year," though he expected the company finances to recover. In the end the *Library of Humor* was another sales disappointment, earning almost no money. "I imagined that a Library of Humor would go well—but I know better now," Sam allowed to Chatto a year later. "On it we have scored an amusingly distinct failure here. I shan't meddle any more in that direction." Of course, Sam blamed Webster for the botch. "He suppressed a compilation made by Howells and me . . . so long and finally issued it so clandestinely," he averred in his autobiography, "that I doubt if anybody in America ever did find out that there was such a book."[6]

Webster was perfectly aware of his uncle's caviling and diagnosed the problem in a note to him in early April 1887. Theirs was "a strained relationship and no business can succeed where partners deal with each other at arms length," he admitted. "Such a condition of affairs is wholly repugnant to my feelings." He asked to renegotiate his contract again both to protect his own interests in the company and to be shielded from his uncle's losses on the typesetter. Sam thought he had Webster trapped and proceeded to tighten the screws. "I could never interfere before" in the management of the company, Sam explained, because the contract William Hamersley had drafted and Sam and Webster had signed in 1886 "was so ingeniously contrived that for two years I have had no more say in the concern than the errand-boy; & to ask a question was to invoke contemptuous silence, & to make a suggestion was to have it coolly ignored." But, he chortled to Orion, their nephew "made one grab too many" when he asked for a new contract

> & turned the tables on himself. He knew I had been spending $5,000 a month here for a year on a project of mine, & that this was to continue for another year; so he got frightened & demanded & *required* that I put up a permanent cash capital of $75,000 for the publishing-house to save it from destruction in case I ruined myself. (Formerly I had to furnish *limitless* Capital & be responsible for everything.) It was offering me my emancipation-papers & I did not lose any time in signing the contract. Up to that time he had been all insolence; but he is the gentlest spirit in this region since—perfectly tame & civil. And stands criticism like a pupil; stands being reminded of the numerous ways in which he has betrayed the fact that he is not the miracle of a publisher he supposed he was, but a blundering, ignorant apprentice.

Before long, however, Sam regretted signing this new contract. Under the terms of the earlier agreements, he decided, "Webster had been my paid servant; under the new one I was his slave, his absolute slave, and without salary. I owned nine-tenths of the business; I furnished all the capital; I shouldered all the losses; I was responsible for everything—but Webster was sole master." As the editors of Sam's autobiography observe, "the clause that Clemens evidently objected to put Webster in charge of the 'entire management of the active business of the said firm,' including 'the employment and discharge of clerks and other employees . . . and the making of all contracts for work or material.'" The only action required of Sam was his consent to publish each book issued by the firm. As Webster later explained to Sam's lawyer Daniel Whitford, while Sam "now complains of a clause placing all business in my hands," the same clause had "appeared in every contract he ever made with me." Before the end of 1887, moreover, Sam tried to persuade Webster to forfeit the eight-hundred-dollar annual raise he had received to compensate him for Frank Scott's embezzlement. Charley predictably objected, insisting to Sam on December 28 that his salary had "always been too small. I think I can say without fear of contradiction that no man in the City of New York having anywhere near the cares and responsibilities that I do works for a salary of less than $5,000 a year." Moreover, he reminded his uncle, "you talk as though you were paying my salary" but "this is not so. I earn it myself. You forget that every dollar invested by you in the firm was earned by the firm." Then the final plea for compassion: "I am not whining but I have actually ruined my health by the hard work which I did" on Grant's *Memoirs*.[7]

In Webster's defense, he suffered from acute neuralgia during the summer of 1887; he was often absent from the office, and Sam did not know it. On September 7, two days after Sam wrote Orion that the *Library of Humor* was "going into the works," his nephew finally wrote his first letter to Sam since June to explain "the reason for this long silence on my part." He had been "laid up here for weeks, most of the time confined to bed unable to consider or attend to any business whatever and this is the first letter I have been able to write anyone in that time." He expressed the hope that he would soon return to his desk "as in better days." Sam replied with sympathy and understanding; he had not realized Webster was "seriously ailing" until that time. "It is plain that you have had an exceedingly hard summer of it," he added, "& we are all glad to know that you are getting up out of it at last."[8]

Despite the failed and aborted projects and missed opportunities, Sam remained upbeat, at least to outward appearances. "We've got a safe full of MS books that are as good as government bonds," he insisted to Orion in March 1887. In fact, most of those manuscripts were duds. Whereas he wrote Fred Hall in July 1887 that the firm wanted Congressman Sunset Cox's *Diversions of a Diplomat in Turkey*, "especially if we can get it at 7 or 8% royalty," a month later he decided they had overpaid for the book because he feared Cox's "sale won't go above 12,000 copies." King David Kalākaua's *The Legends and Myths of Hawaii*, edited by Sam's friend Rollin Daggett, "barely paid for the cost of manufacture," as Paine noted. Webster and Company issued at half profits *Lectures on Preaching and Other Writings* by Nathaniel

Burton, Sam's friend in the Monday Evening Club, over Webster's objection and in violation of the contract the two men had signed. Although Burton's son remembered that "the royalty to my mother was ten times better than if it had been brought out in the usual ten percent trade way," the book earned little money for the firm.[9]

Similar issues plagued a seven-volume series of cookbooks by Alessandro Filippini, the chef of Delmonico's in New York, issued by Webster and Company between 1888 and 1893—first among them *The Table: How to Buy Food, How to Cook It, and How to Serve It* (1888). "I think it is the very book we want," Sam wrote Hall on September 8, 1887. His decision to publish this book was neither rash nor ill informed: "Make [Filippini] an offer of 5 per cent [royalties]. If he agrees, close the contract. If he doesn't, keep at him & yield a little till you get him. . . . Begin the canvass & delivery June 1st—at people's houses; afterward at all the watering places & summer resorts, east & west. *They* concentrate the very people we want." The Delmonico folks were "willing to do anything in their power to forward the sale" of *The Table*, Hall assured Sam, and he planned to deploy a "corps of lady canvassers" to peddle it.[10]

In the mythology that has accreted around Sam Clemens like a pearl around a grain of sand, he has been portrayed as a down-home diner with chuck-wagon tastes. Those who claim that he subsisted on simple fare point to the menu of several dozen of his favorite foods in chapter 49 of *A Tramp Abroad* (1880)—a list that includes pumpkin pie, southern fried chicken, and Virginia bacon. Evan Jones notes approvingly that the menu "mentions no adornments or sauces except 'real cream,' 'clear maple syrup,' and 'American butter.'" To be sure, Sam enjoyed such simple dishes as corned beef and cabbage, but in *Twain's Feast* (2010) Andrew Beahrs wrongly insists that he "detested" gourmet European dishes and considered them "monotonous, a hollow sham, a base counterfeit." Not so. Sam relished fine dining, especially after marrying into the Langdon family, and he routinely reveled in French haute cuisine at Delmonico's, the finest and most famous restaurant in the country. Beahrs "regretfully" concedes that the dinner parties Sam hosted in his Hartford home "owed a great deal to the rich, elevated food served at Delmonico's," including "one 1887 dinner at Twain's house involved creamed asparagus, creamed sweetbreads, and creamed shad sauce over shad-roe balls." But why "regretfully"? Beahrs no doubt referred to the dinner Sam and his wife Olivia hosted in honor of Grace King and Lucius Fairchild in June 1887. As King remembered in her autobiography, the dishes were cooked and delivered by Boston and New York caterers. "The courses filed past our plates in the usual routine," she wrote. "Not a delicacy, not a luxury, in the way of eating, was missing from the menu." In her diary, she was more detailed: "Olives, salted almonds, and bonbons in curious dishes were on the table and decanters of quaint shape and color held the wine. The soup was 'Claire'—the Clairest you ever saw, delicious flavor-sherry. Then fresh salmon, white wine sauce—Apollinaris water—Sweet breads in cream."[11] Filippini's cookbooks may not have earned much money but their publication at least belies the claim that Sam preferred pumpkin pie to crème brûlée.

Then there were the books Webster and Company failed or refused to accept for a variety of reasons, foremost among them Webster's chronic illness: the autobiographies of Guiseppe Garibaldi, Lillie Langtry, and Arthur Orton, the Tichborne Claimant; a history of the Grand Army of the Republic by Lucius Fairchild; William Franklin Dana's *The Optimism of Ralph Waldo Emerson*; William Waldorf Astor's historical romance *Valentino*; and Moncure Conway's novel *Pine and Palm*. Ignatius Donnelly, best known today as the author of the utopian romance *Caesar's Column* (1890), offered the press the manuscript of *The Great Cryptogram*, a study that purported to prove Francis Bacon was the author of the plays attributed to Shakespeare. On July 9, 1887, Sam queried Fred Hall: "Couldn't we get Ignatius Don[n]elly's Shakspeare-cipher book?" But he then he changed his mind, almost in midsentence: "No—we don't want it." Hall answered that Webster had already refused the manuscript because "the author wanted all the profits." A month later Sam had forgotten that both he and Webster had declined the project, instead blaming his nephew for rejecting the submission without first consulting him. He whined to Orion that their nephew "had the hardihood to turn Don[n]elly's Shakspeare book away without asking me anything about it. . . . Of course he didn't know he was throwing away $50,000; he was merely ignorant; had probably never heard of Bacon & didn't know there was a controversy" over the authorship of the plays. Sam ended his letter to his brother on an ominous note: "This won't happen again." In 1909 Sam claimed in a stunning lapse of memory that he *had*, in fact, not only read Donnelly's book in 1887—"an ingenious piece of work"—but published it.[12]

Then there were the Grant-related books Webster and Company solicited but were never submitted to the press, such as the correspondence of Ulysses and Julia Grant and Grant's diary of his round-the-world tour. Sam also proposed to issue a limited deluxe edition of Grant's memoirs that would have featured a page of Grant's manuscript tipped into the binding, a marketing technique Houghton Mifflin exploited successfully over twenty years later in issuing the Manuscript Edition of Henry David Thoreau's *Writings*, though Fred and Jesse Grant eventually quashed the idea. None of these projects reached fruition because of disagreements with the Grant family, though Sam blamed Webster for the failure of the firm to reach terms with them.[13]

Sam also projected a "Royalty & Nobility Exposed" series of reprints to include Thomas Carlyle's *History of the French Revolution*, *The Memoirs of the Duke of Saint-Simon*, George Standring's *The People's History of the English Aristocracy*, Hippolyte Taine's *The Ancient Régime*, and Frederica Sophia Wilhelmina's *Memoirs*, but it never materialized. Webster and Company issued reprints of five Henry George books, including *Progress and Poverty* (1879), George's classic argument for a single tax on unearned increment or appreciation in land values. Though the market for these reprints had largely been exhausted by their earlier printings, Sam apparently had become a convert to George's economic doctrines. The Connecticut Yankee agrees to become King Arthur's "perpetual minister and executive" and manage the kingdom of Camelot not for a salary but for the income from a single tax, "one per cent of such actual increase of revenue over and above its present amount as I may succeed in creating for the state." In all, on August 3, 1887, Sam confessed to Webster that, with a cash shortfall and the loss of the Grant letters, "our outlook is disturbing" and that he held his nephew responsible. He was still writing every day in his Quarry Farm study but "the fun, which was abounding in the Yankee at Arthur's Court up to three days ago, has slumped into funereal seriousness, & this will not do—it will not answer at all. The very title of the book requires fun, & it must be furnished. But it can't be done, I see, while this cloud hangs over the workshop."[14]

Webster's health had so deteriorated by mid-February 1888 that he agreed to a yearlong leave of absence. He withdrew "from business, from all authority, and from the City, till April 1, 1889," in a vain effort to recover his health. "How long he has been a lunatic I do not know," Sam confided in his journal, "but several facts suggest that it began in the summer or very early in the fall of '85,—while the 1st vol. of the Grant *Memoirs* was in preparation." For the remainder of his life, Webster was addicted to the analgesic phenacetin and, according to Fred Hall, he consumed "the drug all the time." It helped to relieve the pain, but only temporarily. Or as Sam remembered in his autobiography, "The physicians limited his use of it but he found a way to get it in quantity. . . . He took this drug with increasing frequency and in increasing quantity. It stupefied him and he went about as one in a dream. He ceased from coming to the office except at intervals."[15] In 1983, after nearly a century on the market, the drug was banned by the U.S. Food and Drug Administration.

Webster never returned to work after his leave of absence. Sam essentially forced him to retire by promoting Fred Hall from factotum to underling to Webster's replacement and then fronting Hall the money to buy Webster's interest in the business. "It is idle to try to convince me that Uncle Sam is not interested and in back of Mr. Hall's proposition," Webster realized. Though Sam had assessed the value of Webster and Company in February 1886 at a half million dollars, Webster estimated his share of the business at only about twenty thousand dollars. He offered to sell out for fifteen thousand, an agreement that he could not be sued for his past management decisions, and a limit of five years on the use of his name. He admitted to his uncle—albeit in passive voice—that "mistakes have been made" in the administration of the company "but they were mutual on our part for *not a move*" was made "up to the time I left" on his leave of absence "that was not acquiesced in by you." Sam confided in his journal at about the same time that "since the spring of '86" the enterprise had "gone straight downhill toward sure destruction" and he wanted Webster dismissed. Only after Webster was permanently incapacitated did Sam realize how sick he was.[16]

Webster was removed from the company in December 1888 when he sold his share in the firm to Hall for a mere twelve thousand dollars, cash on the barrel. Webster conceded to Whitford on December 31 that he had "sold out my interest for far less than I believe it to be worth but it is done and that is the end of it." Six months later, Sam's anger had not dissipated. He had consigned Webster, like Bret Harte, John Raymond, Whitelaw Reid, Dan Slote, and others, to the not-so-exclusive club of former friends, partners, collaborators, and colleagues. He wrote Pamela that her son-in-law was "not a man but a hog" and he was "so bitter that I could not even endure the idea of addressing a letter whose mere envelope could pass under the defilement of his eye." That same day he admitted to Orion that he had "never hated any creature with a hundred thousandth fraction of the hatred I bear for that human louse Webster." Sam's enmity was so intense that he coined a word to describe his nephew: "Charles L. Webster was one of the most assful persons I have ever met—perhaps the most assful."[17]

When Hall became manager of Webster and Company in February 1888, he inherited Webster's title, his annual salary of thirty-eight hundred dollars, and his duties. Sam was initially pleased with his performance. "The substitution of brains for guesswork was accomplished when you took Webster's place," he wrote Hall on January 11, 1889. "I cordially approve, detail by detail, of what you have done, & of what you have planned to do. You & I will never have any trouble." He also took a swipe at Webster, who became the convenient scapegoat for all looming threats to the company: "We are not sailing a pirate ship any longer; we have discarded the pirate ways & the inalterable pirate laws, along with the pirate himself." Yet it was also a distressed business, nearing bankruptcy, often with a cash balance in the coffers of less than two thousand dollars. That same day Hall notified Sam that he had found receipts for a desk and a chair totaling nearly two hundred dollars. Webster had taken the furniture with him when he retired, and Hall reported that "they were paid for by the firm and so really belong *to the firm.*" Sam underlined the final phrase.[18] The incident is reminiscent of the accusations by the comptroller of the U.S. Treasury in 1865 that Orion had cheated the government of wastebaskets and spittoons when he left his territorial office in Nevada.

Charles L. Webster died early in the morning of April 26, 1891, from a self-administered overdose of phenacetin, though publicly his death was attributed to inflammation of the bowels. Sam refused to attend the funeral in Fredonia, though he wrote his niece Annie a letter of consolation: "Charlie was a great sufferer & to him death is peace, a grateful release from intolerable pain. When death takes this merciful form it is a benefaction, & the grave a refuge."[19]

Sam was occasionally mistaken in person and in the press with Bret Harte, much to his chagrin. The annoyance was never greater than in October 1887 when Edmund Yates, editor of the London *World*, reported "on the authority of supposedly trustworthy sources" that Sam had rented Buckenham Hall near Norwich and would reside there for the next year while completing a book. The item was reprinted in the New York *World* and within the week Yates received both a telegram from Sam asking that anybody "personating me in England" be exposed as an impostor and a letter from Madame Hydeline Van de Velde, wife of the secretary of the Belgian legation in England, expressing "her astonishment at the paragraph." As the New York *Sun* observed, "In the annals of journalism more errors have never been crowded in five lines." In fact, the Van de Veldes had leased Buckenham Hall for two months and invited Harte, their houseguest, to join them. "From the hour when the paragraph" appeared, according to the *Sun*, "their quiet autumn quarters knew no further peace or seclusion." Harte recorded in his diary that "understandably Madame Van de Velde was not amused by the newspaper paragraph." On his part, Sam assured London publishers Chatto & Windus that he "was not in England, and if I had been I wouldn't have been at Buckenham Hall anyway but at Buckingham Palace, or I would have endeavored to find out the reason why."[20]

The reason Sam was unable to sustain writing projects during the nine months a year he lived in Hartford was never more obvious than in late 1887 and early 1888. His calendar was simply too cluttered with other activities. Even as Webster and Company staggered toward insolvency, he raised money for several charities and campaigned for copyright. During the same period, he and Livy hosted a multitude of visitors and he attended a host

of social events. He had been elected a life member of the Hartford Putnam Phalanx of the Ancient and Honorable Artillery Company of Boston
in June 1886—"the rest of the phalanx can always be depended upon in time
of war, and I shall never fail you in time of peace," he wrote in accepting
the honor—and he accompanied the brigade to Washington, D.C., in early
October to watch the 125 uniformed soldiers march in parade. Grace King
arrived in Hartford on October 10, lodging with the Clemenses for four
weeks and with the George Warners for three. The British writer and evangelist Henry Drummond passed through Hartford in late September and
called on Sam and Harriet Beecher Stowe. After a musical benefit for the
Union for Home Work at Unity Hall the afternoon of October 24, Sam
and Livy hosted a formal dinner for the entertainers and a few other guests,
among them Hjalmar Hjorth Boyesen and Boyesen's friend Count Claës
Lewenhaupt, a first lieutenant of Hussars in the Swedish king's bodyguard,
who wore his uniform to dine; Joe Hawley; Ned and Koto House; Grace
King; Joe Twichell; and Charles and Susan Warner. Charles Dickens the
younger, his wife Bessie, and their daughter were also the Clemenses' guests
the second week of November.[21]

On November 26 Sam was back in Washington, where he and George
Washington Cable lobbied Congress for copyright regulations. Attired "in
a wrinkled sack suit of gray goods," according to the New York *Sun*, Sam
read a pair of old chestnuts at Chickering Hall in New York the afternoon of
November 28 to benefit the American Copyright League: the tale of Hank
Monk and Horace Greeley from *Roughing It* (1872) and an anecdote about
a man cured of stammering by whistling. With him onstage were George
William Curtis, Edward Eggleston, Howells, James Russell Lowell, the humorist Bill Nye, the Hoosier poet James Whitcomb Riley, Stedman, and
Charley Warner. Another group of authors performed the following afternoon and the two events raised four thousand dollars for the cause. The next
evening the Clemenses hosted a dinner in their Hartford home in honor
of Joe Hawley attended by Koto House, Joe Twichell, and George and Lilly Warner. He appeared at a farewell dinner for the English actor Henry
Irving at the Star Theatre in New York the evening of December 9. Along
with Chauncey Depew and Governor Oliver Ames, Sam spoke at the Forefathers' Day celebration at the Congregational Club in Boston on December
20 and introduced his "universal climate proof, automatically adjustable oration," the template for an elastic after-dinner speech that could be adjusted
to suit any occasion, including "a granger gathering, a wedding breakfast,
or the funeral of a friend." A week later he met with forty other men at
the Parker House in Boston to organize a local association akin to the Authors Copyright League of New York. Among the attendees were Richard

Henry Dana, President Charles W. Eliot of Harvard University, Edward Everett Hale, and Lowell. Sam spent New Year's Eve entertaining friends and admirers at the Authors' Club in New York. The next night he dined with the Lambs Club at their quarters on West Twenty-Sixth Street in the company of such other celebrities as Albert Bierstadt, Léon Paul Blouet (aka Max O'Rell), Charles A. Dana, Parke Godwin, Mayor Abram Hewitt, theatrical managers A. M. Palmer and Lester Wallack, James Pond, and William Winter. By January 1888, in fact, Sam was so well known in theatrical circles that he was invited by Edwin Booth and Augustin Daly to become a founding member of the Players Club, a fraternity of theatrical professionals. The organizational meeting of the group, with Lawrence Barrett and Palmer in attendance, was held over lunch at Delmonico's on January 6. Other founding members included Thomas Bailey Aldrich, Judge Joseph F. Daly, John Drew, Laurence Hutton, Joe Jefferson, Brander Matthews, and William Tecumseh Sherman.[22] Sam entertained the local chapter of Yale University alumni at Seminary Hall in Hartford the evening of February 3 by reciting "An Encounter with an Interviewer" and "Buck Fanshaw's Funeral" from *Roughing It*. He returned to New York on March 10 for a dinner honoring Henry Irving at Charles A. Dana's home the following evening and was promptly trapped by the Great Blizzard of 1888, which dumped twenty-two inches of snow on the city and snarled rail service along the East Coast for the next several days. He was largely confined to the Murray Hill Hotel until March 16, when he left for Washington on the first train south after the storm. "Blast that blasted dinner party at Dana's!" he complained to Livy. Had he not left Hartford to attend it, he reflected, "I would have been at home all this time."[23]

After settling into a suite of rooms at the Arlington Hotel on Vermont Avenue, a block from the White House, Sam again read at the Soldiers' Home and on behalf of the American Copyright League before a crowd of about seven hundred at the Congregational church. Though not originally scheduled to speak, he replaced Charley Warner, who was snowbound in Hartford. First Lady Frances Folsom Cleveland and Frances Willard, founder of the Women's Christian Temperance Union, were in the audience and, according to the *Springfield Republican*, he "convulsed Mrs Cleveland and the other women with laughter" when he read "How I Escaped Being Killed in a Duel." The church was so full, Sam remembered, that "the air would have been very bad only there wasn't any. I can see that mass of people yet, opening and closing their mouths like fishes gasping for breath." As usual, several of the readers had "overloaded." Thomas Nelson Page "read forty minutes by the watch, and he was no further down than the middle of the list." Later that afternoon, along with many of the writers who had traveled with him from New York, including Boyesen, R. W. Gilder, Laurence Hutton, James Whitcomb Riley, Stedman, and Frank Stockton, Sam went to tea at the White House, where they were welcomed by the president and first lady and Juliet Lamont, wife of Secretary of War Daniel Lamont. That evening Sam attended a dinner at Joe Hawley's home and the next day he and the other authors were feted by Phoebe Hearst, the wife of Sam's Nevada friend George Hearst, now a U.S. senator from California, at the Hearst mansion on New Hampshire Avenue. He did not meet "young Mr. Hearst," however, as he wrote Sam Moffett two weeks later. In 1887, at the age of twenty-four, William Randolph Hearst had become the owner and publisher of the *San Francisco Examiner*. The twenty-seven-year-old Moffett, who had edited the student newspaper at the University of California while working as a stringer for the *Oakland News*, was working for the *San Francisco Post* and apparently had asked his Uncle Sam to recommend him for a job with the *Examiner*. Whether or not Sam intervened, Moffett joined the editorial staff of the newspaper later that year. Livy joined her husband at the Arlington the next day and, in company with the authors, they were entertained during the afternoon by John Hay at his new home on Lafayette Square across the street from the White House. That evening Sam read a second time at the Congregational church on behalf of the Copyright League, this time on the same program with Eggleston, Gilder, Howells, Riley, and Stedman; in the audience were the president and first lady, George Bancroft, Senator Jonathan Chace of Rhode Island, John Hay, and Phoebe Hearst.[24]

Sam and some of the authors tarried in Washington a few days longer to lobby on behalf of copyright regulation. During this break in his schedule, Sam and Livy were entertained at the home of Representative Robert H. Hitt of Illinois, where they were joined by Senators Shelby Moore Cullom and Charles B. Farwell of Illinois and Representative William Walter Phelps of New Jersey. At the Capitol on March 22 Sam was escorted by his friend Samuel Cox to the Speaker of the House's private pew in the gallery, where Cox identified for Sam the "various legislative characters" in the chamber. Later in the day Representative John Davis Long of Massachusetts received unusual permission from the Speaker to conduct Sam onto the floor, where he met "all the Congressional celebrities from [Thomas Brackett] Reed of Maine to [William Harrison] Martin of Texas," beginning on the Democratic side and gradually sidling "over to the heart of the Republican camp, shaking hands, telling stories, cracking jokes, and getting in his fine work." That evening, Sam and Livy were guests at a dinner hosted by Secretary of the Navy William Whitney in honor of the financier Ogden Mills.[25]

The next day, March 23, Sam testified before the House Judiciary Committee on behalf of the Chace-Breckinridge Copyright Bill. As in January

1886, he contended that "authors were the persons least concerned in international copyright," that the interests of "many other people" were at stake, including "the printer, the binder, and publisher," and that he understood that "all these . . . were in favor of the Chace-Breckinridge bill" because it contained a printing clause. He believed, not very logically, that copyright laws would "tend to cheapen books, on the same principle that a man owning a patent" and thus "protected from pirates" would "produce the article at the cheapest possible rate," as if the telephone or local gas company and other monopolies always operated in the public interest. He concluded to laughter in the hearing room that he was pleased the author had been demoted "from his Alpine altitude" and "made to take his place among the foothills where he properly belongs."[26]

On Saturday, March 24, Sam attended the meeting of the local literary society where he heard the American investigative journalist George Kennan discuss the plight of Russian serfs banished to Siberia. During the discussion following Kennan's talk, Sam expressed sympathy for the exiles. According to legend, in a "voice choked with tears" he exclaimed, "If such a government cannot be overthrown otherwise than by dynamite, then thank God for dynamite!"[27] In any event, Sam became a fierce critic of the Russian policy of banishing political dissidents. When in chapter 21 of *A Connecticut Yankee in King Arthur's Court* (written during the summer of 1888) the Yankee encounters a procession of slaves, he seems, according to Howard Baetzhold, "almost surely to have been inspired" by Kennan's *Century* articles about the plight of Russian serfs and exiles, particularly "Siberia and the Exile System" in the May 1888 issue. In chapter 30, in fact, the Yankee insists that "there is plenty good enough material for a republic in the most degraded people that ever existed—even the Russians." Sam returned to New York to attend the closing performance of John Drew and Ada Rehan in *A Midsummer Night's Dream* at the Star Theatre the evening of April 7 and afterward a midnight supper at Delmonico's hosted by Augustin Daly in the actors' honor. Sam railed back to the city two weeks later to meet Robert Louis Stevenson for the first and only time. Stevenson had been vacationing at Saranac Lake in upstate New York and had contacted Sam on April 13 to suggest they rendezvous the third week in the month. He added—in the type of note designed to melt Sam's heart—that he had read *Huck Finn* four times and was "quite ready to begin [it] again tomorrow." The two men walked from Stevenson's hotel on East Eleventh Street to Washington Square, where they spent a "very pleasant and sociable" afternoon on a park bench, probably on April 27, chatting "like a couple of characters out of story by Henry James," as Stevenson later put it. Sam also remembered their conversation in 1904: Stevenson's "business in the square was to absorb the sunshine," which accentuated the "special distinction" of his "splendid eyes," which burned with a "smoldering rich fire under the penthouse of his brows" and "made him beautiful.'"[28]

In the spring of 1888 Sam was burned by another ill-advised investment. In early 1883 he had bought ten thousand dollars' worth of "rose-colored stock" in the London branch of American Exchange in Europe, a forerunner of American Express, through the Hartford brokerage of George P. Bissell and Company. He invested on the basis of Bissell's claim that Joe Hawley "was the president of the exchange in every sense of the word." In October 1884, after hearing "whispered doubts" about fiscal health of the firm, he asked Charley Webster to investigate the rumors "& if you find the thing shaky, drop me a line & I will sell out my $10,000 worth." Whatever Webster learned, or whether he learned anything, Sam held the stock and its value collapsed in April 1888. "I was duped and now that the crash has come I can easily see that the concern had been rotten for some months," he noted. He blamed Henry Gillig, the general manager of American Exchange, "a supercilious, light-headed, crack-brained fool, upon whom is written 'jackass,'" who had recently fled the United States for London—"and it is good riddance to bad rubbish." The company declared bankruptcy two months later and Sam lost his entire investment.[29]

Sam was on the road again in May. He was one of the speakers the evening of May 3 at the dinner of the American Watercolor Society at the Hotel Brunswick in New York. Among the others on the dais were the painter J. G. Brown, Charles A. Dana, Mayor Abram Hewitt, and Bishop Henry Codman Potter, with Frank Millet in the audience. The Clemenses left Hartford on May 8 for a two-week holiday, pausing overnight in New Haven, before continuing to the Montowese House in Branford, Connecticut. The New York correspondent of the *Kansas City Star* reported that Sam was considering the publication of a book of war jokes by Ulysses S. Grant, though Sam admitted that such a project might be "unseemly." In any case, the book never appeared. Back in Hartford, Sam spoke at the Asylum Street Congregational Church the evening of May 28, when Joe Twichell was presented with the deed to the parsonage and a check for ten thousand dollars, gifts Sam and Livy helped to fund. In a private letter of thanks to Sam, Twichell acknowledged that he had just "learned to what extent Harmony and I are beholden to Livy and you for our sudden elevation in point of material fortune." The next evening, at a Grover Cleveland reelection rally sponsored by the National Civil Service Reform League, Sam was seated on the stage of Chickering Hall in New York with George William Curtis; E. L. Godkin, founder of the *Nation* and editor of the New York *Evening Post*;

Senator John Coit Spooner of Wisconsin; and architect and art historian Russell Sturgis.[30]

Sometime in early June, during one of his several trips to New York, Sam met the inventor Thomas Edison at his laboratory in West Orange, New Jersey. Sam's right hand had been cramping—much as the hero of *A Connecticut Yankee* is "crippled with rheumatism"—and it was frustrating his hope of completing the novel during his summer in Elmira. He was eager to experiment with dictating the remaining chapters into one of Edison's phonographs. He called on Edison in his office on Dey Street in New York on May 22, but his telegram scheduling an appointment miscarried so Edison was not present. Nonetheless, Sam "spent an hour & a half" noodling with the phonograph there "with vast satisfaction." From Hartford on May 25 Sam again wrote Edison to request a meeting: "I had had the hope that if I could see you I might possibly get my hands on a couple of phonographs *immediately*, instead of having to wait my turn," he allowed. "My case is pretty urgent & if you can give it a puissant push I shall be unspeakably obliged to you." If he could rent, borrow, or buy two of the devices, he told Edison, "all summer long I could use one of them in Elmira, N.Y., & express the wax cylinders to my helper in Hartford to be put into the phonograph here & the contents transferred to paper by type-writer." While he had missed seeing Edison on May 22, he promised to "try again soon & shall hope to find you on deck & still open to invasion." Edison replied on June 5 that he was at that very moment "conducting a series of experiments in connection with Phonograph cylinders for mailing purposes" and "just as soon as these are completed I will see that you are supplied with a couple of Phonographs." Sam soon visited Edison in West Orange, probably the next day, to inspect the machine in operation. Colonel Sellers's description of his workshop in *The American Claimant* (1892)—"apparently a junk-shop; apparently a hospital connected with a patent office—in reality, the mines of Golconda in disguise"—was no doubt inspired by Sam's visit to Edison's lab. During his visit, Sam "told a number of funny stories, some of which I recorded on the phonograph records," Edison recalled in 1927. "Unfortunately, these records were lost in the big fire which we had at the plant in 1914." Edison's agent George Edward Gouraud, who was present when the two men met, also believed that to the literary man the phonograph "must prove an inestimable blessing as regards the saving of the manual labour of writing." Gouraud illustrated the point by recalling that Sam had asked "to have one of the first phonographs, said that he 'had been carrying a book round inside of himself for more than a year, delaying deliverance only through sheer dread of the labour of writing.'" Unfortunately, phonographs were in such short supply that even Edison was unable to find a pair of them to loan Sam, who as a result was compelled to compose in longhand during his summer at Quarry Farm.[31]

In the spring of 1888 Sam also conducted another rearguard action against the imputations of Matthew Arnold. In his essay "Civilisation in the United States" in the April number of *Nineteenth Century*, Arnold censured the American nation for the mediocrity of its middlebrow culture: "Everything is against distinction in America. . . . The glorification of the 'average man,' who is quite a religion with statesmen and publicists there, is against it. The addiction to 'the funny man,' who is a national misfortune there, is against it."[32] Sam construed this last sentence as a personal attack on him and he soon replied in kind, even though Arnold had died suddenly on April 15, only days after the article appeared. The editor of *Forum*, Lorettus S. Metcalf, urged Sam to respond to Arnold in the pages of his magazine and Sam weighed the invitation but ultimately declined: "I believe there is only one detail to Mr. Arnold's article that I want to especially answer," he wrote Metcalf, "& I mean to answer that one in so friendly a way that it may even be called affectionate—loving—sloppy." He found the right opportunity when, two months later and upon the recommendation of Joe Twichell, he was awarded an honorary master of arts degree by Yale University. In a letter to Yale president Timothy Dwight accepting the honor bestowed by "this great and venerable University," which gratified him "quite as much as if I deserved it," he denounced Arnold for rebuking "the guild of American 'funny men.'" On the contrary, Sam declared, humorists practiced

> a useful trade, a worthy calling that with all its lightness and frivolity it has one serious purpose, one aim, one specialty, and it is constant to it—the deriding of sham, the exposure of pretentious falsities, the laughter of stupid superstitions out of existence; and that whoso is by instinct engaged in this sort of warfare is the natural enemy of royalties, nobilities, privileges and all kindred swindles, and the natural friend of human rights and human liberties.

Dwight read Sam's letter aloud at the Yale alumni dinner in New Haven the day he received it; it was reprinted in its entirety in the *New Haven Register* the following day and in the *Hartford Courant* on June 29. Sam cherished the recognition conferred upon him. As he wrote Charley Clark, "I am the only literary animal of my particular sub-species [humor writing] who has ever been given a degree by any College in any age of the world, as far as I know." He briefly considered elaborating his rejoinder to Arnold in an entire book-length essay to be entitled "English Criticism on America: Letters to an English Friend" and jotted nearly a hundred pages of notes for it (e.g., "Matthew Arnold's civilization is *superficial polish*"; what "Arnold regards as a 'civilization'" is a "worm-eaten & dilapidated social structure"). Rather than write that book, Sam responded to Arnold in his next two novels, implicitly in *A Connecticut Yankee* (1889) and explicitly in *The American Claimant* (1892).[33]

Sam resumed work on *A Connecticut Yankee* as soon as he arrived in Elmira with his family on June 23, 1888. Much as he had composed most of the latter half of *Huck Finn* at Quarry Farm during the summer of 1883, he wrote chapters 21–36 of his new novel that summer. In his octagonal study overlooking the city, he assayed a number of social theories in the crucible of his imagination. He perused yet again Carlyle's *History of the French Revolution* that summer and glossed on the flyleaf of his copy: "The Revolution had a *result*—a superb, a stupendous, a most noble & sublime result—to wit, *French Liberty*, & in a degree, *Human* Liberty—& was worth a million times what it cost, of blood, & terror, & various suffering, & titanic labor." In a preface to the novel drafted that summer, he suggested that "human liberty—for white people—may fairly be said to be one hundred years old this year," the centenary of the French Revolution. Under the influence of Carlyle's and William E. H. Lecky's histories, Sam wrote and interpolated chapter 10, "Beginnings of Civilization," into the narrative to forestall the criticism that he had not adequately described the advances the Yankee had introduced to sixth-century Camelot. Eventually named Hank Morgan (after the German adverb *morgen*, meaning "tomorrow"), the man from the future with historical hindsight "started a teacher-factory and a lot of Sunday-schools the first thing" to educate the people. He nationalized the mines, a pipe dream in Orion Clemens's Nevada. He founded "man-factories" modeled on the U.S. Military Academy at West Point to train experts and technicians, though he kept them out of sight lest they attract the attention of vassals and varmints. In brief, Morgan hails the imminent inauguration of the millennium in a paragraph studded with metaphors of violence and assault better suited to apocalypse:

> My works showed what a despot could do with the resources of a kingdom at his command. Unsuspected by this dark land, I had the civilization of the nineteenth century booming under its very nose! It was fenced away from the public view, but there it was, a gigantic and unassailable fact—and to be heard from, yet, if I lived and had luck. There it was, as sure a fact and as substantial

a fact as any serene volcano, standing innocent with its smokeless summit in the blue sky and giving no sign of the rising hell in its bowels. . . . I stood with my hand on the cock, so to speak, ready to turn it on and flood the midnight world with light at any moment.

Henry Nash Smith and others have argued, partly on the basis of this paragraph, that Sam was an agnostic about the inevitability of progress. As Everett Carter puts it, this passage in particular betrays Sam's fear that human evolution "through technology is the wrong course for humanity. Comparing technology to a hell the metaphor seems on the face of it to be loaded with negative feelings about the beneficence of applied science." Rather than contributing to the material comfort of the nation, technology is almost without exception deployed in the novel as an instrument of murder and mayhem: the destruction of Merlin's tower, the assassination of knights with hand grenades and guns, the electrocution of knights during the holocaust of the Sand Belt, and so forth. Or as Smith explains, Sam "had planned a moral fable illustrating how the advance of technology fosters the moral improvement of humanity. But when he puts his belief to the test by attempting to realize it in fiction" he discovered "that his belief in progress and human perfectibility was groundless." Neither a dystopian romance set in the future like George Orwell's *1984* (1949) nor a utopian romance set in the future like Edward Bellamy's *Looking Backward* (1888), *A Connecticut Yankee* is best described, in the words of James M. Cox, as an "inverted utopian fantasy" set in the past. Whereas Bellamy affirmed the perfectibility of human nature and the inevitability of progress, Sam fundamentally questioned "the beneficient effect of industrialism" and insinuated that nineteenth-century civilization had "threatened rather than fulfilled human happiness."[34]

A case in point: Sam's revision at the conclusion of chapter 22 of Lecky's tale about St. Simeon Stylites in *History of European Morals* (1869). According to Lecky, "the chief of the anchorites" stood on a sixty-foot pillar "scarcely two cubits in circumference" for thirty years, "ceaselessly and rapidly bending his body in prayer almost to the level of his feet. A spectator attempted to number these rapid motions, but desisted from weariness when he had counted 1,244. For a whole year, we are told, St. Simeon stood upon one leg, the other being covered with hideous ulcers." In Sam's parody, the saint's pedestal "was a pillar sixty feet high, with a broad platform on the top of it," where for twenty years he bowed "his body ceaselessly and rapidly almost to his feet. It was his way of praying. I timed him with a stop watch, and he made 1,244 revolutions in 24 minutes and 46 seconds." The technocrat Morgan thought it "a pity to have all this power going to waste. It was one of the most useful motions in mechanics, the pedal movement; so I made a note in my memorandum book, purposing someday to apply a system of elastic cords to him and run a sewing machine with it." In perhaps the best illustration of a worker's alienation from the product of his labor before Charlie Chaplin's film *Modern Times* (1936), the Yankee

> afterwards carried out that scheme and got five years' good service out of him; in which time he turned out upward of eighteen thousand first-rate tow-linen shirts, which was ten a day. I worked him Sundays and all; he was going, Sundays, the same as weekdays, and it was no use to waste the power. These shirts cost me nothing but just the mere trifle for the materials—I furnished those myself, it would not have been right to make him do that—and they sold like smoke to pilgrims at a dollar and a half apiece.

The shirts were advertised by every knight with a "paint-pot and stencil-plate" so that "there was not a cliff or a bowlder or a dead wall in England but you could read on it at a mile distance: 'Buy the only genuine St. Stylite; patronized by the Nobility. Patent applied for.'" Morgan was such an astute businessman that he eventually introduced the marketing concept of product extension, adding to the shirts "a line of goods suitable for kings and a nobby thing for duchesses and that sort." Unfortunately, the depersonalized "motive power" finally began to stand "on one leg, and I found that there was something the matter with the other one," so Morgan (in this case like his capitalist namesake, J. P. Morgan), "stocked the business and unloaded" just in time because "the works stopped within a year."[35]

According to Harold Aspiz, moreover, *A Connecticut Yankee* in general is a "laboratory novel . . . best understood" when read through a Leckyan lens. Like Huck Finn, who believes "a person's conscience ain't got no sense," Morgan is driven by the desire for pleasure or the avoidance of pain—the perspective Lecky labels "utilitarian" in opposition to the "intuitivist" view that morality is innate or instinctual. Like *Huck Finn*, Sam's new novel warred on the conscience. As the hero declares, "If I had the remaking of man, he wouldn't have any conscience. It is one of the most disagreeable things connected with a person; and although it certainly does a great deal of good, it cannot be said to pay, in the long run; it would be much better to have less good and more comfort." But this ethical position also permits Morgan to manage Camelot as if it were a third world country ripe for exploitation, to "disseminate soap and civilization" to an unwashed and benighted nation in the style of yet another namesake, the seventeenth-century Welsh privateer Henry Morgan, famous for his colonial raids.[36]

The chapters Sam added to *A Connecticut Yankee* in 1888 were rich with sarcastic asides and topical satire, especially on political and economic issues. In chapter 10, "Beginnings of Civilization," he condemned (in Hank's voice) the burden on the poor of regressive taxation. In chapter 25, "A Competitive Examination," he endorsed robust civil service reform—the idea that civil servants should be hired on the basis of merit, not appointed to office under a spoils system by corrupt politicians who reward their friends. In chapter 30, "The Tragedy of the Manor House," he excoriated the emergence of the Ku Klux Klan and its terrorist tactics, particularly lynch law. In chapter 40, "Three Years Later," he advocated "unlimited suffrage," sincerely though satirically, for "men and women alike—at any rate to all men, wise or unwise, and to all mothers who at middle age should be found to know nearly as much as their sons at twenty-one."[37]

As the father of gifted daughters, Sam had become to all appearances a convert to gender equality when he wrote these words. As he affirmed in his notebook in 1895, "No civilization can be perfect until exact equality between man and woman is included." In truth, however, as Guy Cardwell concludes, Sam largely paid lip service to gender equality. He never considered that black women as well as black men deserved reparations for centuries of slavery, for example. His advocacy of suffrage for educated white women was based less on a conviction to empower them than on a willingness to negate the votes of "every ignorant whisky-drinking foreign-born savage in the land [who] may hold office" and "help[s] to make the laws." He revered not "new" women like Isabella Beecher Hooker but "true" women like Livy, Mary Jane Wilks in *Huck Finn*, and Alisande la Carteloise (aka Sandy) in *A Connecticut Yankee*. He proudly asserted that his daughters Susy, Clara, and Jean had been "carefully raised" to be more ornamental than useful, "young ladies who don't know anything and can't do anything." As if to fulfill prophecy, Susy became a college dropout; Clara studied music, including piano in New York with Jessie Pinney, "an old & brilliant pupil of Liszt & Clara Schumann"; and Jean was, like her mother, an invalid most of her life.[38]

In a reversion to the anti-Catholicism inculcated in him in boyhood, moreover, Sam expressed a virulent religious bias in the novel that had been reinforced by his reading of Lecky. As he glossed in a copy of *History of European Morals*, Catholicism was "an odious religion" and he thought its missionaries "ought to be burned." More to the point, in his satire of the established church, Sam regarded Roman Catholicism in the same light as did many nineteenth-century non-Catholics: as the Antichrist or the beast mentioned in chapter 13 of the book of Revelation. That "awful power," the Catholic Church, Hank declares, has "converted a nation of men to a nation

of worms" and "poisoned" the "blood of Christendom." Much as noncon-
formists were demanding public schools free of Catholic influence in the
1880s and criticizing parochial school education, Hank Morgan founds
teacher factories untainted by theological training. "Let me educate your
children & I will determine your ultimate form of gov't," Sam had jotted in
his notebook while writing the novel. In the interpolated chapter 10, Hank
admits that "a united Church" represents "a mighty power, the mightiest
conceivable, and then when it by and by gets into selfish hands, as it is always bound to do, it means death to human liberty and paralysis to human
thought." In fact, he adds later, "an Established Church is only a political
machine; it was invented for that; it is nursed, cradled, preserved for that;
it is an enemy to human liberty." Such remarks anticipate Sam's criticism
of Mary Baker Eddy and the Church of Christian Science a few years later
in such tales as "The Secret History of Eddypus" (written 1901–2) and his
essay *Christian Science* (1907). To check the threat of theocracy, Morgan becomes a Protestant reformer, a fragmented church militant, with plans "to
overthrow the Catholic Church" and to establish a multitude of dissenting
sects "on its ruins—not as an Established Church, but a go-as-you-please
one." Sam acknowledged in his notebook that he "used compulsion in establishing my several breeds of Prot[estant] Churches, because no missionary-
ing has ever been accomplished except by force." To be sure, a "good priest"
volunteers to raise the child of a young mother who is lynched for petty theft
in chapter 35, and technically it is not the interdict but a bull market ma-
nipulated by Launcelot that topples the first domino in the chain of events
that destroys Camelot. On October 8, still two months before the novel was
issued by Webster and Company, Hall reassured Sam that his anti-Catholic
rants would not damage sales because only Catholics would object to them
and, as Sam had painfully learned by publishing the authorized biography
of Pope Leo, "they were not book buyers."[39]

In chapter 33, "Sixth-Century Political Economy," Sam expounded on the
increased purchasing power of money in a laissez-faire or free-trade economy and the damage wrought by the protective tariff. As in his talk "The New
Dynasty" before the Monday Evening Club in March 1886, he defended
labor "combines" for their role in fixing wages. The "vast hive" of "nobles, rich
men, the prosperous generally" had long colluded "to force their lowly brother to take what they choose to give." For what it's worth, the chapter number,
33, was the age at which, according to tradition, the working-class Christ was
crucified. But in the nineteenth century after "a couple of thousand years"
of wage slavery, Hank predicts, laborers will organize, "the 'combine' will be
the other way, and then how these fine people's posterity will fume and fret

and grit their teeth over the insolent tyranny of trade unions." In effect, Sam anticipated John Kenneth Galbraith's notion of organized labor as a "countervailing force" to capital and corporate power. The chapter was occasionally cited in labor newspapers and magazines, including Edward Bellamy's *Nationalist*, and Sam considered selling the novel at a discount through labor clubs. Though Sam had opposed tariff reform and the Wood Bill in 1880, he favored tariff reform and the Mills Bill to reduce tariffs in 1888. About this time he also noted in his journal that the person who "invented protection belongs in hell." Moreover, on October 30, after returning to Hartford at the end of the summer, he was elected one of the vice presidents of the affiliated Connecticut, Massachusetts, and New York tariff reform clubs. He spoke at a Grover Cleveland rally at Allyn Hall the next day organized by the cluster of clubs and attended by Secretary of the Treasury Charles Fairchild and Francis Goodwin, where he decried the "everlasting howl in the Republican papers about the wages of the laboring class."[40]

In addition to these topical allusions, Sam elaborated in *A Connecticut Yankee* a doctrine of determinism or a "theory of progressive heredity" to which he adhered for the rest of his life. In his essay "The Character of Man" (ca. 1885) Sam had described the evolved human being as "the tail-end of a tape-worm eternity of ancestors extending in linked procession back—and back—and back—to our source in the monkeys, with this so-called individuality of ours a decayed and rancid mush of inherited instincts and teachings derived, atom by atom, stench by stench, from the entire line of that sorry column." Just as Sam had insisted to Francis Wayland in December 1885 that "we have ground the manhood out of" African Americans, basing his belief on an anachronistic Lamarckian notion that "they" as a race had transmitted debased traits inherited through generations of oppression, Hank famously broadcast his opinion in the new novel that character was the product of both individual and ancestral training. As Hank announces in chapter 18,

> Training—training is everything; training is all there is *to* a person. We speak of nature; it is folly; there is no such thing as nature; what we call by that misleading name is merely heredity and training. We have no thoughts of our own, no opinions of our own; they are transmitted to us, trained into us. All that is original in us, and therefore fairly creditable or discreditable to us, can be covered up and hidden by the point of a cambric needle, all the rest being atoms contributed by, and inherited from, a procession of ancestors that stretches back a billion years to the Adam-clam or grasshopper or monkey from whom our race has been so tediously and ostentatiously and unprofitably developed. And as for me, all that I think about in this plodding sad

pilgrimage, this pathetic drift between the eternities, is to look out and humbly live a pure and high and blameless life, and save that one microscopic atom in me that is truly *me*: the rest may land in Sheol and welcome for all I care.

Henry Nash Smith observes that this paragraph is "curiously out of tone with the immediate context and with the book as a whole" because it "is not really [Hank's opinion] but the author's."[41]

Gregg Camfield adds that Sam "did not clearly understand the most important aspect of Darwin's theory" and "espoused a Lamarckian theory of evolution while attributing its proof to Darwin." Still, the passage contains the essence of Sam's budding belief in determinism. Elsewhere in *A Connecticut Yankee* the narrator announces that King Arthur's veins "were full of ancestral blood that was rotten" with "unconscious brutality, brought down by inheritance from a long procession of hearts that had each done its share toward poisoning the stream." As Sam noted in his journal while in the final stages of writing the novel, "the thing in man which makes him cruel to a slave is in him permanently & will not be rooted out for a million years." In *Adventures of Huckleberry Finn* (1885) Huck must "learn" to be a girl before impersonating "Sarah Williams" at the home of Judith Loftus, just as Arthur must practice walking like a serf before he and Hank travel incognito. Sam's most overt public embrace of Lamarckian ideas, however, appears in *The American Claimant*, where Colonel Sellers asserts that "every man is made up of heredities, long-descended atoms and particles of his ancestors" and "there's a contribution in him from every ancestor he ever had. In him there's atoms of priests, soldiers, crusaders, poets, and sweet and gracious women—all kinds and conditions of folk who trod this earth in old, old centuries, and vanished out of it ages ago." Sam expressed a radically Lamarckian view in "A Family Sketch," written in the late 1890s but not published until 2014, in which he suggested that breast milk "imparts to the child certain details of the mother's make-up . . . such as character, disposition, tastes, inclination, traces of nationality, and so on."[42]

Buoyed by his belief in the potentially ameliorating influence of "training," Sam presumed to imagine the founding of a just republic by reenacting the Civil War in sixth-century England. Morgan dreams of "a rounded and complete governmental revolution without bloodshed," the "first of its kind in the history of the world." Like St. Petersburg in *The Adventures of Tom Sawyer* (1876) and *Huck Finn*, Camelot is another portrait of antebellum Hannibal down to the litters of pigs rooting in the streets. But Sam no longer romanticized the South of his childhood. Instead, as James M. Cox argues, Camelot is "a projection of the benighted South," a "negative image of Hannibal, of Hannibal as Bricksville." The Yankee invades and occupies this region "to free the people from religion, aristocracy, and slavery," though in the end he fails at this quixotic mission. As Sam jotted in his notebook in September 1888, "I make a peaceful revolution and introduce advanced civilization" but "the Church overthrows it" in a twinkling "with a 6 year interdict. A revolution cannot be established under 30 years—the men of old ideas must die off." When Hank Morgan declares war on the church and its minions, only fifty-two boys from the man factory ("a darling fifty-two!") and his factotum Clarence remain loyal. Clarence asks Morgan, "Did you think you had educated the superstition out of those people?" Morgan replies,

> "I certainly did think it."
> "Well, then, you may unthink it. They stood every strain easily—until the Interdict. Since then, they merely put on a bold outside—at heart they are quaking." . . .
> "From our various works I selected all the men—boys I mean—whose faithfulness under whatsoever pressure I could swear to, and I called them together secretly and gave them their instructions. There are fifty-two of them; none younger than fourteen, and none above seventeen years old."
> "Why did you select boys?"
> "Because all the others were born in an atmosphere of superstition and reared in it. It is in their blood and bones. We imagined we had educated it out of them; they thought so, too; the Interdict woke them up like a thunderclap! . . . Such as have been under our training from seven to ten years have had no acquaintance with the Church's terrors, and it was among these that I found my fifty-two."[43]

Why exactly fifty-two? The number associates the boys who remain loyal to the republic in *A Connecticut Yankee* to the number of playing cards in the deck in Lewis Carroll's *Alice's Adventures in Wonderland* (1865), loyal servants to the Queen of Hearts—all of whom, like Hank's fifty-two, are eventually discarded too.

Sam also recast in the novel his daughter Clara's infection at the age of seven with membranous croup, the same disease that had killed her brother Langdon. As Sam wrote his mother Jane, on New Year's Day 1881 "Bay was taken alarmingly ill" and for three days "we kept two croup-kettles going"—an alcohol lamp heating "a vessel filled with lactic acid and lime" that discharged "medicated steam" into a tent of blankets over her crib. The treatment succeeded "& our fears were at an end." In chapter 40 of *A Connecticut Yankee*, similarly, Hank diagnoses his daughter's malady "almost at a glance—membranous croup! I bent down and whispered: 'Wake up, sweetheart! Hello-Central.' She opened her soft eyes languidly, and made out to say: 'Papa' [the only word Langdon Clemens learned to speak before his death]. That was a comfort. She was far from dead yet." Much as Sam had assembled a croup kettle for Clara, Hank constructs one for his daughter. He and Sir Launcelot "loaded up the kettle with unslaked lime and carbolic acid, with a touch of lactic acid added thereto, then filled the thing up with water and inserted the steam-spout under the canopy. Everything was ship-shape now, and we sat down on either side of the crib to stand our watch. Well, he stood watch-and-watch with me, right straight through, for three days and nights, till the child was out of danger."[44]

Despite his best efforts, Sam was unable to complete the novel at Quarry Farm during the summer of 1888. The family postponed their normal early-September departure from Elmira when Theodore Crane suffered a stroke on September 6. It was complicated by his diabetes and he was left paralyzed on one side. Sam took his turn sitting beside his brother-in-law's sickbed for the next two weeks. "I had a sort of half-way notion that I might possibly finish the Yankee at King Arthur's Court this summer," he wrote Andrew Chatto on September 17, "but I began too late & so I don't suppose I shall finish it till next summer. We go home to Hartford a week hence; & if at that time I find I am two-thirds done, I mean to try to persuade myself to do that other third before spring."[45]

That is exactly what happened. The family took their belated leave from Elmira on September 24 and, upon Sam's return to Hartford, in order to escape the frequent distractions at the mansion, he sought asylum or at least seclusion in the nearby Twichell home so that he could write the last chapters of A Connecticut Yankee without interruption. As Twichell noted in his diary, on October 1 Sam asked "if we had a room to spare him as a hiding place he could use while finishing a book." The family was "willing enough and glad to accommodate him" but their house was in such a state of disrepair with carpenters and painters "infesting it and adding their racket to the natural Twichell tumult" that it "seemed about the last place to be selected as a literary retreat." Nevertheless, Joe offered him an upper room where he might write. As Sam wrote his brother Orion two days later, "I am finishing a book begun three years ago. I see land ahead; if I stick to the oar without intermission I shall be at anchor in thirty days; if I stop to moisten my hands I am gone." Two more days later, he wrote his brother-in-law Crane that he was at work in Twichell's house amid "the noise of the children & an army of carpenters. . . . It's like a boiler-factory for racket and in nailing a wooden ceiling onto the room under me the hammering tickles my feet amazingly sometimes and jars my table a good deal, but I never am conscious of the racket at all." On October 9 Sam admitted that during most of his waking hours he was "in strict hiding, a mile from home—during the daytime—finishing a book." He wrote eighty pages of the novel during his first week sequestered in Twichell's attic.[46]

Still, Sam met with a multitude of distractions as he struggled to complete the manuscript. He was besieged by a steady stream of old friends throughout the fall of 1888, including Henry Mills Alden, the editor of *Harper's Monthly*, and Will Bowen. Grace King paid another long visit in November 1888 that included an excursion with the Clemenses to New York. They left Hartford the morning of November 20 and registered in early afternoon at the Murray Hill Hotel in the city, where they rendezvoused with Susan and the hobbled Theo Crane. Sam introduced King to Augustin Daly, and the two discussed the dramatization of King's novel *Monsieur Motte*. Daly hosted the Clemens party in his personal box at his theater that evening for a performance of the comedy *The Lottery of Life*, John Brougham's translation of *Les surprises du divorce*, starring Drew and Rehan. The next morning the Clemenses and King called on the Howellses at their new apartment on Stuyvesant Square and a week or so later King joined the Clemenses on a jaunt to Smith College in Northampton, Massachusetts, one of the schools Susy was considering.[47]

On November 6, 1888, President Grover Cleveland was defeated for reelection despite outpolling the Republican candidate Benjamin Harrison by nearly a hundred thousand votes. "The Clemenses and I were deeply grieved at Cleveland's defeat," King remembered. Sam had walked to the polls that day with Charley Warner, who voted a straight Republican ticket. According to King, "in his secret heart" Warner wanted to follow Sam's example and cast a ballot for Cleveland, "but he has been whipped into line by his wife and Gen. Hawley." Sam lamented Cleveland's loss and he quipped in October 1889 that "I would have my leg sawed off right there at the knee to see Cleveland President again." He praised him in later years as "a very great President" who was "all that a President ought to be." He conceded that Cleveland had been "a drinker in Buffalo and loose morally. But since then? I have to doubt it. . . . Of all the public men of today he stands first in my reverence and admiration, and the next one stands two-hundred-and-twenty-fifth." Put another way, "Cleveland *drunk* is a more valuable asset to this country than the whole batch of the rest of public men *sober*."[48]

Susan and Theodore Crane joined the Clemenses in Hartford on November 28 rather than spend the frigid months atop a mountain at Quarry Farm or with Livy and Sue's aged and increasingly infirm mother in Elmira. "We are her mits, now, & must doubtless remain so the rest of the winter," Sam wrote Mary Mason Fairbanks on December 30. His brother-in-law was "in a precarious state," confined to a bed or wheelchair. While "sometimes he picks up a little, & then for a day or two it is a cheerful home; after that, he drops back again & the gloom & the apprehension return. It is pulling Susie Crane down a good deal & Livy also, of course. These two women will get sick if this continues." Christmas 1888 in the Clemens home was no more merry than Christmas 1887 had been. After years of lavish living, the family subsisted in reduced circumstances. The drain on their budget represented by the monthly check to James Paige was evident in their holiday gifts that year to friends and relatives. Rather than spend money, Sam sent Orion and Mollie a set of the *Library of American Literature*, roughly the equivalent of a chunk of coal in its impact on his pocketbook. "The [typesetting] machine is apparently almost done—*but* I take no privileges on that account. It must *be* done before I will spend a cent that can be avoided. I have kept this family on very short commons for 2 years & they must go on scrimping until the machine is finished, no matter how long it may be." Sam thanked his mother-in-law for sending a check to him for his fifty-third birthday in late November and promised to "buy me something nice & warm with it—whisky, or something like that."[49]

The fate of the typesetter was curiously interwoven with the fate of the novel in Sam's imagination. On October 5 he wrote, "I want to finish the day the machine finishes [in the Pratt & Whitney workshop]. A week ago the closest calculations for that, indicated Oct 22—but experience teaches me that their calculations will misfire, as usual."[50] He wanted to complete the novel, that is, on the forty-fourth anniversary of the day the Millerites expected the world to end in fire. Just as their calculations "misfired," however, the novel would not be completed until the following spring and the typesetting machine, obsolete before it could be perfected, was never finished.

CHAPTER 16

Camelot

To write a book one must have great learning, high moral
qualities and—some other little things like that.
But to make a play requires genius.

—Samuel L. Clemens, curtain speech, January 20, 1890

THE SAGA OF the dueling stage productions of Sam Clemens's *The Prince
and the Pauper* (1881) by his soon-to-be-former friends Abby Sage Richardson and Ned House is another comedy of errors and misunderstandings.
Although both Sam and the producer Daniel Frohman claimed to have recruited Richardson to adapt the novel, in truth Richardson struck on the
idea entirely on her own. She wrote Sam a fan letter in early December 1888
pronouncing the tale "one of the most beautiful stories and most exquisite
in treatment of anything I had ever read" and requested his permission to
dramatize it. He replied a day or two later, expressing skepticism that she
would succeed where he, Will Gillette, and House had each failed, but he
suggested that "she try to get House to help her." He also disliked her notion
of casting a single child actor in both roles and employing a "silent double"
in scenes where both characters appeared onstage, an idea both Gillette and
House had floated. Nevertheless, he granted her request. On December 9
she thanked him and added she thought she had found the child star for
her play in Elsie Leslie, who was about to open in the title role of *Little Lord
Fauntleroy* at the Broadway Theater in New York. Richardson went so far
as to consult with Frohman, the manager of the Broadway—who as a cub
reporter for the *New York Tribune* had witnessed the murder of her husband
A. D. Richardson twenty years earlier—and Frohman encouraged her to
script the play and formally contract with Sam for exclusive rights to the
story. Meanwhile, Sam entertained Elsie Leslie when she and her mother
visited Gillette in Hartford. Richardson and Sam signed a contract on January 3, 1889, that divided the profits from the play equally between the two
parties. Soon enough Sam regretted the terms. "Contracts should be of mutual benefit, not be made solely in the interest of one party. In this one the

advantages are all on one side," he complained. "It confers upon [party] B *nothing* but loss: loss of time, loss of liberty, loss of money."[1]

Nevertheless, Sam not only honored the agreement but publicized it. Less than a month after signing it, according to the New York *Evening World*, he joked with a friend that a "dramatization of a book of mine will intrude upon the stage in the Spring or next Fall and that will afford me all the discomfort I shall need for several years. I have had to do with plays before and I've got my sackcloth and ashes ready. I know what to expect." Ned House was alarmed when he read the news because he believed he enjoyed an exclusive privilege to adapt the unnamed book, which he correctly surmised was *The Prince and the Pauper*. House contacted Sam several times, as he claimed on February 14, 1889, to express his concerns and to remind him of their verbal contract. He copyrighted his script the next day and deposited a single typewritten draft of it in the Library of Congress. As Paul Fatout notes, however, this copy "has many longhand alterations, as if it were a preliminary draft rather than a finished work, as if it might have been hastily thrown together to bolster a claim." In his answer to House on February 26 Sam explained that he had believed his friend had long since abandoned his adaptation of the novel. If not, Sam would have welcomed the news before "about the middle of December when I gladly took the first offer that came and made a contract. I remembered that you started once to map out the framework for me to fill in, and I suggested to [Richardson] that possibly you would collaborate with her, but she thought she could do the work alone." He promised to look into the matter.[2]

Sam observed in his notebook that "House seems to have a claim—I will go & see what it [is]. I can't imagine myself." To his credit, Sam was initially disposed to resolve any legal conflicts he may have inadvertently caused. "If I have heedlessly, ignorantly, forgetfully, gone & made a contract which I had no right to make," he wrote House on March 2, "it is a serious thing & I must move in the matter without loss of time. Send me the evidence at once; & send me copy of any & all writings, notes, letters, that throw light upon the thing." To the extent Sam had an agreement with House, however, it was a verbal agreement and no ironclad documentary evidence of a contract existed. When House admitted as much, Sam chose to honor the written contract he had signed. As he insisted to House,

> The case is quite plain, quite simple: I have lately made a contract for the dramatization of the Prince & Pauper. I must live up to it unless there is an earlier contract in existence. If you have one, send me a copy of it, so that I can take measures to undo my illegal action, & I will at once proceed in the matter. . . . I have never lost the desire to see the book dramatized; it has

always been present with me. I was always ready to welcome any comer, & *did* close with the first one that offered. I did not know whether she had had any experience in dramatic writing or not. I would naturally have preferred you, who I knew *could* write plays. . . . I supposed I had a full right to make that late contract, & I made it. If you have a previous one, I beg you to send me a copy, & I will come as near setting things exactly right as possible.[3]

Meanwhile, William Gillette volunteered to arbitrate the dispute.

For House the case was not nearly as "plain" and "simple" as Sam described it. He responded with a proverbial shot across the bow. On April 25 this item appeared in the New York *Sun* and was soon reprinted in the *New York Clipper*, a theatrical newspaper: "Mark Twain's story 'The Prince and the Pauper' has been dramatized at the author's request, by Edward H. House, a journalist and writer of this city, and is now in course of preparation for the stage." The warning shot failed to deter Sam, Frohman, and Richardson from reaching an agreement on May 13 to produce the play, however. Their contract, according to Fatout, reiterated Richardson's right to half the royalties, specified a completion date of October 1 for the script, and required her to submit it to both Frohman and Sam for their approval. Despite his unhappy experience as the would-be producer of Sam and W. D. Howells's *Colonel Sellers as a Scientist* two years earlier, Frohman obtained the exclusive right to stage the theatrical adaptation of *The Prince and the Pauper*—House's or Richardson's version, it made no difference—for five years on the condition he mount it at least seventy-five times a year with Elsie Leslie in the starring roles. As it happened, this clause in the contract became a sticking point when Frohman tried to appease House. The producer took House to a performance of the child star in *Little Lord Fauntleroy*, hoping to find a way out of the impasse. If House would agree to cast Leslie in the lead roles, all four principals in the kerfuffle would be on the same side and perhaps they could compromise on a script, but House insisted that Leslie was ill-suited to the parts. He also rebuffed Sam's attempts to settle the squabble out of court, rejecting Sam's attorney Daniel Whitford's offers of five hundred, eight hundred, and a thousand dollars for rights to his adaptation. Like Gillette, Frohman tried to arbitrate the quarrel by proposing to pay House a royalty on Richardson's play adapted from Sam's novel, but to no avail. "After about eighteen months of petrified absence of interest in this dramatization," Sam complained, "House's condition instantly unpetrified itself when he found that somebody else was willing to undertake the work. He not only imagines that he has an agreement with me for a dramatization, but that the term of it is eternal. . . . Mr. House is never so entertaining as when he has a grievance." Though he claimed to have completed his adaptation of Sam's novel, House was unable to place it with any other theatrical manager because it was in such rough shape. On June 21, over a month after Sam, Frohman, and Richardson signed their contract, the Broadway producer Horace Wall expressed interest in the House script but allowed he could not judge its merits "until it is completed." Not to worry, Sam assured the producer: House "has no rights or anything in the matter."[4]

"During 1886 and the four succeeding years, while Webster and others were sitting on my financial nest and were hatching ruin for me," Sam recalled in his autobiography, "I was assisting in the work at my end of the line, Hartford. I entered into an arrangement with a descendent of Judas Iscariot by the name of J. W. Paige, a national liar and thief, to build a type-setting machine, I to furnish the money." Sam continued to subsidize development of the compositor to the tune of three or four thousand dollars a month and Paige was content to tweek and tinker and issue evergreen reports of its imminent completion. At the peak of his enthusiasm for the machine Sam believed, as he wrote Whitmore, that it was "wholly without a competitor & is quite easily worth fifty millions of dollars." In January 1888 he expected the typesetter to "be finished & exhibiting its powers or its lack of them April 1st. Then my expenses on it will suddenly shrink to $300 a week & I shall be glad." He was so convinced that he had wagered on a winning horse that, in the spring of 1888, he refused an offer of a half interest in the Mergenthaler Linotype in exchange for a half interest in the Paige. By invitation he made "a minute & critical inspection" of the Mergenthaler but remained unwavering in his belief that the Paige was superior to it. "It is possible that my machine will be finished in a few days, now—but we never prophecy anymore," he wrote Will Bowen on December 29, 1888. Two days later Paige telegraphed that the typesetter was "O.K." and Sam announced to his wife Livy that "the machine is finished." On January 5, 1889, he declared in a note to his brother Orion that "at 12.20 this afternoon a line of movable types was spaced and justified by machinery for the first time in the history of the world! And I was there to see. It was done automatically—instantly—perfectly. This is indeed the first line of movable types that ever was perfectly spaced and perfectly justified on this earth." From Sam's perspective, this was a monumental event in human history, the greatest leap forward in printing technology since the Gutenberg printing press. All of the men present at the creation "seemed drunk—well, dizzy, stupefied, stunned." Sam personified the machine and gendered it (in this instance) as male, comparing it to a "cunning devil" more knowledgeable "than any man that ever lived." His account of its development reads like a gothic tale featuring a "gigantic vampire of inventions—that remorseless Frankenstein monster—the machine," voraciously devouring tens of thousands of dollars. Yet he also waxed wondrous:

> All the other wonderful inventions of the human brain sink pretty nearly into commonplace contrasted with this awful mechanical miracle. Telephones, telegraphs, locomotives, cotton gins, sewing machines, Babbitt Babbage calculators, Jacquard looms, perfecting presses, Arkwright's frames—all mere toys, simplicities! The Paige Compositor marches alone and far in the lead of human inventions. In two or three weeks we shall work the stiffness out of her joints [Sam gendered the machine here as a servile female, a type of helpmate or charwoman] and have her performing as smoothly and softly as human muscles.

"She will do the work of six men and do it better than any six men that ever stood at a case," he wrote George Standring. Sam noted in his journal that "the first proper name ever set" by the machine "was William Shakspeare" and that "the space-bar did its duty by the electric connections & steam & separated the two words preparatory to the reception of the space."[5]

Within a month the *Pall Mall Gazette* credited Sam with inventing the machine, not merely subsidizing its development, though he was quick to correct the record. "You do me quite too much honour!" he notified the paper. "I did not invent that typesetting machine. . . . J. W. Paige invented it, and has spent eighteen toilsome years upon it. . . . I have built this machine at my private expense and have been three formidable years at it. I do claim a good deal of credit for that." But the machine also tended to break type and Paige disassembled it for repair in mid-January. On February 13 the machine was up and running again and Whitmore expected to exhibit it to potential investors and buyers within a week or so, as soon as it had been "worked several days by power to permit the oil to run freely & to limber up all parts." Whitmore's son Fred was setting six thousand ems an hour on it, a rate of composition nearly equal to three manual typesetters. On February 15 Sam reported that there were still "several small matters to fix about the machine before it would be wise to give an exhibition. . . . In my opinion it will take from 2 to 3 weeks more before the machine will be entirely done." In the meantime, he sold royalties on sales of the machine to Charley Langdon and Sue Crane. In particular, he offered a 1 percent interest to his brother-in-law for twenty-five thousand dollars. He assured his sister-in-law that the "carping, scoffing, cast-iron skeptic" William Laffan of the New York *Sun* had "inspected the machine in minute detail for an hour" and operated it "for another half hour" before announcing that "the Sun wants 15 of these as soon as she can get them." On March 2 Sam confided to a friend that "we take the machine apart today; & when it goes together again, weeks hence, it shall be without flaw." A week later, Sam barked in his notebook, *"No more experiments. Definite work alone left to do."* The next day he set a deadline for completion of the typesetter: "4 months, sure, that is, July 10." On April 3 he wrote Orion that "we are still poking along at the machine" and he admitted that "sometimes I almost wished we had not taken it down again; it was plenty good enough, just it was. However, it will be still better when we finish it this time—& about perfect, I reckon." In the meantime, "we are still a little cramped for money; & shall continue so for some time yet. But it ain't any matter. All things arrive unto them that wait—& don't die in the meantime." Eight days later, on April 11, he wrote that "the machine was finished (in the rough, so to speak,) six weeks ago, & performed all its functions perfectly. We are now removing temporary devices from it & substituting permanent ones—a tedious job, but necessary. I require that it be done thoroughly, let the cost in delay be what it may. To succeed, a type-setting machine must be blemishless; it is a severe requirement, but we shall meet it." Three months later, in early July, he was still forecasting its imminent completion: "It will be ready for inspection and criticism the 15th of July and will then be complete in all details and without blemish." But the Paige was losing the competition for orders to the Mergenthaler Linotype, which by June had been installed in the print shops of the *New York Tribune*, *Chicago Daily News*, and *Louisville Courier-Journal*. Sam continued to argue for the superiority of the Paige to every other typesetter in development. In a head-to-head competition with the Mergenthaler, he insisted, the speed of the Paige compositor "would show up more and more conspicuously the longer the contest lasted."[6]

Expecting to complete his novel by late 1888, Sam accepted invitations to appear at over a dozen public functions during the first quarter of 1889. On January 17 he replaced Thomas Nelson Page, whose wife had just died, at a benefit reading in the Concert Hall at the Academy of Music in Baltimore before "a very large audience" with Richard Malcolm Johnston, the former professor of rhetoric and belles-lettres at the University of Georgia. Sam declaimed excerpts from the first chapters of *A Connecticut Yankee in King Arthur's Court* and as an encore his essay "How I Escaped Being Killed in a Duel." He donated his share of the box office receipts, seven hundred dollars, to Johnston. "We had an excellent audience," Johnston wrote Page. "I never saw Mark so fine. It was most generous in him to volunteer to come to my help." The *Baltimore American* ("his reading was a feast") and *Baltimore Sun* ("a great go") agreed. On January 21 Sam read from Robert Browning's poetry, specifically "Andrea del Sarto" and "Mulykeh," at Smith College as Susy continued to shop for a school. On January 31 he returned to Washington, D.C., with Johnston to work for copyright legislation. He called on Grover Cleveland at the White House on February 2, a month before the president left office and, with Edward Eggleston and Johnston, he spoke that evening at a reception hosted by the Ladies' Literary Association at the home of William D. Cabell, the principal of the Norwood Institute, a girls' academy. According to the *Washington Post*, "every sentence was punctuated with laughter and applause." Among the other guests were Secretary of War William Crowninshield Endicott and his wife Ellen Peabody Endicott. Sam spent the entire day of February 4 in the Capitol galleries and buttonholing congressmen in the corridors and even on the floor of the House of Representatives. He approached his friend Samuel Sullivan "Sunset" Cox, he told an interviewer in 1906, "and told him I wanted the privilege of going on the floor" in defiance of the rules. Cox "took me on the floor, and introduced me to all the Democrats. I told them about the bill. They said they'd vote for it. John D. Long introduced me to all the Republicans. They promised to vote for it. And the next session"—that is, two years later—"they did." In February 1889 the bill was again killed by filibuster. The opposition to copyright was premised on a false analogy: that intellectual property was the same as manufactured goods or that copyright protection was a kind of protective tariff on books, so the absence of copyright was the equivalent of free trade. The New York *Evening World* pointed to this supposed contradiction in Sam's thinking, declaring him "a Free-Trader, but he wants American authors protected. There is more human nature in Mark than most people imagine."[7]

Back in Hartford the evening of February 6 Sam spoke briefly at the annual banquet of the local chapter of the Yale Alumni Association at Armory Hall. The lineup of prominent speakers also included Timothy Dwight, the president of Yale University; E. C. Stedman; and Charles Dudley Warner. Sam remarked that he "had just returned from Washington where he had been engaged in advocating the international copyright bill" and "then narrated his experience in Washington in an amusing manner," according to the *New Haven Register*. Three nights later, he inaugurated "The People's Lecture Course" at the South Baptist Church in Hartford by reading selections from *Adventures of Huckleberry Finn* (1885). "The audience was large and appreciative, but there was no applause, and no boisterous laughter," according to one of his auditors. The lack of response "proved the wettest kind of blanket to the humorist, and his pique found vent at the conclusion of the performance in these words, 'I never did like churches,' he said, 'and I will never enter another one under any circumstances whatever.'" On February 11 Sam and Livy left for Albany to visit Dean Sage and his wife Sara for two days and they returned to New York in time for Sam to attend the third

annual banquet of the American Newspaper Publishers' Association at the
Hoffman House the evening of February 14, where he and Carl Schurz were
featured speakers.[8] The Clemenses remained in the city over the weekend
and probably went to a matinee of *Tannhäuser*, Sam's favorite Wagner opera,
performed in German at the Metropolitan Opera House the afternoon of
February 16, before returning to Hartford the next day. Back in New York
the evening of February 25 Sam addressed an audience of about a hundred
men at the seventh annual Trinity College Alumni dinner at Delmonico's.
He devoted his remarks to praising his friend from the Monday Evening
Club, the Reverend Dr. George Williamson Smith, the president of the
school. Smith had been elected bishop of a diocese in Maryland in 1886 and
assistant bishop of a diocese in Ohio in the autumn of 1888 but both times
declined the "promotions." Sam, for one, approved his decisions to remain in
Hartford: "Tell those Ohio people—& make it sharp & strong, so that they
will understand—that people are very well satisfied with you where you are
& are tired of this intermeddling. *We* can't afford to furnish bishops for every Maryland & Ohio that comes along." Sam addressed the Trinity alumni
facetiously as if they were another "diocesan electoral college in disguise"
attempting to steal Smith and he was duty bound to foil the conspiracy.
"We want our president and we will not let any man take him away," he declared. "Where should we find his match again?" Bishoprics were common
compared to a college, Sam insisted, and bishops were ordinary compared to
Smith who, he declared, as an educator was "a builder of men and a master
builder. Promote him? There is no promotion for such a man; his is the highest office in the gift of the children of this earth; he stands at the summit of
human usefulness—and above that is nothing but air and the vacant skies!
Away with your minor gauds and titles, he is a Builder of Men!—leave him
where he is."[9] Smith remained in Hartford until 1904, when he left to become assistant rector at St. John's Episcopal Church in Washington.

Sam read before the Wadsworth Athenaeum in Hartford on February
27, raising $170 for the organization. The next evening, after registering at
the Parker House in Boston, he introduced Bill Nye and James Whitcomb
Riley at their reading at Tremont Temple.[10] Afterward, he was a guest of
honor, along with Nye and Riley, at a Boston Press Club reception where,
as James Pond remembered, "a shower of jokes, stories unpublished (and
that never will be published), poems, and epigrams were poured into the
Boston writers until all were full." The next afternoon, after registering at
the Murray Hill Hotel, he delivered his "New England Weather" talk at
an authors' reading sponsored by the International Copyright Association.

Among the others on the program at the Boston Museum were many of the usual suspects: Thomas Bailey Aldrich, George Washington Cable, Annie Fields, Thomas Wentworth Higginson, Oliver Wendell Holmes, Julia Ward Howe, Sarah Orne Jewett, Richard Malcolm Johnston, Louise Chandler Moulton, landscape architect Frederick Law Olmsted, and Charley Warner. According to the *Boston Advertiser*, Sam "kept the house laughing from the time he rose." The benefit raised $2,000 for the cause. A week later Sam joined Cable and Warner at a reception at the St. Botolph (aka St. Bottle) clubhouse in Back Bay Boston and dined at Young's Hotel with Charles H. Taylor, the publisher of the *Boston Globe*. The entire family spent the following weekend in New York, staying at the Murray Hill Hotel; dining with Will Gillette, Elsie Leslie, and her mother; and attending a performance of *The Taming of the Shrew* starring Ada Rehan and John Drew at Daly's Theatre.[11]

Sam returned to New York again for a midnight supper at Delmonico's on March 30 hosted by Augustin Daly and A. M. Palmer in honor of Edwin Booth, who had bought a brownstone for the Players Club facing Gramercy Park. After the building was redesigned by the architect Stanford White, it opened on the last day of 1888; it remains at the same location today. Among the other seventy-four attendees, including White, were Aldrich, Dion Boucicault, Chauncey Depew, Drew, Daniel Frohman, Parke Godwin, New York ex-mayor William Russell Grace, Laurence Hutton, George Parsons Lathrop, Brander Matthews, James R. Osgood, Augustus Saint-Gaudens, and Stedman. In addition to Sam, the speakers included Lawrence Barrett and General Horace Porter. Sam was seated between Daly and W. T. Sherman and, as he joked to his family in Iowa, "We had a good many men at that supper . . . whom I had not met for five, seven, ten years—& meantime how it has been snowing on them!" In his autobiography, Sam claimed he was absent from the dinner because he was ill but his comment masks his failure to entertain the audience. According to the *New York Tribune*, Sam "read a doleful disquisition on the effects of a diet of Connecticut 'long clams,' which sent his hearers into mild hysterics of laughter." Matthews remembered the event differently. Sam "did not say a word about the distinguished guest; he actually took for his topic the long clam of New England—and what was worse, this inappropriate offering was read from manuscript!" James Morgan Appleton, the founder of the Shakespeare Society of New York, also recalled that "We hung our heads, hoping that it would soon be over." The dinner lasted until dawn and before it ended, the *New York Times* reported, "Gen. Porter dropped gracefully into poetry" and William Winter, the drama critic for the *New York Tribune*, "fell into it with a dull thud." A day later, back in Hartford, Sam read before the Monday Afternoon Club, a type of women's auxiliary of the Monday Evening Club.[12]

The evening of April 8, 1889, Sam spoke at a dinner at Delmonico's in honor of two professional baseball clubs that had barnstormed about the world under the management of A. G. Spaulding. Among the other two-hundred-plus men present were Hall of Fame player Cap Anson, Depew, Theodore Roosevelt and his younger brother Elliott Roosevelt, Frank Millet, John A. Sullivan, and the mayors of Brooklyn and Jersey City. Joseph Twichell said grace before the banquet, which was served in nine courses or innings. According to the New York *World*, Sam was "an old timer" knowledgeable about the game "and it was no surprise to the spectators to see him play his position without an error." He toasted "the boys who plowed a new equator round the globe stealing bases on their bellies!" During his speech, which was he devoted to the splendors of Hawaii because the teams had played a game there, New York state senator Jacob Cantor telegraphed the restaurant that the legislature had passed a bill saving the Polo Grounds, the home of the New York Giants baseball team. Abraham G. Mills, former president of the National League and the master of ceremonies at the dinner, congratulated Sam afterward: "You never made an address in your life that has made you so many new friends." Anson recalled that Sam "may have been better than he was that night, but if so I should like someone to mention the time and place." In a couple of late chapters in *A Connecticut Yankee*, Hank Morgan converts the Knights of the Round Table into a baseball team and describes the action on the playing field in the jargon of an expert (e.g., "My peerless short-stop! I've seen him catch a daisy-cutter in his teeth"). Five nights after speaking at the baseball banquet, Sam read on behalf of the Society of Collegiate Alumnae at a private home in New York.[13] Then he retired from travel and public appearances for two weeks.

He briefly resurfaced in New York the weekend of April 28. That evening Sam and Livy attended another performance of *The Taming of the Shrew* at Daly's Theater and he dined in august company the next night at the Metropolitan Opera House. An assemblage of perhaps the most distinguished group of white male Americans in history marked the centennial of George Washington's first inauguration, among them President Benjamin Harrison, Vice President Levi Morton, former presidents Grover Cleveland and Rutherford B. Hayes, future president Theodore Roosevelt, and former vice president Hannibal Hamlin; Chief Justice Melville Fuller and three associate justices of the U.S. Supreme Court; Secretary of the Treasury Ellis Roberts; former secretaries of the Treasury George Boutwell and Charles

Fairchild, former secretary of state Thomas Bayard, and former secretary of state and U.S. senator William Evarts; several state governors, including David Hill of New York; Mayor Hugh Grant of New York; both John Jacob Astor III and William Waldorf Astor, as well as Cornelius Vanderbilt; university presidents Charles Eliot of Harvard and Timothy Dwight of Yale; Archbishop Michael Corrigan of New York; and George Bancroft, Joseph Choate, George William Curtis, Depew, John C. Frémont, Richard Watson Gilder, James Russell Lowell, Frank Millet, Schurz, Sherman, Richard Henry Stoddard, Warner, and Henry Watterson. A week later Sam and Livy were joined by her mother, who was spending part of the spring with them, at a "grand charity ball" in Hartford hosted by Elizabeth Colt on behalf of the Union for Home Work.[14]

By the end of 1888 Sam's/Hank Morgan's dream of a peaceful revolution had long since faded. As early as December 1884 Sam had made a note about a conflagration between a "modern army, with gatling guns" firing "600 shots a minute," equipped with "torpedoes, balloons, 100-ton cannon, iron-clad fleet &c" on the one hand and "Prince de Joinville's Middle Age Crusaders" on the other. In keeping with his reenactment of the Civil War in the novel, Sam modeled events in the penultimate chapter of A Connecticut Yankee, "The Battle of the Sand-Belt," written between mid-April and mid-May 1889, on the Siege of Vicksburg. Perhaps more accurately, he depicted the battle as a cross between Vicksburg as he described it in chapter 35 of Life on the Mississippi (1883) and a commercial for a backyard bug light. In the most obvious sense, the battle joins an army of nobles defending an aristocratic, slaveholding nation and the forces of "a modern, technologically advanced republic led by a general-president." Hank and his boys seek shelter in a cave after provisioning it for a siege much as the noncombatants in Vicksburg during the six-week siege of the city—May 18 to July 4, 1863—sought protection in the caves along the Mississippi River. Hank demands that the knights "surrender unconditionally to the Republic" much as Grant required unconditional surrender of the Confederates at Vicksburg.[15]

In a larger sense, however, Sam modeled "The Battle of the Sand-Belt"—or "the Battle of the Broken Hearts" as he called it in a letter to Mary Mason Fairbanks—on the battle of Armageddon envisioned by the prophet John in the book of Revelation. According to Ernest Lee Tuveson, Sam described "the slaughter of the knights" in terms more biblical than topical. Their front ranks consist of horsemen whose advance to the Sand Belt is announced, like the scourges in Revelation, by "the blare of trumpets." The knights are blown to fragments "with a thundercrash" like the thunder that peals in the eighth chapter of Revelation. After he pushes a button and destroys "all our noble civilization-factories," Morgan endures "one of the dullest quarter hours" of his life, much as silence reigns for a half hour after the Lamb of God opens the seventh seal. The battle ends when Morgan electrocutes twenty-five thousand knights by running current through wire fences they try to cross. Incredibly, when Howells read this chapter, he thought it was "titanic." Sam continued to tinker with the manuscript until late September, when he wrote Howells that he had completed it. But if he were to write it "over again," he added, "there wouldn't be so many things left out. They burn in me; & they keep multiplying & multiplying; but now they can't ever be said. And besides, they would require a library—& a pen warmed up in hell." His remark is reminiscent of Nathaniel Hawthorne's description of his 1850 novel *The Scarlet Letter* ("positively a hell-fired story into which I found it almost impossible to throw any cheering light") and Herman Melville's comment to Hawthorne about *Moby-Dick* ("I have written a wicked book and feel spotless as the lamb").[16]

When the Clemenses arrived at Quarry Farm on June 13, 1889, Theodore Crane was on the threshold of death. "Mr. Crane can hardly last many days; he is very weak, & begs pitifully for release," Sam wrote his sister Pamela. He was "a half wreck, physically," and suffering "a good deal of pain of a bodily sort, together with a mental depression & hopelessness that made him yearn for death every day & break into impatience every time the sun went down on his unsatisfied desire." He had been dissuaded while in Hartford over the winter from taking his own life by Thomas Beecher, whose intervention shaped Sam's conclusion to *A Connecticut Yankee*. In his early notes for the novel, the Yankee "mourns his lost land—has come to England & revisited it, but it is all changed & become old, so old!—& it was so fresh & new, so virgin before. . . . Has lost all interest in life is found dead next morning—suicide." Much as Crane chose not to take his own life, Sam chose to allow Hank Morgan to die naturally, too. In Sue Crane he discovered "an argument against suicide: the grief of the worshipers left behind, the awful famine in their hearts, these are too costly terms for the release."[17]

He escaped the deathwatch for a couple of days in late June, railing to New Haven to speak at a Yale alumni dinner attended by seven hundred in Alumni Hall the afternoon of June 26. Sam was seated onstage with Depew, Dwight, Johns Hopkins University president Daniel Coit Gilman, and Joe Hawley. Sam followed Gilman in the order of speakers and in his remarks he joked that he was "always delighted to listen to the smooth, beautiful English of President Gilman, for I find myself almost ready to believe all he says; but I cannot help wonder how so learned a man has failed to learn how to spell John."[18]

Back at Quarry Farm the evening of July 2, Sam received a telegram from James Paige that "the machine is finished" and he should "come & see it work." But Crane was in his final throes and, "a man who had always hoped for a swift death," he died at the farm the next evening "after ten months of pain." Livy and the children "were in a gloom," Sam wrote Howells, and Susan Crane was heartbroken. "Sue bears up under her calamity with a great and fine fortitude," he wrote Mother Fairbanks. Sam eulogized his brother-in-law as "a thoroughly good man, as genial, charitable and whole souled as he was able and active in business," and he remained in Elmira for several days to comfort the family and assist in funeral arrangements before leaving for Hartford to inspect the typesetter.[19]

Sam was buoyant when he returned to Elmira. He wanted to schedule a public exhibition of the machine in operation in early September. "I have been back here from Hartford ten or twelve days," he wrote Orion on August 2. "The machine has been idle for 7 days to permit the addition" of an accessory to prevent operators from setting two letters in a single stroke. "Not 5 persons in the country know that the machine is done & no more will know it for a month yet, if we can help it." His boast is reminiscent of Hank Morgan's brag that he had the civilization of the nineteenth century "booming" secretly under the nose of the sixth-century British. But the same day Sam penned this letter, the contraption broke down. "The mach[ine] stopped Aug 2—not a line from [Whitmore] to say why or how much is to be done on it," he noted in his journal. As it happened, the stoppage lasted only ten days but as a result the public demonstration of the machine on September 1 was canceled. Charley Langdon had promised to invest in the machine on the condition that it was finished before he left for a year in Europe. When Sam returned from Hartford "& said it was finished . . . once more I was mistaken," he wrote. "I promised another finish for Aug. 12 & another for Sept. 1 & failed twice more." Charley refused to gamble on mere promises, leaving Sam in dire straits. He owed Pratt & Whitney six thousand dollars on September 20 and, he fretted, if Charley "fails me I do not know of any way to raise the money. . . . Time is short & the corner I am in is distressingly tight." Fortunately, Livy received fifteen thousand dollars in partial repayment of a loan just in time to pay the bill.[20]

In late September Sam negotiated with Paige for a five-hundred-dollar royalty on every machine sold, whereupon he once again announced that the prototype was finished and he offered investors a one-dollar royalty on the sale of every machine per thousand dollars of stock purchased. "I have just completed the great undertaking which I began 3½ years ago and in which I have paid out $3,000 every month," Sam informed Frank Fuller in October.

Similarly, he notified Howells a week later that "after patiently & contentedly spending more than $3,000 a month on it for 44 consecutive months, I've got it done at last & it's a daisy!" Then, true to form, he again anthropomorphized the machine, this time as a male titan: "Come & see this sublime magician of iron & steel work his enchantments."[21]

On August 15, 1889, Rudyard Kipling, at the time a virtually unknown writer, called on Sam at the Langdon mansion in Elmira. He wrote on the card he presented at the door, Sam remembered, that he "had come from Allahabad or some such place, fourteen thousand miles away, to see me." The two men spent a couple of hours together and, after Kipling left, Sam told Livy's mother that the stranger was "a most remarkable man." After Kipling published such works as *Plain Tales from the Hills* (1890), Sam became his admirer. "Kipling's name and Kipling's words always stir me now, stir me more than do any other living man's," he noted in August 1906, the year before Kipling received the Nobel Prize in Literature at the age of forty-two. On his part, Kipling was no less impressed with Sam. He wrote the publisher Frank Doubleday in 1903 that he regarded "the great and God-like Clemens" the "biggest man you have on your side of the water by a damn sight" and he proclaimed to Nicholas Murray Butler, president of Columbia University, that Sam "was the largest man of his time, both in the direct outcome of his work, and, more important still, as an indirect force in an age of iron Philistinism."[22]

Sam still needed to commission an artist to illustrate *A Connecticut Yankee*. He wanted to hire the best artist, he wrote Fred Hall on July 19. "This time I want pictures, not blackboard outlines & charcoal sketches. If [E. W.] Kemble's illustrations for my last book [the *Library of Humor*, 1888] were handed me today, I could understand how tiresome to me that sameness would get to be when distributed through a whole book, & I would put them promptly in the fire." He admired the pen-and-ink drawings that accompanied "Wu Chih Tien, the Celestial Empress," a "charming Chinese story" that was then appearing in serialization in *Cosmopolitan*. He instructed Hall to locate the artist, the thirty-nine-year-old socialist Dan Beard, a future founder of the Boy Scouts of America, and offer him the job. As Beard recalled in his autobiography, Hall "came to my studio in the old Judge Building and told me that Mark Twain wanted to meet the man who had made the illustrations for a Chinese story in the *Cosmopolitan* and he wanted that man to illustrate his new book. . . . The manuscript was sent to me to read. I read it through three times with great enjoyment. Then I met Mr. Clemens by appointment in his little office on Fourteenth Street," probably in July 1889. By his own testimony, Beard had "never met Mr. Clemens until I started in to illustrate his book." Sam's directions to the artist were simple and to the point: "I have endeavored to put in all the coarseness & vulgarity into the Yankee in King Arthur's court that is necessary & rely upon you for all that refinement & delicacy of humor your facile pen can depict." The titular character was an unclassed liminal figure, both a master mechanic and a manager, who "has neither the refinement nor the weakness of a college education; he is a perfect ignoramus; he is boss of a machine shop; he can build a locomotive or a Colt's revolver, he can put up and run a telegraph line, but he's an ignoramus nevertheless." Sam advised Beard "to obey his *own* inspiration" because "I want his genius to be wholly unhampered. I sha'n't have any fear as to results." Beard drew about 400 pictures, 220 of them reproduced in the novel, in seventy working days for which he was paid three thousand dollars, two thousand more than he was promised and a thousand more than Kemble received to illustrate *Huck Finn*.[23]

Sam began to read proof of *A Connecticut Yankee*, which included reproductions of Beard's sketches, while at Quarry Farm in late August. "I have examined the pictures a good many times," he commended the artist, "& my pleasure in them is as strong & fresh as ever. I do not know of any quality they lack. Grace, dignity, poetry, spirit, imagination, these enrich them and make them charming and beautiful; and wherever humor appears it is high and fine." Sam was particularly impressed by Beard's depictions of Arthur and Morgan—"you have expressed the King as I wanted him expressed"— and "I like the Yankee every time." According to M. Thomas Inge, moreover, Beard expanded on Sam's topical satire or "included ideas not found in the text" in about one-fourth of the images. By Beard's own testimony, he modeled the heroine Sandy and the page Clarence on the actresses Annie Russell and Sarah Bernhardt. He caricatured Queen Victoria as an old sow and the Prince of Wales as a "chuckleheaded" nobleman. He gave Merlin the countenance of Alfred, Lord Tennyson, and a slave driver the face of Jay Gould.

Not that Sam disapproved. "Jay Gould taught the entire nation to make a god of the money and the man, no matter how the money might have been acquired," he opined. A couple of Beard's images contain phrases, such as "anti-monopolist" and "absorber of unearned increment," that nowhere appear in the narrative. The cartoons that ornament chapter 33, "Sixth-Century Political Economy," emphasize, according to Gregg Camfield, "the allegorical nature of the chapter." In brief, Beard's illustrations constitute a complementary and parallel text to the novel and Sam approved them wholeheartedly. "Hold me under permanent obligations," Sam wrote Beard on November 11, a month before the release of the book. "What luck it was to find you! There are hundreds of artists who could illustrate any other

Figure 28. Dan Beard's illustration of Jay Gould as a slave driver, from *A Connecticut Yankee in King Arthur's Court*, 1889.

book of mine, but there was only one who could illustrate this one. Yes, it was a fortunate hour that I went netting for lightning-bugs and caught a meteor. Live forever!" Before the end of the year, Sam went so far as to tell a correspondent that "to my mind the illustrations are better than the book—which is a good deal for me to say." As late as 1905, in a speech to the Society of Illustrators in New York with Beard in the audience, Sam praised the pictures in *A Connecticut Yankee* without stint. "From the first page to the last" the book ridiculed "the trivialities, the servilities of our poor human race," and "the professions and the insolence of priestcraft and kingcraft—those creatures that make slaves of themselves and have not the manliness to shake it off. Beard put it all" into his sketches. "I meant it to be there. I put a lot of it there and Beard put the rest."[24]

At Sam's request, both Howells and Stedman read *A Connecticut Yankee* prior to publication. In Stedman's opinion, it was "a great book, in some respects [Sam's] most original, most imaginative,—certainly the most effective and sustained." He considered *The Prince and the Pauper* and *A Connecticut Yankee* first cousins, though the former novel "was checkers" whereas the latter "is chess." He understood, too, that Sam's new novel was his most ambitious work ("you have let your whole nature loose in it, at the prime of your powers") and that the targets of Sam's satire were not medieval but modern ("you are going at the *still existing* radical principles or fallacies which made 'chivalry' possible once, & servility & flunkeyism & tyranny possible now"). At the granular level, Stedman also suggested some minor stylistic revisions—in particular the deletion of references to the "homogeneous protoplasm" that falls from the sky after Hank Morgan bombs a gang of knights and "the 4,000,000-lbs.-of-meat" that sizzle at the close of the Battle of the Sand-Belt. Howells was even more enthusiastic about the novel than Stedman. When Sam sent the proof, he assured Howells he had deleted everything from it that might "repel instead of persuade," including a passage in which Morgan plans to build monuments to royal mistresses and such words as "bastard," "prostitute," "rump," "buttocks," "damn," "nipple," and "disemboweled." Much as he had advised Mother Fairbanks almost three years earlier that *A Connecticut Yankee* would be his last book, Sam told Howells it was his "swan-song, my retirement from literature permanently, and I wish to pass to the cemetery unclodded." After reading the tale, Howells showered it with praise. "It's a mighty great book," he announced, "and it makes my heart burn with wrath. It seems God did not forget to put a soul into you." Six days later, he was even more fervent in his admiration:

"The book is glorious—simply noble; what masses of virgin truth never touched in print before!" Sam was relieved that Howells approved "of what I say about the French Revolution. . . . Next to the 4th of July & its results, it was the noblest & the holiest thing & the most precious that ever happened in this earth. And its gracious work is not done yet—not anywhere in the remote neighborhood of it."[25]

Given its satire of monarchy and its English setting, Sam feared his British publisher would decline to issue *A Connecticut Yankee* without heavy editing. "I have already revised the story twice," he notified Andrew Chatto in mid-July 1889, following the recommendations of Howells, Stedman, Livy, and even some Englishmen who had heard him read excerpts in public. "I have taken all [these] pains because I wanted to say a Yankee mechanic's say against monarchy and its several natural props and yet make a book which you would be willing to print exactly as it comes to you, without altering a word." An unapologetic defender of American exceptionalism, Sam claimed that the novel was in a sense a long-winded reply to the aspersions on America of Matthew Arnold, though Arnold's name nowhere appears in it. "We are spoken of (by Englishmen) as a thin-skinned people," Sam contended to Chatto, but

it is you who are thin-skinned. An Englishman may write with the most brutal frankness about any man or institution among us and we republish him without dreaming of altering a line or a word. But England cannot stand that kind of a book written about herself. It is England that is thin-skinned. . . . Now, as I say, I have taken laborious pains to so trim this book of offense that you might not lack the nerve to print it just as it stands. I am going to get the proofs to you just as early as I can. I want you to read it carefully. If you can publish it without altering a single word, go ahead. Otherwise, please hand it to J. R. Osgood [who had emigrated to England to work for Harper & Brothers] in time for him to have it published at my expense. This is important, for the reason that the book was not written for America; it was written for England. So many Englishmen have done their sincerest to teach us something for our betterment that it seems to me high time that some of us should substantially recognize the good intent by trying to pry up the English nation to a little higher level of manhood in turn.

In an interview with the *New York Times* five months later, four days after the novel was issued in England and the same day it appeared in the United States, Sam insisted again that his purpose in writing it was "to get at the Englishman." But "English publishers are cowards, and so are the English newspapers," he alleged, "so I have had to modify and modify my book to suit the English publishers' taste until I really cannot cut it anymore." Even

Chatto, "one of the bravest" of English bookmakers, "will cut my book. All I could do was to appeal to him to cut it as little as possible." So confident was he that Chatto would edit the British edition that he suggested the publisher delete several paragraphs at the close of chapter 25 about royal grants. In the end, fortunately, all that Chatto expurgated was "a little playful remark of mine about the divine right of Kings" in the preface, a sarcastic admission of Sam's failure to settle in the story the question "whether there is such a thing." In any case, he exaggerated in both his letter to Chatto and his interview with the *Times* the extent to which *A Connecticut Yankee* "was written for England." Its targets were more contemporary than medieval, more specifically American than British, though he allowed neither "civilization" to escape unscathed.[26]

During his summer in Elmira, Sam also arranged for some prepublication publicity for the novel. In late July 1889 Robert Underwood Johnson of the *Century* reminded him of his "promise to allow the Century to publish excerpts" of his next book. Sam soon sent him several thousand words of excerpts from the introduction and chapters 7, 10, and 39 that were subsequently printed in the November issue of the magazine accompanied by five of Beard's illustrations. In a headnote, Sam described the novel as "a bitter struggle for supremacy in magic" between the wizard Merlin "using the absurd necromancy of the time" and a Yankee technocrat "beating it easily and brilliantly with the more splendid necromancy of the nineteenth century—that is, the marvels of modern science." Like the excerpts from *Huck Finn* in the *Century* five years earlier, these passages were widely reprinted in papers around the country, including the *Hartford Courant* (November 2); Lawrence, Kansas, *Journal* (November 3); and Wilmington, Delaware, *Post* (November 9). But the excerpts were not universally well received. According to the *Pittsburgh Dispatch*, "By some kind of fatality the dullest" passages in the book were "printed by way of sample in the November *Century*" and the San Francisco *Argonaut* complained that the extracts read "very much like an advertisement."[27]

As soon as the selections appeared in the *Century*, moreover, Sam was accused of plagiarism. According to the New York *World* for November 4 he had "appropriated the entire plot and most of the incidents" in the novel from *The Fortunate Island* (1881) by Charles Heber Clarke (aka Max Adeler), a Philadelphia journalist and humorist. In a telegram to the *World*, Adeler alleged "that no one could help noting" the similarity between the two tales. The "charge was not an isolated incident in Mark Twain's career, and should come as no surprise," Walter Blair avers. In Adeler's story the protagonist, Professor Bafflin, is shipwrecked on an island that literally split off from England and drifted away in the sixth century and remains fixed in time. Bafflin (that is, Hank Morgan) learns that the residents "live here pretty much as King Arthur and his subjects lived." Adeler's cast of characters includes Sir Dinadan and Prince Sagramor, Father Anselm, a Merlin-like sorcerer, and a pair of lovers, Sir Bleoberis and Ysolt, who are Launcelot and Guenever types. Adeler's and Sam's fables also share several similar plot points, such as Bafflin's murder of a knight with a modern revolver, the introduction of the telephone, and the "slow torture" of armor. As David Ketterer concludes, "Many of the incidents depend on Baffin's applying his nineteenth-century knowledge, attitudes, and artifacts to the sixth-century situation," exactly the way Hank Morgan governs Camelot.[28]

To be sure, Sam and others could not understand how Adeler could infer from only ten pages of excerpts in the *Century* that so much of *A Connecticut Yankee* was derived from *The Fortunate Island*. But Sam never definitively denied that he had "borrowed" from Adeler. On the contrary, in an interview in January 1890, he both allowed that he had read Adeler's tale ("how the chapter might have lingered in my mind I could faintly conceive") and attributed the similarity between the two works to his old theory of "unconscious plagiarism": "to repeat another man's thoughts is to pay him the highest compliment you can. It shows what a grip his mind has taken on yours. I never charge anyone with plagiarism, for to do so would prove me incapable of gratitude for the highest compliment a man can pay me." Three months later, he once more insisted that he had "never had an original idea in my life and never have met anybody that *had* had" and offered a narrow definition of plagiarism:

> If a man takes that from me (knowingly, purposely) he is a thief. If he takes it unconsciously—snaking it out of some secluded corner of his memory and mistaking it for a new birth instead of a mummy—he is no thief, and no man has a case against him. Unconscious appropriation is utterly common; it is *not* plagiarism and is no crime; but *conscious* appropriation, i.e. plagiarism, is as rare as parricide. Of course there *are* plagiarists in the world . . . but bless you, they are few and far between.

But some observers were not so sanguine: "If Mark Twain is a literary thief," declared the *Washington Post*, "then he has displayed a barrenness of fancy, a stupidity of method, and a meanness of spirit that belies the characteristics of his former productions and reflect upon his manliness and honesty." At about the same time, Sam scored this comment in his copy of Henry Breen's *Modern English Literature* (1857): "The man of genius does not steal; he conquers; and what he conquers, he annexes to his empire." Sam then glossed in the margin: "A good deal of truth in it. Shakespeare took other people's quartz and extracted the gold from it—it was a nearly valueless commodity before." Or as Pap Finn might have said, good writers borrow and bad writers steal. In the long run, Sam suffered no significant consequences for "borrowing." But Adeler reiterated the accusation as late as 1914 in a footnote to a reprinting of *The Fortunate Island*: "It is necessary to say that this tale was first published in 1881 and antedates a story with a similar theme by a noted author."[29]

At the same moment Sam was accused of plagiarizing Adeler, by a bizarre twist of fate he tried to forestall the claim that he had ripped a critical part of his final pages from the headlines. While sheltered in the cave in chapter 42 of *A Connecticut Yankee*, just before the Battle of the Sand-Belt, Hank Morgan issues a decree establishing his republic. With the death of Arthur in the civil war that destroys the kingdom, the monarchy is abolished, "there is no longer a nobility, no longer a privileged class, no longer an Established Church; all political power has reverted to its original source, the people of the nation." Coincidentally, on November 15, less than two weeks after Adeler accused Sam of plagiarism, the Brazilian military overthrew the government of Emperor Dom Pedro II in a coup d'état and nationalists there issued a "Manifesto of the Republican Government of Brazil." Sam was delighted, of course, and he briefly considered printing "some extracts from the Yankee that have in them this new (sweet) breath of republics." But he also worried that, in the wake of Adeler's charges, he would again be accused of "borrowing." As he wrote his friend Sylvester Baxter, the editor of the *Boston Herald*, who had already received a review copy of his novel,

> If you will turn to about the five hundredth page, you will find a state paper of my Connecticut Yankee in which he announces the dissolution of King Arthur's monarchy and proclaims the English Republic. Compare it with the state paper which announces the downfall of the Brazilian monarchy and proclaims the Republic of the United States of Brazil, and stand by to defend the Yankee from plagiarism. There is merely a resemblance of ideas, nothing more. The Yankee's proclamation was already in print a week ago. This is merely one of those odd coincidences which are always turning up. Come, protect the Yank from that cheapest and easiest of all charges—plagiarism.

Sam also told the interviewer for the *New York Times* on the day Charles L. Webster and Company issued the U.S. edition of the novel that "curiously enough, the short proclamation in which my hero abolishes the monarchy is similar—I don't mean the language, but the ideas—to the proclamation establishing the Brazilian Republic."[30]

As it happened, Sam's fear was misplaced. No critic accused him of copying the Brazilian proclamation nor, for that matter, did any reviewer—save one—defend him against the charge he might have copied it in the novel. In his notice, printed in the *Boston Herald* for December 15, Baxter ignored entirely the similarity between the declaration of Brazilian independence and Hank Morgan's proclamation. The only critic to defend Sam preemptively from a charge of plagiarism was Charley Clark in the *Hartford Courant* on the eve of the book's release.[31] Clark notes, unlike every other reviewer of the novel and presumably at Sam's direction, the "odd coincidence" that, though "written a year in advance," it reads "like today's happenings in Brazil." Three weeks later, ironically, Sam published a thirteen-hundred-word essay in Baxter's *Boston Herald* decrying "the absence of American newspaper interest" in the recent Brazilian revolution. "Here at our elbow occurs an event which, to Americans, should be by all odds the greatest, the most grateful and the most joyful that has happened on the globe" since the French Revolution, he suggested, "and yet they exhibit not nearly as much interest in it as they do in the antics of the complacent young kangaroo who squats upon the German throne and wags his gracious paws." The same day this piece appeared in the *Herald*, Howells wrote Sam that he had "just heated myself up with your righteous wrath about our indifference to the Brazilian Republic" and Thomas Wentworth Higginson sent him a "bravo! For you & Brazil."[32]

Through Baxter's agency, Sam also met the utopian novelist Edward Bellamy. Active in the nationalist movement inspired by Bellamy's *Looking Backward* (1888) and two of the founding members of the First Nationalist Club of Boston, Baxter and Howells both encouraged Sam's interest in this brand of Fabian socialism. At Howells's suggestion, six weeks after completing *A Connecticut Yankee* Sam read Bellamy's "fascinating book" and in late November he welcomed Baxter's offer to introduce him to "the man who has made the accepted heaven paltry by inventing a better one on earth" and "the maker of the latest & best of all the Bibles." As he bluntly allowed, "I vastly want to know Bellamy." Baxter solicited a contribution from Sam to the *Nationalist*, a magazine nominally edited by Bellamy: "If you could write us a bit of something when you felt like giving vent to yourself in our direction it would help the cause," though Sam declined the invitation on the grounds he needed to "let my tank fill up before I do any more writing." In his notice of *A Connecticut Yankee*, moreover, Baxter pronounced the novel "another and very instructive sort of 'Looking Backward.'" Baxter and Bellamy visited Sam in Hartford on January 3, 1890, and although no details of this meeting survive, Sam told an interviewer in 1896 that he knew Bellamy "well."

Howells in 1910 recalled that Sam was "fascinated with *Looking Backward*" and that Bellamy had once visited him.[33]

In mid-October 1889 Sam hit on a new tactic to fund the Paige typesetter, ironically during the same period he was consorting with Baxter and Bellamy. Rather than peddling royalties on sales of the compositor, he planned to form a corporation and sell stock to finance the factory to build the machines; that is, he would hawk shares in the typesetter like subscription books, the only marketing model he understood. He was particularly keen on enticing Andrew Carnegie and other financiers with deep pockets to invest. With this object in view and at the invitation of its president Richard Watson Gilder, Sam spoke in New York the evening of October 15 before the members and guests of the newly organized Fellowcraft Club, including Joseph Choate, Depew, Thomas Edison, John La Farge, Bill Nye, Pond, Horace Porter, and Augustus Saint-Gaudens. His talk was not new, merely a rehash of his Pilgrims' Day speech in Boston two years earlier when he introduced a plan for an extemporaneous after-dinner address that could be adapted to all circumstances—but he offered to teach classes "and charge a high rate" to anyone who wished to learn the trick.[34] Around this time, too, Carnegie presented Sam with a copy of his book *Triumphant Democracy* (1886) inscribed with the "regards of his fellow Republican." In his note of thanks, Sam assured Carnegie that the volume was "a favorite of mine & helped to fire me up" to write *A Connecticut Yankee in King Arthur's Court*. The inscription was doubly ironic: Sam, a self-described mugwump, refused to hew the party line and Carnegie was more a privileged aristocrat like the knights Sam satirized in the novel than a card-carrying small-business Republican. In the end, neither Carnegie nor Edison invested in the Paige company, though Sam was able to entice some small investors, such as Henry Irving and his manager Bram Stoker, later the author of *Dracula* (1897), to buy stock.[35]

Abby Richardson completed the dramatization of *The Prince and the Pauper* before the October 1, 1889, deadline, though she failed to submit her script to Sam for his approval as their contract specified. David Belasco doctored the script and began to direct daily rehearsals of the play on December 1, 1889, at the Lyceum Theater in New York and, produced by Daniel Frohman and starring Elsie Leslie, it premiered at the New Park Theatre in Philadelphia on December 23 for a fifteen-performance, monthlong, out-of-town tryout. The run was a modest success, earning box office receipts of about twenty-three thousand dollars and favorable reviews in the *Philadelphia Inquirer* ("the most successful novelty of the season") and *North American* ("the most picturesque and pathetic play that has been seen in Philadelphia for a long time").[36]

On January 11, nine days before the play was booked to open for a seven-week run in New York, Ned House applied to the Court of Common Pleas of New York for a temporary injunction to restrain the Richardson production pending the resolution of his suit against Sam for breach of contract. Until a judge ruled on House's request, however, the play appeared at the Broadway Theater as scheduled. With the entire Clemens family in the audience, it opened on January 20 to modestly favorable reviews and strong ticket sales. Between the third and fourth acts on opening night, Sam appeared before the curtain hand in hand with Elsie Leslie to compliment in absentia Abby Richardson, to whom "the honor of this curtain call" rightfully belonged.

No doubt Sam was infatuated with the adolescent actress and three weeks later he sent her a hackneyed rhyme:

> I'll be your friend, your thrall, your knave
> I'll be your elder brother
> I'll be, for love, your very slave
> Or anything you'd druther.

In truth, though he was infatuated with young Leslie and "bewitched" by her performance, he was disgusted by the "burlesque" play and its "ludicrous" dialogue. The script added insult to litigation. He told Frohman the first night that the "play hasn't anything of mine in it" and, as he wrote Frohman in an unsent letter, Richardson "carefully & deliberately got as far away from the book as she could. . . . Whenever she meddled with a high character she lowered its tone," and "whenever she took an incident from the book, she distorted & damaged it." Moreover,

> whenever she transferred dialogue from the book she changed the language—& degraded it. The literature of this play is beneath criticism. For baldness, poverty, & windy & meaningless grandiloquence, its language is a curiosity. Its ludicrous attempts to imitate the quaint speech of those in a bygone age would break up the gravity of a graven image. . . . The one incontestably original thing in this play is its language. It is absolutely new. It was never spoken anywhere in the earth—not even in the Bowery. . . . Is the contract fulfilled? Is this mess of idiotic rubbish & vapid twaddle a "dramatization" of the book? It resembles it about as a riot in a sailor boarding-house resembles a Sunday-school.

Figure 29. Elsie
Leslie as the
pauper Tom Canty
in the stage version
of *The Prince and
the Pauper*, 1890.
Courtesy of the
Museum of the
City of New York.

In a note to Moncure Conway, Sam amplified his criticism as if he were shouting into a megaphone: "I think it is by long odds the most ignorant piece of literature & the poorest rubbish the world has ever seen; & it is not a dramatization of the book, but merely uses the book's names, distorts the book's incidents, copies nothing from me, & is wholly original, thank God." Livy was also disappointed "that the Prince & Pauper is not better put upon the stage," as she diplomatically wrote Grace King. "In the main it is poor and does not in the least do the book, we think, justice. Such inferior English is put into the mouths of the actors in many places."[37]

While Elsie Leslie "did beautifully in the double part of Prince & Pauper," Sam decided "to rewrite certain parts" of the script before it was staged in London. "I cannot consent to have this amazing burlesque played in England," he barked in his unsent letter to Frohman. "The very cattle would laugh at it." He reportedly told Frohman, "I'll rewrite it and keep the same structure you have there," but Frohman believed, with some justice, that "writers can't dramatize their own books." Certainly Sam was no dramaturge. He "brought me a script that would have taken two nights to perform," according to the producer. "It was not so suited to acting requirements as the adaptation I was using, so I returned it to the author with my very adequate but, to him, unconvincing reasons for its rejection." The rebuff fractured the united but fragile front the three principals had presented to the public. As Sam fumed to Richardson, "Your dramatization was not submitted to me at all but my emendations of it are submitted [by Frohman] to you for *your* approval." So far as he was concerned, both Frohman and Richardson had overstepped their bounds. "My MS. was submitted to [Frohman] alone. I needed no one's approval, not even his," to rewrite the play.[38] Inasmuch as the dramatic rights to *The Prince and the Pauper* in England were the property of Chatto & Windus, however, Sam soon abandoned his attempt to polish Richardson's script.

More than the plot and characters adapted from Sam's novel, the supporting cast, or the costumes and scenery, eight-year-old Elsie Leslie was credited with the success of the stage production on Broadway. "But for Elsie Leslie's charming acting, the awful piece would have died the first night," Sam conceded to Conway. And the reviewers agreed—for example, Alan Dale in the New York *Evening World* ("her efforts [were] little less than herculean"), the *Critic* ("would have but a poor chance of success without a public favorite like Elsie Leslie to play the two principal characters"), the *New York Herald* ("played almost faultlessly by little Elsie Leslie"), and the *New York Times* (though a "jumble of odds and ends of old melodrama," the play "will draw great crowds because the public likes to see a pretty child as hero").[39]

House's application for a temporary injunction to halt further production of the play was heard by Joseph F. Daly, judge in the New York Court of Common Pleas and brother of Augustin Daly, on January 21. The judge knew Sam socially and probably should have recused himself. None of the principals was present but all submitted affidavits as required by January 27. Frohman protested in his deposition that he should never have been sued because Sam had never told him about his oral agreement with House and he had invested about fourteen thousand dollars in the play. Sam and his attorney Whitford insisted that the author of the novel had never agreed, either orally or in writing, to allow House an exclusive right to dramatize it and that House had simply read the manuscript in 1881 while confined to bed in Hartford "to satisfy his own curiosity." The document submitted by

House's team of lawyers portrayed "the patient and long-waiting invalid" as a victim of a mendacious and venal adversary: Sam "had been growing rich, while the poor writer, now confined closely to his room and with the last term of his slender annuity nearly at hand, had no resources except in his pen." The same day the affidavits were to be submitted, the *New York Times*, still harboring the animus toward Sam that originated in Sam's feud with Charles C. Duncan in 1883—even House acknowledged "the generous interest which the *Times* has shown in the lawsuit brought by me against Mark Twain"—described the quarrel as a David-and-Goliath battle between "a playwright, dependent on his pen for a livelihood, robbed of his ideas, which are his stock in business, and of his labor" by a "prosperous author and owner of the book on which the play is based." Indeed, "the case appeals all the more to public sympathy" because "for years Mr. House has been an invalid." The press coverage of the case routinely included a note of pity for the "invalid playwright" struggling for justice against a "millionaire author." The legal clash seemed to epitomize a type of class conflict, on one side "the most popular author of the day, in the flush of active health and strength, with unbounded resources of influence, wealth, and established position" and "on the other, a well-nigh forgotten writer, condemned by illness to years of seclusion, crippled by a torturing disease, and—as Mr. Clemens knew better than any living being—utterly unprepared to bear the stress of a protracted legal struggle." As the *Boston Advertiser* averred, House was "making a plucky fight here against physical weakness and distress that would incapacitate most men for work of any sort." The *Boston Post* editorialized that "no sane man, and especially no literary man, and still more no bedridden man, reads a voluminous manuscript 'to satisfy his own curiosity.'" While the judge was weighing the evidence, House's attorneys chose to "try their case in the newspapers," as Sam complained to Whitford on February 4, the same day another piece appeared in the *Times* that outlined the basis for the plaintiff's suit.[40]

Over the course of his life, Sam Clemens lost more friends than he made or, as his grandnephew Samuel Charles Webster put it, he "never forgave anyone he had injured." Both Howells ("if he thought you had in any way played him false you were anathema and maranatha forever") and Pond ("injure him, and he is merciless") echoed the sentiment. Predictably, House's suit to restrain production of *The Prince and the Pauper* ended their friendship and, in addition, Sam attempted to defend his behavior in the papers no less than the plaintiff who tried to prosecute the case in public. The *New York Tribune* printed a front-page piece on January 17, six days after House filed his application for a temporary injunction, that summarized Sam's side of the dispute. According to this account, Sam had offered House "$5,000 as compensation" in an attempt to settle the matter "but he declined it."[41] The parties had submitted to arbitration "without success." Frohman was quoted to the effect, moreover, that "he did not regard the affair as anything serious." Sam also sat for an interview with the *Hartford Courant* published the next day in which he challenged at length House's version of events. He asserted a point in it that he had not made before and never asserted again: that he had reached a verbal agreement with Will Gillette to dramatize the novel and he had not rescinded this permission even after Gillette abandoned the project. According to House's own logic, if Sam had no right to grant permission to Richardson to adapt the novel in 1888 because of his prior oral agreement with House, he had no right to grant permission to House to adapt the novel in 1886 because of his earlier understanding with Gillette. Whitford also argued, to no avail, that the New York Court of Common Pleas had no jurisdiction in the case because Richardson's play was protected by federal copyright and, in a nondenial denial, that if House would only produce all the letters he had received from Sam "they would show that House was never authorized to write the play." In truth, the opposite was also true: House's attorneys contended that Sam's affidavit betrayed "ingenious duplicity." If he would only produce all the letters he claimed he had never received from their client—"but none of those quoted in House's complaint"—they would prove the two men had a binding agreement.[42]

Daly's decision turned not on the question of whether House had finished a first act by June 1887 or a complete draft of the play by the fall of that year but whether Sam and House had a valid contract authorizing House to write the play. Based on the two letters the men exchanged in December 1886, the judge concluded they had reached such an agreement. Sam again blamed his attorney Whitford, "an ignorant, blethering gas-pipe," for fumbling the case. Charley Webster had hired him on a thousand-dollar-a-year retainer in 1882 and "indeed Whitford was worth part of it—the two-hundredth part of it." Daly granted the injunction on March 8, 1890, in a verdict buttressed by a curious if not tortured slice of judicial logic: Daly reasoned that, as an invalid confined to a bed and wheelchair, House was "more likely to remember exactly what was said . . . while Clemens was a busy and popular author" and thus "much may have escaped his recollection." The *New York Times* portrayed the ruling as a triumph of the downtrodden, the correction of an "injustice done to an author and playwright in straitened circumstances because of physical infirmity by a very wealthy author and publisher. Like the majority of writers, Mr. House is not eminent in commercial ability and business shrewdness. Mr. Clemens is a writer who is a notable exception to his rule. He is possessed of business sagacity that has made him a million-aire." It was, as Sam told an interviewer, "an extraordinary opinion." The court "declared that as Mr. House was a sick man and had been confined to his bed and had time to think and to revolve the facts in his mind and freshen up his memory" his memory was more reliable than Sam's. "According to that it would seem that sickness is an admirable way to win a lawsuit." The "lowest down of all polecats & liars" had "worked" his invalidism "so effectively that he made the judge believe that the sicker a man is, the nearer he can come to speaking the truth." Sam's carefully cultivated reputation for "business sagacity" was invoked in defense of the decision. He insisted, on the other hand, that the only "rational explanation of my conduct" was that "I did not know that I was under contract with anybody. And that is the truth." Seventeen years later, Sam was still bitter about the judgment: "Daly's decision went against me, upon one ground and upon one ground only—to wit, that the testimony upon the two sides utterly disagreeing, the veracity of a sick man, confined to his chamber, was more to be depended upon than the oath of a man who was well and at large." He was as disgusted by the ruling as he was by Richardson's adaptation. "I want to get far, very far away from plays, just now," he wrote Howells on April Fools' Day 1890, "for any mention of the stage brings House to my mind & turns my stomach. What a gigantic liar that man is!—& what an inconceivable hound." A week later he pledged that he would never "go to law" again with "a rancid adventurer like that scoundrel" because House was "willing to tell lies & swear to them. It gives me no fair chance." As late as August he ranted that "House never thought of making a play out of my book . . . until he heard that Mrs. Richardson had done it."[43]

Within seventy-two hours after Judge Daly issued the temporary injunction, Frohman and House reached an agreement that permitted the play written by Richardson to be performed so long as House received a royalty from it and so long as Sam's and most of Richardson's profits were deposited in an escrow account pending the resolution of the breach-of-contract suit. But when Sam read the correspondence between Frohman and House, he discovered that the theater manager was sending his share of the proceeds "to House for permission" to continue staging Richardson's play. As Sam wrote Whitford,

Now if House has any right to *any* piece, it is to his own, not *this* one. Why cannot I enjoin Frohman from playing this piece, & force him (if he must have a piece), to either play House's version or none. . . . Frohman acknowledges that Mrs. Richardson has rights by continuing to pay a portion of her royalties to her. Is not that a confession that I have rights also? Am I to be insulted in this brutal way by this son of a bitch & have no recourse?

Frohman not only threw Sam under the proverbial bus lest he become the target of a suit but he spun an alternative and exculpatory production history of the play in which he appeared as a fair-minded arbiter of everyone's interests:

> When I was looking for a new play for little Elsie Leslie, I went to Mark Twain and offered him a royalty for the privilege of having his book dramatized. Mr. Clemens consented, but stipulated that the dramatization should be made under his direction. I agreed to that on condition that I need not accept the play if it should prove unsatisfactory. Mr. Clemens employed Mr. House to write the play, agreeing to pay him a part of the royalty he was to receive from me. The play was not satisfactory, and I then engaged Mrs. Richardson to dramatize the book.

When Richardson's version proved successful on the stage, Frohman claimed, he had generously paid royalties to her, House, and Sam. In his 1937 autobiography, published nearly half a century after these events, moreover, Frohman asserted that his production of Richardson's *The Prince and the Pauper* had been "a great success."[44]

As if this web of legal disputes were not already a veritable Gordian knot, after agreeing to permit Frohman to continue to stage Richardson's adaptation of the novel House proposed in the spring of 1890 to stage his version, too—a step that sparked a dispute between the two men. In an open letter to Frohman in August, House protested that he had "voluntarily conferred upon you at a time when you were in sore need of my indulgence"—albeit for a price—"the right of continuing to perform Mrs. Richardson's piece." Frohman regarded House's maneuver not only as betrayal but as an "indiscreet" and "unbusiness-like" act of "meanness" and "contrary to law." Though the press reported that the dueling dramatizations "would be played this season under a harmonious arrangement," no such deal was reached. In an open letter of reply, Frohman reminded House that Sam considered his "several schemes" to dramatize the novel "unsatisfactory," that Sam had "naturally supposed you had long since abandoned your unsuccessful efforts to get the book into dramatic shape," and that "his early and friendly letters to you were regarded by the court as fixing your prior claim," and as a result an "injunction against me, an innocent party, was granted." As for House's "indulgence" in permitting him to continue to stage Richardson's play, "I paid and am paying to you (for this supposed exclusive right) all of Mark Twain's royalties weekly, and a large share of Mrs. Richardson's moiety of royalties for her adaptation." Despite the squabble, House's adaptation debuted at the Amphion Academy in Brooklyn on October 6 with the child actor Tommy Russell, who had costarred with Elsie Leslie on alternating evenings in *Little*

Lord Fauntleroy a year earlier, in the leading roles of Tom Canty and Edward VI. "There are two Prince & Pauper plays—one in the hands of a pirate, the other in the hands of a person who is the same thing without the name," Sam wrote James Pond. "God be thanked I have no influence with either." In an ironic reversal of fortunes, Frohman successfully filed for an injunction to halt the Brooklyn production, issued by Judge Daly on October 8. The play closed only twelve days after it opened, whereupon the actors sued House for failing to pay them. Tommy Russell's parents were eventually awarded a default verdict against him in absentia in the amount of fourteen thousand dollars.[45]

Faced with extradition to France on an unrelated charge "of swindling the Crédit Lyonnais out of a considerable sum," according to Sam, House fled to Japan to escape litigation on two continents. As a result, the case of *House v. Clemens et al.* never came to trial. It was dismissed in January 1894, the temporary injunction was finally lifted, and Richardson was paid her share of the royalties on not only its earnings at the Broadway Theater but its profit during its two years on tour. The next month Sam sued Frohman for his share, an amount he estimated at five or six thousand dollars. Two years later he complained that he would "never collect the money that is owing to me by that Lyceum Theatre Jew," though in 1906 he remembered that he and Frohman "met in the Lotus Club & chaffed each other about it, each claiming that the other owed money," but they played billiards with "unruffled amity" and ignored the elephant in the room.[46] Sam was the author of a novel that inspired a moderately popular play, yet he earned nothing from it except the pittance he received before Daly issued the original injunction.

CHAPTER 17

Nadir

I was the bulk of the firm of Charles L. Webster & Co., publishers.
That is, I furnished the money, not the brains. Nobody furnished the
brains.

—"Frank Fuller and My First New York Lecture"

THE RELEASE OF *A Connecticut Yankee in King Arthur's Court* was prolonged in part by a recalcitrant copy editor hired by Fred Hall bent on im-
proving Samuel Clemens's punctuation. "I telegraphed orders to have him
shot without giving him time to pray," Sam alerted W. D. Howells in late
August 1889. He was also alarmed by the languid pace at which proofs were
sent to publisher Andrew Chatto, who complained in mid-November that
he ought to have already received "the whole of book and illustrations."[1]

A Connecticut Yankee was finally issued without much fanfare in England
on December 6—Sam made a flying trip across the border at Niagara Falls
to secure British copyright on it—and it was published in the United States
four days later. In his autobiography, he blamed his nephew Charley Webster for postponing its publication "as long as he could" and then offering
it for sale "so surreptitiously that it took two or three years to find out that
there was any such book."[2] As usual, rather than recognizing his own complicity in the long-delayed appearance of the novel, Sam found a convenient
scapegoat for the poor sales of the book. But by the time the novel appeared,
Webster had had virtually nothing to do with Charles L. Webster and Company for nearly two years and he had had absolutely nothing to do with the
firm since Sam finished the manuscript the previous spring.

Most of the reviews of the novel in the Commonwealth—in the venues
that deigned to notice it at all—were predictably hostile. As Louis J. Budd
concludes, "The Conservative magazines were the most clearly offended." Most
of the choir sang from the same sheet music—for example, the *Academy* ("utterly unworthy of him"), *London Telegraph* ("a vulgar travesty"), *Scots Observer*
("misleading and offensive"), *Saturday Review* ("a triumph of dullness, vulgarity, and ignorance"), *Spectator* ("coarse and clumsy burlesque"), *Manchester
Guardian* ("the vulgarisation of what some hold romantic"), London *Star* (its

"frankly Philistine humor ... will shock many Tennysonians, who will lift their hands in horror at the profanation of the grave sanctities of the *Idylls* and the *Morte d'Arthur*"), *Athenaeum* ("a rather laborious piece of fun" and "very trite comment"), *New Review* (a "huge Colossus of a joke"), *Montreal Gazette* ("pretty flat"), and London *Speaker* ("he is not only dull when he is offensive, but perhaps even more dull when he is didactic"). The *Speaker* was even critical of Dan Beard's illustrations: "We hope ... that we have seen the artist at his worst; we certainly have not seen the author at his best." The half-penny dreadful London *Echo* complained that Sam had "made an exhibition of himself" and "furnished another painful illustration that irreverence—the caricature of what other people hold sacred—is one of prime elements in what is commonly known as Yankee humor." Even Reginald Brett, Second Viscount Esher, was "cool" in the liberal *Pall Mall Gazette*: "There is a certain sense of profanation about the idea which forms the motif of the new book and we cannot but deplore that Mark Twain should have used his undoubted genius to vulgarize and defile the Arthurian Legend." Henry Labouchère's radical weekly *Truth* waffled no less: "His fooling is admirable and his preaching is admirable, but they are mutually destructive." Even Sam's friend Andrew Lang in the *Illustrated London News* admitted he had "abstained from reading" the novel and refrained from praising it. Sam "has not the knowledge which would enable him to be a sound critic of the Middle Ages," Lang explained, and so he "often sins against good taste" and "some of his passages" are only fit "for the corner of a newspaper." Both the Melbourne *Leader* ("surely Sir Thomas Malory's immortal tale and the glorious legends of the Arthurian Cycle might have been tabooed as subjects of his comic muse") and Victoria, British Columbia, *Colonist* (satirizes "knight errantry of the King Arthur days as effectively as did Cervantes the inanities of chivalry in his immortal Don Quixote") agreed that the novel "is really not in good taste." Both the *Glasgow Herald* ("scarcely less sacrilegious than a parody of the Testament would be") and the *Montreal Witness* ("a great deal of irreverence toward religion") accused Sam of blasphemy. On the other hand, the *Edinburgh Scotsman* ("undoubtedly one of the funniest, if not absolutely the funniest, [book] that he has ever written"), *Manchester Examiner and Times* ("many a genuinely uproarious laugh to be found between the covers"), and *Sydney Bulletin* ("far and away the best work the author has produced") were more charitable in their assessments. The most favorable notice, however, appeared from the pen of William T. Stead in the *Review of Reviews*. In addition to reprinting ten pages of excerpts from the novel, Stead asserted that Sam more directly appealed to "the masses than any of the blue-china set of nimminy-pimminy criticasters." The Chatto & Windus edition of the novel sold about fifteen thousand copies during its first year in print, about average for Sam's books in the Commonwealth.[3]

As both the author and the publisher of the novel in the United States, Sam was better able to control its initial reception by commissioning the first reviews. "I don't care to have [the critics] paw the book at all," he told Howells. As early as October 8 the *New Haven Register* summarized the plot in its prepublication notice. Only two reviews appeared in the United States during the month of December, both of them by critics handpicked by Sam: Sylvester Baxter, a nationalist stalwart, in the *Boston Herald* and Howells in his "Editor's Study" in *Harper's Monthly*. Sam admonished Baxter to ignore his "slurs at the Church or Protection" because he wished to catch the reader unawares "& modify his views if I can." The tone of Baxter's encomium was suggested by its title: "Mark Twain's Masterwork." Sam's "rich humor never coursed more freely than here," he announced. "But there is much more than this; the sources of the claims of aristocratic privileges and royal prerogatives that yet linger in the world are so exposed to the full glare of the sun of nineteenth-century common sense, are shown in so ridiculous an aspect, that the work can hardly fail to do yeoman service in destroying the still existing remnants of respect for such pretensions." Baxter was likewise assiduous in his praise for the "beautiful pen-and-ink drawings by Dan Beard. . . . These drawings are graceful, picturesque and thoroughly characteristic of the spirit of the book. Many of them embody instructive allegories." Sam immediately thanked Baxter for his "admirable notice" and his "appreciative word for Beard's excellent pictures." On his part, Howells in his notice pronounced the novel Sam's best work, no small tribute from the so-called dean of American letters. "In this book our arch-humorist imparts more of his personal quality than in anything else he has done," Howells asserted. Sam's "strong, indignant, often infuriate hate of injustice, and his love of equality, burn hot through the manifold adventures and experiences of the tale," which functions "at every moment" as an eloquent "object-lesson in democracy." As soon as Howells's notice appeared, Sam also wrote to thank him: "The satisfaction it affords us could not be more prodigious if the book deserved every word of it; and maybe it does; I hope it does, though of course I can't realize it and believe it. But I am your grateful servant, anyway and always." As late as 1908, after rereading the novel, Howells declared to Sam it was "the most delightful, truest, most humane, sweetest fancy that ever was."[4]

As Sam hoped, most of the other reviews in the United States approvingly echoed Baxter and Howells. Among proponents of the novel were the *American Hebrew* ("his fame will rest to a greater extent upon the present volume than upon all his previous literary efforts"), *Hartford Times* ("a series of vivid pictures of the brutality of the nobles and the wealthy towards the working people"), *Charleston News* ("one of the strongest and best of Mark Twain's books"), *Brooklyn Times* ("one of the quaintest and most original of this quaint and original writer's works"), *San Francisco Chronicle* (a "bitter satire that in places reminds one of Swift"), Philadelphia *Public Ledger* ("a *sauce piquant* of unsparing satire"), *Utica Herald* ("a keen and witty satire"), *Elmira Advertiser* ("exhaustless wells of rich fun"), *Epoch* ("told in Mark Twain's own inimitable style"), *Critic* ("very naughty indeed" but "we cannot help laughing at it"), *Public Opinion* ("sometimes a little coarse and misplaced, but a great deal of it is very enjoyable"), Keokuk *Gate City* ("a supreme performance of witty imagination"), Keokuk *Constitution-Democrat* ("the acme of wit, humor, sarcasm, and imagination"), San Francisco *Argonaut* ("uncompromising hatred of monarchical institutions"), and San Francisco *American Standard* ("a terrible indictment against priestcraft, kingcraft, and aristocracy"). No less enthusiastic were the *Portland Oregonian* ("a strong vein of satire"), *New York Tribune* ("under its fun and amid its wild anachronisms the book contains a lesson in democracy which is worth noting"), and *Pittsburgh Dispatch* ("Mark Twain has never written anything better"). The *Dispatch* also recognized Beard's contributions to the novel ("as good as the work of the writer").[5]

Not all of the reviewers were so upbeat, of course. Others were more ambivalent, such as the *Providence Journal* ("though sometimes coarse" it "is not so low in tone as in *Tom Sawyer* or *Huckleberry Finn*"), *Boston Advertiser* ("Mark Twain's humor is not of the most subtle or delicate sort, but it is genuine and effective"), *Brooklyn Eagle* ("too much of the didactic and the labored imported into its execution"), *Boston Globe* ("invades sacred precincts of literature and no particular good comes to the author for his trepass"), and *Atlanta Constitution* ("not so fine a piece of literature" as *The Prince and the Pauper*). The *Baltimore Sun* revived the old charge that Sam's writings were irreverent ("among these poetic and religious traditions he cuts his way . . . like a butcher running amuck with a meat axe"). A couple of American reviewers were as harsh as the Brits, though for different reasons, accusing Sam of writing *A Connecticut Yankee* solely for the money. The Boston *Literary World* not only dismissed the novel as "the poorest of all his productions thus far" but alleged that "he prostitutes his humorous gift" in "this tiresome travesty." The *Milwaukee Sentinel* also censured Sam for permitting "the commercial spirit to overwhelm him."[6]

Predictably, the more progressive reviewers extolled the novel—for example, the *St. Louis Republic* ("Mark Twain's masterpiece," which "ought to be in the library of every labor union, free reading-room, and progressive institution in the land"). The notice in the *New York Standard*, a single-tax paper owned and edited by Henry George, averred that "the great American humorist has been moved by the spirit of democracy" and Hamlin Garland, a Henry George disciple, hailed in the *Boston Transcript* "the spirit of reform which animates the book," calling it distinctively the work "of a radical."

Edward Bellamy's *Nationalist* similarly contended that *A Connecticut Yankee* "deserves extensive circulation among Nationalists. It is a nobly earnest, as well as a deliciously humorous work." The revolutionary Cuban poet and politician José Martí hailed the novel in *La Nación*: "with the simple technique of the contrast between the free Yankee and the knights of the Round Table, he makes obvious, with rage that verges on the sublime, the vileness of some people who try to raise themselves above others and eat from their misery and drink from their misfortune." Just as predictably, on the other hand, a pair of religious magazines scorned the book. It "will not do much to elevate his reputation as a humorist," the *Catholic World* professed, "while it shows him to be more ignorant of history than one could have believed." The Boston *Congregationalist* similarly complained that it was "often tedious and sometimes coarse" and "greatly lacking in refinement."[7]

Sam's managed prepublication publicity for the novel yielded meager benefits. Only about twenty-four thousand copies of the novel were sold in the United States during its first six months in print and only about thirty-two thousand during its first year, producing an influx of cash sufficient to keep Webster and Company temporarily afloat but not to pay Sam any royalties.[8]

Sam continued to champion copyright regulation in the Fifty-First Congress in December 1889, though he was convinced new tactics were required. "I have worked for copyright in all the ways that its friends have suggested ever since 1872, seventeen or eighteen years," he indicated, but he no longer thought the strategy of lobbying individual politicians was effective. The Democrats had lost the presidency and forty-two seats in the House of Representatives in the election of 1888 and Sam was dubious the Republicans would enact copyright law. "I don't know the feeling of the present Congress," he told an interviewer, but "I have not much faith in a Republican Congress anyway. They are more likely to slap on more protection where it isn't needed than to pass a measure which would do some good." At least he was no longer equivocal on the benefits of international copyright. It was not, he had concluded, a question of the accessibility of American readers to cheap literature but "a question of maintaining in America a national literature, of preserving national sentiment, national politics, national thought, and national morals."[9]

Rather than appear in person, Sam sent a letter to be read aloud from the stage at an authors' benefit on behalf of copyright at the Brooklyn Academy of Music the evening of December 16, 1889. He had participated in many of the twelve authors' readings organized to date by the American Copyright League, he observed, "but we cannot point to a single one of them and say it was rationally conducted" and so he had concluded to refrain from participating in them in future. "An Authors' Reading conducted in the customary way turns what ought to be the pleasantest of entertainments into an experience to be forever remembered with bitterness by the audience," he explained, and in truth the events were waning in popularity. Sam recalled in particular the foul air in the Congregational Church in Washington, D.C., in March 1888 and the program that ran over schedule. "There are now living but four persons who paid to get into that house," he joked. "It is also a fact, however privately it has been kept, that twenty-two died on the premises and eighty-one on their way home. I am miserable when I think of my share in that wanton, that unprovoked massacre." Not that he objected to public readings in general, however. Less than a month later, on January 11, 1890, he read in Grant Hall at the U.S. Military Academy at West Point passages from *A Connecticut Yankee*, including the chapter "A Competitive Examination," in the course of "a lecture on aristocracy" he delivered to the cadets.[10]

Sam persuaded his old Nevada friend Joe Goodman to become his consigliere and sell stock in his typesetter company on commission in the West. In 1871 Goodman had invested in a Comstock silver mine with John Percival Jones and struck pay dirt. Since selling the *Territorial Enterprise* in 1874, he had been a member of the San Francisco Stock and Exchange Board and lost his fortune before buying a raisin farm near Fresno. In October 1889 Sam outlined an offer to his former editor: for over three years he had financed a mechanical compositor "at a cost of $3,000 a month & in so private a way that Hartford has known nothing about it." The machine had been "finished several weeks ago & has been running ever since in the machine shop. It is a magnificent creature of steel, all of Pratt & Whitney's super-best workmanship." He planned to test the machine "two or three months in New York 24 hours a day 7 days in the week" until it proved it would run "without an infelicity in any of its functions & without causing 5 minutes delay." He invited Goodman to come to Hartford, examine it in detail for "a week & satisfy yourself" of its workability, and then approach his former partner Jones or "whom you please & sell me a hundred thousand dollars' worth of [stock in] this property." Sam assured Goodman that the company was unencumbered by debt—"I have never borrowed a penny to use on the machine"—and that he expected to sell no fewer than fifteen thousand units over the next fifteen years. He was no more prescient a prophet than Chicken Little. "A month ago I couldn't have raised a dollar on the machine," he admitted in mid-October, when suddenly his friend John Russell Young of the *New York Herald* claimed "first place in the list of orders for machines" and "a single individual in New York wants to put up the several millions of capital required" to build the factory. Jones had in fact promised to "take entire charge" of the project if, upon witnessing a demonstration, it "was particularly favorable." The immediate sale of six hundred machines at a cost of two thousand dollars per machine, Sam estimated to Goodman on November 16, would pay all outstanding bills "& leave 2,000,000 [dollars] in the treasury." Moreover, the factory he planned to build could manufacture the six hundred machines in only eight months. By the time ten thousand typesetters had been constructed and sold, he predicted, "the market will have greatly enlarged." Two weeks later, Sam's projections had become even more grandiose: "At the lowest conceivable estimate (2,000 machines a year,) we shall sell 34,000 in the life of the patent—17 years." He also promised Goodman that the Paige typesetter faced no real competition because the money saved by the Mergenthaler Linotype was "absolutely *nothing*." Sam's contention was largely corroborated by an independent study by W. W. Pasko, who reported to the newspaper publishers who commissioned his study that the Mergenthaler "would save only one half of a man's wages, while the Paige, when fully operational, would save the wages of six men." By that calculation, Sam figured, the cost "to set a page of a N.Y. daily" on the Paige was virtually the same "that it now costs to set a column by hand." Whereas the top speed a compositor could set type on a Mergenthaler was three thousand ems per hour, "the limit of our machine is *24,000 ems* per hour."[11]

He was so optimistic that he heeded none of the warning signs that should have restrained his reckless spending. As early as October 1887 William Laffan of the New York *Sun* advised him that the Mergenthaler "had surmounted all obstacles" and was ready to be put into production. Dean Sage repeatedly cautioned him during the last months of 1889 to temper his passion for the project. "I heard lately that the Mergenthaler machine was turning out a great success," Sage notified Sam in October 1889, and that Amos Whitney, the cofounder of Pratt & Whitney, "& others were buying up the stock." A month later Sage again warned Sam about "the enormous cost of the manufacturing plant" he projected to build for the Paige and offered a bit of unsolicited advice: if he were "a part of the corporation I should look about a good while before I should consent to be persuaded that a plant of near $2,000,000 was required to produce $1500 worth of work a day." Sage suggested that Sam's company initially outsource the manufacturing rather than build a two-million-dollar plant "before getting $1 back." He alerted Sam that, in his opinion, the cost of constructing the factory was "vastly out of proportion to the work it is expected to perform" and urged him to revise his plans "for the business management of your machine to *insure* its success." Later in November, Sage reiterated his "anxiety at the enormous outlay in [the] plant you propose" and again recommended that Sam "contract with some one of the many well equipped machine shops of New England to deliver you the first few hundreds of the machines you may need at as low a cost as you can make them." Lest he seem to throw cold water on the entire enterprise, Sage affirmed that Sam had either "a great bonanza or nothing" but cautioned they would not know which was true "until you have a good number of the machines actually turning out successfully the work they are expected to do." Moreover, James Paige was uncertain as late as August 1890 that the typesetter was "equal to a long day-&-night pull" of an endurance test, but Sam was soothed by the thought the inventor "may be mistaken."[12]

In any case, Sam was in such straitened circumstances at the end of 1889 that he sent his brother Orion a check for only fifteen dollars to buy three Christmas "trifles" for the family in Keokuk, "which shows that the machine still has its grip on our purse. But it's a great machine." Though he cultivated a reputation for dressing well, during the Christmas season of 1889 Sam's winter clothing also betrayed his distress. A columnist for the New York *Evening World* reported that Sam had become "careless in his attire" and wore "a pair of low congress gaiters and a pepper-colored suit of the thinest quality." Still, the Clemenses spent several days in November at the Parker House in Boston, where Sam spoke at a dinner meeting of the Press Club, and on November 12 he and his wife Olivia attended a matinee performance of Alessandro Salvini, Tommaso's son, in Howells's failing and "friendless" play *A Foregone Conclusion* at the Tremont Theater. "He stayed my fainting spirit with a cheer beyond flagons, joining me in my joke at the misery of it," Howells recalled. The family spent the last week of December in New York, where they attended Ada Rehan's debut as Rosalind in *As You Like It* at Daly's Theater and Sam rang in the new year at a meeting of the Authors' Club. For the record, moreover, Sam never skimped on money to pay for his mother's nursing care and, early in the new year, he contributed his mite to a fund for the care of the widow and children of a New York journalist who had recently died.[13]

Sam roared past all of these red flags with the overweening self-confidence of a gambling addict. For a few weeks in late 1889 and early 1890 his optimism seemed warranted. He convinced the Elmira banker and businessman Matthias Arnot to purchase fifty thousand dollars' worth of stock in the company conditioned on Jones's even larger investment and in mid-January 1890, soon after Paige had reassembled the typesetter for the umpteenth time, Goodman arrived in Hartford to discuss plans to capitalize the company. Over the next year or so, Goodman traveled east from California at least three times to consult with Sam and to browbeat such potential investors as Jones and the "bonanza king" John Mackay. He conceded to Sam on January 3 that his "negotiations with Jones do not thicken as rapidly or well as I could wish" but Arnot and Jones were scheduled to witness a demonstration of the machine in operation at the Pratt & Whitney factory in Hartford on January 12. The exhibition was postponed, however, when Paige decided to add an air blast. "When [Jones] was ready, we were not," Sam explained two months later, "& now we have been ready more than a month, while he has been kept in Washington by the Silver bill. He said the other day that to venture out of the Capitol for a day at this time could easily chance to hurt *him* if the bill came up for action." In late February, according to press reports, Sam and Goodman played billiards at the Murray Hill Hotel while in New York to pitch the machine to the local print shops. Sam returned to New York on the same mission in mid- and late March. He returned to Washington the first week of April to try to raise money for the typesetter and to lobby Secretary of the Senate Anson G. McCook and Senator George F. Edmunds of Vermont on behalf of copyright despite his doubts about the efficacy of this strategy. His personal finances were in such sad shape that, while he promised Paige to "scrape together $6,000 to meet the March and April expenses" on the machine much as he had scrambled to pay his mining assessments in the West, he could not continue to subsidize its development past April unless he secured some "relief." He admitted to Goodman on March 31 that he was "in as close a place today as ever I was; $3,000 due for the last month's machine-expenses and the purse empty." He arranged for potential investors to witness a demonstration of the machine in operation on April 18 but the air blast was not yet working properly. According to Fred Hall, Sam "used to say the machine could do all things a human typesetter could do and do them faster and better except talk, eat, drink, smoke, and go on a strike. He should have omitted the last qualification. The machine seemed to have an infinite capacity for striking."[14]

The *American Bookseller* announced in May 1890 that Paige had completed his typesetter and that Sam was organizing "a joint stock company for the construction of the machines on an economical scale." But like the famous reports of Sam's death in 1897, all reports that the machine was perfected were premature. Nevertheless, Sam returned to Washington in mid-June in another vain attempt to raise money to manufacture it. He dined with the Hearst family, no doubt hoping to interest his friend Senator George Hearst and/or his son, the newspaper magnate William Randolph Hearst, in buying stock. He also attended a reception at the White House hosted by President Benjamin Harrison and First Lady Caroline Harrison and attended by Attorney General W. H. H. Miller and Senator Joseph Dolph of Oregon. But another scheduled visit to Hartford by Jones that month was canceled when Paige disassembled the prototype to fix "type-breakage," a problem he once had claimed was already solved. As a result, Sam and

Goodman were able to persuade Jones to invest a mere five thousand dollars rather than twenty times that amount. Mackay was impressed when he saw the typesetter in operation in late July, though he left for Europe a few days later and apparently did not invest further. Goodman was dejected: "God damn this going round hat in hand and begging pennies!" he raged in a note to Sam, who feebly attempted to monitor Paige's expenses for a time. "As we are going to do nothing whatever but *set type* henceforth till the company is formed," Sam informed his lawyer Daniel Whitford, "we shall need no one for some little time but our 4 operators." Beginning in September 1890 he budgeted only six hundred dollars a month to the project to cover "salaries, rent, sundries, & *everything*." Still, three months after he seemed ready to deny Paige further financial support, Sam pledged to "stick tight to the thing till I haven't any money left." He allowed to Goodman that on paper he was fabulously rich, a major stockholder in an invention with a worldwide market of one hundred and fifty million dollars, "one of the wealthiest grandees in America—one of the Vanderbilt gang, in fact—& yet if you asked me to lend you a couple of dollars I would have to ask you to take my note." The admission was reminiscent of his confession in *Roughing It* (1872) that while he owned a paper fortune in the Humboldt mining district in 1862 his "credit was not good at the grocer's." Ironically, in the same letter he compared the typesetter to the mineral strikes on the Comstock in the 1870s: "There is no mistake about it, it is the Big Bonanza." Yet in the end, Sam and Goodman could not raise a quarter million dollars to buy Paige's patents, to say nothing of the two million dollars required to build a factory. In July 1890 Sam and William Hamersley clashed over their failing venture. Sam advised Hamersley, who had initially stoked his interest in the machine, that he could no longer bear "the whole burden of expense" to build it. Sam told Hamersley he was "in all fairness in my debt to the amount of some $30,000" and that "another heavy bill from Pratt & Whitney will soon be due & I wish to look to you for your proper share of it." Hamersley took umbrage at the suggestion: "I can hardly believe that you realized what you were writing as you have perfectly well understood all along that I could not and was not expected to invest a dollar in this matter." In a section of his autobiography composed around this time, Sam exacted his revenge. Hamersley, he wrote, "is a great fat good-natured, kind-hearted, chicken-livered slave; with no more pride than a tramp, no more sand than a rabbit, no more moral sense than a wax figure, and no more sex than a tape-worm."[15]

At a breakfast hosted by James Pond at the Everett House in Boston the morning of April 27, 1890, to honor the French journalist Max O'Rell, Sam exploited the opportunity again to slam the late Matthew Arnold for his criticism of American journalism. In his talk "On Foreign Critics" before an audience that included Augustin Daly, Richard Watson Gilder, George Kennan, Horace Porter, and E. C. Stedman he applauded the benefits of free speech and a free press: "Who woke that printing press out of its trance of three hundred years? Let us be permitted to consider that we did it." Sam later re-created the scene in the Mechanics' Club dinner depicted in chapter 10 of *The American Claimant* (1891).[16]

Even as Sam protested that he wanted "to get far, very far away from plays," and in the midst of the litigation over the stage adaptation of his 1881 *The Prince and the Pauper*, he granted rights to his old Nevada friend Howard P. Taylor to dramatize *A Connecticut Yankee in King Arthur's Court*. In collaboration with the theatrical agent Clara Beaumont Packard, Taylor completed a script in July 1890 and read it aloud to Sam, who was underwhelmed. As Sam wrote his daughter Clara, it "bored the very soul out of me." Taylor "made a rattling, stirring & spectacular, & perhaps taking play, & has shown dramatic talent & training," Sam allowed, "*but* his handling of archaic English is as ignorant & dreadful as poor Mrs. Richardson's; & he has captured but one of the Yankee's characters—his rude animal side, his circus side; the good heart & the high intent are left out of him; he is a mere boisterous clown, & oozes slang from every pore. I told Taylor he had degraded a natural gentleman to a low-down blackguard." Sam again vowed that Taylor's adaptation, which was never performed, was "the very last play that I ever mean to have anything to do with."[17]

After Theodore Crane's death, Susan Crane shuttered the house at Quarry Farm. The Clemenses initially planned to sail to Europe in June 1890 and settle in "some pleasant place on the Northern Coast of France" for the summer where Sam's daughter Susy could perfect her French before sitting for the Smith College entrance exam. But Sam soon realized that "on account of business connected with the [typesetting] machine" he would be compelled to accompany his family but then leave them, and Livy objected. "Youth [Livy's pet name for her husband] don't let the thought of Europe worry you one bit because we will give that all up," she wrote on May 20. "I want to see you happy much more than I want anything else even the children's lessons." Livy "did not at all fancy the idea of putting the ocean between us" so they abandoned those plans. Instead, the Clemenses, joined by Sue Crane, summered in 1890 at Onteora Park and hired Delphine Duvall, professor of French at Smith, to tutor Susy. Before departing for the Catskills, however, Sam fulfilled an obligation to perform on behalf of the Union for Home Work in Hartford. He chose to read "The Golden Arm," with dire results.

He asked that the gaslights in the auditorium "be turned down" and his face illuminated by a reflector, then told the story "in a deep, sepulchral voice." The Band of Workers voted afterward "not to ask Mark Twain to tell any more stories."[18]

The family arrived at Onteora Park the first week of July, as Susy recalled, "dreary from a tiresome journey; but the dreariness did not last." Mary Mapes Dodge "provided a home-made banquet." Among the other guests at the mountain retreat that summer were Elizabeth Custer; engineer James Mapes Dodge; Laurence Hutton; the muralist Dora Wheeler Keith; Brander Matthews; the journalist Lucia Runkle and her ten-year-old daughter Bertha, a future novelist; and Charles Dudley Warner and his wife Susan. "We were all boys together that summer," Matthews remembered, though Sam spent much of his time traveling on business to Hartford, New York, Philadelphia, and Washington. He returned to New York and registered at the Hoffman House in mid-July and did not rejoin his family until the end of the month. Two weeks later he was summoned to Keokuk when Jane Lampton Clemens suffered a stroke, though his mother soon improved. Sam hurried to Elmira when Franklin Whitmore notified him that Livy's mother was ill. "I was mighty sorry to have to leave [Keokuk] when I did," Sam wrote Orion and his wife Mollie, "for I had entirely enjoyed my visit until that fool Whitmore sent that idiotic & nerve-stretching dispatch." Livy tarried a week at her infirm mother's bedside before also returning to Onteora.[19]

On August 13, 1890, in the midst of his summer vacation, Sam reached yet another partnership agreement with Paige, who consented to transfer his entire interest in the compositor to Sam for a quarter of a million dollars to be paid no later than February 13, 1891. Should Sam fail to make payment by the deadline, he would forfeit his stock in the machine and instead receive a modest royalty on future sales and rentals. As usual, the contract was flawed: it failed to specify a date for the transfer of the patents to Sam after he paid the $250,000, though Paige refused to reconsider these draconian terms.[20] In the end, of course, his refusal did not matter: there was no difference between ownership of a worthless machine and royalties on sales of a worthless machine.

Sam spent the last several days of August in Washington, where he hounded John Percival Jones to honor his promise to help. He reported to Fred Hall that he "failed with the monumental humbug of the century," though he was more upbeat in describing their meeting to Mollie and Orion; Jones had promised to "set himself seriously to work to raise" almost a million dollars both to build a factory and to pay Paige the quarter million before Sam's option lapsed. On September 8 Sam assured Jones that even in the hands of an apprentice the Paige typesetter, unlike the inferior Mergenthaler, "will *set* 8,000 [ems] in an hour, & *distribute* 8,000 in the same hour, making an aggregate of 16,000 ems." He had returned to Onteora where, on September 2, he read from the works of Robert Browning to his friends and, on a pleasant evening later in the month, according to Matthews, the vacationers gathered around the fireplace in Candace Wheeler's cabin to swap ghost stories and Sam again related "the harrowing tale of the 'Golden Arm.'" The Clemens family's "lovely sojourn" in the Catskills ended on September 22 when they returned to Hartford.[21]

Ten days later Sam was back in Washington to shake the money tree. On this occasion he contended that the Paige was "seven times as good as the Mergenthaler" in wage saving and he seemed to have convinced the senator. "Jones seems quite well satisfied, & evidently expects to make our scheme go," he wrote Goodman. "He will leave for California pretty soon, now, & will be ready to boom the machine." He admonished Goodman to take "a day off" and persuade Jones and his rich friends to invest because "I'm going to need money before long." While in Washington, he also entertained at the banquet of the National Wholesale Druggists Association at the Arlington Hotel the evening of October 2. His address was a slightly revised version of the Nicodemus Dodge story that had appeared in *A Tramp Abroad* (1880) and, according to the Washington *Critic*, the "witty speech . . . kept the company in a constant roar of laughter." The U.S. Marine Band under the direction of John Philip Sousa also entertained.[22]

From Washington, Sam railed to Bryn Mawr College, on the Main Line west of Philadelphia, where Susy, whom Sam considered a prodigy at eighteen, was matriculating. Though only founded in 1885, the school was, Sam bragged, "the best female college in the world," though he considered it mostly a finishing school. After carefully weighing her options, Susy had decided she preferred it to both Smith and Vassar. She had been prepared for admission by Lilly Gillette Foote, who became the girls' governess in 1880, though Susy and Clara also attended a year of public high school in Hartford. Susy was, Grace King recalled, "exquisitely pretty, but frail-looking. Her health was always an anxiety to her mother and father" and from the start she was intensely homesick. "The last time I saw her was a week ago on the platform at Bryn Mawr," Sam wrote his sister Pamela on October 12. "Our train was moving away & she was drifting collegeward afoot, her figure blurred & dim in the rain & fog, & she was crying." "It's about the longest week the almanac has ever furnished to this family," he added in a note to Mary Mason Fairbanks. Susy registered for five courses, three in Latin (prose, Horace, and Sallust and Livy), French, and the requisite physical education, and she insisted in a note to her grandmother Olivia Lewis Langdon three weeks into her freshman year that she was "glad of course" to have been admitted. "There is a great great deal that I enjoy most thoroughly. The work is delightful and the people are lovely and altogether Bryn Mawr is an ideal place, but oh! it *does* not, *can* not compare with home! or with Elmira! our Summer home. I do long and hope for next Summer to come, when it does seem as if we must all be together again, in the beautiful old way." To her parents she wrote "homesick letters" so poignant that Sam and Clara visited her the weekend of October 24, only three weeks into the term. They arrived in the middle of a dance in Susy's dormitory and Sam joined the party. For the next two hours he frolicked "& looked on & talked the rest of the time. It was very jolly & pleasant." A month later Livy went to see Susy but her depression did not lift. As King conceded, "a very short time proved the utter impossibility of hard study for Susy. She did not care for what she experienced and merely submitted to a slow torture by remaining." As Livy reluctantly concluded, "If she remains well I shall keep her there this year, but if she is not more contented I shall not send her back next year but make other plans." The evening of October 9, between his visits to Bryn Mawr, Sam attended a dinner at the Astor House in New York celebrating former Confederate general Roger Pryor's appointment to the New York Court of Common Pleas. He did not address the group, which included former president Grover Cleveland, Daly, Henry George, Murat Halstead, Senators Arthur Pue Gorman and Hearst, Thomas Nast, Union generals William Tecumseh Sherman and Daniel Sickles, and John Russell Young. Sam was seated with Chauncey Depew and Joe Jefferson and the three of them, as the *Hartford Courant* reported, "had too much fun by themselves." After the dinner Sam smoked with Edwin Booth in the actor's hotel room until midnight.[23]

Sam had championed revolution in Russia since hearing George Kennan discuss czarist despotism in March 1888. As he told an interviewer in the wake of the Russian Revolution of 1905, "I sympathize with these Russian revolutionists" and "I hope that they will succeed." While Sam was working on *A Connecticut Yankee* he often fulminated in his notebook about tyranny (e.g., "assassination of a crowned head whenever & wherever opportunity offers should be the first article of all subjects' religion"), though he usually muted his opinion in public. In one of his unused prefaces to the novel, Sam referred derisively to the "twin civilizations of hell and Russia" and asserted that exile to Siberia "concentrated all the bitter inventions of all the black ages for the infliction of suffering upon human beings." In the summer of 1890 he drafted a letter to the editor of *Free Russia*, the organ of Russian liberation parties issued in London, that typified his liberal politics. "What is the Czar of Russia but a house afire in the midst of a city of eighty millions of inhabitants?" he asked. "The properest way to demolish the Russian throne would be by revolution. But it is not possible to get up a revolution there; so the only thing left to do, apparently, is to keep the throne vacant by dynamite until a day when candidates shall decline with thanks. Then organize the Republic." Over the next few months Sam became a founding member of the Society of American Friends of Russian Freedom and befriended Sergei Stepnyak-Kravchinsky (aka Sergius Stepniak), a Ukrainian revolutionary who had assassinated the head of the Russian secret police in 1878. Stepniak spent a "most delightful" day with Sam and Joseph Twichell in Hartford in mid-April 1891, Sam inscribed a copy of *Huck Finn* to him, and Stepniak presented him with a copy of his book *Underground Russia* (1883). Sam read it "with profound & painful interest. What sublime men & women! Nothing milder than Russian despotism could breed such, I suppose." Around the same time, in his unpublished sketch "Letters from a Dog to Another Dog Explaining and Accounting for Man," written in early 1891, Sam again disparaged the czar:

> His powers are a theft today, just as they were when they came originally into his family. His portrait hangs everywhere that you may go, throughout his dominions. His eighty million slaves, instead of being privileged to clod it with mud wherever they find it, and say "This is the posterity of that highwayman that robbed our fathers," are actually required to take their hats off when they come into its presence, and humbly salute it. . . . The Czar requires every Russian to spend the fifteen best and most efficient years of his life in the army; and then turns him adrift without pension and ignorant of all ways of sustaining life except by killing people.

In *The American Claimant* (1891), the novel Sam loosely based on *Colonel Sellers as a Scientist*, the Earl of Rossmore (i.e., Sellers) plans "to buy Siberia" and enfranchise the exiles, "the very finest and choicest material on the globe for a republic.'"[24]

"We had a very sad Fall," Livy wrote Alice Hooker Day in May 1891 in a remarkable understatement. Sam and Livy learned from Charley Langdon the previous October that they would not receive a dividend of ten thousand dollars from J. Langdon and Company they "had counted uncommonly" upon to keep Webster and Company afloat on a sea of red ink. Livy expressed a rare lament about their luxurious lifestyle: "I wish there was some way to change our manner of living, but that seems next to impossible unless we sell our house." Olivia Lewis Langdon then offered to loan her daughter and son-in-law ten thousand dollars to help them stave off the bankruptcy of Webster and Company and Livy appreciated the gesture. "It seems so much easier and better to borrow in the family than out of it," she wrote in thanking her mother. "At any rate it is easier for us whether it is for you or not." Sam instructed Fred Hall to "send her the firm's note & make it a year."[25]

On October 27, the day after Charley Langdon notified the Clemenses that the dividend was not forthcoming, Sam's mother died in Keokuk at the age of eighty-seven. He left Hartford early the next morning and arrived in Hannibal for her funeral and burial twenty-six hours later. "After eighty her memory failed" and her physical condition had steadily deteriorated, he wrote his friend William Winter,

> with intervals of vigorous recuperation between; but her restorations to bodily health were not to her own profit, because they gave new lease to mental tortures—hallucinations which as often took the form of malignant persecutions & insult as any other. And so for eight years she had as a rule a worn & hunted look. It appeased my sorrow to see that that look was wholly gone from her face when she lay in her coffin & that in its place was serenity & peace.

Immediately after her interment the afternoon of October 30 in Mount Olivet Cemetery beside John Marshall Clemens, dead forty-three years, and her son Henry, dead thirty-two years, Sam began his journey back east. He stopped in Elmira on Sunday, November 2, to visit Livy's mother, "talk over his affairs" with Livy's brother, and collect the check for ten thousand dollars. Jane Clemens had saved a few hundred dollars over the years "and she left it to me," Sam recalled, "because it had come from me." He in turn gave it to Orion, who "proceeded to use up that money in building a considerable addition to the house" in Keokuk "with the idea of taking boarders and getting rich. We need not dwell upon this venture. It was another of his failures" along with his attempts to invent a combination windmill and paddle wheel, a hat that would prevent sunstroke, a flying machine, and a wood-sawing machine.[26]

While in New York on November 8, trolling for money from investors to save his publishing company and/or his investment in the Paige machine only nine days after burying his mother, Sam was in a so(m)ber mood. During this trip, the story goes, one of the porters at the Murray Hill Hotel remarked when he saw Sam, "There goes the solemnest and dismalest gent as ever stopped at this 'ouse. I don't b'lieve he ever knowed what it was to larf." While in the city Sam also erupted in rage on a crowded Sixth Avenue horsecar. After boarding, he was accosted by a rude conductor, who cursed at him for blocking the door. Sam described this person as if filing a police report: he was "about 30 years old, I should say, five feet nine, with blue eyes, a small, dim unsuccessful mustache, and the general expression of a chicken thief—you may probably have seen him." Sam "urged him to modify his language" and then tried to file a report with his supervisor but no one "seemed to want to converse with me." So he addressed a letter to the editor of the New York *Sun* about the matter, suggesting that the horsecar conductors "ought to be instructed never to swear at country people except when there are no city ones to swear at and not even then except for practice."[27]

Sam probably did not anticipate the furor that followed. The offending conductor, Thomas F. Shields, was fired. The *New York Tribune* editorialized that Sam's letter "bristles with inaccuracies" and urged him to issue "a general retraction and an apology" by "an early mail." The *Philadelphia Inquirer* wondered "whether Mark Twain isn't losing his wit as well as his temper." The St. Louis *Globe-Democrat* accused Sam of "a large piece of smallness" and conjectured that he "must be hard pushed for a free advertisement of his fading talent when he resorts to such devices to get notoriety." Frank Curtiss, president of the Sixth Avenue Railroad Company, publicly replied to Sam's grievance on November 12. Shields had admitted to "the charges you make" and in extenuation of his misbehavior had explained "that he had been annoyed by a drunken passenger" and "was not in good humor when you boarded the car." Nevertheless, the company had "taken the conductor off." Curtiss only regretted that Sam had not filed his gripe directly with the company. "The result would have been the same, except that the conductor would not have gone from us with the brand you have placed upon him—'chicken thief,' etc., which we, a corporation, think does him a great wrong." Shields wrote Sam a letter of apology on November 15 and begged him to withdraw his complaint. Sam apparently repented his rush to judgment. At his direction, Fred Hall wrote to Curtiss and Shields was reinstated.[28]

In the midst of all this *mishigas*, Livy was summoned to Elmira to stand vigil at the bedside of her own dying mother. Sam accompanied her, leaving Clara and Jean in the care of the servants, but he hastily returned to Hartford when ten-year-old Jean became severely ill, the first onset of the seizure disorder that would afflict her for the rest of her life. "I ought to be there to [be] a support to Mrs. Clemens in this unspeakable trouble," he wrote Howells, "& so ought Susy & Clara; but Jean pleads to be not wholly forsaken; so, when the death-telegram falls, I think I shall stay with Jean & send Susy & Clara to their mother." He appended a self-pitying postscript: "I have fed so full on sorrows these last weeks that I seem to have become hardened to them—benumbed." Olivia Lewis Langdon died on November 28 at the age of eighty. "Death has smitten this family a double blow in the last 31 days," Sam wrote James Pond the next day. "I am here taking care of Jean who is recovering from a dangerous fever; the other children are in Elmira with the mother, who has been watching by the sick bed for eight or nine days." Six weeks later, Thomas K. Beecher—"one of the best men" and "best citizens I have ever known"—delivered a eulogy for Olivia Lewis Langdon at the Park Church in Elmira that was transmitted by long-distance telephone hundreds of miles via Syracuse, Albany, and Springfield to the Clemens home in Hartford. At the end of the year, Sam sent hopes for a merry Christmas to Fred Hall and added the wish he "could have one myself before I die."[29]

When Hall assumed the management of Webster and Company, he faced myriad problems. As early as May 1888 he warned Sam about "certain glaring defects in the organization of our Subscription Department." An organizational diagram of the firm would have placed Sam alone at the top and Hall immediately beneath him, but all lines of responsibility below that level would resemble a bowl of tangled spaghetti—printers, managers, authors, proofreaders, and book agents. Yet the most serious difficulty faced by the company was undercapitalization. It had released no commercially successful book since the memoirs of Ulysses S. Grant in 1885, its backlist consisted of several military memoirs "whose sales were rapidly declining," and production of its latest project, the eleven-volume *Library of American Literature*, required large subsidies prior to sale. The *Library* sold well, prompting Hall to report optimistically to Sam in May 1888 that he thought the series was "going to pan out big eventually." E. C. Stedman insisted to Sam six months later that the *Library* was "the most valuable & *substantial* property the firm possesses" and that so far "we have scarcely *scratched* the end of the buying elephant's nose." He was so confident in its success that he soon urged Hall to increase the royalty paid to him and his coeditor from 3 to 5 percent.[30]

On paper (like the supposed fortune in the Paige typesetter) the company earned money in the late 1880s. "There was a gross profit made out of the business last year [1889] of fifty thousand dollars," Hall notified Sam in April 1890. Of this amount, $12,250 was paid to buy out Charley Webster's interest and $22,234 was plowed back "into the Library of [American] Literature." That is, nearly half of the profit for the year was spent bankrolling a single project, not in dividends nor in other new books. "I am pushing my publishing house. It has turned the corner," Sam boasted to Goodman in April 1891, and he was "piling every cent" of profit possible "into one book—Library of American Literature" but the company needed to earn an additional $50,000 over the next year to underwrite it. "The truth is," Hall advised Sam in April 1890, "we are trying to do too large a business on too small a cash capital." He estimated that the sale of 2,905 copies a month would be required "for us to have the 'L.A.L' on a paying basis." The business model was unsustainable. The more volumes of the *Library* sold, the greater the immediate drain on available capital. The company absorbed all the profit from *A Connecticut Yankee*, $20,000 in loans from Livy and her mother, and an additional $15,000 loan from the Mount Morris Bank in New York. Hall asked Sam in mid-March 1891, a month before he bragged that the company had "turned the corner," for another $20,000 to pay production costs on the *Library* and put the firm "on the high road to prosperity." Whatever his misgivings about the series, Sam wrote an advertisement for it that was widely printed in April 1891: "The 'Library of American Literature' is monumental. I don't suppose that so able and conscientious and all-sampling a piece of culling was ever done before. . . . With it on the shelf, one may say to anybody, name your mood, and I will satisfy its appetite for you."[31]

As the titular head of Webster and Company, moreover, Hall was no better at selecting popular book projects than Webster (or Sam, for that matter). The firm rejected most of the projects proposed for publication. "We can't take any more books for a long time yet," Sam advised Frank Fuller in December 1888, the same moment Webster was retiring, because "we are overcrowded and must wait till we work the list down." During Hall's tenure the company considered but failed to accept autobiographies by Generals Ben Butler, Nelson A. Miles, and Oliver Howard; and the historian Charles Gayarré; a collection of Chauncey Depew's speeches; books by Andrew Carnegie, Thomas Edison, and Ward McAllister; an exposé of the Freemasons; and a travel book by DeWitt Talmage. The firm solicited Henry Stanley's *In Darkest Africa* (1890) but was outbid by Scribner's. Instead, between 1890 and 1892 the firm issued several books by Sam's friends and relatives: Sam Moffett's *The Tariff: What It Is and What It Does*, Dan Beard's *Moonblight and Six Feet of Romance*, Richard Malcolm Johnston's *Mr. Billy Downs and His Likes*, and (probably at Howells's recommendation) English translations of Leo Tolstoy's *Ivan the Fool* and *Life Is Worth Living*. Sam also arranged to reprint General Sherman's *Memoirs*, though he was persuaded of its appeal only after Sherman died. As he wrote Sherman on February 13, 1891, the day before the general's death, "You have been a good friend to me, & I, like all the rest of this nation, grieve to think that the kindest heart & the most noble spirit that exist to-day are about to be taken away from us." Two weeks later he notified Hall that he was "feeling better about" their acquisition of rights to the Sherman book and asked "what is the very *quickest* you can issue it? Its market is best for the next 30 days, I think, then nearly as good for 30 more; then comes the fading quickly out." Despite his finagling, Sam in the end blamed Webster's successor almost as much as he did Webster for the company's problems. As he indicated in his autobiography, "Poor Hall meant well, but he was wholly incompetent for the place. He carried it along for a time with the heroic hopefulness of youth, but there was an obstruction [debt] which was bound to defeat him sooner or later."[32]

To be sure, Webster and Company also released a pair of volumes of Walt Whitman's selected prose and poetry in the Fiction, Fact, and Fancy Series under the general editorship of Arthur Stedman, though Sam was contemptuous by that time of both the editor and his father, "that pair of quite too wonderful people." As he put it to Hall, "idiotcy runs in the family." But he venerated the bard. They had exchanged books in 1889, Sam sending Whitman *A Connecticut Yankee* and Whitman mailing Sam his *Complete Poems & Prose* (1888). Invited by Whitman's disciple Horace Traubel to address a tribute to the poet on his seventieth birthday in May 1891, Sam "sent a longer letter than anybody else," the *New York Tribune* reported, "and one in an unusual vein for a boisterous humorist." Traubel did not know what to make of it—it was "full of generalities, with practically no word about W.W. Have not yet referred to it in W.'s presence." In fact, it was another version of the "Methuselah" homily Sam had delivered for over twenty years, since at least Hannah Duncan's birthday in 1867. In Whitmanesque fashion, Sam cataloged the "great births" of his era: "the steam press, the steamship, railroad, the perfected cotton gin, the telegraph, the telephone, the phonograph, the photograph, photogravure, the electrotype, the gaslight, the electric light, the sewing machine," and so on. Neither man was, in the end, unqualifiedly enthusiastic about the writing of the other. As Whitman confided to Traubel in February 1889, "I think [Sam] mainly misses fire: I think his life misses fire: he might have been something: he comes near to being something: but he never arrives." On his part, Sam wrote in February 1907 that if he was regarded as "a Whitmanite I'm sorry—I never read 40 lines of him in my life."[33]

Meanwhile, Paige continued to tinker with the typesetter. Sam notified Goodman in late October that he thought the machine was perfect "at last," because it no longer damaged type and Paige had installed a "new device for enabling the operator to touch the last letters & justify the line simultaneously," though five weeks later it failed again and required a major repair. Sam screamed into his notebook on December 20 that "about 3 weeks ago, the machine was pronounced 'Finished,' by Paige, for certainly half dozenth time in the past twelvemonth." Then "it was discovered" that no one had inspected

the *period, & it* sometimes refused to perform properly. But to correct that error would take just one day & *only* one day—the "merest trifle in the world."

I said this sort of mere trifle had interfered often before & had always cost ten times as much time & money as their loose calculations promised. P[aige] & [the mechanical engineer Charles E.] Davis *knew* (they always "know," never guess) that this correction would cost but one single day. Well, the best part of two weeks went by. I dropped in (last Monday noon) & they were still tinkering. Still tinkering, but just *one hour*, now, would see the machine at work, blemishless, & never stop again for a generation: the hoary old song that has been sung to weariness in my ears by these frauds & liars! Four days & a half elapsed, & still that "one hour's" work was still going on, & another hour's work still to be done. I have not heard how things stand today. I wish they would get down to where one minute's work would make a finish. In that case we should see the end, certainly, in, say, 15 years.

The "one hour" required for the final repair lasted until Christmas, when Whitmore reported "that it got to work again" but "the machine broke down again *that* day! Remains so, still." Back up and running on January 2, 1891, according to the inventor, it performed perfectly "without bruising, breaking, or damaging a type of any sort and gives promise of working continuously without delays of any kind."[34]

Sam had bet all his marbles on John Percival Jones to fund the typesetter. Or to mix the metaphor, as Sam observed ironically enough in one of Pudd'nhead Wilson's maxims, "the wise man saith, 'Put all your eggs in the one basket and—WATCH THAT BASKET.'" He rushed to the U.S. Capitol on January 13, only a month before his option to organize the company to build and market the machine was set to expire, and Jones promised he would be "foot-loose & free" to beat the drum for investors after a final vote on the Silver Bill the next evening. Sam listened intently to the debate over the bill from the visitor's galley of the Senate chamber the following day. He applauded in particular the speech of Senator John James Ingalls of Kansas, but the opponents of the bill refused to permit it to come to a vote. Jones snubbed Sam after the proceedings adjourned for the day, so he returned to Hartford on January 16. A week later, with the clock winding down and Jones still incommunicado, Sam reminded him of the selling points of the Paige with unmistakable desperation in his voice; either of the two apprentices trained on it, he reminded the senator, could do a manual typesetter's entire day's work

in three quarters of an hour. . . . There is no other machine that can reduce N[ew] Y[ork] composition as low as 20 cents per 1000 ems. . . . The American business can earn $35,000,000 a year on 10,000 machines rented at a royalty of 12 cents per 1000 ems. The European business can earn $20,000,000 a

> year. . . . This business, in America alone, can be made to pay $100,000 a day;
> & two years from the organizing of the company the European patents will
> be promptly saleable at nearly any figure you please. We are offering hundred-
> dollar bills at a penny apiece.

Jones had mentioned the possibility "of having people of moderate means subscribe for the stock. Which suggests this idea to me: If you & Mr. Carnegie & one other—possibly Mackay?—should organize yourselves into a company & head the list with good-sized subscriptions" the expression of confidence in the project would prompt others to buy.[35]

This last-gasp attempt to save the machine flopped miserably. Jones finally cabled Sam on February 11, two days before the deadline for Sam to redeem his option, that he had been unable to raise any money. The same day Jones sent a letter detailing the reasons for his failure: not only were the financiers he had contacted timid to invest given the uncertainties in the market, but they were particularly loath to invest in the Paige given its reputation for unreliability. In fact, two of them were already "large stock holders in the Mergenthaler." After five years of increasing outlays, Sam was undone by "Jones's promises—promises made to me not merely once but every time I talked with him." By the end of the year, twenty-three American newspapers had bought or leased about three hundred Linotype machines. In all, Sam lost between $170,000 and $190,000 (between $4 million and $4.5 million in twenty-first-century money) on an impractical invention.[36]

What began in 1886 with a drum roll ended in 1891 with a rim shot. Whereas Sam had bragged in his salad days that he was endowed with the Midas touch, by 1889 everything he touched turned to dross. "I watched over one dear project of mine for years, spent a fortune on it, and failed to make it go," Sam wrote, "and the history of that would make a large book in which a million men would see themselves as in a mirror." He was gobsmacked by the news. The same day he received Jones's letter, he drafted but may not have sent a reply in which he lambasted Jones for his false pledges of cooperation. "For a whole year you have breathed the word of promise to my ear to break it to my hope at last," he remonstrated, as if shouting into the wind. "It is stupefying, it is unbelievable. . . . If you had given me half an hour of your time instead of two minutes"—this apparently back on January 13, when Sam met him at the Capitol—

> I would have shown you two ways, by either of which you would have been
> totally relieved of work until work should take the aspect of play. . . . I have the
> *proofs* that that [Mergenthaler] machine cannot save the wages of two men
> while I also have the proofs that in the hands of even a green apprentice ours
> can save the wages of ten *men*. . . . I have spent forty thousand dollars that I

could not have dared to spend if I had not valued your word above other men's written promises. . . . You say you will do anything you can to help me. Then take $75,000 worth of royalties for $50,000 & pay it in instalments of $1,000 a month; or take $50,000 worth for $25,000 & pay cash down. You will get your money back ten times over—& I shall be ~~saved from destruction~~ saved from any further worry.

Sam was so angered and frustrated by Jones's cable that the next day he penned another even more famous letter, likewise apparently never sent, in which he excoriated the local gas company for interrupting service to the Clemens home without warning: "Some day you will move me almost to the verge of irritation by your chuckle-headed Goddamned fashion of shutting your Goddamned gas off without giving any notice to your Goddamned parishioners. Several times you have come within an ace of smothering half of this household in their beds and blowing up the other half by this idiotic, not to say criminal, custom of yours. And it has happened again today. Haven't you a telephone?"[37]

Jones's negligence at least saved Sam from throwing any more good money after bad like the blue jay in *A Tramp Abroad*'s "Baker's Blue Jay Yarn" who drops acorn after acorn into a bottomless pit. "Think of this penny-worshiping humbug & shuffler" swindling them with "the lofty silent-contempt dodge," he wrote Goodman on February 22, with Goodman's wife Mary all the while scoffing at them "for believing in that fraud's promises." Three days later Sam notified Orion privately that he had "shook the machine" and "never wish to see it or hear it mentioned again. It is superb, it is perfect, it can do 10 men's work. It is worth billions; & when the pig-headed lunatic, its inventor, dies, it will instantly be capitalized & make the Clemens children rich." Though he no longer squandered hard cash on the typesetter, he still believed in its potential and he was still owed royalties if the machine ever went into production. If Paige could only finish and patent it, Sam might yet recoup or even profit from his investment. But he did not advance Paige another dime. The inventor solicited more money from Sam on March 18 but was bluntly refused: "when you declined to sign a contract [in the winter of 1891] which expressed the real ownership of the invention I advised you that I could lend you no more money. I know of no reason for doing so now." In consequence, in an ironic turn of events, Paige later blamed Sam for the failure of the typesetter. When they crossed paths two years later, Paige told Sam that his heart had broken when Sam "left him and the machine to fight along the best way they could."[38]

Sam's first priority in the wreck of his prosperity was "to rebuild my wasted fortunes." He adjured Hall to economize on postage and shipping. He scrambled to find vendible manuscripts and other properties that he could sell quickly, if not sooner. By February 20, over two weeks after he had last seen Paige, Sam was "deep in work" on "the Date & Fact Game." During "the general house-cleaning" that occurred after the bursting of the "Jones bubble," as Albert Bigelow Paine called it, Sam marketed *Mark Twain's Memory Builder*, which he had invented at Quarry Farm in 1883 and patented in 1885. The game was a bust, however—"the trade sees no promise [in it]"—because he had devised a bewildering array of rules and instructions for playing it, including "Populations, boundaries of countries, length of rivers, specific gravity of various metals, astronomical facts—*anything that is worth remembering* is admissible, and you can score for it" and "One may play the Authors, Artists, Inventors, Scientists, Philosophers, Generals, etc., of all times—each vocation in its turn—naming dates of birth and death, and principal deeds or works." (Reference books not included.) "I am sorry I put my *name* to the Game; I wish I hadn't," he admitted to Hall in March 1892. Sam also suggested to Hall the prospect of reprinting a cheap edition of his works. He jotted a premise for a new Tom-Huck sequel that betrayed his brooding melancholy: "Huck comes back, 60 years old, from nobody knows where—& crazy. Thinks he is a boy again, & scans always every face for Tom & Becky &c. Tom comes, at last, 60 from wandering the world & tends Huck, & together they talk the old times; both are desolate, life has been a failure, all that was lovable, all that was beautiful is under the mould. They die together."[39]

Sam also retrieved a brace of manuscripts from the pigeonholes where he had shoved them years before. The short sketch "Luck," written in April 1886, based on an anecdote Twichell had related to him about a British military hero who was "an absolute fool," the beneficiary of good luck rather than tactical skill during the Crimean War, appeared in *Harper's Monthly* for August 1891. A second piece retrieved from his files, the essay "Mental Telegraphy," had been written while he was living in Heidelberg in 1878 but deleted from *A Tramp Abroad* prior to its publication. He had submitted it to the *North American Review* in 1881 in testimony of his belief in clairvoyance or "mind-telegraphing" or mental telepathy. "The subject is entirely worth of the Review," he wrote James R. Osgood, "& besides I have treated it with the seriousness which it deserves," though he "feared that the public would treat the thing as a joke." He withdrew the manuscript when the editor insisted he sign his name to the essay rather than publish it anonymously. Sam had long been interested in psychic phenomena or clairvoyance, a vestige of his curiosity about spiritualism in the 1850s and 1860s. He had, in fact, read the paper on mental telegraphy before a club of young women in New Haven on October 22, 1881; before a club of young women in Boston on April

15, 1882, with Thomas Bailey Aldrich, Howells, and Osgood present; and again before a club of young ladies in Pittsfield, Massachusetts, on October 7, 1885. He joined the Society for Psychical Research in England in 1884, and as late as March 1906 Sam insisted that "mental telegraphy is an industry which is always silently at work—oftener than otherwise, perhaps, when we are not suspecting that it is affecting our thought." In his essay Sam described his frequent experiences over the years with "thought-transference." It was finally published in *Harper's Monthly* for December 1891 and Sam was paid five hundred dollars for it. Sam recovered a third manuscript from his personal archives; in "The Californian's Tale," based on Sam's conversation with a crazed widower in Tuttletown, California, in 1865, a deranged miner believes that his wife, captured by Indians nineteen years earlier, is simply away on a visit to her family. It finally appeared in *Harper's Monthly* in March 1902.[40]

Most important, Sam salvaged the script of *Colonel Sellers as a Scientist*, written in collaboration with Howells, from its pigeonhole on February 20 and began to convert it into a novel. He had resolved "to earn $75,000 in three months from Feb. 13," the date he had received Senator Jones's devastating letter, and by February 25 he had completed nine thousand words. "I think it will simply howl with fun," he assured Orion. "I wake up in the night laughing at its ridiculous situations." Two days later he notified Hall that the canvass for his new novel should "begin *September 1* and issue Dec. 10 with 75,000 orders—and not a single one short of that." Hall gleefully responded the next day, "I am glad you are writing a new book and I have a plan to propose regarding its sale whereby we think we will have the 75,000 orders by the time we issue it, and what's more there will be some money in it— the profits will not be all swallowed up in getting the book out and on the market, as it was to a great extent on the 'Yankee.'" But by then Sam's right hand throbbed with rheumatism and "every pen-stroke," he complained, "gives me the lockjaw." Just as he had wanted to dictate into a phonograph while composing *A Connecticut Yankee* during an attack of rheumatism two years earlier, he was confident that he could dictate *The American Claimant* "into a phonograph if I don't have to yell. I write 2,000 words a day; I think I can dictate twice as many." He was duty-bound to finish the novel "and sell 100,000 copies of it—no, I mean a million—next fall" so he asked Howells to "drop in at the Boylston Building (New England Phonograph Co) & talk into a phonograph in an ordinary conversation-voice and see if another person (who didn't hear you do it) can take the words from the thing without difficulty & repeat them to you." If the experiment was successful, Howells was to ask "on what terms they will rent me a phonograph for 3 months & furnish me cylinders enough to carry 175,000 words." Sam was so determined to relieve the strain on his writing hand that he presumed on their friendship. "If this is going to be too much trouble to you," he admonished Howells, "go ahead & do it, all the same."[41]

Ever the faithful friend, Howells followed Sam's instructions to the letter. "I talked your letter into a fonograf in my usual tone at my usual gait of speech," he reported, adding,

> Then the fonograf man talked his answer in at his wonted swing and swell. Then we took the cylinder to a type-writer in the next room, and she put the hooks into her ears and wrote the whole out. I send you the result. There is a mistake of one word. I think that if you have the cheek to dictate the story into the fonograf, all the rest is perfectly easy. It wouldn't fatigue me to talk for an hour as I did.

Howells rented the machine and it was delivered to Sam in Hartford on March 11. The first day Sam filled six wax cylinders with about two hundred words per cylinder in an hour and a half and the next day twenty-two cylinders in five hours. But, as he recalled in his autobiography, he soon realized that while a voice recorder was "good enough for mere letter-writing" he could not "write literature with it." He "could have said about as much with the pen & said it a deal better" so he abandoned the trial.[42] He eventually learned to dictate to an amanuensis but not to a machine.

Sam completed the sixty-five-thousand-word novel on May 2, only seventy-one days after he began it. Set largely in a microcosmic boarding-house or "world in little" like the "world in a man o' war" in Herman Melville's *Redburn* (1849), *The American Claimant* consists of an inordinate amount of dialogue, betraying its origin in a playscript. Howells was understandably puzzled how Sam "managed to fight clear of my part in the plot, if you followed the lines of the play at all," in transforming their script into a novel. Sam explained that he "found I couldn't use the play—I had departed too far from its lines when I came to look at it. I thought I might get a great deal of dialogue out of it, but I got only 15 loosely written pages"—mostly cracks about zombies and sewer gas—and they only "saved me half a day's work."[43] He paid Howells nothing for his part of the story.

But Sam benefited mightily from the sale of its serial rights. He was initially offered four thousand dollars, soon increased to six thousand, by Edward Bok of the *Ladies' Home Journal*. At Sam's direction, however, Hall offered the story to John Cockerill of the New York *World* for ten thousand dollars and conferred on May 21 with Samuel S. McClure, who bid twelve thousand dollars for both U.S. and international serial rights—ironically, almost exactly the amount Webster had been paid for his interest in Webster and Company—and Sam accepted the tender with alacrity. McClure sold the story in syndication to several American newspapers, including the New York *Sun*, which serialized it between January and March 1892, and to the *Idler* in England, where it appeared between February 1892 and June 1893. McClure also sweetened the deal by contracting with Sam to write six travel letters for a thousand dollars each.[44]

The publication of *The American Claimant* belies the old saw that a watched pot never boils. It was undoubtedly a potboiler. The best that might be said of it is that it was not as bad as it could have been. A meditation on social class, rank, and nationality, the novel in the most superficial sense represents another reply to Matthew Arnold's indictment of American sniv-elization. In chapter 10 of the novel, one of the "claimants," Lord Berkeley, attends a meeting of the Mechanics' Club where he hears the assistant editor of a local daily defend American journalism from Arnold's charge in *Civilization in the United States* (1888) that "if one were searching for the best means to efface and kill in a whole nation the discipline of respect, one could not do better than take the American newspapers." Sam inserted here as the assistant editor's response to Arnold a speech entitled "The American Press" he had prepared several years earlier but never delivered; that is, he salvaged another vagrant manuscript from his files. In Sam's voice, the editor contends that the "frank and cheerful irreverence" of American journalism is "by all odds the most valuable of all its qualities" because "its mission—overlooked by Mr. Arnold—is to stand guard over a nation's liberties, not its humbugs and shams." He continues,

> Our press does not reverence kings, it does not reverence so-called nobilities, it does not reverence established ecclesiastical slaveries, it does not reverence laws which rob a younger son to fatten an elder one, it does not reverence any fraud or sham or infamy, howsoever old or rotten or holy, which sets one citizen above his neighbor by accident of birth: it does not reverence any law or custom, howsoever old or decayed or sacred.

After hearing this speech, the putative hero Berkeley concludes that the "prodigious results" of American civilization have been "brought about almost wholly by common men, not some Oxford-trained aristocrats."[45]

The episode is all the more ironic in light of Sam's characterization of Mulberry Sellers's daughter Sally, a student at "Rowena-Ivanhoe College." Much as Sam had bragged to Joe Goodman that Bryn Mawr was "the best female college in the world," Sellers declares in the novel that Rowena-Ivanhoe "is the selectest and most aristocratic seat of learning for young ladies in our country." Much as Sam's oldest daughter dropped the diminutive Susy and adopted her given first name Olivia when she left Hartford for Bryn Mawr, Sally Sellers changes her name to Lady Gwendolen when her father assumes the title of the Earl of Rossmore. More to the point, when Mulberry Sellers mocks the "silly college" with its castellated buildings to which he had sent his daughter, Sam betrayed his own cynical opinion of Bryn Mawr and its brand-new Denbigh Hall, opened in 1891 and designed in blatant imitation of Oxbridge buildings in England. Sellers likely speaks for Sam, too, when he complains that the young women students "don't learn a blessed thing, . . . not a single blessed thing but showy rubbish and un-american pretentiousness."[46] Olivia Susan had dropped out of Bryn Mawr only two weeks before Sam finished the novel.

From all indications, Susy had gradually adjusted to college life over the winter. Her daughter "enjoys the work extremely," Livy noted in late January 1891, "and when she is not consumed with homesickness she feels that she should like to remain there three or four years although she only entered for two." Dorm life, however, was another matter. "She finds the food poor and has at times eaten and slept so badly that we have felt that we should be compelled to give it up and bring her home," her mother allowed. "The poor table and the late hours are so far the only objections that I find to the school. There is no rule about the lights being out at night, consequently the girls sit up too late. Even those who desire to retire early are kept up late by those who do not."[47]

At the invitation of the president of Bryn Mawr, Sam addressed the students the afternoon of March 23. No doubt he thought his appearance would lift Susy's spirits. "I have been elected an honorary member of the class of '94," he began. "I feel deeply grateful to my fellow classmates for the compliment they have done me, the more so because I feel I have never deserved such treatment. I will reveal a secret to you. I have an ambition: that I may go up and up on the ladder of education until at last I may be a professor of Bryn Mawr College. I would be a professor of telling anecdotes." For the next hour or so he told stories and read poetry, including Rudyard Kipling's "Gunga Din." Clara, who had accompanied her father, recalled in her biography of him that she would never forget "the ring of awe in his voice as he read the last words" of Browning's "Clive." Susy had begged him not to end his program with his customary rendition of "The Golden Arm," however. Because Sam performed it in "the negro dialect" with "weird wailing, the rising & falling cadences of the wind," she considered it vulgar and in poor taste for "the sophisticated group at Byrn Mawr College." He remembered that she pleaded with him, "Please don't tell the ghost story, Father—promise not to tell the ghost story" and he admitted "I could think of *nothing* else." When he began to tell it she fled from the room in tears.[48]

Three weeks later, in mid-April, Livy visited Bryn Mawr and decided to withdraw her daughter from school. Perhaps Susy believed she had been irrevocably humiliated by her father. Sam claimed in his notebook that during her residence at Bryn Mawr "her health was undermined," perhaps a reference to the poor food she ate and her irregular hours in the dormitory. In any case, Susy's belongings were packed by April 18 and she returned to Hartford no later than April 26. But these explanations overlook a crucial element in Susy's adjustment to college, her willingness to "remain there three or four years" despite her longing for home.[49]

"To my private regret," Sam had confided to Howells in February, Susy was "beginning to love Bryn Mawr." The reason, no doubt, was named Louise Sheffield Brownell. While correspondents at the time often expressed affection in their letters in ways no longer fashionable, the evidence is compelling that Susy and Louise were infatuated and passionate in ways that trespassed the norms. Louise was away from Bryn Mawr during the week in mid-April when Livy was deciding Susy's fate, apparently to avoid shocking Susy's mother with an overt display of their affection. Nevertheless, Susy wrote Louise on April 20 that she yearned "to see you with my whole heart, because I love you so with my whole heart. Often at night I feel myself touching your dear soft cheek. If I could only see you the minute!" Louise had asked Susy to share a room with her the next academic year, an arrangement that surely would have alarmed Susy's parents. After Susy left Bryn Mawr, she continued to bare her soul in letters to Louise. "If I could only look in on you!" she once wrote,

> We would sleep together tonight—and I would allow you opportunities for those refreshing little naps you always indulged in when we passed a night together. . . . My darling I do love you so and I feel so separated from you. If you were here I would kiss you *hard* on that little place that tastes so good just on the right-hand side of your nose. . . . I give myself to you over & over again to make sure there is no mistake we belong to each other.

As Linda Morris and others have speculated, Sam and Livy likely "insisted that Susy accompany them to Europe in order to put distance between their daughter and Louise." As he reminisced in 1898, "we had to take her away from Bryn Mawr College to her deep and lasting grief. She was never in really promising health again." In his story "How Nancy Jackson Married Kate Wilson" (written circa 1902), Sam later imagined two straight women in a secret but satisfying same-sex marriage, apparently a coded account of Susy and Louise's union. That is, like his tale "Wapping Alice" (written in 1907), "Nancy Jackson" is to gender-bending what *The Tragedy of Pudd'nhead Wilson* (1894) is to racial masking.[50]

The Clemenses beat a strategic retreat to Europe in the spring of 1891. Sam and Livy each claimed to friends that the other needed to travel for her or his health. Livy had been diagnosed with a heart condition and, as Sam explained to Howells on May 20, she "must try baths somewhere, and this it is that has determined us to go to Europe... I don't know how long we shall be in Europe—I have a vote, but I don't cast it." On her part, Livy noted to Alice Hooker Day a week later, "Mr Clemens is greatly troubled with rheumatism" and "we want first of all to get him cured up if possible." The real reason they moved to Europe, of course, was to economize. They could no longer afford to live stylishly in the mansion on Farmington Avenue with a retinue of servants and also subsidize the publishing house. Sam and Livy had concluded the previous fall to "spend the next year in Europe," where they could live more frugally than in the United States, like the American expatriates in the 1920s, given the strength of the dollar. They paid a parting visit to the Howellses in New York in early March, a month before Susy withdrew from college and at the nadir of the family fortunes, and they found other employment for their servants. Sam offered the services of their coachman Patrick McAleer, "who has been with us 21 years, and is sober, active, diligent, and unusually bright and capable," to Fred Hall, who was seeking a worker in the Webster and Company warehouse. Their butler George Griffin, who "was in our service 18 years," took a job at the Union League Club in New York, where he worked from 1891 until his death in 1897. Sam hired John and Ellen O'Neil, their gardener and his wife, at a salary of seventy dollars a month to maintain the mansion and grounds for the duration of their absence. In late March and April, while preparing to leave the country, Sam participated along with Hjalmar Hjorth Boyesen, Will Carleton, Robert Underwood Johnson, and Frank Stockton in a couple of authors' readings—even though he had come to despise them—to benefit the YWCA at its hall on East Fifteenth Street in New York. "He was the most perfect reader I have ever known," Johnson recalled. "His voice was peculiarly musical and had its own attraction, while his clear renderings of meanings in the most involved versification was sometimes like the opening of a closed door."[51]

The imminent departure of the Clemens family was publicly announced in Edward Bok's syndicated column on May 16. "In about three weeks," according to Bok, the clan "will sail for the other side, not to return to America for two years." After vacationing for a month or two they planned to nest in "some secluded and remote French village." Bok added,

> "The children," said the humorist to me a few days ago, "will have their tutors, Mrs. Clemens will enjoy the luxury of a complete rest from housekeeping and kindred evils, while I want nothing but my pipe and my pen. I have no special literary plans in mind, but shall probably do a little something. . . . We are going to live in quiet fashion somewhere away from everybody, where no one knows us, and enjoy each other's company."

Their passage had been booked "some time ago on the French line . . . under fictitious names," Bok added. The article contained no hint that the journey was anything other than a long-planned family holiday rather than a semi-permanent exile required by the jaws of the financial vise in which he was gripped. Sam assured his sister Pamela that Bok's report was wrong in a couple of particulars: "The 'fictitious' name we travel under is S. L. Clemens & family. The 'French village' has not yet been decided upon, but it will be Berlin part of the time—all of next winter, no doubt." Sam allowed that he might write a book while in Europe; but then again, he might not; certainly he would not write another travel book. "Travel has no longer any charm for me," he wrote Howells. "I have seen all the foreign countries I want to see except heaven & hell, & I have only a vague curiosity as concerns one of those." Moreover, after completing *The American Claimant* he had no major project on the boards. As he told a reporter in late May,

> Writing is a curious thing with me nowadays. It requires the conjunction of time, inclination, and ideas. Once in a while the ideas come floating gently along, but I am either too lazy to write or have no time. Then again I get off and deliberately loaf, and after a bit I feel an inclination to write, but the idea won't come. So I am waiting placidly until the conjunction of the three comes about.

In fact, Sam jealously guarded his reputation for laziness. The joke circulated at the time that his doctor had prescribed laxative pills "to make his bowels move" and his nurse had replied, "I don't believe he'd take 'em, sir, if he knew it."[52]

Sam sold the piano, horses, and carriage and canceled his club memberships. Livy concluded her farewell letters to neighbors on a somber note: "I am so truly fond of my home and I love so tenderly my Hartford friends that I cannot bear to think of leaving them." Clara recalled that the family "regarded this break in a hitherto smooth flow of harmonious existence as something resembling a tragedy." Sam, Livy, and Jean quit their home on Farmington Avenue on June 5. Livy was the last to close the door. They railed to New York, where they rendezvoused with Susy, Clara, Katy Leary, and Sue Crane at the Murray Hill Hotel. At five the next morning the seven embarked aboard the French steamer *La Gascoigne* for Le Havre.[53] Exiles and expatriates for the next nine years, Sam and Livy never lived in Hartford again.

Abbreviations

AMT	Autobiography of Mark Twain	My MT	My Mark Twain
		N&J	Notebooks and Journals
BA	Boston Advertiser	NHJC	New Haven Journal and Courier
BE	Brooklyn Eagle		
BH	Boston Herald	NHR	New Haven Register
BJ	Boston Journal	NYEP	New York Evening Post
CC	Cincinnati Commercial	NYH	New York Herald
CIO	Chicago Inter Ocean	NYS	New York Sun
CT	Chicago Tribune	NYT	New York Times
HC	Hartford Courant	NYTrib	New York Tribune
LMT&JHT	Letters of Mark Twain and Joseph Hopkins Twichell	SFB	San Francisco Bulletin
		SLC	Samuel Langhorne Clemens
MT&GWC	Mark Twain and G. W. Cable	SR	Springfield Republican
MTB	Mark Twain: A Biography	TA	A Tramp Abroad
MTCI	Mark Twain: The Complete Interviews	UCCL	Union Catalog of Clemens Letters, ed. Paul Machlis (Berkeley: University of California Press, 1986); letters are cited by catalog number
MTCR	Mark Twain: The Contemporary Reviews		
MTHL	Mark Twain–Howells Letters		
MTL	Mark Twain Letters	UCLC	Union Catalog of Letters to Clemens, ed. Paul Machlis (Berkeley: University of California Press, 1992); letters are cited by catalog number
MTLP	Mark Twain's Letters to His Publishers		
MTMF	Mark Twain to Mrs. Fairbanks		
MTP	Mark Twain Papers and Project, Bancroft Library, University of California–Berkeley	WC	Washington Critic
		WS	Washington Star
MTSpk	Mark Twain Speaking		

Notes

Chapter 1

1. Howells, *Literary Friends and Acquaintances*, 299.

2. *MTL*, 4:367–68, 4:371–72, 4:374, 4:377, 4:379, 4:381; SLC to James Redpath, 2 May 1871, UCCL 1986.

3. *A Family Sketch*, 41.

4. *MTL*, 6:436; Berkove, *Insider Stories*, 1036–38; *MTCI*, 272; "Jos. Goodman's Memories of Humorist's Early Days," *San Francisco Examiner*, 22 April 1910, 3.

5. *MTL*, 4:375–76, 4:386.

6. *MTL*, 4:318, 4:376, 4:386–89; "The Magazines," *CT*, 27 February 1871, 3; "The Magazines for April," *Nation*, 6 April 1871, 243.

7. *MTL*, 4:389–90; Hill, *Mark Twain and Elisha Bliss*, 47.

8. *MTL*, 4:390, 4:395; "Home News," *NYTrib*, 1 June 1871, 8; *Roughing It*, 803; Smith, *Mark Twain: The Development*, 71.

9. *MTL*, 4:419; Fields, "Bret Harte and Mark Twain," 345; Reade, *Study and Stimulants*, 120; Cardwell, *Twins of Genius*, 122.

10. "Prominent Arrivals," *NYTrib*, 4 August 1871, 8; Hill, *Mark Twain and Elisha Bliss*, 69; Wonham, "Mark Twain's Short Fiction," 363; *N&J*, 3:407; *MTL*, 4:443, 4:447, 4:499.

11. Wonham, *Mark Twain and the Art of the Tall Tale*, 110; W. D. Howells, "Recent Literature," *Atlantic Monthly* 29 (June 1872): 754–55; *MTHL*, 10–11; *Roughing It*, iv, 376.

12. SLC's famous essay "Fenimore Cooper's Literary Offenses" (1895) ought also to be read in this context—not as a realist manifesto or defense of realism per se but as a humorous critique of western romance.

13. Smith, *Mark Twain: The Development*, 63; *Roughing It*, 295, 330, 332.

14. "From the Sandwich Islands," *Sacramento Union*, 6 September 1866, 2; *Roughing It*, 45; Wister, *The Virginian*, 29; Scharnhorst, *Owen Wister*, 20.

15. Hill, "Introduction," in *RI* (1981), 16; Bellamy, *Mark Twain as a Literary Artist*, 274; *Roughing It*, 147, 397; Wu, "The Siamese Twins," 41.

16. Quirk, *Mark Twain and Human Nature*, 79; Gibson, *The Art of Mark Twain*, 39; *Roughing It*, 343, 398–99.

17. *MTL*, 4:431, 4:477; "The King's Impressions of America," *NYTrib*, 24 December 1874, 1; Paine, *MTB*, 452.

18. *MTL*, 4:374, 4:396, 4:438, 4:442, 4:452.

19. "Mark Twain Takes Out a Patent," *Washington National Republican*, 21 September 1871, 2; *MTL*, 4:459, 4:465, 4:509–11, 5:44; Csicsila, "Langdon Clemens and *The Adventures of Tom Sawyer*," 65; Doyno, "Samuel Clemens as Family Man," 34.

20. *MTL*, 4:459; SLC to C. C. Duncan, 26 September 1871, *UCCL* 12650; "Prominent Arrivals," *NYTrib*, 4 October 1871, 8; "Mark Twain Takes Out a Patent," *Washington National Republican*, 21 September 1871, 2.

21. *MTL*, 3:221; "Letter from 'Mark Twain,'" *San Francisco Alta California*, 6 September 1868, 1; Andrews, *Nook Farm*, 101; "Has Lost His Curiosity," *Jackson (Mich.) Citizen Patriot*, 20 February 1885, 3; SLC to Jacob H. Burrough, 1 November 1876, *UCCL* 01384; Bush, *Mark Twain and the Spiritual Crisis*, 103; Steinbrink, "Mark Twain and Joe Twichell."

22. Orion Clemens to Mollie Clemens, 3 October 1871 *UCLC* 47049; *MTL*, 4:208; David, *Mark Twain and His Illustrators*, 1:133–34; Hill, *Mark Twain and Elisha Bliss*, 58; Stewart, *Reminiscences*, 224.

23. *MTL*, 4:362, 4:392, 4:410, 4:413, 4:420; "Town Talk," *Boston Traveller*, 13 June 1871, 2; *NYEP*, 15 June 1871, 2; "Personal," *Albany Journal*, 16 June 1871, 2; *Cincinnati Gazette*, 17 June 1871, 4; *WS*, 19 June 1871, 4; Hill, "The Composition and Structure of *Tom Sawyer*," 381.

24. *MTL*, 4:408, 4:420, 4:423, 4:425; *MTMF*, 154; *Albany Journal*, 1 July 1871, 2; Paine, *MTB*, 441.

25. *MTL*, 4:399–400, 4:434, 4:438, 4:460.

26. *MTL*, 4:xxix, 4:469, 4:471, 4:474–75, 5:44; "Prominent Arrivals," *NYTrib*, 14 October 1871, 7; "Local Intelligence," *Allentown (Penn.) Chronicle*, 18 October 1871, 4.

27. *MTL*, 4:476–78; *Ithaca Journal*, 21 November 1871, 2; Orion Clemens to Mollie Clemens, 26 October 1871, *UCLC* 47063.

28. "Mark Ward on Artemus Twain," *WS*, 24 October 1871, 1; "Amusements," *Washington Chronicle*, 23 October 1871, 4; "Mark Twain's Lecture at Lincoln Hall," *Washington Chronicle*, 24 October 1871, 4; *MTL*, 4:480.

29. Fatout, *Mark Twain on the Lecture Circuit*, 254; "Twain," *BE*, 1 September 1871, 4; "Mark Twain in the Lyceum Course," *BA*, 2 November 1871, 1; *MTL*, 4:491.

30. "The Lecture Last Evening," *Wilmington Every Evening*, 25 October 1871, 4; "The Lecture Field," *Wilmington Commercial*, 25 October 1871, 1; *MTL*, 4:481–83; "Mark Twain's Lecture," *Wilmington Delaware Gazette*, 27 October 1871, 3; Lorch, *The Trouble Begins at Eight*, 118; Fatout, *Mark Twain on the Lecture Circuit*, 154–56.

31. Fatout, *Mark Twain on the Lecture Circuit*, 156; "Brattleboro," *Manchester (N.H.) Journal*, 16 November 1871, 3; *MTL*, 4:483.

32. *MTL*, 4:401n4, 4:484–85; "Lectures Last Evening," *Boston Post*, 2 November 1871, 3; "Artemus Ward the Humorist," *BJ*, 2 November 1871, 4; "Town Talk," *Boston Traveller*, 2 November 1871, 2; "Mark Twain's Lecture on Artemus Ward," *Boston Transcript*, 2 November 1871, 4; "Mark Twain in the Lyceum Course," *BA*, 2 November 1871, 1.

33. Howells, *My MT*, iv; *MTHL*, 3; *MTL*, 4:489; *AMT*, 1:151.

34. "Mark Twain's Lecture," *Malden (Mass.) Mirror*, 11 November 1871, 4; Fatout, *Mark Twain on the Lecture Circuit*, 157; "Mark Twain's Lecture," *Malden (Mass.) Messenger*, 11 November 1871, n.p.; Wuster, *Mark Twain: American Humorist*, 186, 191; "Mark Twain's Lecture," *Worcester (Mass.) Spy*, 10 November 1871, 1; *MTL*, 4:487–88, 5:11; Lorch, "Mark Twain's 'Artemus Ward' Lecture," 332; "Mark Twain's Lecture," *HC*, 9 November 1871, 2.

35. Kruse, "A Matter of Style," 235; *MTL*, 4:510–11; 5:121; James Redpath to SLC, 12 July 1872, *UCLC* 31814; *MTL*, 4:500; Olivia Langdon Clemens to Olivia Lewis Langdon, 19 January 1873, *UCCL* 00859.

36. *MTL*, 4:488, 4:490–91; "Men and Things," *BH*, 14 November 1871, 4; "The Boston Press Club," *Boston Transcript*, 13 November 1871, 4.

37. Aldrich, *Crowding Memories*, 129–31; SLC to Susy Clemens, 27 December 1893, *UCCL* 04540; *AMT*, 3:242.

38. *Ogdensburg (N.Y.) Journal*, 18 November 1871, 2; Fatout, *Mark Twain on the Lecture Circuit*, 159; "Artemus Ward," *Portland (Maine) Eastern Argus*, 17 November 1871, 3; *MTL*, 4:401, 4:494–95, 4:497; Kruse, "A Matter of Style," 235; *MTL*, 4:494; "Town Talk," *Boston Traveller*, 23 October 1871, 2; "Mark Twain," *Philadelphia Inquirer*, 21 November 1871, 3; *Philadelphia Bulletin*, 21 November 1871, 8; "Mark Twain," *Philadelphia Press*, 21 November 1871; "Mark Twain," *BE*, 22 November 1871, 3; "Mark Twain," *Brooklyn Times*, 22 November 1871, n.p.; "Mark Twain on Artemus Ward," *Brooklyn Union*, 22 November 1871, 2.

39. *MTL*, 4:498, 4:507, 4:515–16; Fatout, *Mark Twain on the Lecture Circuit*, 161; "Mark Twain on Artemus Ward," *Albany Journal*, 29 November 1871, 2; "Personal," *Cincinnati Gazette*, 5 December 1871, 6; "Personal," *New York Commercial Advertiser*, 1 December 1871, 1; *Geneva (N.Y.) Gazette*, 8 December 1871, 3; W. H. Merrill, "When Mark Twain Lectured," *Harper's Weekly*, 10 February 1906, 199.

40. *MTL*, 4:511–12, 4:563.

41. Fatout, *Mark Twain on the Lecture Circuit*, 162; Simpson and Simpson, *Jean Webster*, 11; *MTL*, 4:513–14.

42. *MTL*, 4:513; Lorch, *The Trouble Begins at Eight*, 119.

43. Lorch, *The Trouble Begins at Eight*, 179; *MTL*, 4:515–16; "Entertainments," *Toledo Blade*, 12 December 1871, 3; Moffett, "Mark Twain's Lansing Lecture," 145; Fatout, *Mark Twain on the Lecture Circuit*, 164; "Mark Twain," *Jackson (Mich.) Citizen Patriot*, 14 December 1871, 5.

44. Moffett, "Mark Twain's Lansing Lecture," 153–54; *MTSpk*, 49; "University of Michigan," *CT*, 18 December 1871, 6; "Mark Twain," *Grand Rapids Democrat*, 16 December 1871; Fatout, *Mark Twain on the Lecture Circuit*, 164.

45. "Mark Twain," *Kalamazoo Gazette*, 22 December 1871, 3; Lorch, "Mark Twain's Lecture from *Roughing It*," 291.

46. *MTL*, 4:517–19, 4:562–63; "Mark Twain," *CT*, 20 December 1871, 4; "Mark Twain as a Lecturer," *Melbourne Age*, 6 July 1872, 6; "Mark Twain Last Night," *Chicago Post*, 19 December 1871, 4; "Substantial Donations," *CT*, 14 January 1872, 5.

47. "Mark Twain," *CT*, 20 December 1871, 4, and *CT*, 24 December 1871, 3; "Mark Twain," *Cincinnati Gazette*, 28 December 1871, 3; *MTL*, 4:522.

48. *Cairo (Ill.) Bulletin*, 30 December 1871, 2; Fatout, *Mark Twain on the Lecture Circuit*, 168.

49. SLC to Jane Lampton Clemens, 3 January 1872, *UCCL* 12773; *MTL*, 4:521–24, 4:526, 4:530, 5:43; Lorch, *The Trouble Begins at Eight*, 129; Fatout, *Mark Twain on the Lecture Circuit*, 168.

50. *MTL*, 5:1; Fatout, "Mark Twain Lectures in Indiana"; Lorch, *The Trouble Begins at Eight*, 119.

51. Fatout, "Mark Twain Lectures in Indiana," 366.

52. "From Dayton," *Cincinnati Gazette*, 5 January 1872, 1; *MTL*, 5:3, 5:11, 5:14, 5:19, 5:54; "Mark Twain's Lecture," *Dayton Journal*, 5 January 1872; "Mark Twain's Lecture," *Columbus Ohio State Journal*, 6 January 1872, 4; "Lecture of Mark Twain," *Wooster (Ohio) Republican*, 11 January 1872, 2; Fatout, *Mark Twain on the Lecture Circuit*, 170; "Mark Twain," *Wheeling Intelligencer*, 11 January 1872, 4.

53. Fatout, *Mark Twain on the Lecture Circuit*, 170–71; *MTL*, 5:18, 5:26; "Mark Twain," *Pittsburgh Commercial*, 12 January 1872, 4; "Mark Twain," *Pittsburgh Gazette*, 12 January 1872, 4; "Brevities," *Pittsburgh Gazette*, 15 January 1872, 4.

54. Fatout, *Mark Twain on the Lecture Circuit*, 171; *MTL*, 5:29–30.

55. *MTL*, 5:29–34; "Men and Women," *Portland (Maine) Press*, 5 May 1877, 1; "Mark Twain's Lecture," *NYT*, 25 January 1872, 5; "Mark Twain's Lecture," *NYH*, 25 January 1872, 3; John Hay, "Mark Twain at Steinway Hall," *NYTrib*, 25 January 1872, 5; *N&J*, 2:311; *Life on the Mississippi*, 482.

56. *MTL*, 5:37, 5:315–16, 6:406; Ward, *Dark Midnight*, 164–65; "The Jubilee Singers," *HC*, 29 January 1872, 2.

57. *Jersey City American Standard*, 31 January 1872, 1; *MTL*, 5:37–39, 43; "Twain Talk," *Jersey City Journal*, 31 January 1872, 1; "Prominent Arrivals," *NYTrib*, 31 January 1872, 8; "City and Vicinity," *Paterson (N.J.) Press*, 1 February 1872, 3; "'Roughing It' by Mark Twain," *Troy (N.Y.) Press*, 2 February 1872, 3.

58. *MTL*, 4:11, 5:1, 5:2, 5:11, 5:36, 5:44.

59. "Prominent Arrivals," *NYTrib*, 31 January 1872, 8; "Horace Greeley's Sixty-First Birthday," *NYTrib*, 5 February 1872, 5; "Personal," *HC*, 10 February 1872, 2; *MTL*, 5:40–41; "The Sage of Chappaqua," *CT*, 8 February 1872, 5; Scharnhorst, "The Bret Harte–Mark Twain Feud."

60. "Mark Twain," *Danbury News*, 28 February 1872, 2; *MTL*, 5:46.

61. "The Aldine Dinner," *NYTrib*, 24 February 1872, 5, and *NYTrib*, 26 February 1872, 8; "Mark Twain," *Cleveland Leader*, 1 March 1872, 3; "Mark Twain," *CT*, 2 March 1872, 5; "The 'Aldine' Dinner," *New York Commercial Advertiser*, 24 February 1872, 3; "New York," *BA*, 27 February 1872, 2; *MTL*, 5:47.

62. Higginson, *Thomas Wentworth Higginson*, 259–60; *MTL*, 5:30; Berkove, *Insider Stories*, 1034; SLC to Orion Clemens, 23 March 1878, UCCL 01547.

63. *MTL*, 5:36, 5:48–49; *Amherst (Mass.) Student*, 9 March 1872, 38; "Mark Twain's Lecture," *Amherst (Mass.) Record*, 28 February 1872, 4; "A Collation," *Amherst (Mass.) Record*, 28 February 1872, 4; Fike, "Frank Mayo," 45.

Chapter 2

1. Ganzel, "Samuel Clemens and John Camden Hotten," 238; *MTL*, 4:368, 4:386, 5:17, 5:45.

2. *MTL*, 5:308; SLC to David Gray, 10 June 1880, UCCL 11405.

3. Budd, *MTCR*, 101, 104–5; *MTL*, 5:108, 5:293–94; Louise Chandler Moulton, "Boston Literary Notes," *NYTrib*, 10 June 1872, 6.

4. Budd, *MTCR*, 100, 104, 106; "Mark Twain's Last Book," *Auburn (N.Y.) Bulletin*, 2 January 1872, 1; "New Publications," *Portland (Maine) Press*, 28 March 1872, 2; "Roughing It," *Nashville Union and American*, 20 June 1872, 4; Machor, "A Trying Five Years," 14; "Mark Twain's New Book," *Quincy (Mass.) Whig*, 25 March 1872, 4; "Notes of Travel," *Quincy (Mass.) Whig*, 7 December 1872, 3; "Mark Twain as Editor-in-Chief," *San Francisco Examiner*, 30 April 1872, 1.

5. "Book Notices," *Portland (Maine) Transcript*, 6 April 1872, 2; Budd, *MTCR*, 99, 102–5, 107–8; "Roughing It," *San Francisco Alta California*, 15 July 1872, 2; "Uncivilised America," *Manchester (N.H.) Guardian*, 6 March 1872, 7; Mary Mason Fairbanks to Olivia Langdon Clemens, 1 April 1872, UCLC 48795; "Greeley in the Woods," *NYH*, 25 August 1872, 5; "The Horace Greeley Statue Fund," *NYTrib*, 14 October 1889, 7.

6. *MTL*, 5:59, 5:70, 5:83, 5:271, 5:308, 5:346–47, 6:426; Paine, *MTB*, 455; *Mark Twain's Correspondence with Henry Huttleston Rogers*, 249; Hill, "Mark Twain's Book Sales," 379; *MTCI*, 80; Hill, *Mark Twain and Elisha Bliss*, 63.

7. *AMT*, 2:50–51, 2:143; Hill, *Mark Twain and Elisha Bliss*, 67.

8. SLC to Pamela Moffett, 28 April 1873, *UCCL* 12784; *MTL*, 5:55, 5:68–69.

9. *MTL*, 5:88, 6:442; Orion Clemens to SLC, 17 May 1872, *UCLC* 47067; SLC to Orion Clemens, 24 October 1880, *UCCL* 01845.

10. Hill, *Mark Twain and Elisha Bliss*, 18; Hill, "Mark Twain's Quarrels," 455; *AMT*, 1:50–51, 1:371–72, 2:527–28.

11. *MTL*, 5:50, 5:57, 5:79, 5:86, 6:155.

12. Paine, *MTB*, 456; *AMT*, 1:433; *MTL*, 5:94, 5:97; Lilly Warner to George Warner, 31 May 1872, *UCLC* 31799; Lilly Warner to George Warner, 3 June 1872, *UCLC* 31807.

13. Lilly Warner to George Warner, 3 June 1872, *UCLC* 31807; *MTL*, 5:100.

14. Clemens, *My Father*, 6–7; *AMT*, 1:433; Howells, *My MT*, 12; *MTL*, 5:100.

15. *MTL*, 5:105, 5:128, 5:150–51, 6:112, 6:413; "Brief Mention," *HC*, 9 July 1872, 2, and *HC*, 31 July 1872, 2; "Fenwick Hall," *HC*, 29 July 1872, 2; Joseph L. Blamire to SLC, 6 August 1872, *UCLC* 31828; Olivia Langdon Clemens to Mary Mason Fairbanks, 25 September 1872, *UCCL* 05859.

16. *A Family Sketch*, 11; Olivia Langdon Clemens to Mollie Clemens, 7 July 1872, *UCCL* 00763; Olivia Langdon Clemens to Susan Crane, 27 July 1872, *UCCL* 12778.

17. *AMT*, 2:434; Camfield, *Oxford Companion* 152; Paine, *MTB*, 459.

18. Rodney, *Mark Twain Overseas*, 74–75; Millais, *Life and Letters*, 422; "Civic Changes," *London Telegraph*, 30 September 1872, 3; McWilliams, *Ambrose Bierce*, 100; *MTSpk*, 73; "Mark Twain in London," *HC*, 19 September 1872, 2; Crews, *The Critics Bear It Away*, 157; "Mark Twain at the Whitefriars Club," *South London Press*, 14 September 1872, 4; *MTL*, 5:155; *WS*, 21 September 1872, 2; "London," *CT*, 27 September 1872, 4.

19. John Camden Hotten to Ambrose Bierce, 7 September 1872, *UCLC* 41304; "Mark Twain and His English Editor," *London Spectator*, 21 September 1872, 2301–2; George W. Smalley, "British Topics," *NYTrib*, 12 October 1872, 4; Paine, *MTB*, 464; Baetzhold, *Mark Twain and John Bull*, 8.

20. *MTL*, 5:155, 5:159–60, 5:175, 5:215–16, 5:540, 5:564; *MTCI*, 19.

21. *Mark Twain's Speeches*, 120. SLC elsewhere maligned this memorial to "a most excellent foreign gentleman who was a happy type of the Good, & the Kind, the Well-Meaning, the Mediocre, the Commonplace" (*MTL*, 5:594).

22. Conway, *Autobiography*, 2:143; *MTSpk*, 71; Moncure D. Conway, "Mark Twain in London," *CC*, 10 October 1872, 4.

23. Moncure D. Conway, "Mark Twain in London," *CC*, 10 October 1872, 4; *AMT*, 2:435; *MTL*, 5:169; Conway, *Autobiography*, 2:166; Mary Mason Fairbanks to SLC, 26 October 1872, *UCLC* 31834; Watson, *The Savage Club*, 133–34.

24. *MTL*, 5:159, 5:179, 5:201, 5:629; "Shad'd," *NYH*, 11 July 1873, 3.

25. *MTL*, 5:183; Franc B. Wilkie, "Twain's Best Joke," *Chicago Times*, 17 November 1879, 1.

26. *MTL*, 5:182, 5:184, 5:191–92; *AMT*, 3:503.

27. *MTL*, 5:189, 5:195–96, 5:213; J. Ross Browne to Lucy Browne, 16 October 1872, *UCLC* 48579.

28. *MTL*, 5:614–19.

29. *MTL*, 5:199–201, 5:205, 5:208, 5:214, 5:216, 5:221; *MTCI*, 202; "The Lord Mayor Elect," *London Times*, 5 November 1872, 10.

30. J. Ross Browne to Lucy Browne, 29 October 1872, *UCLC* 48580; Moncure D. Conway, "Mark Twain in London," *CC*, 5 December 1872, 2; Lorch, "Mark Twain's Public Lectures in England in 1873," 297.

31. *N&J*, 2:486.

32. Martin, "Letters and Remarks by Mark Twain"; *MTL*, 5:240; "Mark Twain at Sea," *NYTrib*, 27 November 1872, 1; "Perils of the Sea," *HC*, 27 November 1872, 1; "British Benevolence," *NYTrib*, 27 January 1873, 4.

33. Budd, *MTCR*, 1:541–42; *MTL*, 5:249–50. Ron Powers misinterprets SLC's comment: "In 1872, Samuel Clemens still believed in Civilization and progress" (Powers, *Mark Twain*, 327). SLC simply quoted tongue in cheek the motto on the masthead of the *Weekly*: "A Journal of Civilization and Progress."

34. "The New Cock Robin," *CT*, 2 January 1873, 3; *N&J*, 2:419; Whitelaw Reid to SLC, 28 December 1872, *UCLC* 31842; *MTL*, 5:264, 5:269–71; Whitelaw Reid to SLC, 11 January 1873, *UCLC* 31847.

35. *MTL*, 5:208–9, 5:319; "Personal," *Cincinnati Enquirer*, 9 December 1872, 4; Olivia Langdon Clemens to Olivia Lewis Langdon, 19 January 1873, *UCCL* 00859; "A Card," *Hartford Post*, 29 January 1873, scrapbook 6, MTP; *AMT*, 2:281–82, 2:583–84; "The Poor of Hartford and the Sandwich Islands," *HC*, 29 January 1873, 2; "Mark Twain and Father Hawley," *HC*, 29 January 1873, 2, and *HC*, 1 February 1873, 2; *MTL*, 290.

36. "Personal Intelligence," *NYH*, 2 February 1873, 7, and *NYH*, 10 February 1873, 7; "Lectures and Meetings," *NYTrib*, 1 February 1873, 12; *MTCI*, 501; Elderkin, *A Brief History of the Lotos Club*, 15; "Fun at the Lotos," *WS*, 22 February 1873, 2; John D'Arme, "New York Letters," *Portland Oregonian*, 26 December 1886, 2. See also *MTL*, 5:297.

37. *NYTrib*, 10 February 1873, 4; "Mark Twain," *New York World*, 6 February 1873, 8; "Mark Twain's Lecture on the Sandwich Islands," *NYT*, 6 February 1873, 5; "Mark Twain's Lecture," *NYTrib*, 6 February 1873, 5; "Mark Twain's Lecture on the Sandwich Islands," *Troy (N.Y.) Times*, 7 June 1873, 4; Fatout, *Mark Twain on the Lecture Circuit*, 176–77; "Mark Twain," *BE*, 10 February 1873, 4; SLC to Thomas Nast, 12 November 1877, *UCCL* 02518; "Mark Twain on the Sandwich Islands," *Jersey City Journal*, 14 February 1873, 1; "Mark Twain's Cold," *NYT*, 9 October 1874, 8; Orion Clemens to Mollie Clemens, 3 November 1873, *UCLC* 47085.

38. *MTL*, 5:235–36, 5:251; "New York," *CT*, 23 February 1873, 7; Thomas Nast to SLC, 15 December 1872, *UCLC* 31839; Hill, *Mark Twain and Elisha Bliss*, 76.

39. See, e.g., "A Storm at Sea: Mark Twain's Recollections of It," *CT*, 5 February 1876, 11; Udo Brachvogel, "Rogers," *Die Gegenwart*, 8 July 1882, 26–29; and Regan, "'English Notes,'" 169.

40. Csicsila, "Langdon Clemens and *The Adventures of Tom Sawyer*"; *AMT*, 3:102; Tracy, "Myth and Reality in *The Adventures of Tom Sawyer*," 531.

41. Stoddard, *Exits and Entrances*, 70–71; French, *Mark Twain and the Gilded Age*, 25–27; "Mark Twain and Sellers," *NYS*, 3 September 1878, 3.

42. Paine, *MTB*, 477; *MTL*, 4:185, 5:259–60, 6:53, 6:172; *AMT*, 1:207; *MTHL*, 184; "Eminent Authors at Home," *New York Graphic*, 23 December 1876, 377; *The Gilded Age*, vi; *MTCI*, 214.

43. *MTL*, 5:339, 5:344, 5:414; Camfield, *Oxford Companion*, 299; Cortissoz, *The Life of Whitelaw Reid*, 1:273; *NYTrib*, 19 April 1873, 6.

44. *MTL*, 5:346–47, 5:351.

45. *NYTrib*, 23 April 1873, 4; Hill, "Mark Twain's Book Sales," 380.

46. *MTL*, 5:356; *AMT*, 1:339; Budd, *Our Mark Twain*, 106.

47. *MTL*, 5:568; Whiting, *Kate Field*, 308–9; *MTHL*, 92; Orion Clemens to Mollie Clemens, 1 January 1874, *UCLC* 47111; *AMT*, 3:113–14.

48. *MTL*, 5:362; SLC to Pamela Moffett, 28 April 1873, *UCCL* 12784; "'Mark Twain' to the Editor of 'The Daily Graphic,'" *New York Graphic*, 22 April 1873, 8; Hill, *Mark Twain and Elisha Bliss*, 13, 76; Jerry W. Thomason, "Dramatist, Mark Twain as," in LeMaster and Wilson, *The Routledge Encyclopedia of Mark Twain*, 228–29; Wesley Britton, "Trumbull, James Hammond," in LeMaster and Wilson, *The Routledge Encyclopedia of Mark Twain*, 752.

49. Paine, *MTB*, 477; SLC to George MacDonald, 9 March 1883, *UCCL* 02356; *The Gilded Age*, 552; E. J. Edwards, "The Literary World," *Ogdensburg (N.Y.) Journal*, 28 May 1891, 3; Hill, "Toward a Critical Text," 142; *MTL*, 5:357–58, 6:47; Charles Dudley Warner to Thomas Wentworth Higginson, 31 December 1873, *UCLC* 31920; "Views and Interviews," *Galveston News*, 8 April 1886, 5.

50. "The Revised Catechism," *NYTrib*, 27 September 1871, 1; *MTL*, 5:245, 335–36.

51. Baetzhold, "Mark Twain: England's Advocate," 329; *AMT*, 1:209.

52. *The Gilded Age*, 407.

53. *The Gilded Age*, 493, 510, 547; French, *Mark Twain and the Gilded Age*, 45.

54. French, "Mark Twain, Laura D. Fair, and the New York Criminal Courts"; Kitzhaber, "Mark Twain's Use of the Pomeroy Case," 56; Daufenbach, "'Corruptionville,'" 165.

55. *MTL*, 5:411; Watterson, "Mark Twain—An Intimate Memory," 372; *AMT*, 1:206; "The Tribe of Sellers," *NYTrib*, 19 November 1874, 4.

56. Charles Dudley Warner to Mrs. Goodwin, 29 March 1896, *UCLC* 48203; Hill, *Mark Twain and Elisha Bliss*, 75, 78; Lampton, "Hero in a Fool's Paradise," 51.

57. "Mark Twain in Court," *BA*, 31 May 1873, 2.

58. "Europe," *New York Commercial Advertiser*, 10 June 1873, 4; "Mark Twain's Suit," *NYT*, 12 June 1873, 2; Glass, *Authors, Inc.*, 59; *N&J*, 2:271, 3:307; SLC to Charles L. Webster, 23 September 1882, *UCCL* 10938; Feinstein, "Mark Twain's Lawsuits," 67–68; *Mark Twain on Potholes and Politics*, 88.

59. Olivia Langdon Clemens to SLC, 2–3 December 1871, *UCCL* 00683; Kaplan, *Mr. Clemens and Mark Twain*, 142; *MTL*, 5:269–70; Olivia Langdon Clemens to Theodore Crane, 12 January 1873, *UCCL* 12782.

60. Howells, *If Not Literature*, 187; "The Comic Castle of Mark Twain," *Sacramento Union*, 1 November 1873, 8; "A Few Wooden Nutmegs," *Geneva (N.Y.) Gazette*, 30 January 1874, 2; Blair, "When Was *Huckleberry Finn* Written?," 16; Kaplan, *Mr. Clemens and Mark Twain*, 181; *MTCI*, 58; Harris, *Courtship*, 170.

61. Kaplan, *The Singular Mark Twain*, 289; Pettit, *Mark Twain and the South*, 195; "Personal Items," *Boston Traveller*, 6 April 1875, 4; *AMT*, 2:504; Olivia Langdon Clemens to Susan Crane, 23 March 1873, *UCCL* 12783; SLC to Pamela Moffett, 28 April 1873, *UCCL* 12784.

Chapter 3

1. "Personal Intelligence," *NYH*, 17 May 1873, 6; *MTL*, 5:366, 368; "New York," *Boston Traveller*, 19 May 1873, 2; Olivia Langdon Clemens to Olivia Lewis Langdon, 23–26 May 1873, *UCCL* 00918.

2. "Joaquin Miller's Letter," *CC*, 24 December 1882, 2; Olivia Langdon Clemens to Susan Crane, 31 May 1873, *UCCL* 00921; "Trollope and Mark Twain," *NYT*, 25 December 1882, 3; *MTL*, 5:371, 5:377–78, 5:381, 5:402; SLC to Richard Bentley, 26 April 1876, *UCLC* 32376; Paine, *MTB*, 461, 465.

3. *MTL*, 5:315–16, 5:371, 5:375, 5:385–86, 6:406; *N&J*, 1:570; Bush, *Mark Twain and the Spiritual Crisis*, 146; Ward, *Dark Midnight*, 225; "City and Vicinity," *Lowell (Mass.) Citizen and News*, 22 March 1875, 2; Olivia Langdon Clemens to Susan Crane, 31 May 1873, UCCL 00921; Olivia Langdon Clemens to Jane Lampton Clemens and Pamela Moffett, 15 June 1873, UCCL 00926; Fears, *Mark Twain Day-by-Day*, 1:419; Field, "Receiving the Shah," 4; Rodney, *Mark Twain Overseas*, 82; Baetzhold, *Mark Twain and John Bull*, 9.

4. *MTL*, 5:394; Field, "Receiving the Shah," 4; *Europe and Elsewhere*, 31–86; "The Visit of the Shah of Persia to Portsmouth," *Hampshire Telegraph and Sussex Chronicle*, 25 June 1873, 2. See also *N&J*, 3:92–93.

5. *MTL*, 5:425, 5:430; SLC to Frank Millet, 7 August 1877, UCCL 01468; *AMT*, 3:114.

6. "Political Movements," *Pomeroy's Democrat*, 26 July 1873, 5; "Editorial Notes," *New York Commercial Advertiser*, 28 July 1873, 2; "Editorial Notes," *New York Commercial Advertiser*, 28 July 1873, 2; *Richmond Whig*, 22 July 1873, 2; "Twain," *BE*, 14 July 1873, 2; Whiting, *Kate Field*, 308.

7. *MTL*, 5:385–86, 5:388, 5:393; "Personalities," *CC*, 13 August 1873, 3; Rodney, *Mark Twain Overseas*, 82; Paine, *MTB*, 484.

8. *MTL*, 5:395, 5:402, 6:57; *N&J*, 1:533; "Personal Intelligence," *NYH*, 8 July 1873, 6; "Topics of the Day," *Melbourne Herald*, 28 August 1873, 2.

9. Budd, "Mark Twain Sounds Off." In spring 1878, when addressing the graduating class at Hartford's West Middle School in his slow drawl, SLC said, "You boys and girls will see more in the next fifty years than Methuselah saw in his whole lifetime" (Phelps, *Autobiography*, 67).

10. *MTSpk*, 74–76; *N&J*, 1:557, 1:561, 1:564; "Joaquin Miller's Letter," *CC*, 24 December 1882, 2; Anthony Trollope to Kate Field, in Trollope, *Letters*, 591; *AMT*, 3:491, 3:593; Conway, *Autobiography*, 2:145; "The London Scottish Corporation," *Glasgow Herald*, 2 December 1873, 4; Charles Warren Stoddard to SLC, 12 December 1874, UCLC 32076; *MTL*, 5:415. SLC attended another concert by the Jubilee Singers at the Asylum Hill Congregational Church on 16 November 1890. Katy Leary remembered that the singers performed "all them negro airs they called Spirituals, and Mr. Clemens loved it and begun to sing with 'em, too—he had a lovely voice and was very dramatic in his singing" (Leary, quoted in Lawton, *A Lifetime*, 212).

11. *MTL*, 5:418.

12. *AMT*, 1:186, 1:328–29; Baetzhold, *Mark Twain and John Bull*, 16; *MTL*, 5:419, 5:439, 6:54–55; Paine, *MTB*, 467, 486; Kaplan, *The Singular Mark Twain*, 300–301; Gribben, *Mark Twain's Library*, 618; SLC to George H. Fitzgibbon, 28 November 1873, UCCL 00990; Olivia Langdon Clemens to Olivia Lewis Langdon, 10–15 August 1873, UCCL 00790; Olivia Langdon Clemens to Susan Crane, 18–20 July 1873, UCCL 12785; SLC to Dean Sage, 5 February 1890, UCCL 04012; *MTCI*, 128.

13. *MTL*, 5:435; *AMT*, 3:239, 3:570. See also *MTHL*, 412: "You didn't intend [the protagonist] Bartley [Hubbard] for me, but he is me, just the same." Hubbard's quotation from Emerson was carved on the mantelpiece of SLC's library (Howells, *A Modern Instance*, 348).

14. Olivia Langdon Clemens to Olivia Lewis Langdon, 10–15 August 1873, UCCL 00790.

15. Clemens, *Mark Twain: His Life and Work*, 128; Olivia Langdon Clemens to Olivia Lewis Langdon, 31 August–2 September 1873, UCCL 00801; *N&J*, 2:67; Hastings MacAdam, "Mark Twain Visits His Old Sweetheart," *St. Louis Republic*, 1 June 1902, sec. 3, p. 1; SLC to Richard Watson Gilder, 5 October 1889, UCCL 03945; *MTL*, 5:432, 5:435, 5:440,

5:490–91; *Following the Equator*, 159; Olivia Langdon Clemens to Susan Crane, 24 August 1873, *UCCL* 10595; Olivia Langdon Clemens to Susan Crane, 7 September 1873, *UCCL* 12788.

16. *MTL*, 5:439; SLC to Charles L. Webster, 17 November 1886, *UCCL* 03482.

17. Olivia Langdon Clemens to Olivia Lewis Langdon, 25–28 September 1873, *UCCL* 00964

18. Howells, *My MT*, 12; Olivia Langdon Clemens to Susan Crane, 4 October 1873, *UCCL* 12790.

19. Kaplan, *The Singular Mark Twain*, 449; Conway, *Autobiography*, 2:142; Lorch, *The Trouble Begins at Eight*, 140; Lorch, "Mark Twain's Public Lectures in England in 1873," 299; "Mark Twain on the Sandwich Islands," *London Standard*, 9 October 1873, 5; Moncure D. Conway, "London Letter," CC, 15 August 1881, 5; *MTL*, 5:452; "Odds and Ends," *Melbourne Leader*, 27 December 1873, 5.

20. Lorch, *The Trouble Begins at Eight*, 141; scrapbook, 12:14, 12:15, MTP; Wuster, *Mark Twain: American Humorist*, 421; "Mark Twain on the Sandwich Islands," *London Standard*, 14 October 1873, 6; *London Observer*, 19 October 1873; "Cracking Jokes," *Once a Week*, 8 November 1873, 402–5; "Mark Twain as a Lecturer," *London Times*, 14 October 1873, 12; "Mark Twain as a Lecturer," *Bradford (England) Observer*, 16 October 1873, 5; "Mark Twain on Savages," *Lloyd's Weekly Newspaper*, 19 October 1873, 5; "The London Press on Mark Twain," *HC*, 5 November 1873, 1; Tom Hood, "Mark Twain," *Fun*, 25 October 1873, 170; "Current Events," *London Examiner*, 18 October 1873, 1046; "Mr. Mark Twain's Lecture," *London Post*, 14 October 1873, 6; "Mark Twain on the Sandwich Islands," *London Illustrated Police News*, 18 October 1873, 3; "Our Fellow Savages of the Sandwich Islands," *London Court Journal*, 18 October 1873, 1223; "Summary of News," *Sheffield & Rotherham Independent*, 17 October 1873, 2; "From Our London Correspondent," *Manchester (N.H.) Guardian*, 14 October 1873, 5.

21. "Legal," *London Graphic*, 18 October 1873, 375; "London Theatres," *Penny Illustrated Paper and Illustrated Times*, 18 October 1873, 251; scrapbook, 12:13, MTP; Wuster, *Mark Twain: American Humorist*, 232; "Mark Twain," *Spectator*, 18 October 1873, 1302–3; *MTL*, 5:453–54.

22. "Liverpool Institute," *London Era*, 26 October 1873, 5; "Mark Twain," *New York Graphic*, 8 November 1873, 6; Lorch, "Mark Twain's Public Lectures in England in 1873," 303; *MTL*, 6:182; "Mark Twain on the Sandwich Island Savages," *Liverpool Mercury*, 21 October 1873, 7; Lorch, *The Trouble Begins at Eight*, 142.

23. *Letters from the Earth*, 261–62; Henry recalls the birthday of his son Harry, June 8 (273). Olivia Langdon Clemens was pregnant with their daughter Clara, born on 8 June 1874, before leaving England in 1873.

24. *MTL*, 5:459; "Personal Intelligence," *NYH*, 3 November 1873, 6; Orion Clemens to Mollie Clemens, 3 November 1873, *UCLC* 47085.

25. Paine, *MTB*, 495. Walter Blair erroneously states that this conversation occurred "in London in 1873" (Blair, *Mark Twain and Huck Finn*, 301).

26. *MTL*, 6:47; *MTHL*, 369.

27. Orion Clemens to Mollie Clemens, 3 November 1873, *UCLC* 47085; Kaplan, *The Singular Mark Twain*, 476; *MTL*, 5:473–75; SLC to Olivia Langdon Clemens, 8 November 1873, *UCCL* 12791; Gribben, *Mark Twain's Library*, 578; "Mark Twain," *Bradford (England) Observer*, 20 November 1873, 8.

28. *MTL*, 5:196.

29. SLC to Charles Warren Stoddard, 20 September 1876, *UCCL* 01366. Peter Messent expresses a consensus opinion that Stoddard was homosexual (Messent, *Mark Twain and Male Friendship*, 24). Nevertheless, SLC harbored a conventional bias against "inverts" or the so-called Cleveland street cohort, so named for a "private club at 19 Cleveland Street in London catering to the homosexual and perverse tastes of a number of titled personages" (*N&J*, 3:540). As he noted in his journal, "For some centuries [British] laws have been made by the King, Cleveland-street & the Commons" (*N&J*, 3:542).

30. Stoddard, *Exits and Entrances*, 63–64; *MTL*, 6:3; James, "Charles Warren Stoddard," 669.

31. Stoddard, *Exits and Entrances*, 70; *MTHL*, 154; *AMT*, 1:161; James, "Charles Warren Stoddard," 670; *MTL*, 5:479–80.

32. *MTL*, 5:508, 6:1, 6:3–4, 6:11; Krauth, *Proper Mark Twain*, 76.

33. *MTHL*, 154; *Following the Equator*, 157; *N&J*, 1:550–51.

34. *MTL*, 6:546; SLC to James R. Osgood, 7 March 1881, *UCCL* 01924; SLC to James R. Osgood, 30 March 1881, *UCCL* 02551; *MTHL*, 583; SLC to John W. Chapman, 15 February 1887, *UCCL* 03529.

35. "Remarkable Imposture," *NYS*, 21 July 1889, 10.

36. Howells, *My MT*, 46; *AMT*, 1:161–62; Andrew Chatto to SLC, 25 November 1873, *UCLC* 41299; *MTL*, 5:491, 5:512–13; "Mark Twain on Scotland," *Cleveland Herald*, 26 December 1873, 4; *New Haven Columbian Register*, 13 December 1873, 3; "Mark Twain as a Scotchman," *Cincinnati Gazette*, 26 December 1873, 5.

37. "Scottish Corporation of London," *London Post*, 2 December 1873, 6; "Mark Twain on Woman," *Alexandria (Va.) Gazette*, 29 December 1873, 1; Kaplan, *The Singular Mark Twain*, 490.

38. McWilliams, *Mark Twain in the St. Louis Post-Dispatch*, 10; Kaplan, *The Singular Mark Twain*, 496; *MTL*, 5:508–9.

39. Charles Warren Stoddard, "An Anglo-American City," *San Francisco Chronicle*, 8 February 1874, 1; *MTL*, 5:532; Lorch, "Mark Twain's Public Lectures in England in 1873," 298; Kaplan, *The Singular Mark Twain*, 494; "Mr. Mark Twain," *London Post*, 2 December 1873, 6.

40. Stoddard, *Exits and Entrances*, 64–70; James, "Charles Warren Stoddard," 669; *AMT*, 1:161–62; Paine, *MTB*, 496; Lorch, *The Trouble Begins at Eight*, 147.

41. Stoddard, "Selections," 278; *MTL*, 5:512–13, 5:527; George W. Smalley, "British Topics," *NYTrib*, 25 December 1873, 1; Bright, *Diaries*, 59; Haweis, *American Humorists*, 157–58; "London Gossip," *NYH*, 5 January 1874, 3; *Bradford (England) Observer*, 17 January 1874, 7; "Nottingham's Mechanics Institution," *Nottinghamshire Guardian*, 27 March 1874, 5.

42. *MTL*, 5:496–97; Stoddard, *Exits and Entrances*, 69.

43. *MTL*, 5:500; "Mr. Mark Twain's New Lecture," *London Post*, 9 December 1873, 2; "Mr. Mark Twain," *London Times*, 12 December 1873, 5; Rodney, *Mark Twain Overseas*, 90; "Hanover Square Rooms," *London Telegraph*, 9 December 1873; scrapbook, 12:41, 12:49, MTP; "Mark Twain on a Fresh Trail," *London Standard*, 10 December 1873, 3; "Entertainments," *London Orchestra*, 12 December 1873, 165; "Mark Twain's Lecture," *London Era*, 14 December 1873, 11; "Mark Twain on Nevada," *London Figaro*, 17 December 1873, 51; *MTL*, 6:5.

44. "Mr. Mark Twain," *London Daily News*, 9 December 1873, 3; "Mark Twain's Second Lecture," *London Globe*, 9 December 1873, scrapbook 12:51, MTP.

45. George W. Smalley, "British Topics," *NYTrib*, 25 December 1873, 1; George W. Smalley to SLC, 9 December 1873, *UCLC* 31902; *MTL*, 5:502.

46. Lorch, *The Trouble Begins at Eight*, 144; *MTL*, 5:503.

47. *MTL*, 5:512–13, 5:527; "Brief Mention," *HC*, 29 December 1873, 2; Prentice Mulford, "Notes from London," *SFB* supplement, 24 January 1874, 2; "Mark Twain," *Bradford (England) Observer*, 3 January 1874, 6; *MTL*, 6:188.

48. *MTL*, 5:525, 5:529–32; "Mark Twain's Last Night in London," *HC*, 13 January 1874, 2; "Dramatic," *New York Clipper*, 10 January 1874, 327. SLC also met Alexandra of Denmark, the consort of Prince Albert, the future King Edward VII of England, around this time (see Sydney Brooks, "England's Ovation to Mark Twain," *Harper's Weekly*, 27 July 1907, 1086); this may have been the occasion.

49. Charles Warren Stoddard, "Christmas in New Sarum," *San Francisco Chronicle*, 25 January 1874, 2; *MTL*, 5:534–35; Stoddard, "Selections," 278–79; Sturdevant, "Mark Twain's Unpublished Letter."

50. Layard, *Shirley Brooks of Punch*, 576; *MTL*, 6:2, 6:11, 6:19; "Mark Twain in Leicester," *Leicester Chronicle*, 10 January 1874, 10; Stoddard, "An Anglo-American City"; "Mr. Mark Twain on the Silver Frontier," *Liverpool Post*, 10 January 1874, 5; Stoddard, *Exits and Entrances*, 73–74.

Chapter 4

1. Kaplan, *The Singular Mark Twain*, 421; Hill, *Mark Twain and Elisha Bliss*, 83; *MTL*, 6:53–55; Hill, "Mark Twain's Book Sales," 381–82; Welland, *Mark Twain in England*, 43.

2. *MTL*, 6:12, 6:89; *MTLP*, 121; Woodfield, "The 'Fake' Title-Page."

3. W. D. Howells to Charles Dudley Warner, 28 December 1873, UCLC 49846.

4. Welland, *Mark Twain in England*, 44; *MTL*, 6:53–55; Camfield, *Oxford Companion*, 470.

5. *MTL*, 6:27; Budd, *MTCR*, 122–23; *AMT*, 1:339.

6. Budd, *MTCR*, 139–40; *Marysville (Calif.) Appeal*, 11 April 1874, 2.

7. "New Publications," *SFB*, 7 March 1874, 1; "Gadabout's Column," *WS*, 17 January 1874, 1; McWilliams, *Mark Twain in the St. Louis Post-Dispatch*, 15; Budd, *MTCR*, 125; *MTL*, 5:362.

8. "The Gilded Age," *Saturday Review*, 14 February 1874, 223–24; "New Publications," *Sacramento Union*, 14 March 1874, 4; "The Gilded Age," *Cleveland Herald*, 17 December 1873, 3; "Jeff Thompson Twenty Years Ago," *New Orleans Republican*, 19 April 1874, 6; "Editor's Table," *Ohio Farmer*, 7 March 1874, 152; Budd, *MTCR*, 125.

9. "American Satire," *NYH*, 22 December 1873, 6; "The Gilded Age," *SFB*, 21 March 1874, 2; Budd, *MTCR*, 123, 125, 131, 138–39, 141, 143–45; "Literary Notices," *Alexandria (Va.) State Journal*, 12 February 1874, 2; "Mrs. Burnham after Twain and Warner," *Providence Press*, 2 February 1874, 4.

10. Budd, *MTCR*, 120–22, 125–26, 129; "The Gilded Age," *London Post*, 26 January 1874, 3.

11. Ambrose Bierce to Charles Warren Stoddard, 15 January 1874, UCLC 50202; Budd, *MTCR*, 124, 141; "The Gilded Age," *Spectator*, 21 March 1874, 371–72; "The Gilded Age," *London Post*, 26 January 1874, 3; "The Gilded Age," *Melbourne Australasian*, 11 April 1874, 8; "Review," *New Zealand Evening Post*, 19 September 1874, 2; "Review," *Otago (New Zealand) Times* supplement, 30 January 1875, 6.

12. "The Gilded Age," *Melbourne Argus*, 28 March 1874, 4; "News of the Day," *Melbourne Age*, 19 March 1874, 2; *Brisbane Courier*, 24 March 1874, 3; *Brisbane Courier*, 25 April 1874, 3; "The Gilded Age," *Melbourne Australasian*, 11 April 1874, 8; "Review," *Sydney Empire*, 21

August 1874, 4; "The Gilded Age," *Brisbane Queenslander*, 16 May 1874, 7; "The Gilded Age," *Auckland Star*, 6 October 1876, 3.

13. *New Orleans Southwestern Advocate*, 15 January 1874, 2; Budd, *MTCR*, 119–20, 137–38; "Some New Books," *San Francisco Chronicle*, 15 March 1874, 2; Kaplan, *The Singular Mark Twain*, 467; "New Publications," *Philadelphia Press*, 13 January 1874, 6; "New Publications," *Portland Oregonian*, 21 March 1874, 2; "The Gilded Age," *Alexandria (La.) Caucasian*, 18 April 1874, 3; "The Gilded Age," *SFB*, 21 March 1874, 2.

14. *Waco Examiner*, 22 April 1874, 2; Budd, *MTCR*, 117–19, 132–34; "Paragraphical," *Nashville Union and American*, 31 December 1873, 3; "Mrs. Burnham after Twain and Warner," *Providence Press*, 2 February 1874, 4; Machor, "A Trying Five Years," 17.

15. Budd, *MTCR*, 130–31; Crowley, "A Note on *The Gilded Age*," 117.

16. Hill, "Mark Twain's Book Sales," 382; *MTL*, 6:32, 6:34, 6:47, 6:53–54; "Tributes to Poet by Men of Letters," *NYT*, 24 February 1907, pictorial sec., 4; Higginson, *Thomas Wentworth Higginson*, 259; "The Massachusetts Press," *BA*, 18 February 1874, 4; *MTSpk*, 83–87.

17. *MTL*, 5:364, 5:523, 5:539–40; Paine, *MTB*, 502; *MTL*, 6:43; "Roughing It," *BJ*, 6 March 1874, 1; "Mark Twain's Reappearance in America," *BA*, 6 March 1874, 1; "Mark Twain's 'Roughing It,'" *BH*, 6 March 1874, 4; "Roughing It," *Boston Globe*, 6 March 1874, 5.

18. Aldrich, *Crowding Memories*, 145; *AMT*, 1:229, 3:241; Howells, *My MT*, iv–v, 187.

19. W. D. Howells to J. M. Comly, 21 March 1874, UCLC 48588; Cardwell, *The Man Who Was Mark Twain*, 50; *MTHL*, 71; Aldrich, *Crowding Memories*, 158–59; Kaplan, *Mr. Clemens and Mark Twain*, 174.

20. Budd, *MTCR*, 108; "Personal," *NYEP*, 8 April 1874, 2, and *NYEP*, 15 April 1874, 2; *MTL*, 6:102–5; "Mark Twain's Banquet," *HC*, 14 April 1874, 2.

21. *CIO*, 24 April 1874, 4; "A Cruel Hoax," *Sacramento Union*, 29 April 1874, 1; "The Jumping Frog," *Dubuque Herald*, 21 April 1874, 4; "Clemmens' [sic] Arrival, *Dubuque Herald*, 22 April 1874, 4; "The Clemmens [sic] Trial," *Dubuque Herald*, 24 April 1874, 4; "The Jumping Frog Swindle," *Dubuque Herald*, 25 April 1874, 1; "Caught on the Fly," *Dubuque Herald*, 24 April 1874, 4, and *Dubuque Herald*, 25 April 1874, 4; *MTL*, 6:117, 6:122–23, 6:143–44; *MTCI*, 98–99.

22. *MTCI*, 98–99; "Today's Amusements," *CIO*, 2 July 1875, 4; SLC to Percy F. Sinnett, 24 July 1881, UCCL 09442; *Following the Equator*, 158–60; "Letter from Mark Twain," *Christchurch (New Zealand) Press*, 12 February 1890, 5; "A Fraud That Failed to Pan Out," *Cincinnati Commercial Tribune*, 26 July 1888, 1.

23. *MTL*, 6:109, 6:127, 6:498n4; *MTHL*, 16; *MTMF*, 184–86; Cardwell, *The Man Who Was Mark Twain*, 150; *N&J*, 2:370.

24. *MTL*, 6:157, 6:196, 6:416; Salsbury, *Susy and Mark Twain*, 186; *MTHL*, 71; *AMT*, 3:44–45.

25. *MTL*, 6:158, 6:222; Clark, "Mark Twain at 'Nook Farm,'" 25; *MTMF*, 205–9.

26. *MTL*, 6:221–25, 6:540; *AMT*, 2:196; *MTHL*, 89, 92; Smith, *Mark Twain: The Development*, 90.

27. *MTL*, 6:126–27, 6:267.

28. E. J. Edwards asserts that SLC "bought Warner's rights to the dramatic representation for a few hundred dollars, and Warner for a time thought he had made the best of the bargain" (Edwards, "The Literary World," *Ogdensburg [N.Y.] Journal*, 28 May 1891, 3). But both Joe Twichell and Frank Bliss, Elisha's son, testified that SLC had paid Warner "nothing for

relinquishing his right to share the profits of 'The Gilded Age' play" (Jerry W. Thomason, "Colonel Sellers," in LeMaster and Wilson, *The Routledge Encyclopedia of Mark Twain*, 165). Twichell informed Paine in June 1911 that the pact sparked "some unpleasantness" between the two (*MTL*, 6:129), though Paine in his authorized biography insisted that there had been "no bitterness" at all, "no semblance of an estrangement of any sort" (Paine, *MTB*, 518).

29. Harte, *Letters*, 252; Murphy, *American Realism and American Drama*, 51.

30. *MTL*, 6:267–73; Paine, *MTB*, 518; John T. Raymond, "The Gilded Age," *NYS*, 3 November 1874, 2.

31. Lawrence Barrett to SLC, 25 May 1874, UCLC 31992; *AMT*, 1:207; "Colonel Sellers," *Boston Globe*, 23 March 1876, 3; "Col. Sellers," *New York Sunday Mercury*, 22 August 1875, 1.

32. Hill, "Toward a Critical Text," 147; "The Gilded Age," *HC*, 1 May 1874, 2; *MTL*, 6:267–72; *NYH*, 19 July 1874, 9; *MTHL*, 20, 26.

33. *MTHL*, 22–23; Sedgwick, *A History of the Atlantic Monthly*, 127.

34. *MTHL*, 24; *The Innocents Abroad*, 602. This view is perhaps best expressed in fiction by Marie St. Clair in chapter 16 of *Uncle Tom's Cabin* by SLC's Hartford neighbor Harriet Beecher Stowe: "Mammy couldn't have the feelings that I should. It's a different thing altogether" (252). Rhett S. Jones notes that "white Americans" were comforted by the belief that slave mothers "were much like bitches deprived of their litter. The dog might miss them for a few days, but soon forgot her pups" (Jones, "Nigger and Knowledge," 30).

35. "A True Story," *Atlantic Monthly* 34 (November 1874): 591–94; *MTHL*, 22–23. See also Conroy and Sloane, "'A True Story' Confirmed."

36. Quirk, *Mark Twain: A Study of the Short Fiction*, 18; *MTHL*, 24, 26; "Sociable Jimmy," 7; *Huckleberry Finn* (1885), 201.

37. *MTHL*, 25, 32; Paine, *MTB*, 516.

38. *MTL*, 6:349, 6:658; W. D. Howells, "Recent Literature," *Atlantic Monthly* 36 (December 1875): 750; "The Atlantic," *NYEP*, 19 October 1874, 1; "The November Magazines," *NYT*, 22 October 1874, 2; "Literary Chit Chat," *NYH*, 26 October 1874, 5; Louise Chandler Moulton, "Boston Literary Notes," *NYTrib*, 15 October 1874, 6; *Western Christian Advocate*, 21 October 1874, 333; Wuster, *Mark Twain: American Humorist*, 436.

39. "Lyceum Notes," *BA*, 30 September 1874, 1; *MTL*, 6:216, 6:221; "Stage Affairs," *NYTrib*, 30 August 1876, 4; "Colonel Sellers," *Boston Globe*, 23 March 1876, 3; "Miscellaneous Notes," *CIO*, 6 September 1874, 2; "The 'Gilded Age,'" *Buffalo Express*, 8 September 1874, 1; Wuster, *Mark Twain: American Humorist*, 225; "City Summary," *New York Clipper*, 19 September 1874, 198.

40. "Colonel Sellers," *Boston Globe*, 23 March 1876, 3; Wuster, *Mark Twain: American Humorist*, 230; *MTL*, 6:238, 6:271; "Raymond on 'Sellers,'" *Cleveland Plain Dealer*, 24 March 1876, 1; French, "Mark Twain, Laura D. Fair, and the New York Criminal Courts," 558; "Another Speech from Mark Twain," *New Orleans Times*, 21 September 1874, 6; "Col. Sellers," *New York Sunday Mercury*, 22 August 1875, 1.

41. William Winter, "The Drama," *NYTrib*, 18 September 1874, 4; "Park Theatre," *NYT*, 17 September 1874, 6; "Park Theatre," *NYH*, 17 September 1874, 10; "New York Letter," *Baltimore Bulletin*, 26 September 1874, 1; "Park Theatre," *New York Graphic*, 17 September 1874, 3; "Critical Opinions," *NYH*, 21 September 1874, 2; "Amusements," *New York Commercial Advertiser*, 22 September 1874, 1.

42. "The Park Theatre," *NYEP*, 29 September 1874, 2; "Musical and Dramatic Notes," *NYH*, 29 September 1874, 7; *MTHL*, 32.

43. "Personal," *NYEP*, 20 April 1875, 2; W. D. Howells, "Drama," *Atlantic Monthly* 35 (June 1875): 749–51.

44. "Park Theatre," New York *Evening Express*, 17 September 1874, 2; "The Academy of Music," *CT*, 14 March 1875, 8; "Dramatic, Musical, Etc.," *Philadelphia North American*, 5 October 1875, 2; "Mark Twain's New Play," *HC*, 25 September 1874, 2; "Mark Twain's Simple Play and the Way It Was Spoiled," *SFB*, 22 October 1874, 1; Field, "Notes from the United States," *Athenaeum*, 9 January 1875, 53.

45. *MTL*, 6:267–73, 6:328; John T. Raymond, "The Gilded Age," *NYS*, 3 November 1874, 2; Matthews, *The Tocsin of Revolt*, 254; "Amusements," *NYT*, 24 December 1874, 4.

46. "Amusements," *New York Commercial Advertiser*, 29 August 1876, 1.

47. *MTL*, 6:232, 6:643; Nym Crinkle [Andrew C. Wheeler], "Ah Sin," *NYS*, 5 August 1877, 5; Nym Crinkle [Andrew C. Wheeler], "Park Theatre," *NYS*, 8 January 1878, 1; Nym Crinkle [Andrew C. Wheeler], "John T. Raymond," *NYS*, 9 June 1878, 5; Nym Crinkle [Andrew C. Wheeler], "Mark Twain's Plays," *Kansas City Star*, 8 October 1887, 2.

48. Wagenknecht, *Mark Twain: The Man and His Work*, 375; "The Park Theatre," *NYH*, 24 December 1874, 5; Paine, *MTB*, 540.

49. "Col. Sellers," *New York Sunday Mercury*, 22 August 1875, 1; *MTL*, 6:241; Howells 783; *MTHL*, 81–82; *AMT*, 1:207.

50. "Another Speech from Mark Twain," *New Orleans Times*, 21 September 1874, 6; *AMT*, 1:206; "Colonel Sellers," *Boston Globe*, 23 March 1876, 3.

51. Andrews, *Nook Farm*, 98; Annie Moffett to Samuel Moffett, 12 January 1875, *UCLC* 31580; "Colonel Sellers," *HC*, 12 January 1875, 2; Paine, *MTB*, 539.

52. "Coulisse Chat," *NYH*, 17 January 1875, 12; Scharnhorst, "He Is Amusing," 199–200.

53. "Theatres, *London Graphic*, 24 July 1880, 87; "The London Theatres," *London Era*, 25 July 1880, 12; "The Examiner of Plays," *London Examiner*, 24 July 1880, 889; "The Gaiety Theatre," *London Times*, 22 July 1880, 4; "Music and the Drama," *Glasgow Herald*, 26 July 1880, 5; "The London Dramatic Season of 1880," *Melbourne Argus*, 9 October 1880, 4; Kate Field, "London Stage Gossip," *New York Graphic*, 19 August 1880, 361; *LMT&JHT*, 101; "Music and Drama," *Sydney Mail*, 5 October 1878, 546.

54. Field, *Memories*, 253; Howells, *My MT*, 23; *MTL*, 6:525–29; "Mark Twain's Rights," *CIO*, 30 September 1876, 6; "The Theatres," *NYTrib*, 29 January 1888, 12; Schirer, *Mark Twain and the Theatre*, 56; *MTHL*, 159, 372. See also *N&J*, 3:455: "R[aymond] & I divided $140,000."

55. "Hartford Accident Insurance Co.," *HC*, 20 June 1874, 4; *AMT*, 2:55, 490; Paine, *MTB*, 726; *N&J*, 2:38; "Personal Intelligence," *NYH*, 1 July 1874, 4, and *NYH*, 5 July 1874, 6; "Mark Twain on Accident Insurance," *BA*, 17 October 1874, 1.

56. *MTHL*, 22; Simpson and Simpson, *Jean Webster*, 11; *MTL*, 6:207–8, 6:515.

57. "Arrivals at the Hotels," *NYT*, 12 September 1874, 12; *MTL*, 6:237–38, 6:244–47; *MTHL*, 26, 49.

58. Paine, *MTB*, 522; Andrews, *Nook Farm*, 82; Howells, *My MT*, 37; Willis, *Mark and Livy*, 94; *Hartford Times*, 23 March 1874; Mary Mason Fairbanks, "Letter from 'Myra,'" *Cleveland Herald*, 4 May 1874, 4; Conway, *Autobiography*, 2:143; *MTL*, 5:173–76; *LMT&-JHT*, 191.

59. *MTL*, 6:89, 6:156, 6:238, 6:583; *A Family Sketch*, 17, 20–21; Kaplan, *The Singular Mark Twain*, 306; Paine, *MTB*, 573; Howells, *My MT*, 34; *MTHL*, 158.

Chapter 5

1. Courtney, *Joseph Hopkins Twichell*, 157; Twichell, "Mark Twain," 820; *TA*, 221; *LMT&-JHT*, 74; "Mark Twain as a Pedestrian," *BJ*, 14 November 1874, 2.

2. *MTCI*, 3–4; *MTL*, 6:275; Camfield, *Oxford Companion*, 456.

3. *MTCI*, 2, 4; *MTL*, 6:278; Courtney, *Joseph Hopkins Twichell*, 158; Kolb, *Mark Twain: The Gift of Humor*, 170; *N&J*, 2:87; *AMT*, 2:620; Messent, *Mark Twain and Male Friendship*, 49.

4. "Mine Host and Mark Twain," *Kansas City Times*, 28 February 1889, 2; *MTL*, 6:282–85; Andrews, *Nook Farm*, 257; *MTL*, 6:280; "About Town," *BA*, 14 November 1874, 1; *MTHL*, 36; "Mark Twain as a Pedestrian," *BJ*, 14 November 1874, 2.

5. *MTL*, 6:282, 6:284–85; Howells, *My MT*, 45; *MTHL*, 87.

6. *MTHL*, 34, 62; Harte, *Selected Letters*, 101; Howells, *Life in Letters of William Dean Howells*, 1:194; W. D. Howells to M. M. Hurd, 7 November 1874, UCLC 48590.

7. *MTL*, 4:498–500; *MTCI*, 161; *MTHL*, 42–44, 46, 47, 49, 62.

8. *AMT*, 1:222; *MTL*, 6:324–26; Louise Chandler Moulton, "Boston Literary Notes," *NYTrib*, 12 December 1874, 8; Louise Chandler Moulton, "Boston Literary Notes," *NYTrib*, 18 March 1875, 8; "The January Magazines," *NYEP*, 19 December 1874, 6; "January Magazines," *CIO*, 20 December 1874, 5; "Old Times on the Mississippi," *CIO*, 21 February 1875, 6.

9. "An 'Atlantic Monthly' Dinner," *SFB*, 2 January 1875, 4.

10. "A Dinner on Parnassus," *NYTrib*, 18 December 1874, 3; George Parsons Lathrop, "The Atlantic Dinner," *NYEP*, 17 December 1874, 2; W. D. Howells to W. C. Howells, 20 December 1874, UCLC 49315.

11. Howells, *Literary Friends and Acquaintance*, 324–25.

12. Cox, *Mark Twain: The Fate of Humor*, 106, 109; Branch, "Old Times on the Mississippi," 85; Hugo D. Johnson, "Labor," in LeMaster and Wilson, *The Routledge Encyclopedia of Mark Twain*, 436; *MTHL*, 85.

13. "The February Atlantic," *BA*, 16 January 1875, 2; "Literary News and Gossip," *SFB*, 24 July 1875, 1; "Magazine Notices," *Portland (Maine) Press*, 20 March 1875, 2; *New Orleans Bulletin*, 9 April 1875, 6; "Personal," *CT*, 3 April 1875, 9; "March Magazines," *Milwaukee Sentinel*, 6 March 1875, 2; "The Atlantic," *Cincinnati Star*, 31 March 1875, 1; "The June Magazines," *CIO*, 29 May 1875, 6; "Literary Notes," *New York Evangelist*, 27 May 1875, 6.

14. "Old Times on the Mississippi," 219, 288–89, 446.

15. "Lecture by Mark Twain," *HC*, 22 February 1875, 2; *MTL*, 6:392, 6:395; "Mark Twain's Lecture," *HC*, 23 February 1875, 2.

16. "Mark Twain's Lecture," *HC*, 6 March 1875, 1; "Father Hawley's Acknowledgment," *HC*, 8 March 1875, 2; *MTL*, 6:393, 6:403, 6:603; "Liberal Mark Twain," *Milwaukee Sentinel*, 11 December 1875, 2; "A Book of Autographs," *New York Graphic*, 8 December 1875, 6.

17. Lynn, *William Dean Howells*, 103–4; Willis, *Mark and Livy*, 96; *MTL*, 6:413; *MTHL*, 70–71, 290.

18. *MTL*, 5:235–38; "Mr. Theodore Tilton Tells All He Knows," *BE*, 21 July 1874, 2; *MTL*, 6:202.

19. *MTHL*, 227; *MTL*, 6:427–28, 6:446, 6:449; "Ragged Edge in Earnest," *NYS*, 15 April 1875, 2; "Mark Twain Non-Committal," *New York Graphic*, 15 April 1875, 3.

20. Gribben, *Mark Twain's Library*, 56; Howells, *My MT*, 68; Bush, *Mark Twain and the Spiritual Crisis*, 105; *MTMF*, 192; Isabel Lyon diary, 27 February 1906, MTP.

21. *MTL*, 6:452, 6:455; Howells, *My MT*, 39–41; *MTHL*, 76.

22. SLC to Frank M. Etting, 23 February 1876, *UCCL* 01339; "Francis Lightfoot Lee," *Pennsylvania Magazine of History and Biography* 1 (1877): 343–45; *N&J*, 2:126; *MTMF*, 202.

23. *MTL*, 6:460–63; Leon, *Mark Twain and West Point*, 41; Lorch, *The Trouble Begins at Eight*, 153–54; "Personal," *NHJC*, 8 March 1881, 2; *N&J*, 2:126; *Tom Sawyer*, 269.

24. *MTHL*, 92; *MTL*, 6:379; Melville, *Correspondence*, 191.

25. DeVoto, *Mark Twain at Work*, 13; *MTHL*, 110–12; *Tom Sawyer*, viii; *MTLP*, 96–97; Stone, *The Innocent Eye*, 60; Hill, *Mark Twain and Elisha Bliss*, 118; Hill, "Mark Twain's Book Sales," 385.

26. *MTHL*, 122, 124.

27. *MTL*, 6:424, 426, 432, 436.

28. *MTL*, 6:486–88, 585; "Personal," *NYEP*, 25 May 1875, 2; "Dan DeQuille's Book," *Virginia City (Nev.) Territorial Enterprise*, 23 February 1876, 2; "Something Regarding Twain," *Carson (Nev.) Appeal*, 23 March 1881, 2; *MTLP*, 99.

29. Loomis, "Dan De Quille's Mark Twain"; *AMT*, 2:418; *MTL*, 6:521; Salsbury, *Susy and Mark Twain*, 43; *AMT*, 2:385.

30. Roche, "Making a Reputation." John Seelye has asserted that SLC first wore an iconic white suit when he "appeared before a congressional committee [in 1906] to argue for international copyright" (Seelye, "What's in a Name," 412). However, Louis J. Budd contends that SLC had "sported white summer 'ducks' or linen suits since the early 1870s" (Budd, "Mark Twain's Visual Humor," 470). Similarly, Clara Clemens noted, "From the earliest moment that I can remember, Father wore white linen suits in summer" (Clemens, *My Father, Mark Twain*, 78).

31. "In General," *BA*, 24 August 1875, 1; "Newport," *BJ*, 26 August 1875, 2; Briden, "Mark Twain's Rhode Island Lectures," 37; "Watering-Place Gossip," *Boston Traveller*, 27 August 1875, 2; "Brief Mention," *HC*, 9 September 1875, 2.

32. Longfellow, *Letters*, 6:75; Howells, *My MT*, 47.

33. *MTHL*, 99.

34. *MTL*, 6:488, 6:494–95, 6:511; *MTHL*, 91; *MTLP*, 93–95.

35. *MTL*, 6:349–50; *Sketches, New and Old*, 96.

36. Harrington and Jenn, *Mark Twain and France*, 93; Dumas, "Some Remarks," 149; *MTL*, 5:357–59; Paine, *MTB*, 550; "He Saw No Humor," *Portland Oregonian*, 4 August 1889, 9; "At the Home of Daudet," *NYT*, 26 April 1885, 6; *MTCI*, 146–47.

37. *MTL*, 5:72–74, 6:380.

38. Feinstein, "Mark Twain's Lawsuits," 82; *MTHL*, 106–7; W. D. Howells, "Recent Literature," *Atlantic Monthly* 36 (December 1875): 749–50; Budd, *MTCR*, 149–53; "Mark Twain's Sketches," *Mining & Scientific Press*, 1 January 1876, 12; "Mark Twain's Sketches, New and Old," *Moore's Rural New-Yorker*, 4 December 1875, 370; Hill, "Mark Twain's Book Sales," 384.

39. George Barclay to SLC, 28 February 1876, *UCLC* 32297; SLC to James Redpath, 17 March 1876, *UCCL* 01314; "News Notes," *New York Commercial Advertiser*, 25 March 1876, 3.

40. "Personal," *New York Graphic*, 29 March 1876, 6; "Mark Twain's Lecture," *NYH*, 30 March 1876, 10; "Twain Again," *New York World*, 29 March 1876, 5; Fields, *Memories*, 256; "New York Press Club Reception," *NYT*, 31 March 1876, 5; "People and Things," *CIO*, 6 April 1876, 4; Fields, "Bret Harte and Mark Twain'"; George Barclay to SLC, 5 May 1876, *UCLC* 32344.

41. *MTHL*, 130, 133, 147, 158, 160.

42. "Hartford Dramatic Association," *HC*, 13 November 1875, 2; Daly, *The Life of Augustin Daly*, 146; SLC to Moncure D. Conway, 5 May 1876, *UCCL* 01332; "The Amateur Theatricals," *HC*, 27 April 1876, 2; Ellsworth, *A Golden Age*, 223; Andrews, *Nook Farm*, 98; Fredericks, "The Profane Twain," 9; Salsbury, *Susy and Mark Twain*, 50; Fields, "Bret Harte and Mark Twain," 346; Fields, *Memories*, 246–47; Paine, *MTB*, 571. See also Lawton, *A Lifetime*, 36.

43. Fields, "Bret Harte and Mark Twain," 348; Salsbury, *Susy and Mark Twain*, 53; *MTHL*, 136; SLC to Moncure D. Conway, 5 May 1876, *UCCL* 01332.

44. Young, "Anna Dickinson, Mark Twain, and Bret Harte," 41; *MTL*, 3:66; Fields, *Memories*, 250; *CC*, 11 May 1876, 8; Daly, *The Life of Augustin Daly*, 233; Howells, *My MT*, 57; SLC to W. D. Howells, 4 May 1876, *UCCL* 02502.

45. William Winter, "Anna Dickinson's Debut in Boston," *NYTrib*, 9 May 1876, 5; "Miss Dickinson's Debut," *New York Commercial Advertiser*, 9 May 1876, 6; "Anna Dickinson's Debut," *WC*, 9 May 1876, 4; "Anna Dickinson's Debut," *CIO*, 12 May 1876, 2; "Amusements," *NYT*, 9 May 1876, 7; "Pour Les Dames," *St. Louis Globe-Democrat*, 14 May 1876, 2; "Anna Dickinson's Debut," *NYH*, 9 May 1876, 3; "Anna Scalps the Critics," *NYS*, 10 April 1977, 1; "Miss Dickinson's Debut," *Connecticut Courant*, 6 May 1876, 1.

46. "Contributor's Club," *Atlantic Monthly* 39 (January 1877): 108; *MTMF*, 234.

47. Fields, "Bret Harte and Mark Twain," 347; *Europe and Elsewhere*, 142; *AMT*, 1:269; Andrews, *Nook Farm*, 139.

48. Budd, *MTCR*, 551–53, 565; Wagenknecht, *Mark Twain: The Man and His Work*, 230.

49. "The Curious Republic of Gondour," *Atlantic Monthly* 36 (October 1875): 461–63; Fields, *Memories*, 252; Julian Hawthorne, "When Mark Twain Miscued," 5. Six years later SLC complained to his lawyer Charles Enoch Perkins that the city authorities had "jumped my tax up in such a lively fashion . . . that I sold every taxable thing I had, & put the money into manufacturing-stocks & such like. Next year I'll put a mortgage on the house & not have a damned thing that's taxable." If he could not cast plural votes, he at least wanted to save money. SLC to Charles Enoch Perkins, 2 September 1882, *UCCL* 02262.

50. SLC to Mollie Fairbanks, 6 August 1877, *UCCL* 01467; Howells, *My MT*, 77; "New England News," *Worcester (Mass.) Spy*, 28 May 1875, 3; "Mark Twain as Mayor," *Virginia City (Nev.) Territorial Enterprise*, 6 February 1876, 2.

51. *MTHL*, 143; "Political Notes," *NYTrib*, 18 August 1876, 4; "Our Hartford Letter," *SR*, 31 March 1881, 4.

52. *MTHL*, 145–46, 151, 154; *MTCI*, 5–6; Budd, *Mark Twain: Social Philosopher*, 65.

53. "Meeting of the Missionaries," *New York Graphic*, 3 October 1876, 3; "Mark Twain in Politics," *NYT*, 2 October 1876, 1; *MTSpk*, 97–99; Kohn, "Mark Twain and Joseph Roswell Hawley," 72; "Mark Twain in Politics," *CT*, 7 October 1876, 2; *MTHL*, 156; *Boston Transcript*, 3 October 1876, 4; "Mark Twain's Last Joke," *New Orleans Times*, 11 October 1876, 3.

54. Messent, "Mark Twain, Joseph Twichell," 386; *AMT*, 2:419, 2:424–25, 2:519; *MTHL*, 259–62.

55. *MTHL*, 162, 172, 187; *AMT*, 2:424.

56. Camfield, *Oxford Companion*, 330; Quirk, *Mark Twain and Human Nature*, 98; Doyno, *Writing Huck Finn*, 163.

57. Quirk, *Mark Twain: A Study of the Short Fiction*, 65; Baetzhold, *Mark Twain and John Bull*, 58–59; Messent, "Mark Twain, Joseph Twichell," 386; *MTHL*, 119, 123.

58. Gibson, *The Art of Mark Twain*, 181; *Collected Tales*, 644–60; Cardwell, *The Man Who Was Mark Twain*, 42: Howells, *Selected Letters*, 127; Howells, "Mark Twain," 782; "The Atlantic Monthly," *NYEP*, 16 May 1876, 1; "The Magazines," *Louisville Courier-Journal*, 23 May 1876, 3; "Books and Authors," *Christian Union*, 31 May 1876, 442; Mary Mason Fairbanks to SLC, 1 June 1876, *UCLC* 32367; "June Magazines," *Literary World*, 1 June 1876, 10.

59. SLC to Moncure D. Conway, 5 January 1876, *UCCL* 01295; Moncure D. Conway to Ellen Conway, 18 January 1876, *UCLC* 32267; *MTLP*, 96–97; Welland, *Mark Twain in England*, 31.

60. *MTHL*, 111, 121, 127–28; *MTLP*, 95; "Items," *Boston Transcript*, 28 April 1876, 6.

61. *MTLP*, 98, 100–102; Schirer, *Mark Twain and the Theatre*, 55; *MTLP*, 99; Hill, *Mark Twain and Elisha Bliss*, 124; SLC to the Board of Editors, American Publishing Company, 24 June 1876, *UCCL* 01346.

62. *MTLP*, 100–102; SLC to Charles Warren Stoddard, 20 September 1876, *UCCL* 01366; Hill, *Mark Twain and Elisha Bliss*, 118.

63. Welland, *Mark Twain in England*, 78; W. D. Howells, "Recent Literature," *Atlantic Monthly* 37 (May 1876): 621–22; *MTHL*, 128, 134; *MTLP*, 96–97,104–5; *MTHL*, 134.

64. Welland, *Mark Twain in England*, 237; SLC to Chatto & Windus, 1 May 1880, *UCCL* 00783; Moncure D. Conway, "Mark Twain's New Book," *London Examiner*, 17 June 1876, 687–88; Budd, *MTCR*, 158, 160–61; "Tom Sawyer," *London Post*, 18 September 1876, 3; "New Books and New Editions," *Pall Mall Gazette*, 28 October 1876, 11; "Novels of the Week," *Athenaeum*, 24 June 1876, 851; Scharnhorst, *Critical Essays on* The Adventures of Tom Sawyer, 26, 38–41, 43.

65. Moncure D. Conway, "London Letter," *CC*, 26 June 1876, 5; SLC to Moncure D. Conway 24 July 1876, *UCCL* 01351. Both the *CT* (3 July 1876) and the *HC* (8 July 1876) reprinted Conway's letter in full. The following papers reprinted excerpts from the novel cited in Conway's column prior to U.S. publication (all dates are 1876): *NYEP*, 28 June; *Boston Transcript*, 29 and 30 June, 6 July; *HC*, 30 June, 26 July; *Cincinnati Gazette*, 3 July; *Cincinnati Enquirer*, 5 July; *Boston Globe*, 6 and 11 July; *New York Graphic*, 6 July; *SR*, 7 and 12 July; *SFB*, 8 and 15 July; *St. Louis Globe-Democrat*, 8 July and 19 August; San Francisco *Call*, 9, 13, and 16 July; St. Louis *Post-Dispatch* 10 July and 28 August; *American Socialist*, 13 July; *CT*, 15 July; *New York Commercial Advertiser*, 15 July; *Lowell (Mass.) Citizen*, 15 July; *Wisconsin State Register*, 15 July; *Portland (Maine) Transcript*, 15 July, 26 August; *New Orleans Picayune*, 21 July; Philadelphia *Sunday Republic*, 23 July; *San Francisco Alta California*, 28 July; *Portland (Maine) Eastern Argus*, 31 July; *Concord (N.H.) Independent Statesman*, 3 August; *Providence Press*, 3 August; *Portland Oregonian*, 4 August; *Cincinnati Times*, 5 August; and *Christian Union*, 23 August. In addition, at least nine papers in Australia copied excerpts from the novel in September and October 1876, including the *Sydney Mail* (2 September), *Hobart Tribune* and *Portland Guardian* (13 October), *Queensland Times* (14 October), and *Warwick Examiner* (21 October); the entire novel was later serialized in the *Brisbane Week* between March and June 1878. At least five papers in New Zealand copied excerpts from the novel prior to publication: *Christchurch (New Zealand) Star*, 15 September; *New Zealand Times*, 16 September; *Christchurch (New Zealand) Globe*, 22 September; *Hokitika (New Zealand) West Coast Times*, 23 September; and *Thames Advertiser*, 28 December. A passage from the novel was also reprinted by a Paris newspaper (Welland, "A Note on Some Early Reviews of *Tom Sawyer*," 102).

66. "The Adventures of Tom Sawyer," *Toronto Mail*, 25 July 1876, 3; *MTLP*, 105–6; SLC to Chatto & Windus, 1 May 1880, *UCCL* 00783.

67. *MTLP*, 105–6; Belford Bros. to W. D. Howells, 29 November 1876, *UCCL* 00783; *MTHL*, 167; Hill, *Mark Twain and Elisha Bliss*, 126.

68. SLC to Bernhard von Tauchnitz 14 September 1876, *UCCL* 01364; SLC to Bernhard von Tauchnitz, 7 October 1880, *UCCL* 01837; Griffin, "'American Laughter.'"

69. Elisha Bliss to SLC, 11 December 1876, *UCLC* 32451; *MTLP*, 106–7.

70. SLC to Moncure D. Conway, 10 January 1877, *UCCL* 01400; Roper, "Mark Twain and His Canadian Publishers," 49; "Mark Twain in a Lawsuit," *CT*, 26 April 1879, 3; "Canadian Book Bushwhackers," *CC*, 26 April 1879, 7.

71. Feinstein, "Mark Twain's Lawsuits," 102–3, 107; "'Mark Twain' Confirmed," *CT*, 20 May 1878, 8.

72. *MTHL*, 95–96; *Hannibal, Huck, and Tom*, 245; SLC to Moncure D. Conway, 24 July 1876, *UCCL* 01351; Schirer, *Mark Twain and the Theatre*, 49.

73. William Bowen to SLC, 25 August 1876, *UCLC* 32410; SLC to William Bowen, 31 August 1876, *UCCL* 01360; SLC to Jacob Burrough, 1 November 1876, *UCCL* 01384.

74. "Mark Twain in Brooklyn," *NYS*, 14 November 1876, 1; "Musical," *BE*, 14 November 1876, 3; "The Star Course," *Philadelphia Inquirer*, 15 November 1876, 2; "'Mark Twain' in Philadelphia," *HC*, 16 November 1876, 2; SLC to Thomas Nast, 12 November 1877, *UCCL* 02518.

75. "Mark Twain and Miss Thursby at Music Hall," *Providence Press*, 24 November 1876, 2; "About Town," *BA*, 22 November 1876, 4; "Chelsea," *BA*, 24 November 1876, 4; Briden, "Mark Twain's Rhode Island Lectures."

76. SLC to Bayard Taylor, 24 January 1877, *UCCL* 01403; *AMT*, 2:418–20; SLC to Hjalmar Hjorth Boyesen, 17 January 1877, *UCCL* 12673.

Chapter 6

1. Camfield, *Oxford Companion*, 17; Hill, *Mark Twain and Elisha Bliss*, 117, 120; Schirer, *Mark Twain and the Theatre*, 55; Dreiser, "Mark the Double Twain," 622; Paine, *MTB*, 586.

2. C. D. Warner, "Literary Notices," *HC*, 27 December 1876, 1; "New Publications," *Baltimore Sun*, 29 December 1876, 2; *SR*, 13 January 1877, 8; "Tom Sawyer," *San Francisco Alta California*, 15 January 1877, 2; "Mark Twain's Latest Book," *Boston Globe*, 29 December 1876, 4; *NHJC*, 21 December 1876, 1; "New Publications," *NYT*, 13 January 1877, 3; Budd, *MTCR*, 161–66; "Among Children's Books," *Sydney Herald*, 15 December 1880, 8; "Literature," *Adelaide Observer*, 13 March 1880, 33; "Literature for Children," *Brisbane Courier*, 28 December 1881, 3; "Literature," *Melbourne Australasian*, 30 September 1876, 8.

3. Harris, "Mark Twain's Response to the Native American," 495; Howells, "A Sennight of the Centennial," 103; "Mr. Beecher's Anticipations," *NYT*, 10 October 1885, 5; *MTCI*, 287; *Connecticut Yankee*, 40, 556.

4. *MTMF*, 198–200; SLC to Jane Lampton Clemens and Pamela Moffett, 22 June 1876, *UCCL* 12738; *MTHL*, 138–39, 144; *MTLP*, 102–4; Smith, *Mark Twain: The Development*, 119; *Huckleberry Finn* (1885), 121.

5. Lynn, *William Dean Howells*, 404; Quirk, *Mark Twain's Adventures of Huckleberry Finn*, 125.

6. *AMT*, 2:155–56; SLC to Charles Orr, 30 July 1906, *UCCL* 07486; *N&J*, 2:303; Howells, *Life in Letters of William Dean Howells*, 1:398–99; Fears, *Mark Twain Day-by-Day*, 2:38. The other three convicted "anarchists" were granted pardons by the governor of Illinois in June 1893.

7. Kaplan, *The Singular Mark Twain*, 337; Howells, *My MT*, 4; Harris, "Mark Twain and Gender," 188; *AMT*, 2:155; *1601*, 16; *MTHL*, 147–48; *N&J*, 2:303; Paine, *MTB*, 581; Kohn, "Mark Twain's *1601*," 50; SLC to William Bowen, 31 August 1876, *UCCL* 01360.

8. Stahl, *Mark Twain, Culture and Gender*, 92; *LMT&JHT*, 98; John Hay to Alexander Gunn, 24 June 1880, *UCLC* 39194; SLC to Orion Clemens, 28 February 1880, *UCCL* 01764; SLC to Pamela Moffett, 28 February 1880, *UCCL* 01765; Fears, *Mark Twain Day-by-Day*, 1:817; Leon, *Mark Twain and West Point*, 57; *AMT*, 2:155; *Connecticut Yankee*, 204.

9. SLC to Charles E. S. Wood, 21 February 1882, *UCCL* 02161; SLC to Charles E. S. Wood, 3 April 1882, *UCCL* 02196; *AMT*, 2:155, 2:535–36; Leon, *Mark Twain and West Point*, 59.

10. Paine, *MTB*, 581; Meine, "Introduction," in *1601* (1938), 17, 27–28; Ferguson, *Mark Twain*, 185; Stone, *The Innocent Eye*, 75; Folsom and Loving, "The Walt Whitman Controversy," 126; Stahl, *Mark Twain, Culture and Gender*, 57; Blair, *Mark Twain and Huck Finn*, ix; Wood, "Introduction," in *1601* (1925), n.p.; *AMT*, 2:156.

11. "The Sorosis Ribbons," *NYH*, 22 December 1876, 2; "Forefathers," *BA*, 23 December 1876, 1; "The Morning's News," *NYEP*, 23 December 1876, 1; "The Dinner and the Speeches," *NYTrib*, 23 December 1876, 7; "Notes," *Chicago Advance*, 28 December 1876, 298; "Forefathers' Day," *NYT*, 23 December 1876, 1; Budd, *MTCR*, 673; "Life in New York City," *BE*, 8 March 1885, 2; *MTSpk*, 263; "Our Hartford Letter," *SR*, 15 December 1877, 3; Messent, *Mark Twain and Male Friendship*, 56.

12. *MTMF*, 228; Paine, *MTB*, 583; *AMT*, 3:47, 3:461, 3:463–64.

13. "Mark Twain as an Auctioneer," *Albany Journal*, 18 December 1876, 1; "Connecticut," *BA*, 19 January 1877, 2; "The Press Club's Entertainment," *NYTrib*, 7 February 1877, 8; "The Press Club Entertainment," *NYT*, 7 February 1877, 5.

14. *MTHL*, 173, 253, 269; *Mark Twain's Satires and Burlesques*, 145, 163.

15. Paine, *MTB*, 611; SLC to Elinor Howells, 26 October 1877, *UCCL* 10846; *MTL*, 5:145, 6:221–27; "Literary Chit Chat," *NYH*, 11 December 1876, 8; *MTL*, 5:145; SLC to Charles L. Webster, 18–20 July 1884, *UCCL* 10899; Clark, "Mark Twain at 'Nook Farm'"; *MTCI*, 39; *MTMF*, 219–20; "Editor's Literary Record," *Harper's Monthly* 55 (June 1877): 149; Johnson, *Remembered Yesterdays*, 323; Budd, *MTCR*, 171; "The President," *CIO*, 8 July 1881, 1.

16. *MTMF*, 219; "Humor Reduced to Algebra," *NYS*, 19 May 1878, 2; Budd, *MTCR*, 179.

17. *AMT*, 1:55; "Local Miscellany," *NYTrib*, 19 July 1878, 8; "Personal," *BJ*, 6 August 1878, 2; SLC to Charles L. Webster, 1 May 1881, *UCCL* 01944; SLC to Frank Fuller, 20 August 1878, *UCCL* 02526; Powers, *Mark Twain*, 436; SLC to Charles L. Webster, 3 October 1882, *UCCL* 02285; SLC to Charles L. Webster, 24 September 1882, *UCCL* 02279.

18. "About Mark Twain," *New York World*, 12 January 1877, 5; "The Bickerings of the Innocents," *NYEP*, 12 January 1877, 1; "The Ship-Owners and Mr. Duncan," *NYT*, 15 February 1877, 8; "Shipowners Swindled," *NYH*, 3 May 1873, 5; "The Shipping Act," *NYH*, 10 March 1876, 8.

19. SLC to the *New York World*, 16–17 February 1877, *UCCL* 12683.

20. "Mark Twain on His Muscle," *New York World*, 18 February 1877, 5.

21. "Mark Twain Once More," *New York World*, 25 February 1877, 5; SLC to George W. McCrary, 27 February 1877, *UCCL* 09190; "To the Editor of the World Concerning Captain Duncan," *DV* 18, *MTP*.

22. "C. C. Duncan on Mark Twain," *New York Graphic*, 2 March 1877, 11; *MTHL*, 173; *MTMF*, 213.

23. *AMT*, 2:418; Harte, *Selected Letters*, 134; *MTHL*, 157.

24. *AMT*, 2:407; SLC to Jane Lampton Clemens, 12 July 1877, *UCCL* 12739; Driscoll, "Mark Twain's Music Box," 144; Andrews, *Nook Farm*, 86–87; *MTLP*, 106–7; Frank Fuller to SLC, 20 July 1877, *UCLC* 32518; Duckett, *Mark Twain and Bret Harte*, 127–29.

25. SLC to Pamela Moffett, 27 February 1877, *UCCL* 01409; *MTHL*, 189; SLC to Jane Lampton Clemens, 12 July 1877, *UCCL* 12739.

26. Everett Emerson, for example, suggests that "the determining source for their break-up seems to have been Harte's criticism of Mrs. Clemens" (Emerson, *Authentic Mark Twain*, 93). DeLancey Ferguson suggests that SLC "endured" Harte's offensive comments until he "uttered a witticism" about Olivia Langdon Clemens, whereupon "fireworks followed" (Ferguson, "Mark Twain's Lost Curtain Speeches," 266). Leland Krauth adds that Harte "apologized rather glibly" to Sam, but this apology is dated 16 December 1876, two months before his presumed offense occurred (Krauth, *Mark Twain and Company*, 17).

27. *AMT*, 2:420–21; Duckett, *Mark Twain and Bret Harte*, 140–51 and passim; Scharnhorst, "The Bret Harte–Mark Twain Feud"; Scharnhorst, *Bret Harte*, 199–201; *Mark Twain's Letters* (1917), 293; SLC to Edwin Booth, 7 April 1877, *UCCL* 01411; "Amusements," *HC*, 6 April 1877, 1.

28. *Love Letters of Mark Twain*, 194; *MTCI*, 12–13; *MTHL*, 176; scrapbook 10, MTP.

29. *MTHL*, 192; SLC to Moncure D. Conway, 6 August 1877, *UCCL* 01466; Duckett, *Mark Twain and Bret Harte*, 151; Anderson, "Introduction," in *Ah Sin*, 5.

30. Duckett, *Mark Twain and Bret Harte*, 144; Scharnhorst, *Bret Harte*, 126; John T. Ford to SLC, 8 May 1877, *UCLC* 32487; Gilder, "Mark Twain Detested the Theatre," 112; "Ah Sin," *SFB*, 21 May 1877, 1; SLC to Moncure D. Conway, 6 August 1877, *UCCL* 01466; Henrickson, "Author, Author," 156; *N&J*, 2:9; SLC to Charles Enoch Perkins, 15 May 1877, *UCCL* 01432.

31. "Ah Sin," *Washington National Republican*, 8 May 1877, 1; *Baltimore Bee*, 14 May 1877, 2; "Ah Sin on the Stage," *Denver Rocky Mountain News*, 19 May 1877, 3; "Mark Twain and Bret Harte's Play," *SFB*, 16 May 1877, 1; "City Summary," *New York Clipper*, 19 May 1877, 62; "Ah Sin," *SFB*, 21 May 1877, 1; C. T. Parsloe to SLC, 11 May 1877, *UCLC* 32489

32. SLC to Susan Crane, 23 April 1877, *UCCL* 01415; *N&J*, 2:16; Hoffmann, *Mark Twain in Paradise*, 30; *The Stolen White Elephant Etc.*, 64, 67–68; *MTHL*, 179; *AMT*, 2:612.

33. *MTHL*, 178; Hoffmann, *Mark Twain in Paradise*, 59; *The Stolen White Elephant Etc.*, 70, 79, 85.

34. *Mark Twain on Potholes and Politics*, 106–10; "More about the 'Ocean Tramp,'" *NYH*, 21 September 1877, 4; *MTHL*, 179; *LMT&JHT*, 61–62; Andrews, *Nook Farm*, 97.

35. "New Publications," *NYT*, 22 October 1877, 3; Emerson, *Authentic Mark Twain*, 93; *LMT&JHT*, 62; *MTHL*, 184.

36. SLC to Thomas Bailey Aldrich, 3 June 1877, *UCCL* 01437; Gribben, *Mark Twain's Library*, 552.

37. Chandos Fulton to SLC, 12 March 1877, *UCLC* 32478; *MTHL*, 184, 187–89.

38. *Simon Wheeler, Detective*, 111; *Mark Twain's Satires and Burlesques*, 261, 272.

39. Paine, *MTB*, 595–96; SLC to Jane Lampton Clemens, 12 July 1877, *UCCL* 12739; SLC to Mollie Fairbanks, 6 August 1877, *UCCL* 01467; Baetzhold, *Mark Twain and John Bull*, 33; *MTHL*, 187, 189, 200, 246.

40. "Twain's Latest," *BH*, 22 July 1877, 6; *Love Letters of Mark Twain*, 199–201; *AMT*, 3:39; Hill, "Introduction," in *Wapping Alice*, 8.

41. *Collected Tales*, 837–43; *How Nancy Jackson Married Kate Wilson*, 242–43; *AMT*, 3:24, 3:457–58.

42. *AMT*, 2:423.

43. Olivia Langdon Clemens to SLC, 29 July 1877, *UCCL* 01458; SLC to Olivia Langdon Clemens, 30 July 1877, *UCCL* 01459; SLC to Olivia Langdon Clemens, 27 July 1877, *UCCL* 01456.

44. "Mark Twain on His New Heathen Chinee Play," *SR*, 2 August 1877, 8; *MTSpk*, 103–5; Gilder, "Mark Twain Detested the Theatre," 114; Olivia Langdon Clemens to Mollie Clemens, 29 July and 1 August 1877, *UCCL* 01435.

45. Lai-Henderson, *Mark Twain in China*, 28, emphasis added; Ou, "Mark Twain, Anson Burlingame," 60; Ou, "The Chinese Stereotypical Signification," 147; Wu, "The Siamese Twins," 53.

46. Hall, *Performing*, 91; "'Ah Sin'-gular Drama," *CIO*, 7 August 1877, 2; "Ah Sin," *Ithaca Journal*, 21 September 1877, 4; Nym Crinkle [Andrew C. Wheeler], "Ah Sin," *NYS*, 5 August 1877, 5; "The Fifth Avenue Theatre," *NYEP*, 1 August 1877, 3; "Amusements," *NYH*, 1 August 1877, 6; "Our New York Letter," *Hartford Times*, 3 August 1877, 1; "Amusements," *NYT*, 1 August 1877, 5; "The Drama," *NYTrib*, 1 August 1877, 5; SLC to Moncure D. Conway, 6 August 1877, *UCCL* 01466; *AMT*, 2:420; Duckett, *Mark Twain and Bret Harte*, 157.

47. SLC to Mollie Fairbanks, 6 August 1877, *UCCL* 01467; *Ithaca Journal*, 31 July 1877, 4; *Ithaca Journal*, 8 August 1877, 4; *Ithaca Journal*, 10 August 1877, 4; *MTHL*, 193; SLC to Charles Enoch Perkins, 3 August 1877, *UCCL* 01464; SLC to Moncure D. Conway, 6 August 1877, *UCCL* 01466; SLC to Frank Millet, 7 August 1877, *UCCL* 01468; Daly, *The Life of Augustin Daly*, 237; Scharnhorst, *Bret Harte*, 129.

48. Kaplan, *The Singular Mark Twain*, 332–33; Henrickson, "Author, Author," 157; Gilder, "Mark Twain Detested the Theatre," 112.

49. Duckett, *Mark Twain and Bret Harte*, 157; "Amusements," *St. Louis Globe-Democrat*, 2 September 1877, 5, and *St. Louis Globe-Democrat*, 9 September 1877, 3; "Ah Sin a Decided Hit," *Cincinnati Gazette*, 5 September 1877, 4; "Dramatic," *New York Clipper*, 15 September 1877, 198, and *New York Clipper*, 22 September 1877, 207; "Ah Sin," *Ithaca Journal*, 21 September 1877, 4; "The Grand Opera House," *NYS*, 25 September 1877, 3; Henrickson, "Author, Author," 157; *MTHL*, 206; Pittsburgh *Chronicle*, 8 November 1877, 1; "Amusements," *Pittsburgh Commercial Gazette*, 9 November 1877, 4; "Robinson's Opera-House," *Cincinnati Star*, 10 November 1877, 3; "Amusements," *CC*, 25 November 1877, 3.

50. Bush, *Mark Twain and the Spiritual Crisis*, 144; *Columbus Enquirer-Sun*, 4 January 1878, 2.

51. SLC to W. D. Howells, 21 June 1877, *UCCL* 01066 and 11173; *MTHL*, 185–86.

52. "New York," *Cincinnati Gazette*, 10 January 1878, 5; *MTHL*, 139, 235, 308; Scharnhorst, "The Bret Harte–Mark Twain Feud."

53. *MTHL*, 195–97; "Diamond Cut Diamond," *Virginia City (Nev.) Territorial Enterprise*, 26 September 1877, 1; *AMT*, 2:543.

54. *MTCI*, 491; *Mark Twain's Correspondence with Henry Huttleston Rogers*, 545–46; Paine, *MTB*, 600.

55. *Elmira (N.Y.) Bazoo*, 7 September 1877, 4; Quirk, *Coming to Grips*, 77; *Mark Twain's Satires and Burlesques*, 356; Berger, "Emendations of the Copy-Text," in *Pudd'nhead Wilson and Those Extraordinary Twins*, 190; *Devil's Race-Track*, 355.

56. Robinson, *The Author-Cat*, 66; *New York World*, 25 January 1877, 4; *Portland Oregonian*, 12 February 1877, 2; "Brevities," *San Francisco Alta California*, 4 February 1877, 1.

57. "News of the Morning," *BJ*, 3 October 1877, 2; "Personal," *NYTrib*, 6 October 1877, 4; "The Ancients' Visit to Hartford," *BJ*, 3 October 1877, 4.

58. "W. D. Howells at Seminary Hall," *HC*, 12 December 1877, 3; "Brief Mention," *HC*, 13 December 1877, 2; Messent, "Mark Twain, Joseph Twichell," 55; *MTHL*, 246, 674–75.

59. "Boston," *CT*, 30 December 1877, 10; "Whittier's Birthday," *BA*, 18 December 1877, 1. Most primary sources (e.g., "Whittier's Birthday," *BJ*, 18 December 1877, 4; "Twain at the Whittier Dinner," *NYT*, 20 December 1877, 2) agree that fifty-eight men attended the dinner.

60. Smith, "That Hideous Mistake," 151; "The Whittier Dinner," *Boston Globe*, 18 December 1877, 8. In much the same way that the dialogue in *Roughing It* ("son of a bitch") anticipates a famous exchange between the hero and villain in Owen Wister's *The Virginian*, a line in SLC's Whittier speech ("Mr. Longfellow, if you'll be so kind as to hold your yawp for about five minutes") points back to Walt Whitman's "Song of Myself."

61. "Tramp! Tramp! Tramp!", *Philadelphia Inquirer*, 21 December 1877, 1; Denning, *Mechanic Accents*, 150; Wayland, *A Paper on Tramps*, 10. See also "Contributors' Club," *Atlantic Monthly* 45 (May 1880): 717–19.

62. Lowry, "*Littery Man*," 31; Smith, *Mark Twain: The Development*, 55, 98; "The Whittier Dinner," *Boston Globe*, 18 December 1877, 8; "A Bard's Birthday Banquet," *Boston Traveller*, 18 December 1877, 1; "The Atlantic Dinner," *Boston Transcript*, 18 December 1877, 3; "Whittier's Birthday," *BJ*, 18 December 1877, 4; "The Whittier Testimonial," *Portland (Maine) Press*, 19 December 1877, 1; "Twain at the Whittier Dinner," *NYT*, 18 December 1877, 1; "Whittier's Birthday," *Hartford Times*, 18 December 1877, 2; "Brevities," *San Francisco Alta California*, 3 January 1878, 1; "Boston," *CT*, 23 December 1877, 16; "Whittier's Birthday," *BA*, 18 December 1877, 1; "The Atlantic Dinner," *Boston Transcript*, 18 December 1877, 3; Smith, "That Hideous Mistake," 155; Ballou, *The Building of the House*, 215–19.

63. The dates of reprintings of SLC's Whittier speech in December 1877 are as follows: December 18: *BA*, *Boston Globe*, *BJ*, *Boston Post*, *Boston Transcript*, and *CIO*; December 19: *HC*, *Hartford Times*, *New York Graphic*, *Philadelphia Bulletin*, and *Portland (Maine) Press*; December 20: *Cincinnati Gazette* and *NYT*; December 21: *St. Louis Globe-Democrat*; December 22: *CT*; December 23: *Washington Capital*; December 24: *Lowell (Mass.) Citizen*; December 25: *Milwaukee Sentinel*; December 29: *Portland (Maine) Transcript*; December 30: *Galveston News* and *New Orleans Picayune*.

64. "Boston," *CT*, 30 December 1877, 10; "Wine at the Whittier Banquet," *Boston Post*, 19 December 1877, 4.

65. Wuster, *Mark Twain: American Humorist*, 333–34; Smith, "That Hideous Mistake," 157.

66. "Brevities," *San Francisco Alta California*, 8 January 1878, 1; "Personal Intelligence," *NYH*, 26 December 1877, 4; "People and Things," *Denver Rocky Mountain News*, 9 January 1878, 3; Smith, "That Hideous Mistake," 159; "Mark Twain's Mistake at the Whittier Dinner," *SR*, 27 December 1877, 8.

67. "Mark Twain's Mistake at the Whittier Dinner," *SR*, 27 December 1877, 8; "Boston," *CT*, 30 December 1877, 10; "Mark Twain's Latest," *CC*, 23 December 1877, 4; "The Burdens of a Humorist," *Cincinnati Gazette*, 24 December 1877, 4; *Cleveland Plain Dealer*, 21 December 1877, 1; McWilliams, *Mark Twain in the St. Louis Post-Dispatch*, 81; "Minor Notes," *Washington Capital*, 6 January 1878, 4; "Brevities," *San Francisco Alta California*, 16 January 1878, 1; "Mark Twain," *Denver Rocky Mountain News*, 5 January 1878, 2; Wuster, *Mark Twain: American Humorist*, 332, 443; "Gail Hamilton Once More," *NYTrib*, 5 February 1878, 2; "Literary News," *Independent*, 10 January 1878, 12; "General Notes," *NYT*, 21 December 1877, 4.

68. Smith, "That Hideous Mistake," 156; "A Thundering Row about That Whittier Dinner," *SFB*, 10 January 1878, 1; Howells, *Selected Letters* 182; *MTHL*, 213; Vanderbilt, *The Achievement*, 135–36; Goodman and Dawson, *Howells: A Writer's Life*, 192.

69. "Summary of the News," *BA*, 24 December 1877, 1; "Society Meetings," *Philadelphia Inquirer*, 19 January 1878, 1; "Twain Won't Come," *CIO*, 7 January 1878, 8; *MTHL*, 212–13; "Current Notes," *BJ*, 18 February 1878, 2.

70. *MTHL*, 214; *MTCI*, 578; Smith, "That Hideous Mistake," 162.

71. SLC to Ralph Waldo Emerson, Oliver Wendell Holmes, and Henry Wadsworth Longfellow, 27 December 1877; *MTHL*, 214; *BH*, 13 January 1878, 4.

72. Ellen Emerson to Olivia Langdon Clemens, 31 December 1877, UCLC 32620; Henry Wadsworth Longfellow to SLC, 6 January 1878, UCLC 32626; Oliver Wendell Holmes to SLC, 29 December 1877, UCLC 32619.

73. Howells, *My MT*, 62; *MTMF*, 217; *MTHL*, 398; *AMT*, 1:266–67; Underwood, *John Greenleaf Whittier*, 310.

74. *AMT*, 1:112, 1:265–67.

75. *AMT*, 1:310; *MTCI*, 578; Robinson, *The Author-Cat*, 83.

76. Smith, "That Hideous Mistake," 146; Howells, *My MT*, 63.

Chapter 7

1. Blair, *Mark Twain and Huck Finn*, 160; *MTMF*, 222; *MTCI*, 15.

2. *N&J*, 2:56; *Mark Twain's Letters* (1917), 319–20; SLC to Charles Warren Stoddard, 20 March 1878, UCCL 01546; Cardwell, *The Man Who Was Mark Twain*, 75.

3. *MTHL*, 216.

4. *MTMF*, 218; SLC to Thomas Nast, 12 November 1877, UCCL 02518.

5. Paine, *MTB*, 726; *AMT*, 2:55–56, 2:490, 3:17.

6. *AMT*, 2:57; "Mark Twain as a Journalist," *Vicksburg (Miss.) Commercial*, 6 September 1879, 3; "Mark Twain's Enterprise," *NYS*, 7 January 1878, 2; Orion Clemens to SLC, 24 January 1878, UCLC 47155; "In the Harnass [*sic*] Again," *Virginia City (Nev.) Territorial Enterprise*, 15 January 1878, 2; "A Note from 'Mark Twain,'" *Virginia City (Nev.) Territorial Enterprise*, 3 February 1878, 2; "Not Quite an Editor," *NYS*, 26 January 1878, 2.

7. SLC to James Pond, 30 November 1888, UCCL 02687; *MTCI*, 9; "The Moody and Sankey Meetings," *Hartford Times*, 15 January 1878, 1, *Hartford Times*, 26 January 1878, 1, and *Hartford Times*, 6 February 1878, 1; SLC to Jane Lampton Clemens, 7 April 1878, UCCL 01553; Andrews, *Nook Farm*, 253; *Huckleberry Finn* (1885), 161.

8. *N&J*, 2:42, 2:49; *MTMF*, 218; Andrews, "Mark Twain and James W. C. Pennington"; Hill, "Mark Twain's Quarrels," 451; David, *Mark Twain and His Illustrators*, 1:72; *AMT*, 1:597; *MTHL*, 259–62; *MTCI*, 31.

9. *MTHL*, 340; *MTCI*, 15; Schultz, "New Letters of Mark Twain," 47; *N&J*, 2:65; SLC to George Haven Putnam, 16 March 1878, UCCL 01544.

10. "Honors to Bayard Taylor," *NYTrib*, 5 April 1878, 1; SLC to Jane Lampton Clemens, 7 April 1878, UCCL 01553. Ironically, Taylor had offered a low opinion of SLC's humor two and a half years earlier, noting that his wit "is wholly superficial, without any underlying current of sentiment and thought" (B[ayard] T[aylor], "American Humor," *SFB*, 1 November 1875, 1).

11. "Bayard Taylor Honored," *NYT*, 5 April 1878, 2; *AMT*, 1:417.

12. SLC to Jane Lampton Clemens, 7 April 1878, UCCL 01553; SLC to Frank Fuller, 5 April 1878, UCCL 01552; *LMT&JHT*, 65; "Departure of Hon. Bayard Taylor," *New York*

Mail, 11 April 1878, 1; "The Start for Germany," *NYT*, 12 April 1878, 8; "The Departure of Bayard Taylor and Mark Twain," *Baltimore Sun*, 13 April 1878, 3; *AMT*, 3:575; "Personal," *BJ*, 15 April 1878, 2.

13. *MTHL*, 4 May 1878; *N&J*, 2:67; SLC to Olivia Lewis Langdon, 20 April 1878, *UCCL* 01556; Olivia Langdon Clemens to Susan Crane, 3–4 May 1878, *UCCL* 12743; "Personal Intelligence," *NYH*, 23 April 1878, 6.

14. Olivia Langdon Clemens to Olivia Lewis Langdon, 26 April 1878, *UCCL* 01557; *MTHL*, 227–28; *N&J*, 2:71.

15. Olivia Langdon Clemens to Susan Crane, 3–4 May 1878, *UCCL* 12743; *AMT*, 1:388; *N&J*, 2:75; *MTHL*, 227; Hemminghaus, *Mark Twain in Germany*, 16, 42.

16. Olivia Langdon Clemens to Olivia Lewis Langdon, 7 May 1878, *UCCL* 01559; *MTHL*, 230; *TA*, 27–28.

17. Olivia Langdon Clemens to Susan Crane, 7 and 19 May 1878, *UCCL* 12744; *MTHL*, 229–30; Olivia Langdon Clemens to Olivia Lewis Langdon, 7 May 1878, *UCCL* 01559; *TA*, 31.

18. SLC to Olivia Langdon Clemens, 1 January 1885, *UCCL* 03097; Susy Clemens to Olivia Lewis Langdon, 12 and 18 May 1878, *UCCL* 01561; *N&J*, 2:76, 2:82, 2:85–86, 2:256, 2:265, 2:273; *TA*, 62, 84, 86; *AMT*, 1:288.

19. *TA*, 607–8, 618; *N&J*, 2:80, 2:82, 2:121; *Mark Twain's Speeches*, 194; Phipps, *Mark Twain's Religion*, 256–57; SLC to Jane Lampton Clemens, 1 December 1878, *UCCL* 01610.

20. Howells, *My MT*, 17; SLC to Jane Lampton Clemens and Pamela Moffett, 1 December 1878, *UCCL* 01610.

21. *MTHL*, 231; SLC to David Gray, 2 June 1878, *UCCL* 11403; Olivia Langdon Clemens to Olivia Lewis Langdon, 26 May 1878, *UCCL* 01564; SLC to Charles Dudley Warner, 16 June 1878, *UCCL* 01572; Schultz, "New Letters of Mark Twain," 48–49; *N&J*, 2:104; Olivia Langdon Clemens to Charles Langdon, 21 July 1878, *UCCL* 01578; *TA*, 591; SLC to Frank Bliss, 13 July 1878, *UCCL* 01576.

22. Olivia Langdon Clemens to Olivia Lewis Langdon, 9 June 1878, *UCCL* 01569; Blair, *Mark Twain and Huck Finn*, 165; *N&J*, 2:182; *MTHL*, 236–37.

23. *N&J*, 2:163; Davis, *Mark Twain in Heidelberg*, 23; *Mark Twain in His Own Time*, 125; *TA*, 618; Olivia Langdon Clemens to Charles Langdon, 21 July 1878, *UCCL* 01578.

24. *LMT&JHT*, 426; Courtney, *Joseph Hopkins Twichell*, 196; *N&J*, 2:113; SLC to Charles Dudley Warner, [1?] August 1878, *UCCL* 01581; Rodney, *Mark Twain Overseas*, 101; *TA*, 188; SLC to Mervyn Drake, 9 October 1884, *UCCL* 03005; Lawton, *A Lifetime*, 179.

25. Gibson, *The Art of Mark Twain*, 153; *TA*, 200, 210, 213; *N&J*, 2:120, 2:123, 2:128, 2:129; *Mark Twain's Letters* (1917), 332–34.

26. SLC to Mr. Tyler, 30 July 1878, *UCCL* 01580; *TA*, 27, 589–90; *Connecticut Yankee*, 88, 91, 294. The Yankee's plumbing repair of the Fountain of Holiness in chapter 23 similarly alludes to the castle illumination. Whereas the Heidelberg castle is enveloped first in a mass of "red fires," followed by "vaporous green fire," then "dazzling purple" fire, and finally "a mixture of many colors" (*TA*, 590), Hank Morgan caulks a leak in the fountain and ignites red and green fire, next a "purple glare," and finally all of them "going at once, red, blue, green, purple" (*Connecticut Yankee*, 292). Even the sequence of colors is the same.

27. SLC to Olivia Langdon Clemens, 7 August 1878, *UCCL* 11926; SLC to Jane Lampton Clemens and Pamela Moffett, 20 August 1878, *UCCL* 01587; Courtney, *Joseph Hopkins Twichell*, 197; *TA*, 163; Schultz, "New Letters of Mark Twain," 50–51; Messent, *Mark Twain and Male Friendship*, 70.

28. *TA*, 126, 183; *Huckleberry Finn* (1885), 156.

29. Olivia Langdon Clemens to Olivia Lewis Langdon, 4–5 August 1878, UCCL 01582; Olivia Langdon Clemens to Olivia Lewis Langdon, 18 August 1878, UCCL 01584; Olivia Langdon Clemens to Susan Crane, 11 August 1878, UCCL 12749; *TA*, 245; SLC to Jane Lampton Clemens and Pamela Moffett, 20 August 1878, UCCL 01587.

30. *TA*, 340, 358; *N&J*, 2:141, 2:318; *TA*, 345, 355; *MTLP*, 111; Olivia Langdon Clemens to Susan Crane, 25 August 1878, UCCL 12750.

31. *Mark Twain's Letters* (1917), 334–35; David, *Mark Twain and His Illustrators*, 1:127; *N&J*, 2:143, 2:148, 2:153, 2:165, 2:167, 2:169; *TA*, 399, 489; *N&J*, 2:167.

32. *N&J*, 2:169; *TA*, 405, 490.

33. *N&J*, 2:170, 2:177; *TA*, 532; *Switzerland: Handbook for Travellers*, 260.

34. Olivia Langdon Clemens to Susan Crane, 8 September 1878, UCCL 12751; Courtney, *Joseph Hopkins Twichell*, 199; *LMT&JHT*, 68–69, 74.

35. SLC to Olivia Lewis Langdon, 13 September 1878, UCCL 01595; Olivia Langdon Clemens to Olivia Lewis Langdon, 15 September 1878, UCCL 01596; *N&J*, 2:177, 2:182; *TA*, 543.

36. *N&J*, 2:139, 2:176, 2:212–13; Lawton, *A Lifetime*, 8; Driscoll, "Mark Twain's Music Box" 160, 164; *LMT&JHT*, 82.

37. *N&J*, 2:182–87; Olivia Langdon Clemens to Olivia Lewis Langdon, 18 August 1878, UCCL 01584; Olivia Langdon Clemens to Olivia Lewis Langdon, 15 September 1878, UCCL 01596; *TA*, 546, 550; Driscoll, "Mark Twain's Music Box," 157.

38. *The Innocents Abroad*, 172; *TA*, 557–58, 586; Gibson, *The Art of Mark Twain*, 159; *N&J*, 2:139, 2:188–92.

39. *N&J*, 2:193–94; Olivia Langdon Clemens to Olivia Lewis Langdon, 29–30 September 1878, UCCL 01598.

40. *N&J*, 2:195, 2:202, 2:223; *TA*, 563, 567; *MTHL*, 239.

41. Gibson, *The Art of Mark Twain*, 150–51, 155; Olivia Langdon Clemens to Olivia Lewis Langdon, 19 January 1879, UCCL 01621; Olivia Langdon Clemens to Olivia Lewis Langdon, 16 March 1879, UCCL 01640; *N&J*, 2:340; *AMT*, 1:347; Paine, *MTB*, 633; *MTMF*, 230.

42. *TA*, 238; *Mark Twain on Potholes and Politics* 117; *LMT&JHT*, 82; *N&J*, 2:201.

43. Olivia Langdon Clemens to Olivia Lewis Langdon, 29–30 September 1878, UCCL 01598; Olivia Langdon Clemens to Olivia Lewis Langdon, 13 October 1878, UCCL 01600; *N&J*, 2:215, 226.

44. *N&J*, 2:231. Justin Kaplan mistakenly locates the painting in the Louvre (*Mr. Clemens and Mark Twain*, 221), and Andrew Hoffman parrots the error (*Inventing Mark Twain*, 267).

45. *N&J*, 2:319; *TA*, 578.

46. *N&J*, 2:216, 2:230, 2:236, 2:239, 2:242, 2:250, 2:245, 2:259; Olivia Langdon Clemens to Olivia Lewis Langdon, 10 November 1878, UCCL 01605; *LMT&JHT*, 81; Wagenknecht, *Mark Twain: The Man and His Work*, 154; Soria, "Mark Twain and Vedder's Medusa," 603.

47. *N&J*, 2:248, 2:266; Jackson, "A German Landlady"; *MTHL*, 240; Olivia Langdon Clemens to Mollie Clemens, 15 December 1878, UCCL 01615; Raeithel, "Mark Twain in Munich," 88; Olivia Langdon Clemens to Olivia Lewis Langdon, 22 December 1878, UCCL 01616; *Mark Twain's Letters* (1917), 343–44.

48. Kersten, *Von Hannibal nach Heidelberg*, 304; *LMT&JHT*, 81, 86.

49. *LMT&JHT*, 84; SLC to Susan Crane, 1 December 1878, UCCL 01609; *LMT&JHT*, 86–87; Olivia Langdon Clemens to Mollie Clemens, 15 December 1878, UCCL 01615; SLC

to Frank Bliss, 20 August 1878, *UCCL* 02525; *MTHL*, 249; *MTCI*, 17; Krauth, *Proper Mark Twain*, 72–73; Melton, *Mark Twain, Travel Books, and Tourism*, 82.

50. *Mark Twain on Potholes and Politics*, 114. SLC recycled this little joke from the title of his poem "To Mary in H--l" in the *Hannibal Journal* in 1853 and would reuse it again in his story "The Man That Corrupted Hadleyburg" (1899), in which the answer to the stranger's test question includes the phrase "go to hell or Hadleyburg."

51. *LMT&JHT*, 84, 86; SLC to Frank Bliss, 9 February 1879, *UCCL* 01629; *MTMF*, 226; Courtney, *Joseph Hopkins Twichell*, 196; Messent, "Mark Twain, Joseph Twichell," 50; *LMT&JHT*, 94.

52. *LMT&JHT*, 92; *MTHL*, 248–50; *Huckleberry Finn* (1885), 304; David, *Mark Twain and His Illustrators*, 1:131; Hill, *Mark Twain and Elisha Bliss*, 145; *N&J*, 2:164; *TA*, 545.

53. *N&J*, 2:266; *LMT&JHT*, 87; *MTHL*, 248.

54. "Pitcairn Island," *London Times*, 4 December 1878, 9. The next year Robert Brown inadvertently perpetuated the hoax by accepting SLC's false identification of the invader as an American in volume 4 of *The Countries of the World* (4:79).

55. "The Great Revolution in Pitcairn," *Atlantic Monthly* 43 (March 1879): 295–302; Herm, "'Truth Is Stranger than Fiction.'"

56. A decade later, Julian Hawthorne collaborated with Byrnes, whom he considered "the greatest detective in world," on five "true crime" novels: *A Tragic Mystery* (1887), *The Great Bank Robbery* (1887), *An American Penman* (1887), *Section 558* (1888), and *Another's Crime* (1888).

57. Baetzhold, "'Of Detectives and Their Derring-Do,'" 186–89; *MTHL*, 246; *The Stolen White Elephant Etc.*, 7–35.

58. Byers, *Twenty Years in Europe*, 160–62; Olivia Langdon Clemens to Olivia Lewis Langdon, 22 December 1878, *UCCL* 01616; Olivia Langdon Clemens to Olivia Lewis Langdon, 1–5 January 1879, *UCCL* 01620; Olivia Langdon Clemens to Olivia Lewis Langdon, 19 January 1879, *UCCL* 01621; Olivia Langdon Clemens to Olivia Lewis Langdon, 16 February 1879, *UCCL* 01634; *N&J*, 2:261; Kersten, *Von Hannibal nach Heidelberg*, 307.

59. Olivia Langdon Clemens to Olivia Lewis Langdon, 16 February 1879; *UCCL* 01634; Olivia Langdon Clemens to Olivia Lewis Langdon, 2 March 1879, *UCCL* 01636; Olivia Langdon Clemens to Olivia Lewis Langdon, 16 March 1879, *UCCL* 01640; *MTMF*, 226, 230; *N&J*, 2:292, 2:294; SLC to Elisha Bliss, 6 March 1879, *UCCL* 11673; *AMT*, 3:240; Mary Mason Fairbanks to SLC, 26 July 1880, *UCLC* 32822.

60. "Personal Intelligence," *NYH*, 27 March 1879, 6; Harrington and Jenn, *Mark Twain and France*, 112; SLC to Olivia Langdon Clemens, 25 August 1881, *UCCL* 12729; *AMT*, 3:46–47; "Personal," *NYTrib*, 2 April 1879, 4; SLC to Elisha Bliss, 6 March 1879, *UCCL* 11673; Olivia Langdon Clemens to Charles Langdon, 9 March 1879, *UCCL* 01638; SLC to Frank Bliss, 15 April 1879, *UCCL* 02531; SLC and Olivia Langdon Clemens to Jane Lampton Clemens and Pamela Moffett, 30 March 1879, *UCCL* 12755; *N&J*, 2:288.

61. *MTMF*, 225, 230; *LMT&JHT*, 91; *N&J*, 2:311–12, 2:328.

62. Olivia Langdon Clemens to Olivia Lewis Langdon, 16 March 1879, *UCCL* 01640; Olivia Langdon Clemens to Olivia Lewis Langdon, 13–16 May 1879, *UCCL* 01579; Gibson, *The Art of Mark Twain*, 150–51; *MTHL*, 426.

63. "Fact and Fancy Focused," *New York Clipper*, 10 May 1879, 54; "Too Late for Roger M'Pherson," *NYT*, 11 April 1879, 5; Paine, *MTB*, 643; *MTSpk*, 126; *N&J*, 1:164.

64. *MTLP*, 110; "Mark Twain as a Presidential Candidate," *NYEP*, 9 June 1879, 1.

65. "Mark Twain in Paris," *Oregon State Journal*, 23 August 1879, 3; Rodney, *Mark Twain Overseas*, 120–21; Harrington and Jenn, *Mark Twain and France*, 114; *N&J*, 2:288, 2:299–300, 2:304, 2:306, 2:309, 2:313; Kruse, *Mark Twain and Life on the Mississippi*, 104; *MTCI*, 17–22; "Latest Cable News," *NYH*, 2 May 1879, 7; H. H. Boyesen, "Russia's Manifest Destiny," *BH*, 24 May 1885, 13.

66. *N&J*, 2:287, 2:315, 2:492; *Who Is Mark Twain?*, 131–43. Justin Kaplan erroneously asserts they attended the races at Chantilly (Kaplan, *Mr. Clemens and Mark Twain*, 221).

67. *MTLP*, 113–16; Olivia Langdon Clemens to Olivia Lewis Langdon, 6 July 1879, *UCCL* 01676; Paine, *MTB*, 643; SLC to Lucius Fairchild, 28 April 1880, *UCCL* 01794.

68. Greenslet, *The Life of Thomas Bailey Aldrich*, 137; Aldrich, *Crowding Memories*, 230–31; *N&J*, 2:321; SLC to Thomas Bailey Aldrich, 15 September 1880, *UCCL* 01834.

69. *N&J*, 2:320, 2:324–25; *Letters from the Earth*, 186, 188; *Huckleberry Finn* (1885), 120.

70. *N&J*, 2:271, 2:309, 2:316, 2:318, 2:322, 2:326, 2:346–47; *Who Is Mark Twain?*, 143; Gribben, *Mark Twain's Library*, 797; SLC to Orion Clemens, 21 February 1878, *UCCL* 01531; SLC to Jane Lampton Clemens, 23 February 1878, *UCCL* 01535.

71. *MTMF*, 208; SLC to Mollie Fairbanks, 6 August 1877, *UCCL* 01467; Gribben, *Mark Twain's Library*, 192; Paine, *MTB*, 644; *TA*, 261; *N&J*, 2:321.

72. *N&J*, 2:327–31; *TA*, 354.

73. Olivia Langdon Clemens to Olivia Lewis Langdon, 20 July 1879, *UCCL* 01677; "Latest London Gossip," *Cincinnati Gazette*, 6 August 1879, 5; *N&J*, 2:334; *AMT*, 1:433, 1:635.

74. *N&J*, 2:336; Paine, *MTB*, 647; Olivia Langdon Clemens to Olivia Lewis Langdon, 3 August 1879, *UCCL* 01679.

75. *MTHL*, 261; Scharnhorst, "The Bret Harte-Mark Twain Feud."

76. *N&J*, 2:311–12, 2:342; *MTHL*, 261; *TA*, 322; "Unlearnable Things," *Atlantic Monthly* 45 (June 1880): 849–52.

77. Dunne, *Mr. Dooley Remembers*, 244; Paine, *MTB*, 646; Anesko, *Letters, Fiction, Lives*, 139.

78. Paine, *MTB*, 646; SLC to Andrew Chatto, 7 August 1879.

79. *MTCI*, 30; *N&J*, 2:335, 2:338–39; Olivia Langdon Clemens to Olivia Lewis Langdon, 17 August 1879, *UCCL* 01680.

80. *MTL*, 4:429; *N&J*, 2:339, 2:486; Howells, *My MT*, 51; Higginson, *Cheerful Yesterdays*, 284–85; Jeannette Gilder, "The Lounger," *Critic*, 14 January 1888, 211; Darwin, *Life and Letters*, 81. See also *MTSpk*, 559–60.

81. SLC to John Brown Jr., 1 June 1882, *UCCL* 02212; *Mark Twain's Letters* (1917), 359–60; *AMT*, 1:435; *TA*, 580; *MTCI*, 24, 26; *N&J*, 2:341, 2:370; "Mark Twain," *New York Mail*, 2 September 1879, 4; SLC to Dan Slote, 4 September 1879, *UCCL* 10434; "Arrivals at the Hotels," *NYT*, 3 September 1879, 8.

Chapter 8

1. SLC to Frank Bliss, 8 September 1879, *UCCL* 01684; SLC to the Hartford Flag Committee, 8 September 1879, *UCCL* 01685; SLC to Pamela Moffett, 15 September 1879, *UCCL* 01690.

2. *MTMF*, 232; *MTHL*, 269; *LMT&JHT*, 93.

3. SLC to Pierre Peltier, 14 October 1879, *UCCL* 01699; *MTSpk*, 128–29; *MTHL*, 277; "Mark Twain," *NHR*, 20 October 1879, 4; SLC to Hjalmar Hjorth Boyesen, 6 November 1879, *UCCL* 01707.

4. *LMT&JHT*, 93; SLC to John Brown, 14 and 15 August 1880, *UCCL* 02814.

5. *AMT*, 1:371, 1:597, 2:51; *N&J*, 2:42; SLC to Orion Clemens, 24 October 1880, *UCCL* 01845.

6. "Mark Twain's New Book," *Cleveland Plain Dealer*, 22 November 1879, 2; "Mark Twain's 'Boom,'" *Chicago Times*, 15 November 1879, 3.

7. *AMT*, 1:371–72, 2:52.

8. Blair, *Mark Twain and Huck Finn*, 222; *MTHL*, 274; *Mark Twain's Letters* (1917), 364–65; SLC to William E. Strong, 6 November 1879, *UCCL* 01708; SLC to Blackburn Jones, 30 October 1879, *UCCL* 12006; 7 November 1879, *UCCL* 01710; SLC to Thomas Bailey Aldrich, 7 November 1879, *UCCL* 01709.

9. "Personal," *CIO*, 11 November 1879, 8; SLC to Olivia Langdon Clemens, 11 November 1879, *UCCL* 01712; SLC to Melville Stone, 3 April 1880, *UCCL* 01781; Fisher, *Abroad with Mark Twain and Eugene Field*, xvii.

10. Gold, "Mark Twain and General Grant in Chicago," 155.

11. *MTHL*, 280; *MTL*, 4:168; "The Review," *CIO*, 13 November 1879, 2; *MTSpk*, 130; *Mark Twain's Letters* (1917), 368–70; "Mark Twain's 'Boom,'" *Chicago Times*, 15 November 1879, 3; *N&J*, 2:357; Wilkie, "Twain's Best Joke," *Chicago Times*, 17 November 1879, 1; "Parting Compliments to Mark Twain," *CC*, 15 November 1879, 2.

12. "The Banquet," *CIO*, 15 November 1879, 1; *AMT*, 1:69; "Robert G. Ingersoll: The Volunteer Soldiers," *CT*, 14 November 1879, 3.

13. SLC to Olivia Langdon Clemens, 14 November 1879, *UCCL* 01715; *MTHL*, 279; SLC to Robert Ingersoll, 9 December 1879, *UCCL* 01737; *Mark Twain's Letters* (1917), 373–74; Schwartz, "Mark Twain and Robert Ingersoll"; Gribben, *Mark Twain's Library*, 344; SLC to N. F. Griswold, 20 December 1900, *UCCL* 05937; Howells, *My MT*, 31.

14. *AMT*, 3:117; *Mark Twain's Letters* (1917), 370–73; *MTSpk*, 131–34; "Mark Twain on Babies," *CT*, 14 November 1879, 1; "About Mark Twain," *WS*, 27 June 1896, 16; "Banquet of the Army of the Tennessee," *NYT*, 15 November 1879, 1; "His Funniest Speech," *CT*, 20 April 1890, 10.

15. *Mark Twain's Letters* (1917), 370–73; *MTHL*, 280; SLC to Orion Clemens, 14 November 1879, *UCCL* 01716.

16. "Parting Compliments to Mark Twain," *CC*, 15 November 1879, 2; "Mark Twain's 'Boom,'" *Chicago Times*, 15 November 1879, 3; *MTHL*, 279.

17. SLC to James Pond, 25 November 1879, *UCCL* 10797; Paine, *MTB*, 727; SLC to Olivia Langdon Clemens, 9 November 1879, *UCCL* 11718; SLC to Elisha Bliss, 10 June 1879, *UCCL* 01664; SLC to Elisha Bliss, 20 March 1880, *UCCL* 02540; SLC to Frank Fuller, 22 November 1879, *UCCL* 01723; SLC to Frank Fuller, 5 December 1879, *UCCL* 01733; Olivia Langdon Clemens to Olivia Lewis Langdon, 30 November 1879, *UCCL* 01730; SLC to Orion Clemens, 26 February 1880, *UCCL* 01763; Webster, *Mark Twain: Business Man*, 145; SLC to Dan Slote, 29 June 1880, *UCCL* 01817.

18. SLC to Frank Fuller, 26 November 1879, *UCCL* 01747; SLC to Andrew Dawson, 26 November 1879, *UCCL* 09849; *MTHL*, 280–81, 283.

19. "Honoring Dr. Holmes," *NYTrib*, 4 December 1879, 5; "A Grand Array of Writers," *Sacramento Record-Union*, 26 December 1879, 1; "Poet and Autocrat," *Philadelphia Inquirer*, 4 December 1879, 1; "Our Autocrat," *Philadelphia North American*, 4 December 1879, 1; Wuster, *Mark Twain: American Humorist*, 445; "Oliver Wendell Holmes," *NYH*, 4 December

1879, 4; *MTSpk*, 134–35; "The Holmes Breakfast," *Christian Union*, 10 December 1879, 490; "The Holmes Breakfast," *Literary World*, 20 December 1879, 435.

20. Olivia Langdon Clemens to Olivia Lewis Langdon, 30 November 1879, *UCCL* 01730; Howells, *My MT*, 42; *MTHL*, 284.

21. Webster, *Mark Twain: Business Man*, 140–41; *MTHL*, 286–88, 290; Olivia Langdon Clemens to Olivia Lewis Langdon, 1 November 1879, *UCCL* 01705. Livy's pregnancy required SLC to cancel a cross-country trip to the West that he had been planning. The news broke in October 1879 that he would "probably visit San Antonio this winter" ("Southern States News," *New Orleans Picayune*, 7 October 1879, 2), and SLC notified his old Nevada mining partner Bob Howland two weeks later that "we are planning to come to San Francisco sometime next year" (SLC to Robert Howland, 27 October 1879, *UCCL* 07428). He abandoned these plans when Livy became pregnant, though he still harbored the hope sometime "to see San Francisco once more!" (SLC to Charles Warren Stoddard, 17 June 1880, *UCCL* 01813).

22. *AMT*, 3:24.

23. The precise date in 1880 that Katy Leary joined the Clemenses' household staff has been a matter of some debate. But Leary revealed in an interview in 1925 that she "went to Hartford" soon after the Clemenses installed a telephone in the mansion. SLC wrote his brother Orion on 28 February 1880 that he had a "telephone wire up, now, all to myself" (SLC to Orion Clemens, 28 February 1880, *UCCL* 01764). That is, Leary very likely was hired while SLC and Livy were in Elmira in mid-January 1880.

24. "Mark Twain as Seen by His Housemaid," *NYT*, 15 March 1925, sec. 20, p. 5; Lawton, *A Lifetime*, 74; Clemens, *My Father, Mark Twain*, 29; *A Family Sketch*, 38.

25. *MTHL*, 286; *MTLP*, 190; *TA*, 580; Emerson, *Authentic Mark Twain*, 104; Hill, *Mark Twain and Elisha Bliss*, 146.

26. Paine, *MTB*, 665; SLC to Moncure D. Conway, 31 March 1880, *UCCL* 01778; SLC to Moncure D. Conway, 20–21 April 1880, *UCCL* 01787; *MTHL*, 290, 294; Ratner, "Two Letters of Mark Twain," 9; SLC to Charles Warren Stoddard, 17 June 1880, *UCCL* 01813; Hill, "Mark Twain's Book Sales," 389; SLC to John Brown, 14–15 August 1880, *UCCL* 02814; SLC to Pamela Moffett, [14?] November 1880, *UCCL* 11995; Emerson, *Authentic Mark Twain*, 106; SLC to Elisha Bliss, 30 May 1881, *UCCL* 01960; "Current Opinion," *Macon Telegraph*, 8 March 1881, 2; *MTHL*, 293; "Mark Twain's New Book," *Atlantic Monthly* 45 (May 1880): 686–88; SLC to David Gray, 10 June 1880, *UCCL* 11405; "New Books," *BE*, 25 June 1880, 1; "New Publications," *San Francisco Alta California*, 24 May 1880, 2; Hill, "Mark Twain: Audience and Artistry," 32.

27. Budd, *MTCR*, 183, 190–91; Woodward, "A Selection," 18–19.

28. *MTLP*, 124; *MTHL*, 290, 302, 320; Feinstein, "Mark Twain's Lawsuits," 105; SLC to Moncure D. Conway, 20–21 April 1880, *UCCL* 01787; SLC to Chatto & Windus, 1 December 1880, *UCCL* 01863.

29. SLC to Rollin Daggett, 1 May 1880, *UCCL* 01798; SLC to Rollin Daggett, 24 May 1880, *UCCL* 02811; *MTHL*, 295, 307. Nothing came, at least in the short run, of SLC's proposed change to the law.

30. "The Reader," *London Graphic*, 1 May 1880, 450; "Mark Twain's Last Book," *London Standard*, 23 April 1880, 2; "A Tramp Abroad," *London Post*, 4 May 1880, 3; Cardiff *Western Mail*, 17 May 1880, 2; "Current Literature," *London Daily News*, 13 October 1880, 6; W. E. Henley, "Literature," *Athenaeum*, 24 April 1880, 529–30; Budd, *MTCR*, 193–94; "A Tramp Abroad," *Adelaide Observer*, 28 August 1880, 42; "Mark Twain's New Book," *Sydney Mail*, 26 June 1880, 1142; "Current Literature," *Melbourne Argus*, 14 August 1880, 4; "Mark Twain's

New Book," *Melbourne Herald*, 5 July 1880, 2; "Literature," *Melbourne Australasian*, 31 July 1880, 8; "A Tramp Abroad," *Rockhampton (Australia) Capricornian*, 28 August 1880, 4; "Occasional Notes," *Perth Inquirer and Commercial News*, 20 October 1880, 1; "A Tramp Abroad," *Auckland Star*, 2 August 1880, 2; "A New Book by Mark Twain," *New Zealand Herald*, 7 August 1880, 7.

31. Budd, *MTCR*, 185–86, 189, 191–92; "About Europe and Elsewhere," *Pall Mall Gazette*, 26 April 1880, 1576; "A Tramp Abroad," *London Times*, 7 September 1880, 5; "Belles Lettres," *Westminster Review*, n.s., 58 (July 1880): 290; SLC to Andrew Chatto, 3 March 1882, *UCCL* 02169.

32. SLC to David Gray, 18 September 1879, *UCCL* 11404; SLC to Orion Clemens, 26 February 1880, *UCCL* 01763; *MTHL*, 290–92.

33. Towers, *"The Prince and the Pauper*: Mark Twain's Once and Future King," 194; *MTHL*, 291–92; *AMT*, 1:272; Peters, *General History of Connecticut*, 72; Trumbull, *The True-Blue Laws* v, vi; *The Prince and the Pauper*, 410; Ingersoll, *Ghosts*, 24.

34. Dickinson, "The Sources of *The Prince and the Pauper*," 104.

35. *The English Rogue* 1:62; *The Prince and the Pauper*, 155.

36. Cummings, *Mark Twain and Science*, 117; *The Prince and the Pauper*, 223.

37. SLC to F. V. Christ, 28 August 1908, *UCCL* 08092; Paine, *MTB*, 597. Franklin R. Rogers contends, however, that neither of these Yonge books "offers any hints as to [SLC's] source for the total structure" of *The Prince and the Pauper* (Rogers, *Mark Twain's Burlesque Patterns*, 173).

38. *The Prince and the Pauper*, 126; "A Royal Compliment," *Galaxy* 10 (September 1870): 429–30; SLC to David Gray, 18 September 1879, *UCCL* 11404.

39. *MTHL*, 292; "Amusements," *NYS*, 21 December 1880, 3.

40. Smith, *Mark Twain: The Development*, 116; *Simon Wheeler, Detective*, 9; *Huckleberry Finn* (1885), 147–48.

41. *Huckleberry Finn* (2010), 730; *Huckleberry Finn* (1885), 151, 166.

42. *MTHL*, 306–7; *Huckleberry Finn* (1885), 175, 188.

43. SLC to Jeannette Gilder, 14 May 1887, *UCCL* 03572; Webster, *Mark Twain: Business Man*, 142–44; Paine, *MTB*, 675; *MTHL*, 296.

44. Paine, *MTB*, 676; *Mark Twain's Letters* (1917), 378–79; Fanning, *Mark Twain and Orion Clemens*, 187.

45. *MTHL*, 312–13, 315; Jane Lampton Clemens to SLC, October 1880; Paine, *MTB*, 676; Orion Clemens to SLC, 3 June 1880, *UCLC* 47205; Paine, *MTB*, 676; *MTCI*, 122; SLC to Orion Clemens, 22 February 1883, *UCCL* 02350; SLC to Orion Clemens, 26 March 1882, *UCCL* 12734; *AMT*, 1:599, 2:27.

46. *Dublin Freeman's Journal and Commercial Advertiser*, 12 April 1880, 3; Webster, *Mark Twain: Business Man*, 145–46; *The Stolen White Elephant Etc.*, 224; Andrews, *Nook Farm*, 129–30, 303; *MTHL*, 290, 299; "Amusement Notes," *New York Graphic*, 12 May 1880, 627; "The Bazar," *HC*, 7 June 1880, 2; *The American Claimant*, 166.

47. "Mark Twain a Valuable Contribution to the Buffalo Homeopathic Fair," *Indianapolis Sentinel*, 21 December 1880, 4; "Latest News Items," *SFB*, 27 September 1881, 4; "Local Mention," *WS*, 27 January 1882, 4.

48. "Arrivals at the Hotels," *NYT*, 16 June 1880, 8; SLC to Susan and Lilly Warner, 17 June 1880, *UCCL* 01814; SLC to Franklin G. Whitmore, 15 June 1880, *UCCL* 11814; *MTHL*, 320; *LMT&JHT*, 98; *Collected Tales*, 747–52; "Mark Twain's Romance," *BH*, 4 December 1881, 4; *Tom Sawyer*, 255.

49. SLC to Pamela Moffett, 11 December 1880, *UCCL* 01870; *MTHL*, 319–20, 323–24; Mary Mason Fairbanks to SLC, 26 July 1880, *UCLC* 32822; E. P. Parker to SLC, 22 December 1880, *UCLC* 32903; SLC to E. P. Parker, 24 December 1880, *UCCL* 02547; Joe Goodman to SLC, 24 October 1881, *UCLC* 40889.

50. SLC to Ned House, 31 August–1 September 1880, *UCCL* 01828; SLC to Harriet Whitmore, 13 September 1880, *UCCL* 01832; *Mark Twain's Letters* (1917), 385–86; "Prominent Arrivals," *NYTrib*, 29 September 1880, 8; Gribben, *Mark Twain's Library*, 126; SLC to David Gray, 23 September 1880, *UCCL* 11406.

51. *N&J*, 2:420–21; *MTHL*, 316; "From Many Points of View," *NYTrib*, 24 March 1888, 5.

52. *AMT*, 1:483; "Gen. Grant in Hartford," *NYT*, 17 October 1880, 7; *MTHL*, 329, 332.

53. *MTSpk*, 138–43; Budd, *Mark Twain: Social Philosopher* 82; "German Republican Meeting," *HC*, 29 October 1880, 20.

54. "The Returns in Hartford," *NHJC*, 4 November 1880, 2; Kohn, "Mark Twain and Joseph Roswell Hawley," 75; *MTSpk*, 147; "Mark Twain," *CT*, 4 November 1880, 5; SLC to Herbert Hill, 3 November 1880, *UCCL* 09943.

55. "The Middlesex," *BA*, 8 November 1880, 1.

56. "Personal and Political," *Trenton State Gazette*, 14 December 1880, 2; Burdette and Burdette, *Robert J. Burdette: His Message*, 135–36; *N&J*, 3:233.

57. Simpson and Simpson, *Jean Webster*, 19; Clark, "Mark Twain at 'Nook Farm'"; *MTHL*, 62, 165; Emerson, *Mark Twain: A Literary Life*, 299; Howells, *My MT*, 46; Berkove, *Insider Stories*, 1040.

58. Gribben, "Mark Twain, Business Man," 25; SLC to Pamela Moffett, 10 January 1881, *UCCL* 01890; Hill, *Mark Twain and Elisha Bliss*, 157; *MTL*, 6:461; *MTLP*, 126.

59. SLC to Pamela Moffett, 10 January 1881, *UCCL* 01890; SLC to Orion Clemens, 26 March 1882, *UCCL* 12734; *AMT*, 2:470; SLC to Franklin G. Whitmore, 8 January 1895, *UCCL* 04834.

60. Gates 78–81; *AMT*, 1:241, 2:52–53; SLC to George W. Cable, 4 June 1883, *UCCL* 08821.

61. *AMT*, 1:372, 2:53–54, 2:527–8; *MTHL*, 349; SLC to James R. Osgood, 17 November 1880, *UCCL* 01854; "Current Opinion," *Macon Telegraph*, 8 March 1881, 2; SLC to Joel Chandler Harris, 10 August 1881, *UCCL* 01997; SLC to Joel Chandler Harris, 12 December 1881, *UCCL* 02114.

62. "Author's Readings," *NYT*, 17 December 1889, 3; *MTHL*, 334–36; *MTCI*, 18–19; *Colonel Sellers as a Scientist*, 236.

63. *N&J*, 2:426; SLC to Franklin G. Whitmore, 30 November 1880, *UCCL* 01860.

Chapter 9

1. SLC to Ned House, 19 February 1881, *UCCL* 01910; SLC to James R. Osgood, 26 November 1880, *UCCL* 01856; SLC to Henry Wadsworth Longfellow, 4 June 1877, *UCCL* 01438.

2. Phelps, *Autobiography*, 83; "The Chinese in Connecticut," *Sacramento Union*, 22 April 1879, 2.

3. *MTHL*, 339–40; Courtney, *Joseph Hopkins Twichell*, 206; *Mark Twain's Letters* (1917), 392.

4. *AMT*, 1:71; SLC to Ned House, 19 February 1881, *UCCL* 01910.

5. Bush, *Mark Twain and the Spiritual Crisis*, 137; SLC to Ulysses S. Grant, 15 March 1881, UCCL 01927; Ou, "Mark Twain, Anson Burlingame," 62; "China's Educational Mission," *NYT*, 16 July 1881, 5; "China's Backward Step," *NYT*, 2 September 1881, 5.

6. "The Papyrus Club," *BH*, 25 February 1881, 1; "The Papyrus Club's Guests," *NYT*, 25 February 1881, 4; *MTSpk*, 148–50.

7. *Mark Twain on Potholes and Politics*, 94–95, 127; SLC to Frank Fuller, 24 February 1880, UCCL 01762; Driscoll, "Mark Twain's Music Box," 182; Grace King to Nancy King, 19 June 1887, UCLC 43330. The titular character in W. D. Howells's *The Rise of Silas Lapham* also serves the German mineral water Apollonaris at the dinner in his home when he becomes drunk, a scene Howells apparently modeled at a remove on the Whittier birthday speech.

8. "Mark Twain's Drink," *WS*, 14 October 1889, 7; Gold, *"Hatching Ruin,"* 84; *MTHL*, 304.

9. "Personal," *BJ*, 7 November 1881, 4; "The Advertiser," *Adelaide South Australian Advertiser*, 18 March 1882, 2; "The War Correspondent," *HC*, 18 November 1881, 2; "Our Hartford Letter," *SR*, 19 November 1881, 5; *MTHL*, 304; *Mark Twain on Potholes and Politics*, 147; SLC to John Kinney, 16 October 1888, UCCL 03792 and 10592.

10. SLC to Dean Sage, 5 February 1890, UCCL 04012. SLC advised House in January 1884, when Koto's legal legitimacy as his daughter was questioned, that "To our minds, no course is left you for Koto's protection but the marriage" (SLC to Ned House, 14 January 1884, UCCL 02889).

11. "Is His Word Twain Also or Has Mark's Memory Been Wrecked?," *NYT*, 31 January 1890, 9; SLC to Ned House, 21 October 1881, UCCL 02057.

12. SLC to Pamela Moffett, [14?] November 1880, UCCL 11995. Three years later, SLC considered publishing *Huck Finn* together with *Tom Sawyer* "since Huck is in some sense a continuation of the former story," but *Huck* was still incomplete.

13. *MTHL*, 339–40, 446; SLC to E. P. Parker, 24 December 1880, UCCL 02547; *MTCI*, 229, 262; Andrews, *Nook Farm*, 375; SLC to Chatto & Windus, 25 August 1881, UCCL 01591.

14. SLC to Dan Slote, 16 December 1880, UCCL 01872; SLC to Rose Terry Cooke, 17 December 1880, UCCL 01875; *MTHL*, 339–40; Gribben, *Mark Twain's Library*, 648. Incidentally, SLC enjoyed the oyster dinner in company with Rose Terry Cooke, the writer and artist Francis Hopkinson Smith, and the actor Lawrence Barrett.

15. SLC to Dan Slote, 26 January 1881, UCCL 01898; SLC to Dan Slote, 19–21 February 1881, UCCL 01911; SLC to Charles L. Webster, 5 June 1881, UCCL 01970; SLC to Charles L. Webster, 10–11 January 1882, UCCL 02148; SLC to Charles L. Webster, 18–20 July 1884, UCCL 10899.

16. Pamela Moffett to Mollie Clemens, 25 May 1875, UCLC 47129; Gold, *"Hatching Ruin,"* 86, 99; Pamela Moffett to Sam Moffett, 17–20 April 1881, UCLC 30197; SLC to Charles L. Webster, 29 April 1881, UCCL 01940; SLC to Charles L. Webster, 28 October 1881, UCCL 02077; SLC to Charles L. Webster, 24 November 1881, UCCL 02098; Charles L. Webster to SLC, 9 April 1883, UCLC 41523; *MTLP*, 180.

17. Blair, *Mark Twain and Huck Finn*, 267; Charles L. Webster to SLC, 18 April 1881, UCLC 40757; Charles L. Webster to SLC, 26 April 1881, UCLC 40761; Charles L. Webster to SLC, 4 May 1881, UCLC 40763; Charles L. Webster to SLC, 5 May 1881, UCLC 40765; Charles L. Webster to SLC, 11 May 1881, UCLC 40769; Charles L. Webster to SLC, 18 May 1881, UCLC 40773; Charles L. Webster to SLC, 19 May 1881, UCLC 40774; *N&J*, 2:391; SLC to

Charles L. Webster, 6 May 1881, *UCCL* 01948; SLC to Charles L. Webster, 14 May 1881, *UCCL* 01953; SLC to Charles L. Webster, 20 May 1881, *UCLC* 40775; SLC to Charles L. Webster, 30 May 1881, *UCCL* 01962; SLC to Charles L. Webster, 5 June 1881, *UCCL* 01970.

18. SLC to Charles L. Webster, 20 June 1881, *UCCL* 01975; Gold, "Hatching Ruin," 86.

19. Kaplan, *The Singular Mark Twain*, 364; SLC to Charles L. Webster, 7 September 1881, *UCCL* 02031; SLC to Charles L. Webster, 8 August 1882, *UCCL* 02249; SLC to Charles L. Webster, 9 August 1882, *UCCL* 02250; SLC to James R. Osgood, 31 July 1882, *UCCL* 12448.

20. "Funeral of Daniel Slote," *NYS*, 17 February 1882, 4; Ganzel, *Mark Twain Abroad*, 303; *MTMF*, 247.

21. SLC to Charles L. Webster, 24 September 1882, *UCCL* 02279; SLC to Charles L. Webster, 3 October 1882, *UCCL* 02285; Mary Mason Fairbanks to SLC, 13 March 1882, *UCLC* 41073.

22. Gold, "Hatching Ruin," 30; Kaplan, *The Singular Mark Twain*, 365; SLC to Charles L. Webster, 2 March 1882, *UCCL* 02168; *AMT*, 1:101.

23. *N&J*, 3:147, 3:191–92, 3:230, 3:385.

24. *MTHL*, 597; SLC to Brander Matthews, 31 March 1885, *UCCL* 03200; *N&J*, 3:437; *The American Claimant*, 102; *MTCI*, 327.

25. *AMT*, 1:101; SLC to J. R. Young, 29 April 1881, *UCCL* 01941; SLC to Orion Clemens, 5 January 1889, *UCCL* 03847; SLC to Charles L. Webster, 26 October 1881, *UCCL* 02072; SLC to Charles L. Webster, 24 November 1881, *UCCL* 02098; Blair, *Mark Twain and Huck Finn*, 37.

26. *MTHL*, 351–54; "Springfield," *SR*, 28 February 1881, 5; *MTMF*, 243; *Simon Wheeler, Detective*, 243; *AMT*, 1:87; Josephine Gerhardt to SLC, 24 May 1881, *UCLC* 40777.

27. SLC to Annie Lucas, 31 January 1881, *UCCL* 01899; *The Prince and the Pauper*, 90.

28. SLC to Dan Slote, 16 March 1881, *UCCL* 01929; *N&J*, 3:428.

29. Wagenknecht, *Mark Twain: The Man and His Work*, 138; SLC to Pamela Moffett, 16 March 1881, *UCCL* 01928; SLC to Karl Gerhardt, 30 May 1881, *UCCL* 10064; *N&J*, 2:399; Salsbury, *Susy and Mark Twain*, 146; SLC to Dan Slote, 19–21 February 1881, *UCCL* 01911; Willis, *Mark and Livy*, 143.

30. "Gone to West Point," *Washington National Republican*, 10 June 1881, 1; *MTSpk*, 151, 153.

31. Leon, *Mark Twain and West Point*, 51, 53–55; Bush, *Mark Twain and the Spiritual Crisis*, 162.

32. SLC to Karl and Josephine Gerhardt, 26 June 1881, *UCCL* 01978; SLC to Karl and Josephine Gerhardt, 31 July 1881, *UCCL* 01991; *LMT&JHT*, 107; *N&J*, 2:396; Bikle, *George W. Cable*, 69; SLC to George W. Cable, 17 July 1881, *UCCL* 01985; *Following the Equator*, 159; "New England Notes," *BA*, 27 August 1881, 8; Howells, *If Not Literature*, 237; "State Correspondence," *NHJC*, 23 July 1881, 4.

33. "Branford," *NHJC*, 3 August 1881, 4; *MTHL*, 359; SLC to James R. Osgood, 7 March 1881, *UCCL* 01924; *N&J*, 2:439; *Letters from the Earth*, 193.

34. "Mark Twain," *Sydney Evening News*, 18 January 1882, 6; "Mark Twain / His Latest Oddity—a New Version of 'Hamlet,'" *Portland Oregonian*, 29 December 1881, 4; *Mark Twain's Satires and Burlesques*, 49–86; "Holiday Fun," *CIO*, 24 December 1881, 13; Rogers, *Mark Twain's Burlesque Patterns*, 25.

35. SLC to Jane Lampton Clemens, 19 September 1881, *UCCL* 02038; Howells, *If Not Literature*, 237; SLC to C. E. Norton, 30 August 1881, *UCCL* 02018; SLC to Karl and Josephine

Gerhardt, 9 October 1881, *UCCL* 02049; SLC to Ned House, 4 October 1881, *UCCL* 02043; SLC to Ned House, 27 December 1881, *UCCL* 02126; Salsbury, *Susy and Mark Twain*, 146; *MTHL*, 28 January 1882; Wheeler, *Yesterdays*, 325; Paine, *MTB*, 729.

36. Ticknor, *Glimpses*, 140; SLC to James R. Osgood, 23 August 1881, *UCCL* 02013.

37. *MTHL*, 338–49, 376; SLC to E. P. Parker, 24 December 1880, *UCCL* 02547; SLC to James R. Osgood, 16 December 1880, *UCCL* 01873.

38. SLC to James R. Osgood, 21 January 1881, *UCCL* 01894; SLC to Annie Lucas, 31 January 1881, *UCCL* 01899; *MTCI*, 39.

39. *MTHL*, 373; Taliaferro, *All the Great Prizes*, 221; *MTL*, 5:368; David, *Mark Twain and His Illustrators*, 1:237, 1:242.

40. Howells, *Life in Letters of William Dean Howells*, 1:303; "New Publications," *NYTrib*, 25 October 1881, 6; SLC to James R. Osgood, 27 October 1881, *UCCL* 09947; SLC to David Gray, 9 November 1881, *UCCL* 11409.

41. SLC to Olivia Langdon Clemens, 28 November 1881, *UCCL* 02103 and 11717; SLC to Olivia Langdon Clemens, 29 November 1881, *UCCL* 02105; SLC to Olivia Langdon Clemens, 1 December 1881, *UCCL* 02107; SLC to Olivia Langdon Clemens, 2 December 1881, *UCCL* 02108; *N&J*, 2:413.

42. "Telegraphic Jottings," *NHJC*, 9 December 1881, 3; *N&J*, 2:405, 2:414; SLC to Olivia Langdon Clemens, 7 December 1881, *UCCL* 02111; *MTSpk*, 157–60.

43. "Canada Surprises Mark Twain," *NYT*, 17 December 1881, 2; "Prince and Pauper," *WC*, 20 December 1881, 1; *SR*, 17 December 1881, 4.

44. "Mark Twain Explains," *SR*, 20 December 1881, 4; "Twain's Copyright Claim Refused," *BH*, 17 December 1881, 4; "Sunbeams," *NYS*, 22 December 1881, 2.

45. "Mark Twain's Copyright," *NYT*, 29 December 1881, 1; "Local Intelligence," *SR*, 2 May 1882, 5; "Local Varieties," *BH*, 30 April 1882, 11, and *BH*, 3 October 1882, 2; Feinstein, "Mark Twain's Lawsuits," 119–20; "'Mark Twain' Loses a Suit," *BH*, 9 January 1883, 4; "A Decision against 'Mark Twain,'" *NYTrib*, 10 January 1883, 1; Doyno, *Writing Huck Finn*, 189.

46. Feinstein, "Mark Twain's Lawsuits," 125; *Huckleberry Finn* (1885), 206.

47. "Lecture Facts," *SFB*, 17 October 1878, 1; "Editorial Notes," *Buffalo Courier*, 26 May 1880, 1; *Ithaca Journal*, 15 July 1880, 4; "The Living Obelisk," *NYS*, 28 December 1880, 2. Ironically, three years later SLC contributed a piece to an album sold on behalf of the Pedestal Fund ("Mark Twain on 'Liberty,'" *Macon Telegraph*, 14 December 1883, 1). SLC's interest in the Statue of Liberty dates to 1883, when he contributed work to be auctioned off to raise funds for the construction of the statue's pedestal (Felder and Rosen, *Fifty Jewish Women*, 45).

48. "Ladies' Column," *Adelaide Journal*, 29 July 1882, 2; "All Sorts," *SFB*, 21 November 1882, 4; McWilliams, *Mark Twain in the St. Louis Post-Dispatch*, 121, 123; E. W. Howe, "News and Notes," *Atchison (Kans.) Globe*, 31 December 1881, 3; "Specimens of German Criticism," *WS*, 25 June 1887, 6; Tenney, "About Mark Twain," *Mark Twain Journal* 42 (April 2004): 4; "Our Forty 'Immortals,'" *Critic*, 12 April 1884, 169; "Hartford (Ct.) Authors," *BH*, 26 December 1881, 2; SLC to Osgood and Company, 28 December 1881, *UCCL* 02128.

49. SLC to Orion Clemens, 9 February 1879, *UCCL* 01631; *N&J*, 3:122–23; "Mark Twain's Statement," *Albany Journal*, 22 July 1885, 2; Henry Clay Lukens, "American Literary Comedians," *Harper's Monthly* 80 (April 1890): 796; SLC to Charles Fairbanks, 25 June 1890, *UCCL* 04056.

50. "A Curious Experiment," *Century* 23 (November 1881): 35–46; "A Curious Episode," *Critic*, 3 December 1881, 339; SLC to Jeannette Gilder, 12 December 1881, *UCCL* 02113; SLC to Hjalmar Hjorth Boyesen, 11 January 1882, *UCCL* 02149.

51. Howells, "Mark Twain" 782; *MTHL*, 405.

52. David, *Mark Twain and His Illustrators*, 1:246; Ballou, *The Building of the House*, 280–83; SLC to James R. Osgood, 4 January 1882, *UCCL* 02142; SLC to James R. Osgood, 12 February 1882, *UCCL* 02159; *MTLP*, 150; SLC to Joel Chandler Harris, 10 August 1881, *UCCL* 01997; *AMT*, 1:372; Paine, *MTB*, 729; Welland, *Mark Twain in England*, 125.

53. *MTMF*, 245; *MTCI*, 39; Budd, *MTCR*, 199–201, 204–7; *N&J*, 3:287, 3:290; SLC to Charles L. Webster, 25 April 1887, *UCCL* 02658; Joe Goodman to SLC, 29 January 1882, *UCLC* 41003.

54. "New Publications," *BJ*, 17 December 1881, 5; "Mark Twain's Romance," *NYH*, 4 December 1881, 4; "The Prince and the Pauper," *Sacramento Union*, 28 March 1882, 1; "Mark Twain's Romance," *BH*, 4 December 1881, 4; Budd, *MTCR*, 202, 208, 210–12, 214–15; *NYS*, 19 September 1896, 7.

55. SLC to Andrew Chatto, 3 March 1882, *UCCL* 02169; "Christmas Books," *London Times*, 20 December 1881, 3; "The Prince and the Pauper," *Spectator*, 21 January 1882, 95; "Christmas Books," *London Standard*, 16 December 1881, 2, and *London Standard*, 2 January 1882, 4; "Recent Novels," *London Daily News*, 1 March 1882, 6; "Our London Letter," *Leicester Chronicle*, 17 December 1881, 5; "Novels of the Quarter," *British Quarterly Review* 75 (January 1882): 233–34; "Amongst the Books," *Melbourne Leader*, 21 January 1882, 2; "Mark Twain's 'The Prince and the Pauper,'" *Brisbane Courier*, 25 February 1882, 5; "The Prince and the Pauper," *Lyttelton (New Zealand) Times*, 3 May 1882, 6; "New Novels," *Academy*, 24 December 1881, 469; Budd, *MTCR*, 201–3, 209, 212–14; SLC to Ned House, 23 February 1882, *UCCL* 02164.

56. *MTSpk*, 162–66; "Forefathers' Day," *Philadelphia North American*, 23 December 1881, 1; "The Pilgrims," *Philadelphia Inquirer*, 23 December 1881, 8; Michelson, *Mark Twain on the Loose*, 20; "Persons and Things," *NHR*, 28 December 1881, 2; *CIO*, 29 December 1881, 4; *Cleveland Plain Dealer*, 24 December 1881, 4.

57. *MTHL*, 386–88; *MTLP*, 151; Budd, *Mark Twain: Social Philosopher* 390; *N&J*, 2:417, 2:423, 2:439–42, 2:444.

58. SLC to Charles L. Webster, 21 January 1882, *UCCL* 02152; "Foreign Notes," *NYTrib*, 17 December 1881, 1; "Personal," *NYTrib*, 10 December 1881, 4; "Memories of the Pilgrims," *NYTrib*, 23 December 1881, 5; SLC to J. R. Young, 3 February 1882, *UCCL* 02156; Howells, *My MT*, 70; *AMT*, 3:112–13; *MTHL*, 385–90; SLC to Whitelaw Reid, 6–28 January 1882, *UCCL* 02140.

59. *N&J*, 2:447, 3:234; SLC to James R. Osgood, 12 February 1882, *UCCL* 02159; "Concerning the Scoundrel Edward H. House," DV 305, MTP; Messent, "Mark Twain, Joseph Twichell," 56.

60. SLC to J. R. Young, 13 March 1882, *UCCL* 02171; Howells, *My MT*, 70–72.

61. "Twain Interviews Himself," *Wheeling Register*, 29 March 1882, 3; SLC to John Brown, 14–15 August 1880, *UCCL* 02814; "Men and Things," *BH*, 13 March 1882, 4; *Mark Twain's Notebook*, 382.

Chapter 10

1. Goodman and Dawson, *Howells: A Writer's Life*, 170; Bikle, *George W. Cable*, 132; SLC to George W. Cable, 20 June 1882, *UCCL* 02222; *MTCI*, 77.

2. *MTL*, 6:298, 6:381; *MTHL*, 56, 81.

3. *N&J*, 2:432, 2:459; *MTHL*, 399; Emerson, *Authentic Mark Twain*, 119; Cardwell, "Life on the Mississippi," 288.

4. *MTHL*, 403; *N&J*, 2:466; SLC to Joel Chandler Harris, 2 April 1882, *UCCL* 02194; *MTCI*, 401.

5. SLC to Olivia Langdon Clemens, 21 April 1882, *UCCL* 02203; SLC to Olivia Langdon Clemens, 22 April 1882, *UCCL* 02204; *N&J*, 2:465, 2:529; "Local Personals," *St. Louis Globe-Democrat*, 18 April 1882, 6; "Mark Twain at the Yorick," *Melbourne Australasian*, 5 October 1895, 43; *Life on the Mississippi*, 321; "Hotel Arrivals," *Memphis Appeal*, 25 April 1882, 4.

6. *N&J*, 2:476, 2:530, 2:539, 2:570; *Life on the Mississippi*, 95, 291; "Mark Twain at the Yorick," *Melbourne Australasian*, 5 October 1895, 43.

7. SLC to Olivia Langdon Clemens, 25 April 1882, *UCCL* 02205; Wager, "A Critical Edition," 361; "Personals," *Memphis Appeal*, 29 April 1882, 4.

8. SLC to Olivia Langdon Clemens, 27 April 1882, *UCCL* 02208; Kruse, *Mark Twain and Life on the Mississippi* 70; *Life on the Mississippi*, 417; "A Trip on the Charles Morgan," *New Orleans Picayune*, 10 May 1882, 10; *N&J*, 2:555.

9. SLC to Olivia Langdon Clemens 29 April 1882, *UCCL* 02208; *N&J*, 2:550, 2:553; *Life on the Mississippi*, 445; Parsons, "Down the Mighty River," 6–7.

10. Bikle, *George W. Cable*, 75; Grace King to Nancy King, 10 June 1887, *UCLC* 43316; *Life on the Mississippi*, 458; *N&J*, 2:485, 2:551–52.

11. "Personal and General Notes," *New Orleans Picayune*, 1 May 1882, 1; New Orleans *Times-Democrat*, 4 May 1882, 4; Howells, *My MT*, 99; SLC to Olivia Langdon Clemens 2 May 1882, *UCCL* 02184; *N&J*, 2:552, 2:554; "Tea Table Talk," *New Orleans Picayune*, 7 May 1882, 15; *Life on the Mississippi*, 251, 256, 354, 500.

12. SLC to Olivia Langdon Clemens, 2 May 1882, *UCCL* 02184; "New Orleans Items," *CC*, 6 May 1882, 7; *N&J*, 2:468; "Society Notes," New Orleans *Times-Democrat*, 7 May 1882, 15; *Life on the Mississippi*, 446.

13. Parsons, "Down the Mighty River," 11; Loges, "The Life and Death," 6; *Life on the Mississippi*, 475.

14. "Mark Twain in Town," *New Orleans Picayune*, 29 April 1882, 3; New Orleans *Times-Democrat*, 5 May 1882, 4; *Life on the Mississippi*, 475.

15. *N&J*, 2:470, 2:558.

16. *Life on the Mississippi*, 500, 503; SLC to Olivia Langdon Clemens, 6 May 1882, *UCCL* 02188; Turner, *MT&GWC*, 8. Cable retold this story at SLC's seventieth birthday celebration at Delmonico's in New York twenty-three years later ("Mark Twain's 70th Birthday," *Harper's Weekly*, supplement, 23 December 1905, 1888).

17. Kaplan, *The Singular Mark Twain*, 386; "Dull and Raining at St. Louis," *CC*, 13 May 1882, 7; "Mark Twain's Travels," *St. Louis Globe-Democrat*, 13 May 1882, 8; Paine, *MTB*, 739–40.

18. *Life on the Mississippi*, 524, 540; Smith, "Mark Twain's Images of Hannibal," 12; *N&J*, 2:478–79, 2:513; SLC to Olivia Langdon Clemens, 17 May 1882, *UCCL* 02190; SLC to John Robards, 10 June 1882, *UCCL* 02217.

19. Ironically, Guy Cardwell in an essay expressly devoted to correcting earlier scholars' mistakes asserts that SLC visited "his mother in Keokuk" during his Mississippi River tour in the spring of 1882 (Cardwell, "*Life on the Mississippi*," 289). But Jane Lampton Clemens did not move to Keokuk until August 1882 (*AMT*, 2:470).

20. SLC to Olivia Langdon Clemens, 17 May 1882, *UCCL* 02190; *N&J*, 2:434, 2:480; Paine, *MTB*, 740.

21. *N&J*, 2:486; SLC to John Brown Jr., 1 June 1882, *UCCL* 02212.

22. *N&J*, 2:480–81; *MTCI*, 42; "Personal Intelligence," *NYT*, 25 May 1882, 8; *MTHL*, 403.

23. SLC to Caleb F. Davis, 8 July 1882, *UCCL* 02233; Trumbull, *Memorial History*, 151; SLC to Jane Lampton Clemens, 8 July 1882, *UCCL* 02228; SLC to George W. Cable, 20 June 1882, *UCCL* 02222; *A Family Sketch*, 85; *AMT*, 2:100; SLC to Joel Chandler Harris, 5 September 1882, *UCCL* 02264; "Personal Gossip," *Frank Leslie's Illustrated Newspaper*, 28 July 1883, 371.

24. *AMT*, 2:54; Feinstein, "Mark Twain's Lawsuits," 165; "The Stolen White Elephant," *CT*, 10 June 1882, 9; Paine, *MTB*, 734; Emerson, *Authentic Mark Twain*, 118.

25. Lilian Whiting, "Letter from Boston," *St. Louis Globe-Democrat*, 18 June 1882, 3; "Note from London," *Sheffield & Rotherham Independent*, 24 June 1882, 6; "Literature," *Leeds Mercury*, 12 July 1882, 3; "The Stolen White Elephant," *London Morning Post*, 22 August 1882, 2; "Novels of the Week," *Athenaeum*, 24 June 1882, 794; Budd, *MTCR*, 220–21, 224–31; "Literary Notes," *WS*, 17 June 1882, 2.

26. "Late Publications," *Philadelphia North American*, 28 June 1882, 4; Machor, "Reading," 145–46; "Current Literature," *SFB*, 15 July 1882, 1; "Some Novels and Stories," *Independent*, 3 August 1882, 11; "Book Notes," *Our Continent*, 19 July 1882, 59; "Literature," *Melbourne Australasian*, 30 September 1882, 8; "Mark Twain's New Book," *Atchison (Kans.) Globe*, 16 June 1882, 1; "Mark Twain as a Humorist," *NHR*, 6 September 1882, 2; "Personals," *CT*, 16 July 1882, 5; Budd, *MTCR*, 226, 228–29; Anderson and Hill, "How Samuel Clemens Became Mark Twain's Publisher," 133.

27. "Mark Twain's Summer Home," *NYT*, 10 September 1882, 3; Olivia Langdon Clemens to Sam Moffett, 13 August 1882, *UCCL* 02251; *LMT&JHT*, 123; *MTLP*, 157–58; SLC to Joel Chandler Harris, 5 September 1882, *UCCL* 02264.

28. *MTLP*, 158; Gribben, *Mark Twain's Library*, 788; Ganzel, "Twain, Travel Books, and *Life on the Mississippi*," 42; Ganzel, "Samuel Clemens and Captain Marryat"; Cardwell, "*Life on the Mississippi*," 290; David, "Mark Twain, the War, and *Life on the Mississippi*," 237; *Life on the Mississippi*, 386.

29. SLC to Charles L. Webster, 19 September 1882, *UCCL* 02276; *N&J*, 2:506.

30. *MTHL*, 417–18; SLC to Ned House, 2 December 1882, *UCCL* 02313; SLC to James R. Osgood, 29 December 1882; SLC to Charles L. Webster, 3 January 1883, *UCCL* 02330; SLC to George W. Cable, 15 January 1883, *UCCL* 02336.

31. "Musical Notes," *BH*, 16 November 1882, 2; *NHR*, 22 December 1882, 4; "Postmaster-General Howe at Hartford," *SR*, 8 December 1882, 8; "The Visiting Soldiery," *HC*, 20 October 1882, 2; "Military Courtesies," *BH*, 20 October 1882, 2.

32. SLC to George W. Cable, 5 October 1882, *UCCL* 02286; *MTHL*, 419.

33. "On Plymouth Rock Again," *NYT*, 23 December 1882, 1–2; "New England Day," *SFB*, 23 December 1882, 1; "The Dinner in This City," *NYTrib*, 22 December 1882, 2; *Collected Tales*, 834–36.

34. *NYTrib*, 24 December 1882, 6; *NYTrib*, 3 May 1883, 2; *New Orleans Picayune*, 4 January 1883, 4; *Macon Telegraph*, 31 March 1883, 2; *St. Louis Globe-Democrat*, 27 December 1882, 4; SLC to George W. Cable, 15 January 1883, *UCCL* 02336.

35. Feinstein, "Mark Twain's Lawsuits," 60, 70–71, 76; Whitford to Charles L. Webster, 25 September 1882, *UCLC* 41312; "Mark Twain's Injunction," *NYS*, 17 October 1882, 1; SLC to Clinton Parkhurst, 25 January 1883, *UCCL* 09242; SLC to Andrew Chatto, 1 March 1883, *UCCL* 12923.

36. *N&J*, 2:498; Paine, *MTB*, 513, 744; Blair, *Mark Twain and Huck Finn*, 138; Quirk, *Coming to Grips*, 35; *AMT*, 3:127.

37. SLC echoed this idea in his notebook three years later: "In my opinion these myriads of globes are merely the blood-corpuscles ebbing & flowing through the arteries of God, & we but animalculae that infest them, disease them, pollute them: & God does not know we are there, & would not care if He did" (*N&J*, 3:54, 3:56, 3:246–47).

38. Lease, "Mark Twain and the Publication of *Life on the Mississippi*"; SLC to James R. Osgood, 15 January 1883, *UCCL* 02334. While some scholars have asserted that SLC and Osgood tailored the narrative to avoid offending southern subscribers, the evidence fails to substantiate the claim. On the contrary, rather than an effort to pander to southern readers, SLC's depiction of the South reflected his nostalgia for the region.

39. *N&J*, 2:300, 2:482–83; Wager, "A Critical Edition," 414, 497; Ticknor, "Mark Twain's Missing Chapter," 307–8. Everett Emerson also notes "the author's distress at Southern violence and the tendency to resort to lynch mobs, as he indicated in a chapter written for *Life on the Mississippi* but deleted from it" (Emerson, *Authentic Mark Twain*, 140).

40. Ticknor, "Mark Twain's Missing Chapter," 306; Turner, "Mark Twain and the South," 505–6; *N&J*, 3:45, 3:88.

41. Railton, "The Twain-Cable Combination," 172; "George W. Cable," *HC*, 30 March 1883, 2; *Life on the Mississippi*, 442, 472.

42. Turner, *MT&GWC*, 12, 15, 17–19; "Nutmeg Gratings," *SR*, 8 April 1883, 8; Bikle, *George W. Cable*, 96–97; Moore, *Talks in a Library*, 416; Phelps, *Autobiography*, 68; Turner, *MT&GWC*, 173; *AMT*, 3:527–28; SLC to Frances A. Cox, 6 April 1883, *UCCL* 02367; SLC to James R. Osgood, 6 April 1883, *UCCL* 02803.

43. Bikle, *George W. Cable*, 96–97; SLC to James R. Osgood, 6 April 1883, *UCCL* 02803; Turner, *MT&GWC*, 17–18; SLC to Frances A. Cox, 6 April 1883, *UCCL* 02367; George W. Cable to Louise Cable, 7 April 1883, *UCLC* 41519.

44. "Vignaux, 300; Sexton, 141," *BH*, 6 March 1883, 2; *AMT*, 1:548; Matthews, *The Tocsin of Revolt*, 255; Moore, "Mark Twain and Don Quixote," 326.

45. Fears, *Mark Twain Day-by-Day*, 1:732; *N&J*, 3:205; G. E. Montgomery, "New York Gossip," *Philadelphia North American*, 28 April 1883, 1; "Jottings about Town," *NYS*, 24 April 1883, 1; "A Farewell to Salvini," *NYT*, 27 April 1883, 5; "More Honors to Irving," *BH*, 17 December 1883, 2; Julian Hawthorne, "At a London Publisher's," *Collier's Weekly*, 24 June 1897, 22–23; "A Busy Day for the Irving Company," *NYTrib*, 26 April 1884, 5; "Hail and Farewell," *BH*, 30 April 1884, 8.

46. "Personal," *BJ*, 9 May 1883, 1; SLC to Charles L. Webster, 7 May 1883, *UCCL* 02383; "An Innocent Abroad," *Victoria (B.C.) Daily Colonist*, 31 May 1883, 1; SLC to Olivia Langdon Clemens, 8 May 1883, *UCCL* 02385; SLC to George W. Cable, 4 June 1883, *UCCL* 08821.

47. "Telegraphic Brevities," *BH*, 24 May 1883, 4; "Our Boston Letter," *SR*, 18 May 1883, 2; "Cushion Carrom [*sic*] Billiards," *BH*, 20 May 1883, 6; Webster, *Mark Twain: Business Man*, 214; SLC to Olivia Langdon Clemens, 23 May 1883, *UCCL* 02393; "Mark Twain and Louise on a Raft," *Philadelphia Inquirer*, 30 May 1883, 1; "In Brief," *Carson (Nev.) Appeal*, 26 May 1883, 3; "Pleasant Paragraphs," *Troy (N.Y.) Times*, 21 June 1883, 4; *MTHL*, 438–41.

48. "Our Authors," *BH*, 11 March 1883, 14; SLC to Osgood and Company, 6 January 1883, *UCCL* 02331; David, *Mark Twain and His Illustrators*, 1:316, 322; James R. Osgood to SLC, 5 April 1882, *UCLC* 41234; *AMT*, 2:492; SLC to Charles L. Webster, 9 September 1882, *UCCL* 02268.

49. "Literature," *NYH*, 20 May 1883, 10; "New Publications," *CC*, 27 May 1883, 1; "Recent Publications," *NHJC*, 21 June 1883, 1; "Literature," *NYEP*, 1 September 1883, 4; "New Books," *St. Louis Globe-Democrat*, 21 May 1883, 8; "The Book World," *Milwaukee Sentinel*, 10 June 1883, 10; "Mark Twain's New Book," *Atlanta Constitution*, 17 June 1883, 6; "New Publications," *Sacramento Union*, 29 September 1883, 4; *MTL*, VI, 326; Brodwin, "The Useful and Useless River," 196; Melton, *Mark Twain, Travel Books, and Tourism*, 137; Budd, *MTCR*, 237–37, 239–41, 243, 245, 247–49, 250–52, 254; *NYS*, 19 September 1896, 7.

50. Budd, *MTCR*, 246–47, 253; "Mark Twain's New Book," *Derby Mercury*, 23 May 1883, 6; Tenney, *Mark Twain: A Reference Guide*, 12; "Literature," *Leeds Mercury*, 30 May 1883, 3; "Life on the Mississippi," *London Morning Post*, 13 August 1883, 3; "Life on the Mississippi," *Adelaide South Australian Register*, 4 August 1883, 1; "Contemporary Literature," *British Quarterly Review* 78 (July 1883): 226–27; Henley, "Literature," *Athenaeum*, 2 June 1883, 694–95.

51. *MTLP*, 5, 129, 165, 166, 267; *N&J*, 3:2; Charles L. Webster to SLC, 17 January 1884, *UCLC* 41745; SLC to James R. Osgood, 21 December 1883, *UCCL* 02872; Ballou, *The Building of the House*, 280–83; *MTHL*, 468, 527–28; *AMT*, 1:372, 2:53–54.

52. SLC to George W. Cable, 16 April 1883, *UCCL* 02371; *MTHL*, 442; SLC to Charles L. Webster, 14 April 1884, *UCCL* 02951.

53. SLC to Karl and Josephine Gerhardt, 2 July 1883, *UCCL* 02300; *Huckleberry Finn* (2010), 461–516; *N&J*, 3:358–59; Eliot, "Introduction," in *Huckleberry Finn* (1999), 350; *Huckleberry Finn* (1885), 190.

54. SLC to James R. Osgood, 1 September 1883, *UCCL* 04139; Olivia Langdon Clemens to Harriet Whitmore, 16 July 1883, *UCCL* 02451; *MTHL*, 435, 438; SLC to Orion Clemens, [24?] July 1883, *UCCL* 02326

55. Mary Jane Wilks, Huck's femme ideal, was a portrait of his mother as a young woman with her flaming red hair and her telltale middle name.

56. Andrews, "Mark Twain and James W. C. Pennington," 104–5; MacKethan, "Huck Finn and the Slave Narratives," 255–56.

57. *MTHL*, 465; *A Family Sketch*, 86.

58. Charles L. Webster to SLC, 21 April 1884, *UCLC* 42021. In the omitted passage, Huck learns he and Jim have drifted past Cairo in the fog. But it could be omitted "by heaving in a paragraph to say that Huck visited the raft to find out how far it might be to Cairo." Yet this paragraph was not added. As Bernard DeVoto observed, SLC lacked "the discipline of revision" (DeVoto, *Mark Twain at Work*, 10).

59. SLC to Robert Underwood Johnson, 6 July 1885, *UCCL* 03252.

60. *Huckleberry Finn* (2010), 511; Quirk, *Coming to Grips* 66, 102, 161, 253; SLC to Andrew Chatto, 1 September 1883, *UCCL* 02829.

61. Wallace, "The Case against *Huckleberry Finn*," 16; Cardwell, *The Man Who Was Mark Twain*, 199; Quirk, *Coming to Grips*, 158; Messent, *Mark Twain*, 88; Foner, *Mark Twain: Social Critic*, 205.

62. Smith, "Huck, Jim, and American Racial Discourse," 7; *Huckleberry Finn* (1885), 24.

63. Lionel Trilling, quoted in Geoffrey Hughes, *Political Correctness: A History of Semantics and Culture*, 152; Emerson, *The Journals and Miscellaneous Notebooks*, 9:195.

64. Blair, *Mark Twain and Huck Finn*, 107; *Huckleberry Finn* (1885), 50; Smith, "Huck, Jim, and American Racial Discourse," 5; Schmitz, "Twain, *Huckleberry Finn*, and the Reconstruction," 65.

65. *Mark Twain's Letters* (1917), 434; *LMT&JHT*, 129.

66. *LMT&JHT*, 130; "Mark Twain's Vacation," *HC*, 24 July 1883, 2; "Mark Twain's Vacation," *BE*, 7 August 1883, 1; "Mark Twain's Historical Game," *SFB*, 2 August 1883, 4; SLC to Ned House, 1 October 1883, *UCCL* 02844; *MTHL*, 437, 439.

67. SLC to Jane Lampton Clemens, Orion Clemens, and Mollie Clemens, [24?] July 1883, *UCCL* 02326; *LMT&JHT*, 131–32; SLC to Ned House, 1 October 1883, *UCCL* 02844.

Chapter 11

1. "Commissioner Duncan's Sons," *NYT*, 9 June 1883, 8.

2. *MTCI*, 43–47; "New York," *NHJC*, 11 June 1883, 3.

3. "Mark Twain and Capt. Duncan," *BH*, 17 June 1883, 1; SLC to Charles L. Webster, 11–17 June 1883, *UCCL* 01888; SLC to Charles L. Webster, 18 June 1883, *UCCL* 02143; SLC to Charles L. Webster, 20 June 1883, *UCCL* 01562; "Hartford and Vicinity," *HC*, 18 June 1883, 1; *N&J*, 3:24, 3:58; SLC to Noah Brooks, 23 July 1883, *UCCL* 02351; *MTHL*, 865–67; Charles L. Webster to SLC, 27 December 1883, *UCLC* 41727; Budd, *Our Mark Twain*, 108.

4. "A Government Investigation," *NYTrib*, 22 June 1883, 4; "He Should Be Removed," *NYT*, 9 March 1884, 6. SLC might have claimed some of the credit for exposing this travesty if he had not in a spasm of self-interest repudiated the interview that refocused public attention on it.

5. "Mark Twain as a Witness," *SFB*, 25 August 1883, 4.

6. "Big Libel Suit," *BH*, 4 March 1884, 2; "Mark Twain / He Disclaims the Article Libeling Captain Duncan," *BE*, 7 March 1884, 4; "Captain Duncan's Suing 'The Times,'" *NYTrib*, 4 March 1884, 3; "Duncan's Case," *BE*, 5 March 1884, 10; "The Defence in the Duncan Suit," *NYTrib*, 7 March 1884, 3; "Capt. Duncan," *BE*, 7 March 1884, 2.

7. "Capt. C. C. Duncan," *NYT*, 21 April 1884, 4; "He Should Be Removed," *NYT*, 9 March 1884, 6; *MTHL*, 867.

8. "The Case of Capt. Duncan," *NYT*, 20 March 1884, 8; "He Should Be Removed," *NYT*, 9 March 1884, 6; "Capt. C. C. Duncan," *NYT*, 21 April 1884, 4; "The Four Duncans," scrapbook 8:113, MTP; "Duncan's Woe," *NYT*, 13 May 1884, 4; "A Shipping Commissioner Dismissed," *SFB*, 13 May 1884, 2; "The Laurel Park Chautauqua," *SR*, 19 July 1890, 4.

9. Arnold, "A Word about America," *Nineteenth Century* 11 (May 1882): 689, 693; Baetzhold, *Mark Twain and John Bull*, 97–98; Andrews, *Nook Farm*, 92; Howells, *My MT*, 28; Paine, *MTB*, 759.

10. Hoben, "Mark Twain's *A Connecticut Yankee*," 205; Arnold, *Civilization in the United States*, 92; "Personal Intelligence," *NYH*, 20 November 1883, 6.

11. SLC to Olivia Langdon Clemens, 11 March 1877, *UCCL* 02863; *MTHL*, 232, 246, 269–70.

12. W. D. Howells to John Hay, 18 March 1882; *MTHL*, 372, 415, 419.

13. *MTHL*, 429–30, 444; Howells, *My MT*, 23; Paine, *MTB*, 756; Messent, *Mark Twain and Male Friendship*, 88.

14. Budd, "Twain, Howells, and the Boston Nihilists," 352; *MTHL*, 453; Frohman, *Memories*, 50; *Colonel Sellers as a Scientist*, 215, 217.

15. *AMT*, 1:584; "Theatrical Record," *New York Clipper*, 17 January 1880, 339; "Amusements," *Cleveland Plain Dealer*, 30 March 1880, 4; SLC to Karl and Josephine Gerhardt, 26 June 1881, *UCCL* 01978; "Mark Twain's Shrewd Promise," *BE*, 5 March 1882, 6; *MTHL*, 432; SLC to George and Marshall Mallory, 19 September 1883, *UCCL* 02838.

16. SLC to Charles L. Webster, 30 November 1883, *UCCL* 02860; SLC to Charles L. Webster, 2 January 1884, *UCCL* 02885; Schirer, *Mark Twain and the Theatre*, 71; Webster, *Mark Twain: Business Man*, 253–54.

17. SLC to Charles L. Webster, 8 February 1884, *UCCL* 02912; SLC to Charles L. Webster, 10 February 1884, *UCCL* 02883; *MTHL*, 469.

18. *MTLP*, 175; "News, Notes, and Gossip," *BH*, 3 August 1884, 10, and *BH*, 21 September 1884, 10; "Actors Come to Town," *NYH*, 25 August 1884, 8; *MTHL*, 503; *Mark Twain's Letters* (1917), 544; SLC to Charles L. Webster, 15 September 1884, *UCCL* 02954; John T. Raymond to Charles L. Webster, 9 September 1884, *UCLC* 42275; *MTHL*, 504, 507; "New Plays Begging," *WC*, 13 November 1884, 2. If Raymond intended this statement as an invitation to the authors to reopen discussions, the tactic did not work.

19. *MTHL*, 460; *MTMF*, 255; Sumida, "Reevaluating."

20. "City Briefs," *HC*, 8 June 1883, 2; "Carnival of Authors," *NHJC*, 6 December 1883, 2; "The Authors' Carnival," *HC*, 5 December 1883, 2; "Personal," *NHR*, 29 August 1883, 1; *MTHL*, 467.

21. Webster, *Mark Twain: Business Man*, 251; "Barnay in Farce and Tragedy," *NYT*, 21 March 1883, 8; Salsbury, *Susy and Mark Twain*, 178; SLC to E. C. Stedman, 6 February 1883, *UCCL* 02344; *MTHL*, 448–49, 465, 477, 531; "Our Hartford Letter," *SR*, 22 November 1883, 5; Messent, *Mark Twain and Male Friendship*, 55; Andrews, *Nook Farm*, 87.

22. SLC to James Pond, 31 January 1884, *UCCL* 13080; Turner, *George W. Cable*, 150; Lawton, *A Lifetime*, 81–82.

23. SLC to James Pond, 3 February 1884 and 31 January 1884, *UCCL* 13080; "George W. Cable," *CT*, 3 February 1884, 9; Olivia Langdon Clemens to Louise Cable, 1 February 1884, *UCCL* 02902; Olivia Langdon Clemens to Louise Cable, 6 February 1884, *UCCL* 02909; Bikle, *George W. Cable*, 116; Turner, *MT&GWC*, 30.

24. SLC to Charles L. Webster, 8 February 1884, *UCCL* 02912; Turner, *MT&GWC*, 30; SLC to Augustin Daly, 17 February 1884, *UCCL* 02918; Augustin Daly to SLC, 27 February 1884, *UCLC* 39351; *MTHL*, 520; "News, Notes, and Gossip," *BH*, 1 March 1885, 10; Norton, *Writing Tom Sawyer*, 122; SLC to W. R. Ward, 8 September 1887, *UCCL* 03773.

25. Turner, *MT&GWC*, 30; SLC to Charles L. Webster, 10 February 1884, *UCCL* 02883; *MTSpk*, 256; *MTHL*, 485; "A Talk with Mr. Clemens," *NYT*, 31 January 1890, 9; Will Gillette to SLC, 27 May 1884, *UCLC* 42160; *MTCI*, 115.

26. SLC to Ned House, 27 February 1884, *UCCL* 02923; SLC to Karl and Josephine Gerhardt, 5 March 1884, *UCCL* 02926; *MTHL*, 478.

27. Bikle, *George W. Cable*, 118; Conrad 187; "Mark Twain and His Book," *NYT*, 10 December 1889, 5; *N&J*, 3:14.

28. "Mark Twain's April Fool," *NHR*, 14 April 1884, 2; "Mark Twain's April Fool," *NYS*, 4 April 1884, 1; "Mark Twain in a Rage," *Richmond Dispatch*, 5 April 1884, 4; "The Joker Joked," *WC*, 8 April 1884, 3; Myrick and Ohge, "Mark Twain: April Fool"; Bikle, *George W. Cable*, 121; Cutter to SLC, 29 March 1884, *UCLC* 41834; SLC to Miss Perkins, 30 April 1880, *UCCL* 01796.

29. "Mark Twain's April Fool," *NHR*, 14 April 1884, 2; Turner, *MT&GWC*, 36; Fears, *Mark Twain Day-by-Day*, 1:940; "Mark Twain's April Fool," *NYS*, 4 April 1884, 1.

30. Turner, *MT&GWC*, 24–25; SLC to Karl Gerhardt, 24 September 1884, *UCCL* 00297; SLC to Hamlin Garland, 28 July 1883, *UCCL* 02063; *Mark Twain's Letters* (1917), 476; Budd, "Color Him Curious," 31.

31. SLC to James R. Osgood, 21 December 1883, *UCCL* 02872; SLC to Charles L. Webster, 20 January 1884, *UCCL* 02893; Blair, *Mark Twain and Huck Finn*, 356–57.

32. *N&J*, 3:64–65; Gold, "*Hatching Ruin*," 93; SLC to Charles L. Webster, 12 April 1884, *UCCL* 02950; SLC to Charles L. Webster, 14 April 1884, *UCCL* 02951; SLC to Charles L. Webster, 1 July 1884, *UCCL* 02413; *MTLP*, 173, 175.

33. SLC to Karl and Josephine Gerhardt, 4 May 1884, *UCCL* 02969; *N&J*, 3:55; SLC to Charles L. Webster, 7 May 1884, *UCCL* 02972; SLC to Charles L. Webster, 6 June 1884, *UCCL* 02990; SLC to Charles L. Webster, 1 September 1884, *UCCL* 01293; SLC to Charles L. Webster, 3 October 1884, *UCCL* 03003; *MTCI*, 642; SLC to William T. Sherman, 19 September 1885, *UCCL* 01606.

34. Webster, *Mark Twain: Business Man*, 246; SLC to Charles L. Webster, 12 April 1884, *UCCL* 02950; SLC to Charles L. Webster, 24 May 1884, *UCCL* 02984; SLC to Charles L. Webster, 11 June 1884, *UCCL* 02993; Beverly David and Lester Crossman, "Illustrators," in LeMaster and Wilson, *The Routledge Encyclopedia of Mark Twain*, 383; *MTLP*, 174.

35. Briden, "Kemble's 'Speciality,'" 398, 405; Wonham, "'I Want a Real Coon,'" 139.

36. *MTHL*, 493; SLC to Charles L. Webster, 11 August 1884, *UCCL* 01516; SLC to Charles L. Webster, 14 August 1884, *UCCL* 02944; *Mark Twain's Notebook*, 235; Ferguson, *Mark Twain*, 220.

37. *Huckleberry Finn* (1885), 365; SLC to Charles L. Webster, 6 July 1884, *UCCL* 08930; Gribben, *Mark Twain's Library*, 150, 450; *Hannibal, Huck, and Tom*, 85; Stone, *The Innocent Eye*, 176.

38. Gribben, *Mark Twain's Library*, 71; *Huck Finn and Tom Sawyer among the Indians*, 61; SLC to Charles L. Webster, 1 September 1884, *UCCL* 01293; *MTHL*, 496.

39. SLC to Buffalo Bill Cody, 10 September 1884, *UCCL* 12811; SLC to Charles L. Webster, 20 September 1884, *UCCL* 01325; "The Connecticut Capital," *SR*, 16 September 1883, 8. SLC remained a devotee of circuses and other entertainment spectacles. He attended the Grand London Circus in Hartford in May 1880 and S. H. Barrett's circus sometime in late 1886 or early 1887. He enjoyed the "fascinating" acts and regarded Jo-Jo the Dog-Faced Boy "the most remarkable human phenomenon of the age" ("Endorsed by 'Mark Twain,'" *Bozeman [Mont.] Chronicle*, 17 August 1887, 1). In New York in mid-June 1890, moreover, SLC and Joe Goodman "went to a ten-cent dive" or dime museum "where we saw a variety performance. . . . It lasted 2 hours: there was a Punch & Judy; & a very small dwarf; & some Zulus in native lack of costume," and "& a girl who had 25 alligators & crocodiles for pets, & they crawled all over her" (SLC to Olivia Langdon Clemens, 14 June 1890, *UCCL* 04051). Goodman recalled that they "spent a whole day going from one dime museum to another, finally returning to the one where a beautiful girl performed with live young alligators—twining the clammy things around her neck and body, and kissing and petting them" (Berkove, *Insider Stories*, 1038).

40. Quirk, *Mark Twain's* Adventures of Huckleberry Finn, 179; SLC to Charles L. Webster, 8 September 1884, *UCCL* 01357; Bird, "Mark Twain, Karl Gerhardt," 32.

41. *MTCI*, 80; McWilliams, *Mark Twain in the St. Louis Post-Dispatch*, 171; Quirk, *Mark Twain's* Adventures of Huckleberry Finn, 172; "Mark Twain in a Dilemma," *New York World*, 27 November 1884, 1; "Tampering with Mark Twain's Book," *NYTrib*, 29 November 1884, 3; "Mark Twain in a Dilema [*sic*]," *CT*, 30 November 1884, 23; "Mean Joke on Twain," *Carson (Nev.) Appeal*, 2 December 1884, 3; "Current Literature," *SFB*, 14 March 1885, 1. Justin Kaplan misquotes the Webster interview: "Had the first edition [of *Huckleberry Finn*,

with the damaged plate] been run off, our loss would have been $250,000" (Kaplan, *Mr. Clemens and Mark Twain*, 264).

42. "Tampering with Mark Twain's Book," *NYTrib*, 29 November 1884, 3.

43. SLC to Charles L. Webster, 15 July 1884, *UCCL* 01499; SLC to James Pond, 8 July 1884, *UCCL* 02581; Bikle, *George W. Cable*, 132; "News, Notes, and Gossip," *BH*, 20 July 1884, 10; "The Lounger," *Critic*, 9 August 1884, 66; 26 September 1884; 45–46; SLC to Chatto & Windus, 5 November 1884, *UCCL* 03020.

44. Olivia Langdon Clemens to SLC, 3 January 1885, *UCCL* 03100. The excerpts from *Huck Finn* in the *Century* were widely copied in Australia, New Zealand, and the United States. The dates are as follows: 4 January 1885: *Boston Budget* and *Louisville Journal-Courier*; 11 January 1885: *NYTrib*, *BH*, *Chicago Times*, *Cleveland Leader*, and *New Orleans Picayune*; 18 January 1885: *Portland Oregonian*; 31 January 1885: *Melbourne Weekly Times*; 7 February 1885: *Melbourne Weekly Times*; 14 February 1885: *NYS*; 20 February 1885: *Chicago Herald*; 22 February 1885: *Cleveland Herald*; 14 March 1885: *Cleveland Plain Dealer*; 21 March 1885: *Brisbane Queenslander*; 22 March 1885: *Trenton Times*; 28 March 1885: *Auckland Star*, *Melbourne Weekly Times*; 4 April 1885: *Melbourne Weekly Times*; 11 April 1885: *Adelaide Observer*, *Adelaide Journal*, *Melbourne Weekly Times*.

45. Scharnhorst, *Bret Harte*, 223; Scott, "The *Century Magazine* Edits *Huckleberry Finn*"; Richard Watson Gilder to SLC, 17 October 1884, *UCLC* 42310; *AMT*, 3:58; SLC to Richard Watson Gilder, 14 October 1884, *UCCL* 11816; SLC to Olivia Langdon Clemens, 3 February 1885, *UCCL* 03150; SLC to Olivia Langdon Clemens, 13 February 1885, *UCCL* 03165; DeVoto, *Mark Twain at Work*, 300. Eric Sundquist suggests that Cable regularly delivered a talk on "The Freedman's Case in Equity" on the lecture circuit with SLC, but there is no evidence he ever included it in his program (Sundquist, "Mark Twain and Homer Plessy," 115).

46. "New Publications," *New England Farmer*, 29 November 1884, 2; "The Magazines for February," Sydney *Herald*, 9 March 1885, 4; *SR*, 17 March 1885, 4; Fischer, "Huck Finn Reviewed," 30; Paine, *MTB*, 793; Henry M. Alden to SLC, 28 February 1885, *UCLC* 42422; Henry M. Alden to SLC, 15 March 1885, *UCLC* 40724.

47. *MTCI*, 10; *WC*, 28 July 1884, 2; *MTHL*, 501; *N&J*, 3:77.

48. Tom Powers, "New York Gossip," *St. Louis Republic*, 27 October 1889, 21; *MTSpk*, 182–84, 188, 267; *AMT*, 1:316, 1:346; Sproat, *The Best Men*, 128; SLC to Henry Pierce, 22 October 1884, *UCCL* 03011.

49. *MTSpk*, 184, 186; *AMT*, 1:316; *MTHL*, 500–502; SLC to Ned House, 31 October 1884, *UCCL* 03015.

50. Goodman and Dawson, *Howells: A Writer's Life*, 252; *MTHL*, 503, 508; Scharnhorst and Hofer, *Sinclair Lewis Remembered* 3; SLC to Chatto & Windus, 5 November 1884, *UCCL* 03020; Fulton, *The Reconstruction of Mark Twain*, 164; Leonard, "Mark Twain and Politics," 103; Budd, *Mark Twain: Social Philosopher*, 110.

51. "Connecticut Independents," *BA*, 13 October 1884, 5; "The Independents' Address," *NHR*, 13 October 1884, 2; Andrews, *Nook Farm*, 115–16; "Connecticut Independents," *BH*, 19 October 1884, 1. Neither could Twichell countenance Cleveland's carnal crime, however, so he eventually voted for the Prohibition candidate for president and a straight Republican ticket down ballot.

52. "Schurz at Hartford," *BH*, 21 October 1884, 1; *BA*, 20 October 1884, 4; "Connecticut Independents," *BH*, 19 October 1884, 1; *MTSpk*, 186.

53. *AMT*, 1:315, 1:318, 1:389; *MTSpk*, 184; SLC to Ned House, 31 October 1884, *UCCL* 03015; SLC to Grover Cleveland, 23 September 1885, *UCCL* 03290; Paine, *MTB*, 1655; *Mark Twain's Notebook*, 203.

54. SLC to Ned House, 31 October 1884, *UCCL* 03015.

Chapter 12

1. *MTCI*, 79; *AMT*, 3:166; "Twain and Cable," *NHJC*, 6 November 1884, 2; Bikle, *George W. Cable*, 133; Turner, *George W. Cable*, 173; Turner, *MT&GWC*, 51–52; "Mark Twain and George W. Cable," *East Orange (N.J.) Gazette*, 13 November 1884; "The Twain-Cable Evening," *SR*, 8 November 1884, 4; SLC to Olivia Langdon Clemens, 12 November 1884, *UCCL* 03024; Briden, "Mark Twain's Rhode Island Lectures"; "'Mark Twain'–Cable Readings," *BJ*, 11 November 1884, 3; *Lowell (Mass.) Courier*, 12 November 1884; *Waltham (Mass.) Free Press*, 13 November 1884, n.p.

2. *MTHL*, 513; "Readings by Twain and Cable," *BA*, 14 November 1884, 8; "Lectures and Readings," *Boston Transcript*, 14 November 1884, 1; "The 'Union' Entertainment," *BH*, 14 November 1884, 5; "Mark Twain and Mr. Cable," *Boston Globe*, 14 November 1884, 8; "Mark Twain and Geo. Cable," *Boston Traveller*, 14 November 1884; "Mark Twain and George W. Cable," *Boston Post*, 14 November 1884, 4; *MTCI*, 50; Stronks, "Mark Twain's Boston Stage Debut"; "Mark Twain and the Police," *BH*, 16 November 1884, 16; Turner, *MT&GWC*, 58–59.

3. Kaplan, *The Singular Mark Twain*, 404; "Personal Intelligence," *NYT*, 18 November 1884, 2; "Some of Mark Twain's Fun," *NYS*, 19 November 1884, 1; "The Cable-Twain Readings," *NYH*, 19 November 1884, 7; "Readings by Clemens and Cable," *NYTrib*, 20 November 1884, 5; "Amusements," *Cleveland Plain Dealer*, 15 December 1884, 1; "Genius and Versatility," *NYT*, 19 November 1884, 5; Olivia Langdon Clemens to SLC, 21 November 1884, *UCCL* 03029; Olivia Langdon Clemens to SLC, 24 November 1884, *UCCL* 03038; *MTCI*, 50–51.

4. SLC to Susy Clemens, 23 November 1884, *UCCL* 03035; *AMT*, 1:77.

5. *AMT*, 1:484; *N&J*, 3:418; Perry, *Grant and Twain*, 139.

6. *N&J*, 3:97. James Pond claimed that SLC paid Grant an advance of thirty thousand dollars ("Amongst the Books," *Melbourne Leader*, 26 December 1885, 35); Paine reported it was twenty-five thousand dollars (Paine, *MTB*, 802).

7. Perry, *Grant and Twain*, 115; *AMT*, 1:79, 2:60, 2:64; Flood, *Grant's Final Victory*, 102; "Amongst the Books," *Melbourne Leader*, 26 December 1885, 35.

8. Bikle, *George W. Cable*, 133; SLC to Olivia Langdon Clemens, 22 November 1884, *UCCL* 03030; SLC to Olivia Langdon Clemens, 23 November 1884, *UCCL* 03032; "The Mark Twain–Cable Readings," *Philadelphia Inquirer*, 22 November 1884, 3; Trautmann, "The Twins of Genius," 220; "Fun on the Stage," *BE*, 23 November 1884, 12; "Personal Intelligence," *Washington Post*, 25 November 1884, 2; "From Grave to Gay," *Washington National Republican*, 25 November 1884, 1; "Another Pleased Audience," *WC*, 26 November 1884, 4; Turner, *MT&GWC*, 1.

9. *Ithaca Journal*, 29 November 1884, 3; *MTCI*, 52; Kohn, "Mark Twain and Joseph Roswell Hawley," 75; "The President's Popularity," *WS*, 6 August 1883, 1; Kaplan, *The Singular Mark Twain*, 405; SLC to Olivia Langdon Clemens, 25 November 1884, *UCCL* 03037; Turner, *MT&GWC*, 62; "Mark Twain's Humorous Sayings," *Philadelphia Inquirer*, 27 November 1884, 3; Cardwell, *Twins of Genius*, 122.

10. Wagenknecht, *Mark Twain: The Man and His Work*, 77; SLC to Olivia Langdon Clemens, 28 November 1884, *UCCL* 03040; Turner, *MT&GWC*, 63; Turner, *George W. Cable* 173; Paine, *MTB*, 787; Lawton, *A Lifetime*, 78–80.

11. "Cable and Twain," *Baltimore Sun*, 29 November 1884, 4; Turner, *MT&GWC*, 61, 63; SLC to Olivia Langdon Clemens, 29 November 1884, *UCCL* 03041; SLC to Olivia Langdon Clemens, 3 December 1884, *UCCL* 03044; Ross Winans to SLC, 18 August 1876, *UCLC* 46865; *N&J*, 3:198; "Personal," *Baltimore Sun*, 3 December 1885, 4; "Congratulating the Governor," *NYTrib*, 3 December 1884, 2; "Twain and Cable at Albany," *BA*, 5 December 1884, 1.

12. "Places for Pleasure," *Troy (N.Y.) Times*, 3 December 1884, 3; Turner, *MT&GWC*, 64–66; "Twain and Cable," *Rochester Herald*, 8 December 1884, 4; "Rochester," *NYTrib*, 13 December 1884, 7; *MTCI*, 57.

13. Gribben, "The Master Hand of Old Malory," 34; Turner, *MT&GWC*, 135–36; Railton, "The Twain-Cable Combination," 177; Ekström, "Extracts from a Diary," 112; SLC to Charles L. Webster, 14 December 1884, *UCCL* 10853; *N&J*, 3:78–79; SLC to Susy Clemens, 8 February 1885, *UCCL* 03159; Paine, *MTB*, 1320.

14. "Twain and Cable," *Toronto Globe*, 10 December 1884, 2; Turner, *MT&GWC*, 67; SLC to Olivia Langdon Clemens, 9 December 1884, *UCCL* 03052; "Twain and Cable," *Toronto Mail*, 9 December 1884, 2, and *Toronto Mail*, 10 December 1884, 8; Roberts, "Mark Twain in Toronto"; Fatout, "The Twain-Cable Readings in Indiana," 23; Cardwell, *Twins of Genius*, 27–28; "Personal Intelligence," *Toronto Mail*, 10 December 1884, 8.

15. Turner, *MT&GWC*, 68–69; "The Innocents Abroad," *Cleveland Plain Dealer*, 12 December 1884, 4; "Mark Twain and Cable," *Buffalo Times*, 11 December 1884; "The Scattering of Mark Twain's Friends," *Atchison (Kans.) Globe*, 8 January 1885, 3; "The Innocents Abroad," *Cleveland Plain Dealer*, 12 December 1884, 4; SLC to Olivia Langdon Clemens, 12 December 1884, *UCCL* 03055; *MTCI*, 468.

16. "Literature," *London Post*, 3 February 1885, 3; "Current Literature," *London Congregationalist* 14 (March 1885): 251; "Book Notice," *Otago (New Zealand) Star*, 11 April 1885, 1; Matthews, *The Tocsin of Revolt*, 255; SLC to Charles L. Webster, 1 February 1885, *UCCL* 10898; Quirk, *Mark Twain's Adventures of Huckleberry Finn*, 218; Lang, "The Art of Mark Twain," 222; Besant, "My Favorite Novelist," 661; Budd, *MTCR*, 259, 262, 264, 275–76.

17. *MTCI*, 73; SLC to Olivia Langdon Clemens, 12 December 1884, *UCCL* 03055; Turner, *MT&GWC*, 1, 70; SLC to James Pond, 22 December 1884, *UCCL* 02601.

18. "Personal Mention," *Jackson (Mich.) Citizen Patriot*, 15 December 1884, 4; Turner, *MT&GWC*, 72–73; SLC to Olivia Langdon Clemens, 14 December 1884, *UCCL* 03057; "The Mark Twain–Cable Readings," *Grand Rapids Democrat*, 14 December 1884; "Twain and Cable," *Toledo Blade*, 16 December 1884, 1; Turner, *George W. Cable*, 174.

19. Denney, "Next Stop Detroit"; Clemens, *Mark Twain: His Life and Work*, 147; "Amusements," *Cleveland Plain Dealer*, 18 December 1884, 4; Jerome, Wisbey, and Snedecor, *Mark Twain in Elmira*, 69; SLC to James Pond, 22 December 1884, *UCCL* 02601.

20. SLC to Charles L. Webster, 23 December 1884, *UCCL* 03068; "Mark Twain as a Litigant," *BJ*, 30 December 1884, 1; "Put Him on the Witness Stand," *NYT*, 31 December 1884, 3; Feinstein, "Mark Twain's Lawsuits," 155–56.

21. Olivia Langdon Clemens to SLC, 3 January 1885, *UCCL* 03100; SLC to Estes & Lauriat, 7 January 1885, *UCCL* 03103; SLC to Olivia Langdon Clemens, 17 January 1885, *UCCL* 03119; Feinstein, "Mark Twain's Lawsuits," 177.

22. "Mark Twain a Plaintiff," *NYT*, 15 January 1885, 1; Feinstein, "Mark Twain's Lawsuits," 168, 172; Fischer, "Huck Finn Reviewed," 36.

23. Feinstein, "Mark Twain's Lawsuits," 185, 187; "One of 'Mark Twain's' Woes," *NHJC*, 13 February 1885, 1; Budd, *MTCR*, 267; "Generalities," *Adelaide Observer*, 11 July 1885, 43; "Mark Twain and Massachusetts," *BA*, 2 April 1885, 2; Webster, *Mark Twain: Business Man*, 318; *MTCI*, 120.

24. SLC to Olivia Langdon Clemens, 29 December 1884, *UCCL* 03077; Turner, *MT&GWC*, 77; Trautmann, "The Twins of Genius," 218, 221; Quirk, *Mark Twain's* Adventures of Huckleberry Finn, 197.

25. Stoneley, "Mark Twain and Gender," 76; Olivia Langdon Clemens to SLC, 30 December 1884, *UCCL* 11853; Baker, "Mark Twain in Dayton"; "Twain-Cable," *Dayton Democrat*, 31 December 1884; Turner, *George W. Cable* 183; Turner, *MT&GWC*, 78, 132; Cardwell, *Twins of Genius*, 32; "Mark Twain's 70th Birthday," *Harper's Weekly*, supplement, 23 December 1905, 1889; Weaver, "Samuel Clemens Lectures in Kentucky," 20–22.

26. *MTCI*, 65; Fatout, *Mark Twain on the Lecture Circuit*, 209; SLC to Olivia Langdon Clemens, 2 January 1885, *UCCL* 03098; SLC to Olivia Langdon Clemens, 9 February 1885, *UCCL* 03160; Turner, *MT&GWC*, 81–82.

27. "Another Delighted Audience," *Cincinnati Enquirer*, 4 January 1885, 2; "Distinguished Guests," CC, 4 January 1885, 6; SLC to Olivia Langdon Clemens, 3 January 1885, *UCCL* 03099.

28. "Cable's and Twain's Reading," *Louisville Courier-Journal*, 6 January 1885, 6; Turner, *MT&GWC*, 84–85, 99; Turner, *George W. Cable*, 175; Fatout, "The Twain-Cable Readings in Indiana," 21.

29. SLC to Olivia Langdon Clemens, 8 January 1885, *UCCL* 03107; "'Twain' and Cable," Springfield *Illinois State Journal*, 9 January 1885, 37; "'Mark Twain'–Cable," *St. Louis Globe-Democrat*, 11 January 1885, 12; "The Twain-Cable Readings," *St. Louis Missouri Republican*, 10 January 1885, 8; Turner, "James Lampton"; Paxton, "A Cousin's Recollection," 4.

30. Cardwell, *Twins of Genius*, 42; "Twain and Cable," *Quincy (Mass.) Herald*, 13 January 1885, 4.

31. SLC to Olivia Langdon Clemens, 13 January 1885, *UCCL* 03114; *N&J*, 3:90; Ekström, "Extracts from a Diary," 111; Cardwell, *Twins of Genius*, 44; McParland, *Mark Twain's Audience*, 72; "Twain-Cable," *Keokuk (Iowa) Gate City*, 15 January 1885, 8; Turner, *MT&GWC*, 88; SLC to Orion Clemens, 16 January 1885, *UCCL* 03118. See also "The Humorist," *Keokuk (Iowa) Gate City*, 16 January 1885, 8.

32. Turner, *MT&GWC*, 88–90; Cardwell, *Twins of Genius*, 46; "Twain and Cable," *Burlington (Iowa) Hawkeye*, 16 January 1885; SLC to Orion Clemens, 16 January 1885, *UCCL* 03118.

33. "The Equality of the Negro," *CT*, 17 January 1885, 8; SLC to Olivia Langdon Clemens, 17 January 1885, *UCCL* 03119; "Amusements," *CT*, 17 January 1885, 5; Fatout, *Mark Twain on the Lecture Circuit*, 218, 223; Turner, *MT&GWC*, 88–90.

34. "Twain and Cable," *Evanston (Ill.) Index*, 24 January 1885, 1; "Clemens and Cable," *Janesville (Wis.) Recorder*, 21 January 1885, 3; Turner, *MT&GWC*, 90–91; *Duluth (Minn.) Tribune*, 23 January 1885, 2; "The Mark Twain–Cable Readings," *St. Paul Globe*, 24 January 1885, 4; Cardwell, *Twins of Genius*, 48–49; "Amusements," *Minneapolis Tribune*, 25 January 1885, 4; *MTLP*, 182; "Innocents Abroad," *Winona (Minn.) Republican*, 27 January 1885; Ekström, "Extracts from a Diary," 112.

35. Turner, *MT&GWC*, 91; "Stage and Rostrum," *Madison Wisconsin State Journal*, 28 January 1885; *MTCI*, 79; Fatout, *Mark Twain on the Lecture Circuit*, 224; Cardwell, *Twins of Genius*, 52; James Pond to George W. Cable, 2 February 1885, *UCLC* 42402.

36. "Mark Twain and George W. Cable at the Academy," *Milwaukee Sentinel*, 29 January 1885, 4; "Theatrical News and Notes," *Milwaukee Journal*, 30 January 1885, 1; Turner, *MT&GWC*, 93, 95; SLC to Olivia Langdon Clemens, 1 February 1885, UCCL 03148; Wagenknecht, *Mark Twain: The Man and His Work*, 83.

37. SLC to Olivia Langdon Clemens, 5 February 1885, UCCL 03154; *MTCI*, 199; Fatout, "The Twain-Cable Readings in Indiana," 21–22; Cardwell, *Twins of Genius*, 55; Fatout, *Mark Twain on the Lecture Circuit*, 220.

38. Lorch, *The Trouble Begins at Eight*, 172–73; SLC to Olivia Langdon Clemens, 5 February 1885, UCCL 03154; to Olivia Langdon Clemens, 9 February 1885, UCCL 03160; Cardwell, *Twins of Genius*, 55; Bush, "Grace King and Mark Twain," 32; Olivia Langdon Clemens to SLC, 11 February 1885, UCCL 03163.

39. "Twain and Cable," *CT*, 3 February 1885, 5; SLC to Olivia Langdon Clemens, 4 February 1885, UCCL 03153.

40. Turner, *MT&GWC*, 97–98; SLC to Olivia Langdon Clemens, 4 February 1885, UCCL 03153; SLC to Olivia Langdon Clemens, 5 February 1885, UCCL 03154; SLC to Olivia Langdon Clemens, 6 February 1885, UCCL 03155; Cardwell, *Twins of Genius*, 55; Fatout, "The Twain-Cable Readings in Indiana," 24–25.

41. SLC to Olivia Langdon Clemens, 2 January 1885, UCCL 03098; SLC to Olivia Langdon Clemens, 7 February 1885, UCCL 03156; *N&J*, 3:39, 3:88; Fatout, "The Twain-Cable Readings in Indiana," 27–28; "The Twain-Cable Combination," *Indianapolis Journal*, 8 February 1885, 8; Cardwell, *Twins of Genius*, 10.

42. SLC to Olivia Langdon Clemens, 8 February 1885, UCCL 03158; Fatout, "The Twain-Cable Readings in Indiana," 23; Turner, *George W. Cable* 187; Turner, *MT&GWC*, 99.

43. Fatout, *Mark Twain on the Lecture Circuit*, 226–27; Turner, *MT&GWC*, 99–100, 103; SLC to Olivia Langdon Clemens, 10 February 1885, UCCL 03161; "Twain-Cable," *Columbus Times*, 10 February 1885, n.p.

44. Turner, *MT&GWC*, 101; Cardwell, *Twins of Genius*, 59.

45. Turner, *MT&GWC*, 107–8; Susy Clemens, *Papa*, 171; Bikle, *George W. Cable*, 140; Cardwell, *Twins of Genius*, 237; SLC to Olivia Langdon Clemens, 17 February 1885, UCCL 03171.

46. Bikle, *George W. Cable*, 142; "Notes," *BH*, 23 February 1885, 4; Cardwell, *Twins of Genius*, 62; Fatout, *Mark Twain on the Lecture Circuit*, 228.

47. "In the Academy of Music," *BE*, 22 February 1885, 12; SLC to Olivia Langdon Clemens, 1 February 1885, UCCL 03148; Turner, *MT&GWC*, 113; "Twain and Cable," *Philadelphia North American*, 27 February 1885, 1; "The Star Course," *Philadelphia Inquirer*, 27 February 1885, 3; *MTHL*, 520; *MTCI*, 53; "Amusements," *Washington Post*, 1 March 1885, 4; *N&J*, 3:99; Turner, "Mark Twain, Cable, and 'a Professional Newspaper Liar'"; Fatout, *Mark Twain on the Lecture Circuit*, 228.

48. Cardwell, "Mark Twain's 'Row'" 367–68; Turner, "Mark Twain, Cable, and 'a Professional Newspaper Liar,'" 18–33; Turner, *MT&GWC*, 121; SLC to James Pond, 4 January 1886, UCCL 02628; *MTHL*, 528.

49. Turner, *George W. Cable*, 210; Cardwell, *Twins of Genius*, 108–9; "Twain and Cable," *Atlanta Constitution*, 28 May 1885, 2.

50. "Northampton," *SR*, 16 April 1887, 6; *MTCI*, 184; Bikle, *George W. Cable*, 197; SLC to Cable, 25 June 1895, UCCL 04897; "Mark Twain's 70th Birthday," *Harper's Weekly*, supplement, 23 December 1905, 1889. See also "Memories of Great Men," *Seattle Post-Intelligencer*, 30 April 1899, 16.

51. *AMT*, 1:82, 1:84, 1:92; *MTLP*, 185; *N&J*, 3:95, 3:182–83; Gold, *"Hatching Ruin,"* 63; Paine, *MTB*, 803, 806. Two bits of evidence lend credence to the speculation that SLC meant to refer to General Grant as "G.G.," the "chief of ordnance" who cosigns the preface to *Huckleberry Finn* (1885): SLC remarked in his notebook about the "bogus biogs of GG" and in a piece entitled "A Suggestion" he alluded to "S.L.C. of the firm of Pubs. of G.G's P[ersonal] M[emoirs]" (*Mark Twain in Eruption*, 348–49).

52. *N&J*, 3:182; *AMT*, 1:80–81; Johnson, *Remembered Yesterdays*, 217–19.

53. Johnson, *Remembered Yesterdays*, 217–29; "Gen. Grant, Mark Twain and the Century," *SR*, 9 March 1885, 4; "Grant's Reminiscences," *BH*, 10 March 1885, 3; Ellsworth, *A Golden Age*, 239; Moyne, "Mark Twain and Baroness Alexandra Gripenberg," 373.

54. "Gen. Grant," *BH*, 22 June 1885, 2; SLC to editor of *BH*, 6 July 1885, UCCL 03254; SLC to Ned House, 21 July 1885, UCCL 03263.

55. *N&J*, 3:169; Perry, *Grant and Twain*, 160; SLC to Olivia Langdon Clemens, 4 March 1885, UCCL 03183; Paine, *MTB*, 807.

Chapter 13

1. "New York Book Notes," *BA*, 21 January 1884, 4; "Literary Notes," *BH*, 28 January 1884, 6; "Literary Notes," *BE*, 10 February 1884, 3; "Mark Twain's Latest," *Mexico (N.Y.) Independent*, 12 November 1884, 4; SLC to Charles L. Webster, 23 January 1885, UCCL 03130; SLC to Charles L. Webster, 26 January 1885, UCCL 03137; SLC to Charles L. Webster, 8 February 1885, UCCL 03157; SLC to Charles L. Webster, 10 February 1885, UCCL 03162; Webster, *Mark Twain: Business Man*, 297; Charles L. Webster to SLC, 30 January 1885, UCLC 42397; Charles L. Webster to SLC, 14 February 1885, UCLC 42414; Charles L. Webster to SLC, 24 October 1885, UCLC 42731.

2. "Recent Publications," *San Francisco Alta California*, 24 March 1885, 2; "Current Literature," *SFB*, 14 March 1885, 1; Charles L. Webster to SLC, 4 February 1885, UCLC 42405; Charles L. Webster to SLC, 14 March 1885, UCLC 42435; Gold, *"Hatching Ruin,"* 98; Blair, *Mark Twain and Huck Finn*, 370; *N&J*, 3:115; SLC to Chatto & Windus, 8 September 1885, UCCL 03286; *AMT*, 1:372, 2:59.

3. *N&J*, 3:130, 3:135–36, 3:157; Fischer, "Huck Finn Reviewed," 10; Robert Bridges, "Mark Twain's Blood-Curdling Humor," *Life*, 26 February 1885, 119; "Editorial Notes," *NHJC*, 18 March 1885, 1; "February Magazines," *BH*, 1 February 1885, 17; "Jottings," *Boston Transcript*, 19 March 1885, 4; Emerson, *Authentic Mark Twain*, 144; Budd, *MTCR*, 265–68; "The Humourist," *Melbourne Australasian*, 11 April 1885, 42.

4. "Mark Twain's New Story," *NYS*, 15 February 1885, 3; "Huckleberry Finn," *Port Jervis (N.Y.) Gazette*, 27 April 1885, 1; "New Publications," *Baltimore Sun* supplement, 7 March 1885, 1; "Mark Twain's New Book," *Montreal Gazette*, 17 February 1885, 7; "Literature," *San Francisco Chronicle*, 15 March 1885, 6; "Books of the Month," *Atlantic Monthly* 55 (April 1885): 576; T. S. Perry, "Mark Twain," *Century* 30 (May 1885): 172; Budd, *MTCR*, 240, 259, 263, 268–70, 272–74, 278–79; Fischer, "Huck Finn Reviewed," 9, 12–16, 31.

5. *MTHL*, 117, 499; W. D. Howells to Charles L. Webster, 27 December 1884, UCLC 42368.

6. Budd, *Our Mark Twain*, 17–18; Kaplan, *Mr. Clemens and Mark Twain*, 268; Fischer, "Huck Finn Reviewed," 17–18; "Explosion of the Boiler of the 'Mark Twain,'" *BH*, 28 March 1885, 2.

7. "Jottings," *Boston Transcript*, 25 March 1885, 4; *St. Albans (Vt.) Messenger*, 20 March 1885, 2; "A Virginia Verdict," *BA*, 4 April 1885, 4; "News and Notes," *Literary World*, 21 March 1885, 106; "Newspaper Waifs," *NYEP*, 31 March 1885, 2; Fischer, "Huck Finn Reviewed," 16–17, 19, 31–32.

8. "The Tide Turning," *BA*, 2 April 1885, 4; *SR*, 17 March 1885, 4; Fischer, "Huck Finn Reviewed," 21.

9. SLC to Charles L. Webster, 4 April 1885, UCCL 03205; SLC to Charles L. Webster, 5 April 1885, UCCL 03207; *MTLP*, 188.

10. "Current Notes," *BJ*, 4 April 1886, 2; *WC*, 18 March 1885, 2; Fischer, "Huck Finn Reviewed," 19–20, 29–30; Kaplan, *The Singular Mark Twain*, 410; SLC to Charles L. Webster, 18 March 1885, UCCL 03192.

11. Budd, *MTCR*, 270–72, 274–77, 280; Griska, "Two New Joel Chandler Harris Reviews"; Joel Chandler Harris, "To the Editors," *Critic*, 28 November 1885, 253; *AMT*, 2:577; *Sacramento Record-Union*, 26 March 1885, 2; SLC to Pamela Moffett, 15 April 1885, UCCL 03219.

12. Kaplan, *The Singular Mark Twain*, 410; *NYS*, 18 March 1885, 2; Fischer, "Huck Finn Reviewed," 18.

13. Riley, *Letters*, 54; John Hay to SLC, 14 April 1885, UCLC 42477; Joel Chandler Harris to SLC, 1 June 1885, UCLC 42521; Krauth, *Mark Twain and Company*, 204.

14. *MTHL*, 519; "Mark Twain and Massachusetts," *BA*, 2 April 1885, 2.

15. *SR*, 3 April 1885, 4; Fischer, "Huck Finn Reviewed," 26–27.

16. SLC to Harriet Whitmore, 7 February 1907, UCCL 07645; "The Ban on Mark Twain," *Fort Worth Register*, 28 May 1902, 4; "Mark Twain's Boys Disliked," *Philadelphia Inquirer*, 5 Dec 1904, 16. The first recorded banning of any of SLC's works occurred in Colchester, England, in 1873: "The committee of the YMCA at Colchester have just decreed the banishment from their library three of the works of the illustrious 'Mark Twain,'" including *The Innocents Abroad*, on the grounds they were "unfit reading for Colchester 'young Christians'" ("Our Innocent Abroad," *HC*, 13 October 1873, 2).

17. *MTCI*, 135, 265, 474; Booker T. Washington, "Tributes to Mark Twain," *North American Review* 191 (June 1910): 828–30; George Bernard Shaw to SLC, 3 July 1907, UCLC 36914; Foner, *Mark Twain: Social Critic*, 51; Budd, *MTCR*, 604; Hemingway, *Green Hills of Africa*, 29.

18. "Gen. Grant Sleeps Badly," *NYS*, 10 March 1885, 1; SLC to Andrew Chatto, 11 March 1885, UCCL 01672; SLC to Olivia Langdon Clemens, 8 April 1885, UCCL 03208; "Demand for Gen. Grant's Book," *NYT*, 3 December 1885, 5; Feinstein, "Mark Twain's Lawsuits," 208; Paine, *MTB*, 810; Perry, *Grant and Twain*, 141; *AMT*, 3:312, 3:587; *MTHL*, 539; *N&J*, 3:124.

19. Paine, *MTB*, 808; *AMT*, 1:90; "Mark Twain's Statement," *Albany Journal*, 22 July 1885, 2; *N&J*, 3:110; "Metropolitan Gossip," *NHR*, 18 July 1887, 1; SLC to Karl Gerhardt, 5 September 1885, UCCL 11710; "News of the Day," *Melbourne Age*, 11 April 1885, 9.

20. "Gen. Grant Growing Weaker Hourly," *Jackson (Mich.) Citizen Patriot*, 31 March 1885, 1; "Gen. Grant's Condition," *NYTrib*, 31 March 1885, 1; "General Grant Easier," *NYH*, 1 April 1885, 10; SLC to Brander Matthews, 31 March 1885, UCCL 03200; "Bright and Cheery," *BH*, 9 April 1885, 1; "Resting Well," *CC Gazette*, 9 April 1885, 1; "The General Much Refreshed," *WC*, 20 April 1885, 1; "Rapidly Gaining Ground," *Wheeling Register*, 22 April 1885, 1.

21. Perry, *Grant and Twain*, 196, 198; *AMT*, 1:98; Feinstein, "Mark Twain's Lawsuits," 195–98; SLC to Charles L. Webster, 6 June 1886, *UCCL* 03408; "Badeau's Book," *New Orleans Picayune*, 8 March 1889, 3.

22. Susy Clemens, *Papa*, 120–21; *N&J*, 3:130; *A Family Sketch*, 113, 117; SLC to Charles L. Webster, 3 May 1885, *UCCL* 03085.

23. SLC to Orion Clemens, 16 May 1885, *UCCL* 03228; SLC to William T. Sherman, 19 September 1885, *UCCL* 01606; Flood, *Grant's Final Victory*, 130; "The Publisher of Grant's Book," *Kansas City Star*, 25 June 1887, 1; SLC to Henry Ward Beecher, 11 September 1885, *UCCL* 03288; *MTHL*, 528; *N&J*, 3:152.

24. Powers, *Mark Twain*, 503; *AMT*, 1:487; SLC to Olivia Langdon Clemens, 30 June 1885, *UCCL* 03248; SLC to Olivia Langdon Clemens, 1 July 1885, *UCCL* 03249; "The Season at Saratoga," *NYT*, 3 July 1885, 4; Cantacuzene, *My Life*, 40–41; Paine, *MTB*, 815.

25. SLC to William Smith, 3–4 February 1887, *UCCL* 03522; SLC to Olivia Langdon Clemens, 24 July 1885, *UCCL* 03266.

26. "General Grant," *HC*, 24 July 1885, 2; *N&J*, 3:159, 168.

27. SLC to Karl Gerhardt, 6 July 1885, *UCCL* 03253; SLC to Karl Gerhardt, 18 July 1885, *UCCL* 03260; "Art Notes," *NYT*, 25 October 1885, 6; *N&J*, 3:127; Feinstein, "Mark Twain's Lawsuits," 181.

28. "American Sculpture," *NYH*, 30 April 1884, 9; "Honors to Karl Gerhardt," *HC*, 20 October 1885, 2; Fears, *Mark Twain Day-by-Day*, 2:79; "Metropolitan Gossip," *NHR*, 18 July 1887, 1.

29. SLC to Olivia Langdon Clemens, 6 August 1885, *UCCL* 03277; *N&J*, 3:171–72, 3:174; "Mark Twain on the Future National Capital," *NYS*, 30 July 1885, 2.

30. *AMT*, 3:312; *N&J*, 3:204; "Demand for Gen. Grant's Book," *NYT*, 3 December 1885, 5; *MTHL*, 540; SLC to William Smith, 3–4 February 1887, *UCCL* 03522.

31. Feinstein, "Mark Twain's Lawsuits," 195–98, 222; *MTCI*, 136; *N&J*, 3:316; *AMT*, 2:498; *MTLP*, 252. See also Mark Twain's Correspondence with Henry Huttleston Rogers, 290.

32. *MTCI*, 332; *MTSpk*, 226; "Mark Twain," *San Francisco Chronicle*, 15 June 1885, 2; *Theatre*, 31 May 1886, 312; *N&J*, 3:123.

33. Fred J. Hall to SLC, 29 September 1885, *UCLC* 42691; Charles L. Webster to SLC, 29 October 1885, *UCLC* 42733; SLC to the editor of the *NYS*, 17–21 November 1885, *UCCL* 03087; *N&J*, 3:127; SLC to Charles L. Webster, 1 February 1886, *UCCL* 03363; *AMT*, 2:500.

34. Howells, *My MT*, 73; Charles L. Webster to SLC, 24 December 1886, *UCLC* 43173; SLC to Olivia Langdon Clemens, 26 July 1887, *UCCL* 03615; SLC to Fred J. Hall, 20 August 1886, *UCCL* 12818; "Sheridan's Memoirs," *HC*, 30 May 1888, 8; Fred J. Hall to SLC, 15 October 1888, *UCLC* 44198; *AMT*, 2:500.

35. Feinstein, "Mark Twain's Lawsuits," 216; *Philadelphia Press*, 15 May 1886, 8; *Philadelphia Times*, 19 May 1886, 4; SLC to Charles L. Webster, 11 June 1886, *UCCL* 03313; SLC to Fred J. Hall, 14 July 1886, *UCCL* 03416; *MTHL*, 572; "Twain Goes to Law," *Philadelphia Press*, 4 August 1886, 5; Feinstein, "Mark Twain and the Pirates," 11; *N&J*, 3:250.

36. *MTLP*, 266; "Mark Twain Must Pay Up," *WS*, 6 June 1887, 1; "Jottings about Town," *NYS*, 12 October 1887, 1; *MTLP*, 266; SLC to Fred J. Hall, 27 December 1890, *UCCL* 04121; *N&J*, 3:598; Feinstein, "Mark Twain's Lawsuits," 195–98.

37. *MTLP*, 218; *N&J*, 3:298; "Personal Mention," *BE*, 6 February 1889, 4; Feinstein, "Mark Twain's Lawsuits," 195–98; *AMT*, 2:499

38. *N&J*, 3:105; Robert Underwood Johnson to SLC, 11 May 1885, UCLC 42500; SLC to Robert Underwood Johnson, 18 March 1885, UCCL 03191; Ellsworth, *A Golden Age*, 233; *MTLP*, 178; Robert Underwood Johnson to SLC, 13 November 1885, UCLC 42756.

39. "Mark Twain's War Experiences," *NYT*, 7 October 1877, 10; "Personals," *Indianapolis Sentinel*, 25 April 1881, 4; McWilliams, *Mark Twain in the St. Louis Post-Dispatch*, 135; Gerber 38; "Mark Twain and Quantrill's Band," *St. Louis Globe-Democrat*, 17 March 1885, 2; "Mark Twain on Pensions," *Washington Post*, 18 July 1885, 2; Loving, *Confederate Bushwhacker*, 110; Schmitz, "Mark Twain, Traitor," 26; Feinstein, "Mark Twain's Lawsuits," 303–4.

40. Pettit, *Mark Twain and the South*, 183; SLC to Robert Underwood Johnson, 8 September 1885, UCCL 03285; SLC to James Redpath, 12 September 1885, UCCL 12813.

41. "The Private History of a Campaign That Failed," *Century* 31 (December 1885): 203.

42. *MTHL*, 541; "New Magazines," *Bangor (Maine) Whig and Courier*, 10 December 1885, 1; "Literature and Art," *Kansas City Times*, 7 December 1885, 5; "Literary Notes," *Memphis Appeal*, 15 November 1885, 3; "Mark Twain as a Guerilla," *BH*, 13 December 1885, 16; "Mark Twain's 'War Paper,'" *CT*, 13 December 1885, 4; "Mark Twain's 'War Paper,'" *Washington Post*, 13 December 1885, 4; McWilliams, *Mark Twain in the St. Louis Post-Dispatch*, 196; "Mark Twain," *BA*, 13 February 1886, 8. See also "Mark Twain a Deserter," *Adelaide Express and Telegraph*, 16 June 1886, 4.

43. Salsbury, *Susy and Mark Twain*, 203; Janice J. Beaty, "Cats at Quarry Farm," in Jerome, Wisbey, and Snedecor, *Mark Twain in Elmira*, 296; Gribben, *Mark Twain's Library*, 606; Susy Clemens, *Papa*, 215; *A Family Sketch*, 124; *MTHL*, 533; *N&J*, 3:167, 379; *Hannibal, Huck, and Tom*, 113; Albert E. Stone Jr., "Mark Twain's Joan of Arc: The Child as Goddess," *American Literature* 31 (March 1959): 4.

44. Matthews, *The Tocsin of Revolt*, 259; "Mark Twain," *Dundee Courier & Argus*, 17 April 1882, 3; Clemens, *My Father, Mark Twain*, 24; *A Family Sketch*, 51, 57, 87; SLC and Olivia Langdon Clemens to Susan Crane, 2 June 1878, UCCL 12745.

45. "What Ought John to Have Done?," *Christian Union*, 25 June 1885, 4; Kiskis, *Mark Twain at Home*, 98; *A Family Sketch*, 152; SLC and Olivia Langdon Clemens to Susan Crane, 2 June 1878, UCCL 12745; *AMT*, 2:327.

46. "What Ought He to Have Done?," *Christian Union*, 16 July 1885, 4.

47. "Personal," *NHR*, 5 July 1885, 4; *AMT*, 2:329.

48. Wagenknecht, *Mark Twain: The Man and His Work*, 132; Simpson and Simpson, *Jean Webster*, 19.

49. *WS*, 31 July 1885, 2; "Tribunets," *Washington National Tribune*, 10 September 1885, 4; *Carson (Nev.) Appeal*, 2 December 1885, 2.

50. "Philanthropic: Advertising," *Newcastle (Australia) Morning Herald and Miners' Advocate*, 20 February 1880, 4; "Mark Twain Tells a 'Chestnut,'" *NYH*, 22 March 1885, 11.

51. "Life in a Great City," *NHR*, 5 April 1885, 4; Moore, *Talks in a Library*, 19–22; *N&J*, 3:115; "Musical and Dramatic Notes," *NYH*, 10 April 1885, 6; SLC to Olivia Langdon Clemens, 9 April 1885, UCCL 03210.

52. *N&J*, 3:137, 3:139–40; "Cornell Alumni Banquet," *WC*, 24 April 1885, 3; "Authors' Readings," *BH*, 30 April 1885, 1; *MTHL*, 527, 530; *AMT*, 1:395; Susy Clemens, *Papa*, 131; "Mark Twain at Vassar," *Cincinnati Commercial Tribune*, 10 May 1885, 13; Driscoll, *Mark Twain among the Indians*, 233–36. The Clemenses hosted a lecture on George Meredith by Richard E. Burton, a benefit for the Connecticut Indian Association, in their home in mid-November 1890 ("Mr. Burton's Lecture for the Indian Association," *HC*, 14 November 1890, 5). It was likely the last occasion SLC assisted in a fund-raiser in Hartford.

53. "Two Readings by Mark Twain," *HC*, 2 June 1885, 1; *N&J*, 3:156; *MTSpk*, 656; Salsbury, *Susy and Mark Twain*, 202; "Notes," *Critic*, 26 September 1885, 155; SLC to Thomas Donaldson, 6 August 1885, *UCCL* 02620; "Pittsfield," *SR*, 7 October 1885, 6; SLC to James Pond, 30 December 1887, *UCCL* 02681.

54. Johnson, *Remembered Yesterdays*, 324; *AMT*, 2:571; Elizabeth B. Custer, "A Catskill Cabin," *CT*, 20 September 1885, 12; "Mark Twain and His Wife," *Jackson (Mich.) Citizen Patriot*, 15 October 1885, 6; Wheeler, *Yesterdays*, 337; *A Family Sketch*, 103; *N&J*, 3:193; Salsbury, *Susy and Mark Twain*, 212.

55. *MTHL*, 241; "Contributor's Club," *Atlantic Monthly* 42 (November 1878): 643; Berger, "Emendations of the Copy-Text," in *Pudd'nhead Wilson and Those Extraordinary Twins*, 191; SLC to Karl and Josephine Gerhardt, 1–3 May 1883, *UCCL* 02380; "The Whittaker Case," *Buffalo Courier*, 31 May 1880, 1; Howells, *My MT*, 36.

56. *CC*, 28 June 1882, 8; "General Notes," *Sacramento Record-Union*, 17 August 1882, 3; SLC to Rev. J. Chester, 10 September 1886, *UCCL* 03454; *N&J*, 3:255.

57. Budd, "A Supplement," 60; McDowell, "From Twain, a Letter," 1, 16.

58. Paine, *MTB*, 701; Lorch, *The Trouble Begins at Eight*, 153; *MTHL*, 356, 509–10; *N&J*, 3:486, 3:489; Fears, *Mark Twain Day-by-Day*, 2:33.

59. "The Pope's Autobiography," *BH*, 16 March 1886, 4; SLC to Olivia Langdon Clemens, 5 May 1886, *UCCL* 03389; Paine, *MTB*, 855; Henry B. Wonham, "Webster and Company, Charles L.", in LeMaster and Wilson, *The Routledge Encyclopedia of Mark Twain*, 781.

60. "Charles L. Webster," *NYH*, 27 April 1891, 7; Fred J. Hall to SLC, 19 July 1889, *UCLC* 44599; Webster, *Mark Twain: Business Man*, 364; SLC to Charles L. Webster, 17 June 1886, *UCCL* 03411; *MTLP*, 212; SLC to Charles L. Webster, 1 March 1887, *UCCL* 03534.

61. SLC to Charles L. Webster, 3 August 1887, *UCCL* 02667; SLC to Fred J. Hall, 16 July 1886, *UCCL* 02637; Howells, *My MT*, 73–74.

Chapter 14

1. *MTHL*, 439; Webster, *Mark Twain: Business Man*, 178; *AMT*, 2:490; *N&J*, 3:29; Camfield, "A Republican Artisan," 117; Kaplan, *The Singular Mark Twain*, 365.

2. Hill, *Mark Twain and Elisha Bliss*, 124, 153; SLC to Charles L. Webster, 8 July 1882, *UCCL* 02232; *N&J*, 2:495; "An Intelligent Watch," *Middletown (Conn.) Constitution*, 31 January 1877, 2; Howells, *My MT*, 79; SLC to Joe Goodman, 29 November 1889, *UCCL* 03980.

3. Mott, *American Journalism*, 411; Johanningsmeier, *Fiction and the American Literary Marketplace*, 2, 15; Tebbel, *A History of Book Publishing*, 154.

4. *N&J*, 2:395; SLC to Jane Lampton Clemens, 9 October 1882, *UCCL* 02289; SLC to Charles L. Webster, 19 September 1882, *UCCL* 02276; *AMT*, 2:505.

5. Lawton, *A Lifetime*, 104–5; *AMT*, 1:494; *MTLP*, 185–86; SLC to Charles L. Webster, 8 April 1883, *UCCL* 02876; *N&J*, 3:144, 3:148, 3:155, 3:198.

6. SLC to Mollie Fairbanks, 6 August 1877, *UCCL* 01467; *N&J*, 2:302; "Persons and Things," *NHR*, 25 March 1886, 2; "The New Dynasty," *New England Quarterly* 30 (September 1957): 387.

7. SLC to Charles L. Webster, 4–6 April 1885, *UCCL* 03206; *MTLP*, 186; *N&J*, 3:191; Gold, "Hatching Ruin," 33; *AMT*, 3:103–4.

8. SLC to Charles L. Webster, 28 July 1885, *UCCL* 03270; Andrews, *Nook Farm*, 124; "Colonel Sellers: A Drama in Five Acts," 127; Howells, *My MT*, 80.

9. SLC to Ned House, 11–12 August 1886, *UCCL* 03437; William Laffan to SLC, 25 January 1886, *UCLC* 42869.

10. Charles L. Webster to SLC, 19 February 1886, *UCLC* 42881; *N&J*, 3:219; 3:241.

11. *AMT*, 3:103–5; Paine, *MTB*, 906; Gold, "Hatching Ruin," 38.

12. Gold, "Hatching Ruin," 103; SLC to Fred J. Hall, 19 August 1886, *UCCL* 02642; SLC to Fred J. Hall, 28 August 1886, *UCCL* 02643; Hill, *Mark Twain and Elisha Bliss*, 203–6; SLC to Andrew Chatto, 12 August 1886, *UCCL* 12175.

13. *N&J*, 3:225; SLC to Franklin G. Whitmore, 13 August 1887, *UCCL* 03626; SLC to Franklin G. Whitmore, 18 August 1887, *UCCL* 03629; SLC to Orion Clemens, 18 December 1887, *UCCL* 03680; *AMT*, 1:105–6.

14. *AMT*, 2:601; *N&J*, 3:230–31, 3:234; *A Family Sketch*, 158; Susy Clemens, *Papa*, 187; SLC to Charles L. Webster, 16 December 1885, *UCCL* 03334; SLC to Charles L. Webster, 13 February 1886, *UCCL* 02425; *MTHL*, 550; *Connecticut Yankee*, 27.

15. Budd, *Mark Twain: Social Philosopher*, 134; *Connecticut Yankee*, 22, 45, 498; *AMT*, 2:307; Moore, "Mark Twain and Don Quixote"; Boewe, "Smouching towards Bedlam," 8–12; *MTMF*, 257–58.

16. "'Mark Twain' on International Copyright," Boston *Musical Record*, 262 (November 1883): 9; "State Correspondence," *NHR*, 21 March 1884, 4; *MTCI*, 80; "Topics of the Times," *Century* 31 (February 1886): 634.

17. Scharnhorst, "Mark Twain and Julian Hawthorne," 48–49.

18. SLC to Olivia Langdon Clemens, 17 November 1885, *UCCL* 03309; SLC to Olivia Langdon Clemens, 25 November 1885, *UCCL* 03314; "Personal," *WS*, 20 November 1885, 1; *N&J*, 3:177, 3:211; Salsbury, *Susy and Mark Twain*, 213.

19. "Authors in Public," *St. Louis Post-Dispatch*, 18 March 1888, 10.

20. "Mark Twain a Cub Printer," *NYS*, 19 January 1886, 3; *MTSpk*, 200–202, 205; Camfield, "A Republican Artisan," 99; Walker, *Ambrose Bierce*, 26.

21. "International Copyright," *NYTrib*, 29 January 1886, 3; "Fruits of the Brain," *BH*, 29 January 1886, 3; Johnson, *Remembered Yesterdays*, 267; *MTSpk*, 208; Vandersee, "The Mutual Awareness"; Gath [George Alfred Townsend], "The Protection of Authorship," *Cincinnati Enquirer*, 2 February 1886, 1; SLC to Olivia Langdon Clemens, 28 January 1886, *UCCL* 03361; "Social Life in Washington," *NYS*, 31 January 1886, 1; *MTLP*, 211.

22. Anderson and Hill, "How Samuel Clemens Became Mark Twain's Publisher," 125; *MTLP*, 137; *MTHL*, 347, 361, 427, 493, 539, 544.

23. Duckett, *Mark Twain and Bret Harte*, 216–17; SLC to Charles L. Webster, 20 December 1885, *UCCL* 03339; SLC to Charles L. Webster, 3 January 1886, *UCCL* 03353; SLC to Kate Field, 8 March 1886, *UCCL* 03375; *MTLP*, 226.

24. Zwarg, "Woman as a Force," 62; Leland, *The Alternate Sex*, 11.

25. *AMT*, 2:43; Field, *Selected Letters*, 190; Whiting, *Kate Field*, 429; Scharnhorst, "He Is Amusing"; *Huck Finn and Tom Sawyer among the Indians*, 98.

26. *MTHL*, 555, 559; "The Press Club Entertainment," *NYT*, 7 February 1877, 5; "Mr. Burbank's Recitals," *NYTrib*, 1 April 1879, 5; SLC to A. P. Burbank, [19?] February 1886, *UCCL* 13076; *MTLP*, 196.

27. "Musical and Dramatic Notes," *NYH*, 6 May 1886, 6; *MTHL*, 556, 557, 561; *N&J*, 3:237; Howells, *My MT*, 26; "The New Play by Mark Twain and W. D. Howells," *BJ*, 13 May 1886, 4.

28. *MTHL*, 550–60, 570; Howells, *My MT*, 26.

29. "Table Talk," *Literary World*, 5 May 1886, 172; *MTHL*, 567.

30. SLC to Franklin G. Whitmore, 15 June 1886, *UCCL* 03410; Reigstad, *Scribblin' for a Livin'*, 193; *AMT*, 2:356; Flanagan, "Mark Twain on the Upper Mississippi," 375–76; *MTCI*, 89; "Independence Day," *St. Louis Globe-Democrat*, 4 July 1886, 2.

31. *N&J*, 3:242; SLC to Franklin G. Whitmore, 12 July 1886, *UCCL* 03413; *AMT*, 2:357; "Personal Mention," *CIO*, 10 July 1886, 6; "Mark Twain," *CIO*, 10 July 1886, 13.

32. Salsbury, *Susy and Mark Twain*, 231; Skandera-Trombley, *Mark Twain in the Company of Women*, 117; SLC to Olivia Langdon Clemens, 1 August 1886, *UCCL* 03431; SLC to Franklin G. Whitmore, 16 September 1886, *UCCL* 03458; *MTCI*, 93; *N&J*, 3:256.

33. *AMT*, 2:197; *Collected Tales*, 573–77; *MTL*, 6:368–71; *St. Louis Globe-Democrat*, 18 October 1875, 3.

34. *Mark Twain's Letters* (1917), 322–25; *N&J*, 2:55, 2:69; *Simon Wheeler, Detective*, xvii, 134; *MTHL*, 376; Ferguson, *Mark Twain*, 217; Susy Clemens, *Papa*, 187; SLC to Jeannette Gilder, 14 May 1887, *UCCL* 03572; *AMT*, 2:550.

35. "Yankee Smith of Camelot," *NYS*, 12 November 1886, 1; "Mark Twain's New Lecture," *New York World*, 12 November 1886, 2; "Mark Twain's Yankee," *Boston Globe*, 12 November 1886, 2; "Mark Twain to the Military," *BH*, 12 November 1886, 2; "A Yankee in Camelot," *Washington Post*, 13 November 1886, 2; *MTCI*, 110; Leon, *Mark Twain and West Point*, 80; *N&J*, 3:264.

36. *MTHL*, 576; Andrews, *Nook Farm*, 94; *MTSpk*, 215; "Press Club Reception," *BH*, 10 December 1886, 4.

37. *N&J*, 3:278; "The Authors' Club," *NYH*, 19 February 1887, 8; "New York Clubs," *SFB*, 28 January 1888, 1; "He Was Fly," *Wheeling Register*, 30 March 1888, 3; "Mayor Hewitt's Views on the Strike," *NYTrib*, 11 February 1887, 5; *MTSpk*, 216–18; Eleanor Kirk, "Our New York Letter," *Washington Bee*, 5 March 1887, 1; "English as She Is Taught," *Century* 33 (April 1887): 932–36; Oscar Wilde, "The Child-Philosopher," *Court and Society Review*, 20 April 1887, 380; Julian Ralph, "What New York Talks Of," *Galveston News*, 15 May 1887, 4.

38. SLC to Annie Fields, 1 April 1887, *UCCL* 03553; "Wit and Wisdom," *BH*, 1 April 1887, 8; "Authors Seen and Heard," *NYTrib*, 1 April 1887, 5; Aldrich, *Crowding Memories*, 255; "Letter from Boston," *Congregationalist*, 7 April 1887, 10; *MTCI*, 578; Howells, *My MT*, 52; "Longfellow," *BA*, 1 April 1887, 5; "Among the Collegians," *NHJC*, 30 March 1887, 4.

39. SLC to James Pond, 25 April 1887, *UCCL* 02659; "Gymnasium Exhibition," *HC*, 2 April 1887, 3; *N&J*, 3:283, 3:315; "Mark Twain's Bookkeeper," *NYS*, 13 March 1887, 1, and *NYS*, 18 March 1887, 4; "Did Scott Destroy Cash Books?," *NYTrib*, 19 March 1887, 4; Webster, *Mark Twain: Business Man*, 380–81, 390; Charles L. Webster to SLC, 15 November 1887, *UCLC* 43827; *MTLP*, 216; *AMT*, 2:75–76, 499.

40. *MTSpk*, 221.

41. *MTSpk*, 222; "The Good Gray Poet," *NHJC*, 15 April 1887, 3; Ellsworth, *A Golden Age*, 64; SLC to Sylvester Baxter, 28 May 1887, *UCCL* 03577; Folsom and Loving, "The Walt Whitman Controversy," 124.

42. Matthew Arnold, "General Grant," *Murray's* 1 (January 1887): 131; *MTSpk*, 225–27; Leon, *Mark Twain and West Point*, 65–66, 69, 72–73.

43. Lawton, *A Lifetime*, 8, 40; *MTMF*, 258–60; Bellamy, *Mark Twain as a Literary Artist*, 46; SLC to Cordelia Welsh Foote, 2 December 1887, *UCCL* 03672; Mary Bushnell Cheney, "Mark Twain as a Reader," *Harper's Weekly*, 7 January 1911, 6; Paine, *MTB*, 847; Salsbury, *Susy and Mark Twain*, 181; *MTMF*, 261; Wecter, *Samuel Clemens of Hannibal*, 260–61; Wheeler, *Yesterdays*, 328; *N&J*, 3:422, 3:435–37.

44. Howells, *My MT*, 26; Schirer, *Mark Twain and the Theatre*, 83–85.

45. William Winter, "Mr. Burbank as Col. Sellers," *NYTrib*, 24 September 1887, 4; "Amusements," *NYT*, 24 September 1887, 5; Nym Crinkle [Andrew C. Wheeler], "Down on Mark Twain," *BE*, 2 October 1887, 15; "Music and Drama," *NYEP*, 24 September 1887, 3; "Amusements," *NYS*, 24 September 1887, 4; "New York," *New York Clipper*, 1 October 1887,

455; "The Lyceum," *Theatre*, 11 October 1887, 267; "A Petition," *BH*, 26 September 1887, 4; "Amusements," *NYH*, 24 September 1887, 4; Schirer, *Mark Twain and the Theatre*, 84; Frohman, *Encore*, 107–8. The error in Clemens biography that *Colonel Sellers as a Scientist* was never produced in New York originated with W. D. Howells (*My MT*, 27) and was perpetuated by Albert Bigelow Paine (*MTB*, 762) and Ron Powers (*Mark Twain*, 480).

46. W. A. Croffut, "A Capital Boss," *Milwaukee Sentinel*, 23 October 1887, 10; SLC to A. P. Burbank, October 1887, *UCCL* 03656; Schirer, *Mark Twain and the Theatre*, 89–90; SLC to Augustin Daly, 12 February 1892, *UCCL* 04269; *MTHL*, 628.

47. *MTL*, 4:149; SLC to Ned House, 14 January 1884, *UCCL* 02889; SLC to Ned House, 17 December 1886, *UCCL* 03499; SLC to Ned House, 26 December 1886, *UCCL* 03502; Kaplan, *The Singular Mark Twain*, 444; SLC to Irving Putnam, 26 January 1889, *UCCL* 03854; *MTCI*, 114; *AMT*, 3:499; "Affidavits That Clash," *NYT*, 28 January 1890, 8; "Mark Twain Hauled Up," *NYT*, 27 January 1890, 5; "Mr. House in Reply," *NYT*, 31 January 1890, 9.

48. SLC to Ned House, 7 May 1887, *UCCL* 03568; SLC to Charles L. Webster, 9 May 1887, *UCCL* 03571; "Suit against Mark Twain," *BH*, 18 January 1890, 2; "Mr. House in Reply," *NYT*, 31 January 1890, 9; Fatout, "Mark Twain, Litigant," 35.

49. *AMT*, 3:115; SLC to Dean Sage, 5 February 1890, *UCCL* 04012; *MTCI*, 115; "Affidavits That Clash," *NYT*, 28 January 1890, 8; "Concerning the Scoundrel Edward H. House," DV 305, MTP; Fatout, "Mark Twain, Litigant," 38; SLC to Ned House, 19 March 1889, *UCCL* 03873.

50. Bush, "Grace King and Mark Twain," 32–33; SLC to Frederic Edwin Church, 11 June 1887, *UCCL* 03582.

51. King, *Memories*, 94; Bush, "Grace King and Mark Twain," 36–37.

52. Fears, *Mark Twain Day-by-Day*, 2:181; SLC to Joseph B. Gilder, 16 May 1886, *UCCL* 11414; Britton, "Carlyle, Clemens, and Dickens"; Fulton, *Mark Twain in the Margins*, 11; SLC to Olivia Langdon Clemens, 26 July 1887, *UCCL* 03615; *MTHL*, 595.

53. *Connecticut Yankee*, 31, 39, 56, 157, 242; SLC to Franklin G. Whitmore, 21 July 1887, *UCCL* 03607; SLC to Franklin G. Whitmore, 14 August 1887, *UCCL* 11473; SLC to Dora Wheeler, 12 September 1887, *UCCL* 02435; SLC to Fred J. Hall and Charles L. Webster, 15 August 1887, *UCCL* 02668.

54. *Mark Twain on Potholes and Politics*, 85; Salsbury, *Susy and Mark Twain*, 43; *Letters from the Earth*, 70–71; Brock, "Mark Twain's 'Mysterious Scoresheet'"; Scharnhorst, "Mark Twain on Baseball"; "Hartford's New Amusement Enterprise," *NHR*, 7 February 1887, 3; "Mark Twain as an Umpire," *NYTrib*, 3 July 1887, 2; "Elmira's Great Ball Game," *NYS*, 3 July 1887, 1–2; "Mark Twain," *Los Angeles Times*, 16 July 1887, 10; "Notes and Comments," *Sporting Life*, 20 June 1888, 7; Williams, "Revision and Intention," 294.

Chapter 15

1. Gold, *"Hatching Ruin,"* 97, 113; Simpson and Simpson, *Jean Webster*, 18; Feinstein, "Mark Twain's Lawsuits," 224; *N&J*, 3:322; Paine, *MTB*, 858; Charles L. Webster to SLC, 23 April 1887, *UCLC* 43275; *MTLP*, 216, 244, 267.

2. SLC to Charles L. Webster, 19 January 1887, *UCCL* 03513; SLC to Charles L. Webster, 15 February 1887, *UCCL* 03528; *MTLP*, 212; SLC to Orion Clemens, 16 March 1887, *UCCL* 03380; *LMT&JHT*, 141; SLC to Fred J. Hall, 2 September 1887, *UCCL* 02673; Paine, *MTB*, 856.

3. Gribben, *Mark Twain's Library*, 740; SLC to Charles L. Webster, 13 January 1887, *UCCL* 03506; SLC to Charles L. Webster, 19 January 1887, *UCCL* 03513; SLC to Charles L. Webster, 5 September 1887, *UCCL* 02672; *AMT*, 2:77.

4. SLC to Charles L. Webster, 11 May 1887, *UCCL* 03355; SLC to Charles L. Webster, 28 May 1887, *UCCL* 08918; *MTLP*, 218; SLC to Fred J. Hall and Charles L. Webster, 15 August 1887, *UCCL* 02668; *AMT*, 2:74, 2:76.

5. SLC to Charles L. Webster, 1 March 1887, *UCCL* 03534; *AMT*, 2:78, 2:503; Paine, *MTB*, 857; Gold, "Hatching Ruin," 132; *N&J*, 3:612; "Fred J. Hall Tells the Story," *Twainian* 6 (November–December 1947): 2.

6. Howells, *My MT*, 18; SLC to Charles L. Webster, 3 August 1887, *UCCL* 02667; SLC to Fred J. Hall and Charles L. Webster, 15 August 1887, *UCCL* 02668; *MTLP*, 229; Gold, "Hatching Ruin," 117; SLC to Andrew Chatto, 19 September 1887, *UCCL* 01851; Welland, *Mark Twain in England*, 149; *AMT*, 2:77, 2:501.

7. Gold, "What Happened," 12–13; *MTLP*, 229; *AMT*, 2:65, 2:495; Charles L. Webster to SLC, 28 December 1887, *UCCL* 03685.

8. Charles L. Webster to SLC, 7 September 1887, *UCLC* 43750; SLC to Charles L. Webster, 9 September 1887, *UCCL* 03646.

9. SLC to Orion Clemens, 16 March 1887, *UCCL* 03380; SLC to Fred J. Hall, 9 July 1887, *UCCL* 03597; SLC to Fred J. Hall and Charles L. Webster, 15 August 1887, *UCCL* 02668; Fred J. Hall to SLC, 4 June 1888, *UCLC* 44052; Paine, *MTB*, 856; Gribben, *Mark Twain's Library*, 118; Burton, "Mark Twain in the Hartford Days," 5.

10. SLC to Fred J. Hall, 8 September 1887, *UCCL* 02674; Jones, *American Food*, 115; SLC to Olivia Langdon Clemens, 6 May 1886, *UCCL* 03390; Fred J. Hall to SLC, 7 September 1887, *UCCL* 43751; *MTLP*, 252.

11. Beahrs, *Twain's Feast*, 1, 24; King, *Memories*, 94; Bush, "Grace King and Mark Twain," 36.

12. *MTHL*, 546; *MTLP*, 218–19, 230; SLC to Charles L. Webster, 28 December 1885, *UCCL* 03345; SLC to Charles L. Webster, 29 December 1885, *UCCL* 03194; *N&J*, 3:216; SLC to Moncure D. Conway, 12 July 1886, *UCCL* 02636; *AMT*, 3:299, 3:603–4.

13. Hill, "Mark Twain and His Enemies," 523–24; *MTLP*, 221.

14. *N&J*, 3:295; Gribben, *Mark Twain's Library*, 600, 656–57, 683, 772; *Connecticut Yankee*, 77; *MTLP*, 221.

15. *N&J*, 3:374; Fred J. Hall to SLC, 30 October 1888, *UCLC* 44211; Gold, "What Happened?," 17; *AMT*, 2:78.

16. Eble, *Old Clemens and W.D.H.*, 19; SLC to Charles L. Webster, 8 February 1886, *UCCL* 03273; Simpson and Simpson, *Jean Webster*, 22; Gold, "Hatching Ruin," 129; Charles L. Webster to SLC, 6 November 1888, *UCLC* 44223; *N&J*, 3:431; SLC to Pamela Moffett, 12 July 1887, *UCCL* 03602.

17. Gold, "Hatching Ruin," 130; Webster, *Mark Twain: Business Man*, viii; *MTHL*, 610; SLC to Pamela Moffett, 1 July 1889, *UCCL* 03905; SLC to Orion Clemens, 1 July 1889, *UCCL* 03904; *AMT*, 2:74, 2:503. SLC had earlier used the phrase "human louse" to describe Cable and he did not use the word "assful" here for the first time. As Huck remarks to Tom in "Tom Sawyer's Conspiracy" (written in 1897), "have it your own way, but I think it's an assful way" (*Huck Finn and Tom Sawyer among the Indians*, 177).

18. *N&J*, 3:615; SLC to Fred J. Hall, 11 January 1889, *UCCL* 03850; *MTLP*, 243; Gold, "Hatching Ruin," 132.

19. Mac Donnell, "Who Killed Charlie Webster?," 18; Fred J. Hall to SLC, 30 April 1891, *UCLC* 45545.

20. Edmund Yates, "Mark Twain Set Right," *NYTrib*, 11 October 1887, 5; "Mark Twain in England," *NYS*, 19 October 1887, 4; Duckett, *Mark Twain and Bret Harte*, 335; *Mark Twain's Letters* (1917), 494.

21. "New England News," *Worcester (Mass.) Spy*, 5 June 1886, 3; "The Putnam Phalanx," *WC*, 4 October 1887, 1; Smith, *Life of Henry Drummond*, 380; Bush, "Grace King and Mark Twain," 38; "General State News," *NHJC*, 27 October 1887, 4; "Personal and General Notes," *New Orleans Picayune*, 30 October 1887, 6; "Personal," *BJ*, 14 November 1887, 4; "People and Events," *CIO*, 19 November 1887, 4. Both the *NHJC* ("Count John Lillichurtz") and the *New Orleans Picayune* ("Count Leitedolf") badly misspell Lewenhaupt's name.

22. "Personal and General Notes," *New Orleans Picayune*, 3 December 1887, 4; "Readings by American Authors," *NYS*, 29 November 1887, 5; "Letter from New York," *Congregationalist*, 8 December 1887, 1; *N&J*, 3:353; "Interesting Gossip of the Day," *NYS*, 12 December 1887, 4; "Pilgrims' Day in Boston," *NYTrib*, 21 December 1887, 15; "The Copyright Laws," *BJ*, 28 December 1887, 1; "New York Clubs," *SFB*, 28 January 1888, 1; "The Lambs Honor Their Shepherd," *NYTrib*, 2 January 1888, 5; Paine, *MTB*, 866.

23. "Merry Yale Alumni," *NHR*, 4 February 1888, 4; *N&J*, 3:379; SLC to Olivia Langdon Clemens, 16 March 1888, *UCCL* 03709.

24. Fears, *Mark Twain Day-by-Day*, 2:257; "At the National Capital," *SR*, 18 March 1888, 1; "International Copyright," *CIO*, 18 March 1888, 9; "Authors' Readings," *NYH*, 18 March 1888, 11; *AMT*, 1:384–85, 1:602; "Personalities," *Washington National Republican*, 17 March 1888, 1; Gilder, *Letters*, 196; *N&J*, 3:301, 376; SLC to Olivia Langdon Clemens, 16 March 1888, *UCCL* 03709; "Authors in Public," *St. Louis Post-Dispatch*, 18 March 1888, 10; SLC to Sam Moffett, 30 March 1888, *UCCL* 03711.

25. "Dinner Given to Miss Montgomery," *Portland Oregonian*, 8 April 1888, 3; "Mark Twain's Visit to the Capitol," *Baltimore Sun*, 23 March 1888, 1; "Tariff Reports," *BA*, 23 March 1888, 1; "The Insolence of Office," *CT*, 29 March 1888, 9; "Live Washington Topics," *NYS*, 23 March 1888, 1; "Social Chit Chat," *WC*, 23 March 1888, 4.

26. "The Copyright Hearing," *Washington Post*, 24 March 1888, 4; "Mark Twain Heard," *Kansas City Times*, 24 March 1888, 2.

27. "Society Notes," *WS*, 27 March 1888, 5; Budd, "Twain, Howells, and the Boston Nihilists," 351. SLC has long been rumored to have exclaimed these words after hearing Kennan lecture at the Lowell Institute, but no evidence SLC attended such a lecture has ever been located.

28. *N&J*, 3:377; Baetzhold, "The Course of Composition" 207–11; George Kennan, "Siberia and the Exile System," *Century* 36 (May 1888): 3–24; *Connecticut Yankee*, 390; SLC to Frederick Hawley, 27 June 1887, *UCLC* 43338; Paine, *MTB*, 794; *AMT*, 1:228–29; *N&J*, 3:301; SLC to Augustin Daly, 5 April 1888, *UCCL* 03713. See also "Robert Louis Stevenson's Retreat," *NYS*, 27 November 1887, 4.

29. SLC to Karl and Josephine Gerhardt, 26 March 1883, *UCCL* 02364; SLC to J. Chipchase, 2 March 1885, *UCCL* 03181; *N&J*, 3:8; SLC to Charles L. Webster, 31 October 1884, *UCCL* 03014; "Was Hawley a Figure Head?" *NHR*, 17 April 1888, 1; "Mark Twain a Heavy Loser," *SFB*, 17 April 1888, 3.

30. "Artists and Their Friends Dine," *NYTrib*, 4 May 1888, 7; "Brief Mention," *NHJC*, 9 May 1888, 2; *N&J*, 3:385; "News about Town," *NHR*, 23 May 1888, 4; "Gossip from New York," *Kansas City Star*, 4 August 1888, 3; *LMT&JHT*, 144; "Curtis on Cleveland," *NYH*, 30 May 1888, 3.

31. *Connecticut Yankee*, 153; SLC to Thomas A. Edison, 25 May 1888, *UCCL* 11326; *The American Claimant*, 176; Thomas A. Edison to Cyril Clemens, 10 January 1927, *UCLC* 47863; *AMT*, 3:545; "The First Interview Recorded by the Phonograph," *Pall Mall Gazette*, 24 July 1888, 2. No audio recordings of SLC's voice are known to survive.

32. Arnold, *Civilization in the United States*, 177.

33. SLC to Lorettus S. Metcalf, 13 April 1888, *UCCL* 03714; SLC to Timothy Dwight, 26 June 1888, *UCCL* 03725; "The Alumni Dinner," *NHR*, 28 June 1888, 3; SLC to Charles Clark, 2 July 1888, *UCCL* 03728; *N&J*, 3:383, 3:406.

34. *N&J*, 3:424; Baetzhold, "The Course of Composition," 211; Fulton, *Mark Twain in the Margins*, 179; Carter, "The Meaning of *A Connecticut Yankee*," 428, 435; *Connecticut Yankee*, 118–20; Smith, *Mark Twain: The Development*, 155, 170; Cox, *Mark Twain: The Fate of Humor*, 203.

35. Lecky, *History of European Morals*, 2:119; *Connecticut Yankee*, 282. Of course, Hank Morgan's title "the Boss" also evokes the nickname of William M. (Boss) Tweed of Tammany Hall.

36. Aspiz, "Lecky's Influence on Mark Twain," 17; *Huckleberry Finn* (1885), 292; *Connecticut Yankee*, 191, 219.

37. *Connecticut Yankee*, 514.

38. *Mark Twain's Notebook*, 255; Cardwell, *The Man Who Was Mark Twain*, 223; "The Temperance Insurrection," *London Standard*, 26 March 1874, 1; *A Family Sketch*, 9; *MTMF*, 266.

39. Blair, *Mark Twain and Huck Finn*, 136; *Connecticut Yankee*, 100, 118, 216, 245, 514, 532; Budd, *Mark Twain: Social Philosopher*, 129; *N&J*, 3:405, 3:416; Quirk, *Mark Twain and Human Nature*, 185; *MTLP*, 258.

40. *Connecticut Yankee*, 428; Tenney, *Mark Twain: A Reference Guide*, 17; Fulton, *Mark Twain's Ethical Realism*, 92; Foner, *Mark Twain: Social Critic*, 97; "For Tariff Reform," *NHR*, 30 October 1888, 1; "A Great Tariff Reform Rally," *NHR*, 31 October 1888, 1; "The Talk of the Day," *NYTrib*, 3 November 1888, 9.

41. *AMT*, 1:313; Camfield, *Sentimental Twain*, 170; *Connecticut Yankee*, 217; Smith, *Mark Twain: The Development*, 171.

42. Camfield, *Oxford Companion*, 153; *N&J*, 3:414; *The American Claimant*, 193, 195; *A Family Sketch*, 31.

43. *Connecticut Yankee*, 514, 540; Cox, *Mark Twain: The Fate of Humor*, 218; *N&J*, 3:415.

44. *AMT*, 2:240; Webster, *Mark Twain: Business Man*, 149–50; *Connecticut Yankee*, 518.

45. SLC to Orion Clemens, 16 September 1888, *UCCL* 03765; SLC to Pamela Moffett, 15 September 1888, *UCCL* 03763; SLC to Andrew Chatto, 17 September 1888, *UCCL* 03766.

46. *N&J*, 3:424; Courtney, *Joseph Hopkins Twichell*, 228; SLC to Orion Clemens, 3 October 1888, *UCCL* 03781; SLC to Christen Christensen, 9 October 1888, *UCCL* 03786.

47. SLC to William Bowen, 4 November 1888, *UCCL* 03826; Olivia Langdon Clemens to Olivia Lewis Langdon, 19 November 1888, *UCCL* 03834; Bush, "Grace King and Mark Twain," 42–43; King, *Memories*, 81, 85–86; *N&J*, 3:435.

48. King, *Memories*, 86–87; Bush, "Grace King and Mark Twain," 41; Tom Powers, "New York Gossip," *St. Louis Republic*, 27 October 1889, 21; *AMT*, 3:238; Moser, "Mark Twain: Mugwump."

49. *MTMF*, 263; SLC to Orion Clemens, 23 November 1888, *UCCL* 03835; SLC to Olivia Lewis Langdon, *UCCL* 03797.

50. SLC to Theodore Crane, 5 October 1888, *UCCL* 03782.

Chapter 16

1. *AMT*, 3:115, 3:500; "Daniel Frohman Begins a Suit," *NYTrib*, 11 July 1890, 6; *N&J*, 3:435; "Affidavits That Clash," *NYT*, 28 January 1890, 8; Fatout, "Mark Twain, Litigant," 30; "Elsie Leslie," *NYTrib*, 2 December 1888, 17; "Elsie Amended the Play," *New York Evening World*, 22 March 1889, 3; "Remarks on Richardson Contract," DOC 06768, MTP.

2. Fatout, "Mark Twain, Litigant," 37, 40. No letter House sent SLC dated after May 1, 1888, survives in the Mark Twain Papers.

3. *N&J*, 3:454; SLC to Ned House, 2 March 1889, *UCCL* 12176; SLC to Ned House, 19 March 1889, *UCCL* 03873.

4. *NYS*, 25 April 1889, 4; "Dramatic and Musical Notes," *New York Clipper*, 4 May 1889, 123; *N&J*, 3:487; Fatout, "Mark Twain, Litigant," 31; "Author against Author," *NYTrib*, 17 January 1890, 1; Schirer, *Mark Twain and the Theatre*, 88; "A Talk with Mr. Clemens," *NYT*, 31 January 1890, 9; SLC to Horace Wall, 21 June 1889, *UCCL* 09181; Chandos Fulton to Ned House, 21 June 1889, *UCLC* 44571.

5. *AMT*, 2:80; SLC to Franklin G. Whitmore, 14 August 1887, *UCCL* 03627; SLC to Orion Clemens, 22 January 1888, *UCCL* 03698; SLC to Orion Clemens, 5 January 1889, *UCCL* 03847; Paine, *MTB*, 906; SLC to Stilson Hutchins, April 1888, *UCCL* 09125; SLC to William Bowen, 29 December 1888, *UCCL* 03810; SLC to Olivia Langdon Clemens, 31 December 1888, *UCCL* 03815; Paine, *MTB*, 909.

6. "A Letter from Mark Twain," *Pall Mall Gazette*, 16 February 1889, 3; Paine, *MTB*, 910; *N&J*, 3:448, 3:460–61; SLC to Susan Crane, 1 March 1889, *UCCL* 03856; SLC to Charles Taylor, 2 March 1889, *UCCL* 11015; SLC to Jane Lampton Clemens, 3 April 1889, *UCCL* 03879; SLC to unidentified, 11 April 1889, *UCCL* 11426; SLC to unidentified, 1–10 July 1889, *UCCL* 12082.

7. "Readings by Authors," *Baltimore Sun* supplement, 18 January 1889, 1; Gribben, *Mark Twain's Library*, 91, 94, 357; "Two Authors Give a Treat," *Baltimore American*, 18 January 1889, 6; *N&J*, 3:444; *AMT*, 2:597; Tucker 184; "Late Department News," *WC*, 2 February 1889, 1; "Mark Twain in the City," *Washington Post*, 2 February 1889, 1; "Mark Twain," *Washington Post*, 4 February 1889, 2; "Society Events in Washington," *New York Evening World*, 4 February 1889, 4; "Invited to Meet Authors," *WC*, 2 February 1889, 1; Budd, "A Rediscovered Mark Twain Speech"; "Opposition to the Copyright," *Pittsburgh Dispatch*, 5 February 1889, 1; *MTCI*, 560; "Personal and Pertinent," *New York Evening World*, 8 February 1889, 4.

8. "A Sextette of Items," *WC*, 7 February 1889, 3; "Yale's Hartford Alumni," *NHR*, 7 February 1889, 4; "Eleanor Kirk's Letter," *Plattsburgh Sentinel*, 22 February 1889, 5; "Newspaper Men in Council," *NYT*, 14 February 1889, 8; "Newspaper Circulation," *NYEP*, 14 February 1889, 8; *N&J*, 3:448.

9. "Trinity College Alumni," *BH*, 26 February 1889, 2; "A Bishopric Goes A-Begging," *SFB*, 15 October 1886, 4; *N&J*, 3:449; *Ravenna (Ohio) Democratic Press*, 8 November 1888, 3; SLC to George Williamson Smith, 6 November 1888, *UCCL* 03829; "The College President," *HC*, 26 February 1889, 3.

10. *N&J*, 3:447, 3:457, 3:461; "The Hotel Guests," *BA*, 27 February 1889, 1. Though Albert Bigelow Paine asserts in his biography (*MTB*, 876) that SLC spoke extemporaneously and Paul Fatout claims SLC introduced Riley and Nye "on rather short notice" (*MTSpk*, 238), their claims are not accurate. SLC's introduction of Nye and Riley was advertised nearly a month in advance ("Local Varieties," *BH*, 3 February 1889, 6).

11. *N&J*, 3:448; "Mark Twain," *WC*, 14 March 1889, 2; "Reading Their Works," *BA*, 8 March 1889, 5; "Readings by Authors in Boston," *NYTrib*, 8 March 1889, 7; "Authors and

Their Works," *BH*, 8 March 1889, 5; "A Reception at the St. Botolph," *BA*, 8 March 1889, 5; *AMT*, 2:224; SLC to Augustin Daly, 13 March 1889, *UCCL* 03872.

12. "Banquet to Edwin Booth," *NYH*, 31 March 1889, 15; SLC to Jane Lampton Clemens, 3 April 1889, *UCCL* 03879; "Honors to Edwin Booth," *NYTrib*, 31 March 1889, 7; Matthews, *The Tocsin of Revolt*, 273; *AMT*, 2:348–39, 2:607; "The Booth Supper," *NYT*, 1 April 1889, 4; "The Connecticut Capital," *SR*, 3 March 1889, 1.

13. "Hob-Nobbing with Nobs," *BH*, 9 April 1889, 4; "'Round the Dinner Plate," *New York World*, 9 April 1889, 2; "A Brilliant 'Innings,'" *NYTrib*, 9 April 1889, 1; Abraham Mills to SLC, 12 April 1889, *UCLC* 44483; Anson, *A Ball Player's Career*, 280; *Connecticut Yankee*, 534; *N&J*, 3:468.

14. Fears, *Mark Twain Day-by-Day*, 2:163; "A Memorable Occasion," *BA*, 4 May 1889, 9; SLC to Olivia Lewis Langdon, 17 April 1889, *UCCL* 03885.

15. *N&J*, 3:86; Baetzhold, "The Course of Composition," 213; Dalrymple, "Just War," 9; *Connecticut Yankee*, 540, 558.

16. *MTMF*, 258; Tuveson, *Redeemer Nation*, 230; *Connecticut Yankee*, 554; *MTHL*, 613, 619; Nathaniel Hawthorne 312; Melville, *Correspondence*, 212.

17. SLC to Pamela Moffett, 1 July 1889, *UCCL* 03905; *MTMF*, 264; Gretchen Sharlow, "Love to All the Jolly Household," in Jerome, Wisbey, and Snedecor, *Mark Twain in Elmira*, 329; *N&J*, 3:216; *MTHL*, 605.

18. "The Alumni Hall," *NHR*, 26 June 1889, 1; "The Alumni Dinner," *New Haven Morning Journal and Courier*, 27 June 1889, 2; "Bidding Yale Farewell," *NYTrib*, 27 June 1889, 4.

19. *MTHL*, 604; *MTMF*, 264; Gretchen Sharlow, "Theodore Crane: A New Perspective," in Jerome, Wisbey, and Snedecor, *Mark Twain in Elmira*, 269; *N&J*, 3:49, 3:478.

20. *N&J*, 3:506, 3:511–12, 3:515–16; SLC to Orion Clemens, 2 August 1889, *UCCL* 03920; SLC to William Hamersley, 31 August 1889, *UCCL* 03934. Justin Kaplan alleges that SLC "began to use the publishing house as a private bank to finance the machine" (Kaplan, *Mr. Clemens and Mark Twain*, 291) but, as Hamlin Hill demonstrates, he never diverted funds from the company to subsidize development of the typesetter (Hill, *MTLP*, 6).

21. *N&J*, 3:579; SLC to Frank Fuller, 12 October 1889, *UCCL* 03951; *MTHL*, 615. SLC's comment to Fuller in October 1889, specifying that he had spent thousands of dollars on the typesetter "for 44 consecutive months," is one explanation for the name of "No. 44," the protagonist of the third version of "The Mysterious Stranger" (written between 1902 and 1908).

22. *MTCI*, 203; Paine, *MTB*, 881; *AMT*, 2:175, 2:544.

23. *MTLP*, 254; *N&J*, 3:457; Beard, *Hardly a Man Is Now Alive*, 336–37; "Mark Twain and His Illustrator," *Success* 3 (June 1900): 205; SLC to Dan Beard, 21–24 July 1889, *UCCL* 12552; Paine, *MTB*, 887–88; Camfield, *Oxford Companion*, 134.

24. *N&J*, 3:512; SLC to Dan Beard, 28 August 1889, *UCCL* 03933; SLC to Dan Beard, 11 November 1889, *UCCL* 03965; M. Thomas Inge, "Beard, Daniel Carter," in LeMaster and Wilson, *The Routledge Encyclopedia of Mark Twain*, 64; Beard, *Hardly a Man Is Now Alive*, 337; *AMT*, 1:364; Camfield, *Sentimental Twain*, 122; SLC to L. E. Parkhurst, 20 December 1889, *UCCL* 03991; *MTSpk*, 473–74.

25. E. C. Stedman to SLC, 7 July 1889, *UCLC* 44587; Williams, "Revision and Intention," 294; *MTHL*, 609, 610–11, 613, 616, 618.

26. SLC to Andrew Chatto, 16 July 1889, *UCCL* 03913; *MTSpk*, 253; Webster and Company to Chatto & Windus, 5 August 1889, *UCLC* 36118; *Connecticut Yankee*, xv.

27. *N&J*, 3:502; "A Connecticut Yankee in King Arthur's Court," *Century* 39 (November 1889) 74–83; "Mark Twain Accused of Plagiarism," *New York World*, 4 November 1889, 7; "The Critic's Review," *Pittsburgh Dispatch*, 23 December 1889, 4; Budd, *MTCR*, 289.

28. Blair, *Mark Twain and Huck Finn*, 111; "Mark Twain Accused of Plagiarism," *New York World*, 4 November 1889, 4; Ketterer, "'The Fortunate Island,'" 31.

29. *MTCI*, 110–11; Burdette and Burdette, *Robert J. Burdette: His Message*, 136; "Is Mark Twain a Plagiarist?" *Washington Post*, 6 November 1889, 4; Blair, *Mark Twain and Huck Finn*, 59–60; Adeler, *By the Bend of the River*, 98.

30. *Connecticut Yankee*, 544; *MTHL*, 621; SLC to Sylvester Baxter, 20 November 1889, *UCCL* 02699; *MTCI*, 104.

31. "Curiously Timely Book," *HC*, 9 December 1889, 3. Horst Kruse also argues that this notice mirrors SLC's views (Kruse, "Mark Twain's *A Connecticut Yankee*," 476). In addition, almost all of the notice consists of excerpts from the novel, including Hank's proclamation of the republic. SLC had two years earlier insisted that "it isn't a newspaper's *review* of a book that makes the book sell; it is the *extracts* copied from the book that does it" (SLC to Charles L. Webster, 16 August 1887, *UCCL* 02669).

32. "The Brazilian Republic," *BH*, 29 December 1889, 12; *MTHL*, 626–27; Thomas Wentworth Higginson to SLC, 29 December 1889, *UCLC* 44851.

33. *N&J*, 3:526; SLC to Sylvester Baxter, 24 November 1889, *UCCL* 02701; SLC to Sylvester Baxter, 3 December 1889, *UCCL* 02703; SLC to Sylvester Baxter, 19 December 1889, *UCCL* 02705; Sylvester Baxter to SLC, 30 November 1889, *UCLC* 44794; Sylvester Baxter, "Mark Twain's Masterwork," *BH*, 15 December 1889, 17; Howells, *My MT*, 43.

34. *N&J*, 3:240, 3:530–31, 3:561; "Personal Notes," *Philadelphia Inquirer*, 12 October 1889, 4; "The Fellowcraft Club Banquets," *BJ*, 16 October 1889, 3; "At the Fellowcraft Club," *BE*, 16 October 1889, 1; Matthews, *The Tocsin of Revolt*, 275.

35. Williams, "The Use of History," 107; SLC to Andrew Carnegie, 17 March 1890, *UCCL* 04027; Gribben, *Mark Twain's Library*, 668.

36. Fatout, "Mark Twain, Litigant," 31; "The Theatre in America," *New York Clipper*, 14 December 1889, 662; "Park Theatre," *New York Clipper*, 28 December 1889, 696; "Prince and Pauper a Success," *Philadelphia North American*, 18 January 1890; "A New and Successful Play," *Philadelphia Inquirer*, 25 December 1889, 5; "Prince and Pauper," *Philadelphia North American*, 25 December 1889.

37. Fatout, "Mark Twain, Litigant," 32–33; *N&J*, 3:543; *MTSpk*, 256; SLC to Elsie Leslie, 2 February 1890, *UCCL* 09505; SLC to Daniel Frohman, 2 February 1890, *UCCL* 04010; Gilder, "Mark Twain Detested the Theatre," 114; SLC to Moncure D. Conway, 25 April 1890, *UCCL* 09176; Olivia Langdon Clemens to Grace King, 25 February 1890, *UCCL* 04021.

38. Olivia Langdon Clemens to Pamela Moffett, 27 January 1890, *UCCL* 03997; SLC to Daniel Frohman, 2 February 1890, *UCCL* 04010; Gilder, "Mark Twain Detested the Theatre," 114; Frohman, *Memories*, 52–53; SLC to Abby Richardson, 19 February 1890, *UCCL* 04019.

39. SLC to Moncure D. Conway, 25 April 1890, *UCCL* 09176; Alan Dale, "The Prince and the Pauper," *New York Evening World*, 21 January 1890, 2; "The Prince and the Pauper," *Critic*, 25 January 1890, 43; "Rags and Royalty," *NYH*, 21 January 1890, 8; "Amusements," *NYT*, 21 January 1890, 4.

40. "But Mr. House Had No Contract," *NYS*, 22 January 1890, 5; "Prince and Pauper," *NYH*, 28 January 1890, 8; Fatout, "Mark Twain, Litigant," 37; "Is His Word Twain Also or Has Mark's Memory Been Wrecked?," *NYT*, 31 January 1890, 9; "Mark Twain Hauled Up," *NYT*, 27 January 1890, 5; "Mr. House in Reply," *NYT*, 31 January 1890, 9; Henry R. Elliot, "Poor of New York," *BA*, 20 January 1890, 5; "Twain's Reputation Needs Repairs," *NYT*, 5

February 1890, 4; Daniel Whitford to SLC, 4 February 1890, *UCLC* 44940; "House against Clemens," *NYT*, 4 February 1890, 9.

41. Webster, *Mark Twain: Business Man*, viii; Pond, *Eccentricities of Genius*, 197; Howells, *My MT*, 69. Even SLC's offer to Ned House of a thousand dollars to drop his claim became a bone of contention: "In one of his lying affidavits, House swears I offered him $5,000 to 'compromise' a claim which never existed save in his own laudanum-soaked imagination," he complained (SLC to Dean Sage, 5 February 1890, *UCCL* 04012).

42. "Author against Author," *NYTrib*, 17 January 1890, 1; "A Talk with Mr. Clemens," *NYT*, 31 January 1890, 9; "A Suit over 'Prince & Pauper," *NYH*, 17 January 1890, 10; "But Mr. House Had No Contract," *NYS*, 22 January 1890, 5; "Affidavits That Clash," *NYT*, 28 January 1890, 8.

43. SLC to Fred J. Hall, 27 December 1890, *UCCL* 04121; *AMT*, 2:66, 3:115, 3:502; "Mark Twain Enjoined," *WS*, 10 March 1890, 8; "Mark Twain Is Defeated," *NYT*, 9 March 1890, 1; *MTCI*, 129–30; SLC to Moncure D. Conway, 25 April 1890, *UCCL* 09176; "Concerning the Scoundrel Edward H. House," DV 305, MTP; *MTHL*, 632; SLC to John J. McCook, 8 April 1890, *UCCL* 04038.

44. "House Makes Terms," *NYT*, 12 March 1890, 2; SLC to Daniel Whitford, 16 October 1890, *UCCL* 04102; "A Stay of Proceedings," *NYT*, 11 March 1890, 8; "Daniel Frohman Begins a Suit," *NYTrib*, 11 July 1890, 6; Frohman, *Encore*, 107–8.

45. "Daniel Frohman Begins a Suit," *NYTrib*, 11 July 1890, 6; E. H. House, "The Prince and Pauper," *New York Dramatic Mirror*, 9 August 1890, 5; Daniel Frohman, "The Prince and Pauper," *New York Dramatic Mirror*, 16 August 1890, 5; SLC to James Pond, 17 October 1890, *UCCL* 04558; " 'Prince and Pauper' Enjoined," *BE*, 9 October 1890, 6; "Tommy Russell's Parents Recover $14,000," *NYS*, 7 March 1893, 2.

46. SLC to Olivia Langdon Clemens, 7 February 1894, *UCCL* 04689; *Mark Twain's Correspondence with Henry Huttleston Rogers*, 241–42; *AMT*, 3:116, 3:503–4; Frohman, *Memories*, 52.

Chapter 17

1. *MTHL*, 610; Welland, *Mark Twain in England*, 140.

2. *MTCI*, 102; *AMT*, 2:77; Tenney, "About Mark Twain," 18.

3. "Book for the Season," *Saturday Review*, 4 January 1890, 23; Budd, *MTCR*, 286–87, 290–92, 295, 299, 301–3, 307–8, 310, 314, 316–17; "Folios and Footlights," *New Review* 2 (February 1890): 188; Seymour, Australia, *Express*, 28 March 1890, 2; Budd, *Mark Twain: Social Philosopher* 131; Melton, "The British Reception of 'A Connecticut Yankee,'" 10; Lang, "The Art of Mark Twain," 222; "Amongst the Books," *Melbourne Leader*, 8 February 1890, 35; "Scraps," *Victoria (B.C.) Colonist*, 16 March 1890, 6; Camfield, *Oxford Companion*, 135; Baetzhold, *Mark Twain and John Bull*, 353–54; London *Telegraph*, 13 January 1890, 7; Welland, *Mark Twain in England*, 142.

4. *MTHL*, 610, 624, 833–84; "Mark Twain's New Book," *NHR*, 8 October 1889, 3; SLC to Sylvester Baxter, 22 November 1889, *UCCL* 02700; SLC to Sylvester Baxter, 19 December 1889, *UCCL* 02705; Sylvester Baxter, "Mark Twain's Masterwork," *BH*, 15 December 1889, 17; "Editor's Study," *Harper's Monthly* 80 (January 1890): 319–20.

5. "Literary," *American Hebrew*, 7 March 1890, 93–94; Budd, *MTCR*, 283–85, 287–89, 291, 298–99, 305, 315, 316, 313, 314, 317; "Review of New Books," *Portland Oregonian*, 30

March 1890, 12; "Mark Twain's New Book," *NYTrib*, 22 December 1889, 14; "The Critic's Review," *Pittsburgh Dispatch*, 23 December 1889, 4; *NYS*, 19 September 1896, 7.

6. "Mark Twain's Latest Work," *BA*, 7 March 1890, 4; "Mark Twain's New Book," *Atlanta Constitution*, 23 February 1890, 14; "New Publications," *Baltimore Sun*, 30 December 1889, 2; *Milwaukee Sentinel*, 20 August 1890, 4; Budd, *MTCR*, 287, 296–97, 304, 310–11.

7. "Literary News," *St. Louis Republic*, 1 November 1890, 10; Smith, *Mark Twain: The Development*, 147; Budd, *MTCR*, 303–4; McParland, *Mark Twain's Audience*, 112; Budd, *MTCR*, 306, 310; Schnirmajer, "Poetics, Justice, and Style," 121.

8. *N&J*, 3:481.

9. "Authors' Readings," *NYT*, 17 December 1889, 3; "Mark Twain and His Book," *NYT*, 10 December 1889, 5.

10. "Authors' Readings," *NYT*, 17 December 1889, 3; Leon, *Mark Twain and West Point*, 77; *MTHL*, 625.

11. *AMT*, 1:104, 1:545, 3:597; SLC to Sam Moffett, 28 November 1889, *UCCL* 03979; SLC to Joe Goodman, 7 October 1889, *UCCL* 03948; SLC to Joe Goodman, 16 November 1889, *UCCL* 03968; SLC to Joe Goodman, 29 November 1889, *UCCL* 03980; SLC to Joe Goodman, 4 December 1889, *UCCL* 03982; SLC to Karl Gerhardt, 16 October 1889, *UCCL* 03952; Goble, "Mark Twain's Nemesis," 7; *N&J*, 3:474.

12. *N&J*, 3:333; Dean Sage to SLC, 7 October 1889, *UCLC* 44699; Dean Sage to SLC, 4 November 1889, *UCLC* 44744; Dean Sage to SLC, 8 November 1889, *UCLC* 44754; Dean Sage to SLC, 19 November 1889, *UCLC* 44772; SLC to Franklin G. Whitmore, 5 August 1890, *UCCL* 04072.

13. SLC to Orion Clemens, 16 December 1889, *UCCL* 03987; "Authors' Shabby Clothes," *New York Evening World*, 25 December 1889, 2; *MTHL*, 621; Howells, *My MT*, 56; Clara Clemens to Olivia Lewis Langdon, 25 December 1889, *UCCL* 03996; Eggleston, *Reminiscences*, 281; "The List Closed," *BE*, 6 March 1890, 4.

14. *N&J*, 3:546, 566; Gold, "*Hatching Ruin*," 41; *AMT*, 1:104; SLC to Matthias Arnot, 31 March–2 April 1890, *UCCL* 04035; Joe Goodman to SLC, 3 January 1890, *UCCL* 44867; "Tritle's Metamorphosis," *Carson (Nev.) Appeal*, 25 February 1890, 3; "What Mark Twain Said," *CIO*, 8 April 1890, 4; SLC to Joe Goodman, 31 March 1890, *UCCL* 04033; Olivia Langdon Clemens to Olivia Lewis Langdon, 20 April 1890, *UCCL* 04042; "Fred J. Hall Tells the Story," *Twainian* 6 (November–December 1947): 2.

15. "Stationery and Other Notes," *American Bookseller*, 1 May 1890, 250; *N&J*, 3:549, 3:560, 3:564, 3:567, 3:599; "The Senate Is Captured," *Salt Lake Tribune*, 19 June 1890, 8; "Social Matters," *WS*, 16 June 1890, 2; Kaplan, *The Singular Mark Twain*, 439; Joe Goodman to SLC, 26 July 1890, *UCLC* 45178; SLC to Franklin G. Whitmore, 28 July 1890, *UCCL* 08914; SLC to Joe Goodman, 23 June 1890, *UCCL* 04053; SLC to William Hamersley, 11 July 1890, *UCCL* 04062; *AMT*, 1:103; Budd, *Our Mark Twain*, 83.

16. *N&J*, 3:547; *MTSpk*, 259.

17. "Players Who Amuse the Town," *SR*, 19 January 1890, 3; "Amusements," *SFB*, 30 August 1890, 2; SLC to Clara Clemens, 20 July 1890, *UCCL* 04064.

18. Olivia Langdon Clemens to Grace King, 25 February 1890, *UCCL* 04021; Olivia Langdon Clemens to Grace King, 10 September 1890, *UCCL* 04093; Olivia Langdon Clemens to SLC, 20 May 1890, *UCCL* 04049; "Mark Twain's Story," *Sausalito News*, 4 July 1890, 3.

19. *N&J*, 3:562, 582; Salsbury, *Susy and Mark Twain*, 250–51; Paine, *MTB*, 900; "Second Prize Letter," *NYH*, 14 September 1890, 11; Matthews, *The Tocsin of Revolt*, 260; SLC to Mollie and Orion Clemens, 21 August 1890, *UCCL* 04083; *AMT*, 2:571, 575.

20. *AMT*, 1:495, 3:576, 3:578, 3:595; *N&J*, 3:595n80.

21. SLC to Fred J. Hall, 30 August 1890, *UCCL* 12047; SLC to Mollie and Orion Clemens, 31 August 1890, *UCCL* 04090; SLC to John Percival Jones, 8 September 1890, *UCCL* 12240; Matthews, *The Tocsin of Revolt*, 260; SLC to James Mapes Dodge, 27 September 1890, *UCCL* 13599; Fears, *Mark Twain Day-by-Day*, 2:534; Wheeler, *Yesterdays*, 338.

22. SLC to John Percival Jones, 27 September 1890, *UCCL* 12242; SLC to Joe Goodman, 4 October 1890, *UCCL* 11281; *Mark Twain's Letters* (1917), 538; "A Kind-Hearted Druggist," *New Orleans Picayune*, 14 December 1890, 18; "Closed Its Labors," *WC*, 3 October 1890, 4; *Proceedings of the National Wholesale Druggists Association*, 16 (1890): 206.

23. SLC to Joe Goodman, 4 October 1890, *UCCL* 11281; Lovell, "Clara Clemens: The 'Bay,'" 92; SLC to Orion Clemens, 5 May 1887, *UCCL* 03566; King, *Memories*, 173; SLC to Pamela Moffett, 12 October 1890, *UCCL* 04100; *MTMF*, 265–66; Salsbury, *Susy and Mark Twain*, 283; Susy Clemens to Olivia Lewis Langdon, 20 October 1890, *UCCL* 04104; Olivia Langdon Clemens to Olivia Lewis Langdon, 3 November 1890, *UCCL* 04109; SLC to Olivia Langdon Clemens, 24 October 1890, *UCCL* 04106; SLC to Olivia Langdon Clemens, 25 November 1890, *UCCL* 08631; Olivia Langdon Clemens to Grace King, 14 January 1891, *UCCL* 04159; "In Honor of Judge Pryor," *NYS*, 10 October 1890, 3; *MTSpk*, 263; SLC to Fred J. Hall, 15 October 1890, *UCCL* 04557.

24. "Gorky Evicted Twice in a Day from Hotels," *New York World*, 15 April 1906, 1; *N&J*, 3:540; *Mark Twain on Potholes and Politics*, 157–58; James S. Leonard, "Russia," in LeMaster and Wilson, *The Routledge Encyclopedia of Mark Twain*, 645; SLC to Sergei Stepniak-Kravchinsky, 23 April 1891, *UCCL* 06149; *Mark Twain's Book of Animals*, 106; *The American Claimant*, 186.

25. Olivia Langdon Clemens to Alice Hooker Day, 28 May 1891, *UCCL* 04211; Olivia Langdon Clemens to Olivia Lewis Langdon, 26 October 1890, *UCCL* 04107; Olivia Langdon Clemens to Olivia Lewis Langdon, 8 November 1890, *UCCL* 04112; *N&J*, 3:572; SLC to Fred J. Hall, 11 November 1890, *UCCL* 04113.

26. *N&J*, 2:592; *Huck Finn and Tom Sawyer among the Indians*, 91; SLC to William Winter, 5 November 1890, *UCCL* 08604; Olivia Langdon Clemens to Olivia Lewis Langdon, 3 November 1890, *UCCL* 04109; *AMT*, 2:25; Orion Clemens to Mollie Clemens, 29 September 1871, *UCLC* 47046.

27. "Bric-a-Brac," *HC*, 28 February 1891, 2; "An Appeal against Injudicious Swearing," *NYS*, 9 November 1890, 6.

28. *BH*, 13 November 1890, 4; *N&J*, 3:593–94; "Mark Twain's Letter," *NYTrib*, 11 November 1890, 6; "Speaking of Politics," *Philadelphia Inquirer*, 12 November 1890, 4; "An Opinion of Mark Twain," *Cincinnati Commercial Tribune*, 1 December 1890, 4; "Mark Twain and the Conductor," *NYS*, 12 November 1890, 6; *New York Evening World*, 6 December 1890, 2.

29. *MTHL*, 633; SLC to James Pond, 29 November 1890, *UCCL* 04560; *AMT*, 3:3; "Minister Was 450 Miles Away," *BH*, 12 January 1891, 1; *Mark Twain's Letters* (1917), 705.

30. *N&J*, 3:388, 3:464; "Fred J. Hall Tells the Story," *Twainian* 6 (November–December 1947): 2; Fred J. Hall to SLC, 12 May 1888, *UCLC* 44019; E. C. Stedman to SLC, 2 November 1888, *UCLC* 44214.

31. Fred J. Hall to SLC, 16 April 1890, *UCLC* 45057; Fred J. Hall to SLC, 17 March 1891, *UCLC* 45472; SLC to Joe Goodman, April 1891, *UCCL* 04186; Fears, *Mark Twain Day-by-Day*, 2:547; "Mark Twain on the 'Library of American Literature,'" *New Orleans Picayune*, 26 April 1891, 5.

32. SLC to Frank Fuller, 29 December 1888, *UCCL* 03812; *N&J*, 3:376, 3:549; Bush, "Grace King and Mark Twain," 45; SLC to Fred J. Hall, 15 October 1890, *UCCL* 04557; *MTLP*, 247, 258–59; SLC to Webster and Company, 11 February 1891, *UCCL* 12835; SLC to William T. Sherman, 13 February 1891, *UCCL* 13117; *AMT*, 2:78.

33. SLC to Fred J. Hall, 30 June 1890, *UCCL* 04553; "Walt Whitman's Birthday," *NY Trib*, 1 June 1889, 7; Folsom and Loving, "The Walt Whitman Controversy"; Traubel, *Camden's Compliment to Walt Whitman*, 64–65; Gribben, *Mark Twain's Library*, 764.

34. *N&J*, 3:596–97; James Paige to SLC, 2 January 1891, *UCLC* 45377.

35. SLC to Olivia Langdon Clemens, 13 January 1891, *UCCL* 04157; "Mark Twain as a Listener," *Harrisburg (Penn.) Patriot*, 17 January 1891, 1; SLC to Kate Foote, 16 January 1891, *UCCL* 04160; SLC to John Percival Jones, 20 January 1891, *UCCL* 04162.

36. SLC to Joe Goodman, April 1891, *UCCL* 04186; Goble, "Mark Twain's Nemesis," 8; *AMT*, 3:496–97; Kolb, *Mark Twain: The Gift of Humor*, 246. Howells asserts that SLC invested "three hundred thousand dollars in the beautiful miracle" (Howells, *My MT*, 80).

37. Paine, *MTB*, 542–43; SLC to John Percival Jones, 13 February 1891, *UCCL* 04172; SLC to gas company, 12 February 1891, *UCCL* 04171.

38. SLC to Joe Goodman, 22 February 1891, *UCCL* 04573; SLC to Orion Clemens, 25 February 1891, *UCCL* 04175; SLC to James Paige, 19 March 1891, *UCCL* 04182; *AMT*, 1:495.

39. Fears, *Mark Twain Day-by-Day*, 2:584; Paine, *MTB*, 917; *MTLP*, 307; SLC to Fred J. Hall, 9 April 1891, *UCCL* 04583.

40. SLC to James R. Osgood, 24 October 1881, *UCCL* 02060; "Mental Telegraphy," *Harper's Monthly* 84 (December 1891): 95; SLC to Rutherford B. Hayes, 10 April 1882, *UCCL* 02198; *N&J*, 2:359, 2:455, 2:620; *AMT*, 1:429; SLC to William Fletcher Barrett, 4 October 1884, *UCLC* 03004.

41. SLC to Orion Clemens, 25 February 1891, *UCCL* 04175; SLC to Fred J. Hall, 27 February 1891, *UCCL* 04574; Fred J. Hall to SLC, 28 February 1891, *UCLC* 45444; *MTCI*, 307; *MTHL*, 637.

42. *MTHL*, 638–40; *AMT*, 1:20.

43. *N&J*, 3:621; *MTHL*, 645.

44. *N&J*, 3:625.

45. *The American Claimant*, 96, 98, 102.

46. *The American Claimant*, 53–54.

47. Olivia Langdon Clemens to Georgina Sullivan Jones, 25 January 1891, *UCCL* 12244.

48. "Mark Twain's Coveted Professorship," *SFB* supplement, 4 April 1891, 1; Clemens, *My Father, Mark Twain*, 66; SLC to Joel Chandler Harris, 10 August 1881, *UCCL* 01997; Willis, *Mark and Livy*, 181, 187; *N&J*, 3:605, 3:617; "The Woman with the Golden Arm," *CIO*, 28 March 1891, 14.

49. *Mark Twain's Notebook*, 320; SLC to Olivia Langdon Clemens, 18 April 1891, *UCCL* 04191; SLC to Sergei Stepniak-Kravchinsky, 23 April 1891, *UCCL* 06149.

50. *MTHL*, 635; Susy Clemens to Louise Brownell, 20 April 1891, *UCCL* 09128; Susy Clemens to Louise Brownell, 6–7 October 1891, *UCCL* 09134; Morris, *Gender Play*, 16; Cooley, "Mark Twain, Rebellious Girls, and Daring Young Women," 239–41; Kiskis, "Dead Man Talking," 103.

51. *MTHL*, 645; Olivia Langdon Clemens to Alice Hooker Day, 28 May 1891, *UCCL* 04211; Eble, *Old Clemens and W.D.H.*, 137–38; SLC to Fred J. Hall, 14 April 1891, *UCCL*

04584; Salsbury, *Susy and Mark Twain*, 113; *A Family Sketch*, 28; *MTLP*, 275; *N&J*, 3:611, 3:624; Willis, *Mark and Livy*, 189; "Lectures and Entertainments," *NYTrib*, 30 March 1891, 5; "Authors Read for the Y.W.C.A.," *NYS*, 23 April 1891, 3; Wheeler, *Yesterdays*, 338; Wagenknecht, *Mark Twain: The Man and His Work*, 46.

52. Edward W. Bok, "Mark Twain's Plans," *Chicago Herald*, 17 May 1891, 26; SLC to Pamela Moffett, 3 June 1891, *UCCL* 04215; *MTHL*, 645; "Lazy Mark Twain," *Cleveland Plain Dealer*, 31 May 1891, 11; *Pomeroy's Democrat*, 14 April 1877, 1.

53. SLC to Franklin G. Whitmore, 18 July 1891, *UCCL* 04221; Olivia Langdon Clemens to Sarah Trumbull, 31 May 1891, *UCCL* 11039; Clemens, *My Father, Mark Twain*, 87; Paine, *MTB*, 920; *N&J*, 3:634; SLC to Pamela Moffett, 3 June 1891, *UCCL* 04215.

Bibliography

Writings by Samuel L. Clemens, aka Mark Twain

Adventures of Huckleberry Finn. New York: Webster, 1885.

Adventures of Huckleberry Finn. Edited by Victor Fischer, Lin Salamo, Harriet E. Smith, and Walter Blair. Berkeley: University of California Press, 2010.

The Adventures of Tom Sawyer. Hartford: American Publishing, 1876.

Ah Sin: A Dramatic Work. San Francisco: Book Club of California, 1961. With Bret Harte.

The American Claimant. New York: Webster, 1892.

"An Appeal against Injudicious Swearing." *NYS*, 9 November 1890, 6.

Autobiography of Mark Twain. 3 vols. Vol. 1 edited by Harriet Elinor Smith; vols. 2–3 edited by Benjamin Griffin and Harriet Elinor Smith. Berkeley: University of California Press, 2010–15.

"The Brazilian Republic." *BH*, 29 December 1889, 12.

"British Benevolence." *NYTrib*, 27 January 1873, 4.

"A Card." *Hartford Post*, 29 January 1873, scrapbook 6, MTP.

Collected Tales, Sketches, Speeches, and Essays 1852–90. Edited by Louis J. Budd. New York: Library of America, 1992.

"Colonel Sellers: A Drama in Five Acts." Edited by Jerry Thomason and Tom Quirk. *Missouri Review* 18 (1995): 109–51.

Colonel Sellers as a Scientist. In *The Complete Plays of William Dean Howells*. Edited by Walter J. Meserve. New York: New York University Press, 1960. With W. D. Howells.

"A Connecticut Yankee in King Arthur's Court." *Century* 39 (November 1889): 74–83.

A Connecticut Yankee in King Arthur's Court. New York: Webster, 1889.

"Contributor's Club." *Atlantic Monthly* 39 (January 1877): 108.

"A Curious Experiment." *Century* 23 (November 1881): 35–46.

"The Curious Republic of Gondour." *Atlantic Monthly* 36 (October 1875): 461–63.

The Devil's Race-Track: Mark Twain's Great Dark Writings. Edited by John S. Tuckey. Berkeley: University of California Press, 1980.

"English as She Is Taught." *Century* 33 (April 1887): 932–36.

Europe and Elsewhere. Edited by Albert Bigelow Paine. New York: Harper, 1923.

A Family Sketch and Other Private Writings. Edited by Benjamin Griffin. Berkeley: University of California Press, 2014.

Following the Equator. Hartford: American Publishing, 1897.

"Francis Lightfoot Lee." *Pennsylvania Magazine of History and Biography* 1 (1877): 343–45.

"General Grant." *HC*, 24 July 1885, 2.

The Gilded Age. Hartford: American Publishing, 1873. With Charles Dudley Warner.

"The Great Revolution in Pitcairn." *Atlantic Monthly* 43 (March 1879): 295–302.

Hannibal, Huck, and Tom. Edited by Walter Blair. Berkeley: University of California Press, 1969.

How Nancy Jackson Married Kate Wilson and Other Tales of Rebellious Girls and Daring Young Women. Edited by John R. Cooley. Lincoln: University of Nebraska Press, 2001.

Huck Finn and Tom Sawyer among the Indians and Other Unfinished Stories. Edited by Dahlia Armon, Paul Baender, Walter Blair, et al. Berkeley: University of California Press, 1989.

The Innocents Abroad. Hartford: American Publishing, 1869.

"Letter from Mark Twain." *Christchurch (New Zealand) Press*, 12 February 1890, 5.

"A Letter from Mark Twain." *Pall Mall Gazette*, 16 February 1889, 3.

"Letter from 'Mark Twain.'" *San Francisco Alta California*, 6 September 1868, 1.

Letters from the Earth. Edited by Bernard DeVoto. New York: Harper and Row, 1962.

Letters of Mark Twain and Joseph Hopkins Twichell. Edited by Harold K. Bush, Steve Courtney, and Peter Messent. Athens: University of Georgia Press, 2017.

Life on the Mississippi. Boston: Osgood, 1883.

Love Letters of Mark Twain. Edited by Dixon Wecter. New York: Harper, 1949.

Mark Twain: The Complete Interviews. Edited by Gary Scharnhorst. Tuscaloosa: University of Alabama Press, 2006.

"Mark Twain and His English Editor." *London Spectator*, 21 September 1872, 2301–2.

Mark Twain–Howells Letters. Edited by Henry Nash Smith and William Gibson. Cambridge, Mass.: Belknap, 1960.

Mark Twain in Eruption. Edited by Bernard DeVoto. New York: Harper, 1940.

Mark Twain Letters. 6 vols. Vol. 1, *1853–1866*, edited by Edgar Marquess Branch, Michael B. Frank, Kenneth M. Sanderson, Harriet Elinor Smith, Lin Salamo, and Richard Bucci; vol. 2, *1867–1868*, edited by Harriet Elinor Smith, Richard Bucci, and Lin Salamo; vol. 3, *1869*, edited by Victor Fischer, Michael B. Frank, and Dahlia Armon; vol. 4, *1870–1871*, edited by Victor Fischer, Michael B. Frank, and Lin Salamo; vol. 5, *1872–1873*, edited by Lin Salamo and Harriet Elinor Smith; vol. 6, *1874–1875*, edited by Michael B. Frank and Harriet Elinor Smith. Berkeley: University of California Press, 1988–2002.

"Mark Twain on Pensions." *Washington Post*, 18 July 1885, 2.

Mark Twain on Potholes and Politics. Edited by Gary Scharnhorst. Columbia: University of Missouri Press, 2014.

"Mark Twain on the Future National Capital." *NYS*, 30 July 1885, 2.

"Mark Twain on the 'Library of American Literature.'" *New Orleans Picayune*, 26 April 1891, 5.

Mark Twain Speaking. Edited by Paul Fatout. Iowa City: University of Iowa Press, 1976.

Mark Twain to Mrs. Fairbanks. Edited by Dixon Wecter. San Marino, Calif.: Huntington Library, 1949.

"'Mark Twain' to the Editor of 'The Daily Graphic.'" *New York Graphic*, 22 April 1873, 8.

Mark Twain's Book of Animals. Berkeley: University of California Press, 2011.

Mark Twain's Correspondence with Henry Huttleston Rogers, 1893–1909. Edited by Lewis Leary. Berkeley: University of California Press, 1969.

"Mark Twain's Letter." *NY Trib*, 11 November 1890, 6.

Mark Twain's Letters. Edited by Albert Bigelow Paine. 2 vols. New York: Harper, 1917.

Mark Twain's Letters to His Publishers, 1867–1894. Edited by Hamlin Hill. Berkeley: University of California Press, 1967.

Mark Twain's Memory Builder. New York: Webster, 1891.

Mark Twain's Notebook. Edited by Albert Bigelow Paine. New York: Harper, 1935.

Mark Twain's Satires and Burlesques. Edited by Franklin R. Rogers. Berkeley: University of California Press, 1967.

Mark Twain's Speeches. Edited by Albert Bigelow Paine. New York: Harper, 1923.

"Mental Telegraphy." *Harper's Monthly* 84 (December 1891): 95–104.

"The New Cock Robin." *CT*, 2 January 1873, 3.

"The New Dynasty." *New England Quarterly* 30 (September 1957): 383–88.

"A Note from 'Mark Twain.'" *Virginia City (Nev.) Territorial Enterprise*, 3 February 1878, 2.

"Old Times on the Mississippi." *Atlantic Monthly* 35 (January 1875): 69–74; 35 (February 1875): 217–24; 35 (March 1875): 283–89; 35 (April 1875): 446–52; 35 (May 1875): 567–74; 35 (June 1875): 721–30; 36 (August 1875): 190–96.

The Prince and the Pauper. New York: Harper, 1881.

"The Private History of a Campaign That Failed." *Century* 31 (December 1885): 193–204.

"The Revised Catechism." *NY Trib*, 27 September 1871, 6.

Roughing It. Hartford: American Publishing, 1872.

"A Royal Compliment." *Galaxy* 10 (September 1870): 429–30.

"Shad'd." *NYH*, 11 July 1873, 3.

Simon Wheeler, Detective. Edited by Franklin R. Rogers. New York: New York Public Library, 1963.

1601. 1880; rpt. San Francisco: Grabhorn, 1933.

Sketches New and Old. Hartford: American Publishing, 1875.

"Sociable Jimmy." *NYT*, 29 November 1874, 7.

The Stolen White Elephant Etc. Boston: Osgood, 1882.

"A Storm at Sea: Mark Twain's Recollections of It." *CT*, 5 February 1876, 11.

"The Temperance Insurrection." *London Standard*, 26 March 1874, 1.

A Tramp Abroad. Hartford: American Publishing, 1879.

"A True Story." *Atlantic Monthly* 34 (November 1874): 591–94.

What Is Man? and Other Philosophical Writings. Edited by Paul Baender. Berkeley: University of California Press, 1973.

"What Ought He to Have Done?" *Christian Union*, 16 July 1885, 4.

Who Is Mark Twain? Edited by Robert H. Hirst. New York: HarperStudio, 2009.

Major Print Sources

Anderson, Frederick. "Introduction." In Mark Twain and Bret Harte, *Ah Sin: A Dramatic Work*. Edited by Frederick Anderson. San Francisco: Book Club of California, 1961.

Anderson, Frederick, and Hamlin Hill. "How Samuel Clemens Became Mark Twain's Publisher: A Study of the James R. Osgood Contracts." *Proof* 2 (1972): 117–43.

Andrews, Kenneth R. *Nook Farm: Mark Twain's Hartford Circle*. Cambridge, Mass.: Harvard University Press, 1950.

Andrews, William L. "Mark Twain and James W. C. Pennington: Huckleberry Finn's Smallpox Lie." *Studies in American Fiction* 9 (Spring 1981): 103–12.

Arac, Jonathan. *Huckleberry Finn as Idol and Target.* Madison: University of Wisconsin Press, 1997.

Aspiz, Harold. "Lecky's Influence on Mark Twain." *Science and Society* 26 (Winter 1962): 15–25.

Baetzhold, Howard G. "The Course of Composition of *A Connecticut Yankee*: A Reinterpretation." *American Literature* 33 (May 1961): 195–214.

———. *Mark Twain and John Bull.* Bloomington: Indiana University Press, 1970.

———. "Mark Twain: England's Advocate." *American Literature* 28 (November 1956): 328–46.

———. "'Of Detectives and Their Derring-Do': The Genesis of Mark Twain's 'The Stolen White Elephant.'" *Studies in American Humor* 2 (January 1976): 183–95.

Baker, William. "Mark Twain in Dayton." *Mark Twain Journal* 19 (Summer 1979): 13, 23.

Beard, Dan. *Hardly a Man Is Now Alive.* New York: Doubleday, 1939.

Bellamy, Gladys. *Mark Twain as a Literary Artist.* Norman: University of Oklahoma Press, 1950.

Berger, Sidney E. "Emendations of the Copy-Text." In Mark Twain, *Pudd'nhead Wilson and Those Extraordinary Twins.* New York: Norton, 1980.

Besant, Walter. "My Favorite Novelist and His Best Book." *Munsey's* 18 (February 1898): 659–64.

Bird, John. "Mark Twain, Karl Gerhardt, and the *Huckleberry Finn* Frontispiece." *American Literary Realism* 45 (Fall 2012): 28–37.

Blair, Walter. *Mark Twain and Huck Finn.* Berkeley: University of California Press, 1960.

———. "When Was *Huckleberry Finn* Written?" *American Literature* 30 (Spring 1958): 1–25.

Boewe, Mary. "Smouching towards Bedlam; or, Mark Twain's Creative Use of Some Acknowledged Sources." *Mark Twain Journal* 29 (Spring 1991): 8–12.

Branch, Edgar M. "Old Times on the Mississippi: Biography and Craftsmanship." *Nineteenth-Century Literature* 45 (June 1990): 73–87.

Briden, Earl F. "Kemble's 'Speciality' and the Pictorial Countertext of *Huckleberry Finn*." *Mark Twain Journal* 26 (Fall 1988): 2–14.

———. "Mark Twain's Rhode Island Lectures." *Mark Twain Journal* 24 (Spring 1986): 35–40.

Bridgman, Richard. *Traveling in Mark Twain.* Berkeley: University of California Press, 1987.

Britton, Wesley. "Carlyle, Clemens, and Dickens: Mark Twain's Francophobia, the French Revolution, and Determinism." *Studies in American Fiction* 20 (Autumn 1992): 197–204.

Brock, Darryl. "Mark Twain's 'Mysterious Scoresheet.'" *Nine* 19 (Spring 2011): 101–13.

Brodwin, Stanley. "The Useful and Useless River: *Life on the Mississippi* Revisited." *Studies in American Humor* 2 (January 1976): 196–208.

Budd, Louis J. "Color Him Curious about Yellow Journalism: Mark Twain and the New York City Press." *Journal of Popular Culture* 15 (Fall 1981): 25–33.

———. *Mark Twain: Social Philosopher.* Bloomington: Indiana University Press, 1962.

———. "Mark Twain Sounds Off on the Fourth of July." *American Literary Realism* 34 (Spring 2002): 265–80.

———. "Mark Twain's Visual Humor." In *A Companion to Mark Twain*, edited by Peter Messent and Louis J. Budd. Malden, Mass.: Blackwell, 2005.

———. *Our Mark Twain*. Philadelphia: University of Pennsylvania Press, 1983.

———. "A Rediscovered Mark Twain Speech: New Laws and Old Yarns." *Essays in Arts and Sciences* 23 (October 1994): 59–66.

———. "The Southward Currents under Huck Finn's Raft." *Mississippi Valley Historical Review* 66 (September 1959): 222–37.

———. "A Supplement to 'A Chronology' in 'Mark Twain Speaking.'" *Essays in Arts and Sciences* 29 (October 2000): 57–68.

———. "Twain, Howells, and the Boston Nihilists." *New England Quarterly* 32 (September 1959): 351–71.

———. "W. D. Howells and Mark Twain Judge Each Other 'Aright.'" *American Literary Realism* 38 (Winter 2006): 97–114.

———, ed. *Mark Twain: The Contemporary Reviews*. New York: Cambridge University Press, 1999.

Burton, Richard. "Mark Twain in the Hartford Days." *Mark Twain Quarterly* 1 (Summer 1937): 5.

Bush, Harold K., Jr. *Mark Twain and the Spiritual Crisis of the Age*. Tuscaloosa: University of Alabama Press, 2007.

———. "The Mythic Struggle between East and West: Mark Twain's Speech at Whittier's 70th Birthday Celebration and W. D. Howells' *A Chance Acquaintance*." *American Literary Realism* 27 (Winter 1995): 53–73.

Bush, Robert. "Grace King and Mark Twain." *American Literature* 44 (March 1972): 31–51.

Camfield, Gregg. *The Oxford Companion to Mark Twain*. New York: Oxford University Press, 2003.

———. "A Republican Artisan in the Court of King Capital: Mark Twain and Commerce." In *A Historical Guide to Mark Twain*. New York: Oxford University Press, 2002.

———. *Sentimental Twain: Samuel Clemens in the Maze of Moral Philosophy*. Philadelphia: University of Pennsylvania Press, 1994.

Cardwell, Guy. "The Bowdlerizing of Mark Twain." *ESQ* 21 (1975): 179–93.

———. "*Life on the Mississippi*: Vulgar Facts and Learned Errors." *ESQ* 19 (1973): 283–93.

———. *The Man Who Was Mark Twain*. New Haven, Conn.: Yale University Press, 1991.

———. "Mark Twain, James R. Osgood, and Those 'Suppressed' Passages." *New England Quarterly* 46 (June 1973): 163–88.

———. "Mark Twain's 'Row' with George Cable." *Modern Language Quarterly* 13 (December 1952): 363–71.

———. *Twins of Genius*. East Lansing: Michigan State College Press, 1953.

Carter, Everett. "The Meaning of *A Connecticut Yankee*." *American Literature* 50 (November 1978): 418–40.

Carter, Paul J., Jr. "Mark Twain and the American Labor Movement." *New England Quarterly* 30 (September 1957): 382–88.

Cheney, Mary Bushnell. "Mark Twain as a Reader." *Harper's Weekly*, 7 January 1911: 6.

Clark, Charles H. "Mark Twain at 'Nook Farm' (Hartford) and Elmira." *Critic*, n.s. 3 (January 1885): 25–26.

Clemens, Clara. *My Father, Mark Twain.* New York: Harper, 1931.

Clemens, Susy. *Papa: An Intimate Biography of Mark Twain.* Edited by Charles Neider. Garden City, N.Y.: Doubleday, 1985.

Clemens, Will M. *Mark Twain: His Life and Work.* San Francisco: Clemens, 1892.

Conrad, Eric. "'Anything Honest to Sell Books': Walt Whitman and the Autograph Monster." *Walt Whitman Quarterly Review* 32 (2015): 187–214.

Conroy, Terry, and David E. E. Sloane. "'A True Story' Confirmed: 'How a Slave Mother Found Her Son.'" *Studies in American Humor* 22 (2010): 147–53.

Cooley, John R. "Mark Twain, Rebellious Girls, and Daring Young Women." In *Mark Twain, How Nancy Jackson Married Kate Wilson and Other Tales of Rebellious Girls and Daring Young Women,* edited by John R. Cooley. Lincoln: University of Nebraska Press, 2001.

Cox, James M. *Mark Twain: The Fate of Humor.* Princeton, N.J.: Princeton University Press, 1966.

Crowley, John W. "A Note on *The Gilded Age.*" *English Language Notes* 10 (1972): 116–18.

Csicsila, Joseph. "Langdon Clemens and *The Adventures of Tom Sawyer.*" In *Mark Twain and Youth,* edited by Kevin Mac Donnell and R. Kent Rasmussen. London: Bloomsbury, 2016.

Cummings, Sherwood. *Mark Twain and Science.* Baton Rouge: Louisiana State University Press, 1988.

Dalrymple, Scott. "Just War, Pure and Simple: *A Connecticut Yankee* and the American Civil War." *American Literary Realism* 29 (Fall 1996): 1–11.

Daufenbach, Claus. "'Corruptionville': Washington, D.C., and the Portrait of an Era in Mark Twain's 'The Gilded Age.'" In *Washington, D.C.: Interdisciplinary Approaches,* edited by Lothar Hönnighausen and Andreas Falke. Tübingen, Germany: Francke, 1993.

David, Beverly R. *Mark Twain and His Illustrators.* 2 vols. Troy, N.Y.: Whitson, 1986.

———. "The Pictorial *Huckleberry Finn.*" *American Quarterly* 26 (October 1974): 331–51.

David, Steve. "Mark Twain, the War, and *Life on the Mississippi.*" *Southern Studies* 18 (1979): 231–39.

Davis, Harry B. *Mark Twain in Heidelberg.* Heidelberg: Brausdruck, 1985.

Denney, Lynn. "Next Stop Detroit: A City's Views of Mark Twain's Evolution as a Literary Hero, 1868–1895." *Mark Twain Journal* 31 (Spring 1993): 22–28.

DeVoto, Bernard. *Mark Twain at Work.* Cambridge, Mass.: Harvard University Press, 1942.

Dickinson, Leon T. "The Sources of *The Prince and the Pauper.*" *Modern Language Notes* 64 (1949): 103–6.

Doyno, Victor A. "Samuel Clemens as Family Man and Father." In *Constructing Mark Twain,* edited by Laura E. Skandera-Trombley and Michael Kiskis. Columbia: University of Missouri Press, 2001.

———. *Writing Huck Finn: Mark Twain's Creative Process.* Philadelphia: University of Pennsylvania Press, 1991.

Dreiser, Theodore. "Mark the Double Twain." *English Journal* 24 (October 1935): 615–27.

Driscoll, Kerry. *Mark Twain among the Indians and Other Indigenous Peoples.* Berkeley: University of California Press, 2018.

———. "Mark Twain's Music Box: Livy, Cosmopolitanism, and the Commodity Aesthetic." In *Cosmopolitan Twain*, edited by Ann M. Ryan and Joseph B. McCullough. Columbia: University of Missouri Press, 2008.

Duckett, Margaret. *Mark Twain and Bret Harte*. Norman: University of Oklahoma Press, 1964.

Dumas, Frédéric. "Some Remarks on Mark Twain and Translation." *Acta Universitatis Danubius* 9 (2015): 143–50.

Eble, Kenneth. *Old Clemens and W.D.H.* Baton Rouge: Louisiana State University Press, 1985.

Ekström, Kjell. "Extracts from a Diary Kept by Ozias W. Pond during the Clemens-Cable Tour of Readings in 1885." *Archiv für das Studium der Neueren Sprachen und Literaturen* 188 (1951): 109–13.

Eliot, T. S. "Introduction." In Mark Twain, *Adventures of Huckleberry Finn*, 3rd ed., edited by Thomas Cooley. New York: Norton, 1999.

Emerson, Everett. *The Authentic Mark Twain*. Philadelphia: University of Pennsylvania Press, 1984.

———. *Mark Twain: A Literary Life*. Philadelphia: University of Pennsylvania Press, 2000.

Fanning, Philip Ashley. *Mark Twain and Orion Clemens*. Tuscaloosa: University of Alabama Press, 2003.

Fatout, Paul. "Mark Twain Lectures in Indiana." *Indiana Magazine of History* 46 (December 1950): 363–67.

———. "Mark Twain, Litigant." *American Literature* 31 (March 1959): 30–45.

———. *Mark Twain on the Lecture Circuit*. Bloomington: Indiana University Press, 1960.

———. "The Twain-Cable Readings in Indiana." *Indiana Magazine of History* 53 (March 1957): 19–28.

Fears, David H. *Mark Twain Day-by-Day: An Annotated Chronology of the Life of Samuel L. Clemens*. 4 vols. Banks, Ore.: Horizon Micro, 2007–2013.

Feinstein, Herbert. "Mark Twain and the Pirates." *Harvard Law School Bulletin* 13 (April 1962): 6–18.

———. "Mark Twain's Lawsuits." PhD diss., University of California–Berkeley, 1968.

Felder, Deborah G., and Diana Rosen. *Fifty Jewish Women Who Changed the World*. New York: Citadel, 2003.

Ferguson, DeLancey. *Mark Twain: Man and Legend*. Indianapolis: Bobbs-Merrill, 1943.

———. "Mark Twain's Lost Curtain Speeches." *South Atlantic Quarterly* 42 (1943): 262–69.

Fields, Annie. "Bret Harte and Mark Twain in the 'Seventies.'" Edited by M. A. DeWolfe Howe. *Atlantic Monthly* 130 (September 1922): 344–45.

Fischer, Victor. "Huck Finn Reviewed: The Reception of *Huckleberry Finn* in the United States, 1885–1897." *American Literary Realism* 16 (1983): 1–57.

Flanagan, John T. "Mark Twain on the Upper Mississippi." *Minnesota History* 17 (December 1936): 369–84.

Folsom, Ed, and Jerome Loving. "The Walt Whitman Controversy: A Lost Document." *Virginia Quarterly Review* 83 (Spring 2007): 123–38.

Foner, Philip S. *Mark Twain: Social Critic*. New York: International, 1958.

"Fred J. Hall Tells the Story of His Connection with Charles L. Webster & Co." *Twainian* 6 (November–December 1947): 2.

Fredericks, Sarah. "The Profane Twain: His Personal and Literary Cursing." *Mark Twain Journal* 49 (Spring–Fall 2011): 9–66.

French, Bryant M. *Mark Twain and the Gilded Age.* Dallas: Southern Methodist University Press, 1965.

———. "Mark Twain, Laura D. Fair, and the New York Criminal Courts." *American Quarterly* 16 (Winter 1964): 545–61.

Fulton, Joe B. *Mark Twain in the Margins.* Tuscaloosa: University of Alabama Press, 2000.

———. *Mark Twain's Ethical Realism: The Aesthetics of Race, Class, and Gender.* Columbia: University of Missouri Press, 1998.

———. *The Reconstruction of Mark Twain.* Baton Rouge: Louisiana State University Press, 2010.

Ganzel, Dewey. *Mark Twain Abroad.* Chicago: University of Chicago Press, 1968.

———. "Samuel Clemens and Captain Marryat." *Anglia* 80 (1962): 405–16.

———. "Samuel Clemens and John Camden Hotten." *Library: A Quarterly Journal of Bibliography* 20 (1965): 230–42.

———. "Twain, Travel Books, and *Life on the Mississippi.*" *American Literature* 34 (March 1962): 40–55.

Gates, William B. "Mark Twain to His English Publishers." *American Literature* 11 (1939): 78–81.

Gerber, John. "Mark Twain's 'Private Campaign.'" *Civil War History* 1 (March 1955): 37–60.

Gibson, William M. *The Art of Mark Twain.* New York: Oxford University Press, 1976.

Gilder, Rodman. "Mark Twain Detested the Theatre." *Theatre Arts* 28 (February 1944): 109–16.

Glass, Loren. "Trademark Twain." *American Literary History* 13 (Winter 2001): 671–93.

Goble, Corban. "Mark Twain's Nemesis: The Paige Compositor." *Printing History* 18 (1998): 2–16.

Gold, Charles H. *"Hatching Ruin"; or, Mark Twain's Road to Bankruptcy.* Columbia: University of Missouri Press, 2003.

———. "Mark Twain and General Grant in Chicago." *Chicago History* 7 (Fall 1978): 150–60.

———. "What Happened to Charley Webster?" *Mark Twain Journal* 32 (Fall 1994): 11–22.

Goodman, Susan, and Carl Dawson. *William Dean Howells: A Writer's Life.* Berkeley: University of California Press, 2005.

Gribben, Alan. "'I Kind of Love Small Game': Mark Twain's Library of Literary Hogwash." *American Literary Realism* 9 (Winter 1976): 65–76.

———. "Mark Twain, Business Man: The Margins of Profit." *Studies in American Humor* 1 (June 1982): 24–43.

———. *Mark Twain's Library: A Reconstruction.* 2 vols. Boston: Hall, 1980.

———. "'The Master Hand of Old Malory': Mark Twain's Acquaintance with *Le Morte d'Arthur.*" *English Language Notes* 16 (1978): 32–40.

———. "'A Splendor of Stars & Suns': Twain as a Reader of Browning's Poems." *Browning Institute Studies* 6 (1978): 87–103.

Griffin, Benjamin. "'American Laughter': Nietzsche Reads Tom Sawyer." *New England Quarterly* 83 (March 2010): 129–41.

Griska, Joseph M., Jr. "Two New Joel Chandler Harris Reviews of Mark Twain." *American Literature* 48 (January 1977): 584–89.

Harrington, Paula, and Ronald Jenn. *Mark Twain and France: The Making of a New American Identity.* Columbia: University of Missouri Press, 2017.

Harris, Helen L. "Mark Twain's Response to the Native American." *American Literature* 46 (January 1975): 495–505.

Harris, Susan K. *The Courtship of Olivia Langdon and Mark Twain.* New York: Cambridge University Press, 1996.

Hemminghaus, Edgar G. *Mark Twain in Germany.* New York: Columbia University Press, 1939.

Henrickson, Gary P. "Author, Author: Mark Twain and His Collaborators." *North Dakota Quarterly* 69 (Winter 2002): 156–65.

Herm, Gerd. "'Truth Is Stranger than Fiction': The Historiographical Hoax of Mark Twain's 'The Great Revolution in Pitcairn.'" In *Re-visioning the Past: Historical Self-Reflexivity in American Short Fiction*, edited by Bernd Engler and Oliver Scheiding. Trier, Germany: Wissenschaftlicher, 1998.

Hill, Hamlin. "Barnum, Bridgeport, and *A Connecticut Yankee.*" *American Quarterly* 16 (Winter 1964): 615–16.

———. "The Composition and Structure of *Tom Sawyer.*" *American Literature* 32 (January 1961): 379–92.

———. "Introduction" to Mark Twain, *Roughing It.* New York: Penguin, 1981.

———. "Introduction" to Mark Twain, *Wapping Alice.* Berkeley: Friends of the Bancroft Library, 1981.

———. *Mark Twain and Elisha Bliss.* Columbia: University of Missouri Press, 1964.

———. "Mark Twain and His Enemies." *Southern Review* 4 (1968): 520–29.

———. "Mark Twain: Audience and Artistry." *American Quarterly* 15 (Spring 1963): 25–40.

———. "Mark Twain's Book Sales, 1869–1879." *Bulletin of the New York Public Library* 65 (June 1961): 371–89.

———. "Mark Twain's Quarrels with Elisha Bliss." *American Literature* 33 (January 1962): 442–56.

———. "Toward a Critical Text of *The Gilded Age.*" *Papers of the Bibliographical Society of America* 59 (1965): 142–49.

Hoben, John. "Mark Twain's *A Connecticut Yankee*: A Genetic Study." *American Literature* 18 (November 1946): 197–218.

Hoffman, Andrew. *Inventing Mark Twain.* New York: Morrow, 1997.

Hoffmann, Donald. *Mark Twain in Paradise.* Columbia: University of Missouri Press, 2006.

Howe, Lawrence. *Mark Twain and the Novel.* New York: Cambridge University Press, 1998.

Howells, W. D. *Literary Friends and Acquaintance.* New York: Harper, 1900.

———. "Mark Twain." *Century* 24 (September 1882): 780–83.

———. *My Mark Twain.* New York: Harper, 1910.

James, George Wharton. "Charles Warren Stoddard." *National Magazine* 34 (August 1911): 659–72.

Jerome, Robert D., Herbert A. Wisbey, and Barbara Snedecor, eds. *Mark Twain in Elmira.* Elmira, N.Y.: Elmira College Center for Mark Twain Studies, 2013.

Jones, Alexander E. "Mark Twain and the Determinism of *What Is Man?*" *American Literature* 29 (March 1957): 1–17.

Jones, Rhett S. "Nigger and Knowledge: White Double Consciousness in *Adventures of Huckleberry Finn.*" *Mark Twain Journal* 22 (Fall 1984): 28–37.

Kaplan, Fred. *The Singular Mark Twain.* New York: Doubleday, 2005.

Kaplan, Justin. *Mr. Clemens and Mark Twain.* New York: Simon and Schuster, 1966.

Kersten, Holger. *Von Hannibal nach Heidelberg: Mark Twain und die Deutschen.* Würzburg, Germany: Königshausen und Neumann, 1993.

Ketterer, David. "'The Fortunate Island' by Max Adeler: Its Publication History and *A Connecticut Yankee.*" *Mark Twain Journal* 29 (Fall 1991): 28–32.

King, Grace. *Memories of a Southern Woman of Letters.* New York: Macmillan, 1932.

Kiskis, Michael J. "Dead Man Talking: Mark Twain's Autobiographical Deception." *American Literary Realism* 40 (Winter 2008): 95–113.

———. *Mark Twain at Home: How Family Shaped Twain's Fiction.* Tuscaloosa: University of Alabama Press, 2016.

Kitzhaber, Albert R. "Mark Twain's Use of the Pomeroy Case in *The Gilded Age.*" *Modern Language Quarterly* 25 (1954): 42–56.

Kohn, Henry S. "Mark Twain and Joseph Roswell Hawley." *Mark Twain Journal* 53 (Fall 2015): 67–84.

Kohn, John S. Van E. "Mark Twain's *1601.*" *Princeton University Library Chronicle* 18 (Winter 1957): 49–54.

Kolb, Harold H., Jr. *Mark Twain: The Gift of Humor.* Lanham, Md.: University Press of America, 2015.

Krauth, Leland. *Mark Twain and Company: Six Literary Relations.* Athens: University of Georgia Press, 2003.

———. *Proper Mark Twain.* Athens: University of Georgia Press, 1999.

Kruse, Horst. *Mark Twain and Life on the Mississippi.* Amherst: University of Massachusetts Press, 1981.

———. "'Mark Twain's *A Connecticut Yankee*: Reconsiderations and Revisions." *American Literature* 62 (September 1990): 464–83.

———. "A Matter of Style: How Olivia Langdon Clemens and Charles Dudley Warner Tried to Team and to Tame the Genius of Mark Twain." *New England Quarterly* 72 (June 1999): 232–50.

Lai-Henderson, Selina. *Mark Twain in China.* Stanford, Calif.: Stanford University Press, 2015.

Lampton, Lucius M. "Hero in a Fool's Paradise: Twain's Cousin James J. Lampton and Colonel Sellers." *Mark Twain Journal* 27 (Fall 1989): 1–56.

Lang, Andrew. "The Art of Mark Twain." *Illustrated London News,* 14 February 1891, 222.

Lawton, Mary. *A Lifetime with Mark Twain: The Memories of Katy Leary.* New York: Harcourt, Brace, 1925.

Lease, Benjamin. "Mark Twain and the Publication of *Life on the Mississippi*: An Unpublished Letter." *American Literature* 26 (May 1954): 248–50.

LeMaster, J. R., and J. D. Wilson, eds. *The Routledge Encyclopedia of Mark Twain.* New York: Routledge, 2011.

Leon, Philip W. *Mark Twain and West Point.* Toronto: ECW, 1996.

Leonard, James S. "Mark Twain and Politics." In *A Companion to Mark Twain,* edited by Peter Messent and Louis J. Budd. Malden, Mass.: Blackwell, 2005.

Loges, Max L. "The Life and Death of the 'City of Baton Rouge.'" *Mark Twain Journal* 42 (Fall 2004): 2–8.

Loomis, C. Grant. "Dan De Quille's Mark Twain." *Pacific Historical Review* 15 (September 1946): 336–47.

Lorch, Fred W. "Mark Twain and the 'Campaign That Failed.'" *American Literature* 12 (January 1941): 454–70.

———. "Mark Twain's 'Artemus Ward' Lecture on the Tour of 1871–72." *New England Quarterly* 25 (September 1952): 327–43.

———. "Mark Twain's Lecture from *Roughing It*." *American Literature* 22 (November 1950): 290–307.

———. "Mark Twain's Public Lectures in England in 1873." *American Literature* 29 (November 1957): 297–304.

———. *The Trouble Begins at Eight*. Ames: Iowa State University Press, 1968.

Lovell, Cindy. "Clara Clemens: The 'Bay.'" In *Mark Twain and Youth*, edited by Kevin Mac Donnell and R. Kent Rasmussen. London: Bloomsbury, 2016.

Loving, Jerome. *Confederate Bushwhacker: Mark Twain in the Shadow of the Civil War*. Lebanon, N.H.: University Press of New England, 2013.

———. *Mark Twain: The Adventures of Samuel L. Clemens*. Berkeley: University of California Press, 2010.

Lowry, Richard. *"Littery Man": Mark Twain and Modern Scholarship*. New York: Oxford University Press, 1996.

Mac Donnell, Kevin. "Who Killed Charlie Webster?" *Mark Twain Journal* 51 (Spring–Fall 2013): 9–37.

Machor, James L. "Reading for Humor or Realism: W. D. Howells and Mark Twain's Early Reception in the U.S. Public Sphere." *American Literary Realism* 47 (Winter 2015): 136–50.

———. "A Trying Five Years: The 1870s Reception of *Roughing It*, *The Gilded Age*, and *Sketches New and Old*." *Mark Twain Annual* 13 (2015): 10–28.

MacKethan, Lucinda H. "Huck Finn and the Slave Narratives: Lighting Out as Design." *Southern Review* 20 (April 1984): 247–64.

Martin, Willard E., Jr. "Letters and Remarks by Mark Twain from the *Boston Daily Journal*." *Mark Twain Journal* 18 (1975–76): 1–5.

McParland, Robert. *Mark Twain's Audience: A Critical Analysis of Reader Responses to the Writings of Mark Twain*. Lanham, Md.: Lexington, 2014.

McWilliams, James. *Mark Twain in the St. Louis Post-Dispatch, 1874–1891*. Troy, N.Y.: Whitson, 1997.

Meine, Franklin. "Introduction." In Mark Twain, *1601*. New York: privately printed, 1938.

Melton, Jeffrey Alan. *Mark Twain, Travel Books, and Tourism*. Tuscaloosa: University of Alabama Press, 2002.

Melton, Quimby, IV. "The British Reception of 'A Connecticut Yankee': Contemporary Reviews." *Mark Twain Journal* 39 (Spring 2001): 2–24.

Merrill, W. H. "When Mark Twain Lectured." *Harper's Weekly*, 10 February 1906, 199.

Meserve, Walter J. "*Colonel Sellers as a Scientist*: A Play by Samuel Langhorne Clemens and William Dean Howells." *Modern Drama* 1 (1958): 151–56.

Messent, Peter. *Mark Twain*. New York: St. Martin's, 1997.

———. *Mark Twain and Male Friendship: The Twichell, Howells, and Rogers Friendships*. New York: Oxford University Press, 2009.

————. "Mark Twain, Joseph Twichell, and Religion." *Nineteenth-Century Literature* 58 (December 2003): 368–402.

————. "Tramps and Tourists: Europe in Mark Twain's *A Tramp Abroad*." *Yearbook of English Studies* 34 (2004): 138–54.

Michelson, Bruce. *Mark Twain on the Loose*. Amherst: University of Massachusetts Press, 1995.

Moffett, Wallace B. "Mark Twain's Lansing Lecture on *Roughing It*." *Michigan History* 34 (1950): 144–70.

Moore, Olin Harris. "Mark Twain and Don Quixote." *PMLA* 37 (June 1922): 324–46.

Morris, Linda A. *Gender Play in Mark Twain*. Columbia: University of Missouri Press, 2011.

Moser, Kay R. "Mark Twain: Mugwump." *Mark Twain Journal* 21 (Summer 1982): 1–4.

Moyne, Ernest J. "Mark Twain and Baroness Alexandra Gripenberg." *American Literature* 45 (November 1973): 370–78.

Myrick, Leslie, and Christopher Ohge. "Mark Twain: April Fool, 1884." *Scholarly Editing* 38 (2017). http://scholarlyediting.org/2017/editions/aprilfools/intro.html.

Norton, Charles A. *Writing Tom Sawyer*. Jefferson, N.C.: McFarland, 1983.

Ou, Hsin-yun. "The Chinese Stereotypical Signification in *Ah Sin*." *Mosaic* 46 (December 2013): 145–61.

————. "Mark Twain, Anson Burlingame, Joseph Hopkins Twichell, and the Chinese." *ARIEL* 42 (April 2011): 43–74.

Paine, Albert Bigelow. *Mark Twain: A Biography*. New York: Harper, 1912.

Parsons, Coleman O. "Down the Mighty River with Mark Twain." *Mississippi Quarterly* 22 (1969): 1–18.

Paxton, Katharine Lampton. "A Cousin's Recollection of Mark Twain." *Twainian* 33 (November–December 1974): 4.

Phipps, William E. *Mark Twain's Religion*. Macon, Ga.: Mercer University Press, 2003.

Powers, Ron. *Mark Twain: A Life*. New York: Free Press, 2005.

Quirk, Tom. *Coming to Grips with Huckleberry Finn*. Columbia: University of Missouri Press, 1993.

————. *Mark Twain: A Study of the Short Fiction*. New York: Twayne, 1997.

————. *Mark Twain and Human Nature*. Columbia: University of Missouri Press, 1997.

————, ed. *Mark Twain's* Adventures of Huckleberry Finn: *A Documentary Volume*. Farmington Hills, Mich.: Gale, 2009.

Raeithel, Gert. "Mark Twain in Munich." In *Images of Central Europe in Travelogues and Fiction by North American Writers*, edited by Waldemar Zacharasiewicz. Tübingen, Germany: Stauffenburg, 1995.

Railton, Stephen. "The Twain-Cable Combination." In *A Companion to Mark Twain*, edited by Peter Messent and Louis J. Budd. Malden, Mass.: Blackwell, 2005.

Ratner, Marc L. "Two Letters of Mark Twain." *Mark Twain Journal* 12 (Spring 1964): 9, 17.

Regan, Robert. "'English Notes': A Book Mark Twain Abandoned." *Studies in American Humor* 2 (1976): 157–70.

Reigstad, Thomas J. *Scribblin' for a Livin': Mark Twain's Pivotal Period in Buffalo*. Amherst, N.Y.: Prometheus, 2013.

Roberts, Taylor. "Mark Twain in Toronto, Ontario, 1884–1885." *Mark Twain Journal* 36 (Fall 1998): 18–25.

Robinson, Forrest G. *The Author-Cat: Clemens's Life in Fiction.* New York: Fordham University Press, 2007.

Roche, John. "Making a Reputation: Mark Twain in Newport." *Mark Twain Journal* 25 (Fall 1987): 23–27.

Rodney, Robert M. *Mark Twain Overseas.* Washington, D.C.: Three Continents, 1993.

Rogers, Franklin R. *Mark Twain's Burlesque Patterns.* Dallas: Southern Methodist University Press, 1960.

Roper, Gordon. "Mark Twain and His Canadian Publishers." *American Book Collector* 10 (1960): 13–29.

Ryan, Ann M., and Joseph B. McCullough, eds. *Cosmopolitan Twain.* Columbia: University of Missouri Press, 2008.

Salsbury, Edith. *Susy and Mark Twain.* New York: Harper and Row, 1965.

Scharnhorst, Gary. "The Bret Harte–Mark Twain Feud: An Inside Narrative." *Mark Twain Journal* 31 (Spring 1993): 29–32.

———, ed. *Critical Essays on* The Adventures of Tom Sawyer. New York: Hall, 1993.

———. "'He Is Amusing but Not Inherently a Gentleman': The Vexed Relations of Kate Field and Samuel Clemens." *Legacy* 18 (Spring 2002): 193–204.

———. "Mark Twain and Julian Hawthorne." *Mark Twain Annual* 10 (2012): 47–54.

———, ed. *Mark Twain in His Own Time: A Biographical Chronicle of His Life, Drawn from Recollections, Interviews, and Memoirs by Family, Friends, and Associates.* Iowa City: University of Iowa Press, 2010.

———. "Mark Twain on Baseball: A Recovered Letter to the Editor." *American Literary Realism* 51 (Winter 2018–19): 180–81.

Schirer, Thomas. *Mark Twain and the Theatre.* Nuremberg: Carl, 1984.

Schmitz, Neil. "Mark Twain, Traitor." *Arizona Quarterly* 63 (Winter 2007): 25–37.

———. "Twain, *Huckleberry Finn*, and the Reconstruction." *American Studies* 12 (Spring 1971): 59–67.

Schultz, John Richie. "New Letters of Mark Twain." *American Literature* 8 (March 1936): 47–51.

Schwartz, Thomas. "Mark Twain and Robert Ingersoll: The Freethought Connection." *American Literature* 48 (May 1976): 183–93.

Scott, Arthur L. "The *Century Magazine* Edits *Huckleberry Finn*, 1884–1885." *American Literature* 27 (November 1955): 356–62.

Seelye, John. "What's in a Name: Sounding the Depths of *Tom Sawyer*." *Sewanee Review* 90 (Summer 1982): 408–29.

Sharlow, Gretchen. "Love to All the Jolly Household." In *Mark Twain in Elmira*, edited by Robert D. Jerome, Herbert A. Wisbey, and Barbara Snedecor. Elmira, N.Y.: Elmira College Center for Mark Twain Studies, 2013.

———. "Theodore Crane: A New Perspective." In *Mark Twain in Elmira*, edited by Robert D. Jerome, Herbert A. Wisbey, and Barbara Snedecor. Elmira, N.Y.: Elmira College Center for Mark Twain Studies, 2013.

Skandera-Trombley, Laura. *Mark Twain in the Company of Women.* Philadelphia: University of Pennsylvania Press, 1997.

Skandera-Trombley, Laura, and Michael Kiskis, eds. *Constructing Mark Twain: New Directions in Scholarship.* Columbia: University of Missouri Press, 2001.

Smith, David L. "Huck, Jim, and American Racial Discourse." *Mark Twain Journal* 22 (Fall 1984): 4–12.

Smith, Henry Nash. *Mark Twain: The Development of a Writer.* Cambridge, Mass.: Belknap, 1962.

———. "Mark Twain's Images of Hannibal." *Texas Studies in English* 37 (1958): 3–23.

———. "That Hideous Mistake of Poor Clemens." *Harvard Library Bulletin* 9 (Spring 1955): 145–80.

Soria, Regina. "Mark Twain and Vedder's Medusa." *American Quarterly* 16 (Winter 1964): 602–6.

Stahl, J. D. *Mark Twain, Culture and Gender.* Athens: University of Georgia Press, 1994.

Steinbrink, Jeffrey. "Mark Twain and Joe Twichell: Sublime Pedestrians." *Mark Twain Journal* 20 (Winter 1980–81): 1–6.

Stoddard, Charles W. "Selections from Letters." *University of California Magazine* 2 (November 1896): 276–87.

Stone, Albert E., Jr. *The Innocent Eye: Childhood in Mark Twain's Imagination.* New Haven, Conn.: Yale University Press, 1961.

———. "Mark Twain's Joan of Arc: The Child as Goddess." *American Literature* 31 (March 1959): 1–20.

Stoneley, Peter. "Mark Twain and Gender." In *A Companion to Mark Twain,* edited by Peter Messent and Louis J. Budd. Malden, Mass.: Blackwell, 2005.

Stronks, James B. "Mark Twain's Boston Stage Debut as Seen by Hamlin Garland." *New England Quarterly* 36 (March 1963): 85–86.

Sturdevant, James R. "Mark Twain's Unpublished Letter to Tom Taylor." *Mark Twain Journal* 14 (1969): 8–9.

Sumida, Stephen H. "Reevaluating Mark Twain's Novel of Hawaii." *American Literature* 61 (December 1989): 586–609.

Sundquist, Eric J. "Mark Twain and Homer Plessy." *Representations* 24 (Autumn 1988): 102–28.

Tenney, Thomas. "About Mark Twain." *Mark Twain Journal* 42 (April 2004): 1–48; 45 (Fall 2007): 1–40.

———. *Mark Twain: A Reference Guide.* Boston: Hall, 1977.

Ticknor, Caroline. "Mark Twain's Missing Chapter." *Bookman* 39 (May 1914): 298–309.

Towers, Tom. "*The Prince and the Pauper*: Mark Twain's Once and Future King." *Studies in American Fiction* 6 (Autumn 1978): 193–202.

Tracy, Robert. "Myth and Reality in *The Adventures of Tom Sawyer*." *Southern Review* 4 (Spring 1968): 530–41.

Trautmann, Fredrick. "The Twins of Genius: Readings by George Washington Cable and Mark Twain in Pennsylvania." *Pennsylvania History* 43 (1976): 215–25.

Tucker, Edward L. "The Clemens-Johnston Reading of 17 January 1889: Further Documents." *Resources for American Literary Study* 24 (1998): 177–86.

Turner, Arlin. "James Lampton, Mark Twain's Model for Colonel Sellers." *Modern Language Notes* 70 (December 1955): 592–94.

———. *Mark Twain and G. W. Cable: The Record of a Literary Friendship.* East Lansing: Michigan State University Press, 1960.

———. "Mark Twain and the South: An Affair of Love and Anger." *Southern Review* 4 (Spring 1968): 493–519.

———. "Mark Twain, Cable, and 'a Professional Newspaper Liar.'" *New England Quarterly* 28 (March 1955): 18–33.

Twichell, Joseph H. "Mark Twain." *Harper's Monthly* 92 (May 1896): 817–27.

Vandersee, Charles. "The Mutual Awareness of Mark Twain and Henry Adams." *English Language Notes* 5 (1968): 285–92.

Vogelback, Arthur L. "Mark Twain and the Fight for Control of the *Tribune*." *American Literature* 26 (November 1954): 374–83.

———. "*The Prince and the Pauper*: A Study in Critical Standards." *American Literature* 14 (March 1942): 48–54.

Wagenknecht, Edward. *Mark Twain: The Man and His Work*. Norman: University of Oklahoma Press, 1961.

Wager, Willis. "A Critical Edition of the Morgan Manuscript of Mark Twain's *Life on the Mississippi*." PhD diss., New York University, 1942.

Wallace, John H. "The Case against Huckleberry Finn." In *Satire or Evasion? Black Perspectives on "Huckleberry Finn,"* edited by Thadious Davis, Thomas Tenney, and James S. Leonard. Durham, N.C.: Duke University Press, 1992.

Watterson, Henry. "Mark Twain—an Intimate Memory." *American Magazine* 70 (July 1910): 372–75.

Weaver, William. "Samuel Clemens Lectures in Kentucky." *Mark Twain Journal* 17 (1974): 20–22.

Webster, Samuel Charles, ed. *Mark Twain: Business Man*. Boston: Little, Brown, 1946.

Wecter, Dixon. *Samuel Clemens of Hannibal*. Boston: Houghton Mifflin, 1952.

Welland, Dennis. *Mark Twain in England*. London: Chatto and Windus, 1978.

———. "A Note on Some Early Reviews of *Tom Sawyer*." *Journal of American Studies* 1 (1967): 99–103.

Williams, James D. "Revision and Intention in Mark Twain's *A Connecticut Yankee*." *American Literature* 36 (November 1964): 288–97.

———. "The Use of History in Mark Twain's *A Connecticut Yankee*." *PMLA* 80 (March 1965): 102–10.

Willis, Resa. *Mark and Livy*. New York: Routledge, 2003.

Wonham, Henry B. "'I Want a Real Coon': Mark Twain and Late-Nineteenth-Century Ethnic Caricature." *American Literature* 72 (March 2000): 117–52.

———. *Mark Twain and the Art of the Tall Tale*. New York: Oxford University Press, 1993.

———. "Mark Twain's Short Fiction." In *A Companion to Mark Twain*, edited by Peter Messent and Louis J. Budd. Malden, Mass.: Blackwell, 2005.

Wood, C. E. S. "Introduction." In Mark Twain, *1601*. San Francisco: Grabhorn, 1925.

Woodfield, Denis. "The 'Fake' Title-Page of *The Gilded Age*: A Solution." *Papers of the Bibliographical Society of America* 50 (1956): 292–96.

Woodward, Robert. "A Selection of Harold Frederic's Early Literary Criticism." *American Literary Realism* 5 (Winter 1972): 1–22.

Wu, Cynthia. "The Siamese Twins in Late-Nineteenth-Century Narratives of Conflict and Reconciliation." *American Literature* 80 (March 2008): 29–55.

Wuster, Tracy. *Mark Twain: American Humorist*. Columbia: University of Missouri Press, 2016.

Young, James Harvey. "Anna Dickinson, Mark Twain, and Bret Harte." *Pennsylvania Magazine of History and Biography* 76 (January 1952): 39–46.

Zwarg, Christina. "Woman as a Force in Mark Twain's *Joan of Arc*: The Unwordable Fascination." *Criticism* 27 (1985): 57–72.

Reviews and Other Print Sources

"About Europe and Elsewhere." *Pall Mall Gazette*, 26 April 1880, 1576.

"About Mark Twain." *New York World*, 12 January 1877, 5.

"About Mark Twain." *WS*, 27 June 1896, 16.

"About Town." *BA*, 14 November 1874, 1; 22 November 1876, 4.

"The Academy of Music." *CT*, 14 March 1875, 8.

"Actors Come to Town." *NYH*, 25 August 1884, 8.

"The Adventures of Tom Sawyer." *Toronto Mail*, 25 July 1876, 3.

"The Advertiser." *Adelaide South Australian Advertiser*, 18 March 1882, 2.

"Affidavits That Clash." *NYT*, 28 January 1890, 8.

"Ah Sin." *Ithaca Journal*, 21 September 1877, 4.

"Ah Sin." *San Francisco Bulletin*, 21 May 1877, 1.

"Ah Sin." *Washington National Republican*, 8 May 1877, 1.

"Ah Sin a Decided Hit." *Cincinnati Gazette*, 5 September 1877, 4.

"Ah Sin on the Stage." *Denver Rocky Mountain News*, 19 May 1877, 3.

"'Ah Sin'-gular Drama." *CIO*, 7 August 1877, 2.

Albany Journal, 1 July 1871, 2.

"The 'Aldine' Dinner." *New York Commercial Advertiser*, 24 February 1872, 3.

"The Aldine Dinner." *NYTrib*, 24 February 1872, 5; 26 February 1872, 8.

"All Sorts." *San Francisco Bulletin*, 21 November 1882, 4.

"The Alumni Dinner." *New Haven Morning Journal and Courier*, 27 June 1889, 2.

"The Alumni Dinner." *NHR*, 28 June 1888, 3.

"The Alumni Hall." *NHR*, 26 June 1889, 1.

"The Amateur Theatricals." *HC*, 27 April 1876, 2.

"American Satire." *NYH*, 22 December 1873, 6.

"American Sculpture." *NYH*, 30 April 1884, 9.

Amherst (Mass.) Student, 9 March 1872, 38.

"Among Children's Books." *Sydney Herald*, 15 December 1880, 8.

"Among the Collegians." *NHJC*, 30 March 1887, 4.

"Amongst the Books." *Melbourne Leader*, 21 January 1882, 2; 26 December 1885, 35; 8 February 1890, 35.

"Amusement Notes." *New York Graphic*, 12 May 1880, 627.

"Amusements." *CC*, 25 November 1877, 3.

"Amusements." *Cleveland Plain Dealer*, 30 March 1880, 4; 15 December 1884, 1; 18 December 1884, 4.

"Amusements." *CT*, 17 January 1885, 5.

"Amusements." *HC*, 6 April 1877, 1.

"Amusements." *Minneapolis Tribune*, 25 January 1885, 4.

"Amusements." *New York Commercial Advertiser*, 22 September 1874, 1; 29 August 1876, 1.

"Amusements." *NYH*, 1 August 1877, 6; 24 September 1887, 4.

"Amusements." *NYS*, 21 December 1880, 3; 24 September 1887, 4.

"Amusements." *NYT*, 24 December 1874, 4; 9 May 1876, 7; 1 August 1877, 5; 24 September 1887, 5; 21 January 1890, 4.

"Amusements." Pittsburgh *Commercial Gazette*, 9 November 1877, 4.

"Amusements." *San Francisco Bulletin*, 30 August 1890, 2.

"Amusements." *St. Louis Globe-Democrat*, 2 September 1877, 5; 9 September 1877, 3.

"Amusements." *Washington Chronicle*, 23 October 1871, 4.

"Amusements." *Washington Post*, 1 March 1885, 4.

"The Ancients' Visit to Hartford." *BJ*, 3 October 1877, 4.

"Anna Dickinson's Debut." *CIO*, 12 May 1876, 2.

"Anna Dickinson's Debut." *NYH*, 9 May 1876, 3.

"Anna Dickinson's Debut." *WC*, 9 May 1876, 4.

"Anna Scalps the Critics." *NYS*, 10 April 1977, 1.

"Another Delighted Audience." *Cincinnati Enquirer*, 4 January 1885, 2.

"Another Pleased Audience." *WC*, 26 November 1884, 4.

"Another Speech from Mark Twain." *New Orleans Times*, 21 September 1874, 6.

Arnold, Matthew. "General Grant." *Murray's* 1 (January 1887): 130–44.

"Arrivals at the Hotels." *NYT*, 12 September 1874, 12; 3 September 1879, 8; 16 June 1880, 8.

"Art Notes." *NYT*, 25 October 1885, 6.

"Artemus Ward." *Portland (Maine) Eastern Argus*, 17 November 1871, 3.

"Artemus Ward the Humorist." *BJ*, 2 November 1871, 4.

"Artists and Their Friends Dine." *NYTrib*, 4 May 1888, 7.

"At the Fellowcraft Club." *BE*, 16 October 1889, 1.

"At the Home of Daudet." *NYT*, 26 April 1885, 6.

"At the National Capital." *SR*, 18 March 1888, 1.

"The Atlantic." *Cincinnati Star*, 31 March 1875, 1.

"The Atlantic." *NYEP*, 19 October 1874, 1.

"The Atlantic Dinner." *Boston Transcript*, 18 December 1877, 3.

"The Atlantic Monthly." *NYEP*, 16 May 1876, 1.

"An 'Atlantic Monthly' Dinner." *San Francisco Bulletin*, 2 January 1875, 4.

"Author against Author." *NYTrib*, 17 January 1890, 1.

"Authors and Their Works." *BH*, 8 March 1889, 5.

"The Authors' Carnival, *HC*, 5 December 1883, 2.

"The Authors' Club." *NYH*, 19 February 1887, 8.

"Authors in Public." *St. Louis Post-Dispatch*, 18 March 1888, 10.

"Authors Read for the Y.W.C.A." *NYS*, 23 April 1891, 3.

"Authors' Readings." *BH*, 30 April 1885, 1.

"Authors' Readings." *NYH*, 18 March 1888, 11.

"Authors' Readings." *NYT*, 17 December 1889, 3.

"Authors Seen and Heard." *NYTrib*, 1 April 1887, 5.

"Authors' Shabby Clothes." *New York Evening World*, 25 December 1889, 2.

BA, 20 October 1884, 4.

"Badeau's Book." *New Orleans Picayune*, 8 March 1889, 3.

Baltimore Bee, 14 May 1877, 2.

"The Ban on Mark Twain." *Fort Worth Register*, 28 May 1902, 4.

"The Banquet." *CIO*, 15 November 1879, 1.

"Banquet of the Army of the Tennessee." *NYT*, 15 November 1879, 1.

"Banquet to Edwin Booth." *NYH*, 31 March 1889, 15.

"A Bard's Birthday Banquet." *Boston Traveller*, 18 December 1877, 1.

"Barnay in Farce and Tragedy." *NYT*, 21 March 1883, 8.

Baxter, Sylvester. "Mark Twain's Masterwork." *BH*, 15 December 1889, 17.

B[ayard] T[aylor]. "American Humor." *San Francisco Bulletin*, 1 November 1875, 1.

"Bayard Taylor Honored." *NYT,* 5 April 1878, 2.

"The Bazar." *HC,* 7 June 1880, 2.

"Belles Lettres." *Westminster Review,* n.s. 58 (July 1880): 290.

BH, 13 January 1878, 4; 13 November 1890, 4.

"The Bickerings of the Innocents." *NYEP,* 12 January 1877, 1.

"Bidding Yale Farewell." *NYTrib,* 27 June 1889, 4.

"Big Libel Suit." *BH,* 4 March 1884, 2.

"A Bishopric Goes A-Begging." *San Francisco Bulletin,* 15 October 1886, 4.

Bok, Edward W. "Mark Twain's Plans." *Chicago Herald,* 17 May 1891, 26.

"Book for the Season." *Saturday Review,* 4 January 1890, 23.

"Book Notes." *Our Continent,* 19 July 1882, 59.

"Book Notice." *Otago (New Zealand) Star,* 11 April 1885, 1.

"Book Notices." *Portland (Maine) Transcript,* 6 April 1872, 2.

"A Book of Autographs." *New York Graphic,* 8 December 1875, 6.

"The Book World." *Milwaukee Sentinel,* 10 June 1883, 10.

"Books and Authors." *Christian Union,* 31 May 1876, 442.

"Books of the Month." *Atlantic Monthly* 55 (April 1885): 576.

"The Booth Supper." *NYT,* 1 April 1889, 4.

"Boston." *CT,* 23 December 1877, 16; 30 December 1877, 10.

"The Boston Press Club." *Boston Transcript,* 13 November 1871, 4.

Boston Transcript, 3 October 1876, 4.

Boyesen, H. H. "Russia's Manifest Destiny." *BH,* 24 May 1885, 13.

Brachvogel, Udo. "Rogers." *Die Gegenwart,* 8 July 1882, 26–29.

Bradford (England) Observer, 17 January 1874, 7.

"Branford." *NHJC,* 3 August 1881, 4.

"Brattleboro." *Manchester (N.H.) Journal,* 16 November 1871, 3.

"Brevities." *Pittsburgh Gazette,* 15 January 1872, 4.

"Brevities." *San Francisco Alta California,* 4 February 1877, 1; 3 January 1878, 1; 8 January 1878, 1; 16 January 1878, 1.

"Bric-a-Brac." *HC,* 28 February 1891, 2.

Bridges, Robert. "Mark Twain's Blood-Curdling Humor." *Life,* 26 February 1885, 119.

"Brief Mention." *HC,* 9 July 1872, 2; 31 July 1872, 2; 29 December 1873, 2; 9 September 1875, 2; 13 December 1877, 2.

"Brief Mention." *NHJC,* 9 May 1888, 2.

"Bright and Cheery." *BH,* 9 April 1885, 1.

"A Brilliant 'Innings.'" *NYTrib,* 9 April 1889, 1.

Brisbane Courier, 24 March 1874, 3; and 25 April 1874, 3.

Brooks, Sydney. "England's Ovation to Mark Twain." *Harper's Weekly,* 27 July 1907, 1086.

"The Burdens of a Humorist." *Cincinnati Gazette,* 24 December 1877, 4.

"A Busy Day for the Irving Company." *NYTrib,* 26 April 1884, 5.

"But Mr. House Had No Contract." *NYS,* 22 January 1890, 5.

"Cable and Twain." *Baltimore Sun,* 29 November 1884, 4.

"Cable's and Twain's Reading." *Louisville Courier-Journal,* 6 January 1885, 6.

"The Cable-Twain Readings." *NYH,* 19 November 1884, 7.

Cairo (Ill.) Bulletin, 30 December 1871, 2.

"Canada Surprises Mark Twain." *NYT,* 17 December 1881, 2.

"Canadian Book Bushwhackers." *CC*, 26 April 1879, 7.

"Capt. C. C. Duncan." *NYT*, 21 April 1884, 4.

"Capt. Duncan." *BE*, 7 March 1884, 2.

"Captain Duncan's Suing 'The Times.'" *NYTrib*, 4 April 1884, 3.

Cardiff Western Mail, 17 May 1880, 2.

"Carnival of Authors." *NHJC*, 6 December 1883, 2.

Carson City (Nev.) Appeal, 2 December 1885, 2.

"The Case of Capt. Duncan." *NYT*, 20 March 1884, 8.

"Caught on the Fly." *Dubuque Herald*, 24 April 1874, 4; 25 April 1874, 4.

CC, 11 May 1876, 8; 28 June 1882, 8.

"C. C. Duncan on Mark Twain." *New York Graphic*, 2 March 1877, 11.

"Charles L. Webster." *NYH*, 27 April 1891, 7.

"Chelsea." *BA*, 24 November 1876, 4.

Cheney, Mary Bushnell. "Mark Twain as a Reader." *Harper's Weekly*, 7 January 1911, 6.

"China's Backward Step." *NYT*, 2 September 1881, 5.

"China's Educational Mission." *NYT*, 16 July 1881, 5.

"The Chinese in Connecticut." *Sacramento Union*, 22 April 1879, 2.

"Christmas Books." *London Standard*, 16 December 1881, 2; 2 January 1882, 4.

"Christmas Books." *London Times*, 20 December 1881, 3.

Cincinnati Gazette, 17 June 1871, 4.

CIO, 24 April 1874, 4; 29 December 1881, 4.

"City and Vicinity." *Lowell (Mass.) Citizen and News*, 22 March 1875, 2.

"City and Vicinity." *Paterson (N.J.) Press*, 1 February 1872, 3.

"City Briefs." *HC*, 8 June 1883, 2.

"City Summary." *New York Clipper*, 19 September 1874, 198; 19 May 1877, 62.

"Civic Changes." *London Telegraph*, 30 September 1872, 3.

"Clemens and Cable." *Janesville (Wis.) Recorder*, 21 January 1885, 3.

"Clemmens' [*sic*] Arrival, *Dubuque Herald*, 22 April 1874, 4.

"The Clemmens [*sic*] Trial." *Dubuque Herald*, 24 April 1874, 4.

Cleveland Plain Dealer, 21 December 1877, 1; 24 December 1881, 4.

"Closed Its Labors." *WC*, 3 October 1890, 4.

"Col. Sellers." *New York Sunday Mercury*, 22 August 1875, 1.

"A Collation." *Amherst (Mass.) Record*, 28 February 1872, 4.

"The College President." *HC*, 26 February 1889, 3.

"Colonel Sellers." *Boston Globe*, 23 March 1876, 3.

"Colonel Sellers." *HC*, 12 January 1875, 2.

Columbus Enquirer-Sun, 4 January 1878, 2.

"The Comic Castle of Mark Twain." *Sacramento Union*, 1 November 1873, 8.

"Commissioner Duncan's Sons." *NYT*, 9 June 1883, 8.

"Congratulating the Governor." *NYTrib*, 3 December 1884, 2.

"Connecticut." *BA*, 19 January 1877, 2.

"The Connecticut Capital." *SR*, 16 September 1883, 8; 3 March 1889, 1.

"Connecticut Independents." *BA*, 13 October 1884, 5.

"Connecticut Independents." *BH*, 19 October 1884, 1.

"Contemporary Literature." *British Quarterly Review* 78 (July 1883): 226–27.

"Contributor's Club." *Atlantic Monthly* 42 (November 1878): 643; 45 (May 1880): 717–19.

Conway, Moncure D. "London Letter." *CC*, 26 June 1876, 5; 15 August 1881, 5.

———. "Mark Twain in London." *CC*, 10 October 1872, 4; 5 December 1872, 2.

———. "Mark Twain's New Book." *London Examiner*, 17 June 1876, 687–88.

"The Copyright Hearing." *Washington Post*, 24 March 1888, 4.

"The Copyright Laws." *BJ*, 28 December 1887, 1.

"Cornell Alumni Banquet." *WC*, 24 April 1885, 3.

"Coulisse Chat." *NYH*, 17 January 1875, 12.

"Cracking Jokes." *Once a Week*, 8 November 1873, 402–5.

Crinkle, Nym [Andrew C. Wheeler]. "Ah Sin." *NYS*, 5 August 1877, 5.

———. "Down on Mark Twain." *BE*, 2 October 1887, 15.

———. "John T. Raymond." *NYS*, 9 June 1878, 5.

———. "Mark Twain's Plays." *Kansas City Star*, 8 October 1887, 2.

———. "Park Theatre." *NYS*, 8 January 1878, 1.

"Critical Opinions." *NYH*, 21 September 1874, 2.

"The Critic's Review." *Pittsburgh Dispatch*, 23 December 1889, 4.

Croffut, W. A. "A Capital Boss." *Milwaukee Sentinel*, 23 October 1887, 10.

"A Cruel Hoax." *Sacramento Union*, 29 April 1874, 1.

"Current Events." *London Examiner*, 18 October 1873, 1046.

"Current Literature." *London Congregationalist* 14 (March 1885): 251.

"Current Literature." *London Daily News*, 13 October 1880, 6.

"Current Literature." *Melbourne Argus*, 14 August 1880, 4.

"Current Literature." *San Francisco Bulletin*, 15 July 1882, 1; 14 March 1885, 1.

"Current Notes." *BJ*, 18 February 1878, 2; 4 April 1886, 2.

"Current Opinion." *Macon Telegraph*, 8 March 1881, 2.

"A Curious Episode." *Critic*, 3 December 1881, 339.

"Curiously Timely Book." *HC*, 9 December 1889, 3.

"Curtis on Cleveland." *NYH*, 30 May 1888, 3.

"Cushion Carrom [*sic*] Billiards." *BH*, 20 May 1883, 6.

Custer, Elizabeth B. "A Catskill Cabin." *CT*, 20 September 1885, 12.

Dale, Alan. "The Prince and the Pauper." *New York Evening World*, 21 January 1890, 2.

"Dan DeQuille's Book." *Virginia City (Nev.) Territorial Enterprise*, 23 February 1876, 2.

"Daniel Frohman Begins a Suit." *NYTrib*, 11 July 1890, 6.

D'Arme, John. "New York Letters." *Portland Oregonian*, 26 December 1886, 2.

"A Decision against 'Mark Twain.'" *NYTrib*, 10 January 1883, 1.

"The Defence in the Duncan Suit." *NYTrib*, 7 March 1884, 3.

"Demand for Gen. Grant's Book." *NYT*, 3 December 1885, 5.

"The Departure of Bayard Taylor and Mark Twain." *Baltimore Sun*, 13 April 1878, 3.

"Departure of Hon. Bayard Taylor." *New York Mail*, 11 April 1878, 1.

"Diamond Cut Diamond." *Virginia City (Nev.) Territorial Enterprise*, 26 September 1877, 1.

"Did Scott Destroy Cash Books?" *NYTrib*, 19 March 1887, 4.

"The Dinner and the Speeches." *NYTrib*, 23 December 1876, 7.

"Dinner Given to Miss Montgomery." *Portland Oregonian*, 8 April 1888, 3.

"The Dinner in This City." *NYTrib*, 22 December 1882, 2.

"A Dinner on Parnassus." *NYTrib*, 18 December 1874, 3,

"Distinguished Guests." *CC*, 4 January 1885, 6.

"The Drama." *NYTrib*, 1 August 1877, 5.

"Dramatic." *New York Clipper,* 10 January 1874, 327; 15 September 1877, 198; 22 September 1877, 207.

"Dramatic and Musical Notes." *New York Clipper,* 4 May 1889, 123.

"Dramatic, Musical, Etc." *Philadelphia North American,* 5 October 1875, 2.

Dublin Freeman's Journal and Commercial Advertiser, 12 April 1880, 3.

"Dull and Raining at St. Louis." CC, 13 May 1882, 7.

Duluth (Minn.) Tribune, 23 January 1885, 2.

"Duncan's Case." *BE,* 5 March 1884, 10.

"Duncan's Woe." *NYT,* 13 May 1884, 4.

"Editorial Notes." *Buffalo Courier,* 26 May 1880, 1.

"Editorial Notes." *NHJC,* 18 March 1885, 1.

"Editorial Notes." *New York Commercial Advertiser,* 28 July 1873, 2.

"Editor's Literary Record." *Harper's Monthly* 55 (June 1877): 149.

"Editor's Study." *Harper's Monthly* 80 (January 1890): 319–20.

"Editor's Table." *Ohio Farmer,* 7 March 1874, 152.

Edwards, E. J. "The Literary World." *Ogdensburg (N.Y.) Journal,* 28 May 1891, 3.

"Eleanor Kirk's Letter." *Plattsburgh (N.Y.) Sentinel,* 22 February 1889, 5.

Elliot, Henry R. "Poor of New York." *BA,* 20 January 1890, 5.

Elmira (N.Y.) Bazoo, 7 September 1877, 4.

"Elmira's Great Ball Game." *NYS,* 3 July 1887, 1–2.

"Elsie Amended the Play." *New York Evening World,* 22 March 1889, 3.

"Elsie Leslie." *NYTrib,* 2 December 1888, 17.

"Eminent Authors at Home." *New York Graphic,* 23 December 1876, 377.

"Endorsed by 'Mark Twain.'" *Bozeman (Mont.) Chronicle,* 17 August 1887, 1.

"Entertainments." *London Orchestra,* 12 December 1873, 165.

"Entertainments." *Toledo Blade,* 12 December 1871, 3.

"The Equality of the Negro." *CT,* 17 January 1885, 8.

"Europe." *New York Commercial Advertiser,* 10 June 1873, 4.

"The Examiner of Plays." *London Examiner,* 24 July 1880, 889.

"Explosion of the Boiler of the 'Mark Twain.'" *BH,* 28 March 1885, 2.

"Fact and Fancy Focused." *New York Clipper,* 10 May 1879, 54.

Fairbanks, Mary Mason. "Letter from 'Myra.'" *Cleveland Herald,* 4 May 1874, 4.

"A Farewell to Salvini." *NYT,* 27 April 1883, 5.

"Father Hawley's Acknowledgment." *HC,* 8 March 1875, 2.

"The February Atlantic." *BA,* 16 January 1875, 2.

"February Magazines." *BH,* 1 February 1885, 17.

"The Fellowcraft Club Banquets." *BJ,* 16 October 1889, 3.

"Fenwick Hall." *HC,* 29 July 1872, 2.

"A Few Wooden Nutmegs." *Geneva Gazette,* 30 January 1874, 2.

"The Fifth Avenue Theatre." *NYEP,* 1 August 1877, 3.

"The First Interview Recorded by the Phonograph." *Pall Mall Gazette,* 24 July 1888, 2.

"Folios and Footlights." *New Review* 2 (February 1890): 188.

"For Tariff Reform." *NHR,* 30 October 1888, 1.

"Forefathers." *BA,* 23 December 1876, 1.

"Forefathers' Day." *NYT,* 23 December 1876, 1.

"Forefathers' Day." *Philadelphia North American,* 23 December 1881, 1.

"Foreign Notes." *NYTrib,* 17 December 1881, 1.

"The Four Duncans." Scrapbook 8:113, MTP.

"A Fraud That Failed to Pan Out." *Cincinnati Commercial Tribune*, 26 July 1888, 1.

Frohman, Daniel. "The Prince and Pauper." *New York Dramatic Mirror*, 16 August 1890, 5.

"From Dayton." *Cincinnati Gazette*, 5 January 1872, 1.

"From Grave to Gay." *Washington National Republican*, 25 November 1884, 1.

"From Many Points of View." *NYTrib*, 24 March 1888, 5.

"From Our London Correspondent." *Manchester (N.H.) Guardian*, 14 October 1873, 5.

"From the Sandwich Islands." *Sacramento Union*, 6 September 1866, 2.

"Fruits of the Brain." *BH*, 29 January 1886, 3.

"Fun at the Lotos." *WS*, 22 February 1873, 2.

"Fun on the Stage." *BE*, 23 November 1884, 12.

"Funeral of Daniel Slote." *NYS*, 17 February 1882, 4.

"Gadabout's Column." *WS*, 17 January 1874, 1.

"The Gaiety Theatre." *London Times*, 22 July 1880, 4.

"Gail Hamilton Once More." *NYTrib*, 5 February 1878, 2.

"Gen. Grant." *BH*, 22 June 1885, 2.

"Gen. Grant, Mark Twain and the Century." *SR*, 9 March 1885, 4.

"Gen. Grant Growing Weaker Hourly." *Jackson (Mich.) Citizen Patriot*, 31 March 1885, 1.

"Gen. Grant in Hartford." *NYT*, 17 October 1880, 7.

"Gen. Grant Sleeps Badly." *NYS*, 10 March 1885, 1.

"Gen. Grant's Condition." *NYTrib*, 31 March 1885, 1.

"General Grant." *HC*, 24 July 1885, 2.

"General Grant Easier." *NYH*, 1 April 1885, 10.

"The General Much Refreshed." *WC*, 20 April 1885, 1.

"General Notes." *NYT*, 21 December 1877, 4.

"General Notes." *Sacramento Record-Union*, 17 August 1882, 3.

"General State News." *NHJC*, 27 October 1887, 4.

"Generalities." *Adelaide Observer*, 11 July 1885, 43.

Geneva Gazette, 8 December 1871, 3.

"Genius and Versatility." *NYT*, 19 November 1884, 5.

"George W. Cable." *CT*, 3 February 1884, 9.

"George W. Cable." *HC*, 30 March 1883, 2.

"German Republican Meeting." *HC*, 29 October 1880, 20.

"The Gilded Age." *Alexandria (La.) Caucasian*, 18 April 1874, 3.

"The Gilded Age." *Auckland Star*, 6 October 1876, 3.

"The Gilded Age." *Brisbane Queenslander*, 16 May 1874, 7.

"The 'Gilded Age.'" *Buffalo Express*, 8 September 1874, 1.

"The Gilded Age." *Cleveland Herald*, 17 December 1873, 3.

"The Gilded Age." *HC*, 1 May 1874, 2.

"The Gilded Age." *London Post*, 26 January 1874, 3.

"The Gilded Age." *Melbourne Argus*, 28 March 1874, 4.

"The Gilded Age." *Melbourne Australasian*, 11 April 1874, 8.

"The Gilded Age." *San Francisco Bulletin*, 21 March 1874, 2.

"The Gilded Age." *Saturday Review*, 14 February 1874, 223–24.

"The Gilded Age." *Spectator*, 21 March 1874, 371–72.

Gilder, Jeannette. "The Lounger." *Critic*, 14 January 1888, 211.

"Gone to West Point." *Washington National Republican*, 10 June 1881, 1.

"The Good Gray Poet." *NHJC*, 15 April 1887, 3.

"Gorky Evicted Twice in a Day from Hotels." *New York World*, 15 April 1906, 1.

"Gossip from New York." *Kansas City Star*, 4 August 1888, 3.

"A Government Investigation." *NYTrib*, 22 June 1883, 4.

"A Grand Array of Writers." *Sacramento Record-Union*, 26 December 1879, 1.

"The Grand Opera House." *NYS*, 25 September 1877, 3.

"Grant's Reminiscences." *BH*, 10 March 1885, 3.

"A Great Tariff Reform Rally." *NHR*, 31 October 1888, 1.

"Greeley in the Woods." *NYH*, 25 August 1872, 5.

"Gymnasium Exhibition." *HC*, 2 April 1887, 3.

"Hail and Farewell." *BH*, 30 April 1884, 8.

"Hanover Square Rooms." *London Telegraph*, 9 December 1873.

Harris, Joel Chandler. "To the Editors." *Critic*, 28 November 1885, 253.

"Hartford Accident Insurance Co.." *HC*, 20 June 1874, 4.

"Hartford and Vicinity." *HC*, 18 June 1883, 1.

"Hartford (Ct.) Authors." *BH*, 26 December 1881, 2.

"Hartford Dramatic Association." *HC*, 13 November 1875, 2.

Hartford Times, 23 March 1874.

"Hartford's New Amusement Enterprise." *NHR*, 7 February 1887, 3.

"Has Lost His Curiosity." *Jackson (Mich.) Citizen Patriot*, 20 February 1885, 3.

Hawthorne, Julian. "At a London Publisher's." *Collier's Weekly*, 24 June 1897, 22–23.

———. "When Mark Twain Miscued." *Pasadena Star-News*, 31 October 1931, 5.

Hay, John. "Mark Twain at Steinway Hall." *NYTrib*, 25 January 1872, 5.

"He Saw No Humor." *Portland Oregonian*, 4 August 1889, 9.

"He Should Be Removed." *NYT*, 9 March 1884, 6.

"He Was Fly." *Wheeling Register*, 30 March 1888, 3.

Henley, W. E. "Literature." *Athenaeum*, 24 April 1880, 529–30; 2 June 1883, 694–95.

"His Funniest Speech." *CT*, 20 April 1890, 10.

"Hob-Nobbing with Nobs." *BH*, 9 April 1889, 4.

"Holiday Fun." *CIO*, 24 December 1881, 13.

"The Holmes Breakfast." *Christian Union*, 10 December 1879, 490.

"The Holmes Breakfast." *Literary World*, 20 December 1879, 435.

"Home News." *NYTrib*, 1 June 1871, 8.

"Honoring Dr. Holmes." *NYTrib*, 4 December 1879, 5.

"Honors to Bayard Taylor." *NYTrib*, 5 April 1878, 1.

"Honors to Edwin Booth." *NYTrib*, 31 March 1889, 7.

"Honors to Karl Gerhardt." *HC*, 20 October 1885, 2.

Hood, Tom. "Mark Twain." *Fun*, 25 October 1873, 170.

"Horace Greeley's Sixty-First Birthday." *NYTrib*, 5 February 1872, 5.

"Hotel Arrivals." *Memphis Appeal*, 25 April 1882, 4.

"The Hotel Guests." *BA*, 27 February 1889, 1.

House, E. H. "The Prince and Pauper." *New York Dramatic Mirror*, 9 August 1890, 5.

"House against Clemens." *NYT*, 4 February 1890, 9.

"House Makes Terms." *NYT*, 12 March 1890, 2.

Howe, E. W. "News and Notes." *Atchison (Kans.) Globe*, 31 December 1881, 3.

Howells, W. D. "Drama." *Atlantic Monthly* 35 (June 1875): 749–51.

———. "Recent Literature." *Atlantic Monthly* 29 (June 1872): 754–55.

———. "Recent Literature." *Atlantic Monthly* 36 (December 1875): 749–50.

———. "Recent Literature." *Atlantic Monthly* 37 (May 1876): 621–22.

"Huckleberry Finn." *Port Jervis (N.Y.) Gazette*, 27 April 1885, 1.

"Humor Reduced to Algebra." *NYS*, 19 May 1878, 2.

"The Humorist." *Keokuk (Iowa) Gate City*, 16 January 1885, 8.

"The Humourist." *Melbourne Australasian*, 11 April 1885, 42.

"In Brief." *Carson City (Nev.) Appeal*, 26 May 1883, 3.

"In General." *BA*, 24 August 1875, 1.

"In Honor of Judge Pryor." *NYS*, 10 October 1890, 3.

"In the Academy of Music." *BE*, 22 February 1885, 12.

"In the Harnass [*sic*] Again." *Virginia City (Nev.) Territorial Enterprise*, 15 January 1878, 2.

"Independence Day." *St. Louis Globe-Democrat*, 4 July 1886, 2.

"The Independents' Address." *NHR*, 13 October 1884, 2.

"An Innocent Abroad." *Victoria (B.C.) Daily Colonist*, 31 May 1883, 1.

"The Innocents Abroad." *Cleveland Plain Dealer*, 12 December 1884, 4.

"Innocents Abroad." *Winona (Minn.) Republican*, 27 January 1885.

"The Insolence of Office." *CT*, 29 March 1888, 9.

"An Intelligent Watch." *Middletown (Conn.) Constitution*, 31 January 1877, 2.

"Interesting Gossip of the Day." *NYS*, 12 December 1887, 4.

"International Copyright." *CIO*, 18 March 1888, 9.

"International Copyright." *NYH*, 29 January 1886, 2.

"International Copyright." *NYTrib*, 29 January 1886, 3.

"Invited to Meet Authors." *WC*, 2 February 1889, 1.

"Is His Word Twain Also or Has Mark's Memory Been Wrecked?" *NYT*, 31 January 1890, 9.

"Is Mark Twain a Plagiarist?" *Washington Post*, 6 November 1889, 4.

"Items." *Boston Transcript*, 28 April 1876, 6.

Ithaca Journal, 21 November 1871, 2; 31 July 1877, 4; 8 August 1877, 4; 10 August 1877, 4; 15 July 1880, 4; 29 November 1884, 3.

"January Magazines." *CIO*, 20 December 1874, 5.

"The January Magazines." *NYEP*, 19 December 1874, 6.

"Jeff Thompson Twenty Years Ago." *New Orleans Republican*, 19 April 1874, 6.

Jersey City American Standard, 31 January 1872, 1.

"Joaquin Miller's Letter." *CC*, 24 December 1882, 2.

"The Joker Joked." *WC*, 8 April 1884, 3.

"Jos. Goodman's Memories of Humorist's Early Days." *San Francisco Examiner*, 22 April 1910, 3.

"Jottings." *Boston Transcript*, 19 March 1885, 4; 25 March 1885, 4.

"Jottings about Town." *NYS*, 24 April 1883, 1; 12 October 1887, 1.

"The Jubilee Singers." *HC*, 29 January 1872, 2.

"The Jumping Frog." *Dubuque Herald*, 21 April 1874, 4.

"The Jumping Frog Swindle." *Dubuque Herald*, 25 April 1874, 1.

"The June Magazines." *CIO*, 29 May 1875, 6.

"June Magazines." *Literary World*, 1 June 1876, 10.

"A Kind-Hearted Druggist." *New Orleans Picayune*, 14 December 1890, 18.

"The King's Impressions of America." *NYTrib*, 24 December 1874, 1.

Kirk, Eleanor. "Our New York Letter." *Washington Bee*, 5 March 1887, 1.

"Ladies' Column." *Adelaide Journal*, 29 July 1882, 2.

"The Lambs Honor Their Shepherd." *NYTrib*, 2 January 1888, 5.

"Late Department News." *WC*, 2 February 1889, 1.

"Late Publications." *Philadelphia North American*, 28 June 1882, 4.

"Latest Cable News." *NYH*, 2 May 1879, 7.

"Latest London Gossip." *Cincinnati Gazette*, 6 August 1879, 5.

"Latest News Items." *San Francisco Bulletin*, 27 September 1881, 4.

Lathrop, George Parsons. "The Atlantic Dinner." *NYEP*, 17 December 1874, 2.

"The Laurel Park Chautauqua." *SR*, 19 July 1890, 4.

"Lazy Mark Twain." *Cleveland Plain Dealer*, 31 May 1891, 11.

"Lecture by Mark Twain." *HC*, 22 February 1875, 2.

"Lecture Facts." *San Francisco Bulletin*, 17 October 1878, 1.

"The Lecture Field." *Wilmington Commercial*, 25 October 1871, 1.

"The Lecture Last Evening." *Wilmington Every Evening*, 25 October 1871, 4.

"Lecture of Mark Twain." *Wooster (Ohio) Republican*, 11 January 1872, 2.

"Lectures and Entertainments." *NYTrib*, 30 March 1891, 5.

"Lectures and Meetings." *NYTrib*, 1 February 1873, 12.

"Lectures and Readings." *Boston Transcript*, 14 November 1884, 1.

"Lectures Last Evening." *Boston Post*, 2 November 1871, 3.

"Legal." *London Graphic*, 18 October 1873, 375.

"Letter from Boston." *Congregationalist*, 7 April 1887, 10.

"Letter from New York." *Congregationalist*, 8 December 1887, 1.

"Liberal Mark Twain." *Milwaukee Sentinel*, 11 December 1875, 2.

"Life in a Great City." *NHR*, 5 April 1885, 4.

"Life in New York City." *BE*, 8 March 1885, 2.

"Life on the Mississippi." *Adelaide South Australian Register*, 4 August 1883, 1.

"Life on the Mississippi." *London Morning Post*, 13 August 1883, 3.

"The List Closed." *BE*, 6 March 1890, 4.

"Literary." *American Hebrew*, 7 March 1890, 93–94.

"Literary Chit Chat." *NYH*, 26 October 1874, 5; 11 December 1876, 8.

"Literary News." *Independent*, 10 January 1878, 12.

"Literary News." *St. Louis Republic*, 1 November 1890, 10.

"Literary News and Gossip." *San Francisco Bulletin*, 24 July 1875, 1.

"Literary Notes." *BE*, 10 February 1884, 3.

"Literary Notes." *BH*, 28 January 1884, 6.

"Literary Notes." *Memphis Appeal*, 15 November 1885, 3.

"Literary Notes." *New York Evangelist*, 27 May 1875, 6.

"Literary Notes." *WS*, 17 June 1882, 2.

"Literary Notices." *Alexandria (Va.) State Journal*, 12 February 1874, 2.

"The Literary World." *Ogdensburg (N.Y.) Journal*, 28 May 1891, 3.

"Literature." *Adelaide Observer*, 13 March 1880, 33.

"Literature." *Leeds Mercury*, 12 July 1882, 3; 30 May 1883, 3.

"Literature." *London Post*, 3 February 1885, 3.

"Literature." *Melbourne Australasian*, 30 September 1876, 8; 31 July 1880, 8; 30 September 1882, 8.

"Literature." *NYEP*, 1 September 1883, 4.

"Literature." *NYH*, 20 May 1883, 10.

"Literature." *San Francisco Chronicle*, 15 March 1885, 6.

"Literature and Art." *Kansas City Times*, 7 December 1885, 5.

"Literature for Children." *Brisbane Courier*, 28 December 1881, 3.

"Live Washington Topics." *NYS*, 23 March 1888, 1.

"Liverpool Institute." *London Era*, 26 October 1873, 5.

"The Living Obelisk." *NYS*, 28 December 1880, 2.

"Local Intelligence." *Allentown (Penn.) Chronicle*, 18 October 1871, 4.

"Local Intelligence." *SR*, 2 May 1882, 5.

"Local Mention." *WS*, 27 January 1882, 4.

"Local Miscellany." *NYTrib*, 19 July 1878, 8.

"Local Personals." *St. Louis Globe-Democrat*, 18 April 1882, 6.

"Local Varieties." *BH*, 30 April 1882, 11; 3 October 1882, 2; 3 February 1889, 6.

"London." *CT*, 27 September 1872, 4.

"London Gossip." *NYH*, 5 January 1874, 3.

London Observer, 19 October 1873; 14 December 1873.

"The London Press on Mark Twain." *HC*, 5 November 1873, 1.

"The London Scottish Corporation." *Glasgow Herald*, 2 December 1873, 4.

London Sportsman, 12 December 1873.

London Telegraph, 13 January 1890, 7.

"The London Theatres." *London Era*, 25 July 1880, 12.

"London Theatres." *Penny Illustrated Paper and Illustrated Times*, 18 October 1873, 251.

"Longfellow." *BA*, 1 April 1887, 5.

"The Lord Mayor Elect." *London Times*, 5 November 1872, 10.

"The Lounger." *Critic*, 9 August 1884, 66; 26 September 1884, 45–46.

Lowell (Mass.) Courier, 12 November 1884.

Lukens, Henry Clay. "American Literary Comedians." *Harper's Monthly* 80 (April 1890): 783–97.

"The Lyceum." *Theatre*, 11 October 1887, 267.

"Lyceum Notes." *BA*, 30 September 1874, 1.

MacAdam, Hastings. "Mark Twain Visits His Old Sweetheart." *St. Louis Republic*, 1 June 1902, sec. 3, p. 1.

Macon Telegraph, 31 March 1883, 2.

"Magazine Notices." *Portland (Maine) Press*, 20 March 1875, 2.

"The Magazines." *CT*, 27 February 1871, 3.

"The Magazines." *Louisville Courier-Journal*, 23 May 1876, 3.

"The Magazines for April." *Nation*, 6 April 1871, 243.

"The Magazines for February." *Sydney Herald*, 9 March 1885, 4.

"March Magazines." *Milwaukee Sentinel*, 6 March 1875, 2.

"Mark Twain." *BA*, 13 February 1886, 8.

"Mark Twain." *BE*, 22 November 1871, 3; 10 February 1873, 4.

"Mark Twain." *Bradford (England) Observer*, 20 November 1873, 8; 3 January 1874, 6.

"Mark Twain." *Brooklyn Times*, 22 November 1871, n.p.

"Mark Twain." *Cincinnati Gazette*, 28 December 1871, 3.

"Mark Twain." *CIO*, 10 July 1886, 13.

"Mark Twain." *Cleveland Leader*, 1 March 1872, 3.

"Mark Twain." *CT*, 20 December 1871, 4; 24 December 1871, 3; 2 March 1872, 5; 4 November 1880, 5.

"Mark Twain." *Danbury News*, 28 February 1872, 2.

"Mark Twain." *Denver Rocky Mountain News*, 5 January 1878, 2.

"Mark Twain." *Dundee Courier & Argus*, 17 April 1882, 3.

"Mark Twain." *Grand Rapids Democrat*, 16 December 1871.

"Mark Twain." *Jackson (Mich.) Citizen Patriot*, 14 December 1871, 5.

"Mark Twain." *Kalamazoo Gazette*, 22 December 1871, 3.

"Mark Twain." *Los Angeles Times*, 16 July 1887, 10.

"Mark Twain." *New York Graphic*, 8 November 1873, 6.

"Mark Twain." *New York Mail*, 2 September 1879, 4.

"Mark Twain." *New York World*, 6 February 1873, 8.

"Mark Twain." *NHR*, 20 October 1879, 4.

"Mark Twain." *Philadelphia Inquirer*, 21 November 1871, 3.

"Mark Twain." *Philadelphia Press*, 21 November 1871.

"Mark Twain." *Pittsburgh Commercial Gazette*, 12 January 1872, 4.

"Mark Twain." *San Francisco Chronicle*, 15 June 1885, 2.

"Mark Twain." *Spectator*, 18 October 1873, 1302–3.

"Mark Twain." *Sydney Evening News*, 18 January 1882, 6.

"Mark Twain." *Washington Post*, 4 February 1889, 2.

"Mark Twain." *WC*, 14 March 1889, 2.

"Mark Twain." *Wheeling Intelligencer*, 11 January 1872, 4.

"Mark Twain a Cub Printer." *NYS*, 19 January 1886, 3.

"Mark Twain a Deserter." *Adelaide Express and Telegraph*, 16 June 1886, 4.

"Mark Twain a Heavy Loser." *San Francisco Bulletin*, 17 April 1888, 3.

"Mark Twain a Plaintiff." *NYT*, 15 January 1885, 1.

"Mark Twain a Valuable Contribution to the Buffalo Homeopathic Fair." *Indianapolis Sentinel*, 21 December 1880, 4.

"Mark Twain Accused of Plagiarism." *New York World*, 4 November 1889, 4.

"Mark Twain and Bret Harte's Play." *San Francisco Bulletin*, 16 May 1877, 1.

"Mark Twain and Capt. Duncan." *BH*, 17 June 1883, 1.

"Mark Twain and the Conductor." *NYS*, 12 November 1890, 6.

"Mark Twain and Father Hawley." *HC*, 29 January 1873, 2; 1 February 1873, 2.

"Mark Twain and Geo. Cable." *Boston Traveller*, 14 November 1884.

"Mark Twain and George W. Cable." *Boston Post*, 14 November 1884, 4.

"Mark Twain and George W. Cable." *East Orange (N.J.) Gazette*, 13 November 1884.

"Mark Twain and George W. Cable at the Academy." *Milwaukee Sentinel*, 29 January 1885, 4.

"Mark Twain and His Book." *NYT*, 10 December 1889, 5.

"Mark Twain and His Illustrator." *Success* 3 (June 1900): 205.

"Mark Twain and His Wife." *Jackson (Mich.) Citizen Patriot*, 15 October 1885, 6.

"Mark Twain and Louise on a Raft." *Philadelphia Inquirer*, 30 May 1883, 1.

"Mark Twain and Massachusetts." *BA*, 2 April 1885, 2.

"Mark Twain and Miss Thursby at Music Hall." *Providence Press*, 24 November 1876, 2.

"Mark Twain and Mr. Cable." *Boston Globe*, 14 November 1884, 8.

"Mark Twain and Quantrill's Band." *St. Louis Globe-Democrat*, 17 March 1885, 2.

"Mark Twain and Sellers." *NYS*, 3 September 1878, 3.

"Mark Twain and the Police." *BH*, 16 November 1884, 16.

"Mark Twain as an Auctioneer." *Albany Journal*, 18 December 1876, 1.

"Mark Twain as a Guerilla." *BH*, 13 December 1885, 16.

"Mark Twain as a Humorist." *NHR*, 6 September 1882, 2.

"Mark Twain as a Journalist." *Vicksburg (Miss.) Commercial*, 6 September 1879, 3.

"Mark Twain as a Lecturer." *Bradford (England) Observer*, 16 October 1873, 5.

"Mark Twain as a Lecturer." *London Times*, 14 October 1873, 12.

"Mark Twain as a Lecturer." *Melbourne Age*, 6 July 1872, 6.

"Mark Twain as a Listener." *Harrisburg Patriot*, 17 January 1891, 1.

"Mark Twain as a Litigant." *BJ*, 30 December 1884, 1.

"Mark Twain as Mayor." *Virginia City (Nev.) Territorial Enterprise*, 6 February 1876, 2.

"Mark Twain as a Pedestrian." *BJ*, 14 November 1874, 2.

"Mark Twain as a Scotchman." *Cincinnati Gazette*, 26 December 1873, 5.

"Mark Twain as Seen by His Housemaid." *NYT*, 15 March 1925, sec. 20, p. 5.

"Mark Twain as a Witness." *San Francisco Bulletin*, 25 August 1883, 4.

"Mark Twain as an Umpire." *NYTrib*, 3 July 1887, 2.

"Mark Twain at Sea." *NYTrib*, 27 November 1872, 1.

"Mark Twain at Vassar." *Cincinnati Commercial Tribune*, 10 May 1885, 13.

"Mark Twain at the Whitefriars Club." *South London Press*, 14 September 1872, 4.

"Mark Twain at the Yorick." *Melbourne Australasian*, 5 October 1895, 43.

"'Mark Twain'–Cable." *St. Louis Globe-Democrat*, 11 January 1885, 12.

"'Mark Twain'–Cable Readings." *BJ*, 11 November 1884, 3.

"The Mark Twain–Cable Readings." *Grand Rapids Democrat*, 14 December 1884.

"The Mark Twain–Cable Readings." *Philadelphia Inquirer*, 22 November 1884, 3.

"The Mark Twain–Cable Readings." *St. Paul Globe*, 24 January 1885, 4.

"'Mark Twain' Confirmed." *CT*, 20 May 1878, 8.

"Mark Twain Enjoined." *WS*, 10 March 1890, 8.

"Mark Twain Explains." *SR*, 20 December 1881, 4.

"Mark Twain Hauled Up." *NYT*, 27 January 1890, 5.

"Mark Twain / He Disclaims the Article Libeling Captain Duncan." *BE*, 7 March 1884, 4.

"Mark Twain Heard." *Kansas City Times*, 24 March 1888, 2.

"Mark Twain / His Latest Oddity—A New Version of 'Hamlet.'" *Portland Oregonian*, 29 December 1881, 4.

"Mark Twain in Brooklyn." *NYS*, 14 November 1876, 1.

"Mark Twain in the City." *Washington Post*, 2 February 1889, 1.

"Mark Twain in Court." *BA*, 31 May 1873, 2.

"Mark Twain in a Dilema [*sic*]." *CT*, 30 November 1884, 23.

"Mark Twain in a Dilemma." *New York World*, 27 November 1884, 1.

"Mark Twain in England." *NYS*, 19 October 1887, 4.

"Mark Twain in a Lawsuit." *CT*, 26 April 1879, 3.

"Mark Twain in Leicester." *Leicester Chronicle*, 10 January 1874, 10.

"Mark Twain in London." *CC*, 5 December 1872, 2.

"Mark Twain in London." *HC*, 19 September 1872, 2.

"Mark Twain in the Lyceum Course." *BA*, 2 November 1871, 1.

"Mark Twain in Paris." *Oregon State Journal*, 23 August 1879, 3.

"'Mark Twain' in Philadelphia." *HC*, 16 November 1876, 2.

"Mark Twain in Politics." *CT*, 7 October 1876, 2.

"Mark Twain in Politics." *NYT*, 2 October 1876, 1.

"Mark Twain in a Rage." *Richmond Dispatch*, 5 April 1884, 4.

"Mark Twain in Town." *New Orleans Picayune*, 29 April 1882, 3.

"Mark Twain Is Defeated." *NYT*, 9 March 1890, 1.

"Mark Twain Last Night." *Chicago Post*, 19 December 1871, 4.

"'Mark Twain' Loses a Suit." *BH*, 9 January 1883, 4.

"Mark Twain Must Pay Up." *WS*, 6 June 1887, 1.

"Mark Twain Non-Committal." *New York Graphic*, 15 April 1875, 3.

"Mark Twain on Accident Insurance." *BA*, 17 October 1874, 1.

"Mark Twain on Artemus Ward." *Albany Journal*, 29 November 1871, 2.

"Mark Twain on Artemus Ward." *Brooklyn Union*, 22 November 1871, 2.

"Mark Twain on Babies." *CT*, 14 November 1879, 1.

"Mark Twain on a Fresh Trail." *London Standard*, 10 December 1873, 3.

"Mark Twain on His Muscle." *New York World*, 18 February 1877, 5.

"Mark Twain on His New Heathen Chinee Play." *SR*, 2 August 1877, 8.

"'Mark Twain' on International Copyright." *Boston Musical Record* 262 (November 1883): 9.

"Mark Twain on 'Liberty.'" *Macon Telegraph*, 14 December 1883, 1.

"Mark Twain on Nevada." *London Figaro*, 17 December 1873, 51.

"Mark Twain on the Sandwich Island Savages." *Liverpool Mercury*, 21 October 1873, 7.

"Mark Twain on the Sandwich Islands." *Jersey City Journal*, 14 February 1873, 1.

"Mark Twain on the Sandwich Islands." *London Illustrated Police News*, 18 October 1873, 3.

"Mark Twain on the Sandwich Islands." *London Standard*, 9 October 1873, 5; 14 October 1873, 6.

"Mark Twain on Savages." *Lloyd's Weekly Newspaper*, 19 October 1873, 5.

"Mark Twain on Scotland." *Cleveland Herald*, 26 December 1873, 4.

"Mark Twain on Woman." *Alexandria Gazette*, 29 December 1873, 1.

"Mark Twain Once More." *New York World*, 25 February 1877, 5.

"Mark Twain Takes Out a Patent." *Washington National Republican*, 21 September 1871, 2.

"Mark Twain Tells a 'Chestnut.'" *NYH*, 22 March 1885, 11.

"Mark Twain to the Military." *BH*, 12 November 1886, 2.

"Mark Twain's April Fool." *NHR*, 14 April 1884, 2.

"Mark Twain's April Fool." *NYS*, 4 April 1884, 1.

"Mark Twain's Banquet." *HC*, 14 April 1874, 2.

"Mark Twain's Bookkeeper." *NYS*, 13 March 1887, 1; 18 March 1887, 4.

"Mark Twain's 'Boom.'" *Chicago Times*, 15 November 1879, 3.

"Mark Twain's Boys Disliked." *Philadelphia Inquirer*, 5 December 1904, 16.

"Mark Twain's Cold." *NYT*, 9 October 1874, 8.

"Mark Twain's Copyright." *NYT*, 29 December 1881, 1.

"Mark Twain's Coveted Professorship." *San Francisco Bulletin* supplement, 4 April 1891, 1.

"Mark Twain's Drink." *WS*, 14 October 1889, 7.

"Mark Twain's Enterprise." *NYS*, 7 January 1878, 2.

"Mark Twain's Historical Game." *San Francisco Bulletin*, 2 August 1883, 4.

"Mark Twain's Humorous Sayings." *Philadelphia Inquirer*, 27 November 1884, 3.

"Mark Twain's Injunction." *NYS*, 17 October 1882, 1.

"Mark Twain's Last Book." *Auburn (N.Y.) Bulletin*, 2 January 1872, 1.

"Mark Twain's Last Book." *London Standard*, 23 April 1880, 2.

"Mark Twain's Last Joke." *New Orleans Times*, 11 October 1876, 3.

"Mark Twain's Last Night in London." *HC*, 13 January 1874, 2.

"Mark Twain's Latest." *CC*, 23 December 1877, 4.

"Mark Twain's Latest." Mexico (N.Y.) *Independent*, 12 November 1884, 4.

"Mark Twain's Latest Book." *Boston Globe*, 29 December 1876, 4.

"Mark Twain's Latest Work." *BA*, 7 March 1890, 4.

"Mark Twain's Lecture." *Amherst (Mass.) Record*, 28 February 1872, 4.

"Mark Twain's Lecture." *Columbus Ohio State Journal*, 6 January 1872, 4.

"Mark Twain's Lecture." *Dayton Journal*, 5 January 1872.

"Mark Twain's Lecture." *HC*, 9 November 1871, 2; 23 February 1875, 2; 6 March 1875, 1.

"Mark Twain's Lecture." *London Era*, 14 December 1873, 11.

"Mark Twain's Lecture." *Malden (Mass.) Messenger*, 11 November 1871.

"Mark Twain's Lecture." *Malden (Mass.) Mirror*, 11 November 1871, 4.

"Mark Twain's Lecture." *NYH*, 25 January 1872, 3; 30 March 1876, 10.

"Mark Twain's Lecture." *NYT*, 25 January 1872, 5.

"Mark Twain's Lecture." *NYTrib*, 6 February 1873, 5.

"Mark Twain's Lecture." *Wilmington Delaware Gazette*, 27 October 1871, 3.

"Mark Twain's Lecture." *Worcester (Mass.) Spy*, 10 November 1871, 1.

"Mark Twain's Lecture at Lincoln Hall." *Washington Chronicle*, 24 October 1871, 4.

"Mark Twain's Lecture on Artemus Ward." *Boston Transcript*, 2 November 1871, 4.

"Mark Twain's Lecture on the Sandwich Islands." *NYT*, 6 February 1873, 5.

"Mark Twain's Lecture on the Sandwich Islands." *Troy (N.Y.) Times*, 7 June 1873, 4.

"Mark Twain's Mistake at the Whittier Dinner." *SR*, 27 December 1877, 8.

"Mark Twain's New Book." *Atchison (Kans.) Globe*, 16 June 1882, 1.

"Mark Twain's New Book." *Atlanta Constitution*, 17 June 1883, 6; 23 February 1890, 14.

"Mark Twain's New Book." *Atlantic Monthly* 45 (May 1880): 686–88.

"Mark Twain's New Book." *Cleveland Plain Dealer*, 22 November 1879, 2.

"Mark Twain's New Book." *Derby Mercury*, 23 May 1883, 6.

"Mark Twain's New Book." Melbourne Herald, 5 July 1880, 2.

"Mark Twain's New Book." *Montreal Gazette*, 17 February 1885, 7.

"Mark Twain's New Book." *NHR*, 8 October 1889, 3.

"Mark Twain's New Book." *NYTrib*, 22 December 1889, 14.

"Mark Twain's New Book." *Sydney Mail*, 26 June 1880, 1142.

"Mark Twain's New Lecture." *New York World*, 12 November 1886, 2.

"Mark Twain's New Play." *HC*, 25 September 1874, 2.

"Mark Twain's New Story." *NYS*, 15 February 1885, 3.

"Mark Twain's 'The Prince and the Pauper.'" *Brisbane Courier*, 25 February 1882, 5.

"Mark Twain's Reappearance in America." *BA*, 6 March 1874, 1.

"Mark Twain's Rights." *CIO*, 30 September 1876, 6.

"Mark Twain's Romance." *BH*, 4 December 1881, 4.

"Mark Twain's Romance." *NYH*, 4 December 1881, 4.

"Mark Twain's 'Roughing It.'" *BH*, 6 March 1874, 4.

"Mark Twain's Second Lecture." *London Globe*, 9 December 1873.

"Mark Twain's 70th Birthday." *Harper's Weekly* supplement, 23 December 1905, 1888–89.

"Mark Twain's Shrewd Promise." *BE*, 5 March 1882, 6.

"Mark Twain's Simple Play and the Way It Was Spoiled." *San Francisco Bulletin*, 22 October 1874, 1.

"Mark Twain's Sketches." *Mining & Scientific Press*, 1 January 1876, 12.

"Mark Twain's Sketches, New and Old." *Moore's Rural New-Yorker*, 4 December 1875, 370.

"Mark Twain's Statement." *Albany Journal*, 22 July 1885, 2.

"Mark Twain's Story." *Sausalito News*, 4 July 1890, 3.

"Mark Twain's Suit." *NYT*, 12 June 1873, 2.

"Mark Twain's Summer Home." *NYT*, 10 September 1882, 3.

"Mark Twain's Travels." *St. Louis Globe-Democrat*, 13 May 1882, 8.

"Mark Twain's Vacation." *BE*, 7 August 1883, 1.

"Mark Twain's Vacation." *HC*, 24 July 1883, 2.

"Mark Twain's Visit to the Capitol." *Baltimore Sun*, 23 March 1888, 1.

"Mark Twain's War Experiences." *NYT*, 7 October 1877, 10.

"Mark Twain's 'War Paper.'" *CT*, 13 December 1885, 4.

"Mark Twain's 'War Paper.'" *Washington Post*, 13 December 1885, 4.

"Mark Twain's Yankee." *Boston Globe*, 12 November 1886, 2.

"Mark Ward on Artemus Twain." *WS*, 24 October 1871, 1.

Marysville (Calif.) Appeal, 11 April 1874, 2.

"The Massachusetts Press." *BA*, 18 February 1874, 4.

"Mayor Hewitt's Views on the Strike." *NYTrib*, 11 February 1887, 5.

McDowell, Edwin. "From Twain, a Letter on Debt to Blacks." *NYT*, 14 March 1985, 1, 16.

"Mean Joke on Twain." *Carson City (Nev.) Appeal*, 2 December 1884, 3.

"Meeting of the Missionaries." *New York Graphic*, 3 October 1876, 3.

"A Memorable Occasion." *BA*, 4 May 1889, 9.

"Memories of Great Men." *Seattle Post-Intelligencer*, 30 April 1899, 16.

"Memories of the Pilgrims." *NYTrib*, 23 December 1881, 5.

"Men and Things." *BH*, 14 November 1871, 4; 13 March 1882, 4.

"Men and Women." *Portland (Maine) Press*, 5 May 1877, 1.

"Merry Yale Alumni." *NHR*, 4 February 1888, 4.

"Metropolitan Gossip." *NHR*, 18 July 1887, 1.

"The Middlesex." *BA*, 8 November 1880, 1.

"Military Courtesies." *BH*, 20 October 1882, 2.

Milwaukee Sentinel, 20 August 1890, 4.

"Mine Host and Mark Twain." *Kansas City Times*, 28 February 1889, 2.

"Minister Was 450 Miles Away." *BH*, 12 January 1891, 1.

"Minor Notes." *Washington Capital*, 6 January 1878, 4.

"Miscellaneous Notes." *CIO*, 6 September 1874, 2.

"Miss Dickinson's Debut." *Connecticut Courant*, 6 May 1876, 1.

"Miss Dickinson's Debut." *New York Commercial Advertiser*, 9 May 1876, 6.

Montgomery, G. E. "New York Gossip." *Philadelphia North American*, 28 April 1883, 1.

"The Moody and Sankey Meetings." *Hartford Times*, 15 January 1878, 1; 26 January 1878, 1; 6 February 1878, 1.

"More about the 'Ocean Tramp.'" *NYH*, 21 September 1877, 4.

"More Honors to Irving." *BH*, 17 December 1883, 2.

"The Morning's News." *NYEP*, 23 December 1876, 1.

Moulton, Louise Chandler, "Boston Literary Notes." *NYTrib*, 10 June 1872, 6; 15 October 1874, 6; 12 December 1874, 8; 18 March 1875, 8.

"Mr. Beecher's Anticipations." *NYT*, 10 October 1885, 5.

"Mr. Burbank's Recitals." *NYTrib*, 1 April 1879, 5.

"Mr. Burton's Lecture for the Indian Association." *HC*, 14 November 1890, 5.

"Mr. House in Reply." *NYT,* 31 January 1890, 9.

"Mr. Mark Twain." *London Daily News,* 9 December 1873, 3.

"Mr. Mark Twain." *London Post,* 2 December 1873, 6.

"Mr. Mark Twain." *London Times,* 12 December 1873, 5.

"Mr. Mark Twain on the Silver Frontier." *Liverpool Post,* 10 January 1874, 5.

"Mr. Mark Twain's Lecture." *London Post,* 14 October 1873, 6.

"Mr. Mark Twain's New Lecture." *London Post,* 9 December 1873, 2.

"Mr. Theodore Tilton Tells All He Knows." *BE,* 21 July 1874, 2.

"Mrs. Burnham after Twain and Warner." *Providence Press,* 2 February 1874, 4.

Mulford, Prentice. "Notes from London." *San Francisco Bulletin* supplement, 24 January 1874, 2.

"Music and Drama." *NYEP,* 24 September 1887, 3.

"Music and Drama." Sydney Mail, 5 October 1878, 546.

"Music and the Drama." *Glasgow Herald,* 26 July 1880, 5.

"Musical." *BE,* 14 November 1876, 3.

"Musical and Dramatic Notes." *NYH,* 29 September 1874, 7; 10 April 1885, 6; 6 May 1886, 6.

"Musical Notes." *BH,* 16 November 1882, 2.

"A New and Successful Play." *Philadelphia Inquirer,* 25 December 1889, 5.

"A New Book by Mark Twain." *New Zealand Herald,* 7 August 1880, 7.

"New Books." *BE,* 25 June 1880, 1.

"New Books." *St. Louis Globe-Democrat,* 21 May 1883, 8.

"New Books and New Editions." *Pall Mall Gazette,* 28 October 1876, 11.

"New England Day." *San Francisco Bulletin,* 23 December 1882, 1.

"New England News." *Worcester (Mass.) Spy,* 28 May 1875, 3; 5 June 1886, 3.

"New England Notes." *BA,* 27 August 1881, 8.

New Haven Columbian Register, 13 December 1873, 3.

"New Magazines." *Bangor (Maine) Whig and Courier,* 10 December 1885, 1.

"New Novels." *Academy,* 24 December 1881, 469.

New Orleans Bulletin, 9 April 1875, 6.

"New Orleans Items." *CC,* 6 May 1882, 7.

New Orleans Picayune, 4 January 1883, 4.

New Orleans Southwestern Advocate, 15 January 1874, 2.

New Orleans Times-Democrat, 4 May 1882; 5 May 1882, 4.

"The New Play by Mark Twain and W. D. Howells." *BJ,* 13 May 1886, 4.

"New Plays Begging." *WC,* 13 November 1884, 2.

"New Publications." *Baltimore Sun,* 29 December 1876, 2; supplement, 7 March 1885, 1; 30 December 1889, 2.

"New Publications." *BJ,* 17 December 1881, 5.

"New Publications." *CC,* 27 May 1883, 1.

"New Publications." *New England Farmer,* 29 November 1884, 2.

"New Publications." *NYT,* 13 January 1877, 3; 22 October 1877, 3.

"New Publications." *NYTrib,* 25 October 1881, 6.

"New Publications." *Philadelphia Press,* 13 January 1874, 6.

"New Publications." *Portland Oregonian,* 21 March 1874, 2.

"New Publications." *Portland (Maine) Press,* 28 March 1872, 2.

"New Publications." *Sacramento Union,* 14 March 1874, 4; 29 September 1883, 4.

"New Publications." *San Francisco Alta California*, 24 May 1880, 2.

"New Publications." *San Francisco Bulletin*, 7 March 1874, 1.

"New York." *BA*, 27 February 1872, 2.

"New York." *Boston Traveller*, 19 May 1873, 2.

"New York." *Cincinnati Gazette*, 10 January 1878, 5.

"New York." *CT*, 23 February 1873, 7.

"New York." *New York Clipper*, 1 October 1887, 455.

"New York." *NHJC*, 11 June 1883, 3.

"New York Book Notes." *BA*, 21 January 1884, 4.

"New York Clubs." *San Francisco Bulletin*, 28 January 1888, 1.

New York Evening World, 6 December 1890, 2.

"New York Letter." *Baltimore Bulletin*, 26 September 1874, 1.

"New York Press Club Reception." *NYT*, 31 March 1876, 5.

New York World, 25 January 1877, 4.

"Newport." *BJ*, 26 August 1875, 2.

"News about Town." *NHR*, 23 May 1888, 4.

"News and Notes." *Literary World*, 21 March 1885, 106.

"News Notes." *New York Commercial Advertiser*, 25 March 1876, 3.

"News, Notes, and Gossip." *BH*, 20 July 1884, 10; 3 August 1884, 10; 21 September 1884, 10; 1 March 1885, 10.

"News of the Day." *Melbourne Age*, 19 March 1874, 2; 11 April 1885, 9.

"News of the Morning." *BJ*, 3 October 1877, 2.

"Newspaper Circulation." *NYEP*, 14 February 1889, 8.

"Newspaper Men in Council." *NYT*, 14 February 1889, 8.

"Newspaper Waifs." *NYEP*, 31 March 1885, 2.

NHJC, 21 December 1876, 1.

NHR, 22 December 1882, 4.

"Northampton." *SR*, 16 April 1887, 6.

"Not Quite an Editor." *NYS*, 26 January 1878, 2.

"Note from London." *Sheffield & Rotherham Independent*, 24 June 1882, 6.

"Notes." *BH*, 23 February 1885, 4.

"Notes." *Chicago Advance*, 28 December 1876, 298.

"Notes." *Critic*, 26 September 1885, 155.

"Notes and Comments." *Sporting Life*, 20 June 1888, 7.

"Nottingham's Mechanics Institution." *Nottinghamshire Guardian*, 27 March 1874, 5.

"Novels of the Quarter." *British Quarterly Review* 75 (January 1882): 233–34.

"Novels of the Week." *Athenaeum*, 24 June 1876, 851; 24 June 1882, 794.

"The November Magazines." *NYT*, 22 October 1874, 2.

"Nutmeg Gratings." *SR*, 8 April 1883, 8.

NYEP, 15 June 1871, 2.

NYH, 19 July 1874, 9.

NYS, 18 March 1885, 2; 25 April 1889, 4; 19 September 1896, 7.

NYTrib, 10 February 1873, 4; 19 April 1873, 6; 24 December 1882, 6; 3 May 1883, 2.

"Occasional Notes." *Perth Inquirer and Commercial News*, 20 October 1880, 1.

"Odds and Ends." *Melbourne Leader*, 27 December 1873, 5.

Ogdensburg (N.Y.) Journal, 18 November 1871, 2.

"Old Times on the Mississippi." *CIO*, 21 February 1875, 6.

"Oliver Wendell Holmes." *NYH*, 4 December 1879, 4.

"On Plymouth Rock Again." *NYT*, 23 December 1882, 1–2.

"One of 'Mark Twain's' Woes." *NHJC*, 13 February 1885, 1.

"An Opinion of Mark Twain." *Cincinnati Commercial Tribune*, 1 December 1890, 4.

"Opposition to the Copyright." *Pittsburgh Dispatch*, 5 February 1889, 1.

"Our Authors." *BH*, 11 March 1883, 14.

"Our Autocrat." *Philadelphia North American*, 4 December 1879, 1.

"Our Boston Letter." *SR*, 18 May 1883, 2.

"Our Fellow Savages of the Sandwich Islands." *London Court Journal*, 18 October 1873, 1223.

"Our Forty 'Immortals.'" *Critic*, 12 April 1884, 169.

"Our Hartford Letter." *SR*, 15 December 1877, 3; 31 March 1881, 4; 19 November 1881, 5; 22 November 1883, 5.

"Our Innocent Abroad." *HC*, 13 October 1873, 2.

"Our London Letter." *Leicester Chronicle*, 17 December 1881, 5.

"Our New York Letter." *Hartford Times*, 3 August 1877, 1.

"The Papyrus Club." *BH*, 25 February 1881, 1.

"The Papyrus Club's Guests." *NYT*, 25 February 1881, 4.

"Paragraphical." *Nashville Union and American*, 31 December 1873, 3.

"Park Theatre." *New York Clipper*, 28 December 1889, 696.

"Park Theatre." *New York Evening Express*, 17 September 1874, 2.

"Park Theatre." *New York Graphic*, 17 September 1874, 3.

"The Park Theatre." *NYEP*, 29 September 1874, 2.

"Park Theatre." *NYH*, 17 September 1874, 10; 24 December 1874, 5.

"Park Theatre." *NYT*, 17 September 1874, 6.

"Parting Compliments to Mark Twain." *CC*, 15 November 1879, 2.

"People and Events." *CIO*, 19 November 1887, 4.

"People and Things." *CIO*, 6 April 1876, 4.

"People and Things." *Denver Rocky Mountain News*, 9 January 1878, 3.

"Perils of the Sea." *HC*, 27 November 1872, 1.

Perry, T. S. "Mark Twain." *Century* 30 (May 1885): 171–72.

"Personal." *Albany Journal*, 16 June 1871, 2.

"Personal." *Baltimore Sun*, 3 December 1885, 4.

"Personal." *BJ*, 15 April 1878, 2; 6 August 1878, 2; 7 November 1881, 4; 9 May 1883, 1; 14 November 1887, 4.

"Personal." *Cincinnati Enquirer*, 9 December 1872, 4.

"Personal." *Cincinnati Gazette*, 5 December 1871, 6.

"Personal." *CIO*, 11 November 1879, 8.

"Personal." *CT*, 3 April 1875, 9.

"Personal." *HC*, 10 February 1872, 2.

"Personal." *New York Commercial Advertiser*, 1 December 1871, 1.

"Personal." *New York Graphic*, 29 March 1876, 6.

"Personal." *NHJC*, 8 March 1881, 2.

"Personal." *NHR*, 29 August 1883, 1, 5 July 1885, 4.

"Personal." *NYEP*, 8 April 1874, 2; 15 April 1874, 2; 20 April 1875, 2; 25 May 1875, 2.

"Personal." *NYTrib*, 6 October 1877, 4; 2 April 1879, 4; 10 December 1881, 4.

"Personal." *WS*, 20 November 1885, 1.

"Personal and General Notes." *New Orleans Picayune*, 1 May 1882, 1; 30 October 1887, 6; 3 December 1887, 4.

"Personal and Pertinent." *New York Evening World*, 29 January 1889, 4; 8 February 1889, 4.

"Personal and Political." *Trenton State Gazette*, 14 December 1880, 2.

"Personal Gossip." *Frank Leslie's Illustrated Newspaper*, 28 July 1883, 371.

"Personal Intelligence." *NYH*, 2 February 1873, 7; 17 May 1873, 6; 8 July 1873, 6; 3 November 1873, 6; 1 July 1874, 4; 5 July 1874, 6; 26 December 1877, 4; 23 April 1878, 6; 27 March 1879, 6; 20 November 1883, 6.

"Personal Intelligence." *NYT*, 25 May 1882, 8; 18 November 1884, 2.

"Personal Intelligence." *Toronto Mail*, 10 December 1884, 8.

"Personal Intelligence." *Washington Post*, 25 November 1884, 2.

"Personal Items." *Boston Traveller*, 6 April 1875, 4.

"Personal Mention." *BE*, 6 February 1889, 4.

"Personal Mention." *CIO*, 10 July 1886, 6.

"Personal Mention." *Jackson (Mich.) Citizen Patriot*, 15 December 1884, 4.

"Personal Notes." *Philadelphia Inquirer*, 12 October 1889, 4.

"Personalities." *CC*, 13 August 1873, 3.

"Personalities." *Washington National Republican*, 17 March 1888, 1.

"Personals." *CT*, 16 July 1882, 5.

"Personals." *Indianapolis Sentinel*, 25 April 1881, 4.

"Personals." *Memphis Appeal*, 29 April 1882, 4.

"Persons and Things." *NHR*, 28 December 1881, 2; 25 March 1886, 2.

"A Petition." *BH*, 26 September 1887, 4.

Philadelphia Bulletin, 21 November 1871, 8.

Philadelphia Press, 15 May 1886, 8.

Philadelphia Times, 19 May 1886, 4.

"Philanthropic: Advertising." *Newcastle (Australia) Morning Herald and Miners' Advocate*, 20 February 1880, 4.

"The Pilgrims." *Philadelphia Inquirer*, 23 December 1881, 8.

"Pilgrims' Day in Boston." *NYTrib*, 21 December 1887, 15.

"Pitcairn Island." *London Times*, 4 December 1878, 9.

Pittsburgh Chronicle, 8 November 1877, 1.

"Pittsfield." *SR*, 7 October 1885, 6.

"Places for Pleasure." *Troy (N.Y.) Times*, 3 December 1884, 3.

"Players Who Amuse the Town." *SR*, 19 January 1890, 3.

"Pleasant Paragraphs." *Troy (N.Y.) Times*, 21 June 1883, 4.

"Poet and Autocrat." *Philadelphia Inquirer*, 4 December 1879, 1.

"Political Movements." *Pomeroy's Democrat*, 26 July 1873, 5.

"Political Notes." *NYTrib*, 18 August 1876, 4.

Pomeroy's Democrat, 14 April 1877, 1.

"The Poor of Hartford and the Sandwich Islands." *HC*, 29 January 1873, 2.

"The Pope's Autobiography." *BH*, 16 March 1886, 4.

Portland Oregonian, 12 February 1877, 2.

"Postmaster-General Howe at Hartford." *SR*, 8 December 1882, 8.

"Pour Les Dames." *St. Louis Globe-Democrat*, 14 May 1876, 2.

Powers, Tom. "New York Gossip." *St. Louis Republic*, 27 October 1889, 21.

"The President." *CIO*, 8 July 1881, 1.

"The President's Popularity." *WS*, 6 August 1883, 1.

"The Press Club Entertainment." *NYT*, 7 February 1877, 5.

"Press Club Reception." *BH*, 10 December 1886, 4.

"The Press Club's Entertainment." *NYTrib*, 7 February 1877, 8.

"Prince and Pauper." *NYH*, 28 January 1890, 8.

"Prince and Pauper." *Philadelphia North American*, 25 December 1889.

"Prince and Pauper." *WC*, 20 December 1881, 1.

"Prince and Pauper a Success." *Philadelphia North American*, 18 January 1890.

"'Prince and Pauper' Enjoined." *BE*, 9 October 1890, 6.

"The Prince and the Pauper." *Critic*, 25 January 1890, 43.

"The Prince and the Pauper." *Lyttelton (New Zealand) Times*, 3 May 1882, 6.

"The Prince and the Pauper." *Sacramento Union*, 28 March 1882, 1.

"The Prince and the Pauper." *Spectator*, 21 January 1882, 95.

Proceedings of the National Wholesale Druggists Association 16 (1890): 206.

"Prominent Arrivals." *NYTrib*, 4 August 1871, 8; 4 October 1871, 8; 14 October 1871, 7; 31 January 1872, 8; 29 September 1880, 8.

"The Publisher of Grant's Book." *Kansas City Star*, 25 June 1887, 1.

"Put Him on the Witness Stand." *NYT*, 31 December 1884, 3.

"The Putnam Phalanx." *WC*, 4 October 1887, 1.

"Ragged Edge in Earnest." *NYS*, 15 April 1875, 2.

"Rags and Royalty." *NYH*, 21 January 1890, 8.

Ralph, Julian. "What New York Talks Of." *Galveston News*, 15 May 1887, 4.

"Rapidly Gaining Ground." *Wheeling Register*, 22 April 1885, 1.

Ravenna (Ohio) Democratic Press, 8 November 1888, 3.

Raymond, John T. "The Gilded Age." *NYS*, 3 November 1874, 2.

"Raymond on 'Sellers.'" *Cleveland Plain Dealer*, 24 March 1876, 1.

"The Reader." *London Graphic*, 1 May 1880, 450.

"Reading Their Works." *BA*, 8 March 1889, 5.

"Readings by American Authors." *NYS*, 29 November 1887, 5.

"Readings by Authors." *Baltimore Sun* supplement, 18 January 1889, 1.

"Readings by Authors in Boston." *NYTrib*, 8 March 1889, 7.

"Readings by Clemens and Cable." *NYTrib*, 20 November 1884, 5.

"Readings by Twain and Cable." *BA*, 14 November 1884, 8.

"Recent Literature." *Atlantic Monthly* 36 (December 1875): 750.

"Recent Novels." *London Daily News*, 1 March 1882, 6.

"Recent Publications." *NHJC*, 21 June 1883, 1.

"Recent Publications." *San Francisco Alta California*, 24 March 1885, 2.

"A Reception at the St. Botolph." *BA*, 8 March 1889, 5.

"Remarkable Imposture." *NYS*, 21 July 1889, 10.

"Resting Well." *CC Gazette*, 9 April 1885, 1.

"The Returns in Hartford." *NHJC*, 4 November 1880, 2.

"The Review." *CIO*, 13 November 1879, 2.

"Review." *New Zealand Evening Post*, 19 September 1874, 2.

"Review." *Otago (New Zealand) Times*, 30 January 1875, supplement 6.

"Review." *Sydney Empire*, 21 August 1874, 4.

"Review of New Books." *Portland Oregonian*, 30 March 1890, 12.

Richmond Whig, 22 July 1873, 2.

"Robert G. Ingersoll: The Volunteer Soldiers." *CT*, 14 November 1879, 3.

"Robert Louis Stevenson's Retreat." *NYS*, 27 November 1887, 4.

"Robinson's Opera-House." *Cincinnati Star*, 10 November 1877, 3.

"Rochester." *NYTrib*, 13 December 1884, 7.

"Roughing It." *BJ*, 6 March 1874, 1.

"Roughing It." *Boston Globe*, 6 March 1874, 5.

"Roughing It." *Nashville Union and American*, 20 June 1872, 4.

"'Roughing It' by Mark Twain." *Troy (N.Y.) Press*, 2 February 1872, 3.

"'Round the Dinner Plate." *New York World*, 9 April 1889, 2.

Sacramento Record-Union, 26 March 1885, 2.

"The Sage of Chappaqua." *CT*, 8 February 1872, 5.

"The Scattering of Mark Twain's Friends." *Atchison (Kans.) Globe*, 8 January 1885, 3.

"Schurz at Hartford." *BH*, 21 October 1884, 1.

"Scottish Corporation of London." *London Post*, 2 December 1873, 6.

"Scraps." *Victoria (B.C.) Daily Colonist*, 16 March 1890, 6.

"The Season at Saratoga." *NYT*, 3 July 1885, 4.

"Second Prize Letter." *NYH*, 14 September 1890, 11.

"The Senate Is Captured." *Salt Lake Tribune*, 19 June 1890, 8.

"A Sextette of Items." *WC*, 7 February 1889, 3.

Seymour (Australia) Express, 28 March 1890, 2.

"Sheridan's Memoirs." *HC*, 30 May 1888, 8.

"The Ship-Owners and Mr. Duncan." *NYT*, 15 February 1877, 8.

"Shipowners Swindled." *NYH*, 3 May 1873, 5.

"The Shipping Act." *NYH*, 10 March 1876, 8.

"A Shipping Commissioner Dismissed." *San Francisco Bulletin*, 13 May 1884, 2.

Smalley, George W. "British Topics." *NYTrib*, 12 October 1872, 4; 25 December 1873, 1.

"Social Chit Chat." *WC*, 23 March 1888, 4.

"Society Events in Washington." *New York Evening World*, 4 February 1889, 4.

"Social Life in Washington." *NYS*, 31 January 1886, 1.

"Social Matters." *WS*, 16 June 1890, 2.

"Society Meetings." *Philadelphia Inquirer*, 19 January 1878, 1.

"Society Notes." *New Orleans Times-Democrat*, 7 May 1882, 15.

"Society Notes." *WS*, 27 March 1888, 5.

"Some New Books." *NYS*, 19 May 1878, 2.

"Some New Books." *San Francisco Chronicle*, 15 March 1874, 2.

"Some Novels and Stories." *Independent*, 3 August 1882, 11.

"Some of Mark Twain's Fun." *NYS*, 19 November 1884, 1.

"Something Regarding Twain." *Carson City (Nev.) Appeal*, 23 March 1881, 2.

"The Sorosis Ribbons." *NYH*, 22 December 1876, 2.

"Southern States News." *New Orleans Picayune*, 7 October 1879, 2.

"Speaking of Politics." *Philadelphia Inquirer*, 12 November 1890, 4.

"Specimens of German Criticism." *WS*, 25 June 1887, 6.

"Springfield." *SR*, 28 February 1881, 5.

SR, 13 January 1877, 8; 17 December 1881, 4; 17 March 1885, 4; 3 April 1885, 4.

St. Albans (Vt.) Messenger, 20 March 1885, 2.

St. Louis Globe-Democrat, 18 October 1875, 3; 27 December 1882, 4.

"Stage Affairs." *NYTrib*, 30 August 1876, 4.

"Stage and Rostrum." *Madison Wisconsin State Journal*, 28 January 1885.

"The Star Course." *Philadelphia Inquirer*, 15 November 1876, 2; 27 February 1885, 3.

"The Start for Germany." *NYT*, 12 April 1878, 8.

"State Correspondence." *NHJC*, 23 July 1881, 4.

"State Correspondence." *NHR*, 21 March 1884, 4.

"Stationery and Other Notes." *American Bookseller*, 1 May 1890, 250.

"A Stay of Proceedings." *NYT*, 11 March 1890, 8.

Stoddard, Charles Warren. "An Anglo-American City." *San Francisco Chronicle*, 8 February 1874, 1.

———. "Christmas in New Sarum." *San Francisco Chronicle*, 25 January 1874, 2.

"The Stolen White Elephant." *CT*, 10 June 1882, 9.

"The Stolen White Elephant." *London Morning Post*, 22 August 1882, 2.

"Substantial Donations." *CT*, 14 January 1872, 5.

"Suit against Mark Twain." *BH*, 18 January 1890, 2.

"A Suit over 'Prince & Pauper.'" *NYH*, 17 January 1890, 10.

"Summary of News." *Sheffield & Rotherham Independent*, 17 October 1873, 2.

"Summary of the News." *BA*, 24 December 1877, 1.

"Sunbeams." *NYS*, 22 December 1881, 2.

"Table Talk." *Literary World*, 5 May 1886, 172.

"The Talk of the Day." *NYTrib*, 3 November 1888, 9.

"A Talk with Mr. Clemens." *NYT*, 31 January 1890, 9.

"Tampering with Mark Twain's Book." *NYTrib*, 29 November 1884, 3.

"Tea Table Talk." *New Orleans Picayune*, 7 May 1882, 15.

"Telegraphic Brevities." *BH*, 24 May 1883, 4.

"Telegraphic Jottings." *NHJC*, 9 December 1881, 3.

Theatre, 31 May 1886, 312.

"The Theatre in America." *New York Clipper*, 14 December 1889, 662.

"Theatres." *London Graphic*, 24 July 1880, 87.

"The Theatres." *NYTrib*, 29 January 1888, 12.

"Theatrical News and Notes." *Milwaukee Journal*, 30 January 1885, 1.

"Theatrical Record." *New York Clipper*, 17 January 1880, 339.

"A Thundering Row about that Whittier Dinner." *San Francisco Bulletin*, 10 January 1878, 1.

"The Tide Turning." *BA*, 2 April 1885, 4.

"Today's Amusements." *CIO*, 2 July 1875, 4.

"Tom Sawyer." *London Post*, 18 September 1876, 3.

"Tom Sawyer." *San Francisco Alta California*, 15 January 1877, 2.

"Tommy Russell's Parents Recover $14,000." *NYS*, 7 March 1893, 2.

"Too Late for Roger M'Pherson." *NYT*, 11 April 1879, 5.

"Topics of the Day." *Melbourne Herald*, 28 August 1873, 2.

"Topics of the Times." *Century* 31 (February 1886): 634.

"Town Talk." *Boston Traveller*, 13 June 1871, 2; 2 November 1871, 2; 23 October 1871, 2.

Gath [George Alfred Townsend]. "The Protection of Authorship." *Cincinnati Enquirer*, 2 February 1886, 1.

"A Tramp Abroad." *Adelaide Observer*, 28 August 1880, 42.

"A Tramp Abroad." *Auckland Star*, 2 August 1880, 2.

"A Tramp Abroad." *London Post*, 4 May 1880, 3.

"A Tramp Abroad." *London Times*, 7 September 1880, 5.

"A Tramp Abroad." *Rockhampton (Australia) Capricornian*, 28 August 1880, 4.

"Tramp! Tramp! Tramp!" *Philadelphia Inquirer*, 21 December 1877, 1.

"The Tribe of Sellers." *NY Trib*, 19 November 1874, 4.

"Tribunets." *Washington National Tribune*, 10 September 1885, 4.

"Tributes to Poet by Men of Letters." *NYT*, 24 February 1907, pictorial sec., 4.

"Trinity College Alumni." *BH*, 26 February 1889, 2.

"A Trip on the Charles Morgan." *New Orleans Picayune*, 10 May 1882, 10.

"Tritle's Metamorphosis." *Carson City (Nev.) Appeal*, 25 February 1890, 3.

"Trollope and Mark Twain." *NYT*, 25 December 1882, 3.

"Twain." *BE*, 1 September 1871, 4; 14 July 1873, 2.

"Twain Again." *New York World*, 29 March 1876, 5.

"Twain and Cable." *Atlanta Constitution*, 28 May 1885, 2.

"Twain and Cable." *Burlington Hawkeye*, 16 January 1885.

"Twain and Cable." *CT*, 3 February 1885, 5.

"Twain and Cable." *Evanston Index*, 24 January 1885, 1.

"Twain and Cable." *NHJC*, 6 November 1884, 2.

"Twain and Cable." *Philadelphia North American*, 27 February 1885, 1.

"Twain and Cable." *Quincy Herald*, 13 January 1885, 4.

"Twain and Cable." *Rochester Herald*, 8 December 1884, 4.

"'Twain' and Cable." *Springfield Illinois State Journal*, 9 January 1885, 37.

"Twain and Cable." *Toledo Blade*, 16 December 1884, 1.

"Twain and Cable." *Toronto Globe*, 10 December 1884, 2.

"Twain and Cable." *Toronto Mail*, 9 December 1884, 2; 10 December 1884, 8.

"Twain and Cable at Albany." *BA*, 5 December 1884, 1.

"Twain at the Whittier Dinner." *NYT*, 20 December 1877, 2.

"Twain-Cable." *Columbus Times*, 10 February 1885.

"Twain-Cable." *Dayton Democrat*, 31 December 1884.

"Twain-Cable." *Keokuk (Iowa) Gate City*, 15 January 1885, 8.

"The Twain-Cable Combination." *Indianapolis Journal*, 8 February 1885, 8.

"The Twain-Cable Evening." *SR*, 8 November 1884, 4.

"The Twain-Cable Readings." *St. Louis Missouri Republican*, 10 January 1885, 8.

"Twain Goes to Law." *Philadelphia Press*, 4 August 1886, 5.

"Twain Interviews Himself." *Wheeling Register*, 29 March 1882, 3.

"Twain Talk." *Jersey City Journal*, 31 January 1872, 1.

"Twain Won't Come." *CIO*, 7 January 1878, 8.

"Twain's Copyright Claim Refused." *BH*, 17 December 1881, 4.

"Twain's Latest." *BH*, 22 July 1877, 6.

"Twain's Reputation Needs Repairs." *NYT*, 5 February 1890, 4.

"Two Authors Give a Treat." *Baltimore American*, 18 January 1889, 6.

"Two Readings by Mark Twain." *HC*, 2 June 1885, 1.

"The 'Union' Entertainment." *BH*, 14 November 1884, 5.

"University of Michigan." *CT*, 18 December 1871, 6.

"Unlearnable Things." *Atlantic Monthly* 45 (June 1880): 849–52.

"Views and Interviews." *Galveston News*, 8 April 1886, 5.

"Vignaux, 300; Sexton, 141." *BH*, 6 March 1883, 2.

"A Virginia Verdict." *BA*, 4 April 1885, 4.

"The Visit of the Shah of Persia to Portsmouth." *Hampshire Telegraph and Sussex Chronicle*, 25 June 1873, 2.

"The Visiting Soldiery." *HC*, 20 October 1882, 2.

Waco Examiner, 22 April 1874, 2.

"Walt Whitman's Birthday." *NYTrib*, 1 June 1889, 7.

Waltham (Mass.) Free Press, 13 November 1884, n.p.

"The War Correspondent." *HC*, 18 November 1881, 2.

Warner, C. D. "Literary Notices." *HC*, 27 December 1876, 1.

"Was Hawley a Figure Head?" *NHR*, 17 April 1888, 1.

Washington, Booker T. "Tributes to Mark Twain." *North American Review* 191 (June 1910): 828–30.

"Watering-Place Gossip." *Boston Traveller*, 27 August 1875, 2.

WC, 28 July 1884, 2; 18 March 1885, 2.

"W. D. Howells at Seminary Hall." *HC*, 12 December 1877, 3.

Western Christian Advocate, 21 October 1874, 333.

"What Mark Twain Said." *CIO*, 8 April 1890, 4.

"What Ought John to Have Done?" *Christian Union*, 25 June 1885, 4.

Whiting, Lilian. "Letter from Boston." *St. Louis Globe-Democrat*, 18 June 1882, 3.

"The Whittaker Case." *Buffalo Courier*, 31 May 1880, 1.

"The Whittier Dinner." *Boston Globe*, 18 December 1877, 8.

"The Whittier Testimonial." *Portland (Maine) Press*, 19 December 1877, 1.

"Whittier's Birthday." *BA*, 18 December 1877, 1.

"Whittier's Birthday." *BJ*, 18 December 1877, 4.

"Whittier's Birthday." *Hartford Times*, 18 December 1877, 2.

Wilde, Oscar. "The Child-Philosopher." *Court and Society Review*, 20 April 1887, 380.

Wilkie, Franc B. "Twain's Best Joke." *Chicago Times*, 17 November 1879, 1.

"Wine at the Whittier Banquet." *Boston Post*, 19 December 1877, 4.

Winter, William. "Anna Dickinson's Debut in Boston." *NYTrib*, 9 May 1876, 5.

———. "The Drama." *NYTrib*, 18 September 1874, 4.

———. "Mr. Burbank as Col. Sellers." *NYTrib*, 24 September 1887, 4.

"Wit and Wisdom." *BH*, 1 April 1887, 8.

"The Woman with the Golden Arm." *CIO*, 28 March 1891, 14.

WS, 19 June 1871, 4; 21 September 1872, 2; 31 July 1885, 2.

"Yale's Hartford Alumni." *NHR*, 7 February 1889, 4.

"A Yankee in Camelot." *Washington Post*, 13 November 1886, 2.

"Yankee Smith of Camelot." *NYS*, 12 November 1886, 1.

Yates, Edmund. "Mark Twain Set Right." *NYTrib*, 11 October 1887, 5.

Manuscripts and Scrapbooks

Unless otherwise noted, transcriptions of SLC's letters dated between 1876 and 1880 are available online at the Mark Twain Project website, http://www.marktwainproject.org. Unless otherwise noted, transcriptions of SLC's letters dated between 1881 and 1910 are available on-site at the Mark Twain Papers and Project, Bancroft Library, University of California–Berkeley.

"Concerning the Scoundrel Edward H. House." DV 305, MTP.

Isabel Lyon, diaries and daily reminders, MTP.

"Remarks on Richardson Contract." DOC 06768, MTP.
Scrapbooks 6, 8, 10, and 12, MTP.
"To the Editor of the World Concerning Captain Duncan." DV 18, MTP.

General Studies

Adeler, Max. *By the Bend of the River*. Philadelphia: Winston, 1914.
Aldrich, Lilian. *Crowding Memories*. Boston: Houghton Mifflin, 1920.
Anesko, Michael. *Letters, Fiction, Lives: Henry James and William Dean Howells*. New York: Oxford University Press, 1997.
Anson, A. C. *A Ball Player's Career*. Chicago: Era, 1900.
Arnold, Matthew. *Civilization in the United States*. Boston: Cupples, 1888.
––––––. "A Word about America." *Nineteenth Century* 11 (May 1882): 680–96.
Ballou, Ellen B. *The Building of the House: Houghton Mifflin's Formative Years*. Boston: Houghton Mifflin, 1970.
Beahrs, Andrew. *Twain's Feast*. New York: Penguin, 2010.
Berkove, Lawrence I., ed. *Insider Stories of the Comstock Lode and Nevada's Mining Frontier, 1859–1909*. 2 vols. Lewiston, N.Y.: Mellen, 2007.
Bikle, Lucy L. C. *George W. Cable: His Life and Letters*. New York: Scribner's, 1928.
Bright, John. *Diaries*. Edited by R. A. J. Walling. New York: Morrow, 1931.
Britton, Wesley, "Trumbull, James Hammond." In *The Routledge Encyclopedia of Mark Twain*, edited by J. R. LeMaster and J. D. Wilson. New York: Routledge, 2011.
Brown, Robert. *The Countries of the World*. 6 vols. London: Cassell, 1876–1881.
Burdette, Robert J., and Clara Bradley Burdette. *Robert J. Burdette: His Message*. Philadelphia: Winston, 1922.
Byers, S. H. M. *Twenty Years in Europe*. Chicago: Rand McNally, 1900.
Cantacuzene, Julia. *My Life Here and There*. New York: Scribner's, 1921.
Conway, Moncure D. *Autobiography*. 2 vols. Boston: Houghton Mifflin, 1905.
Cortissoz, Royal. *The Life of Whitelaw Reid*. 2 vols. New York: Scribner's, 1921.
Courtney, Steve. *Joseph Hopkins Twichell*. Athens: University of Georgia Press, 2008.
Crews, Frederick. *The Critics Bear It Away*. New York: Random House, 1992.
Daly, Joseph Francis. *The Life of Augustin Daly*. New York: Macmillan, 1917.
Darwin, Charles. *Life and Letters*. Edited by Francis Darwin. London: Murray, 1887.
David, Beverly, and Lester Crossman, "Illustrators." In *The Routledge Encyclopedia of Mark Twain*, edited by J. R. LeMaster and J. D. Wilson. New York: Routledge, 2011.
Denning, Michael. *Mechanic Accents: Dime Novels and Working-Class Culture in America*. London: Verso, 1998.
Dunne, Finley Peter. *Mr. Dooley Remembers*. Edited by Philip Peter Dunne. Boston: Little, Brown, 1963.
Eggleston, George Cary. *Reminiscences of a Varied Life*. New York: Holt, 1910.
Elderkin, John. *A Brief History of the Lotos Club*. New York: Club House, 1895.
Ellsworth, William W. *A Golden Age of Authors*. Boston: Houghton Mifflin, 1919.
Emerson, Ralph Waldo. *The Journals and Miscellaneous Notebooks*. Edited by Ralph H. Orth and Alfred R. Ferguson. 16 vols. Cambridge, Mass.: Belknap, 1960–82.
Field, Kate. "London Stage Gossip." *New York Graphic*, 19 August 1880, 361.
––––––. "Notes from the United States." *Athenaeum*, 9 January 1875, 53.
––––––. "Receiving the Shah." *NY Trib*, 9 July 1873, 4.

———. *Selected Letters*. Edited by Carolyn Moss. Carbondale: Southern Illinois University Press, 1996.

Fields, Annie. *Memories of a Hostess*. Edited by M. A. DeWolfe Howe. Boston: Atlantic Monthly Press, 1922.

Fike, Duane Joseph. "Frank Mayo: Actor, Playwright, and Manager." PhD diss., University of Nebraska Press, 1980.

Fisher, Henry W. *Abroad with Mark Twain and Eugene Field*. New York: Brown, 1922.

Flood, Charles Bracelen. *Grant's Final Victory*. Cambridge: Da Capo, 2011.

Frohman, Daniel. *Encore*. New York: Furman, 1937.

———. *Memories of a Manager*. Garden City, N.Y.: Doubleday, Page, 1911.

Gilder, Richard Watson. *Letters*. Edited by Rosamond Gilder. Boston: Houghton Mifflin, 1916.

Glass, Loren. *Authors, Inc.* New York: New York University Press, 2004.

Greenslet, Ferris. *The Life of Thomas Bailey Aldrich*. Boston: Houghton Mifflin, 1908.

Hall, Roger. *Performing the American Frontier*. New York: Cambridge University Press, 2001.

Harte, Bret. *Letters*. Edited by Geoffrey Bret Harte. Boston: Houghton Mifflin, 1926.

———. *Selected Letters*. Edited by Gary Scharnhorst. Norman: University of Oklahoma Press, 1997.

Haweis, H. R. *American Humorists*. New York: Funk and Wagnalls, 1883.

Hawthorne, Nathaniel. *Letters, 1843–53*. Edited by Thomas Woodson. Columbus: Ohio State University Press, 1985.

Hemingway, Ernest. *Green Hills of Africa*. New York: Scribner's, 1935.

Higginson, Mary Potter Thacher. *Thomas Wentworth Higginson: The Story of His Life*. Boston: Houghton Mifflin, 1914.

Higginson, Thomas Wentworth. *Cheerful Yesterdays*. Boston: Houghton Mifflin, 1898.

Howells, Elinor Mead. *If Not Literature*. Edited by Ginette De B. Merrill and George Arms. Columbus: Ohio State University Press, 1988.

Howells, W. D. *Life in Letters of William Dean Howells*. Edited by Mildred Howells. 2 vols. Garden City, N.Y.: Doubleday, Doran, 1928.

———. *Selected Letters, 1873–1881*. Edited by George Arms and Christoph K. Lohmann. Boston: Twayne, 1979.

———. "A Sennight of the Centennial." *Atlantic Monthly* 38 (July 1876): 92–107.

Hughes, Geoffrey. *Political Correctness: A History of Semantics and Culture*. Malden, Mass.: Wiley-Blackwell, 2010.

Inge, M. Thomas. "Beard, Daniel Carter." In *The Routledge Encyclopedia of Mark Twain*, edited by J. R. LeMaster and J. D. Wilson. New York: Routledge, 2011.

Ingersoll, Robert. *Ghosts and Other Lectures*. Washington, D.C.: Farrell, 1878.

Jackson, Helen Hunt. "A German Landlady." *Atlantic Monthly* 26 (October 1870) 441–56.

Johanningsmeier, Charles. *Fiction and the American Literary Marketplace*. Cambridge: Cambridge University Press, 1997.

Johnson, Hugo D. "Labor." In *The Routledge Encyclopedia of Mark Twain*, edited by J. R. LeMaster and J. D. Wilson. New York: Routledge, 2011.

Johnson, Robert Underwood. *Remembered Yesterdays*. Boston: Little, Brown, 1923.

Jones, Evan. *American Food*. New York: Dutton, 1975.

Kennan, George. "Siberia and the Exile System." *Century* 36 (May 1888): 3–24.

Layard, George S. *Shirley Brooks of Punch: His Life, Letters, and Diaries.* New York: Holt, 1907.

Lecky, William E. H. *History of European Morals.* New York: Appleton, 1869.

Leland, Charles Godfrey. *The Alternate Sex.* New York: Funk and Wagnalls, 1904.

Leonard, James S. "Russia." In *The Routledge Encyclopedia of Mark Twain,* edited by J. R. LeMaster and J. D. Wilson. New York: Routledge, 2011.

Longfellow, Henry Wadsworth. *Letters.* Edited by Andrew Hilen. 6 vols. Cambridge, Mass.: Belknap, 1966–82.

Lynn, Kenneth S. *William Dean Howells: An American Life.* Boston: Houghton Mifflin, 1971.

Matthews, Brander. *The Tocsin of Revolt and Other Essays.* New York: Scribner's, 1922.

McWilliams, Carey. *Ambrose Bierce: A Biography.* New York: Boni, 1929.

Melville, Herman. *Correspondence.* Edited by Lynn Horth. Evanston, Ill.: Northwestern University Press, 1993.

Millais, John. *Life and Letters.* New York: Stokes, 1899.

Moore, Isabel. *Talks in a Library with Laurence Hutton.* New York: Putnam's, 1905.

Mott, Frank Luther. *American Journalism: A History, 1690–1960.* New York: Macmillan, 1962.

Murphy, Brenda. *American Realism and American Drama, 1880–1940.* New York: Cambridge University Press, 2008.

Perry, Mark. *Grant and Twain.* New York: Random House, 2004.

Peters, Samuel. *General History of Connecticut.* New York: Appleton, 1877.

Phelps, William Lyon. *Autobiography with Letters.* New York: Oxford University Press, 1939.

Pond, James B. *Eccentricities of Genius: Memories of Famous Men and Women of the Platform and Stage.* New York: Dillingham, 1900.

Reade, A. Arthur. *Study and Stimulants.* Manchester, England: Heywood, 1883.

Riley, James Whitcomb. *Letters.* Edited by William Lyon Phelps. Indianapolis: Bobbs-Merrill, 1930.

Scharnhorst, Gary. *Bret Harte: Opening the American Literary West.* Norman: University of Oklahoma Press, 1992.

———. *Owen Wister and the West.* Norman: University of Oklahoma Press, 2015.

Scharnhorst, Gary, and Matthew Hofer, eds. *Sinclair Lewis Remembered.* Tuscaloosa: University of Alabama Press, 2012.

Schnirmajer, Ariela. "Poetics, Justice, and Style: José Martí Reads Mark Twain." In *Syncing the Americas: José Martí and the Shaping of National Identity,* edited by Ryan Anthony Spangler and Georg Michael Schwarzmann. Lewisburg, Penn.: Bucknell University Press, 2018.

Sedgwick, Ellery. *A History of the "Atlantic Monthly."* Amherst: University of Massachusetts Press, 1994.

Simpson, Alan, and Mary Simpson. *Jean Webster, Storyteller.* Union Vale, N.Y.: Stinehour, 1984.

Smith, George Adam. *Life of Henry Drummond.* New York: Doubleday and McClure, 1898.

Sproat, John G. *The Best Men: Liberal Reformers in the Gilded Age.* New York: Oxford University Press, 1982.

Stewart, William M. *Reminiscences.* New York: Neale, 1908.

Stoddard, Charles W. *Exits and Entrances*. Boston: Lothrop, 1903.

Stowe, Harriet Beecher. *Uncle Tom's Cabin*. Boston: Jewett, 1852.

Switzerland: Handbook for Travellers. Leipzig: Baedeker, 1889.

Taliaferro, John. *All the Great Prizes: The Life of John Hay from Lincoln to Roosevelt*. New York: Simon and Schuster, 2013.

Tebbel, John. *A History of Book Publishing in the United States*. New York: Bowker, 1972.

Thomason, Jerry W. "Colonel Sellers." In *The Routledge Encyclopedia of Mark Twain*, edited by J. R. LeMaster and J. D. Wilson. New York: Routledge, 2011.

——. "Dramatist, Mark Twain as." In *The Routledge Encyclopedia of Mark Twain*, edited by J. R. LeMaster and J. D. Wilson. New York: Routledge, 2011.

Ticknor, Caroline. *Glimpses of Authors*. Boston: Houghton Mifflin, 1922.

Traubel, Horace, ed. *Camden's Compliment to Walt Whitman*. Philadelphia: McKay, 1889.

Trollope, Anthony. *Letters*. Edited by N. John Hall. Stanford, Calif.: Stanford University Press, 1983.

Trumbull, J. Hammond. *The Memorial History of Hartford County, Connecticut, 1633–1884*. Boston: Osgood, 1886.

——. *The True-Blue Laws of Connecticut and New Haven*. Hartford: American Publishing, 1876.

Turner, Arlin. *George W. Cable*. Baton Rouge: Louisiana State University Press, 1966.

Tuveson, Ernest Lee. *Redeemer Nation: The Idea of America's Millennial Role*. Chicago: University of Chicago Press, 1968.

Underwood, F. H. *John Greenleaf Whittier*. Boston: Osgood, 1884.

Vanderbilt, Kermit. *The Achievement of William Dean Howells*. Princeton, N.J.: Princeton University Press, 1968.

Walker, Franklin. *Ambrose Bierce: The Wickedest Man in San Francisco*. San Francisco: Colt, 1941.

Ward, Andrew. *Dark Midnight When I Rise: The Story of the Jubilee Singers*. New York: Farrar, Straus and Giroux, 2000.

Watson, Aaron. *The Savage Club: A Medley of History, Anecdote, and Reminiscence*. London: Unwin, 1907.

Wayland, Francis. *A Paper on Tramps*. New Haven, Conn.: Hoggson and Robinson, 1877.

Wheeler, Candace. *Yesterdays in a Busy Life*. New York: Harper, 1918.

Whiting, Lilian. *Kate Field: A Record*. Boston: Little, Brown, 1899.

Wister, Owen. *The Virginian*. New York: Macmillan, 1902.

Index

M